CANADA STUDENT EMPLOYMENT GUIDE

CANADA'S MOST VALUABLE
EMPLOYMENT RESOURCE FOR STUDENTS

Toronto, Ontario

Published By:
SEN Publishing, a division of Student Employment Network
117 Gerrard Street East, Suite 1002
Toronto, Ontario
M5B 2L4
Tel: (416) 971-5090
Fax: (416) 977-3782
E-mail: sen@studentjobs.com

Internet: http://www.studentjobs.com

Kevin E. Makra, Publisher/Editor

Cover Design: Matthew Labutte

Tri-Graphic Printing (Ottawa) Limited

Printed in Canada

All rights reserved. No part of this book may be reproduced or transmitted in any form or by any means, electronic or mechanical, including photocopying, recording or by any information storage and retrieval system without prior written permission from the Student Employment Network.

Canadian Cataloguing in Publication (CIP):

Main entry under title:

The ... Canada student employment guide

Annual.
1996-
ISSN 1204-6191
ISBN 1-896324-34-7 (2001)

1. College students - Employment - Canada - Directories. 2. Business enterprises – Canada - Directories. I. Student Employment Network (Toronto, Ont.).

HF5382.75.C32052   331.12'4'02571   C96-300-377-1

© Copyright 2001 by Student Employment Network
First Printing 2001

THE NAVAL RESERVE IS NOW HIRING!
LA RÉSERVE NAVALE EMBAUCHE!
1-800-856-8488

www.dnd.ca

If you wish to play an active role in protecting Canada's maritime interests and sovereignty, join the Naval Reserve today! Whether you are unemployed, employed, or a student, the Naval Reserve offers you an opportunity to learn a trade and sail onboard the new Kingston-class vessels while being paid.

WHO ARE NAVAL RESERVISTS?

Naval Reservists are individuals engaged in their civilian lives while pursuing a military career. They work selected evenings, weekends, and during the summer period in a trade of their choice. They can be students, teachers, lawyers, secretaries, etc. They serve on a part time basis, and there is no obligation to participate in any mission overseas. Release can be authorized on 30 days' notice.

TO APPLY, CANDIDATES MUST

- Be a Canadian citizen or permanent resident;
- Hold a minimum of high school grade 10 for non-commissioned member occupations or have completed a high school diploma for officer positions;
- Be in good health and physical condition.

TRAINING

With the exception of musicians, no previous formal training or experience is required. The Naval Reserve will train you, both as a member of the military and in the trade you have selected. All trades are open equally to men and women.

SALARY

As a member of the Naval Reserve, you will receive a salary based on your rank. If you are a full time student, this is certainly a good summer employment opportunity to consider.

THE NAVAL RESERVE HAS POSITIONS AVAILABLE IN THE FOLLOWING TRADES

Non-commissioned members: Boatswain, Naval Communicator, Naval Combat Information Operator, Marine Engineering Systems Operator, Inspection Diver, Cook, Resource Management Support Clerk, Supply Technician, Musician.

Officers: Maritime Surface and Sub-surface, Naval Control of Shipping, Logistics, Chaplain, Director of Music.

For more information contact your local Naval Reserve unit, a Canadian Forces Recruiting Centre, or call **1-800-856-8488**.

You can also visit our Web Site through **www.dnd.ca**

www.mdn.ca

Vous désirez jouer un rôle actif dans la protection des intérêts et de l'intégrité territoriale maritimes du Canada? Eh bien, joignez-vous à la Réserve navale dès aujourd'hui! Peu importe que vous déteniez un emploi ou non, ou encore que vous soyez étudiant, la Réserve navale vous offre la possibilité d'apprendre un métier tout en exerçant un emploi rémunéré à bord des nouveaux navires de défense côtière de la classe Kingston.

QUI EST LE RÉSERVISTE DE LA MARINE?

Un réserviste est avant tout un citoyen doublement impliqué à sa vie civile tout en exerçant une carrière militaire en travaillant certains soirs et fins de semaine ainsi que pendant l'été dans un métier de son choix. Dans la Réserve navale, on retrouve entre autres des étudiants, des enseignants, des avocats, des secrétaires, etc. Le service est à temps partiel et le réserviste n'est pas obligé de quitter le Canada. Également, il peut être libéré à 30 jours d'avis.

VOICI LES CRITÈRES D'ADMISSIBILITÉ

- être citoyen canadien ou résident permanent;
- avoir complété la 3ᵉ année du Secondaire pour les métiers des militaires du rang ou posséder un diplôme d'études secondaires pour les postes d'officiers;
- être en bonne santé et posséder une bonne condition physique.

FORMATION

Aucune formation préalable dans le métier n'est nécessaire, à l'exception de celui de musicien. La Réserve navale se charge tant de la formation militaire que de l'instruction pour le métier choisi. Il est à noter que tous les postes sont également ouverts aux hommes et aux femmes.

SALAIRE

En qualité de membres des Forces canadiennes, les réservistes reçoivent un salaire qui varie selon le grade. Il s'agit d'une excellente perspective d'emploi d'été pour les étudiants à temps plein.

POSTES DISPONIBLES DANS LA RÉSERVE NAVALE

Militaires du rang: Manœuvrier, communicateur naval, opérateur (information de combat naval), opérateur (systèmes de mécanique navale), plongeur d'inspection portuaire, cuisinier, commis de soutien de gestion des ressources, technicien en approvisionnement, musicien.

Officiers: Opérations maritimes de surface et sous-marines, contrôle naval de la navigation commerciale, logistique, aumônerie, directeur musical.

Pour plus de renseignements, communiquez avec l'unité de Réserve navale de votre localité ou avec le Centre de recrutement de votre région au **1 800 856-8488**.

Vous pouvez également visiter notre site Web à travers **www.mdn.ca**

Canada

The place to go to find work

Youth Employment Service
TORONTO

- YES has many full-time job listings, as well as subsidized jobs for youth through the Job Connect program.

- YES expert staff provides assistance for job searchers of all ages, plus FREE voicemail, computer use, Internet, faxing, photocopying, resume help and TTC tickets.

- YES helps thousands of students find summer work every year.

- The Youth Business Centre (YBC) is a YES program that helps 18-30 year-olds start their own businesses.

Youth Employment Service
call YES: **(416) 504-5516**
555 Richmond Street West,
Suite 711 (7th floor), Toronto
www.yes.on.ca
email:yes@yes.on.ca

www.WorkinfoNET.ca

Targeting career, learning and labour market information you need to S U C C E E D. Free, complete and up-to-date.

WorkinfoNET
info-Emploi

Sponsored by:
Human Resources Development Canada   Développement des ressources humaines Canada

Creation

The 2001 Edition of *The Canada Student Employment Guide* has been compiled and produced by the Student Employment Network. This organization has been created to provide high school, college, and university students with a practical, on-going source of employment information.

In today's ever-changing labour market, students continue to represent one of the largest groups of unemployed individuals within our population. This, coupled with the fact that there exists a large communication gap between what employers look for and what job seekers expect, has made the search for employment more difficult than ever.

This publication has been designed to help minimize these obstacles while giving readers a greater understanding of the ever-changing job market upon which they will soon be entering. We surveyed hundreds of companies across the country, and asked them the simple question of what they look for in a potential candidate. This book is a compilation of their responses. It is our hope that when equipped with this type of information the chances of finding employment can be significantly increased.

The Canada Student Employment Guide will be updated annually in order to provide the most current information. Please write us with any comments or suggestions you may have, as your feedback is important to us.

Table of Contents

Introduction	9
Acknowledgment	10
User's Guide	11

Part I:

Ten Essential Strategies for a Successful Job Search	16

Part II:

Company Index	40
Industry Index	50
Geographical Index	62

Part III:

Company Profiles	74

Part IV:

College Index	550
University Index	606
Chartered Accounting Index	697
Part Time/Summer Index	713
Co-op/Internship Index	731

Warning - Disclaimer

While every effort has been made to make this book as complete and accurate as possible, this is not guaranteed. The publisher and its contributors do not accept any responsibility for any omissions or errors in information found in this book. Report of any omissions or inaccuracies to the Student Employment Network would be appreciated for future annual editions.

Introduction

Welcome to the 2001 edition of *The Canada Student Employment Guide*. Over the past year we have been working hard to update the information on almost 1,000 company profiles contained in the book. We have also added a new section entitled **Co-ops and Internships**. In response to some of your suggestions we have been conducting research on various co-operative and internship opportunities across Canada. More and more firms are offering these kinds of programs, so make sure to investigate them. We will continue to expand this section in future editions of the book.

Unlike other directories, we have included a unique section called **Ten Essential Strategies For A Successful Job Search**. A valuable component of the book, this section will guide you through all the important steps of looking for work and provide you with a wealth of information to help jump-start your job search. Make sure you have a look! In addition to making the book more value-added than ever before, you'll notice that we have kept the cost of the book down….way down! In order to make the book as accessible as possible for young people we have not increased the price from last year. No other directory with so much information comes close to this price!

For those of you that have not seen *The Canada Student Employment Guide* - it is truly a unique publication. Many resources today illustrate the "how to" of finding a job: how to prepare your resume, how to be effective in an interview, and how to succeed in the job market. Although this is important information individuals, especially youth, also need the practical information about **where** companies are located, **who** to apply to, and specifically **what** these firms look for in a potential candidate. We believe this book can help close the communication gap between individuals and companies and, ultimately increase a job seeker's chances of securing meaningful employment.

When we first published this book in 1995 we had to 'chase' employers across the country to confirm their inclusion. However, the tide has changed! In recent years, companies have actively contacted us to be a part of our publication. Feedback suggests that the success of our book is a result of its win-win format. Employers get their message out to candidates for free, in turn getting a better pool of applicants, and youth get a clearer picture of a firm's expectations in the labour market through essential company information. What a concept!

Keep in mind that that the information outlined in this book is a directory of company information to help you get started in your job hunt – it is not a listing of current job openings. Use the information in this book as a tool, in conjunction with other resources to get the most out of your job search. By conducting research on other companies, and understanding the career field you plan on entering, you will have a far greater chance of finding success in the job market.

What's new with us? Our company, Student Employment Network, has been growing by leaps and bounds! In addition to producing *The Canada Student Employment Guide* we have updated and released our second edition of *The Canadian Job Directory*. As well, we are excited to introduce another new resource for young people – *Ten Way's to Straight A's*. This new book is sure to be popular as it helps youths understand the skills necessary to achieve success in school… and beyond! You can order these titles by completing the order form at the back of this book, or by visiting our website at www.studentjobs.com.

Acknowledgment

Each year this book represents the culmination of hard work by many individuals. Thank you to Douglas Duke at Dash Communications for his wonderful editing skills, Matthew Labutte for another outstanding cover design, and Lou Chenier for his superb assistance in making sure you're orders get to you! To all of you a great big thank you! A special thanks to Maureen Makra, Eileen Mucci, Darcie Sherman and Daniel Kerzner for all of your support, encouragement, and most of all inspiration. Without you this book would not be possible.

User's Guide

Scope

The Canada Student Employment Guide presents information in a variety of ways to allow readers to obtain a broad overview of career opportunities, as well as reference specific information quickly and easily.

The information found in this guide was collected from employer surveys mailed out to human resource departments between April and September, 2000. Firms have provided this data with the intent of illustrating specific characteristics they consider to be important in the selection of potential candidates. Therefore, the presence of a firm's profile in this guide does not necessarily imply the current availability of positions within the company. *The Canada Student Employment Guide* is a directory of major employers across the country, not a directory of current jobs available.

Use this book to help put your job search strategy on the right path. It contains a wide array of valuable information that will assist you in looking for employment and launching your career. Remember, this book is a starting point. It is not intended to replace any effort that you, the jobseeker, should devote to your job hunt.

While we have worked hard to make this book as accurate as possible, please keep in mind that inevitably some of the company information will have changed. This is especially true in regards to contact names, and telephone/fax numbers. It is wise to verify some of this data before you apply to a firm. Take a few minutes to read the next few pages, and learn how best to put *The Canada Student Employment Guide* to work for you.

Format

PART I

Ten Essential Strategies for a Successful Job Search

This section provides job seekers with valuable employment strategies and tips that are beneficial to all. Readers will learn step-by-step some of the most important methods to power up the job search and ultimately increase their chances of finding employment. We are confident that these strategies will be both helpful and informative! Be sure to read this section in order to maximize the use of the more than 900 employer profiles contained in this book.

PART II

Company Index

This index refers the reader to the pages on which company profiles can be found. The firms are arranged alphabetically for quick reference.

Industry Index

This section alphabetically lists companies according to industry sector, and provides the page numbers of where organizational profiles can be found. An outline of specific industry areas is included at the beginning of the index.

Geographical Index

Refers the reader to the province in which the firm's head office is located. Companies are listed alphabetically within each province.

PART III

Company Profiles

The company profiles describe each organization in detail, providing information that is of most interest to the job applicant. The addresses indicated within each profile are in most cases the firm's head office, unless otherwise specified. Although only one address appears, this does not mean that individuals should not apply elsewhere. To get the most out of your job search, individuals are encouraged to check for, and apply to, branches or regional offices that are near them.

Each Company Profile contains the following information:

- **Company Location** - The address, phone number, and fax number of the company's head office and a contact name. E-mail and website addresses are also included in many of the profiles.

- **Company Description** - An outline of what the firm does including the number of employees.

- **Academic Fields** - Those educational backgrounds that desirable candidates are most likely to have.

- **Critical Skills** - Non-academic or personal skills that the firm considers important.

- **Types of Positions** - Entry-level positions or departments where potential candidates could work.

- **Starting Salary** - The average annual salary a recent graduate could expect.

- **Company Benefits** - What the company offers in terms of employee benefits and the type of training and development opportunities available.

- **Method of Correspondence** - How potential applicants should inquire about job opportunities.

- **Part Time/Summer Employment** - Whether a company generally hires for part time and summer job opportunities; some potential summer positions; and the best time to apply.

- **Co-op/Internship** - Whether a company provides co-op or internship opportunities. This is a new section of the book and will be continually updated and expanded.

PART IV

College Index

This index lists popular College Diploma Programs that firms consider important in the selection of candidates. The section summarizes those academic qualifications found within the company profiles. Page numbers where individual company profiles are located are listed to the right of the firm's name.

University Index

This index lists popular University Degree Programs that firms consider important in the selection of candidates. The section summarizes those academic qualifications found within the company profiles. Page numbers where individual company profiles are located are listed to the right of the firm's name.

Chartered Accounting Index

This index lists Chartered Accounting designations that firms consider important in the selection of candidates. The section summarizes those academic qualifications found within the company profiles. Page numbers where individual company profiles are located are listed to the right of the firm's name.

Part Time/Summer Index

This index alphabetically lists companies that occasionally or regularly hire candidates for part time or summer employment. In this section firms that potentially hire for part time work are listed first, and firms that potentially hire for the summer months are listed second. Page numbers where individual company profiles can be found are listed to the right of the firm's name.

Co-op/Internship Index

This index alphabetically lists companies that currently have a co-op or internship opportunities within their organization, or are interested in establishing a program in the near future. Page numbers where individual company profiles can be found are listed to the right of the firm's name.

The Canada Student Employment Guide

PART I

Ten Essential Strategies For A Successful Job Search

Ten Essential Strategies
For A Successful Job Search

Strategy One: Develop a Career Plan

Strategy Two: Take an Inventory of Your Skills

Strategy Three: Network to Create Opportunities

Strategy Four: Research Your Industry

Strategy Five: Dynamite Résumés

Strategy Six: A Great Cover Letter

Strategy Seven: Winning the Interview

Strategy Eight: The Follow-up Letter

Strategy Nine: Effective Job Search Methods

Strategy Ten: Maintain a Proper Attitude

The Successful Job Search

Despite all the obstacles you may face, finding a job does not have to be a painstaking, overwhelming process! While most everyone agrees that looking for employment is not an easy task, there are a number of relatively easy steps you can take to increase your odds of landing that perfect job.

During our correspondence with thousands of companies across the country this past year, we came up with several ideas to help guide you through the job search process. So, before you start blindly sending your résumé out to all the employers listed in this book (which will, in most cases, lead to a stack of rejection letters), take a moment to read through these **"Ten Essential Job Search Strategies"**.

Doing some groundwork now will save you a lot of time and money down the road. For your own reference, try to make some personal notes on how these steps can best be incorporated into your particular job search. While no one step is sufficient on its own, a healthy combination of as many of these strategies as possible is your best chance to securing a meaningful, fulfilling job.

Strategy One: Develop a Career Plan

Looking for employment can be an extremely challenging and intimidating task. Let's face it, finding work is a big exercise in marketing yourself. Some of you may have been exposed to the basics of marketing in the past, either through formal education or prior work experience. Remember, when selling a product to a specific target market, you must choose what your product will be, who your customer is, and how you will get your product into the customers' hands. A good job search should involve much of the same research and planning used in marketing to bring your product to 'life'. In this case however, the product is you!

When preparing to look for work, you must first decide how you are going to market your 'product'. *What are you going to sell?* Learn to recognize all of the skills you possess (taking an inventory of your skills is discussed in the next step). *Who are you selling to?* Decide which employers you are going to target. *How are going to get your product to the customer?* Determine which methods you are going to use to ensure potential employers are aware of you.

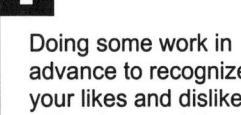

Know Yourself

Doing some work in advance to recognize your likes and dislikes will make your job search easier.

Achieving success in the marketing of any product is no easy task. There is a tremendous amount of competition out there! If you hastily choose a product without giving it some thought, or if you send out marketing material without considering your target market, you will certainly have wasted a lot of valuable time and money. What's worse, however, is that your product simply will not sell.

The Canada Student Employment Guide

These marketing pitfalls apply to your job search as well. If you do not give the proper thought to what you are offering to an employer, or if you do not educate yourself about the companies you're attempting to sell your talents to, then it's very likely that your product will not sell. That is, you will not be hired! You *must* develop a 'plan of attack' to ensure that you are setting realistic goals for yourself and following a clear direction. It is important to take the time to think about what you want and then go after it!

Deciding what it is that you want to do takes some real soul searching. Think about the jobs or tasks you did in the past. If you separate those that you liked from those that you disliked, you will begin to have a clearer picture of where your interests lie. Make a list of these 'likes' and 'dislikes' and update it frequently. There are no easy choices and some of it will undoubtedly be hit and miss. The best thing you can do for yourself though, is to try as many different types of jobs as possible so that you can realistically assess their merits. The old cliché rings true: "You'll never know until you try!"

Start Your Job Search Early

Placing time restrictions on your job search leads to increased stress and disappointing choices.

Whatever you do, make a concerted effort to think about your career choices now! Do some research to educate yourself about different industries and occupations. If you can, talk to people already working in an area that interests you. If you remain conscious of your environment and work to continually upgrade your job search skills, you will be able to set clear, concise goals. This is half the battle to finding gainful employment.

A career plan does not have to be a formal document with every imaginable contingency attached. Your plan can be as simple as mapping out a few experiences which have allowed you to learn some valuable skills and listing some specific ideas as to how to best utilize your job search efforts. If necessary, visit your high school guidance department or your college or university career centre to obtain assistance in this area. As well, there are a number of useful career planning books that can help you in this regard. Do the planning now and you are certain to save time and frustration in the future!

Strategy Two: Take an Inventory of Your Skills

This step easily could have been incorporated into the career planning step above. However, taking inventory of your skills is of such great importance to a good job search, that it needs more clarification. Once again, we can relate this concept to the field of marketing.

Let's say that you are selling a car. If you are unclear as to the benefits and features of the car, or don't have good reasons why someone should buy it, then why would anyone make the purchase? In other words, if you don't know what you're selling, how are you going to sell it? This applies to the job search as well. An employer wants to know what features or benefits (i.e. skills) you have to offer. They will not search for these answers themselves. You must make it clear and concise and this is why taking an inventory of your skills is so very important.

What skills do you have to offer an employer? The answer to this question will be different for each individual. Be aware, however, that your skills are made up of both academic qualifications *and* personal attributes. Based on the contact we've had with employers, it's interesting to note that personal skills such as *communication skills, leadership skills* and *workplace adaptability,* are considered to be just as important – and in some cases more important – than the academic degree or diploma you obtained. So, what does this mean for you, the job seeker? Quite simply, make sure you sell your personal skills as actively as your academic background. Employers want to know that you have these skills!

Listed below are some of the more common personal skills that employers consider important. While there are many others not listed here, this is a good starting point. Look through the list and try to come up with past experiences that have allowed you to gain some of these valuable skills.

Adaptable	*Dependable*	*Good Communication*	*Patient*
Analytical	*Diligent*	*Good With Figures*	*Personable*
Artistic	*Diplomatic*	*Good Written Skills*	*Productive*
Confident	*Efficient*	*Innovative*	*Professional*
Creative	*Enthusiastic*	*Leadership*	*Responsible*
Decisive	*Flexible*	*Organized*	*Team Player*

Most of you can probably think of many experiences, either from school or previous employment, that have given you the opportunity to use most of the skills listed above. Don't short-change yourself! Having leadership skills does not necessarily mean that you have supervised employees. For example, have you ever been a lifeguard? Or, have you ever been in charge of a group assignment to ensure that all of the work gets done in a timely fashion? Both of these examples illustrate ways in which you may have obtained important leadership skills. Make sure you dig deep into your work history to come up with a few examples for each of the skills listed above.

Put Yourself In An Employer's Shoes

If you were looking to hire, what strengths and qualities would you look for in a potential candidate?

When you have found your examples, choose the ones you feel best about. Which of the personal skills listed best describe you as a person? Be sure to include these skills on your résumé in addition to your academic achievements. Your résumé will be a much better snapshot of exactly who you are and will give potential employers a more concise picture of your strengths and accomplishments.

Strategy Three: Network to Create Opportunities

Networking is a term we hear much about but often don't use nearly enough to benefit from its enormous potential. In most cases, networking can be the best strategy to a successful job search. In a recent survey of more than 1,000 young people, greater than two out of three individuals attributed finding their current job to having known someone, usually through family or friends.

In essence, networking is an ongoing process to establish and maintain a rapport or relationship with individuals in your field. It is not a short-term process, but its long-term effects can be dramatic as unforeseen opportunities can arise in areas you may never have thought possible. The key to smart networking is to let as many people as possible know about your skills and your availability.

Network As Much As Possible

Talk to friends, relatives, teachers, etc. Get out into your professional and local community and meet people who share similar interests as yourself.

As a job seeker, you can begin this process by getting your name recognized within your industry. Joining a trade association and talking to others already 'on the job' is a great way to learn about a particular field. Once people see that you are committed and hardworking, they will identify with you and want to help you in your job search efforts.

Make sure that you are sincere with people. Show a genuine interest in their industry and in other people's personal experiences. Most individuals can tell very easily when you are using them simply to get information. Remember, your approach is the most important aspect of networking. Be polite and courteous and realize there are no shortcuts to finding a job using this strategy. However, the more that people know you're looking for work, the greater the chance you'll find employment through one of these contacts.

Strategy Four: Research Your Industry

Researching prospective employers within your industry is an important strategy towards finding a job in today's competitive market. A lot of job seekers do not conduct this background research and are, therefore, unaware of which companies best match their skills and qualifications. By completing this research, not only will you become more aware of what the company is looking for, but also you may learn valuable information that can be of vital importance during a potential interview.

Research Firms Before Applying To Them

You will better understand a company's needs and impress prospective employers. Write to companies and ask them to send you more information.

At the beginning of your research you may want to spend a bit of time reading about your industry and finding the answers to some important questions. *Is the industry growing? Which are some of the key firms within the industry? Are there any regulations within the industry you should be aware of? What are some of the industry's pros and cons?* These are just a few examples that will help guide you when you are looking for employment. As well, they will set the proper expectations for your job search.

At some point, you will want to develop a list of potential employers. This list will be comprised of those companies that, through your research, you have identified as ones you wish to apply to. Prepare a file that contains your list along with contact information and any pertinent background data on these companies that might be useful should you be given an interview. As your job search continues, update and add to this file often.

The Canada Student Employment Guide

Where are you going to get this information, you ask? Perhaps the best place to begin is your high school guidance department or your college or university career centre. The government employment centres can also be very helpful. Finally, don't forget your local public library. All of these establishments are excellent sources of employer information. If you don't find what you're looking for yourself, be sure to ask someone for assistance! You'll be surprised how much information you uncover.

Read Your Local Newspaper

Keep abreast of current news items relating to firms and employment. This will help you to uncover industry trends and seek out new opportunities.

You can also obtain a wealth of employer information on the Internet. Most major firms have a web page soliciting their products or services and, in some cases, even providing you with the opportunity to apply for available positions online. Joining a trade or association is another valuable method of learning about prospective employers and will help you to stay on top of the latest industry trends. There are a number of employer directories (other than this great resource, of course!) that you may find useful and worth checking out. Below is a short list of just a few of them.

Associations Canada
Canadian Almanac & Directory
The Canadian Job Directory
The Financial Post 500
Guide to Canadian Manufacturers
Scott's Industrial Directory

The Blue Book of Canadian Business
Canadian Company Handbook
Canadian Key Business Directory
Fraser's Canadian Trade Directory
International Business & Trade Directory
Survey of Industrials

As you can see, there are many terrific resources to help get you started in your research. However, another great way to learn about employers is to speak directly to individuals who already work in the industry you plan to enter. Some of the information discovered in this may be even more valuable than the literature you read since a lot of published data is produced by the industry itself. In other words, talking informally to individuals may provide some extra insight that you could not obtain otherwise.

Strategy Five: Dynamite Résumés

The résumé is one of the most important tools of the job seeker. It is a vital part of your marketing strategy and when written properly, will jump out at prospective employers in a way that says, "Hire me!" The résumé is basically a written summary of your educational history, work experience, past achievements and interests that are constructed in a positive manner. When putting together your résumé it is important to keep it short, focused, concise and accurate.

The résumé itself contains specific components that are common to all types. These include contact information such as name, address, and phone number; a career objective statement (optional); educational history; skills and abilities; work experience and volunteer work (optional); activities and interests; and references.

The Canada Student Employment Guide

Each component of the résumé is of significant importance to the final package. Following is a brief description of each of these components:

Contact Information: Place your full name at the top of your résumé and include your address and telephone number. If you have a fax number or e-mail address, you can include it as well.

Career Objective: This is a statement that outlines your career goals. It should be very brief – perhaps a sentence or two – and give a strong sense of what direction you plan to take on your career path.

Education: All relevant education should be included here such as college, university or any technical schools that you may have attended. Your high school education can be included as well, however, do not include elementary school. Any awards or scholarships can be outlined separately.

Skills and Abilities: This section allows you to highlight all those impressive skills and abilities that you obtained through school, past employment, volunteer work, and personal activities. To write this section you must complete step two – *Identify Your Skills*.

 Have a Professional Resume

Nothing puts your resume at the bottom of an employer's pile – or worse yet in the garbage – than a hand-written or illegible resume. The resume format has to contain all of your information in a concise and easy-to-read manner.

Work Experience: In point form, list your past jobs in chronological order. Include dates, company names and locations and the responsibilities and duties you had in each position. Any volunteer experience you may have acquired can also be included in this section.

Activities and Interests: The best type of candidate is one who appears well-rounded and has varied interests. Including some diverse activities is a signal to employers that you have gained some effective personal skills.

References: Simply indicating "References available on request" is appropriate. However, ensure that you have prepared these references from your academic, employment, or personal background should you be asked to supply them.

There are different résumé formats depending on the components you would like to emphasize. The two most common styles are the **chronological** résumé and the **functional** résumé. An example of each type of résumé (chronological, functional and **combination** format) is on the next few pages.

Chronological Résumé: Organized in reverse chronological order so that your latest schooling and last job are listed first. This style emphasizes job duties and should be used if you have a steady work history and if your most recent experiences relate to your desired field.

Functional Résumé: Focuses on skills and abilities while de-emphasizing job titles and employers. It should be used if you have been out of the work force for some time, or if you want to highlight specific skills and strengths that your most recent jobs don't necessarily reflect.

Combination Résumé: As a modified version of the above formats, this style emphasizes both work-related duties and skills so that you can highlight strengths acquired from past experiences.

Keep your résumé organized, easy to read and brief. Use point form beginning with action verbs that accentuate your strengths and positive experiences and avoid the use of "I" when emphasizing your accomplishments. Below is a brief list of some of the more common résumé verbs that can be used to accurately describe your acquired abilities.

Achieved	Determined	Initiated	Produced
Administered	Directed	Launched	Promoted
Analyzed	Established	Maintained	Provided
Arranged	Evaluated	Managed	Researched
Assisted	Examined	Motivated	Reviewed
Completed	Executed	Organized	Scheduled
Conducted	Facilitated	Planned	Sold
Coordinated	Generated	Prepared	Supervised
Delivered	Identified	Presented	Trained
Designed	Implemented	Processed	Updated

Remember, your résumé is the first contact that you will likely make with an employer – so make it a good one! Keep it on standard 8-1/2" x 11" premium paper and ensure that you are using a printer that is capable of producing good quality print. In addition, your résumé must be 100% grammatically accurate and free of spelling errors.

Post Your Resume on the Internet

The more exposure your resume gets, the better. Many firms use the Internet to actively recruit candidates and advertise job openings. Make sure you tap into this medium.

Be sure to show your résumé to a lot of people and allow them to critique it for you. One advantage to having your family, friends, and others close to you look at your résumé is that they can pick up on important skills and strengths that you may have failed to mention. It may also be a good idea to post your résumé on the Internet, either through a job board or by having it placed on a home page of your own. The more exposure your résumé receives the better!

As well, if you are having trouble preparing your résumé, or need some extra guidance, make sure you visit your school's guidance department or career centre. They offer a wealth of information and can help you to overcome some of the stumbling blocks you may encounter. There are also a number of very useful résumé books that contain everything you'll need to know on the subject. Some books will also provide hundreds of sample résumés for every type of situation. Check them out!

The Canada Student Employment Guide

Chronological Résumé Sample

JAMES ROBERTS
102 Pape Ave.,
Toronto, Ontario
M79 3B4
(416) 555-9233
jroberts@interlog.com

EDUCATION

1992 – 1997   **BACHELOR OF COMMERCE**
York University
North York, Ontario

        Relevant courses include: Sales/Marketing   Management Accounting
                                                Business Law   Mircoeconomics

WORK EXPERIENCE

May 1996 –   **ACCOUNTING ASSISTANT**
Present   Drake Office Systems, Mississauga, Ontario
- processed orders and prepared end-of-month statements for
regular client base
- assisted in designing new accounting software package for the firm
- knowledgeably answered customer inquiries concerning their account

Summers   **TELEPHONE REPRESENTATIVE**
1992-1995   Triumph Advertising, Scarborough, Ontario
- conducted telephone interviews with clients regarding new, innovative
  consumer products
- achieved top sales award for the month of June in 1995
- diligently performed routine duties such as filing and photocopying

PROFESSIONAL
MEMBERSHIPS   Canadian Business Association – Associate Member

INTERESTS
- Enjoy reading many business magazines including 'Canadian Business' and
'Fortune'

- Recently awarded first prize in Grade 12 business simulation project at
York University

- Active member of the Toronto East Softball Association

REFERENCES   Available on request

Functional Résumé Sample

MARY ALICE FISHER

885 Robson St., Vancouver, B.C., V8T 4N6
(604) 555-8744

OBJECTIVE

To contribute over 3 years experience in graphic design, communications and administration to an entry-level position in advertising.

SKILLS AND ABILITIES

- Effectively performed advertising duties for small public relations firm.

- Gained experience in many creative aspects including storyboard layout and the development of marketing strategies for clients.

- Demonstrated ability to work well in a team setting, and assist others to meet their deadlines.

- Thoroughly researched sales and industry guidelines for advertising convention held last year.

- Experience in business writing and accounting procedures within department.

- Recognized by firm for ability to communicate effectively with clients and keep them up-to-date on their accounts.

EDUCATION

BACHELOR OF ARTS - ENGLISH
University of Victoria, Victoria, B.C.

ADDITIONAL INFORMATION

Keep abreast of latest industry information by reading various publications such as *Marketing Today*
Awarded Most Valuable Player at university basketball meet in 1996
Completed Saint John's First Aid Course in December of 1995

REFERENCES

Supplied upon request

Combination Résumé Sample

MICHELLE CASGRAIN

3600 Avenue du Parc, Apt 323 Tel: (514) 555-3921
Montreal, Quebec Fax: (514) 555-6497
H2X 3R2

EDUCATION

1993 – 1995 **BUSINESS ACCOUNTING DIPLOMA**
Ecole Polytechnique de Montreal
Montreal, Quebec

WORK EXPERIENCE

June 1994 – Present
JUNIOR ACCOUNTING ASSISTANT
Premador Installations, Montreal, Quebec
- organized accounts payable and accounts receivable procedures
- helped prepare annual accounting statements including balance sheet
- trained new employees on relevant accounting software

May 1991 - Sept. 1993
SALES ASSOCIATE
Hudson's Bay Company, Montreal, Quebec
- sold sporting goods to customers and responded to customer inquiries
- achieved sales well above quotas that were established for each month
- participated in year-end inventory of products

SKILLS AND ABILITIES

COMMUNICATION
- Effectively instructed and presented staff with new accounting applications
- Diligently responded to customer needs and generated high levels of sales

ANALYTICAL
- Demonstrated ability to work well with numbers in preparing accounting statements
- Researched and formulated amounts for various expense accounts

ORGANIZATIONAL
- Assisted in preparing sales floor and department for inventory procedures
- Coordinated the accumulation of sales and costs figures for each department in order to meet strict time deadlines

ADDITIONAL INFORMATION

- Active member of the Montreal Board of Trade
- Volunteer annually in the Variety Village Walkathon
- Enjoy chess and reading science fiction novels

REFERENCES AVAILABLE ON REQUEST

The Canada Student Employment Guide

Strategy Six: A Great Cover Letter

The cover letter is an important job search tool that must always accompany your résumé. So much time is focused on a dynamic résumé that we often ignore, or hastily put together, our cover letters. Take the time to prepare your cover letter just as carefully as you would your résumé.

The benefit of the cover letter is that it provides you with an extra marketing tool to sell yourself to a company. In the cover letter you can show interest in an employer that you can't show in a résumé. As well, you have the opportunity to point out one or two key skills or achievements that may pique the interest of the company and lead to a more thorough examination of your résumé.

While each cover letter should be unique and personal, there are specific components that form each paragraph. They are as follows:

First Paragraph: Keeping it short with the intent of generating interest, outline the position you are applying for (or why you would benefit the organization) and what prompted you to write (i.e. want ad, article in the newspaper, career fair, networking contact, etc.).

 Always Include a Cover Letter

Nothing is more frustrating to employers than receiving a resume with no indication of its purpose, position you are applying for, or person the resume should be directed to.

Second Paragraph: Explain how the organization would benefit from your qualifications and highlight any skills or accomplishments that may set you apart from other candidates.

Third Paragraph: Incorporate any relevant education or past experience that might make you a more attractive candidate to the employer.

Fourth Paragraph: Express your interest in the company and make a request for an interview (or informational interview). Suggest how you will follow up and ensure that your last sentence thanks the employer for their consideration.

An example of a cover letter is provided on the following page. It is meant to illustrate all of the components of a 'typical' cover letter, however, feel free to adapt them to meet your specific needs. Most importantly, write the cover letter to sound as personal as possible. Avoid using form letters as employers can pick up on this very quickly.

Keep your cover letter brief and to the point. Don't just repeat information verbatim from your résumé, but strive to explain what you can offer a company and not what you can gain from them. As with your résumé, do not overuse the personal pronoun "I", and make sure that your cover letter is error-free.

Cover Letter Sample

4680 Leeds St..
Halifax, Nova Scotia
B3J 3C4

May 15, 1999

Ms. R. Taylor
Manager of Human Resources
Envision Graphics Inc.
54 Sylvia Ave.
Halifax, Nova Scotia
B3R 1J9

Dear Ms. Taylor,

I recently attended a career fair at Dalhousie University and was extremely impressed when I visited your company's innovative booth and discovered some new design services that you had on display. I am currently in my last year of a four-year graphics arts program and am familiar with most of the techniques that you demonstrated. I would be very interested in obtaining a position within your graphic design firm.

My last job entailed working as an assistant to the boss in a small graphic arts company. In addition to handling several projects at once, I was responsible for learning the latest graphics software packages. I was also in charge of many bookkeeping tasks so that customer accounts were kept up-to-date. Since the firm was small, I gained a large amount of hands-on experience from this position.

Through my university studies I have been involved in many assignments that have allowed me to add to my personal skills. One project in particular involved working with classmates to interview firms and assisting them in creating in-house graphics departments. During this project, I was able to enhance my communication and team player skills.

I am confident that my strong academic background and past experience would make me an ideal candidate for a graphics design position within your company. I look forward to meeting you at some point in the near future to discuss any employment possibilities that may exist. I will contact you next week to arrange a time. Thank you for your consideration.

Yours truly,

Jonathan Andrews

Strategy Seven: Winning the Interview

For many people, the interview is the most daunting and intimidating part of the job search process. Your chances of landing a position within any company depend almost entirely on the impression they get of you during an interview. What will you do? Fortunately, there is hope! A little preparation before the interview goes a long way.

Jobs Are Won In Interviews

Anticipate questions that may be asked and plan honest, high-impact answers. Go through mock interviews to become more prepared for various interview situations.

Once the interview has been arranged, you should do some in-depth research on the company. Find out its main products or services, types of customers, principal locations, size, parent company, and rank in the industry. These are just a few important points to consider. The more you can find out the better. If possible, speak to someone at the firm before the interview as their insight could be invaluable.

Before the interview, make sure that you remind yourself of everything on your résumé and that you are able to expand on any points that are listed on it. The interviewer will likely refer to it many times during the interview while asking their questions. Since you wrote it, this shouldn't be a problem.

Depending on how many interviews you have attended in the past, it's a good idea to try some role-playing so that you gain confidence and feel a bit more at ease. With a trusted individual, act out a full interview, trying to make it as realistic as possible. The more you practice, the better prepared you will be when the real interview occurs. Give it a try!

As for the interview itself, there are a few tips to keep in mind. First and foremost, be on time! Nothing will jeopardize your chances more than showing up late to an interview! Allow yourself lots of extra time in case of unforeseen circumstances and make sure you dress professionally. Bring along a pen and a notepad, and carry a briefcase or a professional folder containing extra copies of your résumé.

When you meet your interviewer, smile and extend your hand for a firm handshake. During the interview try to be attentive and relaxed. On the following page is a list of interview questions to help you prepare.

Set Up Informational Interviews

Even if a company is not hiring, ask people if you may take 30 minutes of their time to talk to them about their business. Most people are willing to speak with you because it's non-threatening.

Answer questions concisely and honestly. There is nothing to fear; the interviewer is on your side. When appropriate, ask questions about the company (but not those relating to salary!) When the interview is finally over, consider it to have been a learning experience. Remember, the first interview is always the hardest. The most important piece of advice is to be confident. You can do it!

The Canada Student Employment Guide

30 Common Interview Questions

1. Why do you want to work in this field?
2. Why do you specifically want to work for this company?
3. What do you know about our company?
4. Why do you feel you are the right candidate for this job? What do you think you can bring to this company?
5. What things are important to you in the type of position you want?
6. How has your education prepared you for this type of job?
7. Which school subjects did you like the most and why?
8. Do you plan to continue your education?
9. What are some extracurricular activities that you enjoy?
10. What are your short-term goals?
11. Where do you see yourself in 5 years?
12. What do you like to do in your leisure time?
13. What are a couple of accomplishments in your life that have given you the most satisfaction and why?
14. What are some important decisions that you have made? What was the result?
15. Which part time/summer job that you have had did you like most?
16. What did you like least about this past job?
17. What are some skills that you feel you have gained from your past employment and education?
18. What motivates you to put forth your best effort?
19. What stands out in your mind as your most successful achievement to date?
20. Explain an important decision you have had to make in the past? How did you make it? What was the result?
21. What are some examples where you have had to work with others? What were some of your experiences in this regard?
22. What is your greatest strength?
23. What is your greatest weakness?
24. What are your salary expectations?
25. Tell me about a time when you were faced with conflict and how you resolved it?
26. Tell me about a time when you were upset with someone? How did you handle it?
27. Tell me about a time when you were stressed? How did you handle it?
28. What hours are you willing to work?
29. Are you flexible in these hours? Can you work overtime if necessary?
30. Are you willing to travel?

Strategy Eight: The Follow-Up Letter

After the interview is completed, it's always a good idea to send out a follow-up letter. Even if you feel unhappy with the way you performed during the interview, it is still recommended that you follow things up with a brief letter. This allows you not only to thank the interviewer for their time, but also to re-emphasize a couple of your key strengths. If the interviewer has not yet decided who is to be hired, this letter could be very beneficial.

In your letter, tell the employer that you are still very interested in their organization and the position. As well, if you feel something was missed during the interview, you can mention it in this letter, however, make sure you keep it brief. The follow-up letter should be no more than a half-page. A sample follow-up letter is shown on the next page.

In the closing paragraph, mention your phone number and the hours that you can be reached. Alternatively, you may wish to let the organization know that you will again be following up with a telephone call in several days. Thank the interviewer once more for meeting with you and state that you would be happy to provide any additional information they might require.

Follow-up, Follow-up, Follow-up

Every contact you make should be followed up in some way, either with a phone call, thank you letter, or a card. Following up will make you stand out in the employers' minds and help get you noticed.

Strategy Nine: Effective Job Search Methods

When looking for work, many people only consider the most traditional methods of landing a job. They may look through the job classified section in their local newspaper or they might aimlessly pull out the names of a few companies in their industry and send them their résumé. Some may even limit themselves simply to mentioning it to others, like parents and friends, and then expect that they'll take on the burden of their job search for them. If only job hunting were so easy!

To find a job, you have to be a good detective. Conduct as much investigation and research as possible while ensuring that you leave "no major stone unturned". The most effective job seeker uses these keen detective-like skills. To increase your chances of securing employment, try as many different tactics as possible – don't just rely on one or two traditional methods.

In financial planning, one fundamental rule is to diversify your savings and not put it all in one place. In other words, do not "keep all your eggs in one basket". The same holds true for the job search. Don't concentrate all your efforts in one area. Try many different approaches for the best possible results.

Follow-Up Letter Sample

2408 11th Ave.
Regina, Saskatchewan
S4P 0K1
May 15, 1999

Ms. T. Pasquale
Personnel Manager
Design Stores Inc.
220 College Ave.
Regina, Saskatchewan
S4P 3V7

Dear Ms. Pasquale,

Thank you very much for taking the time to meet with me on July 7th concerning the position of associate buyer within your organization. I enjoyed our conversation immensely and appreciated your unique insight into the fashion industry. Having studied fashion for three years it has definitely become a great passion of mine.

I'm certain that your firm would benefit tremendously from my past education and employment experiences. My communication and organizational skills would provide a wonderful addition to the "team environment" upon which you placed such great emphasis during our conversation. In short, I am very eager to be a part of your organization.

If you need any additional information please do not hesitate to contact me at (416) 555-7967. Thank you once again for the opportunity to meet with you. I look forward to hearing from you in the near future.

Yours truly,

Linda Delaware

The Canada Student Employment Guide

To help you get started, we have provided insight into a few areas to consider when looking for employment. Some effective job search strategies include: *Tap Into the Hidden Job Market, Get on the Internet, Use a Recruiter, Think About Volunteering, Look Into Internship Programs*, and *Consider Self Employment*.

Tap Into the Hidden Job Market

It has been said before: More than 80% of positions are found in the hidden job market. What is the hidden job market? It is simply job openings that exist, but have not yet been advertised. This type of situation occurs within a company more often than not as hiring managers sometimes wait a period of time to see if they can fill the position before launching a full-scale search.

Imagine that your neighbour was looking to find someone to mow the lawn or baby-sit. They would likely spend some time asking colleagues or friends to recommend a candidate before placing an ad in a local newspaper. It is at this stage that job seekers have the greatest chance of landing the best positions since there is far less competition. However, a large effort on your part still needs to be administered at this point.

Research The Hidden Job Market

Statistics show that 80% of jobs are not advertised. Use this book, along with other directories and resources to find companies in the industry you wish to enter. Send them correspondence and remember to follow up.

To find work in the hidden job market, it is best to make many contacts within your industry. By networking constantly, you'll eventually meet someone who's looking for a person with your skills or who knows of someone else who is. As mentioned previously, consider joining a relevant professional association. During their meetings you can network with decision-makers. As long as you are sincere and professional, you will gain a credible reputation and become a wonderful referral for someone in the industry.

Be Realistic In Your Expectations

Don't turn down employment just because it doesn't fit your 'ideal job'. As well, don't apply for positions that you are not qualified for. Keep an open mind and realistically assess all job opportunities.

The hidden job market in a lot of cases is about being in the right place at the right time. The more people you talk to, the better your chances of finding work in this market. Rather than just sending your résumé out to companies that have advertised openings, get to know the key people within organizations through networking.

As well, don't overlook smaller companies for the sake of the larger ones. Nowadays, more job growth occurs within smaller firms and they don't necessarily have the big budgets to spend on advertising job openings. They are a perfect example of the kind of companies that you should seek out in the hidden job market.

The Canada Student Employment Guide

Get on the Internet

With the advent of the "information highway" comes a relatively new way to look for employment. The Internet provides the job seeker with a truly global search, removing all geographic boundaries. There is a massive amount of company and job search information that can be uncovered using this medium. Individuals who are currently "surfing the net" can gain a large competitive advantage over those who are not.

Post Your Resume on the Internet

The more exposure your resume gets, the better. Many firms use the Internet to actively recruit candidates and advertise job openings.

In certain industries, the Internet is a perfect vehicle for finding a job. Many companies listed in this book have indicated that they actively recruit candidates on the Internet and use e-mail as a predominant method of correspondence. Don't let these potential opportunities pass you by – get on the Internet!

Use the Internet to complement your overall job search efforts. There are literally thousands of employment sites that can be found on the Internet. Below, we have listed a few of the more popular Canadian Internet sites to help you get started.

CACEE's WorkWeb	www.cacee.com
Campus Access	www.campusaccess.com
Campus WorkLink	www.campusworklink.com
Canadian Career Page	www.canadiancareers.com
Canada Employment Weekly	www.mediacorp2.com/
Canadian Jobs Catalogue	www.kenevacorp.mb.ca/
Career Edge	www.careeredge.org
Career Owl	www.careerowl.ca
CareerMosaic	www.careermosaic.com
Mazemaster	www.mazemaster.on.ca/
The Monster Board Canada	www.monster.ca
NextSteps	www.cadvision.com/next/
Student Employment Network	www.studentjobs.com
Youth Resource Network of Canada	www.youth.gc.ca/

In order to view other exciting job sites, use one of the popular on-line search engines (i.e. Yahoo, Lycos, Excite, Infoseek, etc.) and conduct a search using keywords (i.e. job, career, employment, Canada, etc.) that focus on your specific needs.

Newsgroups can also provide a wonderful way to learn more about an industry and to network with others. Many firms – especially those in the high technology sector – actively post positions on employment newsgroups. Some of the more popular Canadian employment newsgroups include: ab.jobs (Alberta jobs), bc.jobs (British Columbia jobs), can.jobs (Canada jobs), mtl.jobs (Montreal jobs), nb.jobs (New Brunswick jobs), nf.jobs (Newfoundland jobs), ns.jobs (Nova Scotia jobs), ont.jobs (Ontario jobs), qc.jobs (Quebec jobs), and sk.jobs (Saskatchewan jobs).

Use a Recruiter

Among other names, recruiters are also known as headhunters, executive search firms, placement firms, or employment agencies. A recruiter is a commercial enterprise engaged in the business of brining together the employer and the employee candidate. The employment agency can provide to an organization a large choice of efficient applicants, and thus promote a recruiting program that is faster and, in some cases, cheaper.

Talk to a Recruiter

In certain industries recruiters are extremely successful in placing qualified candidates. Do some research on recruiters and see if they are right for you.

Simply put, a recruiter works for a company to find "well-suited" individuals for contract, part-time, or permanent employment. Many recruiters specialize in certain industries or only fill special positions. It is important to contact the proper recruiter for the type of industry or position you wish to enter.

A recruiter is not for everyone, however, a lot of people use them successfully to find employment. Depending on the industry you plan to enter, recruiters can be the perfect job search vehicle. They are most commonly used to fill administrative or office positions as well as jobs in factories or involving more industrial-type work.

When contacting a recruiter, remember that they are not set up to find you employment. Instead, they work to find qualified applicants to suit the needs of the party that pays their fees – the employer. Your objective is to make a recruiting company interested in your skills and qualifications. The most common method of contact is to phone a recruiter, spark their interest, send them your résumé, and then follow up.

Some recruiters may charge a fee to the candidate for their services. As with any company, never give money up-front without researching them thoroughly and making sure that they are not only legitimate, but also that their services best suit your needs. This will alleviate any unnecessary problems down the road. For a listing of some of the major recruiters in Canada, check out our other popular publication *The Canadian Job Directory*. Information on ordering it is located at the back of this book.

Think of Volunteering

Volunteering is a unique way to build upon your skills and gain valuable experience to add to your résumé. It also gives you wonderful insight into various jobs to help you in your career exploration process. One other benefit to volunteering is that it offers you the chance to get your foot in the door. If you do a good job and they like your work, who knows . . . sooner or later they may offer you a paid position. When conducting your job search always be on the lookout for good volunteering opportunities.

How do you get a volunteer position? Most likely, there are many volunteering opportunities within your own community, you'll just have to do some research to find them. Firstly, visit your local career centre or guidance department and see if they know of any opportunities. Many times, organizations will go directly to your school looking for interested candidates. As well, visit your local library and try to get a list of community service organizations located close to you. They could probably refer you to large numbers of places that look for volunteers in your own area.

Finding a volunteer position with a larger employer is a little more difficult. Each company has their own rules and regulations concerning volunteer work. Quite simply, some welcome them, and some don't. The best approach is to call an employer and ask them if they have a volunteer coordinator on staff or if they would ever consider hiring a volunteer.

Volunteer Your Time

You'll gain valuable experience and become more marketable in the future. Remember to treat your volunteer work as a regular job.

Volunteering can be a wonderful experience and provide you with very valuable contacts. As long as you keep your options open, this form of employment can be a great complement to your other job search strategies. Whatever you do, don't turn down any opportunities to expose yourself to a new skill or task. Give volunteering a chance!

Look Into Internship Programs

There are many internship programs that are worth looking into for valuable employment opportunities. National programs such as *Career Edge* are becoming increasingly popular and have met with great success. Similar to volunteering, internship candidates generally receive wonderful employment experience and great networking opportunities. Unlike volunteering though, internship programs will usually offer a base salary!

While youth internship is becoming increasingly popular, it will take time before the mainstream private sector commits to such initiatives. As a result, there is not nearly the amount of internship opportunities as there should be. Many of the programs only accept a handful of applicants. However, this does not mean you shouldn't apply; just don't rely too heavily on this form of employment and maintain the proper expectations.

To find out more about the internship programs available in your area, visit your local career centre or guidance department. While some programs are national in scope, others are provincially based. Visit the HRDC (Human Resource Development Canada) site nearest you and ask about programs in your province.

Consider Self Employment

Increasingly, young Canadians are becoming entrepreneurs and choosing to work for themselves. The trend toward self-employment is growing at a dramatic rate and is expected to continue to rise. A combination of both technology and the outsourcing of work by firms is creating a vast amount of self-employment opportunities. Nowadays, developments in technology are such that anyone can set up an efficient and productive home-based business for a relatively low cost.

Create Your Own Job

Starting your own company provides wonderful hands-on experience. Consider whether this option is feasible for you.

Before you decide to dive into the job market and seek a position with an employer, consider whether self-employment is a viable option for you. There are many start-up programs that can provide you with a loan to begin your business venture. As long as you are willing to work hard, don't mind absurd hours, and can handle the reality of not receiving a regular weekly paycheque, self-employment can be an ideal career choice. The risks may be high, but so too are the rewards!

Talk to others who are currently self-employed and gain a better understanding of this type of work. A lot of people who are self-employed would never consider working full time for a company again. According to Statistics Canada, over 2.55 million people, or approximately 18% of our workforce is self-employed.

Don't Give Up!

If your resume is not getting you interviews, consider rewriting it or asking people you know and trust to review it. Don't allow rejections to deflate you sense of self-worth and self-confidence.

There are a number of interesting self-employment books that can provide a wealth of information on the topic. As well, some organizations such as the *Young Entrepreneurs Association*, provide wonderful support to young people. Don't feel you have to do it alone. Part of the fun of being self-employed is the great contacts that you can develop.

To be a successful entrepreneur, you have to learn to recognize opportunity and be passionate about what you want to do. While obviously not everyone's employment solution, self-employment should not totally be ruled out without careful consideration. The important skills and experience that you will gain – even by trying it out for only a summer – will be invaluable. If nothing else, it will do wonders for your résumé!

Strategy Ten: Maintain a Positive Attitude

In the nine previous career steps, we have covered many aspects of the job search and have hopefully provided you with some useful insight. While this information is crucial to an effective job hunting experience, it's extremely important to recognize that, unless you maintain the proper attitude throughout your search, this advice cannot help you. Let's face it, you could have the greatest résumé and cover letter in the world, but if you are not willing to exert the time and effort that is necessary to find a job, then you will simply be out of luck. Looking for a job is really a full-time job in itself. Be prepared for the challenge!

Believe in Yourself!

Self-confidence is key to any successful job search. Believing in yourself is the first step to getting others to believe in you!

Understand from the beginning that rejection is inevitable in the job search process. In most cases, the hiring of an individual is a business decision – nothing more. Don't take things personally! The more firms you apply to, the better your chances of landing a position. Realize that with each rejection you are one step closer to finding employment. Be persistent!

There are a lot of people who are willing to help you in your quest for employment. Visit your local library and career centre and don't be afraid to ask for help. They can provide you with useful information and they often make workshops available that highlight various stages of the job search process. Take advantage of as many of these opportunities as possible.

Finally, the most important piece of advice for your job search is to remain positive. Don't be afraid to try new things and don't be afraid to dream. Once you find where your passions lie, things that you never thought possible are all of a sudden attainable. Show commitment to your job search and don't give up! The challenges you face may seem enormous, but remember, the rewards you gain will be just as large.

Good luck to all of you!

PART II

Company Index

Industry Index

Geographical Index

Company Index

1-800-GOT-JUNK?	74	Allstate Insurance Co. of Canada	96
A C A Cooperative Limited	74	Alpine Oil Service Corporation	96
A E McKenzie Co. Inc.	75	Altona Community Memorial Health Centre	97
A.G. Simpson Co. Ltd.	75	Alumicor Limited	97
Aar-Kel Moulds Ltd.	76	Amcan Castings Limited	98
ABC Group	76	Amcor Twinpak North America Inc.	98
Aberdeen Hospital	77	AMEC Inc.	99
Abitibi-Consolidated Inc.	77	American Airlines Inc.	99
Acadia University	78	Amram's Distributing Ltd.	100
Access Communications	78	Ancast Industries Ltd.	100
Accucaps Industries Limited	79	Andersen Consulting	101
ACE INI Insurance	79	Anjura Services Inc.	101
Acier Leroux Inc.	80	Antamex International Inc.	102
Acklands-Grainger Inc.	80	Anthony Insurance Inc.	102
Addictions Foundation of Manitoba, The	81	Aon Reed Stenhouse Inc.	103
Adherex Technologies Inc.	81	Apex Land Corp.	103
ADI Group Inc.	82	Apotex Fermentation Inc.	104
ADT Canada Inc.	82	Apple Canada Inc.	104
Advanta Seeds	83	Aqua-Power Cleaners Ltd.	105
AGF Management Limited	83	Aquatic Sciences Inc.	105
Agricultural Credit Corp. of Saskatchewan	84	Arbor Care Tree Service Ltd.	106
Aimtronics	84	Arbor Memorial Services Inc.	106
Air Canada	85	Arctic Co-operatives Limited	107
Air Liquide Canada Inc.	85	Armor Personnel	107
Air Nova Inc.	86	Armtec Limited	108
Air Ontario Inc.	86	ArvinMeritor	108
Akita Drilling Ltd.	87	Assiniboine Community College	109
Alberta Alcohol and Drug Abuse Commission	87	Assumption Mutual Life Insurance	109
Alberta Blue Cross	88	Assure Health Inc.	110
Alberta Cancer Board	88	AstraZeneca	110
Alberta Energy & Utilities Board	89	ATCO Electric	111
Alberta Energy Company Ltd.	89	ATCO Frontec Corp.	111
Alberta Gaming & Liquor Commission	90	ATCO Gas Services Ltd.	112
Alberto Culver Canada Inc.	90	Athabasca, Town of	112
Alcan Aluminium Limited	91	Atlantic Blue Cross Care	113
Alexandra Hospital	91	Atlantic Lottery Corporation Inc.	113
Algoma Child & Youth Services Inc.	92	Atlantic Packaging Products Ltd.	114
Algoma District Home For The Aged	92	Atlantic Wholesalers Ltd.	114
Algoma Steel Inc.	93	Atlas Ideal Metals Inc.	115
Aliant Telecom Inc.	93	Atlas Van Lines (Canada) Ltd.	115
Alias	Wavefront	94	ATS Automation Tooling Systems Inc.	116
Allcolour Paint Limited	94	Aurizon Mines Ltd.	116
Allianz Canada	95	Aurum Ceramic Dental Laboratories Ltd.	117
Allmar Distributors Ltd.	95	Aventis Pasteur Limited	117

The Canada Student Employment Guide

Company Index

AXA Insurance (Canada)	118
Axidata Inc.	118
Babcock and Wilcox Canada	119
Bakemark Ingredients Ltd.	119
Ballard Power Systems Inc.	120
Banff Centre for Continuing Education, The	120
Bargain Finder Press Ltd.	121
Barton Place Long Term Care Facility	121
BASF Canada Inc.	122
Basic Technologies Corporation	122
Battlefords Health District	123
Baycrest Centre for Geriatric Care	123
Bayer Inc.	124
Baytex Energy Limited	124
BBM Bureau of Measurement	125
BC Hydro	125
BC Research Inc.	126
BC Telecom Inc.	126
BCG Services	127
BDO Dunwoody	127
Bearskin Lake Air Service Ltd.	128
Bechtel Canada Co.	128
Becker Milk Company Ltd., The	129
Beckman Coulter Canada Inc.	129
Behlen Industries	130
Bell & Howell Ltd.	130
Bell Canada	131
Bell Mobility	131
Belleville General Hospital	132
Benwell Atkins Ltd.	132
Best Western Carlton Place Hotel	133
Betel Home Foundation	133
Bethania Mennonite Personal Care Home Inc.	134
Bethesda Hospital	134
Bettis Canada Ltd.	135
BFGoodrich Landing Gear Division	135
Bic Inc.	136
Biomira Inc.	136
Bio-Research Laboratories Ltd.	137
Biovail Corporation International	137
Birks Jewelry	138
BJ Services Company	138
Black Photo Corporation	139
Blaney McMurty LLP	139
Bloorview Childrens Hospital	140
Bloorview MacMillan Centre, The	140
Blue Giant Equipment of Canada Ltd.	141
Blue Mountain Resorts Limited	141
Blue Wave Seafoods Inc.	142
Bluewater District School Board	142
BNP PARIBAS (Canada)	143
Bombardier Aerospace	143
Bonus Resource Services Corp.	144
Boréal Assurances Inc.	144
Bosal Canada Inc.	145
BOVAR Waste Management	145
Bowater Mersey Paper Company Limited	146
Brandon, City of	146
Brantcorp Inc.	147
Bratty & Partners LLP	147
Brewers Retail Inc.	148
British Columbia Assessment	148
British Columbia Ferry Corporation	149
British Columbia Transit	149
Brookfield Properties Corporation	150
Browning Harvey Limited	150
Buck Consultants Limited	151
Buckeye Canada Inc.	151
Budd Canada Inc.	152
Bugbusters Pest Management Inc.	152
Bullock Associates Design Consultants Inc.	153
Burger King Restaurants of Canada Inc.	153
Burns International Security Services Ltd.	154
C B C L Limited	154
C MAC Industries Inc.	155
C.S.T. Consultants Inc.	155
Cabre Exploration Ltd.	156
Cadith Entertainment Ltd.	156
CAE Newness	157
Calgary Co-operative Association Limited	157
Calgary, City of	158
Cambior Inc.	158
Cambridge Memorial Hospital	159
Cambridge Suites	159
Cameco Corporation	160
Camp Hill Hospital	160
Canada Brick Limited	161
Canada Catering Co. Ltd.	161
Canada Games Aquatic Centre	162
Canada Post Corporation	162
Canada Safeway Limited	163
Canada Starch Company Inc.	163
Canadian Broadcasting Corporation	164
Canadian Cancer Society	164
Canadian Commercial Corp.	165
Canadian Dairy Commission	165
Canadian Depository for Securities Ltd.	166
Canadian General Tower Limited	166

The Canada Student Employment Guide

Company Index

Canadian Museum of Civilization Corporation	167
Canadian National Institute For The Blind	167
Canadian Occidental Petroleum Ltd.	168
Canadian Thermos Products Inc.	168
Canadian Tire Corporation Ltd.	169
Canadian Western Bank	169
Canbra Foods Ltd.	170
Cancarb Limited	170
CancerCare Manitoba	171
Cancore Industries Inc.	171
Cangene Corporation	172
Canon Canada Inc.	172
Canpar Transport Ltd.	173
CanWel Distribution Ltd.	173
Cape Breton Development Corporation	174
Capilano Suspension Bridge	174
Carbone of America (LCL) Ltd.	175
Cargill Limited	175
Carlson Marketing Group Canada Ltd.	176
Carte International Inc.	176
Casa Loma	177
Cassels Brock & Blackwell	177
Catholic Children's Aid Society Foundation	178
CCL Industries Inc.	178
Cegelec Enterprises Ltée	179
Celestica International Inc.	179
CenAlta Energy Services Inc.	180
Centra Gas British Columbia Inc.	180
Centra Gas Manitoba Inc.	181
Central Park Lodges Ltd.	181
Centre de Santé de St-Henri Inc.	182
Century Sales and Service Limited	182
Ceridian Canada	183
CFCF Inc.	183
CFCN Communications Inc.	184
CGI	184
CGU Group Canada Ltd.	185
CH2M Gore and Storrie Limited	185
Challenger Motor Freight Inc.	186
Chapters Inc.	186
Charlottetown Driving Park	187
Cheticamp Packers Ltd.	187
Chevron Canada Resources Ltd.	188
Children's Aid Society of Metro Toronto	188
Children's Hospital of Eastern Ontario	189
Chilliwack General Hospital	189
Chinook Health Region	190
Christian Horizons	190
Cineplex Odeon Corporation	191
Citibank Canada	191
CKF Inc.	192
Clarica	192
Club Monaco International	193
Coast Mountain Bus Company Ltd.	193
COBI Foods Inc.	194
Cobourg District General Hospital	194
Coca Cola Foods Canada Inc.	195
Cognis Canada Corporation	195
Cognos Incorporated	196
Colgate-Palmolive Canada Inc.	196
Columbia House	197
COM DEV International	197
Comcare Health Services	198
Communications & Power Industries Canada	198
Community Savings Credit Union	199
Compaq Canada Inc.	199
Compu-Quote Inc.	200
Computalog Ltd.	200
Computer Associates Canada Ltd.	201
Comstock Canada	201
Comtronic Computer Inc.	202
Conair Aviation Ltd.	202
Connors Bros, Limited	203
Co-op Atlantic	203
Coppley Apparel Group	204
Coquitlam, City of	204
Corel Corporation	205
Corner Brook, City of	205
Cornwall Electric	206
Cosmair Canada Inc.	206
Cosyn Technology	207
Cotton Ginny Ltd.	207
Cougar Helicopters Inc.	208
Credit Union Central of Canada	208
Crestar Energy Inc.	209
Culinar Inc.	209
Custom Trim Ltd.	210
D.A. Stuart Inc.	210
D.H. Howden	211
DaimlerChrysler Canada Ltd.	211
Dana Corporation - Long Manufacturing	212
David Thompson Health Region	212
DDM Plastics Inc.	213
Deer Lodge Centre Inc.	213
Degussa - Huls Canada Inc.	214
Dell Computer Corporation	214
Delphi Solutions Inc.	215
Delta Hotels	215

The Canada Student Employment Guide

Company Index   43

Delta Toronto Airport Hotel	216	Finning	240
Derlan Industries Limited	216	Fisher Scientific Limited	241
Develcon Electronics Ltd.	217	Fishery Products International	241
Directwest Publishers Ltd.	217	Flakeboard Company Limited	242
Dofasco Inc.	218	Fletcher's Fine Foods	242
Domtar Inc.	218	Flint Energy Services Ltd.	243
Drug Trading Company Ltd.	219	FM Global	243
Druxy's Inc.	219	Foremost Industries Inc.	244
Ducks Unlimited Canada	220	Forzani Group Ltd., The	244
Duha Color Services	220	Foster Wheeler Limited	245
Dun & Bradstreet Canada	221	Foyer Valade Inc.	245
DuPont Canada Inc.	221	Friesens Corporation	246
Dura Automotive Systems (Canada) Ltd.	222	Future Shop Ltd.	246
Dylex Limited	222	Gallup Canada Inc.	247
Dynacare Laboratories	223	Gay Lea Foods Co-Operative Ltd.	247
Dynapro Systems Inc.	223	Gencorp Vehicle Sealing	248
Dynasty Furniture Manufacturing Ltd.	224	Gendis Inc.	248
Dynatek Automation Systems Inc.	224	General Chemical Canada Ltd.	249
E B A Engineering Consultants Ltd.	225	General Electric Canada Inc.	249
Earth Tech Canada Inc.	225	General Mills Canada Inc.	250
Echo Bay Mines Ltd.	226	George Jeffrey Children's Treatment Centre	250
Economic Development Edmonton	226	Gienow Building Products Ltd.	251
Economical Insurance Group, The	227	Giffels Associates Limited	251
Eddie Bauer Inc.	227	Gilbey Canada Inc.	252
Edmonton Home Services Ltd.	228	Gimbel Eye Centre	252
EDS of Canada Ltd.	228	Gisborne Design Services Ltd.	253
Elco	229	Glaxo Wellcome Canada	253
Electronics Arts (Canada) Inc.	229	Glentel Inc.	254
Eli Lilly Canada Inc.	230	Goepel McDermid Securities	254
Emco Limited	230	Golder Associates Ltd.	255
EMJ Data Systems Ltd.	231	Goodman and Carr	255
Endpoint Research Ltd.	231	Goodwill Industries of Toronto	256
EnerFlex Systems Ltd.	232	Goodyear Canada Inc.	256
Entreprises Premier Canadien Ltée	232	Gov't of Newfoundland – Dept. of Finance	257
Environics Research Group Ltd.	233	Grand & Toy Ltd.	257
Epson Canada Limited	233	Grant MacEwen Community College	258
Ernst & Young	234	Grant Thornton	258
Espial Group Incorporated	234	Great-West Life Assurance Company, The	259
Exfo	235	Grenville Management Ltd.	259
Exide Canada Inc.	235	Groupe Savoie Inc.	260
Explorer Hotel, The	236	Grouse Mountain Resorts Ltd.	260
Export Development Corporation	236	H A Simmons Ltd.	261
Extendicare (Canada) Inc.	237	H.H. Angus & Associates Ltd.	261
FAG Bearings Limited	237	Haley Industries Limited	262
Family Day Care Service	238	Haliburton Energy Services	262
Farm Credit Corp. Canada	238	Halifax County Regional Rehabilitation Centre	263
Farmers Co-operative Dairy Limited	239	Halifax Regional Municipality	263
Federated Co-operatives Limited	239	Halifax Water Commission	264
FedEx Express	240	Halliburton Energy Services	264

The Canada Student Employment Guide

Company Index

Hallmark Tools	265	Industries Lassonde Inc.	289
Harry Rosen Inc.	265	InfoInterActive Inc.	290
Hasbro Canada Inc.	266	Information Gateway Services	290
HB Studios Multimedia Ltd.	266	ING Canada Financial Services International	291
Health Authority 5	267	Insurance Corp. of B.C.	291
Health Care Corporation of St. John's	267	Intercon Security Ltd.	292
Health Sciences Centre	268	Interforest Ltd.	292
Helijet Airways Inc.	268	Interior Savings Credit Union	293
Hemosol Inc.	269	InterOne Marketing Group	293
Hermes Electronics Inc.	269	Intertape Polymer Group Inc.	294
Hill & Knowlton Canada Ltd.	270	IPL Energy Inc.	294
Hippodrome de Montréal	270	Island Savings Credit Union	295
HMV Canada	271	Island Telecom Inc.	295
Hockey Hall of Fame	271	IST Group Inc.	296
Hoffman-La Roche Limited	272	Ivaco Inc.	296
Holiday Inn Select Toronto Airport	272	IWK Grace Health Centre	297
Holland College	273	Izaak Walton Killam Hospital, The	297
Home Oil Co. Ltd.	273	J.D. Barnes Limited	298
Homewood Corp.	274	J.D. Irving Limited	298
Honda Canada Inc.	274	J.S. Redpath Limited	299
Honeywell Ltd.	275	Jacques Whitford Consulting Engineers	299
Horseshoe Resort Corporation	275	James Richardson International Limited	300
Hôtel Dieu de Montréal	276	JDS Uniphase Corporation	300
Household Movers & Shippers Limited	276	Jim Pattison Group	301
Housesitters Canada, The	277	Jo-Ann Trucking Ltd.	301
HSBC Bank Canada	277	John P. Robarts Research Institute	302
Hub Meat Packers Ltd.	278	Johnson Controls Ltd.	302
Hubbell Canada Inc.	278	Johnson Incorporated	303
Hudon & Deaudelin Ltée	279	Jostens Canada Ltd.	303
Hudson's Bay Company, The	279	Kawneer Company Canada Limited	304
Humber River Regional Hospital	280	Kelowna Home Support	304
Huronia Regional Centre	280	Kelowna, City of	305
Husky Energy Inc.	281	Kennametal Ltd.	305
Hydro Electric Commission of Thunder Bay	281	Kennedy Lodge Nursing Home Inc.	306
Hydro Mississauga Corporation	282	Keyano College	306
Hydro One Inc.	282	KFC Canada	307
Hydro Québec	283	Kimberly-Clark Inc.	307
I M P Group International Inc.	283	Kings Regional Rehabilitation Centre	308
I P L Plastics Ltd.	284	Kinross Gold Corp.	308
IBM Canada Ltd.	284	Kitchener, City of	309
ICI Canada Inc.	285	Kodak Canada Inc.	309
IDEA Associates Inc.	285	Kraft Canada Inc.	310
Ilco Unican Inc.	286	Krug Inc.	310
Imperial Oil Limited	286	Kvaerner Metals	311
Imprimerie Interweb Inc.	287	La Confiserie Comete Ltee	311
INCO Limited	287	Laidlaw Inc.	312
Indalex Limited	288	Lakeside Farm Industries Ltd.	312
Industrial Equipment Co. Ltd.	288	Lambert Somec Inc.	313
Industrial-Alliance Life Insurance Company	289	Leduc, City of	313

The Canada Student Employment Guide

Company Index   45

Lego Canada Inc.	314	McLaren-McCann Advertising of Canada Ltd.	338
Leica Geosystems Canada Inc.	314	McMillan & Associates Inc.	339
Lenbrook Industries Limited	315	MDS Nordion	339
Leo Burnett Co. Ltd.	315	Mediacom Inc.	340
Leon's Manufacturing Company Inc.	316	Mediasynergy	340
Les Centres Jeunesse de Montréal	316	Medical Laboratories of Windsor Limited	341
Les Distilleries Corby Ltée	317	Memotec Communications Inc.	341
Les Forges de Sorel Inc.	317	Metro Richelieu Inc.	342
Les Modes Smart Inc.	318	Metro Toronto Convention Centre	342
Liberty Health	318	Metro Toronto West Detention Centre	343
Lick's Ice Cream & Burger Shops Inc.	319	Metroland Printing, Publishing & Dist. Ltd.	343
Lifetouch Canada Inc.	319	Metropolitan Life Insurance Company	344
Linmor Technologies	320	Meyers Norris Penny & Co.	344
Litton Systems Canada Ltd.	320	Michaels of Canada Inc.	345
LM Architectural Group	321	Midland Walwyn Inc.	345
Loewen Windows	321	Midwest Food Products Inc.	346
London Goodwill Industries Association	322	Millwork & Building Supplies Limited	346
Loss Prevention Group Inc.	322	Milne & Craighead Inc.	347
Lovat Inc.	323	Minas Basin Pulp and Power Company Ltd.	347
M M Industra Ltd.	323	Ministry of Northern Development and Mines	348
M. McGrawth Canada Limited	324	Misericordia General Hospital	348
MAAX Inc.	324	Mississauga, City of	349
MacDonald Dettwiler and Associates Ltd.	325	Mitchell's Gourmet Foods	349
MacDonald Steel Ltd.	325	Mitel Corporation	350
Mactac Canada Ltd.	326	Mitra Imaging Inc.	350
MacViro Consultants Inc.	326	Mitsubishi Electric Sales Canada	351
Magna International Inc.	327	Mobile Computing Corporation	351
Manitoba Agriculture and Food	327	Moen Inc.	352
Manitoba Hydro	328	Moffat Communications Limited	352
Manitoba Pool Elevators	328	Monarch Communications Inc.	353
Manitoba Public Insurance Corporation	329	Montreal Trust Co.	353
Manitoba Telecom Services Inc.	329	Moosehead Breweries Limited	354
Maple Leaf Consumer Foods	330	Morrison Hershfield Limited	354
Marcam Canada	330	Mortice Kern Systems Inc.	355
Marine Atlantic Inc.	331	MOSAID Technologies Inc.	355
Maritime Life Assurance Company, The	331	Motorola Canada Ltd.	356
Mark Anthony Group Inc.	332	Mountain Equipment Co-op	356
Marks & Spencer Canada Inc.	332	MSM Transportation Inc.	357
Mark's Work Warehouse	333	Multi-Languages	357
Marshall Macklin Monaghan Ltd.	333	Multitech Electronics Inc.	358
Marystown Shipyard Limited	334	Mustang Survival Corp.	358
Maryvale Adolescent and Family Services	334	N B S Card Services	359
Matrox Electronic Systems Ltd.	335	Nanaimo Credit Union	359
Maxxam Analytics Inc.	335	Natco Canada Ltd.	360
McBee Systems of Canada Inc.	336	National Grocers Co. Ltd.	360
McCarney Greenwood	336	National Life	361
McGraw Hill Ryerson Ltd.	337	National Manufacturing of Canada Inc.	361
McInnes Cooper & Robertson	337	National Sports Centre	362
McKay-Cocker Construction Limited	338	Neles Automation, Scada Solutions Ltd.	362

The Canada Student Employment Guide

Company Index

Nelvana Limited	363		Owen Bird	387
Neptune Food Suppliers Ltd.	363		Paladin Security & Investigations Limited	388
Nesbitt Burns Inc.	364		Panorama Mountain Village	388
Nestle Canada Inc.	364		Paperboard Industries International Inc.	389
Netron Inc.	365		Paramount Canada's Wonderland Inc.	389
New Brunswick Power Corporation	365		Parkland Industries Ltd.	390
New Brunswick Telephone Company	366		Patheon Inc.	390
New Holland Canada Ltd.	366		Paul Revere Life Insurance Company, The	391
Newfoundland and Labrador Credit Union	367		PavCo	391
Newfoundland and Labrador Hydro	367		PCL Constructors Inc.	392
Newness Machine Ltd.	368		Peacock Inc.	392
News Marketing Canada	368		Pearson Education Canada	393
NewTel Communications	369		Peel Board of Education	393
Niagara Parks Commission, The	369		Peel Children's Centre	394
Nichirin Inc.	370		Peel Regional Police	394
Nielsen Marketing Research	370		Pelmorex Inc.	395
Nike Canada Ltd.	371		Pembina Pipeline Corporation	395
Nissan Canada Inc.	371		PennCorp Life Insurance Company	396
NLK Consultants Inc.	372		Peter Kiewit Sons Co.	396
Norbord Industries	372		Petro-Canada	397
Norcen Energy Resources Ltd.	373		Petromont & Co. Ltd. Partnership	397
North American Life Assurance Company	373		Pharma Plus Drugmarts Ltd.	398
North West Company Inc.	374		Phillips & Tempro Industries Ltd.	398
North York Community Care Access Centre	374		Phoenix International	399
Northern Lights Regional Health Centre	375		Pilot Insurance Company	399
Northern Mountain Helicopters Inc.	375		Pine Falls Paper Company Limited	400
Northwestel Inc.	376		Pioneer Village Special Care Corp.	400
Norwich Union Life Insurance Society	376		Pitney Bowes of Canada Ltd.	401
Nova Scotia Liquor Commission	377		Pizza Pizza Ltd.	401
Nova Scotia Power Corp.	377		Placer Dome Inc.	402
Novartis Consumer Health Canada Inc.	378		Poco Petroleums Ltd.	402
Novotel Canada Inc.	378		Pollack Rentals Limited	403
NPS Allelix Corp.	379		Polygram Group Canada Inc.	403
Numac Energy Inc.	379		Pool People Ltd.	404
Nygard International Ltd.	380		Positron Industries Inc.	404
Oceanis Seafoods Ltd.	380		Potacan Mining Company	405
Ocelot Energy Inc.	381		Powell Equipment Ltd.	405
Oetiker Limited	381		Power Measurement Ltd.	406
Okanagan Skeena Group Limited	382		Powertech Labs Inc.	406
Oland Breweries Limited	382		PPG Canada Inc.	407
Omstead Foods Limited	383		Pratt & Whitney Canada Inc.	407
Ontario Guard Services Inc.	383		Premdor Inc.	408
Ontario Jockey Club, The	384		PRI Automation	408
Ontario Legislative Offices	384		Pricewaterhouse Coopers	409
Ontario March of Dimes	385		Prince Albert Credit Union	409
Opinion Search Inc.	385		Prince Albert, City of	410
Oracle Corp. Canada Inc.	386		Prince George, City of	410
Ottawa Hospital	386		Proctor and Redfern Ltd.	411
Overlander Hospital	387		Progressive Financial Strategy	411

The Canada Student Employment Guide

Company Index

Providence Centre	412
Prudential Insurance Co. of America, The	412
Public Utilities of Kingston	413
Purolator Courier Ltd.	413
QEII Health Sciences Centre	414
QIT-Fer et Titane Inc.	414
Québéc Cartier Mining Company	415
Quebecor Inc.	415
Quesnel River Pulp Company	416
Ramada Inn	416
Rasco Specialty Metals Inc.	417
Raylo Chemicals Inc.	417
Raymond Industrial Equipment Ltd.	418
Raymond Rebar Inc.	418
Raytheon Systems Canada Ltd.	419
Reader's Digest Association of Canada Ltd.	419
Ready Bake Foods Inc.	420
Recochem Inc.	420
Red Deer Co-op Limited	421
Reena	421
Regal Capital Planners Ltd.	422
Regal Constellation Hotel Ltd.	422
Regal Greeting and Gifts	423
Regina Health District	423
Regional Municipality of Niagara	424
Regional Residential Services Society	424
Regis Pictures and Frames Ltd.	425
Rehabilitation Institute of Toronto	425
Reid Crowther	426
Reliable Engine Services Ltd.	426
Renaissance Energy Ltd.	427
Rentway Inc.	427
Replicon Inc.	428
Reuters Information Services (Canada) Ltd.	428
Revenue Properties Company Limited	429
Revy Home Centres Inc.	429
Reynolds and Reynolds (Canada) Limited	430
Rhone-Poulenc Canada Inc.	430
Rich Products of Canada Limited	431
Richmond, City of	431
Richter Usher & Vineberg	432
Rimrock Resort Hotel	432
Rio Algom Limited	433
Riverside Fabricating Ltd.	433
Riverside Hospital of Ottawa, The	434
Rivtow Marine Ltd.	434
Rockwell Automation	435
Roctest Ltée	435
Rogers AT&T Wireless Inc.	436
Rogers Media, Publishing	436
Rothmans, Benson and Hedges Inc.	437
Royal & Sun Alliance Insurance Co. of Cda.	437
Royal Bank of Canada	438
Royal Canadian Mint	438
Royal Inland Hospital	439
Royal Philips Electronics	439
Royal Victoria Hospital	440
Rubbermaid Canada Inc.	440
Ryerson Polytechnic University	441
Saan Stores Ltd.	441
Sales & Merchandising Group	442
Salisbury House of Canada Ltd.	442
Sandman Hotels and Inns	443
Sandwell Inc.	443
Sara Lee Corporation of Canada Limited	444
Saskatchewan Centre of the Arts	444
Saskatchewan Economic Development	445
Saskatchewan Government Insurance	445
Saskatchewan Research Council, The	446
Saskatchewan Transportation Company	446
Saskatchewan Wheat Pool	447
Saskatoon Co-operative Association Limited	447
Saskatoon, City of	448
Saskferco Products Inc.	448
SaskTel	449
SC Infrastructure Inc.	449
Scarborough General Hospital	450
Schlumberger Canada Ltd.	450
Schneider Electric Canada Inc.	451
Scholastic Canada Ltd.	451
Science North	452
SCIEX MDS Health Group	452
SCL Technologies Inc.	453
SED Systems	453
Seprotech Systems Incorporated	454
Sharp Electronics of Canada Ltd.	454
Shaw Communications	455
Shaw Industries Ltd.	455
Sheraton Fallsview Hotel	456
Sheraton Toronto East Hotel and Towers	456
Sherbrooke Community Centre	457
Shermag Inc.	457
Sherwood Credit Union	458
Shoppers Drug Mart Limited	458
Shopping Channel, The	459
Shorewood Packaging Corp. of Canada Ltd.	459
Siemens Electric Ltd.	460
Signature Vacations Inc.	460

The Canada Student Employment Guide

Company Index

Silicon Graphics Canada Inc.	461
Skiing Louise Ltd.	461
Skills Training & Support Services Association	462
Slocan Forest Products Ltd.	462
SNC-Lavalin	463
Sobeys Inc.	463
Société des Alcools du Québec	464
Sodexho Marriott Services Canada	464
SolutionInc Limited	465
Sony Music Canada	465
Southam Inc.	466
Southern Railway of British Columbia Ltd.	466
Southland Canada	467
Spar Aerospace Limited	467
Spectra Premium Industries	468
Spectrum Signal Processing Inc.	468
Speedware Corp. Inc.	469
Sportsco International	469
Sprint Canada	470
SRI Homes Inc.	470
SSQ Life	471
St. Amant Centre Inc.	471
St. Joseph's Care Group	472
St. Lawrence Parks Commission	472
St. Lawrence Seaway Mgmt. Corp., The	473
St. Vincent's Hospitals	473
Standard Knitting Limited	474
Standen's Limited	474
Stanley Canada Inc.	475
Stantec Consulting Ltd.	475
Star Data Systems Inc.	476
State Farm Insurance Companies	476
Steelcraft Industries Ltd.	477
Steelpipe Ltd.	477
Sterling Marking Products Inc.	478
Stitches	478
Stone Consolidated Inc.	479
StorageTek Canada Inc.	479
StressGen Biotechnologies Corp.	480
Sudbury Regional Hospital	480
Sun Peaks Resort Corporation	481
Sun Rype Products Ltd.	481
Sundog Printing Limited	482
Sunoco Inc.	482
Supreme Tooling Group	483
Surrey Memorial Hospital	483
Surrey Place Centre	484
Surrey, City of	484
Swift Current Health District	485
Sydney Steel Corporation	485
Symantec Corporation	486
Syncrude Canada Ltd.	486
Talisman Energy Inc.	487
TCG International Inc.	487
TCT Logistics	488
TD Waterhouse Investor Services (Canada)	488
Teck Corp.	489
Teklogix Inc.	489
Teldon International Inc.	490
Telebec Ltée	490
Telegraph Journal	491
Telesat Canada	491
Telus Corporation	492
The Arthritis Society	492
The Barn Fruit Markets Inc.	493
The Co-operators	493
The Garland Group	494
The McElhanney Group Ltd.	494
Thomas & Betts Ltée	495
Thomas Cook Group (Canada) Ltd.	495
Thomas J. Lipton	496
Thompson's Moving and Storage	496
Thomson - CSF Systems Canada Inc.	497
Thunder Bay Regional Hospital	497
Ticketmaster Canada Inc.	498
Tiger Brand Knitting Company Limited	498
Timmins, City of	499
Tippet-Richardson Ltd.	499
Today's Business Products Ltd.	500
Top Producers Systems Inc.	500
Toronto and Region Conservation Authority	501
Toronto Association For Community Living	501
Toronto Catholic District School Board	502
Toronto Cricket Skating & Curling	502
Toronto District School Board	503
Toronto East General Hospital	503
Toronto Fire Services	504
Toronto French School, The	504
Toronto General Hospital	505
Toronto Hydro	505
Toronto Police Service	506
Toronto Public Library Board	506
Toronto Sun Publishing Corp., The	507
Toronto Zoo	507
Toronto, City of	508
Toshiba of Canada Ltd.	508
Toyota Canada Ltd.	509
TransAlta	509

The Canada Student Employment Guide

Company Index

Transcontinental Digital Services Inc.	510
Triumf	510
Trojan Technologies Inc.	511
Trow Consulting Engineers Ltd.	511
TSC Stores Ltd.	512
Turnbull & Turnbull Ltd.	512
Uni Select Inc.	513
Union Gas Ltd.	513
Union Pacific Resources Group	514
Unisys Canada Inc.	514
United Parcel Service Canada Ltd.	515
Universal Rehabilitation Service Agency	515
University College of Cape Breton	516
Urban Systems Ltd.	516
US Filter BCP	517
USF WaterGroup	517
Vacances Air Transat Inc.	518
Valley First Credit Union	518
Value Village Stores	519
VanCity Credit Union	519
Vancouver International Airport	520
Vancouver Sun	520
Versa Services Ltd.	521
VIA Rail Canada Inc.	521
Villa Providence Shediac Inc.	522
Visteon Canada Inc.	522
Volkswagen Canada Inc.	523
Volvo Cars of Canada Ltd.	523
W C I Canada Inc.	524
Waterloo Furniture Components Ltd.	524
Waterloo Inn	525
Waverly & York Corporation	525
WebCanada	526
Wegu Canada Inc.	526
Weldco-Beales Manufacturing Inc.	527
Wendy's Restaurants of Canada Inc.	527
West Coast Apparel	528
West Kootenay Power Ltd.	528
Westbury Life	529
Westcliff Management Ltd.	529
Westcoast Energy Inc.	530
Western Glove Works	530
Westin Bayshore Resort and Marina, The	531
Westin Prince Hotel, The	531
Westinghouse Canada Inc.	532
WestJet Airlines	532
Westminster Savings Credit Union	533
Weston Produce Inc.	533
Westport Innovations Inc.	534
Westshore Terminals Ltd.	534
Weyerhaeuser Company Limited	535
Whistler Blackcomb Mountain	535
White Rose Crafts and Nursery Sales Limited	536
White Spot Limited	536
Whitehill Technologies Inc.	537
Wilderness Reforestation	537
Wilson Auto Electric Ltd.	538
Windsor, City of	538
Winners Apparel Ltd.	539
Winpak Ltd.	539
Wire Rope Industries Ltd.	540
Workfire Development Corp.	540
World of Vacations Ltd.	541
XCAN Grain Pool Ltd.	541
xwave solutions	542
Yamaha Motor Canada Ltd.	542
Yanke Group of Companies	543
Yarmouth Regional Hospital	543
Yellowknife, City of	544
YFactor	544
York Regional Police	545
YTV Canada Inc.	545
Zeidler Roberts Partnership Architects	546
Zellers Inc.	546
Zenastra	547
Zenon Environmental Inc.	547
Zurich Canada	548

The Canada Student Employment Guide

Industry Index

Industry Sectors

Accounting & Legal

Aerospace & High Technology

Biotechnology & Pharmaceutical

Business Services

Consumer Manufacturing

Diversified

Educational Institutions

Energy

Engineering & Architectural

Entertainment & Leisure

Financial Institutions

Food Manufacturers & Wholesalers

Government

Hospitality

Hospitals & Medical

Industrial Manufacturing

Insurance

Investment

Management & Consulting

Merchandisers

Oil & Mining

Printing, Publishing & Forestry

Social Services

Telecommunications & Media

Transportation

Industry Index

Accounting & Legal

BDO Dunwoody	127
Blaney McMurty LLP	139
Bratty & Partners LLP	147
Cassels Brock & Blackwell	177
Goodman and Carr	255
McCarney Greenwood	336
McInnes Cooper & Robertson	337
Meyers Norris Penny & Co.	344
Owen Bird	387
Pricewaterhouse Coopers	409
Richter Usher & Vineberg	432

Aerospace & High Technology

Advanta Seeds	83
Aimtronics	84
Alias	Wavefront	94
Apple Canada Inc.	104
Axidata Inc.	118
BC Research Inc.	126
Beckman Coulter Canada Inc.	129
BFGoodrich Landing Gear Division	135
Bombardier Aerospace	143
C MAC Industries Inc.	155
CAE Newness	157
Canon Canada Inc.	172
Carte International Inc.	176
Celestica International Inc.	179
CGI	184
Cognos Incorporated	196
COM DEV International	197
Compaq Canada Inc.	199
Compu-Quote Inc.	200
Computer Associates Canada Ltd.	201
Comtronic Computer Inc.	202
Conair Aviation Ltd.	202
Corel Corporation	205
Dell Computer Corporation	214
Develcon Electronics Ltd.	217
Dynapro Systems Inc.	223
Dynatek Automation Systems Inc.	224
Electronics Arts (Canada) Inc.	229
EMJ Data Systems Ltd.	231
Epson Canada Limited	233
Espial Group Incorporated	234
Fisher Scientific Limited	241

HB Studios Multimedia Ltd.	266
Hermes Electronics Inc.	269
IBM Canada Ltd.	284
IDEA Associates Inc.	285
InfoInterActive Inc.	290
Information Gateway Services	290
JDS Uniphase Corporation	300
Linmor Technologies	320
Litton Systems Canada Ltd.	320
MacDonald Dettwiler and Associates Ltd.	325
Matrox Electronic Systems Ltd.	335
Mediasynergy	340
Mitel Corporation	350
Mitra Imaging Inc.	350
Mobile Computing Corporation	351
Mortice Kern Systems Inc.	355
MOSAID Technologies Inc.	355
Motorola Canada Ltd.	356
Multitech Electronics Inc.	358
Neles Automation, Scada Solutions Ltd.	362
Netron Inc.	365
Oracle Corp. Canada Inc.	386
Power Measurement Ltd.	406
Powertech Labs Inc.	406
Pratt & Whitney Canada Inc.	407
PRI Automation	408
Raytheon Systems Canada Ltd.	419
Saskatchewan Research Council, The	446
SCL Technologies Inc.	453
SED Systems	453
Silicon Graphics Canada Inc.	461
SolutionInc Limited	465
Spar Aerospace Limited	467
Spectrum Signal Processing Inc.	468
Speedware Corp. Inc.	469
Symantec Corporation	486
Teklogix Inc.	489
Thomson - CSF Systems Canada Inc.	497
Top Producers Systems Inc.	500
Toshiba of Canada Ltd.	508
Triumf	510
Trojan Technologies Inc.	511
Unisys Canada Inc.	514
WebCanada	526
Westport Innovations Inc.	534
Whitehill Technologies Inc.	537
Workfire Development Corp.	540
xwave solutions	542
YFactor	544

The Canada Student Employment Guide

52 Industry Index

Zenastra 547

Biotechnology & Pharmaceutical

Accucaps Industries Limited	79
Adherex Technologies Inc.	81
Apotex Fermentation Inc.	104
AstraZeneca	110
Aventis Pasteur Limited	117
Bayer Inc.	124
Biomira Inc.	136
Bio-Research Laboratories Ltd.	137
Biovail Corporation International	137
Cangene Corporation	172
Eli Lilly Canada Inc.	230
Endpoint Research Ltd.	231
Glaxo Wellcome Canada	253
Hemosol Inc.	269
Hoffman-La Roche Limited	272
Novartis Consumer Health Canada Inc.	378
NPS Allelix Corp.	379
Patheon Inc.	390
Phoenix International	399
Raylo Chemicals Inc.	417
StressGen Biotechnologies Corp.	480

Business Services

1-800-GOT-JUNK?	74
Apex Land Corp.	103
Arbor Care Tree Service Ltd.	106
Arctic Co-operatives Limited	107
Armor Personnel	107
Bell & Howell Ltd.	130
BOVAR Waste Management	145
Brookfield Properties Corporation	150
Bugbusters Pest Management Inc.	152
Burns International Security Services Ltd.	154
Canpar Transport Ltd.	173
Ceridian Canada	183
FedEx Express	240
Flint Energy Services Ltd.	243
Grenville Management Ltd.	259
Ilco Unican Inc.	286
Intercon Security Ltd.	292
Krug Inc.	310
Lambert Somec Inc.	313

Loss Prevention Group Inc.	322
M. McGrawth Canada Limited	324
Maxxam Analytics Inc.	335
McBee Systems of Canada Inc.	336
McMillan & Associates Inc.	339
Milne & Craighead Inc.	347
Multi-Languages	357
N B S Card Services	359
News Marketing Canada	368
Ontario Guard Services Inc.	383
Paladin Security & Investigations Limited	388
PavCo	391
Peter Kiewit Sons Co.	396
Pitney Bowes of Canada Ltd.	401
Pollack Rentals Limited	403
Purolator Courier Ltd.	413
Replicon Inc.	428
Revenue Properties Company Limited	429
Reynolds and Reynolds (Canada) Limited	430
SC Infrastructure Inc.	449
Today's Business Products Ltd.	500
Waverly & York Corporation	525
Westcliff Management Ltd.	529

Consumer Manufacturing

A E McKenzie Co. Inc.	75
ADT Canada Inc.	82
Alberto Culver Canada Inc.	90
Alcan Aluminium Limited	91
Allcolour Paint Limited	94
Amram's Distributing Ltd.	100
Aurum Ceramic Dental Laboratories Ltd.	117
BASF Canada Inc.	122
Bic Inc.	136
Canada Starch Company Inc.	163
Canadian Thermos Products Inc.	168
CCL Industries Inc.	178
CKF Inc.	192
Colgate-Palmolive Canada Inc.	196
Coppley Apparel Group	204
Cosmair Canada Inc.	206
DuPont Canada Inc.	221
Dynasty Furniture Manufacturing Ltd.	224
Federated Co-operatives Limited	239
Gienow Building Products Ltd.	251
Hasbro Canada Inc.	266
I P L Plastics Ltd.	284

The Canada Student Employment Guide

Industry Index

Interforest Ltd.	292	Grant MacEwen Community College	258
Intertape Polymer Group Inc.	294	Holland College	273
Jostens Canada Ltd.	303	Keyano College	306
Kimberly-Clark Inc.	307	Peel Board of Education	393
Kodak Canada Inc.	309	Ryerson Polytechnic University	441
Lego Canada Inc.	314	Toronto Catholic District School Board	502
Lenbrook Industries Limited	315	Toronto District School Board	503
Les Modes Smart Inc.	318	Toronto French School, The	504
Lifetouch Canada Inc.	319	Toronto Public Library Board	506
MAAX Inc.	324	University College of Cape Breton	516
Mitsubishi Electric Sales Canada	351		
Mustang Survival Corp.	358		
Nike Canada Ltd.	371	## Energy	
Nygard International Ltd.	380		
Phillips & Tempro Industries Ltd.	398	Alberta Energy & Utilities Board	89
Polygram Group Canada Inc.	403	Alberta Energy Company Ltd.	89
Premdor Inc.	408	ATCO Electric	111
Rothmans, Benson and Hedges Inc.	437	Ballard Power Systems Inc.	120
Royal Philips Electronics	439	BC Hydro	125
Rubbermaid Canada Inc.	440	Cornwall Electric	206
Sara Lee Corporation of Canada Limited	444	Crestar Energy Inc.	209
Sharp Electronics of Canada Ltd.	454	Hydro Electric Commission of Thunder Bay	281
Shermag Inc.	457	Hydro Mississauga Corporation	282
Sony Music Canada	465	Hydro One Inc.	282
SRI Homes Inc.	470	Hydro Québec	283
Standard Knitting Limited	474	IPL Energy Inc.	294
Sterling Marking Products Inc.	478	Manitoba Hydro	328
Tiger Brand Knitting Company Limited	498	New Brunswick Power Corporation	365
USF WaterGroup	517	Newfoundland and Labrador Hydro	367
W C I Canada Inc.	524	Norcen Energy Resources Ltd.	373
West Coast Apparel	528	Nova Scotia Power Corp.	377
Western Glove Works	530	Numac Energy Inc.	379
		Ocelot Energy Inc.	381
		Renaissance Energy Ltd.	427
## Diversified		Talisman Energy Inc.	487
		Toronto Hydro	505
General Electric Canada Inc.	249	TransAlta	509
I M P Group International Inc.	283	West Kootenay Power Ltd.	528
J.D. Irving Limited	298	Westcoast Energy Inc.	530
James Richardson International Limited	300		
Jim Pattison Group	301	## Engineering & Architectural	
## Educational Institutions		ADI Group Inc.	82
		AMEC Inc.	99
Acadia University	78	Aquatic Sciences Inc.	105
Assiniboine Community College	109	Basic Technologies Corporation	122
Banff Centre for Continuing Education, The	120	Bechtel Canada Co.	128
Bluewater District School Board	142	C B C L Limited	154

The Canada Student Employment Guide

Industry Index

CH2M Gore and Storrie Limited	185
Cosyn Technology	207
E B A Engineering Consultants Ltd.	225
Earth Tech Canada Inc.	225
Giffels Associates Limited	251
Gisborne Design Services Ltd.	253
Golder Associates Ltd.	255
H A Simmons Ltd.	261
H.H. Angus & Associates Ltd.	261
J.D. Barnes Limited	298
Jacques Whitford Consulting Engineers	299
Kvaerner Metals	311
MacViro Consultants Inc.	326
Marshall Macklin Monaghan Ltd.	333
Morrison Hershfield Limited	354
NLK Consultants Inc.	372
PCL Constructors Inc.	392
Proctor and Redfern Ltd.	411
Reid Crowther	426
Sandwell Inc.	443
SNC-Lavalin	463
The McElhanney Group Ltd.	494
Trow Consulting Engineers Ltd.	511
Urban Systems Ltd.	516
Zeidler Roberts Partnership Architects	546
Zenon Environmental Inc.	547

Entertainment & Leisure

Blue Mountain Resorts Limited	141
Cadith Entertainment Ltd.	156
Canadian Museum of Civilization Corp.	167
Capilano Suspension Bridge	174
Casa Loma	177
Charlottetown Driving Park	187
Cineplex Odeon Corporation	191
Columbia House	197
Grouse Mountain Resorts Ltd.	260
Hippodrome de Montréal	270
Hockey Hall of Fame	271
Horseshoe Resort Corporation	275
Ontario Jockey Club, The	384
Panorama Mountain Village	388
Paramount Canada's Wonderland Inc.	389
Pool People Ltd.	404
Rimrock Resort Hotel	432
Saskatchewan Centre of the Arts	444
Science North	452
Skiing Louise Ltd.	461
Sportsco International	469
Sun Peaks Resort Corporation	481
Ticketmaster Canada Inc.	498
Toronto Cricket Skating & Curling	502
Toronto Zoo	507
Whistler Blackcomb Mountain	535

Financial Institutions

Agricultural Credit Corp. of Saskatchewan	84
BNP PARIBAS (Canada)	143
Canadian Depository for Securities Ltd.	166
Canadian Western Bank	169
Citibank Canada	191
Community Savings Credit Union	199
Credit Union Central of Canada	208
Export Development Corporation	236
Farm Credit Corp. Canada	238
HSBC Bank Canada	277
Interior Savings Credit Union	293
Island Savings Credit Union	295
Montreal Trust Co.	353
Nanaimo Credit Union	359
Newfoundland and Labrador Credit Union	367
Prince Albert Credit Union	409
Progressive Financial Strategy	411
Royal Bank of Canada	438
Royal Canadian Mint	438
Sherwood Credit Union	458
Valley First Credit Union	518
VanCity Credit Union	519
Westminster Savings Credit Union	533

Food Manufacturers & Wholesalers

A C A Cooperative Limited	74
Bakemark Ingredients Ltd.	119
Blue Wave Seafoods Inc.	142
Browning Harvey Limited	150
Canada Safeway Limited	163
Canbra Foods Ltd.	170
Cheticamp Packers Ltd.	187
COBI Foods Inc.	194
Coca Cola Foods Canada Inc.	195
Connors Bros, Limited	203
Co-op Atlantic	203

Culinar Inc.	209
Farmers Co-operative Dairy Limited	239
Fishery Products International	241
Fletcher's Fine Foods	242
Gay Lea Foods Co-Operative Ltd.	247
General Mills Canada Inc.	250
Gilbey Canada Inc.	252
Hub Meat Packers Ltd.	278
Hudon & Deaudelin Ltée	279
Industries Lassonde Inc.	289
J.S. Redpath Limited	299
Kraft Canada Inc.	310
La Confiserie Comete Ltee	311
Lakeside Farm Industries Ltd.	312
Manitoba Agriculture and Food	327
Manitoba Pool Elevators	328
Maple Leaf Consumer Foods	330
Mark Anthony Group Inc.	332
Metro Richelieu Inc.	342
Midwest Food Products Inc.	346
Mitchell's Gourmet Foods	349
Moosehead Breweries Limited	354
Neptune Food Suppliers Ltd.	363
Nestle Canada Inc.	364
Oceanis Seafoods Ltd.	380
Oland Breweries Limited	382
Omstead Foods Limited	383
Ready Bake Foods Inc.	420
Rich Products of Canada Limited	431
Sun Rype Products Ltd.	481
Thomas J. Lipton	496
XCAN Grain Pool Ltd.	541

Government

Alberta Gaming & Liquor Commission	90
Athabasca, Town of	112
Atlantic Lottery Corporation Inc.	113
Brandon, City of	146
British Columbia Assessment	148
Calgary, City of	158
Canadian Commercial Corp.	165
Canadian Dairy Commission	165
Coquitlam, City of	204
Corner Brook, City of	205
Economic Development Edmonton	226
Gov't of Newfoundland – Dept. of Finance	257
Halifax Regional Municipality	263
Halifax Water Commission	264
Kelowna, City of	305
Kitchener, City of	309
Leduc, City of	313
Metro Toronto West Detention Centre	343
Ministry of Northern Develop. and Mines	348
Mississauga, City of	349
Niagara Parks Commission, The	369
Nova Scotia Liquor Commission	377
Ontario Legislative Offices	384
Peel Regional Police	394
Prince Albert, City of	410
Prince George, City of	410
Public Utilities of Kingston	413
Regional Municipality of Niagara	424
Richmond, City of	431
Saskatchewan Economic Development	445
Saskatchewan Government Insurance	445
Saskatoon, City of	448
Société des Alcools du Québec	464
St. Lawrence Parks Commission	472
St. Lawrence Seaway Mgmt. Corp., The	473
Surrey, City of	484
Timmins, City of	499
Toronto and Region Conservation Authority	501
Toronto Fire Services	504
Toronto Police Service	506
Toronto, City of	508
Windsor, City of	538
Yellowknife, City of	544
York Regional Police	545

Hospitality

Best Western Carlton Place Hotel	133
Burger King Restaurants of Canada Inc.	153
Cambridge Suites	159
Canada Catering Co. Ltd.	161
Delta Hotels	215
Delta Toronto Airport Hotel	216
Druxy's Inc.	219
Explorer Hotel, The	236
Holiday Inn Select Toronto Airport	272
KFC Canada	307
Lick's Ice Cream & Burger Shops Inc.	319
Metro Toronto Convention Centre	342
Novotel Canada Inc.	378
Pizza Pizza Ltd.	401

Industry Index

Ramada Inn	416	Regina Health District	423
Regal Constellation Hotel Ltd.	422	Riverside Hospital of Ottawa, The	434
Salisbury House of Canada Ltd.	442	Royal Inland Hospital	439
Sandman Hotels and Inns	443	Royal Victoria Hospital	440
Sheraton Fallsview Hotel	456	Scarborough General Hospital	450
Sheraton Toronto East Hotel and Towers	456	St. Joseph's Care Group	472
Versa Services Ltd.	521	St. Vincent's Hospitals	473
Waterloo Inn	525	Sudbury Regional Hospital	480
Wendy's Restaurants of Canada Inc.	527	Surrey Memorial Hospital	483
Westin Bayshore Resort and Marina, The	531	Swift Current Health District	485
Westin Prince Hotel, The	531	Thunder Bay Regional Hospital	497
White Spot Limited	536	Toronto East General Hospital	503
		Toronto General Hospital	505
		Yarmouth Regional Hospital	543

Hospitals & Medical

Aberdeen Hospital	77
Alberta Blue Cross	88
Alexandra Hospital	91
Altona Community Memorial Health Centre	97
Atlantic Blue Cross Care	113
Battlefords Health District	123
Baycrest Centre for Geriatric Care	123
Belleville General Hospital	132
Bethesda Hospital	134
Bloorview Childrens Hospital	140
Bloorview MacMillan Centre, The	140
Cambridge Memorial Hospital	159
Camp Hill Hospital	160
Centre de Santé de St-Henri Inc.	182
Children's Hospital of Eastern Ontario	189
Chilliwack General Hospital	189
Chinook Health Region	190
Cobourg District General Hospital	194
David Thompson Health Region	212
Deer Lodge Centre Inc.	213
Health Authority 5	267
Health Care Corporation of St. John's	267
Health Sciences Centre	268
Hôtel Dieu de Montréal	276
Humber River Regional Hospital	280
IWK Grace Health Centre	297
Izaak Walton Killam Hospital, The	297
John P. Robarts Research Institute	302
Misericordia General Hospital	348
Northern Lights Regional Health Centre	375
Ottawa Hospital	386
Overlander Hospital	387
QEII Health Sciences Centre	414

Industrial Manufacturing

A.G. Simpson Co. Ltd.	75
Aar-Kel Moulds Ltd.	76
ABC Group	76
Acier Leroux Inc.	80
Acklands-Grainger Inc.	80
Air Liquide Canada Inc.	85
Algoma Steel Inc.	93
Allmar Distributors Ltd.	95
Alumicor Limited	97
Amcan Castings Limited	98
Amcor Twinpak North America Inc.	98
Ancast Industries Ltd.	100
Antamex International Inc.	102
Armtec Limited	108
ArvinMeritor	108
ATCO Frontec Corp.	111
Atlantic Packaging Products Ltd.	114
Atlas Ideal Metals Inc.	115
ATS Automation Tooling Systems Inc.	116
Babcock and Wilcox Canada	119
BCG Services	127
Behlen Industries	130
Blue Giant Equipment of Canada Ltd.	141
Bosal Canada Inc.	145
Brantcorp Inc.	147
Buckeye Canada Inc.	151
Budd Canada Inc.	152
Canada Brick Limited	161
Canadian General Tower Limited	166
Cancarb Limited	170
Cancore Industries Inc.	171

The Canada Student Employment Guide

Industry Index

CanWel Distribution Ltd.	173	M M Industra Ltd.	323
Carbone of America (LCL) Ltd.	175	MacDonald Steel Ltd.	325
Cargill Limited	175	Mactac Canada Ltd.	326
Cegelec Enterprises Ltée	179	Magna International Inc.	327
Century Sales and Service Limited	182	Marystown Shipyard Limited	334
Cognis Canada Corporation	195	McKay-Cocker Construction Limited	338
Communications & Power Industries Canada	198	MDS Nordion	339
Computalog Ltd.	200	Moen Inc.	352
Comstock Canada	201	National Manufacturing of Canada Inc.	361
Custom Trim Ltd.	210	New Holland Canada Ltd.	366
D.A. Stuart Inc.	210	Newness Machine Ltd.	368
DaimlerChrysler Canada Ltd.	211	Nichirin Inc.	370
Dana Corporation - Long Manufacturing	212	Nissan Canada Inc.	371
DDM Plastics Inc.	213	Norbord Industries	372
Degussa - Huls Canada Inc.	214	Oetiker Limited	381
Derlan Industries Limited	216	Paperboard Industries International Inc.	389
Dofasco Inc.	218	Peacock Inc.	392
Dura Automotive Systems (Canada) Ltd.	222	Petromont & Co. Ltd. Partnership	397
Elco	229	Positron Industries Inc.	404
Emco Limited	230	Powell Equipment Ltd.	405
EnerFlex Systems Ltd.	232	PPG Canada Inc.	407
Entreprises Premier Canadien Ltée	232	QIT-Fer et Titane Inc.	414
Exide Canada Inc.	235	Quesnel River Pulp Company	416
FAG Bearings Limited	237	Rasco Specialty Metals Inc.	417
Finning	240	Raymond Industrial Equipment Ltd.	418
Flakeboard Company Limited	242	Raymond Rebar Inc.	418
Foremost Industries Inc.	244	Recochem Inc.	420
Foster Wheeler Limited	245	Reliable Engine Services Ltd.	426
Gencorp Vehicle Sealing	248	Rhone-Poulenc Canada Inc.	430
General Chemical Canada Ltd.	249	Rio Algom Limited	433
Goodyear Canada Inc.	256	Riverside Fabricating Ltd.	433
Groupe Savoie Inc.	260	Rockwell Automation	435
Haley Industries Limited	262	Roctest Ltée	435
Hallmark Tools	265	Saskatchewan Wheat Pool	447
Honda Canada Inc.	274	Saskferco Products Inc.	448
Honeywell Ltd.	275	Schlumberger Canada Ltd.	450
Hubbell Canada Inc.	278	Schneider Electric Canada Inc.	451
ICI Canada Inc.	285	Seprotech Systems Incorporated	454
Indalex Limited	288	Shorewood Packaging Corp. of Canada Ltd.	459
Industrial Equipment Co. Ltd.	288	Siemens Electric Ltd.	460
Ivaco Inc.	296	Spectra Premium Industries	468
Johnson Controls Ltd.	302	Standen's Limited	474
Kawneer Company Canada Limited	304	Stanley Canada Inc.	475
Kennametal Ltd.	305	Steelcraft Industries Ltd.	477
Leica Geosystems Canada Inc.	314	Steelpipe Ltd.	477
Leon's Manufacturing Company Inc.	316	Supreme Tooling Group	483
Les Forges de Sorel Inc.	317	Sydney Steel Corporation	485
Loewen Windows	321	TCG International Inc.	487
Lovat Inc.	323	The Garland Group	494

The Canada Student Employment Guide

58   Industry Index

Thomas & Betts Ltée	495
Toyota Canada Ltd.	509
Uni Select Inc.	513
US Filter BCP	517
Visteon Canada Inc.	522
Volkswagen Canada Inc.	523
Volvo Cars of Canada Ltd.	523
Waterloo Furniture Components Ltd.	524
Wegu Canada Inc.	526
Weldco-Beales Manufacturing Inc.	527
Westinghouse Canada Inc.	532
Wilson Auto Electric Ltd.	538
Winpak Ltd.	539
Wire Rope Industries Ltd.	540
Yamaha Motor Canada Ltd.	542

Insurance

ACE INI Insurance	79
Allianz Canada	95
Allstate Insurance Co. of Canada	96
Anthony Insurance Inc.	102
Assumption Mutual Life Insurance	109
Assure Health Inc.	110
AXA Insurance (Canada)	118
Boréal Assurances Inc.	144
CGU Group Canada Ltd.	185
Clarica	192
Economical Insurance Group, The	227
FM Global	243
Great-West Life Assurance Company, The	259
Industrial-Alliance Life Insurance Company	289
ING Canada Financial Services International	291
Insurance Corp. of B.C.	291
Johnson Incorporated	303
Manitoba Public Insurance Corporation	329
Maritime Life Assurance Company, The	331
Metropolitan Life Insurance Company	344
National Life	361
North American Life Assurance Company	373
Norwich Union Life Insurance Society	376
Paul Revere Life Insurance Company, The	391
PennCorp Life Insurance Company	396
Pilot Insurance Company	399
Prudential Insurance Co. of America, The	412
Royal & Sun Alliance Insurance Co. of Cda	437
SSQ Life	471
State Farm Insurance Companies	476
The Co-operators	493
Westbury Life	529
Zurich Canada	548

Investment

AGF Management Limited	83
Aon Reed Stenhouse Inc.	103
Goepel McDermid Securities	254
Midland Walwyn Inc.	345
Nesbitt Burns Inc.	364
Regal Capital Planners Ltd.	422
TD Waterhouse Investor Services Inc.	488

Management & Consulting

Andersen Consulting	101
Anjura Services Inc.	101
BBM Bureau of Measurement	125
Buck Consultants Limited	151
Bullock Associates Design Consultants Inc.	153
C.S.T. Consultants Inc.	155
Carlson Marketing Group Canada Ltd.	176
EDS of Canada Ltd.	228
Environics Research Group Ltd.	233
Ernst & Young	234
Gallup Canada Inc.	247
Grant Thornton	258
Hill & Knowlton Canada Ltd.	270
InterOne Marketing Group	293
IST Group Inc.	296
Leo Burnett Co. Ltd.	315
Marcam Canada	330
McLaren-McCann Advertising of Canada Ltd.	338
Mediacom Inc.	340
Nielsen Marketing Research	370
Opinion Search Inc.	385
Sales & Merchandising Group	442
Stantec Consulting Ltd.	475
StorageTek Canada Inc.	479
Turnbull & Turnbull Ltd.	512

Merchandisers

Aqua-Power Cleaners Ltd.	105
Atlantic Wholesalers Ltd.	114

The Canada Student Employment Guide

Industry Index

Becker Milk Company Ltd., The	129	**Oil & Mining**		
Birks Jewelry	138			
Black Photo Corporation	139	Akita Drilling Ltd.	87	
Brewers Retail Inc.	148	Alpine Oil Service Corporation	96	
Calgary Co-operative Association Limited	157	ATCO Gas Services Ltd.	112	
Canadian Tire Corporation Ltd.	169	Aurizon Mines Ltd.	116	
Chapters Inc.	186	Baytex Energy Limited	124	
Club Monaco International	193	Benwell Atkins Ltd.	132	
Cotton Ginny Ltd.	207	Bettis Canada Ltd.	135	
D.H. Howden	211	BJ Services Company	138	
Drug Trading Company Ltd.	219	Bonus Resource Services Corp.	144	
Dylex Limited	222	Cabre Exploration Ltd.	156	
Eddie Bauer Inc.	227	Cambior Inc.	158	
Forzani Group Ltd., The	244	Cameco Corporation	160	
Future Shop Ltd.	246	Canadian Occidental Petroleum Ltd.	168	
Gendis Inc.	248	Cape Breton Development Corporation	174	
Grand & Toy Ltd.	257	CenAlta Energy Services Inc.	180	
Harry Rosen Inc.	265	Centra Gas British Columbia Inc.	180	
HMV Canada	271	Centra Gas Manitoba Inc.	181	
Hudson's Bay Company, The	279	Chevron Canada Resources Ltd.	188	
Les Distilleries Corby Ltée	317	Echo Bay Mines Ltd.	226	
Marks & Spencer Canada Inc.	332	Halliburton Energy Services	264	
Mark's Work Warehouse	333	Home Oil Co. Ltd.	273	
Michaels of Canada Inc.	345	Husky Energy Inc.	281	
Millwork & Building Supplies Limited	346	Imperial Oil Limited	286	
Mountain Equipment Co-op	356	INCO Limited	287	
National Grocers Co. Ltd.	360	Jo-Ann Trucking Ltd.	301	
National Sports Centre	362	Kinross Gold Corp.	308	
North West Company Inc.	374	Natco Canada Ltd.	360	
Pharma Plus Drugmarts Ltd.	398	Parkland Industries Ltd.	390	
Red Deer Co-op Limited	421	Pembina Pipeline Corporation	395	
Regis Pictures and Frames Ltd.	425	Petro-Canada	397	
Rentway Inc.	427	Placer Dome Inc.	402	
Revy Home Centres Inc.	429	Poco Petroleums Ltd.	402	
Saan Stores Ltd.	441	Potacan Mining Company	405	
Saskatoon Co-operative Association Limited	447	Québéc Cartier Mining Company	415	
Shoppers Drug Mart Limited	458	Shaw Industries Ltd.	455	
Sobeys Inc.	463	Sunoco Inc.	482	
Sodexho Marriott Services Canada	464	Syncrude Canada Ltd.	486	
Southland Canada	467	Teck Corp.	489	
Stitches	478	Union Gas Ltd.	513	
The Barn Fruit Markets Inc.	493			
TSC Stores Ltd.	512			
Value Village Stores	519	**Printing, Publishing & Forestry**		
Weston Produce Inc.	533			
White Rose Crafts and Nursery Sales Limited	536	Abitibi-Consolidated Inc.	77	
Winners Apparel Ltd.	539	Bargain Finder Press Ltd.	121	
Zellers Inc.	546	Bowater Mersey Paper Company Limited	146	
		Directwest Publishers Ltd.	217	

The Canada Student Employment Guide

Industry Index

Domtar Inc.	218
Duha Color Services	220
Dun & Bradstreet Canada	221
Friesens Corporation	246
Imprimerie Interweb Inc.	287
McGraw Hill Ryerson Ltd.	337
Metroland Printing, Publishing & Dist. Ltd.	343
Minas Basin Pulp and Power Company Ltd.	347
Pearson Education Canada	393
Pine Falls Paper Company Limited	400
Quebecor Inc.	415
Reader's Digest Association of Canada Ltd.	419
Regal Greeting and Gifts	423
Rogers Media, Publishing	436
Scholastic Canada Ltd.	451
Slocan Forest Products Ltd.	462
Southam Inc.	466
Stone Consolidated Inc.	479
Sundog Printing Limited	482
Teldon International Inc.	490
Telegraph Journal	491
Toronto Sun Publishing Corp., The	507
Transcontinental Digital Services Inc.	510
Vancouver Sun	520
Weyerhaeuser Company Limited	535
Wilderness Reforestation	537

Social Services

Addictions Foundation of Manitoba, The	81
Alberta Alcohol and Drug Abuse Commission	87
Alberta Cancer Board	88
Algoma Child & Youth Services Inc.	92
Algoma District Home For The Aged	92
Arbor Memorial Services Inc.	106
Barton Place Long Term Care Facility	121
Betel Home Foundation	133
Bethania Mennonite Personal Care Home Inc.	134
Canada Games Aquatic Centre	162
Canadian Cancer Society	164
Canadian National Institute For The Blind	167
CancerCare Manitoba	171
Catholic Children's Aid Society Foundation	178
Central Park Lodges Ltd.	181
Children's Aid Society of Metro Toronto	188
Christian Horizons	190
Comcare Health Services	198
Ducks Unlimited Canada	220

Dynacare Laboratories	223
Edmonton Home Services Ltd.	228
Extendicare (Canada) Inc.	237
Family Day Care Service	238
Foyer Valade Inc.	245
George Jeffrey Children's Treatment Centre	250
Gimbel Eye Centre	252
Goodwill Industries of Toronto	256
Halifax County Regional Rehabilitation Centre	263
Homewood Corp.	274
Housesitters Canada, The	277
Huronia Regional Centre	280
Kelowna Home Support	304
Kennedy Lodge Nursing Home Inc.	306
Kings Regional Rehabilitation Centre	308
Les Centres Jeunesse de Montréal	316
Liberty Health	318
London Goodwill Industries Association	322
Maryvale Adolescent and Family Services	334
Medical Laboratories of Windsor Limited	341
North York Community Care Access Centre	374
Ontario March of Dimes	385
Peel Children's Centre	394
Pioneer Village Special Care Corp.	400
Providence Centre	412
Reena	421
Regional Residential Services Society	424
Rehabilitation Institute of Toronto	425
SCIEX MDS Health Group	452
Sherbrooke Community Centre	457
Skills Training & Support Services Association	462
St. Amant Centre Inc.	471
Surrey Place Centre	484
The Arthritis Society	492
Toronto Association For Community Living	501
Universal Rehabilitation Service Agency	515
Villa Providence Shediac Inc.	522

Telecommunications & Media

Access Communications	78
Aliant Telecom Inc.	93
BC Telecom Inc.	126
Bell Canada	131
Bell Mobility	131
Canada Post Corporation	162
Canadian Broadcasting Corporation	164
CFCF Inc.	183

Industry Index

CFCN Communications Inc.	184
Delphi Solutions Inc.	215
Exfo	235
Glentel Inc.	254
Island Telecom Inc.	295
Manitoba Telecom Services Inc.	329
Memotec Communications Inc.	341
Moffat Communications Limited	352
Monarch Communications Inc.	353
Nelvana Limited	363
New Brunswick Telephone Company	366
NewTel Communications	369
Northwestel Inc.	376
Okanagan Skeena Group Limited	382
Pelmorex Inc.	395
Reuters Information Services (Canada) Ltd.	428
Rogers AT&T Wireless Inc.	436
SaskTel	449
Shaw Communications	455
Shopping Channel, The	459
Sprint Canada	470
Star Data Systems Inc.	476
Telebec Ltée	490
Telesat Canada	491
Telus Corporation	492
YTV Canada Inc.	545
Signature Vacations Inc.	460
Southern Railway of British Columbia Ltd.	466
TCT Logistics	488
Thomas Cook Group (Canada) Ltd.	495
Thompson's Moving and Storage	496
Tippet-Richardson Ltd.	499
Union Pacific Resources Group	514
United Parcel Service Canada Ltd.	515
Vacances Air Transat Inc.	518
Vancouver International Airport	520
VIA Rail Canada Inc.	521
WestJet Airlines	532
Westshore Terminals Ltd.	534
World of Vacations Ltd.	541
Yanke Group of Companies	543

Transportation

Air Canada	85
Air Nova Inc.	86
Air Ontario Inc.	86
American Airlines Inc.	99
Atlas Van Lines (Canada) Ltd.	115
Bearskin Lake Air Service Ltd.	128
British Columbia Ferry Corporation	149
British Columbia Transit	149
Challenger Motor Freight Inc.	186
Coast Mountain Bus Company Ltd.	193
Cougar Helicopters Inc.	208
Helijet Airways Inc.	268
Household Movers & Shippers Limited	276
Laidlaw Inc.	312
Marine Atlantic Inc.	331
MSM Transportation Inc.	357
Northern Mountain Helicopters Inc.	375
Rivtow Marine Ltd.	434
Saskatchewan Transportation Company	446

The Canada Student Employment Guide

Geographical Index

Alberta

Akita Drilling Ltd.	87
Alberta Alcohol and Drug Abuse Commission	87
Alberta Blue Cross	88
Alberta Cancer Board	88
Alberta Energy & Utilities Board	89
Alberta Energy Company Ltd.	89
Alberta Gaming & Liquor Commission	90
Alpine Oil Service Corporation	96
Apex Land Corp.	103
Arbor Care Tree Service Ltd.	106
ATCO Electric	111
ATCO Gas Services Ltd.	112
Athabasca, Town of	112
Aurum Ceramic Dental Laboratories Ltd.	117
Banff Centre for Continuing Education, The	120
Bargain Finder Press Ltd.	121
Baytex Energy Limited	124
Bettis Canada Ltd.	135
Biomira Inc.	136
BJ Services Company	138
Bonus Resource Services Corp.	144
BOVAR Waste Management	145
Cabre Exploration Ltd.	156
Calgary Co-operative Association Limited	157
Calgary, City of	158
Canada Safeway Limited	163
Canadian Occidental Petroleum Ltd.	168
Canadian Western Bank	169
Canbra Foods Ltd.	170
Cancarb Limited	170
CenAlta Energy Services Inc.	180
Century Sales and Service Limited	182
CFCN Communications Inc.	184
Chevron Canada Resources Ltd.	188
Chinook Health Region	190
Computalog Ltd.	200
Cosyn Technology	207
Crestar Energy Inc.	209
David Thompson Health Region	212
Dynasty Furniture Manufacturing Ltd.	224
E B A Engineering Consultants Ltd.	225
Echo Bay Mines Ltd.	226
Economic Development Edmonton	226
Edmonton Home Services Ltd.	228
EnerFlex Systems Ltd.	232
Finning	240
Flint Energy Services Ltd.	243
Foremost Industries Inc.	244
Forzani Group Ltd., The	244
Gienow Building Products Ltd.	251
Gimbel Eye Centre	252
Grant MacEwen Community College	258
Halliburton Energy Services	264
Health Authority 5	267
Home Oil Co. Ltd.	273
Husky Energy Inc.	281
IPL Energy Inc.	294
Jo-Ann Trucking Ltd.	301
Keyano College	306
Lakeside Farm Industries Ltd.	312
Leduc, City of	313
Milne & Craighead Inc.	347
Monarch Communications Inc.	353
Multitech Electronics Inc.	358
Natco Canada Ltd.	360
Neles Automation, Scada Solutions Ltd.	362
Norcen Energy Resources Ltd.	373
Northern Lights Regional Health Centre	375
Numac Energy Inc.	379
Ocelot Energy Inc.	381
Parkland Industries Ltd.	390
PCL Constructors Inc.	392
Pembina Pipeline Corporation	395
Poco Petroleums Ltd.	402
Raylo Chemicals Inc.	417
Red Deer Co-op Limited	421
Reid Crowther	426
Reliable Engine Services Ltd.	426
Renaissance Energy Ltd.	427
Rentway Inc.	427
Replicon Inc.	428
Rimrock Resort Hotel	432
SC Infrastructure Inc.	449
Skiing Louise Ltd.	461
Skills Training & Support Services Association	462
Spar Aerospace Limited	467

The Canada Student Employment Guide

Geographical Index

Standen's Limited	474
Sundog Printing Limited	482
Syncrude Canada Ltd.	486
Telus Corporation	492
TransAlta	509
Union Pacific Resources Group	514
Universal Rehabilitation Service Agency	515
Waverly & York Corporation	525
Weldco-Beales Manufacturing Inc.	527
WestJet Airlines	532

British Columbia

1-800-GOT-JUNK?	74
Aurizon Mines Ltd.	116
Bakemark Ingredients Ltd.	119
Ballard Power Systems Inc.	120
BC Hydro	125
BC Research Inc.	126
BC Telecom Inc.	126
BCG Services	127
Benwell Atkins Ltd.	132
British Columbia Assessment	148
British Columbia Ferry Corporation	149
British Columbia Transit	149
Buckeye Canada Inc.	151
Bugbusters Pest Management Inc.	152
CAE Newness	157
Capilano Suspension Bridge	174
Centra Gas British Columbia Inc.	180
Chilliwack General Hospital	189
Coast Mountain Bus Company Ltd.	193
Community Savings Credit Union	199
Conair Aviation Ltd.	202
Coquitlam, City of	204
Dynapro Systems Inc.	223
Electronics Arts (Canada) Inc.	229
Fletcher's Fine Foods	242
Future Shop Ltd.	246
Gisborne Design Services Ltd.	253
Glentel Inc.	254
Goepel McDermid Securities	254
Grouse Mountain Resorts Ltd.	260
H A Simmons Ltd.	261
Helijet Airways Inc.	268
HSBC Bank Canada	277
Industrial Equipment Co. Ltd.	288
Insurance Corp. of B.C.	291

Interior Savings Credit Union	293
Island Savings Credit Union	295
Jim Pattison Group	301
Kelowna Home Support	304
Kelowna, City of	305
MacDonald Dettwiler and Associates Ltd.	325
Mark Anthony Group Inc.	332
Mountain Equipment Co-op	356
Mustang Survival Corp.	358
Nanaimo Credit Union	359
Neptune Food Suppliers Ltd.	363
Newness Machine Ltd.	368
NLK Consultants Inc.	372
Northern Mountain Helicopters Inc.	375
Okanagan Skeena Group Limited	382
Overlander Hospital	387
Owen Bird	387
Paladin Security & Investigations Limited	388
Panorama Mountain Village	388
PavCo	391
Placer Dome Inc.	402
Power Measurement Ltd.	406
Powertech Labs Inc.	406
Prince George, City of	410
Quesnel River Pulp Company	416
Raytheon Systems Canada Ltd.	419
Regis Pictures and Frames Ltd.	425
Richmond, City of	431
Rivtow Marine Ltd.	434
Royal Inland Hospital	439
Sandman Hotels and Inns	443
Sandwell Inc.	443
Slocan Forest Products Ltd.	462
Southern Railway of British Columbia Ltd.	466
Spectrum Signal Processing Inc.	468
SRI Homes Inc.	470
St. Vincent's Hospitals	473
StressGen Biotechnologies Corp.	480
Sun Peaks Resort Corporation	481
Sun Rype Products Ltd.	481
Surrey Memorial Hospital	483
Surrey, City of	484
TCG International Inc.	487
Teck Corp.	489
Teldon International Inc.	490
The McElhanney Group Ltd.	494
Top Producers Systems Inc.	500
Triumf	510
Valley First Credit Union	518

The Canada Student Employment Guide

64 Geographical Index

Value Village Stores	519
VanCity Credit Union	519
Vancouver International Airport	520
Vancouver Sun	520
West Coast Apparel	528
West Kootenay Power Ltd.	528
Westcoast Energy Inc.	530
Westin Bayshore Resort and Marina, The	531
Westminster Savings Credit Union	533
Westport Innovations Inc.	534
Westshore Terminals Ltd.	534
Weyerhaeuser Company Limited	535
Whistler Blackcomb Mountain	535
White Spot Limited	536
Workfire Development Corp.	540

Manitoba

A E McKenzie Co. Inc.	75
Addictions Foundation of Manitoba, The	81
Advanta Seeds	83
Allmar Distributors Ltd.	95
Altona Community Memorial Health Centre	97
Ancast Industries Ltd.	100
Apotex Fermentation Inc.	104
Arctic Co-operatives Limited	107
Assiniboine Community College	109
Behlen Industries	130
Betel Home Foundation	133
Bethania Mennonite Personal Care Home Inc.	134
Bethesda Hospital	134
Brandon, City of	146
CancerCare Manitoba	171
Cangene Corporation	172
Cargill Limited	175
Carte International Inc.	176
Centra Gas Manitoba Inc.	181
Ceridian Canada	183
Deer Lodge Centre Inc.	213
Ducks Unlimited Canada	220
Duha Color Services	220
Foyer Valade Inc.	245
Friesens Corporation	246
Gendis Inc.	248
Great-West Life Assurance Company, The	259
Health Sciences Centre	268
James Richardson International Limited	300
Jostens Canada Ltd.	303

Lifetouch Canada Inc.	319
LM Architectural Group	321
Loewen Windows	321
Loss Prevention Group Inc.	322
Manitoba Agriculture and Food	327
Manitoba Hydro	328
Manitoba Pool Elevators	328
Manitoba Public Insurance Corporation	329
Manitoba Telecom Services Inc.	329
Maple Leaf Consumer Foods	330
Meyers Norris Penny & Co.	344
Midwest Food Products Inc.	346
Misericordia General Hospital	348
Moffat Communications Limited	352
New Holland Canada Ltd.	366
North West Company Inc.	374
Nygard International Ltd.	380
Phillips & Tempro Industries Ltd.	398
Pine Falls Paper Company Limited	400
Powell Equipment Ltd.	405
Saan Stores Ltd.	441
Salisbury House of Canada Ltd.	442
St. Amant Centre Inc.	471
Standard Knitting Limited	474
TCT Logistics	488
Turnbull & Turnbull Ltd.	512
Western Glove Works	530
Wilson Auto Electric Ltd.	538
Winpak Ltd.	539
XCAN Grain Pool Ltd.	541

New Brunswick

ADI Group Inc.	82
Aqua-Power Cleaners Ltd.	105
Assumption Mutual Life Insurance	109
Atlantic Blue Cross Care	113
Atlantic Lottery Corporation Inc.	113
Canada Games Aquatic Centre	162
Connors Bros, Limited	203
Co-op Atlantic	203
Elco	229
Flakeboard Company Limited	242
Groupe Savoie Inc.	260
Hub Meat Packers Ltd.	278
I P L Plastics Ltd.	284
J.D. Irving Limited	298
New Brunswick Power Corporation	365

The Canada Student Employment Guide

… Geographical Index   65

New Brunswick Telephone Company	366
Oceanis Seafoods Ltd.	380
Potacan Mining Company	405
Shaw Communications	455
Telegraph Journal	491
Villa Providence Shediac Inc.	522
Whitehill Technologies Inc.	537

Newfoundland

Aliant Telecom Inc.	93
Anthony Insurance Inc.	102
Browning Harvey Limited	150
Corner Brook, City of	205
Fishery Products International	241
Gov't of Newfoundland – Dept. of Finance	257
Health Care Corporation of St. John's	267
Household Movers & Shippers Limited	276
Johnson Incorporated	303
Marystown Shipyard Limited	334
Newfoundland and Labrador Credit Union	367
Newfoundland and Labrador Hydro	367
NewTel Communications	369
xwave solutions	542

Nova Scotia

A C A Cooperative Limited	74
Aberdeen Hospital	77
Acadia University	78
Air Nova Inc.	86
Atlantic Wholesalers Ltd.	114
Blue Wave Seafoods Inc.	142
Bowater Mersey Paper Company Limited	146
C B C L Limited	154
Cambridge Suites	159
Camp Hill Hospital	160
Cape Breton Development Corporation	174
Cheticamp Packers Ltd.	187
CKF Inc.	192
Cougar Helicopters Inc.	208
Farmers Co-operative Dairy Limited	239
Halifax County Regional Rehabilitation Centre	263
Halifax Regional Municipality	263
Halifax Water Commission	264
HB Studios Multimedia Ltd.	266
Hermes Electronics Inc.	269

I M P Group International Inc.	283
InfoInterActive Inc.	290
IWK Grace Health Centre	297
Izaak Walton Killam Hospital, The	297
Jacques Whitford Consulting Engineers	299
Kings Regional Rehabilitation Centre	308
M M Industra Ltd.	323
Marine Atlantic Inc.	331
Maritime Life Assurance Company, The	331
McInnes Cooper & Robertson	337
Minas Basin Pulp and Power Company Ltd.	347
Nova Scotia Liquor Commission	377
Nova Scotia Power Corp.	377
Oland Breweries Limited	382
QEII Health Sciences Centre	414
Regional Residential Services Society	424
SCL Technologies Inc.	453
Sobeys Inc.	463
SolutionInc Limited	465
Sydney Steel Corporation	485
Thompson's Moving and Storage	496
University College of Cape Breton	516
Yarmouth Regional Hospital	543

Northwest Territories

Explorer Hotel, The	236
Yellowknife, City of	544

Ontario

A.G. Simpson Co. Ltd.	75
Aar-Kel Moulds Ltd.	76
ABC Group	76
Accucaps Industries Limited	79
ACE INI Insurance	79
Acklands-Grainger Inc.	80
Adherex Technologies Inc.	81
ADT Canada Inc.	82
AGF Management Limited	83
Aimtronics	84
Air Ontario Inc.	86
Alberto Culver Canada Inc.	90
Alexandra Hospital	91
Algoma Child & Youth Services Inc.	92
Algoma District Home For The Aged	92
Algoma Steel Inc.	93

The Canada Student Employment Guide

66 Geographical Index

Alias | Wavefront	94	Black Photo Corporation	139
Allcolour Paint Limited	94	Blaney McMurty LLP	139
Allianz Canada	95	Bloorview Childrens Hospital	140
Allstate Insurance Co. of Canada	96	Bloorview MacMillan Centre, The	140
Alumicor Limited	97	Blue Giant Equipment of Canada Ltd.	141
Amcan Castings Limited	98	Blue Mountain Resorts Limited	141
AMEC Inc.	99	Bluewater District School Board	142
Amram's Distributing Ltd.	100	Bombardier Aerospace	143
Andersen Consulting	101	Bosal Canada Inc.	145
Anjura Services Inc.	101	Brantcorp Inc.	147
Antamex International Inc.	102	Bratty & Partners LLP	147
Aon Reed Stenhouse Inc.	103	Brewers Retail Inc.	148
Apple Canada Inc.	104	Brookfield Properties Corporation	150
Aquatic Sciences Inc.	105	Buck Consultants Limited	151
Arbor Memorial Services Inc.	106	Budd Canada Inc.	152
Armor Personnel	107	Bullock Associates Design Consultants Inc.	153
Armtec Limited	108	Burger King Restaurants of Canada Inc.	153
ArvinMeritor	108	Burns International Security Services Ltd.	154
Assure Health Inc.	110	C.S.T. Consultants Inc.	155
AstraZeneca	110	Cadith Entertainment Ltd.	156
ATCO Frontec Corp.	111	Cambridge Memorial Hospital	159
Atlantic Packaging Products Ltd.	114	Canada Brick Limited	161
Atlas Ideal Metals Inc.	115	Canada Catering Co. Ltd.	161
Atlas Van Lines (Canada) Ltd.	115	Canada Post Corporation	162
ATS Automation Tooling Systems Inc.	116	Canada Starch Company Inc.	163
Aventis Pasteur Limited	117	Canadian Broadcasting Corporation	164
AXA Insurance (Canada)	118	Canadian Cancer Society	164
Axidata Inc.	118	Canadian Commercial Corp.	165
Babcock and Wilcox Canada	119	Canadian Dairy Commission	165
Barton Place Long Term Care Facility	121	Canadian Depository for Securities Ltd.	166
BASF Canada Inc.	122	Canadian General Tower Limited	166
Basic Technologies Corporation	122	Canadian National Institute For The Blind	167
Baycrest Centre for Geriatric Care	123	Canadian Thermos Products Inc.	168
Bayer Inc.	124	Canadian Tire Corporation Ltd.	169
BBM Bureau of Measurement	125	Cancore Industries Inc.	171
BDO Dunwoody	127	Canon Canada Inc.	172
Bearskin Lake Air Service Ltd.	128	Canpar Transport Ltd.	173
Bechtel Canada Co.	128	CanWel Distribution Ltd.	173
Becker Milk Company Ltd., The	129	Carbone of America (LCL) Ltd.	175
Beckman Coulter Canada Inc.	129	Carlson Marketing Group Canada Ltd.	176
Bell & Howell Ltd.	130	Casa Loma	177
Bell Canada	131	Cassels Brock & Blackwell	177
Bell Mobility	131	Catholic Children's Aid Society Foundation	178
Belleville General Hospital	132	CCL Industries Inc.	178
Best Western Carlton Place Hotel	133	Celestica International Inc.	179
BFGoodrich Landing Gear Division	135	Central Park Lodges Ltd.	181
Bic Inc.	136	CGU Group Canada Ltd.	185
Biovail Corporation International	137	CH2M Gore and Storrie Limited	185
Birks Jewelry	138	Chapters Inc.	186

The Canada Student Employment Guide

Geographical Index 67

Children's Aid Society of Metro Toronto	188	Earth Tech Canada Inc.	225
Children's Hospital of Eastern Ontario	189	Economical Insurance Group, The	227
Christian Horizons	190	Eddie Bauer Inc.	227
Cineplex Odeon Corporation	191	EDS of Canada Ltd.	228
Citibank Canada	191	Eli Lilly Canada Inc.	230
Clarica	192	Emco Limited	230
Club Monaco International	193	EMJ Data Systems Ltd.	231
COBI Foods Inc.	194	Endpoint Research Ltd.	231
Cobourg District General Hospital	194	Environics Research Group Ltd.	233
Coca Cola Foods Canada Inc.	195	Epson Canada Limited	233
Cognis Canada Corporation	195	Ernst & Young	234
Cognos Incorporated	196	Espial Group Incorporated	234
Colgate-Palmolive Canada Inc.	196	Exide Canada Inc.	235
Columbia House	197	Export Development Corporation	236
COM DEV International	197	Extendicare (Canada) Inc.	237
Comcare Health Services	198	FAG Bearings Limited	237
Communications & Power Industries Canada	198	Family Day Care Service	238
Compaq Canada Inc.	199	FedEx Express	240
Compu-Quote Inc.	200	Fisher Scientific Limited	241
Computer Associates Canada Ltd.	201	FM Global	243
Comstock Canada	201	Foster Wheeler Limited	245
Comtronic Computer Inc.	202	Gallup Canada Inc.	247
Coppley Apparel Group	204	Gay Lea Foods Co-Operative Ltd.	247
Corel Corporation	205	Gencorp Vehicle Sealing	248
Cornwall Electric	206	General Chemical Canada Ltd.	249
Cotton Ginny Ltd.	207	General Electric Canada Inc.	249
Credit Union Central of Canada	208	General Mills Canada Inc.	250
Custom Trim Ltd.	210	George Jeffrey Children's Treatment Centre	250
D.A. Stuart Inc.	210	Giffels Associates Limited	251
D.H. Howden	211	Gilbey Canada Inc.	252
DaimlerChrysler Canada Ltd.	211	Glaxo Wellcome Canada	253
Dana Corporation - Long Manufacturing	212	Golder Associates Ltd.	255
DDM Plastics Inc.	213	Goodman and Carr	255
Degussa - Huls Canada Inc.	214	Goodwill Industries of Toronto	256
Dell Computer Corporation	214	Goodyear Canada Inc.	256
Delphi Solutions Inc.	215	Grand & Toy Ltd.	257
Delta Hotels	215	Grant Thornton	258
Delta Toronto Airport Hotel	216	Grenville Management Ltd.	259
Derlan Industries Limited	216	H.H. Angus & Associates Ltd.	261
Develcon Electronics Ltd.	217	Haley Industries Limited	262
Dofasco Inc.	218	Harry Rosen Inc.	265
Drug Trading Company Ltd.	219	Hemosol Inc.	269
Druxy's Inc.	219	Hill & Knowlton Canada Ltd.	270
Dun & Bradstreet Canada	221	HMV Canada	271
DuPont Canada Inc.	221	Hockey Hall of Fame	271
Dura Automotive Systems (Canada) Ltd.	222	Hoffman-La Roche Limited	272
Dylex Limited	222	Holiday Inn Select Toronto Airport	272
Dynacare Laboratories	223	Homewood Corp.	274
Dynatek Automation Systems Inc.	224	Honda Canada Inc.	274

The Canada Student Employment Guide

68 Geographical Index

Honeywell Ltd.	275	MacDonald Steel Ltd.	325
Horseshoe Resort Corporation	275	Mactac Canada Ltd.	326
Housesitters Canada, The	277	MacViro Consultants Inc.	326
Hubbell Canada Inc.	278	Magna International Inc.	327
Hudson's Bay Company, The	279	Marcam Canada	330
Humber River Regional Hospital	280	Marks & Spencer Canada Inc.	332
Huronia Regional Centre	280	Mark's Work Warehouse	333
Hydro Electric Commission of Thunder Bay	281	Marshall Macklin Monaghan Ltd.	333
Hydro Mississauga Corporation	282	Maryvale Adolescent and Family Services	334
Hydro One Inc.	282	Maxxam Analytics Inc.	335
IBM Canada Ltd.	284	McBee Systems of Canada Inc.	336
ICI Canada Inc.	285	McCarney Greenwood	336
IDEA Associates Inc.	285	McGraw Hill Ryerson Ltd.	337
Imperial Oil Limited	286	McKay-Cocker Construction Limited	338
INCO Limited	287	McLaren-McCann Advertising of Canada Ltd.	338
Indalex Limited	288	McMillan & Associates Inc.	339
Information Gateway Services	290	MDS Nordion	339
ING Canada Financial Services International	291	Mediacom Inc.	340
Intercon Security Ltd.	292	Mediasynergy	340
Interforest Ltd.	292	Medical Laboratories of Windsor Limited	341
InterOne Marketing Group	293	Metro Toronto Convention Centre	342
J.D. Barnes Limited	298	Metro Toronto West Detention Centre	343
J.S. Redpath Limited	299	Metroland Printing, Publishing & Dist. Ltd.	343
JDS Uniphase Corporation	300	Metropolitan Life Insurance Company	344
John P. Robarts Research Institute	302	Michaels of Canada Inc.	345
Johnson Controls Ltd.	302	Midland Walwyn Inc.	345
Kawneer Company Canada Limited	304	Millwork & Building Supplies Limited	346
Kennametal Ltd.	305	Ministry of Northern Development and Mines	348
Kennedy Lodge Nursing Home Inc.	306	Mississauga, City of	349
KFC Canada	307	Mitel Corporation	350
Kimberly-Clark Inc.	307	Mitra Imaging Inc.	350
Kinross Gold Corp.	308	Mitsubishi Electric Sales Canada	351
Kitchener, City of	309	Moen Inc.	352
Kodak Canada Inc.	309	Montreal Trust Co.	353
Kraft Canada Inc.	310	Morrison Hershfield Limited	354
Krug Inc.	310	Mortice Kern Systems Inc.	355
Kvaerner Metals	311	MOSAID Technologies Inc.	355
Laidlaw Inc.	312	Motorola Canada Ltd.	356
Lego Canada Inc.	314	MSM Transportation Inc.	357
Leica Geosystems Canada Inc.	314	Multi-Languages	357
Lenbrook Industries Limited	315	N B S Card Services	359
Leo Burnett Co. Ltd.	315	National Grocers Co. Ltd.	360
Liberty Health	318	National Life	361
Lick's Ice Cream & Burger Shops Inc.	319	National Sports Centre	362
Linmor Technologies	320	Nelvana Limited	363
Litton Systems Canada Ltd.	320	Nesbitt Burns Inc.	364
London Goodwill Industries Association	322	Nestle Canada Inc.	364
Lovat Inc.	323	Netron Inc.	365
M. McGrawth Canada Limited	324	News Marketing Canada	368

The Canada Student Employment Guide

Geographical Index

Niagara Parks Commission, The	369	Ramada Inn	416
Nichirin Inc.	370	Rasco Specialty Metals Inc.	417
Nielsen Marketing Research	370	Raymond Industrial Equipment Ltd.	418
Nike Canada Ltd.	371	Raymond Rebar Inc.	418
Nissan Canada Inc.	371	Ready Bake Foods Inc.	420
Norbord Industries	372	Reena	421
North American Life Assurance Company	373	Regal Capital Planners Ltd.	422
North York Community Care Access Centre	374	Regal Constellation Hotel Ltd.	422
Norwich Union Life Insurance Society	376	Regal Greeting and Gifts	423
Novartis Consumer Health Canada Inc.	378	Regional Municipality of Niagara	424
Novotel Canada Inc.	378	Rehabilitation Institute of Toronto	425
NPS Allelix Corp.	379	Reuters Information Services (Canada) Ltd.	428
Oetiker Limited	381	Revenue Properties Company Limited	429
Omstead Foods Limited	383	Revy Home Centres Inc.	429
Ontario Guard Services Inc.	383	Reynolds and Reynolds (Canada) Limited	430
Ontario Jockey Club, The	384	Rhone-Poulenc Canada Inc.	430
Ontario Legislative Offices	384	Rich Products of Canada Limited	431
Ontario March of Dimes	385	Richter Usher & Vineberg	432
Opinion Search Inc.	385	Rio Algom Limited	433
Oracle Corp. Canada Inc.	386	Riverside Fabricating Ltd.	433
Ottawa Hospital	386	Riverside Hospital of Ottawa, The	434
Paramount Canada's Wonderland Inc.	389	Rockwell Automation	435
Patheon Inc.	390	Rogers AT&T Wireless Inc.	436
Paul Revere Life Insurance Company, The	391	Rogers Media, Publishing	436
Pearson Education Canada	393	Royal & Sun Alliance Insurance Co. of Cda	437
Peel Board of Education	393	Royal Bank of Canada	438
Peel Children's Centre	394	Royal Canadian Mint	438
Peel Regional Police	394	Royal Philips Electronics	439
Pelmorex Inc.	395	Rubbermaid Canada Inc.	440
PennCorp Life Insurance Company	396	Ryerson Polytechnic University	441
Peter Kiewit Sons Co.	396	Sales & Merchandising Group	442
Petro-Canada	397	Sara Lee Corporation of Canada Limited	444
Pharma Plus Drugmarts Ltd.	398	Scarborough General Hospital	450
Pilot Insurance Company	399	Schlumberger Canada Ltd.	450
Pitney Bowes of Canada Ltd.	401	Schneider Electric Canada Inc.	451
Pizza Pizza Ltd.	401	Scholastic Canada Ltd.	451
Pollack Rentals Limited	403	Science North	452
Polygram Group Canada Inc.	403	SCIEX MDS Health Group	452
Pool People Ltd.	404	Seprotech Systems Incorporated	454
PPG Canada Inc.	407	Sharp Electronics of Canada Ltd.	454
Premdor Inc.	408	Shaw Industries Ltd.	455
PRI Automation	408	Sheraton Fallsview Hotel	456
Pricewaterhouse Coopers	409	Sheraton Toronto East Hotel and Towers	456
Proctor and Redfern Ltd.	411	Shoppers Drug Mart Limited	458
Progressive Financial Strategy	411	Shopping Channel, The	459
Providence Centre	412	Shorewood Packaging Corp. of Canada Ltd.	459
Prudential Insurance Co. of America, The	412	Siemens Electric Ltd.	460
Public Utilities of Kingston	413	Signature Vacations Inc.	460
Purolator Courier Ltd.	413	Silicon Graphics Canada Inc.	461

The Canada Student Employment Guide

Geographical Index

Sony Music Canada	465
Southam Inc.	466
Southland Canada	467
Sportsco International	469
Sprint Canada	470
St. Joseph's Care Group	472
St. Lawrence Parks Commission	472
St. Lawrence Seaway Mgmt. Corp., The	473
Stanley Canada Inc.	475
Stantec Consulting Ltd.	475
Star Data Systems Inc.	476
State Farm Insurance Companies	476
Steelcraft Industries Ltd.	477
Steelpipe Ltd.	477
Sterling Marking Products Inc.	478
Stitches	478
StorageTek Canada Inc.	479
Sudbury Regional Hospital	480
Sunoco Inc.	482
Supreme Tooling Group	483
Surrey Place Centre	484
Symantec Corporation	486
TD Waterhouse Investor Services (Canada)	488
Teklogix Inc.	489
Telesat Canada	491
The Arthritis Society	492
The Barn Fruit Markets Inc.	493
The Co-operators	493
The Garland Group	494
Thomas Cook Group (Canada) Ltd.	495
Thomas J. Lipton	496
Thomson - CSF Systems Canada Inc.	497
Thunder Bay Regional Hospital	497
Ticketmaster Canada Inc.	498
Tiger Brand Knitting Company Limited	498
Timmins, City of	499
Tippet-Richardson Ltd.	499
Today's Business Products Ltd.	500
Toronto and Region Conservation Authority	501
Toronto Association For Community Living	501
Toronto Catholic District School Board	502
Toronto Cricket Skating & Curling	502
Toronto District School Board	503
Toronto East General Hospital	503
Toronto Fire Services	504
Toronto French School, The	504
Toronto General Hospital	505
Toronto Hydro	505
Toronto Police Service	506
Toronto Public Library Board	506
Toronto Sun Publishing Corp., The	507
Toronto Zoo	507
Toronto, City of	508
Toshiba of Canada Ltd.	508
Toyota Canada Ltd.	509
Transcontinental Digital Services Inc.	510
Trojan Technologies Inc.	511
Trow Consulting Engineers Ltd.	511
TSC Stores Ltd.	512
Union Gas Ltd.	513
Unisys Canada Inc.	514
United Parcel Service Canada Ltd.	515
US Filter BCP	517
Vacances Air Transat Inc.	518
Versa Services Ltd.	521
Volkswagen Canada Inc.	523
Volvo Cars of Canada Ltd.	523
W C I Canada Inc.	524
Waterloo Furniture Components Ltd.	524
Waterloo Inn	525
WebCanada	526
Wegu Canada Inc.	526
Wendy's Restaurants of Canada Inc.	527
Westbury Life	529
Westin Prince Hotel, The	531
Westinghouse Canada Inc.	532
Weston Produce Inc.	533
White Rose Crafts and Nursery Sales Limited	536
Wilderness Reforestation	537
Windsor, City of	538
Winners Apparel Ltd.	539
World of Vacations Ltd.	541
Yamaha Motor Canada Ltd.	542
YFactor	544
York Regional Police	545
YTV Canada Inc.	545
Zeidler Roberts Partnership Architects	546
Zenastra	547
Zenon Environmental Inc.	547
Zurich Canada	548

Prince Edward Island

Charlottetown Driving Park	187
Holland College	273
Island Telecom Inc.	295
Domtar Inc.	218

The Canada Student Employment Guide

Geographical Index

Exfo	235
Matrox Electronic Systems Ltd.	335
Speedware Corp. Inc.	469

Québec

Abitibi-Consolidated Inc.	77
Acier Leroux Inc.	80
Air Canada	85
Air Liquide Canada Inc.	85
Alcan Aluminium Limited	91
Amcor Twinpak North America Inc.	98
Bio-Research Laboratories Ltd.	137
BNP PARIBAS (Canada)	143
Boréal Assurances Inc.	144
C MAC Industries Inc.	155
Cambior Inc.	158
Canadian Museum of Civilization Corporation	167
Cegelec Enterprises Ltée	179
Centre de Santé de St-Henri Inc.	182
CFCF Inc.	183
CGI	184
Cosmair Canada Inc.	206
Culinar Inc.	209
Entreprises Premier Canadien Ltée	232
Hasbro Canada Inc.	266
Hippodrome de Montréal	270
Hôtel Dieu de Montréal	276
Hudon & Deaudelin Ltée	279
Hydro Québec	283
Ilco Unican Inc.	286
Imprimerie Interweb Inc.	287
Industrial-Alliance Life Insurance Company	289
Industries Lassonde Inc.	289
Intertape Polymer Group Inc.	294
IST Group Inc.	296
Ivaco Inc.	296
La Confiserie Comete Ltee	311
Lambert Somec Inc.	313
Les Centres Jeunesse de Montréal	316
Les Distilleries Corby Ltée	317
Les Forges de Sorel Inc.	317
Les Modes Smart Inc.	318
MAAX Inc.	324
Memotec Communications Inc.	341
Metro Richelieu Inc.	342
Paperboard Industries International Inc.	389
Peacock Inc.	392
Petromont & Co. Ltd. Partnership	397
Phoenix International	399
Positron Industries Inc.	404
Pratt & Whitney Canada Inc.	407
QIT-Fer et Titane Inc.	414
Québéc Cartier Mining Company	415
Quebecor Inc.	415
Reader's Digest Association of Canada Ltd.	419
Recochem Inc.	420
Roctest Ltée	435
Royal Victoria Hospital	440
Shermag Inc.	457
SNC-Lavalin	463
Société des Alcools du Québec	464
Sodexho Marriott Services Canada	464
Spectra Premium Industries	468
Stone Consolidated Inc.	479
Telebec Ltée	490
Thomas & Betts Ltée	495
Uni Select Inc.	513
VIA Rail Canada Inc.	521
Westcliff Management Ltd.	529
Wire Rope Industries Ltd.	540
Zellers Inc.	546

Saskatchewan

Access Communications	78
Agricultural Credit Corp. of Saskatchewan	84
Battlefords Health District	123
Cameco Corporation	160
Directwest Publishers Ltd.	217
Farm Credit Corp. Canada	238
Federated Co-operatives Limited	239
Leon's Manufacturing Company Inc.	316
Mitchell's Gourmet Foods	349
National Manufacturing of Canada Inc.	361
Pioneer Village Special Care Corp.	400
Prince Albert Credit Union	409
Prince Albert, City of	410
Regina Health District	423
Saskatchewan Centre of the Arts	444
Saskatchewan Economic Development	445
Saskatchewan Government Insurance	445
Saskatchewan Research Council, The	446
Saskatchewan Transportation Company	446
Saskatchewan Wheat Pool	447
Saskatoon Co-operative Association Limited	447

The Canada Student Employment Guide

Geographical Index

Saskatoon, City of	448
Saskferco Products Inc.	448
SaskTel	449
SED Systems	453
Sherbrooke Community Centre	457
Sherwood Credit Union	458
Swift Current Health District	485
USF WaterGroup	517
Yanke Group of Companies	543

Yukon

Northwestel Inc.	376

PART III

Company Profiles

1-800-GOT-JUNK?

201 - 2182 West 12th Ave.
Vancouver, British Columbia, V6K 2N4
Tel: (604) 659-4052   Fax: (604) 738-5880

Shirley Quinn, VP Client Services
Internet: www.1800gotjunk.com

The company concept is simple for 1-800-GOT JUNK? Not everyone has a truck or the time to take their junk to the dump. Since everyone has junk there is a universal need for junk removal. The company has established its North American presence with one name and one phone number: 1-800-GOT-JUNK?

Academic Fields
College: Administration, Advertising, Business, Communications, Human Res., Journalism, Social Work
Bachelor of Arts: General, Business, Economics, English, History, Journalism, Philosophy, Political Science, Psychology, Public Relations, Sociology/Social Work
Bachelor of Comm/Admin: General, Human Resources, Marketing, Public Admin.
Bachelor of Science: General, Psychology
Bachelor of Laws: General, Corporate
Bachelor of Education: General, Adult Education, Childhood
Masters: Business Administration, Arts, Science

Critical Skills
Adaptable, Confident, Dependable, Diligent, Diplomatic, Efficient, Enthusiastic, Flexible, Good Communication, Good Writing Skills, Leadership, Logical, Manual Dexterity, Organized, Patient, Personable, Persuasive, Professional, Responsible, Integrity, Problem Solver

Types of Positions
Customer Service Rep.   Team Leader
Call Centre Manager   Client Services Centre

Starting Salary
$ 25,000 - 30,000

Company Benefits
- Offers an intensive training program

Correspondence
E-mail resume with cover letter
E-mail: jobs@1800gotjunk.com

Part Time/Summer: 1-800-GOT-JUNK? regularly hires for part time and summer work. Potential jobs include customer service representative or project coordinator. Individuals should apply by March of each year.

A C A COOPERATIVE LIMITED

11 Calkin Dr., Unit 1
New Minas, Nova Scotia, B4N 5A5
Tel: (902) 681-6162   Fax: (902) 681-0611

Alexis Grant, Director of Human Resources

A C A Cooperative is a poultry and egg processing plant, including further processing, product development, breeder, and hatchery facilities.

Academic Fields
College: Accounting, Animal Health, Computer Science, Food/Nutrition, Human Resources, Laboratory Tech., Marketing/Sales, Mechanical Tech.
Bachelor of Comm/Admin: Accounting, Finance, Marketing, Info Mgmt., Human Resources
Bachelor of Science: Agriculture, Computer Science
Bachelor of Engineering: Industrial
Chartered Accounting: CA-Finance, CMA-Finance, CGA-Finance

Critical Skills
Good Communication, Creative, Dependable, Efficient, Enthusiastic, Flexible, Innovative, Leadership, Personable, Productive, Responsible, Good Writing Skills

Types of Positions
Production Labourer   Accounting Clerk
Quality Control Asst.   Computer Asst.
Administrative Asst.   Foreperson

Starting Salary
$ 20,000 - 30,000

Company Benefits
- 50% cost shared health, dental and life insurance
- Long term disability
- Extensive job training

Correspondence
Mail or fax resume with cover letter

Part Time/Summer: A C A Cooperative occasionally hires for part time positions and regularly looks for individuals for the summer. Potential jobs in the summer include production labourer and accounting clerk. The best time to apply is in May.

The Canada Student Employment Guide

A E MCKENZIE CO. INC.

30 - 9th St., Suite 100
Brandon, Manitoba, R7A 6E1
Tel: (204) 571-7500   Fax: (204) 728-8671

Human Resources

Operating under the name McKenzie Seeds, it is Canada's largest seed packaging company. Flower and vegetable seeds of all varieties are available. Customization of seed packaging is available for activities such as promotion and fund raising.

Academic Fields
College: Accounting, Administration, Business, Computer Science, Engineering Tech., Laboratory Tech., Marketing/Sales, Secretarial
Bachelor of Arts: Business, Economics
Bachelor of Science: Biology, Horticulture
Bachelor of Engineering: Computer Systems, Mechanical
Chartered Accounting: CGA-Finance
Masters: Business Administration, Engineering

Critical Skills
Adaptable, Confident, Creative, Decisive, Dependable, Diligent, Diplomatic, Efficient, Enthusiastic, Flexible, Good With Figures, Innovative, Leadership, Logical, Organized, Patient, Personable, Productive, Professional, Responsible, Good Writing Skills

Types of Positions
Certified General Accountant

Starting Salary
$ 20,000 - 25,000

Company Benefits
- Full company funded benefit plan
- Life insurance, dental, vision care, health care
- Long term disability, survivor income

Correspondence
Mail or fax resume with cover letter

Part Time/Summer: A E McKenzie Co. does not hire for part time or summer employment due to their unionized environment.

A.G. SIMPSON CO. LTD.

675 Progress Ave.
Scarborough, Ontario, M1H 2W9
Tel: (416) 438-6650   Fax: (416) 431-8766

Human Resources
Internet: www.agsimpson.com

A.G. Simpson Co. Ltd. is a leader in the automotive stamping business. They provide metal framework systems for major vehicle manufacturers in North America. Over the past 50 years, A.G. Simpson has proudly embraced innovation, quality and tradition as important values in the automotive industry.

Academic Fields
College: Accounting, Computer Science, Engineering Tech., Faculty Mgmt., Human Resources, Mechanical Tech., Secretarial
Bachelor of Comm/Admin: Accounting, Marketing
Bachelor of Science: Computer Science, Environmental Studies
Bachelor of Engineering: General, Chemical, Computer Systems, Electrical, Environmental Studies, Industrial, Materials Science, Mechanical
Bachelor of Education: Adult Education
Chartered Accounting: CA-Finance, CMA-Finance, CGA-Finance
Masters: Business Administration, Engineering

Critical Skills
Adaptable, Analytical, Good Communication, Confident, Creative, Decisive, Dependable, Diligent, Efficient, Enthusiastic, Flexible, Good With Figures, Innovative, Leadership, Logical, Manual Dexterity, Organized, Patient, Productive, Professional

Types of Positions
Information Systems   Human Resources
Administration

Starting Salary
$ 40,000 - 55,000

Company Benefits
- Full range of benefits
- Deferred profit sharing, tuition support for training

Correspondence
Mail or fax resume with cover letter

Part Time/Summer: A.G. Simpson occasionally hires for part time and summer opportunities. The best time to apply is in April.

The Canada Student Employment Guide

AAR-KEL MOULDS LTD.

17 Elm Dr. South
Wallaceburg, Ontario, N8A 5E8
Tel: (519) 627-6078   Fax: (519) 627-5925

Serge Granger, HR Manager
Internet: www.aarkel.com

Aar-Kel Moulds Ltd. is in the metal cutting trade, and is a manufacturer of plastic injection, aluminum and magnesium molds and dies.

Academic Fields
College: Accounting, Administration, Engineering Tech., Human Resources, Industrial Design, Marketing/Sales, Quality Assurance
Bachelor of Comm/Admin: Finance

Critical Skills
Adaptable, Analytical, Good Communication, Creative, Dependable, Efficient, Enthusiastic, Good With Figures, Logical, Manual Dexterity, Organized, Productive, Responsible, Good Writing Skills

Types of Positions
Apprentice Mold Maker   Machine Operator

Starting Salary
$ 25,000 - 30,000

Company Benefits
- Drug and dental plan, life insurance
- Short and long term disability
- In house and external technical training

Correspondence
Mail resume with cover letter

Part Time/Summer: Aar-Kel Moulds sometimes hires for part time and summer employment. Most positions would be available for mold making technician students from community college. The best time to apply is in March or April.

ABC GROUP

110 Ronson Dr.
Etobicoke, Ontario, M9W 1B6
Tel: (416) 246-9886   Fax: (416) 246-1780

Corporate Recruiter
Internet: www.abcgroup.com

ABC Group is a tier 1 automotive plastics supplier of interior, exterior and under-hood parts to the OEM markets. The company has over 3,000 employees and 38 subsidiaries worldwide.

Academic Fields
College: Accounting, Business, Human Resources, Information Systems, Purchasing, Secretarial, Statistics, CAD Autocad, Computer Science, Engineering, Mechanical Tech.
Bachelor of Arts: Business, Statistics
Bachelor of Comm/Admin: Accounting, Human Resources
Bachelor of Science: Computer Sciences
Bachelor of Engineering: Design, Industrial, Mechanical
Chartered Accounting: CA-Finance, CGA-Finance, CMA-Finance
Masters: Engineering

Critical Skills
Good Communication, Confident, Decisive, Dependable, Enthusiastic, Professional

Types of Positions
Project Engineering   Process Engineering
Quality Engineering

Starting Salary
$ 25,000 - 40,000 (depending on position)

Company Benefits
- Full benefit package

Correspondence
Fax, e-mail resume with cover letter, or apply through their web site. E-mail: hr@abcgrp.com

Part Time/Summer: ABC Group rarely hires for part time positions but occasionally seeks engineering students for the summer months. The best time to apply is in April or May.

ABERDEEN HOSPITAL

835 East River Road
New Glasgow, Nova Scotia, B2H 3S6
Tel: (902) 755-2356   Fax: (902) 755-2356

John Lalumiere, Director of Human Resources

Established in 1895, Aberdeen Hospital is a government owned health care facility with over 178 beds. The hospital provides services in areas including intensive care, medicine and surgery, gynecology, and pediatrics. The hospital has an employee base of more than 585 individuals.

Academic Fields
College: Accounting, Computer Science, Human Resources, Laboratory Tech., Nursing, Radiology Tech., Secretarial
Bachelor of Arts: Business
Bachelor of Comm/Admin: General, Accounting, Finance, Info Mgmt.
Bachelor of Science: Computer Science, Food Sciences, Health Sciences, Kinesiology, Microbiology, Nursing (RN), Occupational Therapy, Pharmacy, Physiotherapy, Psychology
Chartered Accounting: CA-General
Masters: Business Administration, Science

Critical Skills
Adaptable, Good Communication, Dependable, Efficient, Enthusiastic, Flexible, Leadership, Organized, Productive, Professional, Responsible

Types of Positions
General Worker   Support Staff
Clerical Positions   Switchboard

Starting Salary
$ 20,000 - 40,000 (depending on position)

Company Benefits
- Full package of benefits excluding dental
- Numerous training opportunities

Correspondence
Mail resume with cover letter

Part Time/Summer: Aberdeen Hospital does not hire individuals for part time work, but sometimes hires for summer opportunities. Potential summer positions involve clerical duties. The best time to apply is in the Spring.

ABITIBI-CONSOLIDATED INC.

800 Rene-Levesque Blvd. W.
Montreal, Québec, H3B 1Y9
Tel: (514) 875-2160   Fax: (514) 875-6284

Human Resources

Abitibi-Consolidated Inc. is a pulp and paper firm that has ownership interests in 29 paper mills in Canada, the U.S., the U.K. and Asia, in 24 sawmills and a market pulp mill. The Company markets over 6 million tonnes of newsprint, nearly 2 million tonnes of value-added papers, approximately 440,000 tonnes of high-quality market pulp, and the capacity to produce 2.2 billion board feet of lumber.

Academic Fields
College: Accounting, Admin., Communications, Engineering Tech., Forestry, Human Res., Secretarial
Bachelor of Arts: Business, Economics
Bachelor of Comm/Admin: Accounting, Finance, Marketing, Info Mgmt.
Bachelor of Science: Biology, Chemistry, Computer Science, Forestry, Mathematics
Bachelor of Laws: General, Corporate, Real Estate
Bachelor of Engineering: Computer Systems, Design, Mechanical
Chartered Accounting: CMA - General/Finance, CGA - General/Finance
Masters: Business Administration, Engineering

Critical Skills
Efficient, Flexible, Good Communication, Good Writing Skills, Organized, Productive, Professional

Types of Positions
Internal Audit

Starting Salary
$ 25,000 - 30,000

Company Benefits
- Dental plan, health plan
- Life insurance, pension plan

Correspondence
Mail resume with cover letter

Part Time/Summer: Abitibi-Consolidated occasionally hires for part time and summer work. The best time to apply is in March or April.

The Canada Student Employment Guide

ACADIA UNIVERSITY

Centre for Career Services
Wolfville, Nova Scotia, B0P 1X0
Tel: (902) 585-1232   Fax: (902) 585-1065

Demita Boschel,
Internet: www.acadiau.ca

Considered one of the leading undergraduate universities in Canada, Acadia offers students a unique opportunity to experience an environment which combines outstanding academic programs with a diversity of extracurricular activities. The university has over 200 degree combinations from the Faculty of Arts, Pure and Professional Studies, Management and Education, and Theology. On 250 acres, Acadia University has a full time student population of 3,700 individuals from 35 countries.

Academic Fields
College: Electronics Tech., Human Resources, Secretarial, Security/Law
Bachelor of Comm/Admin: General, Accounting, Info Mgmt., Public Admin.
Bachelor of Science: Biology, Chemistry, Computer Science

Critical Skills
Adaptable, Dependable, Flexible, Good Communication, Innovative, Organized, Professional

Types of Positions
Departmental Secretary   Clerk
Laboratory Technician

Starting Salary
Below $ 20,000 - 25,000 (depending on position)

Company Benefits
- Group health and life insurance
- Long term disability and pension plan, no dental plan

Correspondence
Mail resume with cover letter
E-mail: career.services@acadiau.ca

Part Time/Summer: Acadia University regularly hires for part time and summer work. Potential positions in the summer include research assistants and conference staff. The best time to apply is between January and March for these potential summer positions.

ACCESS COMMUNICATIONS

2250 Park St.
Regina, Saskatchewan, S4N 7K7
Tel: (306) 569-3510   Fax: (306) 565-5395

Debby Kuntz, Manager of Human Resources
Internet: www.accesscomm.com

Access Communications, a non-profit service co-operative, provides cable television services and access to high speed data communications technology to residents of Regina as well as several surrounding communities.

Academic Fields
College: Accounting, Administration, Computer Science, Drafting/Architecture, Electronics Tech., Human Resources, Marketing/Sales, Secretarial, Television/Radio
Bachelor of Comm/Admin: General, Accounting, Finance, Marketing, Info Mgmt.
Bachelor of Science: Computer Science
Bachelor of Engineering: Electrical

Critical Skills
Adaptable, Good Communication, Confident, Dependable, Diligent, Efficient, Enthusiastic, Innovative, Organized, Productive, Professional, Good Writing Skills

Types of Positions
Customer Service Rep.   Service Technician
Production Assistant   Retail Associate
Electronics Technician   Network Support Rep.

Starting Salary
$ 20,000 - 30,000 (depending on the position)

Company Benefits
- Company-paid extended health care, vision care
- Pension plan, company-sponsored training
- Company-paid wage loss replacement

Correspondence
Mail, fax, or e-mail resume with cover letter
E-mail: debby.kuntz@accesscomm.ca

Part Time/Summer: Access Communications occasionally hires for part time or summer work. Potential jobs include service technician or electronics technician. The best time to apply is from January to March. Apply to the Technical Operations Supervisor.

The Canada Student Employment Guide

ACCUCAPS INDUSTRIES LIMITED

2125 Ambassador Dr.
Windsor, Ontario, N9C 3R5
Tel: (519) 969-5404   Fax: (519) 969-5022

Human Resources

Accucaps Industries is a manufacturer of soft gelatin capsules focusing in the areas of pharmaceuticals, over-the-counter products, health and nutritionals, cosmetics and paintballs. They request no phone calls.

Academic Fields
College: Accounting, Administration, Business, Computer Science, Electronics Tech., Engineering Tech., Human Resources, Marketing/Sales, Science
Bachelor of Arts: General, Business, Political Science, Psychology, Public Relations
Bachelor of Comm/Admin: Accounting, Finance, Marketing, Info Mgmt.
Bachelor of Science: General, Biology, Chemistry, Microbiology, Pharmacy
Bachelor of Engineering: Chemical, Computer Systems, Design, Electrical, Mechanical
Chartered Accounting: CA - General/Finance, CGA/CMA -General/Finance
Masters: Business Administration

Critical Skills
Adaptable, Analytical, Good Communication, Confident, Dependable, Diligent, Diplomatic, Efficient, Enthusiastic, Flexible, Good With Figures, Innovative, Leadership, Logical, Manual Dexterity, Organized, Personable, Productive, Professional, Responsible

Types of Positions
Various Positions

Starting Salary
$ 20,000 - 25,000 (depending on position)

Company Benefits
- Full employee benefits
- In-house training

Correspondence
Mail resume with cover letter

Part Time/Summer: Accucaps Industries does not hire for part time work, but regularly hires production assistants and office clerks for the summer months.

ACE INI INSURANCE

The Exchange Tower, 130 King St. W., 12th Flr.
Toronto, Ontario, M5X 1A6
Tel: (416) 368-2911   Fax: (416) 368-9825

Human Resources Administrator
Internet: www.ace-ina-canada.com

The ACE Group has grown rapidly by building long-term partnerships with brokers and clients in each of the world's major insurance markets. ACE brings a wealth of experience and resources to the table. Today, the ACE Group provides a diversified range of products and services in almost 50 countries. The 1999 acquisition of CIGNA's P&C operations has greatly increased ACE's influence in the international insurance industry. With admitted status in all the world's major markets, ACE is today, one of a small group of truly international insurers.

Academic Fields
College: General, Accounting, Administration, Business, Computer Science, Engineering Tech., Human Resources, Insurance, Secretarial
Bachelor of Arts: General, Business, Psychology
Bachelor of Comm/Admin: General, Accounting, Finance, Info Mgmt.
Bachelor of Science: Environmental Studies
Bachelor of Engineering: General, Environ., Studies
Masters: Business Administration

Critical Skills
Analytical, Good Communication, Dependable, Diligent, Flexible, Good With Figures, Logical, Organized, Personable, Professional, Responsible, Good Writing Skills

Types of Positions
Underwriting Assistant   Administrative Assistant

Starting Salary
$ 25,000 - 30,000

Company Benefits
- Medical and dental insurance, life insurance
- Corporate training and development plan

Correspondence
Mail resume with cover letter

Part Time/Summer: ACE INI Insurance does not hire for part time work, but occasionally hires in the summer. Potential summer jobs are clerical in nature. The best time to apply is in the Spring.

The Canada Student Employment Guide

ACIER LEROUX INC.

1331 Graham Bell
Boucherville, Québec, J4B 6A1
Tel: (514) 641-4360   Fax: (514) 641-2403

Human Resources
Internet: www.leroux-steel.com/

Acier Leroux is one of the country's fastest growing steelmakers with an empire soon stretching from the Atlantic Provinces to north-central United States. Acier Leroux employs more than 500 individuals.

Academic Fields
College: Accounting, Administration, Secretarial
Bachelor of Laws: Corporate, Real Estate

Critical Skills
Analytical, Dependable, Enthusiastic, Flexible, Innovative, Responsible, Dynamic

Types of Positions
Various Positions

Starting Salary
$ 20,000 - 30,000

Company Benefits
- Collective benefits
- Training and development opportunities

Correspondence
Fax resume with cover letter

Part Time/Summer: Acier Leroux occasionally looks for individuals for part time work, and regularly seeks people for summer opportunities. A potential position would be an administrative clerk. The best time to apply is in April.

ACKLANDS-GRAINGER INC.

90 West Beaver Creek Rd.
Richmond Hill, Ontario, L4B 1E7
Tel: (905) 731-5516   Fax: (905) 731-2798

Tricia Newton, HR Assistant
Internet: www.acklands.ca

Started in 1889, Acklands-Grainger Inc. is a national distribution company whose products fall into one of three primary categories: industrial, fleet and safety. Their history of reliable service combined with their ability to be a "one stop" supplier, has positioned Acklands-Grainger as the largest distributor of its kind in Canada

Academic Fields
College: Acctg., Admin., Business, Communications, Computer Sci., Engineering Tech., Human Resources, Marketing/Sales, Science, Secretarial, Statistics
Bachelor of Arts: General, Business, Economics, English, Journalism, Psychology, Sociology/Social Work, Statistics
Bachelor of Comm/Admin: General, Accounting, Finance, Marketing, Info Mgmt.
Bachelor of Science: General, Actuarial, Computer Science, Mathematics, Psychology
Bachelor of Laws: Corporate, Real Estate
Bachelor of Engineering: General, Industrial
Chartered Accounting: CA-General, CMA-General, CGA-General
Masters: Business Admin., Science, Engineering

Critical Skills
Adaptable, Good Communication, Confident, Creative, Efficient, Enthusiastic, Flexible, Leadership, Organized, Patient, Productive, Professional

Types of Positions
Warehouse Person

Starting Salary
Below $ 20,000 - 25,000

Company Benefits
- Health and dental for full time
- Tuition reimbursement for some courses

Correspondence
Mail resume with cover letter

Part Time/Summer: Acklands-Grainger occasionally hires for part time and summer work, but it does not happen often. Potential jobs involve clerical or warehouse duties. May or June is the time to apply.

THE ADDICTIONS FOUNDATION OF MANITOBA

1031 Portage Avenue
Winnipeg, Manitoba, R3G 0R8
Tel: (204) 944-6200   Fax: (204) 786-7768

Leslie Vincent, Human Resources Manager
Internet: www.afm.mb.ca

The Addictions Foundation of Manitoba (AFM) is a provincial crown agency providing a broad range of services relating to alcohol, drug, and gambling problems. Substance abuse and gambling prevention, education and treatment programs, and impaired driver services are available through AFM.

Academic Fields
College: Accounting, Administration, Human Resources, Social Work
Bachelor of Arts: Psychology, Sociology/Social Work
Bachelor of Comm/Admin: Accounting, Human Resources, Public Admin.
Bachelor of Science: Health Sciences, Nursing (RN)
Bachelor of Education: Adult Education

Critical Skills
Adaptable, Analytical, Good Communication, Confident, Dependable, Diplomatic, Enthusiastic, Flexible, Innovative, Leadership, Logical, Organized, Patient, Personable, Persuasive, Productive, Professional, Responsible, Good Writing Skills

Types of Positions
Rehabilitation Counsellor   Researcher

Starting Salary
$ 35,000 - 40,000

Company Benefits
- Extended health plan, dental insurance
- Pension and group life insurance, vision plan

Correspondence
Mail, email resume with cover letter, or apply through their web site. E-mail: lvincent@afm.mb.ca

Part Time/Summer: The Addiction Foundation of Manitoba sometimes hires for part time or summer work. Potential jobs include research assistant in a variety of programs. The best time to apply is in the Spring.

Co-op/Internship: Depending on the program and cost, there are practicuums for social work and clinical psychology available. Check their web site for more info.

ADHEREX TECHNOLOGIES INC.

300 - 600 Peter Morand Cres.
Ottawa, Ontario, K1G 5Z3
Tel: (613) 738-8000   Fax: (613) 738-9060

Human Resources
Internet: www.adherex.com

Adherex Technologies is a biotechnology company developing novel therapeutics based on cell adhesion technologies. Adherex is currently developing a portfolio of biologically active small molecules based on the cadherin family of cell adhesion molecules. They employ 16 individuals.

Academic Fields
Bachelor of Science: Biology, Chemistry, Pharmacy
Masters: Science

Critical Skills
Innovative, Productive, Team Player

Types of Positions
Chemistry Technician   Synthetic Chemist (PhD)
Biology Technician   Biologist (PhD)

Starting Salary
$ 30,000 - 50,000

Company Benefits
- Health insurance
- Share options, paid vacation
- Training courses as needed

Correspondence
Mail resume with cover letter
E-mail: info@adherex.com

Part Time/Summer: Adherex Technologies Inc. does not hire part time employees, but regularly hires for summer employment. Potential jobs include lab research involving biology and chemistry.

ADI GROUP INC.

1133 Regent St., Suite 300
Fredericton, New Brunswick, E3B 3Z2
Tel: (506) 452-9000   Fax: (506) 459-3954

Sharon Wilson, Human Resources
Internet: www.adi.ca

An employee-owned, multi-disciplined firm, ADI Group Inc. is comprised of several companies and employs more that 200 highly trained design professionals, scientists, technical staff, managers and office staff. The ADI companies provide consulting services and engineer, procure, construct, and finance capabilities for a wide variety of government and industrial clients.

Academic Fields
College: Drafting/Architecture, Engineering Tech., Laboratory Tech., Science-General, Secretarial
Bachelor of Comm/Admin: Accounting, Marketing
Bachelor of Science: Biology, Chemistry, Environmental Studies
Bachelor of Engineering: Chemical, Civil, Electrical, Environmental Studies, Geotechnical, Mechanical, Transportation, Water Res., Bachelor of Architecture
Chartered Accounting: CA - General/Finance, CGA/CMA - General/Finance
Masters: Engineering

Critical Skills
Confident, Dependable, Flexible, Good Communication, Good Writing Skills, Innovative, Professional, Responsible

Types of Positions
Architecture Division   Mechanical/Electrical Division
Technical Services Div. Administration Division
Public Works Division   Environment Management

Starting Salary
$ 30,000 - 40,000 (university)

Company Benefits
- Health and dental, group RRSP plan
- Life insurance and long term disability

Correspondence
Mail, fax or e-mail resume with cover letter
E-mail: saw@adi.ca

Part Time/Summer: ADI Group sometimes hires for part time work and regularly hires in the summer. Potential jobs may exist for engineering students. The best time to apply is by March or early April.

ADT CANADA INC.

2815 Matheson Blvd. E.
Mississauga, Ontario, L4W 4P7
Tel: 1-800-567-5675   Fax: N/A

Human Resources
Internet: www.adt.ca

ADT Canada Inc. is the Canadian affiliate of ADT Security Systems, the largest supplier of electronic monitoring and surveillance systems in the world. Specializing in computer-based access control, fire alarms, retail loss prevention, closed circuit systems, and large scale custom designed systems, ADT is the largest residential and commercial electronic security firm in Canada. The company employs over 1,100 individuals.

Academic Fields
College: Computer Science, Drafting/Architecture, Electronics Tech., Engineering Tech., Human Resources, Secretarial
Bachelor of Arts: General, Business, Public Relations
Bachelor of Comm/Admin: General, Accounting, Finance, Marketing, Info Mgmt.
Bachelor of Science: Computer Science
Chartered Accounting: CMA-General, CGA-General

Critical Skills
Adaptable, Dependable, Diligent, Good Communication, Flexible, Efficient, Productive, Manual Dexterity, Professional, Responsible, Good Writing Skills

Types of Positions
Secretarial   Accounting Clerk
Data Entry Operator   Telemarketer
Junior Installer   Mail Clerk

Starting Salary
$ 25,000 - 30,000

Company Benefits
- Employer paid health coverage (family or single)
- Dental coverage (shared cost for family)
- Two weeks vacation annually

Correspondence
Mail resume with cover letter

Part Time/Summer: ADT sometimes hires for part time jobs, and regularly hires students for the summer. Potential summer positions include clerical, and computer work. The best time to apply is at the end of April, or beginning of May.

ADVANTA SEEDS

75 Scurfield Blvd., Unit 6
Winnipeg, Manitoba, R3Y 1P6
Tel: (204) 488-4064   Fax: (204) 488-4766

Heather Glaser, Human Resources Co-ordinator
Internet: www.advantacan.com

In Canada, Advanta Seeds is a leader in the research and development of canola, corn and sunflower seed technology. They have a rich history of performance in Canada and are leaders in seed innovation, being the first company to introduce hybrid canola to the Canadian market. Advanta Seeds has sales, research, and production agronomists located across the country to support their broad distributor network and growing list of research and production locations.

Academic Fields
College: Agricultural, Marketing/Sales
Bachelor of Science: Agriculture, Biology, Chemistry
Chartered Accounting: CGA - General/Finance
Masters: Science

Critical Skills
Adaptable, Confident, Dependable, Diplomatic, Efficient, Enthusiastic, Flexible, Good Communication, Good Writing Skills, Manual Dexterity, Personable, Persuasive, Productive, Professional, Team Player

Types of Positions
Administration   Laboratory Research

Starting Salary
Depends on position

Company Benefits
- Health, dental and wellness program
- Pension plan, safety award program

Correspondence
Mail resume with cover letter or apply through web site
E-mail: heatherglaser@advantacan.com

Part Time/Summer: Advanta Seeds occasionally hires for part time work and regularly hires in the summer months. Potential jobs include assistant sales and marketing agronomists, summer casuals in field work, and technical assistants (lab, field assistant). The best time to apply is in February or March.

AGF MANAGEMENT LIMITED

P.O. Box 50, TD Bank Tower
Toronto, Ontario, M5K 1E9
Tel: (416) 367-1900   Fax: (416) 865-4189

Flora Sousa, Coordinator, Recruitment
Internet: www.agf.com

AGF is one of the most diversified, major independent mutual fund companies in Canada. The company manages the assets of mutual funds in Canada, including RRSP and RRIF eligible funds and provides trust services, mortgages, and guaranteed investment certificates. November through April is their busy time due to the RSP season.

Academic Fields
College: Accounting, Administration, Advertising, Communications, Human Resources, Secretarial, Statistics
Bachelor of Arts: Business, Economics, Political Science, Psychology, Public Relations
Bachelor of Comm/Admin: Accounting, Finance, Marketing, Info Mgmt.
Chartered Accounting: CMA-General, CGA-General

Critical Skills
Adaptable, Analytical, Good Communication, Decisive, Dependable, Diligent, Efficient, Enthusiastic, Flexible, Good With Figures, Innovative, Organized, Patient, Personable, Professional, Responsible

Types of Positions
Client Administration Service Rep.
Client Service Research Asst.

Starting Salary
$ 25,000 - 30,000

Company Benefits
- Full benefit package

Correspondence
Mail or fax resume with cover letter
E-mail: resume@agf.com

Part Time/Summer: AGF regularly hires individuals for part time and summer employment opportunities. Individuals should apply in early April.

The Canada Student Employment Guide

AGRICULTURAL CREDIT CORPORATION OF SASKATCHEWAN
1081 Central Ave. N.
Swift Current, Saskatchewan, S9H 4Y7
Tel: (306) 778-8455   Fax: (306) 778-8550

Nancy Gross, Human Resources Consultant

The Agricultural Credit Corporation of Saskatchewan is a financial institution that offers individuals in the province of Saskatchewan with competitive financial services.

Academic Fields
College: Accounting, Administration, Human Resources, Secretarial
Bachelor of Arts: Economics, Public Relations
Bachelor of Comm/Admin: Accounting, Finance, Marketing, Info Mgmt.
Bachelor of Science: Agriculture
Chartered Accounting: CA - General/Finance, CGA/CMA - General/Finance

Critical Skills
Confident, Creative, Flexible, Good Communication, Innovative, Leadership, Personable, Professional

Types of Positions
Credit Advisor   Junior Systems Analyst
Programmer   Junior Research Analyst
Accounting Clerk

Starting Salary
$ 25,000 - 30,000

Company Benefits
- Pension matching 50% of gross
- Dental, disability and limited vision coverage
- 3 weeks vacation at start, plus 12 'extra' scheduled days off per year

Correspondence
Mail resume with cover letter

Part Time/Summer: The Agricultural Credit Corporation of Saskatchewan sometimes hires for part time and summer opportunities. A potential summer position would include credit advisor trainee. The best time to apply is in March.

AIMTRONICS
1245 California Ave.
Brockville, Ontario, K6V 5Y6
Tel: (613) 342-5041   Fax: (613) 342-1774

Human Resources
Internet: www.aimtronics.com

Aimtronics provides a complete range of highly professional electronic manufacturing solutions that help their customers successfully focus on their core business. They have three manufacturing facilities in Ontario (Kanata, Mississauga and Brockville), one in Delta, British Columbia, and one in Ogdensburg, New York.

Academic Fields
College: Accounting, Electronics Tech.
Bachelor of Comm/Admin: Finance, Info Mgmt.
Bachelor of Engineering: Electrical, Mechanical
Chartered Accounting: CGA-Finance

Critical Skills
Dependable, Efficient, Flexible, Innovative, Manual Dexterity, Personable, Productive, Responsible

Types of Positions
Assembler   General Operator
Junior Engineer   Finance
Marketing   Engineering

Starting Salary
below $ 20,000 (clerical) /
$ 30,000 - 40,000 (engineering)

Company Benefits
- Paid dental, extended health and life insurance
- 2 weeks vacation, pension
- Funding for training towards position

Correspondence
Mail resume with cover letter

Part Time/Summer: Aimtronics does not hire individuals for part time employment or summer jobs.

The Canada Student Employment Guide

AIR CANADA

P.O. Box 14000
Ville St. Laurent, Québec, H4Y 1H4
Tel: (514) 422-5641   Fax: (514) 422-5650

Human Resources
Internet: www.aircanada.ca

In our sixty year history, Air Canada has grown from a modest operation (with two 10-passenger airplanes and a crop duster) to a Cdn. $6.5 billion corporation that maintains a fleet of 158 aircraft (excluding Air Canada's Regional fleet). The company has recently taken ownership of Canadian Airlines.

Academic Fields
College: Accounting, Advertising, Communications, Drafting/Architecture, Engineering Tech., Graphic Arts, Journalism, Law Clerk, Marketing/Sales, Secretarial, Travel/Tourism
Bachelor of Arts: Journalism, Public Relations
Bachelor of Comm/Admin: Accounting, Finance, Marketing, Info Mgmt.
Bachelor of Science: Computer Science
Bachelor of Engineering: Computer Systems, Electrical, Environmental Studies
Chartered Accounting: CMA-General, CGA-Finance
Masters: Business Administration, Engineering

Critical Skills
Confident, Leadership, Personable, French is a must

Types of Positions
Flight Attendant   Customer Service Agent
Finance Clerk   Programmer

Starting Salary
$ 25,000 - 45,000

Company Benefits
- Health, dental, life and disability
- Standard package for permanent employees

Correspondence
Mail resume with cover letter

Part Time/Summer: Air Canada regularly seeks part timers, and sometimes hires in the summer. Minimum requirements include English or French and/or Cantonese, Mandarin, Korean, Japanese, German, Arabic, Hebrew. The best time to apply is from November to January.

AIR LIQUIDE CANADA INC.

1250 Rene Levesque W., Suite 1700
Montreal, Québec, H3B 5E6
Tel: (514) 933-0303   Fax: (514) 846-7700

Human Resources Dept.
Internet: www.airliquide.com

Founded in 1902, the Air Liquide operates in 60 countries through 125 subsidiaries and employs more than 29,000 people. Air Liquide provides innovative solutions which improve the industrial performance of its customers while helping to protect the environment.

Academic Fields
College: Engineering Tech., Welding, Mechanical
Bachelor of Comm/Admin: Accounting, Finance, Marketing
Bachelor of Engineering: Chemical, Computer Systems, Electrical, Industrial, Mechanical, Transportation
Chartered Accounting: CMA-Finance, CGA-Finance
Masters: Business Administration, Engineering

Critical Skills
Adaptable, Confident, Enthusiastic, Flexible, Good Communication, Leadership, Personable

Types of Positions
Start Up Engineer   Customer Service Agent

Starting Salary
$ 25,000 - 30,000

Company Benefits
- Medical, dental, life insurance
- Extensive training on products
- Career discussions, succession planning process in place

Correspondence
Mail or fax resume with cover letter

Part Time/Summer: Air Liquide Canada occasionally hires for part time jobs, and regularly hires for the summer. Potential jobs in the summer are in engineering, or involve other plant work. The best time to apply for potential engineering positions is in December or January, while the best time to apply for plant work is in March.

AIR NOVA INC.

310 Gouden Dr., Halifax International Airport
Enfield, Nova Scotia, B2T 1E4
Tel: (902) 873-5000   Fax: (902) 873-5079

Deborah Mason-Browning, Human Resources
Internet: www.airnova.ca

Air Nova employs over 1000 persons; 35 percent are pilots, 20 percent are flight attendants and 18 percent are maintenance employees, primarily based in Halifax. Eleven percent are station personnel employed at airports throughout Québec and Atlantic Canada.

Academic Fields
College: Hospitality, Secretarial, Travel/Tourism
Bachelor of Arts: Business, Public Relations
Bachelor of Comm/Admin: Accounting, Marketing, Info Management
Bachelor of Engineering: Industrial, Transportation
Chartered Accounting: CMA-Finance

Critical Skills
Adaptable, Dependable, Efficient, Good Communication, Enthusiastic, Flexible, Personable, Professional, Responsible

Types of Positions
Finance Agent   Flight Attendant
Receptionist

Starting Salary
$ 20,000 - 25,000

Company Benefits
- Medical, dental, long term disability
- Life insurance policy, RRSP
- Travel privileges

Correspondence
Mail or fax resume with cover letter

Part Time/Summer: Air Nova sometimes hires for part time work and rarely hires for the summer. They accept applications all the time and keep them on file for a six-month period. Applicants should apply every five months.

AIR ONTARIO INC.

1000 Air Ontario Drive
London, Ontario, N5V 3S4
Tel: (519) 453-8440   Fax: (519) 659-5584

Human Resources
Internet: www.airontario.ca

Air Ontario, headquartered in London, Ontario, Canada, is a wholly-owned subsidiary of Air Canada, and one of four Air Canada connectors. Air Ontario carries over one million passengers annually to 22 destinations throughout central Canada and the Northeastern U.S.A., and employs approximately 900 employees. Air Ontario currently operates a fleet of 27 Dash-8 aircraft, making it one of the largest Dash-8 operators in the world today.

Academic Fields
College: Accounting, Administration, Computer Science, Human Resources, Marketing/Sales, Secretarial, Travel/Tourism, Aircraft Maintenance
Bachelor of Comm/Admin: Accounting, Finance, Marketing, Info Mgmt.
Chartered Accounting: CA - General/Finance, CGA/CMA - General/Finance

Critical Skills
Adaptable, Dependable, Efficient, Good Communication, Enthusiastic, Flexible, Good Writing Skills, Good With Figures, Organized, Personable, Professional, Responsible

Types of Positions
Reception   Accounting Clerk
Accounts Payable   Technical Records
Aircraft Cleaner   Ramp Attendant

Starting Salary
$ 20,000 - 25,000

Company Benefits
- Comprehensive benefits coverage

Correspondence
Mail resume with cover letter

Part Time/Summer: Air Ontario sometimes hires for part time and summer positions. Potential positions in the summer would most likely involve being a technical records clerk or involved in maintenance.

AKITA DRILLING LTD.

1110, 505 - 3rd Street SW
Calgary, Alberta, T2P 3E6
Tel: (403) 292-7979   Fax: (403) 292-7990

Craig Kushner, Administrator, Human Resources

Akita Drilling is a medium sized oil and gas well drilling contractor with operations throughout Western Canada. From offices in Calgary and Nisky, Alberta, the company employs up to 600 people operating 26 drilling rigs in all depth ranges. Akita is active in horizontal and directional drilling and provides specialized drilling services to a broad range of independent and multinational oil and gas companies.

Academic Fields
College: General, Accounting, Business, Engineering Tech.
Bachelor of Arts: General, Business
Bachelor of Comm/Admin: General, Accounting, Finance, Marketing
Bachelor of Engineering: General, Electrical, Mechanical
Chartered Accounting: CA - General/Finance, CGA/CMA - General
Masters: Engineering

Critical Skills
Decisive, Dependable, Diligent, Good Communication, Innovative, Organized, Professional

Types of Positions
Data Entry   Reception

Starting Salary
$ 20,000 - 25,000

Company Benefits
- Group insurance and pension
- Tuition policy

Correspondence
Mail resume with cover letter

Part Time/Summer: Akita Drilling sometimes seeks individuals for part time and summer jobs. In the summer months data entry and field employment are the most likely potential positions.

ALBERTA ALCOHOL AND DRUG ABUSE COMMISSION

10909 Jasper Ave., 6th Floor
Edmonton, Alberta, T5J 3M9
Tel: (780) 427-7935   Fax: (780) 427-1436

Michelle Gosselin, Staffing Assistant
Internet: www.aadac.com

The Alberta Alcohol and Drug Abuse Commission (AADAC) is an agency of the Government of Alberta within the Ministry of Health and Wellness. As a public health agency, AADAC is committed to positively contributing to the health and well-being of Albertans. Their strength in prevention and treatment is their ability to help people succeed with their goals in relation to substance abuse and problem gambling issues.

Academic Fields
College: Nursing (RN), Nursing (RNA), Recreation Studies, Social Work
Bachelor of Arts: Psychology, Sociology/Social Work
Bachelor of Science: Nursing (RN), Psychology
Bachelor of Education: General
Masters: Social Work

Critical Skills
Creative, Good Communication, Innovative, Organized, Personable, Professional, Responsible, Non-judgmental, Caring

Types of Positions
Addictions Counsellor

Starting Salary
$ 30,000 - 35,000

Company Benefits
- Alberta Health Care and Alberta Blue Cross
- Dental plan, long term disability, public service pension plan
- Opportunities for training cover a wide range of skills areas

Correspondence
Mail, fax, or e-mail resume with cover letter
E-mail: hr@aadac.gov.ab.ca

Part Time/Summer: Alberta Alcohol and Drug Abuse Commission occasionally hires for part time or summer employment. The best time to apply is in April or May.

The Canada Student Employment Guide

ALBERTA BLUE CROSS

10009 - 108 Street
Edmonton, Alberta, T5J 3C5
Tel: (403) 498-8507   Fax: (403) 498-8029

Mark Razzolini, HR Administrator

Alberta Blue Cross provides supplementary health care and related benefit programs and services to individuals across the province of Alberta.

Academic Fields
College: Accounting, Communications, Computer Science, Graphic Arts, Human Resources, Journalism, Marketing/Sales, Nursing, Secretarial
Bachelor of Arts: General, Business, Economics, English, Journalism, Public Relations, Statistics
Bachelor of Comm/Admin: General, Accounting, Finance, Marketing, Info Mgmt.
Bachelor of Science: Computer Science, Mathematics, Pharmacy
Bachelor of Education: Adult Education
Chartered Accounting: CMA-General, CGA-General
Masters: Business Administration

Critical Skills
Adaptable, Dependable, Efficient, Flexible, Organized, Personable, Productive, Professional, Responsible, Good Writing Skills

Types of Positions
Claims Processor   Administrative Assistant
Sales Representative   Call Centre Reps

Starting Salary
$ 25,000 - 30,000

Company Benefits
- Alberta health care
- Blue Cross health and dental
- Vision, travel, and life insurance

Correspondence
Mail resume with cover letter

Part Time/Summer: Alberta Blue Cross regularly seeks individuals for part time and summer work. Potential jobs in the summer include claims processor, mailroom clerk, and administrative assistant. The best time to apply is in January.

ALBERTA CANCER BOARD

1220, 10405 Jasper Ave., Standard Life Building
Edmonton, Alberta, T5J 3N4
Tel: (780) 412-6300   Fax: (780) 412-6326

Human Resources

Alberta Cancer Board provides a full range of cancer services including treatment, diagnosis, research and prevention.

Academic Fields
College: Computer Science, Food/Nutrition, Laboratory Tech., Secretarial
Bachelor of Comm/Admin: Info Mgmt.
Bachelor of Science: Nursing (RN), Pharmacy
Masters: Science, Medicine, Nursing

Critical Skills
Diligent, Professional

Types of Positions
Secretary   Laboratory Technologist
Radiology Technologist Programmer
Nurse

Starting Salary
Varies depending on position

Company Benefits
- Full health benefits
- Pension, group insurance
- In-house services, technical presentations, work-related courses and conferences

Correspondence
Mail or fax resume with cover letter
E-mail: jiml@cancerboard.ab.ca

Part Time/Summer: Alberta Cancer Board occasionally seeks individuals for part time employment and regularly hires for the summer. Potential work in the summer involves nursing, pharmacy, research, and information systems. Individuals should apply by early March.

ALBERTA ENERGY & UTILITIES BOARD

640 5th Ave. SW
Calgary, Alberta, T2P 3G4
Tel: (403) 297-8333   Fax: (403) 297-6917

Human Resources
Internet: www.eub.gov.ab.ca

Alberta Energy & Utilities is a provincial regulatory board which oversees the province's energy system.

Academic Fields
College: Accounting, Communications, Computer Science, Drafting/Architecture, Engineering Tech., Human Resources, Journalism, Secretarial
Bachelor of Arts: Business, Economics, Public Relations
Bachelor of Comm/Admin: General, Accounting, Finance, Human Resources
Bachelor of Science: Biology, Chemistry, Computer Science, Environmental Studies, Geology
Bachelor of Laws: General
Bachelor of Engineering: General, Civil, Mechanical, Mining, Chemical, Petroleum
Bachelor of Education: General
Chartered Accounting: CA-General, CMA-General, CGA-General
Masters: Business Admin., Engineering, Library Science

Critical Skills
Analytical, Good Communication, Dependable, Efficient, Innovative, Leadership, Personable, Professional, Responsible, Decisive, Good Writing Skills, Organized, Team Player, Customer Focus, Committed

Types of Positions
Accountant   Engineer
Computer Analyst   Geologist

Starting Salary
$ 28,000 - 40,000 (post secondary graduates)

Company Benefits
- Flexible benefits including extended healthcare

Correspondence
Mail, fax or e-mail resume with cover letter
E-mail: human.resources@gov.ab.ca

Part Time/Summer: Alberta Energy & Utilities rarely hires for part time work, but regularly hires for the summer. Apply in November or December.

Co-op/Internship: They offer internships.

ALBERTA ENERGY COMPANY LTD.

421 7th Ave. SW, Suite 3900
Calgary, Alberta, T2P 4K9
Tel: (403) 423-8333   Fax: (403) 266-8256

Jody Klotz, Human Resources
Internet: www.aec.ca

Alberta Energy Company is an oil and gas exploration company which is involved in oil production, transportation and storage.

Academic Fields
College: Accounting, Administration, Computer Science, Electronics Tech., Engineering Tech., Mechanical Tech.
Bachelor of Comm/Admin: Accounting, Finance, Marketing, Info Mgmt.
Bachelor of Science: Chemistry, Computer Science, Geology, Physics
Bachelor of Engineering: General, Electrical, Environmental Studies, Geotechnical, Mechanical
Chartered Accounting: CA-General
Masters: Business Administration, Engineering

Critical Skills
Analytical, Good Communication, Dependable, Efficient, Flexible, Leadership, Personable, Professional, Responsible, Good Writing Skills

Types of Positions
New Grad Engineers (Petroleum)   Geology
Geophysics

Starting Salary
$ 30,000 - 40,000

Company Benefits
- Flexible benefit system to suit employee's needs
- 100% job related training support
- Career development program

Correspondence
Mail, fax, or e-mail resume with cover letter

Part Time/Summer: Alberta Energy Company does not hire for part time work, but regularly looks for individuals for summer work. Summer employment involves all areas including geology, geophysics, accounting, engineering, computer services, and marketing. The best time to apply is October to December.

ALBERTA GAMING & LIQUOR COMMISSION
50 Corriveau Ave.
St. Albert, Alberta, T8N 3T5
Tel: (780) 447-8600   Fax: (780) 447-8918

Human Resources
Internet: www.aglc.gov.ab.ca

On May 25, 1999, the Alberta Gaming and Liquor Commission (AGLC) became part of the Ministry of Gaming. The AGLC is an agent of the Government of Alberta and consists of a Board and a Corporation. The Corporation acts as the operational arm of the organization, while the Board handles policy and regulatory responsibilities.

Academic Fields
College: General, Accounting, Administration, Business, Computer Science, Electronics Tech., Engineering Tech., Human Res., Marketing/Sales, Secretarial, Security/Law
Bachelor of Arts: General, Business, Economics
Bachelor of Comm/Admin: General, Accounting, Finance, Info Mgmt., Public Admin.
Bachelor of Science: General, Computer Science
Bachelor of Engineering: General, Computer Systems
Bachelor of Education: General
Chartered Accounting: CMA-Finance, CGA-Finance
Masters: Business Administration

Critical Skills
Adaptable, Analytical, Good Communication, Dependable, Diligent, Efficient, Enthusiastic, Flexible, Good With Figures, Innovative, Leadership, Manual Dexterity, Organized, Personable, Persuasive, Productive, Professional, Responsible, Writing Skills

Types of Positions
Licensing Inspectors   Field Technicians
Research Officer   Accounting Supervisors

Starting Salary
$ 20,000 - 30,000

Company Benefits
- 50/50 cost sharing benefit package, extended health

Correspondence
Mail or fax resume with cover letter

Part Time/Summer: Alberta Gaming & Liquor Commission regularly hires for part time and summer jobs. Potential work includes field personnel. The best time to apply is in April or May.

ALBERTO CULVER CANADA INC.
506 Kipling Avenue
Toronto, Ontario, M8Z 5E2
Tel: (416) 251-3741   Fax: (416) 251-3062

Joan Madden, Human Resources

Alberto Culver Canada is a subsidiary of The Alberto Culver Company, an international consumer manufacturing firm which produces V05 products, many food products, and operates a chain of Sally Beauty Supply stores. Their core international retail markets are in the United States, United Kingdom, South Africa, Puerto Rico, Australia, New Zealand, Sweden, Norway, Denmark, and Finland.

Academic Fields
College: Accounting, Business
Bachelor of Arts: Business
Bachelor of Comm/Admin: Marketing
Bachelor of Science: Biology, Chemistry
Chartered Accounting: CMA-Finance, CGA-Finance

Critical Skills
Adaptable, Analytical, Good Communication, Dependable, Diligent, Efficient, Enthusiastic, Good Writing Skills, Logical, Organized, Personable, Productive, Professional, Responsible

Types of Positions
Accounting Clerk   Customer Service

Starting Salary
$ 25,000 - 30,000

Company Benefits
- Full benefits
- On-the-job training and development

Correspondence
Mail resume with cover letter

Part Time/Summer: Alberto Culver Canada does not generally hire for part time employment, but occasionally looks for candidates in the summer months. Potential jobs include clerical, accounting, or manufacturing. The best time to apply is in May.

ALCAN ALUMINIUM LIMITED

1188 rue Sherbrooke Ouest
Montréal, Québec, H3A 3G2
Tel: (514) 848-8000   Fax: (514) 848-1275

Human Resources
Internet: www.alcan.com

Alcan Aluminum is the parent company of a multinational industrial group engaged in all aspects of the aluminum business. Through subsidiaries and related companies around the world, the activities of Alcan Aluminum include bauxite mining, alumna refining, aluminum smelting, manufacturing, sales and recycling. The firm employs more than 37,500 individuals.

Academic Fields
College: Computer Sci., Electronics Tech., Engineering Tech., Industrial Design, Mechanical Tech., Secretarial
Bachelor of Arts: Psychology, Public Relations
Bachelor of Comm/Admin: Accounting, Finance, Info Mgmt.
Bachelor of Science: Actuarial, Chemistry, Computer Science, Environmental Studies, Physics, Psychology
Bachelor of Laws: Corporate
Bachelor of Engineering: Chemical, Computer Systems, Electrical, Industrial, Mechanical
Chartered Accounting: CMA - General/Finance
Masters: Business Administration, Science, Engineering

Critical Skills
Analytical, Creative, Dependable, Good Communication, Efficient, Enthusiastic, Flexible, Good Writing Skills, Innovative, Responsible

Types of Positions
Technical Positions   Engineering Positions

Starting Salary
$ 30,000 - 40,000

Company Benefits
- Major medical and dental benefits
- Life insurance, sick pay and vacation pay

Correspondence
Mail resume with cover letter

Part Time/Summer: Alcan Aluminum sometimes hires for part time work and regularly hires for the summer. There are various positions in the summer months. The best time to apply is in February or March.

ALEXANDRA HOSPITAL

29 Noxon St.
Ingersoll, Ontario, N5C 3V6
Tel: (519) 485-1700   Fax: (519) 485-5486

Human Resources
Internet: www.alexandrahospital.on.ca

Alexandra Hospital is a 32 bed health care facility in Ingersoll. They offer a wide range of medical services. The hospital employs approximately 185 individuals.

Academic Fields
College: Administration, Business
Bachelor of Arts: Business
Masters: Business Administration

Critical Skills
Good Communication, Confident, Creative, Dependable, Efficient, Enthusiastic, Flexible, Good With Figures, Leadership, Organized, Patient, Personable, Productive, Professional, Responsible, Good Writing Skills

Types of Positions
Various Positions

Starting Salary
Varies depending on position

Company Benefits
- Full range of benefits

Correspondence
Mail, fax, or submit resume with cover letter in person

Part Time/Summer: Alexandra Hospital does not hire for part time work, but occasionally seeks candidates for the summer. A potential job in the summer is administrative resident.

The Canada Student Employment Guide

ALGOMA CHILD & YOUTH SERVICES INC.

205 McNabb St.
Sault Ste. Marie, Ontario, P6A 3S2
Tel: (705) 945-5050   Fax: (705) 942-9273

Lloyd Beilhartz, Manager HR

Algoma Child & Youth Services is a children's mental health agency that provides counselling services to both children and their families. They have an employee base of approximately 100 individuals.

Academic Fields
College: Child Care
Bachelor of Arts: Sociology/Social Work

Critical Skills
Analytical, Good Communication, Professional, Personable, Responsible, Good Writing Skills

Types of Positions
Various Positions

Starting Salary
$ 25,000 - 30,000 (depending on position)

Company Benefits
- Full range of benefits

Correspondence
Mail resume with cover letter

Part Time/Summer: Algoma Child & Youth Services occasionally hires for part time employment, and regularly seeks candidates in the summer. Jobs in the summer involve being a recreation assistant. The best time to apply is in May.

THE ALGOMA DISTRICT HOME FOR AGED

860 Great Northern Rd.
Sault Ste. Marie, Ontario, P6A 5K7
Tel: (705) 942-2204   Fax: (705) 942-3402

Shirley Mason, HR Coordinator
Internet: www.adhfa.org

Algoma District Home For The Aged operates two homes - Algoma Manor in Thessalon and Davey Home in Sault Ste. Marie. They have an employee base of approximately 300 individuals.

Academic Fields
College: Cooking/Culinary, Food/Nutrition, Human Resources, Nursing, Secretarial
Chartered Accounting: CMA-Finance

Critical Skills
Good Communication, Dependable, Efficient, Organized, Patient, Personable, Productive, Professional, Responsible, Good Writing Skills

Types of Positions
Nursing (Health Care Aide)   Registered Nurse
Housekeeping/Laundry Aide   Dietary Aide
Activities Aide   Office Worker

Starting Salary
$ 25,000 - 30,000 (depends on position)

Company Benefits
- Pension, extended health, dental, vision and sick leave
- Orientation to home
- In-house training

Correspondence
Mail, or submit resume with cover letter in person
E-mail: smason@adhfa.org

Part Time/Summer: Algoma District Homes For The Aged regularly hires for part time work summer opportunities. Potential jobs in the summer include health care aide, office work, housekeeping, maintenance, activities, social work or dietary worker. The best time to apply is in February or March.

ALGOMA STEEL INC.

P.O. Box 1400, Stn Main
Sault Ste. Marie, Ontario, P6A 5P2
Tel: (705) 945-2240   Fax: (705) 945-2270

Gus Kowalski, Supervisor/Co-ordinator
Internet: www.algoma.com

Algoma Steel is Canada's third largest integrated steel producer and a market leader in the manufacturing of hot rolled plate steel. Algoma was the first Canadian steel maker to convert to 100% continuous casting in the 1990's. The company employs 4,300 individuals.

Academic Fields
College: Accounting, Information Systems, Computer Science, Electronics Tech., Engineering Tech., Mechanical Tech., Electrical Technology
Bachelor of Arts: Business, Economics
Bachelor of Comm/Admin: Accounting, Finance, Marketing, Info Mgmt.
Bachelor of Science: Chemistry, Computer Sci., Math
Bachelor of Engineering: Chemical, Computer Systems, Electrical, Materials Science, Mechanical, Metallurgical
Chartered Accounting: CA-General, CGA-General, CMA-General

Critical Skills
Analytical, Confident, Decisive, Enthusiastic, Flexible, Good Communication, Leadership, Organized

Types of Positions
Systems Assistant   Technology Assistant
Engineering Assistant   Operations Assistant

Starting Salary
$ 30,000 - 40,000

Company Benefits
- Major medical and dental plan, pension plan

Correspondence
Mail resume with cover letter
E-mail: gkowalski@algoma.com

Part Time/Summer: Algoma Steel sometimes hires for part time and summer work. Potential jobs involve general production, clerical replacement and technical project assignments. Apply in February and April.

ALIANT TELECOM INC.

P.O. Box 2110
St. John's, Newfoundland, A1C 5H6
Tel: (709) 739-2897   Fax: (709) 739-3602

Charmaine Williams, Career Consultant
Internet: www.aliant.ca

The Aliant group of advanced technology companies and its staff of more than 9,500 professionals delivers full service, integrated solutions through its four core lines of business: wireline and wireless telecommunications, information technology, mobile satellite services, and emerging business solutions.

Academic Fields
Bachelor of Comm/Admin: General, Accounting, Finance, Human Resources, Marketing, Info Mgmt.
Bachelor of Science: Computer Science, Occupational Therapy
Bachelor of Engineering: Civil, Computer Systems, Electrical, Industrial
Masters: Business Administration

Critical Skills
Relationship Building, Solutions Focus, Business Judgment, Performance Focus, Collaboration, Coaching, Self Management, Leadership

Types of Positions
Direct Marketing   Junior Engineer

Starting Salary
$ 25,000 - 40,000

Company Benefits
- Full range, cost shared flexible benefits plan
- Pension, RRSP, employee share purchase

Correspondence
E-mail resume with cover letter
E-mail: hr@newtel.com

Part Time/Summer: Aliant Telecom occasionally hires for part time and summer work. Potential jobs include operator services and building equipment technician. The best time to apply is in early March.

ALIAS | WAVEFRONT

210 King St. E.
Toronto, Ontario, M5A 1J7
Tel: (416) 362-9181   Fax: (416) 369-6142

Human Resources
Internet: www.aw.sgi.com

Alias | Wavefront is a software development company producing 3D animation and design software. Most of their entry level roles do require experience working with their software. The company employs approximately 300 individuals across Canada.

Academic Fields
College: Animation, Information Systems, Industrial Design, Web Design
Bachelor of Science: Computer Science
Masters: Engineering

Critical Skills
Adaptable, Artistic, Good Communication, Confident, Creative, Decisive, Dependable, Diligent, Efficient, Good With Figures, Logical, Organized, Personable, Professional, Responsible, Good Writing Skills

Types of Positions
Product Specialist   Multi-Media Web Designs
Administrative Roles   Software Engineer
Product Tester   Product/Customer Support

Starting Salary
$ 30,000 - 40,000 (depending on position)

Company Benefits
- Full company benefits for permanent employees

Correspondence
Fax or email resume with cover letter
E-mail: careers@aw.sgi.com

Part Time/Summer: Alias | Wavefront rarely seeks individuals for part time and summer employment.

Co-op/Internship: Some internships for industrial design students, web developers/editors, software engineer/computer science students.

ALLCOLOUR PAINT LIMITED

1257 Speers Rd.
Oakville, Ontario, L6L 2X5
Tel: (905) 827-4173   Fax: (905) 827-6487

Mauro LoRusso, Human Resources
Internet: www.allcolour.com

Allcolour Paint Limited is a Canadian manufacturer of industrial coatings including alkyds air dry and baking, two component polyurethanes, epoxy systems and many more custom formulated coating systems.

Academic Fields
College: Administration, Business
Bachelor of Comm/Admin: Accounting, Finance, Marketing
Chartered Accounting: CMA - General/Finance, CGA - General/Finance

Critical Skills
Analytical, Good Communication, Decisive, Dependable, Diligent, Efficient, Good With Figures, Logical, Organized, Personable, Professional, Responsible, Good Writing Skills

Types of Positions
Accounting Clerk   Receptionist
Order Entry Clerk

Starting Salary
$ 25,000 - 30,000

Company Benefits
- Health and long term disability
- 80% dental paid
- RRSP after 1 year matching

Correspondence
Mail, fax or email resume with cover letter

Part Time/Summer: Allcolour Paint occasionally seeks individuals for part time work, and regularly hires for the summer. Jobs in the summer involve working in the plant. The best time to apply is in May or June.

The Canada Student Employment Guide

ALLIANZ CANADA

425 Bloor St. E., Suite 200
Toronto, Ontario, M4W 3R5
Tel: (416) 961-5015   Fax: (416) 961-3088

Human Resources
Internet: www.allianz.ca

Allianz Canada is the Canadian subsidiary of Allianz AG, a large multi-national insurance organization operating in over 70 countries on five continents. They are in all regions of Canada with office locations in Quebec, Ontario, Alberta and British Columbia. They also service the Maritimes through a managing general agent.

Academic Fields
College: General, Accounting, Administration, Business, Computer Science, Human Resources, Insurance, Marketing/Sales
Bachelor of Arts: General, Business
Bachelor of Comm/Admin: General, Accounting, Finance, Info Mgmt.
Bachelor of Science: Actuarial, Computer Science, Mathematics
Chartered Accounting: CA - General/Finance, CGA/CMA - General/Finance
Masters: Business Administration

Critical Skills
Analytical, Good Communication, Leadership, Organized, Personable, Professional, Good Writing Skills

Types of Positions
Claims Clerk   Receptionist
Underwriting Assistant File/Mail Clerk

Starting Salary
$ 25,000 - 30,000

Company Benefits
- Medical and dental coverage
- Company pays for business related training
- Free on-site fitness facility

Correspondence
Mail or fax resume with cover letter

Part Time/Summer: Allianz Canada occasionally hires for part time and summer employment. Potential jobs include filing, underwriting assistant, and special projects. The best time to apply is in June or prior to June.

ALLMAR DISTRIBUTORS LTD.

287 Riverton Ave.
Winnipeg, Manitoba, R2L 0N2
Tel: (204) 688-3000   Fax: (204) 663-3937

Jan Pritchard, Human Resources

Allmar is a wholesale distributor of architectural hardware, building materials and lumber across Western Canada. Their sales divisions are guided by industry norms, customer relationships, and product knowledge.

Academic Fields
College: Accounting, Drafting/Architecture, Graphic Arts, Human Resources, Marketing/Sales
Bachelor of Comm/Admin: General, Marketing
Chartered Accounting: CA-General, CMA-General, CGA-General

Critical Skills
Adaptable, Analytical, Good Communication, Dependable, Diligent, Diplomatic, Efficient, Flexible, Good With Figures, Innovative, Logical, Organized, Patient, Personable, Productive, Professional, Responsible

Types of Positions
Accounting Clerk   Office Clerk
Shipper/Receiver

Starting Salary
$ 20,000 plus

Company Benefits
- Group insurance benefits, salary advancement opportunities
- On-the-job training, profit based incentives
- Benefits for permanent employees

Correspondence
Mail resume with cover letter

Part Time/Summer: Allmar Distributors occasionally looks for people for part time work, and regularly seeks individuals for summer employment. Positions in the summer are mostly in shipping/receiving. The best time to apply is from February to April.

ALLSTATE INSURANCE CO. OF CANADA

10 Allstate Parkway
Markham, Ontario, L3R 5P8
Tel: (905) 477-6900   Fax: (905) 475-4924

Margaret Attamanchuk, HR Representative
Internet: www.allstate.ca

Allstate is a major insurance company in Canada that specializes in personal line services. Employing over 1,600 individuals, Allstate is a wholly owned subsidiary of Allstate Life Insurance Co. of Northbrook, Illinois.

Academic Fields
College: Accounting, Business, Communications, Computer Science, Insurance
Bachelor of Arts: General, Business, Economics, English, Psychology
Bachelor of Comm/Admin: General, Finance, Info Mgmt.
Chartered Accounting: CA - General/Finance, CGA/CMA - General/Finance

Critical Skills
Adaptable, Analytical, Good Communication, Confident, Decisive, Dependable, Diligent, Diplomatic, Efficient, Enthusiastic, Logical, Patient, Personable, Productive, Professional, Responsible, Good Writing Skills

Types of Positions
Market Support Associate
Actuarial Student Position
Record Clerk

Starting Salary
$ 20,000 - 30,000 (depending on position available)

Company Benefits
- Life, dental, extended health care, drug and vision
- Pension and profit sharing programs
- In-house training programs to develop industry skills

Correspondence
Mail, fax, submit resume & cover letter in person

Part Time/Summer: Allstate Insurance sometimes hires for part time and summer positions. Some potential summer opportunities include data entry, filing, and customer service. The best time to apply is January through to March.

ALPINE OIL SERVICE CORPORATION

2460, 240 - 4th Avenue SW
Calgary, Alberta, T2P 4H4
Tel: (403) 263-7800   Fax: (403) 264-7260

Mark Desaunoy, Human Resources
Internet: www.alpineoil.com

With headquarters in Calgary, Alberta, Alpine Oil Service provides specialized technology used during the drilling, testing, completion and production of petroleum reservoirs. Alpine provides various services in North America, South America, North Africa, and sells its equipment worldwide.

Academic Fields
College: Computer Science, Drafting/Architecture
Bachelor of Arts: Business
Bachelor of Comm/Admin: Accounting, Finance, Info Mgmt.
Bachelor of Science: Computer Science
Bachelor of Engineering: Mechanical
Chartered Accounting: CA-General, CMA-General, CGA-General

Critical Skills
Good Communication, Diligent, Efficient, Innovative, Professional, Responsible

Types of Positions
Various Positions

Starting Salary
$ 25,000 - 30,000

Company Benefits
- Health and dental insurance
- Group RRSP

Correspondence
Mail or e-mail resume with cover letter

Part Time/Summer: Alpine Oil Service occasionally looks for individuals for part time or summer work. The best time to apply for summer opportunities is in April or May.

The Canada Student Employment Guide

ALTONA COMMUNITY MEMORIAL HEALTH CENTRE

240 - 5th Avenue N.E.
Altona, Manitoba, R0G 0B0
Tel: (204) 324-6411   Fax: (204) 324-1299

Merrilee Giesbrecht, Human Resources

Altona Community Memorial Health Centre is a general medical and surgical hospital. They have an employee base of approximately 100 individuals.

Academic Fields
College: Accounting, Nursing, Recreation Studies
Bachelor of Science: Nursing (RN)
Chartered Accounting: CA-Finance

Critical Skills
Adaptable, Confident, Creative, Decisive, Dependable, Diplomatic, Efficient, Enthusiastic, Flexible, Innovative, Leadership, Logical, Manual Dexterity, Organized, Patient, Personable, Professional, Responsible

Types of Positions
Nurse Aide	Dietary Aide
Activity Aide	Housekeeping Aide
Activity Worker	Maintenance Worker

Starting Salary
$ 20,000 - 25,000

Company Benefits
- Health and dental insurance
- Long term disability, pension plan
- Training and development as needed

Correspondence
Mail resume with cover letter

Part Time/Summer: Altona Community Memorial Health Centre occasionally hires for part time work, and regularly seeks candidates in the summer. Potential jobs include aides in all departments, especially nursing. Graduate nurses are sometimes hired on a casual basis. The best time to apply is in April or May.

ALUMICOR LIMITED

33 Racine Rd.
Etobicoke, Ontario, M9W 2Z4
Tel: (416) 745-4222   Fax: (416) 745-7759

Jim Shepherd, Human Resources
Internet: www.alumicor.com

Alumicor Limited is a Canadian based architectural aluminum company, in business since 1959. A recognized leader in it's field, Alumicor Limited today operates through four efficient manufacturing plants in Canada, a number of sales offices in North America and a number of partnerships around the world.

Academic Fields
College: Drafting/Architecture
Bachelor of Engineering: Civil, Design, Industrial

Critical Skills
Analytical, Good Communication, Diligent, Enthusiastic, Innovative, Organized, Productive

Types of Positions
Project Coordinator	Drafter

Starting Salary
$ 20,000 - 25,000

Company Benefits
- Health and dental insurance
- Benefits received after completion of 6 month probationary period

Correspondence
Mail or fax resume with cover letter

Part Time/Summer: Alumicor Limited does not hire for part time work, but sometimes seeks candidates for summer opportunities. Potential jobs in the summer include general help in shipping and receiving.

AMCAN CASTINGS LIMITED

P.O. Box 446, L.C.D. 1, 10 Hillyard St.
Hamilton, Ontario, L8L 7X3
Tel: (905) 527-9178   Fax: (905) 527-9150

Human Resources Dept.
Internet: www.amcancastings.com

Amcan Castings is an aluminum die casting firm for the auto industry. They have one large size casting plant in Hamilton, one small size casting plant in Burlington, and one precision machining plant also in Burlington. In total, they employ over 725 individuals.

Academic Fields
College: Accounting, Engineering Tech., Human Resources, Mechanical Engineering
Bachelor of Arts: General, Business, Economics
Bachelor of Comm/Admin: General
Bachelor of Engineering: General, Design, Mechanical
Chartered Accounting: CA - General/Finance,
CGA/CMA - General/Finance
Masters: Business Administration

Critical Skills
Adaptable, Analytical, Good Communication, Confident, Decisive, Dependable, Flexible, Leadership, Productive, Good Writing Skills

Types of Positions
Engineering	Process Control
Designing	Human Resources
Purchasing	Quality

Starting Salary
$ 25,000 - 30,000 (college), $ 30,000 - 40,000 (university)

Company Benefits
- Full health benefit package
- Group RRSP
- Bonus system paid monthly

Correspondence
Mail or fax resume with cover letter

Part Time/Summer: Amcan Castings Limited regularly hires individuals for part time and summer employment. They generally hire co-op students to work in the factory sections of their plants. The best time to apply is in April.

AMCOR TWINPAK NORTH AMERICA INC.

1255 Trans-Canada Hwy, Suite 210
Dorval, Québec, H9P 2V4
Tel: (514) 684-7070   Fax: (514) 684-3128

Human Resources Department
Internet: www.twinpak.com

Amcor Twinpak North America is a Canadian leader in plastic, paper and composite material packaging. The company possess expertise in injection molding, stretch blow molding, extrusion, thermoforming, paper and film converting, laminating, extrusion coating and printing. Amcor Twinpak employs some 1,023 Canadians.

Academic Fields
College: Accounting, Administration, Business, Computer Science, Engineering Tech., Human Resources, Marketing/Sales, Science, Secretarial
Bachelor of Arts: Business, Economics
Bachelor of Comm/Admin: General, Accounting, Finance, Marketing, Info Mgmt.
Bachelor of Science: Chemistry, Comp. Sci., Math
Bachelor of Engineering: Chemical, Computer Systems, Mechanical
Chartered Accounting: CA - General/Finance,
CGA/CMA - General/Finance
Masters: Business Admin., Arts, Science, Engineering

Critical Skills
Adaptable, Analytical, Good Communication, Confident, Creative, Dependable, Diplomatic, Efficient, Enthusiastic, Flexible, Innovative, Leadership, Organized, Personable, Productive, Professional, Responsible, Good Writing Skills

Types of Positions
Accounting Clerk	Receptionist
Salesperson	Laboratory Tech.
Purchasing Clerk	Customer Service

Starting Salary
$ 25,000 - 35,000

Company Benefits
- Very generous pension and group insurance plans

Correspondence
Mail or fax resume with cover letter

Part Time/Summer: They sometimes hire for part time work and regularly hire for the summer. Jobs involve accounting or vacation replacement of regular staff. The best time to apply is in May or June.

The Canada Student Employment Guide

AMEC INC.

36 Toronto Street, Suite 300
Toronto, Ontario, M5C 2C5
Tel: (416) 644-3621   Fax: N/A

Human Resources
Internet: www.amec.com

AGRA Inc. has changed its name to AMEC Inc. and adopted AMEC's new corporate identity. This follows the recently complete merger between AGRA and AMEC plc of the United Kingdom. AGRA's subsidiary companies continue to operate under the AGRA name but will adopt the AMEC identity in January, 2001. With offices throughout the Americas, AMEC provides total life of asset support through professional engineering, construction, environmental and technology services.

Academic Fields
College: Accounting, Administration, Business, Human Resources, Insurance, Law Clerk, Admin., Security/Law
Bachelor of Laws: Corporate
Chartered Accounting: CA-Finance, CGA/CMA - Finance

Critical Skills
Adaptable, Analytical, Good Communication, Confident, Decisive, Dependable, Diligent, Diplomatic, Efficient, Enthusiastic, Flexible, Good With Figures, Logical, Manual Dexterity, Organized, Patient, Personable, Productive, Professional, Responsible, Good Writing Skills

Types of Positions
Payables Clerk   Accounting Clerk
Legal Assistant   Receptionist

Starting Salary
$ 30,000 - 40,000

Company Benefits
- Life, health and dental upon employment
- Group RRSP with company matching contributions

Correspondence
Mail resume with cover letter

Part Time/Summer: AMEC sometimes hires for part time work, but does not hire for the summer.

Co-op/Internship: Open to exploring internship opportunities.

AMERICAN AIRLINES INC.

P.O. Box 6005, L.B. Pearson Int'l Airport
Toronto, Ontario, L5P 1B6
Tel: (905) 612-7266   Fax: (905) 612-0144

Jeffrey D. Ward, Supervisor Administration

AMR Corporation consists of American Airlines, along with American Eagle offer airline service to more than 300 destinations around the world.

Academic Fields
College: Accounting, Business, Marketing/Sales, Travel/Tourism
Bachelor of Arts: Business, Economics, Fine Arts, History, Languages, Public Relations
Bachelor of Comm/Admin: General, Accounting, Marketing
Masters: Business Administration

Critical Skills
Adaptable, Good Communication, Confident, Dependable, Diplomatic, Efficient, Enthusiastic, Flexible, Good With Figures, Manual Dexterity, Organized, Patient, Personable, Professional, Responsible

Types of Positions
Airport Passenger Service Agent
Cargo Service Agent

Starting Salary
$ 25,000

Company Benefits
- Full benefits, travel privileges
- Company paid life insurance, pension plan
- 4 weeks training

Correspondence
Mail resume with cover letter

Part Time/Summer: American Airlines occasionally looks for candidates for part time or summer opportunities. A job in the summer may be passenger assist agent. The best time to apply is in March.

The Canada Student Employment Guide

AMRAM'S DISTRIBUTING LTD.

18 Parkshore Dr.
Brampton, Ontario, L6T 5M1
Tel: (416) 675-1040   Fax: (416) 675-3230

Susan Nowocin, Human Resources

Amram Distributing is a wholesaler and distributor of giftware and toys. They have a sales force of 60 people across Canada, and a Canadian head office in Etobicoke.

Academic Fields
College: General, Business, Communications, Human Resources, Marketing/Sales
Bachelor of Arts: General, Business, Psychology, Public Relations
Bachelor of Comm/Admin: General, Marketing

Critical Skills
Adaptable, Good Communication, Creative, Dependable, Enthusiastic, Flexible, Organized, Personable, Persuasive, Productive, Professional, Responsible

Types of Positions
Customer Service Representative   Sales Representative
Collector

Starting Salary
$ 20,000 - 25,000

Company Benefits
- Medical, dental, health and life insurance
- Deferred profit sharing, stock purchase plan
- Product knowledge, technology training

Correspondence
Mail resume with cover letter

Part Time/Summer: Amram's Distributing does not hire individuals for part time work, but occasionally seeks out people for the summer. However, in recent years they rarely hire for the summer. If they do, the best time to apply is in late July.

ANCAST INDUSTRIES LTD.

1351 Saskatchewan Ave.
Winnipeg, Manitoba, R3E 0L2
Tel: (204) 786-7911   Fax: (204) 786-2548

Human Resources
Internet: www.ancast.mb.ca

Ancast utilizes state of the art technology, equipment and processes to stay on the cutting edge of ductile and grey iron custom casting production. Their plant is in Winnipeg, and they have an employee base of approximately 180 individuals.

Academic Fields
College: Engineering Tech.
Bachelor of Engineering: Industrial, Mechanical

Critical Skills
Dependable, Responsible

Types of Positions
General Utility Person   Grinder

Starting Salary
$ 20,000 - 25,000

Company Benefits
- Standard health and dental, life insurance
- Long and short term disability
- Group RRSP

Correspondence
Mail resume with cover letter
E-mail: ancast@ancast.mb.ca

Part Time/Summer: Ancast Industries occasionally looks for people for part time duties, and regularly looks for candidates for the summer months. Potential work in the summer could be maintenance helper, engineering assistant, or general labourer. The best time to apply is in February.

ANDERSEN CONSULTING

185 The West Mall, Suite 500
Etobicoke, Ontario, M9C 5L5
Tel: (416) 641-5100   Fax: (416) 641-5044

Human Resources
Internet: www.ac.com

Andersen Consulting is a global management and technology consulting firm whose mission is to help its clients create their future. They employ 500 individuals at this location and approximately 1,400 people in Canada.

Academic Fields
Bachelor of Arts: Business, Psychology
Bachelor of Comm/Admin: General, Information Systems
Bachelor of Science: Computer Science, Mathematics, Psychology
Bachelor of Engineering: General, Chemical, Civil, Computer Systems, Design, Electrical, Industrial, Mechanical
Masters: Business Administration, Science, Engineering

Critical Skills
Adaptable, Flexible, Good Communication, Professional,

Types of Positions
Process Analyst
Technology Analyst
Change Management Analyst

Starting Salary
$ 40,000 - 55,000 plus

Company Benefits
- Competitive benefits package
- Industry leading training

Correspondence
Apply through their web site

Part Time/Summer: Andersen Consulting does not hire for part time work but occasionally hires for the summer months. They have a student leadership conference in February. The best time to apply for summer work varies.

Co-op/Internship: Internship opportunities vary. See your career centre for details.

ANJURA SERVICES INC.

6 Gurdwara Rd., Suite 101
Nepean, Ontario, K2E 8A3
Tel: (613) 228-0988   Fax: (613) 228-0366

Human Resources
Internet: www.anjura.com

Anjura Services recruits, trains and manages people for the IT service market. Their client base is a mix of private and public sector organizations. They currently have 70 specialized consultants and over 400 customer service and technical help desk employees.

Academic Fields
College: Accounting, Administration, Business, Communications, Computer Science
Bachelor of Science: Computer Sciences
Bachelor of Engineering: Computer Systems

Critical Skills
Analytical, Confident, Dependable, Diplomatic, Efficient, Enthusiastic, Good Communication, Good Writing Skills, Organized, Patient, Personable, Productive, Professional, Responsible

Types of Positions
Data Entry
Customer Service/Bilingual Agent
Technical Support Agent

Starting Salary
$ 20,000 - 25,000

Company Benefits
- Life insurance, medical, dental plan after 3 months
- Customer service and technical support training

Correspondence
Fax or e-mail resume with cover letter
E-mail: jobs@anjura.com

Part Time/Summer: Anjura Services occasionally seeks candidates for part time employment, but does not hire for the summer months.

The Canada Student Employment Guide

ANTAMEX INTERNATIONAL INC.

125 Villarboit Cres.
Concord, Ontario, L4K 4K2
Tel: (905) 660-4520   Fax: (905) 669-4402

Human Resources
Internet: www.antamex.com

Antamex International is a designer, manufacturer, and installer of curtainwall. Working in a metal fabrication environment, the firm employs about 120 individuals.

Academic Fields
College: Computer Science, Drafting/Architecture
Bachelor of Comm/Admin: General

Critical Skills
Analytical, Responsible, Good Writing Skills

Types of Positions
Architectural Drafting   Industrial Engineering
Production Control

Starting Salary
$ 25,000 - 30,000

Company Benefits
- Basic benefit package, no pension plan
- Seminars and in-house training
- An employee profit sharing company

Correspondence
Mail resume with cover letter E-mail:
nchatee@antamex.com

Part Time/Summer: Antamex International occasionally hires for part time work, and regularly looks for people for the summer. Potential jobs in the summer months involve general labour.

ANTHONY INSURANCE INC.

ICON Building, 187 Kenmount Rd., Box 8130
St. John's, Newfoundland, A1B 3N2
Tel: (709) 758-5600   Fax: (709) 579-4500

Pauline Russell, Human Resources

Anthony Insurance offers personal automobile, home and commercial insurance. They also provide life insurance and many financial products.

Academic Fields
College: General, Accounting, Administration, Advertising, Business, Communications, Computer Sci., Insurance, Law Clerk, Marketing/Sales, Secretarial
Bachelor of Arts: General, Business, English, Psychology
Bachelor of Comm/Admin: General, Accounting, Finance, Marketing, Info Mgmt.
Bachelor of Science: Computer Science
Bachelor of Laws: Corporate
Bachelor of Engineering: Computer Systems
Bachelor of Education: General, Adult Education
Chartered Accounting: CA - General/Finance, CMA-Finance, CGA - General/Finance
Masters: Business Administration, Arts, Education

Critical Skills
Adaptable, Analytical, Good Communication, Confident, Creative, Decisive, Dependable, Diligent, Diplomatic, Efficient, Enthusiastic, Flexible, Good With Figures, Innovative, Leadership, Logical, Organized, Patient, Personable, Persuasive, Productive, Professional, Responsible, Good Writing Skills

Types of Positions
Receptionist   Junior Computer Programmer
Junior Underwriter

Starting Salary
below $ 20,000 - 25,000

Company Benefits
- Dental, drug, vision care, life insurance

Correspondence
Mail, fax, e-mail, or submit resume in person
E-mail: russp@newcomm.net

Part Time/Summer: Anthony Insurance occasionally hires part time workers, and regularly hires in the summer. Potential jobs are most likely listed above. April or May is the best time to apply.

The Canada Student Employment Guide

AON REED STENHOUSE INC.

20 Bay St., Reed Stenhouse Tower
Toronto, Ontario, M5J 2N9
Tel: (416) 868-5500   Fax: (416) 868-5502

Human Resources
Internet: www.aon.ca

Aon is Canada's premier insurance brokerage, consulting services and consumer insurance underwriting organization. With offices in 24 cities across Canada and with a worldwide network of more than 550 offices in 120 countries, Aon has solutions for all your insurance, risk management and human resources consulting needs.

Academic Fields
College: Insurance, Secretarial
Bachelor of Comm/Admin: Finance

Critical Skills
Analytical, Confident, Decisive, Dependable, Good With Figures, Logical, Organized, Professional

Types of Positions
Account Assistant   Clerk/Typist

Starting Salary
$ 20,000 - 30,000

Company Benefits
- Basic benefits outlined
- Insurance courses to upgrade skills

Correspondence
Mail resume with cover letter

Part Time/Summer: Aon Reed Stenhouse occasionally hires for part time or summer employment opportunities. The firm, however, generally goes through co-op programs to fill summer vacancies.

APEX LAND CORP.

500 - 4th Avenue SW, Suite 1100
Calgary, Alberta, T2P 2V6
Tel: (403) 264-3232   Fax: (403) 263-0502

Michelle Romaniuk, Sr. Accountant
Internet: www.apexland.com

Apex Land Corp. is involved with land development, acquisition and sale for the construction of single family and multi-family dwellings, along with specialized housing.

Academic Fields
College: General, Accounting, Administration, Advertising, Business, Engineering Tech., Human Resources, Secretarial, Security/Law
Bachelor of Arts: Business, Public Relations
Bachelor of Comm/Admin: General, Accounting, Finance, Marketing, Info Mgmt.
Bachelor of Engineering: General, Civil, Environmental Studies, Geotechnical
Chartered Accounting: CA - General/Finance, CGA/CMA - General/Finance
Masters: Business Administration, Engineering

Critical Skills
Good Communication, Confident, Dependable, Flexible, Organized, Personable, Self-Managed

Types of Positions
Payables Clerk   Receptionist

Starting Salary
below $ 20,000

Company Benefits
- Medical, health and dental benefits
- Tuition, training, and upgrading reimbursement
- Room for growth and promotion within

Correspondence
Mail, fax, or e-mail resume with cover letter
E-mail: apex@cadvision.com

Part Time/Summer: Apex Land Corp. does not generally hire for part time or summer employment opportunities.

The Canada Student Employment Guide

APOTEX FERMENTATION INC.

50 Surfield Blvd.
Winnipeg, Manitoba, R3Y 1G4
Tel: (204) 989-6830   Fax: (204) 488-4063

Human Resources
Internet: www.apoferm.mb.ca/

Apotex Fermentation Inc. (AFI) is a member of the Apotex Pharmaceutical Group of Companies which includes Apotex Inc., the largest Canadian-owned pharmaceutical firm. AFI is an advanced technology company utilizing state-of-the-art techniques for search and discovery, strain selection and improvement, and bioprocess scale-up. AFI employees are highly qualified and trained in sophisticated chemical, biological and pharmaceutical technologies. Their multi-million dollar facility in Southwest Winnipeg is the largest fermentation-based facility in Canada.

Academic Fields
Bachelor of Science: Chemistry, Microbiology
Bachelor of Engineering: Chemical, Electrical, Industrial, Mechanical
Masters: Science

Critical Skills
Adaptable, Good Communication, Creative, Dependable, Diplomatic, Enthusiastic, Flexible, Productive, Responsible

Types of Positions
Lab Technician   Lab Assistant
Production Technician

Starting Salary
$ 20,000 - 25,000

Company Benefits
- All benefits paid by employer
- Extensive on-the-job training, and pharmaceutical regulatory training

Correspondence
Mail resume with cover letter

Part Time/Summer: Apotex Fermentation occasionally hires individuals for part time work, and sometimes looks for individuals for the summer. They hire Manitoba students. Potential jobs are those listed above, and the best time to apply is usually in March.

APPLE CANADA INC.

7495 Birchmount Road
Markham, Ontario, L3R 5G2
Tel: (905) 513-5596   Fax: (905) 513-5891

Bethany Kopstick, Human Resources
Internet: www.apple.com

Apple Canada is a wholly owned sales and distribution subsidiary of Apple Computer Inc. The company markets a range of professional and consumer hardware and software products. In addition, the company provides complete after sales and service support. Apple Canada has a number of regional sales offices across the country and has an employment base of approximately 135 individuals.

Academic Fields
College: Marketing/Sales, Business
Bachelor of Arts: General
Bachelor of Comm/Admin: Accounting
Bachelor of Engineering: Computer Systems, Electrical
Masters: Business Administration, Marketing, Engineering

Critical Skills
Adaptable, Good Communication, Dependable, Enthusiastic, Flexible, Innovative, Personable

Types of Positions
Office Administration   Customer Service

Starting Salary
$ 30,000 - 35,000

Company Benefits
- A competitive benefit package is offered

Correspondence
Apply through their web site

Part Time/Summer: Apple Canada Inc. sometimes hires individuals for part time and summer opportunities. Potential positions in the summer involve finance, customer support, or are clerical. The best time to apply is in April.

The Canada Student Employment Guide

AQUA-POWER CLEANERS LTD.

P.O. Box 3268, Stn B
Fredericton, New Brunswick, E3A 5H1
Tel: (506) 458-1113   Fax: (506) 459-8895

John Brown, Vice President

Aqua-Power Cleaners is a professional cleaning service for companies and private homes. They provide carpet/furniture cleaning, air ducts/exchanger cleaning, water/fire restoration, janitorial services, and cleaning supplies and equipment. They employ approximately 140 individuals.

Academic Fields
College: Accounting, Administration, Marketing/Sales
Bachelor of Comm/Admin: Accounting, Finance, Human Resources

Critical Skills
Adaptable, Analytical, Confident, Creative, Decisive, Diligent, Diplomatic, Efficient, Enthusiastic, Enthusiastic, Flexible, Leadership, Manual Dexterity, Organized, Patient, Personable, Productive, Professional, Responsible

Types of Positions
Supervisor   Crew Chief
Cleaner

Starting Salary
$ 20,000 - 25,000

Company Benefits
- Health insurance

Correspondence
Submit resume and cover letter in person
E-mail: smfred@nbnet.nb.ca

Part Time/Summer: Aqua-Power Cleaners occasionally seeks candidates for part time and summer employment. Potential jobs for the summer include carpet and furniture cleaning. Janitorial jobs are available year round. The best time to apply is in February.

AQUATIC SCIENCES INC.

P.O. Box 2205 - 250 Martindale Rd.
St. Catharines, Ontario, L2R 7R8
Tel: (905) 641-0941   Fax: (905) 641-1825

Sheila Ingram, Controller
Internet: www.aquaticsciences.com

Aquatic Sciences Inc. (ASI) is an employee owned, wholly Canadian, environmental consulting and engineering firm specializing in industrial water and waste water environmental management and research. Established in 1987, ASI currently employs a staff of fifty professionals within two offices. Their main offices, ecological toxicity laboratory, and R&D facilities are located in St. Catharines, Ontario with a branch office in Sarnia, Ontario, serving the particular needs of the chemical and petroleum industry.

Academic Fields
College: Marketing/Sales, Engineering Tech., Industrial Design, Mechanical Tech.
Bachelor of Comm/Admin: Marketing
Bachelor of Science: Environmental Studies
Bachelor of Engineering: Chemical, Civil, Environmental Studies, Mechanical, Water Resources

Critical Skills
Adaptable, Analytical, Dependable, Efficient, Enthusiastic, Flexible, Good Communication, Good With Figures, Good Writing Skills, Innovative, Leadership, Logical, Manual Dexterity, Organized, Productive, Professional, Responsible

Types of Positions
Technician   Engineering Student

Starting Salary
$ 20,000 - 25,000

Company Benefits
- Full benefit program

Correspondence
Mail, e-mail resume with cover letter, or apply through web site

Part Time/Summer: Aquatic Sciences Inc. regularly hires for part time and summer work. The best time to apply is in April.

ARBOR CARE TREE SERVICE LTD.

Box 105, Site 6, R.R. #5
Calgary, Alberta, T2P 2G6
Tel: (403) 273-6378   Fax: (403) 272-1536

Brad Luft, Safety Supervisor
Internet: www.arborcare.com

Arbor Care Tree Service is an experienced and dynamic tree care company. They offer services in residential, municipal and commercial tree care. Their services include pruning, trimming, fertilization, insect control, stomp, grinding and removals. They are an equal opportunity employer. Year round, full time positions exist.

Academic Fields
College: Administration, Communications, Agriculture, Forestry
Bachelor of Science: Agriculture, Forestry

Critical Skills
Adaptable, Confident, Creative, Decisive, Dependable, Diligent, Efficient, Enthusiastic, Flexible, Good Communication, Good Writing Skills, Leadership, Manual Dexterity, Patient, Personable, Productive, Professional

Types of Positions
Groundsperson
Stomp Grinder
Beginning Tree Worker/Climber
Snow Removal

Starting Salary
$ 20,000 - 25,000

Company Benefits
- Full time employees entitled to benefit package after 6 months
- Training is site specific and usually occurs on the job.

Correspondence
Mail, fax, e-mail resume with cover letter or submit in person. E-mail: trees@arborcare.com

Part Time/Summer: Arbor Care Tree Service Ltd. rarely hires for part time work, but regularly hires in the summer months. Potential jobs include groundsperson, stomp grinder operator, and plant health technician (spray dept). The best time to apply is in March and April.

ARBOR MEMORIAL SERVICES INC.

2 Jane Street
Toronto, Ontario, M6S 4W8
Tel: (416) 763-3230   Fax: (416) 763-8714

Human Resources
Internet: www.arbormemorial.com

Arbor Memorial Services is an Ontario corporation which, through wholly owned subsidiaries, is engaged in providing interment rights, cremations, funerals and associated merchandise and services across Canada. It owns 38 cemeteries and 96 funeral homes.

Academic Fields
College: Accounting, Administration, Business, Marketing/Sales
Bachelor of Arts: General, Business
Bachelor of Comm/Admin: General, Accounting
Bachelor of Science: General, Computer Science, Horticulture
Bachelor of Engineering: Civil, Bachelor of Landscape Architecture
Chartered Accounting: CA-General, CMA-General, CGA-General

Critical Skills
Adaptable, Dependable, Diplomatic, Flexible, Good Communication, Innovative, Leadership, Professional

Types of Positions
Funeral Director   Administrative Assistant
Sales Representative   Accounting Clerk
Property Staff   Information Services Support

Starting Salary
$ 25,000 - 35,000

Company Benefits
- Competitive benefits package

Correspondence
Mail, fax, or e-mail resume with cover letter
E-mail: hrdept@arbormemorial.com

Part Time/Summer: Arbor Memorial Services occasionally hires for part time summer positions. In the summer, a potential job is property staff, which involves seasonal cemetery maintenance. The best time to apply is from January to March. Applications should go directly to the property management offices located on the cemetery.

The Canada Student Employment Guide

ARCTIC CO-OPERATIVES LIMITED

1645 Inkster Blvd.
Winnipeg, Manitoba, R2X 2W7
Tel: (204) 697-1625   Fax: (204) 697-1880

Jim Newman, Human Resources

Arctic Co-operatives are owned by Co-operatives in N.W.T. and Nunavut, and provide management advice, accounting, merchandise procurement, and construction services.

Academic Fields
College: Administration, Business, Human Resources, Secretarial, Travel/Tourism
Bachelor of Comm/Admin: General, Accounting
Chartered Accounting: CGA - General/Finance

Critical Skills
Adaptable, Analytical, Good Communication, Confident, Creative, Dependable, Diligent, Efficient, Enthusiastic, Flexible, Good With Figures, Innovative, Good Writing Skills

Types of Positions
Customer Service   Merchandising
Human Resources   Accounting
Administration   Marketing

Starting Salary
$ 20,000 - 35,000

Company Benefits
- Group insurance, pension (company matched)
- Company pays for 75% of approved training

Correspondence
Mail or fax resume with cover letter

Part Time/Summer: Arctic Co-operatives Limited occasionally looks for individuals for part time or summer positions. In the summer, potential jobs can exist in all departments. The best time to apply is in early April.

ARMETEC LIMITED

15 Campbell Rd.
Guelph, Ontario, N1H 6P2
Tel: (519) 822-0210   Fax: (519) 822-1160

Jan McEwin, Human Resources
Internet: www.armtec.com

Armtec Limited is a manufacturer and marketer of products used in municipal, highway, industrial and water resource projects across Canada. The company has an employee base of 400 individuals.

Academic Fields
College: Engineering Tech., Mechanical Tech.
Bachelor of Engineering: Civil, Design, Mechanical

Critical Skills
Dependable, Enthusiastic, Good Communication, Personable, Productive, Responsible

Types of Positions
Engineering Technologist   Customer Service
Engineering Grad (Design)

Starting Salary
Depends on position

Company Benefits
- Full range of medical, dental, health benefits, RRSP incentive
- Continuing education assistance
- Sales training

Correspondence
Mail, fax resume with cover letter or apply through web site

Part Time/Summer: Armtec Limited rarely hires for part time or summer employment.

The Canada Student Employment Guide

ARMOR PERSONNEL

181 Queen St. E.
Brampton, Ontario, L6W 2B3
Tel: (905) 459-1617   Fax: (905) 459-1704

Professional Recruitment Services
Internet: www.armorpersonnel.com

Armor Personnel is a professional employment organization specializing in recruitment services and job placements for permanent, temporary, and contract positions at no charge to applicants.

Academic Fields
College: General, Accounting, Administration, Business, Computer Science, Drafting/Architecture, Electronics Tech., Engineering Tech., Human Resources, Marketing/Sales, Mechanical Tech., Secretarial
Bachelor of Arts: General, Business, Sociology/Social Work
Bachelor of Comm/Admin: General, Accounting, Finance, Marketing, Info Mgmt., Public Admin.
Bachelor of Science: General
Bachelor of Engineering: Computer Systems, Design, Electrical, Industrial, Mechanical
Bachelor of Education: Adult Education
Chartered Accounting: CA-General, CMA-General, CGA-General

Critical Skills
Confident, Good Communication, Dependable, Efficient, Flexible, Innovative, Manual Dexterity, Organized, Personable, Productive, Professional

Types of Positions
Accounting Clerk   Receptionist
Customer Service Rep.   Junior H.R. Assistant
Data Entry Clerk

Starting Salary
$ 20,000 - 25,000

Company Benefits
- Varies depending on client
- No benefits for temporary employees

Correspondence
Fax or e-mail resume with cover letter
E-mail: info@armorpersonnel.com

Part Time/Summer: Armor Personnel regularly hires for part time and summer employment opportunities. Potential positions include customer service, drivers, dispatchers, filing clerks, clerical work, payroll assistants, and engineering jobs. The best time to apply is in April.

ARVINMERITOR

3600 Lakeshore Blvd. W.
Etobicoke, Ontario, M8W 1N8
Tel: (416) 252-5111   Fax: (416) 252-1472

Jennifer Conte, Human Resources Assistant
Internet: www.arvinmeritor.com

ArvinMeritor is a premier global Tier I supplier to the automotive industry. ArvinMeritor is a leading supplier of complete drivetrain systems, components for medium and heavy-duty trucks, trailers, off-highway equipment and specialty vehicles. In general, the company is dedicated to every commercial vehicle system, aftermarket, light vehicle, exhaust and roll coater market. ArvinMeritor employs approximately 1,500 individuals in Canada.

Academic Fields
College: Human Resources, Marketing/Sales, Purchasing, Aircraft Maintenance, Engineering Tech., Industrial Design, Mechanical Tech., Laboratory Tech.
Bachelor of Comm/Admin: General
Bachelor of Science: Environmental Studies
Bachelor of Engineering: General, Design, Electrical, Environmental Studies, Industrial, Mechanical
Masters: Business Administration, Engineering

Critical Skills
Dependable, Diligent, Efficient, Flexible, Good Communication, Good Writing Skills, Organized, Productive, Professional, Responsible

Types of Positions
Purchasing Department

Starting Salary
$ 30,000 - 40,000

Company Benefits
- Hospital, dental, supplementary health benefit, life insurance
- Pension plan, short and long term disability
- Provides training through academic programs at colleges and universities

Correspondence
Fax or e-mail resume with cover letter
E-mail: jennifer_conte@arvin.com

Part Time/Summer: ArvinMeritor rarely seeks candidates for part time work, but regularly hires for the summer months. They regularly hire students for production work during the summer season. The best time to apply is in the middle of April.

The Canada Student Employment Guide

ASSINIBOINE COMMUNITY COLLEGE

1430 Victoria Avenue E.
Brandon, Manitoba, R7A 2A9
Tel: (204) 726-6714   Fax: (204) 726-7013

Human Resources Division
Internet: www.assinboinec.mb.ca

Assiniboine Community College is an innovative and accessible rural college in Manitoba. The college serves a population of 200,000 in the southwest region of the province. Its main campus is located in Brandon.

Academic Fields
College: Accounting, Business, Child Care, Computer Science, Cooking/Culinary, Electronics Tech., Food/Nutrition, Hospitality, Human Resources, Marketing/Sales, Nursing, Secretarial, Television/Radio
Bachelor of Arts: General, Business, Economics, English, Journalism, Psychology, Public Relations, Sociology/Social Work
Bachelor of Comm/Admin: General, Accounting, Marketing, Info Mgmt.
Bachelor of Science: Agriculture, Biology, Chemistry, Computer Science, Food Sciences, Horticulture, Mathematics, Nursing (RN), Physics, Psychology
Bachelor of Laws: General, Corporate
Bachelor of Engineering: Electrical
Bachelor of Education: Adult Education
Chartered Accounting: CA-General, CMA-General, CGA-General
Masters: Business Administration, Arts, Science, Engineering, Education, Library Science

Critical Skills
Adaptable, Analytical, Good Communication, Creative, Dependable, Diligent, Diplomatic, Efficient, Enthusiastic, Flexible, Good With Figures, Innovative, Leadership, Organized, Productive, Good Writing Skills

Types of Positions
Clerk I and II   Secretary II

Starting Salary
$ 20,000 - 40,000 (depending on position)

Company Benefits
- Life, dental, and group health insurance, vision

Correspondence
Mail or fax resume with cover letter

Part Time/Summer: Assiniboine College regularly hires for part time work and in the summer months. Positions vary during the summer.

ASSUMPTION MUTUAL LIFE INSURANCE

P.O. Box 160
Moncton, New Brunswick, E1C 8L1
Tel: (506) 853-6040   Fax: (506) 853-5421

Rachelle Gagnon, Human Resources

Assumption Mutual Life Insurance is a mutual company that is owned by its members. The company offers individual and group insurance, along with RRSP annuities, and mortgage loans. The head office is located in Moncton, New Brunswick. Assumption Life distributes its products through career officers as well as brokers and career agents in the four Atlantic Provinces, Quebec and Ontario. The company employs approximately 200 individuals.

Academic Fields
College: Accounting, Computer Science, Mechanical Tech., Secretarial
Bachelor of Arts: Public Relations
Bachelor of Comm/Admin: Accounting, Finance, Marketing
Bachelor of Science: Actuarial, Computer Science, Nursing (RN)
Bachelor of Laws: Corporate
Chartered Accounting: CA-Finance, CMA-General/Finance, CGA-General/Finance
Masters: Business Administration, Science

Critical Skills
Adaptable, Analytical, Confident, Creative, Good Communication, Dependable, Enthusiastic, Flexible, Good Writing Skills, Leadership, Organized, Productive, Professional

Types of Positions
Various Positions

Starting Salary
$ 20,000 - 30,000

Company Benefits
- Health and dental coverage
- Short and long term disability, group insurance
- Preferred rates on insurance and mortgages

Correspondence
Mail or fax resume with cover letter

Part Time/Summer: Assumption Mutual Life Insurance sometimes hires for part time and summer work. The best time to apply is in the Spring.

ASSURE HEALTH INC.

5090 Explorer Dr., Suite 1000
Mississauga, Ontario, L9W 4Y6
Tel: (905) 602-7350   Fax: (905) 602-7343

Stacey Adams, HR Specialist

Assure Health is a high tech health care business that is 100% Canadian. They provide adjudication services to insurance companies including drug and dental claim processing.

Academic Fields
College: Business, Information Systems, Insurance
Bachelor of Science: Computer Sciences, Pharmacy

Critical Skills
Creative, Enthusiastic, Flexible, Innovative, Leadership

Types of Positions
Data Entry Clerk   Case Centre Rep.
Junior Programmer Analyst

Starting Salary
$ 25,000 - 30,000

Company Benefits
- Medical, dental, and drug plan
- Group RSP

Correspondence
Fax or e-mail resume with cover letter

Part Time/Summer: Assure Health regularly hires for part time positions and occasionally seeks candidates for the summer months. Potential jobs are within administration in the general office. The best time to apply is in April or May.

Co-op/Internship: They offer co-op programs in pharmacy, information technology, and information services.

ASTRAZENECA

1004 Middlegate Road
Mississauga, Ontario, L4Y 1M4
Tel: (905) 275-7111   Fax: (905) 275-7036

Human Resources Department
Internet: www.astrazeneca.com

AstraZeneca underwent worldwide restructuring following the merger of Astra AB and the Zeneca Group PLC in April 1999, and the majority of the new structure is now in place. AstraZeneca is one of the world's top five ethical pharmaceutical companies, active in more than 100 countries. They have over 47,000 employees worldwide, who are engaged in the research, development, manufacture and marketing of pharmaceuticals and the supply of healthcare services.

Academic Fields
College: Computer Science
Bachelor of Comm/Admin: Accounting, Finance, Marketing, Info. Mgmt.
Bachelor of Science: General, Biology, Chemistry, Computer Science, Environmental Studies, Food Sciences, Health Sciences, Kinesiology, Microbiology, Nursing (RN), Pharmacy, Physiotherapy
Bachelor of Engineering: Biomedical, Chemical, Computer Systems
Masters: Business Administration, Science

Critical Skills
Analytical, Creative, Good Communication, Good Writing Skills, Leadership, Personable, Professional, Responsible

Types of Positions
Sales Representative   Administration

Starting Salary
$ 25,000 - 30,000

Company Benefits
- Full benefits including dental and health
- Drugs, eye care and pension also included

Correspondence
Mail resume with cover letter

Part Time/Summer: AstraZeneca occasionally hires individuals for part time and summer employment. Potential jobs most likely involve those listed above, and generally are for university students only. The best time to apply is in January or February.

The Canada Student Employment Guide

ATCO ELECTRIC

Hanna, Alberta, T0J 1P0
Tel: (403) 854-5141   Fax: N/A

Rod Peake, Human Resources
Internet: www.apl.ca/

ATCO Electric is a member of the ATCO Group of Companies - one of Canada's premier corporations. They are an Albertan, investor-owned utility providing electricity services to customers throughout northern and east-central Alberta. Their service area encompasses nearly two-thirds of the province. More than 160,000 customers in over 200 communities count on them for safe, reliable and affordable power service - as they have for more than 70 years.

Academic Fields
College: Accounting, Administration, Computer Science, Drafting/Architecture, Electronics Tech., Engineering Tech., Human Resources, Mechanical Tech.
Bachelor of Arts: Journalism
Bachelor of Comm/Admin: Accounting, Finance
Bachelor of Science: Computer Science
Bachelor of Engineering: Electrical, Mechanical
Chartered Accounting: CMA - General/Finance, CGA - General/Finance
Masters: Business Administration, Engineering

Critical Skills
Adaptable, Analytical, Creative, Decisive, Dependable, Efficient, Flexible, Good Writing Skills, Good Communication, Innovative, Leadership, Organized, Professional, Responsible

Types of Positions
Engineering	Technologist
Clerical	Apprentice Lineman
Service Man	

Starting Salary
$ 30,000 - 40,000

Company Benefits
- Dental, prescriptions, eyeglasses
- Night school (university, college, etc.)

Correspondence
Mail resume with cover letter

Part Time/Summer: ATCO Electric sometimes looks for part time employees, and regularly seeks individuals for the summer. Positions in the summer involve general labour, or clerk jobs. Apply in February or March.

ATCO FRONTEC CORP.

100 - 170 Laurier Ave. W.
Ottawa, Ontario, K1P 5V5
Tel: (613) 234-9033   Fax: (613) 787-3888

Louise Paquette, HR Coordinator
Internet: wwww.atcofrontec.com

Known for service excellence, cost control and strong relationships, ATCO Frontec is a North American leader in technical services for the resource, telecommunications, transportation, utility and defence sectors.

Academic Fields
College: Accounting, Administration, Business, Human Resources, Information Systems, CAD Autocad, Computer Science, Electronics Tech., Engineering Tech., Mechanical Tech.
Bachelor of Arts: Business
Bachelor of Comm/Admin: Accounting, Finance, Human Resources, Info Mgmt.
Bachelor of Science: Computer Science
Bachelor of Engineering: Civil, Electrical, Environmental Studies, Mechanical
Chartered Accounting: CMA-Finance, CGA-Finance
Masters: Business Administration

Critical Skills
Adaptable, Analytical, Dependable, Diligent, Efficient, Manual Dexterity, Organized, Professional

Types of Positions
Facilities Engineering	Operations
Electrical Engineer	Mechanical Engineer

Starting Salary
Depends on position

Company Benefits
- Competitive salary and comprehensive benefit

Correspondence
E-mail resume with cover letter
E-mail: recruit@atcofrontec.com

Part Time/Summer: ATCO Frontec Corp. regularly hires for part time and summer work. Staff are mainly labourers and trades people. Work period may range from a couple of weeks to a couple of months. Summer works recruitment begins in May.

Co-op/Internship: They have internship opportunities particularly in the engineering dept.

The Canada Student Employment Guide

ATCO GAS SERVICES LTD.

909 - 11 Avenue SW, 10th Floor
Calgary, Alberta, T2R 1L8
Tel: (403) 245-7700   Fax: (403) 245-7200

Human Resources Department

ATCO Gas Services Ltd., a member of the ATCO Group of companies, is a full service mainstream company, providing innovative gathering, processing and storage services to producers.

Academic Fields
College: Computer Science, Cooking/Culinary, Drafting/Architecture, Electronics Tech., Engineering Tech., Graphic Arts, Journalism, Laboratory Tech.
Bachelor of Arts: Business, Journalism, Public Relations
Bachelor of Comm/Admin: Accounting, Finance
Bachelor of Engineering: Civil, Mechanical
Chartered Accounting: CA-Finance, CMA-General, CGA-General
Masters: Business Administration

Critical Skills
Analytical, Confident, Creative, Dependable, Flexible, Productive, Professional, Good Communication, Responsible

Types of Positions
Junior Clerk   Stenographer
Labourer   Meter Reader

Starting Salary
$ 25,000 - 30,000

Company Benefits
- Standard employer paid benefits
- Dental, life insurance, pension

Correspondence
Mail resume with cover letter

Part Time/Summer: ATCO Gas Services sometimes seeks individuals on a part time basis and for jobs in the summer. Potential jobs include labourer and entry level clerks. The best time to apply is in April.

TOWN OF ATHABASCA

4705 49 Avenue
Athabasca, Alberta, T9S 1B7
Tel: (403) 675-2061   Fax: (403) 675-4242

Harold Gyte, Human Resources

The Town of Athabasca is a municipal government involved in the formation of policy and laws in matters under its jurisdiction.

Academic Fields
College: Accounting, Administration, Engineering Tech., Human Resources, Recreation Studies, Secretarial
Bachelor of Arts: Recreation Studies
Bachelor of Comm/Admin: Accounting, Finance, Public Admin.

Critical Skills
Adaptable, Analytical, Artistic, Good Communication, Confident, Creative, Decisive, Dependable, Diligent, Diplomatic, Efficient, Enthusiastic, Flexible, Good With Figures, Innovative, Leadership, Logical, Manual Dexterity, Organized, Patient, Personable, Persuasive, Productive, Professional, Responsible, Good Writing Skills

Types of Positions
General Clerical
Public Works Equipment Operator I
Public Works Labourer I
Public Works Water Treatment

Starting Salary
$ 25,000 - 30,000

Company Benefits
- Part time workers receive no benefits
- Full time staff receive full coverage, all aspects
- On-the-job training, if applicable, and appropriate course and workshops as necessary

Correspondence
Mail or fax resume with cover letter
E-mail: harold@town.athabasca.ab.ca

Part Time/Summer: The Town of Athabasca regularly seeks candidates for part time or summer work. Potential jobs include parks development worker. The best time to apply is in early Spring.

ATLANTIC BLUE CROSS CARE

644 Main St., P.O. Box 220
Moncton, New Brunswick, E1C 8L3
Tel: (506) 853-1811   Fax: (506) 869-9651

John Dallaire, Director Human Resources
Internet: www.atl.bluecross.ca

Atlantic Blue Cross Care is a provider of prepaid health, dental, life, travel and disability insurance programs in the Atlantic provinces. The company employs over 700 individuals.

Academic Fields
College: Accounting, Administration, Communications, Human Resources, Information Systems, Insurance, Purchasing, Secretarial, Graphic Arts, Journalism, Social Work, Travel/Tourism, Computer Science, Dental, Nursing (RN/RNA)
Bachelor of Arts: General, Business, Economics, Journalism, Public Relations, Sociology/Social Work
Bachelor of Comm/Admin: General, Accounting, Finance, Human Resources, Marketing, Info Mgmt.
Bachelor of Science: General, Actuarial, Computer Science, Health Sciences, Kinesiology, Nursing (RN), Occupational Therapy, Pharmacy
Bachelor of Education: Adult Education
Masters: Business Administration

Critical Skills
Adaptable, Analytical, Confident, Creative, Dependable, Diplomatic, Efficient, Flexible, Good Communication, Good Writing Skills, Good With Figures, Innovative, Logical, Personable, Professional, Responsible

Types of Positions
Administrative Asst.	Claims Adjudicator
Customer Service Rep.	Accounting Clerk
HR Assistant	Programmer

Starting Salary
$ 25,000 - 30,000 (depending on position)

Company Benefits
- Health, dental, vision, travel program

Correspondence
Fax or e-mail resume with cover letter
E-mail: humanresources@atl.bluecross.ca

Part Time/Summer: Atlantic Blue Cross Care occasionally hires for part time work, and regularly hires for the summer. Potential jobs in the summer are administration assistant, claims clerk, accounting clerk, or customer service rep. Apply in May.

ATLANTIC LOTTERY CORPORATION INC.

P.O. Box 5500, 922 Main St.
Moncton, New Brunswick, E1C 8W6
Tel: (506) 853-5800   Fax: (506) 867-5710

Human Resources Dept.
Internet: www.alc.ca

Atlantic Lottery Corporation contributes directly to the daily income and well being of almost 7,000 Atlantic Canadians. Since 1976 they have been managing the gaming business on behalf of the governments of Nova Scotia, New Brunswick, Newfoundland & Labrador and Prince Edward Island. Today, they have more than 500 employees throughout the four Atlantic provinces and offer more than 14 games to Atlantic Canadians.

Academic Fields
College: General, Accounting, Administration, Computer Science, Electronics Tech., Graphic Arts, Human Resources, Marketing/Sales
Bachelor of Arts: Business, Public Relations
Bachelor of Comm/Admin: Accounting, Marketing, Info Mgmt.
Bachelor of Science: Computer Science
Bachelor of Engineering: Computer Systems
Chartered Accounting: CA-General
Masters: Business Administration

Critical Skills
Good Communication, Leadership, Professional

Types of Positions
Various Positions

Starting Salary
$ 25,000 - 30,000

Company Benefits
- Medical, dental, and pension plan
- Vacation leave, sick leave

Correspondence
Mail resume with cover letter

Part Time/Summer: Atlantic Lottery Corporation occasionally seeks individuals for part time work, and regularly looks for summer help. Potential jobs in the summer are in marketing and accounting. The best time to apply is in May.

ATLANTIC PACKAGING PRODUCTS LTD.

111 Progress Ave.
Scarborough, Ontario, M1G 2Y9
Tel: (416) 298-8101   Fax: (416) 297-2264

Recruiter

Atlantic Packaging Products Ltd. is a manufacturer of corrugated cardboard. The company employs approximately 1,800 individuals.

Academic Fields
College: Accounting, Administration, Business, Human Resources, Information Systems, Marketing/Sales, Secretarial, CAD Autocad, Industrial Design, Graphic Arts
Bachelor of Arts: Business, Economics
Bachelor of Comm/Admin: Accounting, Finance, Human Resources, Marketing
Bachelor of Engineering: Design, Industrial, Mechanical
Chartered Accounting: CGA-General

Critical Skills
Confident, Dependable, Enthusiastic, Flexible, Good Communication, Good Writing Skills, Innovative, Logical, Organized, Responsible

Types of Positions
Accounting   Administration
Warehouse/Plant

Starting Salary
$ 25,000 - 30,000

Company Benefits
- Benefits include medical and dental after 2 months probation
- Opportunities for further training

Correspondence
Fax or e-mail resume with cover letter
E-mail: recruiter@atlantic.ca

Part Time/Summer: Atlantic Packaging Products Ltd. rarely hires part time workers, but regularly hires summer staff. Potential jobs include general labour (plant, shift work) or general office work. The best time to apply is April to June.

ATLANTIC WHOLESALERS LTD.

120 Eileen Stubbs Avenue, Suite 101
Dartmouth, Nova Scotia, B3B 1Y1
Tel: (902) 481-4216   Fax: (902) 481-4293

Katherine Boinski, Human Resources

Atlantic Wholesalers is a food retailer located in Dartmouth, Nova Scotia. Approximately 250 employees work in our Merchandising, Human Resources, Marketing & Advertising, and Operations Support departments at their head office. The company is a wholly owned subsidiary of Loblaws Companies Limited. Atlantic Wholesalers operates grocery stores throughout the Maritime Provinces with over 11,000 corporate and franchise employees.

Academic Fields
College: Accounting, Administration, Advertising, Business, Communications, Graphic Arts, Human Resources, Marketing/Sales, Photography, Secretarial, Security/Law
Bachelor of Arts: Business, Public Relations
Bachelor of Comm/Admin: Finance, Marketing, Info Mgmt.
Chartered Accounting: CMA-General, CMA-Finance
Masters: Business Administration

Critical Skills
Adaptable, Creative, Dependable, Enthusiastic, Flexible, Good Writing Skills, Leadership, Good Communication, Organized, Productive

Types of Positions
Receptionist   Cashier
Data Entry   Accounts Receivable Clerk

Starting Salary
$ 20,000 - 25,000

Company Benefits
- Complete range of benefits

Correspondence
Mail or fax resume with cover letter

Part Time/Summer: Atlantic Wholesalers regularly employs people for part time and summer positions. A potential summer job may involve the special events cruiser. The best time to apply is in April.

The Canada Student Employment Guide

ATLAS IDEAL METALS INC.

161 The West Mall
Etobicoke, Ontario, M9C 4V8
Tel: (416) 622-3100   Fax: (416) 622-8602

Marilyn Denley, Human Resources

Atlas Ideal Metals is a specialty metals distributor. The company's head office is in Etobicoke, Ontario. Atlas Ideal Metals employs approximately 600 individuals.

Academic Fields
College: Accounting, Administration, Advertising, Business, Communications, Human Resources, Information Systems, Marketing/Sales, Purchasing, Secretarial, CAD Autocad, Computer Science, Mechanical Tech.
Bachelor of Arts: General, Business, Economics
Bachelor of Comm/Admin: General, Accounting, Finance, Human Resources, Marketing, Info Mgmt.
Bachelor of Engineering: Mechanical

Critical Skills
Adaptable, Analytical, Good Communication, Confident, Creative, Decisive, Dependable, Diligent, Diplomatic, Efficient, Enthusiastic, Flexible, Good With Figures, Innovative, Leadership, Logical, Manual Dexterity, Organized, Patient, Personable, Persuasive, Productive, Professional, Responsible

Types of Positions
Sales Trainee	Clerical
Assistant	Accounting
Human Resources	

Starting Salary
$ 20,000 - 25,000

Company Benefits
- Company paid benefits including life insurance, health, dental
- International travel, short and long term disability, pension
- Reimburse continuing education

Correspondence
Mail or fax resume with cover letter

Part Time/Summer: Atlas Ideal Metals Inc. regularly hires for part time and summer employment opportunities. Potential work involves warehouse, clerical, accounting, and sales administration jobs.

ATLAS VAN LINES (CANADA) LTD.

485 North Service Rd. E.
Oakville, Ontario, L6J 5M7
Tel: (905) 844-0701   Fax: (905) 844-5448

Human Resources
Internet: www.atlasvanlines.ca

Atlas Van Lines is a transportation company involved in the transpiration of various movers transporting household goods.

Academic Fields
College: General, Accounting, Administration, Advertising, Communications, Marketing/Sales
Bachelor of Arts: General, Business, Public Relations
Bachelor of Comm/Admin: General, Accounting, Finance, Marketing, Info Mgmt.
Bachelor of Engineering: Transportation

Critical Skills
Adaptable, Analytical, Good Communication, Dependable, Diligent, Efficient, Enthusiastic, Flexible, Organized, Patient, Personable, Productive, Professional, Responsible

Types of Positions
Document Control   Dispatch Assistant

Starting Salary
$ 20,000 - 25,000

Company Benefits
- Health, dental, and disability for full time staff after 3 months

Correspondence
Mail or fax resume with cover letter

Part Time/Summer: Atlas Van Lines occasionally hires for part time work, and sometimes seeks candidates for the summer. Potential jobs in the summer include mail room assistant and document control assistant. The best time to apply is in March or April.

ATS AUTOMATION TOOLING SYSTEMS INC.
250 Royal Oak Rd., Box 32100, Preston Ctr.
Cambridge, Ontario, N3H 5M2
Tel: (519) 653-6500   Fax: (519) 653-6533

Nancy Valla, HR Supervisor
Internet: www.atsautomation.com

ATS Automation Tooling Systems has grown to become the leader in the design, development, and support of advanced automated manufacturing systems, providing solutions that deliver fast payback for their customers worldwide.

Academic Fields
College: Accounting, Administration, Human Resources, Computer Science, Electronics Tech., Engineering Tech., Mechanical Tech.
Bachelor of Arts: Business, Economics
Bachelor of Comm/Admin: Human Resources
Bachelor of Science: Computer Science
Bachelor of Engineering: Computer Systems, Design, Electrical, Industrial, Mechanical
Masters: Business Administration, Engineering

Critical Skills
Analytical, Confident, Decisive, Dependable, Enthusiastic, Good Communication, Good With Figures, Good Writing Skills, Innovative, Leadership, Organized, Productive, Professional, Responsible

Types of Positions
Mechanical Design   Administration
Control Systems Design   Shop

Starting Salary
Depends on position

Company Benefits
- Comprehensive benefits including medical, dental
- Stock purchase plan, RRSP, profit sharing

Correspondence
Mail, fax, e-mail resume with cover letter or apply through web site. E-mail: hr@atsautomation.com

Part Time/Summer: The company rarely hires for part time work, but occasionally seeks candidates for the summer. They hire many co-op students, so they don't have many opportunities for summer students. When they do hire, the majority of jobs would be on the shop floor doing general labour.

Co-op/Internship: They are looking at internships for engineering students.

AURIZON MINES LTD.
Marine Building, 355 Burrard St., Ste. 830
Vancouver, British Columbia, V6C 2G8
Tel: (604) 687-6600   Fax: (604) 687-3912

Alex Caldwell, Human Resources
Internet: www.aurizon.com

Aurizon Mines Ltd. is a Canadian-based gold mining company with operations and exploration activities in the prolific gold producing Abitibi region of north-western Quebec.

Academic Fields
College: Accounting, Computer Science, Engineering Tech., Nursing, Secretarial
Bachelor of Arts: Public Relations
Bachelor of Comm/Admin: Accounting
Bachelor of Science: Geology
Bachelor of Engineering: Design, Electrical, Mining
Chartered Accounting: CA - General/Finance

Critical Skills
Adaptable, Good Communication, Dependable, Leadership, Responsible, Possess Integrity

Types of Positions
Investor Relations Assistant
Administrative Assistant
Accountant

Starting Salary
$ 25,000 - 30,000

Company Benefits
- Extended health, dental, and long term disability
- On the job experience
- Mentoring and recommended industry/job related course work

Correspondence
Mail or fax resume with cover letter in response to company indicated need only.
E-mail: info@aurizon.com

Part Time/Summer: Aurizon Mines occasionally looks for employees for part time and summer positions. Jobs in the summer could potentially involve field geotechnical work, reception, or secretarial duties. The best time to apply is in May or June.

AURUM CERAMIC DENTAL LABORATORIES LTD.
115 17 Avenue SW
Calgary, Alberta, T2S 0A1
Tel: (403) 228-5120   Fax: 1-800-747-1233

Human Resources Department
Internet: www.aurumgroup.com

Aurum Ceramic Dental Laboratories is the largest crown and bridge lab in Canada. With locations across Canada, Aurum's Group of Companies is a leading supplier of all aspects of esthetic and restorative dentistry. An on-going education program keeps them on the cutting edge of dental techniques and technology.

Academic Fields
College: General, Accounting, Administration, Business, Communications, Computer Science, Human Resources, Laboratory Tech., Marketing/Sales, Dental Technology, Science-General
Bachelor of Arts: General, Business, English, Fine Arts, Psychology, Public Relations, Sociology/Social Work
Bachelor of Comm/Admin: General, Accounting, Marketing
Bachelor of Science: General, Biology, Chemistry, Health Sciences
Chartered Accounting: CA-General, CMA-General, CGA-General

Critical Skills
Adaptable, Artistic, Dependable, Diligent, Efficient, Good With Figures, Manual Dexterity, Organized, Productive, Professional, Flexible

Types of Positions
Dental Technician Trainee	Data Entry/Office Clerk
Accounting Clerk	Marketing/Sales
Shipping/Receiving	Reception

Starting Salary
below $ 20,000

Company Benefits
- Extended health, dental, group life insurance

Correspondence
Fax resume with cover letter
E-mail: cerumhr@telusplanet.net

Part Time/Summer: Aurum Ceramic Dental Laboratories regularly hires for part time work, and occasionally hires in the summer. Potential jobs include office/ data entry clerks or model room technicians. The best time to apply is in May.

AVENTIS PASTEUR LIMITED
1755 Steeles Avenue West
North York, Ontario, M2R 3T4
Tel: (416) 667-2701   Fax: (416) 667-2252

John Fantin, Recruiter
Internet: www.aventis.com

Aventis Pasteur is the vaccine division of Aventis, a world leader in life sciences. For over 85 years, Aventis Pasteur has protected Canadians against preventable disease. As Canada's largest vaccine company, Aventis Pasteur employs 1,000 people at its fully integrated facility in Toronto.

Academic Fields
College: Animal Health, Laboratory Tech., Sciences
Bachelor of Comm/Admin: Accounting, Finance, Info Mgmt.
Bachelor of Science: Biology, Chemistry, Computer Science, Health Sciences, Microbiology, Nursing
Bachelor of Laws: Corporate
Bachelor of Engineering: Chemical, Computer Systems, Electrical, Mechanical
Chartered Accounting: CA-Finance, CGA-Finance, CMA-Finance
Masters: Business Administration, Science, Engineering, Library Science

Critical Skills
Adaptable, Analytical, Confident, Good Communication, Enthusiastic, Dependable, Good With Figures, Responsible, Innovative, Leadership, Manual Dexterity, Professional, Good Writing Skills

Types of Positions
Lab Support	Technician/Technologist
Admin. Support	Analyst
Assistant/Coordinator	Programmer

Starting Salary
$ 30,000 (depending on position and skill level)

Company Benefits
- An extensive employee benefit program offered

Correspondence
Mail, fax, e-mail resume with cover letter or apply through web site

Part Time/Summer: Aventis Pasteur regularly hires part time workers in the field of animal health only. They regularly hire for summer positions. Potential summer jobs include technician, operator, admin. support and labourer. Apply in February or March.

AXA INSURANCE (CANADA)

5700 Yonge St., Suite 1400
North York, Ontario, M2M 4K2
Tel: (416) 218-4188   Fax: (416) 218-4174

Andrea Pollon, Recruiter
Internet: www.axa-insurance.ca

AXA Insurance (Canada) is part of the international AXA Group which is the largest insurer and largest asset management company in the world. The AXA Group is active in over 60 countries on five continents. AXA Canada is currently one of the four largest insurers in Canada with over $1.0 billion in sales. AXA Insurance (Canada) serves Ontario and the Atlantic provinces. They employ approximately 550 individuals in Canada.

Academic Fields
College: Accounting, Business, Human Resources, Health Sciences, Insurance, Secretarial
Bachelor of Arts: Business, Economics, Political Science
Bachelor of Comm/Admin: Accounting, Finance, Human Resources
Bachelor of Science: Actuarial, Chemistry, Health Sciences, Kinesiology, Physiotherapy, Psychology
Chartered Accounting: CGA-General, CMA-General

Critical Skills
Adaptable, Analytical, Decisive, Flexible, Good Communication, Good Writing Skills, Logical, Productive, Professional

Types of Positions
Underwriter   Claims Service Rep.
Customer Service Rep.   Junior Accountant
Data Processor

Starting Salary
$ 25,000 - 30,000

Company Benefits
- Comprehensive benefits and pension package
- Profit sharing, extensive training for new employees
- Development plan

Correspondence
Mail, fax, or e-mail resume with cover letter
E-mail: hr@axa-insurance.ca

Part Time/Summer: AXA Insurance (Canada) rarely hires for part time work, but regularly seeks candidates for the summer. Potential work involves Entry level positions in claims, data processing, and clerical work. The best time to apply is in early February.

AXIDATA INC.

45 Commander Blvd.
Scarborough, Ontario, M1S 3Y3
Tel: (416) 291-6400   Fax: (416) 291-6416

Catherine Foti, HR Administrator

Axidata is a diversified computer products company specializing in system storage and computer supplies.

Academic Fields
College: Accounting, Administration, Advertising, Communications, Computer Science, Human Resources, Marketing/Sales
Bachelor of Arts: General, Business, Languages, Public Relations
Bachelor of Comm/Admin: General, Accounting, Finance, Marketing, Info Mgmt., Public Admin.
Bachelor of Science: Computer Science, Mathematics

Critical Skills
Adaptable, Analytical, Good Communication, Confident, Creative, Dependable, Efficient, Organized, Good With Figures, Good Writing Skills, Persuasive, Professional, Responsible

Types of Positions
Customer Service   Accounting I
Collector   Production Helper
Warehouse Worker   Shipping Assistant

Starting Salary
$ 22,000 - 30,000 (depending on position)

Company Benefits
- Health care plan, dental plan, life insurance
- In-house training
- College and university courses

Correspondence
Mail or fax resume with cover letter

Part Time/Summer: Axidata regularly seeks candidates for part time and summer employment opportunities. Potential jobs include warehouse worker, press helper, or office help. The best time to apply is from April to May.

The Canada Student Employment Guide

BABCOCK AND WILCOX CANADA

581 Coronation Blvd.
Cambridge, Ontario, N1R 5V3
Tel: (519) 621-2120   Fax: (519) 624-2532

Human Resources
Internet: www.babcock.com

Babcock and Wilcox Canada is an organization committed to satisfying the diverse steam generation needs of Canadian and overseas clients with a combined commitment to quality, dependability and service. Babcock and Wilcox Canada employs a total of 1,000 individuals.

Academic Fields
College: Accounting, Business, Drafting, Electronics Tech., Engineering Tech., Human Resources, Industrial Design, Journalism, Mechanical Tech., Secretarial
Bachelor of Arts: Journalism
Bachelor of Comm/Admin: Accounting, Finance, Marketing, Info Mgmt., Human Resources
Bachelor of Laws: Corporate
Bachelor of Engineering: Computer Systems, Design, Electrical, Industrial, Materials Sci., Mechanical, Welding
Chartered Accounting: CMA - General/Finance, CGA - General/Finance
Masters: Engineering, Business Develop., Marketing

Critical Skills
Adaptable, Analytical, Good Communication, Confident, Creative, Decisive, Dependable, Enthusiastic, Flexible, Good With Figures, Innovative, Leadership, Organized, Personable, Persuasive, Productive

Types of Positions
Accounting Clerk   Drafting Assistant
Technician/Technologist   Materials Clerk
Document Control Clerk   Graduate Engineer

Starting Salary
Depends on position and qualifications

Company Benefits
- Health, dental care, vision care, life insurance
- Internal and external training, education assistance

Correspondence
Mail, fax or e-mail resume with cover letter
E-mail: resume@pgg.mcdermott.com

Part Time/Summer: Babcock and Wilcox Canada occasionally hires for part time and summer work. Potential jobs involve manufacturing, administration, or engineering. Apply in February or March.

BAKEMARK INGREDIENTS LTD.

2480 Viking Way
Richmond, British Columbia, V6V 1N2
Tel: (604) 303-1700   Fax: (604) 270-8002

Angela Dempsey, Payroll

Bakemark Ingredients Ltd. is a full line bakery supplier. They distribute and manufacture ingredients to the bakery sector of the food industry.

Academic Fields
College: Food/Nutrition
Bachelor of Comm/Admin: Accounting, Info Mgmt.
Bachelor of Science: Food Sciences
Chartered Accounting: CMA-General, CGA - General/Finance

Critical Skills
Adaptable, Dependable, Flexible, Good Communication, Innovative, Logical, Productive

Types of Positions
Technical Food Services   Administration

Starting Salary
$ 25,000 - 30,000

Company Benefits
- Full benefit package including RRSP

Correspondence
Mail resume with cover letter
E-mail: adempsey@bakemarkcanada.com

Part Time/Summer: Bakemark Ingredients Ltd. does not hire for part time employment, but occasionally seeks candidates for the summer months. Potential jobs include food technician or involve systems development. The best time to apply is in April.

BALLARD POWER SYSTEMS INC.

9000 Glenlyon Parkway
Burnaby, British Columbia, V5J 5J9
Tel: (604) 454-0900   Fax: (604) 412-4700

Human Resources
Internet: www.ballard.com

Ballard Power Systems, Inc. was founded in 1979 under the name Ballard Research Inc. to conduct research and development in high energy lithium batteries. In 1983, Ballard began developing proton exchange membrane (PEM) fuel cells. Today, these systems have evolved into pre-commercial prototypes proving the practicality of the Ballard® fuel cell and fuel cells are widely viewed as viable alternatives to conventional technologies.

Academic Fields
College: Computer Science, Electronics Tech., Engineering Tech., Human Resources, Laboratory Tech., Mechanical Tech., Science-General
Bachelor of Comm/Admin: Finance, Marketing, Info Mgmt.
Bachelor of Science: Chemistry, Physics
Bachelor of Engineering: Chemical, Design, Electrical, Industrial, Materials Science, Mechanical
Chartered Accounting: CA - General/Finance
Masters: Business Administration, Science, Engineering

Critical Skills
Good Communication, Dependable, Flexible, Innovative, Productive

Types of Positions
Production Technician Technologist
Engineer

Starting Salary
$ 20,000 - 40,000 (depending on position)

Company Benefits
- Competitive benefits, bonus plan, and pension plan
- Stock option plan
- Many developmental opportunities

Correspondence
Mail, fax, or e-mail resume with cover letter
E-mail: careers@ballard.com

Part Time/Summer: Ballard Power Systems occasionally hires for part time work and regularly hires in the summer. Jobs include production vacation relief, technologist, or analyst.

THE BANFF CENTRE FOR CONTINUING EDUCATION

P.O. Box 1020, Station 19
Banff, Alberta, T0L 0C0
Tel: (403) 762-6173   Fax: (403) 762-6677

Lisa Flierjans, Recruiting & Training Coord.
Internet: www.banffcentre.ab.ca

The Banff Centre for Continuing Education is a unique Canadian Institution playing a special role in the advancement of cultural and professional life. The Banff Centre employs approximately 600 people year round.

Academic Fields
College: General, Accounting, Admin., Business, Communications, Cooking/Culinary, Faculty Management, Graphic Arts, Human Resources, Journalism, Marketing/Sales, Mech. Tech., Performing Arts, Rec. Studies, Television/Radio, Travel/Tourism
Bachelor of Arts: General, Business, English, Fine Arts, Journalism, Music, Public Relations, Recreation Studies, Sociology/Social Work
Bachelor of Comm/Admin: General, Accounting, Finance, Marketing, Info Mgmt.
Bachelor of Science: Environ. Studies, Food Sciences
Bachelor of Engineering: General, Electrical, Mechanical, Bachelor of Landscape Architecture
Bachelor of Education: General, Adult Education
Chartered Accounting: CA - General/Finance, CGA/CMA - General/Finance
Masters: Business Admin., Arts, Educ., Library Sci.

Critical Skills
Most skills considered important

Types of Positions
Housekeeping   Banquet Server Staff
Office Assistant   Front Desk Clerk
Recreation Staff   Festival Assistant

Starting Salary
$ 20,000 - 25,000 (entry-level)

Company Benefits
- Salaried staff receive major medical and dental

Correspondence
Mail, fax or e-mail resume with cover letter
E-mail: lisa_flierjans@banffcentre.ab.ca

Part Time/Summer: Banff Centre occasionally hires for part time work and regularly hires in the summer. Potential jobs are above. Apply in March.

The Canada Student Employment Guide

BARGAIN FINDER PRESS LTD.

11642 - 149 Street NW
Edmonton, Alberta, T5M 3R3
Tel: (403) 420-2200   Fax: (403) 420-2201

Human Resources

Bargain Finder Press is involved in the publishing of a weekly classified and display advertising newspaper, which is on average about 160 pages. The firm employs approximately 140 individuals in total.

Academic Fields
College: Computer Science, Graphic Arts
Bachelor of Arts: Fine Arts
Bachelor of Comm/Admin: Info Mgmt.
Chartered Accounting: CMA-General

Critical Skills
Artistic, Good Communication, Confident, Creative, Dependable, Efficient, Enthusiastic, Leadership, Organized, Personable, Persuasive

Types of Positions
Graphic Artist   Classified Advisor
A/R Administrator   Sales Representative

Starting Salary
$ 20,000 - 25,000

Company Benefits
- Group insurance
- Group RRSP

Correspondence
Fax resume with cover letter

Part Time/Summer: Bargain Finder Press occasionally looks for candidates for part time or summer employment. Potential jobs include classified advisor or graphic artist. The best time to apply is in April.

BARTON PLACE LONG TERM CARE FACILITY

914 Bathurst St.
Toronto, Ontario, M5R 3G5
Tel: (416) 533-9473   Fax: (416) 538-2685

Janet Robinson, Administrator

Barton Place Long Term Care Facility is a 244-bed nursing home located near downtown Toronto.

Academic Fields
College: Accounting, Administration, Computer Science, Food/Nutrition, Nursing, Recreation Studies
Bachelor of Arts: Business, Economics, Gerontology, Music, Psychology, Public Relations, Recreation Studies, Sociology/Social Work
Bachelor of Comm/Admin: Accounting, Finance, Marketing, Info Mgmt., Public Admin.
Bachelor of Science: Computer Science, Environmental Studies, Food Sci., Health Sci., Kinesiology, Nursing (RN), Occupational Therapy, Physiotherapy, Psychology
Chartered Accounting: CA-General, CGA-General
Masters: Business Administration, Science

Critical Skills
Adaptable, Confident, Creative, Dependable, Efficient, Enthusiastic, Flexible, Good Communication, Innovative, Personable, Professional, Client-Centred

Types of Positions
Bookkeeper   Social Services Coordinator
Programs Manager   Receptionist
Registered Nurse   Maintenance Worker

Starting Salary
$ 25,000 - 30,000

Company Benefits
- Health, dental, 4% employee matched pension
- 2 weeks vacation, weekly indemnity

Correspondence
Mail or fax resume with cover letter
E-mail: lborges@responsive.on.ca

Part Time/Summer: Barton Place regularly hires for part time work and occasionally hires for the summer. Jobs include receptionist, housekeeper, dietary aide, programs therapist, porter, or special projects coordinator. Apply from January to March.

Co-op/Internship: They have internship opportunities in social work, theology and nursing.

The Canada Student Employment Guide

BASF CANADA INC.

345 Carlingview Drive
Etobicoke, Ontario, M9W 6N9
Tel: (416) 674-2264   Fax: (416) 674-2939

Louise Ciardullo, Manager of HR
Internet: www.basf.com/basf-canada

BASF Canada manufactures and markets a broad range of chemicals, fibres, polymers, agricultural products, coatings, colourants, and a wide variety of consumer products. BASF Canada Inc. has approximately 975 employees.

Academic Fields
College: General, Accounting, Business, Computer Science, Human Resources, Marketing/Sales, Secretarial
Bachelor of Arts: Business, Economics
Bachelor of Comm/Admin: General, Accounting, Finance, Marketing
Bachelor of Science: Agriculture, Chemistry, Computer Science, Mathematics
Bachelor of Engineering: General, Chemical, Computer Syst., Environ. Studies, Materials Sci., Mech.
Chartered Accounting: CMA - General/Finance, CGA - General/Finance
Masters: Business Administration, Science

Critical Skills
Adaptable, Analytical, Good Communication, Confident, Creative, Decisive, Dependable, Diligent, Diplomatic, Efficient, Enthusiastic, Flexible, Good With Figures, Innovative, Leadership, Logical, Manual Dexterity, Organized, Patient, Personable, Persuasive, Productive, Professional, Responsible, Writing Skills,

Types of Positions
Mail Room   Accounting

Starting Salary
$ 25,000 - 30,000 Univ. / Over $ 50,000 Masters

Company Benefits
- Complete benefit plan
- On-the-job training
- Tuition program

Correspondence
Mail or fax resume with cover letter

Part Time/Summer: BASF Canada regularly hires for part time and summer opportunities. Although many positions are filled from within, possible positions are in the areas of clerical, accounting, or in the warehouse. The best time to apply is in February or March.

BASIC TECHNOLOGIES CORPORATION

P.O. Box 1006, Stn Main
Welland, Ontario, L3B 5R6
Tel: (905) 735-0510   Fax: (905) 735-5646

Human Resources
Internet: www.basic.ca

Basic Technologies Corporation, part of the worldwide Mannesmann Rexroth organization, is a world class provider of motion and motion control products and systems for major applications including special purpose, high speed production machines and heavy industry equipment for the plastics, wood processing, forestry and marine handling equipment industries.

Academic Fields
College: Accounting, Business, Human Resources, Information Systems, Marketing/Sales, Secretarial, CAD Autocad, Computer Science, Electronics Tech., Engineering Tech., Industrial Design, Mechanical Tech., Welding
Bachelor of Comm/Admin: General, Accounting, Finance
Bachelor of Science: Computer Science
Bachelor of Engineering: General, Computer Systems, Mechanical
Chartered Accounting: CGA-General

Critical Skills
Analytical, Good Communication, Dependable, Organized, Personable, Good Writing Skills

Types of Positions
Inside Sales   Technical Sales Consultant
Sales Support   Systems Design (Mechanical)

Starting Salary
$ 25,000 - 30,000

Company Benefits
- Comprehensive benefit package, profit sharing
- Computer purchase program
- Tuition aid, education assistance program

Correspondence
Mail, fax or e-mail resume with cover letter
E-mail: employment@basic.ca

Part Time/Summer: Basic Technologies Corporation occasionally hires for part time work and regularly hires for the summer. Potential jobs are clerical, secretarial, or administrative type positions. The best time to apply is later Winter, or early Spring.

The Canada Student Employment Guide

BATTLEFORDS HEALTH DISTRICT

Box 39
North Battleford, Saskatchewan, S9A 2X8
Tel: (306) 446-6815   Fax: (306) 446-6810

Director of Human Resources

The Battlefords Health District was established in 1993, and provides general health care services to a service area of over 27,000. The District has an employee base of more than 1,450 individuals.

Academic Fields
College: Accounting, Administration, Human Resources, Laboratory Tech., Nursing, Secretarial
Bachelor of Arts: Sociology/Social Work
Bachelor of Science: Health Sciences, Nursing (RN), Occupational Therapy, Pharmacy, Physiotherapy, Psychology
Masters: Business Administration

Critical Skills
Adaptable, Dependable, Flexible, Good Communication, Good Writing Skills, Organized, Productive, Responsible

Types of Positions
Dietary   Housekeeping

Starting Salary
$ 20,000 - 30,000 (depending on position)

Company Benefits
- Unionized environment, therefore benefits vary
- Pension and group life
- Disability and dental

Correspondence
Mail resume with cover letter

Part Time/Summer: The Battlefords Health District sometimes seeks individuals for part time positions, and regularly hires for summer opportunities. Positions in the summer involve housekeeping, dietary, and nursing-auxiliary departments. Summer student program (SEED/Partnership program) is setup and based on government funding. The best time to apply is March through May.

BAYCREST CENTRE FOR GERIATRIC CARE

3560 Bathurst Street
North York, Ontario, M6A 2E1
Tel: (416) 785-2500   Fax: (416) 785-2490

Employment Services
Internet: www.baycrest.org

The Baycrest Centre for Geriatric Care is a fully-affiliated teaching organization with the University of Toronto which provides facilities, services and programs to enrich the quality of life of the elderly through the integration of care, research and education.

Academic Fields
College: Food/Nutrition, Human Resources, Laboratory Tech., Orthotics/Prosthetics, Registered Practical Nurse, Secretarial, Security/Law
Bachelor of Science: Computer Science, Nursing (RN), Occupational Therapy, Physiotherapy
Bachelor of Engineering: Computer Systems
Chartered Accounting: CMA-Finance, CGA-General/Finance
Masters: Education, Library Science, Social Work, Health Administration, Psychology

Critical Skills
Adaptable, Dependable, Diplomatic, Efficient, Enthusiastic, Patient, Organized, Good Communication, Personable, Professional, Responsible, Forward Thinking

Types of Positions
Secretary   Receptionist/Typist
Kitchen Helper   Janitor
Housekeeping Aide   Research Assistant

Starting Salary
$ 22,000 - 28,000

Company Benefits
- A competitive benefit package

Correspondence
Mail or fax resume with cover letter

Part Time/Summer: Baycrest Centre for Geriatric Care sometimes hires for part time and summer work. Potential jobs include program assistant, health care aide, therapeutic recreation, and clerical and secretarial work. Apply in March or April.

BAYER INC.

77 Belfield Road
Etobicoke, Ontario, M9W 1G6
Tel: (416) 240-5233   Fax: (416) 248-1297

Sue Weiler, HR Assistant
Internet: bayer.ca

A research-based, highly diversified company with businesses in specialty chemicals, polymers and life sciences, Bayer Inc. is one of Canada's leading companies. Headquartered in Toronto and with a major manufacturing site in Sarnia, Ontario, Bayer Inc. employs more than 2,200 people.

Academic Fields
College: General, Accounting, Administration, Law Clerk, Secretarial
Bachelor of Arts: General, Business, Public Relations, Sociology/Social Work
Bachelor of Comm/Admin: Accounting, Finance
Bachelor of Science: General, Biology, Chemistry, Health Sciences, Microbiology, Pharmacy
Chartered Accounting: CMA-Finance, CGA-Finance

Critical Skills
Analytical, Dependable, Efficient, Good Communication, Organized, Professional, Responsible

Types of Positions
Accounts Payable Clerk   Administrative Assistant
Credit Services Clerk   Secretary
Warehouse Operator I

Starting Salary
$ 25,000 - 40,000 (depending on position)

Company Benefits
- 100% dental and medical, RRSP savings
- External training reimbursement
- French and German language training

Correspondence
Mail resume with cover letter

Part Time/Summer: Bayer sometimes hires for part time employment and regularly hires for the summer months. Jobs vary depending on the department. Potential positions include market analysts, clerks, or lab assistants among others. The best time to apply is in February.

BAYTEX ENERGY LIMITED

205 - 5th Avenue SW, Suite 2200
Calgary, Alberta, T2P 2V7
Tel: (403) 267-0700   Fax: (403) 267-0777

Human Resources
Internet: www.baytex.ab.ca

Baytex is a Calgary-based, Canadian oil and natural gas exploration, development and production company with a mandate to create shareholder value through exploration, development and asset acquisitions in select core areas.

Academic Fields
College: Accounting, Administration, Computer Science, Engineering Tech.
Bachelor of Comm/Admin: Accounting, Info Mgmt.
Bachelor of Engineering: General, Chemical
Chartered Accounting: CMA-General, CMA-Finance
Masters: Engineering

Critical Skills
Adaptable, Confident, Dependable, Enthusiastic, Good Writing Skills, Innovative, Leadership, Good Communication, Logical, Organized, Persuasive, Productive, Professional

Types of Positions
Accounting Clerk   Data Entry Clerk
File Clerk   Receptionist
Junior Secretary   Field Operator

Starting Salary
$ 20,000 - 25,000

Company Benefits
- Health benefits, life insurance
- Savings plan
- Related courses are reimbursed

Correspondence
Mail or fax resume with cover letter

Part Time/Summer: Baytex Energy Limited does not hire for part time jobs, but regularly seeks candidates for summer employment. Potential positions involve clerical work, computers or being a field operator. The best time to apply is in March.

BBM BUREAU OF MEASUREMENT

1500 Don Mills Road, Suite 305
Don Mills, Ontario, M3B 3L7
Tel: (416) 445-9200   Fax: (416) 445-8644

Anna Petosa, HR Manager
Internet: www.bbm.ca

BBM Bureau of Measurement is the best known media research company in Canada, with over 50 years of experience in supplying radio and television audience ratings and research to broadcasters, advertisers and their agencies. ComQUEST Research operates as their full service market research division.

Academic Fields
College: Accounting, Administration, Computer Sci., Human Res., Marketing/Sales, Statistics, Television/Radio
Bachelor of Arts: Business, Statistics
Bachelor of Comm/Admin: General, Accounting, Finance, Marketing, Info Mgmt.
Bachelor of Science: General, Computer Science
Bachelor of Engineering: Computer Systems
Chartered Accounting: CA - General/Finance, CGA/CMA - General/Finance

Critical Skills
Analytical, Good Communication, Creative, Decisive, Dependable, Diligent, Diplomatic, Efficient, Enthusiastic, Flexible, Good With Figures, Innovative, Leadership, Logical, Organized, Personable, Productive, Professional, Responsible, Writing Skills,

Types of Positions
Data Analyst	Accounting Clerk
Information Technology	Research Assistant

Starting Salary
$ 25,000 - 32,000 (depending on position)

Company Benefits
- Benefits for full time permanent staff
- Life insurance, dental, and extended health included

Correspondence
Mail or fax resume with cover letter
E-mail: info@bbm.ca

Part Time/Summer: BBM Bureau of Measurement hires regularly for part time jobs, but rarely employs in the summer. The best time to send your resume is late April or early May when their summer holiday schedule is finalized.

BC HYDRO

6911 Southpoint Drive
Burnaby, British Columbia, V3N 4X8
Tel: (604) 528-3404   Fax: (604) 528-1733

Human Resource Services
Internet: www.bchydro.bc.ca

BC Hydro is Canada's third largest electric utility and a provincial crown corporation. Their job is to support the economic growth of British Columbia through the efficient supply and distribution of electricity throughout the province. They serve 1.4 million customers in an area containing over 92 per cent of British Columbia's population. BC Hydro offers both men and women a wide variety of exciting careers in many different fields. The corporation employs more than 5,400 individuals.

Academic Fields
College: Engineering Tech.
Bachelor of Arts: Business, Public Relations
Bachelor of Science: Biology, Environmental Studies
Bachelor of Engineering: Civil, Electrical, Mechanical
Chartered Accounting: CA - General/Finance, CGA/CMA - General/Finance
Masters: Business Administration, Engineering

Critical Skills
Adaptable, Dependable, Efficient, Enthusiastic, Flexible, Innovative, Leadership, Good Communication, Organized, Productive, Professional

Types of Positions
Clerical	Apprentice
Engineer in Training	Technologist in Training

Starting Salary
$ 25,000 - 30,000

Company Benefits
- Medical and dental benefits
- Start with 3 weeks annual vacation
- Encourage any education relevant to the job

Correspondence
Mail, fax, submit resume & cover letter in person

Part Time/Summer: BC Hydro sometimes seeks part time people and regularly hires for the summer. Positions usually include meter reader, clerical duties, or student biologist. There are also engineering and business opportunities. The best time to apply is in February and March.

The Canada Student Employment Guide

BC RESEARCH INC.

3650 Westbrook Mall
Vancouver, British Columbia, V6S 2L2
Tel: (604) 224-4331   Fax: (604) 224-0540

Judy Hillier, Human Resources
Internet: www.bcr.bc.ca

BC Research provides technical development and services in environmental sciences and engineering, biotechnology, advanced systems engineering, and ergonomics.

Academic Fields
College: Computer Science, Forestry, Human Resources, Laboratory Tech.
Bachelor of Science: Biology, Chemistry, Environmental Studies, Forestry, Kinesiology
Bachelor of Engineering: Chemical, Environmental Studies, Mechanical
Masters: Science, Engineering

Critical Skills
Adaptable, Analytical, Good Communication, Dependable, Efficient, Enthusiastic, Flexible, Innovative, Leadership, Logical, Productive, Responsible

Types of Positions
Forest Biotechnology   Environmental Chemistry
Ergonomics & Human Factors

Starting Salary
$ 25,000 - 30,000

Company Benefits
- Dental plan
- Group life
- Disability plans

Correspondence
Mail resume with cover letter

Part Time/Summer: BC Research occasionally looks for individuals for part time and summer employment.

BC TELECOM INC.

3777 Kingsway
Burnaby, British Columbia, V5H 3Z7
Tel: (604) 432-2796   Fax: (604) 436-1352

Employment Centre
Internet: www.bctel.com

BC Telecom is a corporate structure made up of BC Tel, Canada's second largest telecommunications company, and BC Tel Services Inc. which is a group of companies focused on emerging communications technologies. BC Tel offers worldwide telecommunications to 99% of B.C.'s population.

Academic Fields
College: General, Accounting, Administration, Electronics Tech., Engineering Tech., Marketing/Sales
Bachelor of Arts: General, Business
Bachelor of Comm/Admin: Marketing, Info Mgmt.
Bachelor of Science: Computer Science
Bachelor of Engineering: General, Computer Systems, Electrical
Masters: Business Administration, Science

Critical Skills
Adaptable, Good Communication, Dependable, Enthusiastic, Flexible, Good Writing Skills, Productive, Responsible

Types of Positions
Traffic Operator   General Clerical
Call Centre Representative

Starting Salary
$ 30,000 - 35,000

Company Benefits
- Full medical and dental benefits
- Internal advancement, fitness facilities
- Continuing education funded and supported

Correspondence
Mail or fax resume with cover letter

Part Time/Summer: BC Telecom regularly hires for part time and summer employment. Potential jobs include traffic operator, customer service rep. and general clerical work. The best time to apply is in January or February.

BCG SERVICES

2691 No. 5 Rd.
Richmond, British Columbia, V6X 2S8
Tel: (604) 232-2063   Fax: (604) 232-2050

Dawn Barnes, HR Manager

BCG Services is an irrigation supply company. They provide professional advice to irrigation design for all types of needs and supply irrigation and plumbing products. The company works with contractors, municipalities, golf courses, and agricultural businesses.

Academic Fields
College: Accounting, Administration, Business, Secretarial, Agricultural, Mechanical Tech., Plumbing
Bachelor of Arts: Business
Bachelor of Comm/Admin: General, Accounting
Bachelor of Engineering: Industrial, Bachelor of Architecture, Bachelor of Landscape Architecture

Critical Skills
Adaptable, Analytical, Dependable, Diligent, Enthusiastic, Flexible, Good Writing Skills, Organized, Personable, Responsible, Computer Skills

Types of Positions
Administration   Warehouse Worker
Accounting - Bookkeeping   Counter Sales

Starting Salary
$ 30,000 - 35,000

Company Benefits
- Full benefit package, pension plan, health, life insurance, dental
- Training on-going in-house for those interested in moving into sales or counter work
- Part time or seasonal employees receive no benefits

Correspondence
Fax resume with cover letter
E-mail: dbarnes@internationalplastics.bc.ca

Part Time/Summer: BCG Services rarely hires for part time work, but regularly seeks candidates in the summer. Potential jobs involve warehouse, shipping, receiving, and yard work. They usually only hire between one and two people at each of their four locations in the Lower Mainland. The best time to apply is in late May.

BDO DUNWOODY

P.O. Box 32, Royal Bank Plaza
Toronto, Ontario, M5J 2J8
Tel: (416) 865-0200   Fax: (416) 865-0887

Gary Wasylow, Human Resources
Internet: www.bdo.ca

BDO Dunwoody is a major accounting firm offering a wide range of accounting, auditing and bookkeeping services to individuals, businesses and other groups. Operating across Canada, the firm provides specific services including taxation, insolvency, bankruptcy, mergers and acquisitions, and litigation support. BDO Dunwoody employs over 2,500 individuals across Canada and has 7 locations in the Toronto region. BDO's focus of expertise is in the mid-market and entrepreneurial sectors.

Academic Fields
Bachelor of Comm/Admin: Accounting
Bachelor of Science: Computer Science, Mathematics

Critical Skills
Adaptable, Analytical, Confident, Good Writing Skills, Diligent, Efficient, Enthusiastic, Good Communication, Flexible, Logical, Dependable, Good With Figures, Organized, Personable, Professional, Responsible

Types of Positions
CA Student

Starting Salary
$ 35,000 - 40,000

Company Benefits
- Standard medical, dental, life insurance, and income protection plans
- Development encouraged and supported

Correspondence
Mail resume with cover letter (include transcripts)
E-mail: gwasylow@toronto.bdo.ca

Part Time/Summer: BDO Dunwoody rarely hires for part time positions, but annually hires for the summer during February and March. These positions are for B.Comm students with 3rd year university completed.

The Canada Student Employment Guide

BEARSKIN LAKE AIR SERVICE LTD.

1475 West Walsh St.
Thunder Bay, Ontario, P7E 4X6
Tel: (807) 577-1141   Fax: (807) 474-2609

Amy Einarson Human Resources
Internet: www.bearskinairlines.com

Bearskin Airlines is Northern Ontario's largest commuter airline. The company serves over 37 destinations, offering 200 scheduled departures daily. They employ nearly 400 employees in Northern Ontario and Manitoba.

Academic Fields
College: Accounting, Administration, Human Resources, Information Systems, Marketing/Sales, Travel/Tourism, Aircraft Maintenance, Aviation
Bachelor of Arts: General
Bachelor of Comm/Admin: General, Human Res.

Critical Skills
Dependable, Efficient, Flexible, Good Communication, Logical, Manual Dexterity, Personable, Professional, Responsible

Types of Positions
Passenger Service Agent   Ramp Attendant
Aircraft Groomer   Parts Clerk
Greeter   Maintenance Helper

Starting Salary
$ 20,000 - 25,000

Company Benefits
- Dental, extended health, life, short term disability
- 3 week classroom training for passenger service agents
- Dangerous goods, WHMIS, cultural awareness

Correspondence
Mail resume with cover letter
E-mail: hresources@bearskinairlines.com

Part Time/Summer: Bearskin Airlines regularly seeks individuals for part time work and occasionally hires for the summer. Potential summer jobs include ramp attendant, greeter, maintenance helper, and aircraft maintenance apprentice. The best time to apply is in April or May.

Co-op/Internship: They have educational institutions sponsored placements for passenger service, aircraft maintenance, ramp attendant, and administration.

BECHTEL CANADA CO.

12 Concorde Place, Suite 200
North York, Ontario, M3C 3T1
Tel: (416) 441-4900   Fax: (416) 441-4941

Human Resources
Internet: www.bechtel.com

Bechtel Canada is an engineering consulting company that is involved in the area of heavy industrial construction. They also work in project management. The firm employs approximately 400 individuals across Canada.

Academic Fields
College: Accounting, Human Resources
Bachelor of Engineering: Civil, Design, Electrical, Mechanical, Mining
Chartered Accounting: CA - General/Finance, CGA - General/Finance, CMA - General/Finance
Masters: Engineering

Critical Skills
Adaptable, Dependable, Diligent, Diplomatic, Enthusiastic, Flexible, Good Communication, Good Writing Skills, Manual Dexterity, Organized, Patient, Personable, Productive, Professional, Responsible

Types of Positions
Project Related Positions   Junior Accountant

Starting Salary
$ 25,000 - 30,000 (non-technical), $ 30,000 - 40,000

Company Benefits
- Comprehensive group benefits
- Retirement plan
- Internal and external career development and training

Correspondence
Mail or fax resume with cover letter or apply through their web site

Part Time/Summer: Bechtel Canada occasionally looks for individuals for part time work and regularly seeks people for summer employment. Potential jobs in the summer include clerical work within engineering and other departments.

The Canada Student Employment Guide

THE BECKER MILK COMPANY LTD.

671 Warden Avenue
Scarborough, Ontario, M1L 3Z7
Tel: (416) 698-2591   Fax: (416) 698-2907

C. Vani, Human Resources Manager

The Becker Milk Company operates a chain of 592 franchised and company owned convenience food stores in Metropolitan Toronto and in communities in southern and eastern Ontario. The company is also engaged in the processing of milk, ice cream, and other dairy items, along with fruit juices at plants in Scarborough, St. Thomas, and Cornwall, Ontario. Many outlets offer food service, lottery sales, gasoline, video rentals, automated banking machines, postage stamps, and other products and services. The company employs approximately 410 people.

Academic Fields
Bachelor of Comm/Admin: Accounting, Info Mgmt.
Bachelor of Science: Food Sciences, Microbiology

Critical Skills
Adaptable, Dependable, Diligent, Good Communication, Flexible, Personable, Responsible, Manual Dexterity

Types of Positions
Data Entry Clerk   Dairy Worker
Shipping Worker

Starting Salary
Below $ 20,000

Company Benefits
- Full benefit package for full time workers
- No benefits available for part time or summer employees

Correspondence
Fax or submit resume & cover letter in person

Part Time/Summer: The Becker Milk Company sometimes hires individuals for part time help and regularly hires for summer opportunities. Potential summer jobs include dairy worker in the plant, and shipping worker. The best time to apply for summer positions is in March, well before the summer season.

BECKMAN COULTER CANADA INC.

6755 Mississauga Rd., Suite 600
Mississauga, Ontario, L5N 7Y2
Tel: (905) 819-1234   Fax: (905) 819-1485

Human Resources

Beckman Coulter Canada Inc. sells and services sophisticated medical instruments including those used in hematology, chemistry coagulation, and flow cytometry. The company employs about 200 people. The firm has very few openings at any given time.

Academic Fields
College: Accounting, Electronics Tech., Engineering Tech., Laboratory Tech., Secretarial
Bachelor of Comm/Admin: Accounting, Info Mgmt.
Bachelor of Science: Chemistry
Chartered Accounting: CMA-General, CGA-General

Critical Skills
Adaptable, Good Communication, Dependable, Flexible, Professional, Responsible

Types of Positions
Clerical Position   Warehouse Position
Electrical Technician   Jr. Service Specialist

Starting Salary
$ 25,000 - 30,000

Company Benefits
- Life, health, dental, long term disability
- Pension plan, group RRSP
- Company training for professional positions

Correspondence
Mail or fax resume with cover letter

Part Time/Summer: Beckman Coulter Canada does not hire individuals for part time work, but occasionally looks for people for the summer. A potential summer job could be in the warehouse. The best time to apply is in April.

The Canada Student Employment Guide

BEHLEN INDUSTRIES

927 Douglas St.
Brandon, Manitoba, R7A 7B3
Tel: (204) 728-1188   Fax: (204) 725-4932

Sharon Leopold, Manager Human Resources
Internet: www.behlen.ca

Behlen Industries manufactures a full line of agricultural and commercial products. They are the largest steel manufacturing company in Canada. They have been awarded one of the 50 Best Managed Companies in Canada. Their in-house engineering and detailing departments offer traditional pre-engineered building systems as well as customized built structures.

Academic Fields
College: Accounting, Information Systems, CAD Autocad, Engineering Tech., Welding
Bachelor of Arts: General
Bachelor of Comm/Admin: General
Bachelor of Science: General
Bachelor of Engineering: General, Civil
Chartered Accounting: CA-General, CMA-General, CGA-General

Critical Skills
Adaptable, Analytical, Creative, Dependable, Diligent, Efficient, Enthusiastic, Flexible, Innovative, Logical, Organized, Patient, Productive, Professional, Responsible

Types of Positions
Draftsperson   Detailing/Design
Engineering

Starting Salary
$ 20,000 - 35,000 (depending on position)

Company Benefits
- Full time perm. staff receive medical and dental
- Training and educational programs covered

Correspondence
Mail, fax or e-mail resume with cover letter
E-mail: sleopold@behlen.ca

Part Time/Summer: Behlen Industries rarely hires individuals for part time work, but regularly seeks candidates for the summer. Potential positions would involve clerical duties, design or detailing work. Individuals can apply anytime.

Co-op/Internship: They offer internship opportunities through government sponsorship.

BELL & HOWELL LTD.

360 Hanlan Rd.
Woodbridge, Ontario, L4L 8V6
Tel: (905) 850-6727   Fax: (905) 850-6710

Human Resources Manager
Internet: www.bellhowell.com

Bell & Howell Ltd. is a sales and service company of mail processing equipment. The company's head office is in Woodbridge, Ontario.

Academic Fields
College: Accounting, Electronics Tech., Marketing/Sales, Mechanical Tech.

Critical Skills
Adaptable, Confident, Decisive, Flexible, Good Communication, Innovative, Personable

Types of Positions
Service Technician I   Accounting Clerk
Entry Level Sales Rep.

Starting Salary
$ 25,000 - 30,000

Company Benefits
- Comparable benefit package
- 80% company paid
- Tuition assistance program

Correspondence
Mail or fax resume with cover letter

Part Time/Summer: Bell & Howell Ltd. occasionally hires candidates for part time or summer employment.

BELL CANADA

483 Bay Street, North Tower, Ground Flr.
Toronto, Ontario, M5G 2E1
Tel: (416) 310-2355   Fax: (416) 586-0929

Bell Staffing Solutions
Internet: www.bell.ca

Bell Canada, the largest Canadian telecommunications operating company, markets a world class portfolio of products and services to more than seven million business and residence customers in Ontario and Quebec. The skilled and committed Bell Ontario team is comprised of 24,500 employees on a corporate mission to be a world leader in helping people communicate and manage information. Bell is looking for forward thinking graduates who have a good academic record, have demonstrated leadership in extracurricular activities or through job experiences, and who can excel in a competitive environment characterized by constant change. The candidate must function effectively as a team player and focus on exceeding customers' needs and expectations.

Academic Fields
College: Computer Science
Bachelor of Comm/Admin: Marketing
Bachelor of Engineering: Electrical
Masters: Marketing

Critical Skills
Adaptable, Confident, Dependable, Flexible, Innovative, Leadership, Organized, Good Communication, Professional, Responsible

Types of Positions
Product Manager   Engineering Consultant
Direct Marketing   Computer Systems Specialist

Starting Salary
$ 24,000 - 35,000 (depending on position)

Company Benefits
- A competitive benefits package
- Comprehensive employee development programs
- An equal opportunity employer

Correspondence
Initial contact can be made by sending your cover letter and resume quoting file BDIR95 or through your campus career planning and placement centre.

Part Time/Summer: A small number of summer and coop students are hired. Individuals are sometimes hired for part time jobs.

BELL MOBILITY

2920 Matheson Blvd. E.
Mississauga, Ontario, L4W 5J4
Tel: (905) 674-2220   Fax: (905) 282-3290

Human Resources
Internet: www.bellmobility.ca

Bell Mobility Cellular is a communications company providing cellular, paging, radio, mobile data and air-to-ground communications to individuals and businesses across Canada.

Academic Fields
College: General, Accounting, Administration, Advertising, Business, Communications, Computer Science, Electronics Tech., Engineering Tech., Human Resources, Marketing/Sales, Secretarial, Security/Law
Bachelor of Arts: General, Business, Economics, Languages, Philosophy
Bachelor of Comm/Admin: General, Accounting, Finance, Marketing, Info Mgmt.
Bachelor of Science: General, Computer Science, Environmental Studies
Bachelor of Engineering: General, Computer Systems, Electrical, Environmental Studies
Chartered Accounting: CA - General/Finance, CGA/CMA - General/Finance
Masters: Business Administration, Engineering

Critical Skills
Adaptable, Analytical, Good Communication, Confident, Creative, Decisive, Dependable, Diligent, Efficient, Enthusiastic, Flexible, Good With Figures, Innovative, Leadership, Logical, Organized, Personable, Productive, Responsible, Writing Skills

Types of Positions
Customer Service   Accounts Payable
Accounts Receivable   Network Operations
Secretarial   Administration

Starting Salary
$ 20,000 - 30,000

Company Benefits
- Flexible benefits program

Correspondence
Mail or fax resume and cover letter
E-mail: careers@mobility.com

Part Time/Summer: Bell Mobility regularly hires part time and summer students. The best time to apply is from January to March.

The Canada Student Employment Guide

BELLEVILLE GENERAL HOSPITAL

P.O. Box 428
Belleville, Ontario, K8N 5A9
Tel: (613) 969-7400   Fax: (613) 969-1451

Janet Roseblade, Human Resources Officer

Established in 1886, Belleville General Hospital is a public health facility with more than 345 beds to serve the community. The hospital provides services in medicine and surgery, maternity, gynecology, intensive and chronic care, pediatric, and psychiatric departments. They employ more than 1,180 people.

Academic Fields
College: Accounting, Child Care, Computer Science, Emergency/Paramedic, Food/Nutrition, Human Resources, Lab. Tech., Nursing, Radiology Tech., Rec. Studies, Secretarial, Health Records, Respiratory Therapy
Bachelor of Arts: General, Business, Gerontology, Psychology, Recreation Studies, Sociology/Social Work
Bachelor of Comm/Admin: Accounting, Info Mgmt.
Bachelor of Science: Computer Science, Food Sciences, Health Sciences, Nursing (RN), Occupational Therapy, Pharmacy, Physiotherapy, Psychology
Bachelor of Engineering: Civil, Computer Systems
Chartered Accounting: CMA-General, CGA-General
Masters: Business Administration, Psychology

Critical Skills
Adaptable, Dependable, Efficient, Enthusiastic, Good Writing Skills, Leadership, Organized, Good Communication, Patient, Productive, Professional, Responsible, Team Player

Types of Positions
Registered Practical Nurse   Radiology Tech.
Physiotherapist   Occupational Therapist
Pharmacist   Social Worker

Starting Salary
$ 25,000 - 40,000 (depending on position)

Company Benefits
- Comprehensive package for full time employees
- Medical and dental plan, pension

Correspondence
Mail, submit resume & cover letter in person

Part Time/Summer: Belleville General Hospital regularly hires for part time and summer work, although there is limited opportunities due to downsizing and restructuring.

BENWELL ATKINS LTD.

901 Great Northern Way
Vancouver, British Columbia, V5T 1E1
Tel: (604) 872-2326   Fax: (604) 872-4235

Steve Cobb, Human Resources
Internet: www.benwell.com

Benwell Atkins is a printing and prepress company. The firm also provides various mailing services.

Academic Fields
College: Graphic Arts, Print Production
Chartered Accounting: CA-General

Critical Skills
Adaptable, Dependable, Diligent, Diplomatic, Flexible, Personable, Productive, Responsible

Types of Positions
Mail Room Clerk   Bindery Person
Shipper

Starting Salary
below $ 25,000

Company Benefits
- 50% medical, 85% dental
- In-house training
- Occasional sponsorship in training outside the company

Correspondence
Mail or fax resume and cover letter
E-mail: ctrevitt@benwell.com

Part Time/Summer: Benwell Atkins occasionally seeks candidates for part time and summer employment opportunities.

BEST WESTERN CARLTON PLACE HOTEL

33 Carlson Court
Etobicoke, Ontario, M9W 6H5
Tel: (416) 675-1234   Fax: (416) 675-3436

Catherine Lynn Cumming, Human Resources

Best Western Carlton Place Hotel, is a hotel establishment with 528 rooms. The hotel offers a wide range of facilities for dining, conventions, banquets, business meetings, or family vacations. The Best Western Carlton Place Hotel employs more than 170 individuals.

Academic Fields
College: Accounting, Cooking/Culinary, Hospitality, Human Resources, Marketing/Sales, Secretarial, Travel/Tourism
Bachelor of Arts: General, Business
Bachelor of Comm/Admin: Accounting

Critical Skills
Confident, Decisive, Dependable, Good Communication, Efficient, Enthusiastic, Diligent, Good With Figures, Leadership, Patient, Personable, Professional, Responsible

Types of Positions
Front Desk Agent   Server
Accounting Clerk   Telephone Operator
Bell Person   Bartender

Starting Salary
$ 20,000 - 25,000

Company Benefits
- Full benefit package
- On-the-job training

Correspondence
Mail, fax, submit resume & cover letter in person

Part Time/Summer: Best Western Carlton Place Hotel regularly hires for part time positions and sometimes hires for summer opportunities. Some potential summer jobs include banquet servers or porters. The best time to apply for these potential positions is in April, May and August.

BETEL HOME FOUNDATION

212 Manchester Avenue
Selkirk, Manitoba, R1A 0B6
Tel: (204) 482-5469   Fax: (204) 482-4651

Karen Still, Human Resources

Betel Home Foundation is a multi-disciplinary residential care facility established in Selkirk, Manitoba, in 1915. The facility uses a team approach to establish common goals regarding the care of residents. Betel houses 93 residents and has six wings accommodating 62 single rooms and 16 double rooms. Physician and nursing care along with occupational therapy is provided on-site. The residential facility employs approximately 100 individuals.

Academic Fields
College: Recreation Studies
Bachelor of Arts: Gerontology, Recreation Studies, Sociology/Social Work

Critical Skills
Adaptable, Artistic, Good Communication, Confident, Creative, Decisive, Dependable, Diligent, Diplomatic, Efficient, Enthusiastic, Flexible, Innovative, Leadership, Organized, Patient, Personable, Productive, Professional, Responsible, Good Writing Skills

Types of Positions
Activity Worker   Health Care Aide
Housekeeping Aide

Starting Salary
below $ 20,000

Company Benefits
- Under union guidelines
- Service Employees International Union (S.E.I.U.)

Correspondence
Mail resume with cover letter

Part Time/Summer: Betel Home Foundation sometimes seeks candidates for part time work, and regularly hires in the summer. In the summer months the most likely position would be activity program assistant. The best time to apply is in April or May.

The Canada Student Employment Guide

BETHANIA MENNONITE PERSONAL CARE HOME INC.
1045 Concordia Avenue
Winnipeg, Manitoba, R2K 3S7
Tel: (204) 667-0795   Fax: (204) 667-7078

Administrator

Bethania Mennonite Personal Care Home is a private, non-profit company founded in 1945 by the Mennonite Benevolent Society, and has been at its present location since 1970. Bethania has rooms to accommodate 140 people, and is funded from sources including the Manitoba government, fees paid by residents, and private donations. The personal care home has a total of 148 long term care beds, and employs approximately 230 individuals.

Academic Fields
College: Cooking/Culinary, Nursing, Recreation Studies
Bachelor of Arts: Gerontology, Recreation Studies, Sociology/Social Work
Bachelor of Comm/Admin: Info Management
Bachelor of Science: Nursing (RN)
Bachelor of Social Work
Chartered Accounting: CMA-General, CGA-General
Masters: Education

Critical Skills
Creative, Dependable, Enthusiastic

Types of Positions
Personal Care Aide	Kitchen Aide
Laundry Aide	Housekeeping Aide
Clerk Typist	Registered Nursing

Starting Salary
$ 20,000 and above

Company Benefits
- Health, dental and life insurance
- Pension, vacation, sick pay and long term disability
- Staff development trainer on site

Correspondence
Mail resume with cover letter

Part Time/Summer: Bethania Mennonite Personal Care Home sometimes looks for individuals for part time employment and regularly seeks candidates for the summer months. Potential positions include grounds maintenance, office support, recreation and music therapy. The best time to apply is early April.

BETHESDA HOSPITAL
P.O. Box 939
Steinbach, Manitoba, R0A 2R0
Tel: (204) 326-6411   Fax: (204) 326-6931

Cheryl Lebleu, Human Resources

Bethesda Hospital is a general medical and health care facility that was established in 1937. The hospital provides services in the areas of medicine and surgery, pediatrics, gynecology, and extended care, among others. Bethesda Hospital has about 80 beds in total, and has a staff of approximately 235 individuals.

Academic Fields
College: Accounting, Cooking/Culinary, Emergency/Paramedic, Food/Nutrition, Human Resources, Laboratory Tech., Nursing, Radiology Tech., Recreation Studies, Secretarial
Bachelor of Arts: Business, Recreation Studies
Bachelor of Comm/Admin: Accounting
Bachelor of Science: Food Sci., Health Sci., Nursing, Occupational Therapy, Pharmacy, Physiotherapy
Chartered Accounting: CA-Finance

Critical Skills
Adaptable, Confident, Dependable, Efficient, Good Communication, Flexible, Good Writing Skills, Manual Dexterity, Organized, Patient, Professional

Types of Positions
Health Care Aide	Dietary Aide
Housekeeping Clerk	Laundry Aide
Maintenance	Nursing

Starting Salary
$ 20,000 - 25,000 (Aides) /
$ 30,000 - 40,000 (Reg. Nurse)

Company Benefits
- Health care, dental and life insurance
- Pension, short term sick benefits
- Continuous nursing training & development

Correspondence
Mail, fax, or submit resume & cover letter in person

Part Time/Summer: Bethesda Hospital regularly hires for part time and summer opportunities. Jobs in the summer may include dietary aide, linen aide, housekeeping aide, health care aide, or registered nurse. The best time to apply is in April.

BETTIS CANADA LTD.

4112 - 91A St. NW
Edmonton, Alberta, T6E 5V2
Tel: (780) 450-3600   Fax: (780) 450-1400

Personnel Administrator
Internet: www.bettiscanada.com

Bettis Canada Ltd. manufacture and market valve actuators, multiport flow selectors and a multitude of pneumatic and hydraulic control components including linebreak systems and pressure pilot valves.

Academic Fields
College: Accounting, Administration, Business, Computer Science, Engineering Tech., Human Resources, Industrial Design, Marketing/Sales, Mechanical Tech.
Bachelor of Arts: Business, Public Relations
Bachelor of Comm/Admin: General, Accounting, Finance, Marketing, Info Mgmt., Public Admin.
Bachelor of Science: Computer Science
Bachelor of Engineering: Computer Systems, Design, Industrial, Materials Science, Mechanical
Chartered Accounting: CA-General, CMA-General, CGA-General
Masters: Business Administration, Engineering

Critical Skills
Adaptable, Analytical, Good Communication, Creative, Dependable, Efficient, Flexible, Innovative, Leadership, Logical, Manual Dexterity, Organized, Productive, Professional

Types of Positions
Receptionist   General Labourer
Document Clerk   Assembler
Accounting Clerk

Starting Salary
$ 20,000-25,000

Company Benefits
- Group insurance, group RRSP
- Outside training based on position

Correspondence
Mail or fax resume and cover letter

Part Time/Summer: Bettis Canada does not hire individuals for part time work, but regularly hires in the summer. Potential jobs in the summer include engineering student or general labourer. The best time to apply is in April or May.

BFGOODRICH LANDING GEAR DIVISION

1400 South Service Road West
Oakville, Ontario, L6L 5Y7
Tel: (905) 827-7777   Fax: (905) 825-1591

Stacey Dow, Human Resources
Internet: www.bfgoodrich.com

BFGoodrich Landing Gear Division, Oakville is a global leader in the design, manufacture and testing of integrated, state-of-the-art landing gear and flight control systems. The company employs more than 600 individuals.

Academic Fields
College: Accounting, Administration, Business, Human Resources, Information Systems, Purchasing, Secretarial, Aircraft Maintenance, CAD Autocad, Computer Science, Electronics Tech., Engineering Tech., Mechanical Tech., Nursing RN
Bachelor of Arts: General, Business, Economics, Psychology, Statistics
Bachelor of Comm/Admin: General, Accounting, Finance, Human Resources, Info Mgmt.
Bachelor of Science: General, Computer Science, Mathematics, Nursing, Occupational Therapy
Bachelor of Engineering: General, Chemical, Computer Systems, Design, Electrical, Industrial, Materials Science, Mechanical, Transportation
Chartered Accounting: CA - General/Finance, CGA/CMA - General/Finance
Masters: Business Admin., Science, Engineering

Critical Skills
Adaptable, Analytical, Good Communication, Dependable, Enthusiastic, Flexible, Innovative, Productive, Responsible

Types of Positions
Plating/Processing   Machine Shop
Office

Starting Salary
$ 35,000 - 40,000

Company Benefits
- Full benefit package

Correspondence
Mail or fax resume with cover letter
E-mail: staceyd@menasco.com

Part Time/Summer: BFGoodrich Landing Gear Division occasionally looks for people for part time work and rarely hires for the summer.

The Canada Student Employment Guide

BIC INC.

155 Oakdale Rd.
Downsview, Ontario, M3N 1W2
Tel: (416) 742-9173   Fax: (416) 741-4965

Monica Parenti, Human Resources
Internet: www.bicworld.com

Bic Inc. is involved in the manufacturing of writing instruments, lighters, and shavers. The company employs approximately 130 individuals.

Academic Fields
College: Accounting, Drafting/Architecture, Electronics Tech., Human Resources, Laboratory Tech., Marketing/Sales, Secretarial, Programming, Purchasing
Bachelor of Arts: Business, Psychology, Public Relations
Bachelor of Comm/Admin: Accounting, Finance, Marketing
Bachelor of Science: Computer Science
Bachelor of Engineering: Electrical, Mechanical
Bachelor of Education: Adult Education
Chartered Accounting: CMA-Finance, CGA-Finance
Masters: Business Administration, Science

Critical Skills
Analytical, Excellent Communication, Creative, Enthusiastic, Leadership, Personable, Professional, Detail Oriented, Second Language Preferable, Reliable, Customer Oriented

Types of Positions
Receptionist   Office Clerk
Order Entry Clerk   Packaging Operator
Maintenance Mechanic   Graphic Artist

Starting Salary
$ 25,000 - 30,000

Company Benefits
- Flexible benefits
- Computer training, tuition fee program
- Other in-house training as needed

Correspondence
Mail or e-mail resume with cover letter
E-mail: monica.parenti@bicworld.com

Part Time/Summer: Bic occasionally looks for people for part time work, and regularly seeks individuals for summer employment. Potential jobs in the summer include office support, marketing, human resources, MIS department, and general labour in plant operations. The best time to apply is in April or May.

BIOMIRA INC.

2011 - 94th Street
Edmonton, Alberta, T6N 1H1
Tel: (780) 450-3761   Fax: (780) 463-0871

Human Resources Department
Internet: www.biomira.com

Biomira Inc. is a biotechnology company applying its leading technology in immunotherapy and organic chemistry for the development of cancer therapeutics. The company's commitment to the development of products for the treatment of cancer is currently focused on synthetic therapeutic vaccines and innovative strategies for immunotherapeutic treatment of cancer.

Academic Fields
College: Paiological Sciences
Bachelor of Science: Chemistry (Organic), Microbiology, Pharmacy, Immunology
Bachelor of Engineering: Biomedical
Masters: Engineering

Critical Skills
Adaptable, Analytical, Dependable, Good Communication, Good Writing Skills, Logical, Organized, Professional

Types of Positions
Technician I   Research Scientist
Clinical Research   Regulatory Affairs

Starting Salary
Salary depends on position and educational level

Company Benefits
- Competitive benefits
- On-the-job training
- Technical and professional career ladders

Correspondence
Mail resume with cover letter
E-mail: hr@biomira.com

Part Time/Summer: Biomira sometimes seeks candidates for part time employment and regularly employs individuals during the summer months. Potential positions involve technical work. The best time to apply is in January or February.

BIO-RESEARCH LABORATORIES LTD.

87 Senneville Road
Senneville, Québec, H9X 3R3
Tel: (514) 630-8200   Fax: (514) 630-8234

Human Resources

Bio-Research Laboratories is a research and development laboratory that operates in the field of biotechnology. The company was established in 1989, and has an employee base of approximately 500 individuals.

Academic Fields
College: Animal Health, Business, Laboratory Tech., Science-General
Bachelor of Comm/Admin: Accounting, Marketing, Info Mgmt.
Bachelor of Science: Biology, Chemistry, Computer Science, Health Sciences, Microbiology, Pharmacy
Bachelor of Engineering: Biomedical, Chemical
Chartered Accounting: CMA-General
Masters: Science

Critical Skills
Adaptable, Analytical, Good Communication, Decisive, Dependable, Diligent, Efficient, Enthusiastic, Flexible, Good With Figures, Innovative, Leadership, Logical, Manual Dexterity, Organized, Patient, Personable, Productive, Professional, Responsible, Good Writing Skills

Types of Positions
Scientist   Technician

Starting Salary
below $ 20,000 - 40,000 (depends on education)

Company Benefits
- Complete benefit package

Correspondence
Mail resume with cover letter

Part Time/Summer: Bio-Research Laboratories regularly looks for individuals on a part time basis, and sometimes seeks candidates for the summer months. The best time to apply is in the Fall.

BIOVAIL CORPORATION INTERNATIONAL

2488 Dunwin Drive
Mississauga, Ontario, L5L 1J9
Tel: (416) 285-6000   Fax: (416) 285-6499

Human Resources
Internet: www.biovail.com

Biovail Corporation International is a full-service pharmaceutical company that applies its proprietary drug delivery technologies in developing "oral controlled-release" products. Biovail engages in the formulation, clinical testing, registration, manufacturing and, in Canada, direct marketing of these oral controlled-release products.

Academic Fields
College: Administration, Industrial Design, Laboratory Tech., Marketing/Sales, Nursing, Orthotics/Prosthetics, Secretarial
Bachelor of Arts: Psychology, Public Relations, Sociology/Social Work, Statistics
Bachelor of Comm/Admin: Info Mgmt., Public Admin.
Bachelor of Science: Biology, Chemistry, Computer Science, Environmental Studies, Food Sciences, Microbiology, Nursing (RN), Occupational Therapy, Pharmacy, Psychology
Bachelor of Laws: Corporate
Bachelor of Engineering: Biomedical, Chemical, Computer Syst., Electrical, Materials Sci., Mechanical
Chartered Accounting: CMA-Finance, CGA-Finance
Masters: Business Administration, Engineering

Critical Skills
Analytical, Creative, Decisive, Diligent, Leadership, Personable, Persuasive, Professional

Types of Positions
Administrative Assistant   Lab Technician
Receptionist

Starting Salary
$ 25,000 - 30,000

Company Benefits
- Full group life and health, group RRSP

Correspondence
Mail resume with cover letter

Part Time/Summer: Biovail Corporation International does not hire for part time or summer employment.

The Canada Student Employment Guide

BIRKS JEWELRY

P.O. Box 210, Eaton Centre, 220 Yonge Street
Toronto, Ontario, M5B 2H1
Tel: (416) 979-9311   Fax: (416) 979-2850

Human Resources Manager

Birks is the sign name for stores operated by Henry Birks and Sons (1993) Inc. The company is a major retailer in the Canadian market of jewelry and giftware. Established in Canada in 1879, Birks currently has 38 outlets across the country, and employs approximately 1,000 individuals. With its head office in Montreal, candidates should apply individually to stores for employment opportunities. The address above reflects the store location at the Eaton Centre in Toronto, Ontario.

Academic Fields
College: General, Business
Bachelor of Arts: General, Business
Bachelor of Comm/Admin: General

Critical Skills
Adaptable, Dependable, Enthusiastic, Good Communication, Leadership, Organized, Productive, Professional

Types of Positions
Sales Associate   Customer Service Repairs
Maintenance   Reception
Management Trainee

Starting Salary
below $ 20,000 - 25,000

Company Benefits
- Full time staff receive benefits and store discount
- Sales training and product knowledge
- Management trainee program

Correspondence
Mail, fax, submit resume & cover letter in person

Part Time/Summer: Birks Jewelry regularly seeks candidates for part time and summer employment. Potential employment includes retail sales. Hiring usually occurs for the summer months and the Christmas season. The best time to apply is by June 1st for summer jobs, and starting after October 15th for Christmas positions.

BJ SERVICES COMPANY

355 - 4 Avenue SW, Suite 1700
Calgary, Alberta, T2P 0J1
Tel: (403) 266-0586   Fax: (403) 256-0550

Sue Levesque, Human Resources
Internet: www.bjservices.com

In Canada, BJ Services operates as Nowsco Well Service Ltd (A BJ Services Company), headquartered in Calgary, Alberta. Nowsco, began drilling with coiled tubing in the mid 90s and now BJ Services is taking this technology around the world. An industry leader in Canada, Nowsco supports the full line of core pumping services as well as BJ Process and Pipeline Services, Unichem and BJ Tubular and Completions Services.

Academic Fields
College: Computer Science, Electronics Tech., Engineering Tech., Laboratory Tech.
Bachelor of Comm/Admin: Accounting
Bachelor of Science: Chemistry
Bachelor of Engineering: Chemical, Mechanical
Chartered Accounting: CMA-General
Masters: Engineering

Critical Skills
Adaptable, Analytical, Decisive, Diplomatic, Efficient, Enthusiastic, Flexible, Good Writing Skills, Innovative, Organized, Patient, Personable, Productive, Professional

Types of Positions
Accounts Receivable   Accounts Payable
Human Resources   Sales
Engineering

Starting Salary
$ 25,000 - 30,000

Company Benefits
- Benefits comparable to most other firms
- Reimbursement for successful completion of job related courses
- Many soft skills courses offered

Correspondence
Fax resume with cover letter

Part Time/Summer: BJ Services occasionally hires for part time jobs, and regularly hires for the summer. A variety of potential positions are offered in the summer months. The best time to apply is in January.

The Canada Student Employment Guide

BLACK PHOTO CORPORATION

371 Gough Rd.
Markham, Ontario, L3R 4B6
Tel: (905) 475-2777   Fax: (905) 475-8814

Renee Dover, HR Manager
Internet: www.blackphoto.com

Black Photo Corporation is a specialty photofinishing company with locations all across Canada. Their stores are known as Black's Camera.

Academic Fields
College: General, Accounting, Advertising, Business, Communications, Computer Science, Electronics Tech., Human Resources, Marketing/Sales, Mechanical Tech., Photography
Bachelor of Arts: General, Business, Economics, English, Fine Arts, Political Science, Psychology, Public Relations, Sociology/Social Work
Bachelor of Comm/Admin: General, Accounting, Finance, Marketing, Info Mgmt.
Bachelor of Science: General, Computer Science
Bachelor of Engineering: Electrical, Mechanical
Chartered Accounting: CMA-Finance, CGA-Finance

Critical Skills
Adaptable, Analytical, Good Communication, Confident, Creative, Decisive, Dependable, Diligent, Diplomatic, Efficient, Enthusiastic, Flexible, Good With Figures, Manual Dexterity, Organized, Personable, Productive, Professional, Responsible

Types of Positions
Accounts Payable Clerk   Sales Associate
Accounts Receivable Clerk   Programmer

Starting Salary
below $ 20,000 - 25,000

Company Benefits
- Health, dental, long term disability
- Tuition reimbursement
- RSP, profit sharing, employee discounts

Correspondence
Mail or fax resume and cover letter

Part Time/Summer: Black Photo Corporation regularly seeks individuals for part time and summer employment opportunities. In the summer months a potential job is sales associate in their retail store. The best time to apply is in the Spring.

BLANEY MCMURTY LLP

20 Queen St. W., Suite 1400
Toronto, Ontario, M5H 2V3
Tel: (416) 593-1221   Fax: (416) 593-5437

Susan Carr, Manager of Human Resources
Internet: www.blaney.com

Blaney McMurty is a full service law firm with approximately 80 lawyers, secretaries and support staff.

Academic Fields
College: Accounting, Business, Human Resources, Marketing/Sales, Legal Assistant
Bachelor of Comm/Admin: Human Resources
Bachelor of Science: Computer Science
Bachelor of Laws: General, Corporate, Real Estate
Chartered Accounting: CA-General, CGA-General

Critical Skills
Dependable, Efficient, Flexible, Good Communication, Good Writing Skills, Organized, Personable, Productive, Professional

Types of Positions
Junior Legal Secretary   Junior Law Clerk
IT Technician   Accounting Clerk
C.A. Assistant

Starting Salary
$ 25,000 - 30,000

Company Benefits
- Health and dental (addt'l fee for family benefits)
- Life insurance, voluntary additional insurance
- Group GRSP (firm does not match contributions)

Correspondence
Mail, fax or e-mail resume with cover letter
E-mail: scarr@blaney.com

Part Time/Summer: Blaney McMurty LLP rarely hires for part time work, but regularly hires in the summer. Potential jobs include billing co-ordinator or assistant to corporate clerks. The best time to apply is in March or April.

Co-op/Internship: Their information technology department regularly hires students for internship programs. Contact Wendy Wiltshire.

The Canada Student Employment Guide

BLOORVIEW CHILDRENS HOSPITAL

25 Buchan Court
North York, Ontario, M2J 4S9
Tel: (416) 494-2222   Fax: (416) 494-9985

Human Resources Department

Established in 1899, Bloorview Children's Hospital is a specialty hospital operating to provide chronic care to young individuals. The public hospital has approximately 87 beds in its facility and employs a total of 285 highly skilled individuals to work in various health care capacities.

Academic Fields
College: Child Care, Electronics Tech., Food/Nutrition, Human Resources, Recreation Studies, Secretarial
Bachelor of Arts: Recreation Studies
Bachelor of Science: Computer Science, Food Sciences, Health Sciences, Nursing (RN), Occupational Therapy, Pharmacy, Physiotherapy
Bachelor of Engineering: Electrical
Chartered Accounting: CA-Finance, CMA-Finance, CGA-Finance
Masters: Business Administration, Arts, Education, Library Science

Critical Skills
Adaptable, Good Communication, Confident, Dependable, Diligent, Efficient, Enthusiastic, Flexible, Patient, Personable, Professional, Responsible

Types of Positions
Various Positions

Starting Salary
Depends on position

Company Benefits
- Group life insurance, health and dental
- Long term disability and pension
- Various education funds available

Correspondence
Mail or fax resume and cover letter

Part Time/Summer: Bloorview Children's Hospital sometimes hires for part time and summer opportunities. A potential summer job would be in recreation, or as an employed nursing student. The best time to apply is in December or January for positions in recreation. Applications are taken year round for the position of employed nursing student.

THE BLOORVIEW MACMILLAN CENTRE

350 Rumsey Rd.
Toronto, Ontario, M4G 1R8
Tel: (416) 424-3824   Fax: (416) 424-3868

Paula Gerolimon, Human Resources

The Bloorview MacMillan Centre helps children with disabilities and special needs achieve their personal best. They are Ontario's largest health-care facility for children and youth with disabilities. As a leader in family-centred rehabilitation and habilitation, as well as advocacy, education and research, Bloorview MacMillan Centre provides care to more than 5,000 clients each year.

Academic Fields
College: Accounting, Administration, Child Care, Computer Science, Electronics Tech., Food/Nutrition, Human Resources, Orthotics/Prosthetics, Recreation Studies, Science-General, Secretarial, Statistics
Bachelor of Arts: Music, Psychology, Recreation Studies, Sociology/Social Work
Bachelor of Comm/Admin: Accounting, Finance
Bachelor of Science: General, Food Sciences, Health Sciences, Kinesiology, Nursing (RN), Occupational Therapy, Psychology
Bachelor of Engineering: Computer Systems, Design, Mechanical
Chartered Accounting: CA - General/Finance
Masters: Science, Engineering

Critical Skills
Adaptable, Confident, Dependable, Diligent, Efficient, Enthusiastic, Flexible, Good Communication, Patient, Personable, Professional, Responsible

Types of Positions
Housekeeping

Starting Salary
$ 20,000 - 25,000

Company Benefits
- Health, dental, and life insurance
- Long term disability and pension

Correspondence
Fax resume and cover letter

Part Time/Summer: The Bloorview MacMillan Centre sometimes hires for part time and summer employment. Potential positions are in recreation and finance. The best time to apply is in January.

The Canada Student Employment Guide

BLUE GIANT EQUIPMENT OF CANADA LTD.

85 Heart Lake Rd. S.
Brampton, Ontario, L6W 3K2
Tel: (905) 457-3900   Fax: (905) 457-2313

Tarryn Copeling, Human Resources
Internet: www.bluegiant.com

Blue Giant Equipment of Canada is a manufacturer of material handling equipment. The firm has an employee base of about 140 people.

Academic Fields
College: Accounting, Administration
Bachelor of Arts: Business, Economics
Bachelor of Comm/Admin: General
Bachelor of Engineering: Design, Electrical, Industrial, Mechanical
Chartered Accounting: CMA-General

Critical Skills
Adaptable, Analytical, Good Communication, Dependable, Efficient, Enthusiastic, Flexible, Organized, Personable, Productive, Professional, Responsible

Types of Positions
Accounting Clerk   Purchasing Clerk

Starting Salary
$ 25,000 - 30,000

Company Benefits
- Extensive medical and basic and preventative dental
- Company RRSP
- Full tuition reimbursement

Correspondence
Fax or e-mail resume with cover letter

Part Time/Summer: Blue Giant Equipment of Canada does not hire for part time work, but regularly seeks people for summer opportunities. Potential summer jobs are on the production floor. The best time to apply is in March.

BLUE MOUNTAIN RESORTS LIMITED

R.R. # 3
Collingwood, Ontario, L9Y 3Z2
Tel: (705) 445-0231   Fax: (705) 444-1751

Celia Beaucage, Human Resources Coordinator
Internet: www.bluemountain.ca

Blue Mountain is located 2 hours north of Toronto bordering the southern shores of Georgian Bay. Originally conceived as a winter playground featuring the province's highest vertical serviced by 15 lifts across 235 acres of skiable terrain and snow-tubing park, the resort has evolved into a 4-seasons destination. Blue Mountain employs 190 year round, 700 winter seasonal, and 225 summer seasonal employees.

Academic Fields
College: Accounting, Administration, Cooking/Culinary, Recreation Studies, Travel/Tourism, Plumbing, Welding
Bachelor of Arts: General, Business
Bachelor of Comm/Admin: General, Accounting, Marketing
Masters: Business Administration, Engineering

Critical Skills
Adaptable, Confident, Creative, Dependable, Diplomatic, Enthusiastic, Flexible, Good Communication, Personable, Professional

Types of Positions
Cafe Attendant   Lift Attendant
Lift Ticket Cashier   Guest Service Attendant
Room Attendant   Ski/Snowboard Rentals

Starting Salary
$ 15,000 or less (seasonal)
$ 20,000 - 25,000 (year round)

Company Benefits
- Benefits for full time year round
- Extended health and dental benefits, life insurance

Correspondence
Mail, fax, e-mail or submit resume with cover letter in person. E-mail: mail@bluemountain.ca

Part Time/Summer: Blue Mountain Resorts regularly hires for part time and summer work. Positions include golf shuttlers, slide ride attendants, cook and dishwasher. Applicants can apply anytime.

BLUE WAVE SEAFOODS INC.

P.O. Box 20
Port Mouton, Nova Scotia, B0T 1T0
Tel: (902) 683-2044   Fax: N/A

Human Resources

Blue Wave Seafoods is engaged in the business of manufacturing fresh and frozen packaged fish and other seafood products. The company was established in 1991, and currently employs approximately 100 individuals to work in various sectors in the food manufacturing industry.

Academic Fields
College: Accounting, Administration, Computer Science, Engineering Tech., Mechanical Tech.
Bachelor of Arts: Business
Bachelor of Comm/Admin: Accounting, Marketing
Bachelor of Science: Biology, Food Sciences, Zoology
Bachelor of Laws: Corporate
Bachelor of Engineering: Electrical, Industrial, Mechanical
Chartered Accounting: CA-General

Critical Skills
Adaptable, Dependable, Diligent, Efficient, Flexible, Logical, Manual Dexterity, Organized, Productive, Responsible

Types of Positions
Labourer   Fish Cutter

Starting Salary
$ 20,000 - 25,000

Company Benefits
- Full time employees receive competitive package
- Health and dental benefits

Correspondence
Mail resume with cover letter

Part Time/Summer: Blue Wave Seafoods sometimes seeks staff for part time and summer opportunities. Potential positions include labourer and herring roe cutter. The best time to apply for these positions is in June through to August.

BLUEWATER DISTRICT SCHOOL BOARD

351 1st Ave. North, Box 190
Chesley, Ontario, N0G 1L0
Tel: (519) 363-2014   Fax: (519) 363-5302

Executive Assistant, Human Resources
Internet: www.bwdsb.on.ca

Bluewater District School Board is a public education board located in Grey and Bruce Countries. They oversee the teaching of grades K to OAC (13).

Academic Fields
College: Child Care, Secretarial
Bachelor of Education: General, Childhood, Special
Chartered Accounting: CMA-General, CGA-General

Critical Skills
Adaptable, Diligent, Efficient, Enthusiastic, Flexible, Good Writing Skills, Organized, Patient, Professional, Responsible

Types of Positions
Teaching   Secretary
Custodian   Educational Assistant

Starting Salary
$ 20,000 - 40,000 (depending on position)

Company Benefits
- Excellent public sector benefit package
- Extensive in-service training

Correspondence
Mail resume with cover letter

Part Time/Summer: Bluewater District School Board occasionally seeks candidates for part time or summer work. A potential job would be custodian assistant in the summer. The best time to apply is early in the calendar year.

The Canada Student Employment Guide

BNP PARIBAS (CANADA)

1981 McGill College Avenue
Montréal, Québec, H3A 2W8
Tel: (514) 285-6000   Fax: (514) 285-6278

Lyne Burnham, Human Resources
Internet: www.bnpparibas.ca

With its head office in Montreal and business centres in Quebec City, Toronto and Vancouver, BNP PARIBAS (Canada) is one of the largest foreign bank subsidiaries doing business in Canada. BNP PARIBAS' (Canada) clients, consisting of companies geared towards world markets as well as private and institutional investors, have access to a full range of products and services that combine quality, security and flexibility.

Academic Fields
College: Accounting, Administration, Computer Science, Law Clerk, Secretarial
Bachelor of Comm/Admin: General, Accounting, Finance, Info Mgmt.
Bachelor of Science: Computer Science
Bachelor of Laws: General, Corporate
Chartered Accounting: CA - General/Finance, CMA-Finance, CGA-Finance
Masters: Business Administration

Critical Skills
Adaptable, Analytical, Creative, Dependable, Diligent, Efficient, Enthusiastic, Good Communication, Flexible, Good Writing Skills, Innovative, Organized, Productive, Responsible

Types of Positions
Credit Trainer   Other Positions

Starting Salary
$ 30,000 - 40,000

Company Benefits
- Medical and dental benefits
- Advantageous social programs
- Personal loans and mortgages

Correspondence
Mail resume with cover letter

Part Time/Summer: BNP PARIBAS (Canada) sometimes seeks people for part time and summer opportunities. Currently, there are no summer positions available.

BOMBARDIER AEROSPACE

123 Garratt Blvd.
Downsview, Ontario, M3K 1Y5
Tel: (416) 633-7310   Fax: (416) 375-4519

Human Resources
Internet: www.bombardier.com

Bombardier Aerospace is a part of Bombardier Inc., a world leader in recreational products, rail transportation equipment and aerospace. Today, they are the world's third largest manufacturer of civil aircraft. They focus on the design, manufacture, sale and support of regional and amphibious aircraft and business jets, as well as airframe components. Bombardier Aerospace combines the resources of four leading aircraft manufacturers: Canadair and de Havilland in Canada, Learjet in the United States and Shorts in the United Kingdom.

Academic Fields
They will look at candidates from many different academic areas.

Critical Skills
Adaptable, Analytical, Confident, Dependable, Enthusiastic, Flexible, Good Communication, Innovative, Leadership

Types of Positions
Engineering   Finance/Human Res.
Work & Material Planning   Procurement
Methods   Business Processes

Starting Salary
$ 35,000 - 40,000

Company Benefits
- Full range of health benefits
- Education reimbursement program
- Graduate development program for new grads

Correspondence
Mail resume with cover letter
E-mail: humanresources@dehavilland.ca

Part Time/Summer: Bombardier does not hire for part time work, but regularly hires for summer employment opportunities.

Co-op/Internship: The company offers internship opportunities.

The Canada Student Employment Guide

BONUS RESOURCE SERVICES CORP.

8112 Edgar Industrial Dr.
Red Deer, Alberta, T4P 3R2
Tel: (403) 347-3737   Fax: (403) 343-6131

Sandra Loxam, Human Resources Manager
Internet: www.bonusgroup.com

Bonus Resource Services Corp. provides oilfield services to both major and independent oil and gas exploration and production companies. Bonus has a fleet of over 212 service rigs available for completion, workover and servicing assignments throughout Saskatchewan, Alberta and British Columbia.

Academic Fields
College: Accounting, Administration, Human Resources, Marketing/Sales, Purchasing, Secretarial, Welding
Bachelor of Comm/Admin: Human Resources, Marketing
Chartered Accounting: CA-General, CGA-General, CMA-General

Critical Skills
Adaptable, Good Communication, Enthusiastic, Good Writing Skills, Innovative, Leadership, Organized, Personable, Productive, Professional

Types of Positions
Accounting Clerk	Receptionist
Administrative Clerk	Safety Clerk
HR Clerk	Operations Assistant

Starting Salary
$ 15,000 - 25,000

Company Benefits
- Comprehensive benefits coverage for full time employees
- Health, dental, vision, life insurance, disability, RRSP
- Internal training provided on-the-job, educational assistance program

Correspondence
Mail, fax resume with cover letter or apply through web site. E-mail: loxams@bonusgroup.com

Part Time/Summer: Bonus Resource Services occasionally looks for individuals for part time and summer employment. Potential jobs involve accounting, administration or general clerical duties. The best time to apply is in April of each year.

BORÉAL ASSURANCES INC.

1100, boul. René-Lévesque Ouest
Montréal, Québec, H3B 4P4
Tel: (514) 392-6000   Fax: (514) 392-7777

Marie-Josée Bisson, Conseillère en ressources humaines

Boreal Insurance provides property and casualty insurance coverage for individuals and organizations. A subsidiary of AXA Canada Inc., Boreal Insurance deals specifically with accident, sickness, liability, mortgage, property, surety, and theft insurance among others. The insurance company employs approximately 850 individuals, and has 11 branches throughout the country.

Academic Fields
College: Accounting, Administration, Business, Insurance, Secretarial
Bachelor of Arts: Business, Psychology, Public Rel.
Bachelor of Comm/Admin: General, Accounting, Finance, Marketing, Info Mgmt.
Bachelor of Science: Actuarial, Computer Science
Bachelor of Laws: Corporate
Bachelor of Engineering: Civil, Computer Systems
Bachelor of Education: Adult Education
Chartered Accounting: CA-General
Masters: Business Administration

Critical Skills
Confident, Dependable, Efficient, Good Communication, Good Writing Skills, Professional

Types of Positions
Secretary	Junior Analyst

Starting Salary
$ 25,000 - 30,000

Company Benefits
- Medical and dental insurance
- Sick leave and vacation pay based on seniority
- Fees paid for courses pertinent to the job

Correspondence
Mail resume with cover letter

Part Time/Summer: Boréal Assurances regularly hires part time and summer candidates. Summer jobs include clerk, secretary, general office worker, and special consulting work. Apply in March or April.

The Canada Student Employment Guide

BOSAL CANADA INC.

1150 Gardiners Rd.
Kingston, Ontario, K7P 1R7
Tel: (613) 384-4150   Fax: (613) 384-2991

Human Resources Dept.

Bosal Canada is involved in the manufacture of automotive exhaust systems for the aftermarket and original equipment market. The firm has approximately 190 employees.

Academic Fields
College: Engineering Tech., Mechanical Tech., Welding Certification (pre. MIG welding)
Bachelor of Engineering: Industrial, Mechanical
Masters: Business Administration, Engineering

Critical Skills
Dependable, Diligent, Efficient, Flexible, Manual Dexterity, Organized, Personable, Productive, Punctual, Professional, Responsible, Motivated, Dedicated

Types of Positions
Production Worker   Customer Service (Bilingual)
Accounting Clerk   Welder

Starting Salary
Varies depending on position

Company Benefits
- Competitive benefits package

Correspondence
Mail resume with cover letter
E-mail: b07hr@bosal.kingston.net

Part Time/Summer: Bosal Canada occasionally looks for individuals for part time work and regularly hires for the summer. Potential jobs are in human resources or the finance dept. The best time to apply is from April to June.

Co-op/Internship: Internships are available in Human Resources.

BOVAR WASTE MANAGEMENT

4 Manning Close N.E.
Calgary, Alberta, T2E 7N5
Tel: (403) 235-8300   Fax: (403) 248-3306

Lori Skerrett Internal HR Consultant
Internet: www.bovar.com

BOVAR Waste Management operates Canada's only fully-integrated hazardous waste treatment facility in Swan Hills, Alberta, designed to treat all types of hazardous waste except explosives, radioactive and pathogenic waste.

Academic Fields
College: Accounting, Administration, Business, Human Resources, Marketing/Sales, CAD Autocad, Computer Science, Mechanical Tech., Plumbing
Bachelor of Arts: Business
Bachelor of Comm/Admin: Accounting, Finance, Human Resources, Marketing, Info Mgmt.
Bachelor of Science: Chemistry, Computer Sciences, Environmental Studies
Bachelor of Laws: Corporate
Bachelor of Engineering: Chemical, Civil, Computer Syst., Design, Electrical, Environ., Industrial, Mech.,
Chartered Accounting: CA - General/Finance, CGA-General, CMA-General
Masters: Business Admin., Science, Engineering

Critical Skills
Most skills important

Types of Positions
Administration   Accounting
Labourer   Human Resources

Starting Salary
Depends on position

Company Benefits
- Full benefit package including pension, dental

Correspondence
Mail, fax, e-mail resume with cover letter or apply through web site. E-mail: bovarinc@bovar.com

Part Time/Summer: BOVAR occasionally hires for part time and summer work. Potential jobs involve administration or being a labourer. Engineering students are also hired. Apply in March.

Co-op/Internship: Have an informal internship program, dependent on the firm's needs at the time.

The Canada Student Employment Guide

BOWATER MERSEY PAPER COMPANY LIMITED
P.O. Box 1150
Liverpool, Nova Scotia, B0T 1K0
Tel: (902) 354-3411   Fax: (902) 354-4240

Arthur Anthony, Human Resources
Internet: www.bowater.com

Bowater Mersey Paper Company is a newsprint manufacturer, which harvests 25% from their own land. They have markets in Canada, the U.S., Europe, the Middle East, South America, and the Pacific Rim.

Academic Fields
College: Computer Science, Drafting/Architecture, Electronics Tech., Forestry, Human Resources, Mechanical Tech., Nursing, Secretarial
Bachelor of Arts: Business, Public Relations
Bachelor of Comm/Admin: General, Accounting, Finance, Info Mgmt.
Bachelor of Science: Chemistry, Computer Science, Environmental Studies, Forestry
Bachelor of Engineering: Chemical, Civil, Computer Systems, Electrical, Environmental Studies, Mechanical
Chartered Accounting: CMA-Finance

Critical Skills
Adaptable, Analytical, Good Communication, Decisive, Dependable, Efficient, Flexible, Innovative, Leadership, Organized, Personable, Productive, Responsible, Good Writing Skills

Types of Positions
Project Engineering   General Accountant
Electronic Technician   Secretarial
Draftsman

Starting Salary
$ 40,000 - 50,000

Company Benefits
- Wide scope of benefits
- Medical, dental, pension, life insurance
- Short and long term disability

Correspondence
Mail resume with cover letter

Part Time/Summer: Bowater Mersey Paper Company occasionally looks for people for part time work, and regularly seeks candidates for the summer. Potential jobs in the summer involve office administration. The best time to apply is mid-March to mid-April.

CITY OF BRANDON
410 - 9th Street
Brandon, Manitoba, R7A 6A2
Tel: (204) 729-2163   Fax: (204) 729-1904

Human Resources Department
Internet: www.city.brandon.mb.ca

The City of Brandon is the municipal government that functions to serve the citizens of Brandon, Manitoba.

Academic Fields
College: Recreation Studies, Security/Law Enforcement, Accounting, Administration, Human Resources, Information Systems, Secretarial, Automotive Maintenance, CAD Autocad, Computer Science, Welding, Emergency/Paramedic
Bachelor of Arts: General, Business, Criminology, Psychology, Public Relations, Sociology/Social Work
Bachelor of Science: General, Agriculture, Computer Science, Horticulture, Zoology
Bachelor of Laws: Real Estate
Bachelor of Engineering: Civil, Computer Systems, Design, Water Resources
Chartered Accounting: CA-General, CGA-General, CMA-General

Critical Skills
Adaptable, Analytical, Good Communication, Confident, Creative, Dependable, Diligent, Efficient, Enthusiastic, Flexible, Good With Figures, Innovative

Types of Positions
Clerk Typist   Purchasing Clerk
Junior Operator   Receptionis

Starting Salary
$ 25,000 - 30,000

Company Benefits
- Extended health and dental, life insurance, pension
- Disability income protection

Correspondence
Check at Brandon Employment Ctr., HRDC, or apply through their site. E-mail: l.volek@city.brandon.mb.ca

Part Time/Summer: The City of Brandon sometimes hires for part time work, and regularly hires in the summer. Potential jobs include grass cutter, casual labourer, by-law enforcement student, computer technician, and lifeguard. Jobs are posted with Human Resources Canada as needed. March or April is the best time to apply.

BRANTCORP INC.

426 Elgin St.
Brantford, Ontario, N3T 5M8
Tel: (519) 751-3810   Fax: (519) 751-2272

Human Resources

Brantcorp Inc. is a manufacturer of small to medium size automotive dies, and computerized attribute and variable gauging services, as well as special purpose machinery.

Academic Fields
College: Electronics Tech., Mechanical Tech.
Bachelor of Engineering: General, Computer Systems, Design, Mechanical

Critical Skills
Analytical, Dependable, Efficient, Enthusiastic, Good Communication, Leadership, Manual Dexterity, Professional, Responsible

Types of Positions
Apprentice Tool & Die Marker   Apprentice Machinist

Starting Salary
below $ 20,000

Company Benefits
- Competitive benefits plan

Correspondence
Mail resume with cover letter

Part Time/Summer: Brantcorp Inc. does not hire for part time work, but occasionally hires for the summer months. A potential job would be odd job person/driver. The best time to apply is early May.

BRATTY & PARTNERS LLP

7501 Keele St., Suite 200
Vaughan, Ontario, L4K 1Y2
Tel: (416) 226-4884   Fax: (416) 226-6395

Alex Zlatanovic, Human Resources
Internet: www.bratty.com

Bratty & Partners is a law firm in North York, which specializes in the areas of real estate, corporate, and municipal law, as well as litigation.

Academic Fields
College: Accounting, Computer Science, Law Clerk
Bachelor of Engineering: Computer Systems

Critical Skills
Good Communication, Confident, Dependable, Diplomatic, Good With Figures, Personable, Responsible, Good Writing Skills

Types of Positions
Legal Secretary

Starting Salary
$ 20,000 - 25,000

Company Benefits
- Medical and dental insurance

Correspondence
Mail or fax resume with cover letter
E-mail: azlatanovic@bratty.com

Part Time/Summer: Bratty & Partners does not generally hire part time workers, but occasionally looks for individuals for the summer months. Potential positions include filing clerk.

The Canada Student Employment Guide

BREWERS RETAIL INC.

1 City Centre Dr., Suite 1700
Mississauga, Ontario, L5B 4A6
Tel: (905) 949-0429   Fax: (905) 277-7533

Dennis H. Fielding, Human Resources

Brewers Retail is a private company which provides efficient beer warehousing, distribution and sales, both retail and wholesale, for any brewer that wishes to use their system. There are 429 Beer Store outlets across Ontario, along with 69 distribution centres, providing 6,000 men and women with full and part time employment.

Academic Fields
College: Computer Science, Human Resources
Bachelor of Arts: General, Business
Bachelor of Comm/Admin: Accounting, Finance, Info Mgmt.
Bachelor of Science: Computer Science
Chartered Accounting: CMA-General, CMA-Finance

Critical Skills
Adaptable, Analytical, Good Communication, Dependable, Diligent, Diplomatic, Efficient, Leadership, Personable, Persuasive, Professional, Good Writing Skills

Types of Positions
Retail Stores (Temporary)   Information Services
Wholesale Distribution

Starting Salary
below $ 20,000 - 25,000

Company Benefits
- Full dental, major medical
- Salary continuance for short term disability
- No benefits for temporary positions

Correspondence
E-mail resume with cover letter
E-mail: dennis.fielding@brewers.com

Part Time/Summer: Brewers Retail regularly hires individuals for part time work, but does not hire people for the summer months only.

BRITISH COLUMBIA ASSESSMENT

1537 Hillside Ave.
Victoria, British Columbia, V8T 4Y2
Tel: (250) 595-6211   Fax: (250) 595-3733

Gwen Shulhan, Human Resources
Internet: www.bcassessment.bc.ca

The mission of BC Assessment is to produce uniform property assessments that form the basis for local and provincial taxation while providing information to assist people when making real estate decisions.

Academic Fields
College: Diploma Program (Appraisal Option or Real Property Assessment)
Bachelor of Comm/Admin: Urban Land Economics
Bachelor of Business in Real Estate

Critical Skills
Accurate, Articulate, Cooperative, Customer-focused, Diplomatic, Enthusiastic, Analytical, Confident, Creative, Decisive, Efficient, Flexible, Approachable, Conscientious, Curious/Inquisitive, Detail-Oriented, Empathetic, Focused, Forward-looking, Honest, Intuitive, Organized, Self-Motivated, Patient, Tactful, Trustworthy

Types of Positions
Appraiser Trainee

Starting Salary
$ 30,000 - 40,000

Company Benefits
- Full benefits
- Promote training and development in related field

Correspondence
Mail or fax application with cover letter.
Resume can also be forwarded.
E-mail: gwen.shulhan@gems7.gov.bc.ca

Part Time/Summer: British Columbia Assessment rarely seeks individuals for part time work, but regularly looks for candidates for the summer. A potential job may be for appraisal students or clerical students. The best time to apply is in January.

Co-op/Internship: Limited internship opportunities are available.

BRITISH COLUMBIA FERRY CORPORATION

1112 Fort Street
Victoria, British Columbia, V8V 4V2
Tel: (604) 381-1401   Fax: (604) 360-1799

Human Resources
Internet: www.bcferries.bc.ca

The British Columbia Ferry Corporation is a crown corporation of the B.C. Government that provides an integral part of the province's coastal transportation system. Among other routes, the ferry system links Vancouver Island to the Lower Mainland, and has 40 vessels, serving 42 ports of call along 24 routes.

Academic Fields
College: General, Accounting, Administration, Communications, Human Resources, Journalism, Marketing/Sales, Secretarial
Bachelor of Arts: General, Business, Economics, Journalism, Public Relations
Bachelor of Comm/Admin: General, Accounting, Finance, Marketing, Info Mgmt., Public Admin.
Bachelor of Science: General, Computer Science
Bachelor of Engineering: General, Civil, Electrical, Mechanical
Chartered Accounting: CA - General/Finance, CGA/CMA - General/Finance
Masters: Business Administration

Critical Skills
Adaptable, Analytical, Good Communication, Decisive, Dependable, Efficient, Logical, Organized, Productive, Professional, Responsible, Good Writing Skills

Types of Positions
Clerk   Seaman
Officer   Catering Attendant
Dock Repair Worker   Terminal Attendant

Starting Salary
$ 20,000 - 25,000

Company Benefits
- Comprehensive benefit package, group life ins.
- Medical and extended health coverage

Correspondence
Mail resume with cover letter

Part Time/Summer: The B.C. Ferry Corp. regularly hires for part time and summer jobs. In the summer, they look for deck attendants and catering attendants. The best time to apply is in January of each year.

BRITISH COLUMBIA TRANSIT

650 - 13401 108th Avenue
Surrey, British Columbia, V3T 5T4
Tel: (604) 540-3010   Fax: (604) 540-3005

Employment Services Advisor
Internet: www.transitbc.com

British Columbia Transit is a crown corporation that serves more than 2.8 million people throughout British Columbia by bus, skytrain, and seabus to the Lower Mainland. The corporation's 29 conventional transit systems, in greater Vancouver, greater Victoria and 27 communities across the province carry more than 151 million passengers annually. The largest contributor to this total is the Vancouver Regional Transit System with 128 million passengers. British Columbia Transit employs approximately 3,830 individuals including temporary staff.

Academic Fields
No specific academic background is required. They will look at candidates from all academic backgrounds.

Critical Skills
Diplomatic, Good Writing Skills, Organized, Good Communication, Personable, Professional, Team Player, Initiative

Types of Positions
Casual Customer Info Clerk
Casual Farebox Attendant
Casual Farebox Receipts Attendant
Casual Traffic Checker

Starting Salary
$ 25,000 - 30,000

Company Benefits
- Medical, dental and income continuance
- Basic group life insurance
- Temporary assignments for employees to develop their skills

Correspondence
Mail resume with cover letter

Part Time/Summer: British Columbia Transit sometimes hires for part time work and regularly hires for the summer. Applications for summer work are accepted in January with most positions filled by April. Positions are most likely include serviceperson, or student engineering assistant.

The Canada Student Employment Guide

BROOKFIELD PROPERTIES CORPORATION

181 Bay Street, Suite 4440, Box 770
Toronto, Ontario, M5J 2T3
Tel: (416) 369-2300   Fax: (416) 369-2301

Cynthia Bautista, Human Resources Dept.
Internet: www.brookfield.ca

Brookfield Properties Corporation owns and manages a portfolio of premier North American office properties and also develops master-planned residential communities.

Academic Fields
College: General, Accounting, Administration, Business, Communications, Computer Science, Emergency/Paramedic, Engineering Tech., Secretarial, Security/Law
Bachelor of Arts: General, Business, Languages, Psychology, Sociology/Social Work
Bachelor of Comm/Admin: General, Accounting, Finance
Bachelor of Science: General
Bachelor of Laws: Real Estate
Bachelor of Engineering: General, Computer Systems, Electrical, Mechanical
Bachelor of Education: General
Chartered Accounting: CA - General/Finance, CGA/CMA - General/Finance
Masters: Business Administration

Critical Skills
Adaptable, Confident, Diplomatic, Good Communication, Efficient, Enthusiastic, Flexible, Good With Figures, Organized, Leadership, Logical, Good Writing Skills, Professional, Positive, Team Skills, People Oriented

Types of Positions
Receptionist   Mail Room Clerk
Loading Dock Staff   Courier Runner
Secretarial   Maintenance Worker

Starting Salary
$ 20,000 - 25,000

Company Benefits
- Medical, and dental coverage, life insurance

Correspondence
Submit resume with cover letter in person

Part Time/Summer: Brookfield Properties Corporation sometimes hires for part time jobs, and regularly hires for the summer. Apply in April or May.

BROWNING HARVEY LIMITED

P.O. Box 455, Stn Main
Grand Falls-Windsor, Newfoundland, A2A 2J8
Tel: (709) 489-2145   Fax: N/A

Human Resources

Browning Harvey Limited is a soft drink bottler of major brands such as Pepsi, Cadbury and Schewppes. The company's head office is in Grand Falls-Windsor, Newfoundland.

Academic Fields
College: Accounting, Business
Bachelor of Arts: Business
Bachelor of Comm/Admin: Marketing
Bachelor of Science: Chemistry

Critical Skills
Adaptable, Dependable, Diligent, Efficient, Logical, Organized, Productive

Types of Positions
Various Positions

Starting Salary
$ 30,000 - 40,000

Company Benefits
- Competitive benefit package

Correspondence
Mail resume with cover letter

Part Time/Summer: Browning Harvey Limited occasionally looks for people for part time jobs, and regularly hires for the summer.

The Canada Student Employment Guide

BUCK CONSULTANTS LIMITED

P.O. Box 1500, Suite 1500, 95 Wellington St. W.
Toronto, Ontario, M5J 2N7
Tel: (416) 865-0060   Fax: (416) 865-1301

Human Resources
Internet: www.buckconsultants.ca

Buck Consultants Limited provides actuarial and benefit plan consulting. Their head office is in Toronto, Ontario.

Academic Fields
College: Computer Science, Insurance
Bachelor of Science: Actuarial, Computer Science, Mathematics

Critical Skills
Adaptable, Analytical, Confident, Decisive, Dependable, Diligent, Diplomatic, Efficient, Enthusiastic, Flexible, Good Communication, Good Writing Skills, Leadership, Logical, Organized, Persuasive, Professional

Types of Positions
Data Entry Clerk

Starting Salary
below $ 20,000

Company Benefits
- Extended health, dental, life insurance
- Long term disability

Correspondence
Mail resume with cover letter
E-mail: hr@buckconsultants.ca

Part Time/Summer: Buck Consultants Limited does not hire for part time positions, but occasionally seeks candidates for the summer months.

BUCKEYE CANADA INC.

7979 Vantage Way
Delta, British Columbia, V4G 1A6
Tel: (604) 946-0677   Fax: (604) 946-3516

Human Resources Dept.
Internet: www.bkitech.com

Buckeye Canada Inc. is a manufacturer of air-laid non-woven products, including paper, which is sold in jumbo roll form to end product manufacturers. This non-woven material is used as the absorbent core in feminine hygiene products, and baby diapers, among other goods.

Academic Fields
College: Administration, Computer Science, Human Resources, Mechanical Tech.
Bachelor of Arts: General, Business, Psychology
Bachelor of Comm/Admin: General, Finance, Marketing, Info Mgmt.
Bachelor of Science: Chemistry, Computer Science, Psychology
Bachelor of Engineering: Chemical, Electrical, Industrial, Mechanical
Chartered Accounting: CMA-General, CGA-General
Masters: Business Administration, Engineering

Critical Skills
Adaptable, Analytical, Good Communication, Dependable, Diligent, Flexible, Good With Figures, Innovative, Leadership, Logical, Manual Dexterity, Organized, Personable, Persuasive, Productive, Professional, Responsible, Good Writing Skills

Types of Positions
Production Worker   Lab Technician
Accounting Clerk   Admin. Assistant

Starting Salary
Varies depending on position

Company Benefits
- Full benefits, profit sharing, RRSP plan

Correspondence
Mail or fax resume with cover letter

Part Time/Summer: Buckeye Canada does not hire for part time work, but regularly hires for the summer. Potential jobs include production worker, warehouse worker, maintenance assistant, admin. assistant, quality assurance assistant, and R & D. The best time to apply is in March or April. Interviews begin in May.

The Canada Student Employment Guide

BUDD CANADA INC.

1011 Homer Watson Boulevard
Kitchener, Ontario, N2G 4G5
Tel: (519) 895-3022   Fax: (519) 895-0152

Tony Collins, Employment & Benefits Manager

Budd Canada is a major automotive stamping plant that provides products to each of three large auto makers. Budd Canada's Plant in Kitchener opened in 1967 to produce full-size chassis frames for Ford and Lincoln-Mercury. Today, the Plant is located on a 124-acre site, occupying 968,368 square feet of manufacturing space. Budd Canada employs over 1,500 individuals.

Academic Fields
College: Accounting, Administration, Computer Science, Electronics Tech., Engineering Tech., Human Resources, Mechanical Tech.
Bachelor of Arts: Economics
Bachelor of Comm/Admin: Accounting, Finance, Human Resources, Info Mgmt.
Bachelor of Science: Chemistry, Computer Science, Environmental Studies, Kinesiology, Nursing (RN)
Bachelor of Engineering: Computer Systems, Environmental Studies, Materials Science, Mechanical
Masters: Engineering

Critical Skills
Adaptable, Confident, Good Communication, Personable, Analytical, Professional, Positive Attitude

Types of Positions
General Clerk   Receptionist
Accounts Payable Clerk Accounts Receivable Clerk
Data Entry Clerk

Starting Salary
$ 40,000 +

Company Benefits
- Excellent compensation package
- Benefits similar to those offered by big three auto makers, internal and external training

Correspondence
Mail or e-mail resume with cover letter

Part Time/Summer: Budd Canada rarely seeks people for part time and summer work. The best time to apply is generally in June.

BUGBUSTERS PEST MANAGEMENT INC.

Box 1750
Prince George, British Columbia, V2L 4V7
Tel: (250) 564-0383   Fax: (250) 562-4885

Michelle Horgos, HR Assistant
Internet: www.bugbusters.ca

Bugbusters Pest Management Inc. is a full service silviculture consulting and contracting company. With their head office in Prince George, B.C., and satellite offices in Mackenzie, Chetwynd and Whitecourt, they service clientele throughout British Columbia, into Alberta, the Yukon and N.W.T. Since incorporation in 1986, their horizons have expanded and diversified within the field of natural resource management. They are able to provide expertise and professional services specializing in: forest management, forest health, vegetation management, reforestation and biology.

Academic Fields
College: Forestry
Bachelor of Science: Forestry

Critical Skills
Adaptable, Analytical, Dependable, Efficient, Enthusiastic, Flexible, Good Communication, Leadership, Manual Dexterity, Organized, Personable, Productive

Types of Positions
Treeplanting   Chemical Spraying

Starting Salary
Piecework

Company Benefits
- For experienced, hard working individuals they may provide additional training

Correspondence
Mail, fax, e-mail resume with cover letter, or submit in person. E-mail: bugbusters@bugbusters.ca

Part Time/Summer: Bugbusters Pest Management Inc. regularly hires for part time and summer employment. Potential jobs involve tree planting or working with herbicide. For tree planting the best time to apply is in February or March. For herbicide work the best time to apply is in July or August.

The Canada Student Employment Guide

BULLOCK ASSOCIATES DESIGN CONSULTANTS INC.
184 Front St. East, Suite 300
Toronto, Ontario, M5A 4N3
Tel: (416) 868-1616   Fax: (416) 868-1619

Donna Wood, Associate
Internet: www.bullockdesign.com

Bullock Associates Design Consultants are interior designers, space planners, and project managers that specialize in corporate offices. Together they form an interior design consulting firm that specializes in the renovation and relocation of corporate offices. They have 16 employees at their location in Toronto.

Academic Fields
College: Accounting, Administration, Human Resources, Marketing/Sales, CAD Autocad
Bachelor of Arts: General, Fine Arts

Critical Skills
Adaptable, Confident, Creative, Dependable, Enthusiastic, Good Communication, Organized, Personable, Productive, Professional, Responsible

Types of Positions
Junior Interior Designer   Receptionist

Starting Salary
Depends on position

Company Benefits
- 50% paid health benefits
- Ongoing computer training
- Ongoing acute CAD training

Correspondence
Mail or e-mail resume with cover letter
E-mail: email@bullockdesign.com

Part Time/Summer: Bullock Associates Design Consultants Inc. occasionally hires for part time or summer employment. Potential jobs involve reception or interior design. The best time to apply is in May.

BURGER KING RESTAURANTS OF CANADA INC.
769 Burnhamthorpe Rd. W.
Mississauga, Ontario, L5C 3A6
Tel: (905) 281-0932   Fax: (905) 896-6928

Julie Seguin, Human Resources Rep.
Internet: www.burgerking.com

Burger King Restaurants of Canada is a fast food restaurant with operations throughout the country. With its parent company being Burger King Corp. of the United States, the restaurant in Canada employs more than 3,200 individuals. A large number of these employees work in a part-time capacity.

Academic Fields
College: General, Business, Hospitality
Bachelor of Arts: Business
Bachelor of Comm/Admin: General
Bachelor of Science: General

Critical Skills
Decisive, Enthusiastic, Flexible, Good Communication, Leadership, Personable, Professional, Entrepreneurial, Show Initiative

Types of Positions
Assistant Manager of Operations
Various Other Positions

Starting Salary
below $ 20,000

Company Benefits
- Health, dental, short/long term disability
- Educational assistance, employee meals
- Full range of training and development

Correspondence
Mail or fax resume with cover letter

Part Time/Summer: Burger King regularly hires for part time openings, and summer opportunities. Part time and summer positions are recruited at the restaurant level for hourly staff positions.

BURNS INTERNATIONAL SECURITY SERVICES LTD.
340 Ferrier St., Unit 2
Markham, Ontario, L3R 2Z5
Tel: (905) 948-2500   Fax: (905) 948-2545

Barbara Tocoacelli Director Human Resources
Internet: www.burnsinternational.com

As one of the largest security service providers in the world, Burns International Security Services provides physical security to a wide variety of clients. Offices across the country allow them to meet the needs of both large and small facilities, local, regional or national.

Academic Fields
College: Security/Law Enforcement
Bachelor of Arts: General

Critical Skills
Adaptable, Confident, Dependable, Diligent, Diplomatic, Flexible, Good Communication, Personable, Persuasive

Types of Positions
Security Officer   Office Staff
Site Supervisor

Starting Salary
below $ 20,000 - 25,000

Company Benefits
- Extended health coverage
- Life insurance

Correspondence
Mail, fax or e-mail resume with cover letter
E-mail: btocoacelli@burnsinternational.com

Part Time/Summer: Burns International Security Services regularly seeks candidates for part time and summer employment. A potential job would be a security officer. Individuals can apply anytime.

C B C L LIMITED
P.O. Box 606, 1489 Hollis St.
Halifax, Nova Scotia, B3J 2R7
Tel: (902) 421-7241   Fax: (902) 423-3938

Human Resources
Internet: www.cbci.ca

C B C L Limited is a multi discipline engineering firm offering design, project management and construction management services.

Academic Fields
College: Computer Science, Drafting/Architecture, Engineering Tech.
Bachelor of Engineering: Civil, Design, Electrical, Environmental Studies, Mechanical, Transportation
Masters: Engineering

Critical Skills
Adaptable, Confident, Dependable, Efficient, Flexible, Good Communication, Organized, Good Writing Skills, Professional, Responsible

Types of Positions
Junior Engineer   CAD Operator
Typist

Starting Salary
$ 20,000 - 25,000

Company Benefits
- Full benefit package
- Pension plan
- Training encouraged for all employees and supported by company

Correspondence
Mail resume with cover letter
E-mail: info@cbci.ca

Part Time/Summer: C B C L Limited occasionally seeks individuals for part time and summer employment opportunities. A potential job would be a junior engineer.

C MAC INDUSTRIES INC.

1010 Sherbrooke St. W., Suite 1610
Montreal, Québec, H3A 2R7
Tel: (514) 282-7229   Fax: (514) 282-3402

Human Resources
Internet: www.cmac.ca

C-MAC is a leading internationally diversified designer and manufacturer of integrated electronic manufacturing solutions, from components to full systems, primarily serving the communications, automotive, instrumentation, defense and aerospace equipment markets worldwide. C-MAC, headquartered in Montreal, Quebec, employs more than 7,300 employees and operates 44 manufacturing facilities located in Belgium, Canada, China, France, Germany, India, Mexico, the United Kingdom and the United States.

Academic Fields
College: Administration, Computer Science, Electronics Tech., Engineering Tech., Mechanical Tech.
Bachelor of Comm/Admin: Accounting, Finance
Bachelor of Science: Computer Science
Bachelor of Engineering: Computer Systems, Electrical, Industrial, Mechanical
Chartered Accounting: CA - General/Finance, CGA/CMA - General/Finance

Critical Skills
Adaptable, Analytical, Creative, Dependable, Diligent, Efficient, Enthusiastic, Flexible, Organized, Productive, Professional, Responsible

Types of Positions
Various positions

Starting Salary
$ 20,000 - 40,000

Company Benefits
- Group health and dental insurance

Correspondence
Submit resume with cover letter in person

Part Time/Summer: C MAC Industries sometimes seeks candidates for part time jobs and regularly looks for individuals in the summer months. Potential jobs are in production, and the best time to apply is in June.

C.S.T. CONSULTANTS INC.

240 Duncan Mill Rd., Suite 600
Don Mills, Ontario, M3B 3P1
Tel: (416) 445-7377   Fax: (416) 445-1708

Carla Moore, HR Administrator
Internet: www.cst.org

C.S.T. Consultants is involved in the distribution and administration of R.E.S.P.'s (Registered Education Savings Plans). The company's head office is in Don Mills, Ontario.

Academic Fields
College: Accounting, Administration, Advertising, Business, Human Resources, Secretarial
Bachelor of Arts: General, Business, English
Bachelor of Comm/Admin: General, Accounting, Finance, Marketing, Info Mgmt.
Chartered Accounting: CA - General/Finance, CGA/CMA - General/Finance
Masters: Business Administration, Arts

Critical Skills
Adaptable, Analytical, Artistic, Good Communication, Confident, Creative, Decisive, Dependable, Diligent, Diplomatic, Efficient, Enthusiastic, Flexible, Good With Figures, Innovative, Leadership, Logical, Manual Dexterity, Organized, Patient, Personable, Persuasive, Productive, Professional, Responsible, Good Writing Skills

Types of Positions
Scholarship Clerk - Data Processing Office
Service Clerk - Data Process
Customer Relations Specialist

Starting Salary
$ 25,000 - 30,000

Company Benefits
- Health insurance, company pension
- Bonus, share plan, in-house training

Correspondence
Fax resume with cover letter
E-mail: hr@cst.org

Part Time/Summer: C.S.T. Consultants regularly seeks candidates for part time and summer work. A potential position would be a scholarship clerk. The best time to apply is in January or February.

CABRE EXPLORATION LTD.

Suite 1400, 700 - 9th Avenue SW
Calgary, Alberta, T2P 3V4
Tel: (403) 231-8800   Fax: (403) 263-4865

Gordon Kirk, Manager, Human Resources
Internet: www.cabrexploration.com

Cabre's exploration focus remains on Western Canada, primarily Alberta, but increasingly northeastern British Columbia. Their acquisition of Jet Energy Corp. in 1999 provides them with deeper-basin prospects, and substantial drilling success was achieved in their deeper natural gas areas in the Western Canadian Sedimentary Basin.

Academic Fields
College: General, Accounting, Administration, Business, Computer Science, Engineering Tech., Human Res.
Bachelor of Arts: General, Business, Economics
Bachelor of Comm/Admin: General, Accounting, Finance, Marketing, Info Mgmt.
Bachelor of Science: Computer Science, Environmental Studies, Geology
Bachelor of Laws: Corporate
Bachelor of Engineering: General, Geotechnical
Bachelor of Education: General
Chartered Accounting: CA - General/Finance, CGA/CMA - General/Finance
Masters: Business Administration, Engineering

Critical Skills
Adaptable, Analytical, Good Communication, Dependable, Diligent, Diplomatic, Efficient, Enthusiastic, Flexible, Good With Figures, Innovative, Leadership, Logical, Organized, Patient, Personable, Productive

Types of Positions
Accounts Payable Clerk   Secretary
Data Entry   Joint Venture Accounts

Starting Salary
$ 25,000 - 30,000

Company Benefits
- Full health, dental benefits, and life insurance

Correspondence
Mail resume with cover letter
E-mail: g-kirk@cabrexploration.com

Part Time/Summer: Cabre Exploration occasionally hires for part time and summer work. Potential jobs involve accounting, clerical, secretarial, engineering, or geology. The best time to apply is in early February.

CADITH ENTERTAINMENT LTD.

800 Upper Canada Dr.
Sarnia, Ontario, N7W 1A4
Tel: (519) 344-0342   Fax: (519) 344-8918

Doug Bestard, HR Manager

Cadith Entertainment employs approximately 1,300 individuals who work in the gaming industry between bingo and casino establishments. The firm's head office is located in Sarnia, Ontario.

Academic Fields
College: General, Accounting, Administration, Business, Communications, Hospitality, Human Resources, Security/Law
Bachelor of Arts: General, Business, Economics, Psychology
Bachelor of Comm/Admin: General, Accounting, Finance, Info Mgmt.
Bachelor of Education: General
Chartered Accounting: CA - General/Finance, CGA/CMA - General/Finance
Masters: Business Administration

Critical Skills
Good Communication, Confident, Dependable, Efficient, Innovative, Organized, Personable, Responsible

Types of Positions
Food Service Positions   Dealers

Starting Salary
below $ 20,000 - 25,000

Company Benefits
- Currently no employee benefits
- Comprehensive training and development opportunities

Correspondence
Mail resume with cover letter

Part Time/Summer: Cadith Entertainment regularly looks for individuals for part time employment, but does not hire people for the summer months.

The Canada Student Employment Guide

CAE NEWNESS

P.O. Box 8
Salmon Arm, British Columbia, V1E 4N2
Tel: (250) 832-7116   Fax: (250) 804-4015

Dwight Guy, Director Human Resources
Internet: www.cae.com

CAE is the world's premier provider of simulation and control technologies for training and optimization solutions for the aerospace, defence and forestry sectors. Headquartered in Canada and operating globally, the company employs over 6,000 people and has revenue in excess of $1 billion.

Academic Fields
Bachelor of Science: Mathematics
Bachelor of Engineering: Computer Systems, Design, Electrical, Industrial, Mechanical
Masters: Engineering

Critical Skills
Adaptable, Analytical, Confident, Decisive, Dependable, Diligent, Efficient, Flexible, Good Communication, Innovative, Leadership, Organized, Patient, Personable, Persuasive, Productive, Professional, Responsible

Types of Positions
Software Tester   GUI Developer
Software Developer   Controls Engineering
Mechanical Engineering
Mechanical & Electrical Design

Starting Salary
$ 35,000 - 40,000

Company Benefits
- Full benefits, best in its class, best in industry

Correspondence
Mail or e-mail resume with cover letter
E-mail: dwight.guy@caenewness.com

Part Time/Summer: CAE Newness regularly hires for part time or summer employment opportunities. Potential summer work involves those positions listed above.

Co-op/Internship: They do offer internship programs. Visit their website.

CALGARY CO-OPERATIVE ASSOCIATION LIMITED

2735 - 39 Avenue N.E.
Calgary, Alberta, T1Y 7C7
Tel: (403) 299-4000   Fax: N/A

Human Resources

Calgary Co-Operative Association is involved in the grocery and retailing business. They also provide a pharmacy, family fashions, hardware, and an auto centre. Candidates should apply to individual stores as opposed to their head office address.

Academic Fields
College: General, Advertising, Business, Communications, Computer Science, Faculty Management, Human Resources, Journalism, Marketing/Sales, Secretarial, Urban Planning
Bachelor of Arts: General, Business, English, Journalism, Psychology, Public Relations, Statistics
Bachelor of Comm/Admin: General, Accounting, Finance, Marketing, Info Mgmt., Public Admin.
Bachelor of Science: General, Computer Science, Health Sciences, Horticulture, Kinesiology, Nursing (RN), Occupational Therapy, Pharmacy, Psychology
Bachelor of Engineering: General, Design
Bachelor of Education: Adult Education
Chartered Accounting: CA - General/Finance, CGA/CMA - General/Finance

Critical Skills
Adaptable, Analytical, Good Communication, Confident, Decisive, Dependable, Efficient, Enthusiastic, Flexible, Leadership, Organized, Productive, Good Writing Skills

Types of Positions
Service Clerk/Cashier   Personnel Assistant

Starting Salary
below $ 20,000 - 25,000 (depending on position)

Company Benefits
- Benefits to employees after qualifying period

Correspondence
Submit resume & cover letter in person to individual store locations.

Part Time/Summer: Calgary Co-operative regularly hires part time workers, and occasionally hires in the summer. Potential summer work would be in the garden centre. Apply from February to April.

CITY OF CALGARY

#8107, P.O. Box 2100, Postal Stn M
Calgary, Alberta, T2P 2M5
Tel: (403) 268-2355   Fax: (403) 268-2471

Human Resources
Internet: www.gov.calgary.ab.ca

The City of Calgary provides a variety of services to Calgarians. Visit their web site for more info.

Academic Fields
College: Accounting, Administration, Business, Communications, Computer Science, Emergency/Paramedic, Faculty Management, Human Resources, Laboratory Tech., Marketing/Sales, Secretarial, Statistics, Urban Planning
Bachelor of Arts: Criminology, Public Relations
Bachelor of Comm/Admin: Accounting
Bachelor of Science: Actuarial, Computer Science, Environmental Studies
Bachelor of Engineering: Chemical, Civil, Computer Syst., Electrical, Environ. Studies, Transportation, Water
Chartered Accounting: CA - General/Finance, CGA/CMA - General/Finance
Masters: Business Admin., Engineering, Library Science

Critical Skills
Adaptable, Analytical, Confident, Creative, Dependable, Diplomatic, Efficient, Enthusiastic, Flexible, Good Communication, Good With Figures, Good Writing Skills, Innovative, Leadership

Types of Positions
Various Positions

Starting Salary
$ 25,000 - 35,000

Company Benefits
- Competitive benefits plan, learning organization

Correspondence
Mail, fax or e-mail resume with cover letter
E-mail: cityjobs@gov.calgary.ab.ca

Part Time/Summer: The City of Calgary occasionally hires for part time or summer work. Potential jobs are in parks and recreation, internships, and co-op opportunities. Students should only apply to specific competitions posted.

Co-op/Internship: Watch their website for internship opportunities.

CAMBIOR INC.

800 René-Lévesque-Ouest, Bureau 850
Montréal, Québec, H3B 1X9
Tel: (819) 878-3166   Fax: (819) 878-0635

Roxanne Hugron, Ressources humaines
Internet: www.cambior.com

Cambior Inc. is an international diversified gold producer with operations, development projects and exploration activities throughout the Americas. Cambior employs approximately 2,300 individuals.

Academic Fields
College: Accounting, Administration, Communication
Bachelor of Arts: Human Resources
Bachelor of Comm/Admin: Accounting, Finance
Bachelor of Science: Actuarial, Chemistry, Computer Science, Geology
Bachelor of Engineering: General, Civil, Electrical, Mechanical, Mining
Chartered Accounting: CA-General, CMA-General, CGA-General
Masters: Business Administration, Engineering

Critical Skills
Adaptable, Dependable, Diligent, Diplomatic, Enthusiastic, Flexible, Good Writing Skills, Leadership, Logical, Organized, Patient, Productive, Professional, Responsible

Types of Positions
Technician   Engineer

Starting Salary
$ 30,000 - 40,000

Company Benefits
- Complete benefit package

Correspondence
Mail or fax resume with cover letter

Part Time/Summer: Cambior sometimes looks for part time employees and regularly seeks individuals for summer employment. Potential positions are most likely involve administration. The best time to apply is mid-February to April.

The Canada Student Employment Guide

CAMBRIDGE MEMORIAL HOSPITAL

700 Cornation Blvd.
Cambridge, Ontario, N1R 3G2
Tel: (519) 740-4920   Fax: (519) 740-4938

Marie Fagan, Human Resources

Cambridge Memorial Hospital is a modern, progressive hospital serving a diverse community of more than 84,000 people on the southern part of the regional municipality of Waterloo. The hospital has 391 beds for acute-care, short-term general and chronic care units.

Academic Fields
College: Computer Science, Cooking/Culinary, Electronics Tech., Emergency/Paramedic, Food/Nutrition, Laboratory Tech., Nursing, Radiology Tech., Secretarial
Bachelor of Arts: Gerontology, Sociology/Social Work
Bachelor of Comm/Admin: Accounting, Finance, Info Mgmt.
Bachelor of Science: Food Sciences, Health Sciences, Nursing (RN), Occupational Therapy, Pharmacy, Physiotherapy
Bachelor of Engineering: Biomedical, Computer Systems
Chartered Accounting: CA-General, CMA-Finance, CGA-Finance
Masters: Business Administration, Science

Critical Skills
Adaptable

Types of Positions
Food Service   Housekeeping
Central Supply   Medical Records
Nursing

Starting Salary
$ 25,000 - 30,000

Company Benefits
- Disability and life insurance
- Dental coverage and pension plan

Correspondence
Mail or submit resume and cover letter in person

Part Time/Summer: Cambridge Memorial Hospital sometimes hires for part time and summer jobs. Potential work includes housekeeping and materials management. The best time to apply is in March.

CAMBRIDGE SUITES

1583 Brunswick Street
Halifax, Nova Scotia, B3J 3P5
Tel: (902) 420-0555   Fax: (902) 420-9379

Gregory Thomson, Human Resources
Internet: www.centennialhotels.com/cambridge

Cambridge Suites is a large hotel establishment with many outlets throughout the country. The hotel provides a wide range of facilities for dining, conventions, banquets, business meetings, and family vacations. The address above is for their location in Halifax, Nova Scotia.

Academic Fields
College: Business, Communications, Travel/Tourism

Critical Skills
Adaptable, Confident, Dependable, Efficient, Enthusiastic, Organized, Patient, Good Communication, Personable, Professional

Types of Positions
Suite Attendant   Houseperson
Laundry Attendant   Switchboard Operator
Guest Service Agent   Housekeeping

Starting Salary
below $ 20,000

Company Benefits
- Complete medical plan, special travel benefits
- Comprehensive job skills training for all positions
- Encourage industry related training courses

Correspondence
Mail resume with cover letter

Part Time/Summer: Cambridge Suites sometimes hires for part time positions and regularly looks for candidates in the summer. Potential positions are most likely those listed above. The best time to apply is in March and April.

The Canada Student Employment Guide

CAMECO CORPORATION

2121 - 11th Street W.
Saskatoon, Saskatchewan, S7M 1J3
Tel: (306) 956-6200   Fax: (306) 956-6539

Human Resources
Internet: www.cameco.com

Cameco Corporation is the world's largest publicly traded uranium company and growing gold producer. Canadian operations include the world's two largest high-grade uranium mines in Saskatchewan and uranium processing facilities in Ontario. Gold operations include mines in Northern Saskatchewan and in Central Asia, with exploration in South America and Australia.

Academic Fields
College: Laboratory Tech., Secretarial
Bachelor of Science: Environmental Studies, Geology
Bachelor of Engineering: Chemical, Design, Electrical, Environmental Studies, Mechanical, Mining, Water Resources
Chartered Accounting: CA-General, CMA-General, CGA-General
Masters: Business Administration

Critical Skills
Adaptable, Good Communication, Dependable, Flexible, Innovative, Leadership, Productive, Professional

Types of Positions
Accounts Payable Clerk   Secretary
Radiation Technician Trainee   Junior Engineer
Chemical Technician Trainee

Starting Salary
$ 30,000 - 40,000

Company Benefits
- Comprehensive benefits, medical, dental
- Disability, eyewear, pension
- Corporate training and education

Correspondence
Mail or fax resume with cover letter

Part Time/Summer: Cameco Corporation does not hire for part time work, but regularly hires for the summer. Potential jobs include engineering technical students, chemistry lab students, or environment students. The best time to apply is in February.

CAMP HILL HOSPITAL

1763 Robie Street
Halifax, Nova Scotia, B3H 3G2
Tel: (902) 496-2700   Fax: N/A

Human Resources

Camp Hill Hospital is a general medical and surgical hospital that is owned and operated by the Camp Hill Medical Centre. Established in 1978, the hospital has a total of 700 beds in various depts. including intensive care, geriatrics, rehabilitation, gynecology, psychiatric, and palliative care.

Academic Fields
College: Accounting, Computer Science, Cooking/Culinary, Emergency/Paramedic, Food/Nutrition, Graphic Arts, Human Res., Lab. Tech., Nursing, Orthotics/Prosthetics, Photography, Radiology Tech., Recreation Studies, Secretarial
Bachelor of Comm/Admin: Accounting, Finance, Info Mgmt.
Bachelor of Science: Computer Sci., Food Sciences, Health Sci., Nursing (RN), Occupational Therapy, Pharmacy, Physics, Physiotherapy, Psychology
Bachelor of Engineering: Biomedical, Computer Systems, Industrial, Mechanical
Bachelor of Education: Adult Education
Chartered Accounting: CA - General/Finance
Masters: Business Admin., Education, Library Science

Critical Skills
Adaptable, Analytical, Good Communication, Confident, Dependable, Diligent, Diplomatic, Efficient, Enthusiastic, Flexible, Innovative, Logical, Manual Dexterity, Organized, Patient, Personable, Productive, Professional, Responsible, Writing Skills

Types of Positions
Food Services   Housekeeping
Clerk/Typist

Starting Salary
Salary depends on position and experience

Company Benefits
- Comprehensive benefits package

Correspondence
Phone job line at (902) 496-4025

Part Time/Summer: Camp Hill Hospital sometimes hires for part time and summer work. Employment is most likely to be in positions listed above.

The Canada Student Employment Guide

CANADA BRICK LIMITED

P.O. Box 668, 2121 Britannia Rd. W.
Mississauga, Ontario, L5M 2C3
Tel: (905) 821-8800   Fax: (905) 821-2754

Laurene Payne, Manager Recruitment

Canada Brick is Canada's oldest and largest manufacturer of genuine burned clay brick. They have one plant in Mississauga, two plants in Burlington, one plant in Ottawa, one plant in Montreal, and one plant being built in Aldershot. The company employs approximately 500 individuals in Canada.

Academic Fields
Bachelor of Engineering: Industrial, Materials Science, Ceramic

Critical Skills
Adaptable, Dependable, Diligent, Enthusiastic, Good Communication, Good Writing Skills, Organized, Personable, Professional, Responsible

Types of Positions
Customer Service   Lab
Administration

Starting Salary
$ 20,000 - 25,000

Company Benefits
- Company paid health, dental, life insurance, long term disability
- Company pension for salaried employees

Correspondence
E-mail resume with cover letter

Part Time/Summer: Canada Brick Limited occasionally hires for part time work and regularly hires for the summer. Potential work would mostly be general labour. The best time to apply is by May 1st.

CANADA CATERING CO. LTD.

5 Southvale Drive
Toronto, Ontario, M4G 1G2
Tel: (416) 421-7474   Fax: (416) 421-5694

Ron Kingsley, Vice President Operations

Canada Catering is engaged in the business of retail eating establishments and merchandising vending machines. With its head office located in East York, Canada Catering has outlets across the country. The company has more than 500 employees from coast to coast and operates in approximately 45 locations in the Toronto region.

Academic Fields
College: Cooking/Culinary, Food/Nutrition

Critical Skills
Adaptable, Artistic, Dependable, Diligent, Diplomatic, Efficient, Enthusiastic, Good Communication, Flexible, Leadership, Organized, Personable, Persuasive, Productive, Professional, Responsible

Types of Positions
Cook   Baker
Cashier   Food Service Supervisor
General Help   Short Order Cook

Starting Salary
below $ 20,000

Company Benefits
- A competitive benefits packaged offered

Correspondence
Mail resume with cover letter

Part Time/Summer: Canada Catering sometimes hires part time positions, and regularly hires for summer opportunities. Potential summer positions include the ones listed above.

The Canada Student Employment Guide

CANADA GAMES AQUATIC CENTRE

50 Union St.
Saint John, New Brunswick, E2L 1A1
Tel: (506) 658-4726   Fax: (506) 658-4730

Human Resource Coordinator
Internet: www.acquatics.nb.ca

The Canada Games Aquatic Centre is a recreation and programs facility in Saint John, New Brunswick. The Centre provides many swimming and fitness programs.

Academic Fields
Bachelor of Arts: Business, Recreation Studies
Bachelor of Science: Kinesiology
Bachelor of Education: Adult Education, Childhood, Physical

Critical Skills
Adaptable, Confident, Creative, Decisive, Dependable, Enthusiastic, Flexible, Good Communication, Innovative, Leadership, Personable

Types of Positions
Lifeguard   Instructor
Front Desk Clerk

Starting Salary
below $ 20,000

Company Benefits
- Benefits offered

Correspondence
Mail resume with cover letter

Part Time/Summer: Canada Games Aquatic Centre regularly hires for part time work and occasionally hires for the summer months.

CANADA POST CORPORATION

1 Dundas Street West, Suite 700
Toronto, Ontario, M5G 2L5
Tel: (416) 204-4441   Fax: N/A

Human Resources Department
Internet: www.canadapost.ca

Canada Post provides one of the country's largest distribution networks servicing over 27 million Canadians, and handling over 10 billion messages and parcels a year. The corporation distributes mail to nearly 11 million points of delivery in Canada, and provides international postal services to virtually every other country worldwide. As one of the country's largest employers, Canada Post is made up of 57,000 full and part time people that operate a network of 22 major mail processing plants and a fleet of approximately 5,300 vehicles.

Academic Fields
College: Electronics Tech., Human Resources, Marketing/Sales, Secretarial, Security/Law
Bachelor of Arts: Business, Economics
Bachelor of Comm/Admin: Accounting, Finance, Marketing, Info Mgmt.
Bachelor of Science: Computer Science
Bachelor of Engineering: Computer Systems, Electrical, Industrial, Mechanical
Chartered Accounting: CA-Finance, CGA/CMA - General/Finance
Masters: Business Administration

Critical Skills
Adaptable, Confident, Dependable, Good Communication, Efficient, Enthusiastic, Innovative, Leadership, Personable, Productive, Professional

Types of Positions
Clerk   Junior Officer
Secretary

Starting Salary
$ 20,000 - 25,000

Company Benefits
- Complete range of benefits

Correspondence
Mail resume with cover letter

Part Time/Summer: Canada Post does not hire for part time work, but sometimes hires for the summer. Potential jobs are most likely those listed above.

The Canada Student Employment Guide

CANADA SAFEWAY LIMITED

401 Manitou Road SE
Calgary, Alberta, T2G 4C2
Tel: (403) 730-3500   Fax: N/A

Employment Office
Internet: www.safeway.com

Canada Safeway is the largest food retailer in Western Canada, operating 238 stores throughout British Columbia, Alberta, Saskatchewan, Manitoba, and north western Ontario. A privately owned company, Canada Safeway employs more than 30,000 individuals across the country to work in various capacities within the grocery industry.

Academic Fields
College: Accounting, Administration, Advertising, Business, Human Resources, Marketing/Sales, Photography, Secretarial, Statistics
Bachelor of Arts: General, Business, Public Relations, Statistics, Urban Geography
Bachelor of Comm/Admin: General, Accounting, Finance, Marketing
Bachelor of Science: Chemistry, Pharmacy
Bachelor of Education: Adult Education
Chartered Accounting: CA-General

Critical Skills
Adaptable, Analytical, Dependable, Diplomatic, Enthusiastic, Leadership, Service Oriented, Good Communication

Types of Positions
Accounting   Purchasing
Cashier   Courtesy Clerk

Starting Salary
$ 20,000 - 30,000 (depending on position)

Company Benefits
- Full range of company benefits

Correspondence
Submit resume and cover letter in person

Part Time/Summer: Canada Safeway occasionally looks for part time and summer candidates. Employment in the summer months are most likely in the warehouse or in retail. The best time to apply for positions in the warehouse is in May or June, while jobs in retail can become available anytime throughout the year.

CANADA STARCH COMPANY INC.

401 The West Mall
Etobicoke, Ontario, M9C 5H9
Tel: (416) 620-2391   Fax: (416) 620-2385

Tracey McManus, Human Resources

Canada Starch Company is a holding company engaged in the manufacture of branded groceries and refined corn products. The company is the parent company of Canada Starch Operating Company, Inc., which manufactures industrial starches, sweeteners, and consumer food products. Canada Starch Company employs more than 1,100 people to work in various fields.

Academic Fields
College: Cooking/Culinary, Food/Nutrition, Human Resources
Bachelor of Comm/Admin: General, Accounting, Finance, Marketing
Bachelor of Engineering: Electrical, Mechanical
Chartered Accounting: CA - General/Finance, CGA/CMA - General/Finance
Masters: Business Administration

Critical Skills
Adaptable, Analytical, Dependable, Efficient, Enthusiastic, Flexible, Good Writing Skills, Good Communication, Innovative, Personable, Professional

Types of Positions
Sales Representative   Accounting Clerk

Starting Salary
$ 25,000 - 30,000

Company Benefits
- Dental, medical and group life coverage
- Pension plan and savings program
- Tuition assistance available

Correspondence
Mail resume with cover letter

Part Time/Summer: Canada Starch Company sometimes hires individuals for part time and summer employment. Jobs in the summer are in customer service and information systems. The best time to apply is in February and March.

The Canada Student Employment Guide

CANADIAN BROADCASTING CORPORATION
P.O. Box 500, Station A
Toronto, Ontario, M5W 1E6
Tel: (416) 205-3294   Fax: (416) 205-2841

The Job Shop

The CBC provides English and French radio and television services throughout Canada. Its objective is to develop and offer a national broadcasting service in television and radio, for Canadians in both official languages. Their mandate is also to provide an international broadcasting service. The CBC offers a 24-hour all news TV service in English, and maintains a short-wave radio service overseas. The company employs over 9,200 individuals across Canada. The company is currently undergoing a large downsizing, and as a result is not accepting any applications at this time.

Academic Fields
College: Law Clerk, Security/Law, Television/Radio
Bachelor of Arts: Journalism
Bachelor of Comm/Admin: Public Admin.
Bachelor of Science: Computer Science
Masters: Business Administration, Arts, Library Science

Critical Skills
Adaptable, Analytical, Creative, Dependable, Efficient, Good Writing Skills, Organized, Good Communication, Productive, Professional

Types of Positions
Security Officer   Receptionist
Clerk/Secretary   Editorial Assistant

Starting Salary
$ 20,000 - 25,000

Company Benefits
- Benefits for full time permanent staff
- Benefits consistent with public sector

Correspondence
Mail resume and cover letter or submit in person

Part Time/Summer: The CBC sometimes hires for part time openings and summer opportunities. Potential positions are most likely among those listed above. Bilingualism with advanced software skills are important characteristics. The best time to apply is between April 1st and May 31st. As the company is currently downsizing, there are not many opportunities available.

CANADIAN CANCER SOCIETY
10 Alcorn Ave., Suite 200
Toronto, Ontario, M6V 3B1
Tel: (416) 961-7223   Fax: (416) 961-4189

Wini Stoddart, Manager HR
Internet: www.cancer.ca

The Canadian Cancer Society is a national, community-based organization whose mission is to eradicate cancer and to improve the quality of life of people living with cancer. Across Canada, the Society's 350,000 volunteers, supported by approximately 450 staff, carry out public education programs, provide services for cancer patients and their families, support healthy public health policies and organize fundraising events.

Academic Fields
College: General, Accounting, Admin., Business, Communications, Computer Science, Food/Nutrition, Human Resources, Journalism, Science, Secretarial
Bachelor of Arts: General, Business, Public Relations
Bachelor of Comm/Admin: General, Accounting, Finance, Marketing, Info Mgmt., Public Admin.
Bachelor of Science: General, Biology, Health Sci.
Chartered Accounting: CA - General/Finance, CGA/CMA - General/Finance
Masters: Science, Library Science

Critical Skills
Adaptable, Good Communication, Dependable, Diligent, Efficient, Enthusiastic, Flexible, Organized, Productive, Professional, Responsible, Writing Skills

Types of Positions
Assistant Clerical   Research Associate
Accounting Assistant

Starting Salary
$ 20,000 - 30,000

Company Benefits
- Life, medical, dental, pension, long term disability
- Seminars, workshops, conferences

Correspondence
Mail or fax resume and cover letter

Part Time/Summer: The Canadian Cancer Society regularly hires part time workers, and occasionally hires for the summer. Potential summer work includes research, nutritional service, and behavioural science. The best time to apply is in April or May.

The Canada Student Employment Guide

CANADIAN COMMERCIAL CORP.

50 O'Connor Street, 11th Floor
Ottawa, Ontario, K1A 0S6
Tel: (613) 995-2120   Fax: (613) 995-2121

Glenda Lalonde, Human Resources
Internet: www.ccc.ca

Canadian Commercial Corp. is fully owned by the Government of Canada and is established to assist Canadian suppliers through the development of trade. The Corporation facilitates the process of exporting to foreign governments and international agencies. Canadian Commercial Corp. employs about 85 people.

Academic Fields
College: Accounting, Administration, Computer Science, Human Resources, Law Clerk, Marketing/Sales
Bachelor of Arts: Business, Economics, Journalism, Sociology/Social Work
Bachelor of Laws: General, Corporate
Bachelor of Engineering: Computer Systems, Civil, Design, Industrial
Chartered Accounting: CA - General/Finance

Critical Skills
Adaptable, Good Communication, Dependable, Enthusiastic, Flexible, Organized, Personable, Productive, Professional, Responsible, Good Writing Skills

Types of Positions
Marketing	Contracting
Human Resources	Administration
Finance	Legal

Starting Salary
$ 25,000 - 40,000 (depending on position)

Company Benefits
- Complete range of benefits

Correspondence
Fax or e-mail resume with cover letter
E-mail: hr@ccc.ca

Part Time/Summer: Canadian Commercial Corp. occasionally hires for part time employment, and regularly hires for summer opportunities. Potential jobs are most likely in positions listed above. Best time to apply is between January and April.

CANADIAN DAIRY COMMISSION

1525 Carling Avenue
Ottawa, Ontario, K1A 0Z2
Tel: (613) 998-9490   Fax: (613) 991-5028

Odette Cyr, Human Resources

The Canadian Dairy Commission is a federal government agency established in the dairy industry to provide regulation and guidance. The Commission is involved with policy development, milk supply management, prediction, surplus removal, and the exportation of dairy products.

Academic Fields
College: Accounting, Administration, Communications, Computer Science, Human Resources, Marketing/Sales, Statistics
Bachelor of Arts: Business, Economics, Statistics
Bachelor of Comm/Admin: General, Accounting, Finance, Marketing, Info Mgmt., Public Admin.
Chartered Accounting: CMA - General/Finance, CGA - General/Finance
Masters: Business Administration

Critical Skills
Adaptable, Analytical, Good Communication, Confident, Dependable, Productive, Professional, Responsible

Types of Positions
Marketing Clerk	Accounting Clerk
Junior Auditor	Junior Programmer

Starting Salary
$ 20,000 - 35,000

Company Benefits
- Medical and dental plan, pension plan
- 3 weeks holidays
- Training available to full time permanent employees

Correspondence
Mail or fax resume with cover letter, and follow up by telephone

Part Time/Summer: The Canadian Dairy Commission occasionally hires for part time jobs, and regularly looks for candidates for the summer months. Potential positions in the summer involve entry level jobs in special projects. The best time to apply is in January or February.

The Canada Student Employment Guide

CANADIAN DEPOSITORY FOR SECURITIES LTD.

85 Richmond Street West
Toronto, Ontario, M5H 2C9
Tel: (416) 365-8612   Fax: (416) 365-0758

Ann Shields, Manager, HR Development

The Canadian Depository for Securities (CDS) is Canada's national securities clearing and depository services organization. Established in 1970 to improve efficiency within the financial industry, the CDS employs over 425 people in regional offices in Toronto, Montreal, Calgary, and Vancouver.

Academic Fields
College: Accounting, Administration, Business, Computer Science, Human Resources, Law Clerk, Secretarial, Security/Law
Bachelor of Arts: Business, Economics
Bachelor of Comm/Admin: General, Accounting, Finance
Bachelor of Engineering: Computer Systems
Chartered Accounting: CA - General/Finance, CGA/CMA - General/Finance
Masters: Business Administration

Critical Skills
Adaptable, Analytical, Decisive, Dependable, Diligent, Efficient, Enthusiastic, Good Communication, Flexible, Responsible, Organized, Good With Figures, Personable, Persuasive, Professional, Good Writing Skills

Types of Positions
Administrative Services   Clearing Operations
Depository Operations   Finance
Information Services

Starting Salary
$ 20,000 - 25,000

Company Benefits
- Health and dental benefits, life & accident insurance
- Technical and professional training provided

Correspondence
Mail, fax or e-mail resume with cover letter
E-mail: ashields@cds.ca

Part Time/Summer: The Canadian Depository for Securities sometimes hires for part time work and regularly hires for the summer. Potential positions are in administration, clearing operations, depository operations, finance, and information services. The best time to apply is in January or February.

CANADIAN GENERAL TOWER LIMITED

52 Middleton Street
Cambridge, Ontario, N1R 5T6
Tel: (519) 623-1630   Fax: (519) 623-5139

Dan Arndt, HR Advisor

Canadian General Tower is a manufacturer of vinyl coated fabrics, film, and related products for many types of industries across the country. A private company, They have 700 employees.

Academic Fields
College: Accounting, Administration, Business, Computer Science, Engineering Tech., Laboratory Tech., Mechanical Tech., Secretarial
Bachelor of Arts: Business
Bachelor of Comm/Admin: Accounting, Marketing, Info Mgmt.
Bachelor of Science: General, Chemistry, Computer Science, Environmental Studies
Bachelor of Engineering: Chemical, Electrical, Environmental Studies, Mechanical
Chartered Accounting: CMA-Finance, CGA-Finance
Masters: Business Admin., Science, Engineering

Critical Skills
Adaptable, Analytical, Confident, Creative, Decisive, Dependable, Efficient, Flexible, Innovative, Leadership, Personable, Productive, Professional, Responsible

Types of Positions
Customer Service Rep.   Logistics Team
Clerical Support   Production Supervisor
Programmer/Analyst   Help Desk Support

Starting Salary
$ 30,000 - 40,000

Company Benefits
- Flexible benefit plans, pension, EAP program

Correspondence
Mail or fax resume with cover letter
E-mail: darndt@cgtower.com

Part Time/Summer: Canadian General Tower rarely hires for part time work, but regularly hires in the summer. Potential jobs are in manufacturing. Applications accepted after January, but prior to April.

Co-op/Internship: They offer co-op opportunities.

The Canada Student Employment Guide

CANADIAN MUSEUM OF CIVILIZATION CORPORATION
100 Laurier St., P.O. Box 3100, Station B
Hull, Québec, J8X 4H2
Tel: (819) 776-7100   Fax: (819) 776-7110

Human Resources Division

The Canadian Museum of Civilization Corporation is a national museum that is located in Hull, Quebec.

Academic Fields
College: Accounting, Administration, Advertising, Communications, Drafting/Architecture, Graphic Arts, Human Resources, Marketing/Sales, Mechanical Tech., Performing Arts, Secretarial, Security/Law, Museum Technology
Bachelor of Arts: General, Fine Arts, History, Recreation Studies
Bachelor of Comm/Admin: General, Accounting, Finance, Marketing
Bachelor of Engineering: Electrical, Mechanical
Bachelor of Education: General, Childhood
Chartered Accounting: CA - General/Finance
Masters: Library Science

Critical Skills
Adaptable, Analytical, Artistic, Creative, Decisive, Dependable, Efficient, Enthusiastic, Flexible, Good Communication, Good Writing Skills, Innovative, Leadership, Logical, Organized, Persuasive, Professional

Types of Positions
Various Positions

Starting Salary
$ 25,000 - 30,000

Company Benefits
- Medical and dental
- Tuition reimbursement

Correspondence
Fax or e-mail resume with cover letter

Part Time/Summer: The Canadian Museum of Civilization Corporation regularly seeks candidates for part time or summer employment. The best time to apply is in February or March.

CANADIAN NATIONAL INSTITUTE FOR THE BLIND
1929 Bayview Avenue
Toronto, Ontario, M4G 3E8
Tel: (416) 480-7490   Fax: (416) 480-7699

John Thompson, Director of Human Resources
Internet: www.cnib.org

The Canadian National Institute for the Blind (CNIB) is a private, voluntary, not-for-profit organization providing rehabilitation and library services to blind, visually impaired and deaf-blind persons across Canada. Approximately 25,000 volunteers and 1,900 staff work at the CNIB.

Academic Fields
College: General, Administration, Child Care
Bachelor of Arts: General, Business, Gerontology, Psychology, Public Relations, Recreation Studies
Bachelor of Comm/Admin: Accounting
Bachelor of Education: Adult Education, Childhood, Special
Chartered Accounting: CA-General, CMA-General, CGA-General
Masters: Library Science

Critical Skills
Adaptable, Good Communication, Confident, Creative, Decisive, Dependable, Diligent, Diplomatic, Efficient, Enthusiastic, Good With Figures, Innovative, Leadership, Manual Dexterity, Organized, Patient, Personable, Persuasive, Productive, Professional, Responsible, Good Writing Skills

Types of Positions
Clerical/Secretarial   Case Worker
District Administrator Junior Accountant

Starting Salary
Depends on position

Company Benefits
- A range of health benefits
- Pension and work related benefits

Correspondence
Mail resume with cover letter

Part Time/Summer: The CNIB sometimes hires for part time positions and regularly hires for summer opportunities. Employment involves counsellor positions at Lake Joseph Holiday Centre. The best time to apply is from January to March.

CANADIAN OCCIDENTAL PETROLEUM LTD.

635 8th Avenue SW, Suite 1500
Calgary, Alberta, T2P 3Z1
Tel: (403) 234-6700   Fax: (403) 234-1050

Staffing Analyst, Corporate HR
Internet: www.cdnoxy.com

Canadian Occidental Petroleum is engaged in the exploration, development, and production of oil, natural gas, and sulphur worldwide. The company is also involved in the production of synthetic crude oil from oil sands and the exploration for and evaluation of minerals, coal and oil sands deposits.

Academic Fields
College: Accounting, Business, Computer Science, Secretarial
Bachelor of Arts: Economics
Bachelor of Comm/Admin: General, Accounting, Finance
Bachelor of Science: General, Corporate
Bachelor of Laws: Actuarial, Computer Sci., Geology
Bachelor of Engineering: General, Civil, Computer Systems, Mechanical
Chartered Accounting: CA - General/Finance, CMA - General/Finance, CGA - General/Finance
Masters: Business Administration, Science, Engineering

Critical Skills
Adaptable, Analytical, Good Writing Skills, Good Communication, Innovative, Leadership, Professional, Team Player

Types of Positions
Accounting Clerk   Computer Operator
Geology/Engineer Tech.   Computer Technician
Analyst   Jr. Accountant

Starting Salary
$ 30,000 - 44,000

Company Benefits
- Medical, dental and disability insurance
- Training through local university, in-house training

Correspondence
Mail or e-mail resume with cover letter
E-mail: hr_staffing.cdnoxy.com

Part Time/Summer: Canadian Occidental Petroleum sometimes hires for part time jobs and regularly hires for the summer. Potential positions include 3rd year accountants, engineers, and geologists. Applications should be received by January 15th.

CANADIAN THERMOS PRODUCTS INC.

2040 Eglinton Ave. E.
Scarborough, Ontario, M1L 2M8
Tel: (416) 757-6231   Fax: (416) 757-6230

Janice Cameron, HR Manager

Canadian Thermos Products Inc. is involved in the plastics/insulated products manufacturing business. They produce hard and soft coolers and lunch kits, and other useful products. The firm employs approximately 180 individuals.

Academic Fields
College: Accounting, Computer Science, Marketing/Sales, Mechanical Tech.
Bachelor of Comm/Admin: Marketing, Info Mgmt.
Bachelor of Science: Computer Science
Bachelor of Engineering: Chemical, Industrial, Mechanical
Chartered Accounting: CGA-General, CGA-Finance

Critical Skills
Adaptable, Good Communication, Diligent, Efficient, Good With Figures, Leadership, Manual Dexterity, Organized, Productive, Professional

Types of Positions
Machine Operator   Assembler

Starting Salary
Varies depending on position

Company Benefits
- Medical, dental, pension, life insurance
- Pension and group RRSP, fitness subsidy

Correspondence
Mail resume with cover letter

Part Time/Summer: Canadian Thermos Products regularly looks for individuals for part time and summer opportunities. Potential jobs are in the plant area or in accounting and credit. The best time to apply is in January or February.

CANADIAN TIRE CORPORATION LTD.

2180 Yonge Street, 8th Floor South, P.O. Box 770,
Toronto, Ontario, M4P 2V8
Tel: (416) 480-3904   Fax: (416) 480-3996

Campus Recruitment
Internet: www.canadiantire.ca

Canadian Tire Corporation is currently "the best place to work in Canada" (Report of Business Magazine). Canadian Tire continues a 78-year history of retail innovation with a successful entrepreneurial spirit. The 38,000 employees of Canadian Tire and the 423 stores nationwide share a common vision: to be the best at what our customers value most.

Academic Fields
College: Accounting, Business, Computer Science
Bachelor of Arts: Business
Bachelor of Comm/Admin: Accounting, Finance
Bachelor of Science: Computer Science, Mathematics
Bachelor of Engineering: Industrial, Materials Science
Chartered Accounting: CA - General/Finance, CGA/CMA - General/Finance
Masters: Business Administration, Engineering

Critical Skills
Adaptable, Analytical, Enthusiastic, Flexible, Good Communication, Innovative, Persuasive, Professional, Interested in Learning

Types of Positions
Supply Chain Analyst (Logistics)
Associate Analyst (Finance)
Buying Analyst (Marketing)

Starting Salary
$ 30,000 - 40,000

Company Benefits
- Medical, dental and life insurance
- Profit sharing, stock purchase, store discount
- Training is provided, development based on individual needs

Correspondence
Mail or fax resume with cover letter

Part Time/Summer: Canadian Tire Corporation sometimes looks for individuals for part time employment, and regularly seeks candidates for summer opportunities. There are a variety of potential positions. Recruiting for summer positions begins in February.

CANADIAN WESTERN BANK

10303 Jasper Avenue, Suite 2100
Edmonton, Alberta, T5J 3X6
Tel: (403) 423-8888   Fax: (403) 423-8899

Uve Knaak, Human Resources
Internet: www.cwbank.com

A western-based full service bank, Canadian Western Bank is the smallest of only seven banks chartered to operate as a Schedule I Bank. They bank employs over 475 people.

Academic Fields
College: Accounting, Administration, Advertising, Business, Communications, Computer Science, Electronics Tech., Human Resources, Marketing/Sales, Secretarial, Security/Law, Urban Planning
Bachelor of Arts: General, Business, Economics, Political Science, Public Relations
Bachelor of Comm/Admin: General, Accounting, Finance, Marketing, Info Mgmt., Public Admin.
Bachelor of Science: Computer Science, Math.
Bachelor of Laws: General, Corporate, Real Estate
Bachelor of Engineering: Computer Systems
Bachelor of Education: General
Chartered Accounting: CA - General/Finance, CGA/CMA - General/Finance
Masters: Business Administration, Arts

Critical Skills
Adaptable, Analytical, Good Communication, Confident, Decisive, Dependable, Diligent, Diplomatic, Efficient, Enthusiastic, Flexible, Good With Figures, Innovative, Leadership, Logical, Organized, Patient, Productive, Professional, Good Writing Skills

Types of Positions
Customer Service	Computer Operator
Secretary	Accounting Officer
Loan Administrator	Payroll Administrator

Starting Salary
$ 20,000 - 25,000

Company Benefits
- Excellent benefit package, 100% prescription

Correspondence
Mail or fax resume with cover letter

Part Time/Summer: Canadian Western Bank occasionally hires for part time and summer work. Summer jobs are most likely to be customer service rep., or secretarial in nature. Apply in March and April.

The Canada Student Employment Guide

CANBRA FOODS LTD.

P.O. Box 99
Lethbridge, Alberta, T1J 3Y4
Tel: (403) 329-5583   Fax: (403) 328-7933

Ryan Miller, Supervisor Human Resources
Internet: www.canbrafoods.com

Canbra Foods, is a Canadian public company trading on the Toronto Stock Exchange with 39 years of experience in vegetable oil processing. They are Canada's largest on site fully-integrated canola processor and packer. Canbra was the first company in the world to market canola oil.

Academic Fields
College: General, Business, Computer Science, Secretarial
Bachelor of Comm/Admin: General, Accounting, Info Mgmt.
Bachelor of Science: Agriculture, Chemistry, Computer Science, Food Sciences
Bachelor of Engineering: General, Computer Systems, Electrical, Mechanical
Chartered Accounting: CMA-General/Finance, CGA-General/Finance

Critical Skills
Adaptable, Enthusiastic, Good Writing Skills, Good Communication, Logical, Organized, Personable

Types of Positions
Labourer
Junior Programmer
Accounts Payable Clerk
Receptionist
Accounts Receivable Clerk
Typist

Starting Salary
$ 20,000 - 25,000

Company Benefits
- Extended health, vision and dental plan
- Employee assistance program
- 100% coverage for job related courses

Correspondence
Mail resume with cover letter
E-mail: hr@canola.com

Part Time/Summer: Canbra Foods sometimes employs candidates for part time and summer jobs. Positions potentially become available for vacation relief of regular employees. These jobs are labour positions in the plant. The best time to apply is in May or June.

CANCARB LIMITED

P.O. Box 310, Stn Main
Medicine Hat, Alberta, T1A 7G1
Tel: (403) 527-1121   Fax: (403) 527-7706

Human Resources

Cancarb Limited manufactures carbon black for end users. The firm puts carbon in rubber products such as wiper blades. They employ approximately 70 individuals.

Academic Fields
College: Accounting, Business, Human Resources, Laboratory Tech., Marketing/Sales, Secretarial
Bachelor of Arts: Business
Bachelor of Comm/Admin: Accounting, Finance, Marketing
Bachelor of Science: Chemistry
Bachelor of Engineering: Chemical
Chartered Accounting: CA-Finance, CMA - General/Finance, CGA - General/Finance

Critical Skills
Adaptable, Analytical, Good Communication, Confident, Creative, Decisive, Dependable, Diligent, Diplomatic, Efficient, Enthusiastic, Good With Figures, Innovative, Leadership, Logical, Manual Dexterity, Organized, Patient, Personable, Persuasive, Productive, Professional, Responsible, Good Writing Skills

Types of Positions
Receptionist
Customer Service Rep.
Accounting Assistant
Lab Technician

Starting Salary
$ 20,000 - 25,000

Company Benefits
- Flexible benefit plan
- Medical, vision, dental, life insurance, pension

Correspondence
Mail resume with cover letter

Part Time/Summer: Cancarb Limited occasionally looks for individuals for part time or summer employment. Potential jobs in the summer include warehouse worker, receptionist, secretary, or lab technician. The best time to apply is between January and April.

CANCERCARE MANITOBA

100 Olivia Street
Winnipeg, Manitoba, R3V 0V9
Tel: (204) 787-2197   Fax: (204) 787-2979

Ardelle Jacques, Human Resources
Internet: www.mctrf.mb.ca

CancerCare Manitoba, formerly The Manitoba Cancer Treatment and Research Foundation, by an act of the legislature, is responsible for cancer prevention, detection, care, research and education throughout Manitoba.

Academic Fields
College: Accounting, Admin., Business, Computer Sci., Electronics Tech., Human Res., Industrial Design, Mech. Tech., Nursing, Radiology Tech., Science, Secretarial
Bachelor of Arts: Business, Sociology/Social Work
Bachelor of Comm/Admin: Accounting, Finance, Info Mgmt., Public Admin.
Bachelor of Science: Chemistry, Computer Science, Health Sciences, Microbiology, Pharmacy, Physics
Bachelor of Engineering: Design, Mechanical
Chartered Accounting: CA-Finance, CMA-Finance, CGA-Finance
Masters: Business Administration, Science, Engineering

Critical Skills
Adaptable, Analytical, Artistic, Good Communication, Confident, Creative, Decisive, Dependable, Diligent, Diplomatic, Efficient, Enthusiastic, Flexible, Good With Figures, Innovative, Logical, Organized, Patient, Personable, Responsible, Good Writing Skills

Types of Positions
Clerical	Computer Programming
Radiation Therapist	Electronic Technologist
Medical Physicist	Nurse

Starting Salary
$ 20,000 - 25,000

Company Benefits
- Health, dental, and vision benefits

Correspondence
Mail resume with cover letter

Part Time/Summer: CancerCare Manitoba sometimes hires for part time work and regularly hires for the summer. Potential jobs include clerical duties, research assistant, and junior programmer. It is best to submit resume in March or early April. Be specific about the type of position you are interested in.

CANCORE INDUSTRIES INC.

624 Parkdale Ave. N.
Hamilton, Ontario, L8H 5Z3
Tel: (905) 549-4181   Fax: (905) 549-4254

Human Resources

Cancore is a manufacturer of automotive radiators, complete with warehouses and retail service shops that offer complete cooling systems services.

Academic Fields
College: Accounting, Administration, Advertising, Business, Engineering Tech., Marketing/Sales, Secretarial
Bachelor of Arts: Business
Bachelor of Comm/Admin: Marketing
Bachelor of Engineering: Mechanical
Chartered Accounting: CMA-General

Critical Skills
Adaptable, Analytical, Good Communication, Diligent, Efficient, Enthusiastic, Flexible, Good With Figures, Logical, Manual Dexterity, Organized, Personable, Productive, Professional, Responsible, Good Writing Skills

Types of Positions
General Labour	Driver
Repair Technician	Office Work

Starting Salary
$ 30,000 - 40,000

Company Benefits
- Dental, health, life insurance, pension
- Company paid courses, on-the-job training

Correspondence
Mail or fax resume with cover letter

Part Time/Summer: Cancore occasionally looks for individuals for part time work, and regularly seeks people for the summer. Potential jobs include general labour in manufacturing or service areas. The best time to apply is April 1st or May 1st.

The Canada Student Employment Guide

CANGENE CORPORATION

104 Chancellor Matheson Rd.
Winnipeg, Manitoba, R3T 5Y3
Tel: (204) 275-4200   Fax: (204) 269-7003

Gisèle Marks, Human Resources
Internet: www.cangene.ca

Cangene is a world leader in the development, manufacture, and distribution of specialty hyperimmune plasma and biotechnology products. The company employs approximately 300 people.

Academic Fields
College: Engineering Tech., Nursing, Science, Secretarial, Chemical, Biosciences Technology
Bachelor of Comm/Admin: General, Marketing
Bachelor of Science: General, Agriculture, Biology, Chemistry, Environmental Studies, Food Sciences, Microbiology, Nursing (RN), Pharmacy
Bachelor of Engineering: General, Chemical, Computer Science, Mechanical
Chartered Accounting: CA-Finance, CMA-Finance, CGA-Finance
Masters: Life Sciences

Critical Skills
Adaptable, Analytical, Good Communication, Creative, Dependable, Enthusiastic, Flexible, Innovative, Organized, Good Writing Skills, Computer Skills

Types of Positions
Production Assistant   Laboratory Assistant
Administrative Assistant   Laboratory Technician I

Starting Salary
$ 26,000 - 30,000

Company Benefits
- Complete employee benefit package
- Health, dental, life insurance, vision, pension

Correspondence
Mail or fax resume with cover letter
E-mail: gmarks@cangene.ca

Part Time/Summer: Cangene Corporation occasionally looks for individuals for part time or summer employment. Potential jobs include administrative assistant, lab assistant, or co-op student in sciences and engineering. The best time to apply is in April to June.

Co-op/Internship: They occasionally have internship opportunities.

CANON CANADA INC.

6390 Dixie Rd.
Mississauga, Ontario, L5T 1P7
Tel: (905) 795-2111   Fax: (905) 795-2046

Human Resources
Internet: www.canon.ca

Canon is one of the world's leading providers of business and consumer imaging solutions. Their commitment to technological innovation in the worlds of imaging, information and industry has been instrumental to their success and continued growth.

Academic Fields
College: Accounting, Administration, Advertising, Business, Communications, Computer Science, Electronics Tech., Engineering Tech., Human Resources, Marketing/Sales, Mechanical Tech., Photography, Secretarial
Bachelor of Arts: Business, Economics, Psychology, Public Relations
Bachelor of Comm/Admin: General, Accounting, Finance, Marketing, Info Mgmt.
Bachelor of Science: Computer Science, Mathematics
Bachelor of Engineering: Computer Systems
Chartered Accounting: CMA-General
Masters: Business Administration

Critical Skills
Adaptable, Creative, Good Communication, Dependable, Efficient, Enthusiastic, Flexible, Logical, Organized, Personable, Productive, Professional

Types of Positions
Customer Relations Technical Rep.
System Support Representative
Accounting Clerk
Sales/Marketing Assistant

Starting Salary
$ 25,000 - 30,000

Company Benefits
- Full benefits package including life and disability
- Health, pension, in-house computer training
- Tuition reimbursement program

Correspondence
Mail or fax resume with cover letter

Part Time/Summer: Canon does not generally hire for part time or summer employment.

CANPAR TRANSPORT LTD.

1290 Central Pkwy W., Suite 500
Mississauga, Ontario, L5C 4R9
Tel: (905) 897-3678   Fax: (905) 276-7520

Vice President, Human Resources
Internet: www.canpar.com

Canpar Transport is a nationally based company with 62 terminal locations across Canada. The firm provides small parcel delivery. They employ approximately 1,600 individuals across the country.

Academic Fields
College: Accounting, Administration, Business, Human Resources, Marketing/Sales
Bachelor of Comm/Admin: Accounting, Finance, Marketing
Bachelor of Engineering: Computer Systems, Transportation
Chartered Accounting: CMA-Finance, CGA-Finance
Masters: Business Administration

Critical Skills
Adaptable, Analytical, Good Communication, Efficient, Leadership, Professional, Good Writing Skills

Types of Positions
Customer Service   Data Entry
Administration   Dockworker

Starting Salary
$ 25,000 - 30,000 (Clerical), $ 30,000 - 40,000 (Driver)

Company Benefits
- Health and dental coverage

Correspondence
Mail or e-mail resume with cover letter

Part Time/Summer: Canpar Transport regularly hires people for part time work and occasionally seeks candidates in the summer. Potential jobs include driver or dockworker. The best time to apply is in May.

CANWEL DISTRIBUTION LTD.

15 West Dr.
Brampton, Ontario, L6T 3T5
Tel: (905) 457-8500   Fax: (905) 457-3668

Joanne Oomen, Finance & Administration
Internet: www.canwel.com

CanWel provides distribution of building materials to retailers and manufacturers across the country. The firm has more than 400 employees.

Academic Fields
College: Accounting, Administration, Business

Critical Skills
Adaptable, Good Communication, Dependable, Efficient, Enthusiastic, Flexible, Productive, Responsible, Good Writing Skills

Types of Positions
Inside Sales   Accounts Payable
Warehouse

Starting Salary
$ 20,000 - 25,000

Company Benefits
- Standard benefits
- Medical, dental, life insurance, pension
- In-house courses, education assistance

Correspondence
Mail resume with cover letter

Part Time/Summer: CanWel Distribution occasionally looks for individuals for part time work, and regularly seeks people for the summer. Potential jobs are in the warehouse or involve administration.

CAPE BRETON DEVELOPMENT CORPORATION

P.O. Box 2500, Stn A
Sydney, Nova Scotia, B1P 6K9
Tel: (902) 842-2226   Fax: (902) 842-2610

Manager of Personnel and Training

Cape Breton Development Corporation is a federal crown corporation that is involved in underground coal mining, and has surface facilities. The company has approximately 1,700 employees.

Academic Fields
College: General, Accounting, Administration, Computer Science, Drafting/Architecture, Electronics Tech., Emergency/Paramedic, Engineering Tech., Human Resources, Mechanical Tech., Nursing, Secretarial, Security/Law
Bachelor of Comm/Admin: Accounting, Finance, Info Mgmt.
Bachelor of Science: Computer Science, Environmental Studies, Geology, Health Sciences, Nursing (RN)
Bachelor of Engineering: Electrical, Geotechnical, Mechanical, Mining
Chartered Accounting: CA - General/Finance, CMA-General, CGA-General

Critical Skills
Adaptable, Analytical, Good Communication, Decisive, Dependable, Diligent, Efficient, Enthusiastic, Good Writing Skills, Good With Figures, Leadership, Organized, Personable, Productive, Professional, Responsible

Types of Positions
Junior Draftsperson   Junior Accounting Clerk
Electricians Helper   Mechanics Helper

Starting Salary
$ 30,000 - 40,000

Company Benefits
- Full benefit and pension packages

Correspondence
Mail resume with cover letter

Part Time/Summer: Cape Breton Development Corporation does not hire individuals for part time or summer employment.

CAPILANO SUSPENSION BRIDGE

3735 Capilano Rd.
North Vancouver, British Columbia, V7R 4J1
Tel: (604) 985-7474   Fax: (604) 985-7479

Kristi Strickland, HR Manager
Internet: www.capbridge.com

Capilano Suspension Bridge is one of Vancouver's top tourist attractions with over 750 000 guests visiting each year. Their company also has four gift shops in Alberta and British Columbia and owns and operates Morraine Lake Lodge in Alberta.

Academic Fields
College: Cooking/Culinary, Hospitality, Travel/Tourism, Accounting, Administration, Human Resources, Information Systems, Marketing/Sales
Bachelor of Arts: General, Business, Public Relations
Bachelor of Comm/Admin: General, Accounting, Human Resources, Marketing, Info Mgmt.

Critical Skills
Adaptable, Dependable, Enthusiastic, Good Communication, Leadership, Organized, Personable

Types of Positions
Tour Guide   Retail
Reception   Administration
Reservations   Information Systems

Starting Salary
$ 25,000 - 30,000

Company Benefits
- Benefits including medical, dental, RRSP, industry passes
- Guest service training, team building, emergency training
- Job specific training, managing for excellence training

Correspondence
Mail resume with cover letter

Part Time/Summer: Capilano Suspension Bridge regularly hires for part time work and summer jobs. They hire 100 summer students in areas such as cafe, grill, guides, gate, retail, maintenance, servers, mascot, cooks, and reception. Apply late February or early March.

CARBONE OF AMERICA (LCL) LTD.

496 Evans Ave.
Etobicoke, Ontario, M8W 2T7
Tel: (416) 251-2334   Fax: (416) 252-1742

Nancy DiBernardo, Human Resources
Internet: www.carbonebrush.com

Carbone of America is a manufacturer of carbon brushes for electric motors. The firm has an employee base of approximately 140 individuals.

Academic Fields
College: Accounting, Administration, Business, Engineering Tech., Human Resources, Marketing/Sales, Mechanical Tech., Secretarial
Bachelor of Arts: Business, Public Relations
Bachelor of Comm/Admin: Accounting, Finance, Marketing, Info Mgmt.
Bachelor of Engineering: Mechanical
Chartered Accounting: CA-Finance
Masters: Business Administration, Engineering

Critical Skills
Adaptable, Analytical, Good Communication, Confident, Decisive, Dependable, Efficient, Enthusiastic, Flexible, Good With Figures, Leadership, Logical, Organized, Patient, Personable, Persuasive, Productive, Professional, Responsible, Good Writing Skills

Types of Positions
Reception   Accounting Clerks
Machine Operators   Junior Buyer
Customer Service Reps

Starting Salary
Depends on position

Company Benefits
- Full medical and dental benefits

Correspondence
Mail, fax, or submit resume & cover letter in person

Part Time/Summer: Carbone of America does not hire individuals for part time work, but regularly looks for people for the summer months. Potential summer jobs include machine operator. The best time to apply is in April.

CARGILL LIMITED

P.O. Box 5900, 300 - 240 Graham Ave.
Winnipeg, Manitoba, R3C 4C5
Tel: (204) 947-0141   Fax: (204) 947-6222

Vik Kail Employee Development Manager
Internet: www.cargill.com

Cargill Limited is the Canadian subsidiary of Cargill Incorporated, an international corporation and respected world leader in agriculture. In Canada, Cargill has over 4,000 employees involved in grain marketing, crop inputs marketing, animal nutrition, canola crushing, fertilizer manufacturing, meat processing, salt, flax fibre, starch and malt barley.

Academic Fields
College: Accounting, Administration, Agricultural, Computer Science, Marketing
Bachelor of Arts: General
Bachelor of Comm/Admin: General, Accounting, Marketing, Info Mgmt.
Bachelor of Science: Agriculture, Computer Sciences
Chartered Accounting: CA-General, CGA/CMA - General/Finance

Critical Skills
Adaptable, Confident, Dependable, Good Communication, Good Writing Skills, Innovative, Leadership, Personable, Productive, Professional

Types of Positions
Farm Service Centre Assistant   Accounting Analyst
Accounting Technician   Production Trainee
Plant Manager Trainee   IT Associate

Starting Salary
$ 20,000 - 25,000 (Diploma) /
$25,000 - 35,000 (Degree)

Company Benefits
- Health, dental, short term disability, insurance
- Strong on-the-job training and development

Correspondence
Mail or fax resume with cover letter
E-mail: vik.kail@cargill.com

Part Time/Summer: Cargill rarely hires for part time work and regularly hires in the summer. Positions are most likely to be summer accounting clerk, or summer field crop scout. Apply in the Fall or Winter.

Co-op/Internship: Co-op placements available in accounting and information technology.

The Canada Student Employment Guide

CARLSON MARKETING GROUP CANADA LTD.

3300 Bloor Street West, Centre Tower, 14th Floor
Toronto, Ontario, M8X 2Y2
Tel: (416) 207-2994   Fax: (416) 236-9915

Karen Spence, HR Generalist
Internet: www.carlsoncanada.com

Carlson Marketing Group Canada Ltd. (CMG) is a leader in developing integrated marketing strategies that build stronger bonds between Canadian companies and their customers, channel partners, and employees. Carlson is committed to helping their clients foster long-term relationships, influence purchasing behaviours, retain their best customers and improve their bottom line.

Academic Fields
College: Administration, Business, Information Systems, Secretarial, Graphic Arts, Travel/Tourism
Bachelor of Science: Computer Science

Critical Skills
Adaptable, Dependable, Efficient, Good Communication, Good Writing Skills, Leadership, Organized, Personable, Productive, Professional, Responsible

Types of Positions
Bilingual Cust. Service Rep.   Program Coordinator
Accounting   Mail Clerk
Administrative Support

Starting Salary
$ 20,000 - 25,000

Company Benefits
- Full benefits provided including health and dental
- Training is not formalized (it is treated on an individual basis)

Correspondence
Mail, fax or e-mail resume and cover letter
E-mail: hr@carlsoncanada.com

Part Time/Summer: Carlson Marketing Group Canada occasionally hires for part time work and regularly seeks candidates in the summer months. Potential jobs include bilingual customer service representative and administrative support. Generally speaking, children of employees are likely to be hired for summer positions.

CARTE INTERNATIONAL INC.

1995 Logan Avenue
Winnipeg, Manitoba, R2R 0H8
Tel: (204) 633-7220   Fax: (204) 694-0614

Harvey Schmidt, Human Resources

Carte International is a high technology company engaged in the business of manufacturing power, distribution, and specialty transformers. Carte International has an employee base of 193 individuals.

Academic Fields
College: Accounting, Administration, Computer Science, Drafting/Architecture, Electronics Tech., Engineering Tech., Human Resources, Marketing/Sales, Mechanical Tech., Security/Law
Bachelor of Arts: Business
Bachelor of Comm/Admin: Accounting, Finance, Marketing
Bachelor of Science: Computer Science
Bachelor of Engineering: Electrical, Industrial, Mechanical
Masters: Business Administration, Engineering

Critical Skills
Adaptable, Good Communication, Confident, Creative, Decisive, Dependable, Diligent, Diplomatic, Efficient, Enthusiastic, Flexible, Innovative, Leadership, Logical, Organized, Patient, Personable, Productive, Professional, Responsible, Good Writing Skills

Types of Positions
Drafting   Engineering
Accounting   Marketing

Starting Salary
$ 20,000 - 35,000

Company Benefits
- Medical, dental, pension plan and life insurance
- Eyeglass coverage and safety shoe payment
- Internal and external training

Correspondence
Mail resume with cover letter

Part Time/Summer: Carte International does not hire for part time positions, but sometimes employs individuals during the summer. Potential summer jobs involve drafting and engineering for factory experience, which could lead to hiring after graduation. Hiring depends on backlog of work.

The Canada Student Employment Guide

CASA LOMA

1 Austin Terrace
Toronto, Ontario, M5R 1X8
Tel: (416) 923-1172   Fax: (416) 923-5734

Maria Pimentel-Cook, Supervisor of Operations

Casa Loma is a well-recognized tourist attraction receiving as many as 350,000 visitors yearly. Once a private home belonging to Sir Henry Pellat, it has been shown on A & E's America's Castles for it's beauty and unique architectural structure. The Club uses its share of the proceeds to support a wide variety of charitable projects.

Academic Fields
College: General, Administration, Business, Child Care, Emergency/Paramedic, Hospitality, Human Resources, Journalism, Marketing/Sales, Performing Arts, Recreation Studies, Security/Law, Television/Radio, Travel/Tourism
Bachelor of Arts: General, Business, English, Fine Arts, History, Journalism, Languages, Music, Psychology, Public Relations, Sociology/Social Work
Bachelor of Science: Environmental Studies, Forestry, Horticulture

Critical Skills
Adaptable, Analytical, Good Communication, Confident, Creative, Decisive, Dependable, Diligent, Diplomatic, Efficient, Enthusiastic, Flexible, Innovative, Leadership, Logical, Organized, Patient, Personable, Productive, Professional, Responsible, Writing Skills

Types of Positions
Audio-Guide Assistant   Interpretive Guide
Sales Clerk-Gift Shop   Security
Market Research Assistant   Front Door Rep.

Starting Salary
below $ 20,000 (part time only)

Company Benefits
- 100% drug plan, vision, dental and life insurance
- RRSP plan, two floating days given

Correspondence
Mail or fax resume with cover letter

Part Time/Summer: Casa Loma regularly hires for part time work and occasionally hires in the summer. Candidates must demonstrate a strong commitment to learn and a desire to enhance the tourism industry through superior customers service skills. The optimal time to apply is from February to April 30.

CASSELS BROCK & BLACKWELL

40 King Street West, Suite 2100
Toronto, Ontario, M5H 3C2
Tel: (416) 869-5300   Fax: (416) 360-8877

Kim Wright, Human Resources Assistance
Internet: www.casselsbrock.com

Cassels Brock and Blackwell is a full service law firm with approximately 300 employees that operate out of their Toronto location. Serving the legal needs of many businesses and individuals, Cassels Brock and Blackwell has affiliated offices in Vancouver, Montreal and Mexico City.

Academic Fields
College: Accounting, Human Resources, Marketing/Sales, Secretarial (Legal)
Bachelor of Comm/Admin: Accounting, Info Mgmt.
Masters: Library Science

Critical Skills
Adaptable, Confident, Dependable, Efficient, Enthusiastic, Flexible, Good Writing Skills, Good Communication, Organized, Personable, Productive, Professional, Responsible

Types of Positions
Accounting Clerk   Payroll Clerk
Records Clerk   Fax Operator
Mail Delivery Clerk   Receptionist

Starting Salary
$ 20,000 - 25,000

Company Benefits
- Full benefits package provided
- New staff are offered training on Mac computers
- Job training is 'hands on'

Correspondence
Mail or fax resume with cover letter

Part Time/Summer: Cassels Brock & Blackwell sometimes hires for part time positions and regularly hires for summer opportunities. Some potential summer jobs include reception, records clerk, secretarial floater, and accounting clerk. The best time to apply is very early in the year.

CATHOLIC CHILDREN'S AID SOCIETY FOUNDATION
26 Maitland Street
Toronto, Ontario, M4Y 1C6
Tel: (416) 395-1500   Fax: (416) 395-1581

Recruitment Officer
Internet: www.ccas.toronto.on.ca/

The Catholic Children's Aid Society Foundation provides child welfare services and family support programs to individuals throughout the community. With 10 locations in the Toronto region, the agency employs approximately 450 people to work in various fields in the social services industry.

Academic Fields
College: Child Care
Bachelor of Arts: Sociology/Social Work
Bachelor of Comm/Admin: Accounting
Bachelor of Science: Computer Science, Nursing (RN)
Bachelor of Laws: General
Chartered Accounting: CA-Finance

Critical Skills
Adaptable, Creative, Dependable, Good Communication, Flexible, Enthusiastic, Leadership, Good Writing Skills, Organized, Professional, Responsible

Types of Positions
Clerical   Secretarial
Data Entry

Starting Salary
$ 20,000 - 30,000

Company Benefits
- Comprehensive benefit package
- Major health and dental
- Vacation pay

Correspondence
Mail or fax resume with cover letter

Part Time/Summer: The Catholic Children's Aid Society Foundation sometimes seeks people for part time and summer employment. Potential positions involve clerical or secretarial duties. Opportunities also exist in data entry or case aide.

CCL INDUSTRIES INC.
105 Gordon Baker Road, Suite 800
Willowdale, Ontario, M2H 3P8
Tel: (416) 756-8500   Fax: (416) 756-8555

Janice Davidge, Human Resources Director
Internet: www.cclind.com

CCL Industries is a diversified operation, engaged in the custom manufacturing of a wide range of consumer goods in North America, Mexico, and Europe. The company is active in three major business segments. The custom manufacturing division produces many household, personal care and cosmetic products. The container division manufactures aluminum spray containers and tubes. The label division produces the labels used in a broad range of products. CCL Industries employs about 7,800 individuals to work in various sectors within the company.

Academic Fields
College: Engineering Tech., Human Resources, Industrial Design, Secretarial
Bachelor of Arts: Business
Bachelor of Comm/Admin: Finance
Bachelor of Science: Chemistry, Environ. Studies
Bachelor of Engineering: Chemical, Computer Systems, Environmental Studies
Chartered Accounting: CMA-Finance, CGA-Finance
Masters: Business Administration

Critical Skills
Adaptable, Good Communication, Creative, Dependable, Good Writing Skills, Innovative, Leadership, Logical, Professional

Types of Positions
Customer Service   Accounting
Purchasing

Starting Salary
$ 25,000 - 30,000

Company Benefits
- Full benefit package including pension plan

Correspondence
Mail or fax resume with cover letter

Part Time/Summer: CCL Industries sometimes looks for candidates for part time and summer employment. Potential jobs vary. The best time to apply is in March.

The Canada Student Employment Guide

CEGELEC ENTERPRISES LTÉE

7151, Jean-Talon est, Bureau 1000
Anjou, Québec, H1M 3R4
Tel: (514) 493-4343   Fax: (514) 493-4330

Guillaume Desnoyers, Human Resources

Cegelec Enterprises Ltée is an electronic equipment manufacturer for the industrial sector. The company is also involved with energy transfer. Their head office is in Anjou, Quebec.

Academic Fields
Bachelor of Engineering: General, Computer Systems, Electrical, Mechanical

Critical Skills
Adaptable, Analytical, Diligent, Efficient, Flexible, Professional

Types of Positions
Various Positions

Starting Salary
$ 25,000 - 30,000

Company Benefits
- Full benefit package
- Reimbursement of company related courses

Correspondence
Fax resume with cover letter

Part Time/Summer: Cegelec Enterprises occasionally looks for candidates for part time and summer employment opportunities. A potential job is a trainee in the design and logistics department.

CELESTICA INTERNATIONAL INC.

844 Don Mills Rd.
Toronto, Ontario, M3C 1V7
Tel: (416) 448-5566   Fax: (416) 448-5895

Ken Lawrence, Manager Human Resources
Internet: www.celestica.com

Celestica International is a custom design and manufacturer of switch mode power supplies.

Academic Fields
College: Accounting, Electronics Tech., Engineering Tech.
Bachelor of Arts: Business
Bachelor of Comm/Admin: Accounting, Finance, Marketing, Info Mgmt.
Bachelor of Science: Chemistry, Computer Science
Bachelor of Engineering: Design, Electrical

Critical Skills
Adaptable, Analytical, Creative, Decisive, Enthusiastic, Flexible, Professional

Types of Positions
Design Engineer   Manufacturing Engineer
Customer Service   Clerical

Starting Salary
$ 30,000 - 50,000 (depending on position)

Company Benefits
- Health and dental plan, group RRSP
- Employee share ownership plan

Correspondence
Mail, fax, or e-mail resume with cover letter

Part Time/Summer: Celestica International occasionally seeks candidates for part time or summer work. Potential jobs in the summer include electronic technician, computer or clerical work.

CENALTA ENERGY SERVICES INC.

407 - 2nd St. SW, Suite 1900
Calgary, Alberta, T2P 2Y3
Tel: (403) 264-6490   Fax: (403) 264-6995

Charlie Hamilton, Organization Development
Internet: www.cenalta.com

Headquartered in Calgary, CenAlta Energy Services Inc. was created in late 1999 through the combination of several oil and gas service companies. CenAlta is a major oil and gas service company currently comprised of two operating divisions: CenAlta Well Servicing and Polar Drilling.

Academic Fields
College: Drafting/Architecture, Engineering Tech.
Bachelor of Comm/Admin: Accounting, Marketing, Info Mgmt.
Bachelor of Science: Geology
Bachelor of Engineering: Design
Chartered Accounting: CA-Finance

Critical Skills
Adaptable, Good Communication, Confident, Dependable, Enthusiastic, Flexible, Leadership, Manual Dexterity, Organized, Personable, Productive

Types of Positions
Floorhand   Roughneck
Shop Labourer

Starting Salary
$ 25,000 - 30,000

Company Benefits
- Complete benefit package
- Health, dental, prescriptions
- Competency based development tool for advancement within the company

Correspondence
Fax resume with cover letter
E-mail: info@cenalta.com

Part Time/Summer: CenAlta Energy Services Inc. occasionally seeks candidates for part time or summer employment. Potential jobs in the summer include roughnecks and ship labourer. The best time to apply is in April.

CENTRA GAS BRITISH COLUMBIA INC.

1675 Douglas St.
Victoria, British Columbia, V8W 3V3
Tel: (250) 480-4300   Fax: (250) 480-4455

Shannon Feeney, Human Resources

Centra Gas British Columbia is responsible for the safe transmission and distribution of natural gas for Vancouver Island, the Sunshine Coast, Whistler and Coquitlam.

Academic Fields
College: Accounting, Business, Communications, Computer Science, Drafting/Architecture, Engineering Tech., Human Resources, Marketing/Sales, Science
Bachelor of Arts: Business, Public Relations, Sociology/Social Work
Bachelor of Comm/Admin: Accounting, Finance, Marketing, Info Mgmt.
Bachelor of Science: Computer Science, Environmental Studies, Mathematics
Bachelor of Laws: Real Estate
Bachelor of Engineering: Civil, Electrical, Environ. Studies, Geotechnical, Mechanical, Transportation
Chartered Accounting: CA-Finance, CMA-Finance, CGA-Finance
Masters: Business Admin., Science, Engineering

Critical Skills
Adaptable, Analytical, Good Communication, Confident, Efficient, Enthusiastic, Flexible, Innovative

Types of Positions
Mail Clerk   Drafting Clerk
Receptionist   Utility Assistant
Labourer   Call Centre Clerk

Starting Salary
$ 30,000 - 40,000

Company Benefits
- Extended health, dental, employee savings plan

Correspondence
Mail resume with cover letter

Part Time/Summer: Centra Gas British Columbia does not hire for part time work, but regularly hires for the summer. Potential summer jobs include file or office clerk, environmental clerk, finance clerk, human resources clerk, measurement student, transmission student, labourer, receptionist/clerk, customer service student. The best time to apply is in February.

CENTRA GAS MANITOBA INC.

444 St. Mary Avenue, Suite 410
Winnipeg, Manitoba, R3C 3T7
Tel: (204) 925-0710   Fax: (204) 925-0732

HR & Education Services

Centra Gas Manitoba distributes natural gas in the greater Winnipeg area and in rural communities in Manitoba. The company serves over 226,000 customers in 88 locations through a total of 1,020 km of transmission mains and 4,125 km of distribution pipeline. Centra Gas Manitoba is 99.9% owned by Westcoast Energy Inc. of Vancouver, British Columbia.

Academic Fields
College: Administration, Advertising, Communications, Computer Science, Drafting/Architecture, Engineering Tech., Human Res., Industrial Design, Mechanical Tech.
Bachelor of Arts: Public Relations
Bachelor of Comm/Admin: General, Accounting, Finance, Info Mgmt.
Bachelor of Engineering: General, Chemical, Civil, Industrial, Mechanical
Chartered Accounting: CA - General/Finance, CGA/CMA - General/Finance
Masters: Business Administration

Critical Skills
Adaptable, Analytical, Creative, Dependable, Diligent, Diplomatic, Efficient, Good Communication, Innovative, Professional, Responsible

Types of Positions
Accts Payable Rep.   Associate Programmer
Credit / Collections   Customer Support Rep.
Secretary

Starting Salary
$ 25,000 - 30,000

Company Benefits
- Full time, permanent staff eligible for benefits
- Comprehensive benefit program
- Educational assistance program

Correspondence
Submit resume and cover letter in person

Part Time/Summer: Centra Gas Manitoba regularly employs individuals for part time and summer work. These jobs are most likely to include labour, administration, drafting, or clerical work. The best time to apply is in March or April.

CENTRAL PARK LODGES LTD.

175 Bloor St. E., South Tower, Ste. 601
Toronto, Ontario, M4W 3R8
Tel: (416) 929-5450   Fax: (416) 929-8695

Human Resources Department
Internet: www.centralparklodges.com

Central Park Lodges is engaged in providing health care in retirement lodges and nursing homes. Offering homecare and staff relief, the company has 7 locations in the Toronto region and employs almost 1,000 individuals in these areas.

Academic Fields
College: Accounting, Administration, Cooking, Food/Nutrition, Home Care, Hospitality, Human Resources, Information Systems, Marketing/Sales, Nursing (RN/RNA), Recreation Studies, Secretarial, Social Work
Bachelor of Arts: General, Gerontology, Psychology, Sociology/Social Work
Bachelor of Comm/Admin: General, Accounting, Finance, Human Resources, Marketing, Info Mgmt., Public Admin.
Bachelor of Science: Food Sci., Health Sci., Nursing
Bachelor of Education: Adult Education
Chartered Accounting: CA - General/Finance, CGA - General/Finance, CMA - General/Finance

Critical Skills
Adaptable, Dependable, Efficient, Good Communication, Enthusiastic, Flexible, Patient, Professional, Responsible

Types of Positions
Activity Worker   Cook
Accounting Clerk   Receptionist
Healthcare Aide   Registered Nurse

Starting Salary
$ 20,000 - 25,000

Company Benefits
- Major medical, dental, and vision
- Training done internally and outside courses

Correspondence
Mail, fax, e-mail resume and cover letter, or apply through their website. E-mail: hr@cplodges.com

Part Time/Summer: Central Park Lodges sometimes hires for part time and summer positions. Stressing that nothing is available at present, the jobs above are most likely to be filled in the summer.

The Canada Student Employment Guide

CENTRE DE SANTÉ DE ST-HENRI INC.

5205 rue Notre-Dame Ouest
Montréal, Québec, H4C 3L2
Tel: (514) 931-0851   Fax: N/A

Ressources humaines

Established in 1977, Centre de Santé de St-Henri is a public health care facility with approximately 240 beds in total. The hospital provides medical facilities for patients with chronic sickness and those that require extended medical care. They employee approximately 330 individuals.

Academic Fields
College: Administration, Computer Science, Faculty Management, Food/Nutrition, Human Resources, Nursing
Bachelor of Comm/Admin: Accounting
Bachelor of Science: Food Sciences, Health Sciences, Nursing (RN), Occupational Therapy, Pharmacy
Chartered Accounting: CA-General

Critical Skills
Adaptable, Creative, Dependable, Diligent, Efficient, Flexible, Organized, Responsible

Types of Positions
Various Positions

Starting Salary
$ 25,000 - 30,000

Company Benefits
- Collective insurance
- Various training programs

Correspondence
Mail resume with cover letter

Part Time/Summer: Centre de Santé de St-Henri sometimes looks for individuals for part time employment, and regularly seeks candidates for summer opportunities. Potential jobs in the summer involve cafeteria service, health worker, and various nursing positions.

CENTURY SALES AND SERVICE LIMITED

P.O. Box 1218, Stn Main
Edmonton, Alberta, T5J 2M6
Tel: (403) 468-3366   Fax: (403) 490-2893

Brenda Cunningham, Human Resources
Internet: www.vallencorp.com

Century Sales and Service is an industrial and safety supply distributor. The firm employs approximately 350 people, and is based in Alberta, Saskatchewan, British Columbia and Ontario.

Academic Fields
College: General, Marketing/Sales
Bachelor of Comm/Admin: General, Marketing

Critical Skills
Adaptable, Good Communication, Confident, Dependable, Diplomatic, Enthusiastic, Organized, Personable, Productive, Responsible

Types of Positions
Junior Buyer   Sales Trainee

Starting Salary
$ 25,000 - 30,000

Company Benefits
- Extended health, dental, life insurance
- Long term disability, RRSP program
- Training allowances and internal programs

Correspondence
Mail resume with cover letter
E-mail: brenda.cunningham@centurysales.com

Part Time/Summer: Century Sales and Service occasionally looks for individuals for part time work, and regularly seeks people for summer employment. Potential summer jobs are usually in the warehouse including material handler, shipper or receiver. The best time to apply is in March.

The Canada Student Employment Guide

CERIDIAN CANADA

125 Garry St.
Winnipeg, Manitoba, R3C 3P2
Tel: (204) 947-9400   Fax: (204) 957-3899

Director Human Resources
Internet: coolblue.ceridian.ca

Ceridian Canada is Canada's leading employer services company, providing payroll and human resource management services to businesses of all sizes, in virtually every industry.

Academic Fields
College: Accounting, Administration, Advertising, Business, Computer Science, Human Resources, Marketing/Sales
Bachelor of Comm/Admin: Accounting, Finance, Marketing
Bachelor of Science: Computer Science
Chartered Accounting: CA-Finance, CMA-Finance, CGA-Finance
Masters: Business Administration

Critical Skills
Adaptable, Analytical, Good Communication, Confident, Dependable, Diligent, Diplomatic, Efficient, Enthusiastic, Flexible, Good With Figures, Leadership, Logical, Organized, Patient, Personable, Persuasive, Productive, Professional, Responsible

Types of Positions
Distribution Clerk   Account Representative
Customer Helpline Rep.   Receptionist
Systems Developer

Starting Salary
below $ 20,000 - 30,000 (depending on position)

Company Benefits
- Complete package of benefits
- Health and dental plan, pension plan

Correspondence
Mail or fax resume with cover letter

Part Time/Summer: Ceridian Canada sometimes looks for part time and summer candidates. Positions are most likely to be clerical in nature. The best time to apply is generally in March.

CFCF INC.

405, av Ogilvy
Montréal, Québec, H3N 1M4
Tel: (514) 273-6311   Fax: (514) 276-9399

Human Resources

CFCF Inc. is involved in TV cable distribution. The company's head office is in Montreal, Quebec. One of the firm's major shareholders is Jevlam Inc. of Montreal. CFCF Inc. has an employee base of 1,196 individuals.

Academic Fields
College: Communications, Electronics Tech., Secretarial, Television/Radio
Bachelor of Arts: Business, English, Fine Arts, Journalism, Political Science
Bachelor of Comm/Admin: General, Accounting
Bachelor of Science: Computer Science
Chartered Accounting: CMA-General, CGA-General
Masters: Business Administration

Critical Skills
Adaptable, Artistic, Creative, Good Communication, Innovative, Leadership, Professional, Responsible

Types of Positions
Researcher   ENG Editor

Starting Salary
$ 20,000 - 25,000

Company Benefits
- Medical and dental coverage
- General hospital, eyeglass, drug insurance
- Training for professional development

Correspondence
Mail resume with cover letter

Part Time/Summer: CFCF Inc. occasionally hires individuals for part time and summer employment opportunities. Potential jobs include researcher, and technical person. The best time to apply is in April.

CFCN COMMUNICATIONS INC.

P.O. Box 760, Station E
Calgary, Alberta, T3C 3L9
Tel: (403) 240-5600   Fax: (403) 240-5773

Manager, Human Resources

CFCN Communications is engaged in the field of television broadcasting in Calgary. A subsidiary of Maclean Hunter Limited, this company was established in 1962, and has approximately 216 employees. Interested candidates should include a resume tape for related positions (i.e. reporter, photographer, etc.). As a mid market TV station, they have very little requirement for entry-level candidates as almost all of their positions would require three to five years of small market television experience.

Academic Fields
College: Accounting, Advertising, Communications, Electronics Tech., Human Resources, Journalism, Marketing/Sales, Secretarial, Television/Radio
Bachelor of Arts: Journalism
Chartered Accounting: CMA-General, CMA-Finance

Critical Skills
Adaptable, Creative, Dependable, Enthusiastic, Flexible, Good Writing Skills, Productive, Good Communication, Professional, Responsible, Good Work Ethic

Types of Positions
Editorial Assistant	Secretary
Reporter/Producer	Master Control Operator
VTR Operator	Accts Payable/Receivable

Starting Salary
$ 20,000 - 25,000

Company Benefits
- Industry comparable benefits including pension
- Extended medical, dental and life insurance
- Educational assistance available

Correspondence
Mail resume with cover letter

Part Time/Summer: CFCN Communications sometimes seeks candidates for part time positions, but does not generally hire for summer employment.

CGI

1130 Sherbrooke St. W., 5th Floor
Montréal, Québec, H3A 2M8
Tel: (514) 841-3200   Fax: (514) 841-3299

Julie Nobert, HR Coordinator
Internet: www.cgi.ca

CGI is a North American leader in information technology (IT) services, with state-of-the-art expertise in three complimentary areas of specialization: information systems, management and telecommunications. The firm has operations in more than 20 countries, and close to 7,500 members. CGI serves more than 2,000 medium-sized and large public and private organizations.

Academic Fields
College: Computer Science
Bachelor of Comm/Admin: Accounting
Bachelor of Science: Computer Science
Chartered Accounting: CMA-General
Masters: Engineering

Critical Skills
Adaptable, Efficient, Good Communication, Organized, Responsible

Types of Positions
Networking	Programming
Telecom	Internet

Starting Salary
$ 25,000 - 30,000

Company Benefits
- Core and flexible benefits
- Share purchase plan

Correspondence
Mail, fax, e-mail resume with cover letter
E-mail: cgi.imprh@cgi.ca

Part Time/Summer: CGI occasionally seeks candidates for part time positions, and regularly looks for people in the summer. The best time to apply is in March or April.

The Canada Student Employment Guide

CGU GROUP CANADA LTD.

2206 Eglinton Ave. E.
Scarborough, Ontario, M1L 4S8
Tel: (416) 288-1800   Fax: (416) 288-9106

Human Resources
Internet: www.cgu.ca

CGU is one of the world's most broadly based insurance groups. Its three major divisions encompass property and casualty insurance, life insurance and asset management. The company has major operations in the U.K., Europe, North America, South Africa, Australia, New Zealand and Asia, as well as significant market presence in other regions. They employ approximately 2,300 individuals across Canada.

Academic Fields
College: Accounting, Business, Computer Science, Information Systems, Insurance, Secretarial
Bachelor of Arts: General, Business, Criminology
Bachelor of Comm/Admin: General, Accounting, Finance, Info Mgmt.
Bachelor of Science: Actuarial, Computer Science
Chartered Accounting: CGA - General/Finance
Masters: Business Administration

Critical Skills
Adaptable, Analytical, Dependable, Enthusiastic, Good Communication, Good With Figures, Innovative, Leadership, Organized, Productive, Professional

Types of Positions
Junior Underwriter   PC Analyst
Accounting Clerk   Claims Adjuster
Assistant Actuarial Analyst   Customer Service Rep.

Starting Salary
$ 25,000 - 30,000

Company Benefits
- Competitive benefit package

Correspondence
Mail or fax resume with cover letter

Part Time/Summer: CGU Group Canada occasionally looks for people for part time work and regularly seeks candidates for the summer. Potential summer jobs include data entry, file clerk, and microfilm clerk. The best time to apply is in February.

CH2M GORE AND STORRIE LIMITED

255 Consumers Road
North York, Ontario, M2J 5B6
Tel: (416) 499-0090   Fax: (416) 499-0168

Human Resources
Internet: www.ch2m.com

CH2M Gore and Storrie is Canada's foremost consulting firm specializing exclusively in environmental engineering and science. CH2M Gore and Storrie employs over 300 individuals.

Academic Fields
College: Business, Computer Science, Drafting/Architecture, Engineering Tech., Laboratory Tech., Mechanical Tech., Statistics, Urban Planning
Bachelor of Arts: Urban Geography
Bachelor of Comm/Admin: Info Mgmt.
Bachelor of Science: Biology, Chemistry, Computer Science, Environmental Studies, Geology, Mathematics, Microbiology, Physics
Bachelor of Engineering: General, Chemical, Civil, Computer Systems, Design, Electrical, Environmental Studies, Geotechnical, Mechanical, Water Resources
Masters: Engineering

Critical Skills
Adaptable, Analytical, Good Communication, Confident, Creative, Decisive, Dependable, Diligent, Diplomatic, Efficient, Enthusiastic, Flexible, Good With Figures, Leadership, Logical, Organized, Patient, Personable, Persuasive, Productive, Professional, Responsible, Good Writing Skills

Types of Positions
Graduate Engineers   CAD Technician
Design Technologist   Administration
Science Grads   Environmental Planners

Starting Salary
$ 25,000 - 40,000 (depending on position)

Company Benefits
- A standard company benefits program
- Technical training with on-the-job mentoring

Correspondence
E-mail resume and cover page
E-mail: cgsresumes@ch2m.com

Part Time/Summer: CH2M Gore & Storrie sometimes hires for part time and summer workl. Potential summer jobs involves field work for specific projects. Apply from March to May.

CHALLENGER MOTOR FREIGHT INC.

50 Groh Avenue
Cambridge, Ontario, N3C 1Y9
Tel: (519) 658-5154   Fax: (519) 658-9112

Sylvia Bordignon, Manager Human Resources
Internet: www.challenger.com

For 25 years, Challenger Motor Freight Inc. has provided customers with truckload, flatbed and logistics services. Their reputation throughout the transportation industry can be attributed to their impressive record of customer satisfaction, safe and knowledgeable drivers, late model, well maintained equipment, and technological applications.

Academic Fields
College: Accounting, Administration, Business, Information Systems, Secretarial

Critical Skills
Analytical, Decisive, Dependable, Efficient, Enthusiastic, Flexible, Good Communication, Good Writing Skills, Innovative, Organized, Personable, Productive, Professional, Responsible

Types of Positions
General Labourer   General Office Clerk

Starting Salary
$ 20,000 - 25,000

Company Benefits
- Health and safety training
- Computer training
- Participation in company functions

Correspondence
E-mail resume with cover letter
E-mail: sylviab@challenger.com

Part Time/Summer: Challenger Motor Freight Inc. occasionally hires for part time and summer employment. Potential positions include general labourer (warehouse, shop), or clerical work (data entry, filing).

Co-op/Internship: They offer an apprentice mechanics program

CHAPTERS INC.

90 Ronson Drive
Etobicoke, Ontario, M9W 1C1
Tel: (416) 243-3138   Fax: (416) 243-5420

Donna Morris, Human Resources
Internet: www.chapters.ca

Chapters Inc. is in the book retailing business. Chapters was formed by the merger of Smithbooks and Coles Book Stores. The firm's head office is located in Etobicoke, Ontario. Retail stores are located across the country. They are the parent of Chapters Online Inc., a Canadian e-commerce company which operates www.chapters.ca and www.villa.ca, leading Canadian destinations for online shoppers.

Academic Fields
College: General, Accounting, Administration, Business, Communications, Human Resources
Bachelor of Arts: English, Journalism, Languages
Bachelor of Comm/Admin: General, Accounting, Finance, Marketing, Info Mgmt.
Bachelor of Education: Childhood
Chartered Accounting: CA - General/Finance

Critical Skills
Adaptable, Confident, Dependable, Efficient, Enthusiastic, Flexible, Good Communication, Organized, Productive, Professional, Responsible

Types of Positions
Various Positions

Starting Salary
$ 20,000 - 25,000

Company Benefits
- Comprehensive benefits package
- Health care, dental, life, long term disability
- Premiums are company paid

Correspondence
Mail resume with cover letter

Part Time/Summer: Chapters regularly hires candidates for part time employment, and occasionally looks for individuals for the summer months.

CHARLOTTETOWN DRIVING PARK

P.O. Box 308
Charlottetown, PEI, C1A 7K7
Tel: (902) 629-6631   Fax: (902) 368-8856

Cathy Scowcroft, Human Resources

Charlottetown Driving Park is involved in harness racing in P.E.I. The firm employs approximately 120 people.

Academic Fields
College: General, Accounting, Administration, Advertising, Business, Journalism, Secretarial
Bachelor of Arts: General, Business, English, Journalism, Public Relations
Bachelor of Comm/Admin: General, Accounting
Bachelor of Science: Agriculture
Bachelor of Engineering: General
Bachelor of Education: General
Chartered Accounting: CA-General

Critical Skills
Adaptable, Confident, Dependable, Efficient, Enthusiastic, Flexible, Good Communication, Good With Figures, Good Writing Skills, Logical, Organized, Patient, Personable, Professional, Responsible

Types of Positions
Office Assistant   Grounds Maintenance

Starting Salary
below $ 20,000

Company Benefits
- Full time employees receive health package and life insurance

Correspondence
Submit resume and cover letter in person

Part Time/Summer: Charlottetown Driving Park regularly looks for candidates for part time or summer employment. Potential summer jobs include marketing assistant, data entry, grounds keeping, or office assistant. The best time to apply is in March.

CHETICAMP PACKERS LTD.

P.O. Box 580
Cheticamp, Nova Scotia, B0E 1H0
Tel: (902) 224-1866   Fax: (902) 224-1894

Stella LeBlanc, Human Resources

Cheticamp Packers is engaged in the business of manufacturing fresh and frozen packaged fish, and other seafood products. The company was established in 1991, and has an employee base of approximately 200 individuals.

Academic Fields
College: Secretarial

Critical Skills
Dependable, Productive

Types of Positions
Various positions

Starting Salary
below $ 20,000

Company Benefits
- Competitive benefit package offered

Correspondence
Submit resume and cover letter in person

Part Time/Summer: Cheticamp Packers does not generally hire for part time positions, but occasionally hires candidates for the summer months. Potential positions involve general labour in the fish plant. The best time to apply is early in May.

CHEVRON CANADA RESOURCES LTD.

500 - 5th Avenue SW
Calgary, Alberta, T2P 0L7
Tel: (403) 234-5664 Fax: (403) 234-5837

Don Riley, Human Resources
Internet: www.chevron.ca

Chevron Canada Resources is engaged in exploration, production and marketing of crude oil, natural gas and related products. The company is a wholly owned subsidiary of the Chevron Corporation of San Francisco, California. Chevron Canada Resources has approximately 785 employees in Canada.

Academic Fields
College: Computer Science, Graphic Arts
Bachelor of Comm/Admin: General, Accounting, Finance
Bachelor of Science: Computer Science, Geology
Bachelor of Laws: Corporate
Bachelor of Engineering: Chemical, Civil, Electrical
Chartered Accounting: CA - General/Finance
Masters: Science, Engineering

Critical Skills
Adaptable, Creative, Enthusiastic, Flexible, Good Communication, Leadership, Ability to Work

Types of Positions
Accountant   Field Engineer
Geologist   Geophysicist
Programmer/Analyst

Starting Salary
$ 30,000 - 40,000

Company Benefits
- Health, dental and pension plan
- Profit sharing, flexible work schedules
- International career development opportunities

Correspondence
Mail resume with cover letter

Part Time/Summer: Chevron Canada Resources occasionally seeks individuals for part time positions, and regularly hires for summer employment. Summer positions are most like to involve geology, geophysics, engineering, or computer science. The best time to apply is in the Fall on college or university campuses.

CHILDREN'S AID SOCIETY OF METROPOLITAN TORONTO

33 Charles Street East
Toronto, Ontario, M4Y 1R9
Tel: (416) 924-4640 Fax: (416) 324-2502

Donna Duke, Human Resources
Internet: www.casmt.on.ca

The Children's Aid Society of Metropolitan Toronto is a child welfare agency that works with foster parents and other organizations in the protection of children. Operating under the Municipality of Metro Toronto, this agency employs approximately 640 people to work in 12 locations in the Toronto region. These individuals work in various capacities within the field of social services. The Children's Aid Society also has a large staff of volunteers within the agency.

Academic Fields
College: Child Care
Bachelor of Arts: Sociology/Social Work
Bachelor of Science: Computer Science

Critical Skills
Adaptable, Good Communication, Dependable, Diplomatic, Enthusiastic, Flexible, Patient, Personable, Professional, Responsible, Good Writing Skills

Types of Positions
Child and Youth Worker   Social Worker

Starting Salary
$ 30,000 - 40,000

Company Benefits
- Extended health care
- Four weeks vacation and income maintenance
- Income maintenance

Correspondence
Mail, fax, e-mail resume with cover letter

Part Time/Summer: The Children's Aid Society sometimes hires for part time and summer employment. Potential positions for the summer include social worker and child and youth care worker, or clerical type work.

CHILDREN'S HOSPITAL OF EASTERN ONTARIO
401 Smyth Rd.
Ottawa, Ontario, K1H 8L1
Tel: (613) 737-7600   Fax: (613) 738-4840

Personnel Department
Internet: www.cheo.on.ca

The Children's Hospital of Eastern Ontario is a 150 bed, pediatric/quaternary care teaching hospital affiliated with the University of Ottawa. As such, the Hospital serves a broad geographic area, including Eastern Ontario and Western Quebec. Founded in 1974, the hospital treats over 6,000 inpatients annually, and its outpatient program, ambulatory clinics and emergency services handle close to 250,000 patient visits each year.

Academic Fields
College: Child Care, Computer Science, Emergency/Paramedic, Food/Nutrition, Laboratory Tech., Nursing, Radiology Tech., Secretarial, Security/Law
Bachelor of Comm/Admin: Accounting, Info Mgmt.
Bachelor of Science: Computer Science, Food Sciences, Health Sciences, Nursing (RN), Occupational Therapy, Pharmacy, Psychology
Bachelor of Engineering: Computer Systems
Bachelor of Education: Childhood
Masters: Business Administration

Critical Skills
Adaptable, Analytical, Creative, Decisive, Enthusiastic, Flexible, Leadership, Good Writing Skills

Types of Positions
Security	Information Systems
Radiology	Secretary
Nurse	Registered Practical Nurse

Starting Salary
$ 25,000 - 30,000

Company Benefits
- Full benefit package

Correspondence
Fax, or e-mail resume with cover letter
E-mail: personnel@cheo.on.ca

Part Time/Summer: Children's Hospital of Eastern Ontario occasionally looks for individuals for part time and summer employment. Potential summer jobs include clerical, housekeeping, and dietary duties. The best time to apply is in March.

CHILLIWACK GENERAL HOSPITAL
46500 Menholm Road
Chilliwack, British Columbia, V2P 1P7
Tel: (604) 795-4120   Fax: (604) 795-4139

Jodi Lenz, Human Resources
Internet: www.cgh.hnet.bc.ca

Chilliwack General Hospital is a public health care facility with approximately 120 acute care beds and 300 long term care beds. Established in 1911, the hospital provides services in medicine and surgery, pediatrics, psychiatric care, intensive care, obstetrics, emergency and long term care. The hospital employs approximately 1,000 individuals.

Academic Fields
College: Cooking/Culinary, Food/Nutrition, Lab. Tech., Nursing, Radiology Tech., Secretarial
Bachelor of Arts: Business, Gerontology, Sociology/Social Work
Bachelor of Comm/Admin: Accounting, Info Mgmt.
Bachelor of Science: Food Sciences, Nursing (RN), Occupational Therapy, Pharmacy, Physiotherapy, Health Science
Bachelor of Engineering: Biomedical, Electrical
Chartered Accounting: CGA-General

Critical Skills
Adaptable, Dependable, Good Communication, Innovative, Leadership, Organized, Productive, Professional, Responsible

Types of Positions
Nursing	Information Systems
Food Services	Laboratory
Radiology	Pharmacy

Starting Salary
$ 30,000 - 40,000

Company Benefits
- Medical and dental benefits
- Disability benefits, pension plan

Correspondence
Mail or fax resume with cover letter

Part Time/Summer: Chilliwack General Hospital sometimes hires for part time work and regularly for the summer. The hospital typically hires students through its cooperative program at the local university and college.

The Canada Student Employment Guide

CHINOOK HEALTH REGION

960 - 19 Street South
Lethbridge, Alberta, T1J 1W5
Tel: (403) 382-6100   Fax: (403) 382-6016

Human Resources
Internet: www.chv.ab.ca

Chinook Health Region is one of 17 regions that provides health care services in the province of Alberta. The health authority is responsible for acute care, long term care, and public health services within its region. Lethbridge Regional Hospital is the corporate headquarters of the Chinook Health Region and is located at the address above.

Academic Fields
College: Nursing, Radiology Tech.
Bachelor of Science: Health Sciences, Nursing (RN), Occupational Therapy, Physiotherapy

Critical Skills
Adaptable, Decisive, Dependable, Efficient, Enthusiastic, Flexible, Good Communication, Good Writing Skills, Organized, Patient, Personable, Professional

Types of Positions
Various Positions

Starting Salary
$ 30,000 - 50,000

Company Benefits
- Full benefits including pension
- Short and long term disability
- In-house training and available funds for outside courses

Correspondence
Mail, fax, e-mail or submit resume and cover letter in person. E-mail: humanres@mail.chv.ab.ca

Part Time/Summer: Chinook Health Region sometimes seeks candidates for part time and summer employment. Positions in the summer are most likely to be clerical, or nursing (RN, LPN). Individuals should apply early. They also offer casual hiring.

CHRISTIAN HORIZONS

384 Arthur St. S.
Elmira, Ontario, N3B 2P4
Tel: (519) 669-1571   Fax: (519) 669-1574

Human Resources
Internet: domino.christian-horizons.org

Christian Horizons is a non-denominational evangelical Christian not-for-profit organization supporting individuals with developmental disabilities across Ontario through the provision of residential and other support services. The organization covers four Districts in Ontario.

Academic Fields
College: Developmental Services Worker, Recreation Studies, Social Work, General, Accounting, Administration, Business, Human Resources
Bachelor of Arts: Psychology, Sociology/Social Work, General, Business, Gerontology
Bachelor of Comm/Admin: General, Accounting, Finance
Bachelor of Science: Psychology, Occupational Therapy, Physiotherapy
Bachelor of Engineering: Computer Systems
Chartered Accounting: CA - General/Finance, CGA/CMA - General/Finance

Critical Skills
Adaptable, Good Communication, Confident, Creative, Dependable, Diligent, Flexible, Leadership, Organized, Patient, Professional, Responsible, Good Writing Skills

Types of Positions
Residential Support Worker
Relief Support Worker

Starting Salary
$ 20,000 - 30,000

Company Benefits
- Extended health and dental
- RRSP after 5 years, extended vacation after 3 years
- Training specific to special needs of client

Correspondence
Mail or submit resume and cover letter in person

Part Time/Summer: Christian Horizons regularly looks for candidates for part time or summer employment. Potential summer work includes relief support worker. Individuals can apply anytime.

CINEPLEX ODEON CORPORATION

1303 Yonge St.
Toronto, Ontario, M4T 2Y9
Tel: (416) 323-6600   Fax: (416) 323-6612

Human Resources Dept.

Cineplex Odeon Corporation is a major motion picture exhibitor offering movie-going entertainment, with a wide range of services (Cinescape Arcade) and food items for the movie-goer.

Academic Fields
College: Accounting, Administration, Business, Electronics Tech., Graphic Arts, Human Resources, Secretarial
Bachelor of Arts: Business, Economics
Bachelor of Comm/Admin: Accounting, Finance, Marketing
Chartered Accounting: CA - General/Finance, CGA/CMA - General/Finance
Masters: Business Administration

Critical Skills
Adaptable, Analytical, Good Communication, Dependable, Diligent, Efficient, Good With Figures, Innovative, Logical, Organized, Productive, Professional

Types of Positions
Junior Accountant   HR Assistant
Junior Technical Analyst   Administrative Assistant

Starting Salary
$ 20,000 - 25,000

Company Benefits
- Full range of benefits
- Educational assistance program
- Development of employees

Correspondence
Mail or fax resume with cover letter

Part Time/Summer: Cineplex Odeon Corporation occasionally looks for individuals for part time or summer employment. The best time to apply is in May.

CITIBANK CANADA

One Toronto Street, Suite 1200
Toronto, Ontario, M5C 2V6
Tel: (416) 947-2900   Fax: (416) 369-3660

Suzanne Rodrigues, Human Resources
Internet: www.citibank.com/canada

Citibank Canada is the country's second largest Schedule II Bank, offering banking services to corporations, government and financial institutions, as well as consumers since 1974. Their team of professionals is made up of over 1000 employees, located in Toronto, Montreal and Calgary.

Academic Fields
College: Accounting, Computer Science, Human Resources
Bachelor of Arts: Business, Economics, Statistics
Bachelor of Comm/Admin: General, Accounting, Finance, Info Mgmt.
Bachelor of Science: Chemistry, Computer Science, Mathematics
Bachelor of Engineering: Computer Systems, Electrical
Chartered Accounting: CA - General/Finance, CGA/CMA - General/Finance
Masters: Business Administration, Engineering

Critical Skills
Analytical, Confident, Decisive, Dependable, Diligent, Efficient, Enthusiastic, Flexible, Good Communication, Good Writing Skills, Innovative, Organized, Productive, Professional

Types of Positions
Operations & Technology

Starting Salary
$ 30,000 - 40,000

Company Benefits
- Dental, medical, vision, short & long term disability
- Life insurance, loan and mortgage benefits
- Training opportunities off site

Correspondence
Mail or fax resume with cover letter

Part Time/Summer: Citibank sometimes hires for part time work and regularly hires for the summer. Potential summer jobs include clerical, computer, and analyst positions. The best time to apply for these potential positions is in early March or April.

The Canada Student Employment Guide

CKF INC.

P.O. Box 419
Hantsport, Nova Scotia, B0P 1P0
Tel: (902) 684-1394   Fax: (902) 684-9703

Carol Forsey, Human Resources Manager

CKF Inc. produces molded pulp products (i.e. Royal Chinet, egg cartons, etc.). The firm is a sister company to Minas Basin Pulp and Power Co. Ltd.

Academic Fields
College: Accounting, Administration, Business, Computer Science, Electronics Tech., Engineering Tech., Faculty Mgmt., Human Resources, Industrial Design, Marketing/Sales, Mechanical Tech., Nursing, Secretarial
Bachelor of Arts: Business
Bachelor of Comm/Admin: Accounting, Finance, Marketing, Info Mgmt.
Bachelor of Science: Chemistry, Comp. Sci., Environ. Studies, Math., Nursing, Occup. Health Nursing
Bachelor of Engineering: Chemical, Computer Syst., Electrical, Environ. Studies, Industrial, Mechanical
Chartered Accounting: CA - General/Finance, CGA/CMA - General/Finance
Masters: Business Administration, Engineering

Critical Skills
Adaptable, Analytical, Confident, Creative, Dependable, Efficient, Enthusiastic, Flexible, Good Communication, Organized, Personable, Productive, Responsible

Types of Positions
General Accounting   Junior Engineer
Information Systems Dept.   Engineering Technologist

Starting Salary
$ 30,000 - 40,000 (new graduate)

Company Benefits
- Medical, dental, life insurance, LTD and STD

Correspondence
Mail or submit resume and cover letter in person
E-mail: cforsey@ckfinc.com

Part Time/Summer: CKF does not hire for part time work, but regularly hires for the summer. Individuals should apply for engineering student or computer science positions in March, July or November.

Co-op/Internship: They have co-op students in engineering and business.

CLARICA

227 King Street South
Waterloo, Ontario, N2J 4C5
Tel: (519) 888-2581   Fax: (519) 888-2727

E-mail: itjobs@clarica.com
Internet: www.clairca.com

At Clarica, one of Canada's fastest growing financial organizations, they've been helping people make clear financial choices for over 130 years. They market a wide range of financial products and services, including investments, insurance and employee benefits. The innovative use of technology is key to maintaining their competitive advantage in the financial services industry. As a proven industry leader in the development and use of state-of-the-art technologies, their information services team provides technology solutions that are fundamental to Clarica's growth and commitment to customers. Clarica's Information Services team looks for innovative people with an aptitude for technology and a desire for life-long learning.

Academic Fields
College: Computer Science
Bachelor of Comm/Admin: Management Information Systems
Bachelor of Science: Computer Science, Math
Bachelor of Engineering: Computer Science

Critical Skills
Results Oriented, Excellent Communicators, Team Players, Able to Manage Change Well, Proven Leaders

Types of Positions
A variety of positions in the field of information technology exist ranging from development roles to hands on technical roles.

Starting Salary
$ 35,000 - 40,000 (depends on position and prior experience)

Company Benefits
- Flexible group life and health benefits, pension
- On-site fitness facilities at Waterloo location
- On-going training and education

Correspondence
E-mail resume with cover letter

Part Time/Summer: Clarica does hire for IT summer positions. Please submit your resume in March or check your career centre on-campus postings.

The Canada Student Employment Guide

CLUB MONACO INTERNATIONAL

430 King Street West
Toronto, Ontario, M5V 1L5
Tel: (416) 585-4101   Fax: (416) 585-4176

Kim O'Neill, Recruitment Team
Internet: www.clubmonaco.com

Club Monaco is a dynamic retailing concept that designs, manufactures and markets internationally. Club Monaco designs modern products such as clothing for men and women, cosmetics, accessories, home furnishings and footwear. Club Monaco employs over 1,000 people with locations in Canada, USA, Malaysia, Israel, Japan and Korea.

Academic Fields
No specific academic fields required.
They will look at individuals from all areas.

Critical Skills
Adaptable, Artistic, Confident, Creative, Dependable, Diligent, Efficient, Enthusiastic, Flexible, Good Communication, Innovative, Leadership, Organized, Personable, Productive, Professional, Responsible

Types of Positions
Sales-Retail Store
Visual Presentation-Retail Store
Stock-Retail Store
Cashier-Retail Store

Starting Salary
$ 20,000 - 35,000

Company Benefits
- Employees are thoroughly trained in product knowledge, exceptional customer service
- Opportunities for promotion exist within all areas
- Encourage employee development, provide benefits

Correspondence
E-mail resume with cover letter or apply through web site. E-mail: recruitment@clubmonaco.com

Part Time/Summer: Club Monaco International regularly hires for part time work and occasionally hires staff for the summer months.

Co-op/Internship: They have various internship positions depending on student's program and department availability.

COAST MOUNTAIN BUS COMPANY LTD.

C650 - 13401 108th Avenue
Surrey, British Columbia, V3T 5T4
Tel: (604) 540-3010   Fax: (604) 540-3005

Employment Services Advisor
Internet: www.coastmountainbus.com

Coast Mountain Bus Company Ltd. is an operating subsidiary of the Greater Vancouver Transportation Authority (TransLink) that serves more than 2.8 million people throughout British Columbia by bus and seabus in the Lower Mainland. The corporation's conventional transit systems, in Greater Vancouver carry more than 120 million passengers annually. Coast Mountain Bus Company Ltd. employs approximately 3,925 individuals including temporary staff.

Academic Fields
No specific academic background is required.
They will look at candidates from all academic backgrounds.

Critical Skills
Diplomatic, Good Communication, Team Player, Good Writing Skills, Personable, Initiative, Organized, Professional

Types of Positions
Casual Customer Information Clerk
Casual Farebox Attendant
Casual Farebox Receipts Attendant
Casual Traffic Checker

Starting Salary
$ 26,000 - 32,000

Company Benefits
- Medical, dental and income continuance
- Basic group life insurance
- Temporary assignments for employees to develop their skills

Correspondence
Mail or fax resume with cover letter

Part Time/Summer: Coast Mountain Bus Company occasionally looks for individuals for part time work and regularly hires for the summer. Potential jobs include serviceperson, student engineering assistant, farebox attendant, and clerical positions. Resumes are accepted in January with most positions filled by April.

COBI FOODS INC.

P.O. Box 176
Ingersoll, Ontario, N5C 3K5
Tel: (519) 485-4410   Fax: (519) 485-1321

Alice Smith, Human Resources

COBI Foods processes and packages frozen vegetables. The company employs approximately 200 full time employees and another 300 people seasonally.

Academic Fields
College: Accounting, Computer Science, Food/Nutrition, Human Resources, Science-General, Secretarial
Bachelor of Science: Agriculture, Food Sciences, Microbiology
Bachelor of Engineering: General
Chartered Accounting: CA-General

Critical Skills
Good Communication, Dependable, Efficient, Flexible, Leadership, Manual Dexterity, Organized, Patient, Productive, Responsible, Honesty

Types of Positions
Various Positions

Starting Salary
$ 26,000 - 40,000

Company Benefits
- Employer paid health and dental
- Life insurance
- Short and long term disability

Correspondence
Fax resume with cover letter

Part Time/Summer: COBI Foods occasionally looks for people for part time work, and regularly seeks staff for the summer. Potential jobs are in the factory, or involve field work. The best time to apply is in March.

COBOURG DISTRICT GENERAL HOSPITAL

240 Chapel St., P.O. Box 340
Cobourg, Ontario, K9A 4K9
Tel: (905) 372-6811   Fax: (905) 372-4243

Joanne Litt, HR Co-ordinator

Cobourg District General Hospital is a community hospital in Cobourg with general medical and surgical facilities. The hospital has an employee base of approximately 320 individuals.

Academic Fields
College: Accounting, Administration, Business, Communications, Computer Science, Emergency/Paramedic, Food/Nutrition, Human Resources, Lab. Tech., Nursing, Orthotics/Prosthetics, Radiology Tech., Science, Secretarial
Bachelor of Arts: Business, Economics, Gerontology, Psychology, Public Relations, Sociology/Social Work
Bachelor of Comm/Admin: General, Accounting, Finance, Public Admin.
Bachelor of Science: General, Biology, Chemistry, Food Sciences, Health Sciences, Kinesiology, Microbiology, Nursing (RN), Occupational Therapy, Pharmacy, Physiotherapy, Psychology
Bachelor of Laws: Corporate
Bachelor of Engineering: Biomedical, Electrical
Chartered Accounting: CA-Finance, CMA-Finance, CGA-Finance
Masters: Business Administration, Science

Critical Skills
Adaptable, Good Communication, Confident, Dependable, Leadership, Organized, Professional, Responsible

Types of Positions
Nurse (RN, RPN, Health Care Aide)

Starting Salary
$ 25,000 - 40,000

Company Benefits
- Full range of benefits

Correspondence
Mail resume with cover letter

Part Time/Summer: Cobourg District General Hospital occasionally seeks people for part time or summer work. Potential summer jobs include dietary aide or laundry attendant.

COCA COLA FOODS CANADA INC.

2550 Victoria Park Avenue, Suite 800
North York, Ontario, M2J 5A9
Tel: (416) 756-8100   Fax: (416) 756-8153

Frances Bilecki, Human Resources
Internet: www.cokecce.com

Coca Cola Foods Canada Inc. is a food manufacturer that produces many products in the beverage industry. The company's head office is in North York, Ontario.

Academic Fields
College: General, Accounting, Administration, Human Resources, Marketing/Sales, Secretarial
Bachelor of Arts: Business
Bachelor of Comm/Admin: General, Accounting, Finance, Info Mgmt.
Bachelor of Education: General
Chartered Accounting: CA - General/Finance, CGA/CMA - General/Finance
Masters: Business Administration

Critical Skills
Adaptable, Analytical, Good Communication, Confident, Creative, Decisive, Dependable, Diligent, Diplomatic, Efficient, Enthusiastic, Flexible, Good With Figures, Innovative, Leadership, Logical, Organized, Personable, Persuasive, Productive, Professional, Responsible, Good Writing Skills

Types of Positions
Accounts Receivables Clerk   Billings Claim Clerk

Starting Salary
$ 25,000 - 40,000

Company Benefits
- Comprehensive benefits package

Correspondence
Mail resume with cover letter

Part Time/Summer: Coca Cola Foods Canada regularly looks for individuals for part time and summer employment opportunities. The best time to apply is in April or May.

COGNIS CANADA CORPORATION

2290 Argentina Rd.
Mississauga, Ontario, L5N 6H9
Tel: (905) 542-7550   Fax: (905) 542-7566

Human Resources
Internet: www.cognis-us.com

Cognis Canada Corporation is involved in the manufacture and distribution of natural-sourced oleochemicals used in every day products. They have a Canadian employee base of approximately 135 unionized and non-unionized individuals.

Academic Fields
College: Laboratory Tech.
Bachelor of Arts: Business
Bachelor of Science: Chemistry, Environmental Studies
Bachelor of Engineering: Chemical, Mechanical
Chartered Accounting: CMA - General/Finance, CGA - General/Finance
Masters: Science

Critical Skills
Adaptable, Good Communication, Dependable, Diplomatic, Good With Figures, Innovative, Organized, Productive, Good Writing Skills

Types of Positions
Production - General Labourer

Starting Salary
$ 35,000 - 40,000

Company Benefits
- Pension, health, dental, life insurance
- Long and short term disability
- Fitness subsidy, computer purchase plan

Correspondence
Mail or fax resume with cover letter
E-mail: linda.crawford@cognis.ca

Part Time/Summer: Cognis Canada Corporation rarely hires for part time or summer opportunities. Potential jobs include switchboard or reception relief, or special projects. The best time to apply is in April.

COGNOS INCORPORATED

3755 Riverside Drive
Ottawa, Ontario, K1G 4K9
Tel: (613) 738-1440   Fax: (613) 738-8882

Sue Zuccala, Human Resources
Internet: www.cognos.com/student

Cognos is the world's largest and most successful vendor of Enterprise Business Intelligence solutions. Their Web-based software delivers the right information to everyone in the enterprise and beyond, to customers and partners across the supply chain.

Academic Fields
College: Computer Science, Electronics Tech., Information Systems
Bachelor of Arts: Psychology
Bachelor of Comm/Admin: General, Info Mgmt.
Bachelor of Science: Computer Science, Kinesiology, Mathematics
Bachelor of Engineering: Computer Systems, Electrical
Masters: Computer Science

Critical Skills
Enthusiastic, Good Communication, Personable, Productive, Team Player

Types of Positions
Software Developer   Quality Control Analyst
Customer Support   Computer Interaction Specialist

Starting Salary
$ 35,000 - 50,000 (depends on position)

Company Benefits
- Extended health, vision, and dental plan for full time employees
- Group RRSP, computer purchase plan
- Stock purchase plan, new exercise facilities

Correspondence
E-mail resume with cover letter through their web site
E-mail: student.recruiter@cognos.com

Part Time/Summer: Cognos Inc. sometimes seeks people for part time jobs and regularly hires for the summer. Potential jobs include engineering co-op placements. Interested candidates should apply through their school.

Co-op/Internship: Internship opportunities exist for Human Computer Interaction Specialist, Software Developer and Quality Control Analyst.

COLGATE-PALMOLIVE CANADA INC.

99 Vanderhoof Ave.
Toronto, Ontario, M4G 2H6
Tel: (416) 421-6000   Fax: (416) 421-0286

Gail Barton, Human Resources
Internet: www.colgate.ca

Colgate Palmolive Canada markets and manufactures consumer products for both personal and household care. Some brand names include Javex, Fleecy, Mennen, Ajax, and Colgate.

Academic Fields
Bachelor of Comm/Admin: Marketing
Masters: Business Administration

Critical Skills
Adaptable, Good Communication, Creative, Decisive, Dependable, Enthusiastic, Flexible, Innovative, Personable, Professional, Responsible

Types of Positions
Product Assistant

Starting Salary
$ 30,000 - 40,000

Company Benefits
- Flexible benefit plan
- Pension plan
- Other programs

Correspondence
Fax resume with cover letter

Part Time/Summer: Colgate-Palmolive Canada occasionally looks for individuals for part time or summer employment. Potential summer jobs include plant vacation relief. The best time to apply is in May.

COLUMBIA HOUSE

5900 Finch Avenue East
Scarborough, Ontario, M1B 5X7
Tel: (416) 299-9400   Fax: (416) 299-7491

Michelle Lopez, Recruitment Manager
Internet: www.columbiahousecanada.com

The Columbia House is a mail order distributor of various types of records, magnetic tapes, and compact discs. A subsidiary of Sony Corp. of Canada, Columbia House employs over 200 individuals.

Academic Fields
College: General, Accounting, Administration, Advertising, Business, Communications, Computer Sci., Graphic Arts, Hospitality, Human Res., Journalism, Marketing/Sales, Security/Law, Stats, Television/Radio
Bachelor of Arts: General, Business, Criminology, Economics, English, History, Journalism, Languages, Music, Philosophy, Political Science, Psychology, Public Relations, Sociology/Social Work, Statistics
Bachelor of Comm/Admin: General
Bachelor of Science: General, Computer Science
Bachelor of Laws: General
Bachelor of Education: General
Chartered Accounting: CA - General/Finance, CGA/CMA - General/Finance
Masters: Business Administration

Critical Skills
Adaptable, Good Communication, Dependable, Diligent, Diplomatic, Efficient, Enthusiastic, Flexible, Good With Figures, Innovative, Manual Dexterity, Organized, Patient, Personable, Productive, Professional, Responsible, Good Writing Skills

Types of Positions
Telephone Representative   Bank Deposit Clerk
Desktop Publishing Artist   Mail Room Clerk

Starting Salary
$ 20,000 - 30,000

Company Benefits
- 100% tuition reimbursement for relevant programs

Correspondence
Mail resume with cover letter

Part Time/Summer: Columbia House regularly hires for part time work, and occasionally hires in the summer. Jobs are within the distribution and warehouse areas. The best time to apply is before April.

COM DEV INTERNATIONAL

155 Sheldon Drive
Cambridge, Ontario, N1R 7H6
Tel: (519) 622-2300   Fax: (519) 622-5543

Mickie Churchill, Human Resources Associate
Internet: www.comdev.ca

COM DEV is a leading global designer, manufacturer and distributor of wireless infrastructure and the largest Canadian owned designer and manufacturer of space satellite hardware.

Academic Fields
College: Human Res., Purchasing, Secretarial, Electronics Tech., Engineering Tech., Mech. Tech.
Bachelor of Arts: Business
Bachelor of Comm/Admin: General, Accounting, Finance, Human Resources, Marketing, Info Mgmt.
Bachelor of Science: Computer Science, Physics
Bachelor of Engineering: Design, Electrical, Materials Science, Mechanical
Bachelor of Education: Adult Education
Chartered Accounting: CGA-General, CMA-General
Masters: Business Admin., Science, Engineering

Critical Skills
Analytical, Dependable, Diligent, Good Communication, Good Writing Skills, Leadership, Organized, Professional, Responsible

Types of Positions
MTS Engineers   Electronics Technologist

Starting Salary
$ 35,000 - 55,000

Company Benefits
- Competitive benefits package
- Training and development is valued highly

Correspondence
E-mail resume with cover letter, or apply through their web site. E-mail: spacetech.resumes@comdev.ca

Part Time/Summer: COM DEV International rarely seeks candidates for part time employment, but regularly hires for the summer. Potential jobs include electronic assemblers and general administrative work. The best time to apply is February to April.

Co-op/Internship: Internship opportunities are available through colleges and universities.

The Canada Student Employment Guide

COMCARE HEALTH SERVICES

G20 - 339 Wellington Rd. S.
London, Ontario, N6C 4P8
Tel: (519) 432-3726   Fax: (519) 432-3731

Mary Lou Arnold, Human Resources

Comcare Health Services delivers home and occupational health services through 43 locations and more than 8,000 nurses and health care aides. Services include visiting nurses, convalescent care, palliative nursing care, home support, and live-in-care. A leader in its field, they also operate a private vocational school dedicated to specialized health care training.

Academic Fields
College: Accounting, Administration, Business, Computer Sci., Human Resources, Nursing, Secretarial
Bachelor of Arts: Business, Public Relations
Bachelor of Comm/Admin: Marketing, Info Mgmt.
Bachelor of Science: Health Sciences, Nursing (RN), Occupational Therapy, Physiotherapy
Bachelor of Engineering: Computer Systems
Chartered Accounting: CA-General, CGA/CMA - General/Finance

Critical Skills
Adaptable, Good Communication, Confident, Creative, Decisive, Dependable, Diligent, Diplomatic, Efficient, Enthusiastic, Flexible, Good With Figures, Innovative, Logical, Organized, Personable, Productive, Professional, Responsible, Good Writing Skills

Types of Positions
Clerical	Accounting
Reception	Home Support Worker
Nurse (RN)	Nurse (RNA)

Starting Salary
$ 20,000 - 25,000 (Clerical)
$ 30,000 - 40,000 (Professional Groups)

Company Benefits
- Comprehensive benefit package to staff working more than 30 hours a week
- Reimbursement for continuing education initiatives

Correspondence
Mail or fax resume with cover letter

Part Time/Summer: Comcare Health Services regularly hires for part time and summer work. Potential positions involve nursing or clerical work. Individuals may apply anytime. Their peak period is May to Sept.

COMMUNICATIONS & POWER INDUSTRIES CANADA INC.

45 River Drive
Georgetown, Ontario, L7G 2J4
Tel: (905) 877-0161   Fax: (905) 877-5327

Dennis R. Foley, Manager of Human Resources
Internet: www.cpii.com/cmp

Communications & Power Industries Canada specializes in producing radio and TV transmitting, signaling and detection equipment, as well as radiographic, fluoroscopic, therapeutic and other x-ray equipment. They employ over 200 people.

Academic Fields
College: Accounting, Drafting/Architecture, Electronics Tech., Engineering Tech., Human Resources, Mechanical Tech.
Bachelor of Comm/Admin: Finance
Bachelor of Science: Chemistry, Comp. Sci., Physics
Bachelor of Engineering: Electrical, Mechanical
Chartered Accounting: CA-Finance, CMA-Finance
Masters: Engineering

Critical Skills
Adaptable, Analytical, Good Communication, Confident, Creative, Decisive, Dependable, Diligent, Efficient, Enthusiastic, Flexible, Innovative, Leadership, Logical, Manual Dexterity, Organized, Personable, Persuasive, Productive, Professional, Responsible

Types of Positions
Machine Shop Helper	Material Handler
Assembler	

Starting Salary
$ 25,000 - 40,000 (depending on position)

Company Benefits
- Major medical, dental, short/long term disability
- Group life, fitness facility, computer purchase plan

Correspondence
Mail, fax or e-mail resume with cover letter
E-mail: denny.foley@cmp.cpii.com

Part Time/Summer: Communications & Power Industries Canada regularly hires for part time work and occasionally hires for the summer. Potential positions involve engineering and computer science. There are also general labourer jobs. April or May is the best time to apply.

Co-op/Internship: They occasionally offer internship opportunities.

COMMUNITY SAVINGS CREDIT UNION

1170 - 8th Avenue
New Westminster, British Columbia, V3M 2R6
Tel: (604) 654-2000   Fax: (604) 654-2017

Judy Towill, Manager HR
Internet: www.comsavings.com

On February 1st, 1999 IWA and Community Credit Union changed its name to Community Savings Credit Union. Community Savings Credit Union is not restricted to any one group of people. Their doors are open to anyone who enjoys personal, friendly service and a wide range of financial services. Membership is not limited to individuals. Societies, partnerships, companies, proprietorships, and trade unions all belong to Community Savings Credit Union.

Academic Fields
College: Accounting, Administration, Advertising, Computer Science, Human Resources, Marketing/Sales, Secretarial
Bachelor of Arts: Business
Bachelor of Comm/Admin: Accounting, Finance, Marketing, Info Mgmt.
Bachelor of Science: Computer Science
Bachelor of Engineering: Computer Systems
Chartered Accounting: CGA-Finance

Critical Skills
Adaptable, Good Communication, Dependable, Efficient, Enthusiastic, Flexible, Organized, Personable, Productive, Professional, Responsible

Types of Positions
Member Service Representative

Starting Salary
$ 20,000 - 25,000

Company Benefits
- Full benefit package
- Incentive program for courses taken from recognized educational institutions

Correspondence
Mail, fax, e-mail, submit resume and cover letter in person. E-mail: jtowill@comsavings.com

Part Time/Summer: Community Savings Credit Union occasionally looks for individual for part time and summer work. Potential positions include member service representative. The best time to apply is in May.

COMPAQ CANADA INC.

675 Cochrane Dr., Suite 300
Markham, Ontario, L3R 0Y7
Tel: 1-888-222-3559   Fax: N/A

Compaq Recruitment Centre
Internet: www.compaq.ca

Compaq Canada Inc., a wholly-owned subsidiary of Compaq Computer Corporation of Houston, Texas, markets NonStop eBusiness offerings comprised of hardware, software, solutions and services, including industry-leading enterprise computing solutions, fault-tolerant, business-critical solutions, enterprise and network storage products, commercial desktop and portable products, and consumer personal computers. With headquarters and distribution facilities in Richmond Hill, Compaq Canada Inc. has 3,000 employees located in 41 offices across Canada.

Academic Fields
College: Information Systems, Electronics Tech.
Bachelor of Arts: Business, Economics
Bachelor of Comm/Admin: General, Accounting, Finance, Info Mgmt.
Bachelor of Science: Computer Science
Bachelor of Engineering: Computer Syst., Electrical
Chartered Accounting: CGA - General/Finance, CMA - General/Finance
Masters: Business Administration, Engineering

Critical Skills
Adaptable, Analytical, Confident, Creative, Decisive, Dependable, Diligent, Efficient, Enthusiastic, Flexible, Good Communication, Good Writing Skills, Innovative, Leadership

Types of Positions
Desktop Support   Entry Level Sales
Channels Marketing   Finance

Starting Salary
$ 30,000 - 40,000 (depending on position)

Company Benefits
- Flexible Benefits, tuition assistance

Correspondence
Apply through web site

Part Time/Summer: Compaq Canada Inc. rarely hires for part time work and occasionally hires for the summer. The best time to apply is in April and May.

The Canada Student Employment Guide

COMPU-QUOTE INC.

4510 Rhodes Dr., Bldg 400
Windsor, Ontario, N8W 5C2
Tel: (519) 974-8111   Fax: (519) 974-7290

Dale Maria, HR Administration

Compu-Quote is a software development company. They provide solutions for firms within the insurance industry.

Academic Fields
College: Accounting, Computer Science, Insurance, Marketing/Sales, Secretarial
Bachelor of Arts: General, Business
Bachelor of Comm/Admin: Marketing
Bachelor of Science: Computer Science, Mathematics
Bachelor of Engineering: Computer Systems
Masters: Business Administration

Critical Skills
Analytical, Confident, Efficient, Enthusiastic, Flexible, Good Communication, Good Writing Skills, Productive, Professional

Types of Positions
Production Clerk   Insurance Services Clerk
Junior Programmer

Starting Salary
$ 20,000 - 30,000

Company Benefits
- Competitive benefit package

Correspondence
Fax resume with cover letter

Part Time/Summer: Compu-Quote occasionally seeks candidates for part time employment and regularly looks for individuals for the summer months. Potential jobs include data entry clerk, production clerk, or junior programmer.

COMPUTALOG LTD.

4200, 150 - 6th Avenue S.W.
Calgary, Alberta, T2P 3Y7
Tel: (403) 265-6060   Fax: (403) 218-2424

Theresa Black, Human Resources
Internet: www.computalog.com

The business of Computalog is to supply directional and horizontal drilling services, provide wireline logging and completion services, and develop and manufacture wireline logging tools and surface computer systems for internal use and in certain instances, resale. Computalog has the second largest share of the wireless services market in Canada, and a growing market share in the United States and Venezuela.

Academic Fields
College: Accounting, Computer Science, Electronics Tech., Engineering Tech., Human Resources, Mechanical Tech., Petroleum Technology
Bachelor of Comm/Admin: Accounting, Finance
Bachelor of Science: Computer Science
Bachelor of Engineering: Chemical, Computer Systems, Electrical, Mechanical, Geological
Chartered Accounting: CMA-Finance, CGA-Finance
Masters: Engineering

Critical Skills
Adaptable, Analytical, Confident, Decisive, Dependable, Enthusiastic, Flexible, Good Communication, Innovative, Leadership, Logical, Organized, Personable, Productive, Professional, Responsible

Types of Positions
Engineer   Accountant
Electronic Technologist   Programmer

Starting Salary
$ 25,000 - 30,000 Bonus payable to certain positions

Company Benefits
- Extended health care, life insurance, group RRSP
- Long term disability, tuition refund
- On the job training, plus classroom programs

Correspondence
Mail resume with cover letter
E-mail: resumes@computalog.com

Part Time/Summer: Computalog occasionally hires for part time and summer jobs, however, maximum ever hired is two or three individuals.

The Canada Student Employment Guide

COMPUTER ASSOCIATES CANADA LTD.

5935 Airport Rd., Suite 115
Mississauga, Ontario, L4V 1W5
Tel: (905) 676-6700   Fax: (905) 676-6734

Human Resources
Internet: www.cai.com

Computer Associates International, Inc. the world's leading business software company, delivers the end-to-end infrastructure to enable eBusiness through innovative technology, services and education. Computer Associates has 20,000 employees worldwide and had revenue of over $6 billion for the fiscal year ended March 31, 2000.

Academic Fields
College: Accounting, Administration, Business, Human Resources
Bachelor of Arts: General, Business, Economics, Political Science, Psychology, Sociology/Social Work
Bachelor of Comm/Admin: General, Accounting, Finance, Marketing
Bachelor of Science: Computer Science
Bachelor of Engineering: Electrical
Bachelor of Education: General
Chartered Accounting: CA-Finance, CMA - General/Finance, CGA - General/Finance
Masters: Business Administration, Arts

Critical Skills
Good Communication, Dependable, Enthusiastic, Flexible, Personable, Professional, Responsible, Good Writing Skills

Types of Positions
Client Base Administrator
Administrative Assistant
Marketing Events Co-ordinator

Starting Salary
$ 20,000 - 25,000

Company Benefits
- Standard benefits
- On-the-job training

Correspondence
Fax resume with cover letter

Part Time/Summer: Computer Associates Canada does not hire individuals for part time work, or summer employment.

COMSTOCK CANADA

3455 Landmark Rd.
Burlington, Ontario, L7M 1T4
Tel: (905) 335-3333   Fax: (905) 335-4265

Denis Flynn, Vice President

Comstock Canada is involved in mechanical and electrical construction in Canada. Their company's head office is in Burlington, Ontario.

Academic Fields
College: Engineering Tech., Law Clerk, Secretarial
Bachelor of Engineering: Electrical, Mechanical

Critical Skills
Dependable, Diligent, Good Writing Skills, Logical, Organized, Productive, Responsible

Types of Positions
Accounting Clerk   Project Administration
Secretary   Junior Estimator
Switch Board / Reception

Starting Salary
$ 30,000 - 40,000

Company Benefits
- All company paid comprehensive health care benefits after 6 months
- Company paid RSP
- Extensive investment in training

Correspondence
Fax resume with cover letter

Part Time/Summer: Comstock Canada occasionally looks for individuals for part time or summer employment. Potential positions are most likely those listed above. The best time to apply is in March.

The Canada Student Employment Guide

COMTRONIC COMPUTER INC.

83 Commerce Valley Dr. E.
Thornhill, Ontario, L3T 7T3
Tel: (905) 881-3606   Fax: (905) 881-6893

Patricia Ardianto, Human Resources
Internet: www.comtronic.ca

Comtronic, established in 1987, has grown to be one of Canada's leading computer distributors. Comtronic is a privately held national distributor of brand name and OEM computer systems, peripherals, key components with full integration services and technical support. Comtronic is Canada's largest Acer and AOpen distribution.

Academic Fields
College: General, Accounting, Computer Science
Bachelor of Arts: General
Bachelor of Comm/Admin: Accounting, Marketing
Bachelor of Science: Computer Science
Masters: Science, Engineering

Critical Skills
Adaptable, Good Communication, Confident, Dependable, Efficient, Enthusiastic, Flexible, Good With Figures, Organized, Patient, Persuasive, Productive, Professional, Good Writing Skills

Types of Positions
Sales Executive   Account Executive
Technical Support

Starting Salary
below $ 20,000 - 25,000

Company Benefits
- Basic health and dental coverage
- In-house training

Correspondence
Mail or submit resume and cover letter in person

Part Time/Summer: Comtronic Computer Inc. does not generally hire individuals for part time or summer positions.

CONAIR AVIATION LTD.

P.O. Box 220
Abbotsford, British Columbia, V2S 4N9
Tel: (604) 855-1171   Fax: (604) 855-6649

Cindy Braslins, Human Resources
Internet: www.conair.ca

Conair Aviation is a specialty aviation firm involved with operations, maintenance, and the aerospace industry. The company works with fixed and rotary wings.

Academic Fields
College: Accounting, Computer Science, Mechanical Tech.
Bachelor of Comm/Admin: Accounting, Marketing, Info Mgmt.
Bachelor of Science: Computer Science
Bachelor of Engineering: Electrical, Mechanical

Critical Skills
Adaptable, Analytical, Enthusiastic, Flexible, Good Communication, Good Writing Skills, Manual Dexterity, Organized, Personable, Productive, Professional, Responsible

Types of Positions
Apprentice Aircraft Mechanic   Apprentice Structures Technician

Starting Salary
below $ 20,000 - 25,000 (depending on position)

Company Benefits
- Full range of benefits
- Healthcare, insurance, pension
- Technical and development training

Correspondence
Mail or fax resume with cover letter
E-mail: work@conair.ca

Part Time/Summer: Conair Aviation rarely seeks candidates for part time or summer employment. The best time to apply is in early Spring.

CONNORS BROS, LIMITED

669 Main St.
Blacks Harbour, New Brunswick, E5H 1K1
Tel: (506) 456-3391   Fax: (506) 456-1569

Alaina Pollock, Recruitment Supervisor

Connors Bros, Limited is a group of companies with over 100 years experience in the production, sales, and marketing of premium quality seafood.

Academic Fields
College: Accounting, Admin., Business, Human Res., Info Syst., Marketing/Sales, Purchasing, Secretarial, Automotive Maintenance, CAD Autocad, Computer Sci., Engineering Tech., Industrial Design, Mech. Tech.
Bachelor of Arts: Business
Bachelor of Comm/Admin: Accounting, Finance, Human Resources, Marketing, Info Mgmt.
Bachelor of Science: Agriculture, Aquaculture, Biology, Computer Science, Food Sciences, Microbiology
Bachelor of Engineering: General, Civil, Computer Systems, Design, Electrical, Industrial, Mechanical
Chartered Accounting: CA - General/Finance, CGA - General/Finance, CMA - General/Finance
Masters: Business Administration

Critical Skills
Adaptable, Dependable, Efficient, Flexible, Innovative, Productive, Responsible

Types of Positions
Accounting   Clerical
Production Facilities   Information Technology
Sales   Aquaculture

Starting Salary
$ 20,000 - 25,000 (depending on position)

Company Benefits
- Offers Blue Cross health care, pension plan
- Training and development opportunities

Correspondence
Fax resume with cover letter. E-mail: cbl2@clb.weston.ca

Part Time/Summer: Connors Bros, Limited occasionally hires for part time work and regularly hires for the summer. The majority of summer jobs are available in their production facilities (both salmon and sardine). There are limited positions available in their administrative team which is reserved for those students who exemplify great ambition in their field of study. Applications should be sent in April and May.

CO-OP ATLANTIC

123 Halifax Street, P.O. Box 750
Moncton, New Brunswick, E1C 8N5
Tel: (506) 858-6028   Fax: (506) 858-6473

Angela Vautour, HR Area Manager

Co-op Atlantic is a regional co-operative wholesaler and supplier of farm inputs, providing services and products to its member-owned co-ops in the Atlantic provinces and the Magdalen Islands. Co-op Atlantic employs over 600 people. All career opportunities are posted internally first.

Academic Fields
College: Accounting, Advertising, Business, Communications, Computer Science, Drafting/Architecture, Engineering Tech., Graphic Arts, Human Res., Journalism, Lab. Tech., Secretarial
Bachelor of Arts: Journalism, Public Relations
Bachelor of Comm/Admin: General, Accounting, Finance, Marketing, Info Mgmt.
Bachelor of Science: Agriculture, Computer Science, Environmental Studies, Horticulture, Mathematics, Psychology
Bachelor of Education: Adult Education
Chartered Accounting: CA - General/Finance, CGA/CMA - General/Finance
Masters: Business Administration

Critical Skills
Adaptable, Analytical, Creative, Dependable, Efficient, Flexible, Good Communication, Good With Figures, Good Writing Skills, Organized, Personable

Types of Positions
Administrative Support   Computer Programmer
Analyst Trainee

Starting Salary
$ 20,000 - 25,000

Company Benefits
- Full benefits including pension plan and medical
- Job related training, continuous prof. development

Correspondence
Mail resume with cover letter

Part Time/Summer: Co-op Atlantic sometimes seeks candidates for part time and summer work. Hiring is done mainly for positions such as warehouse person. The best time to apply is in March or April.

COPPLEY APPAREL GROUP

56 York Blvd., P.O. Box 2024
Hamilton, Ontario, L8N 3S6
Tel: (905) 529-1112   Fax: (905) 529-9304

Norma Coe, HR Manager
Internet: www.coppley.com

Coppley Apparel Group is a world leader in the men's apparel industry. They are a manufacturer of men's fine apparel, specifically suits, sportcoats, jackets and trousers. Their products are distributed to over 1,200 retailers across Canada and the U.S. They are a world leader in the men's apparel industry by combining old world tailoring skills with modern technology. Their brands include Warren K. Cook, Cambridge, Matteo Maas, Alan Flusser, Hardy Amies, and Keithmoor. They employ approximately 600 individuals.

Academic Fields
College: Accounting, Administration, Human Resources, Marketing/Sales, Secretarial
Bachelor of Comm/Admin: General, Accounting, Finance, Human Resources, Marketing
Bachelor of Engineering: Industrial

Critical Skills
Analytical, Decisive, Dependable, Efficient, Good Communication, Good With Figures, Manual Dexterity, Organized, Productive, Professional, Responsible

Types of Positions
Finance   Customer Service
Human Resources   Administration

Starting Salary
Depends on position

Company Benefits
- Medical and dental benefits
- Policy of looking within the organization first when new positions become available
- Encourage continued development through education, seminars and training

Correspondence
Mail, fax resume with cover letter or submit in person.

Part Time/Summer: Coppley Apparel Group rarely hires for part time work, but regularly hires for the summer months. Potential jobs involve inventory, or being a department clerk. The best time to apply is in March or April.

CITY OF COQUITLAM

3000 Guildford Way
Coquitlam, British Columbia, V3B 7N2
Tel: (604) 927-3072   Fax: (604) 927-3075

Human Resources Advisor

The City of Coquitlam is a municipal government in British Columbia. They employ 1,200 individuals.

Academic Fields
College: Legal Asst., Rec. Studies, Security/Law Enforcement, Social Work, Urban Planning, Acctg, Admin., Advertising, Business, Communications, Human Res., Info Syst., Purchasing, Secretarial, Stats, Auto Maintenance, CAD Autocad, Computer Sci., Elec. Tech., Engineering Tech., Forestry, Science, Industrial Design, Mech. Tech., Plumbing, Welding
Bachelor of Arts: Business, Economics, English, Gerontology, Journalism, Public Relations, Sociology/Social Work, Statistics, Urban Geography
Bachelor of Comm/Admin: General, Acctg, Finance, Human Res., Marketing, Info Mgmt., Public Admin.
Bachelor of Science: Computer Science, Environmental Studies, Forestry, Geography
Bachelor of Laws: General, Corporate, Real Estate
Bachelor of Engineering: General, Civil, Computer Systems, Design, Environ. Studies, Geotechnical, Industrial, Mechanical, Transportation, Water Res., Bach. of Architecture, Bach. of Landscape Architecture
Chartered Accounting: CA, CGA, CMA
Masters: Business Admin., Engineering, Library Sci.

Critical Skills
Adaptable, Dependable, Diligent, Diplomatic, Efficient, Enthusiastic, Good Communication, Flexible, Innovative, Leadership, Logical, Organized

Types of Positions
Entry Positions in all Departments

Starting Salary
$ 30,000 - 35,000

Company Benefits
- Competitive benefit package

Correspondence
Mail or fax resume with cover letter

Part Time/Summer: They occasionally hire for part time work, and regularly hire in the summer. Potential jobs are in parks and recreation, engineering, or admin. The best time to apply is in February.

COREL CORPORATION

1600 Carling Ave.
Ottawa, Ontario, K1Z 8R7
Tel: (613) 728-8200   Fax: (613) 761-1146

Tiffanie Jennings, Recruitment Specialist
Internet: www.corel.com

Corel Corporation is an internationally recognized developer of award-winning graphics and business productivity applications. Development of market-leading products such as CorelDRAW line of graphics applications and the Corel WordPerfect Suite of business tools is continually evolving to meet the demands of the corporate, retail and academic markets. They employ approximately 950 individuals.

Academic Fields
College: Computer Science
Bachelor of Comm/Admin: Marketing
Bachelor of Engineering: Computer Systems
Masters: Science, Engineering

Critical Skills
Adaptable, Enthusiastic, Good Communication, Innovative

Types of Positions
Software Developer   Quality Assurance Specialist
Technical Writer

Starting Salary
$ 40,000 - 45,000

Company Benefits
- Medical, dental, vision and alternative health care plans
- Life insurance, disability leaves, employee assistance plan
- Fitness incentive plan, course and seminar reimbursement

Correspondence
Apply through their web site. E-mail: hr@corel.ca

Part Time/Summer: Corel Corporation rarely seeks individuals for part time work, but occasionally hires for the summer months. Potential jobs include software developer, quality assurance specialist, and administrative assistant. The best time to apply is in April.

Co-op/Internship: Interns and co-op students are hired every work term. They typically go through colleges and universities.

CITY OF CORNER BROOK

P.O. Box 1080
Corner Brook, Newfoundland, A2H 6E1
Tel: (709) 637-1563   Fax: (709) 637-1625

Stephen Colbourne, Human Resources Officer

The City of Corner Brook is a municipal government in Newfoundland. There are about 250 employees working for The City of Corner Brook.

Academic Fields
College: Accounting, Administration, Advertising, Business, Computer Science, Drafting/Architecture, Human Resources, Industrial Design, Marketing/Sales, Mechanical Tech., Recreation Studies, Security/Law, Statistics, Travel/Tourism, Urban Planning
Bachelor of Arts: General, Business, Economics, Languages, Public Relations, Recreation Studies, Statistics, Urban Geography
Bachelor of Comm/Admin: General, Accounting, Finance, Marketing, Info Mgmt., Public Admin.
Bachelor of Engineering: General, Civil, Design, Environmental Studies, Transportation, Water Resources, Bachelor of Landscape Architecture
Chartered Accounting: CA - General/Finance
Masters: Business Administration, Engineering

Critical Skills
Adaptable, Analytical, Confident, Diligent, Good Communication, Creative, Dependable, Enthusiastic, Good With Figures, Good Writing Skills, Leadership, Organized, Personable, Professional

Types of Positions
Secretarial   Engineering Technician
Environmental   Labourer

Starting Salary
$ 30,000 - 40,000

Company Benefits
- Life insurance, vacation, pension fund
- Medical and dental insurance

Correspondence
Mail resume with cover letter

Part Time/Summer: The City of Corner Brook regularly hires for part time and summer employees. Potential jobs are in research, environmental technology, recreation, surveying, drafting or clerical work. The best time to apply is in April or May.

CORNWALL ELECTRIC

P.O. Box 1179, 1001 Sydney St.
Cornwall, Ontario, K6H 5V3
Tel: (613) 932-0123   Fax: (613) 932-6498

Susan Richardson, Human Resources
Internet: www.cornwallelectric.com

Cornwall Electric is a city owed utility that has served the families and businesses of the Cornwall area for over 110 years.

Academic Fields
College: General, Accounting, Computer Science, Drafting/Architecture, Electronics Tech., Engineering Tech., Human Resources, Secretarial
Bachelor of Arts: Business
Bachelor of Comm/Admin: Accounting, Finance
Bachelor of Science: Computer Science
Bachelor of Engineering: Electrical
Chartered Accounting: CMA-Finance
Masters: Business Administration, Engineering

Critical Skills
Adaptable, Efficient, Enthusiastic, Productive

Types of Positions
Clerk   Switchboard/Typist
Cashier Attendant Draftsperson
Attendant

Starting Salary
$ 25,000 - 30,000

Company Benefits
- Medical and dental, group insurance
- Life insurance, long term disability
- On-the-job training

Correspondence
Mail or fax resume with cover letter

Part Time/Summer: Cornwall Electric occasionally hires for part time work, and regularly looks for people for summer employment. Potential jobs include labour type positions, drafting, computer tech. and programs, as well as general clerical. The best time to apply is in January.

COSMAIR CANADA INC.

3737 Côte Vertu
St Laurent, Québec, H4R 2C9
Tel: (514) 287-4900   Fax: (514) 335-6554

Céline Roberge, Ressources humaines

Cosmair Canada is a subsidiary of L'Oreal S.A., the world's largest developer, producer and marketer of cosmetic products. The diverse social, national and professional backgrounds of the people at Cosmair Canada make it a stimulating place to work. Their head office is in St Laurent, Quebec.

Academic Fields
College: Accounting, Administration, Laboratory Tech., Marketing/Sales
Bachelor of Comm/Admin: General, Accounting, Marketing
Chartered Accounting: CMA-General, CGA-General
Masters: Business Administration

Critical Skills
Analytical, Decisive, Dependable, Efficient, Flexible, Good Communication, Innovative, Leadership, Organized, Professional

Types of Positions
Marketing Assistant   Accounting Clerk

Starting Salary
$ 30,000 - 40,000

Company Benefits
- Medical, dental, and eye care plan
- Retirement package
- Help program for staff

Correspondence
Mail resume with cover letter

Part Time/Summer: Cosmair Canada does not look for individuals for the summer months, but regularly seeks candidates for summer work. Potential jobs in the summer are in the factory and distribution centre on the production line. These jobs only exist in Ville St-Laurent. The best time to apply is in March or April.

The Canada Student Employment Guide

COSYN TECHNOLOGY

101, 9405 - 50 Street
Edmonton, Alberta, T6B 2T4
Tel: (780) 440-7000   Fax: (780) 462-3897

Laura Barr, HR Leader
Internet: www.colteng.com

Cosyn Technology is a Canadian owned company that is a division of Colt Engineering. They provide EPCM (engineering, procurement and construction management) services to Alberta's oilsands industry. They focus on quality and value, and are ISO-9001 certified. The company employs approximately 205 individuals.

Academic Fields
College: Administration, Business, Secretarial, CAD Autocad, Engineering Tech.
Bachelor of Comm/Admin: Human Resources, Marketing
Bachelor of Engineering: Chemical, Civil, Electrical, Mechanical, Mining, Bachelor of Architecture
Chartered Accounting: CGA-General, CMA-General
Masters: Engineering

Critical Skills
Analytical, Enthusiastic, Flexible, Good Communication, Logical

Types of Positions
Co-op Engineering Student   Drafting Technician
Office Services

Starting Salary
$ 35,000 - 40,000

Company Benefits
- Hourly staff does not receive benefits
- Salaried staff have immediate benefits
- Training determined by department head and staff member together

Correspondence
Mail resume with cover letter
E-mail: barr-laura@syncrude.com

Part Time/Summer: Cosyn Technology occasionally hires for part time and summer work. Potential positions include file clerk, reception coverage, or computer systems/network admin. Apply in early April.

Co-op/Internship: Co-op program to students from Alberta universities. They often go on to hire these individuals after graduation.

COTTON GINNY LTD.

40 Samor Road
Toronto, Ontario, M6A 1J6
Tel: (416) 785-9686   Fax: (416) 785-9687

Human Resources
Internet: www.cottonginnyltd.com

Cotton Ginny Limited is a Canadian based, ladies retail chain with over 200 stores located in major shopping centres across Canada. The major divisions of Cotton Ginny Ltd. are Cotton Ginny, Cotton Ginny Plus and Tabi International.

Academic Fields
College: Accounting, Administration, Advertising, Business, Communications, Human Resources, Information Systems, Marketing, Sales, Fashion, Graphic Arts, Computer Science
Bachelor of Arts: General, Business
Bachelor of Comm/Admin: General, Accounting, Finance, Human Resources, Marketing, Info Mgmt.
Bachelor of Science: Computer Science
Chartered Accounting: CA-General, CGA-General/Finance
Masters: Business Administration, Arts

Critical Skills
Adaptable, Confident, Dependable, Good Communication, Efficient, Enthusiastic, Flexible, Good With Figures, Diligent, Responsible, Logical, Personable, Productive, Good Writing Skills

Types of Positions
Store Management & Sales Associate
                            Human Resources Dept.
MIS Dept.   Distribution Centre
Operations Dept.   Design Dept.

Starting Salary
Depends on position

Company Benefits
- Competitive benefits package
- Exceptional clothing discount

Correspondence
Mail resume with cover letter
E-mail: recruiting@cottonginnyltd.com

Part Time/Summer: Cotton Ginny regularly hires for part time and summer opportunities. A potential summer position would be sales associate.

The Canada Student Employment Guide

COUGAR HELICOPTERS INC.

P.O. Box 248
Waverly, Nova Scotia, B0N 2S0
Tel: (902) 873-3611   Fax: (902) 873-3972

Carol Ann Johnston Human Resources Manager
Internet: www.cougar.ca

Cougar Helicopters Inc. is a helicopter charter service that provides support services for transferring crews and personnel to and from oil rigs, forest fire patrol, aerial photography, power line patrol, executive charter, emergency medical service, search and rescue, herbicide spraying, helideck inspections, and third party maintenance. They employ 85 individuals.

Academic Fields
College: Accounting, Admin., Advertising, Business, Communications, Human Resources, Information Syst., Marketing/Sales, Purchasing, Secretarial, Aircraft Maintenance, Computer Science, Engineering Tech.
Bachelor of Arts: Business
Bachelor of Comm/Admin: Accounting, Finance, Human Resources, Marketing, Info Mgmt.
Bachelor of Engineering: Computer Systems, Design, Electrical

Critical Skills
Adaptable, Analytical, Confident, Creative, Decisive, Dependable, Efficient, Enthusiastic, Flexible, Good Communication, Good With Figures, Good Writing Skills, Innovative, Leadership, Logical, Organized, Patient, Personable, Productive, Responsible

Types of Positions
Aircraft Maintenance Apprentice   Entry Level Pilot
Accounts Payable   Secretary/Receptionist

Starting Salary
$ 20,000 - 25,000

Company Benefits
- Full benefits including medical, dental, vision
- Tool allowance, uniform, clothing allowance
- Recurrent training, seminars and conventions

Correspondence
Mail, fax, e-mail resume with cover letter or apply through web site. E-mail: humanresources@cougar.ca

Part Time/Summer: Cougar Helicopters Inc. occasionally hires for part time and summer work. Potential jobs include ground crew, aircraft maintenance apprentice (AME), and pilots. Pilots can apply anytime. Other positions should apply April to May.

CREDIT UNION CENTRAL OF CANADA

2810 Matheson Blvd. East
Mississauga, Ontario, L4W 4X7
Tel: (905) 238-9400   Fax: (905) 238-3414

Heather Hancock, Human Resources Supervisor
Internet: www.cucentral.ca

Credit Union Central of Canada is the national financial intermediary and trade association for the credit union system. Its activities are national in scope and aim to achieve greater integration among the various members of the credit union system. They employ 60 people.

Academic Fields
College: General, Accounting, Administration, Business, Communications, Computer Science, Human Res., Journalism, Marketing/Sales, Secretarial
Bachelor of Arts: General, Business, Economics, English
Bachelor of Comm/Admin: General, Accounting, Finance, Marketing, Info Mgmt., Public Admin.
Bachelor of Science: General, Computer Science
Bachelor of Laws: Corporate
Bachelor of Engineering: General, Computer Syst.
Bachelor of Education: Adult Education
Chartered Accounting: CA - General/Finance, CGA/CMA - General/Finance

Critical Skills
Adaptable, Analytical, Good Communication, Confident, Dependable, Efficient, Enthusiastic, Flexible, Good With Figures, Logical, Manual Dexterity, Organized, Personable, Productive, Professional, Responsible, Good Writing Skills

Types of Positions
Accounting Clerk   Receptionist
Computer Services   Clearing

Starting Salary
$ 20,000 - 25,000

Company Benefits
- Group benefits plan including health and dental
- Internal training (software and customer service)

Correspondence
Mail or fax resume with cover letter

Part Time/Summer: The Credit Union Central of Canada regularly hires for part time and summer work. Apply between the end of February and end of April.

The Canada Student Employment Guide

CRESTAR ENERGY INC.

333 - 7th Ave. SW, P.O. Box 888
Calgary, Alberta, T2P 2Z1
Tel: (403) 231-6700   Fax: (403) 231-6811

Bob Nadon, Human Resources
Internet: www.crestar-energy.com

Crestar Energy Inc. is a senior Canadian exploration and production company with oil and gas operations in Western Canada. Crestar's main producing assets are geographically focused in two core regions of the Western Canadian Sedimentary Basin - a Southern Region and a Western Region.

Academic Fields
College: Accounting, Computer Science, Secretarial
Bachelor of Arts: Economics
Bachelor of Comm/Admin: Accounting, Marketing, Info Mgmt.
Bachelor of Science: Computer Science, Geology
Bachelor of Engineering: Chemical, Civil, Electrical, Geotechnical, Mechanical
Chartered Accounting: CMA-General

Critical Skills
Adaptable, Analytical, Good Communication, Confident, Creative, Decisive, Innovative, Leadership, Organized, Productive, Professional, Good Writing Skills

Types of Positions
Accounting Clerk   File Clerk
Receptionist

Starting Salary
$ 30,000 - 40,000

Company Benefits
- Flexible benefit plan
- Medical, dental, life insurance
- Long term disability, family coverage

Correspondence
Mail or fax resume with cover letter

Part Time/Summer: Crestar Energy occasionally looks for people for part time work, and regularly seeks applicants for the summer. Potential opportunities are field operators for engineering students, or accounting clerks.

CULINAR INC.

380, rue Notre-Dame Nord
Ste-Marie de Beauce, Québec, G5E 3B3
Tel: (418) 387-5421   Fax: (418) 387-4746

Ressources humaines

Culinar has its head office in Montreal and comprises three divisions. Canadian operations are under the Vachon Division and the Grocery Division. Culinar is a private company with nearly 36,000 points of sale. They employ 2,200 people.

Academic Fields
College: General, Accounting, Administration, Business, Communications, Computer Science, Engineering Tech., Food/Nutrition, Human Resources, Laboratory Tech., Marketing/Sales, Secretarial
Bachelor of Arts: General, Business, Public Relations
Bachelor of Comm/Admin: General, Accounting, Finance, Marketing, Info Mgmt., Public Admin.
Bachelor of Science: Chemistry, Computer Science, Food Sciences
Bachelor of Engineering: General, Electrical, Industrial, Mechanical
Chartered Accounting: CA - General/Finance, CMA-General CGA-General
Masters: Business Administration

Critical Skills
Adaptable, Dependable, Efficient, Enthusiastic, Flexible, Good Communication, Innovative, Leadership, Productive, Professional, Responsible

Types of Positions
Secretary   Human Resources
Marketing & Sales   Logistics
Information Management   Product Development

Starting Salary
$ 20,000 - 25,000

Company Benefits
- Range of fringe benefits
- Employee assistance program

Correspondence
Mail resume with cover letter

Part Time/Summer: Culinar occasionally hires for part time and summer work. Potential positions are most likely those listed above. Apply in April.

CUSTOM TRIM LTD.

550 Parkside Dr., Unit A12
Waterloo, Ontario, N2L 5V4
Tel: (519) 576-3000   Fax: (519) 576-0204

Mary Houle, Human Resources

Custom Trim Ltd. is an auto parts manufacturer. The company has an employee base of about 1,400 individuals.

Academic Fields
College: Accounting, Computer Science, Drafting/Architecture, Engineering Tech., Human Resources, Mechanical Tech., Nursing, Secretarial
Bachelor of Arts: Business
Bachelor of Comm/Admin: Accounting, Finance
Bachelor of Science: Nursing (RN)
Bachelor of Engineering: Design, Industrial, Mechanical
Chartered Accounting: CA - General/Finance, CGA/CMA - General/Finance

Critical Skills
Adaptable, Good Communication, Dependable, Efficient, Enthusiastic, Flexible, Organized, Personable, Productive, Responsible, Good Writing Skills

Types of Positions
Engineering Assistant   CAD Technician

Starting Salary
$ 25,000 - 30,000

Company Benefits
- Extended health, basic dental
- Short and long term disability, life insurance

Correspondence
Mail or fax resume with cover letter

Part Time/Summer: Custom Trim occasionally looks for people for part time positions, and summer employment. Potential work involves engineering or secretarial or clerical duties.

D.A. STUART INC.

43 Upton Road
Scarborough, Ontario, M1L 2C1
Tel: (416) 757-3226   Fax: (416) 757-3220

Human Resources Department
Internet: www.dastuart.com/

D.A. Stuart manufactures high-quality soluble oils, straight oils, rolling oils, semi-synthetic fluids, biostatic fluids, synthetic fluids, unique additives, as well as in-process and production cleaners. They also supply filter media and biocides to work with our fluids.

Academic Fields
College: General, Accounting, Business, Communications, Computer Science, Engineering Tech., Human Resources, Laboratory Tech., Mechanical Tech., Science-General, Secretarial
Bachelor of Comm/Admin: Accounting, Finance, Info Mgmt.
Bachelor of Science: General, Biology, Chemistry, Computer Science, Environmental Studies
Bachelor of Engineering: Chemical, Industrial, Mechanical, Mining
Chartered Accounting: CA-General, CMA-General, CGA-General
Masters: Science, Engineering

Critical Skills
Adaptable, Confident, Dependable, Diligent, Diplomatic, Efficient, Enthusiastic, Flexible, Good Writing Skills, Organized, Patient, Personable, Productive, Professional, Responsible

Types of Positions
Reception   Lab Technician
Labourer

Starting Salary
$ 25,000 - 30,000

Company Benefits
- Medical and dental benefits
- Life insurance, short and long term disability

Correspondence
Mail resume with cover letter

Part Time/Summer: D.A. Stuart occasionally seeks individuals for part time work, and regularly looks for candidates for summer employment. Summer jobs entail working in the plant.

D.H. HOWDEN

P.O. Box 5485
London, Ontario, N6A 4G8
Tel: (519) 686-2200   Fax: (519) 686-2333

Marc Fraser, Human Resources

D.H. Howden is a wholesale hardware supplier. The company's head office is located in London, Ontario.

Academic Fields
College: General, Accounting, Administration, Computer Science, Drafting/Architecture
Bachelor of Arts: General, Business
Chartered Accounting: CA-General

Critical Skills
Adaptable, Dependable, Efficient, Flexible, Good Communication, Organized, Personable, Productive, Professional

Types of Positions
Accounting   Retail Design

Starting Salary
$ 20,000 - 25,000

Company Benefits
- Benefits are industry standard

Correspondence
Mail or fax resume with cover letter

Part Time/Summer: D.H. Howden regularly looks for candidates for part time and summer employment. The best time to apply is in March.

DAIMLERCHRYSLER CANADA LTD.

P.O. Box 1621
Windsor, Ontario, N9A 4H6
Tel: (519) 973-2000   Fax: (519) 561-7043

Salary Employment
Internet: www.daimlerchrysler.ca

DaimlerChrysler Canada manufactures and distributes cars, light duty trucks, and component parts in Canada, the United States and abroad. Plants are located in Windsor and Brampton, Ontario, while sales and service depots are located throughout the country. The company employs about 18,000 people in hourly and salary positions.

Academic Fields
College: Accounting, Administration, Business, Communications, Human Resources, Information Systems, Marketing/Sales, Automotive Maintenance, Computer Science, Electronics Tech., Engineering Tech., Plumbing, Welding, Security/Law Enforcement
Bachelor of Science: Computer Science, Environmental Studies, Nursing (RN)
Bachelor of Laws: General, Corporate
Bachelor of Engineering: General, Chemical, Civil, Electrical, Environmental Studies, Industrial
Chartered Accounting: CA-General
Masters: Business Administration, Engineering

Critical Skills
Adaptable, Analytical, Decisive, Dependable, Efficient, Flexible, Good Communication, Good Writing Skills, Innovative, Leadership, Organized, Productive, Professional, Team Oriented, Mobile

Types of Positions
Human Resources   Finance
Sales/Marketing   Manufacturing

Starting Salary
$ 45,000 - 52,000

Company Benefits
- Health, life insurance and disability after 3 months
- Dental, vision and hearing coverage after 1 year

Correspondence
Mail resume with cover letter, or through web site

Part Time/Summer: DaimlerChrysler Canada sometimes hires for part time and summer positions. Potential jobs include customer service coordinator, engineer in manufacturing, or production work. The best time to apply is in April.

The Canada Student Employment Guide

DANA CORPORATION - LONG MANUFACTURING

656 Kerr St.
Oakville, Ontario, L7K 3E4
Tel: (905) 849-1200   Fax: (905) 849-5862

Tracy Thomson, Human Resources Manager
Internet: www.longmfg.com

Dana Corporation - Long Manufacturing is a manufacturer of heat exchangers for the automotive industry including oil coolers and engine coolers. They request no phone calls please.

Academic Fields
College: Accounting, Administration, Business, Engineering Tech.
Bachelor of Comm/Admin: Accounting
Bachelor of Engineering: Chemical, Mechanical
Masters: Engineering

Critical Skills
Adaptable, Dependable, Enthusiastic, Flexible, Good Communication, Personable, Professional

Types of Positions
Jr. Engineering Technologist   Jr. Engineer
Accounts Payable   Receivables Clerk

Starting Salary
$ 25,000 - 30,000 (clerical/tech.), $ 30,000 - 40,000 (engineering)

Company Benefits
- Full medical, dental, life and disability, pension plan
- Tuition reimbursement plan
- Internal and external training courses

Correspondence
Mail, fax or e-mail resume with cover letter
E-mail: tracy.thomson@longmfg.com

Part Time/Summer: Dana Corporation - Long Manufacturing occasionally hires for part time and summer employment. Potential jobs are in production, or general help in the office or plant. The best time to apply is in March or April.

DAVID THOMPSON HEALTH REGION

3942 - 50A Ave.
Red Deer, Alberta, T4N 4E7
Tel: (403) 343-4857   Fax: (403) 343-4807

Lynette Grose, Human Resources
Internet: www.dthr.ab.ca

The David Thompson Health Region has eight acute care facilities, twelve community health centres, and fourteen long term care facilities. They offer health services to over 193,000 residents in Central Alberta.

Academic Fields
College: Accounting, Admin., Business, Communications, Computer Sci., Engineering Tech., Faculty Mgmt., Food/Nutrition, Graphic Arts, Human Res., Lab. Tech., Nursing, Orthotics/Prosthetics, Radiology Tech., Recreation Studies, Secretarial, Stats
Bachelor of Arts: Business, Gerontology, Psychology, Public Rel., Rec. Studies, Sociology/Social Work, Stats
Bachelor of Comm/Admin: General, Accounting, Finance, Human Res., Info Mgmt., Public Admin.
Bachelor of Science: Biology, Chemistry, Food Sciences, Kinesiology, Microbiology, Nursing (RN), Occup. Therapy, Pharmacy, Physio., Psychology
Bachelor of Engineering: Computer Systems
Masters: Business Administration, Science

Critical Skills
Adaptable, Dependable, Diligent, Diplomatic, Efficient, Enthusiastic, Flexible, Good Communication, Good With Figures, Good Writing Skills, Leadership, Organized, Patient, Personable, Productive

Types of Positions
Food Service Aide   Porter
Office Assistant / Clerical   Aide/Attendant

Starting Salary
$ 30,000 - 40,000

Company Benefits
- Extended health care, dental, pension plan

Correspondence
Mail resume with cover letter

Part Time/Summer: They regularly hires for part time or summer work. Potential summer jobs include office assistant, technical assistant, or unit assistant. The best time to apply is from February to May.

Co-op/Internship: Preceptorships available through nursing schools

---

The Canada Student Employment Guide

DDM PLASTICS INC.

P.O. Box 574, 50 Clearview Dr.
Tillsonburg, Ontario, N4G 4J1
Tel: (519) 688-1060   Fax: (519) 688-0970

Rita Scott, Human Resources Manager
Internet: www.ddmplastics.on.ca

DDM Plastics is an injection moulding auto parts company. They specialize in bumpers, grills and wheel caps. They have a state-of-the-art robotic paint lines. Their main market is the North American auto industry.

Academic Fields
College: Accounting, Information Systems, Purchasing, Industrial Design, Mechanical Tech.
Bachelor of Comm/Admin: Accounting, Finance, Human Resources, Info Mgmt.
Bachelor of Science: Chemistry
Bachelor of Engineering: Chemical, Civil, Industrial, Mechanical

Critical Skills
Adaptable, Confident, Dependable, Diligent, Diplomatic, Good Communication, Good Writing Skills, Organized, Professional

Types of Positions
Accounting Clerk   Paint Process Technician
HR Administrator   PC Support Tech.
Receptionist

Starting Salary
$ 25,000 - 40,000

Company Benefits
- Health benefit plan, pension
- Educational assistance program

Correspondence
Mail, fax resume with cover letter, or apply through web site

Part Time/Summer: DDM Plastics rarely looks for people for part time work and occasionally hires for summer jobs. Potential opportunities include general labour production, project work or vacation relief. Co-op students are hired for the information systems dept., engineering dept., and quality dept. The best time to apply is in May or June.

DEER LODGE CENTRE INC.

2109 Portage Avenue
Winnipeg, Manitoba, R3J 0L3
Tel: (204) 831-2105   Fax: (204) 896-6509

Sandy McIvor, Staffing Officer

Deer Lodge Centre is a large 495 bed assessment and rehabilitation, chronic and personal care facility. Providing expanded out-reach services through its Day Hospital, psychogeriatric program, physiotherapy, occupational therapy and speech language pathology departments.

Academic Fields
College: Recreation Studies, Social Work, Accounting, Administration, Human Resources, Information Systems, Electronics Tech., Plumbing, Home Care, Nursing (RN/RNA), Respiratory Tech.
Bachelor of Arts: Sociology/Social Work
Bachelor of Comm/Admin: Accounting, Finance, Human Resources, Info Mgmt., Public Admin.
Bachelor of Science: Computer Sciences, Nursing (RN), Occup. Therapy, Pharmacy, Physiotherapy
Bachelor of Education: General
Chartered Accounting: CA, CGA, CMA
Masters: Business Administration, Education, Library Science, Nursing

Critical Skills
Adaptable, Dependable, Diligent, Diplomatic, Efficient, Enthusiastic, Flexible, Good Communication, Patient, Professional, Responsible

Types of Positions
Dietary Aide   Housekeeping Aide
Clerk/Typist I

Starting Salary
$ 15,000 - 20,000

Company Benefits
- Full scope of benefits

Correspondence
Mail, fax, e-mail or submit resume with cover letter in person

Part Time/Summer: Deer Lodge Centre regularly hires for part time and summer positions. Positions usually involve dietary or housekeeping duties. The best time to apply is in April.

DEGUSSA - HULS CANADA INC.

235 Orenda Rd.
Brampton, Ontario, L6T 1E6
Tel: (905) 451-3810   Fax: (905) 451-4469

Human Resources Department
Internet: www.degussa-huls.com

Degussa-Hüls Corporation is a wholly-owned subsidiary of Degussa-Hüls AG. Its parent company, located in Frankfurt, Germany, has a 125-year history of providing superior products in the European marketplace. Today, Degussa-Hüls AG and its affiliates employ over 44,000 on five continents and have worldwide annual sales of approximately $10 billion.

Academic Fields
College: General, Accounting, Administration, Business, Human Resources, Laboratory Tech., Marketing/Sales, Science-General
Bachelor of Comm/Admin: General, Accounting
Bachelor of Science: Chemistry
Bachelor of Engineering: Chemical
Masters: Business Administration, Science

Critical Skills
Good Communication, Confident, Flexible, Logical, Personable, Good Writing Skills

Types of Positions
Lab Technician   Administration

Starting Salary
$ 25,000 - 40,000

Company Benefits
- Full benefits
- Life, medical, dental, vision
- Short and long term disability

Correspondence
Mail resume with cover letter

Part Time/Summer: Degussa - Huls Canada Inc. does not hire individuals for part time work, but occasionally looks for people for the summer months. A potential job in the summer is lab technician.

DELL COMPUTER CORPORATION

155 Gordon Baker Rd., Suite 501
North York, Ontario, M2H 3N5
Tel: (416) 758-2100   Fax: (416) 758-2302

Human Resources Department
Internet: www.dell.ca

Dell Canada, one of Canada's fastest growing vendors of PCs, notebooks, workstations and enterprise products, is a premier supplier to major Canadian corporations, educational institutions and governments, as well as small and medium businesses and customers. Dell Canada employs over 460 people in its North York, Ontario headquarters and sales offices in Halifax, Montreal, Ottawa and Vancouver.

Academic Fields
College: Accounting, Computer Science, Electronics Tech., Human Resources, Marketing/Sales
Bachelor of Arts: Business, Languages (French)
Bachelor of Comm/Admin: General, Accounting, Finance, Marketing, Info Mgmt.
Bachelor of Science: Computer Science
Chartered Accounting: CA-General, CMA-General/Finance

Critical Skills
Adaptable, Analytical, Dependable, Good Writing Skills, Efficient, Enthusiastic, Flexible, Good Communication, Diligent, Organized, Professional, Personable, PC Literate, Technology Minded

Types of Positions
Sales   Accounting
Administration   Quality Assurance

Starting Salary
$ 20,000 - 30,000

Company Benefits
- An extensive benefits package is offered

Correspondence
Mail or fax resume with cover letter

Part Time/Summer: Dell Computer Corporation sometimes hires individuals for part time openings and regularly hires to fill summer opportunities. Some potential summer jobs are in administration and finance, or include the positions of sales assistant, or departmental assistant.

DELPHI SOLUTIONS INC.

7550 Birchmount Road
Markham, Ontario, L3R 6C6
Tel: (905) 513-4600   Fax: (905) 513-4714

Human Resources

Delphi Solutions Inc. is involved in the business of telecommunications equipment. The company deals with the sale and service of business phone systems with peripherals such as voice mail, among other features.

Academic Fields
College: Accounting, Administration, Business, Communications, Electronics Tech., Human Resources, Marketing/Sales, Secretarial
Bachelor of Comm/Admin: Accounting, Finance, Info Mgmt.
Bachelor of Engineering: Electrical
Chartered Accounting: CMA-Finance, CGA-Finance
Masters: Business Administration, Engineering

Critical Skills
Adaptable, Analytical, Good Communication, Confident, Decisive, Dependable, Diplomatic, Efficient, Flexible, Leadership, Organized, Patient, Personable, Productive, Professional, Responsible, Good Writing Skills

Types of Positions
Reception   Accounting Clerk
Customer Service Clerk

Starting Salary
$ 25,000 - 30,000

Company Benefits
- Standard benefit package
- In-house and on-the-job training depending on position

Correspondence
Mail resume with cover letter
E-mail: dhr@delphisolutions.com

Part Time/Summer: Delphi Solutions occasionally looks for candidates for part time and summer employment. Potential jobs in the summer most likely entail clerical work to fill in for those vacationing. The best time to apply is in early July.

DELTA HOTELS

350 Bloor Street East, Suite 300
Toronto, Ontario, M4W 1H4
Tel: (416) 926-7800   Fax: (416) 926-7875

Merideth Macfarlane, People Resources Coordinator
Internet: www.deltahotels.com

Delta Hotels manages and franchises a diverse portfolio of urban, airport and resort properties in Canada. Delta hotels are located in most of Canada's primary and secondary cities and excel at servicing the small and medium sized meetings market. Delta Hotels compete in the first class segment of the Canadian hotel market. Candidates should apply directly to individual hotels.

Academic Fields
College: Business, Child Care, Cooking/Culinary, Engineering Tech., Hospitality, Human Resources, Marketing/Sales, Travel/Tourism
Bachelor of Arts: Public Relations
Bachelor of Comm/Admin: Accounting, Finance, Info Mgmt.
Bachelor of Engineering: Electrical, Mechanical
Chartered Accounting: CA - General/Finance, CGA/CMA - General/Finance

Critical Skills
Decisive, Dependable, Efficient, Enthusiastic, Flexible, Good Communication, Organized, Patient, Personable, Professional, Responsible

Types of Positions
Guest Service Agent   Bell Person
Food and Beverage Server   Room Attendant

Starting Salary
$ 20,000 - 25,000

Company Benefits
- Benefits only to full time employees
- One training opportunity per employee per year
- Tuition reimbursement for career related courses

Correspondence
Mail resume with cover letter

Part Time/Summer: Delta Hotels & Resorts occasionally looks for candidates for part time and summer employment opportunities. Potential jobs include entry-level front desk positions, plus food and beverage positions involving the restaurant, room service, or the lounge.

DELTA TORONTO AIRPORT HOTEL

801 Dixon Rd.
Etobicoke, Ontario, M9W 1J5
Tel: (416) 675-6100   Fax: (416) 675-4022

Julie Smith, Director, People Resources

Delta Toronto Airport Hotel is a full service hotel operated under Delta Hotel & Resorts. It contains 250 bedrooms to meet customer demand.

Academic Fields
College: Accounting, Administration, Hospitality, Human Resources
Bachelor of Arts: General, Business
Bachelor of Comm/Admin: General, Accounting
Chartered Accounting: CA - General/Finance, CGA/CMA - General/Finance

Critical Skills
Good Communication, Decisive, Dependable, Efficient, Enthusiastic, Flexible, Organized, Patient, Personable, Professional, Responsible

Types of Positions
Guest Service Agent   Restaurant Server
Banquet Server   Minibar

Starting Salary
$ 20,000 - 25,000

Company Benefits
- Full health and dental package
- Travel benefits, tuition refund policy
- Comprehensive, in-house (on-line) training program

Correspondence
Mail or fax resume with cover letter

Part Time/Summer: Delta Toronto Airport Hotel regularly seeks individuals for part time employment, and occasionally looks for people in the summer months. Potential summer jobs include patio server in the restaurant, guest service agent, or within the children's creative centre.

DERLAN INDUSTRIES LIMITED

145 King St. E., Suite 500
Toronto, Ontario, M5C 2Y7
Tel: (416) 364-5852   Fax: (416) 362-5334

Garry Winkel, Human Resources
Internet: www.derlan.com

Derlan Industries is a North American industrial corporation operating through ten units for the industrial groups aerospace and industrial technologies.

Academic Fields
Bachelor of Comm/Admin: Accounting, Finance
Bachelor of Engineering: Electrical, Mechanical
Chartered Accounting: CA - General/Finance, CGA/CMA - General/Finance

Critical Skills
Adaptable, Confident, Enthusiastic, Logical, Good Writing Skills

Types of Positions
Accounting Clerk   Analyst

Starting Salary
$ 25,000 - 30,000

Company Benefits
- Full benefit package
- All courses paid for by company

Correspondence
Mail resume with cover letter

Part Time/Summer: Derlan Industries occasionally hires people for part time work, but does not look for individuals for the summer months.

The Canada Student Employment Guide

DEVELCON ELECTRONICS LTD.

18 Dyas Rd.
Toronto, Ontario, M3B 1V5
Tel: (416) 385-1390   Fax: (416) 385-1610

Human Resources
Internet: www.develcon.com

Develcon Electronics is a Canadian developer and marketer of local and remote LAN access products. Founded in 1974 to address the need for remote computer access, they now operate offices throughout Canada, and in the United States, Europe and South-East Asia. Their products are sold and supported in 55 countries through over 500 local distributors and resellers.

Academic Fields
College: Electronics Tech.
Bachelor of Science: Computer Science
Bachelor of Engineering: Electrical

Critical Skills
Good Communication, Innovative, Team Skills

Types of Positions
Receptionist   Assembler
Junior Programmer   Test Technician

Starting Salary
below $ 20,000 - 30,000 (depending on position)

Company Benefits
- Full time employee benefits
- Life, health, dental, vision, pension
- Limited budget for training and development

Correspondence
Mail, fax, e-mail, or submit resume and cover letter in person. E-mail: info@develcon.com

Part Time/Summer: Develcon Electronics rarely hires individuals for part time or summer employment.

DIRECTWEST PUBLISHERS LTD.

900 - 1900 Albert Street
Regina, Saskatchewan, S4P 4K8
Tel: 306) 777-0400   Fax: (306) 359-7849

Glen Gabel, Human Resources Manager
Internet: www.directwest.com

DirectWest Publishers is located in Saskatchewan, Canada. We employ nearly 100 people, with a head office in Regina and branch offices in Saskatoon and Prince Albert.
As SaskTel's telephone directory and Yellow PagesTM publishing agent, DirectWest brings all Saskatchewan consumers together with over 46,000 business advertisers in the ten Saskatchewan directory markets.

Academic Fields
College: General, Accounting, Administration, Advertising, Business, Computer Science, Marketing/Sales, Secretarial
Bachelor of Arts: General, Business
Bachelor of Comm/Admin: General, Accounting, Finance, Marketing, Info Mgmt.
Bachelor of Science: Computer Science
Chartered Accounting: CA - General/Finance, CGA/CMA - General/Finance
Masters: Business Administration

Critical Skills
Adaptable, Good Communication, Confident, Dependable, Enthusiastic, Flexible, Leadership, Organized, Personable, Professional, Responsible, Good Writing Skills

Types of Positions
Production   Sales
Finance   Marketing

Starting Salary
$ 20,000 - 25,000

Company Benefits
- Comprehensive benefit plan
- Pension plan
- Financial support for outside training

Correspondence
Mail resume with cover letter

Part Time/Summer: Directwest Publishers occasionally looks for people for part time positions, but does not hire for summer employment.

DOFASCO INC.

P.O. Box 2460
Hamilton, Ontario, L8N 3J5
Tel: N/A   Fax: N/A

Human Resources
Internet: www.dofasco.ca

Dofasco is one of Canada's largest steel producers, serving customers throughout North America with high quality flat rolled and tubular steels and laser welded blanks. The Company has operations in Canada and the United States, and utilizes both oxygen steelmaking and scrap-based electric arc furnace technology.

Academic Fields
College: Computer Science, Electronics Tech., Engineering Tech., Mechanical Tech.
Bachelor of Comm/Admin: Accounting, Finance, Marketing, Info Mgmt.
Bachelor of Science: Computer Science
Bachelor of Engineering: Chemical, Civil, Computer Systems, Design, Electrical, Environmental Studies, Industrial, Materials Science, Mechanical, Metallurgical
Chartered Accounting: CA - General/Finance, CGA - General/Finance, CMA - General/Finance
Masters: Business Administration, Engineering

Critical Skills
Adaptable, Analytical, Enthusiastic, Good Communication, Innovative, Leadership, Organized, Professional, Responsible, Team Player

Types of Positions
Various Types of Positions

Starting Salary
$ 40,000 - 45,000

Company Benefits
- See their web site for information on benefits

Correspondence
Apply through web site

Summer/Co-op/Internship: Work terms for university and college technical/professional programs (engineering, computer science, commerce, etc.)

DOMTAR INC.

P.O. Box 7210, Station A
Montreal, Quebec, H3C 3M1
Tel: (514) 848-5400   Fax: (514) 848-5393

Manager Staffing and HR
Internet: www.domtar.com

Domtar Inc. is Canada's largest producer of specialty and fine papers and is ranked seventh in North America. They have 8,000 employees.

Academic Fields
College: Accounting, Admin., Business, Communications, Human Res., Information Syst., Marketing/Sales, Secretarial, Computer Sci., Elec. Tech., Engineering Tech., Forestry, Mech. Tech.
Bachelor of Comm/Admin: General, Accounting, Finance, Human Resources, Marketing, Info Mgmt.
Bachelor of Science: Chemistry, Computer Science, Environmental Studies, Forestry
Bachelor of Laws: Corporate
Bachelor of Engineering: Chemical, Computer Systems, Electrical, Environmental Studies, Industrial, Mechanical, Water Resources
Chartered Accounting: CA - General/Finance, CGA - General/Finance, CMA - General/Finance
Masters: Business Admin., Science, Engineering

Critical Skills
Adaptable, Creative, Efficient, Good Communication, Leadership, Organized, Productive, Professional, Responsible, Team Work, Commitment

Types of Positions
Many Types of Positions

Starting Salary
$ 30,000 - 35,000

Company Benefits
- Group insurance, medical, dental, life, disability

Correspondence
Mail resume with cover letter

Part Time/Summer: Domtar Inc. rarely hires for part time work and occasionally hires for the summer. Potential work includes clerical jobs, production-related jobs, maintenance, accounting, and information technology.

Co-op/Internship: No official internship program but they welcome students if the need arises.

DRUG TRADING COMPANY LTD.

131 McNabb St.
Scarborough, Ontario, L3R 5V7
Tel: (905) 943-9499   Fax: N/A

Human Resources

The Drug Trading Company is a customer-owned wholesale drug distribution company owned by 1,550 pharmacist shareholders. The company and its subsidiary, Northwest Drug Company Limited, service the majority of pharmacies and hospitals in Canada from eight distribution locations. Through its subsidiary, The Drug Trading Company is involved in drug packaging, manufacturing, and computer services to pharmacies. The company was established in 1965 and has 162 outlets in Ontario, New Brunswick, Nova Scotia, and Prince Edward Island.

Academic Fields
College: Accounting, Business, Human Resources
Bachelor of Comm/Admin: General, Accounting, Marketing, Info Mgmt.
Bachelor of Science: Pharmacy
Masters: Business Administration

Critical Skills
Adaptable, Analytical, Good Communication, Confident, Creative, Decisive, Dependable, Diligent, Diplomatic, Efficient, Enthusiastic, Flexible, Innovative, Leadership, Logical, Manual Dexterity, Organized, Personable, Persuasive, Productive, Professional, Responsible, Good Writing Skills

Types of Positions
File Clerk   Accounting Clerk
Secretary

Starting Salary
$ 30,000 - 40,000 (university)

Company Benefits
- Health, dental and life insurance
- Tuition aid and in-house skills training offered

Correspondence
Mail resume with cover letter

Part Time/Summer: The Drug Trading Company sometimes seeks individuals for part time and summer work. Jobs potentially offered involve warehouse help and clerical work. The best time to apply is in May or June.

DRUXY'S INC.

1200 Eglinton Ave. E., Suite 802
North York, Ontario, M3C 1H9
Tel: (416) 385-9500   Fax: (416) 385-9501

Peter Druxerman, Vice President of Marketing
Internet: www.druxys.com

Druxy's Inc., also known as Druxy's Famous Deli Sandwiches, is a retail eatery with locations across the province and throughout the country. Employing more than 300 people, Druxy's Inc. offers a large number of flexible part time positions at the management level. The company looks for hardworking and outgoing individuals rather than any specific academic skills.

Academic Fields
College: General, Accounting, Hospitality
Bachelor of Arts: General, Business

Critical Skills
Confident, Creative, Dependable, Good Communication, Enthusiastic, Flexible, Efficient, Good Writing Skills, Innovative, Leadership, Organized, Manual Dexterity, Personable, Professional, Responsible, Outgoing

Types of Positions
Restaurant Manager Trainee   Restaurant Worker

Starting Salary
$ 20,000 - 25,000

Company Benefits
- Standard benefits including health and dental
- Opportunity to help with opening own franchise
- Company provides training and support

Correspondence
Mail or fax resume with cover letter

Part Time/Summer: Druxy's regularly hires part time students and sometimes provides summer opportunities for individuals. The positions for the summer months are in customer service.

DUCKS UNLIMITED CANADA

P.O. Box 1160
Stonewall, Manitoba, R0C 2Z0
Tel: (204) 467-3209   Fax: (204) 467-9028

Personnel

Ducks Unlimited is an international, private, non-profit conservation organization dedicated to the perpetuation and increase of North America's waterfowl resources through restoration, preservation and creation of prime breeding habitat in Canada. Development of this habitat on a multi-use concept benefits wildlife and the general environment and provides water for agriculture, domestic and recreational use. Ducks Unlimited works to foster public understanding of the value of wildlife habitat and a healthy environment.

Academic Fields
College: Accounting, Secretarial
Bachelor of Science: Agriculture, Biology, Computer Science
Chartered Accounting: CMA-General, CGA-General
Masters: Science

Critical Skills
Adaptable, Analytical, Good Communication, Confident, Creative, Decisive, Dependable, Diligent, Diplomatic, Efficient, Enthusiastic, Flexible, Innovative, Leadership, Logical, Organized, Patient, Personable, Responsible, Good Writing Skills, Team Player

Types of Positions
Habitat Technician	Computer Programmer
Accounting Clerk	Biologist (Habitat Professional)
Interpreter	Agrologist (Habitat Professional)

Starting Salary
$ 20,000 - 40,000

Company Benefits
- Full time staff receive health, dental benefits
- Life and accident insurance, pension
- Long term disability pension plan

Correspondence
Mail resume with cover letter

Part Time/Summer: Ducks Unlimited Canada regularly hires people for part time and summer work. Potential jobs involve biology positions. The best time to apply is from January to April.

DUHA COLOR SERVICES

750 Bradford St.
Winnipeg, Manitoba, R3H 0N3
Tel: (204) 786-8961   Fax: (204) 885-3762

Pat Fenlon, Human Resources
Internet: www.duhagroup.com

Duha Color Services is a manufacturer of customized merchandising aids (i.e. paint strips and colour cards) for paint and auto industries. The firm has factories in Winnipeg, Selkirk, Gimli, and Lockport, NY. They also have joint ventures in Mexico, Singapore and Columbia. The firm employs approximately 270 individuals in Canada.

Academic Fields
College: Faculty Management, Graphic Arts
Bachelor of Arts: Business
Bachelor of Comm/Admin: General
Bachelor of Science: Environmental Studies, Physics, Chemistry
Bachelor of Engineering: Industrial, Mechanical
Chartered Accounting: CMA-General, CGA-General
Masters: Business Administration

Critical Skills
Good Communication, Decisive, Dependable, Diligent, Diplomatic, Efficient, Enthusiastic, Flexible, Manual Dexterity, Organized, Patient, Personable, Productive, Professional, Responsible, Leadership

Types of Positions
Bindery Worker/Assembler	Paint Mixer

Starting Salary
$ 27,000 - 32,000

Company Benefits
- Group health plan
- Productivity bonus, attendance rewards
- In-house training, tuition reimbursement

Correspondence
Mail, fax or e-mail resume with cover letter E-mail: pfenlon@duhagroup.com

Part Time/Summer: Duha Printers Limited occasionally looks for individuals for part time work, and regularly seeks people for summer employment. Potential summer work includes bindery, assemblers, or paint mixers. The best time to apply is in May or June.

DUN & BRADSTREET CANADA

5770 Hurontario Street
Mississauga, Ontario, L5R 3B5
Tel: (905) 568-6000   Fax: (905) 568-6360

Human Resources
Internet: www.dnb.ca

Dun & Bradstreet Canada is engaged in the provision of information processing services. The company provides consulting and market analysis services to a wide range of individual and business clientele. Dun & Bradstreet Canada employs over 400 individuals.

Academic Fields
College: Accounting, Administration, Business, Computer Science, Human Resources, Insurance, Science, Secretarial
Bachelor of Arts: Business, Economics, English, Public Relations
Bachelor of Comm/Admin: Accounting, Finance
Bachelor of Science: Actuarial, Computer Science, Mathematics
Bachelor of Laws: General
Bachelor of Education: General
Chartered Accounting: CMA-Finance, CGA-Finance
Masters: Business Administration

Critical Skills
Adaptable, Analytical, Good Communication, Confident, Creative, Decisive, Dependable, Diligent, Diplomatic, Efficient, Enthusiastic, Flexible, Good With Figures, Innovative, Leadership, Logical, Organized, Patient, Personable, Persuasive, Productive, Professional, Responsible, Good Writing Skills

Types of Positions
Secretary   Computer Programmer
Reporter

Starting Salary
$ 20,000 - 25,000

Company Benefits
- Full benefits including medical, dental, and pension
- Profit sharing plans

Correspondence
Mail resume with cover letter

Part Time/Summer: Dun & Bradstreet Canada sometimes hires for part time and summer opportunities. A potential summer position may involve telephone interviewing.

DUPONT CANADA INC.

Box 2200, 7070 Mississauga Rd.
Mississauga, Ontario, L5M 2H3
Tel: (905) 821-3300   Fax: (905) 821-5592

Staffing Team
Internet: www.dupont.ca

DuPont Canada produces and markets specialty products and chemicals for use by customers in manufacturing, resource, and service sectors in over 60 countries. Products fall into three different categories which are fibres and intermediates, specialty chemicals and materials, and specialty plastics and films. DuPont Canada employs more than 3,200 people across the country.

Academic Fields
College: Engineering Tech.
Bachelor of Comm/Admin: Accounting, Finance, Info Mgmt.
Bachelor of Science: Agriculture, Chemistry, Computer Science
Bachelor of Engineering: Chemical, Computer Systems, Electrical, Mechanical
Chartered Accounting: CMA-General, CMA-Finance

Critical Skills
Dependable, Efficient, Good Writing Skills, Good Communication, Leadership, Productive, Self-Managed, Team Player

Types of Positions
Process Engineer   Design Engineer
Accounting Analyst   Customer Service Rep.

Starting Salary
$ 35,000 - 45,000

Company Benefits
- Flexible benefit program
- On-site training courses and on-the-job training
- Many development opportunities

Correspondence
Mail or fax resume with cover letter (Please do not call)

Part Time/Summer: Dupont Canada sometimes looks for part time and summer candidates. Those positions listed above are the most likely to be filled, although there are very few jobs available. The best time to apply is by May 1st.

The Canada Student Employment Guide

DURA AUTOMOTIVE SYSTEMS (CANADA) LTD.
P.O. Box 900, 345 Eccelstone Dr.
Bracebridge, Ontario, P1L 1V1
Tel: (705) 645-5272   Fax: (705) 645-2603

Joanne Wobchatiuk, Human Resources Manager

Dura Automotive Systems (Canada) Ltd. is the largest independent designer and manufacturer of driver control systems, and a leading supplier of door systems, window systems, and engineered mechanical components. The Bracebridge, Ontario facility is the North American headquarters for seat systems, researching, designing, testing and manufacturing of manual and power seat adjusters for light passenger vehicles. They employ more than 1,000 individuals.

Academic Fields
College: Engineering Tech.
Bachelor of Comm/Admin: Accounting, Finance
Bachelor of Engineering: Mechanical
Chartered Accounting: CA-Finance, CGA-Finance, CMA-Finance

Critical Skills
Adaptable, Good Communication, Innovative, Leadership, Logical, Productive, Professional, Responsible, Ability to Learn

Types of Positions
Junior Product Engineer Junior Process Engineer
Junior Accountant

Starting Salary
$ 25,000 - 30,000 (secondary school) / $ 40,000 - 45,000 (college and university)

Company Benefits
- Full time employees receive medical, dental, vision
- Education tuition reimbursement, professional development through assignments
- Seminars, in-house training

Correspondence
Mail or fax resume with cover letter

Part Time/Summer: Dura Automotive Systems (Canada) Ltd. rarely hires for part time work and regularly hires for the summer. Potential jobs include college or university engineering or I.T. positions.

Co-op/Internship: They hire engineering interns for a 12 to 16 month period. These students are currently studying engineering.

DYLEX LIMITED
637 Lakeshore Blvd. W.
Toronto, Ontario, M5V 1A8
Tel: (416) 586-7863   Fax: (416) 599-9952

Janine Tadier, Human Resources Manager
Internet: www.dylex.com

Dylex is Canada's premier specialty retailer, offering mainstream fashions and family merchandise under its well-known operating divisions: BiWay, Braemar, Fairweather, Labels, Thriftys, and Tip Top. They employ approximately 1,200 individuals across Canada.

Academic Fields
College: Accounting, Administration, Business, Communications, Human Resources, Marketing/Sales
Bachelor of Arts: Business, Economics, Psychology
Bachelor of Comm/Admin: Finance, Marketing, Info Mgmt.
Bachelor of Science: Computer Science, Mathematics
Bachelor of Laws: General
Bachelor of Education: Adult Education
Chartered Accounting: CA-General, CGA-General, CMA-General
Masters: Business Administration

Critical Skills
Dependable, Efficient, Good Communication, Organized, Personable, Persuasive, Productive, Professional, Responsible

Types of Positions
Input Clerk   Merchandise Assistant
Sales Associate   HR Assistant
A/P / Payroll   Retail Accounting

Starting Salary
$ 25,000 - 30,000

Company Benefits
- Health and dental benefits
- RRSP plan and group life insurance
- Discounts offered

Correspondence
Mail or fax resume and cover letter in person
E-mail: jtadier@dylex.com

Part Time/Summer: Dylex regularly seeks candidates for part time and summer employment. Most positions involve sales and merchandising. The best time to apply is in March.

The Canada Student Employment Guide

DYNACARE LABORATORIES

115 Middair Court
Brampton, Ontario, L6T 5M3
Tel: (905) 790-3000   Fax: (905) 790-3055

Michele Richman, Human Resources
Internet: www.dynacare.com

Dynacare is one of North America's leading providers of medical diagnostic laboratory services, operating in 20 states and two Canadian provinces. Dynacare provides a commitment to the patient by working with our academic medical center partners and affiliates and under the medical direction of some of North America's top pathologists.

Academic Fields
College: Laboratory Tech.
Bachelor of Comm/Admin: Accounting, Info Mgmt.
Bachelor of Science: Biology, Chemistry, Microbiology, Nursing (RN)
Chartered Accounting: CGA-General, CGA-Finance

Critical Skills
Confident, Dependable, Diplomatic, Good Communication, Personable, Leadership, Organized, Good Writing Skills, Productive, Professional, Responsible

Types of Positions
Data Entry Clerk   Lab Assistant
Billing Clerk   Courier Drivers
Venipuncturist   Phlebotomist

Starting Salary
below $ 20,000

Company Benefits
- Health, dental, short/long term disability
- Life and dependent insurance
- Internal posting of jobs, advancement within

Correspondence
Mail or fax resume with cover letter

Part Time/Summer: Dynacare Laboratories sometimes hires students for part time work and summer positions. Some potential summer opportunities includes courier drivers, data entry, and venipuncturist.

DYNAPRO SYSTEMS INC.

800 Carleton Court, Annacis Island
New Westminster, British Columbia, V3M 6L3
Tel: (604) 521-3962   Fax: (604) 521-8474

Debbie Paulsen, Director Human Resources
Internet: www.dynapro.com

Dynapro simplifies interaction by designing and manufacturing world class hardware, software, and touch screen solutions. Dynapro's products include touch computers, terminals, monitors, touch screens, software, and related components for the industrial and non-industrial marketplace.

Academic Fields
College: Accounting, Administration, Communications, Computer Science, Electronics Tech., Engineering Tech., Graphic Arts, Human Res.
Bachelor of Arts: General, English, Public Relations
Bachelor of Comm/Admin: General, Accounting, Finance, Info Mgmt.
Bachelor of Science: Computer Science, Physics
Bachelor of Engineering: Computer Systems, Design, Electrical, Industrial, Mechanical
Chartered Accounting: CA - General/Finance, CGA/CMA - General/Finance
Masters: Business Administration, Science, Engineering, Library Science

Critical Skills
Adaptable, Analytical, Good Communication, Confident, Creative, Decisive, Dependable, Diligent, Efficient, Enthusiastic, Flexible, Innovative, Leadership, Logical, Manual Dexterity, Organized, Patient, Personable, Professional, Responsible, Writing Skills

Types of Positions
Assembler   Office Assistant
Receiver/Shipper   Materials Handler
Help Desk Support

Starting Salary
Depends on level of education

Company Benefits
- Full comprehensive benefits

Correspondence
Mail, fax or e-mail resume with cover letter
E-mail: debbie_paulsen@dynapro.com

Part Time/Summer: Dynapro occasionally hires for part time work, and regularly hires for the summer. Potential jobs are in manufacturing. Apply is in May.

DYNASTY FURNITURE MANUFACTURING LTD.
3344 - 54 Aveneu S.E.
Calgary, Alberta, T2C 0A8
Tel: (403) 271-1932   Fax: (403) 236-3533

Human Resources

Dynasty Furniture Manufacturing Ltd. is a manufacturer of upholstery furniture. The company's head office is in Calgary, Alberta.

Academic Fields
College: General, Accounting, Administration, Business, Drafting/Architecture, Electronics Tech., Engineering Tech., Marketing/Sales
Bachelor of Arts: General, Business
Bachelor of Comm/Admin: General, Accounting, Finance, Marketing, Info Mgmt., Public Admin.
Bachelor of Engineering: Chemical, Civil, Electrical, Mechanical

Critical Skills
Dependable, Diplomatic, Efficient, Good Communication, Innovative, Leadership, Organized, Patient, Personable, Professional, Responsible, Team Player

Types of Positions
Data Entry   Piecework Calculations

Starting Salary
$ 20,000 - 25,000

Company Benefits
- Alberta health care, extended health including prescriptions
- Dental and life insurance
- Continued opportunities for the right individual

Correspondence
Fax resume with cover letter

Part Time/Summer: Dynasty Furniture Manufacturing Ltd. occasionally seeks candidates for part time or summer work. Potential positions include filing, or projects assistant.

DYNATEK AUTOMATION SYSTEMS INC.
11 Kodiak Cres.
North York, Ontario, M3J 3E5
Tel: N/A   Fax: N/A

Human Resources Manager
Internet: www.dynatek.co.uk/

DynaTek Automation Systems' principle market sector is in Information Technology and therefore the company offers a comprehensive line of integrated SCSI mass storage subsystems. DynaTek mass storage products combine the finest chassis and engine components with innovative hardware design, unique software drivers and custom device firmware. The resulting high-performance products have catapulted DynaTek to the forefront of the data storage marketplace.

Academic Fields
College: Drafting/Architecture, Electronics Tech.
Bachelor of Arts: Public Relations
Bachelor of Comm/Admin: Accounting, Finance, Marketing, Info Mgmt.
Bachelor of Science: Computer Science
Bachelor of Engineering: Computer Systems, Electrical
Chartered Accounting: CMA-General
Masters: Engineering

Critical Skills
Adaptable, Analytical, Creative, Enthusiastic, Flexible, Innovative, Productive, Manual Dexterity

Types of Positions
Engineering / R & D   Product Marketing
Production   Materials Mgmt.
Finance & Admin.   Quality Assurance

Starting Salary
$ 20,000 - 25,000 (varies depending on education)

Company Benefits
- Health, dental benefits, group life insurance
- Employee purchases at cost
- On-the-job training, educational assistance

Correspondence
Mail resume with cover letter

Part Time/Summer: Dynatek Automation Systems does not generally hire for part time or summer employment. There are however co-op or work term students from universities or community colleges at various times of the year.

E B A ENGINEERING CONSULTANTS LTD.

14535 - 118 Ave. NW
Edmonton, Alberta, T5L 2M7
Tel: (403) 451-2121 Fax: (403) 454-5688

Greg Goth, Human Resources
Internet: www.eba.ca

E B A Engineering Consultants is a multi-discipline consulting firm that is involved in transportation, geotechnical, geophysical, civil, and environmental engineering. The company employs approximately 300 people.

Academic Fields
College: Engineering Tech.
Bachelor of Engineering: Civil
Masters: Engineering

Critical Skills
Enthusiastic, Dependable, Personable, Responsible

Types of Positions
Construction Services Technician
Engineer

Starting Salary
$ 20,000 - 25,000

Company Benefits
- Full benefit package for full time staff

Correspondence
Mail resume with cover letter

Part Time/Summer: E B A Engineering Consultants does not generally hire for part time work, but regularly looks for individuals for the summer months. The best time to apply is in February.

EARTH TECH CANADA INC.

45 Greenbelt Dr.
Toronto, Ontario, M3C 3K3
Tel: (416) 445-3600 Fax: (416) 445-5276

Human Resources
Internet: www.earthtech.com

Based in Ontario, Earth Tech Canada Inc. is an 88-year old, full service engineering consulting firm, offering services in water/wastewater, environmental services, transportation, civil engineering, architecture, urban development and infrastructure management systems. The firm has extensive experience in design, build, finance, operations and public/private partnerships in water/wastewater, solid waste and transportation infrastructure.

Academic Fields
Bachelor of Engineering: General, Civil, Electrical, Environmental Studies, Mechanical, Transportation, Water Resources
Masters: Engineering

Critical Skills
Analytical, Decisive, Diligent, Efficient, Enthusiastic, Flexible, Good Communication, Good With Figures, Good Writing Skills, Professional

Types of Positions
Trainee Engineer

Starting Salary
$ 35,000 - 40,000

Company Benefits
- Comprehensive benefits plan including, but not limited to, health, dental, life insurance
- Short and long term disability, accidental death and dismemberment
- Retirement savings plan, employee assistance plan

Correspondence
E-mail resume with cover letter
E-mail: hrcanada@earthtech.ca

Part Time/Summer: Earth Tech Canada Inc. rarely seeks candidates for part time and summer employment opportunities.

Co-op/Internship: They offer opportunities through university co-op programs only.

ECHO BAY MINES LTD.

9818 Edmonton International Airport
Edmonton, Alberta, T5J 2T2
Tel: (780) 890-4695   Fax: (780) 890-4692

Human Resources

Echo Bay Mines Ltd. is engaged in the business of mining, exploration and development of gold and silver. The company's head office is in Denver, Colorado. Echo Bay Mines employs over 1,700 individuals. They employ 325 individuals in Canada.

Academic Fields
College: Accounting, Administration, Human Resources, Information Systems, Engineering Tech., Mechanical Tech.
Bachelor of Comm/Admin: Accounting, Finance, Human Resources, Info Mgmt.
Bachelor of Science: Environmental Studies, Geology
Bachelor of Engineering: Environmental Studies, Geotechnical, Mechanical, Mining, Water Resources
Chartered Accounting: CA - CA - General/Finance
Masters: Science, Engineering

Critical Skills
Adaptable, Analytical, Confident, Creative, Dependable, Diligent, Efficient, Good Communication, Good Writing Skills, Enthusiastic, Flexible, Innovative, Logical, Organized, Productive, Responsible

Types of Positions
Accountant   Geologist Technician
Junior Engineer Technician   Occupational Nurse
Safety Coordinator

Starting Salary
$ 30,000 - 35,000

Company Benefits
- Comprehensive benefit plan including medical and dental coverage
- Life insurance, group RRSP
- Short and long term disability

Correspondence
Mail or fax resume with cover letter

Part Time/Summer: Echo Bay Mines does not hire part time workers, but occasionally seeks candidates for summer employment. Potential positions are entry level such as labourer or operator, or professional in nature such as engineering or environmental. The best time to apply is from February to April.

ECONOMIC DEVELOPMENT EDMONTON

9797 Jasper Ave.
Edmonton, Alberta, T5J 1N9
Tel: (780) 424-9191   Fax: (780) 426-0236

Human Resources
Internet: www.ede.org

Economic Development Edmonton works to promote the City of Edmonton and its surrounding area for both economic growth and prosperity. They are involved in tourism and conventions in Edmonton.

Academic Fields
College: Accounting, Business, Computer Science, Hospitality, Human Resources, Marketing/Sales, Secretarial, Travel/Tourism
Bachelor of Arts: General, Business, Economics, Public Relations, Statistics
Bachelor of Comm/Admin: General, Marketing, Info Mgmt., Public Admin.
Bachelor of Science: General, Computer Science
Chartered Accounting: CA-Finance, CMA-Finance
Masters: Business Administration

Critical Skills
Adaptable, Analytical, Artistic, Good Communication, Confident, Creative, Decisive, Dependable, Diligent, Diplomatic, Efficient, Enthusiastic, Flexible, Good With Figures, Innovative, Leadership, Logical, Manual Dexterity, Organized, Patient, Personable, Persuasive, Productive, Professional, Responsible, Good Writing Skills

Types of Positions
Research Assistant   Receptionist
Administrative Assistant

Starting Salary
$ 20,000 - 25,000

Company Benefits
- Complete health care benefits

Correspondence
Mail or fax resume with cover letter

Part Time/Summer: Economic Development Edmonton occasionally looks for individuals for part time work, and regularly seeks people for the summer. Potential summer jobs include research assistant, or visitor counsellor. The best time to apply is in March.

THE ECONOMICAL INSURANCE GROUP

111 Westmount Rd. S.
Waterloo, Ontario, N2J 4S4
Tel: (519) 570-8500   Fax: (519) 570-8239

Human Resources
Internet: www.economicalinsurance.com

The Economical Insurance Group is a Top 10, Canadian-owned property and casualty insurer with a track record spanning over 125 years. Their full range of personal and commercial line products are tailored to rise above and beyond the needs of their customers. They have 1,300 employees in Canada.

Academic Fields
College: Graphic Arts, Journalism, Security/Law Enforcement, Accounting, Administration, Business, Communications, Human Resources, Information Systems, Insurance, Marketing/Sales, Secretarial, CAD Autocad, Computer Science, General Science
Bachelor of Arts: General, Business, Economics, English, Journalism, Psychology, Public Relations
Bachelor of Comm/Admin: General, Accounting, Finance, Human Resources, Marketing, Info Mgmt.
Bachelor of Science: General, Actuarial, Computer Science, Mathematics
Chartered Accounting: CA-General/Finance, CGA/CGA - General/Finance
Masters: Business Administration

Critical Skills
Adaptable, Analytical, Confident, Creative, Decisive, Dependable, Diligent, Diplomatic, Efficient, Enthusiastic, Flexible, Good Communication, Good Writing Skills, Innovative, Leadership, Logical, Organized, Patient, Personable, Persuasive, Productive, Professional

Types of Positions
Support Clerk   Service Clerk
Mail Clerk   Administrator

Starting Salary
$ 20,000 - 25,000

Company Benefits
- Medical, dental, pension, sick leave, vacation

Correspondence
Mail, fax or e-mail resume with cover letter
E-mail: hrd@economicalinsurance.com

Part Time/Summer: The Economical Insurance Group occasionally hires for part time jobs, and regularly hires during the summer. Apply in mid-March.

EDDIE BAUER INC.

201 Aviva Park Dr.
Vaughan, Ontario, L4L 9C1
Tel: (905) 851-6700   Fax: N/A

Kirk Merrett, Human Resources Manager

Eddie Bauer is a retail company providing private label men's and women's casual clothing, accessories and footwear, along with other miscellaneous items. Established in 1920, Eddie Bauer operates in more than 500 stores in Canada and the United States. The store's sales have grown to more than $1 billion a year. In Canada over 1,000 individuals are employed at Eddie Bauer. Applicants should apply to individual store locations.

Academic Fields
College: General
Bachelor of Arts: General
Bachelor of Science: General

Critical Skills
Confident, Enthusiastic, Flexible, Good Communication, Leadership, Organized, Sales Skills, Merchandising Skills, Interpersonal Skills

Types of Positions
Sales Associate   Stock Associate
Management Trainee

Starting Salary
below $ 20,000 (Sales), $ 25,000 - 30,000 (Mgmt. Trainee)

Company Benefits
- Large number of benefits to full time staff
- Very structured in-house training materials
- Onus on the individual for further training

Correspondence
Submit resume and cover letter in person at a store

Part Time/Summer: Eddie Bauer regularly hires for part time openings and sometimes hires for summer opportunities (usually in a part time capacity). Sales associates can work flexible hours (12 - 40 hours per week) depending on store needs. The best time to apply is in May and to keep contact into June with store manager. Stores do not always forward applications to other Eddie Bauer stores, thus feel free to let the manager know and apply to more than one.

EDMONTON HOME SERVICES LTD.

500 - 10050 112 Street
Edmonton, Alberta, T5K 2J1
Tel: (780) 488-7282   Fax: (780) 488-7321

Judy Meadahl, Human Resources

Edmonton Home Services is a community oriented organization providing support service to the community since 1970. It has been designed to supplement the role of parents by providing home support workers in their absence and to undertake responsibility for the care and well being of the young, elderly, and convalescent. Edmonton Home Services employs licensed practical nurses, personal care attendants and home support workers on an hourly or 24 hour live-in basis, or on a flexible schedule tailored to the individual's needs.

Academic Fields
College: Nursing
Bachelor of Science: Nursing (RN)

Critical Skills
Adaptable, Confident, Dependable, Diligent, Efficient, Enthusiastic, Flexible, Good Communication, Organized, Patient, Personable

Types of Positions
Program Coordinator

Starting Salary
$ 20,000 - 25,000

Company Benefits
- Competitive benefits
- Group insurance
- Opportunity to attend workshops and conferences

Correspondence
Mail resume with cover letter

Part Time/Summer: Edmonton Home Services sometimes seeks individuals on a part time basis and regularly hires for summer employment. Students enrolled in nursing programs can apply for personal care attendant positions. The best time to apply is in May. Student nurses may also apply for evening and weekends on a regular basis.

EDS OF CANADA LTD.

33 Yonge St., Suite 500
Toronto, Ontario, M5E 1G4
Tel: (416) 814-4855   Fax: (416) 814-4856

Staffing Services
Internet: www.eds.ca

EDS of Canada provides a full range of management consulting and information technology services including systems management, integration, development, and process management services. They are the world's largest information technology company, and have more than 110,000 employees in 42 countries around the world.

Academic Fields
College: Business, Computer Science, Marketing/Sales
Bachelor of Arts: General, Business
Bachelor of Comm/Admin: Finance, Info Mgmt.
Bachelor of Science: Computer Science
Bachelor of Engineering: Computer Systems, Electrical, Mechanical
Chartered Accounting: CMA-Finance, CGA-Finance

Critical Skills
Adaptable, Analytical, Good Communication, Dependable, Efficient, Enthusiastic, Flexible, Good With Figures, Innovative, Leadership, Organized, Personable, Productive, Professional, Good Writing Skills

Types of Positions
Information Analyst Development Pro

Starting Salary
$ 30,000 - 50,000

Company Benefits
- Generous benefit program
- Dental, glasses, drugs, pension, PC purchase
- Excellent training and development

Correspondence
Mail or fax resume with cover letter

Part Time/Summer: EDS of Canada sometimes hires part time employees and sometimes offers summer opportunities. Potential positions involve administration, finance, or junior positions. The best time to apply is in the February to March timeframe.

ELCO

P.O. Box 626, 1850 Vanier Blvd.
Bathurst, New Brunswick, E2A 3Z6
Tel: (506) 546-8220   Fax: (506) 546-8229

Monica Oliver, Quality Manager
Internet: www.elco.co.il

Elco is involved in the wholesale distribution of electrical, plumbing, industrial, heating and municipal products to the residential, commercial, utility and industrial markets. A division of Gullevin International Inc., Elco employs approximately 115 individuals.

Academic Fields
College: Engineering Tech., Marketing/Sales
Bachelor of Comm/Admin: Marketing
Bachelor of Engineering: Electrical, Industrial, Mechanical

Critical Skills
Good Communication, Confident, Dependable, Efficient, Enthusiastic, Leadership, Logical, Organized, Personable, Professional, Responsible

Types of Positions
Warehouse Clerk

Starting Salary
$ 20,000 - 25,000

Company Benefits
- Medical plan, RRSP
- Product knowledge in warehouse

Correspondence
Submit resume with cover letter in person

Part Time/Summer: Elco does not generally hire people for part time work, but regularly looks for people for the summer months. Potential jobs include warehouse clerk. The best time to apply is mid-March.

ELECTRONICS ARTS (CANADA) INC.

4330 Sanderson Way
Burnaby, British Columbia, V5C 4X1
Tel: (604) 451-3600   Fax: (604) 451-3747

Human Resources Department
Internet: www.ea.com

Electronic Arts ™ (EA) is the leading independent interactive entertainment software company that develops, publishes and distributes products for personal computers and advanced entertainment systems such as the PlayStation ™ and Nintendo ®64. Since its inception, EA has garnered more than 700 awards for outstanding software in the U.S. and Europe.

Academic Fields
College: Computer Science, Engineering Tech. (Computers), Graphic Arts
Bachelor of Arts: Fine Arts (Art Animation)
Bachelor of Science: Computer Science, Math
Bachelor of Engineering: Computer Systems
Masters: Science

Critical Skills
Adaptable, Analytical, Artistic, Creative, Dependable, Enthusiastic, Flexible, Good Communication, Good With Figures, Good Writing Skills, Innovative, Leadership, Logical, Personable, Productive

Types of Positions
Software Engineer   Computer Graphic Artist

Starting Salary
$ 30,000 - 40,000

Company Benefits
- Extended health plan, dental
- Stock options, stock purchase program

Correspondence
Mail, fax, or e-mail resume with cover letter
E-mail: eachr@ea.com

Part Time/Summer: Electronic Arts (Canada) Inc. regularly seeks individuals for part time and summer employment. Potential jobs include game testers to beta test their products over the summer. Co-op programs exist for software engineers and computer graphic artists. The best time to apply is in April.

Co-op/Internship: They have an Electronic Arts' EA Academy Internship Program. Visit their website for more information.

The Canada Student Employment Guide

ELI LILLY CANADA INC.

3650 Danforth Avenue
Scarborough, Ontario, M1N 2E8
Tel: (416) 694-3221   Fax: (416) 699-7241

Marie Walton, Human Resources
Internet: www.lilly.ca

Eli Lilly Canada is a brand name pharmaceutical company specializing in products related to diabetes, infectious diseases, cancer, the central nervous system and gastrointestinal diseases. The company's current research is focused on osteoporosis, the cardiovascular system, the central nervous system, anti-infectives and oncology. Eli Lilly employs 572 people across Canada.

Academic Fields
College: General, Accounting, Engineering Tech., Human Resources
Bachelor of Arts: General, Business, Economics, Public Relations
Bachelor of Comm/Admin: General, Accounting, Finance, Marketing, Info Mgmt.
Bachelor of Science: General, Biology, Chemistry, Computer Science, Microbiology, Nursing (RN), Pharmacy
Bachelor of Engineering: General, Industrial
Chartered Accounting: CA - General/Finance
Masters: Business Administration, Science

Critical Skills
Analytical, Dependable, Good Writing Skills, Good Communication, Leadership, Organized, Personable, Professional

Types of Positions
Sales Representative   Clinical Research Monitor
Analytical Chemist   Financial Analyst

Starting Salary
Depends greatly on education and position

Company Benefits
- Competitive benefits
- Extensive training and development

Correspondence
Mail or fax resume with cover letter (Please do not call)

Part Time/Summer: Eli Lilly Canada sometimes looks for candidates for part time and summer work. Their summer program is offered initially to family members of employees. If qualified candidates cannot be found then an external search is conducted. The best time to apply is in March or April.

EMCO LIMITED

620 Richmond Street
London, Ontario, N6A 5J9
Tel: (519) 645-3900   Fax: (519) 645-2465

Marlene Root, Director of Human Resources
Internet: www.emcoltd.com

Emco is a leading Canadian distributor of plumbing and related products and a major manufacturer of building and home improvement products. In addition, Emco manufactures and distributes worldwide, fluid handling equipment for the petroleum and petro-chemical industries and produces customs components including brass and aluminum forgings. Through manufacturing facilities in Canada, the United States, Germany, England, France, and Japan they distribute product to over 100 countries worldwide.

Academic Fields
College: Accounting, Administration, Business, Human Resources, Law Clerk, Secretarial
Bachelor of Arts: Business
Bachelor of Comm/Admin: Accounting, Finance
Bachelor of Science: Environmental Studies
Bachelor of Laws: Corporate
Bachelor of Engineering: Environ. Studies, Industrial
Chartered Accounting: CA-Finance, CGA/CMA - General/Finance
Masters: Business Administration, Engineering

Critical Skills
Adaptable, Creative, Dependable, Good Communication, Efficient, Enthusiastic, Flexible, Good With Figures, Good Writing Skills, Innovative, Leadership, Personable, Professional, Responsible

Types of Positions
Financial Analyst   Auditor

Starting Salary
$ 20,000 - 25,000

Company Benefits
- Health, dental, life insurance, educational courses
- Company learning centre offers training courses

Correspondence
Mail resume with cover letter

Part Time/Summer: EMCO sometimes hires for part time or summer work. Potential jobs involve general clerical, audit, or finance. The best time to apply is in May or June.

The Canada Student Employment Guide

EMJ DATA SYSTEMS LTD.

P.O. Box 1012
Guelph, Ontario, N1H 6N1
Tel: (519) 837-2444   Fax: (519) 836-1914

Sue Barton, Human Resources Manager
Internet: www.emj.ca

EMJ Data Systems is a publicly owned company established in 1979. EMJ has evolved into one of the nation's leading distributors of Apple, Unix, Point-of-Sale, Internet, Technology and CD Recordable products. Their head office is located in Guelph, Ontario, with five branch offices across the country (B.C., Alberta, Manitoba, Quebec, and Nova Scotia).

Academic Fields
College: General, Accounting, Administration, Business, Computer Science, Electronics Tech., Engineering Tech., Graphic Arts, Human Resources, Marketing/Sales, Science, Secretarial
Bachelor of Arts: General, Business, Economics, English
Bachelor of Comm/Admin: General, Accounting, Finance, Marketing, Info Mgmt.
Bachelor of Science: General, Computer Science, Mathematics
Bachelor of Engineering: General, Computer Systems
Chartered Accounting: CA - General/Finance, CGA/CMA - General/Finance
Masters: Business Administration, Arts, Science

Critical Skills
Adaptable, Analytical, Good Communication, Creative, Dependable, Diligent, Efficient, Enthusiastic, Flexible, Good With Figures, Innovative, Logical, Organized, Productive, Professional, Responsible, Writing Skills

Types of Positions
Shipper   Receptionist
Inside Sales

Starting Salary
below $ 20,000 - 25,000 (depends on position)

Company Benefits
- Health, dental, and life insurance, RRSP
- On-going product training, continuing education

Correspondence
Mail, fax, or e-mail resume with cover letter

Part Time/Summer: EMJ Data Systems occasionally hires for part time work and regularly hires for the summer. Potential summer jobs involve shipping or accounting. The best time to apply is in April.

ENDPOINT RESEARCH LTD.

2595 Skymark Ave., Suite 210
Mississauga, Ontario, L4W 4L5
Tel: (416) 626-0299   Fax: (416) 626-2063

Indira Sattan, Executive & HR Assistant
Internet: www.endpoint.ca

Endpoint Research Ltd. is a mid-sized Canadian contract research organization based in Toronto, Ontario. They offer full service clinical trial management for pharmaceutical and biotechnology clients, from protocol development and clinical trial conduct to report preparation.

Academic Fields
College: Administration, Business, Secretarial, Nursing (RN), Nursing (RNA)
Bachelor of Arts: Business
Bachelor of Comm/Admin: General
Bachelor of Science: General, Biology, Chemistry, Health Sciences, Kinesiology, Microbiology, Nursing (RN), Psychology
Masters: Science

Critical Skills
Adaptable, Analytical, Confident, Decisive, Dependable, Diligent, Diplomatic, Efficient, Enthusiastic, Flexible, Good Communication, Good Writing Skills, Organized, Patient, Personable, Productive, Professional, Responsible, Interpersonal

Types of Positions
Receptionist   Project Coordinator
Project Assistant   Project Manager
Clinical Research Associate   Accounting Clerk

Starting Salary
$ 20,000 - 25,000

Company Benefits
- Comprehensive employee and dependent benefits
- Mentorship training program, computer training

Correspondence
Mail resume with cover letter or apply through web site. E-mail: info@endpoint.ca

Part Time/Summer: Endpoint Research Ltd. occasionally hires for part time and summer work. The best time to apply is from March to May.

Co-op/Internship: They provide work placement opportunities for college graduates and employ students in university programs.

The Canada Student Employment Guide

ENERFLEX SYSTEMS LTD.

4700 - 47 Street S.E.
Calgary, Alberta, T2B 3R1
Tel: (403) 720-4324   Fax: (403) 720-4385

Mark Arthur, HR Planner
Internet: www.enerflex.com

Since their modest beginnings over twenty years ago, EnerFlex Systems Ltd. has grown into a global leader in providing innovative gas compression solutions.

Academic Fields
College: Accounting, Administration, Business, Human Resources, Secretarial, Computer Science, Electronics Tech., Engineering Tech., Mechanical Tech., Plumbing, Welding, Nursing (RN), Graphic Arts
Bachelor of Arts: Business, Economics
Bachelor of Comm/Admin: Finance, Human Resources, Marketing
Bachelor of Science: Computer Science
Bachelor of Engineering: Design, Electrical, Mechanical
Chartered Accounting: CA-Finance, CGA-Finance, CMA-Finance
Masters: Business Administration, Engineering

Critical Skills
Adaptable, Confident, Creative, Decisive, Dependable, Good Communication, Innovative, Leadership, Productive, Professional, Responsible

Types of Positions
Reception
Labourer
Accounting Clerk
Trade Helper

Starting Salary
$ 30,000 - 35,000

Company Benefits
- Full benefit package, profit sharing, tuition assistance
- In-house training, new "world class" building

Correspondence
Mail resume with cover letter or apply through web site
E-mail: mark.arthur@enerflex.com

Part Time/Summer: EnerFlex Systems Ltd. occasionally hires for part time and summer work. Potential jobs include labourer or involve the apprentice program. The best time to apply is in May or June.

ENTREPRISES PREMIER CANADIEN LTÉE

454 ch Temiscouata
Rivière-du-Loup, Québec, G5R 4C9
Tel: (418) 862-6356   Fax: N/A

Serge St. Pierre, Service Ressources Humaines

Entreprises Premier Canadien Ltée is engaged in the horticulture and agriculture business. The company conducts a large amount of research development on the environment as well.

Academic Fields
College: Accounting, Administration, Computer Science, Electronics Tech., Faculty Management, Forestry, Industrial Design, Laboratory Tech., Mechanical Tech., Secretarial
Bachelor of Arts: Business
Bachelor of Comm/Admin: Accounting, Marketing, Info Mgmt.
Bachelor of Science: Agriculture, Biology, Chemistry, Computer Sci., Environmental Studies, Forestry, Microbiology
Bachelor of Engineering: Chemical, Civil, Computer Systems, Design, Electrical, Environmental Studies, Industrial, Mechanical
Chartered Accounting: CA-General, CMA-General
Masters: Science

Critical Skills
Adaptable, Confident, Creative, Decisive, Dependable, Efficient, Flexible, Good Communication, Good Writing Skills, Innovative, Organized, Professional, Responsible

Types of Positions
Engineering
Research and Development

Starting Salary
$ 25,000 - 30,000

Company Benefits
- Full package including dental
- Flexible hours, courses offered if necessary

Correspondence
Mail resume with cover letter, indicating the work you are seeking

Part Time/Summer: Entreprises Premier Canadien sometimes seeks people for part time work, and regularly hires for the summer. Potential summer jobs are in the laboratory, office, engineering dept. and production dept.

The Canada Student Employment Guide

ENVIRONICS RESEARCH GROUP LTD.

33 Bloor Street East, Suite 900
Toronto, Ontario, M4W 3H1
Tel: (416) 920-9010   Fax: (416) 920-3299

Joseph N. Borg, Human Resources
Internet: www.environics.ca

Throughout Environics' history, custom studies (both quantitative and qualitative) and omnibus research surveys using a wide variety of methodologies have been conducted to address specific client issues. With headquarters in Toronto, Environics has offices and affiliates in Ottawa, Calgary (Environics West) and Montreal (CROP Inc.).

Academic Fields
Bachelor of Arts: Political Science, Public Relations, Sociology/Social Work, Statistics
Bachelor of Science: Computer Science, Environmental Studies, Geography, Mathematics, Psychology
Masters: Business Administration, Arts

Critical Skills
Adaptable, Analytical, Dependable, Efficient, Enthusiastic, Good With Figures, Good Writing Skills, Innovative, Logical

Types of Positions
Data Analyst   Research Assistant
Junior Research Associate

Starting Salary
$ 25,000 - 30,000

Company Benefits
- Full range of benefits provided with medical and dental
- Training and development is encouraged
- Training paid for by company

Correspondence
Mail resume with cover letter

Part Time/Summer: Environics Research Group regularly hires for part time jobs and sometimes hires for summer opportunities. Potential positions involve telephone interviewing, research assistant, computer/network needs, report writing, and specialized data analysis.

EPSON CANADA LIMITED

550 McNicoll Ave.
Willowdale, Ontario, M2H 2E1
Tel: (416) 498-9955   Fax: (416) 498-6104

HR Department
Internet: www.epson.com

Epson Canada Limited is a manufacturer and distributor of high quality printers, as well as high tech OEM equipment. The company employs approximately 300 individuals.

Academic Fields
College: Electronics Tech.
Bachelor of Comm/Admin: General, Marketing
Bachelor of Engineering: Electrical

Critical Skills
Adaptable, Analytical, Good Communication, Flexible, Good With Figures

Types of Positions
Customer Service   Technical Support

Starting Salary
$ 20,000 - 25,000

Company Benefits
- Health and dental

Correspondence
Mail, fax or e-mail resume with cover letter
E-mail: hrcanada@eai.epson.com

Part Time/Summer: Epson Canada regularly looks for individuals for part time work and summer employment. Potential summer jobs are in customer service. The best time to apply is in May or June.

The Canada Student Employment Guide

ERNST & YOUNG

55 Metcalfe St., Suite 1600
Ottawa, Ontario, K1P 6L5
Tel: (613) 232-1511   Fax: (613) 232-5324

Human Resources
Internet: www.eycan.com

Ernst & Young is one of the world's leading professional service organizations, helping companies across the globe to identify and capitalize on business opportunities. Their services include auditing, management consulting and corporate finance. They employ over 85,000 people in 701 cities in 133 countries around the world. They have offices in 356 European cities, 175 cities in the Americas, 64 in the Middle East and Africa, and a growing practice in Asia Pacific.

Academic Fields
College: Accounting
Bachelor of Comm/Admin: Accounting

Critical Skills
Confident, Dependable, Organized, Productive, Professional

Types of Positions
Staff Accountant

Starting Salary
$ 25,000 - 30,000

Company Benefits
- Dental and medical
- Courses, fitness training

Correspondence
Mail or fax resume with cover letter

Part Time/Summer: Ernst & Young occasionally hires for part time work and regularly seeks candidates for the summer months.

Co-op/Internship: Ernst & Young does offer some internship opportunities.

ESPIAL GROUP INCORPORATED

200 Elgin St., 3rd Floor
Ottawa, Ontario, S6V 5Z4
Tel: (613) 230-4770   Fax: (613) 230-8498

Lisa S. Brazeau, Manager Human Resources
Internet: www.espial.com

Espial is on the cutting edge of enabling technology for the pervasive internet. What this actually means is that we develop software for smart devices – handhelds, auto PCs, web-enabled TVs, next-generation cell phones and other internet appliances.

Academic Fields
College: Marketing/Sales, Computer Science, Engineering Tech., Industrial Design
Bachelor of Science: Computer Science

Critical Skills
Analytical, Creative, Dependable, Good Writing Skills, Innovative, Leadership, Adaptable to Change, Imagination, Dedication

Types of Positions
Java Developer
Embedded Linux Developer
Quality Assurance Specialist
Professional Service Consultant
Field Application Engineer

Starting Salary
Depends on position

Company Benefits
- Full benefits plan, healthcare, dental, vision, drugs
- Flexible work hours, employer-paid parking

Correspondence
Apply through web site
E-mail: hr@espial.com

Part Time/Summer: Espial Group regularly seeks candidates for part time or summer employment. Potential positions include quality assurance specialist, java developer, web designer, or embedded Linux developer. The best time to apply is in March or April.

Co-op/Internship: They do offer volunteer work programs, where people of exceptional ability and talent can learn and demonstrate their skills. Many of these volunteer situations lead to employment opportunities.

EXFO

465, av Godin
Vanier, Quebec, G1M 3G7
Tel: (418) 683-0211   Fax: (418) 683-2170

Jean-Francios Mathier, HR Specialist
Internet: www.exfo.com

Exfo is a leading designer, marketer, and manufacturer of fibre-optic test, measurement, and monitoring instruments for the telecommunications industry.

Academic Fields
College: Accounting, Administration, Advertising, Business, Communications, Human Resources, Info Syst., Marketing/Sales, Purchasing, Real Estate, Secretarial, CAD Autocad, Computer Sci., Electronics Tech., Engineering Tech., Industrial Design, Mech. Tech.
Bachelor of Arts: General, Business, Economics, English, Languages, Public Relations
Bachelor of Comm/Admin: General, Accounting, Finance, Human Resources, Marketing, Info Mgmt.
Bachelor of Science: Gen., Comp. Sci., Math., Physics
Bachelor of Laws: General, Corporate
Bachelor of Engineering: General, Computer Systems, Electrical, Industrial, Mechanical
Chartered Accounting: CA - General/Finance, CGA - General/Finance, CMA - General/Finance
Masters: Business Administration, Science, Engineering

Critical Skills
Adaptable, Analytical, Confident, Creative, Decisive, Efficient, Enthusiastic, Flexible, Good Communication, Innovative, Leadership, Logical, Manual Dexterity, Organized, Productive, Professional, Responsible

Types of Positions
Management/Admin.   Research & Development
Sales & Marketing   Information Technology

Starting Salary
$ 20,000 - 25,000

Company Benefits
- Salary, stock options, health insurance

Correspondence
E-mail resume with cover letter. E-mail: info@exfo.com

Part Time/Summer: Exfo rarely hires for part time work, but regularly hires for the summer. Potential jobs are in logistics or research and development.

Co-op/Internship: They offer an internship program.

EXIDE CANADA INC.

8301 Keele St.
Maple, Ontario, L6A 1T2
Tel: (905) 669-9326   Fax: (905) 660-6984

Stewart C. Bryan, Human Resources

Exide Canada Inc. is a manufacturer of lead acid automotive batteries. The company employs more than 450 people who work in various capacities.

Academic Fields
College: Accounting, Administration, Business, Computer Science, Engineering Tech., Human Resources, Marketing/Sales
Bachelor of Arts: General, Business
Bachelor of Comm/Admin: Accounting, Finance, Marketing, Info Mgmt.
Bachelor of Science: Computer Science, Environmental Studies
Bachelor of Engineering: Electrical, Mechanical
Chartered Accounting: CA-General, CMA-Finance
Masters: Engineering

Critical Skills
Good Communication, Confident, Dependable, Efficient, Enthusiastic, Good With Figures, Leadership, Organized, Personable, Productive, Professional, Responsible, Good Writing Skills

Types of Positions
Customer Service/Marketing   Accounts Payable

Starting Salary
$ 25,000 - 40,000

Company Benefits
- Group benefits for full time employees
- Life, dental, major medical
- Training developed on an as needed basis

Correspondence
Mail resume with cover letter

Part Time/Summer: Exide Canada occasionally looks for individuals for part time or summer employment. Potential jobs include general office work, or general warehouse duties. The best time to apply is prior to the end of April.

THE EXPLORER HOTEL

Postal Service 7000
Yellowknife, NWT, X1A 2R3
Tel: (867) 873-3531   Fax: (867) 873-2789

Human Resources
Internet: www.explorerhotel.nt.ca

The Explorer Hotel is a 128 bedroom, full service luxury hotel located just steps away from the commercial and government centre of Yellowknife. The hotel has eight conference rooms suitable for groups of up to 350 people and offers full conference facilities. There are also five associated meeting and banquet rooms within the hotel.

Academic Fields
College: Accounting, Administration, Business, Communications, Cooking/Culinary, Human Resources, Travel/Tourism
Bachelor of Arts: Business, Languages
Bachelor of Comm/Admin: Accounting, Finance, Marketing, Info Mgmt., Public Admin.
Bachelor of Laws: Corporate

Critical Skills
Adaptable, Good Communication, Confident, Creative, Decisive, Dependable, Efficient, Enthusiastic, Flexible, Leadership, Organized, Patient, Personable, Productive, Professional

Types of Positions
Cooks	Front Desk Clerk
Waiter/Waitress	Room Attendant
Banquet Porter	Bartender

Starting Salary
$ 20,000 - 25,000

Company Benefits
- Complete benefit package

Correspondence
Mail, fax or submit resume with cover letter in person
E-mail: operations@explorerhotel.nt.ca

Part Time/Summer: The Explorer Hotel regularly seeks candidates for part time and summer employment opportunities. Positions in the summer months are most likely those listed above. The best time to apply is in April or early May.

EXPORT DEVELOPMENT CORPORATION

151 O'Connor St.
Ottawa, Ontario, K2P 2M5
Tel: (613) 598-2500   Fax: (613) 237-2690

Human Resources
Internet: www.edc.ca

Export Development Corporation (EDC) is a Canadian financial institution devoted exclusively to providing trade finance services in support of Canadian exporters and investors in up to 200 countries. Founded in 1944, EDC is a Crown corporation that operates as a commercial financial institution. They employ approximately 850 individuals.

Academic Fields
Bachelor of Arts: Business
Bachelor of Comm/Admin: Accounting, Finance, Info Mgmt.
Bachelor of Science: Mathematics
Chartered Accounting: CA - General/Finance, CGA - General/Finance, CMA - General/Finance
Masters: Business Administration

Critical Skills
Adaptable, Analytical, Dependable, Good Communication, Good Writing Skills, Personable, Professional

Types of Positions
Financial Services

Starting Salary
$ 45,000 - 50,000

Company Benefits
- Very attractive and competitive benefits package
- Opportunity to earn an incentive (over and above base salary)

Correspondence
E-mail resume with cover letter or apply through web site. E-mail: hrrh@edc-see.ca

Part Time/Summer: Export Development Corporation rarely hires for part time work, but regularly hires for the summer. Potential jobs are available in several areas. Visit their web site for more info. Best time to apply is January and February.

Co-op/Internship: They are currently developing an internship program.

EXTENDICARE (CANADA) INC.

3000 Steeles Avenue East, Suite 700
Markham, Ontario, L3R 9W2
Tel: (905) 470-4000   Fax: (905) 470-5588

Jennifer Alexander, Director Employment Services
Internet: www.extendicare.com

Extendicare operates nursing and retirement centres in Canada, the United States, and throughout the United Kingdom. In Canada, Extendicare also provides home care services, health care consulting, hospital management, and development services.

Academic Fields
College: Accounting, Communications, Computer Science, Human Resources, Journalism, Marketing/Sales, Nursing, Recreation Studies, Secretarial
Bachelor of Arts: General, Business, Economics, Gerontology, Journalism, Recreation Studies
Bachelor of Comm/Admin: General, Accounting, Finance, Info Mgmt.
Bachelor of Science: Computer Science, Environmental Studies, Food Sciences, Mathematics, Nursing (RN), Occupational Therapy, Physiotherapy
Bachelor of Engineering: General, Environ. Studies
Bachelor of Education: General
Chartered Accounting: CA - General/Finance, CGA/CMA - General/Finance
Masters: Business Administration, Engineering

Critical Skills
Adaptable, Analytical, Good Communication, Confident, Creative, Decisive, Dependable, Diligent, Diplomatic, Efficient, Enthusiastic, Flexible, Manual Dexterity, Organized, Patient, Personable, Persuasive, Productive, Professional, Responsible, Writing Skills

Types of Positions
Accounts Payable   Accounts Receivable
Payroll   Human Resources

Starting Salary
$ 20,000 - 25,000

Company Benefits
- Medical, dental and vision plan, RRSP plan

Correspondence
Mail or fax resume with cover letter

Part Time/Summer: Extendicare sometimes hires for part time and summer work. Positions are usually in accounts receivable, accounts payable, and payroll. The best time to apply is from February to May.

FAG BEARINGS LIMITED

801 Ontario St.
Stratford, Ontario, N5A 6T2
Tel: (519) 271-3231   Fax: (519) 273-8500

Frances Smeets, Human Resources Leader
Internet: www.fag-bearings.ca

FAG Bearings Limited is a leading manufacturer of bearings in the automotive industry. The automotive markets are served through sales and engineering offices in Southfield, Michigan, Stratford, Ontario, and Schweinfurt, Germany. Customers include General Motors, Chrysler, and Ford. The company employs approximately 1,200 people.

Academic Fields
College: Administration, Human Resources, Information Systems, Engineering Tech.
Bachelor of Science: Computer Science
Bachelor of Engineering: Computer Systems, Electrical, Mechanical

Critical Skills
Good Communication, Dependable, Organized, Productive, Responsible, Team Player

Types of Positions
Engineer   Machine Operator
Administrative Assistant Technician

Starting Salary
$ 35,000 - 40,000

Company Benefits
- Extended health, life insurance, dental
- Profit sharing/scrap bonus, attendance bonus
- On-going training opportunities, continuous improvement programs

Correspondence
Mail, fax, e-mail or submit resume with cover letter in person. E-mail: hr@fag-bearings.ca

Part Time/Summer: FAG Bearings occasionally looks for individuals for part time work, and regularly seeks summer help. Potential summer jobs occur in numerous disciplines including engineering, information systems and human resources. The best time to apply is in February or March.

Co-op/Internship: They do offer internship opportunities.

The Canada Student Employment Guide

FAMILY DAY CARE SERVICE

380 Sherbourne St.
Toronto, Ontario, M4X 1K2
Tel: (416) 922-3434   Fax: (416) 922-5335

N. Wightman, Human Resources
Internet: www.familydaycare.com

Family Day Care Services (Family Day) is a licensed non-profit charitable organization that has been helping children and their families since 1851. Currently, the Agency cares for approximately 4,000 children in twenty-three child care centres and 600 child care homes throughout the Greater Toronto Area.

Academic Fields
College: Accounting, Administration, Child Care, Secretarial
Chartered Accounting: CMA-General

Critical Skills
Adaptable, Good Communication, Confident, Dependable, Efficient, Enthusiastic, Flexible, Good With Figures, Organized, Patient, Personable, Productive, Professional, Responsible, Good Writing Skills

Types of Positions
Various Positions

Starting Salary
$ 25,000 - 40,000

Company Benefits
- Medical, dental, life insurance
- 100% disability, vision plan, pension
- Staff development courses offered each year

Correspondence
Mail or fax resume with cover letter

Part Time/Summer: Family Day Care Services occasionally looks for individuals for part time or summer employment opportunities. However, their organization won't be hiring students this year unless they receive funding.

FARM CREDIT CORP. CANADA

1800 Hamilton Street
Regina, Saskatchewan, S4P 4L3
Tel: (306) 780-8636   Fax: (306) 780-5703

Staffing Consultant, Human Resources
Internet: www.yop-pej.com

Farm Credit Corporation (FCC) is a federal Crown corporation reporting to Parliament through the Minister of Agriculture and Agri-Food. Established in 1959, FCC is Canada's largest agricultural term lender.

Academic Fields
College: Accounting, Administration, Business, Communications, Human Resources, Information Systems, Marketing/Sales, Secretarial, Journalism, Agricultural, Computer Science
Bachelor of Arts: Business, Journalism, Public Rel.
Bachelor of Comm/Admin: General, Accounting, Finance, Human Resources, Marketing, Info Mgmt.
Bachelor of Science: Agriculture, Computer Science
Chartered Accounting: CA-General, CGA-General, CMA-General
Masters: Business Administration

Critical Skills
Adaptable, Analytical, Confident, Creative, Decisive, Dependable, Diligent, Diplomatic, Efficient, Enthusiastic, Flexible, Good Communication, Good With Figures, Good Writing Skills, Innovative, Leadership, Logical, Organized, Personable, Persuasive, Productive, Professional, Responsible

Types of Positions
Credit Advisor   Accounting/Finance
Information Technology   Administration Support

Starting Salary
$ 20,000 - 25,000

Company Benefits
- Flexible benefits package, flexible hours of work

Correspondence
Mail resume with cover letter

Part Time/Summer: FCC Canada occasionally hires for part time and summer work. Potential jobs are in accounting, human resources, communications, and administration.

Co-op/Internship: They offer internship opportunities through the Career Edge Program.

FARMERS CO-OPERATIVE DAIRY LIMITED

P.O. Box 8118
Halifax, Nova Scotia, B3K 5Y6
Tel: (902) 835-3373   Fax: (902) 835-4036

Human Resources Department

Farmers Co-operative Dairy Limited is a manufacturer and distributor of dairy products in Atlantic Canada. Manufacturing and distribution facilities are located in Nova Scotia, Prince Edward Island and Newfoundland. The firm has approximately 550 employees in total.

Academic Fields
College: Computer Science, Food/Nutrition, Industrial Mechanic, Welding, Electrician
Bachelor of Arts: Business
Bachelor of Comm/Admin: General, Accounting, Finance, Marketing, Info Mgmt., Human Resources
Bachelor of Science: Biology, Computer Science, Food Sciences, Microbiology
Bachelor of Engineering: Industrial
Chartered Accounting: CA-General, CMA-General
Masters: Business Administration

Critical Skills
Adaptable, Good Communication, Confident, Dependable, Efficient, Enthusiastic, Flexible, Leadership, Organized, Persuasive, Professional, Responsible

Types of Positions
Sales   Production
Operations   Accounting
Clerical

Starting Salary
$ 30,000 - 40,000

Company Benefits
- Medical, dental, pension
- Christmas bonus, sick days
- Excellent training opportunities and management incentive plans

Correspondence
Mail resume with cover letter

Part Time/Summer: Farmers Co-operative Dairy Limited regularly looks for people for part time and summer employment. Potential jobs include clerical work, labourer, or sales. Apply in February.

FEDERATED CO-OPERATIVES LIMITED

Box 1050, 401 - 22nd Street East
Saskatoon, Saskatchewan, S7K 0H2
Tel: (306) 244-3311   Fax: (306) 244-3403

Rosalynne Tayler, Retail Recruitment
Internet: www.fcl.ca

More than 300 retail co-operatives serve an estimated 900,000 individual co-op members from Thunder Bay in northwest Ontario to the Queen Charlotte Islands on British Columbia's West Coast, and from the U.S. border to the Arctic Circle.

Academic Fields
College: General, Accounting, Administration, Advertising, Animal Health, Business, Computer Science, Forestry, Graphic Arts, Marketing/Sales, Secretarial, Travel/Tourism
Bachelor of Arts: Business
Bachelor of Comm/Admin: General, Accounting, Finance, Marketing, Info Mgmt., Public Admin.
Bachelor of Science: Agriculture, Chemistry, Computer Science, Environmental Studies, Food Sciences, Forestry, Horticulture, Pharmacy
Bachelor of Laws: General, Corporate
Bachelor of Engineering: General, Design, Electrical, Environmental Studies, Industrial, Mechanical
Bachelor of Education: General, Adult Education
Chartered Accounting: CA - General/Finance, CGA/CMA - General/Finance
Masters: Business Administration, Engineering

Critical Skills
Adaptable, Analytical, Artistic, Good Communication, Confident, Creative, Decisive, Dependable, Diligent, Diplomatic, Efficient, Enthusiastic, Flexible, Organized, Patient, Personable, Persuasive, Productive, Professional, Responsible, Writing Skills

Types of Positions
Human Resources Officer   Data Entry
Accounting Clerk   Auditor

Starting Salary
$ 20,000 - 30,000

Company Benefits
- Dental, pension, life insurance, long term disability

Correspondence
Mail or fax resume with cover letter

Part Time/Summer: They occasionally hire for part time work, but do not hire for the summer.

The Canada Student Employment Guide

FEDEX EXPRESS

5985 Explorer Dr.
Mississauga, Ontario, L4W 5K6
Tel: (905) 212-5060   Fax: (905) 212-5653

Human Resources
Internet: www.fedex.com

FedEx Express is involved in the courier business, shipping packages and goods of all sizes across the country. The firm has an employee base of over 4,000 individuals.

Academic Fields
College: Accounting, Secretarial
Bachelor of Arts: Psychology, Public Relations
Bachelor of Comm/Admin: Finance, Marketing, Info Mgmt.
Bachelor of Science: Computer Science, Psychology
Bachelor of Laws: Corporate
Bachelor of Engineering: Computer Syst., Industrial
Chartered Accounting: CA-Finance, CMA-Finance
Masters: Business Administration, Engineering

Critical Skills
Good Communication, Decisive, Dependable, Diligent, Enthusiastic, Flexible, Leadership, Organized, Professional, Responsible, Good Writing Skills

Types of Positions
Marketing Specialist   Recruitment Specialist
Engineering   Account Executive (Sales)

Starting Salary
Varies depending on position

Company Benefits
- Medical, dental, vision, pension
- Group life coverage, tuition refund program
- Airline benefits

Correspondence
Mail resume with cover letter

Part Time/Summer: FedEx Express regularly looks for people for part time work and occasionally seeks individuals for summer opportunities. The company only hires through the co-op program.

FINNING

16830 107th Avenue
Edmonton, Alberta, T5P 4C3
Tel: (780) 930-4800   Fax: (780) 930-4801

Amanda Brandoma, HR Secretary
Internet: www.finning.ca

Finning sells, services and finances the full line of Caterpillar and complimentary equipment throughout Western Canada. Finning is represented in 65 communities in the western part of the country. They employ about 2,400 individuals.

Academic Fields
College: Accounting, Administration, Advertising, Business, Communications, Human Resources, Information Systems, Insurance, Marketing/Sales, Purchasing, Secretarial, Agricultural, Engineering Tech., Mechanical Tech., Welding
Bachelor of Arts: Business
Bachelor of Comm/Admin: General, Accounting, Finance, Human Resources, Marketing, Public Admin.
Bachelor of Engineering: Electrical, Mech., Mining
Chartered Accounting: CA - General/Finance, CGA - General/Finance, CMA - General/Finance
Masters: Business Administration, Engineering

Critical Skills
Adaptable, Analytical, Diligent, Efficient, Good Communication, Good Writing Skills, Organized

Types of Positions
Secretarial/Clerical   Material Supply Assistant
Accounting   Labourer

Starting Salary
$ 25,000 - 30,000

Company Benefits
- Competitive benefits package

Correspondence
Fax, e-mail resume with cover letter or apply through web site

Part Time/Summer: Finning regularly hires for part time and summer work. Potential jobs include material supply assistant (parts dept.), vacation coverage for clerical and receptionist positions, along with various labour positions. Apply in April and May.

Co-op/Internship: They offer internship opportunities. Contact Lisa Graves at (780) 930-4811 for more information.

The Canada Student Employment Guide

FISHER SCIENTIFIC LIMITED

112 Colonnade Rd.
Nepean, Ontario, K2E 7L6
Tel: (613) 226-8874   Fax: (613) 226-2812

Julie Stewart, Human Resources
Internet: www.fishersci.ca

Fisher Scientific Limited is in the business of sales and distribution of scientific and safety products. The firm sells and services all types of laboratory products.

Academic Fields
College: Business, Computer Science, Human Resources, Nursing, Science-General
Bachelor of Comm/Admin: Accounting
Bachelor of Science: Biology, Chemistry, Environmental Studies, Health Sciences, Microbiology, Nursing (RN), Pharmacy, Physics
Bachelor of Engineering: Environmental Studies, Geotechnical
Chartered Accounting: CA - General/Finance, CGA/CMA - General/Finance
Masters: Business Administration

Critical Skills
Adaptable, Analytical, Good Communication, Confident, Decisive, Dependable, Diligent, Diplomatic, Efficient, Enthusiastic, Flexible, Good With Figures, Leadership, Logical, Persuasive, Professional, Good Writing Skills

Types of Positions
Customer Service Representative

Starting Salary
$ 28,000

Company Benefits
- Group insurance (medical, dental, life, long term disability)

Correspondence
Mail, fax, e-mail, or submit resume with cover letter in person

Part Time/Summer: Fisher Scientific Limited regularly looks for individuals for part time or summer employment. Potential jobs are customer service representatives in Ottawa, or warehouse workers in Whitby.

FISHERY PRODUCTS INTERNATIONAL

P.O. Box 550
St. John's, Newfoundland, A1C 5L1
Tel: (709) 570-0000   Fax: (709) 570-0209

Donna Brophy, Industrial Relations
Internet: www.fpil.com

Fishery Products International (FPI) is a global seafood enterprise which produces and markets a full range of seafood products, including shrimp, crab, scallops, cod, sole, redfish, pollock, turbot, and haddock. These products are distributed across a wide network throughout North America, Southeast Asia, South America, and Europe. FPI employs 3,900 people.

Academic Fields
College: Accounting, Business, Computer Science, Electronics Tech., Food/Nutrition, Human Resources, Marketing/Sales, Mechanical Tech., Secretarial
Bachelor of Arts: Business, Economics
Bachelor of Comm/Admin: Accounting, Finance, Marketing, Info Mgmt.
Bachelor of Science: Computer Science, Food Sciences, Nursing (RN)
Bachelor of Laws: Corporate
Bachelor of Engineering: Computer Systems, Mechanical
Chartered Accounting: CA-Finance, CMA - General/Finance, CGA - General/Finance
Masters: Business Admin., Science, Engineering

Critical Skills
Analytical, Good Communication, Enthusiastic, Innovative, Leadership, Productive

Types of Positions
Accounting Assistant   Programmer
Food Technologist   Secretarial
Sales Support

Starting Salary
$ 25,000 - 30,000

Company Benefits
- Group insurance and company pension
- Share purchase plan and profit sharing

Correspondence
Mail or fax resume with cover letter

Part Time/Summer: FPI sometimes hires people for part time and summer work. The best time to apply is in May or June.

The Canada Student Employment Guide

FLAKEBOARD COMPANY LIMITED

P.O. Box 490
St. Stephen, New Brunswick, E3L 3A6
Tel: (506) 466-2370   Fax: (506) 466-7113

Lorraine Matthews, Manager of Human Relations

Flakeboard Company is a major manufacturer of particleboard in New Brunswick. The company also produces painted panels, melamine and fibre board. The company employs approximately 300 individuals.

Academic Fields
College: Accounting, Business, Computer Science, Electronics Tech., Engineering Tech., Forestry, Laboratory Tech., Marketing/Sales, Mechanical Tech., Secretarial
Bachelor of Arts: Business
Bachelor of Science: Chemistry, Environmental Studies, Forestry
Bachelor of Engineering: Chemical, Civil, Computer Systems, Electrical, Environmental Studies, Mechanical
Chartered Accounting: CMA-Finance

Critical Skills
Adaptable, Analytical, Good Communication, Confident, Decisive, Dependable, Diligent, Diplomatic, Efficient, Enthusiastic, Innovative, Logical, Organized, Patient, Personable, Productive, Professional, Responsible, Good Writing Skills

Types of Positions
Receptionist   Accounts Payable
Accounts Receivable   Plant Labourer
Team Worker   Mechanical/Electrical

Starting Salary
$ 25,000 - 30,000

Company Benefits
- Dental and drug plans, life insurance
- Pension plan and long term disability
- Variety of training for plant and office staff

Correspondence
Mail resume with cover letter
E-mail: lorrainem@flakeboard.ca

Part Time/Summer: Flakeboard Company sometimes hires for both part time and summer employment. However, most positions are filled by siblings, relatives of current workforce, or those that best suit the position. Those jobs above are the most likely to be filled. The best time to apply is in early April.

FLETCHER'S FINE FOODS

8385 Fraser Street
Vancouver, British Columbia, V5X 3X8
Tel: (604) 668-5900   Fax: (604) 668-5919

Ian Doyle, Personnel Manager

Fletcher's Fine Foods is a pork producer with operations in Red Deer, Edmonton, Vancouver and the United States. The company is a wholly owned subsidiary of the Alberta Pork Producers Development Corporation. Fletcher's Fine Foods has an employee base of approximately 1,000 people.

Academic Fields
College: Accounting, Communications, Emergency/Paramedic, Engineering Tech., Laboratory Tech., Marketing/Sales, Mechanical Tech., Secretarial
Bachelor of Comm/Admin: Accounting, Finance, Marketing, Info Mgmt.
Bachelor of Science: Food Sciences
Bachelor of Engineering: Electrical, Industrial, Mechanical

Critical Skills
Adaptable, Dependable, Diligent, Good Communication, Efficient, Enthusiastic, Good Writing Skills, Logical, Productive, Manual Dexterity, Responsible

Types of Positions
Maintenance   Secretarial/Clerical
Labourer

Starting Salary
below $ 20,000 -40,000 (depends on position)

Company Benefits
- 80% coverage for dental
- 60% coverage for sick leave
- 80% medication plan

Correspondence
Fill out an application

Part Time/Summer: Fletcher's Fine Foods regularly hires individuals for part time and summer work opportunities. Positions in the summer are most likely to be labourers. Candidates are invited to apply year round.

The Canada Student Employment Guide

FLINT ENERGY SERVICES LTD.

2029 - 87 Avenue
Edmonton, Alberta, T6P 1L5
Tel: (780) 464-4034   Fax: (780) 464-2983

Jason Beaman, HR Advisor

Flint Energy Services Ltd. is one of Canada's largest integrated downstream oilfield services, industrial construction and fabrication components. Flint Energy Services was formed in 1999 as a result of the purchase or merger with five of Canada's premier oilfield service and construction companies including Flint Canada Inc., Reid's Construction Group, Braidnor Construction, HMW Construction, and Titan Electric and Controls.

Academic Fields
College: Accounting, Human Resources, Information Syst., CAD Autocad, Computer Sci. Engineering Tech., Industrial Tech., Mechanical Tech., Plumbing, Welding
Bachelor of Arts: Business
Bachelor of Comm/Admin: Accounting, Finance, Human Resources, Info Mgmt.
Bachelor of Science: Computer Science
Bachelor of Engineering: General, Civil, Elec., Mech.
Chartered Accounting: CA-General, CMA - General/Finance
Masters: Business Administration

Critical Skills
Adaptable, Confident, Decisive, Dependable, Diplomatic, Flexible, Good Communication, Good With Figures, Writing Skills, Leadership, Organized

Types of Positions
Field Engineer   Field Accounting
Assistant Project Manager   Superintendent Trainee

Starting Salary
$ 30,000 - 35,000

Company Benefits
- Comprehensive medical and dental plan

Correspondence
Fax resume with cover letter E-mail: hr@flint-energy.com

Part Time/Summer: Flint Energy Services occasionally hires for part time work and summer opportunities.

FM GLOBAL

165 Commerce Valley Dr. W., Suite 500
Thornhill, Ontario, L3T 7V8
Tel: (905) 763-5555   Fax: N/A

Gloria Frizzell, Administration Manager
Internet: www.fmglobal.com

FM Global is the world's largest commercial and industrial property insurance and risk management organization specializing in property protection.

Academic Fields
College: General, Insurance
Bachelor of Engineering: General, Electrical, Environmental Studies, Industrial

Critical Skills
Analytical, Good Communication, Dependable, Efficient, Flexible, Organized

Types of Positions
Mail/Filing Clerk   Receptionist

Starting Salary
$ 30,000 - 40,000

Company Benefits
- Medical and dental
- Savings plan with company matched pension
- Training department will pay for outside courses related to job

Correspondence
Mail or fax resume with cover letter

Part Time/Summer: FM Global does not hire individuals for part time or summer employment. From time to time they hire employee's children for odd jobs.

The Canada Student Employment Guide

FOREMOST INDUSTRIES INC.

1225 - 64th Avenue N.E.
Calgary, Alberta, T2E 8P9
Tel: (403) 295-5800   Fax: (403) 295-5810

Human Resources

Foremost Industries Inc. is a manufacturer of large terrain vehicles and drills. The company's head office is in Calgary, Alberta.

Academic Fields
College: Accounting, Administration, Business, Communications, Computer Science, Drafting/Architecture, Engineering Tech., Human Resources, Journalism, Marketing/Sales, Mechanical Tech., Secretarial
Bachelor of Arts: Journalism, Public Relations
Bachelor of Comm/Admin: Accounting, Info Mgmt.
Bachelor of Science: General, Computer Science
Bachelor of Engineering: General, Design, Industrial
Chartered Accounting: CMA-Finance, CGA-Finance
Masters: Business Administration, Engineering

Critical Skills
Analytical, Dependable, Diligent, Efficient, Enthusiastic, Good Communication, Good With Figures, Good Writing Skills, Leadership, Logical, Manual Dexterity, Organized, Persuasive, Professional

Types of Positions
Journeyman Mechanic   Journeyman Welder
Drafting Technician   Accounting Clerk
Secretary   Receptionist

Starting Salary
$ 20,000 - 30,000 (depending on position)

Company Benefits
- Alberta health care, extended health, dental
- Short term and long term disability
- Stock options, bonus plan

Correspondence
Mail resume with cover letter

Part Time/Summer: Foremost Industries Inc. occasionally hires for part time or summer work. Potential jobs include reception, filing, yard work, or inventory. The best time to apply is in March or April.

THE FORZANI GROUP LTD.

824 - 41 Avenue NE
Calgary, Alberta, T2E 3R3
Tel: (403) 717-1400   Fax: (403) 717-1491

Human Resources
Internet: www.forzanigroup.com

The Forzani Group Ltd. (FGL) is the leading national sporting goods retailer providing customers with a vast selection of merchandise ranging from clothing to sporting equipment. FGL operates under the banners of Sport Chek, Forzani's, Sports Experts, and Coast Mountain Sports. FGL has a separate office in Laval, Quebec, to oversee its 160 franchise stores across Canada, operating under the banners of RnR Outdoors, Sports Experts, Intersport, and Econosports. FGL will venture into the world of e-commerce in Fall 2000.

Academic Fields
College: General, Accounting, Advertising, Human Resources, Marketing/Sales, Administrative, Information Technology
Bachelor of Arts: Business
Bachelor of Comm/Admin: Accounting, Finance, Marketing, Info Mgmt.

Critical Skills
Adaptable, Enthusiastic, Good Communication, Innovative, Organized, Personable, Team Player

Types of Positions
Implementation Specialist   Accounting Clerk
Marketing

Starting Salary
$ 20,000 - 25,000

Company Benefits
- Above average benefits package

Correspondence
Mail resume with cover letter (office), Submit resume with cover letter in person (stores).
E-mail: hr@forzani.com

Part Time/Summer: The Forzani Group occasionally hires for part time or summer work. Potential opportunities include sales associates within stores. The best time to apply is in early May.

Co-op/Internship: There are some co-op placements in information technology.

FOSTER WHEELER LIMITED

Box 1, 509 Glendale Ave.
Niagara-on-the-Lake, Ontario, L0S 1J0
Tel: (905) 688-4434   Fax: (905) 688-4588

Personnel Department

Foster Wheeler is involved in steam generation and heat transfer equipment design. The company has an employee base of approximately 150 people.

Academic Fields
College: Drafting/Architecture
Bachelor of Engineering: Mechanical

Critical Skills
Good Communication, Dependable, Enthusiastic, Flexible, Professional, Responsible, Good Writing Skills

Types of Positions
Junior Draftsperson   Junior Proposal Engineer

Starting Salary
$ 40,000 - 50,000

Company Benefits
- Comprehensive benefit and training package

Correspondence
Mail resume with cover letter

Part Time/Summer: Foster Wheeler occasionally looks for individuals for part time or summer employment. Potential jobs are in engineering or accounting. The best time to apply is in April.

FOYER VALADE INC.

450 River Road
Winnipeg, Manitoba, R2M 5M4
Tel: (204) 254-3332   Fax: (204) 254-0329

Edith Alards, Human Resources

Foyer Valade is a personal care home facility established in 1976. The care home contains 115 beds and has an employee base of approximately 150 individuals. The facility is mainly French speaking, therefore staff must be at least partially fluent in the French language.

Academic Fields
College: Accounting, Administration, Business, Computer Science, Cooking/Culinary, Faculty Management, Food/Nutrition, Human Resources, Nursing, Recreation Studies, Secretarial
Bachelor of Arts: Gerontology, Music, Public Relations, Recreation Studies, Sociology/Social Work
Bachelor of Comm/Admin: Accounting, Finance, Info Mgmt., Public Admin.
Bachelor of Science: Computer Science, Environmental Studies, Food Sciences, Health Sciences, Nursing (RN), Occupational Therapy
Bachelor of Engineering: Electrical, Environ. Studies
Chartered Accounting: CA-Finance, CGA-General, CGA-Finance

Critical Skills
Adaptable, Good Communication, Confident, Creative, Decisive, Dependable, Diligent, Diplomatic, Efficient, Enthusiastic, Flexible, Good With Figures, Innovative, Leadership, Logical, Manual Dexterity, Organized, Patient, Personable, Productive, Professional, Responsible, Good Writing Skills

Types of Positions
Resident Assistant   Housekeeping Aide
Cook   Dietary

Starting Salary
below $ 20,000

Company Benefits
- Health, dental, pension, disability plan

Correspondence
Mail or fax resume with cover letter

Part Time/Summer: Foyer Valade regularly hires for part time and summer opportunities. Potential summer jobs include resident assistant or dietary aide.

The Canada Student Employment Guide

FRIESENS CORPORATION

One Painters Way
Altona, Manitoba, R0G 0B0
Tel: (204) 324-6401   Fax: (204) 324-1333

Human Resources Manager
Internet: www.friesens.com

Friesens Corporation is a book manufacturing company that is involved in the printing and binding of many different types of books. The firm produces books, calendars, and yearbooks. They employ about 500 individuals.

Academic Fields
College: Accounting, Administration, Business, Communications, Computer Science, Human Resources, Marketing/Sales, Secretarial
Bachelor of Arts: Business, Economics, Public Relations
Bachelor of Comm/Admin: Accounting, Finance, Marketing, Info Mgmt.
Bachelor of Science: Computer Science
Bachelor of Engineering: Computer Systems, Industrial
Chartered Accounting: CA-Finance, CMA-Finance, CGA-Finance
Masters: Business Administration, Science, Engineering

Critical Skills
Adaptable, Good Communication, Confident, Dependable, Efficient, Enthusiastic, Flexible, Innovative, Leadership, Organized, Professional, Responsible

Types of Positions
Accounting Clerk   Estimator
Prepress Plateburning   Press Feeder

Starting Salary
$ 20,000 - 30,000

Company Benefits
- Health plan, group insurance, pension plan
- On-the-job training, computer training

Correspondence
Mail or fax resume with cover letter

Part Time/Summer: Friesens Corporation regularly looks for people for part time or summer work. Potential jobs in the summer include production support in bindery, prepress, and press.

FUTURE SHOP LTD.

8800 Glenyon Pkwy.
Burnaby, British Columbia, V5J 5K3
Tel: (604) 435-8223   Fax: (604) 412-5280

Human Resources
Internet: www.futureshop.com

Future Shop is one of North America's leading specialty retailers of computers and consumer electronics products. Presently they have 90 stores in Canada and the U.S. and annual sales exceeding $1.3 billion.

Academic Fields
College: Accounting, Administration, Advertising, Business, Communications, Computer Science, Graphic Arts, Human Resources, Marketing/Sales, Secretarial
Bachelor of Arts: Business, Economics, Public Relations
Bachelor of Comm/Admin: General, Accounting, Finance, Marketing, Info Mgmt., Public Admin.
Bachelor of Science: Computer Science
Bachelor of Laws: General, Real Estate
Bachelor of Engineering: Computer Systems
Chartered Accounting: CA - General/Finance, CGA/CMA - General/Finance
Masters: Business Administration

Critical Skills
Analytical, Good Communication, Confident, Decisive, Dependable, Diligent, Efficient, Enthusiastic, Good With Figures, Leadership, Organized, Personable, Persuasive, Productive, Professional, Responsible, Good Writing Skills

Types of Positions
Sales Representative   Customer Service Rep.
Advertising Assistant   Marketing Assistant

Starting Salary
below $ 20,000 - 25,000

Company Benefits
- Full medical and dental
- Share purchase plan, employee discount

Correspondence
Fax resume with cover letter

Part Time/Summer: Future Shop occasionally hires for part time and summer work. Potential jobs are in-store merchandiser, customer service, or help desk. The best time to apply is in the Spring.

The Canada Student Employment Guide

GALLUP CANADA INC.

170 University Ave.
Toronto, Ontario, M5H 3B3
Tel: (416) 586-0808   Fax: N/A

R. Gary Edwards, Human Resources
Internet: www.gallup.com

Gallup Canada provides marketing analysis and other consulting services to a wide range of businesses and other enterprises in Ontario. The company employs over 150 individuals at the location above. Some of these staff members work for the company on a part time basis.

Academic Fields
Bachelor of Arts: Business, Statistics
Bachelor of Comm/Admin: Marketing
Bachelor of Science: Mathematics, Psychology
Masters: Business Administration, Arts

Critical Skills
Analytical, Confident, Decisive, Dependable, Diligent, Efficient, Enthusiastic, Good Communication, Flexible, Professional, Logical, Good With Figures, Organized, Persuasive, Productive, Good Writing Skills,

Types of Positions
Support Analyst

Starting Salary
$ 25,000 - 30,000

Company Benefits
- An extensive benefits package is offered

Correspondence
Mail or fax resume with cover letter

Part Time/Summer: Gallup Canada sometimes hires for part time openings, but does not generally hire individuals to work in the summer months.

GAY LEA FOODS CO-OPERATIVE LTD.

100 Clayson Road
North York, Ontario, M9M 2G7
Tel: (416) 741-0261   Fax: (416) 741-4086

Irene Russell, Human Resources
Internet: www.gaylea.com

Gay Lea Foods Co-Operative is a food manufacturer of dairy and related products. The company produces and distributes food products such as cottage cheese, sour cream, butter, skim milk powder, aerosol whips, hard cheeses, and milk and cream products. Gay Lea Foods Co-Operative employs about 450 individuals across the country.

Academic Fields
College: Accounting, Administration, Business, Human Resources, Marketing/Sales
Bachelor of Arts: General, Business, Economics, Psychology, Public Relations, Sociology/Social Work
Bachelor of Comm/Admin: General, Marketing
Bachelor of Science: Agriculture, Food Sciences, Microbiology
Chartered Accounting: CA - General/Finance, CGA/CMA - General/Finance
Masters: Business Administration

Critical Skills
Adaptable, Analytical, Artistic, Good Communication, Confident, Creative, Decisive, Dependable, Diligent, Diplomatic, Efficient, Enthusiastic, Flexible, Good With Figures, Innovative, Leadership, Logical, Productive, Professional, Responsible, Writing Skills

Types of Positions
Credit Collections	Customer Service Rep.
Junior Sales Rep.	Lab Technician
Marketing Planner	Junior Accountant

Starting Salary
$ 30,000 - 40,000

Company Benefits
- 100% medical, dental, and pension
- Vacation package and flexible hours
- Dedicated training in a 'Total Quality' environment

Correspondence
Mail resume and cover letter or telephone

Part Time/Summer: Gay Lea Foods regularly hires for part time and summer opportunities. Potential summer jobs include those noted above. The best time to apply is in November or December.

The Canada Student Employment Guide

GENCORP VEHICLE SEALING

100 Kennedy St.
Welland, Ontario, L3B 5R9
Tel: (905) 735-5631   Fax: (905) 735-7828

Leslie Luczycki, HR Specialist
Internet: www.vs-gencorp.com

GenCorp Vehicle Sealing Div., is a customer focused automotive supplier specializing in isolating vehicle interior systems from the outside environment. As a seamless extension of our customer's development and design team, they provide sealing solutions that eliminate wind noise, water leaks and emission intrusion. In addition, their designs are engineered to work with vehicle styling, thus providing the consumer with sealing systems that are both functional and attractive.

Academic Fields
College: Information Systems, Electronics Tech., Engineering Tech., Mechanical Tech., Nursing (RN)
Bachelor of Science: Chemistry, Computer Science
Bachelor of Engineering: General, Chemical, Industrial, Mechanical
Bachelor of Education: General
Masters: Engineering

Critical Skills
Adaptable, Analytical, Confident, Creative, Decisive, Dependable, Diplomatic, Efficient, Enthusiastic, Flexible, Good Communication, Good With Figures, Innovative, Leadership, Logical, Organized, Patient, Personable, Productive, Professional, Responsible

Types of Positions
Process Engineer   Electronic Engineer
Electrical Engineer   Chemical Engineer
Mechanical Engineer

Starting Salary
$ 40,000 - 45,000

Company Benefits
- Health care, dental, semi-private, basic life insurance
- Certification diplomas (100% paid)

Correspondence
Mail resume with cover letter
E-mail: lluczycki@vs-gencorp.com

Part Time/Summer: Gencorp Vehicle Sealing rarely hires for part time work or summer employment. Potential jobs involve technical or engineering co-ops.

GENDIS INC.

1370 Sony Place
Winnipeg, Manitoba, R3C 3C3
Tel: (204) 474-5200   Fax: (204) 474-5216

Human Resources Department
Internet: www.gendis.ca

Gendis Inc. is active in the retail merchandising industry through SAAN Stores Ltd., a wholly owned subsidiary that operates junior department and family clothing stores across Canada. These retail outlets have a broad geographic base and operate under the names SAAN and Red Apple Clearance Centre.

Academic Fields
College: Accounting, Administration, Advertising, Business, Human Resources, Marketing/Sales, Secretarial
Bachelor of Comm/Admin: General, Accounting, Finance, Marketing, Info Mgmt., Public Admin.
Chartered Accounting: CA - General/Finance, CGA/CMA - General/Finance
Masters: Business Administration

Critical Skills
Adaptable, Good Communication, Decisive, Dependable, Diligent, Efficient, Enthusiastic, Flexible, Good With Figures, Leadership, Organized, Patient, Personable, Productive, Professional, Responsible, Good Writing Skills

Types of Positions
Accounting   Merchandising
Mailroom   Junior Clerical

Starting Salary
Depends on position

Company Benefits
- Comprehensive benefits package
- Company pension, group life, dental
- On-going in house training programs

Correspondence
Mail or fax resume with cover letter

Part Time/Summer: Gendis occasionally seeks individuals for part time and summer employment opportunities. A potential job is a junior clerk in the accounting department. The best time to apply is in April.

GENERAL CHEMICAL CANADA LTD.

P.O. Box 2000
Amherstburg, Ontario, N9V 3R3
Tel: (519) 736-2111   Fax: (519) 736-4236

Human Resources Department

General Chemical is a worldwide supplier of industrial chemicals and derivative products and services. They operate a network of manufacturing plants, technical, warehousing and distribution centres, rail, barge and truck fleets and sales offices linked by one of the industry's most advanced, computer-based customer service systems.

Academic Fields
College: Computer Science, Electronics Tech., Engineering Tech., Human Res., Lab Tech., Mech. Tech.
Bachelor of Arts: Business
Bachelor of Comm/Admin: Accounting, Finance, Marketing
Bachelor of Science: Chemistry, Computer Science, Environmental Studies
Bachelor of Engineering: Chemical, Civil, Electrical, Environmental Studies, Industrial, Mechanical, Mining
Chartered Accounting: CA - General/Finance, CGA/CMA - General/Finance
Masters: Business Administration, Engineering

Critical Skills
Adaptable, Confident, Decisive, Dependable, Diligent, Diplomatic, Efficient, Enthusiastic, Flexible, Leadership

Types of Positions
Various Positions

Starting Salary
$ 40,000 - 60,000

Company Benefits
- Extended health plan, dental, life insurance

Correspondence
Mail resume with cover letter

Part Time/Summer: General Chemical Canada occasionally hires for part time work and regularly hires for the summer. Potential jobs include general labourer, lab technician, and project engineer. The best time to apply is in March.

Co-op/Internship: Internship opportunities are offered as a environmental technician or project engineer.

GENERAL ELECTRIC CANADA INC.

2300 Meadowvale Blvd.
Mississauga, Ontario, L5N 5P9
Tel: (905) 858-5705   Fax: (419) 858-5641

Terry Peach, Human Resources
Internet: www.ge.com

General Electric Canada is a diversified technology, manufacturing and services company that offers many different consumer products. General Electric itself operates in more than 100 countries around the world, including 250 manufacturing plants in 26 different nations. GE employs 300,000 people worldwide. General Electric Canada employs 6,100 people.

Academic Fields
College: Computer Science, Electronics Tech.
Bachelor of Arts: Business
Bachelor of Comm/Admin: General, Accounting, Finance, Marketing, Info Mgmt.
Bachelor of Science: Computer Science
Bachelor of Engineering: Chemical, Computer Systems, Design, Electrical, Mechanical
Masters: Business Administration, Engineering

Critical Skills
Adaptable, Analytical, Confident, Creative, Decisive, Dependable, Enthusiastic, Flexible, Good Communication, Innovative, Leadership, Productive, Professional

Types of Positions
Engineering   Commerce/Business
Computer Science

Starting Salary
below $ 40,000 - 60,000

Company Benefits
- Two year entry level leadership development program

Correspondence
Fax resume with cover letter

Part Time/Summer: General Electric Canada occasionally hires people for part time work and regularly looks for people for summer positions. In the summer a potential job is an engineering intern.

Co-op/Internship: Internship opportunities at available.

The Canada Student Employment Guide

GENERAL MILLS CANADA INC.

1330 Martingrove Road
Etobicoke, Ontario, M9W 4X4
Tel: (416) 743-8110   Fax: (416) 745-3487

Dayna Heesters, Human Resource Manager
Internet: www.generalmills.com

General Mills Canada is a marketer of packaged foods including ready to eat breakfast cereals, Betty Crocker baking mixes, packaged dinner mixes, and snack foods. General Mills was established in 1954 and is headquartered west of Toronto. Regional sales offices are located in Vancouver, Calgary, Toronto, Montreal and Halifax, with distribution centres in Calgary and Brampton.

Academic Fields
Chartered Accounting: CMA-Finance, CGA-Finance
Masters: Business Administration

Critical Skills
Analytical, Creative, Decisive, Dependable, Enthusiastic, Good Communication, Innovative, Leadership, Persuasive, Professional

Types of Positions
Marketing Assistant   Financial Analyst
Accountant   Trade Analyst

Starting Salary
$ 30,000 - 40,000 (Univ.) / $ 40,000 - 50,000 (MBA)

Company Benefits
- Full benefits package provided
- On-site training offered
- Training at General Mills Institute in U.S.

Correspondence
Mail resume with cover letter

Part Time/Summer: General Mills sometimes hires for part time and summer work. A potential summer opportunity may be in accounting. The best time to apply is in March or April.

GEORGE JEFFREY CHILDREN'S TREATMENT CENTRE

507 North Lillie St.
Thunder Bay, Ontario, P7C 4Y8
Tel: (807) 623-4381   Fax: (807) 623-6626

Tuija Puiras, Human Resources
Internet: www.gjctc.on.ca

Their dedicated team of staff and volunteers provide pediatric rehabilitative and habilitative services with children, families and adults in the community of Thunder Bay and Northwestern Ontario. They are a non-profit, charitable organization with community ties dating back to 1948.

Academic Fields
College: Child Care, Communications, Computer Science, Electronics Tech., Human Resources, Orthotics/Prosthetics, Recreation Studies
Bachelor of Arts: Sociology/Social Work
Bachelor of Comm/Admin: Accounting, Finance
Bachelor of Science: Health Sciences, Occupational Therapy, Physiotherapy

Critical Skills
Adaptable, Good Communication, Creative, Dependable, Efficient, Enthusiastic, Flexible, Organized, Patient, Personable, Good Writing Skills

Types of Positions
Occupational Therapist   Social Worker
Physiotherapist   Program Aide
Speech Language   Child Care Worker

Starting Salary
$ 20,000 - 30,000 (depends on position)

Company Benefits
- Extended health benefits
- Unionized environment
- 4 weeks vacation

Correspondence
Mail resume with cover letter

Part Time/Summer: George Jeffrey Children's Treatment Centre occasionally looks for individuals for part time employment, but does not generally seeks people for the summer months.

GIENOW BUILDING PRODUCTS LTD.

7140 - 40 Street S.E.
Calgary, Alberta, T2C 2B6
Tel: (403) 203-8200   Fax: (403) 279-2615

Human Resources
Internet: www.gienow.com

Gienow Building Products is engaged in the business of metal doors, frames, molding, and trim, as well as vinyl, wood and metal clad windows at its location in Calgary, Alberta. The company was established in 1951, and has approximately 450 employees.

Academic Fields
College: General, Accounting, Administration, Business, Computer Science, Drafting/Architecture, Engineering Tech., Marketing/Sales, Secretarial, Statistics
Bachelor of Arts: Business
Bachelor of Comm/Admin: General, Accounting, Finance, Marketing, Info Mgmt., Public Admin.
Bachelor of Science: General, Computer Sci., Math.
Bachelor of Engineering: General, Chemical, Civil, Computer Systems, Design, Industrial, Mechanical
Chartered Accounting: CA - General/Finance, CGA/CMA - General/Finance
Masters: Business Administration

Critical Skills
Analytical, Good Communication, Confident, Decisive, Dependable, Diligent, Efficient, Enthusiastic, Flexible, Good With Figures, Logical, Manual Dexterity, Organized, Patient, Personable, Professional, Responsible, Good Writing Skills

Types of Positions
Inside Sales   Customer Service
Production Worker   Accounts Payable/Receivable Clerk
Data Entry   Administration

Starting Salary
Depends on position

Company Benefits
- Complete benefit package

Correspondence
Mail or e-mail resume with cover letter
E-mail: sbarker@gienow.com

Part Time/Summer: Gienow Building Products sometimes hires part time workers and regularly hires for the summer. Potential jobs involve human resources, marketing, or general administration. April or March is the best time to apply.

GIFFELS ASSOCIATES LIMITED

30 International Boulevard
Toronto, Ontario, M9W 5P3
Tel: (416) 798-5493   Fax: (416) 675-4620

John S. MacDonald, Director of Personnel
Internet: www.giffels.com

Giffels Associates is an engineering and architectural consulting firm, employing between 250 and 300 people. Primary activities include project management, design and construction of major industrial, institutional and commercial buildings, as well as highways and bridges.

Academic Fields
College: Accounting, Administration, Computer Science, Drafting/Architecture, Engineering Tech., Human Resources, Industrial Design, Mechanical Tech., Secretarial, Urban Planning
Bachelor of Comm/Admin: Acctg, Info Mgmt.
Bachelor of Science: Computer Sci., Environ. Studies
Bachelor of Engineering: Chemical, Civil, Computer Systems, Design, Electrical, Environmental Studies, Geotechnical, Industrial, Materials Science, Mechanical, Transportation, Water Resources, Bachelor of Architecture
Chartered Accounting: CA - General/Finance, CMA-Finance, CGA-General/Finance
Masters: Business Administration, Engineering

Critical Skills
Adaptable, Analytical, Creative, Dependable, Diligent, Efficient, Enthusiastic, Good Communication, Flexible, Good Writing Skills, Innovative, Organized, Personable, Productive, Professional, Responsible

Types of Positions
Engineer-In-Training   CADD Designer/Drafter
Computer Programmer   Estimating/Planning

Starting Salary
$ 25,000 - 35,000

Company Benefits
- A full 'flexible' benefit package is offered

Correspondence
Mail, fax or e-mail resume with cover letter
E-mail: info@giffels.com

Part Time/Summer: Giffels Associates regularly hires part time and summer people. Potential work includes surveying, scheduler/planner (computer skills required), drafter, and secretary/administrator.

GILBEY CANADA INC.

401 The West Mall, Suite 700
Etobicoke, Ontario, M9C 5J4
Tel: (416) 626-2000   Fax: (416) 626-2209

Rod Morrison, Vice President, Human Resources

Gilbey Canada is a distillery and agent for brands of alcoholic beverages. Manufacturing whiskies, gins, rums, vodkas, liqueurs and wines, Gilbey Canada's parent company is IDV North America of the United States. The company employs more than 230 people across Canada.

Academic Fields
College: General, Accounting, Administration, Business, Computer Science, Human Resources, Marketing/Sales, Secretarial
Bachelor of Arts: General, Business
Bachelor of Comm/Admin: General, Accounting, Finance, Marketing, Info Mgmt.
Bachelor of Science: Chemistry, Computer Science, Food Sciences
Bachelor of Engineering: General, Chemical, Civil
Chartered Accounting: CA - General/Finance, CMA-General, CGA-General
Masters: Business Administration

Critical Skills
Adaptable, Analytical, Confident, Good Communication, Dependable, Diligent, Efficient, Good Writing Skills, Flexible, Creative, Enthusiastic, Good With Figures, Organized, Personable, Professional, Responsible

Types of Positions
Accounting Clerk   Sales Representative

Starting Salary
$ 20,000 - 30,000

Company Benefits
- A wide range of benefits paid by the company
- Individuals receive extensive training

Correspondence
Mail or fax resume with cover letter

Part Time/Summer: Gilbey Canada sometimes hires for part time positions and summer jobs. Potential summer opportunities are in the office or the plant. The best time to apply is in April.

GIMBEL EYE CENTRE

4935 40 Ave. NW, Suite 450
Calgary, Alberta, T3A 2N1
Tel: (403) 286-6969   Fax: (403) 286-2943

Human Resources

The Gimbel Eye Centre is a progressive, sophisticated ophthalmic medical centre. They are one of the largest and busiest ophthalmic out-of-hospital facilities in the world.

Academic Fields
College: General, Accounting, Administration, Business, Computer Sci., Electrical Tech., Faculty Mgmt., Food/Nutrition, Human Res., Journalism, Marketing/Sales, Nursing, Television/Radio
Bachelor of Arts: General, Business, English, Gerontology, Journalism, Political Science, Public Relations, Sociology/Social Work
Bachelor of Comm/Admin: Accounting, Finance, Marketing, Info Mgmt.
Bachelor of Engineering: Computer Syst., Electrical
Bachelor of Education: General
Chartered Accounting: CA - General/Finance, CGA/CMA - General/Finance
Masters: Business Administration

Critical Skills
Adaptable, Analytical, Good Communication, Confident, Decisive, Dependable, Diligent, Leadership, Logical, Manual Dexterity, Organized, Patient, Personable, Persuasive, Productive, Professional, Responsible, Good Writing Skills

Types of Positions
Ophthalmic Assistant   Administrative Clerk

Starting Salary
$ 20,000 - 25,000

Company Benefits
- Full medical, sick leave

Correspondence
Mail resume with cover letter

Part Time/Summer: Gimbel Eye Centre regularly hires for part time and summer work. Potential jobs are above. Apply from February to April.

Co-op/Internship: They have internship positions medical receptionist or in medical records.

GISBORNE DESIGN SERVICES LTD.

7476 Hedley Ave.
Burnaby, British Columbia, V5E 2P9
Tel: (604) 520-7300   Fax: (604) 522-0425

S. Brydon, Human Resources

Gisborne Design Services is an engineering and construction company that designs and constructs industrial sites such as pulp mills, mining sites, and chemical plants. The firm employs approximately 150 individuals.

Academic Fields
College: General, Business, Communications, Drafting/Architecture, Marketing/Sales
Bachelor of Arts: Public Relations
Bachelor of Engineering: Civil, Design, Industrial, Mechanical
Chartered Accounting: CGA-Finance

Critical Skills
Good Communication, Confident, Creative, Dependable, Enthusiastic, Leadership, Organized, Professional, Responsible, Good Writing Skills

Types of Positions
Field Construction

Starting Salary
$ 25,000 - 40,000

Company Benefits
- Full benefit package after 3 months
- Endless training opportunities

Correspondence
Mail resume with cover letter

Part Time/Summer: Gisborne Design Services does not generally hire for part time work, but occasionally looks for people for the summer months. Potential summer work is in drafting and engineering.

GLAXO WELLCOME CANADA

7333 Mississauga Road
Mississauga, Ontario, L5N 6L4
Tel: (905) 819-3000   Fax: (905) 819-3099

Human Resources
Internet: www.glaxowellcome.ca

Glaxo Wellcome has been providing safe and cost-effective medicines of the highest quality to Canadians for most of the twentieth century. The company was formed in 1995 as a result of the merger of Glaxo Canada Inc. and Burroughs Wellcome Inc.

Academic Fields
College: Accounting, Admin., Communications, Computer Sci., Electronics Tech., Engineering Tech., Faculty Mgmt., Human Resources, Journalism, Lab Tech., Marketing/Sales, Nursing, Secretarial
Bachelor of Arts: Gen., Bus., Journalism, Public Rel.
Bachelor of Comm/Admin: General, Accounting, Finance, Marketing
Bachelor of Science: General, Biology, Chemistry, Computer Science, Environmental Studies, Health Sciences, Kinesiology, Math, Microbiology, Nursing (RN), Occupational Therapy, Pharmacy, Physics
Bachelor of Laws: Corporate
Bachelor of Engineering: General, Chemical, Civil, Electrical, Mechanical
Chartered Accounting: CA - General/Finance, CGA/CMA - General/Finance
Masters: Business Administration, Library Science

Critical Skills
Adaptable, Analytical, Creative, Dependable, Efficient, Enthusiastic, Flexible, Good Communication, Good Writing Skills, Innovative, Leadership, Organized

Types of Positions
Secretarial   Purchasing
Receptionist   Shipper

Starting Salary
$ 25,000 - 30,000

Company Benefits
- Excellent training and benefits

Correspondence
Mail resume with cover letter

Part Time/Summer: Glaxo Wellcome Canada does not usually hire for part time jobs, but sometimes hires for the summer.

GLENTEL INC.

8501 Commerce Court
Burnaby, British Columbia, V5A 4N3
Tel: (604) 415-6500   Fax: (604) 415-6565

Jim Mercer, Human Resources
Internet: www.glentel.com

Glentel is Canada's leader in wireless business communications. No other company offers the full range of wireless services across Canada: from paging and cellular, to two-way radio and wireless data, and now satellite communications. Glentel was founded in 1963 with the goal of providing wireless communications capabilities to all Canadians. After thirty-four years the company is firmly established in its markets, serving the needs of Canadians.

Academic Fields
College: General, Accounting, Administration, Business, Communications, Computer Science
Bachelor of Arts: General, Business
Bachelor of Comm/Admin: General, Accounting, Info Mgmt.
Chartered Accounting: CMA-General

Critical Skills
Adaptable, Analytical, Confident, Good Communication, Creative, Decisive, Dependable, Good With Figures, Diplomatic, Enthusiastic, Flexible, Good Writing Skills, Leadership, Organized, Professional

Types of Positions
Clerical	Programmer/Analyst
Accounting	Property Management
Distribution	Warehouse

Starting Salary
$ 25,000 - 30,000

Company Benefits
- Full range of benefits
- Pension program
- Training and development opportunities

Correspondence
Mail resume with cover letter

Part Time/Summer: Glentel sometimes seeks individuals for part time and summer employment opportunities. Potential positions involve warehouse and office jobs. The best time to apply is in early Spring.

GOEPEL MCDERMID SECURITIES

601 Hastings St. W., Suite 1000
Vancouver, British Columbia, V6B 5E2
Tel: (604) 654-1111   Fax: (604) 654-1476

Peter Brock, Human Resources

Goepel McDermid Securities is an investment dealer with eight offices across Canada. The firm provides investment advice, financial planning, and a full range of investment products. They require candidates to have the Canadian Securities course.

Academic Fields
College: General
Bachelor of Arts: General
Bachelor of Comm/Admin: General
Bachelor of Science: General
Bachelor of Laws: General
Bachelor of Engineering: General
Bachelor of Education: General
Chartered Accounting: CA-General

Critical Skills
Good Communication, Confident, Decisive, Enthusiastic, Personable, Persuasive, Responsible

Types of Positions
Broker's Assistant   Broker

Starting Salary
$ 20,000 - 25,000

Company Benefits
- Full benefits, company stock ownership
- 3 months broker training

Correspondence
Mail resume with cover letter

Part Time/Summer: Goepel McDermid Securities does not hire individuals for part time work, but occasionally looks for people for the summer. Potential jobs for the summer include clerical positions, although this is very rare. The best time to apply is in February or March.

The Canada Student Employment Guide

GOLDER ASSOCIATES LTD.

2550 Argentia Road, Suite 213
Mississauga, Ontario, L5N 5R1
Tel: (905) 819-0600   Fax: (905) 819-9922

Human Resources
Internet: www.golder.com

Golder Associates is an international group providing earth engineering and environmental science services. With over 2000 employees in over 80 offices worldwide, they are one of the largest employee-owned engineering and earth science companies in the world. We have completed assignments in more than 140 countries.

Academic Fields
College: Engineering Tech.
Bachelor of Science: Biology, Environmental Studies, Geology
Bachelor of Engineering: Civil, Environmental Studies, Geotechnical, Mining, Water Resources

Critical Skills
Analytical, Decisive, Innovative, Professional

Types of Positions
Lab   Engineers in Training
Secretarial

Starting Salary
$ 20,000 - 25,000 (clerical)
$ 30,000 - 40,000 (engineering)

Company Benefits
- Complete health and dental insurance
- Company pension plan

Correspondence
Mail resume with cover letter

Part Time/Summer: Golder Associates regularly hires for part time and summer opportunities including university co-op. Summer positions that are potentially hired for include lab technicians. The best time to apply is in February or March.

GOODMAN AND CARR

200 King Street West, Suite 2300
Toronto, Ontario, M5H 3W5
Tel: (416) 595-2300   Fax: (416) 595-0567

Human Resources Department
Internet: www.goodmancarr.com

Goodman and Carr is a full service law firm providing services to individuals, businesses and other institutions. The firm's office is in downtown Toronto and employs about 300 people.

Academic Fields
College: General, Accounting, Administration, Advertising, Communications, Computer Science, Human Resources, Law Clerk, Marketing/Sales, Secretarial, Urban Planning
Bachelor of Arts: General, Business, Economics, Political Sci., Psychology, Public Rel., Urban Geog.
Bachelor of Comm/Admin: General, Accounting, Finance, Marketing, Info Mgmt.
Bachelor of Laws: General
Chartered Accounting: CA - General/Finance, CGA/CMA - General/Finance
Masters: Business Administration, Library Science

Critical Skills
Adaptable, Analytical, Good Communication, Dependable, Diligent, Diplomatic, Efficient, Enthusiastic, Flexible, Good With Figures, Innovative, Leadership, Organized, Personable, Productive, Professional, Responsible, Good Writing Skills

Types of Positions
Law Student   Accounting
Human Resources   Law Clerk
Land Use Planner

Starting Salary
Depends on position

Company Benefits
- Full medical and dental
- 3 month waiting period

Correspondence
Mail or fax resume with cover letter
E-mail: hr@goodmancarr.com

Part Time/Summer: Goodman & Carr sometimes hires for part time and summer work. In the summer months there are limited opportunities for 2nd year law students, secretarial positions, and administrative jobs.

GOODWILL INDUSTRIES OF TORONTO

234 Adelaide Street East
Toronto, Ontario, M5A 1M9
Tel: (416) 362-4711   Fax: (416) 362-0720

Sheila Fitkin, Personnel Officer
Internet: www.goodwill.on.ca

Goodwill Toronto is a Canadian registered charity that funds and provides work training and job-related services to people facing employment barriers. Each year, over 13 million pounds of reusable merchandise is sold in more than 35 Goodwill stores throughout southeastern Ontario.

Academic Fields
College: General, Accounting, Admin., Business, Communications, Comp. Sci., Human Res., Journalism, Marketing/Sales, Nursing, Secretarial
Bachelor of Arts: Business, English, Journalism, Psychology, Public Relations, Sociology/Social Work
Bachelor of Comm/Admin: General, Accounting, Finance, Marketing, Info Mgmt.
Bachelor of Science: General, Computer Science, Nursing (RN), Psychology
Bachelor of Engineering: Computer Systems
Bachelor of Education: Adult Education
Chartered Accounting: CA - General/Finance, CMA-General/Finance
Masters: Business Admin., Social Work (Rehabilitation)

Critical Skills
Adaptable, Good Communication, Confident, Creative, Dependable, Diligent, Diplomatic, Efficient, Enthusiastic

Types of Positions
Rehabilitation	Public Relations
Accounting	Sales & Management
Graphics	Transportation

Starting Salary
$ 20,000 - 40,000 (depending on position)

Company Benefits
- Life insurance, dental, and extended health

Correspondence
Mail, fax or e-mail resume with cover letter
E-mail: info@goodwill.on.ca

Part Time/Summer: Goodwill Industries sometimes employs students for part time and summer jobs. Although they have not had any summer work for the last few years, potential jobs for the future would be in those employment positions outlined above.

GOODYEAR CANADA INC.

450 Kipling Avenue
Toronto, Ontario, M8Z 5E1
Tel: (416) 201-4300   Fax: (416) 253-3030

W.F. Madill, Human Resources
Internet: www.goodyear.com/ca

Goodyear Canada is a tire and rubber company engaged in the production and sale of tires and related transportation products. Products include new tires and tubes, retreads, automotive repair services, auto belts and hoses, auto molded parts, and engineered rubber products. Goodyear Canada has operations in Ontario, Quebec, Alberta and store locations across Canada. The company employs over 4,800 people throughout the country.

Academic Fields
College: General, Business, Computer Science
Bachelor of Arts: General, Business, English
Bachelor of Comm/Admin: General, Accounting, Finance, Marketing
Bachelor of Science: General
Bachelor of Engineering: General
Chartered Accounting: CA - General/Finance, CGA/CMA - General/Finance
Masters: Business Administration

Critical Skills
Adaptable, Creative, Enthusiastic, Good Communication, Flexible, Professional, Responsible

Types of Positions
Sales	Asst. Store Manager
General Technician	Apprentice Mechanic
Tire Retreader	

Starting Salary
$ 30,000 - 40,000

Company Benefits
- Health, dental insurance and pension plan
- Quality training with in-house skills upgrade course
- Mgmt. course on operating independent store

Correspondence
Mail resume with cover letter

Part Time/Summer: Goodyear sometimes hires students for part time and summer positions. Summer opportunities potentially involve in-shop duties, and clerical tasks in their service stores.

The Canada Student Employment Guide

GOVERNMENT OF NEWFOUNDLAND - DEPARTMENT OF FINANCE

P.O. Box 8700
St. Johns, Newfoundland, A1B 4J6
Tel: (709) 729-3837   Fax: (709) 729-0435

Max Baldwin, Human Resources Manager

The Department of Finance within the Government of Newfoundland is responsible for fiscal and economic policy in the province. The department is particularly responsible for the financial resources used in the generation of revenues for the province. These funds are allocated to several areas including the provincial treasury, the management of the provincial debt, the management of pension funds, the payment of employee benefits, and the consolidated fund services. The Department of Finance employs 320 individuals.

Academic Fields
College: Accounting, Computer Science
Bachelor of Comm/Admin: Accounting, Finance
Bachelor of Science: Computer Science
Bachelor of Engineering: Computer Systems
Chartered Accounting: CA - General/Finance, CMA-General/Finance, CGA-Finance
Masters: Business Administration

Critical Skills
Analytical, Dependable, Efficient, Good Communication, Enthusiastic, Good Writing Skills, Organized, Personable, Professional

Types of Positions
Clerk II   Tax Compliance Officer

Starting Salary
$ 20,000 - 30,000

Company Benefits
- Group medical and dental insurance
- Pension upon retirement
- Annual and sick leave

Correspondence
Mail or fax resume with cover letter

Part Time/Summer: The Department of Finance sometimes hires for part time positions, and regularly hires for summer opportunities. Potential summer jobs involve general clerical duties. The best time to apply is between January and April.

GRAND & TOY LTD.

33 Green Belt Drive
Don Mills, Ontario, M3C 1M1
Tel: (416) 445-7255   Fax: (416) 445-4855

Christine Brownlie, Human Resources
Internet: www.grandandtoy.com

Based in Toronto, Canada, Grand & Toy is a wholly-owned subsidiary of Boise Cascade Office Products, a leading North American commercial office products dealer. In addition to serving large corporate customers, Grand & Toy operates a chain of 80 retail stores across Canada. The company sells more than 15,000 products, to a customer base of over 50,000, and posts revenues of approximately $350 million (CDN) annually.

Academic Fields
College: Accounting, Advertising, Business, Computer Science, Graphic Arts, Human Resources, Marketing/Sales, Secretarial
Bachelor of Arts: Business
Bachelor of Comm/Admin: Marketing, Info Mgmt.
Bachelor of Science: Computer Science
Bachelor of Engineering: Computer Systems
Chartered Accounting: CMA-General, CGA-Finance
Masters: Business Administration

Critical Skills
Analytical, Confident, Dependable, Good Communication, Efficient, Enthusiastic, Flexible, Good With Figures, Diligent, Organized, Innovative, Good Writing Skills, Personable, Professional, Responsible

Types of Positions
Sales Rep.   Data Entry Clerk
Secretary   Order Clerk
Word-processing   Receptionist

Starting Salary
$ 20,000 - 25,000

Company Benefits
- Dental, health, short/long term disability
- A competitive RRSP plan (although no pension)

Correspondence
Fax resume with cover letter

Part Time/Summer: Grand & Toy sometimes hires for part time and summer positions. Some potential jobs in the summer include sales clerk in the retail store, project work in the warehouse, or an opportunity in information technology.

The Canada Student Employment Guide

GRANT MACEWEN COMMUNITY COLLEGE

P.O. Box 1796
Edmonton, Alberta, T5J 2P2
Tel: (403) 497-5040   Fax: (403) 497-5001

Human Resources Department
Internet: www.gmcc.ab.ca

Grant MacEwan College is a learning organization that has its aim to optimize human potential as an investment in prosperity.

Academic Fields
College: Accounting, Admin., Advertising, Business, Child Care, Communications, Computer Sci., Graphic Arts, Human Res., Journalism, Insurance, Marketing/Sales, Nursing, Performing Arts, Secretarial, Security/Law, Travel/Tourism
Bachelor of Arts: Business, Criminology, Economics, English, Fine Arts, Gerontology, History, Journalism, Music, Political Science, Psychology, Public Relations, Recreation Studies, Sociology/Social Work
Bachelor of Comm/Admin: Marketing
Bachelor of Science: Biology, Chemistry, Computer Sci., Environ. Studies, Math., Microbiology, Nursing (RN), Occup. Therapy, Physics, Psychology, Zoology
Bachelor of Laws: General, Corporate
Bachelor of Engineering: Computer Systems
Bachelor of Education: Adult Education, Childhood, Physical, Special
Chartered Accounting: CMA-General/Finance, CGA-General/Finance
Masters: Bus. Admin., Arts, Science, Educ., Library Sci.

Critical Skills
Adaptable, Analytical, Creative, Diplomatic, Enthusiastic, Flexible, Good Communication, Good Writing Skills, Innovative, Leadership, Personable

Types of Positions
Custodian   Clerk
Receptionist   Maintenance Worker

Starting Salary
$ 25,000 - 30,000

Company Benefits
- Benefits dependent upon type of position

Correspondence
Mail, fax, or e-mail resume with cover letter

Part Time/Summer: Grant MacEwen College regularly hires for part time and summer jobs. The best time to apply is in early Spring.

GRANT THORNTON

200 Bay Street, Box 55
Toronto, Ontario, M5J 2P9
Tel: (416) 360-0100   Fax: (416) 360-4949

Personnel Partner
Internet: www.grantthornton.ca

Grant Thornton, together with our Quebec-based affiliate Raymond Chabot Grant Thornton, operates as Grant Thornton Canada, the sixth largest firm of chartered accountants in Canada, ranked by revenue. They have 107 offices across Canada. Grant Thornton is one of Canada's leading firms of chartered accountants and management consultants. They bring the strength of advice to growing entrepreneurial businesses and not-for-profit organizations through a wide range of assurance, tax and advisory services.

Academic Fields
Bachelor of Arts: Business, Economics
Bachelor of Comm/Admin: General, Accounting, Finance
Chartered Accounting: CA - General/Finance
Masters: Business Administration

Critical Skills
Analytical, Confident, Professional, Good With Figures, Leadership, Personable, Good Writing Skills

Types of Positions
Staff Accountant

Starting Salary
$ 30,000 - 40,000

Company Benefits
- Health, dental, life and disability insurance
- Financial and training support to gain CA designation
- Training program for professionals at all levels

Correspondence
Mail resume with cover letter (include transcripts)

Part Time/Summer: Grant Thornton occasionally hires individuals to fill part time positions and summer opportunities. In the summer months, staff accountant positions are usually available. The best time to apply is in January.

THE GREAT-WEST LIFE ASSURANCE COMPANY

Box 6000, 100 Osborne St. N.
Winnipeg, Manitoba, R3C 3A5
Tel: (204) 946-8100   Fax: (204) 946-8865

Human Resources Department
Internet: www.gwl.ca

The Great-West Life Assurance Company offers a wide range of insurance, retirement, and investment products and services for individuals, businesses, and organizations.

Academic Fields
College: General, Accounting, Administration, Advertising, Communications, Computer Science, Human Res., Insurance, Marketing/Sales, Secretarial
Bachelor of Arts: General, Business, Economics, English, Psychology, Sociology/Social Work
Bachelor of Comm/Admin: General, Accounting, Finance, Marketing
Bachelor of Science: Actuarial, Computer Science, Mathematics, Nursing (RN), Occupational Therapy
Bachelor of Laws: General, Corporate
Bachelor of Engineering: Computer Systems
Bachelor of Education: General
Chartered Accounting: CA - General/Finance, CGA/CMA - General/Finance
Masters: Business Administration

Critical Skills
Adaptable, Analytical, Good Communication, Confident, Creative, Decisive, Dependable, Diligent, Diplomatic, Efficient, Enthusiastic, Flexible, Good With Figures, Innovative, Leadership, Logical, Organized, Patient, Personable, Persuasive, Productive, Professional, Responsible, Writing Skills

Types of Positions
Administrative Asst.   Contribution Processor
File Clerk   Accounts Assistant
Messenger   Policy Analyst

Starting Salary
$ 25,000 - 30,000

Company Benefits
- Competitive benefit package

Correspondence
Submit resume and cover letter in person

Part Time/Summer: Great-West Life Assurance sometimes looks for individuals on a part time basis and regularly seeks candidates for the summer.

GRENVILLE MANAGEMENT LTD.

25 Scarsdale Road
Don Mills, Ontario, M1B 2R2
Tel: (416) 449-4499   Fax: (416) 449-4119

Debra McLeod, Human Resources Manager

Grenville Management is engaged in providing consulting and public relations services for all types of businesses and other enterprises in the Toronto region and elsewhere. With more than 225 employees, Grenville Management's head office is located in Don Mills, Ontario.

Academic Fields
College: General, Accounting, Faculty Management, Graphic Arts
Bachelor of Arts: General
Bachelor of Comm/Admin: Accounting

Critical Skills
Adaptable, Confident, Dependable, Good Communication, Enthusiastic, Efficient, Organized, Manual Dexterity, Personable, Productive, Professional, Responsible

Types of Positions
Porter   Mail Clerk
Floater

Starting Salary
$ 20,000 - 25,000

Company Benefits
- Employees receive one year full benefits
- Long term disability and school tuition expenses
- Training and development in most departments

Correspondence
Mail, fax, submit resume & cover letter in person

Part Time/Summer: Grenville Management sometimes hires for part time openings and summer opportunities. Potential summer jobs can be found in the areas of distribution and bindery.

GROUPE SAVOIE INC.

251 Route 180
St. Quentin, New Brunswick, E8A 2K9
Tel: (506) 235-2228   Fax: (506) 235-3200

Line C. Simon, Human Resources
Internet: www.groupesavoie.com

Groupe Savoie is engaged in the business of general sawmilling, and planning mills in Saint-Quentin, New Brunswick. The company employs about 300 individuals to work in various sectors in the sawmilling industry.

Academic Fields
College: General, Accounting, Administration, Business, Engineering Tech., Forestry, Human Resources, Industrial Design, Marketing/Sales, Mechanical Tech.
Bachelor of Arts: Business
Bachelor of Comm/Admin: General, Accounting, Finance, Marketing
Bachelor of Science: Forestry
Bachelor of Engineering: General, Industrial, Mechanical
Chartered Accounting: CA - General/Finance, CGA-General, CGA-Finance
Masters: Business Administration, Engineering

Critical Skills
Adaptable, Good Communication, Confident, Decisive, Dependable, Diligent, Diplomatic, Efficient, Enthusiastic, Flexible, Innovative, Leadership, Logical, Manual Dexterity, Organized, Patient, Personable, Productive, Professional, Responsible

Types of Positions
Various positions

Starting Salary
$ 25,000 - 30,000 (labour positions)

Company Benefits
- Health plan
- Pension plan
- Access to training sessions

Correspondence
Submit resume and cover letter in person
E-mail: reshum@nbnet.nb.ca

Part Time/Summer: Groupe Savoie sometimes seeks candidates for part time and summer employment.

GROUSE MOUNTAIN RESORTS LTD.

6400 Nancy Greene Way
North Vancouver, British Columbia, V7R 4K9
Tel: (604) 984-0661   Fax: (604) 984-7234

Louise Adams, Guest Services Manager
Internet: www.grousemountain.com

Grouse Mountain, the peak of Vancouver, is a year-round tourist recreational facility. Grouse Mountain caters to a variety of markets. During the summer, spring and fall, it caters to the rapidly growing Vancouver tourist market. In the winter, Grouse Mountain's main attractions are skiing and sleighrides on terrain of 130 acres, two thirds of which is lit for night skiing, and 1,210 feet of skiing vertical.

Academic Fields
College: General, Hospitality, Marketing/Sales, Travel/Tourism
Bachelor of Arts: General, Public Relations, Recreation Studies
Bachelor of Comm/Admin: Accounting, Marketing
Chartered Accounting: CA-General, CMA-General, CGA-General

Critical Skills
Adaptable, Confident, Creative, Dependable, Efficient, Enthusiastic, Flexible, Good Communication, Good Writing Skills, Leadership, Personable, Professional

Types of Positions
Sales Clerk   Sales Supervisor
Attraction Supervisor   Accounting Clerk
Guest Services

Starting Salary
$ 20,000 - 25,000

Company Benefits
- Health benefits
- Recreational, skiing activities
- Education subsidies

Correspondence
Mail resume with cover letter, or fill out application

Part Time/Summer: Grouse Mountain Resorts regularly employs individuals for part time and summer work. Potential jobs are with guest services, or as escorts. There are also positions as attraction operators. The best time to apply is between May and August.

The Canada Student Employment Guide

H A SIMMONS LTD.

111 Dunsmuir, Suite 400
Vancouver, British Columbia, V6B 5W3
Tel: (604) 664-4300   Fax: (604) 664-4804

Human Resources
Internet: www.hasimmons.com

H A Simmons Ltd. is an international engineering company providing services primarily to the forest industry, mining and environmental sectors.

Academic Fields
College: Accounting, Computer Science, Engineering Tech., Forestry
Bachelor of Science: Forestry
Bachelor of Engineering: Electrical, Mechanical, Mining

Critical Skills
Dependable, Diligent, Enthusiastic, Good Communication, Initiative

Types of Positions
Varies

Starting Salary
$ 36,000 (engineering grad)

Company Benefits
- 3 weeks vacation, RRSP contribution
- Dental, extended health
- Long term disability

Correspondence
Mail resume with cover letter

Part Time/Summer: H A Simmons Ltd. occasionally looks for individuals for part time or summer employment.

H.H. ANGUS & ASSOCIATES LTD.

1127 Leslie Street
Don Mills, Ontario, M3C 2J6
Tel: (416) 443-8312   Fax: (416) 443-8290

Human Resources
Internet: www.hhangus.com

Established in 1919, H.H. Angus & Associates is a full service engineering company. Services involving project management include planning, design, maintenance and operation planning. Process engineering services include consultation, engineering reports, and feasibility studies. As well they offer environmental services including air quality assessment, recycling plans, property redevelopment, environmental inspections and audits. The company employs 250 individuals, including those within affiliate companies. The firm has offices in Canada, the United States and the United Kingdom.

Academic Fields
College: Drafting/Architecture, Engineering Tech.
Bachelor of Engineering: Electrical, Environmental Studies, Mechanical

Critical Skills
Dependable, Diligent, Enthusiastic, Good Communication, Flexible, Leadership, Professional, Responsible

Types of Positions
Project Engineer   Draftsman
Design

Starting Salary
$ 25,000 - 35,000

Company Benefits
- A wide range of competitive benefits is offered

Correspondence
Mail resume with cover letter
E-mail: hr@hhangus.com

Part Time/Summer: H.H. Angus & Associates does not hire for part time positions, but sometimes hires for summer opportunities. The potential positions in the summer are most likely the ones listed above. The best time to apply is in May.

The Canada Student Employment Guide

HALEY INDUSTRIES LIMITED

General Delivery
Haley, Ontario, K0J 1Y0
Tel: (613) 432-8841   Fax: (613) 432-0743

Murray Brown, HR Manager
Internet: www.haley.on.ca

Haley Industries Limited is one of the world's most advanced manufacturers of precision alloy castings primarily for the International aerospace industry.

Academic Fields
College: Accounting, Engineering Tech., Human Resources, Marketing/Sales, Mechanical Tech.
Bachelor of Science: Environmental Studies
Bachelor of Engineering: Environmental Studies, Mechanical
Masters: Business Administration

Critical Skills
Adaptable, Good Communication, Creative, Decisive, Dependable, Diligent, Efficient, Enthusiastic, Flexible, Innovative, Leadership, Manual Dexterity, Organized, Personable, Productive, Professional, Responsible, Good Writing Skills

Types of Positions
General Foundry   Sales & Marketing
Quality Control   Finance
Human Resources   Office & Clerical

Starting Salary
$ 30,000 - 40,000

Company Benefits
- Hospital coverage, dental plan
- Drug plan, vacation

Correspondence
Fax resume with cover letter

Part Time/Summer: Haley Industries Limited occasionally looks for individuals for part time work, and regularly seeks candidates for the summer. Potential jobs include mechanical or metallurgical engineer, general foundry work, or office and clerical duties.

HALIBURTON ENERGY SERVICES

333 - 5th Ave. SW, Suite 1000
Calgary, Alberta, T2P 3B6
Tel: (403) 231-9000   Fax: (403) 231-9369

Michael Solonynko, HR Generalist
Internet: www.halliburton.com

Halliburton Energy Services provides products, services and integrated solutions for oil and gas exploration, development and production. Capabilities range form initial evaluation of producing formations to drilling, completion, production enhancement and well maintenance. The company has over 300 service centers in more than 100 countries.

Academic Fields
College: Electronics Tech., Engineering Tech., Mechanical Tech., Information Systems, Petroleum Engineering, Chemical Engineering
Bachelor of Science: Chemistry, Physics
Bachelor of Engineering: Chemical, Geotechnical, Mechanical

Critical Skills
Analytical, Confident, Flexible, Good With Figures, Good Writing Skills, Manual Dexterity, Professional, Physically Demanding Work, Deal With Inclement Weather

Types of Positions
Field Operations   Maintenance
Support

Starting Salary
$ 25,000 - 30,000

Company Benefits
- One of the most comprehensive and all encompassing benefits programs
- Offer a number of well designed in-house training programs

Correspondence
Fax resume with cover letter

Part Time/Summer: Haliburton Energy Services occasionally seeks people for part time work, but does not generally hire for the summer months.

Co-op/Internship: Internships and coop programs are infrequently filled. However, most would be in the areas of field engineering, when they do occur.

The Canada Student Employment Guide

HALIFAX COUNTY REGIONAL

P.O. Box 1003, Stn Main
Dartmouth, Nova Scotia, B2Y 3Z7
Tel: (902) 434-7660   Fax: (902 434-2405

Caroline Campbell, Human Resources

Halifax County Regional Rehabilitation Centre is a long term care facility serving 89 residents in a psychiatric rehabilitation setting. The centre employs approximately 220 people. This facility is targeted for complete closure in the summer of 2001.

Academic Fields
College: Business, Cooking/Culinary, Electronics Tech., Engineering Tech., Nursing
Bachelor of Arts: General, Business, Gerontology, Psychology, Public Relations, Recreation Studies, Sociology/Social Work
Bachelor of Comm/Admin: General, Accounting, Finance, Public Admin., Human Resources
Bachelor of Science: General, Food Sciences, Health Sciences, Nursing (RN), Occupational Therapy, Pharmacy, Physiotherapy, Psychology
Bachelor of Education: General, Adult Education, Physical, Special
Chartered Accounting: CA - General/Finance, CGA/CMA - General/Finance
Masters: Business Admin., Education, Health Admin.

Critical Skills
Adaptable, Good Communication, Dependable, Efficient, Enthusiastic, Leadership, Patient, Personable

Types of Positions
Nursing Attendant   Utility Worker
Food Service/Housekeeping   Receptionist

Starting Salary
$ 20,000 - 25,000

Company Benefits
- Health, dental, pension, long term disability

Correspondence
Mail resume with cover letter

Part Time/Summer: The Centre regularly hires for part time and summer work. Potential jobs involve nursing, food service, maintenance, or occupational therapy. The best time to apply is from April to June.

Co-op/Internship: They offer internship opportunities.

HALIFAX REGIONAL MUNICIPALITY

5251 Duke St., 3rd Flr
Halifax, Nova Scotia, B3J 3A5
Tel: (902) 490-4300   Fax: (902) 490-4330

Human Resources Services

Halifax Regional Municipality is the local regional government in Halifax, Nova Scotia. The municipal government is responsible for the creation and formation of policy and laws in matters under its jurisdiction. Individuals working for the municipality are employed within many different sectors.

Academic Fields
College: Accounting, Business, Computer Science, Drafting/Architecture, Electronics Tech., Engineering Tech., Hospitality, Human Resources, Recreation Studies, Secretarial, Travel/Tourism, Urban Planning
Bachelor of Arts: Business, Journalism, Public Relations, Recreation Studies, Urban Geography
Bachelor of Comm/Admin: General, Accounting, Finance, Info Mgmt.
Bachelor of Science: Computer Science, Environmental Studies, Geography, Geology, Mathematics
Bachelor of Engineering: General, Chemical, Civil, Electrical, Transportation, Water Resources
Chartered Accounting: CMA-Finance, CGA-Finance
Masters: Business Administration, Engineering

Critical Skills
Adaptable, Creative, Dependable, Diplomatic, Enthusiastic, Flexible, Innovative, Leadership, Logical, Organized, Patient, Personable, Persuasive, Productive, Professional, Responsible, Writing Skills

Types of Positions
Clerical   Secretarial
Labourer

Starting Salary
$ 25,000 - 30,000

Company Benefits
- Flexible benefits, on-the-job training

Correspondence
Mail resume with cover letter

Part Time/Summer: Halifax Regional Municipality regularly looks for candidates for part time and summer employment opportunities. Potential positions include travel counsellor or co-op student.

The Canada Student Employment Guide

HALIFAX WATER COMMISSION

P.O. Box 8338, Stn A
Halifax, Nova Scotia, B3K 5M1
Tel: (902) 490-6930   Fax: (902) 490-6934

Human Resources Department

The Halifax Water Commission provides potable water to customers in serviced areas in the regional municipality of Halifax. The Commission employs 180 people.

Academic Fields
College: General, Accounting, Admin., Business, Computer Sci., Drafting/Architecture, Electronics Tech., Engineering Tech., Human Res., Lab. Tech., Secretarial
Bachelor of Arts: General, Business
Bachelor of Comm/Admin: General, Accounting, Finance, Info Mgmt., Public Admin.
Bachelor of Science: Biology, Chemistry, Computer Science, Forestry
Bachelor of Engineering: Civil, Design, Environmental Studies, Water Resources
Chartered Accounting: CA - General/Finance, CGA/CMA - General/Finance
Masters: Business Administration, Science, Engineering, Public Administration

Critical Skills
Adaptable, Analytical, Good Communication, Confident, Creative, Decisive, Dependable, Diligent, Diplomatic, Efficient, Enthusiastic, Flexible, Good With Figures, Innovative, Leadership, Logical, Manual Dexterity, Organized, Patient, Personable, Persuasive, Productive, Professional, Responsible, Good Writing Skills, Team Player

Types of Positions
Customer Service Representative   Labourer
Meter Reader

Starting Salary
$ 25,000 - 30,000

Company Benefits
- Health, long term disability, sick leave, pension plan

Correspondence
Mail resume with cover letter

Part Time/Summer: Halifax Water Commission occasionally looks for individuals for part time or summer work. Potential jobs include labourer, engineering technician, or meter reader.

HALLIBURTON ENERGY SERVICES

333 - 5th Ave. SW, Suite 1000
Calgary, Alberta, T2P 3B6
Tel: (403) 231-9000   Fax: (403) 231-9369

Michael Solonynko, Human Resources Generalist
Internet: www.halliburton.com

Halliburton Energy Services is the number one global leader in oilfield servicing, including cementing, stimulation, directional and multilateral drilling, measurement systems, and well testing. They employ approximately 1,500 people in Canada.

Academic Fields
College: Information Systems, Electronics Tech., Engineering Tech., Mechanical Tech., Petroleum Engineering, Chemical Engineering
Bachelor of Science: Physics
Bachelor of Engineering: Chemical, Geotechnical, Mechanical

Critical Skills
Analytical, Flexible, Good With Figures, Good Writing Skills, Manual Dexterity, Professional

Types of Positions
Field Operations   Maintenance
Maintenance Support

Starting Salary
$ 25,000 - 30,000

Company Benefits
- One of the most comprehensive and all encompassing benefits programs
- Number of well-designed in-house training programs

Correspondence
Fax resume with cover letter

Part Time/Summer: Halliburton Energy Services occasionally hires for part time work, but does not hire for the summer months.

The Canada Student Employment Guide

HALLMARK TOOLS

2187 Huron Church Rd., P.O. Box 7040
Windsor, Ontario, N9C 2L8
Tel: (519) 966-4050   Fax: (519) 966-8752

J. Master, Manager, HR & Training

Hallmark Tools designs, engineers, and manufactures custom plastic injection molds, primarily for the automotive industry. Their tools are in use worldwide, and they are a recognized leader in the headlamp, taillight, and optic field. The company employs 250 individuals.

Academic Fields
College: CAD Autocad, Engineering Tech., Mechanical Tech.
Bachelor of Science: Mathematics, Physics
Bachelor of Engineering: Mechanical

Critical Skills
Analytical, Dependable, Enthusiastic, Good Communication, Good Writing Skills

Types of Positions
Mold Making Apprentice   Machinist Apprentice
Design Apprentice   Programming Apprentice

Starting Salary
Depends on position

Company Benefits
- Offer in-house training for mold maker apprentices in a certified 3-year course

Correspondence
Mail resume with cover letter
E-mail: hti@mnsi.net

Part Time/Summer: Hallmark Tools rarely hires for part time or summer employment. Potential jobs include painting, cleaning, and filing. Apply in April for students in Windsor and surrounding area only.

HARRY ROSEN INC.

77 Bloor St. W., Suite 1600
Toronto, Ontario, M5S 1M2
Tel: (416) 935-9200   Fax: N/A

Personnel Manager
Internet: www.harryrosen.com

Harry Rosen is a fine men's retail store providing professional apparel, accessories, and casual wear for consumers in Canada. Established in this country in 1956, Harry Rosen has 23 outlets throughout the provinces of British Columbia, Alberta, Winnipeg, Quebec, and Ontario. Harry Rosen is a subsidiary of Dylex Ltd., and employs more than 700 people in these provinces.

Academic Fields
College: Accounting, Administration, Advertising, Marketing/Sales, Secretarial
Bachelor of Arts: General, English, Fine Arts, History, Philosophy, Psychology
Chartered Accounting: CMA-Finance, CGA-General/Finance

Critical Skills
Adaptable, Analytical, Good Communication, Confident, Creative, Decisive, Dependable, Diligent, Diplomatic, Efficient, Enthusiastic, Flexible, Good With Figures, Innovative, Leadership, Logical, Organized, Personable, Productive, Professional, Responsible, Good Writing Skills

Types of Positions
Accounts Payable   Merchandise Control
Sales Audit/Admin.   Advertising Assistant
Human Resources Asst.   Sales Associate

Starting Salary
below $ 20,000 - 25,000

Company Benefits
- Major medical, dental, and life insurance
- Disability, vision care, and clothing discounts
- Formal and on-the-job training

Correspondence
Mail or fax resume with cover letter

Part Time/Summer: Harry Rosen sometimes hires for part time positions and regularly hires for summer opportunities. Potential summer opportunities include accounting clerk, receptionist, file clerk, and data entry clerk. Positions are filled as they become available, thus there is no best time to apply.

The Canada Student Employment Guide

HASBRO CANADA INC.

2350 de la Province
Longueuil, Québec, J4G 1G2
Tel: (450) 670-9820   Fax: (450) 651-4531

Lorette Mazzanti, Human Resources

Hasbro Canada is a worldwide leader in the design, manufacture and marketing of toys, games, interactive software, puzzles and infant products. There are approximately 170 employees in Canada.

Academic Fields
College: General, Accounting, Administration, Advertising, Business, Communications, Faculty Management, Human Resources, Statistics, Television/Radio
Bachelor of Arts: General, Business, Economics, Languages, Public Relations, Statistics
Bachelor of Comm/Admin: General, Accounting, Finance, Marketing, Info Mgmt.
Masters: Business Administration

Critical Skills
Adaptable, Analytical, Dependable, Diligent, Efficient, Enthusiastic, Flexible, Good Communication, Good With Figures, Good Writing Skills, Innovative, Logical, Organized, Responsible

Types of Positions
Sales Administration   Assistant Product Manager
Costing   Accounting
Traffic Coordinator   Media Coordinator

Starting Salary
$ 25,000 - 30,000

Company Benefits
- Medical and dental package
- Pension plan, life insurance
- On going training and development

Correspondence
Mail or fax resume with cover letter

Part Time/Summer: Hasbro Canada occasionally looks for candidates for part time and summer employment. Summer jobs involve clerical duties that relate to your field of studies.

HB STUDIOS MULTIMEDIA LTD.

Box 725
Lunenburg, Nova Scotia, B0J 2C0
Tel: (902) 634-8316   Fax: N/A

Jeremy Wellard, Producer
Internet: www.hb-studios.com

HB Studios is a multimedia company based in Nova Scotia. The company's services include Playstation 2 development, websites and multimedia CD-Roms. They employ 9 individuals.

Academic Fields
College: Computer Science, Graphic Arts
Bachelor of Arts: Fine Arts
Bachelor of Science: Computer Science, Mathematics, Physics

Critical Skills
Adaptable, Artistic, Creative, Dependable, Diligent, Enthusiastic, Innovative, Professional, Responsible

Types of Positions
Graphic Artist   Programmer

Starting Salary
$ 35,000 - 40,000

Company Benefits
- In-house training

Correspondence
E-mail resume with cover letter E-mail: jobs@hb-studios.com

Part Time/Summer: HB Studios Multimedia Ltd. occasionally hires for part time or summer employment. A potential job would be a graphic artist. The best time to apply is in the Spring.

HEALTH AUTHORITY 5

Box 429
Drumheller, Alberta, T0J 0Y0
Tel: (403) 823-7125   Fax: (403) 823-5418

Terry Browning, Position Control Clerk
Internet: www.ha5.ab.ca

Health Authority 5 is a rural health region located in south central Alberta. It encompasses approximately 25,000 km and serves a population of more than 52,000 people. The health authority has a staff of more than 1,100 skilled healthcare workers who provide an array of services intended to maintain, improve and promote the health of their residents.

Academic Fields
College: Accounting, Human Resources, Information Systems, Secretarial, Cooking/Culinary, Recreation Studies, Emergency/Paramedic, Home Care, Lab Tech., Nursing (RN/RNA), Radiology Tech., Respiratory Tech.
Bachelor of Arts: Psychology
Bachelor of Comm/Admin: Accounting, Finance, Human Resources
Bachelor of Science: Food Sciences, Health Sciences, Kinesiology, Nursing (RN), Occupational Therapy, Pharmacy, Physiotherapy, Psychology
Masters: Business Administration

Critical Skills
Dependable, Flexible, Good Communication, Responsible

Types of Positions
Nursing Attendant   Food Services
Laundry/Housekeeping

Starting Salary
$ 20,000 - 25,000

Company Benefits
- Permanent part time and permanent full time staff are entitled to health, dental and insurance
- Various refresher courses and workshops are offered throughout the year

Correspondence
Fax or e-mail resume with cover letter
E-mail: tbrowning@ha5.ab.ca

Part Time/Summer: Health Authority 5 regularly looks for people for part time and summer employment. Potential jobs include nursing attendant, recreation therapy aide, porter, grounds keeper. The best time to apply is in early May.

HEALTH CARE CORPORATION OF ST. JOHN'S

Waterford Bridge Road
St. John's, Newfoundland, A1E 4J8
Tel: (709) 758-1362   Fax: (709) 758-1303

Recruitment Officer
Internet: www.hccsj.nf.ca

Health Care Corporation of St. John's is the corporate "umbrella" or board which administers the operations of 7 Health Care facilities in St. John's and Bell Island. Positions available through human resources would be found at each of their sites, but recruited through corporate office.

Academic Fields
College: Accounting, Communications, Computer Sci., Cooking/Culinary, Electronics Tech., Emergency/Paramedic, Engineering Tech., Food/Nutrition, Industrial Design, Journalism, Lab Tech., Nursing, Orthotics/Prosthetics, Radiology Tech., Recreation Studies, Secretarial
Bachelor of Arts: Business, Psychology, Public Relations, Recreation Studies, Sociology/Social Work
Bachelor of Comm/Admin: General, Accounting, Info Mgmt.
Bachelor of Science: Computer Sci., Food Sciences, Health Sciences, Nursing (RN), Occupational Therapy, Pharmacy, Physiotherapy, Psychology
Bachelor of Engineering: Biomedical, Computer Systems, Industrial
Bachelor of Education: General, Adult, Physical
Chartered Accounting: CA-General, CMA-General, CGA-General
Masters: Business Administration

Critical Skills
Adaptable, Good Communication, Confident, Personable, Professional, Responsible, Writing Skills

Types of Positions
Clerical   Nursing
Dietetics   Materials Management

Starting Salary
below $ 20,000 - 25,000

Company Benefits
- Pension and group insurance

Correspondence
Mail resume with cover letter

Part Time/Summer: They occasionally hire for part time work and regularly hire for the summer.

The Canada Student Employment Guide

HEALTH SCIENCES CENTRE

60 Pearl Street
Winnipeg, Manitoba, R3E 1X2
Tel: (204) 787-3668   Fax: (204) 787-1376

Employment Office
Internet: www.hsc.mb.ca

The five hospitals comprising the Health Sciences Centre occupy 32 acres of land in central Winnipeg. They are one of the largest health care facilities in Canada and the major referral centre in Manitoba for complex health problems requiring expert consultation and sophisticated investigation and management.

Academic Fields
College: Child Care, Computer Science, Drafting/Architecture, Electronics Tech., Food/Nutrition, Graphic Arts, Lab Tech., Nursing, Orthotics/Prosthetics, Photography, Radiology Tech., Secretarial, Security/Law
Bachelor of Arts: Rec. Studies, Sociology/Social Work
Bachelor of Comm/Admin: Finance, Info Mgmt., Public Admin.
Bachelor of Science: Computer Science, Kinesiology, Health Sciences, Nursing, Occupational Therapy, Pharmacy, Physiotherapy
Bachelor of Engineering: Biomedical, Electrical, Computer Systems, Mechanical
Chartered Accounting: CA - General/Finance
Masters: Business Admin., Social Work, Health, Nursing

Critical Skills
Adaptable, Analytical, Good Communication, Confident, Dependable, Diligent, Diplomatic, Efficient, Personable, Productive, Professional, Responsible, Good Writing Skills, Team Player

Types of Positions
Laundry   Housekeeping
Nursing   Marketing

Starting Salary
Depends on position

Company Benefits
- Medical and dental plan

Correspondence
Mail resume with cover letter

Part Time/Summer: Health Sciences Centre sometimes hires for part time and summer work. A potential job could be in the laundry dept or in nursing. The best time to apply is in April.

HELIJET AIRWAYS INC.

5911 Airport Rd. S., Vancouver Int'l Airport
Richmond, British Columbia, V7B 1B5
Tel: (604) 273-4688   Fax: (604) 273-5301

Kala Goodwin, Director of Human Resources
Internet: www.helijet.com

Helijet Airways is a scheduled and charter helicopter service in British Columbia. The firm employs more than 100 people who work in various capacities within the company.

Academic Fields
College: Accounting, Administration, Advertising, Business, Communications, Hospitality, Human Resources, Marketing/Sales, Mechanical Tech., Secretarial, Travel/Tourism
Bachelor of Comm/Admin: General, Accounting, Finance, Marketing, Info Mgmt.
Chartered Accounting: CGA-Finance
Masters: Business Administration

Critical Skills
Adaptable, Analytical, Artistic, Good Communication, Confident, Creative, Decisive, Dependable, Diligent, Diplomatic, Efficient, Enthusiastic, Flexible, Good With Figures, Innovative, Leadership, Logical, Manual Dexterity, Organized, Patient, Personable, Persuasive, Productive, Professional, Responsible, Good Writing Skills

Types of Positions
Agent/Ramp Services   Accounting Clerk
Costing Clerk   Apprentice Engineer
Flight Crew   Marketing & Sales

Starting Salary
Depends on position

Company Benefits
- Medical, dental, travel
- On-the-job training

Correspondence
Mail or fax resume with cover letter

Part Time/Summer: Helijet Airways occasionally seeks individuals for part time and summer work. Potential jobs include hanger and maintenance support, or ramp agent.

HEMOSOL INC.

2 Meridan Rd.
Toronto, Ontario, M9W 4Z7
Tel: (416) 798-0700   Fax: (416) 798-0152

Wendy Forndron, HR Administrator
Internet: www.hemosol.com

Hemosol Inc. is an integrated biopharmaceutical company developing a multi-product pipeline for global markets based on proprietary technologies, used initially in the treatment of hemoglobin deficiencies. The company employs approximately 130 individuals.

Academic Fields
Bachelor of Comm/Admin: Accounting, Human Resources, Marketing
Bachelor of Science: Biology, Chemistry, Health Sciences, Microbiology

Critical Skills
Adaptable, Analytical, Decisive, Dependable, Diligent, Diplomatic, Efficient, Enthusiastic, Good Communication, Manual Dexterity, Productive, Professional, Responsible

Types of Positions
Administrative Assistant
Lab Technician

Starting Salary
$ 25,000 - 30,000

Company Benefits
- Employer paid medical, dental, and life insurance
- Employee PC purchase loan, stock purchase at 10% discount
- Training and development as it pertains to the job

Correspondence
Fax resume with cover letter

Part Time/Summer: Hemosol Inc. rarely hires for part time work and regularly seeks candidates for the summer months. Potential jobs include administrative assistant or lab technician. The best time to apply is February or March.

HERMES ELECTRONICS INC.

40 Atlantic Street, Box 1005
Dartmouth, Nova Scotia, B2Y 4A1
Tel: (902) 461-3309   Fax: (902) 463-6098

Sharon King, Human Resources

Hermes Electronics develops, manufactures, and supplies systems, sub-systems and components for the aerospace, defence and industrial markets. The company also manufactures and distributes mechanical, electronic, and polymer products for the automotive industry.

Academic Fields
College: Accounting, Administration, Business, Drafting/Architecture, Electronics Tech., Engineering Tech., Human Res., Marketing/Sales, Mech. Tech.
Bachelor of Comm/Admin: General, Accounting, Finance, Marketing
Bachelor of Science: Computer Science, Occupational Therapy
Bachelor of Engineering: Electrical, Industrial, Mechanical
Chartered Accounting: CMA-Finance, CGA-Finance
Masters: Business Admin., Science, Engineering

Critical Skills
Adaptable, Analytical, Good Communication, Confident, Creative, Decisive, Dependable, Diligent, Diplomatic, Efficient, Enthusiastic, Flexible, Good With Figures, Innovative, Leadership, Logical, Productive, Professional, Good Writing Skills, Sincere, Candid

Types of Positions
Engineering	Manufacturing
Finance	Marketing
Quality Assurance	Human Resources

Starting Salary
$ 25,000 - 30,000 / $ 30,000 - 40,000 (engineering)

Company Benefits
- Extended health, dental, and life insurance

Correspondence
Mail or fax resume with cover letter

Part Time/Summer: Hermes Electronics sometimes hires for part time and summer work. The best time to apply is in January. Summer positions include engineering technologists for mechanical and electrical engineering students, and computer programmer for info management students.

The Canada Student Employment Guide

HILL & KNOWLTON CANADA LTD.

160 Bloor Street E., Suite 700
Toronto, Ontario, M4W 3P7
Tel: (416) 413-1218   Fax: (416) 413-1550

Human Resources Manager
Internet: www.hillandknowlton.ca

Hill & Knowlton Canada is a public relations, public affairs, and public opinion research firm that serves all types of businesses and enterprises. Decima Research is a division of Hill & Knowlton Canada. They employ more than 130 associates across the country, and have offices in six Canadian cities.

Academic Fields
College: Accounting, Communications, Human Resources, Journalism, Television/Radio
Bachelor of Arts: Journalism, Public Relations
Bachelor of Comm/Admin: Marketing
Chartered Accounting: CA-General
Masters: Business Administration, Arts

Critical Skills
Adaptable, Analytical, Good Communication, Confident, Creative, Decisive, Dependable, Diligent, Diplomatic, Efficient, Enthusiastic, Flexible, Good With Figures, Innovative, Leadership, Logical, Organized, Patient, Personable, Persuasive, Productive, Professional, Responsible, Good Writing Skills

Types of Positions
Account Coordinator   Accounting Clerk
Research Analyst   Research Assistant

Starting Salary
$ 25,000 - 30,000

Company Benefits
- Full employer paid benefits
- Significant investment in training

Correspondence
Mail resume with cover letter

Part Time/Summer: Hill and Knowlton Canada sometimes seeks students for part time and summer opportunities. Potential positions in the summer months are those outlined above.

HIPPODROME DE MONTRÉAL

7440 boulevard Décarie
Montréal, Québec, H4P 2H1
Tel: (514) 739-2741   Fax: (514) 340-2025

Sylvie Gilbert, Ressources humaines

Hippodrome de Montréal is a race track in Quebec that was established in 1962. The race track is host to many events in Montreal, and employs more than 500 people to work in the amusement and recreation industry.

Academic Fields
College: Accounting, Administration, Animal Health, Computer Science, Faculty Management, Human Resources, Insurance
Bachelor of Arts: Public Relations
Bachelor of Comm/Admin: General, Accounting, Finance, Info Mgmt.
Chartered Accounting: CA - General/Finance, CMA-General

Critical Skills
Adaptable, Analytical, Enthusiastic, Good Communication, Flexible, Good Writing Skills, Organized, Professional, Responsible

Types of Positions
Various Positions

Starting Salary
$ 20,000 - 30,000

Company Benefits
- Complete benefit package

Correspondence
Mail resume with cover letter

Part Time/Summer: Hippodrome de Montréal sometimes looks for individuals for part time and summer employment opportunities. Jobs in the summer most likely involve general clerical duties.

The Canada Student Employment Guide

HMV CANADA

5401 Eglinton Avenue West, Suite 110
Etobicoke, Ontario, M9C 5K6
Tel: (416) 620-4470   Fax: (416) 620-5064

Mary Ann Dunlop, Human Resources Manager
Internet: www.hmv.com

With over 75 years of music retailing history and 275 stores worldwide, HMV is the world's premier retailer of music. Continually growing within the international retail music industry, HMV has proven itself as an innovative leader in Canada since 1986.

Academic Fields
No specific academic background is required. Do not look at education for any entry level positions. Look for experience and skill level as more important factors.

Critical Skills
Adaptable, Enthusiastic, Flexible, Good Communication, Innovative, Organized, Productive, Professional, Responsible, Self-Motivated, Problem-Solving

Types of Positions
Full Time Sales Clerk   Part Time Sales Clerk
Receivers

Starting Salary
below $ 20,000

Company Benefits
- Health, dental, life, vision care, disability
- Employee assistance program, savings plan
- no formal training, mgmt. opportunities

Correspondence
Mail, fax, submit resume & cover letter in person

Part Time/Summer: HMV Canada regularly hires for part time openings and summer opportunities. Potential positions include full time and part time sales. The best time to apply is from May to June. Contact the store manager at the location you are interested in working for more information on these opportunities.

HOCKEY HALL OF FAME

BCE Place, 30 Yonge Street
Toronto, Ontario, M5E 1X8
Tel: (416) 360-7735   Fax: (416) 360-1501

Human Resources
Internet: www.hhof.com

The Hockey Hall of Fame was founded in 1943 to establish a memorial to those who have developed Canada's great winter sport - ice hockey. Incorporated in 1983, Hockey Hall of Fame and Museum exists in order to honour and preserve the history of the game of ice hockey and, in particular, those who have made outstanding contributions and achievements in the development of the game.

Academic Fields
No specific academic background is required. They will look at candidates from all academic backgrounds.

Critical Skills
Dependable, Enthusiastic, Patient, Good Communication, Personable

Types of Positions
Guest Services   Building Services
Retail

Starting Salary
below $ 20,000

Company Benefits
- No benefits offered since all employees part time
- Training mandatory for all part time positions

Correspondence
Mail resume and cover letter or submit in person

Part Time/Summer: The Hockey Hall of Fame sometimes hires individuals on a part time basis and regularly hires for summer opportunities. Potential positions in the summer include those listed above. Candidates should apply by January 31st.

HOFFMAN-LA ROCHE LIMITED

2455 Meadowpine Blvd.
Mississauga, Ontario, L5N 6L7
Tel: (905) 542-5555   Fax: (905) 542-7130

Human Resources Dept.
Internet: www.rochecanada.com

Roche Canada is a Canadian company with the strength of a global organization. This gives Canadians the benefit of Roche's international focus on the full spectrum of prevention, diagnosis and therapy. The company has grown both through scientific discovery and strategic acquisition, most recently integrating the pharmaceutical firm Syntex and product from the biotechnology leader Genentech.

Academic Fields
College: Administration, Human Resources, Secretarial
Bachelor of Arts: General, Business
Bachelor of Comm/Admin: Accounting, Finance, Info Mgmt.
Bachelor of Science: General, Kinesiology, Nursing (RN), Pharmacy
Chartered Accounting: CMA - General/Finance
Masters: Business Administration

Critical Skills
Good Communication, Efficient, Enthusiastic, Flexible, Leadership, Organized, Personable, Professional, Responsible

Types of Positions
Administrative Assistant   Sales Representative

Starting Salary
$ 30,000 - 50,000

Company Benefits
- Medical, dental, vision
- Highly competitive pension and benefit package

Correspondence
Mail or fax resume with cover letter

Part Time/Summer: Hoffman - La Roche rarely seeks people for part time and occasionally looks for individuals for the summer. Potential jobs vary throughout the company. They include accounts payable clerk, telemarketing, and administrative assistant. The best time to apply is in March or April.

HOLIDAY INN SELECT TORONTO AIRPORT

970 Dixon Rd.
Etobicoke, Ontario, M9W 1J9
Tel: (416) 675-7611   Fax: (416) 675-9162

Employee Services

Holiday Inn Select Toronto Airport is a large airport hotel with 444 rooms and many conference facilities. The company has hotel locations across the country.

Academic Fields
College: General, Accounting, Administration, Business, Cooking/Culinary, Hospitality, Human Resources, Secretarial, Security/Law, Travel/Tourism
Bachelor of Arts: General, Business, Public Relations
Bachelor of Comm/Admin: General, Accounting, Finance, Marketing
Bachelor of Engineering: General

Critical Skills
Adaptable, Good Communication, Dependable, Diligent, Diplomatic, Efficient, Enthusiastic, Flexible, Innovative, Leadership, Organized, Patient, Personable, Productive, Professional, Responsible

Types of Positions
Front Desk Clerk   Restaurant Server/Busperson
PBX Operator   Dishwasher

Starting Salary
$ 20,000 - 25,000

Company Benefits
- Competitive benefit package

Correspondence
Mail resume with cover letter

Part Time/Summer: Holiday Inn Select Toronto Airport occasionally looks for people for part time work, but does not hire individuals specifically for the summer months.

The Canada Student Employment Guide

HOLLAND COLLEGE

140 Weymouth Street
Charlottetown, PEI, C1A 4Z1
Tel: (902) 566-9680   Fax: (902) 566-9608

Marilyn MacCallum, Human Resources

Holland College provides a wide range of education, particularly in the fields of applied arts and technology, vocational and adult education. The college offers training at 12 centres on an annual basis and responds to training needs in several communities through eastern and western coordinators.

Academic Fields
College: Administration, Computer Science, Secretarial
Bachelor of Comm/Admin: General, Marketing, Public Admin.
Bachelor of Science: Computer Science
Bachelor of Education: General, Adult Education

Critical Skills
Adaptable, Dependable, Efficient, Enthusiastic, Flexible, Good Communication, Good Writing Skills, Innovative, Personable, Productive, Responsible, Pro-Active

Types of Positions
Secretary   Clerical

Starting Salary
$ 25,000 - 30,000

Company Benefits
- Cost shared benefits, health and dental insurance
- Life insurance, long term disability
- Vacation and sick leave accumulation

Correspondence
Mail resume with cover letter

Part Time/Summer: Holland College regularly seeks individuals for part time and summer employment opportunities.

HOME OIL CO. LTD.

324 - 8th Avenue SW, Suite 1600
Calgary, Alberta, T2P 2Z5
Tel: (403) 232-7100   Fax: (403) 232-7221

Human Resources

Home Oil Co. is an oil and gas company that is involved in the production process. The head office of Home Oil is located in Calgary, Alberta.

Academic Fields
College: Accounting, Administration, Business, Communications, Computer Science, Drafting/Architecture, Electronics Tech., Engineering Tech., Human Resources, Secretarial, Statistics
Bachelor of Arts: Business, Economics, Public Relations, Statistics
Bachelor of Comm/Admin: General, Accounting, Finance, Marketing
Bachelor of Science: Actuarial, Computer Science, Environmental Studies, Geology, Mathematics
Bachelor of Laws: Corporate
Bachelor of Engineering: General, Chemical, Civil, Geotechnical, Mechanical
Chartered Accounting: CMA-Finance
Masters: Business Administration, Engineering

Critical Skills
Adaptable, Confident, Creative, Decisive, Dependable, Diligent, Efficient, Flexible, Good Communication, Good Writing Skills, Innovative, Leadership, Logical, Personable, Productive, Professional

Types of Positions
Various Positions

Starting Salary
$ 25,000 - 30,000

Company Benefits
- Full competitive benefit package
- Reimbursement of job-related training and courses

Correspondence
Mail resume with cover letter

Part Time/Summer: Home Oil Co. occasionally hires for part time work, and regularly hires for the summer. Potential jobs in the summer are in field positions, accounting, finance, library, office services, and the information systems area. The best time to apply is at the beginning of the year.

HOMEWOOD CORP.

150 Delhi Street
Guelph, Ontario, N1E 6K9
Tel: (519) 824-1010   Fax: (519) 824-9501

Human Resources
Internet: www.homewoodhealth.com

Homewood Corp. is a privately owned, and publicly funded mental health facility. Homewood Corp. is located in Guelph, Ontario.

Academic Fields
College: Accounting, Administration, Advertising, Business, Communications, Computer Science, Cooking/Culinary, Food/Nutrition, Human Resources, Journalism, Marketing/Sales, Nursing, Recreation Studies, Science, Secretarial, Security/Law
Bachelor of Arts: Business, Journalism, Psychology, Public Rel., Recreation Studies, Sociology/Social Work
Bachelor of Comm/Admin: Finance, Marketing, Info Mgmt., Public Admin.
Bachelor of Science: Computer Science, Environmental Studies, Food Sciences, Health Sciences, Horticulture, Nursing (RN), Occupational Therapy, Pharmacy, Psychology
Bachelor of Education: Adult Education

Critical Skills
Adaptable, Dependable, Diligent, Efficient, Enthusiastic, Good Communication, Good Writing Skills, Leadership, Organized, Personable, Productive, Professional, Responsible, Team Player, Interpersonal Skills

Types of Positions
Finance Clerk   Housekeeping
Nutrition/Diet Aide   Administration
Clinical

Starting Salary
$ 20,000 - 25,000

Company Benefits
- Percentage in lieu of benefits to part time staff
- Extended health, dental, travel insurance
- On site staff development lecture theatre

Correspondence
Mail or fax resume with cover letter

Part Time/Summer: Homewood Corp. occasionally hires for part time and summer work. Jobs in the summer are most likely those listed above. The best time to apply is in early May.

HONDA CANADA INC.

715 Milner Avenue
Scarborough, Ontario, M1B 2K8
Tel: (416) 284-8110   Fax: (416) 286-1322

Marilyn McAllister, Human Resources
Internet: www.honda.ca

Honda Canada is involved in the assembly and distribution of vehicles and the distribution of small engines and parts to dealers throughout Canada. The company is jointly owned by Honda Motor Co. Ltd. of Japan and American Honda Motor Co. Inc. Honda Canada employs more than 2,000 people.

Academic Fields
College: Accounting, Advertising, Business, Engineering Tech., Human Resources, Marketing/Sales, Secretarial
Bachelor of Arts: General, Business, Economics
Bachelor of Comm/Admin: Accounting, Finance, Marketing, Info Mgmt.
Bachelor of Science: General, Computer Sci., Math
Bachelor of Laws: Corporate
Bachelor of Engineering: General, Computer Systems, Electrical, Industrial, Mechanical, Transportation
Chartered Accounting: CA-Finance, CMA-General, CGA-Finance
Masters: Business Administration

Critical Skills
Adaptable, Analytical, Dependable, Good Communication, Enthusiastic, Good Writing Skills, Leadership, Organized, Professional, Responsible

Types of Positions
Sales Training   Distribution Coordinator
Parts Clerk   Accounts Payable
Junior Programmer   Warehouse Person

Starting Salary
$ 25,000 - 30,000

Company Benefits
- Full benefits, medical and dental
- Training and development, on-the-job training

Correspondence
Mail or fax resume with cover letter

Part Time/Summer: Honda Canada regularly hires for part time and summer work. Potential jobs are in the warehouse, or involve being a marketing co-op student. Apply for jobs in the warehouse in March.

HONEYWELL LTD.

155 Gordon Baker Road
North York, Ontario, L1S 3Y3
Tel: (416) 502-5305   Fax: (416) 502-5390

Human Resources
Internet: www.honeywell.com

Honeywell develops, manufactures, and markets control automation systems, and products for the home, commercial buildings, industrial processing and aerospace markets. Honeywell in Canada is one of the country's leading control companies. Honeywell has over 2,700 employees across Canada and has 9 locations in the Toronto region.

Academic Fields
College: Accounting, Computer Science, Electronics Tech., Engineering Tech., Secretarial
Bachelor of Arts: Business, Economics, English, Journalism
Bachelor of Comm/Admin: General, Accounting, Finance
Bachelor of Science: Computer Science
Bachelor of Engineering: Chemical, Computer Systems, Electrical, Materials, Mechanical
Chartered Accounting: CA-General, CMA-General, CGA-General
Masters: Business Administration, Engineering

Critical Skills
Adaptable, Analytical, Confident, Good Communication, Decisive, Enthusiastic, Flexible, Leadership, Good Writing Skills, Team Oriented

Types of Positions
Financial Analyst   Control Engineer

Starting Salary
$ 25,000 - 35,000

Company Benefits
- Full flexible benefit plan
- Tuition aid program

Correspondence
Mail resume with cover letter

Part Time/Summer: Honeywell sometimes hires for part time positions and for summer opportunities.

HORSESHOE RESORT CORPORATION

P.O. Box 10, Stn Main
Barrie, Ontario, L4M 4Y8
Tel: (705) 835-2790   Fax: (705) 835-2149

Katherine Renwick, Manager, Human Resources
Internet: www.horseshoeresort.com

Horseshoe Resort Corporation is a ski and golf resort with a 102 room hotel. The resort has two sit down restaurants, along with banquet and conference rooms. The resort employ about 250 people.

Academic Fields
College: Accounting, Administration, Child Care, Cooking/Culinary, Hospitality, Secretarial, Travel/Tourism
Bachelor of Arts: Recreation Studies
Bachelor of Comm/Admin: General, Accounting, Finance
Bachelor of Science: Forestry, Horticulture, Kinesiology
Bachelor of Education: Childhood
Chartered Accounting: CA - General/Finance, CGA/CMA - General/Finance
Masters: Business Administration

Critical Skills
Adaptable, Good Communication, Confident, Dependable, Enthusiastic, Flexible, Personable, Responsible

Types of Positions
Reservations   Guest Services
Front Desk

Starting Salary
below $ 20,000 - 25,000

Company Benefits
- Medical and dental benefits, resort privileges
- On-going guest service training

Correspondence
Mail or fax resume with cover letter E-mail: humreshrebar.imag.net

Part Time/Summer: Horseshoe Resort Corporation regularly looks for individuals for part time or summer employment. Potential jobs involve sports and adventure camp, groundskeeping, and lifeguard. The best time to apply is in March and April.

HÔTEL DIEU DE MONTRÉAL

3840 rue Saint-Urbain
Montréal, Québec, H2W 1T8
Tel: (514) 843-2643   Fax: N/A

Ressources humaines

Hôtel Dieu de Montréal is a public health care facility that provides general medical and surgical services. The hospital has 570 beds, and employs 2,800 people. Hôtel Dieu de Montréal is affiliated with The University of Montreal.

Academic Fields
College: Accounting, Administration, Computer Science, Electronics Tech., Faculty Management, Food/Nutrition, Human Resources, Laboratory Tech., Nursing, Radiology Tech., Secretarial
Bachelor of Comm/Admin: Accounting, Public Admin.
Bachelor of Science: Food Sciences, Health Sciences, Nursing (RN), Occupational Therapy, Pharmacy, Psychology
Bachelor of Engineering: Biomedical
Chartered Accounting: CA - General/Finance, CGA-Finance
Masters: Business Administration

Critical Skills
Adaptable, Creative, Dependable, Good Communication, Diligent, Diplomatic, Efficient, Flexible, Good Writing Skills, Logical, Organized, Productive, Professional, Responsible

Types of Positions
Various positions

Starting Salary
$ 20,000 - 25,000

Company Benefits
- Full time staff receive benefits
- Part time staff receive some benefits

Correspondence
Mail resume with cover letter

Part Time/Summer: Hôtel Dieu de Montréal regularly seeks candidates for part time and summer employment opportunities. Potential jobs usually involve general office duties, or within the medical field. The best time to apply is in February or March.

HOUSEHOLD MOVERS & SHIPPERS LIMITED

Donovans Industrial Park
St. John's, Newfoundland, A1B 3R9
Tel: (709) 747-4222   Fax: (709) 368-2619

Rick Power, Human Resources

Household Movers and Shippers is a privately owned household goods transportation company which is an agent for North American Van Lines. With branches throughout the Maritimes, the company employs 25 permanent full time individuals, which increases during seasonal times to 200 full and part time staff.

Academic Fields
College: Accounting, Business, Computer Science
Bachelor of Arts: Economics
Bachelor of Comm/Admin: General, Accounting, Finance, Marketing, Info Mgmt.
Chartered Accounting: CA - General/Finance, CGA/CMA - General/Finance

Critical Skills
Diligent, Efficient, Personable

Types of Positions
Clerical   Truck Driver
Helper

Starting Salary
$ 25,000 - 30,000

Company Benefits
- Health and pension plan, group insurance
- Job related courses paid by company

Correspondence
Mail resume with cover letter

Part Time/Summer: Household Movers & Shippers sometimes seeks candidates for part time positions and regularly looks for individuals for summer employment opportunities. Jobs in the summer involve warehouse labour, or helping on trucks. The best time to apply is in April.

The Canada Student Employment Guide

THE HOUSESITTERS CANADA

530 Queen St. E.
Toronto, Ontario, M5A 1V2
Tel: (416) 947-1295   Fax: (416) 947-0468

Human Resources

The Housesitters Canada provides property, home care, pet care, and general property management. The firm employs approximately 500 individuals in total.

Academic Fields
College: Accounting, Secretarial, Travel/Tourism
Bachelor of Arts: Public Relations
Bachelor of Comm/Admin: Accounting, Marketing
Bachelor of Science: Computer Science
Bachelor of Laws: Real Estate

Critical Skills
Analytical, Confident, Creative, Decisive, Dependable, Diligent, Diplomatic, Efficient, Enthusiastic, Flexible, Good With Figures, Leadership, Logical, Organized, Patient, Personable, Productive, Professional, Responsible

Types of Positions
Various Positions

Starting Salary
$ 20,000 - 25,000

Company Benefits
- Health and dental
- Group insurance

Correspondence
Fax resume with cover letter

Part Time/Summer: The Housesitters Canada regularly seeks people for part time work, and occasionally looks for staff in the summer months. Potential jobs include part time customer service.

HSBC BANK CANADA

885 West Georgia Street, Suite 300
Vancouver, British Columbia, V6C 3E9
Tel: (604) 641-2905   Fax: (604) 641-2917

Malcolm Tinsley, Assistant Manager Employee Relations
Internet: www.hkbc.ca

HSBC Bank Canada is a principal member of the HSBC Group, which has more than 5,000 offices in 82 countries and territories and is one of the world's largest banking and financial services organizations.

Academic Fields
College: Business, Computer Science
Bachelor of Arts: General, Business, Economics
Bachelor of Comm/Admin: General, Accounting, Finance, Marketing, Info Mgmt., Public Admin.
Bachelor of Science: General, Computer Science
Bachelor of Engineering: General
Chartered Accounting: CMA - General/Finance, CGA - General/Finance
Masters: Business Administration, Arts

Critical Skills
Adaptable, Analytical, Good Communication, Confident, Creative, Decisive, Dependable, Efficient, Enthusiastic, Flexible, Good With Figures, Leadership, Logical, Organized, Personable, Productive, Professional, Responsible, Good Writing Skills, Mobile

Types of Positions
Secretarial/Customer Service Rep.
Commercial Banking-Management Trainee
Personal Banking-Management Trainee

Starting Salary
$ 20,000 - 25,000 (customer rep.) /
$ 30,000 - 40,000 (mgmt.)

Company Benefits
- Comprehensive employee benefits program
- Competitive salary scales

Correspondence
Mail or fax resume with cover letter

Part Time/Summer: HSBC Bank Canada sometimes looks for part time and summer candidates. Positions most likely involve project work, or branch support. The best time to apply is in April or May.

The Canada Student Employment Guide

HUB MEAT PACKERS LTD.

144 Edinburgh Drive
Moncton, New Brunswick, E1B 3Y3
Tel: (506) 853-8899   Fax: (506) 388-3348

Cynthia Brocks Human Resources
www.sunrise.ca

Hub Meat Packers is a meat packaging and processing plant located in Moncton, New Brunswick. Established in 1965, Hub Meat Packers employs 1,200 individuals in total.

Academic Fields
College: Accounting, Animal Health, Marketing/Sales, Secretarial
Bachelor of Comm/Admin: General, Accounting, Finance, Info Mgmt.
Bachelor of Science: Food Sciences

Critical Skills
Adaptable, Decisive, Dependable, Diligent, Efficient, Enthusiastic, Flexible, Good Communication, Innovative, Logical, Manual Dexterity, Personable, Productive, Responsible

Types of Positions
Labourer   Office Clerk

Starting Salary
below $ 20,000

Company Benefits
- Health and life insurance
- Long term disability

Correspondence
Mail, fax, submit resume & cover letter in person
E-mail: cynthiab@sunrise.ca

Part Time/Summer: Hub Meat Packers regularly looks for individuals for part time work, and occasionally seeks candidates for summer positions. Potential jobs in the summer involve being a labourer. The best time to apply is in March or April.

HUBBELL CANADA INC.

870 Brock Rd. S.
Pickering, Ontario, L1W 1Z8
Tel: (905) 839-1138   Fax: (905) 839-0138

Human Resources Department
Internet: www.hubbell-canada.com

Hubbell Canada's mandate is to market, sell and distribute Hubbell products in Canada. These products are basically: wiring, lighting, and power systems. Hubbell Canada also manufactures power/service poles for commercial applications and plastic outlet boxes for building construction.

Academic Fields
College: Accounting, Administration, Business, Computer Science, Electronics Tech., Engineering Tech., Marketing/Sales, Secretarial
Bachelor of Arts: Business
Bachelor of Comm/Admin: Accounting, Marketing
Bachelor of Engineering: Electrical, Mechanical
Chartered Accounting: CMA-General, CGA-General

Critical Skills
Adaptable, Good Communication, Decisive, Leadership, Professional

Types of Positions
Marketing Assistant   Inside Sales Associate

Starting Salary
$ 30,000 - 40,000

Company Benefits
- Life insurance, extended health, dental
- Short and long term disability
- Sales and marketing focused opportunities

Correspondence
Fax resume with cover letter
E-mail: sbrennan@hubbell-canada.com

Part Time/Summer: Hubbell Canada does not generally hire for part time work, but regularly looks for people in the summer. They usually hire for office or warehouse positions. The best time to apply is January or February.

HUDON & DEAUDELIN LTÉE

11281 boulevard Albert-Hudon
Montréal-Nord, Québec, H1G 3S5
Tel: (514) 324-1010   Fax: N/A

Stephanie B. Beaulieu, Ressources humaines

Hudon & Deaudelin is a food wholesaler located in Montreal, Quebec. The company is a wholly owned subsidiary of The Oshawa Group Limited. Hudon & Deaudelin employs approximately 1,600 individuals to work in various disciplines within the food industry.

Academic Fields
College: Accounting, Advertising, Computer Science, Human Resources, Law Clerk, Marketing/Sales, Mechanical Tech., Secretarial
Bachelor of Arts: Business
Bachelor of Comm/Admin: Accounting, Finance, Info Mgmt.
Bachelor of Science: Computer Science, Food Sciences
Bachelor of Laws: Real Estate
Chartered Accounting: CA - General/Finance, CGA/CMA - General/Finance

Critical Skills
Adaptable, Analytical, Creative, Decisive, Dependable, Diligent, Diplomatic, Good Communication, Good Writing Skills, Logical, Patient, Personable, Professional, Responsible

Types of Positions
Various Positions

Starting Salary
$ 20,000 - 25,000

Company Benefits
- Medical and dental coverage
- Vacation pay
- Christmas bonus

Correspondence
Mail resume with cover letter

Part Time/Summer: Hudon & Deaudelin regularly seeks individuals for part time and summer employment opportunities. Potential jobs include warehouse or office work. The best time to apply is in April.

THE HUDSON'S BAY COMPANY

401 Bay Street, Suite 2009
Toronto, Ontario, M5H 2Y4
Tel: (416) 861-6096   Fax: (416) 861-4180

Shawn Brinson, Human Resources
Internet: www.hbc.com

Hudson's Bay Company, established in 1670, is Canada's oldest corporation and largest department store retailer. Through its major operating divisions, the Bay and Zellers, Hudson's Bay Company covers the Canadian retail market across all price zones from coast to coast. The company is a major employer of more than 65,000 individuals across the country.

Academic Fields
College: Accounting, Business, Computer Science, Drafting/Architecture, Human Resources, Secretarial
Bachelor of Arts: Business
Bachelor of Comm/Admin: General, Accounting, Finance, Marketing
Bachelor of Science: Computer Science
Chartered Accounting: CA-Finance, CMA-General/Finance, CGA-General/Finance
Masters: Business Administration

Critical Skills
Confident, Dependable, Enthusiastic, Good Communication, Leadership, Personable, Productive, Professional

Types of Positions
Sales Associate   Retail Executive Program

Starting Salary
$ 30,000 - 50,000

Company Benefits
- Complete benefit package

Correspondence
Mail or e-mail resume with cover letter
E-mail: careers@hbc.com

Part Time/Summer: The Hudson's Bay Company regularly hires individuals for part time openings, but does not hire for the summer exclusively.

Co-op/Internship: Internship opportunities currently exist in Ontario, across HBC, The Bay and Zellers. In Year 2000 they had 9 student interns.

The Canada Student Employment Guide

HUMBER RIVER REGIONAL HOSPITAL

2111 Finch Ave. W.
Downsview, Ontario, M3N 1N1
Tel: (416) 744-2500   Fax: (416) 747-3758

Reena Pabla, Recruiter, Human Resources
Internet: www.hrrh.on.ca

One of Canada's largest regional community health care centres, Humber River Regional Hospital offers a comprehensive range of diagnostic and treatment. With a staff of more than 2,000, the hospital offers services in dialysis, emergency, diagnostics, cardiology, intensive care, birthing, pediatrics, ambulatory care, mental health, medicine and surgery.

Academic Fields
College: Accounting, Administration, Business, Communications, Human Res., Information Systems, Emergency/Paramedic, Lab Tech., Nursing (RN/RNA), Radiology Tech., Respiratory Tech., Physiotherapy, Occup. Therapy, X-Ray Technology, Nuclear Medicine
Bachelor of Arts: Public Relations
Bachelor of Comm/Admin: Accounting, Finance, Human Resources, Info Mgmt.
Bachelor of Science: Computer Science, Food Science, Health Science, Kinesiology, Microbiology, Nursing, Occupational Therapy, Pharmacy, Physiotherapy
Bachelor of Education: Adult Education
Chartered Accounting: CA - General/Finance, CGA - General/Finance, CMA - General/Finance
Masters: Business Admin., Science, Educ., Library Sci., Nursing

Critical Skills
Adaptable, Confident, Dependable, Diligent, Efficient, Enthusiastic, Flexible, Good Communication, Writing Skills, Responsible, Customer Service, Team Work

Types of Positions
Nurse	Secretary
Laboratory Tech.	Accounting Clerk

Starting Salary
Depends on position

Company Benefits
- Full benefits package for full time staff

Correspondence
Mail, fax or e-mail resume with cover letter
E-mail: recruitment@hrrh.on.ca

Part Time/Summer: The Hospital occasionally hires part timers and summer staff. Apply in March or April.

HURONIA REGIONAL CENTRE

P.O. Box 1000, Stn Main
Orillia, Ontario, L3V 6L2
Tel: (705) 326-7361   Fax: (705) 326-3445

Susan Gilchrist, Human Resources

Huronia Regional Centre is a large facility that provides service and support to people with developmental disabilities. The centre employs about 1,000 individuals in total.

Academic Fields
College: Accounting, Computer Science, Cooking/Culinary, Electronics Tech., Engineering Tech., Food/Nutrition, Human Resources, Mechanical Tech., Nursing, Recreation Studies, Secretarial
Bachelor of Arts: General, Business, Psychology, Recreation Studies, Sociology/Social Work
Bachelor of Comm/Admin: Accounting, Finance, Info Mgmt.
Bachelor of Science: Food Sciences, Health Sciences, Kinesiology, Nursing (RN), Occupational Therapy, Pharmacy, Physiotherapy, Psychology
Bachelor of Education: Childhood

Critical Skills
Good Communication, Dependable, Efficient, Flexible, Organized, Patient, Personable, Productive, Professional, Responsible, Good Writing Skills, Team Player, Customer Skills

Types of Positions
Secretarial	Housekeeping
Landscaping	Food Service
Transportation	Maintenance

Starting Salary
$ 15,000 - 19,000

Company Benefits
- Comprehensive benefits package
- In-house training

Correspondence
Mail resume with cover letter

Part Time/Summer: Huronia Regional Centre does not generally hire part time workers, but regularly seeks people for summer employment. Potential work involves recreation, clerical duties, maintenance, landscaping, transportation, or residential life. Applications should be received by April 30th.

HUSKY ENERGY INC.

707 - 8th Avenue SW
Calgary, Alberta, T2P 3G7
Tel: (403) 298-6111   Fax: (403) 298-6799

Staffing, Human Resources
Internet: www.huskyenergy.ca

Headquartered in Western Canadian Place in Calgary, Alberta, Husky Energy Inc. employs approximately 2,500 people and holds almost $9 billion in quality growth assets. A fully integrated oil and gas company, Husky Energy ranks second in production and third in reserves relative to Canada's four other integrated oil and gas companies.

Academic Fields
College: Accounting, Administration, Business, Computer Science, Engineering Tech., Secretarial
Bachelor of Comm/Admin: Accounting
Bachelor of Engineering: Computer Systems, Design, Electrical, Environmental Studies, Geotechnical
Chartered Accounting: CA-Finance

Critical Skills
Adaptable, Dependable, Efficient, Enthusiastic, Flexible, Innovative, Good Writing Skills, Good Communication, Leadership, Organized, Productive, Professional, Responsible

Types of Positions
Mail Clerk   Accounting Clerk
Junior Engineer

Starting Salary
below $ 20,000 (clerk) / $ 30,000 - 40,000 (engineering)

Company Benefits
- Benefits to permanent staff
- No benefits offered to students
- Training dependent upon position and requirements.

Correspondence
Mail resume with cover letter

Part Time/Summer: Husky Energy sometimes looks for candidates for part time positions, and regularly seeks individuals for summer employment opportunities. Potential jobs are most likely those listed above.

HYDRO ELECTRIC COMMISSION OF THUNDER BAY

34 Cumberland St. N.
Thunder Bay, Ontario, P7A 4L4
Tel: (807) 343-1111   Fax: (807) 344-7520

Joanne Fulkerson, Human Resources

The Hydro Electric Commission of Thunder Bay is a municipal electric utility that serves the City of Thunder Bay. The electric commission employs about 150 individuals.

Academic Fields
College: General, Accounting, Administration, Communications, Computer Science, Drafting/Architecture, Electronics Tech., Engineering Tech., Human Resources, Secretarial
Bachelor of Arts: General, Business, Public Relations
Bachelor of Comm/Admin: General, Accounting, Finance, Info Mgmt., Public Admin.
Bachelor of Science: Computer Science, Environmental Studies
Bachelor of Engineering: Computer Systems, Design, Electrical
Chartered Accounting: CA - General/Finance, CGA/CMA - General/Finance
Masters: Business Administration, Arts, Engineering

Critical Skills
Adaptable, Good Communication, Confident, Creative, Dependable, Diplomatic, Efficient, Enthusiastic, Flexible, Logical, Manual Dexterity, Organized, Personable, Productive, Professional, Responsible, Good Writing Skills

Types of Positions
Various Positions

Starting Salary
$ 30,000 - 40,000

Company Benefits
- Full dental and health, vision, life insurance
- Full tuition reimbursement, on-the-job training

Correspondence
Would prefer co-op application form

Part Time/Summer: The Hydro Electric Commission of Thunder Bay occasionally looks for people for part time work, and regularly seeks candidates for the summer. Potential jobs labour duties, clerical work, or electrical engineering. The best time to apply is in February.

The Canada Student Employment Guide

HYDRO MISSISSAUGA CORPORATION

3240 Mavis Road
Mississauga, Ontario, L5C 3K1
Tel: (905) 273-9050   Fax: (905) 566-2704

Human Resources
Internet: www.hydromiss.com

Hydro Mississauga Corporation is an electrical distribution utility serving approximately 158,000 Mississauga customers. Hydro Mississauga prefers correspondence by mail or fax, and not by telephone. Applicants should not expect to receive a response, as only those candidates under consideration will be contacted. Available positions will be posted on their website.

Academic Fields
College: Accounting, Administration, Engineering Tech., Marketing/Sales, Secretarial, Electrical, Engineering Tech.
Bachelor of Arts: General
Bachelor of Comm/Admin: Accounting, Finance, Marketing, Info Mgmt.
Bachelor of Engineering: Electrical
Chartered Accounting: CA, CMA-Finance, CGA-Finance
Masters: Business Administration

Critical Skills
Adaptable, Analytical, Good Communication, Confident, Decisive, Dependable, Diligent, Diplomatic, Efficient, Enthusiastic, Flexible, Good With Figures, Leadership, Logical, Manual Dexterity, Organized, Responsible, Good Writing Skills

Types of Positions
Mailroom Clerk   Labourer
Telephone Operator   General Clerk

Starting Salary
$ 27,000 - 36,000 (depends on position)

Company Benefits
- Comprehensive benefits with health and dental
- Life insurance, defined benefit pension plan

Correspondence
Mail or fax resume with cover letter

Part Time/Summer: Hydro Mississauga Corporation occasionally hires for part time and regularly hires for summer employment. However, summer positions are usually filled by sons and daughters when a small number are required.

HYDRO ONE INC.

483 Bay St., 10th Floor
Toronto, Ontario, M5G 2P5
Tel: (416) 345-5000   Fax: N/A

Human Resources
Internet: www.hydroone.com

Hydro One Inc. launched the corporate holding company and its five subsidiaries in May 2000. The Hydro One group of companies emerged from the restructuring of Ontario Hydro as the owner and operator of the wires operations formerly provided by the provincially owned utility. During the one-year transition, the company operated under the name Ontario Hydro Services Company.

Academic Fields
College: Accounting, Business, Computer Science, Electronics Tech., Engineering Tech., Laboratory Tech., Mechanical Tech.
Bachelor of Arts: Business, Economics
Bachelor of Comm/Admin: Marketing, Info Mgmt.
Bachelor of Science: Chemistry, Computer Science, Environmental Studies
Bachelor of Engineering: Chemical, Computer Systems, Electrical, Environmental Studies, Mechanical
Chartered Accounting: CA-Finance
Masters: Business Administration

Critical Skills
Adaptable, Analytical, Decisive, Flexible, Innovative, Leadership, Personable, Persuasive, Good Communication

Types of Positions
Clerical   Technical
Trade   Senior Engineering
Plant Operations   Finance

Starting Salary
$ 30,000 - 40,000

Company Benefits
- A very competitive benefits package is offered

Correspondence
Mail or e-mail resume with cover letter

Part Time/Summer: Hydro One Inc. regularly hires individuals for part time and summer opportunities. The best time to apply is in January or February.

The Canada Student Employment Guide

HYDRO QUÉBEC

75, boulevard René-Lévesque Ouest
Montréal, Québec, H2Z 1A4
Tel: (514) 289-3871   Fax: (514) 289-2530

Ressources humaines
Internet: www.hydro.qc.ca

Hydro-Québec's mission is to supply power and to pursue endeavors in energy-related research and promotion, energy conversion and conservation, and any field connected with or related to power or energy. Hydro Québec employs 26,000 individuals.

Academic Fields
College: Admin., Computer Science, Cooking/Culinary, Electronics Tech., Engineering Tech., Law Clerk, Mechanical Tech., Nursing, Secretarial, Security/Law
Bachelor of Arts: Economics, Statistics
Bachelor of Comm/Admin: Accounting, Finance, Info Mgmt.
Bachelor of Science: Biology, Chemistry, Environ. Studies, Geography, Geology, Nursing (RN), Physics
Bachelor of Laws: Corporate
Bachelor of Engineering: Chemical, Computer Syst., Electrical, Environ. Studies, Geotechnical, Mechanical
Chartered Accounting: CA-Finance, CGA/CMA - General/Finance
Masters: Business Admin., Engineering, Library Science

Critical Skills
Adaptable, Analytical, Good Communication, Confident, Creative, Decisive, Dependable, Diligent, Diplomatic, Efficient, Enthusiastic, Flexible, Good With Figures, Innovative, Leadership, Logical, Manual Dexterity, Organized, Patient, Personable, Persuasive, Productive, Professional, Responsible, Writing Skills

Types of Positions
Various positions

Starting Salary
$ 25,000 - 40,000 (depending on position)

Company Benefits
- Comprehensive benefit package
- Retirement package

Correspondence
Mail resume with cover letter

Part Time/Summer: Hydro Québec does not hire individuals for part time or summer employment. Positions are posted within colleges and universities when they become available.

I M P GROUP INTERNATIONAL INC.

2651 Dutch Village Road
Halifax, Nova Scotia, B3L 4T1
Tel: (902) 453-2400   Fax: (902) 455-4481

HR Administrator
Internet: www.impgroup.com

I M P Group International is a diversified company. Their activities are involved in aerospace, the industrial/marine field, petroleum, commercial air travel, medical supplies, foundry, and Canadian and International hotels. The company is fully owned by KCR Holdings Inc. I M P Group employs about 2,500 people. I M P Group employs approximately 3,000 individuals.

Academic Fields
College: Computer Science, Electronics Tech., Engineering Tech., Human Resources, Secretarial
Bachelor of Arts: Business
Bachelor of Comm/Admin: General, Accounting, Finance, Info Mgmt.
Bachelor of Science: Computer Science
Bachelor of Laws: Corporate
Bachelor of Engineering: Civil, Computer Systems, Design, Industrial, Materials Science, Transportation
Chartered Accounting: CMA-Finance, CGA-Finance
Masters: Business Administration, Engineering

Critical Skills
Adaptable, Analytical, Dependable, Diligent, Efficient, Good Communication, Good Writing Skills, Organized, Patient, Personable, Productive, Professional, Responsible

Types of Positions
Accounts Payable   Accounts Receivable
Information Technology   Administrative Assistant
Internal Audit   Sales and Marketing

Starting Salary
$ 20,000 - 25,000

Company Benefits
- Full benefit package

Correspondence
Mail or e-mail resume with cover letter
E-mail: hr@impgroup.com

Part Time/Summer: I M P Group International occasionally hires for part time and summer work. Potential jobs are most likely those listed above. The best time to apply is in March or April.

The Canada Student Employment Guide

I P L PLASTICS LTD.

P.O. Box 213, Stn Main
Edmundston, New Brunswick, E3V 3K8
Tel: (506) 739-9559   Fax: (506) 735-5494

Claude Nadeau, Human Resources

I P L Plastics is a manufacturer of thin wall plastic containers and lids for food packaging. The process uses injection molding. The firm employs approximately 55 individuals, and has annual sales of about $9 million.

Academic Fields
College: Administration, Engineering Tech., Graphic Arts
Bachelor of Engineering: Civil, Industrial, Mechanical

Critical Skills
Adaptable, Artistic, Creative, Efficient, Enthusiastic, Flexible, Innovative, Personable

Types of Positions
Various Positions

Starting Salary
$ 20,000 - 25,000

Company Benefits
- Full insurance package, pension plan
- Profit sharing

Correspondence
Mail or fax resume with cover letter
E-mail: ipl@nbnet.ca.com

Part Time/Summer: I P L Plastics regularly looks for individuals for part time and summer employment. Potential jobs include helper or operator.

IBM CANADA LTD.

3600 Steeles Ave. E.
Markham, Ontario, L3R 2Z1
Tel: (905) 316-2000   Fax: (905) 316-1507

Human Resources Employment
Internet: www.can.ibm.com

IBM Canada Ltd. is a leader in providing total networked solutions to the software, services and hardware portfolios. With more than 16,500 employees delivering the technology that will help change the world, IBM Canada provides attractive opportunities for growth and development for its employees. Browse their IBM Page on the Internet.

Academic Fields
College: Computer Science, Electronics Tech., Engineering Tech.
Bachelor of Arts: Business, Economics, Public Rel.
Bachelor of Comm/Admin: Finance, Marketing, Info Mgmt.
Bachelor of Science: Chemistry, Computer Science, Mathematics, Physics
Bachelor of Engineering: Chemical, Computer Systems, Design, Electrical, Mechanical
Chartered Accounting: CA-Finance, CGA/CMA - General/Finance
Masters: Business Admin., Science, Engineering

Critical Skills
Analytical, Enthusiastic, Good Communication, Leadership

Types of Positions
I/T Developer   I/T Architect
Client Representative Programmer
Entry Consultant

Starting Salary
$ 35,000 - 40,000

Company Benefits
- Competitive compensation and benefits which recognizes and rewards individual performance

Correspondence
Mail, fax, or e-mail resume with cover letter. Use the online application form with cover letter at www.can.ibm.com/hr.

Part Time/Summer: IBM Canada regularly hires for part time and summer work. Potential jobs are in the lab or at IBM Global Services. The best time to apply is in January or February.

The Canada Student Employment Guide

ICI CANADA INC.

2600 Steeles Ave. W.
Concord, Ontario, L4K 3C8
Tel: N/A   Fax: (905) 738-7592

Human Resources

ICI Canada Inc. is a multinational company headquartered in the UK. Manufacturing and distributing industrial and consumer chemicals all over the world, ICI's main businesses in Canada is paint manufacturing and retailing under Colour Your World and Glidden brand names. They have approximately 2,000 employees in Canada. They request no telephone calls.

Academic Fields
College: Marketing, Retailing, Secretarial
Bachelor of Comm/Admin: General, Accounting, Finance
Chartered Accounting: CA - General/Finance

Critical Skills
Adaptable, Dependable, Enthusiastic, Flexible, Good Communication, Good Writing Skills, Organized, Personable, Productive, Professional, Responsible

Types of Positions
Retail Store Clerk   Office/Admin Services
Manufacturing Plant Operator

Starting Salary
$ 23,000 - 28,000

Company Benefits
- Extended health care and dental coverage, life insurance, pension plan
- Discounts on corporate consumer products
- On-the-job training, in-house computer training

Correspondence
Mail or fax resume with cover letter

Part Time/Summer: ICI Canada Inc. occasionally looks for candidates for part time or summer jobs, however, very few are available. The best time to apply is from February to April.

IDEA ASSOCIATES INC.

6620 Kitimat Rd., Unit 1A
Mississauga, Ontario, L5N 2B8
Tel: (905) 826-0685   Fax: (905) 826-4851

Jack Herron, General Manager
Internet: www.ideassociates.com

IDEA Associates is a custom electronic engineering firm of hardware, firmware and software solutions. The company employs 9 individuals at their location.

Academic Fields
College: Accounting, Administration, Information Systems
Bachelor of Engineering: Electrical/Electronics
Masters: Engineering

Critical Skills
Dependable, Efficient, Enthusiastic, Good Communication, Good With Figures, Good Writing Skills, Logical, Manual Dexterity, Organized, Productive, Professional, Responsible, Entrepreneurial

Types of Positions
Junior Engineer   Technologist
Administrative Assistant

Starting Salary
$ 35,000 - 40,000

Company Benefits
- Usual benefits
- Training seminars (in-house and third party)

Correspondence
Mail or e-mail resume with cover letter
E-mail: jack@ideassociates.com

Part Time/Summer: IDEA Associates rarely hires for part time or summer employment opportunities. A potential job could be technical assistant.

ILCO UNICAN INC.

7301 Décarie
Montréal, Québec, H4P 2G7
Tel: (514) 735-5411   Fax: (514) 735-5732

Louise Belanger, Human Resources Consultant
Internet: www.ilcounican.com

Ilco Unican Inc. is a Montreal based firm specializing in the design, manufacturing and international sales and customer support of its security systems. They employ approximately 1,100 individuals in Canada.

Academic Fields
College: Accounting, Information Systems, Secretarial, Electronics Tech., Industrial Design, Mechanical Tech.
Bachelor of Comm/Admin: Accounting, Finance, Human Resources, Marketing
Bachelor of Science: Computer Science
Bachelor of Engineering: Computer Systems, Electrical, Industrial, Mechanical
Chartered Accounting: CA, CGA, CMA
Masters: Business Administration, Engineering

Critical Skills
Adaptable, Creative, Decisive, Enthusiastic, Flexible, Good Communication, Innovative, Leadership, Organized, Professional, Responsible

Types of Positions
Junior Software Programmer   Electronic Technologist
Junior Cost Accountant   Staffing Specialist
Accounts Receivable Clerk   Marketing Coordinator

Starting Salary
$ 30,000 - 35,000

Company Benefits
- Medical and dental coverage, Flexible hours, pension plan, profit sharing

Correspondence
Fax or e-mail resume with cover letter
E-mail: cv@ilcounican.com

Part Time/Summer: Ilco Unican Inc. rarely hires for part time work, but occasionally hires for the summer. Potential jobs involve engineering, human resources, advertising, and management information systems (M.I.S.). The best time to apply is in April.

Co-op/Internship: Internship opportunities in electronics, quality control, management information systems, material mgmt., accounting, manufacturing, mechanical design, and graphics design.

IMPERIAL OIL LIMITED

111 St. Clair Ave. W.
Toronto, Ontario, M5W 1K3
Tel: (416) 968-8312   Fax: (416) 968-4783

Human Resources Department
Internet: www.imperialoil.ca/campus

Imperial is Canada's largest producer of crude oil, a major producer of natural gas and a major supplier of petrochemicals. It is also the largest refiner and marketer of petroleum products sold under the Esso brand, with a coast-to-coast supply network. They employ approximately 6,600 individuals across the country.

Academic Fields
College: Engineering Tech.
Bachelor of Comm/Admin: Accounting, Finance, Marketing, Info Mgmt.
Bachelor of Science: Computer Science, Environmental Studies, Geology, Mathematics
Bachelor of Engineering: Chemical, Civil, Computer Systems, Electrical, Environ., Industrial, Mechanical
Chartered Accounting: CMA-General
Masters: Business Admin., Engineering, Industrial Rel.

Critical Skills
Adaptable, Analytical, Creative, Good Communication, Enthusiastic, Innovative, Leadership, Persuasive, Productive, Professional, Ability to Learn

Types of Positions
Engineering Trainee   Geology Trainee
Research Scientist   Accounting Analyst
Marketing Territory Manager   Info Systems Analyst

Starting Salary
Depends on position

Company Benefits
- Competitive health, dental, physical fitness prog.
- Educational refund program, mentor program

Correspondence
Fax one resume with cover letter, plus copy of most recent transcript and indicate desired positions in order of preference

Part Time/Summer: Imperial Oil does not seek people for part time work, but regularly looks for candidates for the summer. Individuals should see job postings at universities and on the Internet during the Fall and Winter. The best time to apply is in January.

IMPRIMERIE INTERWEB INC.

1603 boulevard Montarville
Boucherville, Québec, J4B 5Y2
Tel: (450) 655-2801   Fax: (450) 641-3650

Lucie Gerin, Ressources humaines

Imprimerie Interweb is a commercial printing company that specializes in the production of magazines, newspapers, and inserts. Founded in 1981, the company is a subsidiary of Groupe Transcontinental Inc. Imprimerie Interweb has about 300 permanent employees that work from their central office in Boucherville, Quebec.

Academic Fields
College: Accounting, Administration, Electronics Tech., Faculty Management, Mechanical Tech., Secretarial
Chartered Accounting: CA - General/Finance

Critical Skills
Creative, Diligent, Enthusiastic, Good Communication, Organized, Productive, Responsible

Types of Positions
Customer Service   Production

Starting Salary
below $ 20,000 - 25,000 (depending on position)

Company Benefits
- Medical and dental insurance, profit sharing
- Life Insurance, retirement plan, vacation pay
- Necessary training and career advancement

Correspondence
Mail resume with cover letter

Part Time/Summer: Imprimerie Interweb regularly looks for candidates for part time and summer employment. Positions usually involve general factory help. The company generally uses an employment agency to find suitable candidates. The best time to apply is in the Spring.

INCO LIMITED

Copper Cliff, Ontario, P0M 1N0
Tel: (705) 682-4211   Fax: (705) 682-5136

N. Gordon, Employee Relations
Internet: www.incoltd.com

INCO Limited is one of the world's premier mining and metals companies. It is a producer of nickel, copper, cobalt, and other precious metals. The company also manufacturers high performance alloy components such as nickel alloys, blades, rings, discs, an other forged and precision machine components for industrial applications. The company also produces sulphuric acid and liquid sulphur dioxide. INCO employs approximately 7,500 individuals and has properties, operations and markets around the world.

Academic Fields
College: Engineering Tech., Mechanical Tech.
Bachelor of Comm/Admin: General, Accounting
Bachelor of Science: Chemistry, Computer Science, Geology
Bachelor of Engineering: Chemical, Civil, Electrical, Mechanical, Mining
Chartered Accounting: CMA-General, CGA-General

Critical Skills
Good Communication, Diligent, Efficient, Leadership, Personable

Types of Positions
Engineer in Training   Technologist
Chemical Analyst

Starting Salary
$ 25,000 - 30,000

Company Benefits
- Full range of benefits

Correspondence
Mail resume with cover letter

Part Time/Summer: INCO Limited does not hire individuals for part time work, but regularly hires for summer employment. The best time to apply is from December to February each year.

The Canada Student Employment Guide

INDALEX LIMITED

5675 Kennedy Rd.
Mississauga, Ontario, L4Z 2H9
Tel: (905) 890-8821 Fax: (905) 890-8385

Human Resources Dept.
Internet: www.indalex.com

Indalex Limited is the Canadian aluminium extrusion company and is part of the Indalex Aluminium Solutions Group, that extends across North America. Their company strives to satisfy their customers through manufacturing of the various products they produce.

Academic Fields
College: General, Accounting, Business, Drafting/Architecture, Human Resources, Sales, Marketing, Information Technology
Bachelor of Arts: Business
Bachelor of Comm/Admin: Accounting, Info Mgmt.
Bachelor of Engineering: Industrial, Mechanical
Chartered Accounting: CMA-General, CGA-General
Masters: Business Administration, Engineering

Critical Skills
Good Communication, Dependable, Enthusiastic, Flexible, Innovative, Leadership, Organized, Responsible, Good Writing Skills, Attention to Detail

Types of Positions
Inside Sales   Plant Labourers

Starting Salary
$ 20,000 - 25,000

Company Benefits
- Medical, drugs, dental and vision care
- Job specific training, WHIMS
- On-the-job training

Correspondence
Fax resume with cover letter

Part Time/Summer: Indalex Limited occasionally looks for people for part time positions, and regularly seeks candidates in the summer. Potential work includes general labourer, or summer office administration jobs for vacation relief of others. The best time to apply is in April.

Co-op/Internship: Provides co-operative education and opportunities arise depending on the needs of individual departments.

INDUSTRIAL EQUIPMENT CO. LTD.

7462 Progress Way
Delta, British Columbia, V4G 1E1
Tel: (604) 946-1675 Fax: (604) 946-1315

Human Resources
Internet: www.ieco.com

Industrial Equipment Co. Ltd. was founded in 1953 when Gordon Lindemere saw a need for broad-range bearing and power transmission distributor with local inventory and staffed by people who understood the reality of running a mill 24 hours a day. They offer their customers the benefit of a single source for the entire scope of industrial replacement parts, engineering talent, and manufacturing, repair and servicing capabilities.

Academic Fields
College: Accounting, Administration, Computer Science, Drafting/Architecture, Marketing/Sales, Mechanical Tech.
Bachelor of Arts: Business
Bachelor of Comm/Admin: Accounting
Bachelor of Science: Computer Science
Bachelor of Engineering: Design
Chartered Accounting: CGA-Finance
Masters: Business Administration

Critical Skills
Confident, Enthusiastic, Good Communication, Good Writing Skills, Leadership, Organized, Professional

Types of Positions
Accounting   Purchasing
Data Entry   Engineering
Clerical

Starting Salary
$ 20,000 - 25,000

Company Benefits
- Medical, 80% dental, life insurance
- Disability, tuition
- In-house training as well as supplier course training

Correspondence
Fax resume with cover letter

Part Time/Summer: Industrial Equipment Co. Ltd. occasionally looks for individuals for part time work, but does not hire for the summer months.

The Canada Student Employment Guide

INDUSTRIAL-ALLIANCE LIFE INSURANCE COMPANY
1080 Saint Louis Road
Québec City, Québec, G1K 7M3
Tel: (418) 684-5182   Fax: (418) 684-5106

Ronald Graham, Ressources humaines
Internet: www.inalco.com

Industrial-Alliance Life Insurance is a major Canadian company that provides individual life and health insurance, group health and life insurance, individual annuities and group pensions. The company has 64 branch offices in Quebec, 28 branch offices in Ontario, and 10 in the Atlantic provinces. The company has 2,500 employees.

Academic Fields
College: General, Accounting, Administration, Business, Computer Sci., Insurance, Marketing/Sales, Secretarial
Bachelor of Arts: Business
Bachelor of Comm/Admin: Accounting, Finance, Marketing, Info Mgmt.
Bachelor of Science: Actuarial, Computer Science
Bachelor of Laws: Corporate
Bachelor of Engineering: Computer Systems
Chartered Accounting: CMA-General/Finance, CGA-General/Finance
Masters: Business Administration

Critical Skills
Adaptable, Analytical, Confident, Good Communication, Creative, Decisive, Diligent, Good With Figures, Efficient, Good Writing Skills, Innovative, Leadership, Logical, Persuasive, Professional

Types of Positions
Actuarial	Programmer
Clerk	Insurance
Secretary	Technician

Starting Salary
$ 25,000 - 30,000

Company Benefits
- Group insurance, group pensio
- General employee development

Correspondence
Mail, e-mail resume with cover letter, or telephone
E-mail: carriere@que.inalco.com

Part Time/Summer: Industrial-Alliance sometimes hires for part time work, and regularly hires for the summer. Work includes low level office jobs, or maintenance positions.

INDUSTRIES LASSONDE INC.
170 5e Avenue
Rougemont, Québec, J0L 1M0
Tel: (514) 469-4926   Fax: (514) 469-2505

Jacques Jardif, Ressources humaines
Internet: www.lassonde.com

Industries Lassonde manufactures, processes and markets a line of food products, which includes juices, fruit juices, fondue bouillon and sauces, for wholesalers and retailers in the industrial and institutional markets. Brand names include Oasis, Rougemont, Mont, Rouge, Del Sol, Fruité, Graves, Avon and Orange Maison for juices and fruit drinks. Industries Lassonde has an employee base of about 500 people.

Academic Fields
College: Accounting, Administration, Computer Science, Electronics Tech., Engineering Tech., Food/Nutrition, Human Resources, Industrial Design, Laboratory Tech., Mechanical Tech., Secretarial
Bachelor of Comm/Admin: Accounting, Finance, Marketing, Info Mgmt.
Bachelor of Engineering: Chemical, Computer Systems, Electrical, Environmental Studies, Industrial, Mechanical
Chartered Accounting: CA-Finance, CGA/CMA - General/Finance
Masters: Business Administration

Critical Skills
Adaptable, Diplomatic, Flexible, Good Communication, Good Writing Skills, Leadership, Innovative, Productive, Professional, Responsible

Types of Positions
Cost Accounting

Starting Salary
$ 30,000 - 40,000

Company Benefits
- Complete benefit package

Correspondence
Mail resume with cover letter

Part Time/Summer: Industries Lassonde regularly hires candidates for part time and summer jobs. Potential positions are most likely to be in finance or within the factory. The best time to apply is in April.

The Canada Student Employment Guide

INFOINTERACTIVE INC.

1550 Bedford Hwy., Suite 600
Bedford, Nova Scotia, B4A 1E6
Tel: (902) 832-1014   Fax: (902) 832-1015

David Keefe, Director of Human Resources
Internet: www.infointeractive.com

InfoInterActive Inc. is a publicly-traded Canadian high-technology corporation which develops and deploys network-based enhanced services that bring telephone, Internet and wireless networks together. The company has an employee base of 80 individuals.

Academic Fields
College: Computer Science
Bachelor of Comm/Admin: General, Accounting, Finance, Marketing
Bachelor of Science: Computer Science, Mathematics
Bachelor of Engineering: Computer Systems
Masters: Business Administration, Science, Engineering

Critical Skills
Adaptable, Creative, Dependable, Enthusiastic, Flexible, Innovative, Leadership, Productive, Responsible, Team Focus

Types of Positions
Software Developer   Technical Support
Customer Support   Marketing Officer
Account Executive

Starting Salary
$ 35,000 - 40,000

Company Benefits
- Competitive salaries, bonuses, stock options
- Unique culture, employee focused
- Professional development opportunities

Correspondence
E-mail resume with cover letter or apply through web site. E-mail: jobs@infointeractive.com

Part Time/Summer: InfoInterActive Inc. rarely hires for part time work and regularly seeks candidates in the summer. A potential job would be in customer service. The best time to apply is in April.

Co-op/Internship: They do offer internship opportunities.

INFORMATION GATEWAY SERVICES

300 March Rd., Suite 101
Kanata, Ontario, K2K 2E2
Tel: (613) 592-5619   Fax: (613) 592-3556

Denise Kahle, V.P. of Operations
Internet: www.ott.igs.net

Information Gateway Services is an Internet service provider that has franchises in 20 different cities in Ontario and one in Vancouver. They provide Internet access of all varieties. Providing their clients with a solution that fits their needs. They employ 20 individuals across the country.

Academic Fields
College: Accounting, Administration, Advertising, Information Systems, Marketing/Sales
Bachelor of Arts: Economics, English
Bachelor of Comm/Admin: Accounting, Info Mgmt.
Bachelor of Science: Computer Science, Mathematics
Bachelor of Engineering: Computer Systems

Critical Skills
Adaptable, Confident, Creative, Dependable, Diplomatic, Efficient, Enthusiastic, Good Communication, Good Writing Skills, Logical, Organized, Personable, Productive, Professional, Responsible

Types of Positions
Technical Support   Accounts Receivable
Reception   Sales

Starting Salary
$ 30,000 - 35,000

Company Benefits
- After 3 months a health plan paid by company
- Different employment advancements

Correspondence
E-mail resume with cover letter
E-mail: denise@igs.net

Part Time/Summer: Information Gateway Services rarely hires for part time employment, but occasionally seeks candidates for the summer months. A potential job would be receptionist. The best time to apply is in June.

The Canada Student Employment Guide

ING CANADA FINANCIAL SERVICES INTERNATIONAL

181 University Ave., Suite 600
Toronto, Ontario, M5H 3M7
Tel: (416) 941-5202   Fax: (416) 941-5198

Alda Haughn HR Consultant

ING companies in Canada are members of the ING Group - one of the world's largest integrated financial services organizations. Together, they form a network of Canadian businesses bringing an expanding range of insurance, financial security and wealth-building solutions to customers across the country.

Academic Fields
College: General, Accounting, Administration, Business, Computer Science, Human Resources, Insurance, Secretarial
Bachelor of Arts: Business, Economics, Political Science, Statistics
Bachelor of Comm/Admin: General, Accounting, Finance, Info Mgmt.
Bachelor of Science: Actuarial, Computer Science, Mathematics
Bachelor of Engineering: Computer Systems
Chartered Accounting: CA - General/Finance, CGA/CMA - General/Finance

Critical Skills
Adaptable, Analytical, Good Communication, Decisive, Efficient, Flexible, Innovative, Leadership, Organized, Personable, Productive, Professional, Good Writing Skills

Types of Positions
Insurance Trainee   Clerical Support

Starting Salary
$ 25,000 - 30,000

Company Benefits
- Health and dental benefits
- Life insurance, pension plan
- Educational reimbursements

Correspondence
Mail or fax resume with cover letter

Part Time/Summer: ING Canada Financial Services occasionally seeks people for part time and summer work. Potential jobs involve clerical support. The best time to apply is in April or May.

INSURANCE CORP. OF B.C.

151 West Esplanade, Room 118
North Vancouver, British Columbia, V7M 3H9
Tel: (604) 661-6200   Fax: (604) 661-6450

Human Resources
Internet: www.icbc.com

Insurance Corp. of B.C. is a major motor vehicle insurance company in the province. The head office of Insurance Corp. is located in North Vancouver, British Columbia.

Academic Fields
College: General, Administration, Business, Human Resources, Insurance
Bachelor of Arts: General, Business, Criminology, Economics, Psychology
Bachelor of Comm/Admin: General, Accounting, Finance, Marketing, Info Mgmt.
Bachelor of Science: General, Actuarial
Bachelor of Laws: General
Bachelor of Education: General, Adult Education
Chartered Accounting: CA-General
Masters: Business Administration

Critical Skills
Adaptable, Analytical, Dependable, Enthusiastic, Flexible, Good Communication, Innovative, Leadership, Organized, Patient, Productive

Types of Positions
Claims Adjuster   Office Assistant
Telephone Adjuster

Starting Salary
$ 30,000 - 40,000

Company Benefits
- Standard benefits offered
- 6 weeks vacation first year
- Both internal and external training available

Correspondence
Mail or fax resume with cover letter

Part Time/Summer: Insurance Corp. of B.C. occasionally looks for individuals for part time and summer employment opportunities.

The Canada Student Employment Guide

INTERCON SECURITY LTD.

40 Sheppard Avenue West
Willowdale, Ontario, M2N 6K9
Tel: (416) 229-6811   Fax: (416) 229-2062

Recruiting Co-Ordinator
Internet: www.interconsecurity.com

Intercon Security provides security personnel and systems to individuals, businesses, and other enterprises across Canada and internationally. Offering detective and protective services, Intercon employs over 2,000 individuals across the country and another 270 personnel work for the company worldwide.

Academic Fields
College: General, Accounting, Administration, Business, Electronics Tech., Emergency/Paramedic, Engineering Tech., Faculty Management, Human Resources, Marketing/Sales, Security/Law
Bachelor of Arts: General, Business, Criminology
Bachelor of Comm/Admin: General, Accounting, Finance, Marketing
Bachelor of Engineering: General, Design
Chartered Accounting: CA - General/Finance, CMA - General/Finance
Masters: Business Administration

Critical Skills
Adaptable, Analytical, Good Communication, Confident, Creative, Decisive, Dependable, Diligent, Diplomatic, Efficient, Enthusiastic, Flexible, Organized, Patient, Personable, Persuasive, Productive, Professional, Responsible, Writing Skills

Types of Positions
Security Officer   Protective Services Operative
Systems Service Tech.   Systems Installation

Starting Salary
$ 20,000 - 40,000 (depending on position)

Company Benefits
- Benefits after 6 months, pension after 1 year
- Most extensive in-house training in the industr

Correspondence
Mail resume and cover letter or submit in person
E-mail: recruiting@interconsecurity.com

Part Time/Summer: Intercon Security regularly hires for part time work and occasionally hires for the summer. Potential positions include security officer or clerical/office jobs. Applications for Security Officer positions must be made in person.

INTERFOREST LTD.

P.O. Box 170
Durham, Ontario, N0G 1R0
Tel: (519) 369-3310   Fax: (519) 369-3316

Human Resources
Internet: www.interforest.com

Interforest Ltd. is the premier wood veneer producer in North America. Their products are used by furniture manufacturers and architectural designers. They employ 1,000 people in North America at six facilities.

Academic Fields
College: Forestry
Bachelor of Arts: Business
Bachelor of Comm/Admin: General, Info Mgmt.

Critical Skills
Dependable, Enthusiastic, Good Communication, Good With Figures, Leadership, Manual Dexterity

Types of Positions
Management Trainee - Production

Starting Salary
$ 25,000 - 30,000 (to start)

Company Benefits
- Dental care, supplementary medical, vision care
- Pension plan, life insurance, tuition reimbursement
- On-the-job training, seminars, conferences

Correspondence
Mail resume with cover letter

Part Time/Summer: Interforest Ltd. occasionally hires for part time work and regularly seeks people for the summer months. In the summer it is usually general help to start. With progressive summers, operator positions in production can be achieved. Other positions could be office support, inventory control or human resources assistant. The best time to apply is in March.

The Canada Student Employment Guide

INTERIOR SAVINGS CREDIT UNION

678 Bernard Ave., Suite 300
Kelowna, British Columbia, V1Y 6P3
Tel: (604) 762-4355   Fax: (604) 762-9581

Joanne Ross, Human Resources Officer
Internet: www.interiorsavings.com

The Interior Savings Credit Union is a financial services institution located in Kelowna, British Columbia. Their financial services include general insurance, life insurance, trust services and portfolio/wealth management. The credit union employs 247 individuals.

Academic Fields
College: Administration, Human Resources, Information Systems, Insurance, Marketing/Sales
Bachelor of Arts: Business, Economics, Psychology, Public Relations
Bachelor of Comm/Admin: General, Finance, Human Resources, Marketing, Info Mgmt.
Bachelor of Science: Computer Science
Chartered Accounting: CA - General/Finance, CGA/CMA - General/Finance

Critical Skills
Adaptable, Confident, Efficient, Enthusiastic, Good With Figures, Personable, Professional

Types of Positions
Customer Services Rep.   Office Assistant
Receptionist/Secretary

Starting Salary
$ 20,000 - 25,000

Company Benefits
- Full benefits to full time, permanent employees
- New employees receive 1 day orientation, 3 days classroom, plus numerous days on-the-job training.
- All jobs posted internally

Correspondence
Fax or e-mail resume with cover letter
E-mail: jross@interiorsavings.com

Part Time/Summer: The Interior Savings Credit Union regularly looks for people for part time work and occasionally hires for the summer. Potential summer jobs include office assistant or customer service representative. The best time to apply is in April or May.

INTERONE MARKETING GROUP

1737 Walker Rd.
Windsor, Ontario, N8Y 4R8
Tel: (519) 258-7584   Fax: (519) 258-0275

Human Resources

InterOne Marketing Group is a marketing and merchandising company working for a major automotive company. The firm's head office is in Windsor, Ontario.

Academic Fields
College: Accounting, Administration, Advertising, Business, Communication, Computer Science, Human Resources, Secretarial
Bachelor of Arts: Business, English, Languages, Public Relations
Bachelor of Science: General, Actuarial, Computer Science
Chartered Accounting: CMA-Finance, CGA-Finance

Critical Skills
Analytical, Artistic, Creative, Dependable, Efficient, Enthusiastic, Good Communication, Good Writing Skills, Leadership, Organized, Productive, Professional, Responsible

Types of Positions
Account Administration   Program Coordinator
Accounts Receivable   Accounts Payable
Payroll Administration

Starting Salary
$ 20,000 - 30,000

Company Benefits
- Full group health benefits
- RRSP, ISO training process

Correspondence
Mail, fax or e-mail resume with cover letter

Part Time/Summer: InterOne Marketing Group regularly hires for part time work and occasionally looks for people in the summer. Potential jobs include French proofreading administration, and shipping and receiving clerk. The best time to apply is in the Spring.

The Canada Student Employment Guide

INTERTAPE POLYMER GROUP INC.

110 montée de Liesse
Montréal, Québec, H4T 1N4
Tel: (514) 731-7591   Fax: (514) 344-0220

Ressources humaines

Intertape Polymer Group Inc., a publicly owned company, is headquartered in Montreal, Canada, with 14 facilities throughout North America and Europe. The IPG team spans the globe to provide strong support through a dedicated network of local representatives. With a unique and broad range of products and industry expertise, IPG brings innovative packaging solutions to customers worldwide.

Academic Fields
College: Accounting, Administration
Bachelor of Comm/Admin: General
Bachelor of Science: Chemistry
Bachelor of Engineering: Mechanical
Chartered Accounting: CA - General/Finance
Masters: Business Administration, Science, Engineering

Critical Skills
Dependable, Diligent, Efficient, Flexible, Organized, Responsible, Bilingual

Types of Positions
Accounts Receivable Clerk   Accounts Payable Clerk
Customer Service Clerk   Assistant Operator
Accounting Clerk

Starting Salary
$ 20,000 - 25,000

Company Benefits
- Group insurance, pension plan
- Courses relating to the company are paid for

Correspondence
Mail resume with cover letter

Part Time/Summer: Intertape Polymer Group rarely looks for people for part time employment, but occasionally seeks candidates for the summer months. In the summer, potential jobs include office clerk and warehouse worker. The best time to apply is in May.

IPL ENERGY INC.

P.O. Box 398
Calgary, Alberta, T5J 2J9
Tel: (403) 420-5210   Fax: (403) 420-5289

Human Resources Department

IPL Energy is engaged in the transportation of liquid hydrocarbons and the distribution of natural gas. The wholly owned subsidiary of Interprovincial Pipe Line Inc., and Lakehead Pipe Line Company combine together under the umbrella of IPL Energy Inc. to provide the world's largest crude oil and liquids pipeline system.

Academic Fields
College: Accounting, Business, Computer Science, Engineering Tech., Lab Tech., Mech. Tech., Secretarial
Bachelor of Arts: General
Bachelor of Comm/Admin: General, Accounting, Finance, Info Mgmt.
Bachelor of Science: Computer Science, Math
Bachelor of Engineering: Civil, Computer Systems, Electrical, Mechanical
Chartered Accounting: CA - General/Finance, CGA/CMA - General/Finance
Masters: Business Administration, Engineering

Critical Skills
Adaptable, Analytical, Good Communication, Confident, Creative, Decisive, Dependable, Diligent, Diplomatic, Efficient, Enthusiastic, Flexible, Good With Figures, Innovative, Leadership, Logical, Organized, Professional, Responsible, Good Writing Skills

Types of Positions
Systems Analyst I   Associate Engineer
Accountant Trainee

Starting Salary
Varies depending on the position

Company Benefits
- Competitive benefits package
- Consistent with industry standards

Correspondence
Mail resume with cover letter

Part Time/Summer: IPL Energy does not hire part time staff, but sometimes hires for the summer. Potential jobs may exist for students of engineering and information systems, however, preference is given to children of current employees.

ISLAND SAVINGS CREDIT UNION

499 Canada Ave., Suite 300
Duncan, British Columbia, V9L 1T7
Tel: (604) 748-4728   Fax: (604) 748-8831

Rhonda Hittinger, Manager Human Resources

Island Savings Credit Union offers its members a full range of financial and insurance products and services. It is owned and operated by its members. The credit union has 9 branches, 9 insurance offices, and an administration office. They have a membership close to 33,000 people, and employ about 280 individuals. To correspond individuals should submit their resume and cover letter in person to manager of member services at the branch, with a copy to Human Resources at the Administration Office. Individuals interested in insurance positions should submit a resume and cover letter in person to Human Resources at the Administration Office.

Academic Fields
College: Accounting, Administration, Business, Marketing/Sales
Bachelor of Arts: Business, Economics
Bachelor of Comm/Admin: General, Accounting, Finance, Marketing
Chartered Accounting: CA - General/Finance, CGA/CMA - General/Finance
Other: Insurance Brokers Association of B.C. Courses, Canadian Securities Course, Mutual Funds Course

Critical Skills
Adaptable, Good Communication, Enthusiastic, Flexible, Organized, Personable, Professional, Good Writing Skills, Team Player, Risk Tolerant, Sales Skills

Types of Positions
Service Representative   Customer Service Rep. Trainee
Computer Operator   Branch Services Rep.

Starting Salary
$ 22,510 - 30,100

Company Benefits
- Extended health, dental, life insurance

Correspondence
See description above. E-mail: rhittinger@iscu.com

Part Time/Summer: Island Savings Credit Union occasionally hires for part time work, and regularly hires for the summer. Potential jobs include service representative. Apply at the end of April.

ISLAND TELECOM INC.

P.O. Box 820
Charlottetown, PEI, C1A 7M1
Tel: (902) 566-0268   Fax: (902) 566-3265

Frances Llewellyn, Personnel Manager

Island Telecom is in the telecommunications industry in PEI. The company serves all of Prince Edward Island. They employ about 330 people.

Academic Fields
College: Electronics Tech., Secretarial, Computer Engineering Technology, Business Info Technology
Bachelor of Arts: General, Bus., Economics, English, History, Journalism, Languages, Philosophy, Public Rel.
Bachelor of Comm/Admin: General, Accounting, Finance, Marketing, Public Admin.
Bachelor of Science: General, Computer Science, Environmental Studies, Psychology
Bachelor of Engineering: Computer Systems, Electrical, Design, Industrial
Bachelor of Education: General
Chartered Accounting: CA-General
Masters: Business Administration, Arts, Engineering

Critical Skills
Adaptable, Good Communication, Confident, Creative, Decisive, Dependable, Diligent, Diplomatic, Efficient, Enthusiastic, Flexible, Good With Figures, Professional, Responsible, Good Writing Skills

Types of Positions
Service Representative   Technical Support Specialist

Starting Salary
$ 25,000 - 40,000

Company Benefits
- All benefits including health, dental, group life

Correspondence
Mail resume with cover letter and complete application form. E-mail: Fllewellyn@islandtel.pe.ca

Part Time/Summer: Island Telecom rarely hires for part time work and occasionally hires for the summer. Only 4 to 5 individuals are hired per summer for entry level positions. Apply in March, April, or May.

Co-op/Internship: They offer internship opportunities through UPEI Internship Business Program.

The Canada Student Employment Guide

IST GROUP INC.

1611 Cremazie Blvd.
Montréal, Québec, H2M 2P2
Tel: (514) 383-1611   Fax: (514) 383-7241

Martine Gendron, Ressources humaines

IST Group offers a wide range of information management services on the Canadian market through its two main corporate branches consisting of IST-Integration and IST-Healthcare. The Integration Division offers outsourcing, consultation, and systems integration services. The Healthcare Division offers delivery of leading edge software, computerized payroll services and development of turnkey systems to health institutions and social service agencies located primarily in Quebec and Ontario. IST Group employs approximately 775 people.

Academic Fields
College: Computer Science
Bachelor of Engineering: Computer Systems

Critical Skills
Analytical, Efficient, Enthusiastic, Good Communication, Good Writing Skills, Innovative, Leadership, Logical, Organized, Professional

Types of Positions
Various positions

Starting Salary
$ 25,000 - 30,000

Company Benefits
- Life, health, and dental insurance
- Group insurance plan
- Personal computer financing program

Correspondence
Mail resume with cover letter

Part Time/Summer: IST Group does not hire part time employees, but sometimes seeks candidates for summer employment. In the summer, a potential job may be that of programmer. The best time to apply is in April or May.

IVACO INC.

770 rue Sherbrooke Ouest
Montréal, Québec, H3A 1G1
Tel: (514) 288-4545   Fax: (514) 284-9414

Andre Cromp, Director Corporate HR
Internet: www.ivaco.com

Ivaco is a Canadian corporation and is a leading North American producer of steel, fabricated steel products and other diversified fabricated products. Ivaco has operations in Canada and in the United States. Shares of Ivaco are traded on the Toronto Stock Exchange and The Montreal Exchange (IVA).

Academic Fields
College: Accounting, Computer Science, Electronics Tech., Industrial Design, Law Clerk, Mechanical Tech., Nursing, Secretarial
Bachelor of Arts: Languages
Bachelor of Comm/Admin: Finance
Bachelor of Science: Nursing, Industrial Hygiene
Bachelor of Laws: Corporate
Bachelor of Engineering: Environmental Studies, Industrial
Chartered Accounting: CMA-Finance, CGA-Finance

Critical Skills
Analytical, Dependable, Diligent, Good Communication, Efficient, Flexible, Good Writing Skills, Leadership, Logical, Organized, Productive, Responsible

Types of Positions
Various positions

Starting Salary
Depends on position

Company Benefits
- Complete benefit package

Correspondence
Mail resume with cover letter

Part Time/Summer: Ivaco sometimes looks for candidates for part time employment and regularly hires individuals for the summer months. Summer job opportunities vary from year to year.

IWK GRACE HEALTH CENTRE

5850 University Ave., P.O. Box 3070
Halifax, Nova Scotia, B3J 3G9
Tel: (902) 428-8012   Fax: (902) 420-6612

Amanda LeBlanc, Recruitment/Selection Consultant
Internet: www.iwk.grace.ns.ca

The IWK Grace Health Centre provides quality care for children, women and families in 3 Maritime provinces.

Academic Fields
College: Accounting, Business, Human Res., Info Syst., Secretarial, Computer Sci., Electronics Tech., Engineering Tech., Stationary Engineer, Dental, Lab Tech., Nursing (RN), Radiology Tech., Respiratory Tech., Child Care, Cooking/Culinary, Sec./Law Enforcement
Bachelor of Arts: Journalism, Psychology, Public Rel.
Bachelor of Comm/Admin: Accounting, Finance, Human Resources, Info Mgmt.
Bachelor of Science: Computer Sci., Food Sci., Health Sci., Microbiology, Nursing (RN), Occupational Therapy, Pharmacy, Physics, Physiotherapy, Psychology
Bachelor of Laws: Labour Relations
Bachelor of Engineering: Biomedical, Computer Syst.
Bachelor of Education: Adult Education, Childhood
Chartered Accounting: CA - General/Finance, CGA - General/Finance, CMA - General/Finance
Masters: Business Administration, Science, Engineering, Education, Library Science, Nursing, Social Work

Critical Skills
Adaptable, Dependable, Enthusiastic, Good Communication, Personable, Productive, Professional

Types of Positions
Nursing Aide   General Worker
Utility Worker   Ward Clerk

Starting Salary
$ 35,000 - 40,000

Company Benefits
- Health and dental plan not supplemented

Correspondence
No preferred method. E-mail: aleblanc@iwkgrace.ns.ca

Part Time/Summer: IWK Grace Health Centre regularly hires for part time and summer work. Check their job line (902-428-2980) by mid-February.

Co-op/Internship: They have accepted co-op and practicum students in a wide variety of programs.

THE IZAAK WALTON KILLAM HOSPITAL

P.O. Box 3070
Halifax, Nova Scotia, B3J 3G9
Tel: (902) 428-8012   Fax: (902) 428-8567

Karen Lyle, Human Resources Consultant

The Izaak Walton Killam Hospital is a pediatric hospital that was established in 1909. The hospital provides general medical and surgical services including rehabilitation and psychiatric facilities. There are a total of 171 beds devoted to children and the hospital has a staff of 1,254 people.

Academic Fields
College: Accounting, Business, Human Resources, Secretarial
Bachelor of Arts: Psychology, Public Relations, Recreation Studies, Sociology/Social Work
Bachelor of Comm/Admin: Accounting
Bachelor of Science: General, Computer Science, Food Sciences, Health Sciences, Nursing (RN), Occupational Therapy, Pharmacy, Physiotherapy, Psychology
Bachelor of Engineering: Biomedical
Masters: Business Administration

Critical Skills
Adaptable, Confident, Dependable, Good Communication,
Flexible, Organized, Professional, Responsible,

Types of Positions
Clerical   General Work

Starting Salary
below $ 20,000

Company Benefits
- Medical, dental, pension plan
- Long term disability
- Training and development department within

Correspondence
Mail resume and cover letter or submit in person

Part Time/Summer: The Izaak Walton Killam Hospital sometimes employs individuals on a part time basis, or for the summer months. Most positions are in nursing or the child life program. Individuals are generally hired through government summer grants.

The Canada Student Employment Guide

J. D. BARNES LIMITED

145 Renfrew Dr., Suite 160
Markham, Ontario, L3R 9R6
Tel: (905) 477-3600   Fax: (905) 477-0892

Catrioria Bark, Human Resources
Internet: www.jdbarnes.com/jdb

J.D. Barnes Limited provides surveying, mapping and land information services. Departments include cadastral, condominium, utilities, engineering, accounting and human resources. They employ approximately 200 individuals and have other offices in Thunder Bay, Mississauga, Hamilton and Whitby.

Academic Fields
College: CAD Autocad
Bachelor of Science: Surveying
Bachelor of Engineering: Civil

Critical Skills
Adaptable, Dependable, Diligent, Efficient, Enthusiastic, Flexible, Good Communication, Good With Figures, Leadership, Logical, Manual Dexterity, Organized, Patient, Personable, Productive, Professional, Responsible

Types of Positions
Survey Assistant

Starting Salary
$ 25,000 - 30,000

Company Benefits
- Benefits for regular full-time employees
- Major medical and extended health, dental, life insurance, and long term disability
- Group RRSP, profit sharing plan, continuing education assistance

Correspondence
Fax or e-mail resume with cover letter
E-mail: cbark@jdbarnes.com

Part Time/Summer: J.D. Barnes Limited rarely hires for part time jobs, but regularly seeks people for summer opportunities. A potential job could be survey assistant. The best time to apply is in early April.

J.D. IRVING LIMITED

P.O. Box 5777
Saint John, New Brunswick, E2L 4M3
Tel: (506) 632-5922   Fax: (506) 632-4598

Human Resources Division
Internet: www.jdirving.com

J.D. Irving Limited is involved in diversified interests in the industrial, commercial and manufacturing sectors.

Academic Fields
College: Accounting, Admin., Computer Science, Engineering Tech., Forestry, Mech. Tech., Secretarial
Bachelor of Arts: Business, Public Relations
Bachelor of Comm/Admin: Gen., Acctg, Finance, Marketing, Info Mgmt., Human Res., E-Commerce
Bachelor of Science: Biology, Chemistry, Computer Science, Environmental Studies, Forestry
Bachelor of Laws: Corporate
Bachelor of Engineering: Chemical, Civil, Computer Systems, Electrical, Industrial, Mechanical
Bachelor of Education: Adult Education
Chartered Accounting: CA-General, CMA - General/Finance, CGA - General/Finance
Masters: Business Admin., Engineering, Public Rel.

Critical Skills
Adaptable, Analytical, Good Communication, Confident, Decisive, Dependable, Diligent, Diplomatic, Efficient, Enthusiastic, Flexible, Personable, Persuasive, Productive, Professional, Responsible

Types of Positions
Sales   Administration

Starting Salary
$ 20,000 - 40,000 (depending on education)

Company Benefits
- Comprehensive benefits, health, dental, life ins.

Correspondence
Mail or e-mail resume with cover letter
E-mail: resumes@jdirving.com

Part Time/Summer: J.D. Irving occasionally hires for part time work and regularly hires in the summer. Potential positions involve accounting, labour, or general business. Apply in February or March.

Co-op/Internship: They have an active Cooperative Education Program.

J.S. REDPATH LIMITED

P.O. Box 810
North Bay, Ontario, P1B 8K3
Tel: (705) 474-2461   Fax: (705) 474-9109

Ron Dion, Human Resources
Internet: www.jsredpath.com

J.S. Redpath Limited is the founding member of The Redpath Group, providing shaft sinking, mine development, underground construction and contract mining services to the mining and civil construction industries.

Academic Fields
College: Accounting, Drafting/Architecture, Engineering Tech.
Bachelor of Comm/Admin: Accounting
Bachelor of Science: Mining
Bachelor of Engineering: Civil, Mining

Critical Skills
Adaptable, Confident, Decisive, Enthusiastic, Good Communication, Good With Figures, Good Written Skills, Leadership, Logical, Persuasive

Types of Positions
Payroll Clerk   Costing Clerk
Site Clerk   Junior Engineer
Junior Technician

Starting Salary
$ 25,000 - 30,000

Company Benefits
- Competitive benefits and pension plan
- Personnel development and training program

Correspondence
Mail resume with cover letter
E-mail: jsrl@jsredpath.com

Part Time/Summer: J.S. Redpath Limited regularly hires for part time and summer positions. Potential jobs include office and construction site positions. The best time to apply is in January.

JACQUES WHITFORD CONSULTING ENGINEERS

3 Spectacle Lake Drive
Dartmouth, Nova Scotia, B3B 1W8
Tel: (902) 468-7777   Fax: (902) 468-9009

C. Marc Bailey, Corporate HR Administrator
Internet: www.jacqueswhitford.com

Jacques Whitford is one of Canada's largest environmental consulting services with offices across Canada and the United States. Founded in 1972, the firm is involved in a spectrum of disciplines including environmental engineering, environmental sciences, geotechnical engineering, hydrogeology, materials engineering and research, and mining engineering. The firm employs over 700 people.

Academic Fields
Bachelor of Comm/Admin: Accounting
Bachelor of Science: Biology, Environmental Studies, Forestry, Geography
Bachelor of Engineering: Civil, Environmental Studies, Geotechnical, Materials Science, Water Resources
Masters: Engineering

Critical Skills
Analytical, Efficient, Enthusiastic, Good Writing Skills, Good Communication, Professional, Responsible, Self Motivated

Types of Positions
Engineering Technician   Engineer in Training
Data Entry Clerk   Administrative Assistant
Accounting Clerk   Environmental Scientist

Starting Salary
$30,000 - 40,000

Company Benefits
- Health, dental insurance, company pension
- Partial payment of tuition for education
- In-house training opportunities

Correspondence
Mail resume with cover letter

Part Time/Summer: Jacques Whitford Consulting Engineers regularly employs individuals for part time and summer job opportunities. Potential positions include student engineer, or student scientist. The best time to apply is in March.

JAMES RICHARDSON INTERNATIONAL LIMITED

2800 One Lombard Place
Winnipeg, Manitoba, R3B 0X8
Tel: (204) 934-5961   Fax: (204) 947-2647

Sherrie Rauth, Human Resources Administrator
Internet: www.jri.ca

James Richardson International is an established Canadian supplier of goods and services to customers in the agriculture and agri-food industries. James Richardson International maintains offices and facilities in six Canadian provinces and conducts business on a world-wide basis.

Academic Fields
College: Accounting, Administration, Business, Computer Science, Faculty Management, Human Resources, Marketing/Sales
Bachelor of Arts: Business
Bachelor of Comm/Admin: Accounting, Finance, Marketing, Info Mgmt.
Bachelor of Science: Agriculture, Computer Science
Chartered Accounting: CA - General/Finance, CGA/CMA - General/Finance
Masters: Business Administration

Critical Skills
Adaptable, Analytical, Decisive, Good Communication, Dependable, Diligent, Efficient, Good With Figures, Flexible, Good Writing Skills, Innovative, Leadership, Logical, Productive, Professional, Responsible

Types of Positions
Mail Clerk   File Clerk
Junior Accounting Clerk   Administrative Assistant
Grain Elevator Assistant

Starting Salary
$ 20,000 - 25,000 (univ.) /
$ 25,000 - 30,000 (univ. plus experience)

Company Benefits
- Flexible benefits program, pension plan
- Employee tailors benefits to their own needs
- Tuition reimbursement program

Correspondence
Mail resume with cover letter

Part Time/Summer: James Richardson & Sons sometimes hires for part time jobs and regularly hires for the summer. Potential work involves junior accounting, or clerical and administrative work. The best time to apply is in February or March.

JDS UNIPHASE CORPORATION

570 West Hunt Club Rd.
Nepean, Ontario, K2G 5W8
Tel: (613) 727-1304   Fax: (613) 727-8284

Michelle McDonell, Recruiter, Student Programs
Internet: www.jdsunph.com

JDS Uniphase is a high technology company that designs, develops, manufactures and distributes a comprehensive range of products for the growing fiberoptic communications market. These products are deployed by system manufacturers worldwide to develop advanced optical networks for the telecommunications and cable television industries.

Academic Fields
College: Electronics Tech., Engineering Tech.
Bachelor of Science: Physics
Bachelor of Engineering: Electrical, Industrial, Mechanical
Masters: Science, Engineering

Critical Skills
Analytical, Decisive, Efficient, Good Communication, Good Writing Skills, Innovative, Leadership, Logical, Organized, Professional

Types of Positions
Product Engineer   Process Engineer
Production Application Engineer Test Engineer
Fibreoptic Designer/Engineer   Quality Engineer

Starting Salary
Depends on position

Company Benefits
- Health care, prescription drug card, dental care
- Life insurance, deferred profit sharing plan

Correspondence
Apply through their web site

Part Time/Summer: JDS Uniphase Corporation occasionally hires for part time jobs and regularly hires for the summer. Potential positions include product engineer, process engineer, production application engineer, test engineer, fibreoptic designer/engineer, or a quality engineer.

Co-op/Internship: They do offer internship opportunities.

JIM PATTISON GROUP

1055 West Hastings Street, Suite 1600
Vancouver, British Columbia, V6E 2H2
Tel: (604) 688-6764   Fax: (604) 687-2601

Human Resources
Internet: www.jimpattison.com

The Jim Pattison Group is a diversified organization with consumer oriented lines of business that include food, broadcasting, packaging, transportation and financial services. Thy employ approximately 15,000 individuals.

Academic Fields
College: General, Accounting, Administration, Business, Computer Science, Science-General, Security/Law, Television/Radio
Bachelor of Arts: General, Business, Economics
Bachelor of Comm/Admin: General, Accounting, Finance, Marketing, Info Mgmt.
Bachelor of Science: General, Chemistry, Computer Science, Environmental Studies
Bachelor of Laws: Corporate
Bachelor of Engineering: General, Chemical, Industrial, Mechanical
Chartered Accounting: CA - General/Finance, CGA/CMA - General/Finance
Masters: Business Administration

Critical Skills
Adaptable, Analytical, Good Communication, Confident, Creative, Decisive, Dependable, Diligent, Diplomatic, Enthusiastic, Flexible, Organized, Patient, Personable, Productive, Professional, Responsible, Good Writing Skills

Types of Positions
Various positions

Starting Salary
Depends on position

Company Benefits
- Comprehensive set of benefits

Correspondence
Mail resume with cover letter

Part Time/Summer: Jim Pattison Group sometimes looks for individuals to fill part time and summer positions. Potential jobs in the summer months vary.

JO-ANN TRUCKING LTD.

P.O. Box 2020, Stn Main
Brooks, Alberta, T1R 1C7
Tel: (403) 362-4215   Fax: (403) 362-4015

Human Resources

Jo-Ann Trucking Ltd. is an oilfield hauling and rig moving company. They also house a pipeyard that supplies, and other hardware used, on oil and gas drilling rigs.

Academic Fields
College: Mechanical Tech.

Critical Skills
Adaptable, Dependable, Diligent, Efficient, Manual Dexterity, Personable

Types of Positions
Welding   Mechanics
Class I Driver   Labourer

Starting Salary
$ 20,000 - 40,000

Company Benefits
- 6 month waiting period
- Premiums paid 100% by company (excluding life insurance and long term disability)
- Class I training and testing reimbursed

Correspondence
Mail or fax resume with cover letter
E-mail: jo-ann@awinc.com

Part Time/Summer: Jo-Ann Trucking Ltd. does not hire individuals for part time work, but regularly seeks candidates for the summer. A potential job could be swamper or labourer. There is no best time to apply. Apply anytime.

JOHN P. ROBARTS RESEARCH INSTITUTE

P.O. Box 5015, 100 Perth Dr.
London, Ontario, N6K 4H5
Tel: (519) 663-5777   Fax: (519) 663-3789

Kathie Cunningham, Director of Human Resources
Internet: www.rri.on.ca

The John P. Robarts Research Institute is a privately directed medical research facility. It is affiliated with the University of Western Ontario and London Health Sciences Centre. It is made up of basic scientists, medical doctors and technical specialists. The Centre has approximately 400 employees.

Academic Fields
College: Accounting, Administration, Business, Communications, Human Resources, Information Systems, Secretarial
Bachelor of Comm/Admin: Accounting, Finance, Human Resources
Bachelor of Science: Biology, Chemistry, Computer Science, Mathematics, Microbiology, Pharmacy, Physics
Bachelor of Engineering: Biomedical, Computer Systems, Design, Electrical
Masters: Science

Critical Skills
Adaptable, Analytical, Confident, Creative, Dependable, Enthusiastic, Flexible, Good Communication, Good Writing Skills, Innovative, Leadership, Personable, Professional, Responsible

Types of Positions
Accounting   Administration
Lab Assistant

Starting Salary
$ 30,000 - 50,000

Company Benefits
- Complete benefit package including a pension plan

Correspondence
Mail, fax, e-mail resume with cover letter or apply through web site. E-mail: kathiec@rri.on.ca

Part Time/Summer: John P. Robarts Research Institute occasionally hires for part time work and summer employment. A potential job would be a lab assistant (genetics, immunology, medical biophysics, pharmacology).

JOHNSON CONTROLS LTD.

7400 Birchmount Rd.
Markham, Ontario, L3R 5V4
Tel: (416) 494-1576   Fax: (416) 474-5433

Human Resources
Internet: www.jci.com

Johnson Controls is a global company with 53 consecutive years of growth and more than a century of commitment to exceeding customer expectations. A Fortune 150 company, the Johnson Controls family has 95,000 employees on six continents. With a proud heritage of innovation and quality, we've achieved outstanding success as a leading supplier of automotive seating, interiors and batteries; facility management and control systems.

Academic Fields
College: Computer Science, Electronics Tech., Engineering Tech.
Bachelor of Science: Computer Science
Bachelor of Engineering: Computer Systems, Electrical, Mechanical
Masters: Engineering

Critical Skills
Good Communication, Professional

Types of Positions
Sales   Performance Contracting
Systems Representative   Systems Designer

Starting Salary
$ 30,000 - 40,000

Company Benefits
- Medical, dental, life insurance
- Long term disability, pension, RRSP
- Tuition assistance, corporate training institute

Correspondence
Mail resume with cover letter

Part Time/Summer: Johnson Controls regularly looks for individuals for part time and summer work. Potential positions involve clerical work. The best time to apply is in April or May.

Co-op/Internship: They do offer internship programs. Visit their website.

The Canada Student Employment Guide

JOHNSON INCORPORATED

95 Elizabeth Ave., P.O. Box 12049
St. John's, Newfoundland, A1B 1R7
Tel: (709) 737-1500   Fax: (709) 737-1580

Sandra Facey, Manager, Personnel Training
Internet: johnsoninc.com

Johnson Incorporated is a personal insurance and benefits consulting/administration company. The firm operates in Ontario, B.C., Alberta and in the Atlantic Provinces with its head office in Newfoundland.

Academic Fields
College: Accounting, Administration, Business, Communications, Computer Science, Human Resources, Insurance, Marketing/Sales, Secretarial
Bachelor of Arts: General, Business, Public Relations
Bachelor of Comm/Admin: General, Accounting, Finance, Marketing, Info Mgmt.
Bachelor of Science: Computer Science
Bachelor of Engineering: Computer Systems
Chartered Accounting: CA - General/Finance, CGA-General
Masters: Business Administration

Critical Skills
Adaptable, Analytical, Good Communication, Creative, Decisive, Dependable, Diligent, Diplomatic, Efficient, Enthusiastic, Flexible, Good With Figures, Innovative, Leadership, Logical, Manual Dexterity, Organized, Responsible, Good Writing Skills

Types of Positions
Branch Service & Develop.   Information Systems
Group Claims   Finance/Administration
Underwriting   Consulting

Starting Salary
$ 30,000 - 50,000

Company Benefits
- Full range of employee benefits
- Group insurance, discounts on insurance
- Formal training for all jobs, study plan for continuing education

Correspondence
Mail resume with cover letter. E-mail: smf@johnson.ca

Part Time/Summer: Johnson Incorporated regularly hires for part time and summer work. Potential positions include telemarketer, service rep. asst., computer programmer asst. and marketing asst. The best time to apply is in April.

JOSTENS CANADA LTD.

1051 King Edward Street
Winnipeg, Manitoba, R3H 0R4
Tel: (204) 633-9233   Fax: (204) 633-9150

Cindy Harrison, Human Resources Specialist

Jostens was founded in 1897 in Owatonna, Minnesota and is one of only a few companies in North America that can say they are over 100 years old. Jostens is internationally recognized as the leader in the manufacture of high quality school photographs, yearbooks, class and championship rings, scholastic awards, diplomas, graduation announcements and other recognition products.

Academic Fields
College: Accounting, Administration, Communications, Computer Science, Engineering Tech., Graphic Arts, Marketing/Sales, Photography
Bachelor of Arts: General, Business
Bachelor of Comm/Admin: General, Accounting, Finance, Marketing, Info Mgmt.
Bachelor of Science: Computer Science
Bachelor of Engineering: Computer Systems, Electrical, Mechanical
Bachelor of Education: Adult Education
Chartered Accounting: CA - General/Finance, CGA/CMA - General/Finance
Masters: Business Administration

Critical Skills
Adaptable, Good Communication, Diligent, Efficient, Enthusiastic, Flexible, Innovative, Leadership, Logical

Types of Positions
Accounting Clerk   Film Checker
Data Entry   Digital Imaging

Starting Salary
below $ 20,000 - 25,000 (depending on position)

Company Benefits
- Full benefits for most positions

Correspondence
Mail or fax resume with cover letter

Part Time/Summer: Jostens Canada occasionally hires for part time and summer work. Summer is generally their 'down time' as they service the educational market. Peak photography season begins late August and ends approx. Christmas. Yearbook season peaks around January and lasts until July.

The Canada Student Employment Guide

KAWNEER COMPANY CANADA LIMITED

1051 Ellesmere Rd.
Scarborough, Ontario, M1P 2X1
Tel: (416) 755-7751   Fax: (416) 755-7683

Jeannine McIlmoyle, Human Resources Manager
Internet: www.alcoa.com

Kawneer Company Canada Limited is a manufacturer of architectural aluminum products including windows, doors, curtain wall, skylights and storefronts. The company employs approximately 600 individuals in Canada.

Academic Fields
College: Accounting, Business, Human Resources, Purchasing, Mechanical Tech., Architectural Technology
Bachelor of Comm/Admin: Accounting, Finance, Human Resources
Bachelor of Engineering: Industrial, Mechanical, Bachelor of Technology Architectural Science
Chartered Accounting: CMA-General

Critical Skills
Adaptable, Analytical, Enthusiastic, Good Communication, Personable, Productive

Types of Positions
Production Controller   Project Coordinator
Customer Service   Engineering
Junior Buyer   Draftsperson

Starting Salary
$ 30,000 - 35,000

Company Benefits
- 100% prescription drug coverage, 80% dental coverage
- Company pension plan, life insurance, tuition reimbursement
- Company goal for training and development is 40 hours per year for each employee

Correspondence
Mail or fax resume with cover letter

Part Time/Summer: Kawneer Company Canada Limited rarely hires for part time employment and occasionally hires for the summer months. The majority of summer jobs are clerical in nature. The best time to apply is in April and May.

Co-op/Internship: They have hired co-op students from Human Resource programs.

KELOWNA HOME SUPPORT

1340 Ellis St.
Kelowna, British Columbia, V1Y 1Z8
Tel: (250) 868-7707   Fax: (250) 868-0739

Stuart Ballard, Human Resources

Kelowna Home Support Society provides in-home support to elderly and physically disabled adults to assist in independent living. The organization employs approximately 180 individuals.

Academic Fields
College: Nursing, Residential Care Aid Certificate, Rehab. Assistant
Bachelor of Science: Nursing (RN)
Chartered Accounting: CA-General, CGA-General

Critical Skills
Adaptable, Analytical, Good Communication, Confident, Creative, Decisive, Dependable, Diligent, Diplomatic, Efficient, Enthusiastic, Flexible, Innovative, Leadership, Organized, Patient, Personable, Professional, Responsible

Types of Positions
Home Support Worker   Rehabilitation Asst.
Clerical/Administration Support

Starting Salary
$ 20,000 - 30,000

Company Benefits
- Excellent full benefit package

Correspondence
Submit resume and cover letter in person

Part Time/Summer: The Kelowna Home Support Society occasionally looks for individuals for part time work, and regularly seeks candidates for the summer. A potential position is a home support worker.

The Canada Student Employment Guide

CITY OF KELOWNA

1435 Water Street
Kelowna, British Columbia, V1Y 1J4
Tel: (604) 763-6011   Fax: N/A

Marsha Keen, Human Resources

The City of Kelowna is a municipal government in British Columbia. The City of Kelowna employs staff to work in various capacities for the betterment of the community.

Academic Fields
College: Accounting, Computer Science, Engineering Tech., Laboratory Tech., Secretarial
Bachelor of Arts: Business, Recreation Studies, Urban Geography
Bachelor of Comm/Admin: Accounting, Finance, Info Mgmt., Public Admin.
Bachelor of Science: Computer Science, Environmental Studies
Bachelor of Engineering: Civil, Electrical, Environmental Studies, Transportation, Water Resources, Bachelor of Architecture
Chartered Accounting: CMA-General, CMA-Finance
Masters: Engineering

Critical Skills
Adaptable, Decisive, Dependable, Good Communication, Flexible, Leadership, Organized, Personable, Productive

Types of Positions
Survey Crew   Plant Operator I
Engineering Technician   Accounting Assistant

Starting Salary
$ 25,000 - 30,000

Company Benefits
- Health, dental, pension plan
- In-house self development courses

Correspondence
Mail resume with cover letter

Part Time/Summer: The City of Kelowna sometimes looks for candidates for part time positions and regularly seeks individuals for summer jobs. In the summertime, potential jobs are most commonly with the outside work crews doing park maintenance. There may be other positions in drafting, computer services, or doing clerical duties. The best time to apply is in April.

KENNAMETAL LTD.

115B Matheson Blvd. W., Suite 211
Mississauga, Ontario, L5R 3L1
Tel: (905) 568-2288   Fax: (905) 568-4955

Grant Adam, Human Resources
Internet: www.kennametal.com

Kennametal Ltd. is a Fortune 1000 U.S. Company supplying tools, tooling systems and supplies to the metalworking industry.

Academic Fields
College: Accounting, Administration, Business, Engineering Tech., Human Resources
Bachelor of Arts: Business, Psychology
Bachelor of Comm/Admin: Accounting, Finance, Marketing
Bachelor of Engineering: Industrial, Mechanical
Chartered Accounting: CMA-General
Masters: Business Administration, Engineering

Critical Skills
Adaptable, Creative, Dependable, Enthusiastic, Good Communication, Innovative, Leadership, Professional, Responsible

Types of Positions
Customer Service Representative   Engineering Technologist

Starting Salary
$ 35,000 - 45,000

Company Benefits
- Usual compliment of benefits
- Health, dental, life and pension, 100% employer paid
- Good opportunity for promotion

Correspondence
Fax or e-mail resume with cover letter
E-mail: grant.adam@kennametal.com

Part Time/Summer: Kennametal Ltd. occasionally hires for part time work and rarely hires for summer employment opportunities. Potential jobs include engineering technologist and design/drafting. The best time apply is in the Spring.

The Canada Student Employment Guide

KENNEDY LODGE NURSING HOME INC.

1400 Kennedy Road
Scarborough, Ontario, M1P 4V6
Tel: (416) 752-8282   Fax: (416) 752-0645

Dan Kaniuk, Administrator

Kennedy Lodge Nursing Home is a private nursing care facility for the elderly. Established in 1976 to meet the needs of the aging, the nursing home has more than 280 beds and provides skilled nursing facilities, social services, and residential care. Kennedy Lodge Nursing Home employs more than 250 individuals to work at its location in Scarborough.

Academic Fields
College: Nursing
Bachelor of Arts: Gerontology, Sociology/Social Work
Bachelor of Comm/Admin: Accounting
Bachelor of Science: Health Sciences, Nursing (RN)
Bachelor of Education: Adult Education
Chartered Accounting: CGA-General

Critical Skills
Dependable, Diplomatic, Efficient, Good Communication, Flexible, Leadership, Organized, Patient, Personable, Productive, Professional

Types of Positions
Health Care Aide   Registered Nurse
Reg. Practical Nurse   Bookkeeper
Accountant

Starting Salary
Depends on position

Company Benefits
- Competitive benefits package offered

Correspondence
Mail resume with cover letter

Part Time/Summer: Kennedy Lodge Nursing Home regularly hires for part time positions and sometimes hires for summer opportunities. Potential openings are most likely those listed above.

KEYANO COLLEGE

8515 Franklin Ave.
Fort McMurray, Alberta, T9H 2H7
Tel: (780) 791-4873   Fax: (780) 791-1555

Human Resources
Internet: www.keyano.ab.ca

Keyano College has gained a solid reputation for its innovative academic programming and quality of instruction. In an affordable, student centered learning environment, Keyano College offers quality programming ranging from university studies transfer and degree completion programs, diploma and certificate programs, academic upgrading, apprenticeship trades and technology programs and heavy equipment training.

Academic Fields
College: Accounting, Child Care, Cooking/Culinary, Graphic Arts, Human Resources, Secretarial
Bachelor of Arts: English, Music, Political Science, Psychology
Bachelor of Comm/Admin: Accounting, Finance, Marketing, Info Mgmt.
Bachelor of Science: Biology, Chemistry, Computer Science, Mathematics, Nursing (RN), Physics
Bachelor of Engineering: Chemical, Civil, Computer Systems, Electrical, Industrial
Bachelor of Education: Adult Education
Chartered Accounting: CMA - General/Finance, CGA - General/Finance
Masters: Business Administration, Arts, Science, Engineering, Education, Library Science

Critical Skills
Decisive, Dependable, Flexible, Good Communication, Professional

Types of Positions
Clerical   Custodial

Starting Salary
$ 20,000 - 25,000

Company Benefits
- Competitive benefits package

Correspondence
Mail or fax resume with cover letter

Part Time/Summer: Keyano College occasionally hires for part time employment, but does not hire for the summer months.

KFC CANADA

10 Carlson Court, Suite 300
Rexdale, Ontario, M9W 6L2
Tel: (416) 674-0367   Fax: (416) 674-5594

Human Resources
Internet: www.kfc.com

KFC Corporation, based in Louisville, Kentucky, is the world's most popular chicken restaurant chain and is part of Tricon Global Restaurants, Inc., which is the world's largest restaurant system with nearly 30,000 KFC, Taco Bell and Pizza Hut restaurants in more than 100 countries and territories.

Academic Fields
Bachelor of Arts: Business
Bachelor of Comm/Admin: General, Accounting, Finance, Marketing, Info Mgmt.
Bachelor of Science: General, Chemistry, Computer Science, Food Sciences, Microbiology, Occupational Therapy
Bachelor of Engineering: Design
Chartered Accounting: CMA-General/Finance, CGA-General/Finance

Critical Skills
Adaptable, Analytical, Confident, Flexible, Good Communication, Good Writing Skills, Leadership, Productive, Professional, Responsible, Team Oriented

Types of Positions
Various Positions

Starting Salary
$ 40,000 - 50,000

Company Benefits
- A choice of benefits offered
- Group insurance, and retirement savings plan
- Pepsi Co. shares and stock options offered

Correspondence
Mail or fax resume with cover letter

Part Time/Summer: KFC Canada sometimes hires for part time employment and summer opportunities. The best time to apply is in April or May.

KIMBERLY-CLARK INC.

50 Burnhamthorpe Road W.
Mississauga, Ontario, L5B 3Y5
Tel: (905) 277-6500   Fax: (905) 277-6508

Louise Plant, Manager Human Resources
Internet: www.kimberly-clark.com

Kimberly-Clark Inc. manufactures a range of products including diapers, baby wipes, training pants, feminine products, facial tissue, bathroom tissue and napkins.

Academic Fields
College: Business, Marketing/Sales
Bachelor of Arts: Business, Economics
Bachelor of Comm/Admin: Marketing
Bachelor of Engineering: Chemical, Electrical, Mechanical
Masters: Business Administration

Critical Skills
Adaptable, Analytical, Flexible, Innovative, Leadership

Types of Positions
Engineer Level I   Marketing Assistant
Sales Representative   Category Analyst
Customer Business Manager

Starting Salary
$ 35,000 - 45,000

Company Benefits
- A wide range of competitive benefits is offered including company car and sales incentives
- Provides extensive training applicable to job
- Promotes and supports employees in their continuing pursuit of professional development

Correspondence
Mail resume with cover letter
E-mail: dchapman@kcc.com

Part Time/Summer: Kimberly-Clark does not hire for part time employment, but regularly hires for summer positions. Co-op engineering students hired regularly at the Huntsville, Ontario and St. Hyacinthe, Quebec manufacturing locations.

Co-op/Internship: They have a sales intern program where they hire 8 to 10 students every summer to manage their own retail territory. It offers great experience for students and a great way for the company to meet future new employees.

KINGS REGIONAL REHABILITATION CENTRE
P.O. Box 128
Waterville, Nova Scotia, B0P 1V0
Tel: (902) 538-3103   Fax: (902) 538-7022

Human Resources
Internet: www.nsnet.org/krrc/

Kings Regional Rehabilitation Centre provides services of educational, social, vocational, and medical nature to adults with psychological and social problems, or mental handicaps. Staff provide services on a team basis by preparing and maintaining clients toward small, integrated environments in home communities. The rehabilitation centre employs a staff of 284 people.

Academic Fields
College: Human Resources, Nursing, Recreation Studies
Bachelor of Science: Nursing (RN), Occupational Therapy, Pharmacy, Physiotherapy, Psychology
Masters: Science

Critical Skills
Adaptable, Decisive, Dependable, Good Communication, Diplomatic, Enthusiastic, Flexible, Professional, Responsible

Types of Positions
Personal Care Worker   Developmental Worker
Certified Nursing Assistant

Starting Salary
$ 20,000 - 25,000

Company Benefits
- 50-50 cost shared health care
- Long term disability, group life, pension
- Provide CPR, first aid, and sexuality training

Correspondence
Mail resume with cover letter

Part Time/Summer: Kings Regional Rehabilitation Centre regularly seeks individuals for part time and summer employment. Applications are generally only accepted upon response to a specific advertisement. Advertisements occur each Spring in local newspapers.

KINROSS GOLD CORP.
40 King Street West, 57th Floor
Toronto, Ontario, M5H 3Y2
Tel: (416) 365-5123   Fax: (416) 363-6622

Human Resources Department
Internet: www.kinross.com

Kinross Gold Corporation is a large North American based gold producer with annualized production estimated at approximately 1 million ounces of gold equivalent at a total cash cost of approximately US$200 per ounce. The Company has five primary operations on four continents with three flagship gold mines in the United States, Canada and Russia.

Academic Fields
Bachelor of Science: Chemistry, Geology
Bachelor of Engineering: Geotechnical, Mining, Geology, Metallurgy

Critical Skills
Adaptable, Analytical, Good Communication, Confident, Dependable, Diligent, Efficient, Enthusiastic, Flexible, Good With Figures, Innovative, Logical, Organized, Personable, Persuasive, Productive, Professional, Responsible, Writing Skills

Types of Positions
Junior Mining Engineer   Junior Geologist

Starting Salary
$ 25,000 - 40,000

Company Benefits
- Full benefits
- On-the-job training
- Leadership training

Correspondence
Mail or fax resume with cover letter

Part Time/Summer: Kinross Gold Corp. occasionally hires individuals for part time employment, and regularly looks for students in the summer months. Potential positions are in mining operations, mill operations, or geological operations. The best time to apply is in February or March.

CITY OF KITCHENER

200 King St. W., City Hall
Kitchener, Ontario, N2G 4G7
Tel: (519) 741-2347   Fax: (519) 741-2400

Human Resources
Internet: www.city.kitchener.on.ca

The City of Kitchener is a municipal government responsible for the formation of policy and laws. The government employs about 2,100 individuals.

Academic Fields
College: General, Accounting, Administration, Advertising, Business, Communications, Computer Science, Drafting/Architecture, Electronics Tech., Engineering Tech., Forestry, Graphic Arts, Human Resources, Law Clerk, Marketing/Sales, Recreation Studies, Secretarial, Security/Law, Urban Planning
Bachelor of Arts: General, Business, Economics, English, Gerontology, Political Science, Psychology, Public Rel., Rec. Studies, Social Work, Urban Geog.
Bachelor of Comm/Admin: General, Accounting, Finance, Marketing, Info Mgmt., Public Admin.
Bachelor of Science: Computer Science, Forestry, Geography, Horticulture, Mathematics
Bachelor of Laws: General, Corporate, Real Estate
Bachelor of Engineering: Civil, Computer Systems, Environ. Studies, Mech., Bach. Landscape Architecture
Chartered Accounting: CA - General/Finance, CGA/CMA - General/Finance

Critical Skills
Adaptable, Good Communication, Dependable, Flexible, Innovative, Professional, Responsible

Types of Positions
Bus Driver	Custodian Trainee
Gardener Trainee	Mechanic
Technician	Accounting Clerk

Starting Salary
$ 25,000 - 40,000

Company Benefits
- Comprehensive benefit package
- Extended health, vision, dental, group life

Correspondence
E-mail their application form along with resume and cover letter

Part Time/Summer: City of Kitchener regularly hires for part time and summer work. Apply in January or February.

KODAK CANADA INC.

3500 Eglinton Ave. W.
Toronto, Ontario, M6M 1V3
Tel: (416) 766-8233   Fax: (416) 760-4462

Human Resources
Internet: www.kodak.com

Kodak is the world leader in imaging. Dedicated to innovative, continuous improvement. To creating more innovative film and digital products than you ever imagined. To thinking outside the box. To changing reality. Kodak is a place where your creativity can virtually explode, in a remarkably advanced technical environment.

Academic Fields
College: Accounting, Computer Science, Electronics Tech., Human Resources, Marketing/Sales, Photography, Radiology Tech., Secretarial, Statistics
Bachelor of Arts: Business, Psychology
Bachelor of Comm/Admin: Finance, Marketing, Info Mgmt.
Bachelor of Science: Chemistry, Computer Science, Health Sciences, Mathematics, Psychology
Bachelor of Engineering: Chemical, Industrial, Mechanical
Chartered Accounting: CA-Finance, CMA - Finance, CGA - Finance
Masters: Business Administration

Critical Skills
Adaptable, Analytical, Confident, Enthusiastic, Flexible, Good Communication, Leadership, Logical, Organized, Personable, Persuasive, Productive

Types of Positions
Sales/Marketing	Information Systems Analysis
Chemical Engineer	Administrative Assistant
Bilingual Dispatch Opr.	

Starting Salary
$ 40,000

Company Benefits
- Supplementary health care, dental
- Non-contributory pension plan
- Wage dividend (quasi profit sharing plan)

Correspondence
Fax resume with cover letter

Part Time/Summer: Kodak Canada Inc. occasionally seeks candidates for part time work, but does not hire for the summer months.

The Canada Student Employment Guide

KRAFT CANADA INC.

95 Moatfield Dr.
Don Mills, Ontario, M3B 3L6
Tel: (416) 441-5000   Fax: (416) 441-5807

Mark Coulter, Human Resources

Kraft is at the forefront of the food industry in Canada, the U.S., and around the world. With products sold in over 100 countries worldwide, Kraft produces everything from confections, desserts and beverages, to refrigerated products, and coffee and main meal products.

Academic Fields
College: Advertising, Food/Nutrition
Bachelor of Arts: Business, Economics
Bachelor of Comm/Admin: Finance, Marketing, Info Mgmt.
Bachelor of Science: Computer Science, Food Sciences, Microbiology
Bachelor of Engineering: General, Chemical, Civil, Computer Systems, Electrical, Mechanical
Chartered Accounting: CMA-Finance, CGA-Finance
Masters: Business Administration

Critical Skills
Adaptable, Analytical, Good Communication, Confident, Creative, Decisive, Dependable, Diligent, Diplomatic, Efficient, Enthusiastic, Flexible, Good With Figures, Innovative, Leadership, Logical, Organized, Responsible, Good Writing Skills

Types of Positions
Product Assistant   Financial Analyst
Consumer Response Associate   Sales Representative

Starting Salary
$ 30,000 - 50,000

Company Benefits
- Medical, dental benefits, life insurance, RRSP

Correspondence
Mail or fax resume with cover letter

Part Time/Summer: Kraft Canada occasionally looks for individuals for part time or summer employment. Potential jobs include consumer response associate. The best time to apply is in March or April.

Co-op/Internship: Internship opportunities are available.

KRUG INC.

421 Manitou Dr.
Kitchener, Ontario, N2C 1L5
Tel: (519) 748-5100   Fax: (519) 748-5177

Human Resources
Internet: www.krug.ca

Krug Inc. is a leading manufacturer of high end business furniture including casegoods, seating and conference tables. The company's head office is in Kitchener, Ontario.

Academic Fields
College: Materials Management, Woodworking, Technician, Marketing
Bachelor of Arts: Business
Bachelor of Engineering: Industrial

Critical Skills
Adaptable, Decisive, Enthusiastic, Good Communication, Good Writing Skills, Leadership, Professional, Flexible, Motivated

Types of Positions
Scheduling Clerk   Product Engineering Tech.
Human Resources Asst.   Marketing Asst.

Starting Salary
$ 20,000 - 30,000

Company Benefits
- Full benefits package, including tuition reimbursement
- Extended health care, life insurance, profit sharing, pension plan

Correspondence
Mail resume with cover letter

Part Time/Summer: Krug Inc. occasionally hires individuals for part time or summer employment. The best time to apply is in April and May.

The Canada Student Employment Guide

KVAERNER METALS

480 University Avenue, Suite 300
Toronto, Ontario, M5G 1V2
Tel: (416) 340-1145   Fax: (416) 343-9300

Janet Kun, Director, Human Resources

Kvaerner Metals is an engineering firm specializing in process and mining technology. Currently employing 150 staff at its Toronto location, the firm targets projects in the non-ferrous market sector in Canada and on an international scale.

Academic Fields
College: Engineering Tech.
Bachelor of Engineering: Civil, Electrical, Geology, Instrumentation, Mechanical, Mining
Chartered Accounting: CGA-General
Masters: Engineering

Critical Skills
Adaptable, Dependable, Efficient, Good Communication, Flexible, Professional, Organized, Good Writing Skills

Types of Positions
Various Positions

Starting Salary
$ 32,000 - 34,000 (College) / $ 35,000 - 38,000 (Univ.)

Company Benefits
- Depends on terms of hire
- Benefits according to position

Correspondence
Mail resume with cover letter
E-mail: janet.kun@kvaerner.com

Part Time/Summer: Kvaerner Metals sometimes hires individuals to work in part time positions and fill summer opportunities.

LA CONFISERIE COMETE LTEE

2950 rue Nelson
Saint Hyacinthe, Québec, J2S 1Y7
Tel: (514) 774-9131   Fax: (514) 774-8335

Jean Thibodeau Human Resources Coordinator

La Confiserie Comete is a food products company that produces chocolate for sales in the United States and Canada. The company has an employee base of 450 individuals in Canada.

Academic Fields
College: General, Accounting, Administration, Business, Computer Science, Electronics Tech., Food/Nutrition, Secretarial
Bachelor of Arts: Business, Economics, Public Relations, Statistics
Bachelor of Comm/Admin: Accounting, Marketing, Info Mgmt.
Bachelor of Science: Chemistry, Computer Science, Food Sciences
Bachelor of Engineering: Computer Systems, Industrial
Masters: Business Administration

Critical Skills
Diligent, Flexible, Good Writing Skills, Leadership, Logical, Organized

Types of Positions
Customer Service Clerk General Clerk
Production Worker

Starting Salary
$ 25,000 - 30,000

Company Benefits
- Group insurance and pension plan
- Complete professional training for factory employees

Correspondence
Mail or fax resume with cover letter

Part Time/Summer: La Confiserie Comete Ltee occasionally hires candidates for part time employment, and regularly seeks individuals for the summer. Potential jobs include clerk, receptionist, or production worker. Applications should be in by the end of February.

LAIDLAW INC.

3221 North Service Road, P.O. Box 5028
Burlington, Ontario, L7R 3Y8
Tel: (905) 336-1800   Fax: (905) 336-0670

Debbie Block, Human Resources
Internet: www.laidlaw.com

Laidlaw Inc.'s 60,000 employees provide high quality, cost-effective transportation management services to municipalities, businesses, industries and individuals. Operating from 900 locations throughout Canada and the U.S., Laidlaw is the largest service company in school bus transportation and health care transportation.

Academic Fields
College: Accounting, Business, Communications, Computer Science, Human Resources, Laboratory Tech., Marketing/Sales, Secretarial
Bachelor of Arts: General, Business, Economics, Political Science
Bachelor of Comm/Admin: General, Accounting, Finance, Marketing, Info Mgmt.
Bachelor of Science: Computer Science
Bachelor of Engineering: General
Chartered Accounting: CA - General/Finance, CGA/CMA - General/Finance

Critical Skills
Adaptable, Analytical, Flexible, Good Communication, Innovative, Leadership, Organized, Professional

Types of Positions
Mail Clerk   Accounting Clerk
Computer Operator

Starting Salary
Depends on education level

Company Benefits
- Health, dental, and life insurance
- Disability and group RRSP
- Tuition reimbursement

Correspondence
Mail or fax resume with cover letter

Part Time/Summer: Laidlaw occasionally seeks candidates for part time jobs, and regularly looks for individuals for summer employment. In the summer, potential jobs include accounting clerk, computer operator, and tax analyst. Candidates are usually hired through college or university co-op programs.

LAKESIDE FARM INDUSTRIES LTD.

P.O. Box 800, Stn Main
Brooks, Alberta, T1R 1B7
Tel: (403) 362-3326   Fax: (403) 362-8231

Glenn Ravnsborg, Director of Human Resources

Lakeside Farm Industries is involved in livestock research, feedlot, feed and fertilizer manufacturing and sales. The firm also operates a beef slaughter plant. Lakeside Feeders employs approximately 550 individuals in total.

Academic Fields
College: Animal Health
Bachelor of Science: Agriculture
Chartered Accounting: CA - General/Finance, CGA/CMA - General/Finance

Critical Skills
Enthusiastic, Responsible

Types of Positions
Fertilizer of Feed Sales Person
Feed Mill Counter Sales
Animal Health Technician

Starting Salary
$ 20,000 - 25,000 (Diploma) /
$ 25,000 - 30,000 (Bach. of Science)

Company Benefits
- Full medical and dental benefits

Correspondence
Mail or fax resume with cover letter

Part Time/Summer: Lakeside Farm Industries occasionally looks for people for part time and summer positions.

LAMBERT SOMEC INC.

1505 rue des Tanneurs
Québec City, Québec, G1N 4S7
Tel: (418) 687-1640   Fax: (418) 688-7571

Ann Martell, Director HR
Internet: www.lambertsomec.com/

Lambert Somec is a construction contractor specializing in the electrical, piping, ventilation and air conditioning, and industrial mechanical fields. The company carries on business primarily in the commercial construction and industrial construction sectors. The construction firm employs approximately 390 individuals. French is their usual language of business.

Academic Fields
College: Engineering Tech., Industrial Design
Bachelor of Science: Computer Science
Bachelor of Engineering: General, Electrical, Industrial, Mechanical

Critical Skills
Dependable, Efficient, Productive, Responsible

Types of Positions
Various Positions

Starting Salary
below $ 20,000

Company Benefits
- Complete benefit package

Correspondence
Mail resume with cover letter

Part Time/Summer: Lambert Somec sometimes seeks individuals for part time and summer employment opportunities. Potential jobs are most likely technical in nature.

CITY OF LEDUC

1 Alexandra Park
Leduc, Alberta, T9E 4C4
Tel: (780) 980-7177   Fax: (780) 980-7127

Human Resources
Internet: www.city.leduc.ab.ca

The City of Leduc is a municipal government involved in the formation of policy, laws and service delivery under its jurisdiction.

Academic Fields
College: General, Accounting, Administration, Business, Communications, Computer Science, Drafting/Architecture, Electronics Tech., Engineering Tech., Faculty Management, Human Resources, Law Clerk, Mechanical Tech., Recreation Studies, Secretarial, Security/Law, Urban Planning
Bachelor of Arts: General, Business, Political Science, Psychology, Public Relations, Recreation Studies, Sociology/Social Work, Urban Geography
Bachelor of Comm/Admin: General, Accounting, Finance, Info Mgmt., Public Admin., HR Mgmt.
Bachelor of Science: General, Computer Science, Environ. Studies, Geography, Health Sci., Horticulture
Bachelor of Laws: General
Bachelor of Engineering: General, Civil, Computer Syst., Design, Electrical, Environ. Studies, Mechanical
Chartered Accounting: CA - General/Finance, CGA/CMA - General/Finance
Masters: Business Administration, Engineering

Critical Skills
Adaptable, Analytical, Good Communication, Confident, Creative, Decisive, Dependable, Professional, Responsible, Writing Skills

Types of Positions
Varies

Starting Salary
Varies

Company Benefits
- Full line of benefits, dental, health, life, pension

Correspondence
Mail, fax or e-mail resume with cover letter
E-mail: human.resources@city.leduc.ab.ca

Part Time/Summer: The City of Leduc regularly hires for part time or summer work. Potential jobs are with the parks crew as a labourer, or in the parks summer programs. Apply in February of March.

LEGO CANADA INC.

45 Mural Street, Unit 7
Richmond Hill, Ontario, L4B 1J4
Tel: (905) 764-5346   Fax: (905) 886 3093

Wendy Lavalle, HR Manager
Internet: www.lego.com

Lego Canada is a distributor of construction toys for children. The company employs about 100 individuals.

Academic Fields
College: General, Accounting, Administration, Business, Marketing/Sales
Bachelor of Arts: General, Business, English
Bachelor of Comm/Admin: General, Accounting, Finance, Marketing, Info Mgmt.
Bachelor of Science: General, Computer Science
Bachelor of Education: General
Chartered Accounting: CA - General/Finance, CGA/CMA - General/Finance
Masters: Business Administration

Critical Skills
Adaptable, Good Communication, Confident, Dependable, Diligent, Efficient, Enthusiastic, Good With Figures, Innovative, Leadership, Organized, Personable, Productive, Professional, Responsible, Good Writing Skills

Types of Positions
Credit Department   Consumer Services
Warehouse

Starting Salary
$ 20,000 - 25,000

Company Benefits
- Extended health and dental
- Life insurance, vision care
- Summer hours, social events

Correspondence
Mail or fax resume with cover letter
E-mail: jobs@lego.com

Part Time/Summer: Lego Canada occasionally seeks people for part time work, but does not hire for the summer, as this is their slowest time of the year.

LEICA GEOSYSTEMS CANADA INC.

513 McNicoll Ave.
Willowdale, Ontario, M2H 2C9
Tel: (416) 497-2460   Fax: (416) 497-2053

Louise Van Paassen, Director of Human Resources
Internet: www.leica-geosystems.com

Leica Geosystems is a globally-active enterprise with a long tradition. It plays a leading role in the development, production and distribution of state-of-the-art systems for the capture and processing of spatial data for surveying, mapping and positioning. To their customers in the engineering, surveying and construction fields, in industry, in telecommunications and in security technology, they offer innovative total solutions based on leading-edge technology.

Academic Fields
College: General, Accounting, Administration, Engineering Tech., Secretarial
Bachelor of Arts: General, Business
Bachelor of Science: Computer Science, Geography, Geology, Mathematics
Bachelor of Engineering: Civil, Geotechnical
Masters: Business Administration

Critical Skills
Adaptable, Analytical, Dependable, Diligent, Flexible, Good Communication, Innovative, Leadership, Organized, Personable, Persuasive, Productive, Professional

Types of Positions
Inside Sales Coordinator   Customer Support

Starting Salary
$ 25,000 - 30,000

Company Benefits
- Comprehensive, competitive benefits package
- Health, dental, vision, life, pension, disability
- On-the-job training, internal courses

Correspondence
Mail or fax resume with cover letter

Part Time/Summer: Leica Geosystems Canada occasionally looks for individuals for part time or summer employment opportunities.

LENBROOK INDUSTRIES LIMITED

633 Granite Court
Pickering, Ontario, L1W 3K1
Tel: (905) 831-6333   Fax: (905) 837-6352

Human Resources Department

Lenbrook Industries is a Canadian based, privately-owned national distribution company. Divisions include audio/video, personal communications, energy systems, and speaker manufacturing. The company employs approximately 110 individuals.

Academic Fields
College: Accounting, Administration, Advertising, Communications, Computer Science, Electronics Tech., Engineering Tech., Human Resources, Marketing/Sales
Bachelor of Arts: Business, Public Relations
Bachelor of Comm/Admin: Accounting, Marketing, Info Mgmt.
Bachelor of Science: Computer Science, Mathematics, Physics
Bachelor of Laws: Corporate
Bachelor of Engineering: General, Computer Systems, Design, Electrical
Chartered Accounting: CA-General, CMA-General, CGA-General
Masters: Business Administration, Engineering

Critical Skills
Adaptable, Good Communication, Creative, Dependable, Efficient, Enthusiastic, Flexible, Innovative, Organized, Personable, Productive, Professional, Good Writing Skills, Self Motivated, High Initiative

Types of Positions
MIS Support
Marketing Coordinator
Sales Administrator/Coordinator

Starting Salary
$ 20,000 - 25,000

Company Benefits
- Benefits vary by position

Correspondence
Mail resume with cover letter

Part Time/Summer: Lenbrook Industries regularly hires for part time and summer work. Potential jobs include MIS support, clerical support, and technical services support. Apply by mid February.

LEO BURNETT CO. LTD.

175 Bloor Street East, North Tower
Toronto, Ontario, M4W 3R9
Tel: (416) 925-5997   Fax: (416) 925-3447

Human Resources
Internet: www.leoburnett.com

Leo Burnett Co. is a holding company with its interests in the provisions of advertising services. A wholly owned subsidiary of Leo Burnett Worldwide Inc., of the United States, the firm in Canada provides a wide range of marketing services to individuals, businesses and other enterprises. The company employs approximately 200 people across the country.

Academic Fields
College: Advertising
Bachelor of Arts: General, Business
Masters: Business Administration

Critical Skills
Creative, Decisive, Organized, Productive, Professional, Responsible

Types of Positions
Assistant Account Executive   Media Buyer

Starting Salary
$ 20,000 - 40,000 (depending on position)

Company Benefits
- Full range of benefits provided

Correspondence
Mail resume with cover letter

Part Time/Summer: Leo Burnett Co. sometimes hires for part time positions and summer opportunities. The company also awards scholarship positions to a handful of students.

LEON'S MANUFACTURING COMPANY INC.

Box 5002, 135 York Road E.
Yorkton, Saskatchewan, S3N 3Z4
Tel: (306) 786-2600   Fax: (306) 782-1884

Suzette deVries, Payroll Officer
Internet: www.leonsmfg.com

Leon's Mfg. Company Inc. is a Canadian company with a history that dates back over forty-five years. From a simple blacksmith and machine shop in the rural community of Bankend, Saskatchewan, the company expanded and grew to its present size. Today, Leon's Mfg. Company Inc. by technical innovation, engineering expertise, and a dedication to product quality and service, has grown to a leading Canadian company of international stature, with factories and warehouses located in Canada and the United States.

Academic Fields
College: Accounting, Administration, Advertising, Information Systems, Marketing/Sales, Purchasing, Secretarial, Agricultural, CAD Autocad
Bachelor of Comm/Admin: General, Accounting, Finance, Human Resources, Marketing, Info Mgmt.
Bachelor of Engineering: Design
Masters: Business Administration

Critical Skills
Dependable, Diligent, Efficient, Enthusiastic, Good Communication, Good Writing Skills, Leadership, Personable, Productive

Types of Positions
Sales Dept.   Administration
Engineering

Starting Salary
$ 15,000 - 20,000 (depending on position)

Company Benefits
- Pension plan
- Group insurance benefits

Correspondence
Mail, fax or e-mail resume with cover letter

Part Time/Summer: Leon's Manufacturing Company Inc. rarely hires for part time workers and occasionally hires in the summer months. Potential jobs would be engineering related.

LES CENTRES JEUNESSE DE MONTRÉAL

9335 St-Huberé
Montréal, Québec, H2M 1Y7
Tel: (514) 858-3903   Fax: (514) 858-3914

Nicole Godfroy, Ressources humaines

Les Centres Jeunesse de Montréal is established to offer psychological services and rehabilitation to children, youth, mothers in difficulty as well as their families. Les Centres Jeunesse de Montréal operates in an urban and multi-ethnic framework.

Academic Fields
College: General, Child Care, Computer Science, Faculty Management, Human Resources, Law Clerk, Nursing, Secretarial
Bachelor of Arts: Criminology, Psychology, Sociology/Social Work
Bachelor of Comm/Admin: General, Accounting, Finance, Info Mgmt., Public Admin.
Bachelor of Science: Computer Science, Nursing (RN), Psychology
Bachelor of Education: Special
Chartered Accounting: CA-General, CMA-General
Masters: Business Administration, Social Work, Criminology

Critical Skills
Analytical, Diligent, Efficient, Flexible, Good Communication, Good Writing Skills, Organized, Patient, Professional, Responsible

Types of Positions
Various Positions

Starting Salary
below $ 20,000 - 30,000 (depending on education)

Company Benefits
- Good benefit package
- Training and development offered

Correspondence
Mail resume with cover letter

Part Time/Summer: Les Centres Jeunesse de Montréal regularly seeks candidates for part time and summer employment. Potential jobs are involved with specialized education, or include being a technician. The best time to apply is in April.

LES DISTILLERIES CORBY LTÉE

1002 Sherbrooke Street West, Suite 2300
Montreal, Québec, H3A 3L6
Tel: (514) 288-4181   Fax: (514) 288-6715

Marielle Daoust, Human Resources

Les Distilleries Corby Ltée is engaged in the consumer goods industry in the sale and manufacture of alcoholic beverages. The company's head office is in Montréal, Québec.

Academic Fields
Bachelor of Arts: Business, Economics
Bachelor of Comm/Admin: General, Accounting, Finance, Marketing, Info Mgmt.
Bachelor of Science: Computer Science, Mathematics
Chartered Accounting: CA-Finance, CMA-Finance, CGA-Finance
Masters: Business Administration

Critical Skills
Adaptable, Analytical, Creative, Efficient, Flexible, Good Communication, Good With Figures, Good Writing Skills, Innovative, Leadership, Persuasive, Productive, Professional, Responsible

Types of Positions
Finance Department   Marketing Department

Starting Salary
Depends on position

Company Benefits
- Comprehensive benefit package

Correspondence
Mail resume with cover letter

Part Time/Summer: Les Distilleries Corby Ltée occasionally looks for individuals for part time and summer jobs. Potential jobs involve analytical work or data entry in the finance or marketing department. The best time to apply is in April or May.

LES FORGES DE SOREL INC.

100 McCarthy
Sorel, Québec, J3R 3M8
Tel: (514) 746-4000   Fax: (514) 746-4118

Ressources humaines

Les Forges de Sorel is an industrial company that is engaged in machining, manufacturing, thermal treatment, inspection, mechanical and electrical maintenance.

Academic Fields
College: Administration, Computer Science, Electronics Tech., Laboratory Tech., Mechanical Tech.
Bachelor of Comm/Admin: Info Mgmt.
Bachelor of Engineering: Industrial, Mechanical, Metallurgist
Chartered Accounting: CMA-Finance

Critical Skills
Adaptable, Creative, Dependable, Efficient, Flexible, Good Communication, Leadership, Productive, Responsible

Types of Positions
Mechanic

Starting Salary
$ 30,000 - 40,000

Company Benefits
- Competitive benefit plan
- Pension plan, profit sharing

Correspondence
Mail resume with cover letter

Part Time/Summer: Les Forges de Sorel regularly seeks individuals for part time and summer employment opportunities. In the summer months, potential jobs include mechanic apprentice, machinist apprentice, bricklayer aid, janitor, or day labourer.

LES MODES SMART INC.

111 Chabanel O., Bureau 601
Montreal, Québec, H2N 1C8
Tel: (514) 381-5911   Fax: (514) 383-0439

Enza Bernardi, Human Resources

Les Modes Smart Inc. has one company that manufactures lingerie and another that manufactures sportswear. Their lingerie company was acquired two years ago and since that time sales and production has tripled.

Academic Fields
College: Accounting, Administration, Business, Human Resources, Information Systems, Marketing/Sales, Secretarial, Fashion, Graphic Arts
Bachelor of Arts: Business
Bachelor of Comm/Admin: Accounting, Finance, Human Resources, Marketing, Info Mgmt.
Bachelor of Engineering: Industrial
Chartered Accounting: CA-Finance, CGA-Finance, CMA-Finance

Critical Skills
Adaptable, Analytical, Confident, Diplomatic, Efficient, Enthusiastic, Flexible, Good Communication, Good Writing Skills, Innovative, Leadership, Logical, Organized, Productive, Professional, Responsible

Types of Positions
Accounting   Design
Production   Engineering
Management

Starting Salary
$ 15,000 - 20,000

Company Benefits
- They do not have employee benefits right now but are looking into it
- Send employees on courses as needed for different departments

Correspondence
Mail resume with cover letter

Part Time/Summer: Les Modes Smart Inc. does not hire part time workers, but occasionally seeks candidates for the summer months.

LIBERTY HEALTH

3500 Steeles Ave. E.
Markham, Ontario, L3R 0X4
Tel: (905) 946-4100   Fax: (905) 946-4129

Human Resources Department
Internet: www.coverme.com

Liberty Health is one of Canada's largest supplementary health benefits firms. Operating in Canada since 1938, they employ more than 23,000 people in 450 offices throughout the world.

Academic Fields
College: General, Accounting, Administration, Business, Communications, Computer Sci., Faculty Mgmt., Human Resources, Insurance, Lab Tech., Marketing/Sales, Nursing, Science, Secretarial, Stats
Bachelor of Arts: General, Business, Economics, English, Journalism, Psychology, Public Rel., Statistics
Bachelor of Comm/Admin: General, Accounting, Finance, Info Mgmt., Public Admin.
Bachelor of Science: General, Actuarial, Computer Science, Health Sciences, Mathematics, Nursing (RN), Occupational Therapy, Pharmacy, Physics, Psychology
Bachelor of Engineering: General, Computer Syst.
Bachelor of Education: General, Adult Education
Chartered Accounting: CA - General/Finance, CGA/CMA - General/Finance

Critical Skills
Analytical, Good Communication, Creative, Dependable, Diligent, Efficient, Enthusiastic, Flexible, Good With Figures, Organized, Personable, Productive, Professional, Responsible, Writing Skills

Types of Positions
Administrative Assistant   Customer Service Rep.
Accounting Clerk   Support Clerk

Starting Salary
$ 20,000 - 30,000

Company Benefits
- Prescriptions, vision, travel, dental

Correspondence
Mail or fax resume with cover letter

Part Time/Summer: Liberty Health occasionally hires for part time work and regularly hires for the summer. Potential jobs include mail room clerk, claims admin., or customer service rep. They usually hire sons and daughters of current employees for summer positions.

LICK'S ICE CREAM & BURGER SHOPS INC.

1962A Queen St. E.
Toronto, Ontario, M4L 1H8
Tel: (416) 362-5425   Fax: (416) 691-6224

Frank Peruzzi, Human Resources
Internet: www.licksburgers.com

LICK'S is popular for its friendly exciting atmosphere, excellent food, and most of all, for our enthusiastic staff. This is a result of our humanistic approach towards our employees. As most of our employees are young, we feel it is important to teach them good work habits and life skills.

Academic Fields
College: Business, Hospitality
Bachelor of Arts: Business
Bachelor of Comm/Admin: General

Critical Skills
Good Communication, Leadership, Personable, Responsible, Good Writing Skills

Types of Positions
Management in Training
New Store Training Crew

Starting Salary
$ 20,000 - 25,000

Company Benefits
- Full benefit plan
- 3 month training program
- Rapid advancement possible for qualified candidates

Correspondence
Fax resume with cover letter

Part Time/Summer: Lick's Ice Cream & Burger Shops regularly looks for individuals for part time and summer employment. The best time to apply is from May 1st to June 30th.

LIFETOUCH CANADA INC.

1395 Inkster Blvd.
Winnipeg, Manitoba, R2X 1P6
Tel: (204) 633-1395   Fax: (204) 694-5226

Human Resources

Lifetouch Canada is a photofinishing company that produces school, grad and professional photographs. Their head office is in Winnipeg, Manitoba.

Academic Fields
College: Animation, Graphic Arts, Journalism, Photography, Accounting, Administration, Advertising, Business, Communications, Human Resources, Information Systems, Insurance, Marketing/Sales, Purchasing, Computer Science, Electronics Tech., Engineering Tech.
Bachelor of Arts: General, Business, Economics
Bachelor of Comm/Admin: General, Accounting, Finance, Human Resources, Marketing, Info Mgmt.
Bachelor of Engineering: Computer Syst., Electrical
Chartered Accounting: CA, CGA-General, CMA
Masters: Business Administration

Critical Skills
Adaptable, Analytical, Artistic, Confident, Dependable, Efficient, Enthusiastic, Good Communication, Logical, Manual Dexterity, Productive, Responsible

Types of Positions
Analyzer   Proof Printer
Paper Processor   Film Developing
Data Entry   Art Work

Starting Salary
$ 20,000 - 25,0000 (depends on position)

Company Benefits
- 80% coverage, dental, hospital (depending on position)
- In-house training opportunities
- Deferred profit sharing

Correspondence
Mail resume with cover letter

Part Time/Summer: Lifetouch Canada occasionally hires for part time or summer work. There are many Fall seasonal opportunities. They are always seeking management trainee candidates. Apply in June.

The Canada Student Employment Guide

LINMOR TECHNOLOGIES

177 Colonnade Rd.
Nepean, Ontario, K2E 7J4
Tel: (613) 727-2757   Fax: (613) 727-2627

Michelle Graham, Director, Human Resources
Internet: www.linmor.com

Linmor Technologies is a network management software developer for the telecommunications industry. The company employs 75 individuals and is growing again.

Academic Fields
College: Computer Science
Bachelor of Comm/Admin: Accounting, Finance, Marketing
Bachelor of Science: Computer Systems
Masters: Business Administration, Engineering

Critical Skills
Adaptable, Analytical, Dependable, Diligent, Efficient, Enthusiastic, Good Communication, Leadership, Organized, Personable, Professional, Responsible

Types of Positions
Accounting Clerk   Jr. Software Developer
Jr. Quality Assurance Specialist   Jr. IS/IT Administrator
Jr. Technical Support Specialist

Starting Salary
$ 35,000 - 55,000

Company Benefits
- Medical, dental, vision care, life insurance, dependent life insurance
- Stock options, performance bonuses, training
- Employee referral award program

Correspondence
Apply through website. E-mail: hr@linmor.com

Part Time/Summer: Linmor Technologies occasionally seeks candidates for part time and summer work. Potential jobs are in information systems, information technology, or in software development. The best time to apply is in the Spring.

Co-op/Internship: Internship placements are available throughout the year, mainly in the software development area.

LITTON SYSTEMS CANADA LTD.

25 City View Drive
Etobicoke, Ontario, M9W 5A7
Tel: (416) 249-1231   Fax: (416) 245-0324

Gayle L. Morrison, Employee Relations Manager
Internet: www.litton.com

Litton Systems Canada is involved in the design and manufacture of airborne and maritime electronics. In addition, the company is engaged in highly sophisticated electronic equipment including navigation systems, naval command control and communications systems, automated test equipment, airborne surveillance radar, flight inspection systems, LED flat panel and multifunctional cockpit designs.

Academic Fields
College: Accounting, Computer Science, Drafting/Architecture, Electronics Tech., Engineering Tech., Mechanical Tech., Security/Law
Bachelor of Comm/Admin: Accounting, Finance, Marketing
Bachelor of Science: Chemistry, Comp. Sci., Physics
Bachelor of Engineering: Chemical, Computer Syst., Design, Electrical, Materials Science, Mechanical
Chartered Accounting: CA - General/Finance, CGA/CMA - General/Finance
Masters: Science, Engineering

Critical Skills
Adaptable, Confident, Dependable, Diligent, Good Communication, Diplomatic, Enthusiastic, Good Writing Skills, Innovative, Organized, Productive, Manual Dexterity, Professional, Responsible

Types of Positions
Electrical Engineering   Computer Science
Mech. Engineering   Chemical Engineering
Financial Analyst   Engineering Technologist

Starting Salary
$ 25,000 - 40,000 (depending on position)

Company Benefits
- Major medical, dental, and life insurance

Correspondence
Mail or fax resume with cover letter

Part Time/Summer: Litton Systems sometimes hires for part time and summer work. They offer a full range of summer jobs depending on the company's requirements at the time.

The Canada Student Employment Guide

LM ARCHITECTURAL GROUP

300 - 290 Vaughan St.
Winnipeg, Manitoba, R3B 2L9
Tel: (204) 942-0681   Fax: (204) 943-8676

Human Resources
Internet: www.lmarchitects.mb.ca

LM Architectural Group provides architectural and interior design services. The company is located in Winnipeg, Manitoba and employs 38 individuals.

Academic Fields
College: CAD Autocad
Bachelor of Engineering: Bachelor of Architecture

Critical Skills
Adaptable, Artistic, Creative, Good Communication, Good Writing Skills, Personable, Professional, Responsible

Types of Positions
Intern Architect   Interior Designer
Graphics Artist   Computer AutoCAD Technician

Starting Salary
$ 25,000 - 30,000

Company Benefits
- Competitive benefits

Correspondence
Mail resume with cover letter
E-mail: lbarkwell@lmarchitects.mb.ca

Part Time/Summer: LM Architectural Group occasionally seeks individuals for part time work and regularly hires in the summer. A potential job would be production assistant. The best time to apply is at the beginning of March.

LOEWEN WINDOWS

P.O. Box 2260
Steinbach, Manitoba, R0A 2A0
Tel: (204) 326-6446   Fax: (204) 326-5347

Personnel Department
Internet: www.loewen.com

Loewen Windows manufactures a full line of premium wood (Douglas Fir) windows and doors distributed by a global network of over one thousand window and door dealers. As Canada's largest manufacturer of wood windows and doors, they have committed ourselves to developing a heritage of customer satisfaction through high-quality, innovative window and door products manufactured by a skilled work force.

Academic Fields
College: Accounting, Drafting/Architecture, Engineering Tech., Secretarial
Bachelor of Comm/Admin: Finance, Marketing
Bachelor of Engineering: Industrial, Mechanical
Chartered Accounting: CMA-General, CMA-Finance

Critical Skills
Adaptable, Dependable, Efficient, Enthusiastic, Flexible, Good Communication, Manual Dexterity, Personable, Responsible

Types of Positions
Office Clerical / Data Entry   Engineering Tech.
Drafting   General Labourer

Starting Salary
Depends on position

Company Benefits
- Dental and health insurance
- Short and long term disability, life insurance
- Profit sharing plan

Correspondence
Mail or fax resume with cover letter

Part Time/Summer: Loewen Windows does not hire for part time work, but regularly seeks candidates for the summer months. A general labour position is the most likely job. The best time to apply is in May.

The Canada Student Employment Guide

LONDON GOODWILL INDUSTRIES ASSOCIATION
544 First St.
London, Ontario, N5V 1Z3
Tel: (519) 645-1455   Fax: (519) 645-8610

Alan Jackson, Human Resources

London Goodwill Industries Association provides employment, education and training for people with physical, mental, emotional or social disabilities. Goodwill aims for their clients to become participating members of the community, working towards self-sufficiency.

Academic Fields
College: Accounting, Human Resources, Marketing/Sales, Secretarial
Bachelor of Arts: Psychology, Sociology/Social Work
Bachelor of Comm/Admin: Accounting
Chartered Accounting: CMA-General, CMA-Finance

Critical Skills
Diplomatic, Efficient, Enthusiastic, Good Communication, Leadership, Persuasive, Productive

Types of Positions
Secretarial   Retail Management

Starting Salary
$ 25,000 - 30,000

Company Benefits
- Drug plan, life insurance, long term disability
- Pension plan with matching costs
- Accumulating sick benefits

Correspondence
Mail resume with cover letter

Part Time/Summer: London Goodwill Industries Association occasionally looks for individuals for part time and summer employment. Potential jobs include labourer, or positions in retail. The best time to apply is in the Spring.

LOSS PREVENTION GROUP INC.
493 Madison St.
Winnipeg, Manitoba, R3J 1J2
Tel: (204) 788-1697   Fax: (204) 788-1563

Dan Nickel, Human Resources
Internet: www.losspreventiongroup.com

Since 1989 the Loss Prevention Group Inc. has provided Canada's retail, hospitality and manufacturing sectors with comprehensive loss prevention and profit retention services that include consulting, training services, in-house and industry seminars.

Academic Fields
Bachelor of Arts: Criminology, Political Science, Psychology, Sociology/Social Work
Bachelor of Laws: General

Critical Skills
Adaptable, Good Communication, Confident, Decisive, Dependable, Efficient, Personable, Productive, Professional, Responsible, Good Writing Skills

Types of Positions
Retail Investigator   Security Person

Starting Salary
below $ 20,000 - 25,000

Company Benefits
- Medical and dental for full time employees
- Full in-house intensive training course

Correspondence
Mail or submit resume with cover letter in person

Part Time/Summer: Loss Prevention Group regularly seeks candidates for part time positions, and occasionally looks for people for summer opportunities. Potential jobs include retail investigator.

LOVAT INC.

441 Carlingview Dr.
Etobicoke, Ontario, M9W 5G7
Tel: (416) 675-3293   Fax: (416) 675-6702

Human Resources
Internet: www.lovat.com

For more than a quarter century, LOVAT has specialized in the custom design and manufacture of Tunnel Boring Machines (TBM) utilized in the construction of metro, railway, road, sewer, water main, penstock, mine access and telecable tunnels. Founded in 1972 by Richard Lovat, the company's extensive experience, advanced technology and continued development provide the solutions for any tunnelling challenge on any project.

Academic Fields
College: Accounting, Administration, Engineering Tech., Mechanical Tech.
Bachelor of Engineering: Electrical, Mechanical
Chartered Accounting: CMA-General, CGA-General

Critical Skills
Adaptable, Analytical, Creative, Dependable, Diligent, Enthusiastic, Flexible, Good With Figures, Innovative, Manual Dexterity, Personable, Productive, Good Writing Skills

Types of Positions
Junior Draftsperson	Junior Designer
Administration Assistant	Marketing Assistant
Receptionist	Plant Helper

Starting Salary
$ 25,000 - 30,000

Company Benefits
- 100% company paid health and dental plan

Correspondence
Mail or fax resume with cover letter

Part Time/Summer: Lovat Inc. does not hire for part time work, but regularly seeks individuals for summer duties. Potential jobs include plant helpers, junior designers and assistants in accounting. The best time to apply is in April or May.

M M INDUSTRA LTD.

61 Estates Road
Dartmouth, Nova Scotia, B2Y 4K3
Tel: (902) 465-7675   Fax: (902) 465-4102

Human Resources

M M Industra Ltd. specializes in custom metal fabrication. The company is involved in the manufacture of pressure vessels, heat exchangers, reactors, and mining equipment among other products. Most of the employees that they hire are tradesman who specialize in welding or fitting. Their workforce fluctuates from 100 to 500 employees, depending upon their work demands.

Academic Fields
College: Accounting, Administration, Drafting/Architecture, Engineering Tech., Human Resources, Marketing/Sales, Mechanical Tech., Secretarial
Bachelor of Comm/Admin: Accounting, Finance, Marketing
Bachelor of Engineering: Mechanical
Chartered Accounting: CMA-General/Finance, CGA-General/Finance

Critical Skills
Flexible, Logical, Organized, Good Communication, Personable, Productive, Responsible, Manual Dexterity

Types of Positions
Drafting	Estimating
Accounting	Quality Control

Starting Salary
$ 25,000 - 30,000

Company Benefits
- Full medical benefits
- 2 weeks holidays with 10 statutory holidays
- 10 sick days per year

Correspondence
Mail resume with cover letter

Part Time/Summer: M M Industra Ltd. sometimes seeks candidates to work on a part time basis, or during the summer months. Potential jobs are related to general labour and manufacturing (i.e. custom metal fabrication), or involve clerical and office duties including accounting.

M. MCGRAWTH CANADA LIMITED

111A Rideau St.
Ottawa, Ontario, K1N 5X1
Tel: (613) 241-8422   Fax: (613) 241-1653

Jan Smith, Director of Personnel

M. McGrawth Canada Limited is a collection agency in Ottawa, Ontario. They collect outstanding accounts for their clients.

Academic Fields
College: General, Administration, Business
Bachelor of Arts: General, Business, Criminology, Economics
Bachelor of Education: General

Critical Skills
Adaptable, Confident, Decisive, Dependable, Diplomatic, Efficient, Enthusiastic, Flexible, Good Communication, Good With Figures, Good Written Skills, Innovative, Leadership, Organized, Patient, Personable, Persuasive, Productive, Professional, Responsible

Types of Positions
Collection Clerk   Telemarketing Clerk

Starting Salary
below $ 20,000

Company Benefits
- Competitive benefits plan

Correspondence
Mail resume with cover letter

Part Time/Summer: M. McGrawth Canada Limited occasionally hires for part time and summer employment.

MAAX INC.

600 rte Cameron
Ste-Marie-De-Beauce, Québec, G6E 1B2
Tel: (418) 387-4155   Fax: (418) 387-3507

Ressources humaines
Internet: www.maax.com

Since its beginning 26 years ago, MAAX Inc. has been known as an innovative manufacturer of bathroom products and of composite material industrial component parts. MAAX has 20 plants and 8 distribution centers across North America to better serve its clientele.

Academic Fields
College: Accounting, Administration, Advertising, Communications, Computer Science, Engineering, Faculty Mgmt., Human Resources, Industrial Design, Marketing/Sales, Mechanical Tech., Secretarial
Bachelor of Comm/Admin: Accounting, Marketing, Info Mgmt.
Bachelor of Science: Chemistry, Computer Science
Bachelor of Engineering: General, Chemical, Computer Systems, Electrical, Mechanical
Chartered Accounting: CA-General, CMA-General, CGA-General

Critical Skills
Adaptable, Analytical, Good Communication, Confident, Creative, Dependable, Diligent, Diplomatic, Efficient, Enthusiastic, Flexible, Good With Figures, Logical, Manual Dexterity, Organized, Patient, Personable, Productive, Professional, Responsible, Good Writing Skills

Types of Positions
Research and Development   Production
Factory

Starting Salary
$ 20,000 - 25,000

Company Benefits
- Complete benefit package
- Life insurance, health plan
- Training offered as needed

Correspondence
Mail or fax resume with cover letter

Part Time/Summer: MAAX occasionally looks for individuals for part time work, and regularly seeks candidates for summer employment.

The Canada Student Employment Guide

MACDONALD DETTWILER AND ASSOCIATES LTD.
13800 Commerce Pkwy.
Richmond, British Columbia, V6V 2J3
Tel: (604) 231-2252   Fax: (604) 278-2281

Recruiting Office
Internet: www.mda.ca

MDA collects data from sources above the Earth and from locations around the world, using high-resolution satellites, aerial photography and technologies that allows them to source, retrieve and convert digital records from private and government sources and databases. They design and deliver information extraction and integration systems that use the data they collect.

Academic Fields
College: Accounting, Administration, Business, Computer Science
Bachelor of Comm/Admin: Accounting, Finance, Marketing
Bachelor of Science: Computer Science, Physics
Bachelor of Engineering: Computer Systems, Electrical
Masters: Science, Engineering

Critical Skills
Adaptable, Analytical, Good Communication, Creative, Innovative, Leadership, Business Awareness

Types of Positions
Various Positions

Starting Salary
$ 30,000 - 40,000

Company Benefits
- Comprehensive benefit package
- Medical, life insurance, income protection
- Training and development programs

Correspondence
Fax or e-mail resume with cover letter
E-mail: jobs@mda.ca

Part Time/Summer: MacDonald Dettwiler and Associates occasionally seeks people for part time work and regularly hires for the summer. Potential jobs include software developer, hardware engineer, co-ops and interns. Individuals should apply year-round.

MACDONALD STEEL LTD.
1556 Industrial Rd.
Cambridge, Ontario, N3H 4S6
Tel: (519) 653-3000   Fax: (519) 621-4995

Human Resources
Internet: www.macdonaldsteel.com

MacDonald Steel is one of the worlds leading diversified manufacturing companies. As one of the largest manufacturers of custom metal fabrication, they provide services in profile cutting, welding, machining, complete finishing and assembly. They currently have 400 employees.

Academic Fields
College: Accounting, Computer Science, Engineering Tech.
Bachelor of Engineering: General, Computer Systems, Industrial, Mechanical
Chartered Accounting: CGA-General

Critical Skills
Adaptable, Good Communication, Dependable, Experienced

Types of Positions
Welder   Machine Operator

Starting Salary
$ 30,000 - 40,000

Company Benefits
- Basic health and dental
- In-house health and safety training
- Job related training for advancement

Correspondence
Mail or submit resume and cover letter in person

Part Time/Summer: MacDonald Steel occasionally looks for people for part time work, and regularly seeks candidate for the summer. Potential jobs include general labourer, painter, or welder. Individuals should apply anytime.

MACTAC CANADA LTD.

100 Kennedy Rd. S.
Brampton, Ontario, L6W 3E8
Tel: (905) 459-3100   Fax: (905) 459-8078

Human Resources
Internet: www.mactac.com

Mactac Canada Ltd. is a manufacturer of pressure sensitive adhesive paper products. The company's head office is in Brampton, Ontario.

Academic Fields
College: Accounting, Business, Marketing/Sales
Bachelor of Arts: Business, Languages
Bachelor of Comm/Admin: Accounting
Chartered Accounting: CMA-Finance, CGA-Finance

Critical Skills
Adaptable, Analytical, Confident, Creative, Decisive, Dependable, Diligent, Diplomatic, Efficient, Enthusiastic, Flexible, Good Communication, Good With Figures, Innovative, Logical, Patient, Personable, Productive, Professional, Responsible

Types of Positions
No Junior Positions

Starting Salary
$ 20,000 - 25,000

Company Benefits
- Full company paid benefit package
- Full educational reimbursement on successful completion of job related study

Correspondence
Mail resume with cover letter

Part Time/Summer: Mactac Canada Ltd. does not hire individuals for part time or summer employment.

MACVIRO CONSULTANTS INC.

90 Allstate Parkway, Suite 600
Markham, Ontario, L3R 6H3
Tel: (905) 475-7270   Fax: (905) 475-5994

Mario Conetta, Senior Engineer
Internet: www.macviro.com

MacViro Consultants Inc. is an Ontario based company providing consulting engineering, planning and scientific services. The company is a multi-discipline engineering services firm directed at creating environmental and energy solutions for clients in both the private and public sectors.

Academic Fields
College: CAD Autocad, Engineering Tech., Industrial Design, Mechanical Tech.
Bachelor of Engineering: Chemical, Civil, Computer Systems, Design, Electrical, Environmental Studies, Water Resources

Critical Skills
Dependable, Diligent, Efficient, Enthusiastic, Good Communication, Good Writing Skills, Responsible

Types of Positions
Water Resources   Water & Wastewater
Municipal Engineering   Waste Management
Mech./Elec. Engineering

Starting Salary
$ 30,000 - 35,000

Company Benefits
- Comprehensive benefit package including drugs, eye care, dental, short and long term disability
- Company is wholly-owned by its employees
- Internal and external training opportunities as required

Correspondence
Mail or fax resume with cover letter
E-mail: mconetta@macviro.com

Part Time/Summer: MacViro Consultants Inc. occasionally hires for part time work and regularly hires for the summer. They hire at least two co-op students from University of Waterloo on a regular basis. Individuals can apply anytime.

Co-op/Internship: They offer internship opportunities working with licensed professional engineers.

The Canada Student Employment Guide

MAGNA INTERNATIONAL INC.

337 Magna Drive
Aurora, Ontario, L4G 7K1
Tel: (905) 726-2462   Fax: (905) 760-7474

Tara Bibby, Human Resources
Internet: www.magnaint.com

Magna International Inc. is a leading global supplier of technologically-advanced automotive systems, components and complete modules. The company employs approximately 59,000 people at 174 manufacturing divisions and 33 product development and engineering centres in 19 countries.

Academic Fields
College: Accounting, Business, Communications, Electronics Tech., Engineering Tech., Human Resources, Industrial Design, Journalism, Marketing/Sales, Mechanical Tech., Nursing
Bachelor of Arts: Business, Public Relations
Bachelor of Comm/Admin: Accounting, Finance, Marketing
Bachelor of Science: Environ. Studies, Mathematics, Nursing (RN), Occupational Therapy, Physiotherapy
Bachelor of Laws: Corporate
Bachelor of Engineering: Chemical, Design, Electrical, Environmental Studies, Industrial, Mechanical
Chartered Accounting: CA-Finance, CMA-Finance, CGA-Finance
Masters: Business Administration, Engineering

Critical Skills
Confident, Decisive, Dependable, Flexible, Good Communication, Personable, Leadership, Logical, Good Writing Skills, Responsible, Professional

Types of Positions
Administrative Asst.   Mail Room Clerk
Receptionist

Starting Salary
$ 20,000 - 25,000

Company Benefits
- Wide range of benefits provided

Correspondence
Mail resume with cover letter

Part Time/Summer: Magna regularly hires for part time and summer work. Potential positions include reception, librarian, inventory clerk, mailroom clerk, and computer operator. Apply in April or May.

MANITOBA AGRICULTURE AND FOOD

401 York Ave., Suite 803
Winnipeg, Manitoba, R3C 0P8
Tel: (204) 945-3308   Fax: (204) 948-4735

Angie Kudlak, Human Resources
Internet: www.gov.mb.ca/agriculture/

Working together for a dynamic sustainable agri-food industry, Manitoba Agriculture and Food seeks progressive individuals to join their team.

Academic Fields
College: Administration, Computer Science, Human Resources, Laboratory Tech.
Bachelor of Comm/Admin: General, Accounting, Finance, Marketing, Public Admin.
Bachelor of Science: Agriculture, Computer Science, Horticulture, Microbiology, Human Ecology
Bachelor of Laws: Corporate
Bachelor of Engineering: Environ., Agricultural
Bachelor of Education: Adult Education
Chartered Accounting: CA - General/Finance, CGA/CMA - General/Finance
Masters: Bus. Admin., Sci., Engineering, Agriculture

Critical Skills
Adaptable, Analytical, Confident, Creative, Decisive, Enthusiastic, Flexible, Innovative, Leadership, Logical, Organized, Personable, Productive, Professional

Types of Positions
Asst. Agricultural Rep.   Asst. Home Economist

Starting Salary
$ 40,000 - 50,000

Company Benefits
- Civil service benefit package

Correspondence
Mail, fax, submit resume and cover letter in person
E-mail: humanresources@agr.gov.mb.ca

Part Time/Summer: Manitoba Agriculture and Food occasionally hires for part time work and regularly hires for the summer. Jobs involve the soils and crop branch, marketing and farm business mgmt., regional offices, veterinary services, human res. and economics. Apply from Dec. to March.

Co-op/Internship: Internships are available occasionally.

The Canada Student Employment Guide

MANITOBA HYDRO

P.O. Box 815, 820 Taylor Avenue
Winnipeg, Manitoba, R3C 2P4
Tel: (204) 474-3211   Fax: (204) 474-4868

Employment Services
Internet: www.hydro.mb.ca

Manitoba Hydro is a major energy utility serving more than 402,000 electric customers throughout Manitoba and 246,000 gas customers in various communities throughout southern Manitoba.

Academic Fields
College: Accounting, Communications, Computer Science, Drafting/Architecture, Electronics Tech., Engineering Tech., Graphic Arts, Journalism, Laboratory Tech., Law Clerk, Mechanical Tech., Secretarial
Bachelor of Arts: Business, Economics, Public Relations, Sociology/Social Work, Statistics
Bachelor of Comm/Admin: Accounting, Finance, Marketing, Human Resources
Bachelor of Science: Chemistry, Computer Science, Environmental Studies, Mathematics
Bachelor of Laws: Corporate
Bachelor of Engineering: Chemical, Civil, Computer Systems, Electrical, Environmental Studies, Geotechnical, Mechanical, Water Resources
Bachelor of Education: Adult Education
Chartered Accounting: CA - General/Finance, CGA/CMA - General/Finance
Masters: Business Admin., Engineering, Library Science

Critical Skills
Adaptable, Analytical, Dependable, Efficient, Flexible, Good Communication, Good With Figures, Organized, Good Writing Skills, Personable, Responsible

Types of Positions
Labourer   Clerk
Apprentice   Engineers-In-Training
Information Systems   Commerce Trainees

Starting Salary
$ 25,000 - 30,000

Company Benefits
- Dental plan, group insurance, disability
- Staff assistance program, voluntary health plan

Correspondence
Mail or submit resume and cover letter in person

Part Time/Summer: Manitoba Hydro sometimes hires for part time jobs and regularly hires for the summer.

MANITOBA POOL ELEVATORS

P.O. Box 9800, Stn Main
Winnipeg, Manitoba, R3C 3K7
Tel: (204) 947-0468   Fax: (204) 934-0485

Jane Cox, Employment Administration

Manitoba Pool Elevators is a wholesaler of grain in the province of Manitoba. The firm has an employee base of approximately 800 people in total.

Academic Fields
College: Accounting, Computer Science, Graphic Arts, Secretarial
Bachelor of Arts: Journalism
Bachelor of Comm/Admin: Accounting, Finance, Marketing
Bachelor of Science: Agriculture, Computer Science
Chartered Accounting: CMA-General, CGA-General
Masters: Science

Critical Skills
Adaptable, Good Communication, Dependable, Diligent, Efficient, Enthusiastic, Flexible, Personable, Productive, Professional

Types of Positions
Mail Room Clerk   Junior Accounting Clerk

Starting Salary
$ 20,000 - 25,000

Company Benefits
- Full benefit package
- Health and dental coverage
- Tuition reimbursement, training opportunities

Correspondence
Mail resume with cover letter

Part Time/Summer: Manitoba Pool Elevators occasionally looks for individuals for part time work, and regularly hires for the summer. Potential jobs involve seasonal agricultural work, or general clerical duties. The best time to apply is by the beginning of March.

MANITOBA PUBLIC INSURANCE CORPORATION

P.O. Box 6300, 330 Graham Ave.
Winnipeg, Manitoba, R3C 4A4
Tel: (204) 985-7000   Fax: (204) 985-8049

Human Resources Dept.

The Manitoba Public Insurance Corporation provides automobile insurance and special risk extension insurance to Manitobans. The insurance company employs more than 1,100 people.

Academic Fields
College: General, Administration, Advertising, Business, Communications, Computer Science, Human Resources, Insurance, Journalism, Secretarial
Bachelor of Arts: General, Business, Journalism, Public Relations
Bachelor of Comm/Admin: General, Accounting, Finance
Bachelor of Science: Computer Science
Bachelor of Laws: General
Chartered Accounting: CA - General/Finance, CGA/CMA - General/Finance
Masters: Business Administration

Critical Skills
Adaptable, Good Communication, Confident, Dependable, Efficient, Enthusiastic, Flexible, Organized, Personable, Productive, Professional, Responsible

Types of Positions
Clerk I   Clerk Typist I
Internal Audit Dept.

Starting Salary
below $ 20,000 - 25,000

Company Benefits
- Extended health, dental
- Company pension, group life insurance
- Educational assistance

Correspondence
Mail resume with cover letter

Part Time/Summer: The Manitoba Public Insurance Corporation occasionally looks for people for part time and summer work. Potential jobs include general clerical, clerk typist, or computer science through co-op programs. The best time to apply is in February.

MANITOBA TELECOM SERVICES INC.

P.O. Box 6666, 333 Main St.
Winnipeg, Manitoba, R3C 3V6
Tel: (204) 941-7314   Fax: (204) 775-0718

Ken Larence, Human Resources
Internet: www.mts.mb.ca

Manitoba Telecom Services Inc. is a telecommunications market leader providing basic and enhanced local, long distance, data and network services through its world class network in addition to serving the rapidly expanding wireless communications industry.

Academic Fields
College: Communications, Computer Science
Bachelor of Comm/Admin: Marketing
Bachelor of Science: Computer Science
Bachelor of Engineering: Electrical
Chartered Accounting: CA-Finance

Critical Skills
Enthusiastic, Good Writing Skills, Innovative, Good Communication

Types of Positions
Clerical Support   Programmer
Sales Person   Engineer

Starting Salary
$ 25,000 - 30,000

Company Benefits
- Normal benefit package including dental and pension
- Extensive in-house training
- Educational assistance available

Correspondence
Not accepting resumes at the present time
E-mail: humanresources@mts.mb.ca

Part Time/Summer: Manitoba Telecom Services sometimes seeks candidates for part time and summer positions. However, at the present time they are not accepting resumes or applications.

The Canada Student Employment Guide

MAPLE LEAF CONSUMER FOODS

P.O. Box 70
Winnipeg, Manitoba, R3C 2G5
Tel: (204) 235-8259   Fax: (204) 233-5413

George Gysel, Human Resources Manager

Maple Leaf Foods is the largest company in Canada in the manufacturing and distribution of food products. Its head offices are in Toronto and the company's operations extend across Canada and into the global village. The firm employs about 11,000 people in Canada. The Winnipeg operation is the hams plant for all of Maple Leaf Foods.

Academic Fields
College: Accounting, Computer Science, Engineering Technology, Food/Nutrition, Human Resources, Industrial Design
Bachelor of Comm/Admin: General, Finance, Marketing, Human Resources
Bachelor of Science: Biology, Chemistry, Computer Science, Food Sciences, Microbiology
Bachelor of Engineering: Design, Industrial
Masters: Business Administration

Critical Skills
Adaptable, Analytical, Creative, Good Communication, Dependable, Diligent, Efficient, Good With Figures, Flexible, Good Writing Skills, Innovative, Organized, Personable, Professional, Punctual

Types of Positions
Accounting   Quality Assurance

Starting Salary
$ 20,000 - 25,000

Company Benefits
- Major medical, dental and pension plan
- Group life insurance and vision care plan
- Education tuition rebate

Correspondence
Mail resume with cover letter

Part Time/Summer: Maple Leaf Consumer Foods regularly hires for part time jobs and in the summer. Positions may be in quality assurance, and a production worker in the plant. Individuals must be at least 18 years of age to work in these positions. The best time to apply is in April or May.

MARCAM CANADA

880 Laurentian Dr.
Burlington, Ontario, L7N 3V6
Tel: (905) 632-6015   Fax: (905) 333-2600

Human Resources
Internet: www.avantis.marcam.com

Marcam is a world-leader in asset management solutions, and our expertise is second to none. For more than 15 years, professionals in diverse industries have relied on the insight and global expertise of Marcam to reach their maintenance management goals.

Academic Fields
College: Business, Computer Science
Bachelor of Arts: Business
Bachelor of Science: Computer Science, Mathematics
Bachelor of Engineering: General, Computer Systems
Masters: Science, Engineering

Critical Skills
Confident, Creative, Dependable, Enthusiastic, Flexible, Good Communication, Innovative, Professional, Responsible

Types of Positions
Jr. Associate Software Developer
Jr. Technical Writer
Jr. Customer Service

Starting Salary
$ 25,000 - 40,000

Company Benefits
- Extended medical benefits, flexible hours
- On-site fitness centre, casual dress
- 100% tuition reimbursement

Correspondence
Mail resume with cover letter

Part Time/Summer: Marcam Canada occasionally seeks candidates for part time work, and regularly hires for the summer. Potential jobs in the summer include systems administrator, technical writer, and quality assurance analyst. The best time to apply is in January or February.

MARINE ATLANTIC INC.

P.O. Box 2000
Sydney, Nova Scotia, B1P 6W4
Tel: (902) 564-2894   Fax: N/A

Michel H. Gratton, Employee Services Officer
Internet: www.marine-atlantic.ca

Marine Atlantic is one of Atlantic Canada's major ferry operator, fulfilling a federal government commitment to provide marine transportation services to Newfoundland. The organization has finished a massive downsizing, thus jobs are severely limited.

Academic Fields
College: Accounting, Computer Science, Engineering Tech., Hospitality, Human Resources
Bachelor of Arts: Business, Journalism, Psychology, Public Relations, Statistics
Bachelor of Comm/Admin: Acctg, Finance, Info Mgmt
Bachelor of Science: Computer Science, Environmental Studies, Psychology
Bachelor of Laws: Corporate
Bachelor of Engineering: Civil, Industrial, Transportation
Bachelor of Education: Adult Education
Chartered Accounting: CA-General, CMA-General, CGA - General
Masters: Business Administration, Engineering

Critical Skills
Adaptable, Analytical, Good Communication, Confident, Creative, Decisive, Dependable, Diligent, Efficient, Enthusiastic, Flexible, Good With Figures, Innovative, Leadership, Logical, Organized, Persuasive, Productive, Professional, Responsible, Writing Skills

Types of Positions
Information Systems   Finance
Accounting

Starting Salary
$ 30,000 - 40,000

Company Benefits
- Comprehensive health care, life insurance

Correspondence
Mail resume with cover letter
E-mail: mcgratton@marine-atlantic.ca

Part Time/Summer: Marine Atlantic sometimes hires for part time work and the summer. Positions are exclusive to Atlantic Canada through co-op education programs.

THE MARITIME LIFE ASSURANCE COMPANY

2701 Dutch Village Rd., P.O. Box 1030
Halifax, Nova Scotia, B3J 2X5
Tel: (902) 453-7415   Fax: (902) 453-7170
Paula Whitman, Human Resources Consultant
Internet: www.maritimelife.ca

Maritime Life has been offering financial security products to Canadians since 1992. Maritime life operates nationally, with offices in Halifax, Montreal, Toronto, Kitchener, Calgary and Vancouver.

Academic Fields
College: Accounting, Admin., Advertising, Business, Communications, Human Res., Info Syst., Insurance, Marketing/Sales, Real Estate, Secretarial, Statistics, Computer Science, Journalism, Legal Assistant
Bachelor of Arts: Business, Journalism, Languages, Public Relations, Statistics
Bachelor of Comm/Admin: General, Accounting, Finance, Human Resources, Marketing
Bachelor of Science: Actuarial, Computer Science, Mathematics, Occupational Therapy
Bachelor of Laws: General
Bachelor of Engineering: Computer Systems
Chartered Accounting: CA - General/Finance, CGA/CMA - General/Finance
Masters: Business Administration

Critical Skills
Adaptable, Analytical, Creative, Decisive, Dependable, Innovative, Leadership, Organized

Types of Positions
Mail Administrator   Administrative Assistant
Claims Processor   Receptionist
Customer Service Rep.   Data Entry Clerk

Starting Salary
$ 25,000 - 30,000

Company Benefits
Full health, dental, vision, pension

Correspondence
Mail, fax or e-mail resume with cover letter

Part Time/Summer: The Maritime Life Assurance Company occasionally hires for part time work and regularly hires for the summer.

Co-op/Internship: Co-op opportunities are available year round.

The Canada Student Employment Guide

MARK ANTHONY GROUP INC.

1750 75th Ave. W., Suite 210
Vancouver, British Columbia, V6P 6G2
Tel: (604) 263-9994   Fax: (604) 263-9913

Gina Repole, Recruiter

Mark Anthony Group is involved in the production, sales and marketing, and distribution of wine, refreshment beverages and beer. The company employs over 350 people throughout Canada and the U.S., with its head office in Vancouver, BC.

Academic Fields
College: General, Accounting, Administration, Business, Communications, Computer Science, Graphic Arts, Human Resources, Marketing/Sales
Bachelor of Arts: General, Business
Bachelor of Comm/Admin: General, Accounting, Finance, Marketing, Info Mgmt.
Bachelor of Science: General
Bachelor of Engineering: General

Critical Skills
Adaptable, Good Communication, Confident, Creative, Dependable, Diplomatic, Enthusiastic, Flexible, Innovative, Leadership, Organized, Personable, Professional

Types of Positions
Administrative Assistant   Entry Level Accounting
Sales Representative

Starting Salary
$ 20,000 - 30,000

Company Benefits
- Solid benefit package
- Medical and dental
- Out of house training, recognition program

Correspondence
Mail resume with cover letter
E-mail: hr@markanthony.com

Part Time/Summer: Mark Anthony Group regularly looks for candidates for part time and summer employment opportunities. Potential work in the summer includes sales representative.

MARKS & SPENCER CANADA INC.

Yorkdale Place, 1 Yorkdale Road, Suite 300
Toronto, Ontario, M6A 3A1
Tel: (416) 782-1910   Fax: (416) 782-6991

Human Resources

Marks & Spencer is a family clothing and food specialty merchandiser operating 42 stores across Canada. Established in Canada in 1972, the department store is a subsidiary of Marks & Spencer plc, of the United Kingdom. Marks & Spencer employs over 700 people across the country, with the majority of these individuals working in a part time capacity.

Academic Fields
College: General, Business, Marketing/Sales
Bachelor of Arts: Business, Public Relations
Bachelor of Comm/Admin: Marketing

Critical Skills
Adaptable, Decisive, Dependable, Diplomatic, Efficient, Enthusiastic, Flexible, Good Communication, Organized, Professional, Responsible

Types of Positions
Part Time Sales Associate   Associate Manager

Starting Salary
below $ 20,000 (part time),
up to $ 20,000 - $ 25,000 (full time)

Company Benefits
- Benefits include group life insurance, medical plan, and pension
- Long term disability and employee discount
- Part time benefits include employee discount and optional membership of pension plan

Correspondence
Apply directly to the store where you wish to work by submitting your resume or completing an application form

Part Time/Summer: Marks & Spencer Canada sometimes hires for part time openings and summer opportunities. Potential positions include part time sales associate.

MARK'S WORK WAREHOUSE

2625 Weston Rd.
North York, Ontario, M9N 3V8
Tel: (416) 241-9305   Fax: (416) 241-8944

Donna Lodu, Human Resources
Internet: www.marks.com

Mark's Work Warehouse is a specialty retail clothing store, selling both work and casual clothing for men. The store also has a small ladies wear department. The company's head office is in North York, Ontario.

Academic Fields
No specific academic background is required. They will look at candidates from all academic backgrounds.

Critical Skills
Adaptable, Dependable, Enthusiastic, Flexible, Good Communication, Innovative, Leadership, Organized, Patient, Personable, Customer Oriented

Types of Positions
Sales Associate
Sales and Product Manager
Associate Store Operator

Starting Salary
below $ 20,000 - 25,000

Company Benefits
- Competitive health and dental plans for permanent staff
- Employee discount on merchandise
- Bonus and incentive programs

Correspondence
Mail, fax, submit resume and cover letter in person

Part Time/Summer: Mark's Work Warehouse regularly looks for candidates for part time jobs, and occasionally seeks people for summer employment.

MARSHALL MACKLIN MONAGHAN LTD.

80 Commerce Valley Drive East
Thornhill, Ontario, L3T 7N4
Tel: (905) 882-1100   Fax: (905) 882-0055

Carolyn Philps, Human Resources Manager
Internet: www.mmm.ca

Established in 1952, Marshall Macklin Monaghan offers services to government and private clients with emphasis on consulting engineering, surveying, planning, project management and development. The firm has carried out assignments in the Caribbean, Africa, the Middle East, India, the Far East, Central America, South America, and the United States.

Academic Fields
College: Urban Planning, Accounting, Information Systems, Secretarial, CAD Autocad, Computer Science, Engineering Tech.
Bachelor of Arts: Urban Geography
Bachelor of Science: Biology, Environmental Studies
Bachelor of Engineering: Civil, Electrical, Environmental Studies, Mechanical, Transportation, Water Resources, Bach. of Landscape Architecture
Masters: Engineering

Critical Skills
Adaptable, Analytical, Confident, Dependable, Enthusiastic, Good Communication, Good With Figures, Good Writing Skills, Leadership, Logical, Organized, Personable, Productive, Professional

Types of Positions
Engineer In Training   Urban Planner
Civil Engineering Tech.   AutoCAD Operator
Designer   Secretary

Starting Salary
$ 30,000 - 40,000 (depending on the position)

Company Benefits
- Comprehensive benefits package

Correspondence
Mail or fax resume with cover letter
E-mail: philpsc@mmm.ca

Part Time/Summer: Marshall Macklin Monaghan sometimes hires for part time and summer work. Potential positions are surveying, designing/drafting, secretarial/word processing, civil engineering technologist in training. Apply from March until May.

The Canada Student Employment Guide

MARYSTOWN SHIPYARD LIMITED

P.O. Box 262
Marystown, Newfoundland, A0E 2M0
Tel: (709) 279-1200   Fax: (709) 279-1408

Human Resources

Marystown Shipyard Limited provides offshore and general industrial fabrication and shipbuilding. They are located in Marystown, Newfoundland.

Academic Fields
College: Accounting, Computer Science, Drafting/Architecture, Electronics Tech., Human Resources, Secretarial
Bachelor of Comm/Admin: Accounting, Finance, Info Mgmt.
Bachelor of Science: Computer Science
Bachelor of Engineering: Computer Systems, Electrical, Mechanical
Chartered Accounting: CA-Finance

Critical Skills
Adaptable, Flexible

Types of Positions
Accounting Clerk   Junior Accountant
Junior Programmer   Engineer
Technologist

Starting Salary
$ 25,000 - 30,000

Company Benefits
- Group insurance coverage
- Group RRSP, vacation, statutory holidays
- Some employer training initiatives

Correspondence
Mail or fax resume with cover letter

Part Time/Summer: Marystown Shipyard Limited occasionally hires for part time and summer employment. Potential jobs include accounting clerk, MIS programmer and systems, technical engineer and technologist.

MARYVALE ADOLESCENT AND FAMILY SERVICES

3640 Wells St.
Windsor, Ontario, N9C 1T9
Tel: (519) 258-0484   Fax: (519) 258-0488

Program Manager

Maryvale Adolescent and Family Services is a children's mental health centre which helps young people towards a better tomorrow. The centre is located in Windsor, Ontario.

Academic Fields
College: Child Care
Bachelor of Arts: Psychology, Sociology/Social Work
Bachelor of Education: General, Special

Critical Skills
Adaptable, Analytical, Decisive, Dependable, Diligent, Diplomatic, Efficient, Enthusiastic, Flexible, Good Communication, Good Writing Skills, Organized, Patient, Personable, Productive, Professional, Responsible

Types of Positions
Relief Child and Youth Worker
Part Time Child and Youth Worker

Starting Salary
$ 30,000 - 40,000

Company Benefits
- Comprehensive benefit package
- Dental, pension, extended medical
- Comprehensive training curriculum

Correspondence
Mail, fax or e-mail resume with cover letter
E-mail: maryvale@wincom.net

Part Time/Summer: Maryvale Adolescent and Family Services regularly looks for candidates for part time or summer employment opportunities. The best time to apply is Early Spring.

The Canada Student Employment Guide

MATROX ELECTRONIC SYSTEMS LTD.

1055, boul St-Regis
Dorval, Quebec, H9P 2T4
Tel: (514) 822-6000   Fax: (514) 822-6274

Patrick Chayer, Recruiting Specialist
Internet: www.matrox.com

Over the last 24 years Matrox has taken its place as leader and innovator in today's hottest, most state-of-the-art technologies - computer graphics, image processing, video and multimedia, and networking.

Academic Fields
College: Administration, Communications, Human Res., Info Syst., Marketing/Sales, Purchasing, Automotive Maintenance, CAD Autocad, Computer Sci., Electronics Tech., Engineering Tech., Graphic Arts, Legal Assistant
Bachelor of Arts: English, Journalism, Languages, Public Relations
Bachelor of Comm/Admin: General, Accounting, Human Resources, Marketing, Info Mgmt.
Bachelor of Science: Computer Science
Bachelor of Laws: General, Corporate
Bachelor of Engineering: Computer Systems, Electrical
Masters: Engineering

Critical Skills
Analytical, Confident, Dependable, Diplomatic, Efficient, Flexible, Good Communication, Good Writing Skills, Innovative, Logical, Manual Dexterity, Organized, Patient, Productive, Responsible

Types of Positions
Sales & Marketing Coord.   Analyst Programmer
Legal Assistant   Electronic Technician
Hardware Designer   Software Designer

Starting Salary
Depends on position

Company Benefits
- Competitive salaries with annual salary reviews

Correspondence
Fax, e-mail resume with cover letter or apply through web site. E-mail: personnel@matrox.com

Part Time/Summer: Matrox Electronic Systems Ltd. occasionally hires for part time work and regularly hires for the summer. The best time to apply is in January.

Co-op/Internship: Matrox takes in about 300 students a year and has built strong ties with univ. and colleges.

MAXXAM ANALYTICS INC.

5540 McAdam Rd.
Mississauga, Ontario, L4Z 1P1
Tel: (905) 890-2555   Fax: (905) 890-0370

Randall Helander, Corp. HR Manager
Internet: www.maxxam.ca

Maxxam Analytics Inc. is one of the largest, multi-disciplinary, independent analytical service companies in Canada. Maxxam conducts over 5 million tests annually in the environmental, industrial, pharmaceutical and food industries. The company operates modern laboratory facilities in 10 Canadian cities and employs more than 600 highly trained people.

Academic Fields
College: Accounting, Information Systems, Laboratory Tech.
Bachelor of Science: Biology, Chemistry, Environmental Studies, Microbiology
Masters: Science

Critical Skills
Efficient, Flexible, Organized, Responsible

Types of Positions
Lab Technician   Microbiologist
Scientist

Starting Salary
$ 20,000 - 25,000

Company Benefits
- Comprehensive benefits including group RRSP
- Opportunity to be trained on state-of-the-art instrumentation

Correspondence
E-mail resume with cover letter or apply through web site. E-mail: hr@on.maxxam.ca

Part Time/Summer: Maxxam Analytics Inc. regularly hires for part time and summer employment. A potential job would be a lab technician. The best time to apply is in April or May.

The Canada Student Employment Guide

MCBEE SYSTEMS OF CANADA INC.

179 Bartley Dr.
Toronto, Ontario, M4A 1E8
Tel: (416) 751-6120   Fax: (416) 751-3029

Peter Ruggiero, Manager Human Resources
Internet: www.mcbee-systems.com

McBee Systems of Canada is a business forms producer and printer. They work with one-write bookkeeping systems. The company employs approximately 200 individuals.

Academic Fields
College: General, Accounting, Administration, Advertising, Business, Communications, Computer Science, Drafting/Architecture, Human Resources, Marketing/Sales, Mechanical Tech.
Bachelor of Arts: General, Business, Fine Arts
Bachelor of Comm/Admin: General, Accounting, Finance, Marketing
Bachelor of Science: General, Computer Science
Bachelor of Engineering: Computer Systems, Industrial, Mechanical
Masters: Business Administration, Arts

Critical Skills
Adaptable, Analytical, Artistic, Good Communication, Confident, Creative, Decisive, Dependable, Diligent, Diplomatic, Efficient, Enthusiastic, Flexible, Good With Figures, Innovative, Leadership, Logical, Manual Dexterity, Organized, Patient, Personable, Persuasive, Productive, Professional, Responsible, Good Writing Skills

Types of Positions
Manufacturing   Sales and Marketing
Human Resources   Finance and Administration

Starting Salary
$ 20,000 - 25,000

Company Benefits
- Standard health and dental

Correspondence
Mail resume with cover letter

Part Time/Summer: McBee Systems of Canada occasionally seeks individuals for part time and summer employment. Potential jobs include temporary office and plant duties. The best time to apply is in May.

MCCARNEY GREENWOOD

1300 Central Pkwy. W., Suite 300
Mississauga, Ontario, L5C 4G8
Tel: (905) 276-3891   Fax: (905) 896-8959

R. Dinshaw, Human Resources

McCarney Greenwood is a chartered accounting firm that is involved in public accounting including audits, review engagements, compilations, tax returns and consulting services.

Academic Fields
College: Accounting, Business
Bachelor of Arts: General, Business, Economics
Bachelor of Comm/Admin: General, Accounting, Finance
Bachelor of Science: General
Masters: Business Administration

Critical Skills
Analytical, Good Communication, Good With Figures, Organized, Personable, Professional, Good Writing Skills

Types of Positions
Student-In-Accounts

Starting Salary
$ 33,000

Company Benefits
- Medical and dental plan
- 2 weeks paid vacation
- In-house training

Correspondence
Mail resume with cover letter

Part Time/Summer: McCarney Greenwood does not hire individuals for part time or summer employment. Summer is generally slow, thus don't hire students. Co-op students are sometimes sought from January through to April.

Co-op/Internship: Co-op opportunities for students in accounting programs.

MCGRAW HILL RYERSON LTD.

300 Water Street
Whitby, Ontario, L1N 9B6
Tel: (905) 430-5049   Fax: (905) 430-5227

Nancy Pavlakovich, Human Resources
Internet: www.mcgrawhill.ca

McGraw Hill Ryerson Ltd. is a publishing company made up of three revenue divisions - higher education, school and trade, professional and medical. The firm has more than 1,000 Canadian produced books in print representing about 800 authors. They employ 290 individuals.

Academic Fields
College: Accounting, Business, Graphic Arts, Human Resources, Marketing/Sales, Secretarial, Book & Magazine Publishing
Bachelor of Arts: English, History, Languages
Bachelor of Comm/Admin: Accounting, Finance, Marketing, Info Mgmt.
Bachelor of Science: Geography, Mathematics
Chartered Accounting: CA-Finance, CGA-Finance
Degrees in other fields may also be suitable.

Critical Skills
Creative, Enthusiastic, Good Communication, Innovative, Professional, Team Player, Customer Focus, Integrity & Values, Continuous Learning

Types of Positions
Sales Representative	Direct Marketing Co-ordinator
Marketing Assistant	Accounting Clerk
Editorial Assistant	Other Clerical

Starting Salary
$ 28,000 - 32,000

Company Benefits
- Flexible benefit plan with health and dental
- Life insurance, long term disability, spousal life

Correspondence
Mail or fax resume with cover letter
E-mail: nancyp@mcgrawhill.ca

Part Time/Summer: McGraw Hill Ryerson occasionally hires for part time and summer jobs. In the summer, potential jobs are in the warehouse, mail room, or involve maintenance. Very occasionally positions become available in the office. Apply early in May.

Co-op/Internship: Internship opportunities occasionally become available.

McINNES COOPER & ROBERTSON

1601 Lower Water St., P.O. Box 730
Halifax, Nova Scotia, B3J 2V1
Tel: (902) 425-6500   Fax: (902) 425-6350

Cathy Roberts, HR Coordinator
Internet: www.mcrlaw.com

McInnes Cooper & Robertson is a law firm with a total of 150 employees, partners and associates. Support staff positions within the company are most likely to be that of legal secretary. However, the firm sometimes hires for some accounting, administrative and computer positions.

Academic Fields
College: Accounting, Administration, Information Systems, Secretarial, Legal Assistant
Bachelor of Arts: Business, Criminology
Bachelor of Comm/Admin: General, Accounting, Info Mgmt.
Bachelor of Laws: General, Corporate, Real Estate, Labour

Critical Skills
Adaptable, Analytical, Confident, Creative, Decisive, Diligent, Diplomatic, Efficient, Enthusiastic, Flexible, Good Communication, Good With Figures, Good Writing Skills, Organized, Personable, Productive, Professional, Responsible

Types of Positions
Receptionist	Junior Legal Secretary
Accounting Clerk	Mail Room Clerk

Starting Salary
$ 20,000 - 25,000

Company Benefits
- Full benefits to full time employees only

Correspondence
Mail, fax or e-mail resume with cover letter

Part Time/Summer: McInnes Cooper & Robertson rarely hires for part time work, but regularly seeks individuals for summer employment opportunities. Positions include mail room relief or secretarial coverage. The best time to apply is in May.

MCKAY-COCKER CONSTRUCTION LIMITED

1665 Oxford St. E., P.O. Box 4037
London, Ontario, N5W 5H3
Tel: (519) 451-5270   Fax: (519) 451-8050

Office Manager
Internet: www.mckaycocker.com

McKay-Cocker is a general contractor involved in industrial and commercial building. The company's construction management team has become recognized in the industry for its thorough pre-construction services on all types of projects. Their ability to provide design coordination, budget control and advice on constructability issues has resulted in more and more contracts from successful pre-construction services.

Academic Fields
College: Accounting, Computer Science, Drafting/Architecture, Engineering Tech., Secretarial
Bachelor of Comm/Admin: Accounting
Bachelor of Engineering: General, Design
Chartered Accounting: CMA-General
Masters: Business Administration

Critical Skills
Adaptable, Confident, Creative, Enthusiastic, Good With Figures, Good Writing Skills, Organized, Professional

Types of Positions
Various Positions

Starting Salary
$ 20,000 - 25,000

Company Benefits
- Pension plan
- Upgrade of computer skills
- Stress seminars

Correspondence
Mail resume with cover letter
E-mail: info@mckaycocker.com

Part Time/Summer: McKay-Cocker Construction Limited occasionally looks for individuals for part time and summer positions. Potential jobs are secretarial or accounting in nature. The best time to apply is in May or June.

MCLAREN-MCCANN ADVERTISING OF CANADA LTD.

10 Bay St., Suite 1300
Toronto, Ontario, M5J 2S3
Tel: (416) 594-6000   Fax: (416) 643-7030

Human Resources Dept.

McLaren-McCann Advertising of Canada is a full service advertising agency in Toronto. The firm employs approximately 140 individuals who work in many different fields.

Academic Fields
College: Advertising, Graphic Arts, Marketing/Sales, Television/Radio
Bachelor of Arts: General, Business, Economics, Journalism
Bachelor of Comm/Admin: General, Marketing
Bachelor of Science: Computer Science
Masters: Business Administration, Arts

Critical Skills
Adaptable, Good Communication, Confident, Creative, Dependable, Innovative, Organized, Personable, Responsible, Good Writing Skills

Types of Positions
Media Estimator   Account Coordinator
Junior Copywriter   Administration Assistant

Starting Salary
Varies depending on position

Company Benefits
- Full group health benefits for full time employees
- Training is limited

Correspondence
Mail resume with cover letter

Part Time/Summer: McLaren-McCann Advertising of Canada occasionally seeks candidates for part time or summer employment. Jobs in the summer involve administrative positions such as reception, secretarial, or the mail room.

MCMILLAN & ASSOCIATES INC.

541 Sussex Drive, 3rd Floor
Ottawa, Ontario, K1N 6Z6
Tel: (613) 789-1234   Fax: (613) 789-2255

Nancy Henry, Controller
Internet: www.thinkup.com

McMillan & Associates Inc. is a full service design, advertising, writing, marketing and web design firm. The company has an employee base of 44 individuals.

Academic Fields
College: Administration, Business, Communications, Human Resources, Animation, Graphic Arts
Bachelor of Arts: Public Relations
Bachelor of Comm/Admin: Marketing

Critical Skills
Adaptable, Artistic, Creative, Dependable, Efficient, Good Communication, Good Writing Skills, Personable, Responsible

Types of Positions
Administration   Production Artist
Junior Designer   Junior Web Developer

Starting Salary
$ 30,000 - 35,000

Company Benefits
- Standard insurance (health and dental)

Correspondence
E-mail resume with cover letter

Part Time/Summer: McMillan & Associates Inc. rarely hires for part time or summer employment.

MDS NORDION

447 March Rd.
Kanata, Ontario, K2K 1X8
Tel: (613) 592-3400   Fax: (613) 592-9117

Anabela Santos, Recruiter
Internet: www.mds.nordion.com

MDS Nordion is a leader in setting standards for working with radioactive materials.

Academic Fields
College: CAD Autocad, Computer Science, Electronics Tech., Engineering Tech., Mechanical Tech., Welding
Bachelor of Arts: Business
Bachelor of Comm/Admin: Human Resources, Marketing, Info Mgmt.
Bachelor of Science: Chemistry, Computer Science, Health Sciences, Microbiology, Physics
Bachelor of Engineering: Biomedical, Chemical, Computer Syst., Electrical, Materials Sci., Mechanical
Masters: Business Admin., Science, Engineering

Critical Skills
Adaptable, Analytical, Creative, Dependable, Efficient, Enthusiastic, Flexible, Good Communication, Innovative, Logical, Organized, Patient, Personable

Types of Positions
Lab Assistant   Administration Assistant
HR Generalist   Technologist
Quality Control Technician   Computer Operator

Starting Salary
Varies depending on position

Company Benefits
- Competitive benefit package, medical, dental

Correspondence
Apply through web site
E-mail: careers@mds.nordion.com

Part Time/Summer: MDS Nordion occasionally looks for individuals for part time work, and regularly seeks candidates for the summer. Potential jobs include technician (life science, engineering, or computer), clerical/administrative, engineering (mechanical and electrical). The best time to apply is starting in February.

MEDIACOM INC.

377 Horner Ave.
Etobicoke, Ontario, M8W 1Z6
Tel: (416) 255-1392   Fax: (416) 255-2063

Human Resources Department
Internet: www.mediacom.ca

Mediacom is an out-of-home advertising company owned by Infinity Outdoor of the U.S. Mediacom sells advertising space to individuals, businesses and other enterprises coast-to-coast and also provides production service for ad campaigns. This out of home company employs approximately 400 people across the country.

Academic Fields
College: Accounting, Business, Human Resources, Marketing/Sales, Secretarial
Bachelor of Comm/Admin: Accounting
Chartered Accounting: CA-General, CMA-Finance, CGA-Finance

Critical Skills
Adaptable, Good Communication, Decisive, Dependable, Diligent, Diplomatic, Efficient, Enthusiastic, Flexible, Innovative, Leadership, Organized, Personable, Productive, Professional, Responsible, Good Writing Skills

Types of Positions
Client Service   Accounting

Starting Salary
$ 25,000 - 30,000

Company Benefits
- Health, dental, insurance, pension

Correspondence
Mail, fax or e-mail resume with cover letter

Part Time/Summer: Mediacom Industries does not hire for part time opportunities, but sometimes hires for summer employment. Potential positions involve construction and general labour. The best time to apply is in April.

MEDIASYNERGY

260 King St. E., Building C
Toronto, Ontario, M5A 1K3
Tel: (416) 369-1100   Fax: (416) 369-9037

Mark Orlow, Human Resources
Internet: www.mediasynergy.com

Mediasynergy is a software development company focused on Email Business Solutions. Its flagship product, The FLO NETWORK, enables clients to communicate with millions of email subscribers at a touch of a button. The software is able to track, personalize and deploy up to 1 million emails per hour. They have approximately 50 employees.

Academic Fields
College: Administration, Communications, Information Systems, Marketing/Sales, Computer Science, Engineering Tech.
Bachelor of Arts: Business, Public Relations
Bachelor of Comm/Admin: Marketing, Info Mgmt.
Bachelor of Science: Computer Sciences, Mathematics
Bachelor of Engineering: Computer Systems
Masters: Business Administration, Science, Engineering

Critical Skills
Confident, Decisive, Dependable, Diligent, Efficient, Enthusiastic, Flexible, Good Communication, Innovative, Leadership, Organized, Personable, Responsible

Types of Positions
Client Services Account Associate   Technical Services
Software Development

Starting Salary
$ 30,000 - 50,000

Company Benefits
- Full medical, health and dental
- Stock options, RRSP matching of $1,000

Correspondence
E-mail resume with cover letter
E-mail: hresources@mediasynergy.com

Part Time/Summer: Mediasynergy regularly looks for candidates for part time and summer positions. Potential jobs are in the operations group, or software development. The best time to apply is in April or May.

MEDICAL LABORATORIES OF WINDSOR LIMITED

1428 Ouellette Ave., Suite 201
Windsor, Ontario, N8X 1K4
Tel: (519) 258-1991   Fax: (519) 258-9505

William Yee, Human Resources

Medical Laboratories of Windsor is involved in the collection and testing of medical laboratory specimens. The company employs about 85 individuals.

Academic Fields
College: Electronics Tech., Nursing
Bachelor of Comm/Admin: Accounting, Finance
Bachelor of Science: Biology, Chemistry, Computer Science, Health Sciences, Microbiology, Nursing (RN)

Critical Skills
Adaptable, Good Communication, Confident, Dependable, Diligent, Innovative, Organized, Productive

Types of Positions
Various Positions

Starting Salary
$ 20,000 - 25,000

Company Benefits
- Complete benefit package

Correspondence
Fax resume with cover letter

Part Time/Summer: Medical Laboratories of Windsor regularly seeks candidates for part time and summer positions. Potential jobs include clerical duties, computer work, or phlebotomist (person that takes blood from individuals).

MEMOTEC COMMUNICATIONS INC.

600 rue McCaffrey
Saint Laurent, Québec, H4T 1N1
Tel: (514) 738-4781   Fax: (514) 738-4436

Sandra Aguzzi, Human Resources
Internet: www.memotec.com

Memotec Communications is involved in the telecommunications industry focusing on frame relay, packet switching CAN/WAN connectivity products. They design and produce a wide range of communications products for voice and the multimedia marketplace.

Academic Fields
College: Electronics Tech.
Bachelor of Comm/Admin: Accounting, Finance, Marketing, Info Mgmt.
Bachelor of Engineering: Design, Electrical
Chartered Accounting: CA-Finance
Masters: Business Administration, Science, Engineering

Critical Skills
Adaptable, Analytical, Confident, Diplomatic, Efficient, Enthusiastic, Flexible, Good Communication, Good With Figures, Good Writing Skills, Innovative, Leadership, Organized, Productive, Professional, Responsible

Types of Positions
Various Positions

Starting Salary
$ 30,000 - 40,000 (depending on education and experience)

Company Benefits
- Full range of benefits including medical and dental
- Life insurance, long term disability, tuition reimbursement
- Training available in-house

Correspondence
Mail, fax, or e-mail resume with cover letter
E-mail: aguzzis@memotec.com

Part Time/Summer: Memotec Communications occasionally seeks individuals for part time and summer employment. Some areas students may be hired for include clerical, finance, or production. The best time to apply is in May.

The Canada Student Employment Guide

METRO RICHELIEU INC.

11011 boul Maurice Duplessis
Montréal, Québec, H1C 1V6
Tel: (514) 643-1000   Fax: (514) 613-1030

Ressources humaines
www.metro-richelieu.com

Metro Richelieu is a large grocery wholesaler in the Province of Québec. The company's ownership is widely held, and the firm employs over 6,200 people across the province. Metro Richelieu's head office is located in Montréal, Québec.

Academic Fields
College: General, Administration, Computer Science, Faculty Management, Food/Nutrition, Law Clerk
Bachelor of Comm/Admin: General, Accounting, Finance, Marketing, Info Mgmt.
Bachelor of Science: Computer Science
Bachelor of Engineering: General
Chartered Accounting: CA - General/Finance, CGA/CMA - General/Finance
Masters: Business Administration

Critical Skills
Adaptable, Analytical, Decisive, Dependable, Leadership, Logical, Persuasive, Productive

Types of Positions
Various positions

Starting Salary
$ 25,000 - 30,000

Company Benefits
- Compete benefit package
- Reimbursement of education costs

Correspondence
Mail resume with cover letter

Part Time/Summer: Metro Richelieu regularly looks for candidates for part time and summer employment. A potential job would be an office clerk. The best time to apply is in March.

METRO TORONTO CONVENTION CENTRE

255 Front Street West
Toronto, Ontario, M5V 2W6
Tel: (416) 585-8000   Fax: (416) 585-8262

Joelle Orban, Assistant Director, Human Resources
Internet: www.mtccc.com

The Metro Toronto Convention Centre is a full service facility offering convention and show services to individuals, businesses and other enterprises. In the heart of downtown Toronto, the Convention Centre employs over 1,000 individuals to work at this location. Most of those employed with the Convention Centre work in casual, call-in positions.

Academic Fields
College: General, Accounting, Administration, Business, Communications, Cooking/Culinary, Faculty Management, Food/Nutrition, Hospitality, Human Resources, Marketing/Sales, Secretarial, Security/Law, Travel/Tourism
Bachelor of Arts: General, Business, English, Journalism, Psychology
Bachelor of Comm/Admin: General, Accounting, Marketing, Info Mgmt.
Chartered Accounting: CA-General, CGA-General

Critical Skills
Adaptable, Good Communication, Confident, Diplomatic, Enthusiastic, Flexible, Good Writing Skills, Personable, Responsible

Types of Positions
Secretarial	Cooks
Event Services	Steward Helpers
Accounting Clerk	Concessions

Starting Salary
$ 30,000 - 35,000

Company Benefits
- Full dental and medical
- Pension plan
- Education assistance programs

Correspondence
Mail or fax resume with cover letter

Part Time/Summer: The Metro Toronto Convention Centre does not hire for part time or summer work. However, they regularly hire for casual work.

METRO TORONTO WEST DETENTION CENTRE
111 Disco Road
Rexdale, Ontario, M9W 5L6
Tel: (416) 675-1806   Fax: (416) 674-7515

Mike Conry, Superintendent

The Metro Toronto West Detention Centre is a correctional services facility located in Etobicoke. Operating under the Ontario Ministry of Correctional Services, The Detention Centre employs almost 500 people to work in various sectors. Some of these individuals are currently employed on a part time basis. Mail resume and cover letter to the Attention: Business Administrator.

Academic Fields
College: Nursing, Recreation Studies, Science, Security/Law
Bachelor of Arts: Psychology, Sociology/Social Work
Bachelor of Science: Nursing (RN)
Bachelor of Education: Physical
Masters: Social Work

Critical Skills
Confident, Decisive, Dependable, Good Communication, Professional, Leadership, Persuasive, Good Writing Skills

Types of Positions
Correctional Officer   Nurse
Switchboard   Receptionist
Filing Clerk

Starting Salary
$ 20,000 - 25,000

Company Benefits
- Extensive medical and dental package
- 9 weeks training the first year for correctional staff
- 3 weeks vacation after first year

Correspondence
Mail resume with cover letter
E-mail: mike.conry@jus.gov.on.ca

Part Time/Summer: The Metro Toronto West Detention Centre does not hire any additional staff on a part time basis. Potential summer positions are sometimes available. They are mostly clerical and are usually placed by Jobs Ontario in the business office, records dept., health care dept., or classification dept.

METROLAND PRINTING, PUBLISHING & DISTRIBUTING LTD.
3125 Wolfdale Road
Mississauga, Ontario, L5C 1W1
Tel: (905) 279-0440   Fax: (905) 279-5103

Human Resources Department
Internet: www.metroland.com

Metroland Printing Publishing and Distributing was formed in 1981 following the amalgamation of Inland Publishing and Metrospan Publishing. It is the publisher of 59 community newspapers and the major distributor of flyers and product samples in greater Toronto and south-central Ontario.

Academic Fields
College: Accounting, Administration, Advertising, Electronics Tech., Graphic Arts, Human Resources, Journalism, Marketing/Sales, Photography
Bachelor of Arts: Business, Journalism
Bachelor of Comm/Admin: Accounting
Chartered Accounting: CA-Finance, CMA-Finance, CGA-Finance

Critical Skills
Adaptable, Analytical, Creative, Dependable, Efficient, Enthusiastic, Flexible, Good Communication, Innovative, Persuasive, Personable, Productive, Manual Dexterity

Types of Positions
Reporter   Advertising Sales Rep.
Accounting Clerk   Human Resources Clerk
Keyboard Operator   Computer Artist

Starting Salary
$ 20,000 - 30,000 (depends on job)

Company Benefits
- All health and dental
- Vision and various insurance plans
- Life insurance, accidental death

Correspondence
Mail or fax resume with cover letter

Part Time/Summer: Metroland Printing, Publishing & Distributing sometimes acquires individuals for part time work, and regularly hires for summer opportunities. Positions in the summer include classified representative, reporter, press operator, and general clerical help. The best time to apply is in the Spring.

The Canada Student Employment Guide

METROPOLITAN LIFE INSURANCE COMPANY

2235 Sheppard Avenue East, Suite 1702
North York, Ontario, M2J 5B5
Tel: (416) 493-1844 Fax: (416) 494-5288

Tamara Humphries, Assistant Sales Manager
Internet: www.metlife.ca

Metropolitan Life is the largest life insurer in North America in terms of life insurance in-force. MetLife has operations throughout the world, with 41,000 associates worldwide, including 2,600 in Canada.

Academic Fields
College: General, Accounting, Administration, Advertising, Business, Communications, Hospitality, Human Resources, Insurance, Law Clerk, Marketing/Sales, Performing Arts, Recreation Studies
Bachelor of Arts: General, Business, Economics, English, Gerontology, Journalism, Languages, Philosophy, Political Science, Psychology, Public Relations, Recreation Studies, Sociology/Social Work
Bachelor of Comm/Admin: General, Accounting, Finance, Marketing, Public Admin.
Bachelor of Science: General, Actuarial, Health Sciences, Kinesiology, Nursing (RN), Occupational Therapy, Physiotherapy, Psychology
Bachelor of Laws: Corporate
Bachelor of Engineering: General
Bachelor of Education: General, Adult Education, Physical, Special
Chartered Accounting: CA - General/Finance, CGA/CMA - General/Finance
Masters: Business Administration, Education

Critical Skills
Adaptable, Good Communication, Confident, Decisive, Dependable, Diligent, Diplomatic, Efficient, Enthusiastic, Flexible, Good With Figures, Innovative, Leadership, Productive, Professional, Responsible, Writing Skills

Types of Positions
Financial Advisor   Sales Person

Starting Salary
$ 30,000 - over 50,000

Company Benefits
- Complete benefits program

Correspondence
Mail or fax resume with cover letter

Part Time/Summer: Metropolitan Life does not hire individuals for part time or summer employment.

MEYERS NORRIS PENNY & CO.

1401 Princess Ave.
Brandon, Manitoba, R7A 7L7
Tel: (204) 727-0661 Fax: (204) 571-7126

Recruitment Coordinator
Internet: www.mnp.ca

Meyers Norris Penny & Co. is one of the top ten chartered accountancy and business advisory firms in Canada. The firm has more than 800 team members from 27 full and 27 part time offices across Manitoba, Saskatchewan, and Alberta.

Academic Fields
College: Accounting, Administration, Business, Human Resources, Information Systems, Marketing/Sales, Agricultural, Computer Science
Bachelor of Arts: Bus., Economics, Psychology, Stats
Bachelor of Comm/Admin: Accounting, Finance, Human Resources, Marketing, Info Mgmt.
Bachelor of Science: Agriculture, Computer Science
Bachelor of Laws: Corporate
Chartered Accounting: CA, CGA, CMA
Masters: Business Administration

Critical Skills
Adaptable, Analytical, Confident, Creative, Dependable, Efficient, Enthusiastic, Good Communication, Good Communication, Good With Figures, Good Writing Skills, Professional, Professional

Types of Positions
Articling Student   Accounting Technician
Information Technology   Business Advisory Serv.
Financial Advisory Services

Starting Salary
$ 25,000 - 30,000 (depends on job for CA students)

Company Benefits
- Flexible benefits including medical, vision, dental

Correspondence
E-mail resume & cover letter. E-mail: careers@mnp.ca

Part Time/Summer: Meyers Norris Penny & Co. occasionally hires for part time work and regularly hires in the summer.

Co-op/Internship: Placements for co-op students are available in accordance with academic institution guidelines.

The Canada Student Employment Guide

MICHAELS OF CANADA INC.

1650 Victoria St. E.
Whitby, Ontario, L1N 9L4
Tel: (905) 438-1750   Fax: N/A

John Garner, Human Resources
Internet: www.michaels.com

Michaels of Canada is an arts and crafts retail company called 'Michaels'. The firm has an employee base of approximately 575 individuals.

Academic Fields
College: Accounting, Administration, Advertising, Business, Communications, Computer Science, Faculty Mgmt., Graphic Arts, Hospitality, Human Resources, Marketing/Sales, Photography, Secretarial, Television/Radio
Bachelor of Arts: Business, Economics, Public Relations
Bachelor of Comm/Admin: Accounting, Finance, Marketing, Info Mgmt., Public Admin.
Bachelor of Science: Computer Science
Bachelor of Laws: Corporate, Real Estate
Bachelor of Engineering: Computer Systems, Design
Chartered Accounting: CA - General/Finance, CGA/CMA - General/Finance
Masters: Business Administration, Arts, Engineering

Critical Skills
Adaptable, Analytical, Artistic, Good Communication, Confident, Creative, Dependable, Diligent, Diplomatic, Efficient, Enthusiastic, Flexible, Innovative, Leadership, Logical, Organized, Patient, Personable, Persuasive, Productive, Professional, Responsible, Good Writing Skills

Types of Positions
Buyer/Assistant   Store Associate

Starting Salary
below $ 20,000

Company Benefits
- Depends on position

Correspondence
Mail or fax resume with cover letter

Part Time/Summer: Michaels of Canada occasionally seeks people for part time and summer positions. Potential jobs include general person Friday (filing, data, entry, phones, faxing). The best time to apply is in mid April.

MIDLAND WALWYN INC.

22 Front Street West
Toronto, Ontario, M5J 2W5
Tel: (416) 681-4808   Fax: (416) 681-4821

Human Resources

Midland Walwyn has 3,240 employees, including 1,275 financial advisors, and 116 retail branch offices throughout Canada. Midland Walwyn also has offices in four other countries.

Academic Fields
College: General, Accounting, Administration, Business, Communications, Computer Science, Engineering Tech., Faculty Management, Human Resources, Insurance, Law Clerk, Marketing/Sales, Secretarial
Bachelor of Arts: General, Business, Economics
Bachelor of Comm/Admin: General, Accounting, Finance, Marketing
Bachelor of Science: Computer Science
Bachelor of Engineering: Computer Syst., Design
Chartered Accounting: CA - General/Finance, CMA-Finance, CGA-Finance
Masters: Business Administration, Engineering

Critical Skills
Adaptable, Analytical, Good Communication, Confident, Creative, Decisive, Dependable, Diligent, Diplomatic, Efficient, Enthusiastic, Flexible, Good With Figures, Innovative, Leadership, Logical, Organized, Professional, Responsible, Good Writing Skills

Types of Positions
Client Service Representative   Data Entry Clerk
Administrative Assistant   RRSP Administrator

Starting Salary
$ 20,000 - 30,000

Company Benefits
- Standard benefits, tuition reimbursement
- Learning library

Correspondence
Mail or fax resume with cover letter

Part Time/Summer: Midland Walwyn regularly looks for candidates for part time and summer employment opportunities. Potential jobs in the summer include mutual fund administrator, trading assistant, and help desk work for computer support. The best time to apply is in April.

MIDWEST FOOD PRODUCTS INC.

P.O. Box 70
Carberry, Manitoba, R0K 0H0
Tel: (204) 834-2136   Fax: (204) 834-3400

Bill Cairney, Human Resources

Midwest Food Products is a food manufacturer of high quality frozen and dry potato products. The company employs between 400 and 600 individuals that work within management or are union employees. Midwest Food Products is a corporation under Nestle Canada Inc. and Simplot Canada Limited.

Academic Fields
College: General, Accounting, Administration, Business, Computer Science, Drafting/Architecture, Electronics Tech., Engineering Tech., Human Resources, Lab Tech.
Bachelor of Arts: General, Business
Bachelor of Comm/Admin: General, Accounting, Finance, Info Mgmt.
Bachelor of Science: Agriculture, Computer Science, Food Sciences, Microbiology, Occupational Therapy
Bachelor of Engineering: General, Computer Systems, Electrical, Industrial, Mechanical, Water Resources
Bachelor of Education: General, Adult Education
Chartered Accounting: CA - General/Finance, CMA - General
Masters: Business Administration, Science, Engineering

Critical Skills
Adaptable, Analytical, Dependable, Good Writing Skills, Leadership, Organized, Personable, Professional, Responsible

Types of Positions
Labourer   Trades

Starting Salary
$ 20,000 - 40,000 (depending on position)

Company Benefits
- Pension plan, sick benefits
- Long term disability
- Trades training

Correspondence
Mail or fax resume with cover letter

Part Time/Summer: Midwest Food Products does not hire for part time positions, but sometimes seeks candidates for summer employment. Most jobs in the summer are labourer positions. The best time to apply is in March or April.

MILLWORK & BUILDING SUPPLIES LIMITED

1279 Simcoe St. N.
Oshawa, Ontario, L1G 4X1
Tel: (905) 728-6291   Fax: (905) 728-8589

Jacky Jordan, Assistant Manager

Millwork & Building Supplies is a home centre and lumber yard in Oshawa. The retail centre offers hardware and electrical products, paint and wallpaper, and door and windows. The firm employs about 185 people.

Academic Fields
No specific academic fields required.
They will look at individuals from all areas.

Critical Skills
Adaptable, Good Communication, Confident, Decisive, Dependable, Efficient, Enthusiastic, Flexible, Manual Dexterity, Organized, Patient, Personable, Productive, Professional, Responsible, Good Writing Skills,

Types of Positions
Yard Helper   Sales Personnel
Cashier

Starting Salary
below $ 20,000 - 25,000

Company Benefits
- Health and benefits for full time employees
- No benefits for part time staff
- Training program offered

Correspondence
Submit resume with cover letter in person

Part Time/Summer: Millwork & Building Supplies occasionally looks for individuals for part time work, and regularly seeks candidates for the summer. Potential jobs include sales personnel, yard help, and cashiers. The best time to apply is in April or May.

MILNE & CRAIGHEAD INC.

10123 99 Street
Edmonton, Alberta, T5J 3H1
Tel: (780) 890-4540   Fax: N/A

Human Resources

Milne & Craighead is a freight forwarding company with international trade services including customs brokerage, freight forwarding, customs consulting, warehousing, distribution, and transportation logistics.

Academic Fields
College: General, Accounting, Administration, Advertising, Human Resources
Bachelor of Arts: General
Bachelor of Comm/Admin: General, Accounting, Finance, Marketing, Info Mgmt.

Critical Skills
Creative, Dependable, Efficient, Enthusiastic, Good Communication, Good Writing Skills, Organized, Productive, Responsible

Types of Positions
Administrator
Receptionist
Data Entry
Release Coordinator
Accounts Receivable Clerk

Starting Salary
$ 25,000 - 30,000

Company Benefits
- Long and short term disability, life insurance
- Pension, group RRSP
- Educational training

Correspondence
Mail or fax resume with cover letter

Part Time/Summer: Milne & Craighead does not hire for part time positions, but occasionally seeks people for the summer months. Potential jobs include data entry or vacation relief.

MINAS BASIN PULP AND POWER COMPANY LTD.

P.O. Box 401
Hantsport, Nova Scotia, B0P 1P0
Tel: (902) 684-1313   Fax: (902) 684-1762

Janet Thomas, Human Resources Assistant
Internet: www.minas.ns.ca

Minas Basin Pulp and Power Company manufactures coreboard and linerboard products from 100% recycled material. The firm employs approximately 185 individuals.

Academic Fields
College: Accounting, Business, Computer Science, Electronics Tech., Engineering Tech., Mechanical Tech., Secretarial, Security/Law
Bachelor of Arts: Business
Bachelor of Comm/Admin: General, Accounting, Info Mgmt.
Bachelor of Science: Chemistry, Computer Science
Bachelor of Engineering: Chemical, Electrical, Industrial, Mechanical, Environment

Critical Skills
Adaptable, Analytical, Good Communication, Dependable, Diligent, Enthusiastic, Flexible, Good With Figures, Innovative, Logical, Organized, Personable, Professional, Responsible, Good Writing Skills

Types of Positions
Accounting Assistant
Engineer
General Labour
Apprentice Trades

Starting Salary
$ 20,000 - 25,000 (clerical), $35,000 - 45,000 (engineering)

Company Benefits
- All basic benefits offered by manufacturing firms
- Health, dental and pension

Correspondence
Submit resume with cover letter in person, along with transcript of school marks

Part Time/Summer: Minas Basin Pulp and Power Company occasionally looks for people for part time and summer positions. Potential jobs involve general labour, business, engineering, computer science or forestry. The best time to apply is in early Spring.

The Canada Student Employment Guide

MINISTRY OF NORTHERN DEVELOPMENT AND MINES
159 Cedar Street, Suite 702
Sudbury, Ontario, P3E 6A5
Tel: (705) 564-7940   Fax: (705) 564-7942

Lynne Martin, Human Resources

The Ministry of Northern Development and Mines is a provincial ministry with a mandate to stimulate the economic and social development of Northern Ontario and to ensure that the special needs of northerners are addressed by the government.

Academic Fields
College: General, Accounting, Administration, Communications, Computer Sci., Drafting/Architecture, Engineering Tech., Graphic Arts, Human Res., Lab Tech., Science, Secretarial
Bachelor of Arts: General, Economics, Public Relations
Bachelor of Comm/Admin: General, Accounting, Finance, Info Mgmt.
Bachelor of Science: General, Chemistry, Computer Science, Environmental Studies, Geology
Bachelor of Engineering: Geotechnical, Mining
Chartered Accounting: CA-General
Masters: Business Administration, Science, Engineering

Critical Skills
Adaptable, Analytical, Good Communication, Creative, Decisive, Dependable, Diligent, Diplomatic, Efficient, Responsible, Good Writing Skills

Types of Positions
Secretarial/Clerical   Accounts Payable
Accounts Receivable   Geological Assistant
Lab Technician   Drafter

Starting Salary
$ 25,000 - 30,000

Company Benefits
- Full benefits package for full time employees

Correspondence
Mail resume and cover letter

Part Time/Summer: They do not hire for part time work, but regularly hires for the summer. Potential positions involve clerical, secretarial and geological field work. The best time to apply is in April.

Co-op/Internship: Internship opportunities are available yearly.

MISERICORDIA GENERAL HOSPITAL
99 Cornish Avenue
Winnipeg, Manitoba, R3C 1A2
Tel: (204) 788-8152   Fax: (204) 783-6776

HR Coordinator

Misericordia Health Centre is a health care facility located in Winnipeg, that is owned and operated by Caritas Health Group. Established in 1905, the health centre has general medical and surgical facilities and offers services in various departments. Misericordia Health Centre has a total of 200 beds, and has an employee base of more than 2,000 individuals.

Academic Fields
College: Child Care, Food/Nutrition, Human Resources, Nursing
Bachelor of Arts: Gerontology, Recreation Studies
Bachelor of Comm/Admin: Accounting, Finance, Info Mgmt.
Bachelor of Science: Nursing (RN), Occupational Therapy, Physiotherapy
Chartered Accounting: CA-General

Critical Skills
Adaptable, Analytical, Good Communication, Confident, Creative, Decisive, Dependable, Diligent, Diplomatic, Efficient, Enthusiastic, Flexible, Good With Figures, Leadership, Logical, Manual Dexterity, Organized, Patient

Types of Positions
Housekeeping   Dietary

Starting Salary
$ 25,000 - 30,000

Company Benefits
- Blue Cross plan
- Dental plan, life insurance
- Pension plan

Correspondence
Mail, fax, submit resume and cover letter in person

Part Time/Summer: Misericordia General Hospital regularly seeks individuals for part time and summer employment opportunities. Potential positions include casual RN and dietary aide, or involve housekeeping duties.

CITY OF MISSISSAUGA

300 City Centre Dr., 5th Flr
Mississauga, Ontario, L5B 3C1
Tel: (905) 896-5035   Fax: (905) 615-4185

Human Resources
Internet: www.city.mississauga.on.ca

The City of Mississauga is a municipal government responsible for the formation of policy and laws in matters under its jurisdiction. The municipality employs approximately 4,100 people in total. More information can be found on their website.

Academic Fields
College: Computer Sci., Electronics Tech., Architectural Technology, Engineering Tech., Forestry, Human Resources, Mechanical Tech., Security, Secretarial
Bachelor of Arts: Urban Geography, Urban Planning
Bachelor of Science: Computer Science, Environ. Studies, Forestry, Geography, Horticulture
Bachelor of Laws: General, Real Estate
Bachelor of Engineering: Civil, Computer Systems, Electrical, Environmental Studies, Mechanical, Transportation, Water Resources

Critical Skills
Good Communication, Confident, Enthusiastic, Personable

Types of Positions
Reception/File Clerk   Assistant Inspector
Information Technology   Realty Services

Starting Salary
Depends on position

Company Benefits
- No benefits for students, part-timers or temp. staff

Correspondence
Mail, fax or submit resume with cover letter in person
E-mail: hr.info@city.mississauga.on.ca

Part Time/Summer: The City of Mississauga occasionally hires for part time work and regularly hires for the summer. Part time jobs are in libraries and community centres. Employment in the summer involves full time positions in parks maintenance, general office, junior engineering and recreation and parks. The best time to apply is in December or January.

Co-op/Internship: Eight month internships are available. They usually hire through universities for planning students.

MITCHELL'S GOURMET FOODS

Box 850
Saskatoon, Saskatchewan, S7K 3V4
Tel: (306) 382-2210   Fax: (306) 931-4296

Human Resources

Mitchell's Gourmet Foods is a value added meat processor including hog killing and cutting. They have approximately 1,300 unionized employees.

Academic Fields
No specific academic fields required.

Critical Skills
Adaptable, Dependable, Diligent, Efficient, Enthusiastic, Good Communication, Manual Dexterity, Organized, Productive, Responsible

Types of Positions
Labourer in processing departments

Starting Salary
$ 15,000 - 20,000

Company Benefits
- Full benefit package
- On-the-job training

Correspondence
Submit resume and cover letter in person

Part Time/Summer: Mitchell's Gourmet Foods does not hire for part time work and regularly hires for the summer months. Potential jobs exist as labourer. The best time to apply is in May or June.

MITEL CORPORATION

350 Legget Dr.
Kanata, Ontario, K2K 1X3
Tel: (613) 592-2122   Fax: (613) 592-4784

Kathy Enright, Director HR Operations
Internet: www.mitel.com

Mitel Corporation is a designer, manufacturer and marketer of telecommunications products. With its headquarters in Kanata, Canada and 74 offices and manufacturing facilities worldwide, Mitel employs more than 6,300 people.

Academic Fields
College: Accounting, Business, Computer Science, Electronics Tech., Engineering Tech., Human Resources, Secretarial, Security/Law
Bachelor of Arts: English, Public Relations
Bachelor of Comm/Admin: General, Accounting, Finance, Marketing, Info Mgmt.
Bachelor of Science: General, Computer Science, Mathematics, Physics
Bachelor of Laws: Corporate
Bachelor of Engineering: Computer Systems, Electrical
Chartered Accounting: CA - General/Finance
Masters: Business Administration, Engineering

Critical Skills
Adaptable, Analytical, Good Communication, Confident, Creative, Decisive, Dependable, Diligent, Diplomatic, Enthusiastic, Innovative, Leadership, Logical, Personable, Persuasive, Professional, Responsible, Good Writing Skills

Types of Positions
Software Designer   Hardware Designer
Product Management

Starting Salary
$ 20,000 - 50,000 (depending on position)

Company Benefits
- Highly competitive flexible benefit plan

Correspondence
Mail resume with cover letter

Part Time/Summer: Mitel Corporation regularly seeks candidate for part time or summer employment. Potential work is most likely technology related. The best time to apply is by March.

MITRA IMAGING INC.

455 Phillip Street
Waterloo, Ontario, N2L 3X2
Tel: (519) 746-2900   Fax: (519) 746-3745

Human Resources
Internet: www.mitra.com

Mitra develops sotfware applications that allows hospitals to capture, store and display medical images and other clinical information on integrated computer networks and web based technology. Their goals are improved productivity, faster access to data, shorter hospital stays, and more rational use of exports and resources, all of which means better care for the patient.

Academic Fields
College: Computer Science
Bachelor of Science: Physics
Masters: Science, Engineering, Computer Science

Critical Skills
Adaptable, Creative, Dependable, Innovative, Leadership, Entrepreneurial, Problem Solving

Types of Positions
Software Development   Software Verification

Starting Salary
Depends on position

Company Benefits
- Competitive compensation, benefit and group RRSP plan
- Various career growth and advancement opportunities

Correspondence
Apply through their web site E-mail: hr@mitra.com

Part Time/Summer: Mitra Imaging Inc. rarely hires for part time work, but regularly seeks candidates for the summer months.

Co-op/Internship: They provide co-op opportunities for both college and university students. They also employ high school students through the Shad Valley Program.

MITSUBISHI ELECTRIC SALES CANADA

4299 14th Ave.
Markham, Ontario, L3R 0J2
Tel: (905) 475-7728   Fax: (905) 475-3833

Gail Brankston, Manager Human Resources
Internet: www.mitsubishi.com

Mitsubishi Electric Sales Canada is a distributor of industrial products and household appliances. The firm employs approximately 120 individuals.

Academic Fields
College: Computer Science, Electronics Tech., Engineering Tech., Human Resources, Laboratory Tech., Marketing/Sales
Bachelor of Comm/Admin: General, Accounting, Finance, Marketing, Info Mgmt.
Bachelor of Science: Computer Science
Bachelor of Engineering: Computer Systems, Design, Electrical
Chartered Accounting: CA - General/Finance, CGA/CMA - General/Finance
Masters: Business Administration, Arts, Science, Engineering

Critical Skills
Good Communication, Leadership, Productive, Professional, Good Writing Skills

Types of Positions
Parts Department   Corporate Service

Starting Salary
$ 20,000 - 25,000

Company Benefits
- Major medical and dental, vision care
- Short and long term disability, group RRSP
- Pay for relevant course work

Correspondence
Fax resume with cover letter

Part Time/Summer: Mitsubishi Electric Sales Canada occasionally looks for people for part time or summer work. Potential jobs involve the warehouse, or corporate services. The best time to apply is in April.

MOBILE COMPUTING CORPORATION

6877 Goreway Dr., Unit 3
Mississauga, Ontario, L4V 1L9
Tel: (905) 676-8900   Fax: (905) 676-9191

Kate Innanen, Human Resources Manager
Internet: www.mobilecom.com

Mobile Computing Corporation (MCC) is the leading supplier of business solutions to the transportation industry. They provide wireless onboard information systems with consulting and support services to increase companies' efficiencies.

Academic Fields
College: Accounting, Administration, Business, Communications, Computer Science, Electronics Tech., Engineering Tech., Mechanical Tech.
Bachelor of Comm/Admin: General, Accounting, Finance, Marketing, Info Mgmt.
Bachelor of Science: Computer Science
Bachelor of Engineering: General, Computer Systems, Design, Electrical, Industrial, Mechanical, Transportation
Chartered Accounting: CA - General/Finance, CGA/CMA - General/Finance
Masters: Business Administration, Science, Engineering

Critical Skills
Adaptable, Analytical, Good Communication, Creative, Dependable, Efficient, Enthusiastic, Flexible, Leadership, Personable, Productive, Professional, Good Writing Skills

Types of Positions
Repair Technician   Business Operations
Administrator

Starting Salary
$ 25,000 - 30,000

Company Benefits
- Full medical, dental, life insurance
- Short and long term disability

Correspondence
Fax resume with cover letter

Part Time/Summer: Mobile Computing Corporation does not generally hire for part time work, but occasionally seeks people for summer positions. Potential positions vary. The best time to apply is in April, May, or June.

The Canada Student Employment Guide

MOEN INC.

2816 Bristol Circle
Oakville, Ontario, L6H 5S7
Tel: (905) 829-3400   Fax: (905) 829-3387

Sandra England, Director Human Resources
Internet: www.moen.com

Moen is North America's number one facet manufacturer and distributor. Their Canadian office is located in Oakville and focuses on sales, marketing, finance, human resources, customer service, information systems, and distribution areas.

Academic Fields
College: Accounting, Communications, Computer Science, Human Resources, Marketing/Sales
Bachelor of Arts: General, Business
Bachelor of Comm/Admin: General, Accounting, Finance, Marketing, Info Mgmt.
Chartered Accounting: CMA - General/Finance, CGA - General/Finance

Critical Skills
Adaptable, Analytical, Good Communication, Creative, Dependable, Enthusiastic, Flexible, Leadership, Productive, Professional, Responsible, Good Writing Skills

Types of Positions
Receptionist   Customer Service
Material Handler   Technical Service
Accounting Clerk   Data Entry

Starting Salary
$ 30,000 - 35,000

Company Benefits
- Full benefit package for full time staff
- Training is provided and is a major part of their development program

Correspondence
Mail, fax or e-mail resume with cover letter
E-mail: sengland@moen.com

Part Time/Summer: Moen Inc. occasionally seeks candidates for part time and summer positions. They hire students from February to April, however, they recruit associates children first. Most positions are in their warehouse as materials handler.

MOFFAT COMMUNICATIONS LIMITED

P.O. Box 2580
Winnipeg, Manitoba, R3C 4B3
Tel: (204) 788-3440   Fax: (204) 956-2710

Scott Wotherspoon, Human Resources
Internet: www.moffat.ca

Moffat Communications Ltd. is involved in the broadcasting industry, in relation to cable television in both Canada and the United States. The company employs approximately 300 people.

Academic Fields
College: Accounting
Bachelor of Arts: Business
Bachelor of Comm/Admin: Accounting, Finance
Bachelor of Science: Actuarial
Bachelor of Laws: Corporate
Chartered Accounting: CA-General, CMA-General, CGA-General

Critical Skills
Adaptable, Decisive, Dependable, Diligent, Efficient, Enthusiastic, Good Communication, Good With Figures, Personable, Productive, Professional, Responsible

Types of Positions
Junior Accountant

Starting Salary
$ 20,000 - 25,000

Company Benefits
- Medical and dental
- Company pension plan
- Share ownership assistance plan

Correspondence
Mail resume with cover letter

Part Time/Summer: Moffat Communications Limited occasionally looks for individuals for part time and summer opportunities. A potential position for the summer is administrative assistant.

MONARCH COMMUNICATIONS INC.

361 First St. SE
Medicine Hat, Alberta, T1A 0A5
Tel: (403) 526-4529   Fax: (403) 526-4000

Human Resources Department
Internet: www.monarch.net

Monarch Communications is involved in the operation of radio and television stations, as well as cable television systems all across the country.

Academic Fields
College: Accounting, Communications, Computer Science, Electronics Tech., Engineering Tech., Journalism, Marketing/Sales, Television/Radio
Bachelor of Comm/Admin: Accounting, Marketing
Bachelor of Science: Computer Science
Bachelor of Engineering: Computer Systems, Electrical
Masters: Business Administration

Critical Skills
Adaptable, Artistic, Good Communication, Creative, Dependable, Efficient, Enthusiastic, Flexible, Innovative, Leadership, Productive, Professional, Responsible, Good Writing Skills

Types of Positions
Creative Writer	Technician
Sales Executive	News Reporter
Customer Service Rep.	Announcer

Starting Salary
$ 20,000 - 25,000

Company Benefits
- Group health benefits
- Group RRSP program
- Disability insurance

Correspondence
Mail resume with cover letter
E-mail: lemeshuk@monarch.net

Part Time/Summer: Monarch Communications regularly looks for individuals for part time work, and occasionally seeks candidates for the summer.

MONTREAL TRUST CO.

151 Front Street West, 8th Flr.
Toronto, Ontario, M5J 2N1
Tel: (416) 981-9500   Fax: (416) 981-9507

Gina Campbell, Human Resources Officer
Internet: www.montrealtrust.com

Montreal Trust is a diversified marketer of financial and trust services to individuals and business. Montreal Trust operates throughout Canada from more than 119 branches and offices in which over 3,000 individuals are employed.

Academic Fields
College: General, Accounting, Administration, Business, Communications, Computer Science, Human Resources
Bachelor of Arts: General, Business, Economics, English
Bachelor of Comm/Admin: General, Accounting, Finance
Bachelor of Science: General, Actuarial, Computer Science, Mathematics, Psychology
Bachelor of Laws: General, Corporate
Bachelor of Engineering: Computer Systems
Chartered Accounting: CA - General/Finance
Masters: Business Administration

Critical Skills
Adaptable, Analytical, Artistic, Good Communication, Confident, Creative, Decisive, Dependable, Diligent, Diplomatic, Efficient, Enthusiastic, Responsible, Good Writing Skills

Types of Positions
PC Operator	Administrator
Administrative Asst.	Data Entry
Accounting Clerk	Asst. Account Manager

Starting Salary
$ 20,000 - 30,000

Company Benefits
- Health and dental plan

Correspondence
Mail resume with cover letter

Part Time/Summer: Montreal Trust sometimes hires students on a part time basis and regularly hires for summer openings. Potential summer jobs involve the mail room, clerical, administration, or data entry.

The Canada Student Employment Guide

MOOSEHEAD BREWERIES LIMITED

P.O. Box 3100, Station B
Saint John, New Brunswick, E2M 3H2
Tel: (506) 635-7000   Fax: (506) 635-7029

Dayle Messer, Human Resources
Internet: www.moosehead.ca

Moosehead Breweries is a family-owned business that is Canada's oldest and only remaining major independent brewery. The company operates two retail outlets in the Maritime provinces.

Academic Fields
College: Accounting, Business, Communications, Computer Science, Drafting/Architecture, Electronics Tech., Engineering Tech., Human Resources, Journalism, Laboratory Tech., Marketing/Sales, Secretarial
Bachelor of Arts: Journalism, Public Relations, Statistics
Bachelor of Comm/Admin: Accounting, Finance, Marketing, Info Mgmt.
Bachelor of Science: Biology, Chemistry, Computer Science, Food Sciences, Microbiology
Bachelor of Engineering: Chemical, Electrical, Mechanical, Transportation
Chartered Accounting: CMA-General, CMA-Finance
Masters: Science, Engineering

Critical Skills
Adaptable, Analytical, Good Communication, Confident, Decisive, Dependable, Diplomatic, Efficient, Good With Figures, Leadership, Logical, Manual Dexterity, Organized, Personable, Productive, Responsible, Good Writing Skills

Types of Positions
Receptionist   Clerk/Typist
Accounting Clerk   Laboratory Technician
Production Worker

Starting Salary
$ 25,000 - 30,000

Company Benefits
- Regular employees receive full range of benefits
- Pension, life insurance, health and dental

Correspondence
Mail resume with cover letter or telephone

Part Time/Summer: Moosehead Breweries regularly hires for part time and summer work. The majority of potential jobs are unskilled or semi-skilled jobs in the production facility. Apply in February or March.

MORRISON HERSHFIELD LIMITED

4 Lansing Square
North York, Ontario, M2J 1T1
Tel: (416) 499-3110   Fax: (416) 499-9658

Human Resources
Internet: www.morrisonhershfield.com

Morrison Hershfield Limited is a prominent consulting engineering firm with offices in Toronto, Ottawa, Calgary, Edmonton, Vancouver, and Atlanta, Georgia. The company employs over 340 staff in a variety of disciplines that include building engineering, communications services, transportation and mechanical/electrical engineering.

Academic Fields
College: Administration, CAD Autocad, Engineering Tech., Mechanical Tech.
Bachelor of Arts: Business
Bachelor of Comm/Admin: General
Bachelor of Engineering: Civil, Design, Electrical, Mechanical, Transportation, Bachelor of Architecture
Masters: Engineering

Critical Skills
Adaptable, Analytical, Confident, Decisive, Dependable, Diligent, Good Communication, Good With Figures, Good Writing Skills, Leadership, Manual Dexterity, Organized, Personable, Productive

Types of Positions
Civil Engineer-In-Training
Elec./Mech. Engineer-In-Training
Administrative Support

Starting Salary
$ 35,000 - 40,000

Company Benefits
- Comprehensive benefits package

Correspondence
Mail, fax or e-mail resume with cover letter
E-mail: hr@morrisonhershfield.com

Part Time/Summer: Morrison Hershfield Limited occasionally hires for part time work and regularly hires for the summer. Potential jobs include administrative support, engineer-in-training (civil, electrical or mechanical). Apply in March or April.

Co-op/Internship: The company offers internship opportunities.

The Canada Student Employment Guide

MORTICE KERN SYSTEMS INC.

185 Columbia St. W.
Waterloo, Ontario, N2L 5Z5
Tel: (519) 884-2251   Fax: (519) 884-8861

Cathy Pollock, Recruiter
Internet: www.mks.com

Mortice Kern Systems provides a wide range of software management and testing solutions for software development teams. For companies transitioning to eBusiness, they offer Web application and management solutions.

Academic Fields
College: Human Resources, Information Systems, Marketing/Sales, Computer Science
Bachelor of Comm/Admin: Human Resources, Marketing, Info Mgmt.
Bachelor of Science: Computer Science, Mathematics
Bachelor of Engineering: Computer Systems
Masters: Science, Engineering

Critical Skills
Adaptable, Analytical, Confident, Dependable, Enthusiastic, Flexible, Good Communication, Innovative, Logical, Patient, Productive, Professional, Responsible

Types of Positions
Product Support   Software Development
Quality Assurance   Human Resources

Starting Salary
$ 45,000 - 50,000 (technical), depends on position

Company Benefits
- Healthcare including paramedical and prescriptions
- Vision care, dental, life insurance, long term disability
- Employee assistance program, stock option program

Correspondence
E-mail resume with cover letter
E-mail: jobs@mks.com

Part Time/Summer: Mortice Kern Systems occasionally hires for part time work and regularly hires for the summer. Potential jobs include administrative assistant in human resources.

Co-op/Internship: MKS offers great opportunities for coop terms. Coop assignments include software development, quality assurance, and technical support, among others.

MOSAID TECHNOLOGIES INC.

11 Hines Rd.
Kanata, Ontario, K2K 2X1
Tel: (613) 599-9539   Fax: (613) 591-8148

France Hong, Recruiting Administrator
Internet: www.mosaid.com

MOSAID Technologies Incorporated is an independent semiconductor company with a 25-year history of design innovation. MOSAID's Semiconductor Division is a provider of high-performance products for the networking market.

Academic Fields
College: General, Accounting, Administration, Business, Computer Science, Drafting/Architecture, Electronics Tech., Engineering Tech., Human Resources, Marketing/Sales
Bachelor of Arts: General, Business
Bachelor of Comm/Admin: General, Accounting, Finance, Marketing, Info Mgmt.
Bachelor of Science: Computer Science
Bachelor of Laws: Corporate
Bachelor of Engineering: Computer Systems, Design, Electrical, Materials Science
Chartered Accounting: CA-Finance, CMA-General, CGA-General
Masters: Business Administration, Engineering

Critical Skills
Adaptable, Analytical, Creative, Dependable, Efficient, Enthusiastic, Flexible, Good Communication, Innovative, Leadership, Organized, Productive, Professional, Responsible

Types of Positions
Integrated Circuit Engineer
Software and Hardware Engineer
Administration/Secretarial

Starting Salary
$ 25,000 - 40,000

Company Benefits
- Full, non-contributory benefits package

Correspondence
Mail or e-mail resume with cover letter
E-mail: human_resources@mosaid.ca

Part Time/Summer: MOSAID occasionally hires for part time work, and regularly hires for the summer. Potential areas include accounting, administration, finance, or electrical engineering.

The Canada Student Employment Guide

MOTOROLA CANADA LTD.

2 East Beaver Creek
Richmond Hill, Ontario, L4B 2N3
Tel: (905) 709-7207   Fax: (905) 709-7220

Agnes Van Haeren, Recruitment Manager
Internet: www.motorolacareers.com

Motorola Canada is engaged in the manufacturing and distribution of electronic equipment, systems and components. The company specializes in production of two-way communication systems for the police and military. A wholly owned subsidiary of Motorola Inc. of the United States, Motorola Canada employs over 1,400 people across the country.

Academic Fields
College: General, Accounting, Administration, Communications, Computer Science, Electronics Tech., Engineering Tech., Human Resources
Bachelor of Arts: General, Business, Economics
Bachelor of Comm/Admin: General, Accounting, Finance, Marketing, Info Mgmt.
Bachelor of Engineering: Computer Systems, Design, Electrical
Chartered Accounting: CA - General/Finance, CMA-General
Masters: Business Administration

Critical Skills
Adaptable, Analytical, Creative, Good Communication, Enthusiastic, Efficient, Leadership, Good Writing Skills, Organized, Professional

Types of Positions
Electrical Engineer   Computer Engineer
Customer Service

Starting Salary
$ 48,000 - 50,000

Company Benefits
- A wide range of benefits offered

Correspondence
Fax or e-mail resume with cover letter

Part Time/Summer: Motorola Canada sometimes hires for part time and summer employment. Potential positions most likely involve those listed above. The best time to apply is in March or April.

Co-op/Internship: Internship opportunities are available.

MOUNTAIN EQUIPMENT CO-OP

149 West 4th Ave.
Vancouver, British Columbia, V5Y 4A6
Tel: (604) 732-1989   Fax: (604) 731-6483

Human Resources
Internet: www.mec.ca

Mountain Equipment Co-op is an outdoor equipment retailer and sporting goods store operating across the country. The retailer has 5 outlets in Canada located in Vancouver, Edmonton, Calgary, Ottawa, and Toronto. All locations are company owned. Mountain Equipment Co-op was established in Canada in 1971, and employs approximately 800 people in total.

Academic Fields
College: Accounting, Administration, Human Resources
Bachelor of Arts: General, Business
Bachelor of Comm/Admin: Accounting, Finance, Info Mgmt.
Chartered Accounting: CA - General/Finance

Critical Skills
Creative, Enthusiastic, Good Writing Skills, Organized

Types of Positions
Retail Sales   Mail Order Clerk
Administrative Asst.   Reception
Merchandise Asst.   Data Entry Clerk

Starting Salary
$ 20,000 - 25,000

Company Benefits
- Complete benefit package

Correspondence
Mail resume with cover letter for head office positions. Submit resume, cover letter plus application in person for retail store positions.

Part Time/Summer: Mountain Equipment Co-op regularly seeks candidates for part time and summer employment opportunities. Positions are most likely to be in their retail stores. The best time to apply is in March or April.

The Canada Student Employment Guide

MSM TRANSPORTATION INC.

124 Commercial Rd.
Bolton, Ontario, L7E 1K4
Tel: (905) 951-6800   Fax: (905) 951-6818

Kathy Andre, Human Resources Manager
Internet: www.shipmsm.com

MSM is a transportation company with a fast paced environment. Selected three years in a row as one of Profit Magazine's 100 Fastest Growing Companies, and also selected by Arthur Andersen as one of Canada's 50 Best Managed Companies. The firm employs approximately 100 individuals.

Academic Fields
Bachelor of Arts: Business
Bachelor of Science: General

Critical Skills
Adaptable, Confident, Creative, Decisive, Dependable, Diligent, Efficient, Enthusiastic, Good Communication, Good Writing Skills, Innovative, Leadership, Personable, Professional, Responsible

Types of Positions
Customer Service   Administration
Sales   Operations

Starting Salary
$ 25,000 - 30,000

Company Benefits
- 100% coverage for health and dental benefits
- Tuition reimbursement for upgrading skills

Correspondence
Mail or e-mail resume with cover letter
E-mail: kandre@sympatico.ca

Part Time/Summer: MSM Transportation occasionally seeks candidates for part time work and regularly hires for the summer. Potential jobs involve filing and other administrative odd jobs.

MULTI-LANGUAGES

55 Town Centre Court, Suite 700
Scarborough, Ontario, M1P 4X4
Tel: (416) 410-5978   Fax: (416) 410-5976

Lola Bendana, Director
Internet: www.multi-languages.com

Multi-Languages is a language service company that provides translations, interpretation and typesetting in virtually every language in the world. They have a team of highly professional translators with many years of experience in the most varied fields of translation and interpretation. They employ approximately 1,500 freelance translators.

Academic Fields
Bachelor of Arts: General, English, Languages, Political Science
Masters: Arts

Critical Skills
Dependable, Flexible, Good Communication, Good Writing Skills, Organized, Professional, Responsible, Punctual

Types of Positions
Translator   Interpreter

Starting Salary
$ 20 per hour, depends on number of hours

Company Benefits
- All translators are insured with the Workplace Safety and Insurance Board (WSIB)
- Some training if head interpreter

Correspondence
Mail, fax or e-mail resume with cover letter
E-mail: translations@multi-languages.com

Part Time/Summer: Multi-Languages regularly seeks candidates for part time and summer opportunities. A potential position would be a translator. Individuals may apply anytime.

Co-op/Internship: They do not have an internship program, but are planning to implement one soon.

MULTITECH ELECTRONICS INC.

114204 - 170 Street
Edmonton, Alberta, T5S 1L7
Tel: (403) 451-5390   Fax: (403) 451-1735

Manager Human Resources

Multitech Electronics Inc. is involved with providing value added sales and servicing of information technology.

Academic Fields
College: Computer Science
Bachelor of Science: Computer Science
Bachelor of Engineering: Computer Systems

Critical Skills
Good Communication, Professional, Quality Conscious

Types of Positions
Production   Service

Starting Salary
$ 20,000 - 25,000

Company Benefits
- Group benefits, life insurance, long term disability
- Major, medical, dental on shared cost basis
- Job related training and development is encouraged

Correspondence
Mail or fax resume with cover letter

Part Time/Summer: Multitech Electronics Inc. occasionally hires for part time and summer employment. Potential jobs include service technician or network support. The best time to apply is in June.

MUSTANG SURVIVAL CORP.

3810 Jacombs Rd.
Richmond, British Columbia, V6V 1Y6
Tel: (604) 270-8631   Fax: (604) 270-0489

Dwight Noda, Director Human Resources
Internet: www.mustangsurvival.com

Mustang Survival is involved in the research, engineering, design, and manufacture of many types of survival apparel. The company produces everything from protective gear worn by sailors to life preservers for NASA space shuttle crews. The company employs over 300 individuals in five locations in three countries.

Academic Fields
College: Communications, Computer Science, Engineering Tech., Human Resources, Marketing/Sales, Mechanical Tech., Secretarial, Operations Mgmt., CAD
Bachelor of Comm/Admin: Accounting, Finance, Marketing, Info Mgmt.
Bachelor of Science: Kinesiology, Physics
Bachelor of Engineering: Industrial, Mechanical
Chartered Accounting: CMA-General, CGA-General

Critical Skills
Adaptable, Analytical, Good Communication, Confident, Creative, Dependable, Diligent, Efficient, Enthusiastic, Flexible, Innovative, Leadership, Manual Dexterity, Organized, Personable, Productive, Responsible

Types of Positions
Customer Service Rep.   Credit Assistant
Engineering Technologist Quality Assurance Tech.

Starting Salary
$ 25,000 - 40,000

Company Benefits
- Group health and medical benefits
- Product discount, profit sharing, professional fees
- Training and development fund

Correspondence
Mail, fax or e-mail resume with cover letter
E-mail: humanresources@mustangsurvival.com

Part Time/Summer: Mustang Survival occasionally hires for part time or summer work. Potential jobs involve clerical relief. The best time to apply is in May.

N B S CARD SERVICES

3206 Orlando Drive
Mississauga, Ontario, L4V 1R5
Tel: (905) 672-3777   Fax: (905) 672-9378

Human Resources Department
Internet: www.nbstech.com

N B S Card Services is one of the world's largest producers of plastic cards. Their Canadian facility is one of their biggest with an annual capacity of 50 million cards. N B S has complete in-house production capabilities, including custom-design, lithography, silk-screen, lamination, die-cutting and other special patented processes. Applications may be filled out at their premises, they would prefer however not to receive any telephone calls.

Academic Fields
College: Accounting, Computer Science, Electronics Tech., Graphic Arts, Human Resources
Bachelor of Arts: Business
Bachelor of Comm/Admin: Accounting, Info Mgmt.
Bachelor of Engineering: Mechanical
Chartered Accounting: CGA-Finance
Masters: Business Administration, Engineering

Critical Skills
Adaptable, Confident, Dependable, Good Communication, Leadership, Productive

Types of Positions
Machine Operator   Production Clerk
Quality Inspector

Starting Salary
below $ 20,000 - 25,000

Company Benefits
- 100% medical and dental benefits
- Life insurance and education reimbursement

Correspondence
Mail or fax resume with cover letter

Part Time/Summer: N B S Card Services regularly seeks candidates for part time and summer opportunities. Jobs in the summer are most likely to be those listed above. Applications are accepted throughout the year for temporary or part time work. The best time to apply for positions in the summer is at the beginning of May.

NANAIMO CREDIT UNION

13 Victoria Cres., Suite 12
Nanaimo, British Columbia, V9R 5B9
Tel: (604) 741-3200   Fax: (604) 741-3223

Kerm Culham, Manager of Human Resources

Nanaimo Credit Union is a member-owned credit union offering full financial services including loans, mortgages, RRSP's, chequing and savings accounts. The credit union employs about 130 people.

Academic Fields
College: Accounting, Business, Electronics Tech., Human Resources, Insurance, Marketing/Sales
Bachelor of Arts: General, Business, Economics
Bachelor of Comm/Admin: General, Accounting, Finance, Marketing
Chartered Accounting: CA-Finance, CMA-Finance, CGA-Finance
Masters: Business Administration

Critical Skills
Adaptable, Good Communication, Creative, Decisive, Dependable, Enthusiastic, Flexible, Innovative, Leadership, Organized, Personable, Persuasive, Productive, Professional, Responsible

Types of Positions
Member Service Representative

Starting Salary
$ 20,000 - 25,000

Company Benefits
- Full benefit program
- Medical, extended health, dental, pension
- 2 weeks training and buddy system

Correspondence
Fax resume with cover letter

Part Time/Summer: Nanaimo Credit Union occasionally looks for individuals for part time or summer employment. A potential job is member service representative. The best time to apply is in late April.

NATCO CANADA LTD.

P.O. Box 751, Stn T
Calgary, Alberta, T2H 2H3
Tel: (403) 236-1850   Fax: (403) 236-0488

Brian Berdusco, Human Resources

Natco Canada is involved in the design and manufacture of oil and gas production equipment. The company employs about 150 individuals.

Academic Fields
College: Accounting, Administration, Computer Science, Drafting/Architecture, Engineering Tech., Industrial Design
Bachelor of Comm/Admin: Accounting
Bachelor of Engineering: Chemical, Computer Systems, Design, Industrial

Critical Skills
Creative, Good Communication, Diplomatic, Enthusiastic, Flexible, Leadership, Personable, Professional

Types of Positions
Engineering   Junior Draftsperson
Quality Control   Accounting

Starting Salary
$ 25,000 - 30,000

Company Benefits
- Medical and dental
- Savings plan
- In-house training

Correspondence
Mail resume with cover letter

Part Time/Summer: Natco Canada occasionally looks for individuals for part time work, and regularly seeks people for summer opportunities. There are various potential positions in the summer months. The best time to apply is in April.

NATIONAL GROCERS CO. LTD.

6 Monogram Place
Weston, Ontario, M9R 4C4
Tel: (416) 235-2173   Fax: (416) 240-3866

Human Resources Department

National Grocers is a full service wholesaler offering a wide range of products, programs and services to grocery retailers across Ontario. These retailers in the province include Freshmart, Hasty Market, Mr. Grocer, Valu-Mart, and Your Independent Grocer.

Academic Fields
College: General, Accounting, Business, Communications, Computer Sci., Cooking/Culinary, Food/Nutrition, Human Resources, Marketing/Sales, Photography, Secretarial, Security/Law, Travel/Tourism, Urban Planning
Bachelor of Arts: General, Business
Bachelor of Comm/Admin: General, Accounting, Finance, Marketing
Bachelor of Science: Computer Science, Health Sciences, Nursing (RN), Pharmacy, Psychology
Bachelor of Laws: General, Corporate, Real Estate
Bachelor of Engineering: Chemical, Civil, Computer Systems, Electrical, Industrial, Mechanical
Bachelor of Education: General, Adult Education
Chartered Accounting: CA - General/Finance, CGA/CMA - General/Finance
Masters: Business Administration, Science, Engineering, Education

Critical Skills
Many skills considered important.

Types of Positions
Accounts Payable   Mailroom
Security   Sales Representative
Marketing Analyst   IT Systems

Starting Salary
$ 20,000 - 40,000

Company Benefits
- Standard benefit package, pension plan

Correspondence
Mail, fax or submit resume with cover letter in person

Part Time/Summer: National Grocers regularly hires on a part time and summer basis. Summer positions include clerical, administrative, or is project based. The best time to apply is in April.

The Canada Student Employment Guide

NATIONAL LIFE

522 University Ave, 7th Flr
Toronto, Ontario, M5G 1Y7
Tel: (416) 598-2122   Fax: (416) 598-4574

Human Resources Dept.
Internet: www.NationalLife.ca

National Life provides life and health insurance products as well as retirement income plans to customers across Canada. The firm employs about 370 individuals, and has earned a spot in the latest edition of "Canada's Top 100 Employers".

Academic Fields
College: General, Accounting, Administration, Advertising, Business, Communications, Computer Science, Human Resources, Insurance, Journalism, Marketing/Sales, Secretarial, Statistics
Bachelor of Arts: General, Business, Economics, Journalism, Languages, Public Relations, Statistics
Bachelor of Comm/Admin: General, Accounting, Finance, Marketing, Info Mgmt.
Bachelor of Science: Actuarial, Computer Sci., Math
Bachelor of Laws: General, Corporate
Bachelor of Engineering: Computer Systems
Chartered Accounting: CA - General/Finance, CA/CGA/CMA - General/Finance
Masters: Business Administration

Critical Skills
Analytical, Good Communication, Decisive, Dependable, Efficient, Enthusiastic, Flexible, Organized, Productive, Professional, Responsible, Writing Skills

Types of Positions
Claims   Human Resources
Individual Service Teams Central Records

Starting Salary
$ 25,000 - 35,000

Company Benefits
- Full comprehensive benefits package
- In-house training, course reimbursement

Correspondence
Mail, fax or e-mail resume with cover letter
E-mail: hr@NationalLife.ca

Part Time/Summer: National Life occasionally looks for people for part time and summer opportunities. Potential jobs involve administrative or office duties. The best time apply is in March or April.

NATIONAL MANUFACTURING OF CANADA INC.

P.O. Box 1808, 600 Fentons Creek
Swift Current, Saskatchewan, S9H 4J8
Tel: (306) 773-2914   Fax: (306) 773-6323

J. Albinet, HR Coordinator

National Manufacturing of Canada Inc. is a leading manufacture of fasteners. They also package and distribute fasteners and hardware items for the retail market across Canada. They employ 200 full time individuals. Their factory is located in Swift Current and they have a sales force throughout Canada. They have an Eastern Distribution Centre in Ontario opening in Aug 1, 2000.

Academic Fields
College: Accounting, Computer Science, Engineering Tech., Human Resources, Marketing/Sales
Bachelor of Comm/Admin: Accounting, Finance, Info Mgmt.
Bachelor of Science: Chemistry, Environmental Studies
Bachelor of Engineering: General, Industrial, Mechanical
Chartered Accounting: CA-Finance, CMA-Finance
Masters: Engineering

Critical Skills
Adaptable, Dependable, Efficient, Enthusiastic, Flexible, Good With Figures, Logical, Manual Dexterity, Organized, Patient, Team Player

Types of Positions
Production Worker   Order Picker
Warehouse Order Picker

Starting Salary
below $ 20,000

Company Benefits
- Full health benefits for permanent employees
- They run the SIAT Warehouse Worker Program
- Send people out for specialized training

Correspondence
Mail or fax resume with cover letter

Part Time/Summer: National Manufacturing of Canada does not hire for part time work, but regularly seeks candidates for the summer. Potential jobs include those listed above. The best time to apply is from March to May.

The Canada Student Employment Guide

NATIONAL SPORTS CENTRE

R.R. #1
Uxbridge, Ontario, L9P 1R1
Tel: (905) 852-3342   Fax: (905) 852-5810

Annette Watson, Administration Assistant

National Sports Centre is a retailer of sporting, recreational and related goods. With 12 outlets, 5 in the Toronto region, National Sports Centre employs over 600 individuals. More than half of these employees work for the company on a part time basis.

Academic Fields
College: Accounting, Administration, Computer Science, Human Resources, Secretarial, Security/Law
Bachelor of Arts: Business
Bachelor of Comm/Admin: Accounting, Finance, Marketing, Info Mgmt.
Chartered Accounting: CGA-General

Critical Skills
Adaptable, Analytical, Good Communication, Confident, Creative, Decisive, Dependable, Diligent, Diplomatic, Efficient, Enthusiastic, Flexible, Good With Figures, Innovative, Leadership, Logical, Organized, Patient, Personable, Persuasive, Productive, Professional, Responsible, Writing Skills

Types of Positions
Accounts Payable   Department Head
Administrative Asst.   Payroll Assistant

Starting Salary
$ 20,000 - 25,000

Company Benefits
- Group insurance coverage, 10 days sick pay
- Staff discounts, selling skills
- In-house management and marketing training

Correspondence
Mail resume with cover letter

Part Time/Summer: National Sports Centre sometimes hires for part time positions and summer opportunities. More individuals are hired in August for the hockey season. A potential position in the summer months is administrative assistant. The best time to apply is in April.

NELES AUTOMATION, SCADA SOLUTIONS LTD.

2nd Flr., 10333 Southport Rd. S.W.
Calgary, Alberta, T2W 3X6
Tel: (403) 253-8848   Fax: (403) 259-2926

Laura Warnock, Strategic Resource Specialist
Internet: www.sage.nelesautomation.com

The SCADA Solutions Division of Neles Automation is a leading worldwide supplier of supervisory control and data acquisition systems for oil & gas pipelines, electrical and water/waste-water utilities.

Academic Fields
College: Accounting, Administration, Advertising, Business, Communications, Human Res., Information Systems, Marketing/Sales, Purchasing, Secretarial, Graphic Arts, Legal Assistant, CAD Autocad, Computer Sci., Electronics Tech., Engineering Tech.
Bachelor of Arts: Business, Economics, Public Rel.
Bachelor of Comm/Admin: General, Accounting, Finance, Human Resources, Marketing, Info Mgmt.
Bachelor of Science: Computer Sci., Mathematics
Bachelor of Laws: Corporate
Bachelor of Engineering: General, Computer Systems, Design, Electrical, Materials Science
Masters: Business Administration, Engineering

Critical Skills
Adaptable, Analytical, Confident, Creative, Dependable, Enthusiastic, Flexible, Good Communication, Professional, Team Oriented

Types of Positions
Administrative Assistant   Technical Writer
Programmer/Analyst   Project Administrator

Starting Salary
$ 50,000 or more

Company Benefits
- Group health and dental, RRSP

Correspondence
Mail, fax, e-mail resume with cover letter

Part Time/Summer: Neles Automation, Scada Solutions rarely hires for part time work, but regularly hires for the summer. Potential jobs include programmer analyst, reception relief, admin., shipper and receiver, or accounting. Apply in March or April.

Co-op/Internship: They participate in co-op programs through the universities.

NELVANA LIMITED

32 Atlantic Ave.
Toronto, Ontario, M6K 1X8
Tel: (416) 588-5571   Fax: (416) 588-5252

Marlene Ferreira, Human Resources
Internet: www.nelvana.com

Nelvana produces animated television shows including Babar, Franklin, Ned's Newt, Bob & Margaret, Little Bear, Care Bears, Pippi LongStocking, and Rupert. They also provide live action shows such as Nancy Drew, Hardy Boys, and Jake & the Kid.

Academic Fields
College: Accounting, Administration, Communications, Computer Science, Human Resources, Performing Arts, Secretarial, Security/Law
Bachelor of Arts: General, Business, Fine Arts, Languages, Music, Public Relations
Bachelor of Comm/Admin: General, Accounting, Info Mgmt.
Bachelor of Laws: General, Corporate
Chartered Accounting: CA-General

Critical Skills
Adaptable, Artistic, Good Communication, Creative, Dependable, Diligent, Enthusiastic, Flexible, Organized, Patient, Personable, Productive, Responsible

Types of Positions
Digital Painter
Production Assistant
Background/Storyboard Coordinator

Starting Salary
$ 20,000 - 25,000

Company Benefits
- 3 tiered benefit system with health, dental and 3 life insurance packages
- Tuition reimbursement program

Correspondence
Fax resume with cover letter
E-mail: hr@nelvana.com

Part Time/Summer: Nelvana occasionally seeks people for part time and summer work. Potential jobs include production coordinator or office administrator. The best time to apply is in mid March. By mid April the jobs have already been filled.

NEPTUNE FOOD SUPPLIERS LTD.

1700 Cliveden Avenue
Delta, British Columbia, V3M 6T2
Tel: (604) 540-3751   Fax: (604) 540-3970

Janet Higgins, Human Resources

Neptune Food Suppliers is a holding company that is engaged in the business of food wholesaling and distribution. There are approximately 375 individuals in total that work in various capacities within the company. The firm's head office is in Delta, British Columbia.

Academic Fields
College: Accounting, Human Resources, Marketing/Sales
Bachelor of Arts: Economics, Psychology
Bachelor of Comm/Admin: Accounting, Finance, Marketing, Info Mgmt.
Chartered Accounting: CA-Finance, CGA-Finance
Masters: Business Administration

Critical Skills
Adaptable, Analytical, Good Communication, Confident, Decisive, Dependable, Diligent, Diplomatic, Efficient, Enthusiastic, Flexible, Good With Figures, Innovative, Leadership, Logical, Manual Dexterity, Organized, Patient, Personable, Persuasive, Productive, Professional, Responsible, Writing Skills

Types of Positions
Material Handler   Customer Service Rep.
Accounts Receivable   Accounts Payable
Truck Driver   Credit Clerk

Starting Salary
$ 20,000 - 25,000

Company Benefits
- Standard medical and dental benefits
- On-the-job training
- College evening programs

Correspondence
Mail or fax resume with cover letter

Part Time/Summer: Neptune Food Suppliers sometimes seeks candidates for part time and summer employment. Potential jobs include material handler or involve clerical work. The best time to apply is in late May or early June.

The Canada Student Employment Guide

NESBITT BURNS INC.

1 First Canadian Place, 14th Floor, P.O. Box 150
Toronto, Ontario, M5X 1H3
Tel: (416) 359-4250   Fax: (416) 359-7499

Donna McKinley, Manager Recruiting
Internet: www.nesbittburns.com

Nesbitt Burns is Canada's leading full-service investment firm, serving the financial needs of individual, institutional, corporate and government clients. A member of the Bank of Montreal Group of Companies, they employ over 3,600 dedicated professionals in more than 130 offices across Canada and 11 international offices.

Academic Fields
College: Accounting, Computer Science, Human Resources, Marketing/Sales, Secretarial
Bachelor of Arts: Business, Economics, Statistics
Bachelor of Comm/Admin: Accounting, Finance, Info Mgmt.
Bachelor of Science: Computer Science, Mathematics
Bachelor of Laws: Corporate
Bachelor of Engineering: Computer Systems
Chartered Accounting: CA - General/Finance, CGA/CMA - General/Finance
Masters: Business Administration

Critical Skills
Analytical, Creative, Diligent, Innovative, Leadership, Productive, Professional, Responsible

Types of Positions
Operations Department   Accounting Clerk
Investment Banking Analyst

Starting Salary
$ 25,000 - 30,000 (depends on education level)

Company Benefits
- Health, dental and vision plans
- Pension, short/long term disability, life insurance
- In-house training, promote from within

Correspondence
Mail resume with cover letter

Part Time/Summer: Nesbitt Burns sometimes hires for part time openings and regularly hires for summer employment. Potential jobs involve general support positions throughout the firm. February or March is the best time to apply.

NESTLE CANADA INC.

25 Sheppard Avenue West
North York, Ontario, M2N 6S8
Tel: (416) 512-9000   Fax: (416) 218-2654

David Martin, Human Resources
Internet: www.nestle.ca

Nestle Canada is engaged in the manufacturing and distribution of food products. The company produces a wide range of food and beverage goods under brand names such as Nescafe, Nestea, Stouffer's, Nestle Quik, Goodhost, Carnation Evaporated Milk, Dr. Ballard, Coffee Crisp, and Smarties among other well known products.

Academic Fields
College: Accounting, Administration, Business, Computer Science, Electronics Tech., Engineering Tech., Food/Nutrition, Human Resources, Laboratory Tech., Marketing/Sales, Secretarial
Bachelor of Arts: Business, Public Relations
Bachelor of Comm/Admin: Accounting, Finance, Marketing
Bachelor of Science: Biology, Computer Science, Food Sciences, Health Sciences, Microbiology
Bachelor of Engineering: Chemical, Computer Systems, Industrial, Mechanical
Chartered Accounting: CA-Finance, CMA-General/Finance, CGA-General/Finance
Masters: Business Administration, Engineering

Critical Skills
Adaptable, Analytical, Good Communication, Confident, Creative, Decisive, Dependable, Diligent, Diplomatic, Efficient, Enthusiastic, Flexible, Good With Figures, Innovative, Leadership, Logical, Organized, Patient, Personable, Productive, Professional, Responsible, Good Writing Skills

Types of Positions
Clerical   Manual Positions

Starting Salary
$ 20,000 - 30,000

Company Benefits
- Flexible, cafeteria style benefits

Correspondence
Mail resume with cover letter

Part Time/Summer: Nestle Canada occasionally hires for part time and summer work. Jobs involve general labour, clerical work, and project work.

The Canada Student Employment Guide

NETRON INC.

99 Saint Regis Cres. N.
Toronto, Ontario, M3J 1Y9
Tel: (416) 636-8333   Fax: (416) 636-4847

Isabel Smith, Manager of Human Resources
Internet: www.netron.com

Netron is a computer service, product and consulting organization specializing in products and services for the information technology industry.

Academic Fields
Bachelor of Comm/Admin: Info Mgmt.
Bachelor of Science: Computer Science, Mathematics, Physics
Bachelor of Engineering: Chemical, Civil, Computer Systems, Design, Electrical, Industrial, Mechanical
Masters: Science, Engineering

Critical Skills
Adaptable, Analytical, Good Communication, Creative, Dependable, Enthusiastic, Productive, Professional, Responsible, Good Writing Skills

Types of Positions
Associate Software Engineering
Software Engineer

Starting Salary
$ 50,000 - 60,000

Company Benefits
- Medical, dental, life insurance
- Short and long term disability
- Initial training program for all technical people

Correspondence
Mail, fax, e-mail resume with cover letter

Part Time/Summer: Netron does not generally hire for part time work. While they don't generally hire summer students, they often bring in students for the summer who have completed internship programs with them.

NEW BRUNSWICK POWER

P.O. Box 2000, 515 King St.
Fredericton, New Brunswick, E3B 4X1
Tel: (506) 458-3611   Fax: (506) 458-4000

Employment Department

New Brunswick Power is in the business of production, distribution, and transmission of electricity. The company utilizes hydro, oil, coal and nuclear energy in their generating plants. New Brunswick Power hires an average of 350 to 400 students each summer. In addition, the company participates in co-op programs for computer science, business administration, and power engineering. They currently employ more than 2,700 individuals to work in various capacities.

Academic Fields
College: General, Accounting, Admin., Business, Computer Sci., Electronics Tech., Mechanical Tech.
Bachelor of Comm/Admin: General, Accounting, Finance, Info Mgmt.
Bachelor of Science: Computer Science
Bachelor of Laws: General
Bachelor of Engineering: General, Chemical, Civil, Computer Systems, Electrical, Mechanical
Bachelor of Education: General, Adult Education
Chartered Accounting: CMA-General, CGA-General
Masters: Business Administration, Engineering

Critical Skills
Adaptable, Decisive, Enthusiastic, Good Writing Skills, Innovative, Leadership, Good Communication

Types of Positions
Clerical   Administrative
Engineering   Computer Science

Starting Salary
$ 20,000 - 30,000

Company Benefits
- Benefits for temporary and regular employees
- Full menu of health, medical and vacation benefits

Correspondence
Mail, fax or e-mail resume with cover letter
E-mail: jdoucett@nbpower.com

Part Time/Summer: New Brunswick Power Corporation sometimes hires for part time work and regularly hires for the summer. Students are hired for all divisions. Apply in January for a start date in May.

The Canada Student Employment Guide

NEW BRUNSWICK TELEPHONE COMPANY

One Brunswick Square, P.O. Box 1430
Saint John, New Brunswick, E2L 4K2
Tel: (506) 694-2132   Fax: (506) 694-2392

Kimberly DeLong, Employment Administrator

A wholly owned subsidiary of Bruncor Inc., New Brunswick Telephone offers choice, convenience and control when it comes to telecommunications. The company supplies individuals and business in New Brunswick with many telecommunications services including local and long-distance voice and data services, cellular telephones and services, closed-circuit television, and other specialized transmission services.

Academic Fields
College: Communications, Engineering Tech.
Bachelor of Comm/Admin: Gen., Mktg., Info Mgmt.
Bachelor of Science: Computer Science
Bachelor of Engineering: Computer Systems, Electrical, Industrial
Chartered Accounting: CA - General/Finance, CGA/CMA - General/Finance
Masters: Business Administration, Engineering

Critical Skills
Adaptable, Analytical, Good Communication, Confident, Creative, Decisive, Dependable, Diligent, Diplomatic, Efficient, Enthusiastic, Flexible, Innovative, Leadership, Logical, Manual Dexterity, Organized, Personable, Persuasive, Productive, Professional, Responsible, Good Writing Skills

Types of Positions
Residential Service Reps   Business Service Reps
Technical Analyst   Programmer
New Manager Program

Starting Salary
$ 30,000 - 40,000

Company Benefits
- Excellent benefit package
- Stock options, no lay off policy
- Many opportunities and career paths

Correspondence
Mail resume with cover letter

Part Time/Summer: New Brunswick Teleph.one regularly hires for part time and ummer work. Potential positions in the summer include teller or operator. The best time to apply is in early January or February.

NEW HOLLAND CANADA LTD.

1260 Clarence Ave., P.O. Box 7300
Winnipeg, Manitoba, R3C 4E8
Tel: (204) 477-2202   Fax: (204) 477-2325

Maureen Thomas, Human Resources

New Holland Canada is a large tractor design and manufacturing company. They predominantly work in the agricultural industry. The company's head office is in Winnipeg, Manitoba.

Academic Fields
Bachelor of Arts: Business
Bachelor of Comm/Admin: Accounting, Finance
Bachelor of Science: Agriculture
Bachelor of Engineering: Design, Electrical, Industrial, Materials Science, Mechanical
Masters: Business Administration, Engineering

Critical Skills
Analytical, Creative, Dependable, Flexible, Good Communication, Good Writing Skills, Innovative, Leadership, Patient, Persuasive, Productive, Professional

Types of Positions
Manufacturing Engineer   Accountant
Engineer-Analyst   Buyer

Starting Salary
$ 30,000 - 40,000

Company Benefits
- Supplemental medical, dental
- Short and long term disability
- Vacation, pension plan, savings plan

Correspondence
Mail resume with cover letter

Part Time/Summer: New Holland Canada occasionally seeks candidates for part time work, and regularly hires for the summer months. Potential jobs are in engineering, and manufacturing engineering. The best time to apply is in April.

The Canada Student Employment Guide

NEWFOUNDLAND AND LABRADOR CREDIT UNION
341 Freshwater Rd.
St. John's, Newfoundland, A1B 1C4
Tel: (709) 754-2630   Fax: (709) 576-8771

Richard Vaillancourt, Human Resources
Internet: www.nlcu.com

Newfoundland and Labrador Credit Union is involved in the financial services industry providing financial products and services to meet individuals and business needs.

Academic Fields
College: General, Accounting, Administration, Business, Computer Science, Human Resources, Marketing/Sales, Secretarial
Bachelor of Arts: General, Business, Economics, Statistics
Bachelor of Comm/Admin: General, Accounting, Finance, Marketing, Info Mgmt.
Bachelor of Science: General
Bachelor of Education: General
Chartered Accounting: CA - General/Finance, CGA/CMA - General/Finance
Masters: Business Administration, Arts

Critical Skills
Adaptable, Analytical, Good Communication, Confident, Creative, Decisive, Dependable, Diligent, Diplomatic, Efficient, Enthusiastic, Flexible, Good With Figures, Innovative, Leadership, Logical, Organized, Patient, Personable, Persuasive, Productive, Professional, Responsible, Good Writing Skills

Types of Positions
Member Service Consultant   Info Tech. Consultant
Accounting Consultant   Secretary
Financial Planner

Starting Salary
$ 20,000 - 30,000

Company Benefits
- 100% employer paid insurance, health and dental
- Employer paid training and development

Correspondence
Mail, fax, e-mail resume with cover letter
E-mail: rvaillancourt@nlcu.com

Part Time/Summer: Newfoundland and Labrador Credit Union occasionally hires for part time and summer work. Potential jobs involve secretarial or accounting duties. Apply in April or May.

NEWFOUNDLAND AND LABRADOR HYDRO
Hydro Place, Columbus Dr., P.O. Box 12400
St. John's, Newfoundland, A1B 4K7
Tel: (709) 737-1400   Fax: (709) 737-1800

Alan Evans, Human Resources
Internet: www.nlh.nf.ca

The mission of the Newfoundland and Labrador Hydro Group of Companies is to provide electrical power and energy, on behalf of the people of the Province, at the lowest cost consistent with reliable service, due consideration for the environment and the safety of their employees and the customers which they serve.

Academic Fields
College: Accounting, Electronics Tech., Engineering Tech., Mechanical Tech.
Bachelor of Arts: Business
Bachelor of Comm/Admin: Accounting, Finance, Info Mgmt.
Bachelor of Science: Biology, Environmental Studies
Bachelor of Engineering: Civil, Electrical, Mechanical
Masters: Business Administration

Critical Skills
Confident, Diligent, Diplomatic, Efficient, Enthusiastic, Good Communication, Good Writing Skills, Innovative, Leadership, Personable, Productive, Cooperative, Team Player

Types of Positions
Mail Room Clerk   Accounting Clerk
Programmer

Starting Salary
$25,000 - 30,000

Company Benefits
- Competitive benefits plan

Correspondence
Mail or fax resume with cover letter
E-mail: aevans@nlh.nf.ca

Part Time/Summer: Newfoundland and Labrador Hydro occasionally hires for part time work and regularly seeks candidates during the summer months. The best time to apply is in March or April.

NEWNESS MACHINE LTD.

P.O. Box 8, Stn Main
Salmon Arm, British Columbia, V1E 4N2
Tel: (250) 832-7116   Fax: (250) 804-4015

Dwight Guy, Corp. Services Manager
Internet: www.newnes.com

Newness Machine is a manufacturer of sawmill and planemill systems and equipment using advanced engineering concepts, software applications, controls, mechanical and electrical design.

Academic Fields
College: Business, Human Resources, Marketing/Sales
Bachelor of Comm/Admin: Accounting
Bachelor of Science: Mathematics, Physics
Bachelor of Engineering: Computer Systems, Design, Electrical, Industrial, Mechanical
Chartered Accounting: CA-General, CGA-Finance

Critical Skills
Adaptable, Analytical, Good Communication, Confident, Creative, Decisive, Dependable, Diligent, Diplomatic, Efficient, Enthusiastic, Flexible, Good With Figures, Innovative, Leadership, Logical, Organized, Patient, Personable, Persuasive, Productive, Professional, Responsible, Good Writing Skills

Types of Positions
Controls Engineer   Mechanical Drafting
Electrical Engineer

Starting Salary
$ 30,000 - 40,000

Company Benefits
- Full employee benefits
- Benefits paid by company with the exception of long term disability premiums

Correspondence
Mail resume with cover letter and follow-up application in person or by phone

Part Time/Summer: Newnes Machine regularly looks for people for part time or summer work. The best time to apply is from January to March.

NEWS MARKETING CANADA

6 - 2400 Skymark Ave.
Mississauga, Ontario, L4W 5L3
Tel: (905) 602-6397   Fax: (905) 602-8823

Human Resources
Internet: www.newsmarketing.ca

News Marketing Canada is a unit of the international division of News America Marketing and part of the News Corporation Company. Affiliated with diverse news, entertainment and media, the News Corporation Co. is parent company to Twentieth Century Fox, HarperCollins Publishers, and Fox Broadcasting, among others.

Academic Fields
College: Accounting, Administration, Advertising, Business, Communications, Human Resources, Info Syst., Marketing/Sales, Statistics, General Science
Bachelor of Arts: General, Business, Criminology, Economics, English, Fine Arts, Gerontology, History, Journalism, Languages, Music, Philosophy, Political Science, Psychology, Public Rel., Sociology/Social Work, Statistics, Urban Geography
Bachelor of Comm/Admin: General, Accounting, Finance, HR, Marketing, Info Mgmt., Public Admin.
Bachelor of Science: General
Bachelor of Engineering: General
Bachelor of Education: General
Chartered Accounting: CA-General, CMA-General, CGA-General
Masters: Business Administration

Critical Skills
Adaptable, Good Communication, Creative, Enthusiastic, Flexible, Innovative, Good Writing Skills

Types of Positions
Account Coordinator, Merchandising
Account Coordinator, Media Sales
Administrative Assistant

Starting Salary
$ 30,000 - 35,000

Company Benefits
- Comprehensive health and dental benefits

Correspondence
Mail, fax or e-mail resume with cover letter
E-mail: recruiting@newsmarketing.ca

Part Time/Summer: They regularly hire for part time work and occasionally hire in the summer.

NEWTEL COMMUNICATIONS

P.O. Box 2110
St. John's, Newfoundland, A1C 5H6
Tel: (709) 739-2897   Fax: (709) 739-3602

Michele Clarke, Human Resources

A wholly owned subsidiary of NewTel Enterprises Limited of St. John's, the Newfoundland Telephone Company provides telecommunications and information handling services throughout Newfoundland and Labrador. The firm operates nationally as a member of the Stentor Group of Companies. The Newfoundland Telephone Company employs about 1,700 individuals.

Academic Fields
College: Computer Science
Bachelor of Arts: Public Relations
Bachelor of Comm/Admin: Marketing, Info Mgmt.
Bachelor of Science: Computer Science
Bachelor of Laws: Corporate
Bachelor of Engineering: Computer Systems, Electrical
Masters: Business Administration

Critical Skills
Analytical, Decisive, Good Communication, Good Writing Skills, Innovative, Leadership, Professional, Responsible

Types of Positions
Junior Electrical Engineer   Computer Programmer
Direct Marketing Rep.

Starting Salary
$ 25,000 - 40,000

Company Benefits
- Full range, cost shared flexible benefits plan
- Pension, RRSP, employee share purchase
- Fully paid training and educational program

Correspondence
Mail or fax resume with cover letter

Part Time/Summer: NewTel Communications sometimes seeks candidates for part time and summer employment opportunities.

THE NIAGARA PARKS COMMISSION

P.O. Box 150, Stn Main
Niagara Falls, Ontario, L2E 6T2
Tel: (905) 356-2241   Fax: (905) 356-9019

Human Resources

The Niagara Parks Commission is an agency of the Ontario Government that is involved in tourism in the Niagara Falls region.

Academic Fields
College: Accounting, Forestry, Travel/Tourism
Bachelor of Arts: General, Criminology, Languages, Public Relations
Bachelor of Comm/Admin: General, Accounting, Finance, Marketing
Bachelor of Science: Agriculture, Environmental Studies, Forestry, Horticulture

Critical Skills
Adaptable, Dependable, Diligent, Diplomatic, Efficient, Enthusiastic, Flexible, Good Communication, Personable, Productive, Professional, Responsible

Types of Positions
Seasonal Positions

Starting Salary
below $ 20,000

Company Benefits
- No benefits for seasonal workers

Correspondence
Submit resume and cover letter in person

Part Time/Summer: The Niagara Parks Commission regularly hires candidates for part time or summer employment. Potential jobs are in tourism, retail attractions, food services, or horticulture. The best time to apply is in December to March.

NICHIRIN INC.

139 Copernicus Blvd.
Brantford, Ontario, N3P 1N4
Tel: (519) 752-2925   Fax: (519) 752-6408

Human Resources

A manufacturer of high pressure hose assemblies for the automotive industry, Nichirin has been located in Brantford since 1987. The Brantford plant was the Japanese company's first overseas manufacturing operation and remains its only wholly-owned overseas location. Housed in 54,000 square feet on Copernicus Blvd, Nichirin's customers include Honda, Nissan, Cami Automotive and Kawasaki.

Academic Fields
College: General, Administration, Human Resources, Industrial Design
Bachelor of Engineering: General, Design, Industrial, Mechanical
Masters: Business Administration, Engineering

Critical Skills
Adaptable, Dependable, Diplomatic, Flexible, Good Communication, Good Writing Skills, Organized, Personable, Professional

Types of Positions
Quality Control   Product Engineering
Sales Department

Starting Salary
$ 30,000 - 40,000

Company Benefits
- 100% medical

Correspondence
Mail resume with cover letter

Part Time/Summer: Nichirin Inc. occasionally seeks candidates for part time or summer employment. The best time to apply is in March.

NIELSEN MARKETING RESEARCH

160 McNabb Street
Markham, Ontario, L3P 4B8
Tel: (905) 475-3344   Fax: (905) 475-8357

Arlene Hoff Human Resources

Nielsen Marketing Research is a consulting firm which provides research and market analysis to a diverse range of businesses and other enterprises across Canada. A subsidiary of A.C. Nielsen Co. of the United States, Nielsen Marketing Research employs over 800 people from coast to coast.

Academic Fields
College: Advertising, Business, Computer Science, Marketing/Sales, Statistics, Television/Radio
Bachelor of Arts: Business, Economics, Statistics
Bachelor of Comm/Admin: General, Marketing, Info Mgmt.
Bachelor of Science: Computer Science, Mathematics
Masters: Business Administration

Critical Skills
Adaptable, Analytical, Good Communication, Confident, Creative, Decisive, Dependable, Diligent, Diplomatic, Efficient, Enthusiastic, Good With Figures, Organized, Personable, Persuasive, Professional, Responsible, Good Writing Skills

Types of Positions
Programmer   Market Analyst
Customer Service Rep.   Statistician

Starting Salary
$ 25,000 - 40,000 (depending on position)

Company Benefits
- Standard benefits
- Nielsen University provides employee training

Correspondence
Mail or fax resume with cover letter

Part Time/Summer: Nielsen Marketing Research sometimes hires for part time and summer employment. They also regularly offer co-op education to students. Potential positions for the summer and for co-op are most likely those outlined above.

NIKE CANADA LTD.

175 Commerce Valley Dr. W.
Thornhill, Ontario, L3T 7P6
Tel: (905) 764-0400   Fax: (905) 764-1266

Human Resources
Internet: www.nike.com

Nike Canada is a global entity that manufactures sport and athletic apparel, equipment and footwear.

Academic Fields
College: Accounting, Advertising, Business, Communications, Human Resources, Marketing/Sales
Bachelor of Arts: General, Public Relations
Bachelor of Comm/Admin: Accounting, Finance, Marketing
Bachelor of Science: Computer Science
Chartered Accounting: CA - General/Finance, CGA/CMA - General/Finance
Masters: Business Administration

Critical Skills
Adaptable, Good Communication, Confident, Creative, Dependable, Enthusiastic, Innovative, Leadership, Personable, Professional, Responsible

Types of Positions
Warehouse Position   Customer Service
Retail Division

Starting Salary
$ 25,000 - 30,000

Company Benefits
- Complete benefits for full time employees
- Training sessions on product knowledge
- Internal posting of positions

Correspondence
Mail resume with cover letter

Part Time/Summer: Nike Canada regularly looks for individuals for part time and summer opportunities. Potential summer work involves co-op students for marketing and sales, and summer staff in their retail operation.

NISSAN CANADA INC.

5290 Orbitor Drive, P.O. Box 1709, Station B
Mississauga, Ontario, L4Y 4H6
Tel: (905) 629-2888   Fax: (905) 629-6526

Carolyn A. Starshuk, Human Resources Specialist
Internet: www.nissancanada.com

Nissan Canada imports and distributes Nissan cars and light trucks, Infinity luxury vehicles, forklift trucks, outboard motors, and associated parts and accessories. Nissan Canada is a wholly owned subsidiary of Nissan Motor Company of Tokyo. The company employs more than 320 individuals across the country.

Academic Fields
College: Accounting, Advertising, Human Resources, Secretarial
Bachelor of Arts: General, Business, Languages
Bachelor of Comm/Admin: General, Accounting, Finance
Chartered Accounting: CMA-General, CGA-General

Critical Skills
Adaptable, Dependable, Efficient, Enthusiastic, Flexible, Good Communication, Innovative, Personable, Professional, Responsible

Types of Positions
Collections Representative   Warehouse Person

Starting Salary
$ 25,000 - 30,000

Company Benefits
- Above average extended health and dental benefits
- Life insurance benefits
- Discounts on vehicle lease and loan

Correspondence
Mail or fax resume with cover letter

Part Time/Summer: Nissan Canada occasionally looks for individuals for part time and summer employment. Potential jobs most likely include marketing coordinator, or collections representative. The best time to apply is in April or May.

NLK CONSULTANTS INC.

855 Homer Street
Vancouver, British Columbia, V6B 5S2
Tel: (604) 689-0344   Fax: (604) 443-1000

Personnel Department
Internet: www.nlkeng.com

NLK is a full service consulting engineering firm serving the pulp and paper industry worldwide. They have developed a full range of high quality services based on their specialized knowledge and understanding of the pulp and paper industry. NLK provides expertise in the two main business areas of engineering and strategic planning/marketing services. In both areas, NLK clients are provided with an experienced industry partner from project conception to completion.

Academic Fields
College: Drafting/Architecture, Engineering Tech.
Bachelor of Engineering: Chemical, Civil, Electrical, Mechanical
Masters: Engineering

Critical Skills
Adaptable, Dependable, Efficient, Enthusiastic, Flexible, Organized, Personable, Good Communication, Productive, Responsible, Team Player, Accurate

Types of Positions
Clerk   Reception
Data Entry   Drafting
Engineering

Starting Salary
$ 27,000 - 30,000 (drafting) /
$ 34,000 - 40,000 (engineering)

Company Benefits
- Extended health, medical, dental and vision care
- Long term disability, life insurance
- In-house lunchtime seminars

Correspondence
Mail, fax or e-mail resume with cover letter
E-mail: humanresources@nlkvcr.nlkeng.com

Part Time/Summer: NLK Consultants sometimes seeks individuals for part time positions, and regularly looks for candidates for summer employment. Positions in the summer are most likely to include engineering students as assisting engineers, and other students to provide summer vacation relief in the office.

NORBORD INDUSTRIES

1 Toronto Street, Suite 500
Toronto, Ontario, M5C 2W4
Tel: (416) 365-0700   Fax: (416) 360-2243

Lisa Antonucci, Coordinator of Recruitment

Norbord Industries is an international manufacturer of wood products for construction and industrial uses. Norbord Industries is a wholly-owned subsidiary of Noranda Forest Inc., which is a publicly traded company.

Academic Fields
College: Accounting, Forestry, Human Resources, Marketing/Sales, Mechanical Tech.
Bachelor of Arts: Business
Bachelor of Comm/Admin: General, Accounting, Finance, Marketing, Info Mgmt.
Bachelor of Science: Environmental Studies, Forestry
Bachelor of Engineering: Computer Systems, Electrical, Environmental Studies, Mechanical
Chartered Accounting: CA - General/Finance, CGA/CMA - General/Finance
Masters: Business Administration, Engineering

Critical Skills
Adaptable, Analytical, Good Communication, Confident, Creative, Decisive, Dependable, Diligent, Diplomatic, Efficient, Enthusiastic, Flexible, Good With Figures, Innovative, Leadership, Logical, Personable, Productive, Professional, Responsible

Types of Positions
Sales Coordinator   Data Entry Clerk
Accounting Clerk

Starting Salary
$ 25,000 - 30,000

Company Benefits
- Excellent benefits and training opportunities
- Philosophy of promoting from within

Correspondence
Mail or fax resume with cover letter

Part Time/Summer: Norbord Industries does not hire candidates for part time employment, but occasionally looks for people for summer opportunities. Potential jobs are most likely those listed above, as well as secretarial duties. The best time to apply is in April.

The Canada Student Employment Guide

NORCEN ENERGY RESOURCES LTD.

715 5th Avenue NW
Calgary, Alberta, T2P 4V4
Tel: (403) 231-0111   Fax: (403) 231-0144

Human Resources Department

Norcen Energy Resources is an oil and gas exploration and development company. Norcen is also involved in the retail sales of propane. The company employs approximately 3,200 individuals.

Academic Fields
College: Accounting, Human Resources, Marketing/Sales
Bachelor of Comm/Admin: Accounting, Marketing
Bachelor of Science: Computer Science, Environmental Studies, Geography, Geology
Bachelor of Engineering: General, Chemical, Civil, Computer Systems, Design, Electrical, Environmental Studies, Geotechnical, Industrial, Mechanical
Chartered Accounting: CA-Finance, CMA-General, CMA-Finance

Critical Skills
Adaptable, Creative, Enthusiastic, Good Communication, Productive

Types of Positions
Mail Centre   Technician

Starting Salary
$ 25,000 - 30,000

Company Benefits
- Flexible benefits
- Related industry courses

Correspondence
Mail, fax, or e-mail resume with cover letter
E-mail: speddie@norcen.com

Part Time/Summer: Norcen Energy Resources occasionally seeks people for part time and summer employment opportunities. A potential position in the summer would be within information services. The best time to apply is in March.

NORTH AMERICAN LIFE ASSURANCE COMPANY

5650 Yonge Street
North York, Ontario, M2M 4G4
Tel: (416) 218-5673   Fax: (416) 229-3073

David Coward, Human Resources Specialist

As one of Canada's major financial services organizations, North American Life has been serving customers with quality financial security products since 1881. These products include individual and group life insurance, health and annuity plans, RRSP's, RRIF's, and association and cardholder benefits. They employ about 2,100 people.

Academic Fields
College: Accounting, Business, Human Resources, Insurance, Secretarial
Bachelor of Arts: General, Business, Economics, Languages, Psychology, Sociology/Social Work, Stats
Bachelor of Comm/Admin: General, Accounting, Finance, Marketing, Info Mgmt.
Bachelor of Science: Actuarial, Computer Science, Mathematics, Psychology
Chartered Accounting: CA - General/Finance, CGA/CMA - General/Finance
Masters: Business Administration, Arts

Critical Skills
Adaptable, Analytical, Good Communication, Creative, Decisive, Dependable, Diligent, Enthusiastic, Flexible, Good With Figures, Innovative, Leadership, Logical, Organized, Personable, Productive, Professional, Writing Skills, Team Oriented

Types of Positions
Customer Service   Clerical
New Business

Starting Salary
$ 25,000 - 30,000

Company Benefits
- Health, dental, life insurance, vision care
- Long term disability, subsidized cafeteria
- In-house PC training, fitness subsidy

Correspondence
Mail resume with cover letter

Part Time/Summer: They occasionally hire part time and summer students. Potential jobs are usually clerical in nature. Apply in March or April.

The Canada Student Employment Guide

NORTH WEST COMPANY INC.

77 Main Street
Winnipeg, Manitoba, R3C 2R1
Tel: (204) 934-1750   Fax: (204) 934-1696

Pat Jacob, Stores Recruitment
Internet: www.northwest.ca

The North West Company is the leading provider of food and everyday products and services to remote communities across northern Canada and Alaska. In Canada, under the trading name "Northern", they are the largest private sector employer of aboriginal people with approximately 4,000 staff members in 150 stores.

Academic Fields
College: Accounting, Administration, Advertising, Business, Computer Science, Drafting/Architecture, Faculty Management, Food/Nutrition, Graphic Arts, Human Resources, Marketing/Sales, Secretarial
Bachelor of Arts: General, Business
Bachelor of Comm/Admin: General, Accounting, Finance, Marketing, Info Mgmt., Public Admin.
Bachelor of Science: Computer Sci., Environ. Studies
Chartered Accounting: CMA - General/Finance, CGA - General/Finance
Masters: Business Administration, Science

Critical Skills
Adaptable, Confident, Creative, Efficient, Enthusiastic, Flexible, Excellent Communication, Written Communication, Innovative, Leadership, Organized, Professional, Responsible, Team Player

Types of Positions
Accounting Clerk   Mail Clerk
Press Operator   Data Entry Clerk
Administrative Assistant Receptionist

Starting Salary
$ 20,000 - 40,000

Company Benefits
- Dental, extended health care, life insurance

Correspondence
Mail, fax, or e-mail resume with cover letter
E-mail: pjacob@northwest.ca

Part Time/Summer: North West Co. sometimes hires for part time work, and regularly hires in the summer. Potential jobs are in the mail room, accounting, human resources, marketing and logistics. The best time to apply is April and May.

NORTH YORK COMMUNITY CARE ACCESS CENTRE

45 Sheppard Avenue East, 7th Floor
North York, Ontario, M2N 5W9
Tel: (416) 222-2241   Fax: (416) 224-1470

Ingrid Roberts, Human Resources Assistant
Internet: www.nyccac.on.ca

The North York Community Care Access Centre is a non-profit organization dedicated to providing residents of North York with a single point of access to in-home health services, long-term care placement or information and referral services. One phone call will get eligible clients and their families the information, referral and personal services they need, whether those needs are best met at home or in a long-term care facility.

Academic Fields
College: Information Systems, Secretarial
Bachelor of Science: Nursing (RN), Occupational Therapy, Physiotherapy
Masters: Social Work

Critical Skills
Adaptable, Decisive, Dependable, Efficient, Flexible, Good Communication, Good Writing Skills, Organized, Professional, Responsible

Types of Positions
Team Assistant

Starting Salary
$ 26,572 - 32,050

Company Benefits
- Extended health and dental, long term disability
- Basic life insurance, company pension

Correspondence
Fax or e-mail resume with cover letter
E-mail: lroberts@nyccac.on.ca

Part Time/Summer: North York Community Care Access Centre occasionally hires individuals for part time work, and regularly looks for people for summer positions. Potential opportunities in the summer are most likely clerical in nature. The best time to apply is in February or March.

NORTHERN LIGHTS REGIONAL HEALTH CENTRE
7 Hospital Street
Fort McMurray, Alberta, T9H 1P2
Tel: (403) 791-6011   Fax: (403) 791-6281

Human Resources
Internet: www.altech.ab.ca/nlrhs

Northern Lights Regional Health Centre is an active treatment hospital, and a public health unit. The centre offers health care services along with educational and preventative programs to ensure a well rounded service is provided.

Academic Fields
College: Communications, Computer Science, Food/Nutrition, Human Resources, Mechanical Tech., Nursing, Radiology Tech., Secretarial, Security/Law
Bachelor of Arts: Public Relations
Bachelor of Comm/Admin: Accounting, Finance
Bachelor of Science: Computer Science, Environmental Studies, Food Sciences, Health Sciences, Nursing (RN), Occupational Therapy, Pharmacy, Physiotherapy, Psychology
Bachelor of Engineering: Computer Systems
Chartered Accounting: CA-Finance, CMA-Finance, CGA-Finance
Masters: Business Administration

Critical Skills
Adaptable, Analytical, Good Communication, Confident, Dependable, Efficient, Enthusiastic, Flexible, Good With Figures, Innovative, Leadership, Organized, Personable, Persuasive, Productive, Professional, Responsible, Good Writing Skills

Types of Positions
Various Nursing Units   Physiotherapy
Occupational Therapy

Starting Salary
$ 30,000 - 40,000

Company Benefits
- Full range of health coverage
- Insurance benefits

Correspondence
Mail or fax resume with cover letter

Part Time/Summer: Northern Lights Regional Health Centre occasionally hires for part time work and regularly hires for the summer. Potential jobs involve computers, kitchen work, speech pathology, and clerical duties. The best time to apply is in April or May.

NORTHERN MOUNTAIN HELICOPTERS INC.
P.O. Box 368, Stn A
Prince George, British Columbia, V2L 4S2
Tel: (250) 963-1272   Fax: (250) 963-1273

Robert Baber, Manager Employee Relations
Internet: www.nmh.net

Northern Mountain Helicopters provides helicopter transportation service to companies throughout Northern B.C., Alberta, N.W.T., Yukon, Marathon, Ontario, and Internationally. The firm employs approximately 170 individuals.

Academic Fields
College: Accounting
Bachelor of Arts: Business
Bachelor of Comm/Admin: General, Accounting, Marketing, Info Mgmt.
Chartered Accounting: CMA-General, CGA-General

Critical Skills
Adaptable, Analytical, Good Communication, Decisive, Dependable, Efficient, Enthusiastic, Flexible, Innovative, Leadership, Organized, Personable, Productive, Professional, Responsible, Good Writing Skills

Types of Positions
Pilot   Aircraft Maintenance Engineer
Accounting

Starting Salary
$ 25,000 - 30,000 (To start)

Company Benefits
- Full competitive benefits

Correspondence
Mail, fax or e-mail resume with cover letter
E-mail: bbaber@nmh.net

Part Time/Summer: Northern Mountain Helicopters occasionally looks for people for part time and summer employment. Potential jobs include general labour, or office duties. The best time to apply is in April.

NORTHWESTEL INC.

Box 2727
Whitehorse, Yukon, Y1A 4Y4
Tel: (800) 661-0824   Fax: (867) 668-3236

Jodi Drury, Human Resources Officer
Internet: www.nwtel.ca

Northwestel provides a complete range of advanced telecommunications services to 110,000 people in Canada's beautiful North. Their services include voice, data, cellular, mobile, cable television and Internet. Their operating area spans Nunavut, Northwest Territories, Yukon Territory and Northern B.C.

Academic Fields
College: Accounting, Communications, Human Resources, Information Systems, Marketing/Sales, Secretarial, CAD Autocad, Computer Science, Electronics Tech., Engineering Tech.
Bachelor of Arts: Business, Public Relations
Bachelor of Comm/Admin: General, Accounting, Finance, Human Resources, Marketing, Info Mgmt.
Bachelor of Laws: General, Corporate
Bachelor of Engineering: General, Civil, Elec., Mech.
Chartered Accounting: CA - General/Finance, CGA - General/Finance, CMA - General/Finance
Masters: Business Administration, Engineering

Critical Skills
Adaptable, Analytical, Decisive, Dependable, Diplomatic, Efficient, Enthusiastic, Flexible, Good Communication, Innovative, Leadership, Responsible, Customer Service Oriented

Types of Positions
Manager Implementation	Customer Service
Human Resources	Operations
Product/Marketing Manager	Account (Sales) Manager

Starting Salary
$ 40,000 - 45,000

Company Benefits
- Attractive compensation package, competitive salary

Correspondence
E-mail resume with cover letter
E-mail: recruitment@nwtel.ca

Part Time/Summer: Northwestel Inc. regularly hires for part time work and occasionally hires for the summer. Summer jobs include telephone operator or technical position. Preference is given to local candidates. Apply between December and May.

NORWICH UNION LIFE INSURANCE SOCIETY

60 Yonge St.
Toronto, Ontario, M5E 1H5
Tel: (416) 362-2961   Fax: (416) 362-0780

Amy Foston, Manager Human Resources
Internet: www.norwich-union.ca

Norwich Union Life Insurance Society is a life insurance company that provides many types of products and services to individuals across the country relating to life insurance plans. The firm employs 150 people.

Academic Fields
College: General, Accounting, Business, Computer Science, Human Resources, Insurance, Marketing/Sales, Secretarial
Bachelor of Arts: General, Business, Economics, English
Bachelor of Comm/Admin: General, Accounting, Finance, Marketing, Info Mgmt.
Bachelor of Science: General, Actuarial, Computer Science, Mathematics
Chartered Accounting: CA - General/Finance, CGA/CMA - General/Finance
Masters: Business Administration

Critical Skills
Adaptable, Analytical, Good Communication, Decisive, Dependable, Diplomatic, Efficient, Enthusiastic, Flexible, Good With Figures, Leadership, Logical, Organized, Patient, Personable, Productive, Professional, Responsible, Good Writing Skills

Types of Positions
Customer Service Rep.	Administrator
Mail Clerk	

Starting Salary
$ 25,000 - 30,000 (depends entirely on position)

Company Benefits
- Full range of benefits, health and dental
- Pension, group life, disability
- Program assists financially with education

Correspondence
Mail resume with cover letter

Part Time/Summer: Norwich Union does not generally hire for part time work, but regularly hires for the summer. Potential jobs would involve clerical work. The best time to apply is in April or May.

NOVA SCOTIA LIQUOR COMMISSION

93 Chain Lake Dr.
Halifax, Nova Scotia, B3S 1A3
Tel: (902) 450-5825   Fax: (902) 450-6025

Leean Amirault, Human Resources Dept.

Nova Scotia Liquor Commission regulates the sale of liquor products in retail outlets throughout Nova Scotia. They employ about 900 people in total.

Academic Fields
College: Accounting, Administration, Computer Science, Human Resources, Marketing/Sales, Secretarial
Bachelor of Arts: Public Relations
Bachelor of Comm/Admin: Accounting, Marketing, Info Mgmt.
Bachelor of Science: Computer Science
Bachelor of Engineering: Civil
Chartered Accounting: CMA-General
Masters: Business Administration

Critical Skills
Adaptable, Creative, Dependable, Efficient, Enthusiastic, Flexible, Good Communication, Logical, Organized, Productive, Professional, Responsible, Good Writing Skills

Types of Positions
Casual Data Entry Clerk   Casual Administrative Clerk
Casual Accounting Clerk   Casual Store Clerk

Starting Salary
below $ 20,000

Company Benefits
- On-the-job training
- Computer skills courses (in-house)

Correspondence
Mail resume with cover letter

Part Time/Summer: Nova Scotia Liquor Commission occasionally looks for individuals for part time work, however does not hire for the summer months.

NOVA SCOTIA POWER CORP.

P.O. Box 910
Halifax, Nova Scotia, B3J 2W5
Tel: (902) 428-6995   Fax: (902) 428-6130

Mary Keddy, Human Resources

Nova Scotia Power Corp. is an electric utility company established to transmit and distribute electricity in Nova Scotia. The company employs over 2,200 individuals.

Academic Fields
College: Accounting, Business, Computer Science, Drafting/Architecture, Engineering Tech., Forestry, Human Resources, Secretarial
Bachelor of Arts: Public Relations
Bachelor of Comm/Admin: Accounting, Finance, Marketing, Info Mgmt.
Bachelor of Science: Biology, Chemistry, Computer Science, Environmental Studies, Forestry, Health Sciences, Mathematics
Bachelor of Laws: Corporate
Bachelor of Engineering: Chemical, Civil, Computer Syst., Electrical, Environ. Studies, Industrial, Mech.l
Chartered Accounting: CMA - General/Finance
Masters: Business Admin., Science, Engineering

Critical Skills
Adaptable, Analytical, Good Communication, Confident, Creative, Decisive, Dependable, Diligent, Diplomatic, Efficient, Enthusiastic, Flexible, Good With Figures, Organized, Patient, Personable, Persuasive, Productive, Professional, Responsible, Writing Skills

Types of Positions
Staff Analyst   Staff Engineer

Starting Salary
$ 25,000 - 40,000

Company Benefits
- Health and dental insurance, life and accident

Correspondence
Mail resume with cover letter

Part Time/Summer: Nova Scotia Power Corp. regularly hires for part time and summer work. There are a range of summer positions depending on departmental needs. Jobs may include labourer, or be related to field's of study such as engineering, info technology, or commerce. January through March is the best time to apply.

NOVARTIS CONSUMER HEALTH CANADA INC.
2233 Argentia Rd., Suite 205
Mississauga, Ontario, L5N 2W5
Tel: (905) 812-4100   Fax: (905) 812-4082

Human Resources & Communications

Novartis Consumer Health Canada is involved in the manufacturing of over the counter pharmaceuticals. The firm has an employee base of approximately 1,500 people.

Academic Fields
College: General, Accounting, Administration, Advertising, Animal Health, Business, Communications, Human Resources, Marketing/Sales, Mechanical Tech., Nursing, Secretarial
Bachelor of Arts: Business, Public Relations
Bachelor of Comm/Admin: General, Accounting, Finance, Marketing, Info Mgmt.
Bachelor of Science: General, Agriculture, Chemistry, Environmental Studies, Health Sciences, Mathematics, Microbiology, Pharmacy
Bachelor of Laws: Corporate
Bachelor of Engineering: Chemical, Computer Systems, Mechanical
Chartered Accounting: CA-General, CMA-Finance, CGA-Finance
Masters: Business Administration, Science, Engineering

Critical Skills
Good Communication, Confident, Creative, Decisive, Dependable, Efficient, Enthusiastic, Flexible, Good With Figures, Innovative, Organized, Personable, Productive, Professional, Responsible

Types of Positions
Sales Representative   Administration
Customer Service   Quality Control

Starting Salary
$ 30,000 - 35,000 (depending on position)

Company Benefits
- Competitive benefit package

Correspondence
Mail resume with cover letter

Part Time/Summer: Novartis Consumer Health Canada regularly seeks people for part time or summer work. Potential summer jobs are in accounting, information technology, customer service or marketing.

NOVOTEL CANADA INC.
135 Carlingview Drive
Etobicoke, Ontario, M9W 5E7
Tel: (416) 798-9800   Fax: (416) 798-3257

Shelley Miller, Human Resources
Internet: www.novotel.com

Novotel Canada is a hotel establishment operating 4 locations in the Toronto region. Providing facilities for business or pleasure, Novotel Canada employs over 700 individuals across the country. The address above is for their Novotel Toronto Airport location, however, candidates are urged to contact individual hotels for employment opportunities. Their largest facility is located in Mississauga, Ontario.

Academic Fields
College: General, Accounting, Business, Engineering, Hospitality, Human Resources, Marketing/Sales
Bachelor of Arts: Business
Bachelor of Comm/Admin: Accounting
Chartered Accounting: CMA-General, CGA-General

Critical Skills
Adaptable, Good Communication, Confident, Creative, Decisive, Dependable, Diplomatic, Efficient, Enthusiastic, Flexible, Innovative, Leadership, Organized, Patient, Personable, Productive, Professional, Responsible

Types of Positions
Guest Service Agent   Reservation Agent
Restaurant Server   Maintenance Helper
Room Attendant   Houseperson

Starting Salary
$ 20,000 - 25,000

Company Benefits
- Medical, dental, group RRSP
- Discounts on rooms and restaurants, free meals
- Management Development Program

Correspondence
Mail or fax resume with cover letter

Part Time/Summer: Novotel regularly hires for part time openings and sometimes hires for summer work. Potential positions include guest service agent, server, and room attendant. The best time to apply is in April or May.

The Canada Student Employment Guide

NPS ALLELIX CORP.

6850 Goreway Dr.
Mississauga, Ontario, L4V 1V7
Tel: (905) 677-0831   Fax: (905) 677-3698

HR Department
Internet: www.npsp.com

In December 1999, NPS Pharmaceuticals and Allelix Biopharmaceuticals Inc. of Toronto, Canada merged. The merged company operates as NPS Pharmaceuticals, Inc. in the U.S. and as NPS Allelix Corp. in Canada. The company is engaged in the discovery and development of novel, small molecule drugs and recombinant peptides that address a variety of important diseases.

Academic Fields
College: Accounting, Computer Science, Electronics Tech.
Bachelor of Comm/Admin: Accounting
Bachelor of Science: Biology, Chemistry, Computer Science, Microbiology
Bachelor of Engineering: Chemical
Chartered Accounting: CA - General/Finance, CGA/CMA - General/Finance
Masters: Science, Engineering, Library Science

Critical Skills
Adaptable, Analytical, Good Communication, Creative, Dependable, Diligent, Efficient, Enthusiastic, Flexible, Productive, Professional, Good Writing Skills

Types of Positions
Technician

Starting Salary
$ 30,000 - 40,000

Company Benefits
- Medical, dental, and life insurance
- Pension plan

Correspondence
Mail, fax or e-mail resume with cover letter

Part Time/Summer: NPS Allelix Corp. occasionally seeks individuals for part time work and regularly looks for individuals for the summer. The best time to apply is from January to March.

NUMAC ENERGY INC.

321 - 6 Avenue SW
Calgary, Alberta, T2P 3H3
Tel: (403) 260-9400   Fax: (403) 260-9561

Patti-Lou Barron, Human Resources
Internet: www.numac.com

Numac Energy Inc. is one of the 25 largest crude oil, and natural gas companies in Canada. The company is engaged in the exploration, development, production and marketing of crude oil, natural gas, and natural gas liquids. The company employs approximately 230 individuals.

Academic Fields
College: Accounting, Computer Science, Human Resources, Secretarial
Bachelor of Arts: Business, Economics
Bachelor of Comm/Admin: Accounting, Finance, Marketing
Bachelor of Science: Computer Science, Geology
Bachelor of Engineering: General, Chemical, Computer Systems, Geotechnical, Mechanical
Masters: Business Administration, Science, Engineering

Critical Skills
Adaptable, Creative, Diligent, Enthusiastic, Innovative

Types of Positions
Earth Science   Engineering
Accounting   Computer Science

Starting Salary
$ 25,000 - 30,000

Company Benefits
- Health and dental plans, life and accident insurance
- Income protection plans, savings plans, bonus program
- Training offered for both technical and soft skills

Correspondence
Mail resume with cover letter

Part Time/Summer: Numac Energy occasionally looks for people for part time work, and regularly seeks candidates for the summer months. Potential jobs in the summer involve geology, geophysics, land, accounting, computer science, and engineering. The best time to apply is in February or March.

NYGARD INTERNATIONAL LTD.

1771 Inkster Blvd.
Winnipeg, Manitoba, R2X 1R3
Tel: (204) 982-5200   Fax: (204) 697-1254

Jack Palmer, Director of Human Resources
Internet: www.nygard.com

Nygard International is a leading manufacturer of ladies sportswear, and a major retailer with 200 stores across Canada and the United States. The firm employs about 2,600 people in total.

Academic Fields
College: Accounting, Business, Human Resources, Information Systems, CAD Autocad, Computer Science, Fashion
Bachelor of Arts: Business
Bachelor of Comm/Admin: General, Accounting, Info Mgmt.
Chartered Accounting: CA-Finance, CGA-Finance, CMA-Finance

Critical Skills
Adaptable, Analytical, Good With Figures, Organized, Personable, Productive, Professional, Responsible

Types of Positions
Merchandising Assistant   Junior Payroll Clerk
Sales Administration Trainee

Starting Salary
$ 20,000 - 25,000

Company Benefits
- Health package
- Basic dental
- Computer training

Correspondence
Mail, fax, or e-mail resume with cover letter

Part Time/Summer: Nygard International occasionally looks for individuals for part time and summer work. Potential positions involve information technology.

OCEANIS SEAFOODS LTD.

P.O. Box 89
Shippagan, New Brunswick, E0B 2P0
Tel: (506) 336-9725   Fax: (506) 336-0945

Human Resources

Oceanis Seafoods is engaged in the manufacturing and packaging of seafood products. The company has a fish plant that produces mainly crab. Established in 1973, Oceanis Seafoods has approximately 375 employees. Jobs within the plant are seasonal from May to July. They employ 350 staff members during this production period.

Academic Fields
College: Secretarial

Critical Skills
Confident, Diplomatic, Efficient, Good Communication, Good Writing Skills, Leadership, Organized, Professional

Types of Positions
Labourer

Starting Salary
below $ 20,000

Company Benefits
- Many benefits offered

Correspondence
Mail resume with cover letter, or fill out application

Part Time/Summer: Oceanis Seafoods sometimes seeks candidates for part time employment and regularly looks for individuals to work during the summer months. In the summer, labour jobs in the crab plant are the most likely to be available.

OCELOT ENERGY INC.

30th Floor, West Tower, Petro-Canada Centre, 150
Calgary, Alberta, T2P 3Y7
Tel: (403) 299-5700   Fax: (403) 299-5750

Heather Coutts, Human Resources Coordinator
Internet: www.ocelot.ca

Ocelot Energy is a growing, financially solid, public Canadian energy company focused primarily on the exploration, production, and marketing of oil and natural gas. The mission of Ocelot Energy is to become one of Canada's senior independent oil and gas producers by pursuing growth initiatives that create substantial long term value for the company's stakeholders. Ocelot Energy employs approximately 100 people.

Academic Fields
College: Drafting/Architecture, Human Resources, Secretarial
Bachelor of Arts: Business, Economics
Bachelor of Comm/Admin: Accounting
Bachelor of Science: Geology
Bachelor of Laws: Corporate
Bachelor of Engineering: Chemical
Chartered Accounting: CMA-General/Finance, CGA-General/Finance
Masters: Engineering

Critical Skills
Adaptable, Dependable, Diligent, Good Communication, Enthusiastic, Good Writing Skills, Innovative, Organized, Personable, Professional, Responsible

Types of Positions
Finance

Starting Salary
$ 30,000 - 40,000

Company Benefits
- Full health and dental coverage
- Share purchase plan, pension plan

Correspondence
Mail resume with cover letter

Part Time/Summer: Ocelot Energy regularly looks for candidates for part time and summer employment. Potential jobs in the summer involve field positions such as mowing grass and painting, or office positions such as junior engineers and geologists.

OETIKER LIMITED

203 Dufferin St. S.
Alliston, Ontario, L9R 1W7
Tel: (705) 435-4394   Fax: (705) 435-3155

Karen Currior Human Resources

Oetiker Limited is a manufacturer of automotive parts and stainless steel clamps. They also produce non-automotive industrial products. The firm employs 130 individuals.

Academic Fields
College: Accounting, Administration, Advertising, Business, Drafting/Architecture, Electronics Tech., Engineering Tech., Human Resources, Marketing/Sales
Bachelor of Arts: Public Relations
Bachelor of Comm/Admin: Marketing, Info Mgmt.
Bachelor of Engineering: General, Design, Electrical, Industrial, Mechanical
Chartered Accounting: CMA-General
Masters: Business Administration

Critical Skills
Adaptable, Analytical, Good Communication, Confident, Creative, Decisive, Dependable, Diplomatic, Enthusiastic, Flexible, Innovative, Leadership, Personable, Productive, Professional, Responsible, Good Writing Skills

Types of Positions
Team Leader   Finance Accountant
Draftsperson

Starting Salary
below $ 20,000

Company Benefits
- Group health and dental, group pension plan
- Annual bonus plan
- Extensive orientation and product training

Correspondence
Mail resume with cover letter

Part Time/Summer: Oetiker Limited occasionally looks for individuals for part time positions, and regularly seeks people in the summer. Potential jobs involve production and shipping, and clerical duties. The best time to apply is in mid-March.

OKANAGAN SKEENA GROUP LIMITED

4625 Lazelle Avenue
Terrace, British Columbia, V8G 1S4
Tel: (604) 635-6316   Fax: (604) 638-6320

Sharon Taylor, Manager of Human Resources

Okanagan Skeena Group Limited is a communications company operating cablevision, radio and television systems in the province of British Columbia. The company serves small and medium size markets in northwest British Columbia, and in the Okanagan.

Academic Fields
College: Communications, Computer Science, Journalism, Marketing/Sales, Television/Radio
Chartered Accounting: CA - General/Finance

Critical Skills
Creative, Dependable, Diligent, Efficient, Flexible, Organized, Patient, Personable, Professional

Types of Positions
News Reporter   Announcer
Creative Writer   Traffic Clerk

Starting Salary
$ 20,000 - 25,000

Company Benefits
- Comprehensive medical, dental & life insurance
- Tuition fees paid on approved courses
- Company & union sponsorship of training

Correspondence
Mail or fax resume with cover letter

Part Time/Summer: Okanagan Skeena Group sometimes seeks individuals for part time positions, but does not hire individuals for the summer months.

OLAND BREWERIES LIMITED

3055 Agricola Street
Halifax, Nova Scotia, B3K 4G2
Tel: (902) 453-3821   Fax: (902) 453-3847

Eleanor Gaudett, Human Resources

For over 130 years, the Oland Brewery has stood for pride of craftsmanship. The Oland Brewery is a subsidiary of Labatt Brewing Company under the family operated Interbrew S.A., one of the most successful brewers in the world for over 400 years.

Academic Fields
College: Accounting, Computer Science, Engineering Tech., Food/Nutrition, Human Resources, Laboratory Tech., Marketing/Sales
Bachelor of Arts: General, Business
Bachelor of Comm/Admin: Accounting, Finance, Marketing
Bachelor of Science: Chemistry, Computer Science, Food Sciences, Microbiology
Bachelor of Laws: Corporate
Bachelor of Engineering: Chemical, Civil, Electrical, Environmental Studies
Bachelor of Education: General
Chartered Accounting: CMA-Finance, CGA-Finance
Masters: Business Admin., Science, Engineering

Critical Skills
Adaptable, Analytical, Creative, Dependable, Diplomatic, Enthusiastic, Flexible, Good Communication, Innovative, Leadership, Personable, Productive, Responsible

Types of Positions
Various positions

Starting Salary
$ 25,000 - 30,000

Company Benefits
- Complete benefits package

Correspondence
Mail or fax resume with cover letter
E-mail: eleanor.gaudett@labatt.com

Part Time/Summer: Oland Breweries occasionally looks for candidates for part time jobs, and regularly seeks candidates for summer employment. Potential positions involve the manufacturing line. The best time to apply is between January and March.

OMSTEAD FOODS LIMITED

P.O. Box 520, 303 Mile Rd.
Wheatley, Ontario, N0P 2P0
Tel: (519) 825-4611   Fax: (519) 825-7144

Carolyn Lang, Human Resources Specialist

Omstead Foods is a food processing facility. It was founded in 1911 and was a family owned and run company until it was sold to John Labatts Foods in 1984. It was then acquired by the H.J. Heinz Co. in 1991 and is still owned by them today. They produce frozen fruit and vegetables, coated products (onion rings, cheese sticks), and fresh and frozen fish products (predominantly perch, smelt and pickerel).

Academic Fields
College: Accounting, Administration, Human Resources, Secretarial, Agricultural, CAD Autocad, Engineering Tech., Mechanical Tech., Nursing (RN)
Bachelor of Arts: Business
Bachelor of Comm/Admin: Accounting, Finance, Human Resources
Bachelor of Science: Agriculture, Biology, Chemistry, Food Sciences, Microbiology
Bachelor of Engineering: Chemical, Electrical
Chartered Accounting: CA-Finance, CGA-Finance, CMA-Finance
Masters: Business Administration, Science, Engineering

Critical Skills
Adaptable, Dependable, Efficient, Enthusiastic, Flexible, Good Communication, Leadership, Personable, Professional

Types of Positions
Secretarial/Admin. Assistant   Accounting Clerk
Lab Technician   Supervisor (Production)

Starting Salary
$ 35,000 - 40,000

Company Benefits
- Health benefits including dental, drug, vision
- Fitness subsidy, global stock purchase plan

Correspondence
Mail or fax resume with cover letter

Part Time/Summer: Omstead Foods Limited rarely hires for part time or summer employment. A potential job includes quality control lab technician. Apply in April or May. Occasionally they require administrative help during the summer months.

ONTARIO GUARD SERVICES INC.

1915 Danforth Avenue
Toronto, Ontario, M4C 1J5
Tel: (416) 690-2827   Fax: (416) 690-5420

Ross Snider, Human Resources

Ontario Guard Services is a security company providing personnel, detective and protective services to individuals, residential establishments, and all types of businesses. Employing about 500 individuals in the Toronto region, Ontario Guard Services has one location in Toronto. Many of the company's employees work on a part time basis.

Academic Fields
College: Business
Bachelor of Arts: General, Business, Criminology, Public Relations
Bachelor of Comm/Admin: Marketing
Bachelor of Laws: General

Critical Skills
Adaptable, Good Communication, Confident, Creative, Decisive, Dependable, Diligent, Diplomatic, Efficient, Enthusiastic, Flexible, Good With Figures, Innovative, Leadership, Logical, Organized, Patient, Personable, Persuasive, Productive, Professional, Responsible, Good Writing Skills

Types of Positions
Security Officer

Starting Salary
$ 25,000 - 30,000

Company Benefits
- 80% medical (drug) and dental
- Two to eight weeks of training

Correspondence
Submit resume with cover letter in person

Part Time/Summer: Ontario Guard Services regularly hires candidates for part time and summer employment. Openings during the summer months are usually for security officers. May or June is usually the best time to apply.

The Canada Student Employment Guide

THE ONTARIO JOCKEY CLUB

555 Rexdale Blvd.
Rexdale, Ontario, M9W 5L2
Tel: (416) 675-3993   Fax: (416) 674-1958

Human Resources
Internet: www.ojc.com

The Ontario Jockey Club is engaged in standard and thoroughbred horse racing including track operation. The Club employs almost 2,000 people at one of its 3 locations in the Toronto region.

Academic Fields
College: Accounting, Business, Computer Science, Human Resources, Marketing/Sales, Secretarial, Security/Law, Television/Radio
Bachelor of Arts: General, Business, Public Relations
Bachelor of Comm/Admin: General, Accounting, Finance, Marketing, Info Mgmt.
Bachelor of Science: Computer Science
Chartered Accounting: CA - General/Finance, CGA/CMA - CA - General/Finance
Masters: Business Administration

Critical Skills
Adaptable, Analytical, Dependable, Good Communication, Flexible, Innovative, Organized, Productive, Responsible

Types of Positions
Accounting   Information Systems
Human Resources   Food and Beverage

Starting Salary
$ 20,000 - 30,000

Company Benefits
- 80% medical, dental
- Vision every two weeks, life insurance, pension
- Short and long term disability

Correspondence
Mail resume and cover letter or submit in person

Part Time/Summer: The Ontario Jockey Club occasionally hires students for part time jobs, and regularly seeks candidates for summer opportunities. Potential positions are in the areas of food and beverage, maintenance, or involve being a customer service representative. The best time to apply is in April, May, or June.

ONTARIO LEGISLATIVE OFFICES

Room 2540 Whitney Block, 99 Wellesley Street
Toronto, Ontario, M7A 1A2
Tel: (416) 325-3556   Fax: (416) 325-3573

Staffing Coordinator

As part of the Finance and Administration Division, The Office of the Controller works to promote good financial management practices of The Ontario Legislative Offices. It provides financial direction for the Legislative Assembly to ensure the smooth operation and the proper financial transactions of departments. The Office of the Controller works with The Ministry of Finance to research and publish information on the province's financial activities.

Academic Fields
College: General, Accounting, Administration, Computer Sci., Cooking/Culinary, Human Resources
Bachelor of Arts: General, Business, Political Science, Public Relations
Bachelor of Comm/Admin: General, Accounting, Finance, Info Mgmt., Public Admin.
Bachelor of Laws: General
Bachelor of Engineering: Computer Syst., Electrical
Bachelor of Education: Adult Education
Chartered Accounting: CA - General/Finance, CGA/CMA - General/Finance
Masters: Business Admin., Education, Library Science

Critical Skills
Adaptable, Analytical, Artistic, Good Communication, Confident, Creative, Decisive, Dependable, Diligent, Diplomatic, Efficient, Enthusiastic, Flexible, Good With Figures, Innovative, Leadership, Logical, Organized, Professional, Responsible, Good Writing Skills

Types of Positions
Receptionist   Administrative Asst.
Payroll Clerk   Accounting Clerk
Library Clerk

Starting Salary
$ 25,000 - 40,000 (depending on position)

Company Benefits
- Full benefits package

Correspondence
Mail resume with cover letter

Part Time/Summer: The Office of the Controller sometimes hires for part time and summer positions.

ONTARIO MARCH OF DIMES

10 Overlea Blvd.
Toronto, Ontario, M4H 1A4
Tel: (416) 425-3463   Fax: (416) 425-1920

Birgit Matthaes, Human Resources
Internet: www.dimes.on.ca

Ontario March of Dimes is a multi-service, charitable organization delivering a wide range of programs that enrich the lives of over 10,000 men and women with physical disabilities each year in communities across Ontario.

Academic Fields
College: General, Accounting, Human Resources, Journalism, Secretarial
Bachelor of Arts: Journalism, Psychology, Public Relations, Recreation Studies, Sociology/Social Work
Bachelor of Comm/Admin: Info Mgmt.
Bachelor of Science: General, Kinesiology, Occupational Therapy, Psychology
Bachelor of Education: Adult Education
Chartered Accounting: CA-General, CGA - General/Finance

Critical Skills
Adaptable, Good Communication, Dependable, Flexible, Personable, Productive

Types of Positions
Support Service Attendant   Clerk/Secretary

Starting Salary
$ 20,000 - 25,000

Company Benefits
- Health, hospital, drug, dental
- Life insurance, pension

Correspondence
Mail or fax resume with cover letter

Part Time/Summer: Ontario March of Dimes occasionally looks for people for part time and summer work. Potential jobs are mostly clerical or secretarial positions. The best time to apply is in February or March.

OPINION SEARCH INC.

160 Elgin St., Suite 1800
Ottawa, Ontario, K2P 2C4
Tel: (613) 230-9109   Fax: (613) 230-3793

Recruitment Coordinator
Internet: www.opinionsearch.com

Opinion Search Inc. is one of North American's leading market research data collection agencies, providing a range of phone, site and Internet interviewing and tabulation services. With a special emphasis on telephone fieldwork, Opinion Search Inc. has developed a strong bilingual and multi-lingual team of trained interviewers, supervisors, analysts and coders.

Academic Fields
No specific academic background required.
They look at individuals from all academic areas. Statistics and Sociology are important.

Critical Skills
Adaptable, Good Communication, Dependable, Flexible, Patient, Personable, Professional

Types of Positions
Research Interviewer

Starting Salary
below $ 20,000

Company Benefits
- Work is part time contract based, thus benefits vary
- Training offered

Correspondence
Mail, fax, e-mail, or submit resume with cover letter in person

Part Time/Summer: Opinion Search regularly looks for people for part time or summer work. The best time to apply is in the middle or end of April.

ORACLE CORP. CANADA INC.

110 Matheson Boulevard West, Suite 100
Mississauga, Ontario, L5R 3P4
Tel: (905) 890-0800   Fax: (905) 890-4034

Aileen Duncan, HR Consultant
Internet: www.oracle.ca

Oracle Corporation Canada Inc., was founded in 1984 to better meet the current and emerging systems architecture and information-management software needs of Canadian companies and organizations. With headquarters in Mississauga, Ontario, the company, through its more than 1,000 employees, develops customized, fully integrated computing solutions for its customers from 13 offices across the country.

Academic Fields
College: General, Accounting, Advertising, Business, Computer Science, Electronics Tech., Engineering Tech., Human Resources, Marketing/Sales, Secretarial
Bachelor of Arts: General, Business, English, Public Rel.
Bachelor of Comm/Admin: Accounting, Marketing, Info Mgmt.
Bachelor of Science: Actuarial, Computer Sci., Math
Bachelor of Engineering: Chemical, Computer Syst.
Bachelor of Education: Adult Education
Chartered Accounting: CA-Finance, CMA-General/Finance, CGA-General/Finance
Masters: Business Admin., Engineering, Education

Critical Skills
Adaptable, Analytical, Good Communication, Confident, Creative, Decisive, Dependable, Diligent, Professional, Responsible, Good Writing Skills

Types of Positions
Accounting Clerk   Technical Analyst
Associate Consultant   Office Clerk
Administrative Support

Starting Salary
$ 20,000 - 30,000

Company Benefits
- Medical and dental benefits including vision
- Under program no deductibles, or waiting period
- Reimbursement for education costs

Correspondence
Mail or e-mail resume with cover letter

Part Time/Summer: Oracle sometimes hires for part time work and for the summer. Potential jobs include office clerk, marketing assistant, and shipping clerk.

OTTAWA HOSPITAL

1053 Carling Ave.
Ottawa, Ontario, K1Y 4E9
Tel: (613) 798-5555   Fax: (613) 761-5374

Rosanna Lashley, Manager, Recruitment

The Ottawa Hospital is the second largest acute care teaching hospital in Canada, with three campuses (Riverside, Civic and General) and is affiliated with universities and colleges in the Ottawa area.

Academic Fields
College: Accounting, Human Resources, Information Systems, Purchasing, Secretarial, CAD Autocad, Computer Science, Engineering Tech., Industrial Design, Mechanical Tech., Plumbing, Dental, Emergency/Paramedic, Nursing (RN/RNA), Radiology Tech., Respiratory Tech.
Bachelor of Comm/Admin: Accounting, Finance, Human Resources, Info Mgmt.
Bachelor of Science: Biology, Computer Science, Food Sciences, Nursing (RN), Occupational Therapy, Pharmacy, Physiotherapy, Psychology
Bachelor of Engineering: Biomedical, Computer Systems, Design
Bachelor of Education: Adult Education
Chartered Accounting: CA - General/Finance, CGA/CMA - General/Finance
Masters: Business Administration

Critical Skills
Adaptable, Analytical, Efficient, Enthusiastic, Flexible, Good Communication, Good Writing Skills, Productive, Professional, Responsible

Types of Positions
Support Staff   Clerical/Secretarial
Junior Specialized Position

Starting Salary
$ 30,000 - 35,000

Company Benefits
- Full benefit package for permanent staff

Correspondence
Mail, fax, e-mail or submit resume with cover letter in person

Part Time/Summer: Ottawa Hospital occasionally hires for part time work and rarely hires for the summer. Potential jobs are most likely those listed above. The best to apply is from February to June.

OVERLANDER HOSPITAL

953 Southill Street
Kamloop, British Columbia, V2B 7Z9
Tel: (250) 554-2323   Fax: (250) 554-3403

Human Resources

Overlander Hospital is a 200 bed geriatric care facility located in Kamloop, British Columbia. They provide numerous extended care services.

Academic Fields
College: Cooking/Culinary, Engineering Tech., Food/Nutrition, Nursing, Unit Clerk, Medical Terminology
Bachelor of Science: Nursing (RN), Physiotherapy, Occupational Therapy, Recreation Therapy, Music Therapy, Dietitian, Cook

Critical Skills
Adaptable, Analytical, Confident, Decisive, Dependable, Diligent, Diplomatic, Efficient, Enthusiastic, Flexible, Good Communication, Good Writing Skills, Leadership, Logical, Manual Dexterity, Organized, Patient, Personable, Productive, Professional, Responsible

Types of Positions
Registered Nurse   Nurse Aide
Cleaner   Dietary Aide
Maintenance

Starting Salary
$30,000 - 40,000

Company Benefits
- Fully paid group life and dental
- Extended health benefits
- Contributory pension plan

Correspondence
Mail or submit resume with cover letter in person

Part Time/Summer: Overlander Hospital occasionally seeks people for part time work, but does not hires specifically for the summer months.

OWEN BIRD

P.O. Box 49130, Bentall III
Vancouver, British Columbia, V7X 1J5
Tel: (604) 688-0401   Fax: (604) 688-2827

Ann Johnston Human Resources
Internet: www.owenbird.com

Owen Bird is a law firm in Vancouver, British Columbia. The company employs over 110 individuals.

Academic Fields
College: Secretarial (Legal)

Critical Skills
Adaptable, Good Communication, Confident, Dependable, Diligent, Diplomatic, Efficient, Enthusiastic, Flexible, Logical, Organized, Personable, Productive, Professional, Responsible, Good Writing Skills

Types of Positions
Mail Clerk   Photocopy/Fax Clerk
Reception

Starting Salary
$ 20,000 - 25,000

Company Benefits
- Employer pays 100% medical, dental and life insurance
- 5 days orientation
- On-going job related courses

Correspondence
Mail resume with cover letter

Part Time/Summer: Owen Bird does not hire individuals for part time work, but occasionally looks for candidates for summer jobs. Potential work involves clerical duties. The best time to apply is in April.

PALADIN SECURITY & INVESTIGATIONS LIMITED

260 West Esplanade, Suite 301
North Vancouver, British Columbia, V7M 3G7
Tel: (604) 980-7550   Fax: (604) 984-7443

Jo-anne Morefield, Human Resources
Internet: www.pinc.com/paladin

Paladin Security and Investigations is a detective agency and offers protective services to individuals and businesses in British Columbia. Established in 1976, the detective agency has an employee base of approximately 300 individuals.

Academic Fields
College: Administration, Communications, Emergency/Paramedic, Hospitality, Journalism, Security/Law
Bachelor of Arts: Criminology

Critical Skills
Analytical, Good Communication, Good Writing Skills, Innovative, Responsible

Types of Positions
Security Guard   First Aid Attendant
Mobile Driver

Starting Salary
below $ 20,000

Company Benefits
- Extended medical, basic dental, life insurance
- On-the-job training

Correspondence
Mail, fax, or submit resume and cover letter in person

Part Time/Summer: Paladin Security & Investigations regularly looks for individuals to work on a part time basis or during the summer months. Potential jobs include security guard and first aid attendants. Applicants can apply year round.

PANORAMA MOUNTAIN VILLAGE

2030 Summit Dr.
Panorama, British Columbia, V0A 1T0
Tel: (250) 342-6941   Fax: (250) 342-3727

Kelly Nadeau, Coordinator Human Resources
Internet: www.panoramaresort.com

Panorama Mountain Village is a four season ski and golf vacation destination undergoing a ten-year development plan. Winter activities including skiing, snowboarding, heli-skiing, soaking in their hot pools, sleigh and snowmobile tours, and nordic skiing. Summer offers golf, rafting, horseback riding, mountain biking, tennis, etc. They recruit employees from across Canada for seasonal career opportunities and offer a great benefits package.

Academic Fields
College: Communications, Marketing/Sales, Cooking/Culinary, Hospitality, Travel/Tourism
Bachelor of Comm/Admin: Info Mgmt.

Critical Skills
Adaptable, Dependable, Efficient, Enthusiastic, Flexible, Good Communication, Personable

Types of Positions
Front Desk   Room Attendant
Lift Operating   Ticket Sales
Server   Cashier

Starting Salary
$ 15,000 - 20,000

Company Benefits
- Benefits plan, medical, dental, vision
- Full time employees receive a free ski pass

Correspondence
Apply through web site
E-mail: knadeau@intrawest.com

Part Time/Summer: Panorama Mountain Village occasionally hires for part time work and regularly hires for the summer. Summer jobs include room attending, lifeguarding/pool attending, groundskeeping, working at the activities desk or day camp, or on the golf course as play or equipment coordinator, or turf care. Also available are positions in food and beverage as servers and cooks, and some positions in retail, reservations, front desk and maintenance.

PAPERBOARD INDUSTRIES INTERNATIONAL INC.
772 Sherbrooke W.
Montreal, Québec, H3A 1G1
Tel: (514) 284-9800   Fax: (514) 289-1773

Human Resources Manager

Paperboard Industries International is a boxboard company in Montreal, Quebec. The company is a subsidiary of Cascades Inc., of Kingsey Falls, Quebec. Cascades Paperboard International has an employee base of approximately 3,200 individuals.

Academic Fields
College: Graphic Arts
Bachelor of Comm/Admin: General
Bachelor of Engineering: Industrial, Mechanical
Chartered Accounting: CA-General
Masters: Business Administration

Critical Skills
Adaptable, Analytical, Good Communication, Confident, Creative, Decisive, Dependable, Efficient, Flexible, Good With Figures, Innovative, Leadership, Organized, Personable, Productive, Professional, Responsible, Good Writing Skills

Types of Positions
Sales   Production

Starting Salary
$ 25,000 - 30,000

Company Benefits
- Full benefit package

Correspondence
Mail resume with cover letter

Part Time/Summer: Paperboard Industries International does not hire for part time employment, but occasionally seeks candidates for summer employment. Potential jobs are in production. The best time to apply is in the Spring.

PARAMOUNT CANADA'S WONDERLAND INC.
9580 Jane St.
Vaughan, Ontario, L6A 1S6
Tel: (905) 832-7000   Fax: (905) 832-7519

Ken Graham, HR Coordinator
Internet: www.canadaswonderland.com

Paramount Canada's Wonderland is an amusement park that caters to families. They also have group events for schools and companies.

Academic Fields
College: General, Accounting, Admin., Advertising, Animal Health, Business, Communications, Computer Sci., Cooking/Culinary, Electronics Tech., Emergency/Paramedic, Food/Nutrition, Graphic Arts, Hospitality, Human Res., Marketing/Sales, Mechanical Tech., Nursing, Performing Arts, Secretarial, Security/Law, Stats, Television/Radio, Travel/Tourism
Bachelor of Arts: General, Business, Criminology, Fine Arts, Music, Public Relations, Statistics
Bachelor of Comm/Admin: General, Accounting, Finance, Marketing, Info Mgmt., Public Admin.
Bachelor of Science: General, Computer Science, Food Sciences, Nursing (RN), Zoology
Bachelor of Laws: General
Bachelor of Engineering: General, Computer Systems, Electrical, Industrial, Mechanical, Water Res., Bach. of Architecture, Bach. of Landscape Architecture
Bachelor of Education: General
Masters: Business Administration, Engineering

Critical Skills
Good Communication, Confident, Dependable, Enthusiastic, Personable, Responsible, Honest

Types of Positions
Food Services Dept.   Merchandising Dept.
Games Dept.   Rides Dept.

Starting Salary
below $ 20,000 - 25,000 (seasonal only)

Company Benefits
- Full medical, dental, life insurance for full time staff
- Seasonal employees get free passes, incentives

Correspondence
Submit resume with cover letter in person

Part Time/Summer: Paramount Canada's Wonderland occasionally hires for part time work, and regularly hires in the summer. Many positions exist. Recruiting begins the second week in January.

The Canada Student Employment Guide

PARKLAND INDUSTRIES LTD.

4959 - 59 Street, Suite 236
Red Deer, Alberta, T4R 2K6
Tel: (403) 357-6400   Fax: (403) 346-3015

Kelly Collier, Controller

Parkland Industries is involved in the refining and marketing of petroleum products in the prairie provinces. They employ about 140 individuals.

Academic Fields
College: Business
Chartered Accounting: CA-General, CMA-General, CGA-General

Critical Skills
Adaptable, Good Communication, Diligent, Efficient, Enthusiastic, Flexible, Good With Figures, Personable, Productive, Professional, Responsible

Types of Positions
Data Entry   Sales Administration

Starting Salary
$ 30,000 - 40,000

Company Benefits
- Life, health, disability, and dental insurance
- Dollar matching long term savings plan
- Reimbursement of company related courses

Correspondence
Submit resume with cover letter in person

Part Time/Summer: Parkland Industries occasionally look for people for part time positions, and regularly seeks candidates in the summer months. A potential job may involve data entry. The best time to apply is in May.

PATHEON INC.

2100 Syntex Court
Mississauga, Ontario, L5N 7K9
Tel: (905) 821-4001   Fax: (905) 812-6709

Human Resources
Internet: www.patheon.com

Patheon is an integrated provider of contract manufacturing and drug development services to the pharmaceutical and biotechnology markets. With 25 years of manufacturing expertise, Patheon is a leader in product formulation, analytical development, and the commercial production of pharmaceutical products. They employ 1,800 individuals worldwide and 900 people in Canada.

Academic Fields
College: Human Resources, General Science, Mechanical Tech., Laboratory Tech.
Bachelor of Comm/Admin: Accounting, Finance, Human Resources
Bachelor of Science: Biology, Chemistry, Food Sciences, Health Sciences, Microbiology, Pharmacy
Bachelor of Engineering: Biomedical, Chemical
Bachelor of Education: General
Chartered Accounting: CA - General/Finance, CGA - General/Finance, CMA - General/Finance
Masters: Science, Engineering

Critical Skills
Adaptable, Analytical, Confident, Dependable, Diligent, Diplomatic, Efficient, Enthusiastic, Flexible, Logical, Manual Dexterity, Organized, Productive, Professional, Responsible

Types of Positions
Lab Technician   Research Chemist
Formulation Technologist   Processing Operator
QC Sampler

Starting Salary
$ 30,000 - 35,000

Company Benefits
- Extensive benefit package

Correspondence
Fax or e-mail resume with cover letter
E-mail: patheon@patheon.com

Part Time/Summer: Patheon does not hire for part time work, but regularly hires for the summer. The best time to apply is in mid March or early April.

The Canada Student Employment Guide

THE PAUL REVERE LIFE INSURANCE COMPANY
5420 North Service Rd., P.O. Box 5044
Burlington, Ontario, L7R 4C1
Tel: (905) 319-9501   Fax: (905) 319-6518

John Grinvalds, Director of Human Resources

The Paul Revere Life Insurance Company is Canada's leading provider of disability insurance. The firm has many offices and provides many types of insurance products and services.

Academic Fields
College: Accounting, Business, Computer Science, Insurance
Bachelor of Arts: Business, Economics
Bachelor of Comm/Admin: General
Bachelor of Science: Actuarial

Critical Skills
Analytical, Good Communication, Dependable, Flexible, Organized, Responsible

Types of Positions
Customer Service   Office Services
Underwriting   Claims

Starting Salary
$ 20,000 - 25,000

Company Benefits
- Comprehensive group benefits
- Pension plan, incentive savings plan
- On-the-job training, self development

Correspondence
Mail or fax resume with cover letter

Part Time/Summer: The Paul Revere Life Insurance Company occasionally looks for people for part time work and summer positions. Potential jobs are general office clerical duties. The best time to apply is from April to June.

PAVCO
375 Water Street, Suite 600
Vancouver, British Columbia, V6B 5C6
Tel: (604) 482-2200   Fax: (604) 482-2248

Human Resources Department
Internet: www.bcpavco.com

PavCo operates the Vancouver Convention and Exhibition Centre, B.C. Place Stadium, Robson Square Conference Centre, The Bridge Studios, and the Fraser Valley Trade and Exhibition Centre (TRADEX). PavCo is a Crown Corporation of The Province of British Columbia and employs approximately 150 full time and 350 part time staff.

Academic Fields
College: General, Accounting, Administration, Business, Communications, Computer Science, Electronics Tech., Emergency/Paramedic, Engineering Tech., Hospitality, Human Resources, Marketing/Sales, Mechanical Tech., Secretarial, Security, Tourism, Event/Facility Management
Bachelor of Arts: Business
Bachelor of Comm/Admin: General, Accounting, Finance, Marketing, Info Mgmt., Public Admin.
Chartered Accounting: CA - General/Finance, CMA-General/Finance, CGA-General/Finance

Critical Skills
Adaptable, Analytical, Confident, Creative, Decisive, Dependable, Diligent, Diplomatic, Efficient, Enthusiastic, Flexible, Good Communication, Innovative, Organized, Personable, Productive, Professional, Responsible

Types of Positions
Housekeeping   Administrative Assistant
Junior Accountant   Hosting
Security   Event Assistant

Starting Salary
$ 25,000 - 35,000

Company Benefits
- Excellent benefits for full time employees
- Includes medical, dental, disability insurance

Correspondence
Mail resume with cover letter

Part Time/Summer: PavCo sometimes hires for part time or summer work. Positions vary depending on the need. The best time to apply is from April to May.

The Canada Student Employment Guide

PCL CONSTRUCTORS INC.

5410 - 99 Street
Edmonton, Alberta, T6E 3P4
Tel: (403) 435-9749   Fax: (403) 436-2247

Mr. Wiens, Human Resources
Internet: www.pcl.ca

PCL Constructors Inc. is a contractor founded in 1906 that offers experience, competitive pricing, financial strength, professionalism, integrity and a commitment to projects that are supported by quality and workplace safety initiatives. PCL is one of the largest contracting organizations in North America.

Academic Fields
College: Accounting, Computer Science, Engineering Tech., Secretarial
Bachelor of Arts: Business
Bachelor of Comm/Admin: Accounting
Bachelor of Science: Computer Science
Bachelor of Engineering: Civil, Mechanical
Chartered Accounting: CA-General, CMA-General, CGA-General
Masters: Business Administration, Engineering

Critical Skills
Adaptable, Analytical, Dependable, Diligent, Good Communication, Good Writing Skills, Innovative, Professional, Responsible, Honest, Team Oriented

Types of Positions
Engineering Trainee   Field Engineer
Estimator   Project Accountant

Starting Salary
$ 30,000 - 40,000

Company Benefits
- Comprehensive flexible benefits plan
- PCL 'College of Construction' offers courses, seminars and workshops
- Mentoring and on-the-job training

Correspondence
Mail, fax or submit resume and cover letter in person

Part Time/Summer: PCL Constructors regularly looks for candidates for part time and summer opportunities. In the summer, potential jobs include construction labourer, engineering trainee, and accounting clerk.

PEACOCK INC.

8600 St. Patrick Street
Lasalle, Québec, H8N 1V1
Tel: (514) 366-0907   Fax: (514) 366-9804

Henry Crochetiere, Director of Human Resources

Peacock Inc., founded in 1897, is a Canadian company supplying a diversified range of products and equipment to meet the needs of the mining, pulp and paper, petrochemical, food and beverage, marine, oil/gas, metallurgical, manufacturing, and process industries and utilities. Allied and complimentary to this is a comprehensive service network for the repair and overhaul of rotating and reciprocating machinery. The company employs over 550 people in its operating divisions.

Academic Fields
College: Accounting, Human Resources, Marketing/Sales
Bachelor of Arts: Business
Bachelor of Comm/Admin: Accounting, Finance, Marketing, Info Mgmt.
Bachelor of Engineering: Computer Systems, Mechanical
Chartered Accounting: CA-General, CMA-General, CGA-Finance

Critical Skills
Dependable, Personable, Manual Dexterity

Types of Positions
Accounting   Sales
Reception

Starting Salary
$ 20,000 - 25,000

Company Benefits
- Complete benefit package
- Group insurance, pension
- Company encourages and supports training

Correspondence
Mail resume with cover letter

Part Time/Summer: Peacock sometimes looks for individuals for part time and summer employment. Potential opportunities in the summer months involve clerical work or reception duties. The best time to apply is in April or May.

PEARSON EDUCATION CANADA

26 Prince Andrew Place
Toronto, Ontario, M3C 2T8
Tel: (416) 447-5101   Fax: (416) 443-0948

Johann Cresswell, Human Resources Manager
Internet: www.pearsoned.ca/

Pearson Education Canada, a division of the world's leading educational and technology publisher, is owned by Pearson plc. As the largest publisher in Canada, Pearson Education Canada has an established reputation for producing market-leading educational products.

Academic Fields
College: Accounting, Advertising, Computer Science, Human Resources, Secretarial
Bachelor of Arts: General, Business, English, History, Journalism, Political Science
Bachelor of Comm/Admin: General, Accounting, Finance, Marketing, Info Mgmt.
Bachelor of Education: General
Chartered Accounting: CA-Finance, CMA-General/Finance, CGA-Finance
Masters: Business Administration, Education

Critical Skills
Adaptable, Analytical, Good Communication, Confident, Creative, Decisive, Dependable, Diligent, Diplomatic, Efficient, Enthusiastic, Flexible, Good With Figures, Innovative, Leadership, Logical, Organized, Responsible, Good Writing Skills

Types of Positions
Clerical   Accounting
Distribution Centre   Sales Team
Editorial

Starting Salary
$ 20,000 - 25,000

Company Benefits
- Comprehensive benefit package
- Group RRSP with company match
- Hands on in-house training, some external training

Correspondence
Mail resume with cover letter

Part Time/Summer: Pearson Education Canada sometimes hires for part time and summer positions. Potential jobs include editorial co-op, customer service or involve duties in the distribution warehouse. The best time to apply is in February or April.

PEEL BOARD OF EDUCATION

5650 Hurontario Street
Mississauga, Ontario, L5R 1C6
Tel: (416) 890-1099   Fax: (416) 890-4955

Human Resources Department
Internet: www.attn.org

The Peel Board of Education is responsible for maintaining quality education in elementary and secondary schools in the Region of Peel.

Academic Fields
College: General, Accounting, Business, Child Care, Computer Science, Drafting/Architecture, Food/Nutrition, Graphic Arts, Human Resources, Secretarial, Urban Planning
Bachelor of Arts: Business, English
Bachelor of Comm/Admin: General, Accounting, Finance, Info Mgmt., Public Admin.
Bachelor of Science: General, Biology, Chemistry, Computer Science, Geography, Mathematics, Physics
Bachelor of Engineering: General, Design, Bachelor of Architecture
Bachelor of Education: General, Adult Education, Childhood, Special
Chartered Accounting: CA - General/Finance, CGA/CMA - General/Finance
Masters: Business Administration, Arts, Science, Education, Library Science

Critical Skills
Adaptable, Analytical, Good Communication, Confident, Creative, Decisive, Dependable, Diligent, Diplomatic, Efficient, Enthusiastic, Flexible, Good With Figures, Innovative, Leadership, Logical, Organized, Patient, Professional, Responsible, Good Writing Skills

Types of Positions
Teacher   Teaching Assistant
Secretarial   School Attendant

Starting Salary
$ 20,000 - 40,000 (depending on position)

Company Benefits
- Extended health, dental, vision care
- Long term disability, pension

Correspondence
Mail resume with cover letter

Part Time/Summer: The Peel Board of Education sometimes hires for part time work, but does not hire in for the summer months.

The Canada Student Employment Guide

PEEL CHILDREN'S CENTRE

101 Queensway West, Suite 500
Mississauga, Ontario, L5B 2P7
Tel: (905) 273-3193   Fax: (905) 273-3664

Lisa Marcy, HR Coordinator
Internet: www.peelcc.org

Peel Children's Centre is an accredited children's mental health centre which provides a wide range of treatment services to children and their families who reside in the Peel region. The Centre employs 167 individuals.

Academic Fields
College: Human Resources, Secretarial, Social Work, CYC Diploma
Bachelor of Arts: Psychology, Sociology/Social Work
Bachelor of Comm/Admin: Human Resources
Bachelor of Science: Psychology
Bachelor of Education: Childhood
Masters: Social Work

Critical Skills
Flexible

Types of Positions
Child & Youth Counsellor   Intake Worker
Child & Family Clinician

Starting Salary
$ 30,000 - 35,000

Company Benefits
- Full benefits package for full time employees
- Pension plan, generous vacation plan
- Professional development is always encouraged

Correspondence
Mail, fax or e-mail resume with cover letter
E-mail: hr@peelcc.org

Part Time/Summer: Peel Children's Centre regularly looks for individuals for part time and summer employment. They hire through HRDC and the YMCA summer jobs program. Check the HRDC website for their postings in early May.

PEEL REGIONAL POLICE

7750 Hurontario Street
Brampton, Ontario, L6V 3W6
Tel: (905) 453-3311   Fax: (905) 453-4722

Human Resources

Peel Regional Police is engaged in the provision of municipal police services. The police division has 5 locations in the area and employs over 1,500 individuals to work in various areas of law enforcement.

Academic Fields
College: Accounting, Administration, Business, Computer Science, Electronics Tech., Engineering Tech., Human Resources, Journalism, Marketing/Sales, Mechanical Tech., Secretarial, Security/Law, Statistics, Television/Radio, Police Studies, Police Management, Police Services
Bachelor of Arts: Business, Criminology, Journalism, Public Relations
Bachelor of Comm/Admin: Finance, Marketing, Public Admin.
Bachelor of Science: Computer Science
Chartered Accounting: CMA-Finance
Masters: Business Administration, Engineering

Critical Skills
Different skills apply depending on the job.
All may apply.

Types of Positions
Records Systems Operator   Switchboard Operator
Headquarters Receptionist   Maintenance
Court Clerk

Starting Salary
$ 20,000 - 40,000 (depending on position)

Company Benefits
- Full health care, dental plan, life insurance, pension
- Short/long term disability, shift premiums
- Race relations training, educational assistance

Correspondence
Mail or fax resume with cover letter

Part Time/Summer: The Peel Regional Police sometimes hires for part time openings and regularly hires for summer jobs. Potential positions include maintenance, groundskeeper, and cleaner. Candidates should apply in mid-February for these positions.

PELMOREX INC.

1 Robert Speck Pkwy., Suite 1600
Mississauga, Ontario, L4Z 4B3
Tel: (905) 566-9511   Fax: (905) 566-9696

Human Resources
Internet: www.theweathernetwork.com

Pelmorex is the owner of The Weather Network (Cable 23). They are a leading provider of multimedia weather information to Canada and around the world.

Academic Fields
College: Advertising, Business, Communications, Computer Science, Engineering Tech., Human Resources, Journalism, Marketing/Sales, Television/Radio
Bachelor of Arts: Business, English, Journalism, Music, Public Relations, Urban Geography
Bachelor of Comm/Admin: Accounting, Finance, Marketing, Info Mgmt., Public Admin.
Bachelor of Science: Computer Science, Environmental Studies, Geography
Bachelor of Engineering: Computer Systems, Electrical
Chartered Accounting: CA-Finance, CMA-Finance, CGA-Finance

Critical Skills
Adaptable, Analytical, Good Communication, Creative, Dependable, Enthusiastic, Leadership, Organized, Professional, Responsible

Types of Positions
Marketing Assistant   Administration Assistant
Radio Operator

Starting Salary
Depends on position

Company Benefits
- On-the-job training

Correspondence
E-mail resume with cover letter
E-mail: hr@on.pelmorex.com

Part Time/Summer: Pelmorex regularly seeks individuals for part time jobs. Potential part time work includes switcher/editor or graphic artist. The company does not generally hire for the summer. They offer internships in all departments.

Co-op/Internship: Internship opportunities are available.

PEMBINA PIPELINE CORPORATION

P.O. Box 1948, 707 - 8th Ave. SW
Calgary, Alberta, T2P 2M7
Tel: (403) 231-7500   Fax: (403) 266-1155

Barbara S. Davies, Human Resources Administrator
Internet: www.pembina.com

Pembina Pipeline is a major owner and operator of petroleum liquids feeds pipeline systems in Alberta. The company employs approximately 260 people.

Academic Fields
College: Accounting, Electronics Tech., Secretarial
Bachelor of Comm/Admin: Accounting
Bachelor of Science: Computer Science, Environmental Studies
Bachelor of Laws: Corporate
Bachelor of Engineering: Chemical, Civil, Environmental Studies, Geotechnical, Mechanical

Critical Skills
Analytical, Good Communication, Diligent, Organized, Flexible, Patient, Responsible, Good Writing Skills, Work Ethic, Problem Solving

Types of Positions
Accounting   Clerical

Starting Salary
$ 25,000 - 40,000 (depending on position)

Company Benefits
- Full benefits including medical and dental
- Vision, long and short term disability, pension
- Training and development program

Correspondence
Mail, or e-mail resume with cover letter
E-mail: valexand@pembina.com

Part Time/Summer: Pembina Corporation occasionally looks for individuals for part time work, and regularly seeks candidates in the summer. Potential jobs include engineer, accountant, or clerical duties. The best time to apply is in the fall in October.

The Canada Student Employment Guide

PENNCORP LIFE INSURANCE COMPANY

90 Dundas St. W., 4th Floor
Mississauga, Ontario, L5B 2T5
Tel: (905) 272-0210   Fax: (905) 272-3797

Nicole Kalloo, Director Human Resources

PennCorp Life Insurance Company provides life, accident and sickness insurance products. Their clients are both blue collar or self-employed. They have been providing home office insurance in Canada for the last 26 years. They have 13 branches across the country.

Academic Fields
College: General, Accounting, Administration, Business, Communications, Graphic Arts, Human Resources, Insurance, Secretarial
Bachelor of Arts: General, Business, Languages, Public Relations
Bachelor of Comm/Admin: General, Accounting, Finance, Marketing, Info Mgmt., Public Admin.
Bachelor of Science: Health Sciences
Chartered Accounting: CA - General/Finance, CGA-General
Masters: Business Administration

Critical Skills
Good Communication, Confident, Decisive, Dependable, Efficient, Enthusiastic, Flexible, Good With Figures, Organized, Patient, Personable, Professional, Responsible, Good Writing Skills

Types of Positions
File Clerk   Accounting Clerk
Policy Typist   Receptionist
Mail Clerk   Claims Clerk

Starting Salary
Depends on position

Company Benefits
- Dental, medical, long term disability

Correspondence
Mail or fax resume with cover letter

Part Time/Summer: PennCorp occasionally seeks people for part time work, and regularly hires for the summer. Potential jobs are mostly clerical to cover vacations. The best time to apply is in March. Occasionally, there may be a need in December as well.

PETER KIEWIT SONS CO.

2600 Skymark Avenue, Suite 201
Mississauga, Ontario, L4W 5B2
Tel: (905) 206-1490   Fax: N/A

Human Resources

Peter Kiewit Sons Co. is engaged in the business of heavy construction. Their projects are often carried out in remote site locations. The head office of Peter Kiewit Sons Co. is located in Mississauga, Ontario.

Academic Fields
Bachelor of Engineering: Civil, Mechanical, Mining

Critical Skills
Adaptable, Analytical, Good Communication, Confident, Creative, Decisive, Dependable, Diligent, Efficient, Enthusiastic, Flexible, Good With Figures, Leadership, Logical, Manual Dexterity, Organized, Personable, Productive, Professional, Responsible, Good Writing Skills

Types of Positions
Cost Engineer   Field Engineer
Mechanical Engineer

Starting Salary
$ 30,000 - 40,000

Company Benefits
- Health and dental benefits
- In-house training programs

Correspondence
Mail resume with cover letter

Part Time/Summer: Peter Kiewit Sons Co. occasionally looks for individuals for part time and summer employment opportunities. Potential jobs are most likely those listed above.

The Canada Student Employment Guide

PETRO-CANADA

5140 Yonge Street, Suite 200
North York, Ontario, M2N 6L6
Tel: (416) 730-2000   Fax: (416) 730-2151

Donna McNeely, Human Resources

Established in 1975, Petro-Canada is the largest Canadian owned oil and gas company and a leader in the petroleum industry. The company is engaged in the exploration, development, production, transportation, and marketing of crude oil, natural gas, field liquids, sulphur and oil sands. Petro-Canada is also involved in the refining of crude oil into oil products and the distribution and sales of these products. Petro-Canada has an employee base of over 7,300 people.

Academic Fields
Bachelor of Comm/Admin: Accounting
Bachelor of Engineering: Chemical, Mechanical
Chartered Accounting: CMA-General, CGA-General
Masters: Business Administration, Engineering

Critical Skills
Adaptable, Creative, Decisive, Good Communication, Flexible, Leadership, Organized, Good With Figures, Team Player, Results Oriented

Types of Positions
Territory Manager Trainee   Engineer
Accountant

Starting Salary
$ 30,000 - 40,000

Company Benefits
- Comprehensive health, dental and life insurance
- Capital accumulation plan
- Special assignments and team work projects

Correspondence
Mail resume with cover letter

Part Time/Summer: Petro Canada sometimes offers opportunities for part time employment and during the summer months.

PETROMONT & CO. LTD. PARTNERSHIP

2931 boulevard Marie-Victorin
Varennes, Québec, J3X 1S7
Tel: (514) 640-6400   Fax: (514) 652-2459

M. Bergeron, Ressources humaines

Petromont & Co. Ltd. Partnership is a chemicals company that has its operations based in Varennes, Quebec. The company has an employee base of about 600 individuals.

Academic Fields
College: Accounting, Laboratory Tech., Mechanical Tech., Science, Secretarial
Bachelor of Engineering: Chemical, Electrical, Industrial, Mechanical

Critical Skills
Decisive, Flexible, Logical, Good Communication, Responsible

Types of Positions
Technical Science   Laboratory Work
Accounting   Maintenance
Human Resources

Starting Salary
$ 30,000 - 40,000

Company Benefits
- Most benefits offered
- Medical, dental, life insurance
- Savings plan, pension plan

Correspondence
Mail resume with cover letter

Part Time/Summer: Petromont & Co. Ltd. Partnership does not hire individuals for part time employment, but sometimes seeks candidates for the summer months. Potential positions most likely involve office duties. The best time to apply is in March.

PHARMA PLUS DRUGMARTS LTD.

5965 Coopers Ave.
Mississauga, Ontario, L4Z 1R9
Tel: (905) 671-5425   Fax: (905) 672-5857

Travis More, Recruitment Co-ordinator

Pharma Plus Drugmarts is involved in the sales of pharmaceutical products and general merchandise. A wholly owned subsidiary of the Oshawa Group Ltd., Pharma Plus operates 106 outlets in Ontario and has over 2,800 employees across Canada. Applications can be dropped off at individual store locations.

Academic Fields
College: General, Accounting, Administration, Advertising, Business, Computer Science, Human Resources, Marketing/Sales, Secretarial
Bachelor of Arts: General, Business, Criminology
Bachelor of Comm/Admin: General, Accounting, Finance, Info Mgmt.
Bachelor of Science: Pharmacy
Chartered Accounting: CA - General/Finance, CGA/CMA - General/Finance
Masters: Business Administration

Critical Skills
Adaptable, Analytical, Dependable, Good Communication, Flexible, Diligent, Logical, Good Writing Skills, Organized, Patient, Productive, Professional, Responsible

Types of Positions
Accounting Clerk   Asst. Category Manager
Administrative Asst. Management Trainee
Traffic Coordinator

Starting Salary
$ 20,000 - 25,000

Company Benefits
- Complete benefit package
- Major medical, dental, insurance, flexible days

Correspondence
Mail resume and cover letter or submit at stores

Part Time/Summer: Pharma Plus regularly hires for part time and summer work. Summer jobs are within the office or the retail stores. Positions in the office include accounting clerks or administrators. The best time to apply is in April. Within the stores potential positions include cashier or stockperson. These opportunities can be applied to year round.

PHILLIPS & TEMPRO INDUSTRIES LTD.

100 Paquin Rd.
Winnipeg, Manitoba, R3C 2V3
Tel: (204) 667-2260   Fax: (204) 667-2041

Shirley Bray-Mak HR Administrator

Phillips & Tempro Industries is a manufacturer of automobile cold weather starting aids for the automotive, heavy duty and industrial industries.

Academic Fields
College: CAD Autocad, Electronics Tech., Engineering Tech., Industrial Design, Mechanical Tech.
Bachelor of Engineering: General, Electrical, Industrial, Mechanical

Critical Skills
Dependable, Diligent, Enthusiastic, Flexible, Good Communication, Good Writing Skills, Manual Dexterity, Personable, Productive, Responsible

Types of Positions
Cord Assembler

Starting Salary
$ 15,000 - 20,000

Company Benefits
- Health, dental, pension plan
- Life insurance, short/long term disability
- Tuition reimbursement of approved courses

Correspondence
Mail or submit resume with cover letter in person
E-mail: bray-mak@thyssenkrupp.com

Part Time/Summer: Phillips & Tempro Industries occasionally looks for individuals for part time work, and regularly seeks candidates for the summer. Potential jobs involve production worker on the shop floor. In addition, there are usually 2 -4 opportunities for engineering students. The best time to apply is in March or April.

PHOENIX INTERNATIONAL

2350 Cohen St.
Montreal, Québec, H4R 2N6
Tel: (514) 333-0033   Fax: (514) 335-8340

Staffing Department
Internet: www.pils.com

Phoenix International is the world's premier provider of bioanalytical services, a leader in clinical studies and a pioneer in drug discover support services. As a contract research organization, they perform clinical and bioanalytical research on new medications. This work is conducted on behalf of their clients who are major players in the international pharmaceutical, biotech and generic drug industries.

Academic Fields
College: Accounting, Human Resources, Marketing/Sales, Computer Science, Electronics Tech., Animal Health, Laboratory Tech., Nursing (RN/RNA)
Bachelor of Arts: English, Public Relations
Bachelor of Comm/Admin: Accounting, Human Resources, Info Mgmt.
Bachelor of Science: Chemistry, Computer Sciences, Health Sciences, Nursing (RN), Pharmacy
Bachelor of Engineering: Computer Systems
Masters: Business Administration, Science

Critical Skills
Analytical, Confident, Dependable, Efficient, Enthusiastic, Flexible, Good Communication, Innovative, Professional, Responsible

Types of Positions
Analyst   Scientist
Software Developer   Project Manager
Phlebotomist   Scientific Sales

Starting Salary
$ 15,000 - 40,000

Company Benefits
- Dental, drug, paternity leave, profit sharing
- Group auto insurance, offsite health club discount

Correspondence
Mail, fax or e-mail resume with cover letter
E-mail: emp-recruit@pils.com

Part Time/Summer: Phoenix International occasionally hires for part time work and regularly hires for the summer. Potential jobs include laboratory analyst (apply in March), or various clerical positions (apply in March or April).

PILOT INSURANCE COMPANY

90 Eglinton Ave. W.
Toronto, Ontario, M4R 2E2
Tel: (416) 487-5141   Fax: (416) 482-0228

Human Resources Department

Pilot Insurance Company is a property and casualty insurance firm which operates in Ontario. Their head office is in Ontario, with 20 branch claim offices throughout the province.

Academic Fields
College: General, Accounting, Human Resources, Insurance
Bachelor of Arts: General, Business
Bachelor of Comm/Admin: General, Accounting

Critical Skills
Adaptable, Analytical, Good Communication, Dependable, Efficient, Enthusiastic, Flexible, Good With Figures, Leadership, Professional, Responsible, Good Writing Skills

Types of Positions
Accounting Clerk   Underwriting Trainee
Adjuster Trainee

Starting Salary
$ 20,000 - 30,000 (depends on position)

Company Benefits
- Standard medical and dental benefits
- Profit sharing and pension plan
- Offer in-house and external training

Correspondence
Mail or fax resume with cover letter

Part Time/Summer: Pilot Insurance Company does not hire people for part time or summer employment.

The Canada Student Employment Guide

PINE FALLS PAPER COMPANY LIMITED

P.O. Box 10
Pine Falls, Manitoba, R0E 1M0
Tel: (204) 367-5205   Fax: (204) 367-2442

Kathy Oakes, Human Resources Department

Pine Falls Paper Company is a pulp and paper manufacturer producing newsprint that is distributed worldwide. They have an employee base of approximately 525 individuals at this location.

Academic Fields
College: Administration, Business, Communications, Human Resources, CAD Autocad, Electronics Tech., Engineering Tech., Forestry, General Science
Bachelor of Arts: Business, Public Relations
Bachelor of Comm/Admin: Accounting, Finance
Bachelor of Science: Biology, Chemistry, Computer Science, Environmental Studies
Bachelor of Engineering: Chemical, Computer Systems, Electrical, Environmental Studies, Mechanical
Masters: Business Administration, Arts, Science, Engineering

Critical Skills
Adaptable, Analytical, Confident, Creative, Efficient, Good Communication, Good Writing Skills, Leadership, Logical

Types of Positions
Office (Engineering/Technical)   Main Mill Labour

Starting Salary
$ 35,000 - 40,000

Company Benefits
- Comprehensive package of medical and disability benefits
- Blue cross, life insurance

Correspondence
Mail resume with cover letter

Part Time/Summer: Pine Falls Paper Company occasionally looks for part time workers, and regularly seeks candidates for summer employment. Potential summer work includes labourer in the papermaking process. The best time to apply is in April.

PIONEER VILLAGE SPECIAL CARE CORP.

430 Pioneer Dr.
Regina, Saskatchewan, S4T 6L8
Tel: (306) 751-5200   Fax: (306) 757-5001

C. Fox, Human Resources

Pioneer Village Special Care Corp. is a nursing home in Regina that provides care to about 390 residents. The home has about 500 staff members.

Academic Fields
College: Food/Nutrition, Nursing
Bachelor of Science: Food Sciences, Nursing (RN)

Critical Skills
Adaptable, Decisive, Dependable, Enthusiastic, Organized, Productive, Professional

Types of Positions
Dietary   Housekeeping
Caretaking

Starting Salary
$ 35,000 - 45,000 (for RN's)

Company Benefits
- Dental plan, group life
- Pension, disability insurance plan

Correspondence
Mail resume with cover letter

Part Time/Summer: Pioneer Village Special Care Corp. occasionally seeks people for part time positions, and regularly looks for candidates in the summer. Potential jobs include special care aides or dietary aides. The best time to apply is before April 15th.

The Canada Student Employment Guide

PITNEY BOWES OF CANADA LTD.

2200 Yonge Street, Suite 100
Toronto, Ontario, M4S 3E1
Tel: (416) 489-2211   Fax: (416) 484-3972

Peter O'Hanley, Staffing and Employment Specialist
Internet: www.pitneybowes.ca/

Pitney Bowes Canada is a subsidiary of Pitney Bowes Inc., located in Stamford, Connecticut. With more than 1150 Canadian employees, working in more than 20 branches in major city centres across the country, Pitney Bowes Canada offers an exceptional range of products.

Academic Fields
College: General, Accounting, Admin., Business, Communications, Comp. Sci., Electronics Tech., Human Res., Marketing/Sales, Mech. Tech., Science, Secretarial
Bachelor of Arts: General, Business, Economics, Psychology, Public Relations, Sociology/Social Work
Bachelor of Comm/Admin: General, Accounting, Finance, Marketing, Info Mgmt.
Bachelor of Science: General, Kinesiology, Mathematics, Psychology
Bachelor of Engineering: Computer Systems
Bachelor of Education: General, Adult Education
Chartered Accounting: CA - General/Finance, CGA/CMA - General/Finance
Masters: Business Admin., Engineering, Education

Critical Skills
Adaptable, Analytical, Confident, Dependable, Diligent, Diplomatic, Efficient, Enthusiastic, Flexible, Good With Figures, Innovative, Leadership, Logical, Manual Dexterity, Organized, Patient, Personable, Persuasive, Productive, Good Writing Skills

Types of Positions
Area Sales Rep.   Administration
Technician   Customer Service

Starting Salary
$ 20,000 - 25,000 / $ 30,000 - 40,000 in sales

Company Benefits
- Comprehensive benefit package
- Group RRSP, stock purchase, educational assistance

Correspondence
Mail or fax resume with cover letter

Part Time/Summer: Pitney Bowes sometimes hires part time and summer employees. Potential positions vary. The best time to apply is in May.

PIZZA PIZZA LTD.

580 Jarvis St.
Toronto, Ontario, M4Y 2H9
Tel: (416) 967-1010   Fax: (416) 967-0891

Michelle Simpson, Human Resources
Internet: www.pizzapizza.ca

Pizza Pizza began in 1967 in a 30 square meter store at Wellsley and Parliament in Toronto. Today, there are over 125 Pizza Pizza stores in the greater Toronto area. This represents a higher degree of concentration than any other pizza company has achieved elsewhere in the world.

Academic Fields
College: Accounting, Advertising, Business, Communications, Engineering Tech., Graphic Arts, Hospitality, Human Resources, Law Clerk, Marketing/Sales, Secretarial
Bachelor of Arts: General, Business, Public Relations
Bachelor of Comm/Admin: General, Accounting, Finance, Marketing, Info Mgmt.
Bachelor of Science: General, Computer Science
Bachelor of Engineering: Bachelor of Architecture
Bachelor of Education: General, Adult Education
Chartered Accounting: CGA-General, CGA-Finance
Masters: Business Administration

Critical Skills
Adaptable, Analytical, Good Communication, Dependable, Enthusiastic, Flexible, Innovative, Leadership, Organized, Personable, Productive, Professional

Types of Positions
Accounting Assistant   Junior Legal Asst.
Group Sales Coordinator   HR Assistant

Starting Salary
$ 20,000 - 25,000

Company Benefits
- Dental, medical, vision care
- Life insurance, travel insurance
- 50 -100% reimbursement of external training

Correspondence
Fax resume with cover letter

Part Time/Summer: Pizza Pizza occasionally looks for individuals for part time and summer work. Potential work is within the special events team. The best time to apply is in February or March.

The Canada Student Employment Guide

PLACER DOME INC.

1600 - 1055 Dunsmuir Street
Vancouver, British Columbia, V7X 1P1
Tel: (604) 682-7082   Fax: (604) 602-3811

Human Resources
Internet: www.placerdome.com

Placer Dome Inc. is an international mining company that is involved in the exploration, development and production of gold. The company employs approximately 12,000 individuals.

Academic Fields
College: Computer Science
Bachelor of Comm/Admin: Accounting
Bachelor of Science: Environmental Studies
Bachelor of Engineering: Mining, Chemical, Electrical, Environmental Studies, Geotechnical
Chartered Accounting: CA-General
Masters: Business Administration

Critical Skills
Adaptable, Analytical, Diligent, Enthusiastic, Flexible, Good Communication, Good Writing Skills, Innovative, Leadership, Personable

Types of Positions
Engineer in Training   Technical Support Role
Financial Analyst

Starting Salary
Depends on position

Company Benefits
- Flexible benefits package including health and dental
- Engineer in training program
- Opportunity to attend many in-house and external courses

Correspondence
Mail or fax resume with cover letter

Part Time/Summer: Placer Dome occasionally looks for candidates for part time and summer employment. Potential positions most likely involve engineering. The best time to apply is in September.

POCO PETROLEUMS LTD.

250 - 6th Avenue S.W., Suite 3500
Calgary, Alberta, T2P 3H7
Tel: (403) 260-8000   Fax: (403) 263-2708

Human Resources Department

Poco Petroleums is a senior Canadian natural gas and crude oil exploration, production and marketing corporation. The company has producing wells and land holding in Alberta, Saskatchewan and northeastern British Columbia.

Academic Fields
College: General, Accounting, Engineering Tech., Human Resources, Marketing/Sales, Secretarial
Bachelor of Arts: General, Business, Economics, Psychology
Bachelor of Comm/Admin: General, Accounting, Finance, Marketing
Bachelor of Science: General, Geology
Bachelor of Engineering: Chemical, Civil, Computer Systems, Mechanical
Chartered Accounting: CA - General/Finance, CGA/CMA - General/Finance
Masters: Business Administration, Engineering

Critical Skills
Adaptable, Analytical, Confident, Creative, Dependable, Flexible, Good Writing Skills, Good Communication, Innovative, Organized, Personable, Productive, Professional

Types of Positions
Administration Clerk   Accounting Clerk
Secretary

Starting Salary
$ 20,000 - 25,000

Company Benefits
- Full and comprehensive benefits program
- Many training and development opportunities

Correspondence
Mail or fax resume with cover letter

Part Time/Summer: Poco Petroleums sometimes hires for part time work and regularly hires for the summer. Potential jobs deal with the areas of geology, engineering, legal, accounting, or clerical duties. The best time to apply is in February or March.

POLLACK RENTALS LIMITED

R.R. # 6, 16 Second St.
Strathroy, Ontario, N7G 3H7
Tel: (519) 245-3000   Fax: (519) 245-3725

Human Resources

Pollack Rentals Limited is a leasing company which leases trucks of all sizes to companies who need them to distribute goods. They are based in Southwestern Ontario.

Academic Fields
College: General, Accounting, Administration, Advertising, Business, Computer Science, Marketing/Sales
Bachelor of Arts: General, Business
Bachelor of Comm/Admin: General, Marketing
Bachelor of Science: General

Critical Skills
Adaptable, Good Communication, Leadership, Responsible

Types of Positions
Vehicle Cleaner   Rental Sales Representative

Starting Salary
$20,000 - 30,000

Company Benefits
- Full range of benefits
- Retirement savings

Correspondence
Mail resume with cover letter

Part Time/Summer: Pollack Rentals Limited occasionally looks for individuals for part time work and regularly hires for the summer. Potential jobs in the summer include groundskeeper or rental sales. The best time to apply is in March or April.

POLYGRAM GROUP CANADA INC.

1345 Denison Street
Markham, Ontario, L3R 5V2
Tel: (905) 415-9900   Fax: (905) 415-7369

Voula Vagdatis, Human Resources
Internet: www.polygramgrop.com

Polygram Group Canada is engaged in the record business and in music publishing. Specifically the company is a manufacturer of compact discs and tapes and is a wholesale distributor of these products. The company operates under the divisions Polygram Records, A & M Records, Island Records of Canada Ltd., Polygram Distribution and Polygram Music Publishing.

Academic Fields
College: Accounting, Admin., Advertising, Business, Computer Sci., Graphic Arts, HR, Journalism, Law Clerk, Marketing/Sales, Secretarial, Television/Radio
Bachelor of Arts: Business, Fine Arts, Music
Bachelor of Comm/Admin: Accounting, Finance, Marketing, Info Mgmt.
Bachelor of Science: Computer Science
Bachelor of Laws: Corporate (Entertainment)
Bachelor of Engineering: Computer Systems
Chartered Accounting: CA - General/Finance, CGA-General/Finance
Masters: Business Administration

Critical Skills
Adaptable, Analytical, Good Communication, Confident, Creative, Decisive, Dependable, Diligent, Diplomatic, Efficient, Enthusiastic, Good With Figures, Productive, Professional, Responsible, Writing Skills

Types of Positions
Warehouse   Office Services
Accounting Clerk

Starting Salary
$ 20,000 - 25,000

Company Benefits
- Group insurance package

Correspondence
Mail or fax resume with cover letter

Part Time/Summer: PolyGram Group sometimes hires for part time work and regularly hires one individual per summer. Potential opportunities involve office services. Apply in April or May.

The Canada Student Employment Guide

POOL PEOPLE LTD.

76 Brydon Drive
Rexdale, Ontario, M9W 4N6
Tel: (416) 746-0233   Fax: (416) 746-8919

Kim Puskas, Human Resources
Internet: poolpeople.com

Pool People provides products including pools, spas, saunas, and offers construction, renovation, and repair services. The company is also a major lifeguard employer for various apartment and condominium complexes throughout greater Toronto and its vicinities. Employing over 150 lifeguards, there are many summer and permanent opportunities offered within this organization.

Academic Fields
College: Child Care, Emergency/Paramedic, Human Resources, Nursing, Recreation Studies, Security/Law
Bachelor of Arts: Public Relations, Recreation Studies
Bachelor of Science: Health Sciences, Kinesiology, Nursing (RN)
Bachelor of Education: Childhood, Physical, Special

Critical Skills
Adaptable, Confident, Creative, Decisive, Dependable, Efficient, Enthusiastic, Good Communication, Flexible, Innovative, Leadership, Organized, Patient, Personable, Professional, Responsible

Types of Positions
Lifeguard   Area Supervisor
Service Person   Recreation Assistant

Starting Salary
below $ 20,000 - 25,000

Company Benefits
- Benefits for full time employees
- Canadian Pension Plan
- Vacation pay

Correspondence
Fax resume with cover letter, or telephone

Part Time/Summer: The Pool People regularly hires students for part time and summer opportunities. Positions in the summer would most likely involve lifeguarding. The best time to apply is in January.

POSITRON INDUSTRIES INC.

5101 Buchan
Montréal, Québec, H4P 2R9
Tel: (514) 345-2200   Fax: (514) 731-8662

Carole Charbonneau, Human Resources
Internet: www.positroninc.com

Positron Industries Inc. is engaged in the business of commercial physical and biological research. The company's head office is located in Montréal, Québec.

Academic Fields
College: Accounting, Advertising, Drafting/Architecture, Electronics Tech., Industrial Design, Secretarial
Bachelor of Comm/Admin: Accounting, Finance, Marketing
Bachelor of Science: Computer Science
Bachelor of Engineering: Computer Systems, Design, Electrical, Mechanical
Chartered Accounting: CA - General/Finance

Critical Skills
Adaptable, Creative, Flexible, Good Writing Skills, Manual Dexterity, Organized, Productive, Responsible

Types of Positions
Secretary   Accounting
Assembler   Shipper

Starting Salary
below $ 20,000

Company Benefits
- Health and medical insurance
- Various training opportunities depending on the job

Correspondence
Mail resume with cover letter

Part Time/Summer: Positron Industries occasionally looks for candidates for part time work, and regularly seeks individuals for summer employment. In the summer, potential positions most likely involve engineering. The best time to apply is around February.

POTACAN MINING COMPANY

P.O. Box 5005
Sussex, New Brunswick, E0E 1P0
Tel: (506) 839-2146   Fax: (506) 839-2808

John E. Mallet, Human Resources

Potacan Mining Company is engaged in the business of mining and quarrying potash, soda, and borate minerals. Located in Sussex, New Brunswick, Potacan Mining Company was established in 1985 and employs approximately 500 individuals that work in many different areas within the mining industry.

Academic Fields
College: General, Accounting, Administration, Business, Computer Science, Drafting/Architecture, Engineering Tech., Human Resources
Bachelor of Arts: General, Business
Bachelor of Comm/Admin: General, Accounting, Finance
Bachelor of Science: Computer Science, Geology, Nursing (RN)
Bachelor of Engineering: General, Computer Systems, Electrical, Mechanical, Mining
Chartered Accounting: CA - General/Finance
Masters: Business Administration, Engineering

Critical Skills
Adaptable, Analytical, Good Communication, Confident, Creative, Decisive, Dependable, Diligent, Diplomatic, Enthusiastic, Flexible, Good With Figures, Innovative, Leadership, Logical, Manual Dexterity, Professional, Responsible, Good Writing Skills

Types of Positions
Clerical	Mine Operator II
Mill Operator	Administration

Starting Salary
$ 30,000 - 40,000

Company Benefits
- Medical benefits offered
- Life insurance

Correspondence
Mail or fax resume with cover letter

Part Time/Summer: Potacan Mining sometimes seeks candidates for part time and summer employment opportunities. Potential jobs are most commonly entry level. The best time to apply is January through to March.

POWELL EQUIPMENT LTD.

1455 Buffalo Pl.
Winnipeg, Manitoba, R3T 1L8
Tel: (204) 453-4343   Fax: (204) 478-3373

Dorothy Callaghan, Human Resources Manager
Internet: www.powell.ca/powell

Powell Equipment is the authorized Caterpillar dealer for Manitoba, Northwestern Ontario and Nunavut. Powlift, their lift truck operation, serves the same area, but also includes all of Ontario. Their divisions include powlift trucks and systems, powell engines systems, powell AC, and powell rentals.

Academic Fields
College: Accounting, Administration, Computer Programming, Marketing, Apprenticeship (Heavy Equipment)
Bachelor of Arts: General, Economics, Management Studies, Marketing
Bachelor of Science: Agriculture

Critical Skills
Analytical, Good Communication, Dependable, Enthusiastic, Flexible, Leadership, Organized

Types of Positions
Office Services	Accounting
Yard	Service/Parts
General Office	

Starting Salary
below $ 20,000 - 35,000 (depending on position)

Company Benefits
- Dental, extended health, pension plan
- Group life insurance, short and long term disability
- On-going training, apprenticeship

Correspondence
Mail , fax or e-mail resume with cover letter
E-mail: humanresources@powell.ca

Part Time/Summer: Powell Equipment occasionally hires for part time work and regularly looks for people for summer opportunities. Jobs in the summer include lab assistant, yard work or administration. The best time to apply is in March or April.

The Canada Student Employment Guide

POWER MEASUREMENT LTD.

2195 Keating Cross Rd.
Saanichton, British Columbia, V8M 2A5
Tel: (250) 652-7100   Fax: (250) 652-0411

Human Resources
Internet: www.pml.com

Power Measurement is the world's leading manufacturer of advanced, multi-function digital power meters and billing meters. For over two decades they have been serving the power monitoring needs of industrial, institutional, and commercial facilities, as well as power utilities, power marketers, and energy service companies around the globe.

Academic Fields
College: Electronics Tech., Engineering Tech.
Bachelor of Arts: Business, English
Bachelor of Comm/Admin: Accounting, Finance, Marketing, Info Mgmt.
Bachelor of Science: Computer Science
Bachelor of Engineering: Computer Systems, Electrical, Mechanical

Critical Skills
Adaptable, Dependable, Diligent, Efficient, Enthusiastic, Flexible, Good Communication, Good Writing Skills, Organized, Manual Dexterity, Patient, Personable, Productive, Professional, Responsible, Composed

Types of Positions
Production   Development

Starting Salary
below $ 20,000 (Production) /
$ 25,000 - 30,000 (Development)

Company Benefits
- A small benefits package including some extended medical and dental
- Training is "on the job"

Correspondence
Submit resume & cover letter in person

Part Time/Summer: Power Measurement regularly hires co-op university work term students for part time positions, and occasionally seeks candidates for summer jobs. It is best to apply 1 or 2 months before desired time of employment and then make sure to follow-up.

POWERTECH LABS INC.

12388 88th Ave.
Surrey, British Columbia, V3W 7R7
Tel: (604) 590-7500   Fax: (604) 599-8269

Lori Finskars, Manager HR
Internet: www.powertechlabs.com

For almost two decades, Power Tech Labs has been the research and technology arm of B.C. Hydro. They have developed a wide range of technical expertise that is now offered to industry at large. They employ approximately 100 individuals.

Academic Fields
College: Computer Science, Electronics Tech., Laboratory Tech.
Bachelor of Science: Chemistry, Physics
Bachelor of Engineering: Civil, Electrical, Mechanical
Masters: Science, Engineering

Critical Skills
Adaptable, Good Communication, Dependable, Efficient, Enthusiastic, Flexible, Innovative, Professional

Types of Positions
Chemical Lab Technician
Engineer-In-Training
Post Doctoral Fellowship

Starting Salary
$ 30,000 - 50,000

Company Benefits
- Dental, medical, group life insurance
- Pension plan
- 3 weeks holidays to start

Correspondence
Fax resume with cover letter

Part Time/Summer: Powertech Labs regularly seeks people for part time work. They mostly hire co-op students for part time duties. The firm occasionally looks for people for summer jobs. Potential jobs include lab technician or engineering student. The best time to apply is in February.

PPG CANADA INC.

2301 Royal Windsor Dr.
Mississauga, Ontario, L5J 1K5
Tel: (905) 823-1100   Fax: (905) 855-5808

Alex Henshaw, Human Resources Supervisor
Internet: www.ppg.com

PPG Canada Inc. is a leading manufacturer and major supplier of high quality automotive and flat glass, automotive and industrial coatings and chemicals. The company employs 350 individuals at this location and 2,200 in total across Canada.

Academic Fields
College: Accounting, Administration, Business, Human Resources, Information Systems, Marketing/Sales, Chemical Technology
Bachelor of Arts: Business, Economics
Bachelor of Comm/Admin: General, Accounting, Human Resources, Marketing, Info Mgmt.
Bachelor of Science: Chemistry, Computer Science, Environmental Studies
Bachelor of Engineering: General, Chemical, Mechanical
Chartered Accounting: CGA-General, CMA-General
Masters: Business Admin., Arts, Science, Engineering

Critical Skills
Adaptable, Analytical, Confident, Decisive, Dependable, Diligent, Diplomatic, Flexible, Good Communication, Leadership, Organized, Good With Figures, Productive, Professional

Types of Positions
Chemist   Engineering
Financial Management   Laboratory Technician
Human Resources   Sales

Starting Salary
$ 35,000 - 40,000

Company Benefits
- Medical, dental, vision care, life insurance
- Employee savings plan, non-contributory pension

Correspondence
Mail, fax or e-mail resume with cover letter
E-mail: henshaw@ppg.com

Part Time/Summer: PPG Canada occasionally hires for part time work and regularly hires for the summer. Potential jobs include laboratory technician, or involve manufacturing, accounting, or technical service. The best time to apply is in March or April.

PRATT & WHITNEY CANADA INC.

1000 route Marie-Victorin
Longueuil, Québec, J4G 1A1
Tel: (514) 677-9411   Fax: (514) 647-3786

Staffing & Selection
Internet: www.pratt-whitney.ca

Pratt & Whitney Canada is engaged in the design, development, and manufacture of gas turbine engines for air, sea and land applications. The company is a wholly owned subsidiary of United Technologies Corporation of the United States. Pratt & Whitney Canada employs about 8,000 people to work in the high technology industry.

Academic Fields
College: Engineering Tech.
Bachelor of Comm/Admin: Accounting, Finance
Bachelor of Science: Computer Science
Bachelor of Engineering: Computer Systems, Industrial, Mechanical
Chartered Accounting: CA-Finance, CMA-Finance, CGA-Finance
Masters: Business Administration

Critical Skills
Adaptable, Efficient, Good Communication, Leadership, Organized, Professional, Responsible

Types of Positions
Engineering Trainee   Finance Trainee
Junior Buyer

Starting Salary
$ 30,000 - 40,000

Company Benefits
- Complete benefit package

Correspondence
Fax or e-mail resume with cover letter

Part Time/Summer: Pratt & Whitney Canada sometimes looks for individuals for part time employment, and regularly seeks candidates for summer jobs. Potential positions are mostly technical in nature. The jobs involve shop skills and include machinists and sheet metal workers. The best time to apply is in February and March of each year.

PREMDOR INC.

1600 Britannia Rd. E.
Mississauga, Ontario, L4W 1J2
Tel: (905) 670-6550   Fax: (905) 670-6540

Human Resources
Internet: www.premdor.com

Premdor has been manufacturing, marketing and merchandising quality door products for over 40 years. Focusing on interior and exterior doors has allowed Premdor to expand geographically while concentrating on both the home and new construction markets. As a result, Premdor is now one of the world's largest door manufacturers, producing in excess of 100,000 doors per day in five countries.

Academic Fields
College: Accounting, Computer Science, Electronics Tech., Engineering Tech., Forestry
Bachelor of Arts: Business, Economics, Languages
Bachelor of Comm/Admin: Accounting, Finance, Marketing
Bachelor of Science: Computer Science, Forestry
Bachelor of Engineering: Industrial, Mechanical
Chartered Accounting: CA-General, CMA-General, CGA-General

Critical Skills
Adaptable, Confident, Diligent, Efficient, Good Communication, Good Writing Skills, Logical, Organized, Professional

Types of Positions
Various Positions

Starting Salary
$20,000 - 30,000

Company Benefits
- Competitive benefit plan

Correspondence
Mail or fax resume with cover letter

Part Time/Summer: Premdor Inc. occasionally seeks individuals for part time work and regularly hires for the summer months. Most positions are mainly manufacturing help, however a few students are employed in administration.

PRI AUTOMATION

170 University Ave., Suite 1200
Toronto, Ontario, M5H 3B3
Tel: (416) 977-0599   Fax: (416) 977-2016

Human Resources
Internet: www.pria.com

PRI Automation is the leader in advanced automation systems and software for the semiconductor industry. They offer complete and flexible solutions that address the widest range of automation requirements for semiconductor and OEM process tool manufacturers.

Academic Fields
College: Computer Science
Bachelor of Comm/Admin: Accounting
Bachelor of Engineering: Computer Systems
Chartered Accounting: CMA - General/Finance, CGA - General/Finance
Masters: Business Administration, Engineering

Critical Skills
Adaptable, Analytical, Creative, Flexible, Good Communication, Innovative, Logical, Productive, Professional

Types of Positions
Entry Software Test Analyst

Starting Salary
$ 30,000 - 40,000

Company Benefits
- Competitive salary and benefits
- Strong corporate commitment to training

Correspondence
Fax resume with cover letter

Part Time/Summer: PRI Automation occasionally looks for individuals for part time and summer opportunities. The best time to apply is in March or April.

PRICEWATERHOUSE COOPERS

145 King Street West, Suite 2300
Toronto, Ontario, M5H 1V8
Tel: (416) 869-1130   Fax: (416) 863-0926

Human Resources
Internet: www.pwcglobal.com

At Pricewaterhouse Coopers, they measure their success by yours. Everyday, their 150,000 people in more than 150 countries go to work to help their clients succeed. From Dublin to Durban, from Minneapolis to Manila, their job is channeling knowledge and value through six lines of service and 22 industry-specialized practices.

Academic Fields
College: Accounting, Engineering Tech., Human Resources, Statistics
Bachelor of Comm/Admin: Accounting, Finance, Marketing, Info Mgmt.
Bachelor of Science: Actuarial, Chemistry, Computer Science, Mathematics
Bachelor of Engineering: General, Chemical, Computer Systems, Design, Electrical, Industrial, Mechanical, Mining, Transportation
Chartered Accounting: CA - General/Finance, CGA/CMA - General/Finance
Masters: Business Administration, Engineering

Critical Skills
Adaptable, Analytical, Artistic, Good Communication, Confident, Creative, Decisive, Dependable, Diligent, Diplomatic, Efficient, Enthusiastic, Flexible, Patient, Personable, Persuasive, Productive, Professional

Types of Positions
Associate Consultant   Staff Accountant

Starting Salary
$ 30,000 - 40,000

Company Benefits
- Standard benefits including drug and dental plan
- Life insurance and disability

Correspondence
Mail or fax resume with cover letter

Part Time/Summer: Coopers & Lybrand regularly hires for part time and summer work. Potential jobs include staff accountants and computer programmers. The best time to apply is in the fall for staff accountant positions, and in early January for computer programmer positions.

PRINCE ALBERT CREDIT UNION

2800 2nd Ave. West
Prince Albert, Saskatchewan, S6V 5Z4
Tel: (306) 953-6147   Fax: (306) 764-4198

Karen Eyre, Human Resources

Prince Albert Credit Union is a community based credit union in Prince Albert, Saskatchewan. They offer many types of financial services to the community.

Academic Fields
College: Accounting, Administration, Marketing/Sales
Bachelor of Comm/Admin: Accounting, Finance, Marketing
Bachelor of Science: Computer Science
Chartered Accounting: CGA - General/Finance

Critical Skills
Adaptable, Efficient, Good Communication, Innovative, Leadership, Organized, Personable, Persuasive, Productive, Professional, Responsible

Types of Positions
Member Service Representative

Starting Salary
$ 15,000 - 20,000

Company Benefits
- Group life, disability, dental, extended health care and vision
- Sales training, cross training various departments
- Member service training, self study courses

Correspondence
Mail, e-mail or submit resume with cover letter in person. E-mail: karen.eyre@pa.cu.sk.ca

Part Time/Summer: Prince Albert Credit Union regularly seeks candidates for part time or summer employment. A potential job would be member service representative. The best time to apply is in March or April.

CITY OF PRINCE ALBERT

1084 Central Ave.
Prince Albert, Saskatchewan, S6V 7P3
Tel: (306) 953-4330   Fax: (306) 953-4353

Human Resources
Internet: www.citypa.com

City of Prince Albert is a municipal government for a city of 35,000 people. They are responsible for the formation of policy and laws in matters under its jurisdiction.

Academic Fields
College: Accounting, Business, Drafting/Architecture, Electronics Tech., Emergency/Paramedic, Engineering Tech., Faculty Mgmt., Recreation Studies, Urban Planning
Bachelor of Arts: Public Relations
Bachelor of Comm/Admin: General, Accounting
Bachelor of Science: Computer Science, Horticulture
Bachelor of Laws: General
Bachelor of Engineering: Civil, Design, Water Resources
Chartered Accounting: CMA-Finance

Critical Skills
Adaptable, Good Communication, Dependable, Enthusiastic, Manual Dexterity, Organized, Productive, Responsible

Types of Positions
Labourer	Engineering Tech.
Secretarial	Administrator
Parks Department	Fire Department

Starting Salary
below $ 20,000 - 25,000

Company Benefits
- Full benefits for permanent employees
- Health, dental, group life, pension
- Seasonal students receive no benefits

Correspondence
Mail or submit resume with cover letter in person

Part Time/Summer: City of Prince Albert occasionally looks for people for part time work, and regularly seeks individuals in the summer. Potential jobs include some of those listed above. The best time to apply is before April 1st.

CITY OF PRINCE GEORGE

1100 Patricia Blvd.
Prince George, British Columbia, V2L 3V9
Tel: (604) 561-7626   Fax: (604) 561-7719

Human Resources Department

City of Prince George is a local government for the city. They are responsible for the formation of policy and laws in matters under its jurisdiction.

Academic Fields
College: Accounting, Administration, Animal Health, Business, Computer Science, Drafting/Architecture, Electronics Tech., Engineering Tech., Faculty Management, Human Resources, Marketing/Sales, Mechanical Tech., Recreation Studies, Urban Planning
Bachelor of Arts: Public Relations, Recreation Studies
Bachelor of Comm/Admin: General, Accounting, Finance, Marketing, Info Mgmt., Public Admin.
Bachelor of Science: Computer Science, Environmental Studies, Horticulture
Bachelor of Laws: Real Estate
Bachelor of Engineering: Civil, Computer Systems, Electrical, Environmental Studies, Mechanical, Water Resources, Bachelor of Landscape Architecture
Chartered Accounting: CGA/CMA - General/Finance
Masters: Engineering

Critical Skills
Adaptable, Confident, Dependable, Diligent, Efficient, Enthusiastic, Flexible, Good Communication, Good With Figures, Good Writing Skills, Organized, Patient, Personable, Productive, Professional, Responsible

Types of Positions
Labourer	Clerk Typist
Clerk II	Truck Driver II
Switchboard Receptionist	Cleaner

Starting Salary
$ 25,000 - 30,000 (depending on position)

Company Benefits
- Comprehensive package

Correspondence
Mail or fax resume with cover letter

Part Time/Summer: City of Prince George regularly hires for part time jobs, and occasionally seeks staff in the summer. Potential positions include labourers. The best time to apply is in March.

The Canada Student Employment Guide

PROCTOR AND REDFERN LTD.

45 Green Belt Drive
Don Mills, Ontario, M3C 3K3
Tel: (416) 445-3600   Fax: (416) 445-5276

Human Resources

Involved in engineering planning and architectural services, Proctor and Redfern employs 250 specialists and operates throughout Ontario.

Academic Fields
College: Industrial Design, Mechanical Tech., Automation/Instrumentation, Electronics Tech., Urban Planning
Bachelor of Engineering: General, Civil, Computer Systems, Electrical, Environmental Studies, Industrial, Mechanical, Transportation, Water and Wastewater
Masters: Engineering

Critical Skills
Good Communication, Confident, Decisive, Dependable, Efficient, Enthusiastic, Flexible, Innovative, Leadership, Productive, Professional, Responsible, Good Writing Skills

Types of Positions
Trainee Engineer   Junior Technologist

Starting Salary
$ 36,000 - 40,000

Company Benefits
- Full range of benefits

Correspondence
Mail or e-mail resume with cover letter
E-mail: recruiting@pandr.com

Part Time/Summer: Proctor and Redfern does not hire for part time work, but occasionally hires for the summer. The best time to apply is in May.

PROGRESSIVE FINANCIAL STRATEGY

5170 Dixie Rd., Suite 203
Mississauga, Ontario, L4W 1E3
Tel: (905) 212-9149   Fax: (905) 212-9201

Deborah Melanson, Director Business Development
Internet: www.financialstrategy.net

Progressive Financial Strategy is a full service comprehensive financial planning firm providing sound advice and solutions to existing and prospective clients. They provide a complete range of financial products and services enabling their advisors to recommend solutions objectively in the full view of the client's best interest.

Academic Fields
College: Accounting, Business, Insurance, Marketing/Sales
Bachelor of Arts: General, Business, Economics
Bachelor of Comm/Admin: General, Finance, Human Resources, Marketing, Info Mgmt.
Bachelor of Laws: General
Bachelor of Engineering: General
Bachelor of Education: Adult Education
Chartered Accounting: CA - General/Finance, CGA - General/Finance, CMA - General/Finance
Masters: Business Administration

Critical Skills
Adaptable, Confident, Decisive, Dependable, Diligent, Diplomatic, Efficient, Enthusiastic, Flexible, Good Communication, Good With Figures, Good Writing Skills, Leadership, Organized, Personable, Persuasive, Productive, Self Directed, Enjoys Learning

Types of Positions
Financial Advisor

Starting Salary
Commission plus bonus

Company Benefits
- Short and long term training in products, sales skills, self marketing, financial planning and more

Correspondence
Mail, fax, e-mail resume with cover letter, or submit in person, or apply through web site.
E-mail: dmelanson@financialstrategy.net

Part Time/Summer: Progressive Financial Strategy rarely hires for part time or summer employment.

PROVIDENCE CENTRE

3276 St. Clair Avenue East
Scarborough, Ontario, M1L 1W1
Tel: (416) 285-3666   Fax: (416) 285-3756

Human Resources Department

Providence Centre is a specialty hospital and skilled nursing care facility that provides chronic care, rehabilitation, self care, and palliative care to individuals. Established in 1855, Providence Centre is operated by the Sisters of St. Joseph of Toronto. The facility has more than 630 beds and employs almost 900 individuals who work in various health care capacities.

Academic Fields
College: Cooking/Culinary, Food/Nutrition, Human Resources, Laboratory Tech., Nursing, Recreation Studies, Secretarial
Bachelor of Arts: General, Gerontology
Bachelor of Science: General, Food Sciences, Health Sciences, Nursing (RN), Occupational Therapy, Pharmacy, Physiotherapy
Bachelor of Engineering: General
Bachelor of Education: General, Adult Education
Chartered Accounting: CA - General/Finance
Masters: Business Administration

Critical Skills
Dependable, Flexible, Good Communication, Good Writing Skills, Leadership, Organized, Personable, Professional

Types of Positions
Various Positions

Starting Salary
$ 20,000 - 25,000

Company Benefits
- Dental and extended health care coverage
- Group life insurance
- Hospital pension plan

Correspondence
Mail or fax resume with cover letter

Part Time/Summer: Providence Centre sometimes hires for part time and summer opportunities. Potential summer jobs are within food services only. The best time to apply is in June.

THE PRUDENTIAL INSURANCE CO. OF AMERICA

200 Consilium Place
Scarborough, Ontario, M1H 3E6
Tel: (416) 296-0777   Fax: (416) 296-3332

Susan McIntyre, Human Resources
Internet: www.prudential.com

The Prudential Insurance Co. of America provides life, health, property and casualty insurance for groups and individuals. The company offers a full range of personal and business investments including RRSP's, RRIF's, mutual funds, fixed term investments and residential mortgages.

Academic Fields
College: Accounting, Administration, Business, Computer Sci., Human Res., Insurance, Secretarial
Bachelor of Arts: Business, Economics, English, Public Relations, Statistics
Bachelor of Comm/Admin: Finance, Marketing, Info Mgmt.
Bachelor of Science: Actuarial, Biology, Computer Science, Mathematics
Bachelor of Engineering: Computer Systems
Chartered Accounting: CA - General/Finance, CGA/CMA - General/Finance
Masters: Business Administration

Critical Skills
Adaptable, Creative, Decisive, Good Communication, Enthusiastic, Flexible, Dependable, Good With Figures, Personable, Leadership, Organized, Good Writing Skills, Productive, Professional

Types of Positions
Claim Examiner   Programmer
Legal Secretary   Group Underwriting
Customer Service Rep.

Starting Salary
$ 25,000 - 30,000

Company Benefits
- Full, cafeteria style benefits
- University of Prudential established for training

Correspondence
Mail or fax resume with cover letter

Part Time/Summer: Prudential Insurance sometimes hires for part time work and regularly hires for the summer. Potential jobs are mostly clerical using Wordperfect 5.1. Applications are accepted after January 1st. for the following summer.

The Canada Student Employment Guide

PUBLIC UTILITIES OF KINGSTON

211 Counter St.
Kingston, Ontario, K7L 4X7
Tel: (613) 546-0000   Fax: (613) 542-1463

Connie Hewitt, Human Resources
Internet: www.utilitieskingston.com

Public Utilities of Kingston supplies electricity, water, natural gas, and transit services to the City of Kingston. For more information, look at their website.

Academic Fields
College: General, Accounting, Administration, Business, Computer Science, Drafting/Architecture, Electronics Tech., Human Resources, Marketing/Sales, Mechanical Tech., Urban Planning
Bachelor of Arts: Business, Public Relations
Bachelor of Comm/Admin: Accounting, Finance, Marketing, Info Mgmt., Public Admin.
Bachelor of Science: Chemistry, Computer Science
Bachelor of Laws: Corporate
Bachelor of Engineering: General, Civil, Computer Syst., Electrical, Mechanical, Transportation, Water Res.
Chartered Accounting: CA - General/Finance, CGA/CMA - General/Finance
Masters: Business Administration, Engineering

Critical Skills
Adaptable, Analytical, Good Communication, Confident, Decisive, Dependable, Diligent, Diplomatic, Efficient, Enthusiastic, Flexible, Good With Figures, Leadership, Logical, Organized, Personable, Persuasive, Productive, Professional, Responsible, Good Writing Skills

Types of Positions
Labourer   Draftsperson
Clerk

Starting Salary
$ 20,000 - 25,000

Company Benefits
- Extended health care, dental, pension
- Group RRSP, life insurance, long term disability

Correspondence
Mail resume with cover letter

Part Time/Summer: Public Utilities of Kingston occasionally looks for individuals for part time or summer opportunities. Potential jobs include part time bus operator, temporary labourer, or draftsperson. The best time to apply is in March.

PUROLATOR COURIER LTD.

11 Morse Street
Toronto, Ontario, M4M 2P7
Tel: (416) 461-9031   Fax: (416) 463-3994

Joe Worden, Metro Recruiter
Internet: www.purolator.com

Purolator Courier is the largest overnight courier in Canada. Over 375,000 envelopes and parcels are funneled through Purolator's system each night. Purolator serves Canadian locations through two regional hubs and a central hub in Toronto. They employ about 13,000 people across Canada.

Academic Fields
College: General, Accounting, Administration, Advertising, Business, Communications, Computer Science, Human Resources, Marketing/Sales
Bachelor of Arts: General, Business
Bachelor of Comm/Admin: Accounting, Finance, Marketing, Info Mgmt.
Bachelor of Laws: Corporate
Bachelor of Engineering: Civil, Computer Systems, Design, Industrial, Transportation
Bachelor of Education: Adult Education
Chartered Accounting: CA - General/Finance, CGA/CMA - General/Finance
Masters: Business Administration, Education

Critical Skills
Adaptable, Good Communication, Confident, Creative, Decisive, Dependable, Diligent, Efficient, Enthusiastic, Flexible, Good With Figures, Innovative, Leadership, Logical, Organized, Productive, Professional, Good Writing Skills

Types of Positions
Relief Courier   Administration
Sorter   Support Representative

Starting Salary
below $ 20,000 - 40,000 (depends on position)

Company Benefits
- Competitive benefits

Correspondence
Mail, fax or submit resume with cover letter in person
E-mail: jworden@purolator.com

Part Time/Summer: Purolator Courier regularly looks for candidates for part time and summer work. Summer jobs are most likely to include sorter, support rep., or administration. Apply is in March or April.

The Canada Student Employment Guide

QEII HEALTH SCIENCES CENTRE

1278 Tower Rd.
Halifax, Nova Scotia, B3H 2Y9
Tel: (902) 473-5757   Fax: (902) 473-8499

HR Customer Service
Internet: www.ge2-hsc.ns.ca

The QEII Health Sciences Centre is the largest health centre east of Montreal. Housed in 10 buildings, it is located in the heart of Halifax.

Academic Fields
College: Accounting, Human Resources, Information Systems, Secretarial, Computer Science, Engineering Tech., Mechanical Tech., Plumbing, Emergency/Paramedic, Laboratory Tech., Nursing (RN), Orthotics/Prosthetics, Radiology Tech., Respiratory Tech., Recreation Studies, Social Work
Bachelor of Arts: General, Business, Psychology, Public Relations, Sociology/Social Work
Bachelor of Comm/Admin: General, Accounting, HR
Bachelor of Science: General, Biology, Chemistry, Computer Science, Food Sciences, Health Sciences, Kinesiology, Nursing (RN), Occupational Therapy, Pharmacy, Physics, Physiotherapy, Psychology
Bachelor of Engineering: General, Biomedical

Critical Skills
Dependable, Flexible, Good Communication, Organized, Professional, Responsible, Team Work

Types of Positions
Food/Nutrition   Housekeeping
Porter   Ward Aide Clerk
Medical Records   Pharmacy

Starting Salary
$ 20,000 - 25,000

Company Benefits
- Comprehensive orientation program
- Have educators devoted to building your clinical, teamwork and technology skills

Correspondence
Mail, fax, e-mail resume with cover letter or apply through web site. E-mail: hrcs@ge2-hsc.ns.ca

Part Time/Summer: QEII Health Sciences Centre regularly hires for part time work and occasionally hires for the summer. They often look for casual staff to cover summer shortages due to vacations. Job openings are posted in human resources every Tuesday and Friday afternoon at 4:00 pm. Apply in May or June.

QIT-FER ET TITANE INC.

1625 route Marie-Victorin
Tracy, Québec, J3R 1M6
Tel: (514) 746-3000   Fax: (514) 742-4495

Victor Cormier, Directeur du personnel
Internet: www.qit.com

QIT-Fer et Titane produces and markets four main products. These are titania slag for the pigment industry, high quality pig iron, high quality steel billets, and ilmenite ore for iron blast furnaces. It also produces high quality iron and steel powders for the powder metallurgy industry through a fully owned subsidiary Quebec Metal Powders Limited. Growing demand for its product over the past two decades has required a continual expansion of production facilities.

Academic Fields
College: Accounting, Computer Science, Laboratory Tech., Mechanical, Secretarial
Bachelor of Comm/Admin: Accounting, Finance, Info Mgmt.
Bachelor of Science: Chemistry, Environ. Studies
Bachelor of Engineering: Chemical, Computer Systems, Electrical, Mechanical, Mining, Water Res.
Chartered Accounting: CA-Finance, CMA-Finance, CGA-Finance
Masters: Business Administration, Engineering

Critical Skills
Analytical, Dependable, Diligent, Efficient, Flexible, Logical, Organized, Productive, Good Communication, Professional, Responsible

Types of Positions
Various Positions

Starting Salary
$ 30,000 - 40,000

Company Benefits
- Medical and dental benefits
- Life insurance
- Retirement plan

Correspondence
Mail resume with cover letter

Part Time/Summer: QIT-Fer et Titane sometimes seeks individuals for part time work and regularly looks for candidates for the summer. The best time to apply is in February.

QUÉBÉC CARTIER MINING COMPANY

Route 138
Port Cartier, Québec, G5B 2H3
Tel: (418) 768-2269   Fax: (418) 768-2105

Adelard Robichaud, Ressources humaines

Québec Cartier Mining Company is an exploration and development mining company. The company's head office is in Port Cartier, Québec.

Academic Fields
College: Accounting, Computer Science, Human Resources, Industrial Design, Laboratory Tech.
Bachelor of Comm/Admin: Accounting, Info Mgmt.
Bachelor of Science: Chemistry
Bachelor of Engineering: Civil, Electrical, Mining
Chartered Accounting: CA-Finance, CMA-General
Masters: Business Administration

Critical Skills
Adaptable, Analytical, Creative, Dependable, Diligent, Flexible, Good Communication, Professional,

Types of Positions
Technician

Starting Salary
$ 30,000 - 40,000

Company Benefits
- Complete benefit package
- In-house and external training courses

Correspondence
Mail resume with cover letter

Part Time/Summer: Québéc Cartier Mining Company does not look for individuals for part time jobs, but regularly seeks candidates for the summer. Potential jobs include office clerk, and factory worker. The best time to apply is in March.

QUEBECOR INC.

612 rue St-Jacques
Montréal, Québec, H3C 4M8
Tel: (514) 877-9777   Fax: (514) 877-0347

Ressources humaines
Internet: www.quebecor.com

Québécor is a communications company with business activities spread throughout North America, Europe, Latin America and Asia. The company operates in four main sectors: printing, newspaper publishing, new media and broadcasting, as well as in the book, magazine and music sectors. Quebecor Inc. employs approximately 60,000 people in 15 countries.

Academic Fields
College: Accounting, Communications, Computer Science, Human Resources, Journalism
Bachelor of Arts: Journalism
Bachelor of Comm/Admin: Accounting, Finance, Info Mgmt.
Bachelor of Science: Computer Science
Bachelor of Laws: Corporate
Bachelor of Engineering: General, Computer Systems, Mechanical
Chartered Accounting: CA-Finance, CGA-General
Masters: Business Administration

Critical Skills
Confident, Creative, Decisive, Good Communication, Diligent, Innovative, Productive, Professional

Types of Positions
Various Positions

Starting Salary
Depends on the field

Company Benefits
- Medical and dental plan, retirement plan

Correspondence
Mail resume with cover letter

Part Time/Summer: Quebecor Inc. sometimes hires candidates for part time and summer employment opportunities. Potential jobs are in manufacturing. The best time to apply is in March.

QUESNEL RIVER PULP COMPANY

1000 Finning Rd.
Quesnel, British Columbia, V2J 6A1
Tel: (250) 992-8919   Fax: (250) 992-2612

Human Resources

Quesnel River Pulp Company is a bleached chemi thermomechanical pulp mill producing approximately 900 tonnes per day. They employ about 140 individuals.

Academic Fields
College: Administration, Engineering Tech.
Bachelor of Arts: Business
Bachelor of Comm/Admin: Accounting, Info Mgmt.
Bachelor of Science: Computer Science
Bachelor of Engineering: Mechanical
Chartered Accounting: CMA-General, CGA-General

Critical Skills
Adaptable, Analytical, Confident, Creative, Decisive, Dependable, Diligent, Efficient, Enthusiastic, Flexible, Logical, Organized, Personable, Productive, Professional, Responsible

Types of Positions
Lab Technician   Casual Labourer
Receptionist

Starting Salary
$ 25,000 - 30,000

Company Benefits
- Medical, dental, group life
- Extended health coverage for full time, permanent employees
- Long term disability

Correspondence
Mail or fax resume with cover letter

Part Time/Summer: Quesnel River Pulp Company does not hire for part time employment, but regularly hires for the summer months. Potential jobs include lab technician, warehouse operation, stores clerk, engineering tech., or reception/admin. assistant. The best time to apply is after January 1st, and before March 1st of the year.

RAMADA INN

185 Yorkland Blvd.
Willowdale, Ontario, M2J 4R2
Tel: (416) 493-9000   Fax: (416) 493-5729

Robin Stephenson, Human Resources
Internet: www.ramada.ca

Ramada Inn is a hotel off the Don Valley Parkway in downtown Toronto. The hotel offers many facilities to the business or vacationing traveller.

Academic Fields
College: General, Accounting, Administration, Advertising, Business, Cooking/Culinary, Food/Nutrition, Hospitality, Human Resources, Marketing/Sales

Critical Skills
Adaptable, Dependable, Enthusiastic, Flexible, Good Communication, Professional, Responsible

Types of Positions
Guest Service Agent   Dining Room Server

Starting Salary
below $ 20,000

Company Benefits
- Competitive benefit package

Correspondence
Mail or fax resume with cover letter

Part Time/Summer: Ramada Inn occasionally seeks candidates for part time or summer employment opportunities. Potential jobs include guest service agent or dining room sever. The best time to apply is in April, May, or June.

RASCO SPECIALTY METALS INC.

2140 Meadowpine Blvd.
Mississauga, Ontario, L5N 6H6
Tel: (905) 567-9900   Fax: (905) 567-8302

Victoria Stamper, HR Manager

RASCO Specialty Metals Inc. is a company involved in the sales and distribution of stainless steel and aluminum. The firm has service centres across Canada.

Academic Fields
College: Advertising, Human Resources, Marketing/Sales
Bachelor of Arts: Business, Economics
Bachelor of Comm/Admin: Accounting, Finance, Marketing, Info Mgmt.
Bachelor of Engineering: Materials Science
Chartered Accounting: CMA-General/Finance, CGA-General/Finance
Masters: Business Administration, Engineering

Critical Skills
Adaptable, Good Communication, Confident, Dependable, Efficient, Flexible, Innovative, Leadership, Organized, Personable, Productive, Responsible

Types of Positions
Inside Sales
Warehouse Materials Handling
Administrative Assistant

Starting Salary
Depends on position

Company Benefits
- Full time, full benefit package
- Pension (after 6 months), incentive plan
- On-going training and development

Correspondence
Mail resume with cover letter
E-mail: vstamper@rmc.com

Part Time/Summer: RASCO Specialty Metals occasionally looks for individuals for part time or summer employment. Potential work include warehouse materials handling, or filing and administration duties. The best time to apply is in May.

RAYLO CHEMICALS INC.

8045 Argyll Rd.
Edmonton, Alberta, T6C 4A9
Tel: (780) 472-6447   Fax: (780) 472-8189

Human Resources

Raylo Chemicals Inc., a Laporte Fine Chemicals company located in Edmonton, is one of the Canadian leaders in developing and manufacturing pharmaceutical activities in intermediates under cGMP. They employ approximately 180 individuals.

Academic Fields
College: Laboratory Tech., Science-General
Bachelor of Science: Biology, Chemistry
Bachelor of Engineering: General, Chemical, Design, Mechanical

Critical Skills
Adaptable, Analytical, Dependable, Efficient, Enthusiastic, Flexible, Organized, Productive, Professional, Responsible, Good Communication

Types of Positions
Laboratory Technologist   Chemical Operator

Starting Salary
$ 25,000 - 30,000

Company Benefits
- Supplemental health and dental insurance
- Pension plan

Correspondence
Mail or e-mail resume with cover letter
E-mail: resumes.raylo@laporteplc.com

Part Time/Summer: Raylo Chemicals occasionally seeks candidates for part time or summer work. A potential job would be laboratory technologist. The best time to apply is in March or April.

RAYMOND INDUSTRIAL EQUIPMENT LTD.

P.O. Box 1325
Brantford, Ontario, N3T 5T6
Tel: (519) 759-0358   Fax: (519) 759-0360

J. Bethune, Human Resources
Internet: www.raymondcorp.com

Raymond Industrial Equipment Ltd. is Canada's leading manufacturer of electric forklifts. Their commitment is to quality and their continuous improvement is demonstrated in their superior product, state-of-the-art facility and advanced manufacturing and business systems.

Academic Fields
College: Accounting, Business, Electronics Tech., Engineering Tech., Human Resources, Industrial Design, Mechanical Tech.
Bachelor of Arts: Business
Bachelor of Comm/Admin: Accounting
Bachelor of Science: Computer Science
Bachelor of Engineering: Computer Systems, Design, Electrical, Mechanical
Chartered Accounting: CMA-General, CGA-General

Critical Skills
Adaptable, Creative, Dependable, Enthusiastic, Flexible, Good Communication, Good Writing Skills, Innovative, Leadership

Types of Positions
Various Positions

Starting Salary
$35,000 - 40,000

Company Benefits
- Comprehensive benefits offered

Correspondence
Mail, fax or e-mail resume with cover letter
E-mail: careers@rie.com

Part Time/Summer: Raymond Industrial Equipment Ltd. does not hire for part time work, but occasionally hires for the summer. Potential positions involve plant work, or computers and engineering. The best time to apply is in January or February.

RAYMOND REBAR INC.

3419 Hawthorne Rd.
Ottawa, Ontario, K1G 4G2
Tel: (613) 736-1500   Fax: (613) 736-0165

Judy Wright, Controller
Internet: www.raymondrebar.com

Raymond Steel is involved in reinforcing steel and provides a steel service centre. The firm employs approximately 325 individuals in total.

Academic Fields
College: Accounting, Administration, Business, Human Resources, Information Systems, Marketing/Sales, Purchasing, Secretarial, CAD Autocad, Industrial Design, Mechanical Tech., Welding
Bachelor of Comm/Admin: General, Accounting, Finance, Human Resources, Marketing
Bachelor of Engineering: Computer Systems, Design, Electrical
Chartered Accounting: CA - General/Finance, CGA - General/Finance, CMA - General/Finance
Masters: Business Administration

Critical Skills
Dependable, Efficient, Good Communication, Good With Figures, Good Writing Skills, Organized, Professional

Types of Positions
Administration   Shop Labour
Detailing

Starting Salary
$ 25,000 - 30,000

Company Benefits
- Full medical and dental benefit package

Correspondence
Fax resume with cover letter

Part Time/Summer: Raymond Rebar occasionally looks for people for part time jobs, and regularly seeks candidates in the summer months. Potential jobs include office and shop help.

RAYTHEON SYSTEMS CANADA LTD.

13951 Bridgeport Rd.
Richmond, British Columbia, V6V 1J6
Tel: (604) 279-5990   Fax: (604) 821-5100

Kareen Sheppard, HR Consultant
Internet: www.raytheon.com

Raytheon Systems Canada Ltd. is modernizing Canada's air traffic control business by developing the industry's safest and most advanced automated systems. They are part of Raytheon Systems Company, a global leader in defence electronics and complex integrated information systems. Their Richmond facility employs more than 300 individuals.

Academic Fields
College: Computer Science, Electronics Tech.
Bachelor of Comm/Admin: Info Mgmt
Bachelor of Science: Computer Science, Mathematics, Physics
Bachelor of Engineering: Computer Systems, Electrical, Mechanical

Critical Skills
Adaptable, Analytical, Flexible, Good Communication, Good Writing Skills, Leadership, Technical Ability, Team Player

Types of Positions
Engineering   Information Technology

Starting Salary
$ 40,000 - 45,000

Company Benefits
- Competitive benefits
- Comprehensive training and development programs
- Extensive computer based training library

Correspondence
E-mail resume with cover letter, or apply through their web site. E-mail: rmd-hr@raytheon.com

Part Time/Summer: Raytheon Systems Canada Ltd. rarely hires for part time employment and does not hire for the summer months.

Co-op/Internship: They do offer internship opportunities. All temporary student employment openings are offered through the co-op programs at local universities.

READER'S DIGEST ASSOCIATION OF CANADA LTD.

1125 Stanley St.
Montreal, Québec, H3B 5H5
Tel: (514) 940-0751   Fax: (514) 940-3637

Patrick Colavecchio, Manager Human Resources
Internet: www.readersdigest.ca

Reader's Digest Association of Canada is the preeminent global leader in publishing and direct marketing, creating and delivering products that inform, enrich, entertain and inspire customers the world over. Reader's Digest operates companies headquartered in 21 countries.

Academic Fields
College: Administration, Advertising, Business, Communications, Computer Science, Graphic Arts, Journalism, Marketing/Sales, Secretarial, Statistics
Bachelor of Arts: English, History, Journalism, Languages, Statistics
Bachelor of Comm/Admin: Accounting, Finance, Marketing, Info Mgmt.
Bachelor of Science: Computer Science, Math.
Chartered Accounting: CA - General/Finance, CMA - General/Finance, CGA - General/Finance
Masters: Business Administration, Arts, Science

Critical Skills
Adaptable, Analytical, Artistic, Creative, Good Communication, Good With Figures, Good Writing Skills, Efficient, Innovative, Leadership, Organized, Flexible, Personable, Productive, Responsible

Types of Positions
Marketing Assistant   Copywriter
Graphic Designer   Programmer
Research Associate   Financial Analyst

Starting Salary
$ 25,000 - 40,000 (depends on position)

Company Benefits
- Full range of dental, medical, and life insurance
- Short and long term disability coverage
- Pension, education assistance program

Correspondence
Mail or fax resume with cover letter

Part Time/Summer: Reader's Digest occasionally hires for part time work, and regularly hires for the summer. Potential jobs most likely involve general work or accounting clerk. The best time to apply is by the end of April, or beginning of May.

READY BAKE FOODS INC.

2095 Meadowvale Blvd.
Mississauga, Ontario, L5N 5N1
Tel: (905) 567-0660　　Fax: (905) 567-0909

Leslie Lauder, Human Resources
Internet: www.readybakefoods.com

Ready Bake Foods is a leading supplier of frozen bakery products and related services to in-store bakeries in the U.S. and Canada. They employ 850 people within their organization.

Academic Fields
College: Food/Nutrition
Bachelor of Arts: Business
Bachelor of Comm/Admin: Accounting
Bachelor of Science: Food Sciences

Critical Skills
Adaptable, Enthusiastic, Persuasive, Professional

Types of Positions
Accounting

Starting Salary
Depends on position

Company Benefits
- Medical, dental, vision, life insurance
- Offer fringe benefits
- Formal and informal training provided

Correspondence
Fax resume with cover letter

Part Time/Summer: Ready Bake Foods regularly seeks individuals for part time and summer positions. Potential jobs include production work, warehouse work, finance, human resource interns, or co-op student jobs. The best time to apply is anytime in the Spring or Summer.

RECOCHEM INC.

850 Montée de Liesse Road
Montréal, Québec, H4T 1P4
Tel: (514) 341-3550　　Fax: (514) 341-1292

Human Resources Department

Recochem Inc., with over 100 years of combined manufacturing experience, is a major producer of napthalene and paradichlorobenzene for world markets. The refining operations are located in Napierville, Quebec, and Marche-les-Dames, Belguim with distribution from Brisbane, Australia. They employ about 500 people to serve markets worldwide.

Academic Fields
College: Accounting, Computer Science, Faculty Mgmt., Laboratory Tech., Mechanical Tech., Secretarial
Bachelor of Comm/Admin: Accounting, Finance, Info Mgmt.
Bachelor of Science: Chemistry, Computer Science
Bachelor of Engineering: Chemical, Mechanical
Chartered Accounting: CA-Finance, CMA - General/Finance
Masters: Science, Engineering

Critical Skills
Adaptable, Analytical, Good Communication, Confident, Creative, Dependable, Diligent, Diplomatic, Efficient, Enthusiastic, Flexible, Good With Figures, Logical, Manual Dexterity, Organized, Productive, Professional, Responsible

Types of Positions
Various Positions

Starting Salary
Depends on area of specialty

Company Benefits
- Group insurance
- DPSP (deferred profit sharing plan)

Correspondence
Mail resume with cover letter

Part Time/Summer: Recochem occasionally looks for individuals for part time and summer employment. Potential positions differ each year. Recently they have been somewhat rare.

RED DEER CO-OP LIMITED

5118 47 Ave.
Red Deer, Alberta, T4N 3P7
Tel: (403) 343-2667 Fax: (403) 341-5811

Human Resources
Internet: www.reddeer.com

Red Deer Co-op Limited is a large grocery retailer, with feed mill and home and garden centre sales. The company has a staff of 215 people.

Academic Fields
College: Accounting, Administration, Food/Nutrition
Bachelor of Arts: Business
Bachelor of Comm/Admin: General, Accounting, Finance
Bachelor of Science: Food Sciences
Bachelor of Education: Adult Education
Chartered Accounting: CMA-General, CGA-General
Masters: Business Administration, Arts

Critical Skills
Good Communication, Confident, Creative, Decisive, Dependable, Diplomatic, Efficient, Enthusiastic, Flexible, Leadership, Organized, Personable, Productive

Types of Positions
Grocery Clerk   Mill Hand
Lumber Yard   Personnel
Sales Personnel   Driver

Starting Salary
$ 25,000 - 30,000

Company Benefits
- Dental, Blue Cross, life insurance, pension
- Accelerated and advanced training
- Educational subsidies

Correspondence
Mail resume with cover letter

Part Time/Summer: Red Deer Co-op Limited regularly seeks candidates for part time and summer employment. Potential summer jobs include home and garden centre sales and yard work, and grocery store jobs. The best time to apply is in April.

REENA

927 Clarke Ave. W.
Thornhill, Ontario, L4J 8G6
Tel: (905) 763-8254 Fax: (905) 763-8272

Wuanita DiLuciano, HR Assistant
Internet: www.reena.org

Reena is a non-profit social service agency dedicated to integrating individuals who have a developmental disability into the mainstream of society. Reena was established in 1973 by parents of children with developmental disabilities, as a practical alternative to institutions. They provide services to close to 1000 people who have a developmentally disability and their families.

Academic Fields
College: Child Care, Social Work, Home Care, Nursing (RN), Nursing (RNA)
Bachelor of Arts: Gerontology, Psychology, Sociology/Social Work
Bachelor of Science: Health Science, Psychology
Bachelor of Education: Special

Critical Skills
Adaptable, Analytical, Dependable, Efficient, Enthusiastic, Flexible, Good Communication, Good Writing Skills, Innovative, Leadership, Logical, Organized, Patient, Personable, Professional

Types of Positions
Part Time Support Worker
Full Time Support Worker
Overnight Awake Support Worker

Starting Salary
$ 25,000 - 30,000

Company Benefits
- Full time employees are eligible to participate in group benefits after three months
- A large number of training and development courses are offered in-house

Correspondence
Fax or e-mail resume with cover letter
E-mail: hr@reena.org

Part Time/Summer: Reena regularly hires for part time and summer employment opportunities. Potential jobs include recreation workers for cottage and respite programs, and administration assistants for several departments. Apply in May.

The Canada Student Employment Guide

REGAL CAPITAL PLANNERS LTD.

319 Bridgeport Rd. E.
Waterloo, Ontario, N2J 2K9
Tel: (519) 885-1980   Fax: (519) 885-6578

Penny Steckly, Human Resources
Internet: www.regal.ca

Regal Capital Planners is a financial planning company which provides services and sales of mutual funds, insurance, and retirement plans. The firm has an employee base of 850 people.

Academic Fields
College: Accounting, Business, Computer Science, Human Resources, Marketing/Sales, Financial Planning
Bachelor of Arts: Economics, Public Relations
Bachelor of Comm/Admin: General, Accounting, Finance, Marketing
Masters: Business Administration

Critical Skills
Good Communication, Efficient, Good With Figures, Financially Inclined

Types of Positions
Data Entry   Sales Representative
Junior Client Services

Starting Salary
$ 20,000 - 25,000

Company Benefits
- Competitive benefit package
- Educational support

Correspondence
Mail or fax resume with cover letter

Part Time/Summer: Regal Capital Planners occasionally looks for people for part time and summer opportunities. Part time opportunities are usually in January or February. Potential jobs in the summer involve data entry, or being in the mail room. The best time to apply is right before the Summer.

REGAL CONSTELLATION HOTEL LTD.

900 Dixon Road
Etobicoke, Ontario, M9W 1J7
Tel: (416) 675-1500   Fax: (416) 675-1737

Janet Crank, Director Human Resources
Internet: www.regalconstellation.com

The Regal Constellation Hotel, located next to Lester B. Pearson International Airport, is an establishment that provides individuals with all types of vacation and business facilities.

Academic Fields
College: General, Accounting, Administration, Advertising, Business, Computer Science, Cooking/Culinary, Engineering Tech., Hospitality, Human Resources, Marketing/Sales, Recreation Studies, Secretarial, Travel/Tourism
Bachelor of Arts: General, Business, Languages, Public Relations, Recreation Studies
Bachelor of Comm/Admin: General, Accounting, Finance, Marketing
Bachelor of Engineering: General, Computer Systems
Chartered Accounting: CA-General, CGA/CMA - General/Finance
Masters: Business Administration

Critical Skills
Adaptable, Analytical, Good Communication, Confident, Dependable, Diligent, Efficient, Flexible, Organized, Patient, Personable, Productive, Professional, Responsible

Types of Positions
Various Positions

Starting Salary
below $ 20,000 - 25,000

Company Benefits
- Health, dental, life insurance
- Meals, parking, dry cleaning
- Customer service training

Correspondence
Submit resume and cover letter in person

Part Time/Summer: The Regal Constellation Hotel regularly hires for part time work and sometimes hires for the summer. Jobs may include front desk clerk, server, busperson, or involve engineering or housekeeping. The best time to apply is in May.

The Canada Student Employment Guide

REGAL GREETING AND GIFTS

7035 Ordan Drive
Mississauga, Ontario, L5T 1T1
Tel: (905) 670-1126   Fax: (905) 670-1478

Christine Klassen, HR Recruiter/Generalist
Internet: www.regalgreetings.com

Regal Greetings & Gifts is a consumer catalogue, mail-order distributor of general merchandise. The company also operates a manufacturing facility for paper products. Regal, and its Quebec subsidiary Prime de Luxe Inc., market a wide range of household and functional products, greeting cards and giftwrap at mostly affordable prices. With its head office in Toronto, Regal has approximately 800 employees across Canada.

Academic Fields
College: Accounting, Information Systems, Marketing/Sales, Purchasing, Graphic Arts
Bachelor of Arts: Business
Bachelor of Comm/Admin: General, Accounting, Finance, Marketing, Info Mgmt.
Chartered Accounting: CGA-General

Critical Skills
Adaptable, Confident, Enthusiastic, Flexible, Good Communication, Good Writing Skills, Organized, Productive, Professional, Responsible

Types of Positions
Merchandising Dept.   Customer Service Dept.
Finance Dept.   Sales & Marketing Dept.

Starting Salary
$ 20,000 - 30,000

Company Benefits
- Medical and dental benefits
- Vision care and pension
- Employee discounts

Correspondence
Mail or fax resume with cover letter

Part Time/Summer: Regal Greeting & Gifts sometimes hires for part time work but rarely hires for the summer. Potential jobs may involve being a customer service representative. The best time to apply is in May or June.

REGINA HEALTH DISTRICT

2180 23rd Ave.
Regina, Saskatchewan, S4S 0A5
Tel: (306) 766-5208   Fax: (306) 766-5147

Recruitment Classification Consultant
Internet: www.reginahealth.sk.ca

The Regina Health District promotes a healthier community by linking the community of people they serve and the community of the Regina Health District service providers.

Academic Fields
College: Child Care, Accounting, Admin., HR, Info Syst., Secretarial, Emergency/Paramedic, Home Care, Lab Tech., Nursing, Orthotics/Prosthetics, Radiology Tech., Respiratory Tech.
Bachelor of Arts: Sociology/Social Work
Bachelor of Comm/Admin: Accounting, Finance, Human Resources
Bachelor of Science: Computer Sciences, Health Sciences, Microbiology, Nursing (RN), Occupational Therapy, Pharmacy, Physiotherapy
Bachelor of Engineering: Biomedical
Chartered Accounting: CA-Finance
Masters: Library Science, Social Work

Critical Skills
Adaptable, Good Communication, Confident, Dependable, Enthusiastic, Flexible, Leadership, Organized, Patient, Personable, Professional, Responsible

Types of Positions
Housekeeping   Nutrition & Food Services
Laundry Services   Distribution
Processing

Starting Salary
$ 23,000 entry level and up

Company Benefits
- Employee benefits depends on status and hours
- Dental plan, group life, pension

Correspondence
Mail, fax, e-mail resume with cover letter, or submit in person. E-mail: jobs@reginahealth.sk.ca

Part Time/Summer: Regina Health District occasionally looks for people for part time and summer jobs. Not many opportunities specifically for the summer, but are always hiring casually. Individuals may apply anytime.

The Canada Student Employment Guide

REGIONAL MUNICIPALITY OF NIAGARA

P.O. Box 1042
Thorold, Ontario, L2V 4T7
Tel: (905) 685-1571   Fax: (905) 641-2232

Karen Consigli, Human Resources
Internet: www.regional.niagara.on.ca

Regional Municipality of Niagara is a regional government spanning water and sewer works, social and senior services, public health, planning and development, waste management, and transportation. They employ approximately 2,500 individuals.

Academic Fields
College: Legal Assistant, Security/Law Enforcement, Social Work, Human Resources, Information Systems, Electronics Tech., Mechanical Tech., Plumbing, Welding, Nursing RN, Nursing RNA
Bachelor of Education: Adult Education
Masters: Education

Critical Skills
Adaptable, Good Communication, Dependable, Efficient, Productive, Responsible

Types of Positions
Office Cleaner   Building Maintenance
Labourer   Dietary Aide
General Clerk

Starting Salary
$ 25,000 - 30,000

Company Benefits
- General drug plan, dental, vision
- Life insurance, pension, semi private hospital

Correspondence
Mail resume with cover letter
E-mail: fnewfeld@regional.niagara.on.ca

Part Time/Summer: Regional Municipality of Niagara occasionally hires for part time work, and regularly hires in the summer. Potential jobs include public health inspector, dietary aide, or labourer.

REGIONAL RESIDENTIAL SERVICES SOCIETY

380 Pleasant Street, Unit 1 & 2
Dartmouth, Nova Scotia, B2Y 3S5
Tel: (902) 465-4022   Fax: (902) 465-3124

Brenda Dixon, Human Resources Manager

The Regional Residential Services Society (RRSS) is a non-profit agency, employing over 300 full time, part time, and casual relief staff. The agency's mission is to meet the residential needs of intellectually disabled adults from within the Metro Halifax area. Prospective employees must be able to do shift work, especially evenings, overnights and weekends.

Academic Fields
College: Child Care, Recreation Studies
Bachelor of Arts: Gerontology, Psychology, Sociology/Social Work
Bachelor of Science: Psychology
Bachelor of Education: General, Adult Education, Childhood, Special

Critical Skills
Confident, Dependable, Efficient, Enthusiastic, Flexible, Good Writing Skills, Patient, Good Communication, Personable, Professional

Types of Positions
Relief Counsellor   Counsellor
Counsellor Assistant

Starting Salary
$ 26,000 - 28,500

Company Benefits
- Group health and disability insurance
- Group RRSP, sick leave program
- Aggressive staff training program

Correspondence
Mail or fax resume with cover letter
E-mail: bdixon@rrss.ns.ca

Part Time/Summer: Regional Residential Services Society regularly seeks individuals for part time and summer employment. Potential jobs include summer recreation counsellor and relief counsellor (covering staff vacations). The best time to apply is in March or April.

REGIS PICTURES AND FRAMES LTD.

102 SE Marine Dr.
Vancouver, British Columbia, V5X 2S3
Tel: (604) 327-3447   Fax: (604) 327-5223

Mandie LaMontagne, Personnel Manager

Regis Pictures and Frames Ltd. is a merchandiser of various styles of pictures and frames. They have locations throughout the Western Provinces.

Academic Fields
College: Graphic Arts, Human Resources
Bachelor of Arts: General, Fine Arts, History, Public Relations

Critical Skills
Artistic, Creative, Dependable, Leadership, Manual Dexterity, Organized, Professional

Types of Positions
Production Fitter   Sales Assistant

Starting Salary
below $ 20,000

Company Benefits
- Basic coverage, medical, dental
- Two weeks on-the-job training, upgrading seminars
- On-going day to day training

Correspondence
Fax resume with cover letter

Part Time/Summer: Regis Pictures and Frames Ltd. regularly hires for part time and summer positions. The best time to apply is in June or July.

REHABILITATION INSTITUTE OF TORONTO

550 University Ave.
Toronto, Ontario, M5G 2A2
Tel: (416) 597-3422   Fax: (416) 597-6626

Andrea Watson, Human Resources
Internet: www.tor-rehab.on.ca

The Rehabilitation Institute of Toronto (RIT) is a public health care facility formed through the voluntary amalgamation of The Queen Elizabeth and Hillcrest Hospitals. RIT has more than 600 beds for complex continuing care, rehabilitation and geriatric assessment and psychiatry.

Academic Fields
College: Accounting, Child Care, Computer Science, Human Resources, Nursing, Radiology Tech., Recreation Studies, Secretarial
Bachelor of Arts: Gerontology, Public Relations, Recreation Studies
Bachelor of Comm/Admin: Info Mgmt.
Bachelor of Science: Computer Sci., Nursing (RN), Occupational Therapy, Pharmacy, Physiotherapy
Bachelor of Engineering: Computer Systems
Chartered Accounting: CA-Finance, CGA-General, CGA-Finance
Masters: Education, Library Science

Critical Skills
Adaptable, Analytical, Confident, Decisive, Dependable, Diligent, Diplomatic, Good Communication, Flexible, Efficient, Innovative, Good Writing Skills, Logical, Organized, Personable

Types of Positions
Various Positions

Starting Salary
$ 25,000 - 30,000

Company Benefits
- Full benefit package

Correspondence
Mail resume with cover letter

Part Time/Summer: The Rehabilitation Institute of Toronto sometimes hires for part time and summer positions. For the summer months, nursing students may be hired. Students should apply in March.

The Canada Student Employment Guide

REID CROWTHER

340 Midpark Way SE, Suite 210
Calgary, Alberta, T2X 1P1
Tel: (403) 254-3304   Fax: (403) 254-3366

Human Resources Coordinator
Internet: www.reid-crowther.com

As a leading Canadian consulting firm, based in Western Canada and active around the world, they employ more than 650 people who are involved in all stages of the project cycle, from feasibility studies through to final design and construction. Whether it's environmental engineering work in biological nutrient removal, instrumentation and control systems for "smart" buildings, or high-end traffic modeling programs to help deal with transportation demands, our people are among the leaders in engineering design.

Academic Fields
College: Accounting, Drafting/Architecture, Engineering Tech., Industrial Design, Mechanical Tech.
Bachelor of Comm/Admin: Accounting
Bachelor of Science: Computer Science
Bachelor of Engineering: Civil, Design, Electrical, Environ. Studies, Industrial, Mechanical, Water Res.
Chartered Accounting: CMA-General, CGA-General

Critical Skills
Adaptable, Analytical, Efficient, Enthusiastic, Good Communication, Innovative, Leadership

Types of Positions
Engineer Level A or B   Technologist
Designer   Drafter

Starting Salary
$25,000 - 40,000

Company Benefits
- Flexible benefit program, health, dental
- Short and long term disability
- Life insurance, pension plan

Correspondence
Mail resume with cover letter
E-mail: info@reid-crowther.com

Part Time/Summer: Reid Crowther regularly hires individuals for part time and summer employment. Potential jobs include technological assistant or involve engineering. The best time to apply is in January or February.

RELIABLE ENGINE SERVICES LTD.

5311 - 86 Street
Edmonton, Alberta, T6E 5T8
Tel: (403) 468-6220   Fax: (403) 468-5777

Human Resources
Internet: www.reliable.ab.ca

Reliable Engine Services Ltd. is a Canadian owned company, originally established in 1966 to serve the automotive engine rebuilding industry. Over the years the business expanded to supply components for diesel and natural gas engines and compressors up to 5000 HP. The main repair facility located in Edmonton is 66,000 square feet with over 80 employees. There is also a 10,000 square foot plant in Calgary employing a staff of 18 individuals.

Academic Fields
College: Engineering Tech., Marketing/Sales, Mechanical Tech
Chartered Accounting: CMA-General

Critical Skills
Dependable, Efficient, Organized, Productive, Responsible

Types of Positions
Various Positions

Starting Salary
$20,000 - 25,000

Company Benefits
- Sick pay program, medical insurance
- Life insurance, pension plan
- Apprenticeships, training assistance

Correspondence
Mail resume with cover letter

Part Time/Summer: Reliable Engine Services Ltd. occasionally seeks candidates for part time or summer work. A potential position is labourer. The best time to apply is in May or June.

The Canada Student Employment Guide

RENAISSANCE ENERGY LTD.

707 - 8th Avenue S.W.
Calgary, Alberta, T2P 3G7
Tel: (403) 750-1447   Fax: (403) 750-5010

Employee Services
Internet: www.renaissance.ca

Renaissance Energy is involved in oil and natural gas exploration, production and marketing. Exploration activities are in the Alberta and Saskatchewan area. They employ over 500 individuals.

Academic Fields
College: Engineering Tech., Marketing/Sales
Bachelor of Comm/Admin: General, Finance, Marketing
Bachelor of Engineering: Transportation
Masters: Business Administration

Critical Skills
Adaptable, Analytical, Good Communication, Confident, Creative, Decisive, Dependable, Enthusiastic, Flexible, Good With Figures, Innovative, Leadership, Organized, Patient, Personable, Productive, Professional, Responsible, Good Writing Skills

Types of Positions
Administrative Clerk   Accounting Clerk
Land Clerk   Junior Secretary
Field Operator Trainee

Starting Salary
$ 25,000 - 30,000

Company Benefits
- Full range of extremely attractive benefits available upon hire
- Ongoing training and development opportunities

Correspondence
Mail or fax resume with cover letter

Part Time/Summer: Renaissance Energy occasionally looks for people for part time jobs, and regularly hires in the summer months. All departments hire summer students. It is excellent training ground for petroleum engineers and technicians.

RENTWAY INC.

800 5th Avenue S.W., Suite 1910
Calgary, Alberta, T2P 3T6
Tel: (403) 298-5230   Fax: N/A

Local Branch Manager
Internet: www.rent-way.com

Rentway is involved in the truck rental and leasing business. The company provides heavy truck fleet management services, including full-service truck leasing, rentals, maintenance and repair services from Quebec to British Columbia. Rentway also provides service through Triway Truck Leasing Inc. in the states of Michigan, Ohio, and Washington. A wholly owned subsidiary of Trimac Limited, Rentway operates a fleet of 4,400 vehicles from 35 locations. Interested candidates should apply to local branches as opposed to head office.

Academic Fields
College: Engineering Tech., Marketing/Sales
Bachelor of Comm/Admin: General, Finance, Marketing
Bachelor of Engineering: Transportation
Masters: Business Administration

Critical Skills
Analytical, Creative, Innovative, Good Communication, Leadership, Personable, Persuasive, Good With Figures, Professional, Responsible

Types of Positions
Sales Coordinator   Branch Administrator
Service Coordinator   Branch Analyst
Service Writer

Starting Salary
$ 20,000 - 30,000 (high school/college)

Company Benefits
- Competitive group benefits and pension plan
- Generous training subsidies
- Individual development plans

Correspondence
Mail, fax, submit resume and cover letter in person

Part Time/Summer: Rentway sometimes looks for individuals for part time and summer employment opportunities. Jobs in the summer are most likely to include those listed above. The best time to apply is in late Spring.

REPLICON INC.

830, 910 - 7th Avenue
Calgary, Alberta, T2P 3N8
Tel: (403) 262-6519   Fax: (403) 233-8046

Velvet Beaumont, Director of HR & Recruiting
Internet: www.replicon.com

Replicon Inc. is the leader in web-based enterprise applications. Web TimeSheet, our flagship product, builds on our successes with web technology software applications. The Web TimeSheet customer base includes more than 250 clients spanning 23 countries. They employ approximately 50 individuals.

Academic Fields
College: Communications, Human Resources, Marketing/Sales, Computer Science, Electronics Tech., Engineering Tech.
Bachelor of Comm/Admin: General, Marketing
Bachelor of Engineering: Computer Systems, Electrical
Masters: Business Administration

Critical Skills
Adaptable, Creative, Dependable, Flexible, Good Communication, Good Writing Skills, Innovative, Personable, Productive, Professional, Multi-task, Good Listener

Types of Positions
Development (Javascript)   Account Executive
Marketing Coordinator   Customer Support
Technical Writer   HR Assistant

Starting Salary
$ 25,000 - 30,000 (sales/marketing) /
$ 35,000 - 40,000 (development)

Company Benefits
- Full benefits at start of employment
- 3 weeks annual holiday

Correspondence
E-mail resume with cover letter or apply through web site. E-mail: career@replicon.com

Part Time/Summer: Replicon Inc. does not hire for part time or summer employment. They tend not to hire for summer only, however, they will look at interns.

Co-op/Internship: They do offer internship opportunities.

REUTERS INFORMATION SERVICES (CANADA) LTD.

130 King St. W., Suite 2000
Toronto, Ontario, M5X 1E3
Tel: (416) 364-5361   Fax: (416) 364-9017

Human Resources
Internet: www.reuters.com

Reuters Information Services is the world's leading provider of financial information. They serve the financial and business community in all of the world's major markets by providing high quality financial information to analysts and key decision makers in business, finance, and government. Located in downtown Toronto, their group builds databases in the areas of equities, energy, commodities, options, fixed income, foreign exchange, money markets and economics. Their data is gathered from hundreds of sources in more than 50 countries.

Academic Fields
Bachelor of Arts: Economics
Bachelor of Comm/Admin: Accounting, Finance, Info Mgmt.
Bachelor of Science: Computer Systems, Mathematics
Bachelor of Engineering: Computer Systems

Critical Skills
Adaptable, Analytical, Enthusiastic, Good Communication, Good With Figures, Good Writing Skills

Types of Positions
Data Analyst   Programmer/Analyst

Starting Salary
$ 35,000 - 44,000

Company Benefits
- Full benefit package
- In-house training and tuition assistance

Correspondence
Fax resume with cover letter

Part Time/Summer: Reuters Information Services does not hire for part time or summer employment.

The Canada Student Employment Guide

REVENUE PROPERTIES COMPANY LIMITED

131 Bloor Street West, Suite 300
Toronto, Ontario, M5S 1R1
Tel: (416) 963-8100   Fax: (416) 963-8512

Human Resources
Internet: www.revprop.com

Revenue Properties is engaged in various segments of the real estate industry, primarily those relating to shopping centres, residential income properties, gaming, and merchant banking activities. Properties are located in Ontario, British Columbia, Alberta, New Brunswick, Oregon, Tennessee, Kentucky, Florida, Connecticut, California, Nevada, New Mexico, and Washington. Income producing investments represent more than 3.4 million square feet of shopping centre leasable area, 1.2 million square feet of residential leasable area, and 239,000 square feet of office and industrial leasable area.

Academic Fields
College: General, Computer Science, Law Clerk, Secretarial
Bachelor of Arts: General, Business
Chartered Accounting: CA-General, CMA-Finance

Critical Skills
Adaptable, Dependable, Efficient, Flexible, Logical, Organized, Personable, Professional, Responsible, Punctual

Types of Positions
Reception   Secretarial
Accounting Clerk

Starting Salary
$ 20,000 - 25,000

Company Benefits
- Extended health and dental
- Group RRSP, life insurance
- Training as required

Correspondence
Mail or fax resume with cover letter

Part Time/Summer: Revenue Properties sometimes seeks individuals for part time employment, and regularly looks for candidates for summer positions. Potential jobs are most likely those listed above.

REVY HOME CENTRES INC.

1170 Martingrove Rd.
Etobicoke, Ontario, M9W 4X1
Tel: (416) 241-8844   Fax: (416) 241-2344

Dave Chevy, Human Resources Administrator
Internet: www.revy.ca

Revy Home Centres Inc. is a retailer of building materials to both do-it-yourself individuals and contractors. Revy was established in 1903 and is the largest home improvement retailer in Western Canada. Revy and Lansing Buildall merged in 1998 and currently operate eight Lansing Buildall and four Revy Home and Garden Warehouse stores in Southern Ontario. They also operate 45 stores in Western Canada.

Academic Fields
College: Construction Technology, Architectural Technology
Bachelor of Engineering: Design, Bachelor of Architecture

Critical Skills
Adaptable, Confident, Creative, Dependable, Diligent, Efficient, Enthusiastic, Flexible, Good Communication, Good With Figures, Leadership, Personable, Productive, Professional, Responsible

Types of Positions
Cashier   Sales Clerk
Shipper

Starting Salary
$ 20,000 - 25,000

Company Benefits
- Medical, dental, life insurance, prescription drugs for full time employees

Correspondence
Fax, e-mail resume with cover letter or apply through web site

Part Time/Summer: Revy Home Centres Inc. regularly hires for part time and summer employment opportunities. The best time to apply is February to April.

REYNOLDS AND REYNOLDS (CANADA) LIMITED
2100 Steeles Ave. E.
Brampton, Ontario, L6T 3X1
Tel: (905) 790-1381   Fax: (905) 791-4400

Human Resources

Reynolds and Reynolds (Canada) Limited is a major provider of computer systems and business forms to automotive dealerships.

Academic Fields
College: Accounting, Business, Computer Science, Electronics Tech.
Bachelor of Arts: General, Business
Bachelor of Comm/Admin: General, Accounting, Marketing
Bachelor of Science: Computer Science

Critical Skills
Adaptable, Enthusiastic, Flexible, Good Communication, Leadership, Organized, Professional

Types of Positions
Hardware Support Trainee
Software Support Trainee
Field Service Trainee

Starting Salary
$30,000 - 40,000

Company Benefits
- Medical, dental, life insurance, pension, prescription drugs
- Tuition refund program
- On-the-job soft skills training and technical training

Correspondence
Mail or fax resume with cover letter

Part Time/Summer: Reynolds and Reynolds (Canada) Limited does not hire individuals for part time or summer employment.

RHONE-POULENC CANADA INC.
2000 Argentina Road, Plaza 3, Suite 400
Mississauga, Ontario, L5N 1V9
Tel: (905) 821-4450   Fax: (905) 821-0867

Lesley Russell, Human Resources

Rhone-Poulenc Canada is a formulator and distributor of chemicals including specialty chemicals, food ingredients, animal nutrition an crop protection products. Rhone-Poulenc is present in over 140 countries, and employs more than 81,000 individuals, while the Canadian subsidiary has a staff of about 300 people.

Academic Fields
College: Accounting, Business, Human Resources, Laboratory Tech., Secretarial
Bachelor of Arts: Business, Economics
Bachelor of Comm/Admin: General
Bachelor of Science: Agriculture, Chemistry, Food Sciences
Bachelor of Engineering: Chemical, Environmental Studies
Masters: Engineering

Critical Skills
Adaptable, Analytical, Good Communication, Confident, Creative, Dependable, Diplomatic, Efficient, Flexible, Good With Figures, Innovative, Leadership, Organized, Productive, Professional, Responsible, Good Writing Skills

Types of Positions
Customer Service   Manufacturing
Production   Finance
Distribution   Administration

Starting Salary
$ 25,000 - 30,000

Company Benefits
- Flexible benefit plan
- Progression to U.S. or France if have high potential

Correspondence
Mail resume with cover letter

Part Time/Summer: Rhone-Poulenc Canada sometimes hires for part time and summer work. Summer positions most likely to include customer service rep., accounting clerk, production operator, field development rep., or human resources administrator.

The Canada Student Employment Guide

RICH PRODUCTS OF CANADA LIMITED

P.O. Box 1008
Fort Erie, Ontario, L2A 5N8
Tel: (519) 871-5341   Fax: (519) 871-1517

Human Resources

Rich Products of Canada Limited is involved in the frozen food industry specializing in frozen dough. The company's head office is in Fort Erie, Ontario.

Academic Fields
Bachelor of Comm/Admin: Marketing
Bachelor of Science: Food Sciences
Bachelor of Engineering: Mechanical
Chartered Accounting: CA-General
Masters: Business Administration

Critical Skills
Adaptable, Confident, Decisive, Flexible, Good Communication, Innovative, Personable

Types of Positions
Various Positions

Starting Salary
$ 25,000 - 30,000

Company Benefits
- Full range of benefits and educational assistance

Correspondence
Mail resume with cover letter

Part Time/Summer: Rich Products of Canada Limited occasionally hires for part time or summer work. Potential jobs involve labour or clerical duties.

CITY OF RICHMOND

6911 No. 3 Road
Richmond, British Columbia, V6Y 2C1
Tel: (604) 276-4105   Fax: (604) 276-4169

Human Resources

City of Richmond is a municipal government responsible for the formation of policy and laws in matters under its jurisdiction.

Academic Fields
College: Accounting, Administration, Business, Computer Science, Drafting/Architecture, Emergency/Paramedic, Engineering Tech., Hospitality, Human Resources, Mechanical Tech., Recreation Studies, Secretarial, Stats, Urban Planning
Bachelor of Arts: Business, Fine Arts, Recreation Studies, Sociology/Social Work, Statistics, Urban Geography
Bachelor of Science: Computer Science
Bachelor of Engineering: Civil, Computer Systems, Design, Transportation
Chartered Accounting: CA - General/Finance, CGA - General/Finance
Masters: Business Admin., Engineering, Library Sci.

Critical Skills
Adaptable, Good Communication, Creative, Decisive, Dependable, Diligent, Diplomatic, Efficient, Flexible, Innovative, Leadership, Patient, Productive, Responsible, Good Writing Skills

Types of Positions
Clerical   Labourer
Administration   Rodman
Traffic Technician I   Attendant

Starting Salary
$ 25,000 - 40,000

Company Benefits
- Comprehensive benefit package

Correspondence
Mail resume with cover letter

Part Time/Summer: The City of Richmond regularly seeks candidates for part time and summer work. Potential jobs in the summer include labourer, clerical duties, or lifeguarding. One may also work as a community centre attendant or facilitator.

The Canada Student Employment Guide

RICHTER USHER & VINEBERG

90 Eglinton Avenue East, Suite 700
Toronto, Ontario, M4P 2Y3
Tel: (416) 932-8000   Fax: (416) 932-6200

Human Resources
Internet: www.richter.ca

Richter is one of the largest independent accounting, business advisory and consulting firms in Canada. Their ability to help owner-managed organizations anticipate and meet complex challenges is why they are still the firm that means business for entrepreneurs.

Academic Fields
Bachelor of Arts: Business
Bachelor of Comm/Admin: Accounting, Finance
Chartered Accounting: CA-General
Masters: Business Administration

Critical Skills
Adaptable, Analytical, Good Communication, Confident, Creative, Decisive, Dependable, Diligent, Diplomatic, Efficient, Enthusiastic, Flexible, Good With Figures, Innovative, Leadership, Logical, Organized, Patient, Personable, Persuasive, Productive, Professional, Responsible, Good Writing Skills

Types of Positions
Student in Accounts

Starting Salary
$ 30,000 - 40,000

Company Benefits
- Standard benefit package
- Professional development for CA degree

Correspondence
Mail resume and cover letter, or use CACEE form

Part Time/Summer: Richter, Usher & Vineberg occasionally hires for part time positions, but regularly looks for people for summer opportunities. The company seeks 3rd year students in a university business or accounting program. Individuals should apply in November of their 3rd year of studies.

RIMROCK RESORT HOTEL

P.O. Box 1110, Mountain Avenue
Banff, Alberta, T0L 0C0
Tel: (403) 762-1824   Fax: (403) 762-1860

Trevor Gomes, Recruiter
Internet: www.rimrockresort.com

Built on the side of Sulphur Mountain, The Rimrock Resort Hotel is nestled high above the picturesque Town of Banff in the heart of the Canadian Rockies. A four diamond resort hotel, the hotel employs between 300 and 390 individuals.

Academic Fields
College: Accounting, Business, Human Resources, Engineering Tech., Mechanical Tech., Cooking/Culinary, Hospitality, Travel/Tourism
Bachelor of Arts: Business
Bachelor of Comm/Admin: Human Resources
Bachelor of Science: Food Sciences, Health Sciences, Kinesiology
Bachelor of Engineering: General, Mechanical
Chartered Accounting: CA-General, CGA-General, CMA-General

Critical Skills
Dependable, Enthusiastic, Leadership, Organized, Personable, Productive, Professional

Types of Positions
Front Desk Agent   Bellman
Health Club Attendant   Server
Reservations   Housekeeping

Starting Salary
$ 20,000 - 25,000

Company Benefits
- Benefit plan (after 6 months)
- Staff accommodation $4.00 per day, meal allowance per day

Correspondence
Mail, fax, e-mail resume with cover letter, or submit in person. E-mail: trevor.gomes@rimrockresort.com

Part Time/Summer: Rimrock Resort Hotel regularly seeks hires for part time and summer work. Summer jobs in all entry level positions as stated above. The best time to apply is April 1st to April 15th.

The Canada Student Employment Guide

RIO ALGOM LIMITED

120 Adelaide St. W., Suite 2600
Toronto, Ontario, M5H 1W5
Tel: (416) 367-4000   Fax: (416) 365-6820

HR Generalist, Corporate Office
Internet: www.rioalgom.com

Rio Algom is a base metal mining company. There are very limited number of positions in Canada. Knowledge of Spanish is a plus. Applicants should research their company and be able to state how they could help them succeed.

Academic Fields
Bachelor of Comm/Admin: General, Accounting, Finance
Bachelor of Science: Chemistry, Geology
Bachelor of Laws: Corporate
Bachelor of Engineering: Geotechnical, Mining
Chartered Accounting: CA-Finance, CMA-Finance, CGA-Finance
Masters: Business Administration, Engineering

Critical Skills
Adaptable, Efficient, Enthusiastic, Productive

Types of Positions
Corporate Finance   Mining Exploration
Environment

Starting Salary
$ 25,000 - 30,000

Company Benefits
- Supplemental health and dental coverage
- Life insurance, employee stock purchase plan

Correspondence
Mail or fax resume with cover letter

Part Time/Summer: Rio Algom occasionally looks for people for part time and summer positions. Potential jobs are involved with the environment, corporate finance, or law. The best time to apply is in March or April.

RIVERSIDE FABRICATING LTD.

1556 Matthew Brandy Blvd.
Windsor, Ontario, N8S 3K6
Tel: (519) 945-2325   Fax: (519) 945-0696

Human Resource Manager

Riverside Fabricating Ltd. is a metal finishing company. The firm's head office is in Windsor, Ontario.

Academic Fields
College: Business, Human Resources, Mechanical Tech., Secretarial
Bachelor of Arts: Business

Critical Skills
Adaptable, Analytical, Dependable, Diligent, Efficient, Enthusiastic, Flexible, Good Communication, Good Writing Skills, Logical, Organized, Personable, Productive

Types of Positions
Various Positions

Starting Salary
$ 30,000 - 40,000

Company Benefits
- Complete benefits including health care
- Dental, life insurance
- On-the-job training, seminar training

Correspondence
Fax resume with cover letter

Part Time/Summer: Riverside Fabricating Ltd. occasionally hires people for part time or summer employment. A potential job could be general labourer. The best time to apply is in June.

THE RIVERSIDE HOSPITAL OF OTTAWA

1967 Riverside Dr.
Ottawa, Ontario, K1H 7W9
Tel: (613) 738-7100   Fax: (613) 738-8522

Human Resources

The Riverside Hospital of Ottawa is a 204 bed acute care community hospital in the City of Ottawa. They can be reached on the Internet at http://www.ochin.on.ca/riverside.

Academic Fields
College: Accounting, Computer Science, Laboratory Tech., Nursing, Radiology Tech., Secretarial
Bachelor of Arts: Public Relations, Sociology/Social Work
Bachelor of Comm/Admin: Finance, Info Mgmt.
Bachelor of Science: Computer Science, Nursing (RN), Occupational Therapy, Pharmacy, Physiotherapy
Chartered Accounting: CMA - General/Finance, CGA - General/Finance
Masters: Business Administration

Critical Skills
Adaptable, Dependable, Diligent, Diplomatic, Efficient, Enthusiastic, Flexible, Patient, Professional, Responsible

Types of Positions
Registered Nurse   Registered Practical Nurse
Clerical

Starting Salary
$25,000 - 30,000

Company Benefits
- Wide range of health benefits
- Dental, vision care, prescription drugs, semi-private hospital
- Extended health, pension plan

Correspondence
Mail resume with cover letter

Part Time/Summer: The Riverside Hospital of Ottawa occasionally hires for part time or summer employment opportunities.

RIVTOW MARINE LTD.

P.O. Box 3650, Stn Terminal
Vancouver, British Columbia, V6B 3Y8
Tel: (604) 255-1133   Fax: (604) 251-0213

Human Resources
Internet: www.rivtow.com

Rivtow Marine Ltd. is a tug boat company. Their company's head office is in Vancouver, British Columbia.

Academic Fields
College: Accounting, Computer Science
Bachelor of Comm/Admin: Accounting, Finance
Chartered Accounting: CA - General/Finance, CGA/CMA - General/Finance

Critical Skills
Adaptable, Dependable, Efficient, Enthusiastic, Flexible, Organized, Professional, Responsible

Types of Positions
Accounting

Starting Salary
$ 20,000 - 25,000

Company Benefits
- Medical, supplementary health, dental, group life insurance
- Pension plan, home plan insurance (optional)
- On the job training, reimbursement for job-related courses

Correspondence
Mail resume with cover letter
E-mail: info@rivtow.com

Part Time/Summer: Rivtow Marine Ltd. occasionally seeks candidates for part time or summer positions. Normally no academic positions available in the summer. There may be openings during the summer for boat maintenance in the Marine Division.

ROCKWELL AUTOMATION

135 Dundas St.
Cambridge, Ontario, N1R 5X1
Tel: (519) 740-4108   Fax: (519) 740-4111

Rob Page, Human Resources
Internet: www.automation.rockwell.com/

Rockwell Automation is an engineering automation products company that specializes in medium voltage drives and starters. The company's head office is in Cambridge, Ontario.

Academic Fields
College: Computer Science, Electronics Tech., Engineering Tech.
Bachelor of Engineering: Electrical, Mechanical

Critical Skills
Creative, Dependable, Enthusiastic, Good Communication, Good Writing Skills, Innovative, Personable, Productive, Responsible

Types of Positions
Jr. Engineering Specialist
Engineering Sales Trainee
Field Support Engineer Trainee

Starting Salary
$35,000 - 42,000

Company Benefits
- Full benefits for full time employees

Correspondence
Mail or fax resume with cover letter
E-mail: racambhumanresources@ra.rockwell.com

Part Time/Summer: Rockwell Automation regularly hires for part time and summer employment. Potential jobs involve shop floor assembly work, and engineering/drafting positions for those in appropriate programs. The best time to apply is 2-3 months in advance of summer.

ROCTEST LTÉE

665 av Pine
St Lambert, Québec, J4P 2P4
Tel: (450) 465-1113   Fax: (450) 465-1938

Direction des Ressources Humaines
Internet: www.roctest.com

Roctest is a Canadian company founded in 1967, specializing in the manufacture of high technology monitoring instruments. These instruments are primarily used in major civil engineering works and geotechnical applications. Roctest owns four manufacturing facilities, one located with the head office in Saint Lambert, just outside of Montreal, one located in Quebec City, one located near Paris, France, and a fourth in Plattsburgh, New York, U.S.A.

Academic Fields
College: Accounting, Electronics Tech., Engineering Tech., Industrial Design, Mechanical Tech.
Bachelor of Engineering: Civil, Electrical, Geotechnical, Mechanical
Chartered Accounting: CMA-General, CGA-General
Masters: Engineering

Critical Skills
Analytical, Creative, Dependable, Efficient, Enthusiastic, Logical, Productive, Professional, Responsible

Types of Positions
Various Positions

Starting Salary
$ 25,000 - 40,000 (depending on job)

Company Benefits
- Competitive benefit program

Correspondence
E-mail resume with cover letter
E-mail: info@roctest.com

Part Time/Summer: Roctest Ltée occasionally looks for candidates for part time employment, and regularly seeks individuals for the summer months. The best time to apply is in April or March.

The Canada Student Employment Guide

ROGERS AT&T WIRELESS INC.

333 Bloor St. E.
Toronto, Ontario, M4W 1G9
Tel: (416) 935-1100   Fax: (416) 935-3330

Human Resources
Internet: www.rogers.com

Rogers AT&T Wireless is Canada's largest national wireless communications service provider offering subscribers a broad spectrum of wireless communications products and services.

Academic Fields
College: Accounting, Administration, Business, Human Resources, Marketing/Sales, Secretarial, Statistics, Computer Science, Electronics Tech., Engineering Tech.
Bachelor of Arts: General, Business, Economics, English, Languages, Public Relations, Statistics
Bachelor of Comm/Admin: General, Accounting, Finance, Human Resources, Marketing, Info Mgmt.
Bachelor of Science: Actuarial, Computer Sci., Math
Bachelor of Engineering: Civil, Computer Systems, Electrical
Bachelor of Education: Adult Education
Masters: Business Admin., Arts, Science, Engineering

Critical Skills
Adaptable, Dependable, Diplomatic, Enthusiastic, Good Communication, Innovative, Leadership, Persuasive, Professional

Types of Positions
Call Centre Consultant	Marketing Coordinator
Finance Analyst	Retail Sales
Network Technician	IT Analyst

Starting Salary
$ 30,000 - 35,000

Company Benefits
- Full benefits, optical, dental, discounted cell phones
- PC loan purchase plan, on-site staff fitness centre

Correspondence
E-mail resume with cover letter, or apply at web site

Part Time/Summer: Rogers AT&T Wireless regularly hires for part time work and occasionally hires for the summer. Potential jobs involve marketing, finance or contract positions. Apply in February or March.

Co-op/Internship: The company will be offering internship opportunities.

ROGERS MEDIA, PUBLISHING

777 Bay Street
Toronto, Ontario, M5W 1A7
Tel: (416) 596-5270   Fax: (416) 596-5967

Personnel Department

Rogers Media, Publishing is Canada's largest publishing company. It owns many of Canada's best-known consumer magazines as well as the country's most respected business and professional publications.

Academic Fields
College: Administration, Advertising, Business, Human Resources, Journalism, Marketing/Sales
Bachelor of Arts: Business, English, Journalism, Political Science, Public Relations
Bachelor of Comm/Admin: Finance, Info Mgmt.
Chartered Accounting: CMA-Finance, CGA-Finance
Masters: Business Administration

Critical Skills
Creative, Dependable, Enthusiastic, Good Communication, Good Writing Skills, Organized, Personable, Professional

Types of Positions
Sales Co-ordinator	Customer Service Rep.
Receptionist	

Starting Salary
$ 20,000 - 25,000

Company Benefits
- 100% dental and medical, life insurance, pension
- 50% discount on publishing
- 100% reimbursement on external training

Correspondence
Mail or fax resume with cover letter

Part Time/Summer: Rogers Media, Publishing sometimes hires for part time and summer employment. Potential opportunities include editorial assistants or administrative support positions. The best time to apply is at the beginning of April.

ROTHMANS, BENSON AND HEDGES INC.

1500 Don Mills Road
North York, Ontario, M3B 3L1
Tel: (416) 442-3676   Fax: (416) 442-3603

Jane Ngimat, Human Resources

Rothmans, Benson and Hedges is a cigarette manufacturer with plants in Quebec City and Brampton, Ontario. A subsidiary of Rothmans Inc., the company carries out marketing activities through 13 sales offices across Canada. Brand names include Craven A, Rothmans, Benson & Hedges, Number 7, Belvedere, Mark Ten, Viscount, Accord, Belmont, Dunhill, Sportsman, Peter Stuyvesant, and Black Cat. The company also manufactures pipe tobaccos.

Academic Fields
College: Accounting, Computer Science, Human Resources, Laboratory Tech., Marketing/Sales, Secretarial
Bachelor of Arts: Business
Bachelor of Comm/Admin: General, Accounting, Finance, Marketing, Info Mgmt.
Bachelor of Science: Biology, Chemistry, Comp. Sci.
Chartered Accounting: CA - General/Finance, CGA/CMA - General/Finance
Masters: Business Administration

Critical Skills
Adaptable, Dependable, Diligent, Good Communication, Enthusiastic, Responsible

Types of Positions
Sales Representative   Accounting Clerk
Lab Technician   Secretarial

Starting Salary
$ 25,000 - 30,000

Company Benefits
- Cafeteria style benefits plan
- Non-contributory pension plan
- Fully paid educational assistance program

Correspondence
Mail resume with cover letter

Part Time/Summer: Rothmans, Benson and Hedges regularly looks for candidates for part time and summer employment. However, their summer student program is generally geared to children of employees.

ROYAL & SUN ALLIANCE INSURANCE CO. OF CANADA

10 Wellington Street East
Toronto, Ontario, M5E 1L5
Tel: (416) 366-7511   Fax: (416) 366-8615

Christina Jones, Human Resources

Royal Insurance Co. of Canada is a property and casualty insurer and provides fire, marine and other insurance services. The insurance company employs more than 2,000 people across the country.

Academic Fields
College: General, Accounting, Administration, Business, Communications, Computer Science, Human Resources, Insurance, Marketing/Sales, Secretarial, Statistics
Bachelor of Arts: General, Business, Economics, Political Science, Statistics
Bachelor of Comm/Admin: General, Accounting, Finance, Marketing, Info Mgmt.
Bachelor of Science: General, Actuarial, Comp. Sci.
Bachelor of Engineering: General, Computer Syst.
Bachelor of Education: General
Chartered Accounting: CA - General/Finance, CGA/CMA - General/Finance
Masters: Business Administration, Education

Critical Skills
Adaptable, Good Communication, Confident, Creative, Decisive, Dependable, Efficient, Enthusiastic, Personable, Responsible, Good Writing Skills

Types of Positions
Underwriting Asst.   Filer
Mail/Supply Asst.   Switchboard Operator

Starting Salary
$ 20,000 - 25,000

Company Benefits
- Competitive benefits offered

Correspondence
Mail or fax resume with cover letter

Part Time/Summer: Royal Insurance sometimes hires for part time work and regularly hires for the summer. Potential jobs include underwriter's assistant and cashier's assistant. Apply in March.

Co-op/Internship: They have co-op programs in the IS dept., actuarial dept., and IT dept.

The Canada Student Employment Guide

ROYAL BANK OF CANADA

970 Lawrence Ave. W., Suite 110
Toronto, Ontario, M6A 3B6
Tel: (905) 256-0088   Fax: (905) 256-0169

Employment Resource Centre
Internet: www.royalbank.ca

The Royal Bank of Canada provides a full range of banking services to individuals, businesses, and other institutions through a large branch network across Canada. The bank offers many personal banking services including deposits, short and long term investments, a wide range of mutual funds, RRSP's, RRIF's, residential and commercial mortgages, and various lines of credit. As one of the country's largest employers, they employ over 54,000 people.

Academic Fields
College: Accounting, Business, Computer Science, Human Resources, Marketing/Sales
Bachelor of Arts: General, Business, Economics
Bachelor of Comm/Admin: General, Accounting, Finance, Marketing, Info Mgmt., Public Admin.
Bachelor of Science: General, Agriculture, Computer Science, Mathematics
Bachelor of Engineering: Computer Systems
Bachelor of Education: Adult Education
Chartered Accounting: CA - General/Finance, CGA/CMA - General/Finance
Masters: Business Administration, Arts, Education

Critical Skills
Adaptable, Analytical, Good Communication, Creative, Decisive, Enthusiastic, Flexible, Innovative, Leadership

Types of Positions
Customer Service Rep./Teller   Personal Banker
Manager of Customer Service   Account Manager

Starting Salary
$ 25,000 - 40,000

Company Benefits
- Basic no-cost health and dental

Correspondence
Mail or fax resume with cover letter

Part Time/Summer: The Royal Bank of Canada regularly hires for part time and summer work. Potential jobs involve the summer undergraduate program. Individuals must have completed their 2nd year of undergraduate studies. The best time to apply is in December or January.

ROYAL CANADIAN MINT

320 Sussex Dr.
Ottawa, Ontario, K1A 0G8
Tel: (613) 993-3500   Fax: (613) 998-0272

Isabel Calheiros, HR Officer
Internet: www.rcmint.ca

The Royal Canadian Mint is a dynamic market-driven industrial organization which competes aggressively for the production and sale of circulation coinage, precious metals, refinery services, collector products and medals in both Canadian and International markets. They employ approximately 750 individuals in Canada.

Academic Fields
College: Administration, Human Resources, Information Systems, Marketing/Sales, Secretarial, CAD Autocad, Engineering Tech., Industrial Design, Mechanical Tech.
Bachelor of Arts: Public Relations
Bachelor of Comm/Admin: Accounting, Finance, Human Resources, Marketing
Bachelor of Science: Environmental Studies
Bachelor of Engineering: Chemical, Industrial, Mechanical
Masters: Business Administration

Critical Skills
Adaptable, Analytical, Artistic, Diplomatic, Flexible, Good Communication, Innovative, Organized, Personable, Professional

Types of Positions
Marketing Generalist   Administration Assistant

Starting Salary
$ 25,000 - 30,000

Company Benefits
- Full benefit package for any permanent position
- Regularly they listen to the needs in training and development

Correspondence
Mail, fax or e-mail resume with cover letter
E-mail: careers@rcmint.ca

Part Time/Summer: Royal Canadian Mint regularly seeks candidates for part time and summer employment. Potential jobs include tour guides, customer service, plant worker, and administration office help. The best time to apply is in March or April.

ROYAL INLAND HOSPITAL

311 Columbia Street
Kamloops, British Columbia, V2C 2T1
Tel: (250) 314-2720   Fax: (250) 314-2337

Human Resources

Royal Inland Hospital is a general medical and surgical health care regional referral facility in Kamloops, British Columbia. Established in 1896, the hospital provides services in medicine and surgery, gynecology, intensive care, pediatrics, psychiatric care, and rehabilitation. There are 260 beds within the facility, and the hospital employs more than 1,440 individuals.

Academic Fields
College: Accounting, Electronics Tech., Food/Nutrition, Laboratory Tech., Nursing, Orthotics, Radiology Tech., Secretarial
Bachelor of Arts: Sociology/Social Work
Bachelor of Comm/Admin: Accounting
Bachelor of Science: Chemistry, Food Sciences, Health Sciences, Microbiology, Nursing (RN), Occupational Therapy, Pharmacy, Physiotherapy
Bachelor of Engineering: Biomedical
Masters: Business Administration

Critical Skills
Adaptable, Dependable, Diplomatic, Good Communication, Efficient, Good Writing Skills, Innovative, Leadership, Organized, Productive, Responsible

Types of Positions
Housekeeping	Textile Services
Distribution	Clerical - Registration
Clerical - Finance	Food & Nutrition

Starting Salary
$ 30,000 - 35,000

Company Benefits
- Benefits per union contract

Correspondence
Mail, fax or submit resume and cover letter in person

Part Time/Summer: Royal Inland Hospital regularly seeks candidates for part time employment, and sometimes looks for individuals for summer positions. Potential jobs most likely include some of those listed above. The best time to apply is before May.

ROYAL PHILIPS ELECTRONICS

601 Milner Ave.
Scarborough, Ontario, M1B 1M8
Tel: (416) 292-5161   Fax: (416) 297-1019

Sharon Leinwand, HR Assistant
Internet: www.philips.com

Royal Philips Electronics is one of the world's biggest electronics companies and Europe's largest, with sales of EUR 31.5 billion in 1999. It is a global leader in color television sets, lighting, electric shavers, color picture tubes for televisions and monitors, and one-chip TV products. Its 232,433 employees (end June 2000) in more than 60 countries are active in the areas of lighting, consumer electronics, domestic appliances, components, semiconductors, medical systems, and IT services (Origin).

Academic Fields
College: Accounting, Administration, Business, Drafting/Architecture, Electronics Tech., Engineering Tech., Human Resources, Marketing/Sales, Secretarial
Bachelor of Comm/Admin: Accounting, Finance, Info Mgmt.
Bachelor of Laws: Corporate
Bachelor of Engineering: Electrical
Chartered Accounting: CMA-Finance, CGA-Finance
Masters: Business Administration, Engineering

Critical Skills
Adaptable, Analytical, Good Communication, Dependable, Diligent, Efficient, Enthusiastic, Flexible, Good With Figures, Logical, Organized, Personable, Productive, Professional, Responsible, Responsible

Types of Positions
Entry Level Sales Rep.	Junior Draftsperson
Receptionist	

Starting Salary
$ 25,000 - 30,000

Company Benefits
- Full benefit coverage, health, dental, life insurance

Correspondence
Mail resume with cover letter

Part Time/Summer: Royal Philips Electronics occasionally hires for part time work and regularly hires for summer work. Potential positions are most commonly found in the warehouse or involve clerical duties. The best time to apply is in March, although they will hire employees children first.

The Canada Student Employment Guide

ROYAL VICTORIA HOSPITAL

687 Pine Avenue West
Montréal, Québec, H3A 1A1
Tel: (514) 842-1231   Fax: (514) 843-1561

Human Resources

Established in 1894, Royal Victoria Hospital is a public health care facility that provides general medical and surgical services. Departments within the hospital include medicine and surgery, geriatric care, acute and chronic psychiatric care, rehabilitation, chronic care, and gynecology. The hospital has a total of 583 beds, and employs about 4,000 people. Royal Victoria Hospital is recognized as a teaching facility and is affiliated with McGill University.

Academic Fields
College: Business, Child Care, Nursing, Radiology Tech.
Bachelor of Arts: Business
Bachelor of Comm/Admin: Accounting
Bachelor of Science: Computer Science, Health Sciences, Nursing (RN), Occupational Therapy, Physiotherapy
Bachelor of Education: Childhood
Masters: Business Administration, Science

Critical Skills
Dependable, Good With Figures, Good Writing Skills, Organized, Professional, Responsible

Types of Positions
Finance Clerk

Starting Salary
$ 20,000 - 25,000 (CEGEP), $ 30,000 - 40,000 (University)

Company Benefits
- Full benefits for permanent employees
- Temporary benefits also available

Correspondence
Mail or fax resume with cover letter

Part Time/Summer: Royal Victoria Hospital regularly seeks candidates for part time work, and sometimes hires for summer employment opportunities. The best time to apply is in March.

RUBBERMAID CANADA INC.

2562 Stanfield Rd.
Mississauga, Ontario, L4Y 1S5
Tel: (905) 279-1010   Fax: (905) 279-2993

Robert Wolf, Human Resources

Rubbermaid Canada is a plastics manufacturer that operates an injection molding operation. Their head office is in Mississauga, Ontario.

Academic Fields
Bachelor of Engineering: Industrial, Mechanical

Critical Skills
Dependable, Good Communication, Leadership, Productive, Professional, Responsible

Types of Positions
Various positions

Starting Salary
Depends on position

Company Benefits
- Competitive benefit package

Correspondence
Mail resume with cover letter

Part Time/Summer: Rubbermaid Canada does not hire for part time candidates but regularly seeks individuals for the summer months.

RYERSON POLYTECHNIC UNIVERSITY

350 Victoria Street
Toronto, Ontario, M5B 2K3
Tel: (416) 979-5076   Fax: (416) 979-5341

Gayle Sutton, Human Resources Advisor

Ryerson Polytechnic University is a post-secondary undergraduate institution that is career oriented and has degree granting status. In addition to academic courses, Ryerson offers business and industry, hotel administration, journalism, and child care programs.

Academic Fields
College: Accounting, Business, Communications, Drafting/Architecture, Human Resources, Laboratory Tech., Mechanical Tech., Secretarial, Security/Law
Bachelor of Arts: Business, Journalism, Recreation Studies
Bachelor of Comm/Admin: Accounting, Finance
Bachelor of Science: Chemistry, Computer Sci., Environ. Studies, Food Sciences
Bachelor of Engineering: Chemical, Civil, Electrical, Bachelor of Architecture, Bachelor of Landscape Arch.
Bachelor of Education: Physical
Chartered Accounting: CMA-General, CGA-General
Masters: Business Administration, Library Science

Critical Skills
Adaptable, Analytical, Confident, Creative, Dependable, Diligent, Diplomatic, Good Communication, Flexible, Enthusiastic, Leadership, Good Writing Skills, Organized, Patient, Personable, Responsible

Types of Positions
Jr. Programmer   Microcomputer Advisor
Recepticnist   Secretarial
Information Clerk

Starting Salary
$ 20,000 - 30,000

Company Benefits
- Medical, eye care, and 100% paid dental plan
- Disability, 3 weeks vacation after 1st year
- On-the-job training plus university courses

Correspondence
Mail resume and cover letter or submit in person

Part Time/Summer: Ryerson Polytechnic University sometimes hires for part time and summer work if the need arises. Potential jobs include admissions clerk, secretary, or clerical support. Apply in April or May.

SAAN STORES LTD.

1370 Sony Place
Winnipeg, Manitoba, R3C 3C3
Tel: (204) 474-5300   Fax: (204) 474-5471

Human Resources
Internet: www.saan.ca

Saan Stores Ltd. is a subsidiary of the parent company Gendis Inc., of Winnipeg, Manitoba. This retail chain has a large number of employees that work on a part time basis in addition to full time staff. Individuals should apply to specific store locations.

Academic Fields
College: Computer Science, Drafting/Architecture, Faculty Mgmt., Human Resources, Marketing/Sales, Secretarial, Statistics
Bachelor of Comm/Admin: Accounting, Finance, Marketing, Info Mgmt.
Chartered Accounting: CA-Finance, CMA-General/Finance, CGA-General/Finance
Masters: Business Administration

Critical Skills
Adaptable, Analytical, Good Communication, Confident, Dependable, Diligent, Efficient, Enthusiastic, Flexible, Good With Figures, Innovative, Leadership, Logical, Manual Dexterity, Organized, Patient, Personable, Productive, Professional, Responsible, Good Writing Skills

Types of Positions
Junior Clerical

Starting Salary
$ 20,000 - 25,000

Company Benefits
- Major medical, dental, pension, group life
- Long term disability, RRSP, employee purchases

Correspondence
Mail or fax resume with cover letter

Part Time/Summer: Saan Stores occasionally looks for candidates for part time employment, and regularly seeks people for summer opportunities. Potential jobs in the summer are junior accounting positions. The best time to apply is in April and May.

The Canada Student Employment Guide

SALES & MERCHANDISING GROUP

2700 Matheson Blvd. E., West Tower, Suite 200
Mississauga, Ontario, L4W 4V9
Tel: (905) 238-8422   Fax: (905) 238-1998

Kara Wheatley, Seasonal Recruitment Manager
Internet: www.jobs.samg.com

Sales and Merchandising Group was formed in 1986 to respond to changes in retail markets and to address the evolution of sales organizations. S&MG is a national firm representing leading organizations and employing more than 300 full and part time people in their year round business.

Academic Fields
College: Business, Marketing/Sales
Bachelor of Arts: Business
Bachelor of Comm/Admin: General, Marketing

Critical Skills
Adaptable, Good Communication, Decisive, Dependable, Enthusiastic, Flexible, Leadership, Organized, Personable, Persuasive, Professional

Types of Positions
Field Coordinator   Summer Representative
Field Representative

Starting Salary
Depends on position

Company Benefits
- Long term personal and career development, targeted learning, individual and team recognition

Correspondence
Apply on-line at their Internet address

Part Time/Summer: Sales and Merchandising Group regularly seeks people for part time and summer employment. Potential jobs include sales representative, public relations representative, merchandising representative, and sampling representative. The best time to apply is in January or February.

SALISBURY HOUSE OF CANADA LTD.

530 Century St., Suite 212
Winnipeg, Manitoba, R3H 0Y4
Tel: (204) 784-7461   Fax: (204) 786-2181

Human Resources Manager

Salisbury House of Canada is a local restaurant chain in Winnipeg, Manitoba which houses a central kitchen, warehouse, and their head office. The firm employs approximately 600 people in total.

Academic Fields
College: Accounting, Administration, Advertising, Business, Computer Science, Food/Nutrition, Human Resources, Marketing/Sales, Secretarial
Bachelor of Arts: Business
Bachelor of Comm/Admin: Accounting, Finance
Bachelor of Science: Computer Science
Chartered Accounting: CMA-General, CGA-General

Critical Skills
Adaptable, Good Communication, Dependable, Good With Figures, Leadership, Productive, Responsible, Good Writing Skills

Types of Positions
Accounting Supervisor   Data Processing
Administrative Assistant   Secretarial

Starting Salary
$ 20,000 - 25,000

Company Benefits
- Group health and life insurance
- RRSP group program
- Training and educational financial assistance

Correspondence
Mail resume with cover letter

Part Time/Summer: Salisbury House of Canada regularly looks for individuals for part time work and summer positions. Potential jobs include administrative assistant involving reception, secretarial duties, and data processing. The best time to apply is in May.

SANDMAN HOTELS AND INNS

1755 West Broadway, Suite 310
Vancouver, British Columbia, V6J 4S5
Tel: (604) 730-6600   Fax: (604) 730-4645

Human Resources
Internet: www.sandman.ca

Sandman is a hospitality company with hotels, inns and family restaurants.

Academic Fields
College: General, Acctg., Admin., Advertising, Business, Communications, Computer Sci., Cooking/Culinary, Food/Nutrition, Hospitality, Human Resources, Journalism, Law Clerk, Marketing/Sales, Mechanical Tech., Nursing, Secretarial, Security/Law, Travel/Tourism
Bachelor of Arts: General, Business, English, Languages, Psychology, Public Relations, Sociology/Social Work
Bachelor of Comm/Admin: General, Accounting, Marketing
Bachelor of Science: General, Nursing (RN), Occupational Therapy
Bachelor of Laws: General
Bachelor of Engineering: General, Transportation, Bach. of Landscape Architecture
Bachelor of Education: General
Chartered Accounting: CA-General, CGA-General
Masters: Business Administration, Education

Critical Skills
Adaptable, Good Communication, Confident, Creative, Enthusiastic, Flexible, Innovative, Leadership, Logical, Responsible, Good Writing Skills

Types of Positions
Sales/Marketing   Front Office
Rooms Division   Food/Beverage

Starting Salary
$ 20,000 - 30,000

Company Benefits
- Extended health plan

Correspondence
Mail or e-mail resume with cover letter
E-mail: sandho@mail.fronet.com

Part Time/Summer: Sandman Hotels regularly hires for part time and summer work. Potential jobs include front desk clerk, housekeeping, food server, or kitchen staff. Apply in March or April.

SANDWELL INC.

1045 Howe St.
Vancouver, British Columbia, V6Z 2H6
Tel: (604) 684-9311   Fax: (604) 688-5913

Keith Land, Human Resources
Internet: www.sandwell.com

Sandwell is an engineering construction company in Vancouver, British Columbia. The firm employs approximately 1,200 individuals in total.

Academic Fields
College: CAD Autocad, Engineering Tech., Industrial Design, Mechanical Tech.
Bachelor of Science: Chemistry, Computer Sciences, Environmental Studies, Mathematics
Bachelor of Engineering: Chemical, Civil, Design, Electrical, Industrial, Mechanical, Mining, Transportation, Water Resources
Masters: Engineering

Critical Skills
Creative, Dependable, Enthusiastic, Flexible, Good Communication, Good Writing Skills, Innovative, Professional

Types of Positions
Engineer-In-Training

Starting Salary
$ 35,000 - 40,000

Company Benefits
- Full range of insured benefits
- In house "college" for development and training
- Opportunities "world-wide"

Correspondence
E-mail resume with cover letter
E-mail: info@sandwell.com

Part Time/Summer: Sandwell occasionally hires individuals for part time work, but rarely looks for people for summer employment. Potential jobs involve engineering projects. The best time to apply is in January.

The Canada Student Employment Guide

SARA LEE CORPORATION OF CANADA LIMITED

335 Pinebush Rd.
Cambridge, Ontario, N1T 1B2
Tel: (519) 622-9800   Fax: (519) 622-3616

Virginia Moore, Human Resources
Internet: www.saralee.com

Sara Lee Corporation of Canada is a distribution centre for shoe care and personal care products. Their head office is in Cambridge, Ontario.

Academic Fields
College: General, Accounting
Bachelor of Arts: Business
Bachelor of Comm/Admin: Accounting, Finance, Marketing
Chartered Accounting: CA - General/Finance

Critical Skills
Adaptable, Confident, Dependable, Efficient, Enthusiastic, Flexible, Good Communication, Good With Figures, Good Writing Skills, Organized, Personable

Types of Positions
Finance Dept.   Marketing Dept.

Starting Salary
$ 20,000 - 25,000

Company Benefits
- Comprehensive benefit package

Correspondence
Mail resume with cover letter

Part Time/Summer: Sara Lee Corporation of Canada regularly looks for individuals for part time and summer work. Potential jobs in the summer involve factory work. The best time to apply is in June.

SASKATCHEWAN CENTRE OF THE ARTS

200 Lakeshore Drive
Regina, Saskatchewan, S4P 3V7
Tel: (306) 565-4500   Fax: (306) 565-3274

Personnel Department

Saskatchewan Centre of the Arts is a 1,900 seat theatre which is located in Regina. The Centre was established in 1969, and houses many theatrical productions that appeal to a diversity of audiences within the community. The Saskatchewan Centre of the Arts has 425 employees.

Academic Fields
College: Accounting, Business, Marketing/Sales
Bachelor of Arts: Business, Economics
Bachelor of Comm/Admin: Marketing
Chartered Accounting: CA-General

Critical Skills
Adaptable, Dependable, Organized, Good Communication, Personable, Professional

Types of Positions
Clerical Support   Client Services Support
Accounting Clerk

Starting Salary
$ 20,000 - 25,000

Company Benefits
- Health, dental, and disability, pension plan

Correspondence
Mail resume with cover letter

Part Time/Summer: The Saskatchewan Centre regularly hires for part time positions, and sometimes seeks candidates for summer employment. However, the summer is generally a slower time for their organization.

SASKATCHEWAN ECONOMIC DEVELOPMENT
1919 Sask Drive, 6th Flr.
Regina, Saskatchewan, S4P 3V7
Tel: (306) 787-8717   Fax: (306) 798-0345

Human Resource Services
Internet: www.gov.sk.ca/pse

The Saskatchewan Economic Development Department is a provincial government department with a mandate to guide, promote, co-ordinate and implement policies, strategies and programs to develop, diversify and renew the Saskatchewan economy. The department works in partnership with all sectors of the economy including enterprises, co-operatives, businesses, entrepreneurs, investors and government.

Academic Fields
College: Administration, Computer Science, Human Resources, Journalism, Secretarial
Bachelor of Arts: General, Economics, Journalism
Bachelor of Comm/Admin: General, Accounting, Finance, Marketing
Bachelor of Science: General, Computer Science
Bachelor of Engineering: General, Civil
Masters: Business Administration, Science

Critical Skills
Adaptable, Creative, Enthusiastic, Good Communication, Flexible, Innovative, Leadership, Personable, Professional

Types of Positions
Clerk I (Level 2)   Clerk Typist 2 (Level 2 or 3)
Accounting Clerk I   Consultant I (Level 9)
Research Officer I

Starting Salary
$ 25,000 - 30,000

Company Benefits
- Medical, dental, pension plan
- Disability income plan, life insurance
- Departments help staff acquire further learning

Correspondence
Mail or fax resume with cover letter

Part Time/Summer: The Saskatchewan Economic Development Department sometimes seeks candidates for part time and summer work. Potential jobs include clerk/typist and research officer.

SASKATCHEWAN GOVERNMENT INSURANCE
2260 - 11th Avenue, 2nd Floor
Regina, Saskatchewan, S4P 0J9
Tel: (306) 751-1644   Fax: (306) 347-0089

Theresa Crook, Human Resources
Internet: www.sgi.sk.ca/

Saskatchewan Government Insurance is involved in the provision of comprehensive, affordable insurance protection to individuals and businesses in the province.

Academic Fields
College: General, Accounting, Admin., Business, Communications, Computer Sci., Electronics Tech., Graphic Arts, Human Res., Insurance, Journalism, Law Clerk, Mechanical Tech., Nursing, Secretarial, Statistics
Bachelor of Arts: General, Business, Criminology, Economics, English, Journalism, Public Rel., Statistics
Bachelor of Comm/Admin: General, Accounting, Finance, Marketing, Info Mgmt., Public Admin.
Bachelor of Science: General, Computer Science, Health Sciences, Mathematics, Nursing (RN)
Bachelor of Laws: General, Corporate
Bachelor of Education: General
Chartered Accounting: CA - General/Finance, CGA/CMA - General/Finance
Masters: Business Administration, Arts, Science

Critical Skills
Dependable, Diligent, Efficient, Good Communication, Enthusiastic, Flexible, Good Writing Skills, Good With Figures, Logical, Organized, Personable, Professional, Responsible, Innovative, Caring, Customer Service Oriented

Types of Positions
Auto Tradesperson I   Building Operator I
Auto Body Repair Tech.   Pick Up & Delivery Driver

Starting Salary
$ 21,000 - 25,000

Company Benefits
- Pension, dental, group insurance, eye plan

Correspondence
Mail, e-mail or submit resume, cover letter and application form in person. E-mail: tcrook@sgi.sk.ca

Part Time/Summer: Saskatchewan Government Insurance sometimes hires for part time work, and regularly hires for the summer. Potential jobs are entry-level. Apply in January or February.

The Canada Student Employment Guide

THE SASKATCHEWAN RESEARCH COUNCIL

15 Innovation Blvd.
Saskatoon, Saskatchewan, S7N 2X8
Tel: (306) 933-5400   Fax: (306) 933-7446

Wendy Lawrence, H.R. Analyst
Internet: www.src.sk.ca

With over 225 scientific, engineering and technical staff, The Saskatchewan Research Council (SRC) provides contract research, technology transfer and analytical services to companies in Saskatchewan and around the world.

Academic Fields
College: Engineering Tech., Laboratory Tech., Chemical Tech., Med Lab Tech.
Bachelor of Science: Chemistry, Geography, Geology, Hydrology, Hydrogeology, Microbiology
Bachelor of Engineering: Electrical, Industrial, Mechanical, Chemical
Chartered Accounting: CA - General/Finance, CA-Finance, CMA-Finance, CGA-Finance
Masters: Science, Engineering, Business Administration

Critical Skills
Adaptable, Analytical, Good Communication, Diligent, Efficient, Flexible, Innovative, Enthusiastic, Patient, Personable, Professional, Good Writing Skills, Leadership, Client Service Focused

Types of Positions
Assistant Research Engineer   Assistant Research Scientist
Research Technician   Research Technologist

Starting Salary
$ 30,000 - 40,000 (engineering and science degrees)
$ 20,000 - 30,000 (technical school diploma)

Company Benefits
- Pension, life insurance, dental, group RRSP
- Health, long and short term disability
- Many training opportunities available

Correspondence
Mail, fax or e-mail resume with cover letter
E-mail: lawrence@src.sk.ca

Part Time/Summer: The Saskatchewan Research Council occasionally hires for part time work, and regularly seeks candidates in the summer. Jobs involve assisting on projects in various areas. January and February is the best time to apply.

SASKATCHEWAN TRANSPORTATION COMPANY

2041 Hamilton Street
Regina, Saskatchewan, S4P 2E2
Tel: (306) 787-3353   Fax: (306) 787-1633

Human Resources

Saskatchewan Transportation Company (STC) was established in 1946 to act as a common carrier providing passenger service and parcel express service throughout the province. It is a provincial coach company which provides affordable, accessible bus passenger and freight service to 276 communities in Saskatchewan.

Academic Fields
College: Accounting, Administration, Human Resources, Marketing/Sales
Bachelor of Arts: Public Relations
Bachelor of Comm/Admin: Finance, Info Mgmt.
Chartered Accounting: CA-Finance, CMA-Finance

Critical Skills
Dependable, Efficient, Good Communication, Good With Figures, Manual Dexterity, Personable, Productive, Professional, Responsible

Types of Positions
Express Service Attendant II   Passenger Attendant
Coach Cleaner   Clerk

Starting Salary
$ 25,000 - 30,000

Company Benefits
- Unionized environment, medical, dental
- Medical, dental, vision coverage, long term disability
- Some on-the-job training

Correspondence
Mail or fax resume with cover letter

Part Time/Summer: Saskatchewan Transportation Company regularly hires people for part time and summer work. In the summer, potential jobs include custodian, coach cleaner, and express service worker. Jobs may also become available during the Christmas season in express services. The best time to apply is in March and April.

SASKATCHEWAN WHEAT POOL

2625 Victoria Avenue
Regina, Saskatchewan, S4T 7T9
Tel: (306) 569-4411   Fax: (306) 569-5070

Nancy Sandberg, Human Resources
Internet: www.swp.com

Saskatchewan Wheat Pool is Canada's biggest agricultural cooperative and the nation's largest grain-handler. The company provides services to about 61,400 farmer-owners annually and is actively engaged in promotion and development of agricultural policy on their behalf. They employ more than 3,600 people in Canada.

Academic Fields
College: Computer Science, Secretarial
Bachelor of Arts: Business, Journalism
Bachelor of Comm/Admin: Accounting, Finance, Marketing, Info Mgmt.
Bachelor of Science: Agriculture, Computer Science
Bachelor of Engineering: Design
Bachelor of Education: Adult Education
Chartered Accounting: CA-General, CGA/CMA - General/Finance
Masters: Business Administration

Critical Skills
Good Communication, Dependable, Flexible, Innovative, Logical, Personable, Productive, Customer Service

Types of Positions
Warehouse Worker   Administrative Assistant
Computer Programmer

Starting Salary
$ 28,000 - 32,000

Company Benefits
- Insurance and dental package
- Disability, retirement package
- Company pays 100% course fees and books

Correspondence
Mail, fax or e-mail resume with cover letter
E-mail: nancy.sandberg@swp.com

Part Time/Summer: Saskatchewan Wheat Pool sometimes seeks people for part time work, and regularly looks for staff in the summer. Potential jobs are in agriculture (apply Dec/Jan), accounting (apply Feb/Mar), and computer science (apply Jan/Feb).

SASKATOON CO-OPERATIVE ASSOCIATION LIMITED

311 Circle Drive West
Saskatoon, Saskatchewan, S7L 4K6
Tel: (306) 933-3810   Fax: N/A

Human Resources

Saskatoon Co-operative Association is a retail co-operative that maintains two supermarkets, two service stations, one agro centre, two home improvement centres, six gas bars, and a travel office. All locations are situated in the Saskatoon area. The co-operative has an employee base of approximately 400 individuals.

Academic Fields
No specific academic background is required. They will look at candidates from all academic backgrounds.

Critical Skills
Dependable, Personable, Productive, Good Communication, Responsible, Customer Service

Types of Positions
Service Station   Grocery Store
Hardware & Lumber   Bakery
Deli

Starting Salary
$ 20,000 - 25,000

Company Benefits
- Dental, life, income guarantee
- Sick leave, superannuation
- Company training for all positions

Correspondence
Pick up job application at any location and return it to any location

Part Time/Summer: Saskatoon Co-operative Association regularly seeks candidates for part time and summer positions. Potential openings occur at their garden centres, hardware and lumber locations. Applicants should apply by May 1st.

The Canada Student Employment Guide

CITY OF SASKATOON

222 3rd Ave. N.
Saskatoon, Saskatchewan, S7K 0J5
Tel: (306) 975-3261   Fax: (306) 975-3073

Human Resources Department
Internet: www.city.saskatoon.sk.ca

The City of Saskatoon is a municipal government which includes administration, engineering, planning, public works, law, recreation, and protective services in the City of Saskatoon.

Academic Fields
College: Accounting, Animal Health, Computer Science, Drafting/Architecture, Electronics Tech., Engineering Tech., Graphic Arts, Human Resources, Laboratory Tech., Marketing/Sales, Recreation Studies
Bachelor of Arts: Business, Criminology, Fine Arts, Journalism, Psychology, Recreation Studies
Bachelor of Comm/Admin: Accounting, Finance, Marketing, Info Mgmt.
Bachelor of Science: Computer Science, Environmental Studies, Horticulture
Bachelor of Laws: General, Corporate
Bachelor of Engineering: Chemical, Civil, Computer Systems, Design, Electrical, Environ. Studies, Mechanical, Transportation, Water Resources, Bach. of Architecture
Chartered Accounting: CA - General/Finance, CGA/CMA - General/Finance

Critical Skills
Adaptable, Analytical, Good Communication, Confident, Decisive, Dependable, Diligent, Diplomatic, Efficient, Good With Figures, Organized, Patient, Productive, Professional, Responsible, Writing Skills

Types of Positions
Clerk I   Programmer Analyst I
Labourer   Lifeguard

Starting Salary
$ 20,000 - 25,000

Company Benefits
- Medical, group life, pension
- In-house training, tuition reimbursement

Correspondence
Mail application form with resume and cover letter

Part Time/Summer: The City of Saskatoon regularly hires for part time and summer work. Potential jobs include labourer, engineering technician, or playground leader. The best time to apply is in February or March.

SASKFERCO PRODUCTS INC.

Box 39, Kalium Rd.
Belle Plaine, Saskatchewan, S0G 0G0
Tel: (306) 345-4200   Fax: (306) 345-2353

Human Resources
Internet: www.saskferco.com

Saskferco Products Inc., located on the Canadian prairie in Saskatchewan, is North America's largest producer of granular urea and anhydrous ammonia. Despite our relative youth, we have established ourselves as one of the top producers in the world.

Academic Fields
College: Accounting, Administration, Business, Computer Science, Engineering Tech., Human Resources, Laboratory Tech., Mechanical Tech.
Bachelor of Arts: Business, Public Relations
Bachelor of Comm/Admin: Accounting, Finance, Human Resources
Bachelor of Science: Agriculture, Chemistry, Computer Science, Environmental Studies
Bachelor of Engineering: Chemical, Electrical, Environmental Studies, Industrial, Mechanical
Chartered Accounting: CA - General/Finance, CMA - General/Finance

Critical Skills
Adaptable, Good Communication, Confident, Dependable, Efficient, Enthusiastic, Flexible, Leadership, Organized, Personable, Productive, Professional, Responsible

Types of Positions
Accounting Technician   Junior Process Engineer
Systems Analyst

Starting Salary
$ 30,000 - 40,000

Company Benefits
- Extended health and dental
- Computer purchase plan, education reimbursement

Correspondence
Fax resume with cover letter

Part Time/Summer: Saskferco Products does not hire for part time work, but occasionally hires for the summer. Students assist in projects in human resources, engineering, information systems, technical duties, and accounting.

The Canada Student Employment Guide

SASKTEL

2121 Saskatchewan Drive, 13th Floor
Regina, Saskatchewan, S4P 3Y2
Tel: (306) 777-2029   Fax: (306) 777-2016

Human Resources
Internet: www.sasktel.com

SaskTel is a provincial crown corporation that provides local and long distance voice, data, image and text services throughout Saskatchewan.

Academic Fields
College: Administration, Business, Communications, Computer Science, Electronics Tech., Engineering Tech., Marketing/Sales, Secretarial, Urban Planning
Bachelor of Arts: Business, Economics
Bachelor of Comm/Admin: Accounting, Finance, Marketing, Info Mgmt.
Bachelor of Science: Computer Science
Bachelor of Laws: General, Corporate
Bachelor of Engineering: Civil, Computer Systems, Design, Electrical
Chartered Accounting: CA-Finance, CGA/CMA - General/Finance
Masters: Business Administration, Engineering

Critical Skills
Adaptable, Analytical, Confident, Creative, Decisive, Enthusiastic, Flexible, Good Communication, Good Writing Skills, Innovative, Leadership, Manual Dexterity, Organized, Personable, Professional, Responsible

Types of Positions
Engineer   Programmer Analyst
Clerical Associate I   Accounting/Marketing
Telephone Operator   Customer Service

Starting Salary
$ 20,000 - 30,000 (trainee) /
$ 30,000 - 45,000 (engineering)

Company Benefits
- Medical, dental, life insurance, superannuation
- Wellness program, relocation assistance

Correspondence
Mail or fax resume and cover letter with application form. E-mail: human.resources@sasktel.sk.ca

Part Time/Summer: SaskTel sometimes hires for part time work, and regularly hires for the summer. Potential jobs include cust. service tech., computer prog., marketing asst, engineering asst., or telephone operator. Apply between December and January.

SC INFRASTRUCTURE INC.

700, 1177 - 11th Ave. SW
Calgary, Alberta, T2R 1K9
Tel: (403) 244-9090   Fax: (403) 228-8643

John Forgeron, Human Resources
Internet: groupsci.com

SC Infrastructure recently completed construction of the Confederation bridge. The company is an infrastructure construction and management construction company. Currently building a grain storage and handling facility in Gdansk, Poland, they bid for several projects in Ontario and the U.S. They currently employ 35 professionals.

Academic Fields
College: Accounting, Computer Science, Drafting/Architecture, Engineering Tech., Laboratory Tech.
Bachelor of Comm/Admin: Accounting
Bachelor of Science: Environmental Studies
Bachelor of Engineering: Civil, Design, Electrical, Environmental, Mechanical, Transportation
Chartered Accounting: CA-Finance
Masters: Engineering

Critical Skills
Adaptable, Analytical, Confident, Dependable, Efficient, Enthusiastic, Leadership

Types of Positions
Field Engineer   Office Engineer

Starting Salary
$ 30,000 - 50,000

Company Benefits
- Regular benefits program
- Life insurance, dental, 100% prescription
- Short and long term disability

Correspondence
Mail or fax resume with cover letter
E-mail: johnf@groupsci.com

Part Time/Summer: SC Infrastructure Inc. does not seek individuals for part time positions, but sometimes looks for candidates for summer jobs. The company has limited opportunities for summer employment. Positions would most likely involve field engineer. The best to apply is in February or March.

SCARBOROUGH GENERAL HOSPITAL

3050 Lawrance Avenue East
Scarborough, Ontario, M1P 2V5
Tel: (416) 438-2911   Fax: (416) 431-8204

Human Resources Department
Internet: tsh.to

Scarborough General Hospital is a public hospital established in 1956 to serve the community.

Academic Fields
College: General, Accounting, Administration, Business, Computer Science, Cooking/Culinary, Engineering Tech., Food/Nutrition, Human Resources, Lab Tech., Nursing, Radiology Tech., Recreation Studies, Secretarial
Bachelor of Arts: General, Business, Psychology, Recreation Studies, Sociology/Social Work
Bachelor of Science: General, Biology, Chemistry, Computer Science, Health Sciences, Microbiology, Nursing (RN), Occupational Therapy, Pharmacy, Physiotherapy, Psychology
Bachelor of Engineering: Computer Systems
Chartered Accounting: CA - General/Finance, CMA - General/Finance
Masters: Business Administration, Science, Education

Critical Skills
Adaptable, Analytical, Creative, Dependable, Efficient, Flexible, Good Communication, Innovative, Good With Figures, Personable, Productive, Leadership, Professional

Types of Positions
Unit Clerk   Secretary
Housekeeping   Dietary Helper
Food Service Aide   Patient Service Associate

Starting Salary
$ 25,000 - 40,000 (depending on position)

Company Benefits
- Benefit package to full time employees

Correspondence
Mail or fax resume with cover letter
E-mail: careers@tsh.to

Part Time/Summer: Scarborough General Hospital regularly seeks part time employees, and sometimes hires for the summer months.

SCHLUMBERGER CANADA LTD.

7275 West Credit Office
Mississauga, Ontario, L5N 5M9
Tel: (905) 858-4211   Fax: (905) 858-0428

Employee Relations
Internet: www.schlumberger.com

Schlumberger Canada is engaged in the manufacturing of power, distribution, and specialty transformers in the electrical industry. The company manufactures instruments for measuring and testing electricity, and is a wholesaler of electrical equipment, wiring supplies, construction materials and a wide range of industrial machinery and equipment. They employ more than 1,000 individuals across Canada.

Academic Fields
College: Accounting, Administration, Business, Electronics Tech., Engineering Tech., Human Resources, Marketing/Sales
Bachelor of Arts: Business
Bachelor of Comm/Admin: Accounting, Finance, Marketing
Bachelor of Engineering: Electrical, Industrial
Chartered Accounting: CA - General/Finance, CGA/CMA - General/Finance

Critical Skills
Adaptable, Analytical, Good Communication, Confident, Creative, Decisive, Dependable, Diligent, Diplomatic, Efficient, Enthusiastic, Flexible, Good With Figures, Innovative, Logical, Organized, Personable, Persuasive, Responsible, Good Writing Skills

Types of Positions
Various Positions

Starting Salary
$ 20,000 - 30,000

Company Benefits
- Full benefit and insurance program

Correspondence
Mail resume with cover letter

Part Time/Summer: Schlumberger Canada sometimes hires for part time and summer positions, however, positions vary. Apply in April or May.

Co-op/Internship: They do offer internship opportunities.

The Canada Student Employment Guide

SCHNEIDER ELECTRIC CANADA INC.

19 Waterman Ave.
Toronto, Ontario, M4B 1Y2
Tel: (416) 752-8020   Fax: (416) 752-8944

Heather Crowe, Human Resources
Internet: www.schneider-electric.ca

Schneider Electric is the world leader in electrical distribution, industrial control and automation products, systems and services, and the only electrical manufacturer dedicated solely to the distribution and control of electricity.

Academic Fields
College: Computer Science, Electronics Tech., Human Resources
Bachelor of Science: Computer Science
Bachelor of Engineering: Computer Systems, Electrical, Mechanical
Masters: Business Administration, Engineering

Critical Skills
Creative, Good Communication, Innovative, Leadership, Responsible

Types of Positions
Engineering Sales   Engineering Marketing
Customer Service

Starting Salary
$ 42,000 - 50,000

Company Benefits
- Full health and dental, pension
- Technical and interpersonal skills training
- 8 month focused entry engineering program

Correspondence
Mail resume with cover letter

Part Time/Summer: Schneider Electric Canada occasionally seeks individuals for part time work, and regularly hires for summer positions. Potential summer opportunities include factory work, office support, and specialized support (engineering, information systems, human resources). The best time to apply is in April.

SCHOLASTIC CANADA LTD.

175 Hillmount Rd.
Markham, Ontario, L6C 1Z7
Tel: (905) 887-7323   Fax: (905) 887-3639

Marlene Long, Director Human Resources
Internet: http: www.scholastic.com

Scholastic Canada is a publisher and distributor of children's books across the country. They have 400 permanent employees and approximately 400 casuals during peak season (October to March). For more information visit their site on the Internet.

Academic Fields
College: Graphic Arts, Journalism
Bachelor of Arts: English, Journalism
Bachelor of Comm/Admin: Info Mgmt.
Bachelor of Science: Computer Science
Bachelor of Education: Childhood
Chartered Accounting: CMA-General, CGA-General

Critical Skills
Artistic, Enthusiastic, Personable, Team Worker

Types of Positions
Graphic Artist   Junior Editor
Programmer/Analyst   Customer Service Reps.

Starting Salary
$ 20,000 - 25,000

Company Benefits
- Medical, dental, life insurance
- Long term disability, service awards
- Picnics, dinners, employee store

Correspondence
Mail resume with cover letter
E-mail: mlong@scholastic.ca

Part Time/Summer: Scholastic Canada occasionally looks for individuals for part time work, but does not generally hire for the summer months.

SCIENCE NORTH

100 Ramsey Lake Rd.
Sudbury, Ontario, P3E 5S9
Tel: (705) 522-3701   Fax: (705) 522-4306

Career Opportunities
Internet: www.sciencenorth.on.ca

Science North is a science, education and entertainment complex which provides science programs and exhibits to schools and the general public. They offer many special events, have a motion simulator, an Imax theatre, and have a small virtual off-site tourist mine.

Academic Fields
College: Animal Health, Child Care, Computer Science, Cooking/Culinary, Electronics Tech., Forestry, Graphic Arts, Hospitality, Marketing/Sales, Science-General, Travel/Tourism
Bachelor of Arts: Music, Public Rel., Recreation Studies
Bachelor of Comm/Admin: Finance, Marketing
Bachelor of Science: General, Biology, Environmental Studies, Forestry, Geology, Health Sciences, Kinesiology, Physics, Astronomy
Bachelor of Engineering: Environmental Studies

Critical Skills
Adaptable, Good Communication, Dependable, Diligent, Diplomatic, Enthusiastic, Flexible, Innovative, Leadership, Organized, Personable, Productive, Professional, Good Writing Skills, Techno Literate

Types of Positions
Science Program	Sales & Operations
Food Services	Finance
Graphics	Children's Camps

Starting Salary
Below $ 20,000 - 35,000 for support positions, higher for supervisory and management jobs

Company Benefits
- Full range of health care and pension for permanent positions
- Disability benefits for permanent positions

Correspondence
Mail, fax, e-mail resume with cover letter, or use resume drop off boxes on-site. E-mail: fera@sciencenorth.on.ca

Part Time/Summer: Science North regularly hires for part time and summer work. Potential jobs involve the science program, food services, visitor services, and children's programming. Apply in February or March.

SCIEX MDS HEALTH GROUP

71 Four Valley Dr.
Concord, Ontario, L4K 4V8
Tel: (905) 660-9005   Fax: (905) 660-2600

Wendy Murphy, Human Resources Assistant
Internet: www.sciex.com

A division of MDS Health Group Ltd., SCIEX produces sophisticated testing equipment used by government and business in Canada and elsewhere in the world. The company employs over 225 highly skilled scientists and technicians. Approximately 95% of their revenues result from exports to over 50 countries.

Academic Fields
College: Administration, Business, Computer Science, Drafting/Architecture, Electronics Tech., Engineering Tech., Human Resources, Mechanical Tech., Science, Secretarial
Bachelor of Comm/Admin: General, Info Mgmt.
Bachelor of Science: Biology, Chemistry, Computer Science, Physics
Bachelor of Engineering: General, Biomedical, Chemical, Computer Systems, Design, Electrical, Mechanical

Critical Skills
Adaptable, Analytical, Efficient, Flexible, Good Communication, Innovative, Logical, Good With Figures, Organized, Productive, Manual Dexterity

Types of Positions
Manufacturing	Accounting
Finance	

Starting Salary
Depends upon position or department

Company Benefits
- Flexible benefits including medical and dental
- Life insurance and long term disability

Correspondence
Mail or fax resume and cover letter

Part Time/Summer: SCIEX sometimes seeks individuals for part time and summer opportunities. Potential positions are in engineering, research and development, administration, and in the warehouse. The best time to apply is in April or May.

SCL TECHNOLOGIES INC.

P.O. Box 370, Stn Main
Amherst, Nova Scotia, B4H 3Z5
Tel: (902) 667-7533   Fax: (902) 667-0747

Human Resources

SCL Technologies Inc. is involved in the manufacture of electronic circuit boards and telephone refurbishing.

Academic Fields
College: Electronics Tech.
Bachelor of Engineering: Electrical, Industrial

Critical Skills
Dependable, Diligent, Enthusiastic, Good Communication, Organized, Personable

Types of Positions
Assembly Line Operator
Assembly Line Operator (Electronic)
Repair Technician (Electronic)

Starting Salary
below $ 20,000

Company Benefits
- Health and dental plan, competitive salary
- Matching RRSP contribution, tuition refund program
- On-going internal and external training

Correspondence
Mail resume with cover letter

Part Time/Summer: SCL Technologies Inc. occasionally hires candidates for part time work and regularly hires for the summer. Potential jobs include engineering students or lawn care people. The best time to apply is in Early Spring.

SED SYSTEMS

18 Innovation Blvd.
Saskatoon, Saskatchewan, S7K 3P7
Tel: (306) 931-3425   Fax: (306) 933-1486

Judy Adams, Human Resources
Internet: www.sedsystems.ca

SED is a Canadian advanced technology company specializing in satellite communications, control and test systems engineering. They have expertise in space, communications, satellite test and control, and custom electronic system manufacturing. The company employs approximately 280 individuals.

Academic Fields
College: Computer Science, Electronics Tech.
Bachelor of Science: Computer Science
Bachelor of Engineering: Electrical
Masters: Engineering

Critical Skills
Adaptable, Dependable, Flexible, Good Communication, Innovative, Personable

Types of Positions
Programmer   Junior Engineer

Starting Salary
$ 35,000 - 40,000

Company Benefits
- Comprehensive employee benefits plan
- Employee share purchase plan, group RRSP
- Social events, same-sex benefits

Correspondence
Mail, fax, e-mail resume with cover letter or submit in person. E-mail: hr@sedsystems.ca

Part Time/Summer: SED Systems rarely hires for part time work, but regularly hires for the summer. Potential jobs include programmer, engineer or assembler. The best time to apply is in March.

Co-op/Internship: They participate in the University of Saskatchewan Internship Program and University of Regina Co-op Program.

SEPROTECH SYSTEMS INCORPORATED

2378 Holly Lane
Ottawa, Ontario, K1V 7P1
Tel: (613) 523-1641   Fax: (613) 731-0851

Human Resources Manager
Internet: www.seprotech.com

Seprotech Systems Inc. designs, manufactures and markets water treatment systems to industrial clients and operates an accredited laboratory for sample analysis. The company employs 25 individuals.

Academic Fields
College: Accounting, Administration, Information Systems, Marketing/Sales, Secretarial, CAD Autocad, Engineering Tech., Industrial Design, Mechanical Tech., Laboratory Tech.
Bachelor of Comm/Admin: Accounting, Finance, Info Mgmt.
Bachelor of Science: Chemistry
Bachelor of Engineering: Chemical, Civil, Computer Systems, Design, Electrical, Industrial, Mechanical, Water Resources
Chartered Accounting: CA-General, CMA-General, CGA-General
Masters: Business Administration, Science, Engineering

Critical Skills
Adaptable, Dependable, Diligent, Enthusiastic, Flexible, Good Communication, Organized, Personable, Productive, Professional

Types of Positions
Lab Technician   Accounting Clerk
Reception/Administration

Starting Salary
$ 25,000 - 30,000

Company Benefits
- Medical and dental benefits to full time and salaried employees after 3 months
- Training and development is reviewed on a case by case basis

Correspondence
Fax resume with cover letter
E-mail: contact@seprotech.com

Part Time/Summer: Seprotech Systems occasionally seeks candidates for part time work and regularly hires for summer employment. A potential job would be lab technician. The best time to apply is in March or April.

SHARP ELECTRONICS OF CANADA LTD.

335 Britannia Road East
Mississauga, Ontario, L4Z 1W9
Tel: (905) 890-2100   Fax: (905) 568-7141

Tracy Savage, Recruitment
Internet: www.sharp.ca/

Sharp Electronics is a wholesaler and marketer of a wide range of consumer and industrial electronic products including household appliances, electrical equipment, and commercial machines and equipment. The company is a leading supplier of product lines such as LCD products, camcorders, electronic organizers, copiers, facsimile machines and calculators.

Academic Fields
College: General, Accounting, Advertising, Business, Electronics Tech., Human Resources, Marketing/Sales
Bachelor of Arts: General, Business
Bachelor of Comm/Admin: General, Accounting, Finance, Marketing, Info Mgmt.
Bachelor of Science: Computer Science
Chartered Accounting: CA - General/Finance, CGA/CMA - General/Finance

Critical Skills
Adaptable, Analytical, Artistic, Good Communication, Confident, Creative, Decisive, Dependable, Diligent, Diplomatic, Efficient, Enthusiastic, Flexible, Good With Figures, Innovative, Leadership, Logical, Manual Dexterity, Organized, Patient, Personable, Persuasive, Productive, Professional, Responsible, Good Writing Skills

Types of Positions
Various Positions

Starting Salary
$ 25,000 - 40,000 (depending on position)

Company Benefits
- Full range of benefits

Correspondence
Mail resume with cover letter

Part Time/Summer: Sharp Electronics does not hire for part time positions, but sometimes hires for summer opportunities.

The Canada Student Employment Guide

SHAW COMMUNICATIONS

10 Commercial St.
Moncton, New Brunswick, E1C 1A1
Tel: (506) 857-8700   Fax: (506) 388-8575

Human Resources
Internet: www.shaw.ca/

Whatever you call it, a single connection to Shaw is a connection to millions of ways to be entertained and informed in every room of your home. It started with television. For millions of Canadians, they have raised the curtain to the best television entertainment for more than 35 years.

Academic Fields
College: General, Accounting, Admin., Advertising, Business, Communications, Computer Sci., Drafting/Architecture, Electronics Tech., Engineering Tech., Faculty Mgmt., Graphic Arts, HR, Journalism, Marketing/Sales, Science, Secretarial, Television/Radio
Bachelor of Arts: General, Business, Economics, Journalism, Psychology, Public Relations
Bachelor of Comm/Admin: General, Accounting, Finance, Marketing, Info Mgmt., Public Admin.
Bachelor of Science: General, Computer Science
Bachelor of Laws: General, Corporate
Bachelor of Engineering: General, Electrical
Chartered Accounting: CA - General/Finance, CGA/CMA - General/Finance
Masters: Business Administration, Engineering

Critical Skills
Adaptable, Analytical, Artistic, Good Communication, Confident, Creative, Decisive, Dependable, Diligent, Diplomatic, Efficient, Enthusiastic, Flexible, Productive, Professional, Responsible, Writing Skills

Types of Positions
Accounting Clerk   Service Technician
Customer Service   Playback Operator

Starting Salary
$ 20,000 - 30,000

Company Benefits
- Comprehensive health and denta

Correspondence
Mail resume with cover letter

Part Time/Summer:
Shaw Communications sometimes hires for part time and summer jobs. Potential jobs include customer service rep., technician, or programmer and producer. Apply in April or May.

SHAW INDUSTRIES LTD.

25 Bethridge Rd.
Etobicoke, Ontario, M9W 1M7
Tel: (416) 743-7111   Fax: (416) 743-8194

Peter Langdon, Human Resources
Internet: www.shawind.com

Shaw Industries provides products and services to the exploration and production, transmission and downstream sectors of the oil and gas industry. The firm employs approximately 1,250 individuals.

Academic Fields
College: Human Resources, Laboratory Tech., Secretarial
Bachelor of Science: Chemistry
Bachelor of Engineering: Chemical, Electrical, Mechanical
Chartered Accounting: CA - General/Finance, CGA/CMA - General/Finance
Masters: Business Administration, Science, Engineering

Critical Skills
Adaptable, Analytical, Good Communication, Confident, Diligent, Efficient, Good With Figures, Innovative, Leadership, Logical, Organized, Persuasive, Productive, Professional, Good Writing Skills

Types of Positions
Various Positions

Starting Salary
$ 30,000 - 40,000

Company Benefits
- 90% medical and dental coverage
- Defined benefit pension plan after 1 year of service

Correspondence
Mail resume with cover letter

Part Time/Summer:
Shaw Industries occasionally looks for people for part time work, and regularly seeks candidates in the summer months. Potential jobs include project engineers, lab technicians, and quality engineers.

The Canada Student Employment Guide

SHERATON FALLSVIEW HOTEL

6755 Oakes Dr.
Niagara Falls, Ontario, L2G 3W7
Tel: (905) 374-1077   Fax: (905) 374-6224

Denise Sutherland, Human Resources
Internet: www.fallsview.com

Sheraton Fallsview Hotel overlooks the fabulous Canadian and American Falls, and is conveniently located between the major airports in Toronto and Buffalo. This hotel is one of more than 500 Sheraton Hotels, Inns, Resorts and All-Suites which provide superior facilities and quality service to business and leisure travellers in 65 countries throughout the world.

Academic Fields
College: General, Accounting, Administration, Business, Cooking/Culinary, Hospitality, Human Resources, Marketing/Sales, Secretarial, Travel/Tourism
Bachelor of Arts: Business, Languages, Music, Public Relations
Bachelor of Comm/Admin: Accounting
Chartered Accounting: CA - General/Finance, CGA/CMA - General/Finance
Masters: Business Administration

Critical Skills
Adaptable, Analytical, Good Communication, Confident, Creative, Decisive, Dependable, Diligent, Diplomatic, Efficient, Enthusiastic, Flexible, Good With Figures, Innovative, Leadership, Logical, Manual Dexterity, Organized, Patient, Personable, Productive, Professional, Responsible, Good Writing Skills

Types of Positions
Front Desk Clerk   Line Cook
Reservation Agent   Room Attendant
House Person

Starting Salary
below $ 20,000

Company Benefits
- Full benefit package

Correspondence
Mail, fax, or submit resume with cover letter in person
E-mail: ISO9002@fallsview.com

Part Time/Summer: Sheraton Fallsview Hotel regularly looks for people for part time and summer employment opportunities. Potential jobs include busperson and housekeeping. The best time to apply is in April or May.

SHERATON TORONTO EAST HOTEL AND TOWERS

2035 Kennedy Rd. N.
Scarborough, Ontario, M1T 3G2
Tel: (416) 299-1500   Fax: (416) 299-8959

Human Resources Department

Sheraton Toronto East Hotel & Towers is a hotel facility located in Scarborough. Employing approximately 500 people, the hotel offers a wide range of facilities for business functions, banquets, conventions or personal vacations.

Academic Fields
College: Accounting, Cooking/Culinary, Hospitality, Security/Law, Travel/Tourism

Critical Skills
Adaptable, Dependable, Responsible, Good Writing Skills, Personable, Professional, Good Communication

Types of Positions
Busperson   Waiter/Waitress
Guest Service Agent Houseperson
Kitchen Helper   Bartender

Starting Salary
below $ 20,000 - 25,000

Company Benefits
- Full health and welfare plan with dental and vision
- Life insurance, discounts, employee wellness program
- Benefits eligible after 6 months of employment

Correspondence
Submit resume and cover letter in person

Part Time/Summer: Sheraton Toronto East Hotel & Towers sometimes seeks part time and summer employees. Potential positions are most likely those outlined above. The best time to apply is in May.

The Canada Student Employment Guide

SHERBROOKE COMMUNITY CENTRE

301 Acadia Drive
Saskatoon, Saskatchewan, S7H 2E7
Tel: (306) 655-3644   Fax: (306) 655-3688

Bill Ellis, Human Resources Coordinator

Sherbrooke Community Centre is a long term care home that provides services for physically and mentally handicapped individuals, along with the elderly. Established in 1966, the facility has a total of 286 long term care beds, and employs approximately 500 individuals.

Academic Fields
College: Food/Nutrition, Nursing, Recreation Studies, Secretarial
Bachelor of Arts: Recreation Studies, Sociology/Social Work
Bachelor of Science: Food Sciences, Health Sciences, Nursing (RN), Occupational Therapy, Physiotherapy

Critical Skills
Adaptable, Confident, Dependable, Diligent, Diplomatic, Enthusiastic, Flexible, Good Communication, Organized, Patient, Personable, Manual Dexterity, Productive, Professional

Types of Positions
Dietary   Nursing
Housekeeping

Starting Salary
$ 20,000 - 25,000

Company Benefits
- Many benefits offered

Correspondence
Mail, fax or submit resume and cover letter in person

Part Time/Summer: Sherbrooke Community Centre regularly seeks candidates for part time and summer employment opportunities. Potential jobs are most likely those listed above. The best time to apply is in April.

SHERMAG INC.

2171 King Street West
Sherbrooke, Québec, J1J 2G1
Tel: (819) 566-1515   Fax: (819) 566-4104

Human Resources
Internet: www.shermag.com/

Shermag is a leader in the production and distribution of high-quality residential furniture. The company enjoys an enviable reputation in the North American market and figures prominently in the design of contemporary-style furniture. Shermag's facilities include a network of medium-size factories equipped with state-of-the-art technology.

Academic Fields
College: Accounting, Business, Engineering Tech., Industrial Design, Marketing/Sales, Secretarial
Bachelor of Comm/Admin: General, Accounting, Finance, Marketing, Info Mgmt.
Bachelor of Engineering: Computer Systems, Design, Electrical
Chartered Accounting: CA-General

Critical Skills
Adaptable, Creative, Dependable, Efficient, Good Communication, Good Writing Skills, Responsible, Bilingual

Types of Positions
Customer Service   Accounting
Technician

Starting Salary
$ 20,000 - 25,000

Company Benefits
- Competitive benefit package

Correspondence
Mail resume with cover letter

Part Time/Summer: Shermag occasionally seeks candidates for part time and summer employment opportunities. Positions in the summer vary. The best time to apply for potential work is in March.

SHERWOOD CREDIT UNION

1960 Albert St.
Regina, Saskatchewan, S4P 4M1
Tel: (306) 780-1700   Fax: (306) 780-1521

Lynn Hunter, Human Resources Department
Internet: www.sherwoodcu.com

Sherwood Credit Union is a financial institution in Saskatchewan providing a wide range of services to their membership. The credit union currently has 13 Service Centres to serve their membership as well as a number of administrative departments. The company employs over 300 staff.

Academic Fields
College: Accounting, Administration, Computer Science, Human Resources, Marketing/Sales, Statistics
Bachelor of Comm/Admin: General, Accounting, Finance, Marketing, Info Mgmt., Public Admin., Human Resources
Bachelor of Science: Computer Science
Bachelor of Education: Adult Education
Chartered Accounting: CGA/CMA - General/Finance

Critical Skills
Adaptable, Dependable, Diligent, Diplomatic, Efficient, Enthusiastic, Flexible, Good Communication, Innovative, Leadership, Personable, Professional, Responsible

Types of Positions
Financial Services Rep.	Marketing Support Office
Mortgage Services Rep.	Corporate Finance Analyst
Internal Auditor	Technology Specialist

Starting Salary
$ 25,000 - 30,000

Company Benefits
- Life insurance, medical, dental, vision
- Superannuation plan
- Education tuition reimbursement

Correspondence
Mail or fax resume with cover letter

Part Time/Summer: Sherwood Credit Union sometimes looks for candidates for part time and summer employment opportunities. Potential jobs include financial service representative, or involve administration. The best time to apply is between the months of February and April.

SHOPPERS DRUG MART LIMITED

243 Consumers Rd.
North York, Ontario, M2J 4W8
Tel: (416) 493-1220   Fax: (416) 490-0145

Don Casey, Human Resources
Internet: www.shoppersdrugmart.ca

What was once a small pharmacy in Toronto has grown into an organization of over 800 stores from coast to coast, becoming an indelible part of the lives of Canadians, young and old. Shoppers Drug Mart has been built on a foundation of professional expertise and personal service.

Academic Fields
College: Accounting, Marketing/Sales, Secretarial
Bachelor of Arts: Business
Bachelor of Comm/Admin: General, Marketing
Bachelor of Science: Pharmacy

Critical Skills
Adaptable, Confident, Dependable, Diplomatic, Efficient, Enthusiastic, Flexible, Good Communication, Good Writing Skills, Innovative, Organized, Personable, Professional, Responsible

Types of Positions
Data Entry	Accounting
Administration	Information Systems

Starting Salary
$ 20,000 - 40,000 (depends on position)

Company Benefits
- Extended health and dental
- Vision care, pension, drug plan
- Employee discounts on purchases

Correspondence
Fax resume with cover letter

Part Time/Summer: Shoppers Drug Mart sometimes looks for individuals on a part time basis and regularly seeks candidates for summer opportunities. Potential jobs are in accounting, info technology, or administration. Applications are received during February and March.

Co-op/Internship: They offer placement opportunities in accounting and information technology. Visit their web site for more information.

THE SHOPPING CHANNEL

1400 Castlefield Avenue
Toronto, Ontario, M6B 4H8
Tel: (416) 785-3500   Fax: (416) 785-1300

Tuula Katz, Human Resources
Internet: www.tsc.ca/

The Shopping Channel is a 24-hour, seven day per week broadcast retailer available on a variety of cable channels as well as Star Choice, ExpressVu and Look TV satellite throughout Canada. They carry both common, brand-name items; as well as unique items new to the market that cannot be found anywhere else. These products range from fashions to jewellery to household appliances. The Shopping Channel is 100% Canadian and employs over 500 people.

Academic Fields
College: Accounting, Administration, Human Resources, Marketing/Sales, Television/Radio
Bachelor of Arts: Fine Arts, Public Relations
Bachelor of Comm/Admin: General, Accounting, Finance, Marketing, Info Mgmt.
Chartered Accounting: CMA-General

Critical Skills
Adaptable, Dependable, Good Communication, Responsible,

Types of Positions
Camera Operator   Accounts Payable Clerk
Computer Operator

Starting Salary
$ 20,000 - 25,000

Company Benefits
- Full benefits package
- Dental, eye care and drugs
- Financial reimbursement for job related training

Correspondence
Mail resume with cover letter

Part Time/Summer: The Shopping Channel regularly hires for part time positions, and occasionally looks for individuals for summer opportunities. Potential summer jobs include freelance T.V. production and order entry clerk. The best time to apply for these positions is in April or May.

SHOREWOOD PACKAGING CORP. OF CANADA LTD.

2200 Midland Ave.
Scarborough, Ontario, M1P 3E6
Tel: (416) 292-3990   Fax: (416) 292-2763

Kathleen McKinney, Human Resources
Internet: www.shorepak.com

Shorewood Packaging Corp. is the largest non-integrated packaging manufacturer in North America, specializing in folding cartons. They also print materials for a variety of industries such as cosmetics, food and beverage, music, video entertainment, women's and men's apparel, and the tobacco industry.

Academic Fields
College: General, Accounting, Administration, Business, Communications, Computer Science, Electronics Tech., Faculty Mgmt., Graphic Arts, Human Resources, Marketing/Sales, Secretarial
Bachelor of Arts: General, Business, English, Fine Arts, Music, Psychology, Sociology/Social Work
Bachelor of Comm/Admin: General, Accounting, Finance, Marketing, Info Mgmt.
Chartered Accounting: CA - General/Finance, CGA/CMA - General/Finance
Masters: Business Administration

Critical Skills
Adaptable, Analytical, Artistic, Good Communication, Confident, Creative, Decisive, Dependable, Diligent, Diplomatic, Efficient, Enthusiastic, Flexible, Good With Figures, Innovative, Leadership, Logical

Types of Positions
Accounting   Customer Service
Press   Die Cutting
Preparation   Finishing

Starting Salary
below $ 20,000 - 25,000

Company Benefits
- Company paid group benefits and pension plan
- Education reimbursement plan

Correspondence
Mail or fax resume with cover letter

Part Time/Summer: Shorewood Packaging Corp. does not hire for part time work, but regularly hires for the summer.

The Canada Student Employment Guide

SIEMENS ELECTRIC LTD.

2185 Derry Road West
Mississauga, Ontario, L5N 7A6
Tel: (905) 819-8000   Fax: (905) 819-5793

Kenneth M. Spence, Manager, Human Resources

Siemens Electric designs, manufactures, markets, and services electrical and electronic products for residential and commercial buildings, as well as many other institutions. Siemens Electric employs 4,000 people across Canada in 14 plants and 40 offices.

Academic Fields
College: General, Accounting, Administration, Advertising, Business, Communications, Computer Science, Electronics Tech., Engineering Tech., Human Resources, Industrial Design, Marketing/Sales, Mechanical Tech., Radiology Tech., Secretarial
Bachelor of Arts: Business, Public Relations
Bachelor of Comm/Admin: General, Accounting, Finance, Marketing, Info Mgmt.
Bachelor of Science: Computer Science
Bachelor of Engineering: Biomedical, Computer Syst., Design, Electrical, Industrial, Materials Science, Mechanical, Mining, Transportation
Chartered Accounting: CA - General/Finance, CMA- General/Finance
Masters: Business Administration, Science, Engineering

Critical Skills
Adaptable, Analytical, Good Communication, Confident, Creative, Decisive, Dependable, Diligent, Diplomatic, Efficient, Enthusiastic, Flexible, Productive, Professional, Responsible, Writing Skills

Types of Positions
Junior Clerk   Junior Secretary
Customer Service   Inside Sales Rep.

Starting Salary
below $ 20,000 - 30,000 (depending on position)

Company Benefits
- Benefits for full time, permanent employees

Correspondence
Mail resume with cover letter

Part Time/Summer: Siemens Electric sometimes hires for part time jobs and regularly hires for the summer. Siemens makes 40-50 summer jobs available in a variety of areas. Apply no later than January 31st for the coming summer.

SIGNATURE VACATIONS INC.

160 Bloor St. E., Suite 400
Toronto, Ontario, M4W 1B9
Tel: (416) 967-1510   Fax: (416) 967-7154

Human Resources
Internet: www.signature.ca

Signature Vacations is Canada's leading wholesale tour operator offering a range of destinations in the United States, Mexico, Central America, the Caribbean, and Canada. Please do not call them for hiring information.

Academic Fields
College: General, Accounting, Administration, Advertising, Business, Communications, Computer Science, Graphic Arts, Hospitality, Human Resources, Journalism, Marketing/Sales, Secretarial, Statistics, Travel/Tourism
Bachelor of Arts: General, Business, Economics, Languages, Public Rel., Statistics, Urban Geography
Bachelor of Comm/Admin: General, Accounting, Finance, Marketing, Info Mgmt., Public Admin.
Bachelor of Science: General, Computer Science, Environ. Studies, Geography, Math, Psychology
Bachelor of Engineering: General
Bachelor of Education: General, Adult Education
Chartered Accounting: CA - General/Finance, CGA/CMA - General/Finance
Masters: Business Admin., Arts, Science, Education

Critical Skills
Adaptable, Analytical, Good Communication, Confident, Creative, Decisive, Diligent, Diplomatic, Efficient, Enthusiastic, Flexible, Good With Figures, Personable, Productive, Professional, Responsible

Types of Positions
Call Centre Representative   Accounting Agent

Starting Salary
below $ 20,000

Company Benefits
- Flexible benefits including health, dental, vision care, and RRSP

Correspondence
Mail resume with cover letter

Part Time/Summer: Signature Vacations occasionally hires for part time or summer work. Potential summer jobs are for graphic artist or cost accountant. The best time to apply is in May.

The Canada Student Employment Guide

SILICON GRAPHICS CANADA INC.

2550 Matheson Blvd. E.
Mississauga, Ontario, L4W 4Z1
Tel: (905) 625-4747   Fax: (905) 625-3144

Human Resources Department
Internet: www.sgi.com

Silicon Graphics is the world's leading supplier of high-performance visual computing systems. The company's full range of computing systems incorporates multi-processing, 3D graphics, multimedia, and processor technologies.

Academic Fields
College: Administration, Business, Computer Science, Electronics Tech., Engineering Tech., Human Resources
Bachelor of Arts: Business
Bachelor of Comm/Admin: Accounting, Finance, Marketing, Info Mgmt.
Bachelor of Science: Computer Science, Mathematics
Bachelor of Engineering: Computer Systems, Electrical
Chartered Accounting: CA-Finance
Masters: Business Administration, Science, Engineering

Critical Skills
Adaptable, Good Communication, Confident, Creative, Enthusiastic, Flexible, Innovative, Leadership, Organized, Personable, Productive, Professional, Responsible, Good Writing Skills

Types of Positions
Systems Support Rep.   Systems Specialist
Logistics Team   Financial Analyst
Accounting Rep.   General Administration

Starting Salary
$ 20,000 - 40,000 (depending on position)

Company Benefits
- Full benefits, paid sabbatical
- Technical and non-technical development

Correspondence
Mail, fax, e-mail resume and cover letter
E-mail: jobs@toronto.sgi.com

Part Time/Summer: Silicon Graphics occasionally looks for people for part time work, and regularly hires in the summer. Potential jobs include general admin., tech. support, and logistics. The best time to apply is March through May.

SKIING LOUISE LTD.

Box 555
Lake Louise, Alberta, T0L 1E0
Tel: (403) 522-3611   Fax: (403) 522-2271

Andrew Radford, Human Resources
Internet: www.skilouise.com

As one of the largest ski resorts in North America, they serve a large number of international destination skiers and snowboarders. They employ approximately 700 individuals.

Academic Fields
College: Accounting, Administration, Advertising, Business, Human Resources, Marketing/Sales, Purchasing, Secretarial, Emergency/Paramedic, Child Care, Cooking/Culinary, Hospitality, Recreation Studies, Security/Law Enforcement, Travel/Tourism
Bachelor of Arts: General, Business, Public Relations
Bachelor of Comm/Admin: General, Accounting, Finance, Human Resources, Marketing
Bachelor of Science: Computer Science, Environmental Studies
Bachelor of Engineering: Electrical, Industrial, Bachelor of Landscape Architecture
Masters: Business Administration

Critical Skills
Adaptable, Confident, Decisive, Diligent, Diplomatic, Efficient, Enthusiastic, Flexible, Good Communication, Leadership, Logical, Organized, Personable, Professional, Responsible

Types of Positions
Lifts/Outdoor Cust. Service   Retail Dept.
Rental/Repair Dept.   Food & Beverage Dept.
Slopes Dept.   Ski/Snowboard School

Starting Salary
$ 15,000 - 20,000

Company Benefits
- Hourly bonus, multi area ski pass
- Subsidized accommodation and staff activities

Correspondence
Mail, fax, e-mail resume with cover letter, apply through web site or submit in person
E-mail: hr@skilouise.com

Part Time/Summer: Skiing Louise Ltd. regularly hires for part time and summer work. Potential jobs include trail crew, lift operator, food & beverage server, and security. Apply by May 1st.

The Canada Student Employment Guide

SKILLS TRAINING & SUPPORT SERVICES ASSOCIATION
10045 - 111 St., Suite 800
Edmonton, Alberta, T5K 2M5
Tel: (403) 496-9686   Fax: (403) 482-6395

Karen Huta, Human Resources Manager

Skills Training & Support Services Association is a non-profit organization which offers services to enable people of all ages with disabilities to realize their potential for growth and independence. They have been providing quality services in the Edmonton area since 1981. Their professional staff and volunteers offer training, support and relief services to individuals and their families.

Academic Fields
College: Child Care, Nursing, Recreation Studies, Rehabilitation Practitioner Programs
Bachelor of Arts: Psychology, Recreation Studies, Sociology/Social Work
Bachelor of Science: Occupational Therapy
Bachelor of Education: Childhood, Physical, Special
Chartered Accounting: CA-General

Critical Skills
Adaptable, Good Communication, Confident, Creative, Dependable, Diplomatic, Enthusiastic, Flexible, Innovative, Leadership, Logical, Organized, Personable, Professional, Responsible, Good Writing Skills

Types of Positions
Rehabilitation Worker

Starting Salary
below $ 20,000 - 25,000

Company Benefits
- Complete benefit package
- Specific training in standard first aid

Correspondence
Mail, fax, submit resume and cover letter in person

Part Time/Summer: Skills Training & Support Services Association regularly seeks candidates for part time and summer job opportunities. A potential position includes rehabilitation worker. The best time to apply is April or early May.

SLOCAN FOREST PRODUCTS LTD.
10451 Shellbridge Way, Suite 240
Richmond, British Columbia, V6X 2W8
Tel: (604) 278-7311   Fax: (604) 278-7316

Manager, Human Resources
Internet: www.slocan.com

Slocan Forest Products is British Columbia's largest lumber manufacturer with lumber, plywood, OSB and pulp and paper. Within B.C. they have 13 divisions. They employ about 2,700 people in total.

Academic Fields
College: Accounting, Business, Human Resources, Information Systems, Marketing/Sales, Secretarial
Bachelor of Arts: General, Business, Economics
Bachelor of Comm/Admin: General, Accounting, Finance, Human Resources, Marketing, Info Mgmt.
Bachelor of Science: Forestry, Horticulture
Chartered Accounting: CA-Finance, CGA-Finance, CMA-Finance
Masters: Business Administration

Critical Skills
Analytical, Creative, Good Communication, Decisive, Flexible, Good Writing Skills, Innovative, Leadership, Professional

Types of Positions
Forest Technician   Forester
Accounting   Human Resources

Starting Salary
$ 35,000 - 40,000

Company Benefits
- Standard benefits
- Training and development done on an individual basis
- Management training is available

Correspondence
Mail resume with cover letter
E-mail: kleech@slocan.com

Part Time/Summer: Slocan Forest Products occasionally looks for people for part time jobs, and regularly seeks individuals in the summer. Potential jobs include forestry student. The best time to apply is in January or February.

The Canada Student Employment Guide

SNC-LAVALIN

455 Boul. Rene-Levesque Ouest
Montréal, Québec, H2Z 1Z3
Tel: (514) 393-1000   Fax: (514) 866-3118

Marlène Tremblay, Manager
Internet: www.snc-lavalin.com

SNC-Lavalin is one of Canada's leading engineering construction companies with worldwide projects. Their sectors of activity include defence, power, environment, infrastructure and facilities management, infrastructure and buildings, mining and metallurgy, pulp and paper, pharmaceuticals and biotechnology, chemicals and petroleum, mass transit systems, and telecommunications. They employ more than 4,750 individuals.

Academic Fields
Bachelor of Engineering: Civil, Design, Electrical, Environmental Studies, Geotechnical, Industrial, Mechanical
Chartered Accounting: CA-Finance, CGA-Finance
Masters: Business Administration

Critical Skills
Flexible, Good Communication, Leadership

Types of Positions
Various Positions

Starting Salary
$ 15,000 - 27,000

Company Benefits
- General benefit plan, group insurance plan
- Vacation, pension plan

Correspondence
E-mail resume with cover letter
E-mail: tremm2@snc-lavalin.com

Part Time/Summer: SNC-Lavalin does not hire for part time work, but occasionally seeks individuals for the summer months. Potential jobs include junior engineer, junior clerk, junior accountant.

SOBEYS INC.

123 Foord Street
Stellarton, Nova Scotia, B0K 1H0
Tel: (902) 752-8371   Fax: (902) 755-4222

Kim MacKinnon, Human Resources Administrator
Internet: sobeysweb.com

Sobeys Inc. is the second largest food distributor in Canada and employs over 32,000 employees throughout Canada.

Academic Fields
College: Accounting, Administration, Advertising, Business, Human Res., Info Syst., Marketing/Sales
Bachelor of Arts: Business, Public Relations
Bachelor of Comm/Admin: Accounting, Finance, Human Resources, Marketing, Info Mgmt.
Bachelor of Science: Pharmacy
Bachelor of Engineering: Civil
Chartered Accounting: CMA-General, CGA-General
Masters: Business Administration

Critical Skills
Adaptable, Analytical, Dependable, Good Communication, Diligent, Good Writing Skills, Organized, Productive, Responsible

Types of Positions
Management Trainee   Marketing Analyst
Computer Programmer   Accounting

Starting Salary
$ 25,000 - 30,000

Company Benefits
- Comprehensive group benefits

Correspondence
Mail resume with cover letter
E-mail: kimmackinnon@sobeys.ca

Part Time/Summer: Sobeys Inc. regularly looks for candidates for part time and summer employment. Potential jobs involve retail, and there may be positions within various departments at their head office. Individuals should apply no later than January.

Co-op/Internship: Sobeys is committed to providing students with internships to enhance and reinforce their education. All internships are located at their head office in Stellarton, Nova Scotia and vary from summer employment to co-ops.

The Canada Student Employment Guide

SOCIÉTÉ DES ALCOOLS DU QUÉBEC

905 av de Lorimier
Montréal, Québec, H2K 3V9
Tel: (514) 873-8215   Fax: (514) 864-3590

Service des Resources humaines
Internet: www.saq.com

Société des Alcools du Québec specializes in the sale and distribution of alcohol, wine, and imported beer. The company's head office is in Montréal, Québec. They have an employee base of 4,000 people.

Academic Fields
College: Accounting, Computer Science, Laboratory Tech.
Bachelor of Arts: Public Relations
Bachelor of Science: Computer Science, Microbiology
Chartered Accounting: CA - General/Finance, CGA/CMA - General/Finance

Critical Skills
Dependable, Efficient, Enthusiastic, Innovative, Organized, Responsible

Types of Positions
Various Positions

Starting Salary
$ 30,000 - 40,000

Company Benefits
- Full benefit package
- Health and dental, group insurance
- Reimbursement for courses relating to job

Correspondence
Mail resume with cover letter

Part Time/Summer: Société des Alcools du Québec regularly looks for individuals for part time work and summer opportunities. Potential jobs in the summer include secretary and outlet workers. The best time to apply for office jobs is in March and April. Outlet positions should be sought in September and October, or March and April.

SODEXHO MARRIOTT SERVICES CANADA

774 rue St-Paul Ouest
Montréal, Québec, H3C 1M5
Tel: (514) 866-7070   Fax: (514) 866-1216

Human Resources Department
Internet: www.sodexhomarriott.com/

Sodexho Marriott Services Canada is a leading international provider of contract food and other management services, with activities in 46 countries worldwide. The company is the world's fourth largest supplier of food and management services for business, schools, and healthcare institutions. Sodexho Canada provides these services to the Canadian market, with its head office in Montreal, Quebec.

Academic Fields
College: Accounting, Administration, Advertising, Cooking/Culinary, Faculty Mgmt., Food/Nutrition, Secretarial
Bachelor of Comm/Admin: General, Marketing
Bachelor of Science: Food Sciences
Chartered Accounting: CA-General
Masters: Business Administration

Critical Skills
Adaptable, Creative, Dependable, Diligent, Efficient, Enthusiastic, Flexible, Productive, Manual Dexterity, Professional, Responsible

Types of Positions
Office Clerk   Secretary
General Help

Starting Salary
$ 25,000 - 30,000

Company Benefits
- Group insurance offered
- Health and safety training (WHIMS)
- On-site training

Correspondence
Mail or fax resume with cover letter

Part Time/Summer: Sodexho Marriott Services Canada regularly seeks individuals for part time and summer employment. Potential positions most likely involve office duties. The best time to apply is in May.

SOLUTIONINC LIMITED

Suite 1506, 1969 Upper Water St., Tower II
Halifax, Nova Scotia, B3J 3R7
Tel: (902) 420-0077   Fax: (902) 420-0233

Lisa Martin, Manager of Human Resources
Internet: www.solutioninc.com

SolutionInc Ltd. develops the SolutionIP (TM) suite of high performance, Linux based server software applications. This application provides a seamless solution for connecting and managing mobile users of broadband and wireless networks in public access areas such as hospitality and conference locations, apartment complexes and condominiums, office buildings, campuses and airports.

Academic Fields
College: Computer Science, Engineering Tech.
Bachelor of Science: Computer Science
Bachelor of Engineering: Computer Systems, Electrical

Critical Skills
Adaptable, Analytical, Decisive, Dependable, Flexible, Responsible

Types of Positions
Software Developer
Product Development & Engineering
System Test & Support

Starting Salary
$ 40,000 - 45,000

Company Benefits
- Excellent health benefits
- Vision, dental, prescriptions, life insurance
- Stock options for full time permanent staff

Correspondence
E-mail resume with cover letter
E-mail: internships@solutioninc.com

Part Time/Summer: SolutionInc Limited rarely seeks candidates for part time work and regularly hires for the summer. Potential jobs involve software development, engineering, test and support. It is best to apply two to four months ahead of hiring dates, which are January, May and September.

Co-op/Internship: They break the year up into three sections: Jan.-April, May-Aug., Sept.-Dec., and dedicate one open position to each of their three technical departments. This gives them a total of nine internships per year.

SONY MUSIC CANADA

1121 Leslie Street
Don Mills, Ontario, M3C 2J9
Tel: (416) 391-3311   Fax: (416) 391-7969

Human Resources

Sony Music Canada is engaged in the manufacture and marketing of phonograph records, pre-recorded magnetic tapes, compact discs and videos.

Academic Fields
College: General, Accounting, Administration, Advertising, Business, Communications, Computer Science, Electronics Tech., Engineering Tech., Faculty Mgmt., Graphic Arts, Human Resources, Journalism, Marketing/Sales, Mechanical Tech., Television/Radio
Bachelor of Arts: General, Business, Fine Arts, Journalism, Music, Psychology
Bachelor of Comm/Admin: General, Accounting, Finance, Marketing, Info Mgmt., Public Admin.
Bachelor of Science: General
Bachelor of Laws: Corporate
Bachelor of Engineering: General, Chemical, Computer Systems, Electrical, Industrial, Mechanical
Bachelor of Education: General
Chartered Accounting: CA - General/Finance, CGA/CMA - General/Finance

Critical Skills
Analytical, Good Communication, Creative, Decisive, Dependable, Diligent, Diplomatic, Efficient, Productive, Professional, Responsible, Writing Skills

Types of Positions
Administrative Asst.   Account Service Rep.
Junior Sales Rep.   Warehouse Clerk

Starting Salary
$ 25,000 - 30,000

Company Benefits
- Extended health care, dental, life insurance

Correspondence
Mail or fax resume with cover letter

Part Time/Summer: Sony Music does not hire for part time work, but regularly hires for the summer. Jobs may include warehouse clerk and admin. asst.

Co-op/Internship: They have some possibilities for internship opportunities.

The Canada Student Employment Guide

SOUTHAM INC.

1450 Don Mills Road
Don Mills, Ontario, M3B 2X7
Tel: (416) 442-2996   Fax: (416) 442-2208

Human Resources Specialist
Internet: www.southam.ca

Southam is a leading Canadian communications and information company whose principal activity is newspaper publishing, business to business information services and book retailing. The company operates 17 daily newspapers in major cities across Canada as well as many community papers. They employ 10,764 people across the country.

Academic Fields
College: Accounting, Administration, Advertising, Business, Computer Science, Graphic Arts, Human Resources, Journalism, Marketing/Sales, Secretarial
Bachelor of Arts: General, Business, English, Journalism, Urban Geography
Bachelor of Comm/Admin: General, Accounting, Finance
Bachelor of Science: Computer Science, Environmental Studies, Geology
Chartered Accounting: CA - General/Finance, CGA/CMA - General/Finance
Masters: Business Administration, Library Science

Critical Skills
Adaptable, Good Communication, Confident, Creative, Decisive, Dependable, Diligent, Efficient, Enthusiastic, Flexible, Good With Figures, Innovative, Leadership, Logical, Organized, Productive, Professional, Good Writing Skills

Types of Positions
Inside Sales Rep.   Clerical
Administrative Asst.   Editorial Assistant

Starting Salary
$ 20,000 - 30,000

Company Benefits
- Competitive benefit package

Correspondence
Fax resume with cover letter

Part Time/Summer:
Southam sometimes hires for part time and summer jobs. Potential positions include clerical duties, administration, data entry, junior accounting, junior programming, or help desk support.

SOUTHERN RAILWAY OF BRITISH COLUMBIA LTD.

2102 River Dr.
New Westminster, British Columbia, V3M 6S3
Tel: (604) 527-6342   Fax: (604) 526-0914

W. Carrey, Director of Human Resources

Southern Railway of British Columbia provides movement of freight cars to customer sidings. They also are involved in locomotive and RR car repair. The firm employs about 150 people in total.

Academic Fields
College: Accounting
Bachelor of Arts: General, Business
Bachelor of Comm/Admin: General, Accounting, Marketing
Bachelor of Engineering: Mechanical, Transportation
Chartered Accounting: CMA-Finance, CGA-Finance
Masters: Business Administration, Engineering

Critical Skills
Adaptable, Analytical, Good Communication, Creative, Dependable, Diligent, Efficient, Enthusiastic, Good With Figures, Innovative, Leadership, Organized, Persuasive, Productive, Responsible, Good Writing Skills,

Types of Positions
Clerical   Mechanical/Helper
Trainman

Starting Salary
$ 35,000 - 50,000

Company Benefits
- Extended health, dental, life insurance, medical services plan
- Short and long term disability, pension
- Tuition reimbursement for courses and books

Correspondence
Mail or fax resume with cover letter
E-mail: bcarrey@sryraillink.com

Part Time/Summer:
Southern Railway of British Columbia occasionally looks for people for part time or summer work. If there is a vacancy the best time to apply is from May to September. Potential jobs are in maintenance or in the locomotive shop.

SOUTHLAND CANADA

3365 Harvester Road, Suite 201
Burlington, Ontario, L7N 3N2
Tel: (905) 634-1711   Fax: (905) 634-2765

Pat Hopkins, Personnel Consultant

Southland Canada is a retail convenience store chain. Southland was established in Canada in 1969 and has a total of 467 outlets across the country. The company employs approximately 10,000 people from coast to coast. Candidates should apply to individual stores.

Academic Fields
College: Accounting, Business
Bachelor of Arts: Business, Economics
Bachelor of Comm/Admin: Accounting, Finance

Critical Skills
Adaptable, Dependable, Diligent, Efficient, Enthusiastic, Flexible, Good Communication, Good With Figures, Innovative, Manual Dexterity, Organized, Patient, Personable, Productive, Professional, Responsible

Types of Positions
Sales Assistant   Store Manager Trainee

Starting Salary
$15,000 or less

Company Benefits
- Hospital, dental, short and long term disability
- Life insurance, educational assistance, profit sharing, pension plan
- All employees receive three days orientation training

Correspondence
Mail or fax resume and cover letter

Part Time/Summer: Southland Canada regularly seeks individuals for part time and summer employment opportunities. In the summer months, a potential job is sales assistant. The best time to apply is in the months of April and May.

SPAR AEROSPACE LIMITED

P.O. Box 9864, Edmonton Int'l Airport
Edmonton, Alberta, T5J 2T2
Tel: (403) 890-6495   Fax: (403) 890-6544

Jim Holtby, Human Resources
Internet: www.spar.ca

Spar Aerospace Limited is involved in both commercial and military aircraft maintenance and repair, overhaul and technical support. They employ approximately 600 individuals.

Academic Fields
College: Accounting, Computer Science, Drafting/Architecture, Electronics Tech., Engineering Tech., Secretarial
Bachelor of Arts: English
Bachelor of Comm/Admin: General, Accounting, Finance
Bachelor of Science: Computer Science
Bachelor of Engineering: Computer Systems, Electrical, Mechanical
Chartered Accounting: CA-General, CMA - General/Finance, CGA - General/Finance
Masters: Business Administration

Critical Skills
Adaptable, Good Communication, Dependable, Efficient, Flexible, Good With Figures, Organized, Professional, Responsible, Good Writing Skills

Types of Positions
Junior Engineer   Contracts Administrator
Business Analyst   Systems Analyst
Draftsperson   Editor

Starting Salary
$ 25,000 - 30,000

Company Benefits
- Alberta health care
- Medical, dental, vision care
- Long and short term disability

Correspondence
Mail or e-mail resume with cover letter
E-mail: humanres@telusplanet.net

Part Time/Summer: Spar Aviation Services occasionally seeks individuals for part time and summer work. Potential jobs include engineering student, desktop assistant, and drafting assistant. The best time to apply is in April.

SPECTRA PREMIUM INDUSTRIES

1421 rue Ampère
Boucherville, Québec, J4B 5Z5
Tel: (450) 641-3090   Fax: (450) 641-6135

Richard J. Grenier, Vice President, HR
Internet: www.spectrapremium.com

Spectra Premium Industries is a leader in the aftermarket automotive industry. The company makes gas tanks, radiators, and components, to name just a few. They employ more than 1,200 individuals in Canada.

Academic Fields
College: Accounting, Administration, Human Resources, Information Systems, Marketing/Sales, Purchasing, Secretarial, Automotive Maintenance, CAD Autocad, Computer Science, Electronics Tech., Engineering Tech., Mechanical Tech., Welding, Graphic Arts
Bachelor of Arts: Economics
Bachelor of Comm/Admin: Accounting, Finance, Human Resources, Marketing, Info Mgmt., Public Admin.
Bachelor of Engineering: Design, Electrical, Industrial, Mechanical

Critical Skills
Adaptable, Decisive, Dependable, Efficient, Flexible, Good Communication, Leadership, Logical, Manual Dexterity, Organized, Productive, Professional

Types of Positions
Labourer   Mechanic
Welder   Machine Shop
Security Agent

Starting Salary
$ 25,000 - 30,000

Company Benefits
- Offer a comprehensive benefit package
- Dental, medical, pension plan

Correspondence
Mail resume with cover letter
E-mail: hr@spectrapremium.com

Part Time/Summer: Spectra Premium Industries rarely hires individuals for part time or summer employment.

SPECTRUM SIGNAL PROCESSING INC.

200 - 2700 Production Way
Burnaby, British Columbia, V5A 4X1
Tel: (604) 421-5422   Fax: (604) 421-1764

My-Linh Truong, Human Resources Assistant
Internet: www.spectrumsignal.com

Spectrum provides high performance, multiprocessing hardware and software computer systems to customers in three market segments - Network Solutions, Wireless Systems, and Sensor Systems. Spectrum is an industry leading supplier of multiprocessing products based on Digital Signal Processing (DSP) technology.

Academic Fields
College: Accounting, Computer Science, Engineering Tech., Graphic Arts
Bachelor of Arts: Business
Bachelor of Comm/Admin: Accounting, Finance, Human Resources, Marketing
Bachelor of Science: Computer Science
Bachelor of Engineering: Computer Systems, Electrical, Mechanical
Masters: Business Administration, Engineering

Critical Skills
Adaptable, Creative, Diligent, Flexible, Good Communication, Innovative, Leadership, Personable

Types of Positions
Software Engineer   Web Designer/Developer
Manufacturing/Operations

Starting Salary
$ 40,000 - 45,000

Company Benefits
- Health, dental, vision care, life insurance

Correspondence
Fax or e-mail resume with cover letter
E-mail: jobs@spectrumsignal.com

Part Time/Summer: Spectrum regularly looks for individuals for part time and summer work. Potential jobs are in marketing, engineering, accounting/finance, human resources. Right before each school semester. (i.e. January, May, September).

Co-op/Internship: They recruit for international interns and have co-op opportunities from colleges and universities.

The Canada Student Employment Guide

SPEEDWARE CORP. INC.

9999 Cavendish Blvd., Suite 100
St. Laurent, Quebec, H4M 2X5
Tel: (514) 747-7007   Fax: (514) 747-3380

Rose Church, Human Resources
Internet: www.speedware.com

Speedware is one of the largest software companies in Canada. They create and market a range of software development tools that enable companies to rapidly produce Internet, Client/server and OLAP systems. Speedware has over 230 employees in 18 offices in seven countries, serving more than 3,000 clients. Their products include Speedware Autobahn, Speedware 4GL, Speedware/Designer, Easy Reporter and Media EIS/OLAP products.

Academic Fields
College: Computer Science, Marketing/Sales, Secretarial
Bachelor of Comm/Admin: Marketing, Info Mgmt.
Bachelor of Science: Computer Science, Mathematics
Bachelor of Engineering: Computer Systems
Chartered Accounting: CMA - General/Finance

Critical Skills
Adaptable, Creative, Dependable, Enthusiastic, Flexible, Good Communication, Good Writing Skills, Innovative

Types of Positions
Telemarketing   Junior Sales Rep.
Customer Support Rep.   Marketing Associate

Starting Salary
$ 30,000 - 40,000

Company Benefits
- Group medical and dental insurance
- Short and long term disability, life insurance
- Educational assistance program

Correspondence
Fax resume with cover letter

Part Time/Summer: Speedware Corp. occasionally looks for individuals for part time positions, and regularly seeks candidates for summer opportunities. In the summer, potential jobs include systems manager, or LAN manager. The best time to apply is in April.

SPORTSCO INTERNATIONAL

1 Blue Jays Way, Suite 3000
Toronto, Ontario, M5V 1J3
Tel: (416) 341-3000   Fax: (416) 341-3102

Rachel Dowling, Administrative Assistant
Internet: www.skydome.com

Sportsco International runs a world class stadium complex at the foot of the C.N. Tower. Opened in June 1989 and costing $580 million to complete, the stadium is the only one in the world with a fully retractable roof. Skydome contains trade show facilities, a 350 room hotel, and a health club. They employ over 600 individuals.

Academic Fields
College: Accounting, Administration, Human Resources, Information Systems, Marketing/Sales, Hospitality, Television/Radio, Engineering Tech., Mechanical Tech., Plumbing, Welding
Bachelor of Arts: General, Business, Public Relations
Bachelor of Comm/Admin: General, Accounting, Finance, Human Resources, Marketing, Info Mgmt.
Bachelor of Engineering: General, Electrical
Chartered Accounting: CA - General/Finance, CGA/CMA - General/Finance
Masters: Business Administration

Critical Skills
Creative, Dependable, Enthusiastic, Good Communication, Good Writing Skills, Innovative, Personable, Productive, Professional, Responsible

Types of Positions
Administrative Assistant   Receptionist
Security Officer   Event Staff

Starting Salary
$ 20,000 - 25,000

Company Benefits
- Complete benefit package for full time employees
- Dental, health, pension, 3 weeks vacation annually
- Continuous in-house and outside training

Correspondence
Mail or fax resume with cover letter

Part Time/Summer: Sportsco International regularly hires for part time jobs, but does not hire for summer positions.

The Canada Student Employment Guide

SPRINT CANADA

2235 Victoria Park Ave. E., Suite 600
North York, Ontario, M2J 5G1
Tel: (416) 496-1644   Fax: (416) 718-6184

Marianne Carruthers, Recruitment Manager
Internet: www.sprintcanada.com

Sprint Canada Inc. is Canada's leading alternative long-distance telecommunications company, offering voice and data services nationwide. With headquarters in Toronto, Sprint Canada operates in 53 locations and employs more than 2,900 Canadians across the country. Visit their website for an online application.

Academic Fields
College: Administration, Communications, Human Resources, Computer Science
Bachelor of Arts: General, Public Relations
Bachelor of Comm/Admin: General, Accounting, Finance, Human Res., Mktg., Info Mgmt., Public Admin.
Bachelor of Science: Actuarial, Computer Sci., Math
Bachelor of Laws: Corporate, Real Estate
Bachelor of Engineering: Computer Systems, Design, Electrical
Chartered Accounting: CA - General/Finance, CGA/CMA - General/Finance
Masters: Business Administration, Engineering

Critical Skills
Analytical, Confident, Creative, Dependable, Efficient, Enthusiastic, Good Communication, Good Writing Skills, Innovative, Logical, Organized, Personable, Professional, Team Player, Balance

Types of Positions
Customer Care Rep.   Administration
Business Analyst   Circuit Designer

Starting Salary
$ 20,000 - 30,000

Company Benefits
- Group benefits plan, RRSP
- Share purchase plan, employee assistance program

Correspondence
Mail, e-mail or submit resume with cover letter in person

Part Time/Summer: Sprint Canada occasionally looks for people for part time work, and regularly seeks people in the summer. They also offer a number of co-op and internships. Potential work involves administration or customer care. The best time to apply is before April.

SRI HOMES INC.

485 Beaver Lake Rd.
Kelowna, British Columbia, V4V 1S5
Tel: (250) 766-0457   Fax: (250) 762-2086

Human Resources
Internet: www.srihomes.com

SRI Homes Inc. is Canada's largest builder of manufactured housing. Operating three manufacturing facilities across Western Canada, they service a dealer network throughout Central and Western Canada as well as the Pacific Northwest, Alaska, Japan, China, New Zealand and Germany. SRI's corporate office is located in Kelowna, British Columbia. The company employs approximately 500 individuals in Canada.

Academic Fields
College: Accounting, Information Systems, Marketing/Sales, CAD Autocad
Bachelor of Comm/Admin: Accounting, Finance, Marketing
Chartered Accounting: CA - General/Finance, CGA - General/Finance, CMA - General/Finance

Critical Skills
Adaptable, Confident, Dependable, Diligent, Good Writing Skills, Personable, Professional

Types of Positions
Accountant   Draftsperson
Sales & Marketing Assistant Network Administrator
Computer Programmer

Starting Salary
Depends on position

Company Benefits
- Competitive salary
- Company paid medical benefits
- Pension plan

Correspondence
Mail resume with cover letter
E-mail: careers@srihomes.com

Part Time/Summer: SRI Homes Inc. does not hire for part time work, but occasionally hires for the summer months. A potential job would be computer programmer (entry-level). The best time to apply is by March 15th.

SSQ LIFE

2525 boulevard Laurier, C.P. 10500
Ste-Foy, Québec, G1V 4H6
Tel: (418) 651-7000   Fax: (418) 652-2737

Daniel Ouellet, Ressources humaines
Internet: www.ssq.qc.ca

SSQ Life is a major insurance company in Quebec that provides group insurance specializing in life, disability, accident and sickness insurance, along with pension plans. The insurance company has one sales office in Quebec City, and one in Montreal. SSQ Life has an employee base of more than 550 individuals.

Academic Fields
College: Accounting, Administration, Computer Science, Insurance, Nursing, Secretary
Bachelor of Comm/Admin: General, Accounting, Finance, Info Mgmt.
Bachelor of Science: Actuarial, Computer Science, Nursing
Bachelor of Laws: General
Bachelor of Engineering: Computer Systems
Chartered Accounting: CA - General/Finance, CGA - General/Finance
Masters: Administration

Critical Skills
Adaptable, Creative, Dependable, Good Communication, Diligent, Efficient, Flexible, Good Writing Skills, Productive, Professional, Responsible

Types of Positions
Various Positions

Starting Salary
$ 20,000 - 30,000

Company Benefits
- Full benefit package

Correspondence
Mail or fax resume with cover letter

Part Time/Summer: SSQ Life sometimes hires candidates for part time employment, and regularly looks for individuals for the summer months. Potential positions in the summer usually vary. The best time to apply is in February.

ST. AMANT CENTRE INC.

440 River Road
Winnipeg, Manitoba, R2M 3Z9
Tel: (204) 254-3768   Fax: (204) 256-4301

Irene Sanchez-Cielen, Human Resources Officer
Internet: www.stamant.nb.ca

The St. Amant Centre is a residential centre and out reach facility for people with severe mental and physical disabilities. There are a total of 236 long term care beds within the facility. The centre also provides an integrated developmental daycare program along with a community out reach program, and has 19 community homes. The St. Amant Centre employs nearly 789 people to work in various capacities within the facility.

Academic Fields
College: Child Care, Nursing, Secretarial
Bachelor of Arts: Psychology, Sociology/Social Work
Bachelor of Science: Food Sciences, Health Sciences, Nursing (RN), Occupational Therapy, Pharmacy, Physiotherapy, Psychology
Bachelor of Education: Special

Critical Skills
Dependable, Good Communication, Patient, Personable, Professional, Responsible

Types of Positions
Resident Assistant   Counsellor

Starting Salary
$ 20,000 - 25,000

Company Benefits
- Health, dental and pension
- Short and long term disability, group RRSP
- Limited funding for training available

Correspondence
Mail, fax or submit resume and cover letter in person
E-mail: employment@stamant.mb.ca

Part Time/Summer: The St. Amant Centre regularly looks for part time and summer candidates. Potential jobs include resident assistant, or involve duties including laundry, housekeeping, and dietary responsibilities. The best time to apply is in the Spring or Fall.

The Canada Student Employment Guide

ST. JOSEPH'S CARE GROUP

P.O. Box 3251
Thunder Bay, Ontario, P7B 5G7
Tel: (807) 343-2419   Fax: (807) 345-8745

Human Resources Department
Internet: www.sjcg.net

St. Joseph's Care Group includes St. Joseph's Heritage, St. Joseph's Hospital and Westmount Hospital. These facilities are owned and operated by the Sisters of St. Joseph of Sault Ste. Marie and managed by a volunteer Board of Directors.

Academic Fields
College: Human Resources, Gerontology, Recreation, Health Records Tech., Computer Tech., Secretarial
Bachelor of Arts: Business, Recreation Studies, Sociology/Social Work
Bachelor of Comm/Admin: Accounting, Info Mgmt.
Bachelor of Science: Food Sciences, Nursing (RN), Occupational Therapy, Pharmacy, Physiotherapy, Psychology
Masters: Arts, Social Work, Speech Language Pathology, Audiology, Psychology, Health Admin.

Critical Skills
Good Communication, Dependable, Diligent, Efficient, Flexible, Leadership, Organized, Patient, Professional, Good Writing Skills, Problem Solving, Team Player

Types of Positions
Nursing   Therapist
Addictions Counsellor   Housekeeping/Dietary Aide
Secretarial   Pharmacist

Starting Salary
$ 30,000 - 60,000 (depending on position)

Company Benefits
- Vacation, sick, drug plan, vision

Correspondence
Mail resume with cover letter. E-mail: hilla@tbh.net

Part Time/Summer: St. Joseph's Care Group regularly hires for part time work and occasionally hires for the summer. Summer positions are primarily in roles working directly with clients as part of rehabilitation or recreation services. Non-client roles have included assisting with grounds work and in the purchasing department. The best time to apply is early in the calendar year.

Co-op/Internship: Internship opportunities vary.

ST. LAWRENCE PARKS COMMISSION

R.R. # 1
Morrisburg, Ontario, K0C 1X0
Tel: (613) 543-3704   Fax: (613) 543-2047

Human Resources

St. Lawrence Parks Commission is the organization that maintains the parks in the St. Lawrence area. Correspondence must be submitted quoting the competition number of the position you are interested in.

Academic Fields
College: Accounting, Administration, Business, Hospitality, Human Resources, Journalism, Marketing/Sales, Mechanical Tech., Recreation Studies, Security/Law, Travel/Tourism
Bachelor of Arts: Business, History, Journalism, Languages, Music, Public Relations, Recreation Studies
Bachelor of Comm/Admin: Finance, Marketing, Info Mgmt.
Bachelor of Science: Environmental Studies, Forestry, Horticulture
Bachelor of Engineering: Civil, Environ. Studies, Industrial, Mechanical, Bach. of Landscape Arch.
Chartered Accounting: CGA-Finance
Masters: Business Administration, Education

Critical Skills
Adaptable, Creative, Decisive, Dependable, Diplomatic, Efficient, Enthusiastic, Flexible, Good Communication, Leadership, Organized, Personable, Productive, Professional, Responsible

Types of Positions
Park Worker   Visitor Attendant
Program Support

Starting Salary
$ 25,000 - 40,000

Company Benefits
- Competitive benefit package
- 80% dental, vision, supplementary health care

Correspondence
Mail resume with cover letter

Part Time/Summer: St. Lawrence Parks Commission occasionally seeks candidates for part time work and regularly hires for the summer months. The best time to apply is before the end of February.

THE ST. LAWRENCE SEAWAY MANAGEMENT CORPORATION
202 Pitt Street
Cornwall, Ontario, K6J 3P7
Tel: (613) 932-5170   Fax: (613) 932-3041

Human Resources Section
Internet: www.seaway.ca

The St. Lawrence Seaway Management Corporation operates a navigable waterway between Montreal, Quebec and Lake Erie. The St. Lawrence Seaway Management Corporation's office is located in Cornwall, Ontario.

Academic Fields
College: Computer Science, Drafting/Architecture, Electronics Tech., Engineering Tech., Mechanical Tech., Secretarial, Urban Planning
Bachelor of Arts: Business, Economics, Psychology
Bachelor of Comm/Admin: Accounting, Marketing
Bachelor of Science: Computer Science
Bachelor of Engineering: Civil, Design, Electrical, Mechanical
Chartered Accounting: CMA-General, CGA-General

Critical Skills
Adaptable, Dependable, Efficient, Flexible, Innovative

Types of Positions
Service Person 4   Clerk/Typist

Starting Salary
$ 30,000 - 35,000

Company Benefits
- Health, dental coverage, pension plan
- Semi-private hospital, long term disability
- On-going multi-skilled training opportunities

Correspondence
Mail or fax resume with cover letter

Part Time/Summer: The St. Lawrence Seaway Management Corporation regularly hires for part time employment and occasionally seeks candidates for summer opportunities. Potential summer positions involve the areas of engineering, computer science, or marketing. The best time to apply is in early March.

ST. VINCENT'S HOSPITALS
749 West 33rd Avenue
Vancouver, British Columbia, V5Z 2K4
Tel: (604) 877-3005   Fax: (604) 877-3185

Human Resources

St. Vincent's Hospitals is a catholic hospital catering to an elderly and geriatric population. The health care facility employs over 5,000 individuals to work in various capacities within the hospital.

Academic Fields
College: Accounting, Business, Computer Science, Food/Nutrition, Human Resources, Laboratory Tech., Nursing, Radiology Tech.
Bachelor of Arts: Business, Gerontology
Bachelor of Comm/Admin: Info Mgmt.
Bachelor of Science: Computer Science, Food Sciences, Nursing (RN), Occupational Therapy, Pharmacy, Physiotherapy
Chartered Accounting: CA - General/Finance, CGA/CMA - General/Finance

Critical Skills
Adaptable, Good Communication, Confident, Dependable, Enthusiastic, Flexible, Leadership, Logical, Organized, Personable, Productive, Responsible, Team Player

Types of Positions
Food Service Worker   Housekeeping Aide
Admitting Clerk   Switchboard Clerk

Starting Salary
$ 25,000

Company Benefits
- Permanent employees only receive benefits
- General, medical, dental, extended health
- On-the-job training, internal services

Correspondence
Mail or fax resume with cover letter

Part Time/Summer: St. Vincent's Hospitals sometimes seeks candidates for part time work and summer employment. Potential jobs include rehabilitation assistant. The best time to apply is in April.

STANDARD KNITTING LIMITED

P.O. Box 946
Winnipeg, Manitoba, R3C 2T3
Tel: (204) 633-5038   Fax: (204) 633-5037

Human Resources
Internet: www.tundrasportswear.com

Standard Knitting Limited is a knitwear manufacturer in Winnipeg, Manitoba. The company employs approximately 200 individuals at this location.

Academic Fields
College: Accounting, Administration, Human Resources, Information Systems, Marketing/Sales, Purchasing, Secretarial, Industrial Design, Mechanical Tech.
Bachelor of Comm/Admin: Accounting, Finance, Human Resources, Marketing, Info Mgmt.
Bachelor of Engineering: Computer Systems, Industrial, Materials Science, Mechanical

Critical Skills
Adaptable, Analytical, Flexible, Good Communication, Dependable, Efficient, Enthusiastic, Personable, Productive, Professional, Responsible

Types of Positions
Various types of positions

Starting Salary
Depends on position

Company Benefits
- Competitive benefits package

Correspondence
Mail resume with cover letter

Part Time/Summer: Standard Knitting Limited occasionally seeks candidates for part time or summer employment.

STANDEN'S LIMITED

P.O. Box 67, Station 'T'
Calgary, Alberta, T2H 2G7
Tel: (403) 258-7800   Fax: (403) 258-7868

Roland Osske, Human Resources Manager
Internet: www.standens.com

Standen's is one of North America's largest full line manufacturers of leaf springs, suspension components, trailer axles, and agricultural tillage components. Established in 1924, Standen's products include leaf springs for all types of vehicles, cultivator shanks and tillage tools for the agricultural implement industry, grouser bars for the tracked vehicle industry, threaded rods, u-bolts and driveshafts.

Academic Fields
College: Computer Science, Drafting/Architecture, Engineering Tech., Industrial Design, Mechanical Tech.
Bachelor of Engineering: Industrial, Materials Science, Mechanical

Critical Skills
Adaptable, Analytical, Good Communication, Dependable, Efficient, Innovative, Organized, Responsible

Types of Positions
Production   Engineering

Starting Salary
$ 20,000 - 25,000

Company Benefits
- Medical and dental benefits with vision care
- Prescriptions, drugs, long and short term disability
- Training related to business needs

Correspondence
Mail, fax or e-mail resume with cover letter
E-mail: employment@standens.com

Part Time/Summer: Standen's Limited occasionally looks for individuals for part time and summer opportunities. Potential jobs include basic engineering roles and help with production. The best time to apply is during May, or in early June.

STANLEY CANADA INC.

1100 Corporate Drive
Brampton, Ontario, L7L 5R6
Tel: (905) 335-0075   Fax: (905) 335-3430

Human Resources

Stanley Canada Inc. is a distributor of consumer and industrial tools. The company's head office is in Brampton, Ontario.

Academic Fields
College: General, Accounting, Administration, Business, Computer Science, Marketing/Sales, Secretarial
Bachelor of Arts: General, Business
Bachelor of Comm/Admin: General, Finance, Marketing, Info Mgmt.
Chartered Accounting: CMA-Finance, CGA-Finance
Masters: Business Administration

Critical Skills
Adaptable, Analytical, Confident, Dependable, Efficient, Enthusiastic, Good Communication, Good With Figures, Good Writing Skills, Leadership, Organized, Personable, Professional, Responsible

Types of Positions
Various Positions

Starting Salary
$ 25,000 - 30,000 (depends on position)

Company Benefits
- Competitive benefits package

Correspondence
Mail resume with cover letter

Part Time/Summer: Stanley Canada Inc. occasionally looks for individuals for part time or summer employment. A potential job would be in the warehouse.

STANTEC CONSULTING LTD.

871 Victoria St. N.
Kitchener, Ontario, N2B 3S4
Tel: (519) 579-4410   Fax: N/A

Heidi Weber, Human Resources Advisor
Internet: www.stantec.com

Stantec provides lifecycle solutions to infrastructure and facilities projects through value-added professional services and technologies. Services are offered through more than 2,500 employees, operating out of 40 locations.

Academic Fields
College: CAD Autocad, Engineering Tech., Mechanical Tech.
Bachelor of Science: Computer Science, Environmental Studies
Bachelor of Engineering: General, Chemical, Civil, Computer Systems, Design, Electrical, Environmental Studies, Geotechnical, Industrial, Mechanical, Transportation, Water Resources, Bachelor of Architecture, Bachelor of Landscape Architecture
Masters: Engineering

Critical Skills
Dependable, Diplomatic, Efficient, Flexible, Good Communication, Good With Figures, Good Writing Skills, Innovative, Leadership, Logical, Organized, Personable, Persuasive, Productive, Professional

Types of Positions
Engineer-In-Training   Technologist
Technician   Field Inspector
Surveyor

Starting Salary
Depends on position

Company Benefits
- Full benefits package

Correspondence
E-mail resume with cover letter

Part Time/Summer: Stantec Consulting Ltd. occasionally hires for part time work and regularly hires for the summer. Potential jobs include surveyor or field inspector. Apply in the New Year.

Co-op/Internship: They offer co-op education for university and college. They participate in local co-op programs.

STAR DATA SYSTEMS INC.

30 Wellington St., W., Suite 300, P.O. Box 283
Toronto, Ontario, M5L 1G1
Tel: (416) 363-7827   Fax: (416) 363-9766

Annabelle Desira, Human Resources

Star Data Systems Inc. is a leading supplier of online, real-time information systems and solutions to Canada's investment community. Star Data is organized under two operating business units, Information Services and Wealth Management Solutions. The company currently has more than 400 employees in offices across Canada. Headquartered in Toronto, Ontario, Star Data also has offices in Markham, Vancouver, Calgary, Winnipeg, Montreal, Halifax, London Ontario and London, U.K.

Academic Fields
College: Accounting, Administration, Computer Sci., Electronics Tech., Engineering Tech., Human Resources
Bachelor of Comm/Admin: General, Accounting, Finance, Info Mgmt.
Bachelor of Science: Computer Science, Mathematics
Bachelor of Engineering: Computer Systems, Electrical
Chartered Accounting: CMA-Finance, CGA-Finance

Critical Skills
Dependable, Flexible, Good Communication, Innovative, Logical, Organized, Personable, Professional

Types of Positions
Administration Assistant
Junior HR Administrator
Customer Service Representative

Starting Salary
Depends on skills, position, and training

Company Benefits
- Group health coverage, group RRSP
- Dental, life and disability insurance
- In-house training on various applications (excel, word, lotus notes, starquote, etc.)

Correspondence
Fax resume with cover letter

Part Time/Summer: Star Data Systems does not hire for part time work and ocassionally hires in the summer. Potential jobs in the summer may involve finance and admin., or product marketing and business develop.

STATE FARM INSURANCE COMPANIES

100 Consilium Place, Suite 102
Scarborough, Ontario, M1H 3G9
Tel: (416) 290-4717   Fax: (416) 290-4716

Human Resources
Internet: www.statefarm.com

State Farm is a multi-line insurance company providing a full range of life and general insurance services including auto, home and health insurance.

Academic Fields
College: General, Accounting, Computer Science, Human Res., Insurance, Marketing/Sales, Security/Law
Bachelor of Arts: General, Business, Criminology, Economics, English, Fine Arts, History, Journalism, Languages, Political Sci., Psychology, Public Relations, Recreation Studies, Sociology/Social Work, Statistics
Bachelor of Comm/Admin: General
Bachelor of Science: General, Actuarial, Biology, Chemistry, Computer Science, Environmental Studies, Geography, Mathematics, Microbiology, Psychology
Bachelor of Laws: General
Bachelor of Engineering: General, Chemical, Civil, Computer Syst., Design, Electrical, Industrial, Mech.
Bachelor of Education: General
Chartered Accounting: CA-General, CMA-General, CMA-Finance
Masters: Business Admin., Arts, Science, Engineering, Education

Critical Skills
Adaptable, Analytical, Artistic, Good Communication, Confident, Creative, Decisive, Dependable, Diligent, Diplomatic, Efficient, Enthusiastic, Personable, Persuasive, Productive, Professional, Responsible

Types of Positions
Data Entry Clerk   Claim Service Assistant
Policy Admin. Asst.   Underwriter Trainee

Starting Salary
$ 20,000 - 30,000

Company Benefits
- Medical, dental, life insurance, long term disability

Correspondence
Mail resume with cover letter

Part Time/Summer: State Farm occasionally hires for part time work and regularly hires in the summer. Potential jobs include data entry. Apply in April.

The Canada Student Employment Guide

STEELCRAFT INDUSTRIES LTD.

P.O. Box 339, 904 Downie Rd.
Stratford, Ontario, N5A 6T3
Tel: (519) 271-4750   Fax: (519) 272-0911

Lori Elliott, Human Resources Manager
Internet: www.steelcraft.on.ca

Steelcraft Industries Limited is a Canadian company incorporated in Ontario in 1972. They are the administrative parent company of three separate sales divisions. They employ about 190 individuals.

Academic Fields
College: Accounting, Advertising, Human Resources, Information Systems, Marketing/Sales, Purchasing, Secretarial, CAD Autocad, Engineering Tech., Industrial Design, Mechanical Tech., Welding
Bachelor of Comm/Admin: Accounting, Finance, Human Resources, Marketing, Info Mgmt.
Bachelor of Engineering: Design, Industrial, Mechanical
Masters: Engineering

Critical Skills
Adaptable, Analytical, Good Communication, Confident, Creative, Decisive, Dependable, Diligent, Diplomatic, Efficient, Enthusiastic, Flexible, Responsible, Good Writing Skills

Types of Positions
Welding   Machine Shop
Engineering   Sales
Quality Assurance   Accounting

Starting Salary
$ 30,000 - 35,000

Company Benefits
- Health and dental coverage
- Apprenticeship opportunities

Correspondence
Mail, fax, or e-mail resume with cover letter
E-mail: lelliott@steelcraft.on.ca

Part Time/Summer: Steelcraft Industries Ltd. occasionally hires for part time or summer work. Potential jobs include general labour, accounting or engineering. The best time to apply is in April.

Co-op/Internship: They offer internships in apprentice programs including general machinist, welder fitter and millwright.

STEELPIPE LTD.

P.O. Box 1010, 200 Dain Ave.
Welland, Ontario, L3B 6E4
Tel: 1-800-263-7473   Fax: (905) 735-3107

Karen Beatty, Human Resources Manager

Steelpipe Ltd. is a pipe and tube manufacturer. The company employs 500 individuals at their location in Welland, Ontario.

Academic Fields
College: Accounting, Human Resources, Information Systems, Purchasing, CAD Autocad, Electronics Tech., Engineering Tech., Industrial Design, Mechanical Tech., Graphic Arts, Welding, Nursing RN, Orthotics/Prosthetics
Bachelor of Arts: General, Economics
Bachelor of Comm/Admin: General, Accounting, Info Mgmt.
Bachelor of Science: Computer Science, Kinesiology, Mathematics, Occupational Therapy
Bachelor of Laws: Corporate
Bachelor of Engineering: Computer Systems, Electrical, Industrial, Mechanical, Water Resources
Bachelor of Education: General, Special
Chartered Accounting: CA-General, CGA-General, CMA-General

Critical Skills
Adaptable, Creative, Dependable, Efficient, Good Writing Skills, Leadership, Logical, Productive, Professional, Responsible

Types of Positions
General Labourer   Purchasing
Payroll   Treasury
Billing/Shipping

Starting Salary
$ 40,000 - 45,000

Company Benefits
- Full range of vision, prescription and dental plans

Correspondence
Mail resume with cover letter
E-mail: karen.beatty@stelco.ca

Part Time/Summer: Steelpipe Ltd. rarely hires for part time work and regularly hires for the summer months. Children of employees are usually hired for the summer.

STERLING MARKING PRODUCTS INC.

349 Ridout St. N., P.O. Box 5055
London, Ontario, N6A 5S4
Tel: (519) 434-5785   Fax: (519) 434-9516

J. Hofmann, Human Resources
Internet: www.sterling.ca

Sterling Marking Products is a stamp and signage manufacturer that produces pre-inked and rubber stamps, indoor and outdoor signs, name badges and desk plates, and printing of box dies.

Academic Fields
College: Accounting, Business, Computer Science, Graphic Arts, Secretarial
Bachelor of Arts: Business
Bachelor of Comm/Admin: Marketing
Bachelor of Science: Computer Science
Chartered Accounting: CGA-General

Critical Skills
Adaptable, Good Communication, Dependable, Efficient, Flexible, Organized, Productive, Professional

Types of Positions
Sales Representative   Customer Service Representative
Graphic Artist   Proofreader

Starting Salary
$ 20,000 - 25,000

Company Benefits
- Health, dental, life insurance
- Benefits after 3 months
- On-the-job training

Correspondence
Mail resume with cover letter

Part Time/Summer: Sterling Marking Products occasionally looks for candidates for part time and summer work. Potential jobs involve labour positions.

STITCHES

50 Dufflaw Rd.
Toronto, Ontario, M6A 2W1
Tel: (416) 789-1071   Fax: (416) 789-1576

Leon Benz, National Recruiter

Stitches is a national clothier with stores across the country. Their Toronto office is the head location for all of their unisex retail clothing stores.

Academic Fields
College: Accounting, Administration, Advertising, Business, Computer Science, Graphic Arts, Human Resources, Marketing/Sales
Bachelor of Arts: General, Business, English, Languages, Public Relations
Bachelor of Comm/Admin: Accounting, Marketing
Bachelor of Science: Computer Science
Chartered Accounting: CA-General
Masters: Business Administration

Critical Skills
Adaptable, Analytical, Good Communication, Confident, Creative, Decisive, Dependable, Diligent, Diplomatic, Efficient, Enthusiastic, Flexible, Good With Figures, Innovative, Leadership, Logical, Manual Dexterity, Organized, Patient, Personable, Productive, Professional, Responsible, Good Writing Skills

Types of Positions
Sales Associate   Computer Data Entry

Starting Salary
$ 20,000 - 25,000

Company Benefits
- Full benefit package
- Training program with opportunity for advancement

Correspondence
Mail or fax resume with cover letter

Part Time/Summer: Stitches regularly looks for people for part time work, and occasionally seeks individuals for the summer. Potential jobs are retail positions. Individuals can apply anytime.

STONE CONSOLIDATED INC.

800 Rene Levesque Ouest
Montreal, Québec, H3B 1Y9
Tel: (514) 394-2347   Fax: (514) 394-2269

Gina Gambini, Human Resources

Stone Consolidated is a forestry company involved in the pulp and paper industry. The firm's head office is in Montreal, Quebec. Stone Consolidated employs more than 4,000 individuals.

Academic Fields
College: Secretarial
Bachelor of Comm/Admin: Accounting
Bachelor of Science: Computer Science
Bachelor of Engineering: Chemical, Civil, Computer Systems, Electrical
Chartered Accounting: CA - General/Finance, CGA/CMA - General/Finance
Masters: Business Administration

Critical Skills
Dependable, Efficient, Flexible, Good Writing Skills, Professional, Responsible

Types of Positions
Internal Auditor   Clerk

Starting Salary
$ 30,000 - 40,000

Company Benefits
- Group insurance, pension
- 3 weeks vacation
- Tuition refund, health club

Correspondence
Mail or fax resume with cover letter

Part Time/Summer: Stone Consolidated occasionally looks for individuals for part time and summer employment. In the summer, potential jobs include mail clerk, or secretarial replacement. The best time to apply is in April.

STORAGETEK CANADA INC.

5580 Explorer Dr., Suite 300
Mississauga, Ontario, L4W 4Y1
Tel: (905) 602-5586   Fax: (905) 602-6010

Human Resources
Internet: www.stortek.com

StorageTek is the preeminent provider of network computing storage. StorageTek products and services store, transport and secure more than 100 petabytes of the world's information, ranging from mainframe data to client/server applications to video, audio and still images.

Academic Fields
College: Computer Science, Electronics Tech.
Bachelor of Comm/Admin: Info Mgmt.
Bachelor of Science: Computer Science
Bachelor of Engineering: Computer Systems
Masters: Business Administration, Science

Critical Skills
Adaptable, Dependable, Enthusiastic, Good Communication, Good Writing Skills, Organized, Personable, Productive, Professional

Types of Positions
Associate Systems Engineer   Associate Marketing Representative

Starting Salary
$ 30,000 - 40,000

Company Benefits
- Comprehensive benefits package
- Medical, dental, life insurance, RRSP, tuition
- Intensive training and development for entry-level positions noted above

Correspondence
Mail resume with cover letter

Part Time/Summer: StorageTek Canada occasionally hires individuals for part time or summer employment.

STRESSGEN BIOTECHNOLOGIES CORP.

350 - 4243 Glanford Ave.
Victoria, British Columbia, V8Z 4B9
Tel: (250) 744-2811   Fax: (250) 744-2877

Dana Quarry, HR Administrator
Internet: www.stressgen.com

StressGen Biotechnologies Corp. is a growing biopharmaceutical company dedicated to the research development and commercialization of innovative products to fight cancer and prevent infectious disease. The Company's research capitalizes on the proven ability of stress proteins to stimulate the body's immune system to fight disease effectively. StressGen's proprietary technology has the potential for wide application in new vaccines, as enhancements to existing vaccines, and in cancer treatments. The company employs 70 individuals.

Academic Fields
Bachelor of Science: Biology, Chemistry, Computer Science, Microbiology

Critical Skills
Analytical, Dependable, Efficient, Flexible, Good Communication, Manual Dexterity, Organized, Productive, Professional, Responsible

Types of Positions
Lab Assistant   Research Assistant

Starting Salary
$ 25,000 - 30,000

Company Benefits
- Medical and dental coverage, excellent plans
- Career path counselling
- In-house training

Correspondence
Mail, fax, e-mail resume with cover letter, or apply through web site. E-mail: jobs@stressgen.com

Part Time/Summer: StressGen Biotechnologies Corp. occasionally hires for part time work and regularly hires for the summer months. Their company hires many students from BSc (Microbiology/Chemistry) program who are in the Co-op Program. Most of their summer work is reserved for these students in a Co-op Program.

Co-op/Internship: They participate in local co-op programs.

SUDBURY REGIONAL HOSPITAL

41 Ramsey Lake Rd.
Sudbury, Ontario, P3E 5J1
Tel: (705) 522-2200   Fax: (705) 523-7062

Wayne Auchinleck, Human Resources Consultant
Internet: www.hrsrh.on.ca

Sudbury Regional Hospital is an acute care hospital and referral centre providing medical services for the Sudbury region and Northeastern Ontario.

Academic Fields
College: Child Care, Cooking/Culinary, Recreation Studies, Social Work, Acctg, Admin., Advertising, Communications, Human Res., Info Syst., Purchasing, Secretarial, Electronics Tech, Engineering Tech., Mech. Tech., Plumbing, Emerg./Paramedic, Lab Tech., Nursing (RN/RNA), Orthotics/Prosthetics, Radiology Tech., Respiratory Tech.
Bachelor of Arts: Business, Gerontology, Psychology, Sociology/Social Work
Bachelor of Comm/Admin: Accounting, Finance, Human Resources, Info Mgmt., Public Admin.
Bachelor of Science: Chemistry, Computer Science, Food Sciences, Health Sciences, Kinesiology, Microbiology, Nursing (RN), Occupational Therapy, Pharmacy, Physiotherapy, Psychology
Bachelor of Engineering: Biomedical, Civil, Computer Systems
Bachelor of Education: Childhood, Physical
Chartered Accounting: CA-Finance, CMA-Finance
Masters: Education, Library Science

Critical Skills
Adaptable, Confident, Dependable, Efficient, Good Communication, Good Writing Skills, Innovative, Productive, Professional, Responsible

Types of Positions
New Graduates of Programs

Starting Salary
$ 30,000 - 35,000

Company Benefits
- Sick benefits, dental, vision

Correspondence
Mail resume and cover letter

Part Time/Summer: Sudbury Regional Hospital regularly hires for part time and summer work. Potential work exists in groundskeeping, kitchen, and housekeeping. Apply is in April or May.

The Canada Student Employment Guide

SUN PEAKS RESORT CORPORATION

1280 Alpine Rd.
Sun Peaks, British Columbia, V0E 1Z1
Tel: (250) 578-7222   Fax: (250) 578-7223

Sandi Hiebert, Human Resources
Internet: www.sunpeaksresort.com

Sun Peaks is BC's fastest growing year round resort. They feature one of BC's best ski experiences as well as a challenging golf course, world class mountain biking and other superb resort activities. If you are interested in working for one of the many hotels, restaurants and other businesses at Sun Peaks Resort, we encourage you to contact them directly.

Academic Fields
College: Accounting, Administration, Advertising, Communications, Human Resources, Marketing/Sales, Real Estate, Secretarial, Automotive Maintenance, Mechanical Tech., Plumbing, Child Care, Cooking/Culinary, Fashion, Hospitality, Photography, Travel/Tourism
Bachelor of Arts: Public Relations
Bachelor of Science: Environmental Studies, Forestry, Horticulture

Critical Skills
Confident, Dependable, Diplomatic, Efficient, Enthusiastic, Good Communication, Logical, Organized, Patient, Personable, Professional, Responsible,

Types of Positions
Lift Operator   Server
Ski School Instructor   Guest Service Clerk
Cashier   Retail/Rental

Starting Salary
$ 20,000 - 25,000

Company Benefits
- Full time employees entitled to full benefit package
- Orientation and training for all new employees
- Apprentice programs

Correspondence
Fax resume with cover letter or visit their job fair in September and October

Part Time/Summer: Sun Peaks Resort Corporation regularly hires for part time and summer work. Potential positions are most likely those listed above.

Co-op/Internship: The company provides many apprenticeship opportunities.

SUN RYPE PRODUCTS LTD.

1165 Ethel Street
Kelowna, British Columbia, V1Y 2W4
Tel: (604) 470-6411   Fax: (604) 470-6435

Denise Shields, Human Resources

Sun Rype Products is a food manufacturer that employs approximately 410 people in total. Their head office is located in Kelowna, British Columbia.

Academic Fields
College: Accounting, Administration, Business, Computer Science, Engineering Tech., Human Resources, Laboratory Tech., Marketing/Sales, Secretarial
Bachelor of Arts: Business, Psychology, Public Relations
Bachelor of Comm/Admin: Accounting, Finance, Marketing, Info Mgmt.
Bachelor of Science: Agriculture, Biology, Chemistry, Computer Science, Food Sciences, Microbiology
Bachelor of Engineering: Chemical, Industrial, Mechanical
Chartered Accounting: CMA-General, CMA-Finance
Masters: Business Administration, Science, Engineering

Critical Skills
Analytical, Good Communication, Confident, Creative, Decisive, Dependable, Diligent, Efficient, Enthusiastic, Flexible

Types of Positions
Various Positions

Starting Salary
$ 30,000 - 40,000

Company Benefits
- Fully paid life insurance
- Medical, extended health and dental
- Short and long term disability

Correspondence
Mail or e-mail resume with cover letter
E-mail: dshield@sunrype.com

Part Time/Summer: Sun Rype Products regularly seeks candidates for part time and summer employment opportunities. The best time to apply is in March or April. Co-op students are often hired. These individuals may apply anytime.

The Canada Student Employment Guide

SUNDOG PRINTING LIMITED

1311 - 9 Avenue SW
Calgary, Alberta, T3C 0H9
Tel: (403) 264-8450   Fax: (403) 294-1496

Brenda Hawkins-Andrews, Human Resources
Internet: www.sundogprint.com

Sundog Printing Limited is Calgary's second largest offset printing company. They offer six colour printing, plus digital Indigo and Docutech.

Academic Fields
College: Accounting, Computer Science, Human Resources, Marketing/Sales, Secretarial
Bachelor of Arts: General, Business
Bachelor of Comm/Admin: Accounting, Finance
Bachelor of Science: Computer Science
Bachelor of Engineering: General, Computer Systems, Mechanical
Chartered Accounting: CGA - General/Finance
Masters: Business Administration

Critical Skills
Adaptable, Good Communication, Dependable, Diligent, Efficient, Enthusiastic, Leadership, Organized, Productive, Professional, Responsible, Good Writing Skills

Types of Positions
Junior Customer Service Rep.   Secretarial Staff
Accounting Department

Starting Salary
below $ 20,000 - 30,000 (depends on position)

Company Benefits
- Full benefits including dental and medical after 3 months probation

Correspondence
Mail or fax resume with cover letter

Part Time/Summer: Sundog Printing Limited occasionally looks for individuals for part time work, but does not hire people specifically for the summer months.

SUNOCO INC.

36 York Mills Road
North York, Ontario, M2P 2C5
Tel: (416) 733-7000   Fax: (416) 733-1233

Julia Anderson, Human Resources Advisor
Internet: www.suncor.com

Sunoco is one of the top petroleum refiners and marketers in Canada and a leader in providing high performing and environmentally friendly fuels and energy solutions to customers. Sunoco is part of Suncor Energy, a unique and sustainable Canadian integrated energy company dedicated to vigorous growth.

Academic Fields
College: Accounting, Administration, Computer Science
Bachelor of Arts: General, Business, Economics
Bachelor of Comm/Admin: Accounting, Finance, Marketing
Bachelor of Science: Computer Science
Bachelor of Engineering: Chemical, Electrical, Environmental Studies, Mechanical
Chartered Accounting: CA-Finance, CMA-Finance, CGA-Finance
Masters: Business Administration

Critical Skills
Adaptable, Dependable, Enthusiastic, Good Communication, Innovative, Leadership, Professional

Types of Positions
Administrator   Accounting Analyst
Business Analyst   Customer Service Rep.

Starting Salary
$ 36,000 - 42,000

Company Benefits
- Full benefits offered
- Opportunity for training as required

Correspondence
Mail or fax resume with cover letter

Part Time/Summer: Sunoco sometimes hires for part time and summer work. Potential summer jobs include accounting assistant, file clerk, junior engineer. January to March is the best time to apply.

The Canada Student Employment Guide

SUPREME TOOLING GROUP

2 Norelco Dr.
North York, Ontario, M9W 1P6
Tel: (416) 742-9600   Fax: (416) 742-8422

Bryan Crisp, Human Resources Coordinator

Supreme Tooling Group is a manufacturer of tooling and equipment for the automotive plastics industry. They employ approximately 150 individuals.

Academic Fields
College: General, Accounting, Administration, Business, Drafting/Architecture, Electronics Tech., Engineering Tech., Human Resources, Mechanical Tech.
Bachelor of Arts: General, Business, Economics, Psychology, Sociology/Social Work
Bachelor of Comm/Admin: General, Accounting, Finance
Bachelor of Science: General, Psychology
Bachelor of Engineering: General, Chemical, Design, Electrical, Industrial, Mechanical
Bachelor of Education: General
Chartered Accounting: CA-General, CMA-General, CGA-General
Masters: Business Administration, Engineering

Critical Skills
Analytical, Confident, Dependable, Good Communication, Efficient, Good With Figures, Manual Dexterity, Organized, Productive, Responsible, Good Writing Skills

Types of Positions
Quality Engineering   Project Engineering
Accounts Payable/Receiving   Payroll Clerk

Starting Salary
$ 25,000 - 40,000

Company Benefits
- Typical benefits package after 3 months
- Educational assistance, tuition refund
- Training as required or requested

Correspondence
Fax resume with cover letter

Part Time/Summer: Supreme Tooling Group occasionally seeks candidates for part time and summer employment. Potential jobs involve general help or labour.

SURREY MEMORIAL HOSPITAL

13750 96 Ave.
Surrey, British Columbia, V3V 1Z2
Tel: (604) 581-2211   Fax: (604) 585-5670

Elaine Ivanic, Human Resources

Surrey Memorial Hospital is a public healthcare facility in Surrey that offers acute and long term care. The hospital employs about 2,200 individuals in total.

Academic Fields
College: Accounting, Computer Science, Food/Nutrition, Human Resources, Nursing
Bachelor of Science: Food Sciences, Nursing (RN), Occupational Therapy, Pharmacy, Physiotherapy
Bachelor of Engineering: Computer Systems
Chartered Accounting: CA - General/Finance
Masters: Library Science

Critical Skills
Adaptable, Analytical, Confident, Dependable, Efficient, Flexible, Organized, Personable, Professional, Responsible, Good Writing Skills

Types of Positions
Food Services   Porter
Housekeeping   Linen Room

Starting Salary
$ 30,000 - 40,000

Company Benefits
- Full and part time employees receive medical, dental and extended benefits

Correspondence
Mail resume with cover letter

Part Time/Summer: Surrey Memorial Hospital does not generally hire for part time work, but occasionally looks for people in the summer months. Potential jobs are most likely those listed above. The best time to apply is in early Spring.

The Canada Student Employment Guide

SURREY PLACE CENTRE

2 Surrey Place
Toronto, Ontario, M5S 2C2
Tel: (416) 925-5141   Fax: (416) 923-8476

Sandra Y. Aiken, Director, Human Resources
Internet: www.surreyplace.on.ca

Surrey Place Centre is an interdisciplinary, community-based agency committed to enabling people with developmental disabilities and their families to enhance their quality of life through integrated service, research and education.

Academic Fields
College: Behaviour Science Tech., Communicative, Nursing
Bachelor of Arts: Psychology, Sociology/Social Work
Bachelor of Comm/Admin: Info Mgmt.
Bachelor of Science: Health Sciences, Nursing (RN), Occupational Therapy, Psychology
Chartered Accounting: CMA-General
Masters: Science (Social Work, Audiology, Psychology)

Critical Skills
Good Communication, Good Writing Skills, Team Player

Types of Positions
Service Coordinator   Research Assistant
Counsellor

Starting Salary
$ 36,000 - 42,000

Company Benefits
- Full health coverage
- Vision, dental, hearing, life insurance, pension
- Continuous in-house training and development

Correspondence
Mail resume with cover letter
E-mail: spc@toronto.planteteer.com

Part Time/Summer: Surrey Place Centre sometimes hires for part time employment, and regularly hires for summer opportunities. Potential positions are most likely to be clerical work, research assistants, or profession disciplines assistant. The best time to apply is in April.

CITY OF SURREY

14245 56th Avenue
Surrey, British Columbia, V3X 3A2
Tel: (604) 591-4117   Fax: (604) 591-4517

Human Resources
Internet: www.city.surrey.bc.ca

The City of Surrey is a municipal government in British Columbia.

Academic Fields
College: Accounting, Admin., Business, Communications, Comp. Sci., Drafting/Architecture, Electronics Tech., Engineering Tech., Graphic Arts, Human Res., Journalism, Law Clerk, Marketing/Sales, Nursing, Performing Arts, Recreation Studies, Secretarial, Security/Law, Travel, Urban Planning
Bachelor of Arts: Business, Fine Arts, History, Journalism, Political Sci., Public Rel., Recreation Studies
Bachelor of Comm/Admin: Accounting, Finance, Marketing, Public Admin.
Bachelor of Science: Agriculture, Biology, Computer Science, Environmental Studies, Geography, Kinesiology, Nursing (RN), Occupational Therapy
Bachelor of Laws: General, Corporate, Real Estate
Bachelor of Engineering: General, Civil, Comp. Syst., Design, Elec., Environ. Studies, Geotechnical, Mechanical, Transportation, Water Res., Bach. of Architecture, Bach. of Landscape Arch.
Bachelor of Education: Adult Education, Childhood, Physical, Special
Chartered Accounting: CA - General/Finance, CGA/CMA - General/Finance
Masters: Business Administration, Science, Engineering, Education, Library Science

Critical Skills
Most skills considered important

Types of Positions
Labourer   Clerk Typist 2

Starting Salary
$ 25,000 - 30,000 (depends on position)

Company Benefits
- Full medical, dental and health benefits

Correspondence
Mail resume with cover letter
E-mail: humanresources@city.surrey.bc.ca

Part Time/Summer: The City occasionally hires for part time and summer work.

The Canada Student Employment Guide

SWIFT CURRENT HEALTH DISTRICT

429 4th Avenue N.E.
Swift Current, Saskatchewan, S9H 2J9
Tel: (306) 778-5100   Fax: (306) 773-9513

Jeff Grant, Director of Human Resources
Internet: ww.scdhb.sk.ca

Swift Current Health District is a multi-faceted health care delivery organization dedicated to excellence in acute care, long term care, home care, and community health services. The district employs approximately 1,000 individuals.

Academic Fields
College: Administration, Human Resources, Information Systems, Emergency/Paramedic, Home Care, Laboratory Tech., Nursing (RN/RNA), Radiology Tech., Social Work
Bachelor of Arts: Gerontology, Psychology, Sociology/Social Work
Bachelor of Comm/Admin: Accounting, Finance, Human Resources, Info Mgmt.
Bachelor of Science: Food Sci., Health Sci., Nursing (RN), Occupational Therapy, Pharmacy, Physiotherapy
Masters: Business Administration

Critical Skills
Adaptable, Confident, Dependable, Diligent, Diplomatic, Efficient, Good Communication, Leadership, Organized, Patient, Personable, Productive, Professional, Responsible

Types of Positions
Nutrition Services Aide   Laundry Aide
Housekeeping Aide

Starting Salary
$ 20,000 - 25,000

Company Benefits
- Dental, pension, group life
- Disability insurance, employee assistance
- Several on-site services (topics depend on need)

Correspondence
Mail resume with cover letter or apply through their web site

Part Time/Summer: Swift Current Health District regularly seeks candidates for part time work and rarely hires for the summer. Potential jobs in the summer include aides (laundry, housekeeping, nutrition), registered nurse, special care aide, and home care aide. The best time to apply is in April.

SYDNEY STEEL CORPORATION

1 Inglis Street, P.O. Box 1450
Sydney, Nova Scotia, B1P 6K5
Tel: (902) 564-7992   Fax: (902) 564-7903

Fred James, Human Resources
Internet: www.sysco.ns.ca

Sydney Steel Corporation is a steel manufacturing company that produces rails and semi-finished products. The firm employs about 600 people.

Academic Fields
College: Drafting/Architecture, Electronics Tech., Human Resources, Mechanical Tech., Secretarial, Security/Law
Bachelor of Comm/Admin: Accounting, Finance, Info Mgmt.
Bachelor of Science: Chemistry, Computer Science, Environmental Studies
Bachelor of Engineering: Civil, Computer Systems, Electrical, Environmental Studies, Mechanical
Chartered Accounting: CA-General

Critical Skills
Adaptable, Good Communication, Dependable, Diligent, Diplomatic, Efficient, Enthusiastic, Logical, Organized, Personable, Productive, Professional

Types of Positions
Accounting   Human Resources
Computer Services   Metallurgical

Starting Salary
$ 25,000 - 30,000

Company Benefits
- Full medical and hospital
- Pension plan
- Training and development opportunities are available

Correspondence
Mail resume with cover letter

Part Time/Summer: Sydney Steel Corporation does not hire for part time or summer work due to recent downsizing.

The Canada Student Employment Guide

SYMANTEC CORPORATION

895 Don Mills Rd., Suite 700
Toronto, Ontario, M3C 1W3
Tel: (416) 441-3676   Fax: (416) 441-0333

Wendy Ducheck, HR Department
Internet: www.symantec.com

Symantec, a world leader in Internet security technology, provides a broad range of content and network security solutions to individuals and enterprises. The company is a leading provider of virus protection, risk management, Internet content and e-mail filtering, and mobile code detection technologies to customers.

Academic Fields
College: Administration, Communications, Computer Science, Graphic Arts, Human Resources, Secretarial
Bachelor of Arts: Business, Economics, English, Journalism
Bachelor of Comm/Admin: Accounting, Finance, Marketing, Info Mgmt.
Bachelor of Science: Computer Science, Mathematics, Psychology
Bachelor of Engineering: Computer Systems, Electrical
Chartered Accounting: CA-Finance
Masters: Business Administration, Arts, Science, Engineering

Critical Skills
Adaptable, Analytical, Good Communication, Creative, Dependable, Flexible, Innovative, Leadership, Logical, Professional

Types of Positions
Technical Support Rep.   Customer Service Rep.
Administrative Assistant   Facilities Coordinator

Starting Salary
$ 25,000 - 35,000

Company Benefits
- Extended health, dental, vision, RRSP program
- Tuition reimbursement, health club reimbursement

Correspondence
Mail or e-mail resume with cover letter
E-mail: jobs@symantec.com

Part Time/Summer: Symantec Corporation does not generally for part time work, but occasionally looks for people in the summer. Potential jobs are most likely those above. The best time to apply is in late February.

SYNCRUDE CANADA LTD.

P.O. Bag 4023, M.D. 3200
Fort McMurray, Alberta, T9H 3H5
Tel: (780) 790-6189   Fax: (780) 790-6186

Pat Cobbledick, Campus Recruiter
Internet: www.syncrude.com

Syncrude Canada is the world's largest producer of synthetic crude oil, producing 13% of Canada's petroleum requirements or 72 million barrels of light sweet crude oil annually. This activity generates over 16,000 jobs indirectly across Canada. In addition, the company spends more than a billion dollars a year on purchased goods, services and salaries. Syncrude currently produces over 200,000 barrels per day, with a proposed expansion towards the end of the decade to 300,000 barrels per day.

Academic Fields
College: Computer Science, Drafting/Architecture, Laboratory Tech.
Bachelor of Comm/Admin: Accounting
Bachelor of Science: Chemistry, Computer Science
Bachelor of Engineering: Chemical, Computer Systems, Electrical, Geotechnical, Mechanical, Mining
Chartered Accounting: CMA-General

Critical Skills
Creative, Flexible, Good Writing Skills, Organized, Personable, Productive

Types of Positions
Chemical Engineering Graduate
Mechanical Engineering Graduate
Mining Engineering Graduate

Starting Salary
$ 30,000 - 40,000

Company Benefits
- Flexible benefits program

Correspondence
Mail resume with cover letter
E-mail: cobbledick.pat@syncrude.com

Part Time/Summer: Syncrude Canada sometimes looks for individuals for part time employment, and regularly seeks candidates for summer opportunities. Co-op programs are offered year round. Individuals should apply to postings on campus in the month of September.

The Canada Student Employment Guide

TALISMAN ENERGY INC.

855 - 3rd Street S.W., Suite 3400
Calgary, Alberta, T2P 5C5
Tel: (403) 237-1234   Fax: (403) 237-1902

Recruiter
Internet: www.talisman-energy.com

Talisman Energy is a senior oil and gas producer and explorer. Talisman explores and operates in the Western Canada Basin, Ontario, the North Sea and Indonesia. Talisman also has high impact exploration programs in a number of other international basins.

Academic Fields
College: Accounting, Administration, Engineering Tech.
Bachelor of Arts: Business
Bachelor of Comm/Admin: Accounting, Finance, Marketing
Bachelor of Science: Environmental Studies, Geology
Bachelor of Laws: Corporate
Bachelor of Engineering: Chemical, Civil, Mechanical
Chartered Accounting: CA - General/Finance, CGA/CMA - General/Finance
Masters: Business Administration, Science, Engineering

Critical Skills
Adaptable, Analytical, Good Communication, Confident, Creative, Decisive, Dependable, Efficient, Enthusiastic, Flexible, Good With Figures, Innovative, Leadership, Logical, Organized, Personable, Productive, Professional, Responsible, Writing Skills

Types of Positions
Engineer In Training   New Grad Geologist

Starting Salary
$ 30,000 - 50,000

Company Benefits
- Flexible benefits system
- Extensive training and development program

Correspondence
Mail resume with cover letter

Part Time/Summer: Talisman Energy sometimes seeks candidates for part time jobs, and regularly looks for individuals for summer opportunities. The best time to apply is in January or February.

TCG INTERNATIONAL INC.

4710 Kingsway, Suite 2800
Burnaby, British Columbia, V5H 4M2
Tel: (604) 431-2300   Fax: (604) 431-2279

Jim Mercer, Human Resources
Internet: www.tcgi.com

TCG International has its operations established in two major industries - the automotive after-market and wireless communications. TCG International is a world leader in the repair and replacement of automotive glass. The company also has interests in manufacturing and distribution of automotive glass and related products. In addition, TCG International operates in the wireless communications business. TCG employs more than 4,500 people.

Academic Fields
College: Accounting, Administration, Advertising, Business, Computer Science
Bachelor of Arts: Business
Bachelor of Comm/Admin: General, Accounting, Finance, Marketing, Info Mgmt.
Chartered Accounting: CMA-Finance, CGA-Finance

Critical Skills
Adaptable, Analytical, Confident, Creative, Decisive, Dependable, Diligent, Good Communication, Efficient, Good Writing Skills, Innovative, Leadership, Logical, Organized, Professional

Types of Positions
Accounting   Computer Science
Purchasing   Retail
Wholesale

Starting Salary
$ 20,000 - 30,000

Company Benefits
- Health and dental coverage, life insurance
- In-house training

Correspondence
Mail resume with cover letter

Part Time/Summer: TCG International sometimes looks for candidates to work part time and fill summer positions. Potential jobs are most likely to involve junior clerical, or warehousing positions. The best time to apply is in June.

The Canada Student Employment Guide

TCT LOGISTICS

2070 Logan Ave.
Winnipeg, Manitoba, R2R 0H9
Tel: (204) 631-1284   Fax: (204) 694-7021

David Rushforth, Manager of Human Resources
Internet: www.tctlogistics.com

TCT Logistics is one of Canada's leading providers of transportation, storage and distributive services for grocery products, specializing in temperature-sensitive freight. The company is dedicated to supply chain management, providing efficient, fully integrated logistics services in an industry that is rapidly consolidating.

Academic Fields
College: Accounting, Administration, Business, Computer Science, Human Resources, Marketing/Sales
Bachelor of Arts: Business
Bachelor of Comm/Admin: General, Accounting, Finance, Marketing, Info Mgmt.
Bachelor of Engineering: Civil, Computer Systems, Industrial, Transportation
Chartered Accounting: CA - General/Finance, CGA/CMA - General/Finance
Masters: Business Administration

Critical Skills
Adaptable, Analytical, Confident, Creative, Decisive, Dependable, Diligent, Diplomatic, Efficient, Enthusiastic, Flexible, Good With Figures, Innovative, Leadership, Organized, Personable, Productive, Professional, Responsible

Types of Positions
Sales/Marketing Rep.   Rate Audit
Pricing Analyst   Billing Clerk
Accounts Receivable   Accounts Payable

Starting Salary
$ 20,000 - 25,000

Company Benefits
- Comprehensive medical and dental
- Training programs developed as need arises

Correspondence
Mail resume with cover letter
E-mail: info@tctlogistics.com

Part Time/Summer: TCT Logistics occasionally looks for candidates for part time and summer employment. Potential jobs in the summer include dock worker or data entry. The best time to apply is in May.

TD WATERHOUSE INVESTOR SERVICES (CANADA) INC.

TD Bank, P.O. Box 1, TD Centre
Toronto, Ontario, M5K 1A2
Tel: (416) 944-6535   Fax: (416) 982-2266

Human Resources
Internet: tdbank.ca

TD Waterhouse Investor Services (Canada) Inc. is a discount brokerage firm and floatation company. With approximately 35 branches across the country, in Ontario they have offices in Toronto, Kitchener, London, Ottawa, Sudbury, Kingston, Hamilton and Windsor. They employ over 700 people across Canada.

Academic Fields
College: General, Accounting, Administration, Business, Computer Science, Electronics Tech., Human Resources, Insurance, Law Clerk, Marketing/Sales, Secretarial
Bachelor of Arts: General, Business, Economics, English, Political Science, Public Relations
Bachelor of Comm/Admin: General, Accounting, Finance, Marketing, Info Mgmt.
Bachelor of Science: Actuarial, Mathematics
Chartered Accounting: CA - General/Finance, CGA/CMA - General/Finance
Masters: Business Administration, Arts

Critical Skills
Adaptable, Analytical, Confident, Good Communication, Decisive, Dependable, Enthusiastic, Good Writing Skills, Creative, Flexible, Innovative, Good With Figures, Leadership, Personable

Types of Positions
Investment Representative

Starting Salary
$ 25,000 - 30,000

Company Benefits
- Health and dental included in the benefits package
- Insurance, short and long term disability

Correspondence
Mail, fax, e-mail, or submit resume & cover letter in person

Part Time/Summer: TD Waterhouse Investor Services (Canada) regularly hires part time individuals, but does not hire for the summer. The best time to apply for part time opportunities is in July and August.

The Canada Student Employment Guide

TECK CORP.

200 Burrard St., Suite 600
Vancouver, British Columbia, V6C 3L9
Tel: (604) 687-1117   Fax: (604) 640-6100

M.J. Guillard, Human Resources
Internet: www.teckcorp.ca

Teck Corp. is a mining company involved in the exploration of gold, copper, coal, zinc and lead. The firm is partially owned by Temagami Mining Co. Ltd. of Toronto, Ontario. Teck Corp has an employee base of 3,259 individuals.

Academic Fields
College: Administration, Computer Science, Drafting/Architecture, Human Resources
Bachelor of Arts: Business
Bachelor of Comm/Admin: General, Accounting
Bachelor of Science: Computer Science, Geology
Bachelor of Engineering: Mining
Chartered Accounting: CA-Finance, CMA-Finance, CGA-Finance
Masters: Library Science

Critical Skills
Adaptable, Analytical, Good Communication, Confident, Creative, Decisive, Dependable, Diligent, Diplomatic, Efficient, Enthusiastic, Flexible, Good With Figures, Innovative, Leadership, Logical, Organized, Patient, Personable, Productive, Professional, Responsible, Good Writing Skills

Types of Positions
Information Systems   Human Resources
Accounting

Starting Salary
$ 25,000 - 30,000

Company Benefits
- Medical, dental, vision care, life insurance
- Long and short term disability
- 3 weeks vacation

Correspondence
Mail resume with cover letter

Part Time/Summer: Teck Corp. occasionally looks for individuals for part time jobs, and regularly seeks candidates for summer employment. Potential summer jobs are most likely those listed above. The best time to apply is in February.

TEKLOGIX INC.

2100 Meadowvale Blvd.
Mississauga, Ontario, L5N 7J9
Tel: (905) 813-9900   Fax: (905) 812-6300

Cheryl Caswell, Human Resources Representative
Internet: www.teklogix.com

Teklogix is a wireless data communications provider, offering a network for real-time communications. Their wireless systems have created major opportunities for reducing distribution costs, improving operational efficiencies, meeting customer expectations for just-in-time order fulfillment, and achieving higher asset utilization.

Academic Fields
College: General, Accounting, Administration, Business, Engineering Tech., Human Resources
Bachelor of Arts: General, Business
Bachelor of Comm/Admin: General, Accounting, Finance, Marketing, Info Mgmt.
Bachelor of Science: Computer Science, Mathematics
Bachelor of Engineering: General, Computer Systems, Design, Electrical, Industrial, Mechanical
Chartered Accounting: CA - General/Finance, CMA-Finance, CGA-Finance

Critical Skills
Adaptable, Good Communication, Confident, Creative, Decisive, Dependable, Efficient, Enthusiastic, Flexible, Innovative, Leadership, Personable, Professional, Responsible, Good Writing Skills

Types of Positions
Engineering   Materials

Starting Salary
Depends on position

Company Benefits
- Basic life, health, and dental
- Tuition reimbursement, profit sharing
- Internal and external training

Correspondence
Mail or fax resume with cover letter

Part Time/Summer: Teklogix occasionally hires for part time work, and regularly hires in the summer. Potential jobs are co-op engineering, materials handler or shipper and receiver. The best time to apply is in January.

The Canada Student Employment Guide

TELDON INTERNATIONAL INC.

3500 Viking Way
Richmond, British Columbia, V6N 1N6
Tel: (604) 273-4500   Fax: (604) 273-6100

Human Resources
Internet: www.teldon.com

Teldon International is a commercial printing, and lithographic organization in Richmond, British Columbia. The company was established in 1975, and employs of 170 individuals to work in various sectors in the printing and publishing industry.

Academic Fields
College: Printing
Bachelor of Arts: Business, Journalism
Bachelor of Comm/Admin: General, Marketing
Bachelor of Engineering: Computer Systems

Critical Skills
Adaptable, Confident, Dependable, Diligent, Diplomatic, Enthusiastic, Good Writing Skills, Good Communication, Leadership, Organized, Personable, Professional

Types of Positions
Order Entry   Customer Service
Production

Starting Salary
$ 20,000 - 25,000

Company Benefits
- Full benefit package after 3 months full time
- On-the-job training
- Apprentice type program for technical jobs

Correspondence
Mail or fax resume with cover letter

Part Time/Summer: Teldon International sometimes seeks candidates for part time and summer employment. However, there is presently no summer job opportunities.

TELEBEC LTÉE

7151 Jean Talon East
Anjou, Québec, H1M 3N8
Tel: (514) 493-5394   Fax: (514) 493-5352

Human Resources

Telebec Ltée is a telecommunications company in Quebec, with its head office in Anjou, Québec. The company has offices in Montreal, and Val Dor, and Bécancour, among other locations across the province. Telebec Ltée is fully owned by Bell Québec.

Academic Fields
College: Computer Science
Bachelor of Arts: Business, Communications
Bachelor of Comm/Admin: Marketing, Info Mgmt.
Bachelor of Engineering: Computer Systems, Electrical
Masters: Business Administration, Engineering, Marketing

Critical Skills
Analytical, Creative, Decisive, Efficient, Enthusiastic, Flexible, Good Communication, Innovative, Leadership, Organized, Persuasive, Professional, Responsible

Types of Positions
Non management positions
Management positions

Starting Salary
Depends on position

Company Benefits
- Full package comparable to other companies
- Assistance program

Correspondence
Mail resume with cover letter

Part Time/Summer: Telebec occasionally looks for individuals for part time employment, and regularly seeks people for the summer months. Potential jobs in the summer are in the office, engineering department, or involve being an information technician. The best time to apply is in the Spring.

TELEGRAPH JOURNAL

210 Crown Street, P.O. Box 2350
Saint John, New Brunswick, E2L 3V8
Tel: (506) 648-2958   Fax: (506) 635-6107

Linda Fleury, Human Resources
Internet: www.telegraphjournal.com

The Telegraph Journal is involved in the newspaper industry. Located in Saint John, New Brunswick, the company employs a total of 220 full time and part time individuals to work in various capacities in the print media industry.

Academic Fields
College: Accounting, Advertising, Computer Science
Bachelor of Arts: Business, Journalism
Bachelor of Science: Computer Science
Bachelor of Engineering: Computer Systems

Critical Skills
Adaptable, Dependable, Diligent, Diplomatic, Flexible, Personable, Professional, Good Communication

Types of Positions
Business Office   Newsroom
Circulation

Starting Salary
Depends on position

Company Benefits
- Complete medical, dental and health insurance
- Group home and auto insurance
- Reduction on aquatic centre membership

Correspondence
Mail resume with cover letter

Part Time/Summer: The Telegraph Journal sometimes seeks candidates for part time and summer employment. Potential positions include collections and credit clerk, reporter, and motor route drivers.

TELESAT CANADA

1601 Telesat Court
Gloucester, Ontario, K1B 5P4
Tel: (613) 748-0123   Fax: (613) 748-8865

Human Resources
Internet: www.telesat.ca

Telesat Canada is a world leader in satellite communications, satellite operations and consulting. The company operates a fleet of satellites for the provision of broadcast distribution and telecommunications services throughout the Americas. For more than thirty years, Telesat's name has been synonymous with high-quality satellite communications. In 1972, the company made history with the launch of the Anik A1 - an event that inaugurated the age of satellite communications. The company employs approximately 500 people.

Academic Fields
College: Electronics Technology
Bachelor of Comm/Admin: Info Mgmt.
Bachelor of Science: Computer Science, Mathematics
Bachelor of Engineering: Electrical, Aerospace
Masters: Business Administration, Engineering

Critical Skills
Analytical, Creative, Dependable, Flexible, Good Writing Skills, Good Communication, Personable

Types of Positions
Technologist   Satellite Engineer
Systems Programmer

Starting Salary
$ 30,000 - 35,000 (Tech.) /
$ 40,000 - 45,000 (Engineer, Computer Programmer)

Company Benefits
- Medical, dental, vision care
- 3 weeks vacation, stock purchase program

Correspondence
Mail, fax or e-mail resume with cover letter
E-mail: resumes@telesat.ca

Part Time/Summer: Telesat Canada sometimes hires for part time work and regularly hires for the summer. Jobs in the summer include administrative support, engineering, or computer science. The best time to apply is in the early Spring.

TELUS CORPORATION

10020 - 100 Street, 32 Floor
Edmonton, Alberta, T5J 0N5
Tel: (403) 493-4728   Fax: (403) 498-7319

Heather Rutkowski, Human Resources
Internet: www.telus.com

Telus Corporation, a widely held public company, is a leading Canadian telecommunications and information management services company. Through its subsidiaries, Telus manages assets of $3.5 billion. Subsidiaries of Telus include AGT Limited, which provides voice, data and video telecommunications services; AGT Mobility which is a leading supplier of wireless mobile communications; AGT Directory which publishes white and Yellow pages and Canadian Mobility Products which provides cellular paging equipment. Telus employs over 7,700 people.

Academic Fields
College: Administration, Business, Communications, Human Res., Journalism, Marketing/Sales, Secretarial
Bachelor of Arts: Business, Public Relations
Bachelor of Comm/Admin: General, Accounting, Finance, Marketing
Chartered Accounting: CA - General/Finance, CMA-Finance, CGA-Finance
Masters: Business Administration

Critical Skills
Creative, Decisive, Flexible, Good Communication, Innovative, Leadership

Types of Positions
Finance   reasury
Corporate Communications

Starting Salary
$ 30,000 - 40,000

Company Benefits
- Medical, dental, vacation, sick leave
- Pension, share purchase plan, group RRSP
- After hours education program (100% books and tuition)

Correspondence
Mail resume with cover letter

Part Time/Summer: Telus sometimes seeks candidates for part time and summer employment opportunities. Potential jobs include administration support, or finance trainee. The best time to apply is in April.

THE ARTHRITIS SOCIETY

1700 - 393 University Ave.
Toronto, Ontario, M5G 1E6
Tel: (416) 979-7228   Fax: (416) 979-8366

Ann Clancy, Director Human Resources
Internet: www.arthritis.ca

The mission of The Arthritis Society is to search for the underlying causes and subsequent cures for arthritis and to promote the best possible care and treatment for people with arthritis. They employ approximately 250 individuals.

Academic Fields
College: Administration, Communications, Marketing/Sales, Fund Raising
Bachelor of Arts: Business, Sociology/Social Work
Bachelor of Science: Occupational Therapy, Physiotherapy

Critical Skills
Adaptable, Dependable, Good Communication, Good With Figures, Good Writing Skills, Leadership, Personable

Types of Positions
Administration
Entry Level Fundraising
Marketing & Communications

Starting Salary
$ 25,000 - 30,000

Company Benefits
- Standard benefits package, health, dental, pension, short and long term disability
- 3 weeks vacation to start for permanent employees
- Training opportunities exist

Correspondence
Fax or e-mail resume with cover letter

Part Time/Summer: The Arthritis Society regularly hires for part time work and occasionally hires for the summer. They usually bring summer students in through HRDC programs. They are bound by their deadlines.

Co-op/Internship: They have no formal internship or co-op programs, however, they are open to ideas.

The Canada Student Employment Guide

THE BARN FRUIT MARKETS INC.

2075 Fairview St.
Burlington, Ontario, L7R 4E8
Tel: (905) 639-1660   Fax: N/A

Human Resources

The Barn Fruit Markets is a wholesaler and retailer grocery store. The company's head office is in Burlington, Ontario.

Academic Fields
College: Accounting, Advertising, Cooking/Culinary, Food/Nutrition, Human Resources, Marketing/Sales, Security/Law
Bachelor of Arts: Business, Sociology/Social Work
Bachelor of Comm/Admin: Accounting, Finance, Marketing, Info Mgmt.
Chartered Accounting: CA-Finance, CMA - General/Finance

Critical Skills
Adaptable, Analytical, Creative, Decisive, Efficient, Enthusiastic, Flexible, Good Communication, Good With Figures, Good Writing Skills, Leadership, Organized, Patient, Personable, Professional, Responsible

Types of Positions
Human Resources   Accounting
Payroll   Marketing

Starting Salary
$ 20,000 - 30,000

Company Benefits
- Standard benefits
- Training dependant upon career path

Correspondence
Mail resume with cover letter

Part Time/Summer: The Barn Fruit Markets regularly seeks candidates for part time work and during the summer months. Potential jobs exist in all positions. The best time to apply is in April or May.

THE CO-OPERATORS

Priory Square, 130 MacDonell St.
Guelph, Ontario, N1H 6P8
Tel: (519) 824-4400   Fax: (519) 767-6615

OE Contact Centre
Internet: www.cooperators.ca

The Co-operators is a group of Canadian companies focusing on insurance, which also provide financial security products, investment counselling, and property management and development services. The company employs 3,100 people across Canada.

Academic Fields
College: Administration, Human Res., Info Syst. CAD Autocad, Graphic Arts, Journalism, Legal Assistant
Bachelor of Arts: Business, Economics, Public Relations, Sociology/Social Work
Bachelor of Comm/Admin: Accounting, Finance, Human Resources, Marketing
Bachelor of Science: Actuarial, Computer Science, Occupational Therapy
Bachelor of Engineering: Computer Systems
Bachelor of Education: Adult Education
Chartered Accounting: CA-General, CMA-General, CGA-General

Critical Skills
Adaptable, Analytical, Creative, Decisive, Dependable, Diplomatic, Enthusiastic, Flexible, Good Communication, Good Writing Skills, Innovative, Productive, Professional, Responsible

Types of Positions
Finance   Accounting
Personal Lines

Starting Salary
$ 20,000 - 25,000

Company Benefits
- Competitive benefits package

Correspondence
Mail, fax, e-mail resume with cover letter, or apply through web site

Part Time/Summer: The Co-operators occasionally hires for part time and summer employment. April and May is the best time to apply.

Co-op/Internship: Most internships are through Career Edge.

THE GARLAND GROUP

1177 Kamato Rd.
Mississauga, Ontario, L4W 1X4
Tel: (905) 624-0260   Fax: (905) 624-5669

Elizabeth O'Keefe, HR Coordinator
Internet: www.garland-group.com

The Garland Group is a manufacturer of commercial cooking equipment including ovens and ranges. The company employs approximately 400 individuals.

Academic Fields
College: Accounting, Administration, Communications, Human Resources, Purchasing, Secretarial, CAD Autocad, Computer Science, Engineering Tech., Mechanical Tech., Welding
Bachelor of Arts: Business
Bachelor of Comm/Admin: Accounting, Finance, Human Resources
Bachelor of Engineering: General, Civil, Design, Electrical

Critical Skills
Dependable, Efficient, Enthusiastic, Flexible, Good Communication, Good Writing Skills, Logical, Organized, Professional, Responsible

Types of Positions
Plant (Steel Room or Production)   Customer Service

Starting Salary
$ 30,000 - 35,000

Company Benefits
- There are a variety of benefit plans
- Currently offering training in health and safety, forklift operations, and leadership

Correspondence
Mail, fax resume with cover letter, or submit in person

Part Time/Summer: The Garland Group does not hire part time workers, but regularly hires for the summer months. Potential jobs include office positions (accounting, purchasing, human resources etc.) and general labour in the plant. The best time to apply is from February to April.

THE MCELHANNEY GROUP LTD.

L100 - 780 Beatty St.
Vancouver, British Columbia, V6B 2M1
Tel: (604) 683-8521   Fax: (604) 683-4350

Human Resources
Internet: www.mcelhanney.com

McElhanney is an employee-owned Canadian consulting company specializing in engineering, surveying, mapping/GIS and technical services. The company has fifteen national offices located throughout British Columbia and Alberta and two international locations. The company employs 435 individuals in Canada.

Academic Fields
College: CAD Autocad, Engineering Tech., Geomatics
Bachelor of Engineering: Civil, Transportation, Geomatics, Survey Technology, Mapping

Critical Skills
Analytical, Creative, Dependable, Enthusiastic, Good Communication, Organized, Productive, Professional

Types of Positions
Survey Assistant   Junior Draftsperson
Clerk   Instrument Person
Mapping Technician   Engineer-In-Training

Starting Salary
Salaries are negotiable

Company Benefits
- Comprehensive benefits package, competitive salaries, matching RRSP contributions
- Will provide training, seminars and workshops for those required to upgrade skills

Correspondence
E-mail resume with cover letter
E-mail: humanresources@mcelhanney.com

Part Time/Summer: The McElhanney Group Ltd. rarely seeks candidates for part time work, but regularly hires for summer employment. The best time to apply is April to June.

THOMAS & BETTS LTÉE

700 av Thomas
Iberville, Québec, J2X 2M9
Tel: (514) 347-5318   Fax: (514) 347-1976

Human Resources

Thomas & Betts Ltée is engaged in the business of electrical machinery equipment and supplies. The company's head office is located in Iberville, Québec.

Academic Fields
College: General, Accounting, Administration, Electronics Tech., Human Resources, Industrial Design, Marketing/Sales, Secretarial
Bachelor of Arts: General, Business
Bachelor of Comm/Admin: General, Accounting, Marketing, Info Mgmt.
Bachelor of Science: General
Bachelor of Engineering: Electrical, Industrial, Mechanical
Chartered Accounting: CMA-Finance, CGA-General

Critical Skills
Adaptable, Decisive, Diplomatic, Enthusiastic, Flexible, Good Communication, Good Writing Skills, Leadership, Logical

Types of Positions
Various Positions

Starting Salary
$ 20,000 - 30,000 (with a college diploma)

Company Benefits
- Dental, medical and life insurance

Correspondence
Mail or fax resume with cover letter

Part Time/Summer: Thomas & Betts Ltée occasionally looks for individuals for part time employment, and regularly seeks people for summer opportunities. All entry positions may be potentially filled during the summer months. The best time to apply is in April.

THOMAS COOK GROUP (CANADA) LTD.

100 Yonge Street, 15th Floor
Toronto, Ontario, M5C 2W1
Tel: (416) 359-3700   Fax: (416) 359-3671

Human Resources

Thomas Cook Group is a leading international travel and financial services group providing services to their customers at more than 3,000 locations around the world. Thomas Cook employs over 13,000 staff world-wide and services to some 20 million customers each year.

Academic Fields
College: General, Accounting, Business, Communications, Hospitality, Human Resources, Marketing/Sales, Travel/Tourism
Bachelor of Arts: General
Bachelor of Comm/Admin: Accounting, Finance, Marketing, Info Mgmt.

Critical Skills
Adaptable, Creative, Diligent, Enthusiastic, Flexible, Leadership, Innovative, Good Communication, Personable, Persuasive, Productive, Professional, Responsible

Types of Positions
Travel Counsellor   Customer Service Rep.
Administrative Asst.   Accounting Clerk

Starting Salary
$ 20,000 - 25,000

Company Benefits
- Competitive benefit package

Correspondence
Mail resume with cover letter

Part Time/Summer: Thomas Cook sometimes hires for part time and summer opportunities. The best time to apply is in March and April.

THOMAS J. LIPTON

160 Bloor Street East, Suite 1500
Toronto, Ontario, M4W 3R2
Tel: (416) 964-7255   Fax: (416) 964-0294

Human Resources Department

Thomas J. Lipton is a food manufacturer of a wide range of consumer products. The company prepares many goods such as dried and dehydrated fruits, vegetables and soup mixes, shortening, table oils, margarine, food preparations, and a wide range of other related products. Employing more than 800 people in the Toronto region, a number of these individuals work for the firm on a part time basis.

Academic Fields
College: Computer Science, Food/Nutrition, Laboratory Tech.
Bachelor of Comm/Admin: Accounting, Finance, Marketing
Bachelor of Science: General, Computer Science, Food Sciences
Bachelor of Engineering: General, Mechanical
Chartered Accounting: CMA - General/Finance, CGA - General/Finance
Masters: Business Administration

Critical Skills
Creative, Flexible, Innovative, Team Oriented

Types of Positions
Assistant Brand Manager   Financial Analyst

Starting Salary
$ 30,000 - 40,000

Company Benefits
- Comprehensive benefit package

Correspondence
Mail resume with cover letter

Part Time/Summer: Thomas J. Lipton sometimes hires for part time and summer positions, however both these opportunities are very rare.

THOMPSON'S MOVING AND STORAGE

P.O. Box 670
Middleton, Nova Scotia, B0S 1P0
Tel: (902) 825-3464   Fax: (902) 825-4635

Kevin Matheson, Human Resources

Thompson's Moving and Storage is engaged in the business of moving services for individuals and businesses in Nova Scotia. The company is located in the city of Middleton in Nova Scotia.

Academic Fields
College: Accounting, Administration, Advertising, Business, Communications, Computer Science, Marketing/Sales, Secretarial, Statistics
Bachelor of Arts: General, Business, English, Public Relations, Sociology/Social Work, Statistics
Bachelor of Comm/Admin: General, Accounting, Finance, Marketing, Public Admin.
Bachelor of Science: General, Computer Science, Health Sciences, Mathematics
Bachelor of Engineering: General, Computer Systems, Industrial, Materials Science, Mechanical, Transportation
Bachelor of Education: General
Masters: Business Administration, Science

Critical Skills
Adaptable, Good Communication, Confident, Creative, Decisive, Dependable, Diligent, Diplomatic, Flexible, Good With Figures, Innovative, Leadership, Responsible, Good Writing Skills

Types of Positions
Freight Dispatch   Accountant
Payroll Administrator   Receptionist
Stock Room Manager   Truck Driver

Starting Salary
$ 20,000 - 25,000

Company Benefits
- Health, dental, pension plan
- 2 weeks vacation, sick days

Correspondence
Submit resume and cover letter in person

Part Time/Summer: Thompson's Moving and Storage sometimes hires for part time work and regularly hires for the summer. Summer jobs mostly involve moving and storage duties. The best time to apply is in late June.

The Canada Student Employment Guide

THOMSON - CSF SYSTEMS CANADA INC.

49 Auriga Dr.
Ottawa, Ontario, K2E 8A1
Tel: (613) 723-7000   Fax: (613) 723-5600

Stanley M. Janas, Manager, Human Resources

Thomson - CSF Systems Canada is one of the country's leading defence companies specializing in the areas of command, control, communications, and countermines. Their area of expertise includes navigation, radar, robotics, command and control, communications, countermines, real-time software, and integrated logistics support. The firm has a staff of 80 persons.

Academic Fields
College: Administration, Computer Science, Human Resources, Mechanical Tech.
Bachelor of Comm/Admin: Finance
Bachelor of Science: Computer Science
Bachelor of Engineering: Computer Systems, Design, Electrical, Mechanical
Chartered Accounting: CGA-Finance
Masters: Engineering

Critical Skills
Adaptable, Analytical, Creative, Flexible, Good Communication, Good Writing Skills, Leadership, Organized, Productive, Professional, Responsible

Types of Positions
Junior Programmer   Software Analyst
Junior Software Designer

Starting Salary
$ 25,000 - 30,000 (college grad) /
$ 30,000 - 40,000 (university grad)

Company Benefits
- Medical, dental, life insurance
- RRSP, flexible hours, bonus plan
- Formal training program, on-the-job training

Correspondence
Mail or e-mail resume with cover letter
E-mail: sjanas@thomson-csf.ca

Part Time/Summer: Thomson - CSF Systems Canada occasionally looks for people for part time and summer work. Potential jobs include secretarial replacement, computer trainee, or manual labourer. The best time to apply is in March.

THUNDER BAY REGIONAL HOSPITAL

460 Court St. N.
Thunder Bay, Ontario, P7A 4X6
Tel: (807) 343-6724   Fax: (807) 343-7179

Human Resources Department

Thunder Bay Regional Hospital is a general medical and surgical hospital serving the Thunder Bay community.

Academic Fields
College: Accounting, Child Care, Computer Science, Electronics Tech., Emergency/Paramedic, Engineering Tech., Food/Nutrition, Human Resources, Nursing, Radiology Tech.
Bachelor of Comm/Admin: Accounting, Info Mgmt.
Bachelor of Science: Chemistry, Computer Science, Health Sciences, Nursing (RN), Occupational Therapy, Pharmacy, Physiotherapy
Bachelor of Engineering: Computer Systems
Chartered Accounting: CGA-Finance
Masters: Business Administration

Critical Skills
Analytical, Good Communication, Good Writing Skills, Leadership, Organized

Types of Positions
Nurse   Any Paramedical Position

Starting Salary
$ 30,000 - 40,000

Company Benefits
- Full benefit package
- Drugs, dental, pension plan

Correspondence
Mail or fax resume with cover letter

Part Time/Summer: Thunder Bay Regional Hospital occasionally looks for people for part time work and regularly hires for the summer months. Potential positions include respiratory therapy, fixed asset clerk, budget analyst, or summer gardener.

TICKETMASTER CANADA INC.

1 Blue Jays Way, Suite 3900
Toronto, Ontario, M5V 1J3
Tel: (416) 345-9200   Fax: (416) 341-8765

Derek Macrae, Human Resources
Internet: www.ticketmaster.ca

Ticketmaster Canada is involved in the sales of entertainment tickets by phone and in person. The firm employs approximately 350 individuals in total.

Academic Fields
College: General, Accounting, Administration, Advertising, Business, Human Resources
Bachelor of Arts: General, Business, Languages, Public Relations
Bachelor of Comm/Admin: General

Critical Skills
Adaptable, Good Communication, Confident, Dependable, Diligent, Diplomatic, Efficient, Enthusiastic, Organized, Patient, Personable, Persuasive, Productive, Professional, Responsible, Customer Service Skills

Types of Positions
Phone Centre Agent

Starting Salary
below $ 20,000

Company Benefits
- All supervisory positions posted
- 35 hours training to start

Correspondence
Mail or fax resume with cover letter

Part Time/Summer: Ticketmaster Canada regularly hires individuals for part time employment, but does not hire for the summer months.

TIGER BRAND KNITTING COMPANY LIMITED

P.O. Box 188, 96 Grand Ave. S.
Cambridge, Ontario, N1R 5S9
Tel: (519) 621-5722   Fax: (519) 621-2695

Robina Dogger, Human Resources Department
Internet: www.tigerbrand.com

Tiger Brand Knitting Company is a manufacturer of cotton leisure-wear garments. The firm employs about 270 people.

Academic Fields
College: General, Accounting, Administration, Business, Computer Science, Electronics Tech., Security/Law
Bachelor of Arts: General, Business
Bachelor of Comm/Admin: General, Accounting, Finance, Marketing
Bachelor of Science: Chemistry, Computer Science
Chartered Accounting: CA-General, CGA-General
Masters: Business Administration

Critical Skills
Good Communication, Creative, Dependable, Diligent, Efficient, Enthusiastic, Flexible, Innovative, Manual Dexterity, Organized, Productive, Professional, Responsible

Types of Positions
Material Handler	Garment Processor
Sewing Operator	Knitter

Starting Salary
below $ 20,000 (high school) /
$ 20,000 - 30,000 (college/university)

Company Benefits
- Prescription, dental, life insurance
- Pension, retail discounts, travel insurance
- Training depends on position

Correspondence
Mail, fax, or submit resume with cover letter in person

Part Time/Summer: Tiger Brand Knitting Company regularly seeks people for part time work, and occasionally looks for individuals in the summer. Potential jobs are mainly general labour. Very few are hired though.

CITY OF TIMMINS

220 Algonquin Blvd. E.
Timmins, Ontario, P4N 1B3
Tel: (705) 264-1331   Fax: (705) 360-1392

Carol Lajeunesse, Personnel Officer

The City of Timmins is a municipal government responsible for the formation of policy and laws in matters under its jurisdiction. The municipality employs more than 780 people.

Academic Fields
College: Accounting, Child Care, Computer Science, Drafting/Architecture, Food/Nutrition, Human Resources, Nursing, Recreation Studies, Secretarial, Urban Planning
Bachelor of Arts: Gerontology, Sociology/Social Work
Bachelor of Science: Computer Science, Environmental Studies, Health Sciences, Nursing (RN)
Bachelor of Engineering: Civil, Computer Systems, Environmental Studies
Bachelor of Education: Childhood
Chartered Accounting: CMA - General/Finance
Masters: Business Administration, Engineering

Critical Skills
Good Communication, Creative, Diplomatic, Enthusiastic, Good With Figures, Leadership, Professional

Types of Positions
Clerk Typist   Cashier
Receptionist

Starting Salary
$ 25,000 - 30,000

Company Benefits
- Extended health care, dental, optical
- Short and long term disability
- Drug, life insurance

Correspondence
Submit City of Timmins application form

Part Time/Summer: The City of Timmins occasionally looks for people for part time work, and regularly seeks candidates in the summer. Potential jobs include labourer or office clerk. The best time to apply is 3-5 months in advance of availability date.

TIPPET-RICHARDSON LTD.

25 Metropolitan Road
Scarborough, Ontario, M1R 2T5
Tel: (416) 291-1200   Fax: (416) 291-2601

Tracey M. Stevens, Human Resources Manager
Internet: tippet-richardson.com

Tippet-Richardson is a local and long distance trucking company that provides service across Canada and the United States. Serving Canada since 1927, Tippet-Richardson is involved in residential moving, office moving, employee relocations, international moving, residential and commercial storage, special products transportation and distribution, trade shows, and records management. Affiliates of the company include Fox Cartage & Storage Ltd., Maritime Warehousing & Transfer Co. Ltd., and The Windsor Truck & Storage Co. Ltd. The moving company employs more than 750 individuals across the country.

Academic Fields
No specific academic background is required. They will look at candidates from all academic backgrounds.

Critical Skills
Dependable, Enthusiastic, Flexible, Manual Dexterity, Patient, Responsible

Types of Positions
Mover   Driver
Various Other Positions

Starting Salary
$ 20,000 - 25,000

Company Benefits
- Dental, health, 80% co-insurance
- Life insurance, pension plan
- Optional life and accidental death

Correspondence
Mail resume with cover letter

Part Time/Summer: Tippet-Richardson regularly hires employees for part time and summer positions. Opportunities in the summer are usually as a helper of household and commercial moving. The best time to apply is in May or June.

The Canada Student Employment Guide

TODAY'S BUSINESS PRODUCTS LTD.

875 Middlefield Rd.
Scarborough, Ontario, M1V 4Z5
Tel: (416) 292-6161   Fax: (416) 292-2537

Human Resources

Today's Business Products Ltd. is involved in the distribution of stationary to many types of business and organizations.

Academic Fields
College: General, Accounting, Administration, Advertising, Business, Communications, Human Resources, Marketing/Sales, Secretarial
Bachelor of Arts: General, Business, Public Relations
Bachelor of Comm/Admin: General, Accounting, Finance, Marketing, Info Mgmt., Public Admin.
Bachelor of Science: Computer Science
Bachelor of Laws: Corporate
Bachelor of Engineering: Computer Systems, Industrial, Transportation
Chartered Accounting: CA - General/Finance, CGA/CMA - General/Finance
Masters: Business Administration

Critical Skills
Adaptable, Analytical, Confident, Creative, Dependable, Efficient, Enthusiastic, Flexible, Good Communication, Good With Figures, Good Writing Skills, Innovative, Leadership, Logical, Organized, Personable, Productive, Professional, Responsible

Types of Positions
Receptionist   Order Entry
File Clerk

Starting Salary
$ 20,000 - 25,000

Company Benefits
- Full benefit package
- Full training

Correspondence
Mail or fax resume with cover letter

Part Time/Summer: Today's Business Products Ltd. occasionally looks for people for part time or summer employment. A potential job could marketing assistant. The best time to apply is late May.

TOP PRODUCERS SYSTEMS INC.

10651 Shellbridge Way, Suite 155
Richmond, British Columbia, V6X 2W8
Tel: (604) 270-8819   Fax: (604) 270-8218

A. Lambert, Human Resources
Internet: www.topproducer.com

Top Producers Systems is a developer of software for the residential real estate industry. They provide the largest selling software for real estate, and offer sales and productivity software for the industry as well.

Academic Fields
College: Computer Science, Marketing/Sales
Bachelor of Comm/Admin: Marketing
Bachelor of Science: Computer Science, Mathematics

Critical Skills
Adaptable, Analytical, Confident, Dependable, Flexible, Innovative, Leadership, Productive

Types of Positions
Technical Telephone Support
Customer Service Representative
In-House Telemarketing/Sales

Starting Salary
$ 20,000 - 30,000

Company Benefits
- Full medical and dental benefits
- Profit sharing, 2 weeks vacation
- In-house technical training

Correspondence
Mail resume with cover letter

Part Time/Summer: Top Producers Systems occasionally looks for people for part time and summer employment. Potential jobs involve clerical, administration, reception, shipping or production.

TORONTO AND REGION CONSERVATION AUTHORITY
5 Shoreham Dr.
Downsview, Ontario, M3N 1S4
Tel: (416) 661-6600   Fax: (416) 661-6898

Carolann Connors, Human Resources
Internet: www.trca.on.ca

The Toronto and Region Conservation Authority is a public agency devoted to the protection, enhancement, and public enjoyment of the renewable natural resources within nine watersheds in the Great Lakes Basin.

Academic Fields
College: Cooking/Culinary, Engineering Tech., Forestry, Hospitality, Recreation Studies, Urban Planning, Secretarial, Marketing/Sales, Fish & Wildlife, Travel/Tourism
Bachelor of Arts: Recreation Studies, Urban Geography
Bachelor of Science: Biology, Environmental Studies, Forestry, Geography, Geology, Horticulture
Bachelor of Engineering: Civil, Environmental Studies, Geotechnical, Water Resources
Bachelor of Landscape Architecture

Critical Skills
Creative, Dependable, Enthusiastic, Good Communication, Flexible, Personable, Leadership, Good Writing Skills, Professional, Responsible, Efficient, Organized, Productive

Types of Positions
Environmental Technician   GIS Technician
Planning Technician   Admin. Assistant
Labourers

Starting Salary
$ 20,000 - 30,000

Company Benefits
- Very competitive benefit package
- Excellent training opportunities provided

Correspondence
Mail or fax resume with cover letter

Part Time/Summer: The Toronto and Region Conservation Authority occasionally looks for candidates for part time jobs and regularly hires for the summer. Potential jobs include labourer, gate attendant, cashier, cleaner, lifeguard, interpreter, wait staff, gift shop clerk, maintenance staff, or conservation area worker. The best time to apply is January to April.

TORONTO ASSOCIATION FOR COMMUNITY LIVING
20 Spadina Road
Toronto, Ontario, M5R 2S7
Tel: (416) 968-0650   Fax: (416) 968-6463

Andrea Costello, Manager, Employee/Labour Relations
Internet: www.taci.on.ca

The Toronto Association for Community Living is a United Way agency addressing the needs of children or adults with developmental disabilities and their families. Services provided through more than 70 program locations across Toronto include early childhood services, employment training and placement, adult residential programs, adult development centres, volunteer services and public education. The organization serves almost 5,000 persons with developmental disabilities, and employs a staff of 1,000 who work at various program locations.

Academic Fields
Bachelor of Arts: Psychology, Sociology/Social Work
Bachelor of Science: Psychology

Critical Skills
Creative, Dependable, Enthusiastic, Good Communication, Flexible, Personable, Leadership, Good Writing Skills, Professional, Responsible

Types of Positions
Residential Counsellor II Instructor II
Part Time Residential Counsellor

Starting Salary
$ 25,000 - 30,000

Company Benefits
- Extended health, dental, vision, life insurance
- Internal training
- Employee assistance program

Correspondence
Mail or fax resume with cover letter
E-mail: acostello@taci.on.ca

Part Time/Summer: The Toronto Association for Community Living regularly hires for part time positions and sometimes hires for summer opportunities. During the summer months they operate a camp and therefore hire camp counsellors, kitchen help, and maintenance. The best time to apply is in early March.

TORONTO CATHOLIC DISTRICT SCHOOL BOARD
80 Sheppard Avenue East
Willowdale, Ontario, M2N 6E8
Tel: (416) 222-8282   Fax: (416) 512-3429

Personnel Department
Internet: www.tcdsb.on.ca

The Toronto Catholic District School Board is proud to serve students from diverse cultural, linguistic and ethnic backgrounds through a broad range of programs and services. Working in partnership with parents, local parishes and the wider school community, TCDSB schools offer a safe and caring learning environment, which reflects Catholic tradition and values.

Academic Fields
College: Accounting, Administration, Computer Science, Drafting/Architecture, Electronics Tech., Engineering Tech., Human Resources, Mechanical Tech., Secretarial
Bachelor of Arts: General, Economics
Bachelor of Engineering: Computer Systems, Industrial, Mechanical
Bachelor of Education: General
Chartered Accounting: CMA-Finance
Masters: Education

Critical Skills
Dependable, Organized, Good Communication, Punctual

Types of Positions
Clerical   Secretarial
Custodial   Teaching
Supply Education Assistant

Starting Salary
$ 20,000 - 25,000

Company Benefits
- A competitive benefits package

Correspondence
Mail resume with cover letter

TORONTO CRICKET SKATING & CURLING
141 Wilson Ave.
Toronto, Ontario, M5M 3A3
Tel: (416) 487-4581   Fax: (416) 487-7595

Human Resources

Toronto Cricket Skating & Curling is a social activities club in Toronto that offers many types of outdoor activities.

Academic Fields
College: General, Accounting, Business, Child Care, Cooking/Culinary, Hospitality, Recreation Studies, Secretarial, Travel/Tourism
Bachelor of Arts: Recreation Studies
Bachelor of Science: Health Sciences
Bachelor of Education: Physical

Critical Skills
Adaptable, Confident, Creative, Dependable, Diligent, Diplomatic, Efficient, Enthusiastic, Flexible, Good Communication, Good Writing Skills, Innovative, Leadership, Organized, Patient, Personable, Productive, Professional, Responsible

Types of Positions
Activities Dept.   Food & Beverage Dept.
Property/Facilities Dept.   General Office Dept.

Starting Salary
$ 20,000 - 30,000

Company Benefits
- Group life, insurance, extended health, 50% dental
- On-going training and development (internal and external)

Correspondence
Mail, fax or submit resume with cover letter in person

Part Time/Summer: Toronto Cricket Skating & Curling regularly looks for candidates for part time work and the summer months. Potential jobs are in the swimming pool, summer day camp, or summer skating school. The best time to apply is in January or February.

TORONTO DISTRICT SCHOOL BOARD

155 College Street
Toronto, Ontario, M5T 1P6
Tel: (416) 397-3322   Fax: (416) 397-3331

Horace Knight, Human Resources
Internet: www.tdsb.on.ca

The Toronto District School Board is responsible for maintaining the operation of elementary and secondary schools in Toronto. Employing over 10,400 individuals to work in various educational fields, the Toronto District School Board oversees approximately 160 schools in the region.

Academic Fields
College: Computer Science, Human Resources
Bachelor of Arts: English, History, Languages, Music, Political Science, Sociology/Social Work, Statistics
Bachelor of Comm/Admin: Accounting, Finance
Bachelor of Science: Biology, Chemistry, Computer Science, Food Sciences, Geography, Mathematics, Physics
Bachelor of Engineering: Civil, Electrical, Mechanical, Bachelor of Architecture
Bachelor of Education: General, Adult Education, Childhood, Physical, Special
Chartered Accounting: CA - General/Finance
Masters: Education, Library Science

Critical Skills
Analytical, Confident, Dependable, Good Writing Skills, Diplomatic, Efficient, Diligent, Good With Figures, Leadership, Organized, Productive, Professional, Responsible

Types of Positions
Human Resources   Maintenance
Administrative Services Purchasing
Computer Services

Starting Salary
$ 25,000 - 30,000

Company Benefits
- Major medical and dental
- Life insurance and pension

Correspondence
Mail resume with cover letter

Part Time/Summer: Toronto District School Board sometimes hires for part time and summer employment.

TORONTO EAST GENERAL HOSPITAL

825 Coxwell Avenue
East York, Ontario, M4C 3E7
Tel: (416) 469-6629   Fax: (416) 469-7982

Recruiter

Toronto East General Hospital is a public health care facility offering a wide range of medical services including pediatric, intensive and coronary care, maternity, orthopedic, geriatric, ophthalmology, gynecology, urology and general surgery. Established in 1929, the hospital has more than 400 beds and employs a total of 2,500 people.

Academic Fields
College: Accounting, Computer Science, Food/Nutrition, Human Resources, Laboratory Tech., Nursing, Radiology Tech., Health Records
Bachelor of Arts: Business, Psychology, Sociology
Bachelor of Comm/Admin: Accounting, Finance, Info Mgmt.
Bachelor of Science: Food Sciences, Health Sciences, Nursing (RN), Occupational Therapy, Pharmacy, Physiotherapy, Speech Language, Computer Science
Bachelor of Engineering: General, Mechanical
Chartered Accounting: CA-Finance
Masters: Business Admin., Science, Social Work, Nursing

Critical Skills
Dependable, Enthusiastic, Flexible, Creative, Innovative, Organized, Professional, Responsible

Types of Positions
Nursing   Pharmacy
Radiology   Lab Technologist
Occupational Therapy   Physiotherapy

Starting Salary
$ 30,000 - 40,000

Company Benefits
- Extended health care, dental, group life

Correspondence
Mail, fax or e-mail resume with cover letter
E-mail: hr@tegh.on.ca

Part Time/Summer: Toronto East General Hospital regularly hires for part time and summer work. Positions include cleaners, food service aides and clerical students. Pharmacy students are also hired for the summer. Apply between February and June.

The Canada Student Employment Guide

TORONTO FIRE SERVICES

895 Eastern Avenue
Toronto, Ontario, M4L 1A2
Tel: (416) 392-0163   Fax: (416) 392-0599

Ron Barrow, Recruitment Officer
Internet: www.city.toronto.on.ca/fire.ht

The City of Toronto Fire Department is responsible for the fire safety for the citizens of the City of Toronto. The Fire Services structure include fire fighting divisions, fire prevention, human resources and training and development. Operating an efficient and effective fire and rescue service, the Toronto Fire Department employs over 3,000 dedicated individuals who work in various capacities that include fire suspension and rescue, fire and emergency planning, fire prevention and inspections, training, health and safety and community outreach. The Toronto Fire Services has a job hot line at 392-FIRE (3473).

Academic Fields
No specific academic background is required. They will look at candidates from all academic backgrounds. Current minimum education required is Grade 12 or equivalent.

Critical Skills
Adaptable, Confident, Decisive, Good Communication, Enthusiastic, Productive, Personable, Manual Dexterity, Responsible

Types of Positions
Probationary Fire Fighter

Starting Salary
$ 30,000 - 40,000 / over $ 40,000 after 6 months

Company Benefits
- Full benefit package
- Major medical and dental
- Short and long term disability

Correspondence
Mail, fax, submit resume with cover letter in person

Part Time/Summer: Toronto Fire Services does not hire individuals for part time positions or summer opportunities. All jobs involve regular, full time employment.

THE TORONTO FRENCH SCHOOL

296 Lawrence Avenue East
Toronto, Ontario, M4N 1T7
Tel: (416) 484-6533   Fax: (416) 481-1447

Inga Lavoie, Human Resources

The Toronto French School is a an educational establishment designed to provide learning skills to children and promote the French language. The school employs approximately 150 individuals and also provides child day care services.

Academic Fields
Bachelor of Arts: General, Economics, English, Fine Arts, History, Languages, Music, Philosophy, Statistics
Bachelor of Science: Chemistry, Computer Science, Environmental Studies, Geography, Mathematics, Physics, Zoology
Bachelor of Education: General, Childhood
Masters: Arts, Science, Education, Library Science

Critical Skills
Adaptable, Decisive, Dependable, Good Communication, Flexible, Efficient, Organized, Good Writing Skills, Professional, Responsible, French Proficiency

Types of Positions
Teacher   Administration
Day-Care

Starting Salary
$ 20,000 - 25,000 ($ 30,000 - 40,000 teaching)

Company Benefits
- Extended health and dental care
- RRSP savings
- Professional development for teachers

Correspondence
Mail resume with cover letter. E-mail: ilavoie@tfs.on.ca

Part Time/Summer: The Toronto French School sometimes hire part time students and regularly hires for summer employment. Positions in the summer are most likely for French-speaking students to act as camp counsellors. The best time to apply is in April.

TORONTO GENERAL HOSPITAL

200 Elizabeth St.
Toronto, Ontario, M5G 2C4
Tel: (416) 340-4141   Fax: (416) 595-5441

Supervisor, Employment Services

Toronto General Hospital was established in 1988. With more than 1,220 beds, Toronto General Hospital offers a wide range of medical services and employs over 7,000 people.

Academic Fields
College: Accounting, Administration, Communications, Computer Science, Cooking/Culinary, Electronics Tech., Emergency/Paramedic, Engineering Tech., Faculty Mgmt., Food/Nutrition, Human Resources, Journalism, Nursing, Radiology Tech., Secretarial, Security/Law
Bachelor of Arts: General, Business, Economics, English, Gerontology, History, Journalism, Psychology, Public Rel., Rec. Studies, Sociology/Social Work, Statistics
Bachelor of Comm/Admin: General, Accounting, Finance, Info Mgmt., Public Admin.
Bachelor of Science: General, Biology, Chemistry, Computer Science, Food Sciences, Health Sciences, Kinesiology, Microbiology, Nursing (RN), Occupational Therapy, Pharmacy, Physiotherapy, Psychology
Bachelor of Engineering: Biomedical, Chemical, Computer Systems, Mechanical
Bachelor of Education: Adult Education
Chartered Accounting: CA - General/Finance, CGA/CMA - General/Finance
Masters: Business Administration, Science

Critical Skills
Adaptable, Analytical, Dependable, Enthusiastic, Good Communication, Good Writing Skills, Organized, Patient, Personable, Professional, Responsible

Types of Positions
Registered Nurse   Registered Nursing Assistant

Starting Salary
$ 25,000 - 30,000

Company Benefits
- Full health benefits

Correspondence
Mail resume with cover letter

Part Time/Summer: Toronto General Hospital regularly hires part time and summer students. Potential jobs are in housekeeping or nutrition.

TORONTO HYDRO

14 Carlton Street
Toronto, Ontario, M5B 1K5
Tel: (416) 599-0400   Fax: (416) 591-4721

Personnel Services Department
Internet: www.torontohydro.com

Toronto Hydro is engaged in the supply of electrical power within the City of Toronto. Also known as Toronto Electric Commissioners, Toronto Hydro employs over 1,600 individuals in 3 locations in the Toronto region. The company is an equal opportunity employer.

Academic Fields
College: General, Accounting, Administration, Business, Communications, Computer Science, Drafting/Architecture, Engineering Tech., Human Resources, Industrial Design, Science, Statistics
Bachelor of Arts: General, Economics, Political Science, Sociology/Social Work, Statistics, Urban Geography
Bachelor of Science: General, Actuarial, Computer Science, Environmental Studies, Geography, Health Sciences, Kinesiology, Physiotherapy
Bachelor of Engineering: General, Civil, Electrical, Environmental Studies

Critical Skills
Adaptable, Analytical, Dependable, Diligent, Diplomatic, Efficient, Enthusiastic, Good Communication, Flexible, Responsible, Organized, Good With Figures, Patient, Productive, Professional, Good Writing Skills

Types of Positions
Cleaner   Labourer
Clerical   Word Processor
Graduate Engineer

Starting Salary
$ 20,000 - 40,000 (depending on position)

Company Benefits
- Full benefits including medical and bereavement
- 3 weeks vacation, same sex, maternity benefits

Correspondence
Mail resume with cover letter

Part Time/Summer: Toronto Hydro does not hire for part time, but regularly hires for summer positions. These jobs would include clerical, technical, and warehouse worker.

The Canada Student Employment Guide

TORONTO POLICE SERVICE

40 College St.
Toronto, Ontario, M5G 2J3
Tel: (416) 808-7134   Fax: (416) 808-7152

Employment Unit
Internet: www.torontopolice.on.ca

The Toronto Police Service is dedicated to delivering police services, in partnership with their communities, to keep Toronto the best and safest place to be. Their service is committed to being a world leader in policing through excellence, innovation, continuous learning, quality leadership and management.

Academic Fields
College: General, Accounting, Administration, Business, Computer Science, Drafting/Architecture, Electronics Tech., Human Resources, Nursing, Secretarial, Security/Law, Police Foundations
Bachelor of Arts: General, Business, Criminology
Bachelor of Comm/Admin: Accounting, Finance
Bachelor of Science: Computer Science, Nursing (RN)
Bachelor of Engineering: Computer Systems
Bachelor of Education: General
Chartered Accounting: CA - General/Finance, CGA/CMA - General/Finance
Masters: Business Administration

Critical Skills
Adaptable, Dependable, Efficient, Enthusiastic, Flexible, Good Communication, Good Writing Skills, Responsible

Types of Positions
Clerical Support   Part Time Court Officer
Police Officer   P/T Communication Operator (911)
Parking Officer

Starting Salary
$ 25,000 - 30,000

Company Benefits
- Complete benefit package

Correspondence
Visit their Internet site

Part Time/Summer: The Toronto Police Service occasionally looks for individuals for part time or summer work. Potential jobs in the summer include lifeguard. The best time to apply is in April and May.

TORONTO PUBLIC LIBRARY BOARD

281 Front Street East
Toronto, Ontario, M5A 4L2
Tel: (416) 393-7580   Fax: (416) 393-7544

Human Resources Dept.

The Toronto Public Library Board is responsible for maintaining the operation of Toronto's public library system. Employing over 2,800 individuals, the Toronto Public Library Board oversees more than 90 public libraries in the region. A large number of employees work for the Board on a part time basis.

Academic Fields
Masters: Library Science

Critical Skills
Adaptable, Dependable, Diplomatic, Efficient, Flexible, Good Communication, Organized, Patient, Personable, Persuasive, Professional, Responsible

Types of Positions
Librarian   Page

Starting Salary
$ 25,000 - 40,000 (depending on position)

Company Benefits
- Extended health care plans after six months
- Life insurance
- Pension plan

Correspondence
Mail or fax resume with cover letter

Part Time/Summer: Toronto Public Library sometimes hires for part time and summer employment. A potential summer job would be a cleaner. The best time to apply is in the Spring. Potential part time hiring would be for pages.

The Canada Student Employment Guide

THE TORONTO SUN PUBLISHING CORP.

333 King Street East
Toronto, Ontario, M5A 4L1
Tel: (416) 947-2222   Fax: (416) 368-0374

Human Resources Department

Toronto Sun Publishing is a newspaper publishing company offering five major dailies in Canada. These newspaper dailies are operated in Toronto, Ottawa, Calgary, and Edmonton. Toronto Sun Publishing has over 2,700 employees.

Academic Fields
College: General, Accounting, Administration, Advertising, Business, Communications, Computer Science, Human Resources, Industrial Design, Insurance, Journalism, Marketing/Sales, Photography, Science, Secretarial, Security/Law, Statistics, Television/Radio
Bachelor of Arts: General, Business, Economics, English, Fine Arts, History, Journalism, Languages, Political Science, Psychology, Public Relations, Sociology/Social Work
Bachelor of Comm/Admin: General, Accounting, Finance, Marketing, Info Mgmt., Public Admin.
Bachelor of Science: General, Actuarial, Chemistry, Comp. Sci., Environ. Studies, Health Sci., Math, Physics
Bachelor of Engineering: Computer Syst., Mechanical
Bachelor of Education: General
Chartered Accounting: CA - General/Finance, CGA/CMA - General/Finance
Masters: Business Administration, Arts, Library Science

Critical Skills
Adaptable, Analytical, Artistic, Good Communication, Confident, Creative, Decisive, Dependable, Diligent, Patient, Personable, Persuasive, Professional, Good Writing Skills

Types of Positions
Accounting   Circulation

Starting Salary
$ 20,000 - 25,000

Company Benefits
- Wide range of benefits

Correspondence
Mail resume with cover letter

Part Time/Summer: Toronto Sun sometimes hires for part time and summer work. Potential jobs involve telemarketing.

TORONTO ZOO

361A Old Finch Ave.
Scarborough, Ontario, M1B 5K7
Tel: (416) 392-5921   Fax: (416) 392-5934

Michelle Jones, Human Resources
Internet: www.torontozoo.com

The Toronto Zoo is a zoological park just east of downtown Toronto that displays a large collection of wildlife. The Zoo has 242 permanent employees. Most hiring is of seasonal work from May to September.

Academic Fields
College: Animal Health, Security/Law
Bachelor of Science: Environ. Studies, Zoology
Bachelor of Education: General, Childhood

Critical Skills
Dependable, Efficient, Personable

Types of Positions
Gardening   Animal Keeper
Visitor Services   Membership Sales

Starting Salary
Depends on position

Company Benefits
- Full time staff receive medical and dental, tuition reimbursement, and in-house training
- Seasonal staff receive no benefits

Correspondence
Mail resume with cover letter

Part Time/Summer: The Toronto Zoo occasionally hires for part time work, and regularly seeks summer candidates. Potential summer jobs include gardening, materials collection, maintenance, visitor services, retail gift shop, or membership sales.

The Canada Student Employment Guide

CITY OF TORONTO

100 Queen Street West, 2nd Floor West, City Hall
Toronto, Ontario, M5N 2N2
Tel: (416) 392-1234   Fax: (416) 392-0131

Joy Isaacs, Special Employment Programs Consultant

The City of Toronto is a municipal government responsible for the formation of policy and laws in matters under its jurisdiction. The City of Toronto employs over 9,000 individuals to work in various fields in local government. Approximately 2,500 of these individuals work on a part time basis.

Academic Fields
College: Accounting, Business, Communications, Computer Science, Drafting/Architecture, Engineering Tech., Forestry, Law Clerk, Nursing, Recreation Studies, Security/Law, Urban Planning
Bachelor of Arts: General, Business, Gerontology, Public Relations, Recreation Studies
Bachelor of Comm/Admin: Accounting, Finance, Info Mgmt., Public Admin.
Bachelor of Science: General, Agriculture, Computer Science, Environ. Studies, Forestry, Health Sciences, Horticulture, Nursing (RN), Occupational Therapy
Bachelor of Laws: General, Corporate
Bachelor of Engineering: Biomedical, Chemical, Civil, Computer Systems, Environmental Studies, Bachelor of Architecture, Bachelor of Landscape Architecture
Chartered Accounting: CA - General/Finance, CGA/CMA - General/Finance

Critical Skills
Adaptable, Analytical, Good Communication, Confident, Creative, Decisive, Dependable, Diligent, Persuasive, Productive, Responsible, Cultural Sensitivity

Types of Positions
Various Positions

Starting Salary
$ 25,000 - 30,000

Company Benefits
- Extended medical and dental

Correspondence
Mail resume and cover letter or submit in person

Part Time/Summer: The City of Toronto does not hire for part time jobs, but sometimes hires for the summer. These positions include clerical, labourer, or technical duties. The best time to apply is in March or early April.

TOSHIBA OF CANADA LTD.

191 McNabb Street
Markham, Ontario, L3R 8H2
Tel: (905) 470-3500   Fax: (905) 470-3521

Marilyn Melnick, Human Resources Specialist
Internet: www.toshiba.ca

Toshiba of Canada is at the forefront of the world's high-technology industry, applying its integrated capabilities to a broad range of businesses. Their expertise in all areas of electronics and electric products has been shown throughout the world.

Academic Fields
College: General, Accounting, Administration, Business, Computer Science, Electronics Tech., Engineering Tech., Human Resources, Marketing/Sales, Secretarial
Bachelor of Arts: General, Business, Languages, Public Relations
Bachelor of Comm/Admin: General, Accounting, Finance, Marketing, Info Mgmt.
Bachelor of Science: Computer Science
Bachelor of Engineering: General, Computer Systems, Design, Electrical
Chartered Accounting: CA-General, CGA/CMA - General/Finance
Masters: Business Administration, Engineering

Critical Skills
Adaptable, Analytical, Artistic, Good Communication, Confident, Creative, Decisive, Dependable, Diligent, Diplomatic, Efficient, Enthusiastic, Personable, Persuasive, Productive, Professional, Responsible

Types of Positions
Junior Accountant   Bench Technician
Administrative Assistant   Technical Support Rep.

Starting Salary
Depends on position

Company Benefits
- Competitive benefit package

Correspondence
Mail, fax or e-mail resume with cover letter
E-mail: resumes@toshiba.ca

Part Time/Summer: Toshiba of Canada does not hires for part time work, but regularly hires for the summer. Summer jobs include parts/warehouse handler, admin. floater, admin. assistant, or bench technician. The best time to apply is in January.

TOYOTA CANADA LTD.

One Toyota Place
Scarborough, Ontario, M1H 1H9
Tel: (416) 438-6320   Fax: (416) 431-1871

Valerie Nodell, Human Resources Coordinator
Internet: www.toyota.ca

Toyota Canada is the Canadian distributor of Toyota and Lexus vehicle parts, and a full range of Toyota industrial equipment. The company has over 475 employees.

Academic Fields
College: General, Accounting, Business, Computer Science, Human Resources, Industrial Design, Marketing/Sales, Secretarial, Statistics
Bachelor of Arts: General, Business, Economics, Journalism, Languages, Psychology, Public Relations, Statistics
Bachelor of Comm/Admin: General, Accounting, Finance, Marketing, Info Mgmt.
Bachelor of Science: Computer Science
Bachelor of Engineering: Industrial
Bachelor of Education: Adult Education
Chartered Accounting: CA - General/Finance, CGA/CMA - General/Finance
Masters: Business Administration

Critical Skills
Adaptable, Analytical, Creative, Good Communication, Efficient, Flexible, Dependable, Good Writing Skills, Innovative, Logical, Organized, Personable, Sales Skills, Customer Oriented

Types of Positions
Warehouse Team Member
Coordinator Administration Asst.
Coordinator Sales/Marketing

Starting Salary
$ 25,000 - 40,000 (depending on position)

Company Benefits
- Above average company paid benefits
- In-house training
- Continuing education reimbursement

Correspondence
Mail or fax resume with cover letter

Part Time/Summer: Toyota Canada sometimes hires for part time and summer opportunities. Potential jobs for the summer are either clerical or in the warehouse. The best time to apply is in February or March.

TRANSALTA

P.O. Box 1900, 110 - 12th Avenue SW
Calgary, Alberta, T2P 2M1
Tel: (403) 267-3600   Fax: (403) 267-4657

Staffing

TransAlta is an international electric energy company with about $6 billion in assets. The company is focused on achieving strong earnings growth and enhancing its competitive edge as a low-cost operator of generation and transmission assets, and a successful developer of gas-fired independent power projects. The company is concentrating its growth in Canada, the United States, Australia and Mexico. They employ 2,679 individuals in Canada.

Academic Fields
College: Communications, Computer Science, Engineering Tech.
Bachelor of Comm/Admin: Accounting, Finance, Human Resources
Bachelor of Engineering: Chemical, Civil, Electrical, Environmental Studies, Mechanical, Mining

Critical Skills
Adaptable, Analytical, Creative, Decisive, Enthusiastic, Flexible, Good Communication, Innovative, Leadership, Organized

Types of Positions
Clerk Typist	Prof. Partnership Program
Customer Service	Clerical Staff
Apprentice Lineman	Labourer

Starting Salary
$ 25,000 - 30,000 (depends largely on position)

Company Benefits
- Full range of benefits
- Various training and development opportunities
- Training depends on individual's needs

Correspondence
Apply through their web site

Part Time/Summer: TransAlta sometimes looks for candidates for part time positions, and regularly seeks individuals for summer opportunities. Potential positions vary from year to year. The best time to apply is in January.

The Canada Student Employment Guide

TRANSCONTINENTAL DIGITAL SERVICES INC.
66 Nuggett Court
Brampton, Ontario, L6T 5A9
Tel: (905) 792-8385   Fax: (905) 792-3731

Marcel Courville, Human Resources

Transcontinental Digital Services is a graphic arts company that is involved in prepress, design, photography, desktop page assembly and film output.

Academic Fields
College: Graphic Arts

Critical Skills
Adaptable, Analytical, Artistic, Good Communication, Confident, Creative, Decisive, Dependable, Diligent, Efficient, Enthusiastic, Flexible, Innovative, Leadership, Logical, Manual Dexterity, Organized, Personable, Productive, Professional, Responsible

Types of Positions
Graphic Artist   Desktop Operator
Customer Service Rep.

Starting Salary
$ 30,000 - 40,000

Company Benefits
- Full benefits
- Training department provides on-the-job training

Correspondence
Mail resume with cover letter
E-mail: courvillem@mail.transcontinental.ca

Part Time/Summer: Transcontinetal Digital Services occasionally hires for part time or summer employment. A potential position would be customer service representative. The best time to apply is in March or April.

Co-op/Internship: They occasionally have internship opportunities.

TRIUMF
4004 Wesbrook Mall
Vancouver, British Columbia, V6T 2A3
Tel: (604) 222-1047   Fax: (604) 222-1074

Charles Davis, Human Resources
Internet: www.triumf.ca

Triumf is an organization involved in nuclear research. Based in Vancouver, British Columbia, this company has approximately 380 individuals that work in a full time capacity, and employs 200 scientists who visit throughout the year.

Academic Fields
College: Electronics Tech., Engineering Tech.
Bachelor of Science: Computer Science, Physics
Bachelor of Engineering: Electrical, Mechanical

Critical Skills
Adaptable, Dependable, Diligent, Good Communication, Efficient, Organized, Productive, Responsible

Types of Positions
Junior Engineer   Junior Technician

Starting Salary
$ 30,000 - 40,000 (university)

Company Benefits
- Medical, dental, extended health
- Group life, pension, long term disability
- Training is sometimes paid for

Correspondence
Mail or fax resume with cover letter

Part Time/Summer: Triumf sometimes hires individuals for part time and summer employment. For the summer months, students are hired through university co-op programs. All summer positions involve highly technical projects. Applications for summer positions are usually received no later than December of the previous year.

The Canada Student Employment Guide

TROJAN TECHNOLOGIES INC.

3020 Gore Rd.
London, Ontario, N5V 4T7
Tel: (519) 457-3400   Fax: (519) 457-0447

Alison Buma, Human Resources
Internet: www.trojanuv.com/

Trojan Technologies is a Canadian based, high technology environmental company operating internationally. With more than 20 years of experience, Trojan has the largest installed base of UV disinfection systems operating around the world.

Academic Fields
College: Information Systems, Marketing/Sales, Purchasing, Computer Science, Electronics Tech., Engineering Tech., Mechanical Tech.
Bachelor of Comm/Admin: Accounting, Human Resources, Marketing, Info Mgmt.
Bachelor of Science: Biology, Chemistry, Comp. Sci.
Bachelor of Engineering: Chemical, Civil, Design, Electrical, Mechanical, Water Resources
Chartered Accounting: CA-General, CGA-General
Masters: Science, Engineering

Critical Skills
Adaptable, Creative, Dependable, Diligent, Enthusiastic, Flexible, Good Communication, Innovative, Leadership, Logical, Organized, Personable, Professional, Responsible

Types of Positions
Engineering Designer   R & D Technologist
R & D Associate Scientist   Sales Engineer
Project Engineer

Starting Salary
$ 30,000 - 35,000

Company Benefits
- Fairly standard health, dental, drug, vision care

Correspondence
Apply through web site

Part Time/Summer: Trojan Technologies occasionally hires for part time work and regularly hires for the summer. Co-op positions in science and technology, as well as their other engineering teams are available on a rotating schedule throughout the year. They partner with various universities across the country to fill co-op and internship opportunities.

Co-op/Internship: See above.

TROW CONSULTING ENGINEERS LTD.

1595 Clark Blvd.
Brampton, Ontario, L6T 4V1
Tel: (905) 793-9800   Fax: (905) 793-0641

Jennifer Jackson, Human Resources Generalist
Internet: www.trow.com

Trow Consulting Engineers is a multi-disciplinary engineering firm offering services in geosciences, the environment, building science, mechanical, electrical, construction materials, pipelines, fire and life safety. They request no phone calls please.

Academic Fields
College: Drafting/Architecture, Engineering Tech., Secretarial
Bachelor of Science: Environmental Studies, Geology
Bachelor of Engineering: General, Chemical, Civil, Design, Electrical, Environmental Studies, Geotechnical, Mechanical, Mining, Transportation

Critical Skills
Adaptable, Analytical, Artistic, Good Communication, Confident, Creative, Decisive, Dependable, Diligent, Diplomatic, Efficient, Enthusiastic, Flexible, Good With Figures, Innovative, Leadership, Logical, Manual Dexterity, Organized, Patient, Personable, Persuasive, Productive, Professional, Responsible, Writing Skills

Types of Positions
Junior Technician   Lab Technician
Junior Hydrogeologist   Jr. Environmental Scientist
Junior Geologist   Engineer-In-Training

Starting Salary
$ 28,000 - 34,000 (Technicians and Clerical) /
$ 34,000 - 42,000 (Engineers)

Company Benefits
- General group benefit package, and group RSP
- Profit sharing, incentive bonuses
- Computer purchase program

Correspondence
Mail or e-mail resume with cover letter
E-mail: resumes@trow.com

Part Time/Summer: Trow Consulting Engineers does not hire people for part time work, but occasionally looks for individuals in the summer. Potential jobs include technicians and engineer-in-training. The best time to apply is March to May.

The Canada Student Employment Guide

TSC STORES LTD.

570 Industrial Dr.
London, Ontario, N5V 1V1
Tel: (519) 453-5270   Fax: (519) 453-6068

Roy Carter, Vice President, Finance & Administration
Internet: www.tscstores.com

TSC Stores offers retail sales of hardware, farm supplies, and garden supplies. There are 17 stores in southwestern Ontario. Individuals should apply to stores individually. The address above is for their administration office only.

Academic Fields
College: General, Accounting, Administration, Advertising, Business, Computer Science, Marketing/Sales, Secretarial
Bachelor of Arts: General, Business, Economics
Bachelor of Comm/Admin: General, Accounting, Finance, Marketing, Info Mgmt.
Chartered Accounting: CA - General/Finance, CGA/CMA - General/Finance
Masters: Business Administration

Critical Skills
Analytical, Dependable, Good With Figures, Logical, Organized, Personable, Productive, Responsible, Good Writing Skills

Types of Positions
Accounting Clerk   Buyer's Assistant
Warehouse Shipper/Receiver

Starting Salary
$ 25,000 - 40,000

Company Benefits
- Full benefit package
- Life, health, dental, vision, pension, RRSP
- Reimbursement for courses related to job

Correspondence
Mail resume with cover letter
E-mail: rcarter@tscstores.com

Part Time/Summer: TSC Stores occasionally hires for part time and summer work. The best time to apply to individual stores is in March or April.

TURNBULL & TURNBULL LTD.

1850 Main St.
Winnipeg, Manitoba, R2V 3J4
Tel: (204) 982-7843   Fax: (204) 694-4025

Human Resources Manager

Turnbull & Turnbull is a consulting actuarial firm. They design and implement pension, health and welfare, and other employee benefit plans. The company also provides technical and administrative services for some plans.

Academic Fields
College: Accounting, Administration, Computer Science
Bachelor of Comm/Admin: General, Accounting, Finance
Bachelor of Science: Actuarial, Nursing (RN)
Bachelor of Laws: General
Chartered Accounting: CMA - General/Finance, CGA - General/Finance

Critical Skills
Adaptable, Analytical, Good Communication, Dependable, Diplomatic, Efficient, Good With Figures, Organized

Types of Positions
Dental Processing Benefits Claims Clerk
RSP Clerk
Person Friday

Starting Salary
below $ 20,000

Company Benefits
- Dental and health benefits, pension plan
- RSP plan, long term disability, life insurance
- Training offered

Correspondence
Mail, fax, or submit resume with cover letter in person

Part Time/Summer: Turnbull & Turnbull occasionally looks for people for part time and summer employment.

The Canada Student Employment Guide

UNI SELECT INC.

170 Boulevard Industriel
Boucherville, Québec, J4B 2X3
Tel: (450) 641-2440   Fax: (450) 641-6566

Jo-Anne Constantin, Human Resources Coordinator
Internet: www.uni-select.com

Uni Select Inc. is Canada's second largest distributor of automotive and heavy duty replacement parts, equipment, tools and accessories. They employ approximately 850 individuals in Canada.

Academic Fields
College: Accounting, Administration, Business, Human Resources, Information Systems, Marketing/Sales, Purchasing/Logistics
Bachelor of Comm/Admin: Accounting, Finance, Human Resources, Marketing, Info Mgmt.
Chartered Accounting: CA - General/Finance, CMA - General/Finance, CGA - General/Finance
Masters: Business Administration

Critical Skills
Analytical, Decisive, Flexible, Innovative, Leadership, Organized, Productive, Professional, Responsible

Types of Positions
Accounting   Computer Science
Clerical

Starting Salary
$ 30,000 - 35,000

Company Benefits
- Collective insurance and pension fund
- Training and development varies depending on department

Correspondence
Fax resume with cover letter specifying the type of position you are seeking.
E-mail: usi.human.resources@sympatico.ca

Part Time/Summer: Uni Select regularly looks for candidates for part time and summer employment. A potential job for the summer may be an accounting clerk. The best time to apply is in April.

Co-op/Internship: They have internship opportunities in computer programming, marketing and accounting.

UNION GAS LTD.

50 Keil Drive North
Chatham, Ontario, N7M 5M1
Tel: (519) 352-3100   Fax: (519) 436-4566

Human Resources Services
Internet: www.uniongas.com

Union Gas Ltd. is an energy delivery and service company. It is engaged in the business of natural gas. The company is fully owned by Westcoast Energy Inc. of Vancouver, British Columbia. Union Gas has an employee base of 2,630 people.

Academic Fields
College: Electronics Tech., Engineering Tech., Mechanical Tech.
Bachelor of Comm/Admin: General, Accounting, Finance, Marketing
Bachelor of Science: Computer Science, Mathematics
Bachelor of Engineering: General, Chemical, Civil, Electrical, Mechanical
Chartered Accounting: CA - General/Finance, CGA/CMA - General/Finance
Masters: Business Administration

Critical Skills
Adaptable, Confident, Creative, Enthusiastic, Flexible, Good Communication, Innovative, Leadership, Persuasive

Types of Positions
Various Positions

Starting Salary
$ 30,000 - 40,000 (with university degree)

Company Benefits
- Full range of benefits

Correspondence
Mail resume with cover letter

Part Time/Summer: Union Gas occasionally seeks individuals for part time or summer work. Positions depend upon the company's needs. A potential position will usually be for an engineering student.

UNION PACIFIC RESOURCES GROUP

15811 - 112 Ave.
Edmonton, Alberta, T5M 2V9
Tel: (403) 452-7360   Fax: (403) 454-3041

Helen Rafters, Human Resources
Internet: www.upr.com

Union Pacific Resources Group is a shipping company that handles the loading and unloading of freight to destinations in Alberta, Northwest Territories, Yukon, and Northern British Columbia. The company employs approximately 80 people.

Academic Fields
College: General, Accounting, Administration, Computer Science, Human Resources

Critical Skills
Adaptable, Good Communication, Dependable, Diligent, Diplomatic, Efficient, Enthusiastic, Flexible, Good With Figures, Logical, Manual Dexterity, Organized, Patient, Personable, Productive, Good Writing Skills

Types of Positions
Various Positions

Starting Salary
$ 20,000 - 25,000

Company Benefits
- Medical and dental
- Long term disability

Correspondence
Fax resume with cover letter

Part Time/Summer: Union Pacific Resources Group occasionally looks for people for part time work and summer positions. Potential summer jobs are in the warehouse. The best time to apply is in May or June.

UNISYS CANADA INC.

2001 Sheppard Ave. E.
North York, Ontario, M2J 4Z7
Tel: (416) 495-0515   Fax: (416) 495-4495

Human Resources
Internet: www.unisys.com

Unisys is one of a select group of global companies with a broad portfolio of services, technologies, and third-party alliances needed to deliver the benefits of information management. They serve clients in some 100 countries around the world. Their 50,000 clients include leading financial services, airlines, transportation companies, government agencies, communications and health care providers, and other commercial market leaders.

Academic Fields
College: Compute Science, Electronics Tech., Engineering Tech.
Bachelor of Arts: Business
Bachelor of Comm/Admin: Info Mgmt.
Bachelor of Science: Computer Science
Bachelor of Engineering: Computer Systems, Mechanical

Critical Skills
Adaptable, Analytical, Decisive, Dependable, Enthusiastic, Flexible, Good Communication, Good Writing Skills, Innovative, Leadership, Personable, Productive, Professional, Responsible

Types of Positions
Client Service Representative
Information Systems Consultant

Starting Salary
$ 25,000 - 30,000

Company Benefits
- Benefits are discussed when an offer of employment is made

Correspondence
Fax or e-mail resume with cover letter

Part Time/Summer: Unisys Canada Inc. occasionally hires for part time or summer employment. Jobs usually go to sons and daughters of current employees first. The best time to apply is in April or May.

UNITED PARCEL SERVICE CANADA LTD.

2900 Steeles Ave. W.
Concord, Ontario, L4K 3S2
Tel: (905) 260-8019   Fax: (905) 660-8529

Isabel Cocomello, Employee Services Supervisor
Internet: www.ups.com/canada

UPS, the world's largest package distribution company, transports more than 3 billion parcels and documents annually. Using more than 500 aircraft, 157,000 vehicles and 1,700 facilities to provide service in more than 200 countries and territories, they have made a worldwide commitment to serving the needs of the global marketplace. In Canada, they employ approximately 6,000 individuals.

Academic Fields
They look at candidates from all areas.
Academic skills are not essential, but an asset.

Critical Skills
Adaptable, Dependable, Diligent, Efficient, Enthusiastic, Flexible, Good Communication, Manual Dexterity, Responsible

Types of Positions
Warehouse (part time)   Drivers (part time)
Airport Entry

Starting Salary
$ 15,000 or less (warehouse)

Company Benefits
- Full employee benefits after 60 days
- Health, dental, vision coverage, life insurance
- Provide on-the-job training

Correspondence
Fax, e-mail resume with cover letter, apply in person, or call their job line at (905) 660-8519

Part Time/Summer: United Parcel Service Canada regularly hires part time workers, but does not hire for the summer months. Drivers are hired for part time work and must be able to driver standard, be over 21 years, and have a valid G driver's license. All warehouse positions are part time.

UNIVERSAL REHABILITATION SERVICE AGENCY

808 Manning Road N.E.
Calgary, Alberta, T2E 7N8
Tel: (403) 272-7722   Fax: (403) 273-7852

Human Resources

Universal Rehabilitation Service Agency (URSA) is a Calgary-based, non-profit agency. Established in 1985, their objective is to meet the needs of individuals with disabilities in community settings. URSA provides residential, vocational, educational, rehabilitation and assessment services to individuals who currently lack the full extent of these services. URSA employs about 110 people to work full time, part time, or as relief staff.

Academic Fields
College: Administration, Child Care, Human Resources, Nursing, Recreation Studies, Rehabilitation
Bachelor of Arts: Psychology, Recreation Studies, Sociology/Social Work
Bachelor of Science: Health Sciences, Kinesiology, Occupational Therapy, Physiotherapy
Bachelor of Education: Adult Education, Childhood, Special

Critical Skills
Analytical, Good Communication, Confident, Decisive, Dependable, Diligent, Diplomatic, Efficient, Enthusiastic, Flexible, Innovative, Leadership, Organized, Patient, Personable, Professional, Responsible, Good Writing Skills

Types of Positions
Program Care Worker   Community Support Worker

Starting Salary
$ 20,000 - 25,000

Company Benefits
- Full health, dental, life insurance
- Long term disability

Correspondence
Mail or fax resume with cover letter

Part Time/Summer: Universal Rehabilitation Service Agency regularly employs candidates for part time and summer work. This agency receives provincial and federal grants for positions. The best time to apply is in April. Candidates must be returning students.

The Canada Student Employment Guide

UNIVERSITY COLLEGE OF CAPE BRETON

P.O. Box 5300
Sydney, Nova Scotia, B1P 6L2
Tel: (902) 563-1158   Fax: (902) 563-1458

Gordon MacLean, Director of Human Resources
Internet: www.uccb.ns.ca

University College of Cape Breton is a large educational institution with many programs for both post-secondary students and adults alike. They have an employee base of approximately 350 individuals.

Academic Fields
College: General, Accounting, Admin., Business, Communications, Computer Sci., Cooking/Culinary, Electronics Tech., Engineering Tech., Hospitality, Law Clerk, Marketing/Sales, Mech. Tech., Science, Secretarial
Bachelor of Arts: General, Business, Economics, English, Fine Arts, History, Languages, Philosophy, Political Science, Psychology, Sociology, Statistics
Bachelor of Comm/Admin: General, Accounting, Finance, Marketing, Info Mgmt., Public Admin.
Bachelor of Science: General, Biology, Chemistry, Computer Science, Environmental Studies, Geology, Mathematics, Physics, Psychology, Zoology
Bachelor of Engineering: General, Civil, Electrical, Environmental Studies
Chartered Accounting: CA-General
Masters: Business Administration, Science, Engineering, Library Science

Critical Skills
Adaptable, Analytical, Artistic, Good Communication, Confident, Creative, Decisive, Dependable, Diligent, Manual Dexterity, Organized, Personable, Productive

Types of Positions
Clerk   Secretary
Computer Data Entry   Lab Assistant
Learning Assistant   Program Coordinator

Starting Salary
Depends on position

Company Benefits
- Extended health, life insurance

Correspondence
Mail resume with cover letter

Part Time/Summer: University College of Cape Breton occasionally hires for part time work, and regularly hires for the summer. Potential jobs include research assistant. The best time to apply is in April.

URBAN SYSTEMS LTD.

286 St. Paul Street West
Kamloops, British Columbia, V2C 6G4
Tel: (250) 374-8311   Fax: (250) 374-5334

Shannon McQuillan, Human Resources Advisor
Internet: www.ubran-systems.com

Urban Systems is a consulting firm of engineers, planners, landscape architects, and local government advisors. The company currently has four branches located in Kamloops, Kelowna, Vancouver, British Columbia, and Calgary, Alberta.

Academic Fields
College: Drafting/Architecture, Engineering Tech., Urban Planning
Bachelor of Engineering: Civil, Environ. Studies, Transportation, Water Res., Bach. of Landscape Arch.
Masters: Business Administration, Arts (Urban Planning), Science, Engineering

Critical Skills
Adaptable, Confident, Creative, Dependable, Diligent, Diplomatic, Efficient, Enthusiastic, Flexible, Good With Figures, Innovative, Leadership, Logical, Personable, Productive, Professional, Responsible, Writing Skills

Types of Positions
Engineer In Training   Junior Planner
Junior Landscape Architect   Engineering Technologist
Junior Support Staff   CAD Drafting

Starting Salary
$ 20,000 - 40,000 (depending on position)

Company Benefits
- Extended medical, dental, and disability

Correspondence
Mail or e-mail resume with cover letter & make sure to follow-up. E-mail: smcquillan@urban-systems.com

Part Time/Summer: Urban Systems regularly seeks people for part time work, and sometimes hires for the summer. Potential summer jobs involve clerical, drafting, and support staff positions. The best time to apply is from January to March. The company also has a co-op program in place for those on a professional career path.

Co-op/Internship: Internship opportunities exist in engineering, planning and landscape architecture staff.

The Canada Student Employment Guide

US FILTER BCP

2180 Speers Rd.
Oakville, Ontario, L6L 2X8
Tel: (905) 827-0643   Fax: (905) 827-3429

Human Resources

US Filter BCP is involved with metal finishing equipment and supplies. The company's head office is in Oakville, Ontario.

Academic Fields
College: Accounting, Computer Science, Drafting/Architecture, Electronics Tech., Engineering Tech., Marketing/Sales
Bachelor of Arts: Business, Public Relations
Bachelor of Comm/Admin: Accounting, Marketing
Bachelor of Science: General, Computer Science, Mathematics
Bachelor of Engineering: General, Computer Systems, Design, Electrical
Chartered Accounting: CMA-General
Masters: Engineering

Critical Skills
Adaptable, Confident, Creative, Decisive, Dependable, Diligent, Efficient, Enthusiastic, Flexible, Good With Figures, Innovative, Logical, Organized, Personable, Productive, Professional, Responsible

Types of Positions
Various Positions

Starting Salary
$ 20,000 - 25,000

Company Benefits
- Medical, dental, life insurance

Correspondence
Mail resume with cover letter

Part Time/Summer: US Filter BCP occasionally hires for part time and summer employment opportunities.

USF WATERGROUP

580 Park St.
Regina, Saskatchewan, S4N 5A9
Tel: (306) 761-3200   Fax: (306) 721-5610

Gerald Mushka, Human Resources
Internet: www.usfilter.com

USF WaterGroup is owned by USFilter/Vivendi and heads up the Consumer Group in Canada, including Culligan. WaterGroup manufactures and markets water treatment equipment for residential and commercial applications. The company's head office is in Regina, Saskatchewan.

Academic Fields
College: Engineering Tech.
Bachelor of Comm/Admin: Accounting
Bachelor of Engineering: Mechanical
Chartered Accounting: CMA-General

Critical Skills
Analytical, Diligent, Good Communication, Manual Dexterity, Professional

Types of Positions
File Clerk   Assembler

Starting Salary
$ 30,000 - 40,000

Company Benefits
- Medical, dental, disability insurance
- Retirement plans
- Product training, professional skills

Correspondence
Mail resume with cover letter
E-mail: gmushka@usfcanada.com

Part Time/Summer: USF WaterGroup occasionally seeks candidates for part time work, and regularly hires for the summer months. Potential jobs include office clerk, or are involved in manufacturing. The best time to apply is in March.

VACANCES AIR TRANSAT INC.

5915 Airport Rd., Suite 1000
Mississauga, Ontario, L4V 1T1
Tel: (905) 405-8585   Fax: N/A

Human Resources Department
Internet: www.vacanceairtransat.com

Vacances Air Transat is engaged in the arrangement of passenger transportation. A subsidiary of Transat A.T. Inc., the company was established in 1989. There are approximately 400 employees in Montreal, Toronto and Vancouver within this travel organization.

Academic Fields
College: Accounting, Administration, Marketing/Sales, Travel/Tourism
Bachelor of Comm/Admin: Accounting, Finance, Marketing
Bachelor of Science: Computer Science, Geography
Chartered Accounting: CA-Finance, CMA - General/Finance, CGA-General

Critical Skills
Enthusiastic, Flexible, Good Communication, Organized, Persuasive, Professional

Types of Positions
Reservation Agent   Operation Agent
Accounting Clerk

Starting Salary
below $ 20,000 - 25,000

Company Benefits
- Medical and dental coverage
- Life insurance
- Travel benefits

Correspondence
Mail resume with cover letter

Part Time/Summer: Vacances Air Transat occasionally seeks individuals for part time and summer opportunities. The company does not usually have many summertime jobs. There are most commonly 1 or 2 positions available in their accounting department. The best time to apply is in the Spring.

VALLEY FIRST CREDIT UNION

184 Main St., 3rd Floor
Penticton, British Columbia, V2A 8G7
Tel: (250) 490-2721   Fax: (250) 490-3661

Asst. Vice President, Human Resources
Internet: www.valleyfirst.com

Valley First Credit Union is a leading and progressive financial institution serving the Okanagan Similkameen Valleys. With its head office in Penticton, 11 retail branches, and 7 insurance offices. Valley First often requires new employees in retail banking, lending, financial planning, and insurance operations.

Academic Fields
College: General, Accounting, Administration
Bachelor of Arts: General, Business
Bachelor of Comm/Admin: General, Accounting, Finance

Critical Skills
Confident, Creative, Decisive, Dependable, Diligent, Diplomatic, Efficient, Enthusiastic, Flexible, Good Communication, Good With Figures, Innovative, Leadership, Logical, Manual Dexterity, Organized, Patient, Personable, Persuasive, Productive, Professional, Responsible, Sales Oriented, Service Driven

Types of Positions
Member Service Rep. (Teller)
Customer Service Rep.

Starting Salary
$ 20,000 - 25,000

Company Benefits
- Medical, dental, life insurance, group RRSP
- Tuition reimbursement
- Full time training department offering various courses and workshops

Correspondence
Mail or e-mail resume with cover letter
E-mail: humanres@valleyfirst.com

Part Time/Summer: Valley First Credit Union regularly hires for part time employment and occasionally seeks individuals for summer positions. March is the best time to apply.

VALUE VILLAGE STORES

30 - 774 Columbia Street
New Westminster, British Columbia, V3M 1B5
Tel: (604) 461-7000   Fax: N/A

Human Resources
Internet: www.vaulevillage.com

Value Village Stores is a privately owned retail company which sells second hand merchandise that is purchased from charities. The company has 57 stores throughout Canada, and 23 locations in Ontario. Hourly positions are offered for retail clerks and production workers, while management trainee programs are set up for individuals with a minimum 2 years supervisory experience in a full time capacity. Valu Village Stores promotes from within whenever possible.

Academic Fields
No specific academic background is required. They will look at candidates from all academic backgrounds. High school education is all that is required.

Critical Skills
Dependable, Diligent, Diplomatic, Efficient, Enthusiastic, Good Communication, Good With Figures, Manual Dexterity, Organized, Patient, Personable, Productive, Responsible

Types of Positions
Sales Clerk   Production Clerk

Starting Salary
below $ 20,000

Company Benefits
- Full package with medical, dental, vision care
- Christmas bonus, attendance bonus
- Service awards

Correspondence
Submit resume and cover letter in person

Part Time/Summer: Value Village Stores regularly looks for individuals for part time and summer employment. Potential jobs include sales clerk and production clerk. Individuals can apply year-round.

VANCITY CREDIT UNION

P.O. Box 2120, Station Terminal
Vancouver, British Columbia, V6B 5R8
Tel: (604) 877-4919   Fax: (604) 877-8299

Personnel Department
Internet: www.vancity.com

As the largest credit union in Canada, VanCity Credit Union offers a full array of financial services including insurance services, mutual funds, RRSP counselling, financial planning and analysis, among others. VanCity Credit Union also supports the community in numerous corporate and social responsibility initiatives that promote the social and economic health and well being of the community.

Academic Fields
College: Business, Financial Management
Bachelor of Comm/Admin: Accounting, Finance, Marketing
Chartered Accounting: CGA/CMA
Masters: Business Administration

Critical Skills
Adaptable, Analytical, Creative, Decisive, Dependable, Diligent, Efficient, Enthusiastic, Good Communication, Good With Figures, Good Writing Skills, Organized, Personable, Productive, Professional, Responsible

Types of Positions
Financial Services Rep.   Accounting Clerk
Administrative Clerk   VISA Customer Service Rep.
Various Administrative

Starting Salary
$ 22,000 - 32,000 (depending on position and qualifications)

Company Benefits
- Full benefits to part time and full time employees, flexible benefits plan
- Dental, extended health, group life, short and long term disability, group RRSP

Correspondence
Mail, fax or e-mail resume with cover letter
E-mail: personnel_resumes@vancity.com

Part Time/Summer: VanCity Credit Union regularly hires for part time work, and occasionally hires for summer work. Potential summer positions include financial services rep.

VANCOUVER INTERNATIONAL AIRPORT

P.O. Box 23750, Airport Postal Outlet
Richmond, British Columbia, V7B 1Y7
Tel: (604) 276-6101   Fax: (604) 276-6538

Mo-Jean Lai, Employment Advisor
Internet: www.yvr.ca

Vancouver International Airport provides transportation facilities and services to airlines travelling in and out of Vancouver. The airport employs approximately 300 individuals in total.

Academic Fields
College: General, Accounting, Advertising, Business, Communications, Computer Science, Drafting/Architecture, Engineering Tech., Human Resources, Marketing/Sales
Bachelor of Arts: Business
Bachelor of Comm/Admin: Accounting, Finance, Marketing, Info Mgmt.
Bachelor of Engineering: Civil
Chartered Accounting: CMA - General/Finance, CGA - General/Finance

Critical Skills
Adaptable, Confident, Creative, Diplomatic, Efficient, Enthusiastic, Innovative, Leadership, Organized, Personable, Productive, Professional, Responsible, Team Player

Types of Positions
Various positions

Starting Salary
Depends on position

Company Benefits
- Very competitive package

Correspondence
Mail or fax resume with cover letter

Part Time/Summer: Vancouver International Airport does not hire for part time work, but occasionally hires for the summer. Potential jobs are in customer service, engineering, or the environment. The best time to apply is between February and March.

Co-op/Internship: Internship opportunities available for students majoring in airport management.

VANCOUVER SUN

2250 Granville Street, Suite 1
Vancouver, British Columbia, V6C 3N3
Tel: (604) 605-2000   Fax: (604) 605-2308

Human Resources
Internet: vancouversun.com

The Vancouver Sun is a daily newspaper in the province of British Columbia. The company has an employee base of more than 1,500 individuals that work in many different areas within the newspaper industry.

Academic Fields
Bachelor of Arts: General, Business, Economics, Journalism, Languages, Political Science, Psychology, Public Relations, Sociology/Social Work, Statistics, Urban Geography
Bachelor of Comm/Admin: General, Accounting, Finance, Marketing, Info Mgmt., Public Admin.
Bachelor of Science: General, Agriculture, Chemistry, Computer Sci., Environ. Studies, Health Sci., Math., Nursing (RN), Occupational Therapy
Bachelor of Laws: Corporate
Bachelor of Engineering: General, Chemical, Civil, Computer Systems, Electrical, Industrial, Mechanical
Chartered Accounting: CA - General/Finance, CMA-Finance, CGA-Finance
Masters: Business Administration, Arts, Science, Engineering, Education, Library Science

Critical Skills
Adaptable, Analytical, Artistic, Good Communication, Confident, Creative, Decisive, Dependable, Diligent, Diplomatic, Efficient, Enthusiastic, Flexible, Good With Figures, Innovative, Leadership, Logical, Manual Dexterity, Organized, Patient, Personable, Persuasive, Productive, Professional, Responsible, Good Writing Skills

Types of Positions
Various positions

Starting Salary
$ 25,000 - 40,000 (depending on position)

Company Benefits
- Complete employee benefits

Correspondence
Mail resume with cover letter

Part Time/Summer: The Vancouver Sun occasionally hires for part time and summer work.

VERSA SERVICES LTD.

P.O. Box 950, Station U
Toronto, Ontario, M8Z 5Y7
Tel: (416) 253-3163   Fax: (416) 255-4706

Human Resources

Versa Services is a diversified management company providing foodservices to business, health care, education, and government institutions. The company also provides dietary, housekeeping, laundry, maintenance, coffee systems, and material management services to all markets areas. Operating across Canada, Versa Services employs a total of 15,000 individuals in most major Canadian cities.

Academic Fields
College: Cooking/Culinary, Food/Nutrition, Hospitality
Bachelor of Science: Computer Science, Food Sciences
Chartered Accounting: CA-General, CGA-General/Finance

Critical Skills
Adaptable, Analytical, Decisive, Good Communication, Flexible, Dependable, Professional, Good With Figures, Leadership, Organized, Personable, Good Writing Skills

Types of Positions
Manager Trainee   Accounting Analyst
Banking Analyst   Cook
Chef

Starting Salary
$ 20,000 - 25,000

Company Benefits
- Major medical and dental
- Life insurance, long term disability
- Training is provided on a variety of topics

Correspondence
Mail resume and cover letter or submit in person

Part Time/Summer: Versa Services sometimes hires students for part time work and regularly hires for summer opportunities. Potential positions are at Wild Water Kingdom in Toronto. The best time to apply is in April.

VIA RAIL CANADA INC.

2 Place Ville Marie
Montreal, Québec, H3B 2C9
Tel: (514) 871-6000   Fax: (514) 871-6658

Human Resources Department
Internet: www.viarail.ca

VIA Rail Canada Inc. is Canada's national passenger rail company, dedicated to providing safe and efficient intercity and transcontinental rail services. VIA operates more than 340 trains weekly and employs fewer than 3,000 people. VIA Rail covers the country from coast to coast, serving more than 500 communities.

Academic Fields
College: General, Hospitality, Secretarial
Bachelor of Arts: General, Business
Bachelor of Comm/Admin: General

Critical Skills
Adaptable, Dependable, Efficient, Enthusiastic, Flexible, Good Communication, Organized, Personable, Productive, Professional, Responsible

Types of Positions
Telephone Sales Agent

Starting Salary
$ 25,000 - 30,000

Company Benefits
- Benefits for permanent employees
- Medical and dental coverage, life insurance
- Free train travel

Correspondence
Mail resume and cover letter or submit in person

Part Time/Summer: VIA Rail Canada occasionally looks for individuals for part time and summer employment opportunities. The best time to apply is in the middle or end of March.

The Canada Student Employment Guide

VILLA PROVIDENCE SHEDIAC INC.

403 Main St.
Shediac, New Brunswick, E4P 2B9
Tel: (506) 532-4484   Fax: (506) 532-8189

Yvon Girouard, Director of Human Resources

Villa Providence Shediac Inc. is a nursing home for seniors and younger persons with physical and mental illnesses.

Academic Fields
College: Nursing
Bachelor of Science: Nursing (RN)

Critical Skills
Adaptable, Confident, Dependable, Diligent, Efficient, Flexible, Good Communication, Patient, Personable, Productive, Professional, Responsible

Types of Positions
Part Time Nurse
Part Time Registered Nurse Asst.
Part Time Resident Assistant

Starting Salary
below $ 20,000 - 45,000 (depending on hours worked and classification)

Company Benefits
- Health and pension benefits for full time staff if they qualify
- Part time employees paid all inclusive rate

Correspondence
Mail resume with cover letter

Part Time/Summer: Villa Providence Shediac Inc. occasionally seeks candidates for part time and summer employment. Potential jobs are in the nursing department or in recreation. The best time to apply is from January to March.

VISTEON CANADA INC.

7455 Birchmount Rd.
Markham, Ontario, L3R 5C2
Tel: (905) 475-8510   Fax: (905) 474-4254

Human Resources
Internet: www.visteon.com

Visteon Automotive Systems is a state-of-the-art manufacturing facility, located in Markham, Ontario. They are a world class supplier of electronic and electro-mechanical components to the global automotive industry.

Academic Fields
College: Electronics Tech., Engineering Tech., Mechanical Tech.
Bachelor of Comm/Admin: Finance, Human Resources
Bachelor of Science: Computer Systems
Bachelor of Engineering: Computer Systems, Electrical, Industrial, Mechanical
Masters: Business Administration, Engineering

Critical Skills
Adaptable, Analytical, Creative, Dependable, Efficient, Enthusiastic, Flexible, Good Communication, Leadership, Professional

Types of Positions
Electrical Engineer   Mechanical Engineer
Industrial Engineer   Product Material Analyst
Financial Analyst   Human Resources Associate

Starting Salary
$ 35,000 - 40,000

Company Benefits
- Comprehensive benefits package

Correspondence
Mail or fax resume with cover letter

Part Time/Summer: Visteon Automotive Systems does not hire candidates for part time positions, but occasionally looks for people for the summer months, usually through universities. A potential job for the summer would be engineering assistant or in finance. The best time to apply is in March.

Co-op/Internship: Eight to sixteen month internships are offered in conjunction with a student's pursuance of a degree program in Engineering or Finance.

VOLKSWAGEN CANADA INC.

777 Bayly Street West
Ajax, Ontario, L1S 7G7
Tel: (905) 428-5807   Fax: (905) 428-5837

Human Resources
Internet: www.vw.com

Volkswagen Canada is a major car manufacturer. The majority of the firm's departments are in the U.S., under its American counterpart. Accounting services are carried out in Canada plus parts machinery for Canadian dealers. The company employs over 700 individuals.

Academic Fields
College: Accounting
Bachelor of Comm/Admin: Accounting
Chartered Accounting: CMA-General, CGA-General

Critical Skills
Adaptable, Confident, Dependable, Diligent, Diplomatic, Enthusiastic, Flexible, Personable, Productive

Types of Positions
Warehouse Person   Accounting Clerk

Starting Salary
$ 30,000 - 40,000

Company Benefits
- Fully paid benefits for permanent employees
- Extended health benefits, pension plan

Correspondence
Fax resume and cover letter

Part Time/Summer: Volkswagen Canada occasionally seeks candidates for part time work, and regularly hires people for the summer months. In the summer, potential positions include warehouse person. Some positions may be available where computer knowledge, or accounting knowledge is required.

VOLVO CARS OF CANADA LTD.

175 Gordon Baker Road
North York, Ontario, M2H 2N7
Tel: (416) 493-3700   Fax: (416) 493-9190

Anne Lake, Human Resources Administration
Internet: www.volvo.com

Volvo Cars of Canada is an automotive manufacturer in North York, Ontario. The company is fully owned by Volvo Canadian Holdings Ltd., and has an employee base of approximately 70 individuals. Volvo makes cars for both the domestic and foreign markets.

Academic Fields
College: General, Administration, Business
Bachelor of Arts: General, Business, Public Relations
Bachelor of Comm/Admin: General, Accounting, Finance, Human Resources, Marketing, Info Mgmt.
Chartered Accounting: CA-Finance, CGA/CMA - General/Finance

Critical Skills
Adaptable, Analytical, Creative, Dependable, Efficient, Enthusiastic, Innovative, Leadership, Personable, Professional

Types of Positions
Accounting   Marketing

Starting Salary
$ 25,000 - 30,000

Company Benefits
- All benefits included
- One pension plan
- Car lease program

Correspondence
Mail or fax resume with cover letter
E-mail: lakea@mail.volvo.com

Part Time/Summer: Volvo Cars of Canada occasionally looks for candidates for part time employment and summer opportunities. A potential summer job would be in finance. The best time to apply is in April.

W C I CANADA INC.

866 Langs Drive
Cambridge, Ontario, N3H 2N7
Tel: (519) 653-8880   Fax: (519) 653-3189

Gerry Lavis, Operations Manager

W C I Canada is a consumer manufacturing company that is made up of products under the name Frigidaire and Eureka. Frigidaire makes appliances, while Eureka produces vacuums. Their Cambridge plant assembles Eureka vacuums, and is a sales and marketing office for both brand name consumer goods.

Academic Fields
College: Accounting, Computer Science, Human Resources, Marketing/Sales
Bachelor of Arts: Business, Economics
Bachelor of Comm/Admin: Accounting, Finance, Marketing, Info Mgmt.
Chartered Accounting: CMA-Finance

Critical Skills
Adaptable, Analytical, Creative, Dependable, Diplomatic, Efficient, Enthusiastic, Flexible, Good Communication, Good With Figures, Innovative, Organized, Personable, Professional

Types of Positions
Mail Room Coordinator   Order Desk
Receptionist

Starting Salary
$ 20,000 - 25,000

Company Benefits
- Good benefit plan including health and dental
- Training and development opportunities

Correspondence
Mail resume with cover letter

Part Time/Summer: W C I Canada occasionally looks for individuals for part time and summer positions. Potential jobs include assembler, or service stock person. The best time to apply is in May.

WATERLOO FURNITURE COMPONENTS LTD.

501 Manitou Dr.
Kitchener, Ontario, N2C 1L2
Tel: (519) 748-5060   Fax: (519) 748-4095

Terri Richardson, Human Resources Coordinator
Internet: www.wfcltd.com

Waterloo Furniture Components is a Canadian manufacturer of components for the global office furniture market. Their product is promoted in 30 countries around the world. They employ over 850 dedicated employees.

Academic Fields
College: Accounting, Electronics Tech., Human Resources, Industrial Design, Marketing/Sales
Bachelor of Arts: Business
Bachelor of Comm/Admin: Accounting, Finance, Marketing, Info Mgmt.
Bachelor of Science: Environmental Studies
Bachelor of Engineering: Mechanical

Critical Skills
Analytical, Good Communication, Confident, Enthusiastic, Flexible, Innovative, Organized, Professional, Good Writing Skills

Types of Positions
CAD Operator   Accounting/Payroll Clerk
Customer Service Rep.

Starting Salary
$ 25,000 - 30,000

Company Benefits
- Extended health care, dental, vision
- Life insurance, pension, long term disability
- Training opportunities to increase skills and knowledge

Correspondence
Mail or fax resume with cover letter
E-mail: trichard@wfcltd.com

Part Time/Summer: Waterloo Furniture Components occasionally looks for people for part time work, and regularly seeks candidates in the summer. Most summer positions are in the factory. The best time to apply is in April.

The Canada Student Employment Guide

WATERLOO INN

475 King St. N.
Waterloo, Ontario, N2J 2Z5
Tel: (519) 884-0220   Fax: (519) 884-0321

Donna Doogan, Human Resources Manager
Internet: www.waterlooinn.com

Waterloo Inn is a hotel and restaurant that offers facilities and services for both business and family travellers. The hotel employs approximately 200 individuals.

Academic Fields
College: Accounting, Cooking/Culinary, Food/Nutrition, Hospitality, Marketing/Sales, Travel/Tourism

Critical Skills
Adaptable, Good Communication, Confident, Dependable, Diligent, Diplomatic, Efficient, Enthusiastic, Flexible, Organized, Personable, Productive, Professional, Multi-Tasking, Ability to Work in Fast Paced Environment

Types of Positions
Banquet Server   Front Desk Clerk
Room Attendant   Kitchen Assistant
Dishwasher

Starting Salary
below $ 20,000

Company Benefits
- Group insurance package
- Co-op work experience, student exchange

Correspondence
Mail or fax resume with cover letter

Part Time/Summer: Waterloo Inn regularly seeks candidates for part time work, but does not hire for the summer months.

WAVERLY & YORK CORPORATION

1010 1st St. SW, Suite 300
Calgary, Alberta, T2R 1K4
Tel: (403) 294-0411   Fax: (403) 266-5735

Angela Bardsley, Personnel

Waverly & York Corporation is involved in real estate and property management. The company employs 300 people in total.

Academic Fields
College: General, Accounting, Administration, Secretarial
Bachelor of Comm/Admin: General, Accounting, Finance, Public Admin.
Bachelor of Laws: Corporate, Real Estate
Chartered Accounting: CA - General/Finance
Masters: Business Administration

Critical Skills
Adaptable, Good Communication, Confident, Dependable, Efficient, Enthusiastic, Flexible, Good With Figures, Organized, Patient, Productive, Professional, Responsible, Good Writing Skills

Types of Positions
Accounting   Property Administration
Filing   Receptionist

Starting Salary
below $ 20,000 - 25,000

Company Benefits
- Competitive benefit package

Correspondence
Mail or fax resume with cover letter

Part Time/Summer: Waverly & York Corporation regularly looks for people for part time jobs, and occasionally hires in the summer months. Potential jobs include landscaping, cleaning, or being a leasing agent. The best time to apply is in May or June.

WEBCANADA

298 Jarvis St., Suite 1008
Toronto, Ontario, M5B 2M4
Tel: (416) 977-4411   Fax: (416) 977-4434

Paul Smith, Human Resources
Internet: www.webcanada.com

WebCanada, founded in 1994, is Canada's premier, full-service web development powerhouse. The company was created on the basis of providing affordable and effective communications structures by utilizing all aspects of the information superhighway. WebCanada's expertise is in the field of web design and development, including database management. Please enclose URLs of your completed HTML or graphic design work when forwarding your resume.

Academic Fields
College: Business, Communications, Computer Science, Graphic Arts
Bachelor of Arts: Fine Arts
Bachelor of Comm/Admin: Marketing
Bachelor of Science: Computer Science
Bachelor of Engineering: Computer Systems

Critical Skills
Analytical, Artistic, Good Communication, Creative, Diplomatic, Efficient, Organized, Productive, Responsible

Types of Positions
Junior Programmer   Junior HTML Designer
Junior Graphic Artist   Flash Developer

Starting Salary
$ 25,000 - 30,000

Company Benefits
- No benefits for part time employees

Correspondence
E-mail resume with cover letter
E-mail: hr@webcanada.com

Part Time/Summer: WebCanada regularly seeks people for part time work, and occasionally hires staff in the summer. Potential jobs are most likely those listed above. The best time to apply is in May or June.

WEGU CANADA INC.

1707 Harbour St.
Whitby, Ontario, L1N 9G6
Tel: (905) 668-2359   Fax: (905) 668-3414

Human Resources
Internet: www.durhammacc.com/wegu

Wegu Canada is a manufacturer of molded rubber and plastic products located in Whitby, Ontario. The company employs approximately 120 individuals in total.

Academic Fields
College: Accounting, Business, Engineering Tech., Marketing/Sales
Bachelor of Comm/Admin: Accounting
Bachelor of Engineering: Chemical, Mechanical
Chartered Accounting: CMA-General, CGA-Finance

Critical Skills
Adaptable, Analytical, Confident, Dependable, Efficient, Good With Figures, Innovative, Organized, Productive, Responsible, Good Writing Skills

Types of Positions
Mechanical Engineering
Quality Technician
Accounting Clerk

Starting Salary
$ 25,000 - 30,000

Company Benefits
- Insurance, drug plan, dental
- Training varies

Correspondence
Mail resume with cover letter
E-mail: wegu@idirect.com

Part Time/Summer: Wegu Canada regularly looks for individuals for part time or summer employment. Positions range from factory work to accounting or sales. The best time to apply is in March.

The Canada Student Employment Guide

WELDCO-BEALES MANUFACTURING INC.

12155 - 154 St. NW
Edmonton, Alberta, T5V 1J3
Tel: (403) 454-5244   Fax: (403) 455-6770

Anne Dingwell, Human Resources
Internet: www.weldco-beales.com

Weldco-Beales Manufacturing specializes in the equipment design and manufacturing of heavy duty equipment. The company has an employee base of about 300 people.

Academic Fields
College: Accounting, Administration, Computer Science, Drafting/Architecture, Engineering Tech., Industrial Design, Marketing/Sales, Secretarial
Bachelor of Comm/Admin: Accounting, Finance, Marketing
Bachelor of Engineering: Design, Mechanical
Chartered Accounting: CGA/CMA - General/Finance
Masters: Engineering

Critical Skills
Adaptable, Dependable, Diligent, Efficient, Enthusiastic, Flexible, Innovative, Organized, Personable, Productive, Professional, Responsible

Types of Positions
Various Positions

Starting Salary
$ 35,000 - 45,000

Company Benefits
- Competitive benefit package
- Includes pension plan
- Apprenticeship program

Correspondence
Mail or fax resume with cover letter
E-mail: adingwell@weldco-beales.com

Part Time/Summer: Weldco-Beales Manufacturing occasionally looks for individuals for part time or summer opportunities.

WENDY'S RESTAURANTS OF CANADA INC.

6715 Airport Road, Suite 301
Mississauga, Ontario, L4V 1X2
Tel: (905) 677-7023   Fax: (905) 677-5297

Human Resources Department
Internet: www.wendys.com

Wendy's Restaurants of Canada is engaged in the operation of fast food outlets. A quick service family restaurant chain, Wendy's Restaurants is a division of Wendy's International Inc. in the United States. With outlets throughout Canada, the restaurant employs over 3,600 individuals from coast to coast. There are over 20 restaurant locations in the Toronto region.

Academic Fields
College: Accounting, Business, Cooking/Culinary, Food/Nutrition, Hospitality
Bachelor of Arts: General, Business, Economics, Psychology, Public Relations
Bachelor of Comm/Admin: General, Accounting
Bachelor of Science: General

Critical Skills
Adaptable, Dependable, Enthusiastic, Good Communication, Flexible, Responsible, Leadership, Good With Figures, Personable, Productive, Professional, Manual Dexterity, Good Writing Skills

Types of Positions
Hourly Crew   Management Trainee
Shift Supervisor

Starting Salary
$ 24,500 - 26,000 (Manager Trainee)

Company Benefits
- Management trainee - 12 weeks training
- In-house school teaches courses for management

Correspondence
Mail resume with cover letter (Mgmt Position)
Fill out application at restaurant (Crew Member)

Part Time/Summer: Wendy's Restaurants regularly hires for part time positions and summer employment. Positions in the summer months include hourly crew members. The best time to apply is in May.

The Canada Student Employment Guide

WEST COAST APPAREL

611 Alexander St.
Vancouver, British Columbia, V6A 1E1
Tel: (604) 251-8609   Fax: (604) 251-8600

Personnel Administrator
Internet: www.jax.ca

West Coast Apparel designs, manufactures, and wholesales women's apparel. The 'Jax' and 'Studio Jax' are designed, developed, and produced at their facility in Vancouver. Koret and Perry Ellis divisions are import lines. The company has an employee base of approximately 350 individuals.

Academic Fields
College: General, Accounting, Administration, Business, Computer Science, Engineering Tech., Pattern Drafting, Marketing/Sales, Secretarial, Purchasing, Costing, Home Economics, Fashion
Bachelor of Engineering: Industrial

Critical Skills
Adaptable, Good Communication, Confident, Creative, Dependable, Efficient, Enthusiastic, Flexible, Good With Figures, Logical, Organized, Responsible

Types of Positions
Receptionist	Data Entry Clerk
Accounting	Warehouse
Quality Assurance Tech.	Pattern Making Assistant

Starting Salary
$ 22,000 - 25,000

Company Benefits
- Group health and medical benefits
- Clothing discount
- Pension membership

Correspondence
Mail, fax or e-mail resume with cover letter
E-mail: jobopportunities@jax.ca

Part Time/Summer: West Coast Apparel sometimes looks for individuals for part time work, and regularly seeks people for summer employment. Potential positions involve engineering or merchandise and design. The best time to apply is in February or March.

WEST KOOTENAY POWER LTD.

P.O. Box 130, Stn Main
Trail, British Columbia, V1R 4L4
Tel: (250) 368-0300   Fax: (250) 368-3211

Diane Brownrigg, Human Resources
Internet: www.wkpower.com

West Kootenay Power is a private utility company that delivers power, maintains and constructs electrical lines, markets energy-efficient products, and maintains and operates dams throughout the West Kootenays and part of the Okanagan.

Academic Fields
College: Accounting, Communications, Drafting/Architecture, Electronics Tech., Engineering Tech., Human Resources, Journalism, Secretarial
Bachelor of Arts: Business, Economics, Public Relations
Bachelor of Comm/Admin: Accounting, Finance, Marketing
Bachelor of Science: Computer Science
Bachelor of Engineering: Civil, Design, Electrical, Mechanical
Chartered Accounting: CMA-Finance, CGA-Finance
Masters: Engineering

Critical Skills
Adaptable, Good Communication, Decisive, Dependable, Enthusiastic, Leadership, Organized, Productive, Professional, Good Writing Skills, Flexible

Types of Positions
Labourer	Customer Service Rep.
Mail Coordinator	Office Assistant
Junior Engineer	

Starting Salary
$ 30,000 - 40,000

Company Benefits
- Flexible benefits including extended health
- Dental, vision care, long term disability

Correspondence
Mail or fax resume with cover letter
E-mail: dbrownrigg@wkpower.com

Part Time/Summer: West Kootenay Power occasionally hires for part time work, and occasionally hires for the summer. Potential jobs include labourer positions, clerical relief jobs, data entry type positions, or meter reading. Apply in early Spring.

WESTBURY LIFE

500 University Ave.
Toronto, Ontario, M5G 1V8
Tel: (416) 598-4321   Fax: (416) 585-5832

Brenda Norman, Human Resources
Internet: www.wendys.com

Westbury Life is a provider of group life and health, individual life, annuities and individual disability insurance products.

Academic Fields
College: Accounting, Administration, Advertising, Business, Communications, Computer Science, Graphic Arts, Human Resources, Insurance, Journalism, Law Clerk, Nursing, Secretarial, Statistics
Bachelor of Arts: General, Business, Languages
Bachelor of Comm/Admin: Accounting, Finance, Info Mgmt.
Bachelor of Science: Actuarial, Computer Science, Mathematics, Nursing (RN)
Bachelor of Laws: General, Corporate
Chartered Accounting: CA - General/Finance, CMA-General, CGA - General/Finance
Masters: Business Administration

Critical Skills
Adaptable, Analytical, Dependable, Diligent, Diplomatic, Efficient, Enthusiastic, Flexible, Good Communication, Good With Figures, Logical, Organized, Personable, Responsible

Types of Positions
Policyowner's Service Dept.   Office Services Dept.
New Business   Individual/Group Claims

Starting Salary
$ 25,000 - 30,000

Company Benefits
- 100% coverage on health and dental
- Company pension, life insurance
- Insurance courses

Correspondence
Mail or fax resume with cover letter

Part Time/Summer: Westbury Life does not hire for part time work, but regularly seeks people in the summer. Jobs include administration assistant, policyowner's service clerk or new business clerk. The best time to apply is in April.

WESTCLIFF MANAGEMENT LTD.

600 de Maisonneuve Ouest, bureau 2600
Montréal, Québec, H3A 3J2
Tel: (514) 499-8300   Fax: N/A

Human Resources Manager
Internet: www.westcliff.com

Westcliff Management is a real estate operator of non-residential buildings. The company is located in Montreal, Quebec, and was established in 1972. Westcliffe Management has an employee base of approximately 500 individuals.

Academic Fields
College: Accounting, Administration, Business, Communications, Engineering Tech., Law Clerk, Secretarial, Information Systems
Bachelor of Arts: Business, Economics, Public Relations
Bachelor of Comm/Admin: Accounting, Finance, Marketing, Info Mgmt.
Bachelor of Laws: Corporate, Real Estate
Chartered Accounting: CA-General, CMA-General, CGA-General
Masters: Business Administration

Critical Skills
Dependable, Efficient, Good Writing Skills, Good Communication, Organized, Personable, Productive, Good With Figures, Professional, Responsible

Types of Positions
Secretarial   Accounting Clerk

Starting Salary
$ 25,000 - 30,000

Company Benefits
- Comprehensive group insurance
- Company pays for courses related to job
- Computer and software training

Correspondence
Mail resume with cover letter

Part Time/Summer: Westcliff Management sometimes seeks individuals for part time and summer employment. Potential summer jobs include filing clerk, office services clerk, and secretarial duties. The best time to apply is in the Spring.

The Canada Student Employment Guide

WESTCOAST ENERGY INC.

1333 West Georgia Street
Vancouver, British Columbia, V6E 3K9
Tel: (604) 488-8000   Fax: (604) 488-8500

Joleene Beaven, Human Resources
Internet: www.westcoastenergy.com

Westcoast Energy is the major natural gas gathering, processing and transportation company in British Columbia. The company's operations are divided into the two main divisions.

Academic Fields
College: Accounting, Administration, Business, Communications, Computer Science, Engineering Tech., Human Resources, Mechanical Tech., Secretarial
Bachelor of Arts: Business, Economics
Bachelor of Comm/Admin: Accounting, Finance
Bachelor of Science: Chemistry, Computer Science, Environmental Studies, Geology, Mathematics
Bachelor of Engineering: Chemical, Civil, Computer Syst., Electrical, Environ. Studies, Geotechnical, Mech.
Chartered Accounting: CA - General/Finance, CGA/CMA - General/Finance
Masters: Business Admin., Engineering, Library Science

Critical Skills
Adaptable, Analytical, Good Communication, Confident, Creative, Dependable, Diligent, Diplomatic, Efficient, Enthusiastic, Flexible, Good With Figures, Leadership, Logical, Manual Dexterity, Organized, Patient, Personable, Productive, Professional, Responsible, Good Writing Skills

Types of Positions
Mail Room Clerk   Receptionist
Accounting Clerk   Field Clerk

Starting Salary
$ 20,000 - 30,000

Company Benefits
- Full range of benefits
- Night school part of training

Correspondence
Mail resume with cover letter

Part Time/Summer: Westcoast Energy regularly hires for part time jobs, and in the summer. Jobs are in all depts. at the entry-level, however, sons and daughters of employees are hired first. Individuals should apply early in February.

WESTERN GLOVE WORKS

555 Logan Ave.
Winnipeg, Manitoba, R3A 0S4
Tel: (204) 788-4249   Fax: (204) 783-9049

Lori Smith, Director of Training
Internet: www.silverjeans.com

Western Glove Works is a leader in the garment manufacturing industry, serving markets throughout North America and overseas. They make private label apparel for high profile names such as Gap International, Thrifty's, Nordstrom's, etc., in addition to their own line of fashion jeans carrying the "Silver" label.

Academic Fields
College: Accounting, Administration, Business, Human Resources, Information Syst., Marketing/Sales, Purchasing, Secretarial, Engineering Tech., Mech. Tech., Plumbing, Human Ecology, Textiles
Bachelor of Arts: General, Business, Fine Arts
Bachelor of Comm/Admin: General, Accounting, Finance, Human Resources, Marketing, Info Mgmt.
Bachelor of Engineering: General, Industrial, Mech.
Bachelor of Education: Adult Education
Chartered Accounting: CA-General, CMA-General, CGA-General

Critical Skills
Adaptable, Analytical, Artistic, Good Communication, Confident, Creative, Decisive, Dependable, Diligent, Diplomatic, Efficient, Enthusiastic, Flexible, Good With Figures, Innovative, Leadership, Responsible

Types of Positions
Merchandising   Accounting
Human Resources   Customer Service
Quality Control   Product Development

Starting Salary
$ 20,000 - 25,000

Company Benefits
- Basic health care plan, dental plan

Correspondence
Mail, fax or e-mail resume with cover letter

Part Time/Summer: Western Glove Works occasionally hires for part time work and regularly hires for the summer. Apply in April, May or June.

Co-op/Internship: They offer a work experience program.

THE WESTIN BAYSHORE RESORT AND MARINA
1601 Georgia St. W.
Vancouver, British Columbia, V6G 2V4
Tel: (604) 691-6995   Fax: (604) 691-6986

Sheila Brock, Manager Human Resources

The Westin Bayshore Resort and Marina is a luxury hotel in downtown Vancouver. The hotel's goal is to be the best and most sought after hotel in Vancouver by delivering exceptional customer service.

Academic Fields
College: Hospitality

Critical Skills
Adaptable, Confident, Dependable, Diplomatic, Enthusiastic, Flexible, Good Communication, Organized, Patient, Personable, Professional

Types of Positions
Front Office   Guest Services
Service Express   Housekeeping
Culinary

Starting Salary
$ 20,000 - 30,000 (depending on position)

Company Benefits
- Comprehensive medical and dental coverage
- Other industry benefits based on hours worked
- In-house training

Correspondence
Mail resume with cover letter

Part Time/Summer: The Westin Bayshore Resort and Marina regularly hires people for part time and summer opportunities. Potential jobs include banquet server, outdoor pool server, lifeguard (bronze certificate required), and refreshment centre attendant. The best time to apply is in March or April.

THE WESTIN PRINCE HOTEL
900 York Mills Road
North York, Ontario, M3B 3H2
Tel: (416) 444-2511   Fax: (416) 444-9597

Isobel Millar, Director of Human Resources

The Westin Prince Hotel is located in North York. A subsidiary of Prince Hotel Inc. of Japan, the Toronto Prince Hotel has a large number of facilities for business meetings, conventions or family retreats. The hotel employs over 340 individuals including part-timers.

Academic Fields
College: Hospitality, Human Resources, Marketing/Sales, Secretarial, Travel/Tourism
Chartered Accounting: CGA-Finance
Masters: Business Administration

Critical Skills
Confident, Dependable, Diligent, Diplomatic, Efficient, Enthusiastic, Flexible, Good Communication, Organized, Innovative, Leadership, Good Writing Skills, Personable, Productive, Professional

Types of Positions
Room Attendant   House Person
Stewards Helper   Potwasher
Cleaner

Starting Salary
$ 20,000 - 25,000

Company Benefits
- Medical, dental and life insurance coverage
- Long term sickness and twelve paid holidays
- Employees trained from department heads

Correspondence
Fax or submit resume with cover letter in person

Part Time/Summer: The Westin Prince Hotel sometimes hires for part time and summer employment depending on business demands. Sample positions include room attendant, and wait staff for the lounge. The best time to apply is in April.

WESTINGHOUSE CANADA INC.

30 Milton Avenue, P.O. Box 2510
Hamilton, Ontario, L8N 3K2
Tel: (905) 528-8811   Fax: (905) 577-0275

Angela Rocci, Human Resources

Westinghouse Canada is involved in the manufacture and sale of electrical, electronic and mechanical products and services for industrial, construction, utility, and defence applications. Competing globally, Westinghouse Canada employs over 2,500 individuals across the country.

Academic Fields
College: Accounting, Business, Computer Science, Drafting/Architecture, Engineering Tech., Mechanical Tech., Secretarial
Bachelor of Arts: Business
Bachelor of Comm/Admin: General, Accounting, Finance
Bachelor of Science: Computer Science
Bachelor of Engineering: Computer Systems, Electrical, Mechanical
Chartered Accounting: CMA - General/Finance, CGA - General/Finance

Critical Skills
Adaptable, Good Communication, Confident, Creative, Decisive, Dependable, Diligent, Efficient, Enthusiastic, Flexible, Innovative, Leadership, Logical, Organized, Personable, Productive, Professional, Responsible, Good Writing Skills

Types of Positions
Production Controller   Jr. Analyst Planner
Accounting Clerk   Administrative Asst.

Starting Salary
$ 30,000 - 40,000

Company Benefits
- Dental and medical, personal accident
- Life insurance, income protection

Correspondence
Mail resume with cover letter

Part Time/Summer: Westinghouse does not hire for part time work, but sometimes offers summer opportunities. Potential positions involve clerical, secretarial, or accounting duties. Individuals could also work as a production controller. The best time to apply is in May.

WESTJET AIRLINES

35 McTavish Place NE
Calgary, Alberta, T2E 7J7
Tel: (403) 717-2146   Fax: (403) 717-2141

Deanna Hunter, Recruiter
Internet: www.westjet.com

Westjet Airlines is the leading low-fare airline that people want to work with, customers want to fly with and shareholders want to invest with.

Academic Fields
College: Accounting, Administration, Advertising, Business, Communications, Human Resources, Information Systems, Marketing/Sales, Purchasing, Secretarial, Aircraft Maint., Computer Sci., Electronics Tech., Engineering Tech., Hospitality, Travel/Tourism
Bachelor of Arts: General, Business, English, Languages, Public Relations
Bachelor of Comm/Admin: General, Accounting, Finance, Human Resources, Marketing
Bachelor of Science: General, Computer Science
Chartered Accounting: CA-General, CMA-General, CGA-General
Masters: Business Administration

Critical Skills
Adaptable, Analytical, Artistic, Good Communication, Confident, Creative, Decisive, Dependable, Diligent, Diplomatic, Efficient, Enthusiastic, Flexible, Organized, Patient, Personable, Persuasive, Productive, Professional, Responsible, Writing Skills

Types of Positions
Agent   Customer Service Agent
Flight Attendant

Starting Salary
$ 20,000 - 25,000

Company Benefits
- Typical health, medical, dental coverage to all staff

Correspondence
Fax resume with cover letter or apply through website

Part Time/Summer: Westjet regularly hires for part time work and rarely hires for the summer. Potential jobs include go getter at the airport or customer service agent. The best time to apply is in April.

Co-op/Internship: They review all internship/work experience requests to determine suitability and whether they can accommodate.

WESTMINSTER SAVINGS CREDIT UNION

108 - 960 Quayside Dr.
New Westminster, British Columbia, V3M 6G2
Tel: (604) 528-3806   Fax: (604) 519-4210

Human Resources
Internet: www.betterbanking.com

Westminster Savings Credit Union is a local credit union serving the citizens of the lower Mainland. The credit union employs approximately 380 individuals in total.

Academic Fields
College: Accounting, Business, Computer Science, Faculty Management, Human Resources, Journalism, Financial, Marketing/Sales
Bachelor of Arts: Business, Economics
Bachelor of Comm/Admin: Finance, Marketing, Info Mgmt.
Bachelor of Engineering: Computer Systems
Chartered Accounting: CGA/CMA - General/Finance
Masters: Business Administration

Critical Skills
Good Communication, Dependable, Enthusiastic, Flexible, Good With Figures, Innovative, Personable, Professional

Types of Positions
Various Positions

Starting Salary
Depends on position

Company Benefits
- Competitive package

Correspondence
Mail or fax resume with cover letter

Part Time/Summer: Westminster Savings Credit Union occasionally looks for people for part time and summer employment opportunities. A potential job would include clerk or in customer service.

WESTON PRODUCE INC.

9625 Yonge St.
Richmond Hill, Ontario, L4C 5T2
Tel: (905) 883-4800   Fax: (905) 883-4330

Human Resources

Weston Produce is a grocery store, otherwise known as F & F Supermarkets. The company has an employee base of approximately 195 individuals.

Academic Fields
College: General
Bachelor of Arts: General, Business
Bachelor of Comm/Admin: General
Bachelor of Science: General
Bachelor of Laws: General
Bachelor of Engineering: General
Chartered Accounting: CA-General

Critical Skills
Adaptable, Analytical, Good Communication, Dependable, Diligent, Diplomatic, Efficient, Enthusiastic, Flexible, Good With Figures, Logical, Patient, Personable

Types of Positions
Accounts Payable   Grocery Clerk
Cashier

Starting Salary
below $ 20,000 - 25,000

Company Benefits
- Dental, medical, life insurance
- Minimum training

Correspondence
Mail or submit resume with cover letter in person

Part Time/Summer: Weston Produce regularly seeks people for part time work, and occasionally seeks candidates for the summer months. Potential jobs include cashier or stock help.

WESTPORT INNOVATIONS INC.

1691 West 75th Avenue
Vancouver, British Columbia, V6P 6P2
Tel: (604) 718-2000   Fax: (604) 718-2001

Duane Radcliffe, Recruiter
Internet: www.westport.com

Westport is developing fuel systems that allow diesel engines to run on natural gas, which is cleaner and usually less expensive than diesel fuel. Westport's patented technology is intended to reduce harmful diesel engine emissions while retaining performance, durability and fuel efficiency.

Academic Fields
College: Accounting, Human Resources, Automotive Maintenance, CAD Autocad, Computer Science, Electronics Tech., Engineering Tech., Mechanical Tech.
Bachelor of Comm/Admin: Accounting, Finance, Human Resources
Bachelor of Engineering: Chemical, Design, Electrical, Industrial, Materials Science, Mechanical
Chartered Accounting: CA-General, CGA-General, CMA-General
Masters: Engineering

Critical Skills
Analytical, Confident, Creative, Dependable, Enthusiastic, Innovative, Leadership, Productive

Types of Positions
Engineering   Administration

Starting Salary
Depends on position

Company Benefits
- Comprehensive benefits including extended health, dental
- Life insurance, disability insurance

Correspondence
E-mail resume with cover letter or apply through web site. E-mail: careers@westport.com

Part Time/Summer: Westport Innovations Inc. rarely hires for part time work and occasionally hires for the summer months. Typically, the company will consider summer employment only for co-op engineering students.

Co-op/Internship: They have on occasion brought in MBA marketing interns for the summer.

WESTSHORE TERMINALS LTD.

1 Roberts Bank Rd.
Delta, British Columbia, V4M 4G5
Tel: (604) 946-4491   Fax: (604) 946-1388

Alan Kazuta, Human Resources

Westshore Terminals is the largest bulk loading terminal on the West Coast of North America. The firm receives coal from mines in Southeastern British Columbia, Alberta, Washington, Montana, and Wyoming. They ship to Japan, Korea, and many European countries. Entry-level positions are hired through the union hiring hall.

Academic Fields
College: Accounting, Administration, Business, Computer Science, Engineering Tech., Human Resources
Bachelor of Comm/Admin: General, Accounting, Finance, Info Mgmt.
Bachelor of Science: Environmental Studies
Bachelor of Engineering: Electrical, Industrial, Mechanical, Mining
Chartered Accounting: CA - General/Finance, CGA/CMA - General/Finance
Masters: Business Administration, Engineering

Critical Skills
Adaptable, Good Communication, Dependable, Efficient, Enthusiastic, Flexible, Good With Figures, Leadership, Organized, Personable, Productive, Professional, Responsible

Types of Positions
Various Positions

Starting Salary
Depends on position

Company Benefits
- Comprehensive benefit package

Correspondence
Mail resume with cover letter

Part Time/Summer: Westshore Terminals occasionally hires for part time and summer work. Potential jobs involve working with management information systems. The best time to apply is in May.

WEYERHAEUSER COMPANY LIMITED

925 Georgia St. W.
Vancouver, British Columbia, V6C 3L2
Tel: (604) 661-8494   Fax: (604) 688-8256

Alex Catterill, Human Resources
Internet: www.weyerhaeuser.com

Weyerhaeuser is an international forest products company whose principal businesses are the growing and harvesting of trees; the manufacture, distribution and sale of forest products; and real estate construction and development.

Academic Fields
College: Accounting, Administration, Business, Communications, Engineering Tech., Forestry, Human Resources, Journalism, Marketing/Sales, Mechanical Tech., Statistics, Legal Assistant, Social Work, Info Syst., Purchasing, Real Estate, Secretarial, Computer Science
Bachelor of Arts: Business, Economics, Journalism, Statistics, Public Relations, Sociology/Social Work
Bachelor of Comm/Admin: General, Acctg, Finance, Marketing, Info Mgmt., Human Res., Public Admin.
Bachelor of Science: General, Biology, Chemistry, Computer Sci., Environ. Studies, Forestry, Geog., Math
Bachelor of Laws: Corporate
Bachelor of Engineering: General, Chemical, Computer Systems, Electrical, Environmental Studies, Geotechnical, Industrial, Mechanical, Transportation
Chartered Accounting: CA - General/Finance, CGA/CMA - General/Finance
Masters: Business Admin., Science, Engineering, Educ.

Critical Skills
Analytical, Good Communication, Confident, Creative, Decisive, Efficient, Flexible, Innovative, Leadership, Productive, Good Writing Skills, Safety Conscious

Types of Positions
Service Centre   Junior Level Accountant

Starting Salary
$ 25,000 - 30,000

Company Benefits
- Competitive pay ranges, flexible benefits

Correspondence
Mail, fax, submit resume & cover letter in person
E-mail: alex.catterill@weyerhaeuser.com

Part Time/Summer: Weyerhaeuser occasionally hires for part time or summer work. Potential jobs are in forestry or engineering. Apply is November.

WHISTLER BLACKCOMB MOUNTAIN

4545 Blackcomb Way
Whistler, British Columbia, V0N 1B4
Tel: (604) 938-7366   Fax: (604) 938-7527

Karen Bauckham, Employment Manager
Internet: www.whistler-blackcomb.com

Whistler Blackcomb Mountain is a four-season mountain resort offering skiing, snowboarding, hiking and mountain biking. They offer guests the best mountain experience around.

Academic Fields
College: Accounting, Administration, Advertising, Business, Child Care, Communications, Computer Science, Cooking/Culinary, Food/Nutrition, Graphic Arts, Hospitality, Human Resources, Marketing/Sales, Secretarial, Travel/Tourism
Bachelor of Arts: General, Business, Public Relations, Recreation Studies
Bachelor of Comm/Admin: General, Accounting, Finance, Marketing, Info Mgmt., Public Admin
Bachelor of Science: Computer Science, Food Sciences, Health Sciences
Bachelor of Education: General, Childhood, Physical
Chartered Accounting: CA - General/Finance, CGA/CMA - General/Finance
Masters: Business Administration

Critical Skills
Creative, Enthusiastic, Leadership, Personable, Good Communication, Positive Attitude, Animated, Customer Skills

Types of Positions
Retail Clerk   Food or Beverage
Guest Relations Host   Lift Operator
Ski School Instructor   Ticket Sellers

Starting Salary
Pay range from $7 to $11 per hour

Company Benefits
- 100% basic medical after 3 months employment

Correspondence
Submit resume with cover letter in person

Part Time/Summer: Whistler Blackcomb Mountain regularly hires for part time work during the Winter season and occasionally hires for the summer. Jobs include lift operator, food and beverage staff, mini golf attendants, slide attendants, and ticket sellers. Apply at the end of May or beginning of June.

The Canada Student Employment Guide

WHITE ROSE CRAFTS AND NURSERY SALES LIMITED
4038 Hwy. #7 East
Unionville, Ontario, L3R 2L5
Tel: (905) 477-3330   Fax: (905) 477-1105

Christine Liddell, Human Resources
Internet: www.whitehorse.ca

White Rose is a retail merchandiser specializing in nursery, home decor and craft products. The company also owns and operates a nursery farming facility in the Township of Uxbridge, that supplies the company's stores with outdoor plants for retail sale. Operating 32 stores in the Ontario region, the company employs 2,000 people.

Academic Fields
College: General, Accounting, Forestry, Business Merchandising
Bachelor of Arts: General, Business, Urban Geography
Bachelor of Science: Agriculture, Environmental Studies, Forestry, Horticulture

Critical Skills
Adaptable, Good Communication, Creative, Decisive, Dependable, Diplomatic, Efficient, Enthusiastic, Flexible, Good With Figures, Leadership, Organized, Patient, Reliable, Productive, Professional, Responsible

Types of Positions
Carry Out Clerk	Cashier
Sales	Bookkeeper
Merchandise Admin.	Admin. Support

Starting Salary
below $ 20,000 - 25,000

Company Benefits
- Health, dental, life insurance
- Short and long term disability, group RRSP, employee discount
- Internal and external training courses

Correspondence
Mail, fax or e-mail resume with cover letter
E-mail: hr@whitehorse.ca

Part Time/Summer: White Rose regularly hires part time employees and individuals for the summer months. Potential positions are most likely store jobs or involve head office clerical work. The best time to apply is in March or April.

WHITE SPOT LIMITED
1126 Marine Drive S.E.
Vancouver, British Columbia, V5X 2V7
Tel: (604) 321-6631   Fax: (604) 325-1499

Denise Buchanan, Director, Human Resources
Internet: www.whitespot.ca

White Spot is a large food service company consisting of over 50 family style restaurants, some of which are corporately owned and operated, the majority of which are franchise operations. White Spot also operates a quick service division, 'Triple O's'. White Spot has operated restaurants in British Columbia since 1928, and between its corporate and franchise locations currently numbers over 2,500 employees.

Academic Fields
College: Hospitality

Critical Skills
Adaptable, Analytical, Confident, Dependable, Flexible, Leadership, Personable, Professional, Responsible, Strong Communication

Types of Positions
Assistant Manager	Server
Cook	

Starting Salary
$ 25,000 - 30,000 (Entry level mgmt. roles)

Company Benefits
- Comprehensive medical, dental and insurance package
- Extensive on-the-job training and workshops
- Opportunities to progress to general manager or franchise opportunity

Correspondence
Mail resume with cover letter

Part Time/Summer: White Spot sometimes looks for candidates for part time and summer employment. Potential jobs in the summer include servers or cooks.

The Canada Student Employment Guide

WHITEHILL TECHNOLOGIES INC.

260 MacNaughton Ave.
Moncton, New Brunswick, E1H 2J8
Tel: (506) 855-0005   Fax: (506) 855-0088

Lisa Moore, HR Coordinator
Internet: www.whitehill.com

Whitehill Technologies, Inc. is a leading provider of e-business infrastructure software for the capture and transformation of legacy data into e-enabled business information. More than 150 companies in 32 countries currently use Whitehill products as part of their e-commerce strategy.

Academic Fields
College: Accounting, Information Systems, Marketing/Sales, Computer Science
Bachelor of Comm/Admin: Accounting, Marketing, Info Mgmt.
Bachelor of Science: Computer Science, Mathematics
Bachelor of Engineering: Civil, Computer Systems
Bachelor of Education: Adult Education
Chartered Accounting: CGA-General
Masters: Business Administration, Engineering

Critical Skills
Adaptable, Analytical, Decisive, Dependable, Efficient, Enthusiastic, Good Communication, Productive, Professional, Responsible

Types of Positions
Accounting   Administration
Junior Network Analyst   Junior Programmer

Starting Salary
$ 30,000 - 35,000

Company Benefits
- Health benefits, employee stock options

Correspondence
E-mail resume with cover letter
E-mail: career@whitehill.com

Part Time/Summer: Whitehill Technologies occasionally hires for part time and summer work. Potential jobs are in the area of administration and client services. The best time to apply is in early Spring.

Co-op/Internship: In conjunction with government sponsored programs, Whitehall occasionally participates in these programs when special projects arise.

WILDERNESS REFORESTATION

36 Montreal Ave.
Wawa, Ontario, P0S 1K0
Tel: (705) 856-2799   Fax: (705) 856-1365

Johanna Rowe, Recruiting Supervisor
Internet: www.wilderness.on.ca

Wilderness Reforestation is a tree planting company based out of Wawa, Ontario. The company began modestly, planting 835,000 trees for Algoma Central Properties and the Ontario Ministry of Natural Resources, in the Wawa District. Since 1986, the company has become a leader in the unique silviculture industry in Ontario.

Academic Fields
Applications will be accepted from candidates from all disciplines.

Critical Skills
Adaptable, Dependable, Diligent, Efficient, Enthusiastic, Leadership, Manual Dexterity, Patient, Personable, Productive, Responsible, Physically Fit

Types of Positions
Tree Planter   Crew Boss
Cook   Cook's Assistant

Starting Salary
$ 15,000 or less (part time) /
$ 25,000 - 40,000 (full time)

Company Benefits
- Offers first aid, CPR, WHMIS, passenger vehicle drivers licensing
- Fire-fighting and pesticide application training
- Offers opportunities to work in forest fire base camps

Correspondence
Mail resume with cover letter or apply through web site. E-mail: wild@onlink.net

Part Time/Summer: Wilderness Reforestation regularly hires for both part time and summer employment. Potential jobs include treeplanting (Feb/March), cooks and cook's assistant (Feb/March), pesticide application (ground and aerial) (May/June), and commercial thinning (Feb/March). The best time to apply is stated above.

The Canada Student Employment Guide

WILSON AUTO ELECTRIC LTD.

600 Golspie St.
Winnipeg, Manitoba, R2K 2V1
Tel: (204) 667-5535   Fax: (204) 668-3438

Cathy Walker, Human Resources
Internet: www.wilsonautoelectric.com

Wilson Auto Electric is a remanufacturer of alternators, starters, generators and their component parts for the automotive, agricultural, industrial, and marine aftermarkets.

Academic Fields
College: Accounting, Administration, Business, Drafting/Architecture, Electronics Tech., Engineering Tech., Human Resources, Marketing/Sales, Mechanical Tech.
Bachelor of Arts: General, Business, Public Relations
Bachelor of Comm/Admin: General, Accounting, Finance, Marketing, Info Mgmt.
Bachelor of Science: Computer Science
Bachelor of Engineering: Computer Systems, Electrical, Industrial, Mechanical
Bachelor of Education: Adult Education
Chartered Accounting: CA - General/Finance, CMA-General
Masters: Business Administration

Critical Skills
Adaptable, Analytical, Creative, Dependable, Diligent, Efficient, Enthusiastic, Flexible, Good With Figures, Innovative, Leadership, Logical, Manual Dexterity, Organized, Patient, Personable, Productive, Professional, Responsible

Types of Positions
Accountant   Operations Engineer
Customer Service

Starting Salary
$ 25,000 - 30,000

Company Benefits
- Life insurance, dental coverage
- Short and long term disability

Correspondence
Mail or fax resume with cover letter

Part Time/Summer: Wilson Auto Electric occasionally seeks people for part time work and summer positions. The best time to apply is in the early Spring.

CITY OF WINDSOR

171 Goyeau St.
Windsor, Ontario, N9A 1G5
Tel: (519) 255-6515   Fax: (519) 255-6874

Human Resources Department
Internet: www.city.windsor.on.ca

The City of Windsor is a municipal government responsible for the formation of policy and laws in matters under its jurisdiction.

Academic Fields
College: Accounting, Administration, Business, Computer Science, Drafting/Architecture, Electronics Tech., Engineering Tech., Food/Nutrition, Hospitality, Mechanical Tech., Nursing, Secretarial
Bachelor of Arts: Business, Sociology/Social Work
Bachelor of Comm/Admin: General, Accounting, Finance, Info Mgmt.
Bachelor of Science: Biology, Chemistry, Computer Science, Environmental Studies, Food Sciences, Forestry, Health Sciences, Horticulture, Nursing (RN)
Bachelor of Engineering: General, Biomedical, Chemical, Civil, Computer Systems, Design, Electrical, Environmental Studies, Geotechnical, Industrial, Mechanical, Transportation, Water Resources
Chartered Accounting: CA - General/Finance, CGA/CMA - General/Finance
Masters: Business Administration, Engineering

Critical Skills
Adaptable, Good Communication, Confident, Decisive, Dependable, Diligent, Diplomatic, Efficient, Responsible, Good Writing Skills

Types of Positions
Junior Clerk   File Clerk
Document Clerk   General Labourer

Starting Salary
$ 30,000 - 40,000

Company Benefits
- Life insurance, green shield, pension plan

Correspondence
Mail resume with cover letter

Part Time/Summer: They do not hire students part time, but regularly hires for the summer. Potential jobs include lifeguard, pool checker, marina attendant, and playground leader (apply December to first week of February). Labourer work may also be offered (apply December to mid-February).

WINNERS APPAREL LTD.

6715 Airport Rd.
Mississauga, Ontario, L4V 1Y2
Tel: (905) 405-8000   Fax: (905) 405-7581

Human Resources
Internet: www.tjx.com

Winners Apparel is Canada's leading "off-price" fashion retailer in men's, ladies', kids' wear, and giftware.

Academic Fields
College: Accounting, Administration, Advertising, Business, Human Resources, Information Systems, Marketing/Sales, Purchasing, Secretarial, Statistics, Security/Law Enforcement, CAD Autocad, Comp. Sci.
Bachelor of Arts: General, Business, Economics, Stats
Bachelor of Comm/Admin: General, Accounting, Finance, Human Resources, Marketing, Info Mgmt.
Bachelor of Science: General, Computer Sci., Math
Chartered Accounting: CA - General/Finance, CGA/CMA - General/Finance
Masters: Business Administration

Critical Skills
Dependable, Good Communication, Productive, Professional, Resourceful, Team Player

Types of Positions
Administrative Asst.   Clerical (Finance Dept.)
Data Entry   Merchandise/Planning Asst.

Starting Salary
$ 20,000 - 25,000

Company Benefits
- Full medical and dental plan, paid for by company

Correspondence
Mail, fax or e-mail resume with cover letter
E-mail: dana-peever@tjx.com

Part Time/Summer: Winners Apparel regularly hires for part time work and occasionally hires for the summer. They rarely hire at their home office for part time, but hire regularly at their stores for the summer. The best time to apply is in July and August for part time work at stores, and March and April for summer work at their home office.

Co-op/Internship: Depending on specific department needs, candidates are interviewed and placed in internship programs around their school schedule, and if successful offered full time employment upon completion of education if available.

WINPAK LTD.

100 Saulteaux Crescent
Winnipeg, Manitoba, R3J 3T3
Tel: (204) 831-2220   Fax: (204) 888-7806

Susan Brucki, Human Resources Coordinator

Through operating companies in Canada and the United States, Winpak manufactures and distributes flexible packaging materials for use in various foods, pharmaceutical, and industrial applications.

Academic Fields
College: General, Accounting, Business, Computer Sci., Electronics Tech., Engineering Tech., Food/Nutrition, Graphic Arts, Human Resources, Science-General, Secretarial
Bachelor of Arts: General, Business
Bachelor of Comm/Admin: General, Accounting, Finance, Marketing
Bachelor of Science: General, Chemistry, Food Sci.
Bachelor of Engineering: Chemical, Industrial, Mechanical
Chartered Accounting: CA - General/Finance, CMA - General/Finance
Masters: Business Administration

Critical Skills
Efficient, Enthusiastic, Flexible, Good Communication, Professional, Responsible

Types of Positions
Sales Coordinator   Quality Control Inspector
Junior Programmer   Data Entry Clerk
Receptionist   Secretarial

Starting Salary
$ 25,000 - 30,000

Company Benefits
- All benefits included, life, disability

Correspondence
Mail or submit resume and cover letter in person

Part Time/Summer: Winpak sometimes hires for part time work and regularly hires for the summer. Potential jobs include entry level assistant, file clerk, quality control inspector, and special projects.

Co-op/Internship: They occasionally have internship opportunities for marketing and technical service.

The Canada Student Employment Guide

WIRE ROPE INDUSTRIES LTD.

5501 Transcanadienne
Pointe-Claire, Québec, H9R 1B7
Tel: (514) 697-9711   Fax: (514) 697-3346

Jacques Fortier, Ressources humaines
Internet: www.wirerope.com

Wire Rope Industries is a manufacturer of wide rope and strand, and is involved in the distribution of industrial supplies and power transmission products. A subsidiary of Noranda Inc., the company has a plant in Surrey, British Columbia, in addition to head office address above. The manufacturer has numerous service centres across the country. Wire Rope Industries employs approximately 550 people.

Academic Fields
College: Accounting, Business, Computer Science, Electronics Tech., Engineering Tech., Industrial Design, Marketing/Sales, Mechanical Tech.
Bachelor of Comm/Admin: Accounting, Finance, Marketing
Bachelor of Science: Computer Science
Bachelor of Engineering: General, Civil, Computer Systems, Electrical, Industrial, Materials Science, Mechanical
Chartered Accounting: CA-Finance, CMA - General/Finance, CGA - General/Finance
Masters: Business Administration

Critical Skills
Adaptable, Confident, Creative, Dependable, Decisive, Leadership, Logical, Productive

Types of Positions
Junior Engineer   Accounting Trainee

Starting Salary
$ 25,000 - 30,000

Company Benefits
- Health and dental benefits
- Career path for young employees
- Training opportunities in every department

Correspondence
Mail resume with cover letter

Part Time/Summer: Wire Rope Industries does not hire for part time employment, but occasionally seeks candidates for the summer. Most positions in the summer are offered first to the families of employees, however, potential jobs usually involve engineering. The best time to apply is in April.

WORKFIRE DEVELOPMENT CORP.

1708 Dolphin Ave., Suite 400
Kelowna, British Columbia, V1Y 9S4
Tel: (250) 717-8966   Fax: (250) 717-8946

Jennifer S. Nyland, V.P. Engineering
Internet: www.workfire.com

Workfire develops and markets software which dramatically improves Internet performance. Workfire's proprietary Genetic Caching technology promises to revolutionize the Internet caching market. They employ 20 individuals in total.

Academic Fields
Bachelor of Science: Computer Sciences, Mathematics
Bachelor of Engineering: Computer Systems, Electrical
Masters: Science, Engineering

Critical Skills
Analytical, Flexible, Good Communication, Good Writing Skills, Logical, Productive

Types of Positions
Software Engineer   Software Test Engineer
Advanced Tech. Engineer   Advanced Technology
Mathematician

Starting Salary
$ 40,000 - 45,000

Company Benefits
- Competitive benefit package

Correspondence
E-mail resume with cover letter
E-mail: resumes@workfire.com

Part Time/Summer: Workfire Development Corp. occasionally looks for individuals for part time jobs, and regularly seeks people for summer work. A potential job could be junior software engineer. The best time to apply is the first week of April for a May 1st start date.

Co-op/Internship: They offer internship opportunities as junior software engineer and advanced technology.

WORLD OF VACATIONS LTD.

191 The West Mall, Suite 600
Etobicoke, Ontario, M9C 5K8
Tel: (416) 620-8050   Fax: (416) 620-8709

Lisa Sukie, Human Resources
Internet: www.worldofvacations.com

World of Vacations has deep roots in the history of Canadian travel industry. From modest beginnings in 1926 in Montreal where Treasure Tours was first created until present where World of Vacations brings an unmatched broad and comprehensive range of quality and value priced vacations to their customers.

Academic Fields
College: Accounting, Administration, Hospitality, Human Resources, Marketing/Sales, Travel/Tourism
Bachelor of Comm/Admin: Accounting, Finance, Marketing
Chartered Accounting: CA - General/Finance

Critical Skills
Adaptable, Decisive, Dependable, Diplomatic, Flexible, Professional, Personable, Good Communication, Responsible

Types of Positions
Reservations   Accounts Payable
Ticketing   Accounts Receivable
Human Resources

Starting Salary
$ 16,000 - 20,000

Company Benefits
- Full time staff receive medical and dental
- Life insurance and travel benefits
- Seasonal/part timers receive travel benefits

Correspondence
Mail or fax resume with cover letter

Part Time/Summer: World of Vacations does not hire for part time or summer work. Their busiest time is during the fall and winter months, therefore hiring is usually done in the summer to ensure everyone is fully trained. Training for reservations is usually 5 weeks in length.

XCAN GRAIN POOL LTD.

1200 - 201 Portage Avenue
Winnipeg, Manitoba, R3B 3K6
Tel: (204) 949-4519   Fax: (204) 949-1057

Lynne Petit, Human Resources

XCAN Grain Pool Ltd. is the marketing arm of Agricore Cooperative Ltd. and the Saskatchewan Wheat Pool. XCAN is the largest exporter of non-board grains, oilseeds, and special crops in Canada.

Academic Fields
College: Administration, Computer Science, Food/Nutrition, Marketing/Sales
Bachelor of Arts: Business
Bachelor of Comm/Admin: Accounting, Finance, Marketing
Bachelor of Science: Agriculture, Food Sciences
Bachelor of Education: General
Chartered Accounting: CA-Finance, CGA/CMA - General/Finance
Masters: Business Administration

Critical Skills
Adaptable, Analytical, Confident, Decisive, Dependable, Diplomatic, Flexible, Good Communication, Good With Figures, Good Writing Skills, Leadership, Organized, Patient, Productive, Professional, Responsible

Types of Positions
General Office Clerk   Switchboard/Receptionist
Logistics Assistant   Fax Clerk

Starting Salary
$ 20,000 - 25,000

Company Benefits
- Employee paid life and long term disability
- Company paid medical, dental, and vision

Correspondence
Mail, fax or e-mail resume with cover letter
E-mail: lpetite@xcan.com

Part Time/Summer: XCAN Grain Pool occasionally looks for individuals for part time employment, but does not hire people for the summer months.

XWAVE SOLUTIONS

40 Higgins Line, Box 13543
St. John's, Newfoundland, A1B 4B8
Tel: (709) 724-7500   Fax: (709) 724-7485

Dawn Burke, HR Consultant
Internet: www.xwave.com

---

xwave, An Aliant Company, delivers complete IT services to clients in three areas: Integration, Infrastructure and Fulfillment Solutions. These areas offer clients, in key sectors where xwave has extensive experience, a broader delivery capability to plan, design, build and operate IT solutions that span both corporate and operational systems, and to fulfill the equipment and infrastructure upon which they are built. With more than $300 million in revenues and 2,300 people, xwave is one of the largest IT companies in Canada, with offices in St. John's, Halifax, Moncton, Saint John, Fredericton, Montreal, Ottawa, Toronto, Calgary, Edmonton and Dallas.

Academic Fields
College: Computer Science
Bachelor of Comm/Admin: General, Information Systems
Bachelor of Science: General
Bachelor of Engineering: General, Computer Systems
Masters: Business Administration

Critical Skills
Adaptable, Analytical, Confident, Good Communication, Good Writing Skills, Innovative, Leadership, Organized, Personable, Professional, Interpersonal

Types of Positions
Various Entry-Level Technical Jobs

Starting Salary
$ 35,000 - 40,000

Company Benefits
- Salary commensurate with qualifications
- Comprehensive range of benefits

Correspondence
E-mail resume with cover letter

Part Time/Summer: As the requirements within each of their business units vary, active recruitment also varies. Please contact the xwave office in your region for more information.

YAMAHA MOTOR CANADA LTD.

480 Gordon Baker Road
North York, Ontario, M2H 3B4
Tel: (416) 498-1911   Fax: (416) 491-3122

Human Resources Department
Internet: www.yamaha-motor.ca

Yamaha Motor Canada is a wholesale distributor of products made by Yamaha Motor Co. of Japan. Its Canadian operation opened in 1973. The company's products include motorcycles, power products, outboard motors, jet-skis, all-terrain vehicles, and parts and accessories. Today, the company has diversified into many new fields, becoming a comprehensive manufacturer of products ranging from sports and leisure goods to industrial equipment. Yamaha Motor Company employs approximately 180 individuals.

Academic Fields
College: Accounting, Business, Engineering Tech., Human Resources, Marketing/Sales
Bachelor of Arts: Economics
Bachelor of Comm/Admin: General, Accounting, Marketing, Info Mgmt.
Bachelor of Science: Computer Science
Chartered Accounting: CMA-General

Critical Skills
Adaptable, Confident, Creative, Decisive, Dependable, Efficient, Enthusiastic, Good Communication, Flexible, Innovative, Leadership, Personable, Professional

Types of Positions
Material Handler   Clerical/Support Staff

Starting Salary
$ 25,000 - 30,000

Company Benefits
- Comprehensive life, disability, health
- Company pension plan
- Tuition assistance plan, in-house training programs

Correspondence
Mail or fax resume with cover letter

Part Time/Summer: Yamaha Motor Canada sometimes hires for part time work and regularly hires for the summer. Potential jobs include warehouse material handler, as well as various clerical positions. Hiring for the summer is done in March of each year.

The Canada Student Employment Guide

YANKE GROUP OF COMPANIES

2815 Lorne Ave.
Saskatoon, Saskatchewan, S7J 0S5
Tel: (306) 664-1515   Fax: (306) 955-5663

Human Resources Manager
Internet: www.yanke.ca

Yanke Group of Companies is a transportation company. Their mission is to be committed to delivering unequalled transportation solutions in partnership with their customers. They will be the example customers and competitors use to establish new standards in service and support.

Academic Fields
College: General, Accounting, Administration, Business, Computer Science, Human Resources, Marketing/Sales
Bachelor of Arts: Business, Psychology, Statistics, Urban Geography
Bachelor of Comm/Admin: General, Info Mgmt., Public Admin.
Bachelor of Science: General, Computer Science, Geography, Psychology
Bachelor of Engineering: Computer Systems, Transportation
Bachelor of Education: Adult Education

Critical Skills
Adaptable, Analytical, Decisive, Good Communication, Innovative, Organized, Productive, Professional, Responsible

Types of Positions
Dispatcher   Driver Service Rep.
Customer Service Rep.

Starting Salary
below $ 20,000 - 25,000

Company Benefits
- Full in-house cross training services
- Extended health, vision, dental, life insurance, short and long term disability

Correspondence
Mail, fax or e-mail resume with cover letter
E-mail: hr@yanke.ca

Part Time/Summer: Yanke Group of Companies does not hire for part time work, but occasionally seeks candidates for the summer. Potential jobs involve project assignments in information systems, administration or accounting.

YARMOUTH REGIONAL HOSPITAL

60 Vancouver Street
Yarmouth, Nova Scotia, B5A 2P5
Tel: (902) 742-3541   Fax: (902) 742-0369

Shirley Watson-Poole, Human Resources

Yarmouth Regional Hospital is a general medical and surgical health care facility serving the community. The hospital also provides an addiction treatment centre, veterans place, a nursing home, and an adult residential centre. The facility is also recognized as a teaching hospital that is affiliated with the nursing programs offered at Dalhousie University in Nova Scotia.

Academic Fields
College: Laboratory Tech., Nursing, Radiology Tech., Secretarial
Bachelor of Arts: Psychology
Bachelor of Comm/Admin: Accounting
Bachelor of Science: Computer Science, Health Sciences, Nursing (RN), Occupational Therapy, Pharmacy, Physiotherapy, Psychology
Bachelor of Engineering: Computer Systems
Masters: Library Science

Critical Skills
Dependable, Efficient, Enthusiastic, Good Communication, Flexible, Innovative, Leadership, Organized, Patient, Personable, Productive

Types of Positions
Housekeeping/Laundry   Personal Care Worker
Laboratory Technologist   Clerical
Radiological Technologist Cook

Starting Salary
$ 25,000 - 30,000

Company Benefits
- Full benefit portfolio
- Pension, health, life insurance, long term disability
- On-the-job training for non-skilled jobs

Correspondence
Complete hospital's application form

Part Time/Summer: Yarmouth Regional Hospital regularly hires for part time work and occasionally hires for the summer. Jobs in the summer include general worker for nutrition and food service. The best time to apply is in March.

The Canada Student Employment Guide

CITY OF YELLOWKNIFE

P.O. Box 580
Yellowknife, NWT, X1A 2N4
Tel: (403) 920-5677   Fax: (403) 669-3463

Sheila Dunn, Human Resources
Internet: www.city.yellowknife.nt.ca

The City of Yellowknife is a municipal government that oversees the formation of policy and laws pertaining to the City.

Academic Fields
College: General, Accounting, Administration, Business, Computer Science, Drafting/Architecture, Emergency/Paramedic, Engineering Tech., Human Resources, Recreation Studies, Secretarial, Urban Planning
Bachelor of Arts: General, Business, Criminology, Economics, Public Relations, Recreation Studies, Urban Geography
Bachelor of Comm/Admin: General, Accounting, Finance, Info Mgmt., Public Admin.
Bachelor of Science: General, Computer Science
Bachelor of Engineering: General, Civil
Chartered Accounting: CA - General/Finance, CGA/CMA - General/Finance
Masters: Business Administration, Library Science

Critical Skills
Adaptable, Decisive, Dependable, Diligent, Diplomatic, Efficient, Enthusiastic, Flexible, Good Communication, Logical, Organized, Personable, Productive, Professional, Responsible

Types of Positions
Road & Sidewalk Maintainer   Sewer Maintenance
Clerical/Reception/Cashier

Starting Salary
$ 30,000 - 40,000

Company Benefits
- Health, dental, life insurance, vision care
- Housing, travel allowance, group RRSP

Correspondence
Fax resume with cover letter
E-mail: sheilaccity.yellowknife.nt.ca

Part Time/Summer: The City of Yellowknife regularly looks for people for part time and summer jobs. They include parks maintainer, playground/childcare worker, labourer, lifeguard, or instructor. The best time to apply is in March of each year.

YFACTOR

2020 Clark Blvd., Suite 1B
Brampton, Ontario, L6T 5R4
Tel: (905) 793-5016   Fax: (905) 792-2065

Cherubie Co, Administrative Assistant
Internet: www.yfactor.com

YFactor Inc. was established in 1997. Recognizing the necessity to provide a high calibre of interactive communication for the corporate environment is the main purpose of YFactor. With services ranging from internet/intranet development, to corporate communications and spatial graphics, they are focused on providing corporations and government with fresh ideas, communication strategy, expertise in technology and large project management.

Academic Fields
College: Advertising, Communications, Information Systems, Marketing/Sales, Graphic Arts
Bachelor of Arts: Business, Public Relations
Bachelor of Comm/Admin: Accounting, Finance, Marketing, Info Mgmt., Public Admin.
Masters: Business Administration, Arts

Critical Skills
Adaptable, Artistic, Confident, Creative, Dependable, Efficient, Good Communication, Good With Figures, Good Writing Skills, Innovative, Logical, Organized, Productive, Professional, Responsible

Types of Positions
Website Designer Assistant
Sales Representative
Marketing Representative

Starting Salary
$ 15,000 - 20,000

Company Benefits
- Full time employees receive group benefit insurance including life, health and dental
- After 3 months eligible to receive support for related training and development courses

Correspondence
Apply through web site.
E-mail: cco@yfactor.com

Part Time/Summer: YFactor occasionally seeks candidates for part time and summer employment. A potential job would be website designer assistant.

YORK REGIONAL POLICE

17250 Yonge Street
Newmarket, Ontario, L3Y 4W5
Tel: (905) 830-0303   Fax: (905) 853-5810

Gilda Sutton, Assistant Manager Human Resources

York Regional Police is engaged in the provision of municipal police services in the Region of York. The police division has 7 locations in the area and employs over 800 individuals to work in various areas of law enforcement.

Academic Fields
College: Security/Law
Bachelor of Arts: Criminology

Critical Skills
Adaptable, Analytical, Confident, Good Communication, Decisive, Professional, Personable, Good Writing Skills

Types of Positions
4th Class Constable   Records Clerk

Starting Salary
$ 30,000 - 40,000

Company Benefits
- Full benefit package
- Recruit training at Ontario Police College
- Significant career path opportunities

Correspondence
Mail or fax resume with cover letter

Part Time/Summer: York Regional Police does not offer part time or summer opportunities due to the nature of the work.

YTV CANADA INC.

64 Jefferson Ave., Unit 18
Toronto, Ontario, M6K 3H4
Tel: (416) 534-1191   Fax: (416) 530-5178

Human Resources Department
Internet: www.ytv.com

YTV Canada is a specialty network which acquires, produces and delivers award-winning Canadian and international programming for children and their families.

Academic Fields
College: Administration, Communications, Television/Radio
Bachelor of Arts: Business
Bachelor of Comm/Admin: Marketing
Chartered Accounting: CMA-General, CGA-General

Critical Skills
Adaptable, Good Communication, Confident, Decisive, Efficient, Flexible, Innovative, Organized, Personable, Productive, Professional, Responsible, Good Writing Skills, Detail Oriented

Types of Positions
Receptionist   Customer Service
Librarian   VTR Operator

Starting Salary
$ 20,000 - 25,000

Company Benefits
- Extended health and dental
- Life insurance, pension plan
- Tuition assistance, workshops, seminars

Correspondence
Fax resume with cover letter

Part Time/Summer: YTV Canada does not hire individuals for part time work, but occasionally seeks people for the summer months.

The Canada Student Employment Guide

ZEIDLER ROBERTS PARTNERSHIP ARCHITECTS

315 Queen Street West
Toronto, Ontario, M5V 2X2
Tel: (416) 596-8200   Fax: (416) 596-1408

David Jefferies, Office Manager
Internet: www.zrpa.com

Zeidler Roberts Partnership Architects provides engineering, architectural, and surveying services to a wide range of businesses and other enterprises in Ontario. Zeidler Roberts Partnership Architects is located in downtown Toronto and employs over 100 individuals at this location.

Academic Fields
Bachelor of Engineering: Materials Science, Bachelor of Architecture

Critical Skills
Adaptable, Analytical, Artistic, Good Communication, Confident, Creative, Decisive, Dependable, Diligent, Diplomatic, Efficient, Enthusiastic, Flexible, Good With Figures, Innovative, Leadership, Logical, Manual Dexterity, Organized, Patient, Personable, Persuasive, Productive, Professional, Responsible

Types of Positions
Model Building   Computer Modeling
Other Various Positions

Starting Salary
$ 25,000 - 30,000

Company Benefits
- Benefits only for full time employees

Correspondence
Mail resume and cover letter (include portfolio)

Part Time/Summer: Zeidler Roberts Partnership regularly hires individuals for part time and summer employment. The best time to apply is in April.

ZELLERS INC.

1125 Boul. Moody
Terrebonne, Québec, J6W 3L2
Tel: (514) 483-7600   Fax: (514) 483-7749

Human Resources
Internet: www.hbc.com/zellers

Zellers began in 1931, when Walter P. Zeller opened 12 stores during his first year of operation. From this modest beginning, Zellers has grown into one of Canada's most progressive and successful retailers with over 350 stores! Zellers is a division of Hudson's Bay Company, Canada's oldest corporation and its largest department store retailer.

Academic Fields
College: General, Accounting, Administration, Advertising, Business, Computer Science, Human Resources, Marketing/Sales, Secretarial
Bachelor of Arts: General, Business
Bachelor of Comm/Admin: General, Accounting, Finance, Marketing, Info Mgmt.
Bachelor of Science: Computer Science
Bachelor of Engineering: Computer Syst., Design
Chartered Accounting: CA - General/Finance, CGA/CMA - General/Finance
Masters: Business Administration

Critical Skills
Adaptable, Analytical, Good Communication, Confident, Creative, Decisive, Dependable, Diligent, Diplomatic, Efficient, Enthusiastic, Flexible, Good With Figures, Leadership, Organized, Personable, Persuasive, Productive, Professional, Responsible, Good Writing Skills

Types of Positions
Sales Clerk   Clerical
Material Handler   Secretary

Starting Salary
$ 20,000 - 25,000

Company Benefits
- Complete benefit package

Correspondence
Mail resume with cover letter to individual store locations

Part Time/Summer: Zellers regularly seeks individuals for part time and summer employment. Potential jobs are most likely those listed above. The best time to apply is in April.

The Canada Student Employment Guide

ZENASTRA

2305 St. Laurent Blvd.
Ottawa, Ontario, K1G 4J8
Tel: (613) 736-8777   Fax: (613) 731-4558

Human Resources
Internet: www.zenastra.com

Zenastra is an emerging global leader in the design, development and manufacture of highly integrated active and passive optical components and sub assemblies for high performance optical networking systems. Zenastra is addressing the needs of a supply constrained optical components market by designing, manufacturing and marketing a portfolio of innovative fiber optic products. For more information visit their website. All positions are based in Ottawa, Canada. Thank you to all who apply however, only selected applicants will be contacted.

Academic Fields
College: Administration, Marketing/Sales, Secretarial, Electronics Tech., Engineering Tech., Mechanical Tech.
Bachelor of Science: Physics
Bachelor of Engineering: Electrical, Mechanical
Masters: Science (Physics), Engineering

Critical Skills
Analytical, Diligent, Efficient, Good Communication, Good Writing Skills, Innovative, Leadership, Organized, Personable, Professional, Responsible

Types of Positions
Assembler	Technician
Technologist	Jr. Administration
Office Clerk	

Starting Salary
Depends on position

Company Benefits
- Full benefits including medical and dental for full-time permanent staff

Correspondence
Mail, fax, e-mail resume with cover letter or apply through web site. E-mail: hr@zenastra.com

Part Time/Summer: Zenastra occasionally looks for candidates for part time work and regularly hires in the summer months. Potential jobs include reception, junior administration (office clerk), technician, or technologist.

ZENON ENVIRONMENTAL INC.

3239 Dundas St. W.
Oakville, Ontario, L6M 4B2
Tel: (905) 465-3030   Fax: (905) 465-3050

Human Resources
Internet: www.zenon.ca

Zenon Environmental is engaged in the developing, manufacturing and marketing of environmental control technologies and operates an environmental testing laboratory. The company produces an extensive range of products and services which help industry purify and recycle water and waste.

Academic Fields
College: Accounting, Engineering Tech., Human Res., Industrial Design, Marketing/Sales, Secretarial
Bachelor of Arts: General, Business
Bachelor of Comm/Admin: General, Accounting, Marketing
Bachelor of Science: Chemistry
Bachelor of Engineering: Design, Electrical, Environmental Studies, Mechanical, Water Resources
Chartered Accounting: CMA-General, CGA-General
Masters: Science, Engineering

Critical Skills
Adaptable, Analytical, Good Communication, Confident, Creative, Decisive, Dependable, Diplomatic, Efficient, Enthusiastic, Flexible, Good With Figures, Innovative, Leadership, Logical, Organized, Patient, Productive, Professional, Responsible, Good Writing Skills

Types of Positions
Operations	Customer Service
Production	Engineering
Drafting	

Starting Salary
$ 25,000 - 30,000

Company Benefits
- Medical, dental, life insurance
- RRSP, health and safety training

Correspondence
Mail or fax resume with cover letter

Part Time/Summer: Zenon Environmental occasionally looks for candidates for part time and summer employment opportunities. Potential jobs are most likely in the production department. The best time to apply is in early May or June.

ZURICH CANADA

400 University Ave.
Toronto, Ontario, M5G 1S7
Tel: (416) 586-3000   Fax: (416) 586-3082

Human Resources
Internet: www.zurichcanada.com

Zurich Canada is a member of Zurich Financial Services, a leading internationally-recognized provider of insurance and financial services in non-life and life insurance, reinsurance and asset management. It offers financial protection and investment solutions to customers in the personal, commercial and corporate market segments. Headquartered in Zurich, Switzerland, the group operates in 50 countries worldwide and employs 47,000 people.

Academic Fields
College: Communications, Computer Science, Human Resources, Insurance, Marketing/Sales
Bachelor of Arts: Public Relations
Bachelor of Comm/Admin: Info Mgmt.
Bachelor of Science: Computer Science

Critical Skills
Confident, Dependable, Enthusiastic, Flexible, Good Communication, Good Writing Skills, Leadership, Personable, Productive, Professional, Responsible

Types of Positions
Accounting	Underwriting
New Business	Marketing
Human Resources	

Starting Salary
$ 25,000 - 30,000

Company Benefits
- All benefits paid at 80% (drugs, dental, etc.)
- Auto and life insurance coverage
- Training and development expenses covered

Correspondence
Mail or fax resume with cover letter

Part Time/Summer: Zurich Canada does not seek candidates for part time work, but occasionally looks for individuals for summer employment. Opportunities are usually filled by Zurich Life employee's contacts.

PART IV

College Index

University Index

Chartered Accounting Index

Part Time/Summer Index

Co-op/Internship Index

College Index

Below are some of the most popular College Diploma Programs in Canada. Use the College Index to find employers listed by the academic areas they consider important in the selection of candidates. The corresponding page number of the firm's profile is also shown.

Accounting	550
Administration	555
Advertising	559
Animal Health	560
Business	560
CAD Autocad	564
Child Care	564
Communications	565
Computer Science	566
Cooking/Culinary	570
Electronics Tech.	571
Emergency/Paramedic	573
Engineering Tech.	573
Faculty Management	576
Forestry	576
General	577
Graphic Arts	578
Hospitality	579
Human Resources	580
Industrial Design	584
Information Systems	585
Insurance	585
Journalism	586
Laboratory Tech.	587
Law	587
Marketing/Sales	588
Mechanical Tech.	591
Nursing (RN/RNA)	593
Performing Arts	594
Plumbing	594
Radiology Tech.	594
Recreation Studies	594
Science (General)	595
Secretarial	599
Security/Law Enforcement	603
Social Work	603
Statistics	603
Television/Radio	604
Travel/Tourism	604
Urban Planning	605
Welding	605

Accounting

A C A Cooperative Limited	74
A E McKenzie Co. Inc.	75
A.G. Simpson Co. Ltd.	75
Aar-Kel Moulds Ltd.	76
ABC Group	76
Aberdeen Hospital	77
Abitibi-Consolidated Inc.	77
Access Communications	78
Accucaps Industries Limited	79
ACE INI Insurance	79
Acier Leroux Inc.	80
Acklands-Grainger Inc.	80
Addictions Foundation of Manitoba, The	81
AGF Management Limited	83
Agricultural Credit Corp. of Saskatchewan	84
Aimtronics	84
Air Canada	85
Air Ontario Inc.	86
Akita Drilling Ltd.	87
Alberta Blue Cross	88
Alberta Energy & Utilities Board	89
Alberta Energy Company Ltd.	89
Alberta Gaming & Liquor Commission	90
Alberto Culver Canada Inc.	90
Algoma Steel Inc.	93
Allianz Canada	95
Allmar Distributors Ltd.	95
Allstate Insurance Co. of Canada	96
Altona Community Memorial Health Centre	97
Amcan Castings Limited	98
Amcor Twinpak North America Inc.	98
AMEC Inc.	99
American Airlines Inc.	99
Anjura Services Inc.	101
Anthony Insurance Inc.	102
Apex Land Corp.	103
Aqua-Power Cleaners Ltd.	105
Arbor Memorial Services Inc.	106
Armor Personnel	107

The Canada Student Employment Guide

College Index 551

Assiniboine Community College	109	Budd Canada Inc.	152
Assumption Mutual Life Insurance	109	Bullock Associates Design Consultants Inc.	153
ATCO Electric	111	C.S.T. Consultants Inc.	155
ATCO Frontec Corp.	111	Cabre Exploration Ltd.	156
Athabasca, Town of	112	Cadith Entertainment Ltd.	156
Atlantic Blue Cross Care	113	Calgary, City of	158
Atlantic Lottery Corporation Inc.	113	Cambior Inc.	158
Atlantic Packaging Products Ltd.	114	Camp Hill Hospital	160
Atlantic Wholesalers Ltd.	114	Canada Safeway Limited	163
Atlas Ideal Metals Inc.	115	Canadian Cancer Society	164
Atlas Van Lines (Canada) Ltd.	115	Canadian Commercial Corp.	165
ATS Automation Tooling Systems Inc.	116	Canadian Dairy Commission	165
Aurizon Mines Ltd.	116	Canadian Depository for Securities Ltd.	166
Aurum Ceramic Dental Laboratories Ltd.	117	Canadian General Tower Limited	166
AXA Insurance (Canada)	118	Canadian Museum of Civilization Corp.	167
Axidata Inc.	118	Canadian Occidental Petroleum Ltd.	168
Babcock and Wilcox Canada	119	Canadian Thermos Products Inc.	168
Banff Centre for Continuing Education, The	120	Canadian Tire Corporation Ltd.	169
Barton Place Long Term Care Facility	121	Canadian Western Bank	169
BASF Canada Inc.	122	Cancarb Limited	170
Basic Technologies Corporation	122	CancerCare Manitoba	171
Battlefords Health District	123	Cancore Industries Inc.	171
Bayer Inc.	124	Canon Canada Inc.	172
Baytex Energy Limited	124	Canpar Transport Ltd.	173
BBM Bureau of Measurement	125	CanWel Distribution Ltd.	173
BC Telecom Inc.	126	Cape Breton Development Corporation	174
BCG Services	127	Capilano Suspension Bridge	174
Bearskin Lake Air Service Ltd.	128	Carbone of America (LCL) Ltd.	175
Bechtel Canada Co.	128	Cargill Limited	175
Beckman Coulter Canada Inc.	129	Carte International Inc.	176
Behlen Industries	130	Cassels Brock & Blackwell	177
Bell & Howell Ltd.	130	Celestica International Inc.	179
Bell Mobility	131	Centra Gas British Columbia Inc.	180
Belleville General Hospital	132	Central Park Lodges Ltd.	181
Best Western Carlton Place Hotel	133	Ceridian Canada	183
Bethesda Hospital	134	CFCN Communications Inc.	184
Bettis Canada Ltd.	135	CGU Group Canada Ltd.	185
BFGoodrich Landing Gear Division	135	Challenger Motor Freight Inc.	186
Bic Inc.	136	Chapters Inc.	186
Black Photo Corporation	139	Charlottetown Driving Park	187
Blaney McMurty LLP	139	Christian Horizons	190
Bloorview MacMillan Centre, The	140	Cineplex Odeon Corporation	191
Blue Giant Equipment of Canada Ltd.	141	Citibank Canada	191
Blue Mountain Resorts Limited	141	CKF Inc.	192
Blue Wave Seafoods Inc.	142	COBI Foods Inc.	194
BNP PARIBAS (Canada)	143	Cobourg District General Hospital	194
Bonus Resource Services Corp.	144	Coca Cola Foods Canada Inc.	195
Boréal Assurances Inc.	144	Columbia House	197
BOVAR Waste Management	145	Comcare Health Services	198
Brandon, City of	146	Communications & Power Industries Canada	198
Bratty & Partners LLP	147	Community Savings Credit Union	199
British Columbia Ferry Corporation	149	Compu-Quote Inc.	200
Brookfield Properties Corporation	150	Computalog Ltd.	200
Browning Harvey Limited	150	Computer Associates Canada Ltd.	201

The Canada Student Employment Guide

College Index

Comtronic Computer Inc.	202	Flakeboard Company Limited	242
Conair Aviation Ltd.	202	Fletcher's Fine Foods	242
Connors Bros, Limited	203	Flint Energy Services Ltd.	243
Co-op Atlantic	203	Foremost Industries Inc.	244
Coppley Apparel Group	204	Forzani Group Ltd., The	244
Coquitlam, City of	204	Foyer Valade Inc.	245
Corner Brook, City of	205	Friesens Corporation	246
Cornwall Electric	206	Future Shop Ltd.	246
Cosmair Canada Inc.	206	Gay Lea Foods Co-Operative Ltd.	247
Cotton Ginny Ltd.	207	Gendis Inc.	248
Cougar Helicopters Inc.	208	Gienow Building Products Ltd.	251
Credit Union Central of Canada	208	Giffels Associates Limited	251
Crestar Energy Inc.	209	Gilbey Canada Inc.	252
Culinar Inc.	209	Gimbel Eye Centre	252
Custom Trim Ltd.	210	Glaxo Wellcome Canada	253
D.A. Stuart Inc.	210	Glentel Inc.	254
D.H. Howden	211	Goodman and Carr	255
DaimlerChrysler Canada Ltd.	211	Goodwill Industries of Toronto	256
Dana Corporation - Long Manufacturing	212	Gov't. of Newfoundland – Dept. of Finance	257
David Thompson Health Region	212	Grand & Toy Ltd.	257
DDM Plastics Inc.	213	Grant MacEwen Community College	258
Deer Lodge Centre Inc.	213	Great-West Life Assurance Company, The	259
Degussa - Huls Canada Inc.	214	Grenville Management Ltd.	259
Dell Computer Corporation	214	Groupe Savoie Inc.	260
Delphi Solutions Inc.	215	H A Simmons Ltd.	261
Delta Toronto Airport Hotel	216	Haley Industries Limited	262
Directwest Publishers Ltd.	217	Halifax Regional Municipality	263
Domtar Inc.	218	Halifax Water Commission	264
Drug Trading Company Ltd.	219	Harry Rosen Inc.	265
Druxy's Inc.	219	Hasbro Canada Inc.	266
Ducks Unlimited Canada	220	Health Authority 5	267
Dun & Bradstreet Canada	221	Health Care Corporation of St. John's	267
Dylex Limited	222	Helijet Airways Inc.	268
Dynapro Systems Inc.	223	Hermes Electronics Inc.	269
Dynasty Furniture Manufacturing Ltd.	224	Hill & Knowlton Canada Ltd.	270
Echo Bay Mines Ltd.	226	Hippodrome de Montréal	270
Economic Development Edmonton	226	Holiday Inn Select Toronto Airport	272
Economical Insurance Group, The	227	Home Oil Co. Ltd.	273
Eli Lilly Canada Inc.	230	Homewood Corp.	274
Emco Limited	230	Honda Canada Inc.	274
EMJ Data Systems Ltd.	231	Honeywell Ltd.	275
EnerFlex Systems Ltd.	232	Horseshoe Resort Corporation	275
Entreprises Premier Canadien Ltée	232	Hôtel Dieu de Montréal	276
Ernst & Young	234	Household Movers & Shippers Limited	276
Exfo	235	Housesitters Canada, The	277
Exide Canada Inc.	235	Hub Meat Packers Ltd.	278
Explorer Hotel, The	236	Hubbell Canada Inc.	278
Extendicare (Canada) Inc.	237	Hudon & Deaudelin Ltée	279
Family Day Care Service	238	Hudson's Bay Company, The	279
Farm Credit Corp. Canada	238	Humber River Regional Hospital	280
Federated Co-operatives Limited	239	Huronia Regional Centre	280
FedEx Express	240	Husky Energy Inc.	281
Finning	240	Hydro Electric Commission of Thunder Bay	281
Fishery Products International	241	Hydro Mississauga Corporation	282

The Canada Student Employment Guide

College Index 553

Hydro One Inc.	282	Marine Atlantic Inc.	331
IDEA Associates Inc.	285	Maritime Life Assurance Company, The	331
Ilco Unican Inc.	286	Mark Anthony Group Inc.	332
Imprimerie Interweb Inc.	287	Marshall Macklin Monaghan Ltd.	333
Indalex Limited	288	Marystown Shipyard Limited	334
Industrial Equipment Co. Ltd.	288	Maxxam Analytics Inc.	335
Industrial-Alliance Life Insurance Company	289	McBee Systems of Canada Inc.	336
Industries Lassonde Inc.	289	McCarney Greenwood	336
Information Gateway Services	290	McGraw Hill Ryerson Ltd.	337
ING Canada Financial Services International	291	McInnes Cooper & Robertson	337
Intercon Security Ltd.	292	McKay-Cocker Construction Limited	338
InterOne Marketing Group	293	Mediacom Inc.	340
Intertape Polymer Group Inc.	294	Metro Toronto Convention Centre	342
IPL Energy Inc.	294	Metroland Printing, Publishing & Dist. Ltd.	343
Island Savings Credit Union	295	Metropolitan Life Insurance Company	344
Ivaco Inc.	296	Meyers Norris Penny & Co.	344
IWK Grace Health Centre	297	Michaels of Canada Inc.	345
Izaak Walton Killam Hospital, The	297	Midland Walwyn Inc.	345
J.D. Irving Limited	298	Midwest Food Products Inc.	346
J.S. Redpath Limited	299	Milne & Craighead Inc.	347
James Richardson International Limited	300	Minas Basin Pulp and Power Company Ltd.	347
Jim Pattison Group	301	Ministry of Northern Develop. and Mines	348
John P. Robarts Research Institute	302	Mitel Corporation	350
Johnson Incorporated	303	Mobile Computing Corporation	351
Jostens Canada Ltd.	303	Moen Inc.	352
Kawneer Company Canada Limited	304	Moffat Communications Limited	352
Kelowna, City of	305	Monarch Communications Inc.	353
Kennametal Ltd.	305	Montreal Trust Co.	353
Keyano College	306	Moosehead Breweries Limited	354
Kitchener, City of	309	MOSAID Technologies Inc.	355
Kodak Canada Inc.	309	Motorola Canada Ltd.	356
La Confiserie Comete Ltee	311	Mountain Equipment Co-op	356
Laidlaw Inc.	312	N B S Card Services	359
Leduc, City of	313	Nanaimo Credit Union	359
Lego Canada Inc.	314	Natco Canada Ltd.	360
Leica Geosystems Canada Inc.	314	National Grocers Co. Ltd.	360
Lenbrook Industries Limited	315	National Life	361
Leon's Manufacturing Company Inc.	316	National Manufacturing of Canada Inc.	361
Les Modes Smart Inc.	318	National Sports Centre	362
Liberty Health	318	Neles Automation, Scada Solutions Ltd.	362
Lifetouch Canada Inc.	319	Nelvana Limited	363
Litton Systems Canada Ltd.	320	Neptune Food Suppliers Ltd.	363
Loewen Windows	321	Nesbitt Burns Inc.	364
London Goodwill Industries Association	322	Nestle Canada Inc.	364
Lovat Inc.	323	New Brunswick Power Corporation	365
M M Industra Ltd.	323	Newfoundland and Labrador Credit Union	367
MAAX Inc.	324	Newfoundland and Labrador Hydro	367
MacDonald Dettwiler and Associates Ltd.	325	News Marketing Canada	368
MacDonald Steel Ltd.	325	Niagara Parks Commission, The	369
Mactac Canada Ltd.	326	Nike Canada Ltd.	371
Magna International Inc.	327	Nissan Canada Inc.	371
Manitoba Hydro	328	Norbord Industries	372
Manitoba Pool Elevators	328	Norcen Energy Resources Ltd.	373
Maple Leaf Consumer Foods	330	North American Life Assurance Company	373

The Canada Student Employment Guide

College Index

North West Company Inc.	374		Quebecor Inc.	415
Northern Mountain Helicopters Inc.	375		Ramada Inn	416
Northwestel Inc.	376		Raymond Industrial Equipment Ltd.	418
Norwich Union Life Insurance Society	376		Raymond Rebar Inc.	418
Nova Scotia Liquor Commission	377		Recochem Inc.	420
Nova Scotia Power Corp.	377		Red Deer Co-op Limited	421
Novartis Consumer Health Canada Inc.	378		Regal Capital Planners Ltd.	422
Novotel Canada Inc.	378		Regal Constellation Hotel Ltd.	422
NPS Allelix Corp.	379		Regal Greeting and Gifts	423
Numac Energy Inc.	379		Regina Health District	423
Nygard International Ltd.	380		Rehabilitation Institute of Toronto	425
Oetiker Limited	381		Reid Crowther	426
Oland Breweries Limited	382		Reynolds and Reynolds (Canada) Limited	430
Omstead Foods Limited	383		Rhone-Poulenc Canada Inc.	430
Ontario Jockey Club, The	384		Richmond, City of	431
Ontario Legislative Offices	384		Rimrock Resort Hotel	432
Ontario March of Dimes	385		Riverside Hospital of Ottawa, The	434
Oracle Corp. Canada Inc.	386		Rivtow Marine Ltd.	434
Ottawa Hospital	386		Roctest Ltée	435
Paramount Canada's Wonderland Inc.	389		Rogers AT&T Wireless Inc.	436
Paul Revere Life Insurance Company, The	391		Rothmans, Benson and Hedges Inc.	437
PavCo	391		Royal & Sun Alliance Insurance Co. of Cda	437
PCL Constructors Inc.	392		Royal Bank of Canada	438
Peacock Inc.	392		Royal Inland Hospital	439
Pearson Education Canada	393		Royal Philips Electronics	439
Peel Board of Education	393		Ryerson Polytechnic University	441
Peel Regional Police	394		Salisbury House of Canada Ltd.	442
Pembina Pipeline Corporation	395		Sandman Hotels and Inns	443
PennCorp Life Insurance Company	396		Sara Lee Corporation of Canada Limited	444
Petromont & Co. Ltd. Partnership	397		Saskatchewan Centre of the Arts	444
Pharma Plus Drugmarts Ltd.	398		Saskatchewan Government Insurance	445
Phoenix International	399		Saskatchewan Transportation Company	446
Pilot Insurance Company	399		Saskatoon, City of	448
Pitney Bowes of Canada Ltd.	401		Saskferco Products Inc.	448
Pizza Pizza Ltd.	401		SC Infrastructure Inc.	449
Poco Petroleums Ltd.	402		Scarborough General Hospital	450
Pollack Rentals Limited	403		Schlumberger Canada Ltd.	450
Polygram Group Canada Inc.	403		Seprotech Systems Incorporated	454
Positron Industries Inc.	404		Sharp Electronics of Canada Ltd.	454
Potacan Mining Company	405		Shaw Communications	455
Powell Equipment Ltd.	405		Sheraton Fallsview Hotel	456
PPG Canada Inc.	407		Sheraton Toronto East Hotel and Towers	456
Premdor Inc.	408		Shermag Inc.	457
Pricewaterhouse Coopers	409		Sherwood Credit Union	458
Prince Albert Credit Union	409		Shoppers Drug Mart Limited	458
Prince Albert, City of	410		Shopping Channel, The	459
Prince George, City of	410		Shorewood Packaging Corp. of Canada Ltd.	459
Progressive Financial Strategy	411		Siemens Electric Ltd.	460
Prudential Insurance Co. of America, The	412		Signature Vacations Inc.	460
Public Utilities of Kingston	413		Skiing Louise Ltd.	461
Purolator Courier Ltd.	413		Slocan Forest Products Ltd.	462
QEII Health Sciences Centre	414		Sobeys Inc.	463
QIT-Fer et Titane Inc.	414		Société des Alcools du Québec	464
Québéc Cartier Mining Company	415		Sodexho Marriott Services Canada	464

College Index 555

Sony Music Canada	465	TSC Stores Ltd.	512
Southam Inc.	466	Turnbull & Turnbull Ltd.	512
Southern Railway of British Columbia Ltd.	466	Uni Select Inc.	513
Southland Canada	467	Union Pacific Resources Group	514
Spar Aerospace Limited	467	University College of Cape Breton	516
Spectra Premium Industries	468	US Filter BCP	517
Spectrum Signal Processing Inc.	468	Vacances Air Transat Inc.	518
Sportsco International	469	Valley First Credit Union	518
SRI Homes Inc.	470	Vancouver International Airport	520
SSQ Life	471	Volkswagen Canada Inc.	523
St. Lawrence Parks Commission	472	W C I Canada Inc.	524
St. Vincent's Hospitals	473	Waterloo Furniture Components Ltd.	524
Standard Knitting Limited	474	Waterloo Inn	525
Stanley Canada Inc.	475	Waverly & York Corporation	525
Star Data Systems Inc.	476	Wegu Canada Inc.	526
State Farm Insurance Companies	476	Weldco-Beales Manufacturing Inc.	527
Steelcraft Industries Ltd.	477	Wendy's Restaurants of Canada Inc.	527
Steelpipe Ltd.	477	West Coast Apparel	528
Sterling Marking Products Inc.	478	West Kootenay Power Ltd.	528
Stitches	478	Westbury Life	529
Sudbury Regional Hospital	480	Westcliff Management Ltd.	529
Sun Peaks Resort Corporation	481	Westcoast Energy Inc.	530
Sun Rype Products Ltd.	481	Western Glove Works	530
Sundog Printing Limited	482	Westinghouse Canada Inc.	532
Sunoco Inc.	482	WestJet Airlines	532
Supreme Tooling Group	483	Westminster Savings Credit Union	533
Surrey Memorial Hospital	483	Westport Innovations Inc.	534
Surrey, City of	484	Westshore Terminals Ltd.	534
Talisman Energy Inc.	487	Weyerhaeuser Company Limited	535
TCG International Inc.	487	Whistler Blackcomb Mountain	535
TCT Logistics	488	White Rose Crafts and Nursery Sales Limited	536
TD Waterhouse Investor Services (Canada)	488	Whitehill Technologies Inc.	537
Teklogix Inc.	489	Wilson Auto Electric Ltd.	538
Telegraph Journal	491	Windsor, City of	538
The Barn Fruit Markets Inc.	493	Winners Apparel Ltd.	539
The Garland Group	494	Winpak Ltd.	539
Thomas & Betts Ltée	495	Wire Rope Industries Ltd.	540
Thomas Cook Group (Canada) Ltd.	495	World of Vacations Ltd.	541
Thompson's Moving and Storage	496	Yamaha Motor Canada Ltd.	542
Thunder Bay Regional Hospital	497	Yanke Group of Companies	543
Ticketmaster Canada Inc.	498	Yellowknife, City of	544
Tiger Brand Knitting Company Limited	498	Zellers Inc.	546
Timmins, City of	499	Zenon Environmental Inc.	547
Today's Business Products Ltd.	500		
Toronto Catholic District School Board	502		
Toronto Cricket Skating & Curling	502	## Administration	
Toronto East General Hospital	503		
Toronto General Hospital	505	1-800-GOT-JUNK?	74
Toronto Hydro	505	A E McKenzie Co. Inc.	75
Toronto Police Service	506	Aar-Kel Moulds Ltd.	76
Toronto Sun Publishing Corp., The	507	Abitibi-Consolidated Inc.	77
Toronto, City of	508	Access Communications	78
Toshiba of Canada Ltd.	508	Accucaps Industries Limited	79
Toyota Canada Ltd.	509	ACE INI Insurance	79

The Canada Student Employment Guide

College Index

Acier Leroux Inc.	80	Brandon, City of	146
Acklands-Grainger Inc.	80	British Columbia Ferry Corporation	149
Addictions Foundation of Manitoba, The	81	Brookfield Properties Corporation	150
AGF Management Limited	83	Buckeye Canada Inc.	151
Agricultural Credit Corp. of Saskatchewan	84	Budd Canada Inc.	152
Air Ontario Inc.	86	Bullock Associates Design Consultants Inc.	153
Alberta Energy Company Ltd.	89	C MAC Industries Inc.	155
Alberta Gaming & Liquor Commission	90	C.S.T. Consultants Inc.	155
Alexandra Hospital	91	Cabre Exploration Ltd.	156
Allcolour Paint Limited	94	Cadith Entertainment Ltd.	156
Allianz Canada	95	Calgary, City of	158
Amcor Twinpak North America Inc.	98	Cambior Inc.	158
AMEC Inc.	99	Canada Safeway Limited	163
Anjura Services Inc.	101	Canadian Cancer Society	164
Anthony Insurance Inc.	102	Canadian Commercial Corp.	165
Apex Land Corp.	103	Canadian Dairy Commission	165
Aqua-Power Cleaners Ltd.	105	Canadian Depository for Securities Ltd.	166
Arbor Care Tree Service Ltd.	106	Canadian General Tower Limited	166
Arbor Memorial Services Inc.	106	Canadian Museum of Civilization Corp.	167
Arctic Co-operatives Limited	107	Canadian National Institute For The Blind	167
Armor Personnel	107	Canadian Western Bank	169
ATCO Electric	111	CancerCare Manitoba	171
ATCO Frontec Corp.	111	Cancore Industries Inc.	171
Athabasca, Town of	112	Canon Canada Inc.	172
Atlantic Blue Cross Care	113	Canpar Transport Ltd.	173
Atlantic Lottery Corporation Inc.	113	CanWel Distribution Ltd.	173
Atlantic Packaging Products Ltd.	114	Cape Breton Development Corporation	174
Atlantic Wholesalers Ltd.	114	Capilano Suspension Bridge	174
Atlas Ideal Metals Inc.	115	Carbone of America (LCL) Ltd.	175
Atlas Van Lines (Canada) Ltd.	115	Cargill Limited	175
ATS Automation Tooling Systems Inc.	116	Carlson Marketing Group Canada Ltd.	176
Aurum Ceramic Dental Laboratories Ltd.	117	Carte International Inc.	176
Axidata Inc.	118	Casa Loma	177
Banff Centre for Continuing Education, The	120	Centra Gas Manitoba Inc.	181
Barton Place Long Term Care Facility	121	Central Park Lodges Ltd.	181
Battlefords Health District	123	Centre de Santé de St-Henri Inc.	182
Bayer Inc.	124	Ceridian Canada	183
Baytex Energy Limited	124	Challenger Motor Freight Inc.	186
BBM Bureau of Measurement	125	Chapters Inc.	186
BC Telecom Inc.	126	Charlottetown Driving Park	187
BCG Services	127	Christian Horizons	190
Bearskin Lake Air Service Ltd.	128	Cineplex Odeon Corporation	191
Bell Mobility	131	CKF Inc.	192
Bettis Canada Ltd.	135	Cobourg District General Hospital	194
BFGoodrich Landing Gear Division	135	Coca Cola Foods Canada Inc.	195
Biovail Corporation International	137	Columbia House	197
Bloorview MacMillan Centre, The	140	Comcare Health Services	198
Blue Giant Equipment of Canada Ltd.	141	Community Savings Credit Union	199
Blue Mountain Resorts Limited	141	Computer Associates Canada Ltd.	201
Blue Wave Seafoods Inc.	142	Connors Bros, Limited	203
BNP PARIBAS (Canada)	143	Coppley Apparel Group	204
Bonus Resource Services Corp.	144	Coquitlam, City of	204
Boréal Assurances Inc.	144	Corner Brook, City of	205
BOVAR Waste Management	145	Cosmair Canada Inc.	206

The Canada Student Employment Guide

College Index 557

Cosyn Technology	207	Helijet Airways Inc.	268
Cotton Ginny Ltd.	207	Hermes Electronics Inc.	269
Cougar Helicopters Inc.	208	Hippodrome de Montréal	270
Credit Union Central of Canada	208	Hoffman-La Roche Limited	272
Culinar Inc.	209	Holiday Inn Select Toronto Airport	272
D.H. Howden	211	Holland College	273
DaimlerChrysler Canada Ltd.	211	Home Oil Co. Ltd.	273
Dana Corporation - Long Manufacturing	212	Homewood Corp.	274
David Thompson Health Region	212	Horseshoe Resort Corporation	275
Deer Lodge Centre Inc.	213	Hôtel Dieu de Montréal	276
Degussa - Huls Canada Inc.	214	Hubbell Canada Inc.	278
Delphi Solutions Inc.	215	Humber River Regional Hospital	280
Delta Toronto Airport Hotel	216	Husky Energy Inc.	281
Directwest Publishers Ltd.	217	Hydro Electric Commission of Thunder Bay	281
Domtar Inc.	218	Hydro Mississauga Corporation	282
Dun & Bradstreet Canada	221	Hydro Québec	283
Dylex Limited	222	I P L Plastics Ltd.	284
Dynapro Systems Inc.	223	IDEA Associates Inc.	285
Dynasty Furniture Manufacturing Ltd.	224	Imprimerie Interweb Inc.	287
Echo Bay Mines Ltd.	226	Industrial Equipment Co. Ltd.	288
Economical Insurance Group, The	227	Industrial-Alliance Life Insurance Company	289
Emco Limited	230	Industries Lassonde Inc.	289
EMJ Data Systems Ltd.	231	Information Gateway Services	290
Endpoint Research Ltd.	231	ING Canada Financial Services International	291
EnerFlex Systems Ltd.	232	Insurance Corp. of B.C.	291
Entreprises Premier Canadien Ltée	232	Intercon Security Ltd.	292
Exfo	235	Interior Savings Credit Union	293
Exide Canada Inc.	235	InterOne Marketing Group	293
Explorer Hotel, The	236	Intertape Polymer Group Inc.	294
FAG Bearings Limited	237	Island Savings Credit Union	295
Family Day Care Service	238	J.D. Irving Limited	298
Farm Credit Corp. Canada	238	James Richardson International Limited	300
Federated Co-operatives Limited	239	Jim Pattison Group	301
Finning	240	John P. Robarts Research Institute	302
Foremost Industries Inc.	244	Johnson Incorporated	303
Foyer Valade Inc.	245	Jostens Canada Ltd.	303
Friesens Corporation	246	Kennametal Ltd.	305
Future Shop Ltd.	246	Kitchener, City of	309
Gay Lea Foods Co-Operative Ltd.	247	La Confiserie Comete Ltee	311
Gendis Inc.	248	Leduc, City of	313
Gienow Building Products Ltd.	251	Lego Canada Inc.	314
Giffels Associates Limited	251	Leica Geosystems Canada Inc.	314
Gilbey Canada Inc.	252	Lenbrook Industries Limited	315
Gimbel Eye Centre	252	Leon's Manufacturing Company Inc.	316
Glaxo Wellcome Canada	253	Les Forges de Sorel Inc.	317
Glentel Inc.	254	Les Modes Smart Inc.	318
Goodman and Carr	255	Liberty Health	318
Goodwill Industries of Toronto	256	Lifetouch Canada Inc.	319
Grant MacEwen Community College	258	Lovat Inc.	323
Great-West Life Assurance Company, The	259	M M Industra Ltd.	323
Groupe Savoie Inc.	260	M. McGrawth Canada Limited	324
Halifax Water Commission	264	MAAX Inc.	324
Harry Rosen Inc.	265	MacDonald Dettwiler and Associates Ltd.	325
Hasbro Canada Inc.	266	Manitoba Agriculture and Food	327

The Canada Student Employment Guide

College Index

Manitoba Public Insurance Corporation	329	Prince George, City of	410
Maritime Life Assurance Company, The	331	Prudential Insurance Co. of America, The	412
Mark Anthony Group Inc.	332	Public Utilities of Kingston	413
Matrox Electronic Systems Ltd.	335	Purolator Courier Ltd.	413
McBee Systems of Canada Inc.	336	Quesnel River Pulp Company	416
McInnes Cooper & Robertson	337	Ramada Inn	416
McMillan & Associates Inc.	339	Raymond Rebar Inc.	418
Mediasynergy	340	Reader's Digest Association of Canada Ltd.	419
Metro Richelieu Inc.	342	Red Deer Co-op Limited	421
Metro Toronto Convention Centre	342	Regal Constellation Hotel Ltd.	422
Metroland Printing, Publishing & Dist. Ltd.	343	Regina Health District	423
Metropolitan Life Insurance Company	344	Richmond, City of	431
Meyers Norris Penny & Co.	344	Rogers AT&T Wireless Inc.	436
Michaels of Canada Inc.	345	Rogers Media, Publishing	436
Midland Walwyn Inc.	345	Royal & Sun Alliance Insurance Co. of Cda	437
Midwest Food Products Inc.	346	Royal Canadian Mint	438
Milne & Craighead Inc.	347	Royal Philips Electronics	439
Ministry of Northern Develop. and Mines	348	Salisbury House of Canada Ltd.	442
Mobile Computing Corporation	351	Sandman Hotels and Inns	443
Montreal Trust Co.	353	Saskatchewan Economic Development	445
Morrison Hershfield Limited	354	Saskatchewan Government Insurance	445
MOSAID Technologies Inc.	355	Saskatchewan Transportation Company	446
Motorola Canada Ltd.	356	Saskferco Products Inc.	448
Mountain Equipment Co-op	356	SaskTel	449
Natco Canada Ltd.	360	Scarborough General Hospital	450
National Life	361	Schlumberger Canada Ltd.	450
National Sports Centre	362	SCIEX MDS Health Group	452
Neles Automation, Scada Solutions Ltd.	362	Seprotech Systems Incorporated	454
Nelvana Limited	363	Shaw Communications	455
Nestle Canada Inc.	364	Sheraton Fallsview Hotel	456
New Brunswick Power Corporation	365	Sherwood Credit Union	458
Newfoundland and Labrador Credit Union	367	Shopping Channel, The	459
News Marketing Canada	368	Shorewood Packaging Corp. of Canada Ltd.	459
Nichirin Inc.	370	Siemens Electric Ltd.	460
North West Company Inc.	374	Signature Vacations Inc.	460
Nova Scotia Liquor Commission	377	Silicon Graphics Canada Inc.	461
Novartis Consumer Health Canada Inc.	378	Skiing Louise Ltd.	461
Oetiker Limited	381	Sobeys Inc.	463
Omstead Foods Limited	383	Sodexho Marriott Services Canada	464
Ontario Legislative Offices	384	Sony Music Canada	465
Paladin Security & Investigations Limited	388	Southam Inc.	466
Paramount Canada's Wonderland Inc.	389	Spectra Premium Industries	468
PavCo	391	Sportsco International	469
Peel Regional Police	394	Sprint Canada	470
PennCorp Life Insurance Company	396	SSQ Life	471
Pharma Plus Drugmarts Ltd.	398	St. Lawrence Parks Commission	472
Pine Falls Paper Company Limited	400	Standard Knitting Limited	474
Pitney Bowes of Canada Ltd.	401	Stanley Canada Inc.	475
Pollack Rentals Limited	403	Star Data Systems Inc.	476
Polygram Group Canada Inc.	403	Stitches	478
Potacan Mining Company	405	Sudbury Regional Hospital	480
Powell Equipment Ltd.	405	Sun Peaks Resort Corporation	481
PPG Canada Inc.	407	Sun Rype Products Ltd.	481
Prince Albert Credit Union	409	Sunoco Inc.	482

The Canada Student Employment Guide

Supreme Tooling Group	483
Surrey, City of	484
Swift Current Health District	485
Symantec Corporation	486
Talisman Energy Inc.	487
TCG International Inc.	487
TCT Logistics	488
TD Waterhouse Investor Services (Canada)	488
Teck Corp.	489
Teklogix Inc.	489
Telus Corporation	492
The Arthritis Society	492
The Co-operators	493
The Garland Group	494
Thomas & Betts Ltée	495
Thompson's Moving and Storage	496
Thomson - CSF Systems Canada Inc.	497
Ticketmaster Canada Inc.	498
Tiger Brand Knitting Company Limited	498
Today's Business Products Ltd.	500
Toronto Catholic District School Board	502
Toronto General Hospital	505
Toronto Hydro	505
Toronto Police Service	506
Toronto Sun Publishing Corp., The	507
Toshiba of Canada Ltd.	508
TSC Stores Ltd.	512
Turnbull & Turnbull Ltd.	512
Uni Select Inc.	513
Union Pacific Resources Group	514
Universal Rehabilitation Service Agency	515
University College of Cape Breton	516
Vacances Air Transat Inc.	518
Valley First Credit Union	518
Volvo Cars of Canada Ltd.	523
Waverly & York Corporation	525
Weldco-Beales Manufacturing Inc.	527
West Coast Apparel	528
Westbury Life	529
Westcliff Management Ltd.	529
Westcoast Energy Inc.	530
Western Glove Works	530
WestJet Airlines	532
Westshore Terminals Ltd.	534
Weyerhaeuser Company Limited	535
Whistler Blackcomb Mountain	535
Wilson Auto Electric Ltd.	538
Windsor, City of	538
Winners Apparel Ltd.	539
World of Vacations Ltd.	541
XCAN Grain Pool Ltd.	541
Yanke Group of Companies	543
Yellowknife, City of	544
YTV Canada Inc.	545
Zellers Inc.	546
Zenastra	547

Advertising

1-800-GOT-JUNK?	74
AGF Management Limited	83
Air Canada	85
Anthony Insurance Inc.	102
Apex Land Corp.	103
Atlantic Wholesalers Ltd.	114
Atlas Ideal Metals Inc.	115
Atlas Van Lines (Canada) Ltd.	115
Axidata Inc.	118
Bell Mobility	131
Black Photo Corporation	139
C.S.T. Consultants Inc.	155
Calgary Co-operative Association Limited	157
Canada Safeway Limited	163
Canadian Museum of Civilization Corp.	167
Canadian Western Bank	169
Cancore Industries Inc.	171
Canon Canada Inc.	172
Centra Gas Manitoba Inc.	181
Ceridian Canada	183
CFCN Communications Inc.	184
Charlottetown Driving Park	187
Columbia House	197
Community Savings Credit Union	199
Co-op Atlantic	203
Coquitlam, City of	204
Corner Brook, City of	205
Cotton Ginny Ltd.	207
Cougar Helicopters Inc.	208
Directwest Publishers Ltd.	217
Exfo	235
Federated Co-operatives Limited	239
Finning	240
Forzani Group Ltd., The	244
Future Shop Ltd.	246
Gendis Inc.	248
Goodman and Carr	255
Grand & Toy Ltd.	257
Grant MacEwen Community College	258
Great-West Life Assurance Company, The	259
Harry Rosen Inc.	265
Hasbro Canada Inc.	266
Helijet Airways Inc.	268
Homewood Corp.	274
Honda Canada Inc.	274
Hudon & Deaudelin Ltée	279
Information Gateway Services	290
InterOne Marketing Group	293

College Index

Kitchener, City of	309
Kraft Canada Inc.	310
Lenbrook Industries Limited	315
Leo Burnett Co. Ltd.	315
Leon's Manufacturing Company Inc.	316
Lifetouch Canada Inc.	319
MAAX Inc.	324
Manitoba Public Insurance Corporation	329
Maritime Life Assurance Company, The	331
McBee Systems of Canada Inc.	336
McLaren-McCann Advertising of Canada Ltd.	338
Metroland Printing, Publishing & Dist. Ltd.	343
Metropolitan Life Insurance Company	344
Michaels of Canada Inc.	345
Milne & Craighead Inc.	347
National Life	361
Neles Automation, Scada Solutions Ltd.	362
News Marketing Canada	368
Nielsen Marketing Research	370
Nike Canada Ltd.	371
Nissan Canada Inc.	371
North West Company Inc.	374
Novartis Consumer Health Canada Inc.	378
Oetiker Limited	381
Oracle Corp. Canada Inc.	386
Paramount Canada's Wonderland Inc.	389
Pearson Education Canada	393
Pelmorex Inc.	395
Pharma Plus Drugmarts Ltd.	398
Pizza Pizza Ltd.	401
Pollack Rentals Limited	403
Polygram Group Canada Inc.	403
Positron Industries Inc.	404
Purolator Courier Ltd.	413
Ramada Inn	416
Rasco Specialty Metals Inc.	417
Reader's Digest Association of Canada Ltd.	419
Regal Constellation Hotel Ltd.	422
Rogers Media, Publishing	436
Salisbury House of Canada Ltd.	442
Sandman Hotels and Inns	443
Sharp Electronics of Canada Ltd.	454
Shaw Communications	455
Siemens Electric Ltd.	460
Signature Vacations Inc.	460
Skiing Louise Ltd.	461
Sobeys Inc.	463
Sodexho Marriott Services Canada	464
Sony Music Canada	465
Southam Inc.	466
Steelcraft Industries Ltd.	477
Stitches	478
Sudbury Regional Hospital	480
Sun Peaks Resort Corporation	481
TCG International Inc.	487
Telegraph Journal	491
The Barn Fruit Markets Inc.	493
Thompson's Moving and Storage	496
Ticketmaster Canada Inc.	498
Today's Business Products Ltd.	500
Toronto Sun Publishing Corp., The	507
TSC Stores Ltd.	512
Vancouver International Airport	520
Westbury Life	529
WestJet Airlines	532
Whistler Blackcomb Mountain	535
Winners Apparel Ltd.	539
YFactor	544
Zellers Inc.	546

Animal Health

A C A Cooperative Limited	74
Aventis Pasteur Limited	117
Bio-Research Laboratories Ltd.	137
Federated Co-operatives Limited	239
Hippodrome de Montréal	270
Hub Meat Packers Ltd.	278
Lakeside Farm Industries Ltd.	312
Novartis Consumer Health Canada Inc.	378
Paramount Canada's Wonderland Inc.	389
Phoenix International	399
Prince George, City of	410
Saskatoon, City of	448
Science North	452
Toronto Zoo	507

Business

1-800-GOT-JUNK?	74
A E McKenzie Co. Inc.	75
ABC Group	76
Accucaps Industries Limited	79
ACE INI Insurance	79
Acklands-Grainger Inc.	80
Akita Drilling Ltd.	87
Alberta Gaming & Liquor Commission	90
Alberto Culver Canada Inc.	90
Alexandra Hospital	91
Allcolour Paint Limited	94
Allianz Canada	95
Allstate Insurance Co. of Canada	96
Amcor Twinpak North America Inc.	98
AMEC Inc.	99
American Airlines Inc.	99
Amram's Distributing Ltd.	100

College Index

Anjura Services Inc.	101	Casa Loma	177
Anthony Insurance Inc.	102	Centra Gas British Columbia Inc.	180
Apex Land Corp.	103	Ceridian Canada	183
Apple Canada Inc.	104	CGU Group Canada Ltd.	185
Arbor Memorial Services Inc.	106	CH2M Gore and Storrie Limited	185
Arctic Co-operatives Limited	107	Challenger Motor Freight Inc.	186
Armor Personnel	107	Chapters Inc.	186
Assiniboine Community College	109	Charlottetown Driving Park	187
Assure Health Inc.	110	Christian Horizons	190
ATCO Frontec Corp.	111	Cineplex Odeon Corporation	191
Atlantic Packaging Products Ltd.	114	CKF Inc.	192
Atlantic Wholesalers Ltd.	114	Cobourg District General Hospital	194
Atlas Ideal Metals Inc.	115	Columbia House	197
Aurum Ceramic Dental Laboratories Ltd.	117	Comcare Health Services	198
AXA Insurance (Canada)	118	Computer Associates Canada Ltd.	201
Babcock and Wilcox Canada	119	Connors Bros, Limited	203
Banff Centre for Continuing Education, The	120	Co-op Atlantic	203
BASF Canada Inc.	122	Coquitlam, City of	204
Basic Technologies Corporation	122	Corner Brook, City of	205
BCG Services	127	Cosyn Technology	207
Bell Mobility	131	Cotton Ginny Ltd.	207
Bettis Canada Ltd.	135	Cougar Helicopters Inc.	208
BFGoodrich Landing Gear Division	135	Credit Union Central of Canada	208
Bio-Research Laboratories Ltd.	137	Culinar Inc.	209
Birks Jewelry	138	D.A. Stuart Inc.	210
Black Photo Corporation	139	DaimlerChrysler Canada Inc.	211
Blaney McMurty LLP	139	Dana Corporation - Long Manufacturing	212
Boréal Assurances Inc.	144	David Thompson Health Region	212
BOVAR Waste Management	145	Degussa - Huls Canada Inc.	214
Brookfield Properties Corporation	150	Delphi Solutions Inc.	215
Browning Harvey Limited	150	Delta Hotels	215
Burger King Restaurants of Canada Inc.	153	Directwest Publishers Ltd.	217
C.S.T. Consultants Inc.	155	Domtar Inc.	218
Cabre Exploration Ltd.	156	Drug Trading Company Ltd.	219
Cadith Entertainment Ltd.	156	Dun & Bradstreet Canada	221
Calgary Co-operative Association Limited	157	Dylex Limited	222
Calgary, City of	158	Dynasty Furniture Manufacturing Ltd.	224
Cambridge Suites	159	Economic Development Edmonton	226
Canada Safeway Limited	163	Economical Insurance Group, The	227
Canadian Cancer Society	164	EDS of Canada Ltd.	228
Canadian Depository for Securities Ltd.	166	Emco Limited	230
Canadian General Tower Limited	166	EMJ Data Systems Ltd.	231
Canadian Occidental Petroleum Ltd.	168	Endpoint Research Ltd.	231
Canadian Tire Corporation Ltd.	169	EnerFlex Systems Ltd.	232
Canadian Western Bank	169	Exfo	235
Canbra Foods Ltd.	170	Exide Canada Inc.	235
Cancarb Limited	170	Explorer Hotel, The	236
CancerCare Manitoba	171	Farm Credit Corp. Canada	238
Cancore Industries Inc.	171	Federated Co-operatives Limited	239
Canon Canada Inc.	172	Finning	240
Canpar Transport Ltd.	173	Fisher Scientific Limited	241
CanWel Distribution Ltd.	173	Fishery Products International	241
Carbone of America (LCL) Ltd.	175	Flakeboard Company Limited	242
Carlson Marketing Group Canada Ltd.	176	Foremost Industries Inc.	244

The Canada Student Employment Guide

College Index

Foyer Valade Inc.	245
Friesens Corporation	246
Future Shop Ltd.	246
Gay Lea Foods Co-Operative Ltd.	247
Gendis Inc.	248
Gienow Building Products Ltd.	251
Gilbey Canada Inc.	252
Gimbel Eye Centre	252
Gisborne Design Services Ltd.	253
Glentel Inc.	254
Goodwill Industries of Toronto	256
Goodyear Canada Inc.	256
Grand & Toy Ltd.	257
Grant MacEwen Community College	258
Groupe Savoie Inc.	260
Halifax County Regional Rehabilitation Centre	263
Halifax Regional Municipality	263
Halifax Water Commission	264
Hasbro Canada Inc.	266
Helijet Airways Inc.	268
Hermes Electronics Inc.	269
Holiday Inn Select Toronto Airport	272
Home Oil Co. Ltd.	273
Homewood Corp.	274
Honda Canada Inc.	274
Household Movers & Shippers Limited	276
HSBC Bank Canada	277
Hubbell Canada Inc.	278
Hudson's Bay Company, The	279
Humber River Regional Hospital	280
Husky Energy Inc.	281
Hydro One Inc.	282
Indalex Limited	288
Industrial-Alliance Life Insurance Company	289
ING Canada Financial Services International	291
Insurance Corp. of B.C.	291
Intercon Security Ltd.	292
InterOne Marketing Group	293
IPL Energy Inc.	294
Island Savings Credit Union	295
Island Telecom Inc.	295
IWK Grace Health Centre	297
Izaak Walton Killam Hospital, The	297
James Richardson International Limited	300
Jim Pattison Group	301
John P. Robarts Research Institute	302
Johnson Incorporated	303
Kawneer Company Canada Limited	304
Kennametal Ltd.	305
Kimberly-Clark Inc.	307
Kitchener, City of	309
La Confiserie Comete Ltee	311
Laidlaw Inc.	312
Leduc, City of	313
Lego Canada Inc.	314
Les Modes Smart Inc.	318
Liberty Health	318
Lick's Ice Cream & Burger Shops Inc.	319
Lifetouch Canada Inc.	319
M. McGrawth Canada Limited	324
MacDonald Dettwiler and Associates Ltd.	325
Mactac Canada Ltd.	326
Magna International Inc.	327
Manitoba Public Insurance Corporation	329
Marcam Canada	330
Maritime Life Assurance Company, The	331
Mark Anthony Group Inc.	332
Marks & Spencer Canada Inc.	332
McBee Systems of Canada Inc.	336
McCarney Greenwood	336
McGraw Hill Ryerson Ltd.	337
McMillan & Associates Inc.	339
Mediacom Inc.	340
Metro Toronto Convention Centre	342
Metropolitan Life Insurance Company	344
Meyers Norris Penny & Co.	344
Michaels of Canada Inc.	345
Midland Walwyn Inc.	345
Midwest Food Products Inc.	346
Minas Basin Pulp and Power Company Ltd.	347
Mitel Corporation	350
Mobile Computing Corporation	351
Montreal Trust Co.	353
Moosehead Breweries Limited	354
MOSAID Technologies Inc.	355
Nanaimo Credit Union	359
National Grocers Co. Ltd.	360
National Life	361
Neles Automation, Scada Solutions Ltd.	362
Nestle Canada Inc.	364
New Brunswick Power Corporation	365
Newfoundland and Labrador Credit Union	367
Newness Machine Ltd.	368
News Marketing Canada	368
Nielsen Marketing Research	370
Nike Canada Ltd.	371
North American Life Assurance Company	373
North West Company Inc.	374
Norwich Union Life Insurance Society	376
Nova Scotia Power Corp.	377
Novartis Consumer Health Canada Inc.	378
Novotel Canada Inc.	378
Nygard International Ltd.	380
Oetiker Limited	381
Ontario Guard Services Inc.	383
Ontario Jockey Club, The	384
Oracle Corp. Canada Inc.	386
Paramount Canada's Wonderland Inc.	389

The Canada Student Employment Guide

College Index

Parkland Industries Ltd.	390	Siemens Electric Ltd.	460
Paul Revere Life Insurance Company, The	391	Signature Vacations Inc.	460
PavCo	391	Silicon Graphics Canada Inc.	461
Peel Board of Education	393	Skiing Louise Ltd.	461
Peel Regional Police	394	Slocan Forest Products Ltd.	462
Pelmorex Inc.	395	Sobeys Inc.	463
PennCorp Life Insurance Company	396	Sony Music Canada	465
Pharma Plus Drugmarts Ltd.	398	Southam Inc.	466
Pine Falls Paper Company Limited	400	Southland Canada	467
Pitney Bowes of Canada Ltd.	401	St. Lawrence Parks Commission	472
Pizza Pizza Ltd.	401	St. Vincent's Hospitals	473
Pollack Rentals Limited	403	Stanley Canada Inc.	475
Polygram Group Canada Inc.	403	Sterling Marking Products Inc.	478
Potacan Mining Company	405	Stitches	478
PPG Canada Inc.	407	Sun Rype Products Ltd.	481
Prince Albert, City of	410	Supreme Tooling Group	483
Prince George, City of	410	Surrey, City of	484
Progressive Financial Strategy	411	TCG International Inc.	487
Prudential Insurance Co. of America, The	412	TCT Logistics	488
Public Utilities of Kingston	413	TD Waterhouse Investor Services (Canada)	488
Purolator Courier Ltd.	413	Teklogix Inc.	489
Ramada Inn	416	Telus Corporation	492
Raymond Industrial Equipment Ltd.	418	Thomas Cook Group (Canada) Ltd.	495
Raymond Rebar Inc.	418	Thompson's Moving and Storage	496
Reader's Digest Association of Canada Ltd.	419	Ticketmaster Canada Inc.	498
Regal Capital Planners Ltd.	422	Tiger Brand Knitting Company Limited	498
Regal Constellation Hotel Ltd.	422	Today's Business Products Ltd.	500
Reynolds and Reynolds (Canada) Limited	430	Toronto Cricket Skating & Curling	502
Rhone-Poulenc Canada Inc.	430	Toronto Hydro	505
Richmond, City of	431	Toronto Police Service	506
Rimrock Resort Hotel	432	Toronto Sun Publishing Corp., The	507
Riverside Fabricating Ltd.	433	Toronto, City of	508
Rogers AT&T Wireless Inc.	436	Toshiba of Canada Ltd.	508
Rogers Media, Publishing	436	Toyota Canada Ltd.	509
Royal & Sun Alliance Insurance Co. of Cda	437	TSC Stores Ltd.	512
Royal Bank of Canada	438	Uni Select Inc.	513
Royal Philips Electronics	439	University College of Cape Breton	516
Royal Victoria Hospital	440	VanCity Credit Union	519
Ryerson Polytechnic University	441	Vancouver International Airport	520
Sales & Merchandising Group	442	Volvo Cars of Canada Ltd.	523
Salisbury House of Canada Ltd.	442	WebCanada	526
Sandman Hotels and Inns	443	Wegu Canada Inc.	526
Saskatchewan Centre of the Arts	444	Wendy's Restaurants of Canada Inc.	527
Saskatchewan Government Insurance	445	West Coast Apparel	528
Saskferco Products Inc.	448	Westbury Life	529
SaskTel	449	Westcliff Management Ltd.	529
Scarborough General Hospital	450	Westcoast Energy Inc.	530
Schlumberger Canada Ltd.	450	Western Glove Works	530
SCIEX MDS Health Group	452	Westinghouse Canada Inc.	532
Sharp Electronics of Canada Ltd.	454	WestJet Airlines	532
Shaw Communications	455	Westminster Savings Credit Union	533
Sheraton Fallsview Hotel	456	Westshore Terminals Ltd.	534
Shermag Inc.	457	Weyerhaeuser Company Limited	535
Shorewood Packaging Corp. of Canada Ltd.	459	Whistler Blackcomb Mountain	535

The Canada Student Employment Guide

College Index

White Rose Crafts and Nursery Sales Limited	536
Wilson Auto Electric Ltd.	538
Windsor, City of	538
Winners Apparel Ltd.	539
Winpak Ltd.	539
Wire Rope Industries Ltd.	540
Yamaha Motor Canada Ltd.	542
Yanke Group of Companies	543
Yellowknife, City of	544
Zellers Inc.	546

CAD Autocad

ABC Group	76
ATCO Frontec Corp.	111
Atlantic Packaging Products Ltd.	114
Atlas Ideal Metals Inc.	115
Basic Technologies Corporation	122
Behlen Industries	130
BFGoodrich Landing Gear Division	135
BOVAR Waste Management	145
Brandon, City of	146
Bullock Associates Design Consultants Inc.	153
Connors Bros, Limited	203
Coquitlam, City of	204
Cosyn Technology	207
Economical Insurance Group, The	227
Exfo	235
Flint Energy Services Ltd.	243
Hallmark Tools	265
J.D. Barnes Limited	298
Leon's Manufacturing Company Inc.	316
LM Architectural Group	321
MacViro Consultants Inc.	326
Marshall Macklin Monaghan Ltd.	333
Matrox Electronic Systems Ltd.	335
MDS Nordion	339
Morrison Hershfield Limited	354
Neles Automation, Scada Solutions Ltd.	362
Northwestel Inc.	376
Nygard International Ltd.	380
Omstead Foods Limited	383
Ottawa Hospital	386
Phillips & Tempro Industries Ltd.	398
Pine Falls Paper Company Limited	400
Raymond Rebar Inc.	418
Royal Canadian Mint	438
Sandwell Inc.	443
Seprotech Systems Incorporated	454
Spectra Premium Industries	468
SRI Homes Inc.	470
Stantec Consulting Ltd.	475
Steelcraft Industries Ltd.	477

Steelpipe Ltd.	477
The Co-operators	493
The Garland Group	494
The McElhanney Group Ltd.	494
Westport Innovations Inc.	534
Winners Apparel Ltd.	539

Child Care

Algoma Child & Youth Services Inc.	92
Assiniboine Community College	109
Belleville General Hospital	132
Bloorview Childrens Hospital	140
Bloorview MacMillan Centre, The	140
Bluewater District School Board	142
Canadian National Institute For The Blind	167
Casa Loma	177
Catholic Children's Aid Society Foundation	178
Children's Aid Society of Metro Toronto	188
Children's Hospital of Eastern Ontario	189
Delta Hotels	215
Family Day Care Service	238
George Jeffrey Children's Treatment Centre	250
Grant MacEwen Community College	258
Health Sciences Centre	268
Horseshoe Resort Corporation	275
IWK Grace Health Centre	297
Keyano College	306
Les Centres Jeunesse de Montréal	316
Maryvale Adolescent and Family Services	334
Misericordia General Hospital	348
Peel Board of Education	393
Pool People Ltd.	404
Reena	421
Regina Health District	423
Regional Residential Services Society	424
Rehabilitation Institute of Toronto	425
Royal Victoria Hospital	440
Science North	452
Skiing Louise Ltd.	461
Skills Training & Support Services Association	462
St. Amant Centre Inc.	471
Sudbury Regional Hospital	480
Sun Peaks Resort Corporation	481
Thunder Bay Regional Hospital	497
Timmins, City of	499
Toronto Cricket Skating & Curling	502
Universal Rehabilitation Service Agency	515
Whistler Blackcomb Mountain	535

The Canada Student Employment Guide

Communications

1-800-GOT-JUNK?	74
Abitibi-Consolidated Inc.	77
Acklands-Grainger Inc.	80
AGF Management Limited	83
Air Canada	85
Alberta Blue Cross	88
Alberta Energy & Utilities Board	89
Allstate Insurance Co. of Canada	96
Amram's Distributing Ltd.	100
Anjura Services Inc.	101
Anthony Insurance Inc.	102
Arbor Care Tree Service Ltd.	106
Atlantic Blue Cross Care	113
Atlantic Wholesalers Ltd.	114
Atlas Ideal Metals Inc.	115
Atlas Van Lines (Canada) Ltd.	115
Aurum Ceramic Dental Laboratories Ltd.	117
Axidata Inc.	118
Banff Centre for Continuing Education, The	120
Bell Mobility	131
Black Photo Corporation	139
British Columbia Ferry Corporation	149
Brookfield Properties Corporation	150
Cadith Entertainment Ltd.	156
Calgary Co-operative Association Limited	157
Calgary, City of	158
Cambridge Suites	159
Canadian Cancer Society	164
Canadian Dairy Commission	165
Canadian Museum of Civilization Corp.	167
Canadian Western Bank	169
Canon Canada Inc.	172
Centra Gas British Columbia Inc.	180
Centra Gas Manitoba Inc.	181
CFCF Inc.	183
CFCN Communications Inc.	184
Chapters Inc.	186
Cobourg District General Hospital	194
Columbia House	197
Co-op Atlantic	203
Coquitlam, City of	204
Cotton Ginny Ltd.	207
Cougar Helicopters Inc.	208
Credit Union Central of Canada	208
Culinar Inc.	209
D.A. Stuart Inc.	210
DaimlerChrysler Canada Ltd.	211
David Thompson Health Region	212
Delphi Solutions Inc.	215
Domtar Inc.	218
Dylex Limited	222
Dynapro Systems Inc.	223

Economical Insurance Group, The	227
Exfo	235
Explorer Hotel, The	236
Extendicare (Canada) Inc.	237
Farm Credit Corp. Canada	238
Finning	240
Fletcher's Fine Foods	242
Foremost Industries Inc.	244
Friesens Corporation	246
Future Shop Ltd.	246
George Jeffrey Children's Treatment Centre	250
Gisborne Design Services Ltd.	253
Glaxo Wellcome Canada	253
Glentel Inc.	254
Goodman and Carr	255
Goodwill Industries of Toronto	256
Grant MacEwen Community College	258
Great-West Life Assurance Company, The	259
Hasbro Canada Inc.	266
Health Care Corporation of St. John's	267
Helijet Airways Inc.	268
Hill & Knowlton Canada Ltd.	270
Home Oil Co. Ltd.	273
Homewood Corp.	274
Humber River Regional Hospital	280
Hydro Electric Commission of Thunder Bay	281
John P. Robarts Research Institute	302
Johnson Incorporated	303
Jostens Canada Ltd.	303
Kitchener, City of	309
Laidlaw Inc.	312
Leduc, City of	313
Lenbrook Industries Limited	315
Liberty Health	318
Lifetouch Canada Inc.	319
MAAX Inc.	324
Magna International Inc.	327
Manitoba Hydro	328
Manitoba Public Insurance Corporation	329
Manitoba Telecom Services Inc.	329
Maritime Life Assurance Company, The	331
Mark Anthony Group Inc.	332
Matrox Electronic Systems Ltd.	335
McBee Systems of Canada Inc.	336
McMillan & Associates Inc.	339
Mediasynergy	340
Metro Toronto Convention Centre	342
Metropolitan Life Insurance Company	344
Michaels of Canada Inc.	345
Midland Walwyn Inc.	345
Ministry of Northern Develop. and Mines	348
Mobile Computing Corporation	351
Moen Inc.	352
Monarch Communications Inc.	353

College Index

Montreal Trust Co.	353
Moosehead Breweries Limited	354
Motorola Canada Ltd.	356
Mustang Survival Corp.	358
National Grocers Co. Ltd.	360
National Life	361
Neles Automation, Scada Solutions Ltd.	362
Nelvana Limited	363
New Brunswick Telephone Company	366
News Marketing Canada	368
Nike Canada Ltd.	371
Northern Lights Regional Health Centre	375
Northwestel Inc.	376
Novartis Consumer Health Canada Inc.	378
Okanagan Skeena Group Limited	382
Paladin Security & Investigations Limited	388
Panorama Mountain Village	388
Paramount Canada's Wonderland Inc.	389
PavCo	391
Pelmorex Inc.	395
PennCorp Life Insurance Company	396
Pine Falls Paper Company Limited	400
Pitney Bowes of Canada Ltd.	401
Pizza Pizza Ltd.	401
Purolator Courier Ltd.	413
Quebecor Inc.	415
Reader's Digest Association of Canada Ltd.	419
Replicon Inc.	428
Royal & Sun Alliance Insurance Co. of Cda	437
Ryerson Polytechnic University	441
Sandman Hotels and Inns	443
Saskatchewan Government Insurance	445
SaskTel	449
Shaw Communications	455
Shorewood Packaging Corp. of Canada Ltd.	459
Siemens Electric Ltd.	460
Signature Vacations Inc.	460
Sony Music Canada	465
Sprint Canada	470
Sudbury Regional Hospital	480
Sun Peaks Resort Corporation	481
Surrey, City of	484
Symantec Corporation	486
Telus Corporation	492
The Arthritis Society	492
The Garland Group	494
Thomas Cook Group (Canada) Ltd.	495
Thompson's Moving and Storage	496
Today's Business Products Ltd.	500
Toronto General Hospital	505
Toronto Hydro	505
Toronto Sun Publishing Corp., The	507
Toronto, City of	508
TransAlta	509
University College of Cape Breton	516
Vancouver International Airport	520
WebCanada	526
West Kootenay Power Ltd.	528
Westbury Life	529
Westcliff Management Ltd.	529
Westcoast Energy Inc.	530
WestJet Airlines	532
Weyerhaeuser Company Limited	535
Whistler Blackcomb Mountain	535
YFactor	544
YTV Canada Inc.	545
Zurich Canada	548

Computer Science

A C A Cooperative Limited	74
A E McKenzie Co. Inc.	75
A.G. Simpson Co. Ltd.	75
ABC Group	76
Aberdeen Hospital	77
Access Communications	78
Accucaps Industries Limited	79
ACE INI Insurance	79
Acklands-Grainger Inc.	80
ADT Canada Inc.	82
Air Ontario Inc.	86
Alberta Blue Cross	88
Alberta Cancer Board	88
Alberta Energy & Utilities Board	89
Alberta Energy Company Ltd.	89
Alberta Gaming & Liquor Commission	90
Alcan Aluminium Limited	91
Algoma Steel Inc.	93
Allianz Canada	95
Allstate Insurance Co. of Canada	96
Alpine Oil Service Corporation	96
Amcor Twinpak North America Inc.	98
Anjura Services Inc.	101
Antamex International Inc.	102
Anthony Insurance Inc.	102
Armor Personnel	107
Assiniboine Community College	109
Assumption Mutual Life Insurance	109
AstraZeneca	110
ATCO Electric	111
ATCO Frontec Corp.	111
ATCO Gas Services Ltd.	112
Atlantic Blue Cross Care	113
Atlantic Lottery Corporation Inc.	113
Atlas Ideal Metals Inc.	115
ATS Automation Tooling Systems Inc.	116
Aurizon Mines Ltd.	116

The Canada Student Employment Guide

College Index

Aurum Ceramic Dental Laboratories Ltd.	117	Ceridian Canada	183
Axidata Inc.	118	CGI	184
Ballard Power Systems Inc.	120	CGU Group Canada Ltd.	185
Bargain Finder Press Ltd.	121	CH2M Gore and Storrie Limited	185
Barton Place Long Term Care Facility	121	Chevron Canada Resources Ltd.	188
BASF Canada Inc.	122	Children's Hospital of Eastern Ontario	189
Basic Technologies Corporation	122	Citibank Canada	191
Baytex Energy Limited	124	CKF Inc.	192
BBM Bureau of Measurement	125	Clarica	192
BC Research Inc.	126	COBI Foods Inc.	194
Bell Canada	131	Cobourg District General Hospital	194
Bell Mobility	131	Cognos Incorporated	196
Belleville General Hospital	132	Columbia House	197
Bettis Canada Ltd.	135	Comcare Health Services	198
BFGoodrich Landing Gear Division	135	Community Savings Credit Union	199
BJ Services Company	138	Compu-Quote Inc.	200
Black Photo Corporation	139	Computalog Ltd.	200
Bloorview MacMillan Centre, The	140	Comtronic Computer Inc.	202
Blue Wave Seafoods Inc.	142	Conair Aviation Ltd.	202
BNP PARIBAS (Canada)	143	Connors Bros, Limited	203
BOVAR Waste Management	145	Co-op Atlantic	203
Bowater Mersey Paper Company Limited	146	Coquitlam, City of	204
Brandon, City of	146	Corel Corporation	205
Bratty & Partners LLP	147	Corner Brook, City of	205
Brewers Retail Inc.	148	Cornwall Electric	206
Brookfield Properties Corporation	150	Cotton Ginny Ltd.	207
Buck Consultants Limited	151	Cougar Helicopters Inc.	208
Buckeye Canada Inc.	151	Credit Union Central of Canada	208
Budd Canada Inc.	152	Crestar Energy Inc.	209
C B C L Limited	154	Culinar Inc.	209
C MAC Industries Inc.	155	Custom Trim Ltd.	210
Cabre Exploration Ltd.	156	D.A. Stuart Inc.	210
Calgary Co-operative Association Limited	157	D.H. Howden	211
Calgary, City of	158	DaimlerChrysler Canada Ltd.	211
Cambridge Memorial Hospital	159	David Thompson Health Region	212
Camp Hill Hospital	160	Dell Computer Corporation	214
Canadian Cancer Society	164	Directwest Publishers Ltd.	217
Canadian Commercial Corp.	165	Dofasco Inc.	218
Canadian Dairy Commission	165	Domtar Inc.	218
Canadian Depository for Securities Ltd.	166	Dun & Bradstreet Canada	221
Canadian General Tower Limited	166	Dynapro Systems Inc.	223
Canadian Occidental Petroleum Ltd.	168	Economic Development Edmonton	226
Canadian Thermos Products Inc.	168	Economical Insurance Group, The	227
Canadian Tire Corporation Ltd.	169	EDS of Canada Ltd.	228
Canadian Western Bank	169	Electronics Arts (Canada) Inc.	229
Canbra Foods Ltd.	170	EMJ Data Systems Ltd.	231
CancerCare Manitoba	171	EnerFlex Systems Ltd.	232
Canon Canada Inc.	172	Entreprises Premier Canadien Ltée	232
Cape Breton Development Corporation	174	Espial Group Incorporated	234
Cargill Limited	175	Exfo	235
Carte International Inc.	176	Exide Canada Inc.	235
Centra Gas British Columbia Inc.	180	Extendicare (Canada) Inc.	237
Centra Gas Manitoba Inc.	181	Farm Credit Corp. Canada	238
Centre de Santé de St-Henri Inc.	182	Farmers Co-operative Dairy Limited	239

The Canada Student Employment Guide

College Index

Federated Co-operatives Limited	239	InterOne Marketing Group	293
Fisher Scientific Limited	241	IPL Energy Inc.	294
Fishery Products International	241	IST Group Inc.	296
Flakeboard Company Limited	242	Ivaco Inc.	296
Flint Energy Services Ltd.	243	IWK Grace Health Centre	297
Foremost Industries Inc.	244	J.D. Irving Limited	298
Foyer Valade Inc.	245	James Richardson International Limited	300
Friesens Corporation	246	Jim Pattison Group	301
Future Shop Ltd.	246	Johnson Controls Ltd.	302
General Chemical Canada Ltd.	249	Johnson Incorporated	303
General Electric Canada Inc.	249	Jostens Canada Ltd.	303
George Jeffrey Children's Treatment Centre	250	Kelowna, City of	305
Gienow Building Products Ltd.	251	Kitchener, City of	309
Giffels Associates Limited	251	Kodak Canada Inc.	309
Gilbey Canada Inc.	252	La Confiserie Comete Ltee	311
Gimbel Eye Centre	252	Laidlaw Inc.	312
Glaxo Wellcome Canada	253	Leduc, City of	313
Glentel Inc.	254	Lenbrook Industries Limited	315
Goodman and Carr	255	Les Centres Jeunesse de Montréal	316
Goodwill Industries of Toronto	256	Les Forges de Sorel Inc.	317
Goodyear Canada Inc.	256	Liberty Health	318
Gov't of Newfoundland – Dept. of Finance	257	Lifetouch Canada Inc.	319
Grand & Toy Ltd.	257	Linmor Technologies	320
Grant MacEwen Community College	258	Litton Systems Canada Ltd.	320
Great-West Life Assurance Company, The	259	MAAX Inc.	324
H A Simmons Ltd.	261	MacDonald Dettwiler and Associates Ltd.	325
Halifax Regional Municipality	263	MacDonald Steel Ltd.	325
Halifax Water Commission	264	Manitoba Agriculture and Food	327
HB Studios Multimedia Ltd.	266	Manitoba Hydro	328
Health Care Corporation of St. John's	267	Manitoba Pool Elevators	328
Health Sciences Centre	268	Manitoba Public Insurance Corporation	329
Hippodrome de Montréal	270	Manitoba Telecom Services Inc.	329
Holland College	273	Maple Leaf Consumer Foods	330
Home Oil Co. Ltd.	273	Marcam Canada	330
Homewood Corp.	274	Marine Atlantic Inc.	331
Honeywell Ltd.	275	Maritime Life Assurance Company, The	331
Hôtel Dieu de Montréal	276	Mark Anthony Group Inc.	332
Household Movers & Shippers Limited	276	Marshall Macklin Monaghan Ltd.	333
HSBC Bank Canada	277	Marystown Shipyard Limited	334
Hubbell Canada Inc.	278	Matrox Electronic Systems Ltd.	335
Hudon & Deaudelin Ltée	279	McBee Systems of Canada Inc.	336
Hudson's Bay Company, The	279	McKay-Cocker Construction Limited	338
Huronia Regional Centre	280	MDS Nordion	339
Husky Energy Inc.	281	Mediasynergy	340
Hydro Electric Commission of Thunder Bay	281	Metro Richelieu Inc.	342
Hydro One Inc.	282	Meyers Norris Penny & Co.	344
Hydro Québec	283	Michaels of Canada Inc.	345
I M P Group International Inc.	283	Midland Walwyn Inc.	345
IBM Canada Ltd.	284	Midwest Food Products Inc.	346
Industrial Equipment Co. Ltd.	288	Minas Basin Pulp and Power Company Ltd.	347
Industrial-Alliance Life Insurance Company	289	Ministry of Northern Develop. and Mines	348
Industries Lassonde Inc.	289	Mississauga, City of	349
InfoInterActive Inc.	290	Mitel Corporation	350
ING Canada Financial Services International	291	Mitra Imaging Inc.	350

The Canada Student Employment Guide

College Index 569

Mitsubishi Electric Sales Canada	351
Mobile Computing Corporation	351
Moen Inc.	352
Monarch Communications Inc.	353
Montreal Trust Co.	353
Moosehead Breweries Limited	354
Mortice Kern Systems Inc.	355
MOSAID Technologies Inc.	355
Motorola Canada Ltd.	356
Multitech Electronics Inc.	358
Mustang Survival Corp.	358
N B S Card Services	359
Natco Canada Ltd.	360
National Grocers Co. Ltd.	360
National Life	361
National Manufacturing of Canada Inc.	361
National Sports Centre	362
Neles Automation, Scada Solutions Ltd.	362
Nelvana Limited	363
Nesbitt Burns Inc.	364
Nestle Canada Inc.	364
New Brunswick Power Corporation	365
Newfoundland and Labrador Credit Union	367
NewTel Communications	369
Nielsen Marketing Research	370
North West Company Inc.	374
Northern Lights Regional Health Centre	375
Northwestel Inc.	376
Norwich Union Life Insurance Society	376
Nova Scotia Liquor Commission	377
Nova Scotia Power Corp.	377
NPS Allelix Corp.	379
Numac Energy Inc.	379
Nygard International Ltd.	380
Okanagan Skeena Group Limited	382
Oland Breweries Limited	382
Ontario Jockey Club, The	384
Ontario Legislative Offices	384
Oracle Corp. Canada Inc.	386
Ottawa Hospital	386
Paramount Canada's Wonderland Inc.	389
Paul Revere Life Insurance Company, The	391
PavCo	391
PCL Constructors Inc.	392
Pearson Education Canada	393
Peel Board of Education	393
Peel Regional Police	394
Pelmorex Inc.	395
Pharma Plus Drugmarts Ltd.	398
Phoenix International	399
Pitney Bowes of Canada Ltd.	401
Placer Dome Inc.	402
Pollack Rentals Limited	403
Polygram Group Canada Inc.	403
Potacan Mining Company	405
Powertech Labs Inc.	406
Premdor Inc.	408
PRI Automation	408
Prince George, City of	410
Prudential Insurance Co. of America, The	412
Public Utilities of Kingston	413
Purolator Courier Ltd.	413
QEII Health Sciences Centre	414
QIT-Fer et Titane Inc.	414
Québéc Cartier Mining Company	415
Quebecor Inc.	415
Raytheon Systems Canada Ltd.	419
Reader's Digest Association of Canada Ltd.	419
Recochem Inc.	420
Regal Capital Planners Ltd.	422
Regal Constellation Hotel Ltd.	422
Rehabilitation Institute of Toronto	425
Replicon Inc.	428
Revenue Properties Company Limited	429
Reynolds and Reynolds (Canada) Limited	430
Richmond, City of	431
Riverside Hospital of Ottawa, The	434
Rivtow Marine Ltd.	434
Rockwell Automation	435
Rogers AT&T Wireless Inc.	436
Rothmans, Benson and Hedges Inc.	437
Royal & Sun Alliance Insurance Co. of Cda	437
Royal Bank of Canada	438
Saan Stores Ltd.	441
Salisbury House of Canada Ltd.	442
Sandman Hotels and Inns	443
Saskatchewan Economic Development	445
Saskatchewan Government Insurance	445
Saskatchewan Wheat Pool	447
Saskatoon, City of	448
Saskferco Products Inc.	448
SaskTel	449
SC Infrastructure Inc.	449
Scarborough General Hospital	450
Schneider Electric Canada Inc.	451
Science North	452
SCIEX MDS Health Group	452
SED Systems	453
Shaw Communications	455
Sherwood Credit Union	458
Shorewood Packaging Corp. of Canada Ltd.	459
Siemens Electric Ltd.	460
Signature Vacations Inc.	460
Silicon Graphics Canada Inc.	461
Société des Alcools du Québec	464
SolutionInc Limited	465
Sony Music Canada	465
Southam Inc.	466

The Canada Student Employment Guide

College Index

Spar Aerospace Limited	467	W C I Canada Inc.	524
Spectra Premium Industries	468	WebCanada	526
Spectrum Signal Processing Inc.	468	Weldco-Beales Manufacturing Inc.	527
Speedware Corp. Inc.	469	West Coast Apparel	528
Sprint Canada	470	Westbury Life	529
SSQ Life	471	Westcoast Energy Inc.	530
St. Lawrence Seaway Mgmt. Corp., The	473	Westinghouse Canada Inc.	532
St. Vincent's Hospitals	473	WestJet Airlines	532
Standen's Limited	474	Westminster Savings Credit Union	533
Stanley Canada Inc.	475	Westport Innovations Inc.	534
Star Data Systems Inc.	476	Westshore Terminals Ltd.	534
State Farm Insurance Companies	476	Weyerhaeuser Company Limited	535
Sterling Marking Products Inc.	478	Whistler Blackcomb Mountain	535
Stitches	478	Whitehill Technologies Inc.	537
StorageTek Canada Inc.	479	Windsor, City of	538
Sun Rype Products Ltd.	481	Winners Apparel Ltd.	539
Sundog Printing Limited	482	Winpak Ltd.	539
Sunoco Inc.	482	Wire Rope Industries Ltd.	540
Surrey Memorial Hospital	483	XCAN Grain Pool Ltd.	541
Surrey, City of	484	xwave solutions	542
Symantec Corporation	486	Yanke Group of Companies	543
Syncrude Canada Ltd.	486	Yellowknife, City of	544
TCG International Inc.	487	Zellers Inc.	546
TCT Logistics	488	Zurich Canada	548
TD Waterhouse Investor Services (Canada)	488		
Teck Corp.	489		
Telebec Ltée	490		

Cooking/Culinary

Telegraph Journal	491		
The Garland Group	494	Algoma District Home For The Aged	92
Thomas J. Lipton	496	Assiniboine Community College	109
Thompson's Moving and Storage	496	ATCO Gas Services Ltd.	112
Thomson - CSF Systems Canada Inc.	497	Banff Centre for Continuing Education, The	120
Thunder Bay Regional Hospital	497	Best Western Carlton Place Hotel	133
Tiger Brand Knitting Company Limited	498	Bethania Mennonite Personal Care Home Inc.	134
Timmins, City of	499	Bethesda Hospital	134
Top Producers Systems Inc.	500	Blue Mountain Resorts Limited	141
Toronto Catholic District School Board	502	Cambridge Memorial Hospital	159
Toronto District School Board	503	Camp Hill Hospital	160
Toronto East General Hospital	503	Canada Catering Co. Ltd.	161
Toronto General Hospital	505	Canada Starch Company Inc.	163
Toronto Hydro	505	Capilano Suspension Bridge	174
Toronto Police Service	506	Chilliwack General Hospital	189
Toronto Sun Publishing Corp., The	507	Delta Hotels	215
Toronto, City of	508	Explorer Hotel, The	236
Toshiba of Canada Ltd.	508	Foyer Valade Inc.	245
Toyota Canada Ltd.	509	Halifax County Regional Rehabilitation Centre	263
TransAlta	509	Health Authority 5	267
Trojan Technologies Inc.	511	Health Care Corporation of St. John's	267
TSC Stores Ltd.	512	Holiday Inn Select Toronto Airport	272
Turnbull & Turnbull Ltd.	512	Homewood Corp.	274
Union Pacific Resources Group	514	Horseshoe Resort Corporation	275
University College of Cape Breton	516	Huronia Regional Centre	280
US Filter BCP	517	Hydro Québec	283
Vancouver International Airport	520	IWK Grace Health Centre	297

The Canada Student Employment Guide

College Index 571

Keyano College	306
Metro Toronto Convention Centre	342
National Grocers Co. Ltd.	360
Ontario Legislative Offices	384
Overlander Hospital	387
Panorama Mountain Village	388
Paramount Canada's Wonderland Inc.	389
Providence Centre	412
Ramada Inn	416
Regal Constellation Hotel Ltd.	422
Rimrock Resort Hotel	432
Sandman Hotels and Inns	443
Scarborough General Hospital	450
Science North	452
Sheraton Fallsview Hotel	456
Sheraton Toronto East Hotel and Towers	456
Skiing Louise Ltd.	461
Sodexho Marriott Services Canada	464
Sudbury Regional Hospital	480
Sun Peaks Resort Corporation	481
The Barn Fruit Markets Inc.	493
Toronto and Region Conservation Authority	501
Toronto Cricket Skating & Curling	502
Toronto General Hospital	505
University College of Cape Breton	516
Versa Services Ltd.	521
Waterloo Inn	525
Wendy's Restaurants of Canada Inc.	527
Whistler Blackcomb Mountain	535

Electronics Tech.

Acadia University	78
Access Communications	78
Accucaps Industries Limited	79
ADT Canada Inc.	82
Aimtronics	84
Alberta Energy Company Ltd.	89
Alberta Gaming & Liquor Commission	90
Alcan Aluminium Limited	91
Algoma Steel Inc.	93
Armor Personnel	107
Assiniboine Community College	109
ATCO Electric	111
ATCO Frontec Corp.	111
ATCO Gas Services Ltd.	112
Atlantic Lottery Corporation Inc.	113
ATS Automation Tooling Systems Inc.	116
Babcock and Wilcox Canada	119
Ballard Power Systems Inc.	120
Basic Technologies Corporation	122
BC Telecom Inc.	126
Beckman Coulter Canada Inc.	129

Bell & Howell Ltd.	130
Bell Mobility	131
BFGoodrich Landing Gear Division	135
Bic Inc.	136
BJ Services Company	138
Black Photo Corporation	139
Bloorview Childrens Hospital	140
Bloorview MacMillan Centre, The	140
Bowater Mersey Paper Company Limited	146
Brantcorp Inc.	147
Budd Canada Inc.	152
C MAC Industries Inc.	155
Cambridge Memorial Hospital	159
Canada Post Corporation	162
Canadian Western Bank	169
CancerCare Manitoba	171
Canon Canada Inc.	172
Cape Breton Development Corporation	174
Carte International Inc.	176
Celestica International Inc.	179
CFCF Inc.	183
CFCN Communications Inc.	184
Cineplex Odeon Corporation	191
CKF Inc.	192
Cognos Incorporated	196
COM DEV International	197
Communications & Power Industries Canada	198
Compaq Canada Inc.	199
Computalog Ltd.	200
Coquitlam, City of	204
Cornwall Electric	206
DaimlerChrysler Canada Ltd.	211
Deer Lodge Centre Inc.	213
Dell Computer Corporation	214
Delphi Solutions Inc.	215
Develcon Electronics Ltd.	217
Dofasco Inc.	218
Domtar Inc.	218
Dynapro Systems Inc.	223
Dynasty Furniture Manufacturing Ltd.	224
Dynatek Automation Systems Inc.	224
EMJ Data Systems Ltd.	231
EnerFlex Systems Ltd.	232
Entreprises Premier Canadien Ltée	232
Epson Canada Limited	233
Exfo	235
Fishery Products International	241
Flakeboard Company Limited	242
Gencorp Vehicle Sealing	248
General Chemical Canada Ltd.	249
General Electric Canada Inc.	249
George Jeffrey Children's Treatment Centre	250
Glaxo Wellcome Canada	253
Haliburton Energy Services	262

The Canada Student Employment Guide

College Index

Halifax County Regional Rehabilitation Centre	263	Neles Automation, Scada Solutions Ltd.	362
Halifax Regional Municipality	263	Nestle Canada Inc.	364
Halifax Water Commission	264	New Brunswick Power Corporation	365
Halliburton Energy Services	264	Newfoundland and Labrador Hydro	367
Health Care Corporation of St. John's	267	Northwestel Inc.	376
Health Sciences Centre	268	NPS Allelix Corp.	379
Hermes Electronics Inc.	269	Oetiker Limited	381
Home Oil Co. Ltd.	273	Oracle Corp. Canada Inc.	386
Honeywell Ltd.	275	Paramount Canada's Wonderland Inc.	389
Hôtel Dieu de Montréal	276	PavCo	391
Hubbell Canada Inc.	278	Peel Regional Police	394
Huronia Regional Centre	280	Pembina Pipeline Corporation	395
Hydro Electric Commission of Thunder Bay	281	Phillips & Tempro Industries Ltd.	398
Hydro One Inc.	282	Phoenix International	399
Hydro Québec	283	Pine Falls Paper Company Limited	400
I M P Group International Inc.	283	Pitney Bowes of Canada Ltd.	401
IBM Canada Ltd.	284	Positron Industries Inc.	404
Ilco Unican Inc.	286	Power Measurement Ltd.	406
Imprimerie Interweb Inc.	287	Powertech Labs Inc.	406
Industries Lassonde Inc.	289	Premdor Inc.	408
Intercon Security Ltd.	292	Prince Albert, City of	410
Island Telecom Inc.	295	Prince George, City of	410
Ivaco Inc.	296	Proctor and Redfern Ltd.	411
IWK Grace Health Centre	297	Public Utilities of Kingston	413
JDS Uniphase Corporation	300	Raymond Industrial Equipment Ltd.	418
Johnson Controls Ltd.	302	Raytheon Systems Canada Ltd.	419
Kitchener, City of	309	Regional Municipality of Niagara	424
Kodak Canada Inc.	309	Replicon Inc.	428
La Confiserie Comete Ltee	311	Reynolds and Reynolds (Canada) Limited	430
Leduc, City of	313	Rockwell Automation	435
Lenbrook Industries Limited	315	Roctest Ltée	435
Les Forges de Sorel Inc.	317	Rogers AT&T Wireless Inc.	436
Lifetouch Canada Inc.	319	Royal Inland Hospital	439
Litton Systems Canada Ltd.	320	Royal Philips Electronics	439
Magna International Inc.	327	Saskatchewan Government Insurance	445
Manitoba Hydro	328	Saskatoon, City of	448
Marystown Shipyard Limited	334	SaskTel	449
Matrox Electronic Systems Ltd.	335	Schlumberger Canada Ltd.	450
MDS Nordion	339	Schneider Electric Canada Inc.	451
Medical Laboratories of Windsor Limited	341	Science North	452
Memotec Communications Inc.	341	SCIEX MDS Health Group	452
Metroland Printing, Publishing & Dist. Ltd.	343	SCL Technologies Inc.	453
Midwest Food Products Inc.	346	SED Systems	453
Minas Basin Pulp and Power Company Ltd.	347	Sharp Electronics of Canada Ltd.	454
Mississauga, City of	349	Shaw Communications	455
Mitel Corporation	350	Shorewood Packaging Corp. of Canada Ltd.	459
Mitsubishi Electric Sales Canada	351	Siemens Electric Ltd.	460
Mobile Computing Corporation	351	Silicon Graphics Canada Inc.	461
Monarch Communications Inc.	353	Sony Music Canada	465
Moosehead Breweries Limited	354	Spar Aerospace Limited	467
MOSAID Technologies Inc.	355	Spectra Premium Industries	468
Motorola Canada Ltd.	356	St. Lawrence Seaway Mgmt. Corp., The	473
N B S Card Services	359	Star Data Systems Inc.	476
Nanaimo Credit Union	359	Steelpipe Ltd.	477

The Canada Student Employment Guide

College Index 573

StorageTek Canada Inc.	479	QEII Health Sciences Centre	414
Supreme Tooling Group	483	Regina Health District	423
Surrey, City of	484	Richmond, City of	431
Sydney Steel Corporation	485	Skiing Louise Ltd.	461
TD Waterhouse Investor Services (Canada)	488	Sudbury Regional Hospital	480
Thomas & Betts Ltée	495	Swift Current Health District	485
Thunder Bay Regional Hospital	497	Thunder Bay Regional Hospital	497
Tiger Brand Knitting Company Limited	498	Toronto General Hospital	505
Toronto Catholic District School Board	502	Yellowknife, City of	544
Toronto General Hospital	505		
Toronto Police Service	506		
Toshiba of Canada Ltd.	508	## Engineering Tech.	
Triumf	510		
Trojan Technologies Inc.	511	A E McKenzie Co. Inc.	75
Union Gas Ltd.	513	A.G. Simpson Co. Ltd.	75
Unisys Canada Inc.	514	Aar-Kel Moulds Ltd.	76
University College of Cape Breton	516	Abitibi-Consolidated Inc.	77
US Filter BCP	517	Accucaps Industries Limited	79
Visteon Canada Inc.	522	ACE INI Insurance	79
Waterloo Furniture Components Ltd.	524	Acklands-Grainger Inc.	80
West Kootenay Power Ltd.	528	ADI Group Inc.	82
WestJet Airlines	532	ADT Canada Inc.	82
Westport Innovations Inc.	534	Air Canada	85
Wilson Auto Electric Ltd.	538	Air Liquide Canada Inc.	85
Windsor, City of	538	Akita Drilling Ltd.	87
Winpak Ltd.	539	Alberta Energy & Utilities Board	89
Wire Rope Industries Ltd.	540	Alberta Energy Company Ltd.	89
Zenastra	547	Alberta Gaming & Liquor Commission	90
		Alcan Aluminium Limited	91
		Algoma Steel Inc.	93
## Emergency/Paramedic		Amcan Castings Limited	98
		Amcor Twinpak North America Inc.	98
Belleville General Hospital	132	Ancast Industries Ltd.	100
Bethesda Hospital	134	Apex Land Corp.	103
Brandon, City of	146	Aquatic Sciences Inc.	105
Brookfield Properties Corporation	150	Armor Personnel	107
Calgary, City of	158	Armtec Limited	108
Cambridge Memorial Hospital	159	ArvinMeritor	108
Camp Hill Hospital	160	ATCO Electric	111
Cape Breton Development Corporation	174	ATCO Frontec Corp.	111
Casa Loma	177	ATCO Gas Services Ltd.	112
Children's Hospital of Eastern Ontario	189	Athabasca, Town of	112
Cobourg District General Hospital	194	ATS Automation Tooling Systems Inc.	116
Fletcher's Fine Foods	242	Aurizon Mines Ltd.	116
Health Authority 5	267	Babcock and Wilcox Canada	119
Health Care Corporation of St. John's	267	Ballard Power Systems Inc.	120
Humber River Regional Hospital	280	Basic Technologies Corporation	122
Intercon Security Ltd.	292	Baytex Energy Limited	124
Ottawa Hospital	386	BC Hydro	125
Paladin Security & Investigations Limited	388	BC Telecom Inc.	126
Paramount Canada's Wonderland Inc.	389	Beckman Coulter Canada Inc.	129
PavCo	391	Behlen Industries	130
Pool People Ltd.	404	Bell Mobility	131
Prince Albert, City of	410	Bettis Canada Ltd.	135

The Canada Student Employment Guide

College Index

BFGoodrich Landing Gear Division	135	Exfo	235
BJ Services Company	138	Exide Canada Inc.	235
Blue Wave Seafoods Inc.	142	FAG Bearings Limited	237
Bosal Canada Inc.	145	Finning	240
Brookfield Properties Corporation	150	Flakeboard Company Limited	242
Budd Canada Inc.	152	Fletcher's Fine Foods	242
C B C L Limited	154	Flint Energy Services Ltd.	243
C MAC Industries Inc.	155	Foremost Industries Inc.	244
Cabre Exploration Ltd.	156	Gencorp Vehicle Sealing	248
Canadian General Tower Limited	166	General Chemical Canada Ltd.	249
Cancore Industries Inc.	171	Gienow Building Products Ltd.	251
Cangene Corporation	172	Giffels Associates Limited	251
Canon Canada Inc.	172	Glaxo Wellcome Canada	253
Cape Breton Development Corporation	174	Golder Associates Ltd.	255
Carbone of America (LCL) Ltd.	175	Groupe Savoie Inc.	260
Carte International Inc.	176	H A Simmons Ltd.	261
CCL Industries Inc.	178	H.H. Angus & Associates Ltd.	261
Celestica International Inc.	179	Haley Industries Limited	262
CenAlta Energy Services Inc.	180	Haliburton Energy Services	262
Centra Gas British Columbia Inc.	180	Halifax County Regional Rehabilitation Centre	263
Centra Gas Manitoba Inc.	181	Halifax Regional Municipality	263
CH2M Gore and Storrie Limited	185	Halifax Water Commission	264
CKF Inc.	192	Halliburton Energy Services	264
COM DEV International	197	Hallmark Tools	265
Communications & Power Industries Canada	198	Health Care Corporation of St. John's	267
Computalog Ltd.	200	Hermes Electronics Inc.	269
Comstock Canada	201	Home Oil Co. Ltd.	273
Connors Bros, Limited	203	Honda Canada Inc.	274
Co-op Atlantic	203	Honeywell Ltd.	275
Coquitlam, City of	204	Hubbell Canada Inc.	278
Cornwall Electric	206	Huronia Regional Centre	280
Cosyn Technology	207	Husky Energy Inc.	281
Cougar Helicopters Inc.	208	Hydro Electric Commission of Thunder Bay	281
Culinar Inc.	209	Hydro Mississauga Corporation	282
Custom Trim Ltd.	210	Hydro One Inc.	282
D.A. Stuart Inc.	210	Hydro Québec	283
DaimlerChrysler Canada Ltd.	211	I M P Group International Inc.	283
Dana Corporation - Long Manufacturing	212	I P L Plastics Ltd.	284
David Thompson Health Region	212	IBM Canada Ltd.	284
Delta Hotels	215	Imperial Oil Limited	286
Dofasco Inc.	218	INCO Limited	287
Domtar Inc.	218	Industries Lassonde Inc.	289
DuPont Canada Inc.	221	Intercon Security Ltd.	292
Dura Automotive Systems (Canada) Ltd.	222	IPL Energy Inc.	294
Dynapro Systems Inc.	223	IWK Grace Health Centre	297
Dynasty Furniture Manufacturing Ltd.	224	J.D. Irving Limited	298
E B A Engineering Consultants Ltd.	225	J.S. Redpath Limited	299
Echo Bay Mines Ltd.	226	JDS Uniphase Corporation	300
Elco	229	Johnson Controls Ltd.	302
Electronics Arts (Canada) Inc.	229	Jostens Canada Ltd.	303
Eli Lilly Canada Inc.	230	Kelowna, City of	305
EMJ Data Systems Ltd.	231	Kennametal Ltd.	305
EnerFlex Systems Ltd.	232	Kitchener, City of	309
Espial Group Incorporated	234	Kvaerner Metals	311

The Canada Student Employment Guide

College Index

Lambert Somec Inc.	313	Pizza Pizza Ltd.	401
Leduc, City of	313	Poco Petroleums Ltd.	402
Leica Geosystems Canada Inc.	314	Potacan Mining Company	405
Lenbrook Industries Limited	315	Power Measurement Ltd.	406
Lifetouch Canada Inc.	319	Pratt & Whitney Canada Inc.	407
Litton Systems Canada Ltd.	320	Premdor Inc.	408
Loewen Windows	321	Pricewaterhouse Coopers	409
Lovat Inc.	323	Prince Albert, City of	410
M M Industra Ltd.	323	Prince George, City of	410
MacDonald Steel Ltd.	325	QEII Health Sciences Centre	414
MacViro Consultants Inc.	326	Quesnel River Pulp Company	416
Magna International Inc.	327	Raymond Industrial Equipment Ltd.	418
Manitoba Hydro	328	Regal Constellation Hotel Ltd.	422
Marine Atlantic Inc.	331	Reid Crowther	426
Marshall Macklin Monaghan Ltd.	333	Reliable Engine Services Ltd.	426
Matrox Electronic Systems Inc.	335	Renaissance Energy Ltd.	427
McKay-Cocker Construction Limited	338	Rentway Inc.	427
MDS Nordion	339	Replicon Inc.	428
Mediasynergy	340	Richmond, City of	431
Midland Walwyn Inc.	345	Rimrock Resort Hotel	432
Midwest Food Products Inc.	346	Rockwell Automation	435
Minas Basin Pulp and Power Company Ltd.	347	Roctest Ltée	435
Ministry of Northern Develop. and Mines	348	Rogers AT&T Wireless Inc.	436
Mississauga, City of	349	Royal Canadian Mint	438
Mitel Corporation	350	Royal Philips Electronics	439
Mitsubishi Electric Sales Canada	351	Sandwell Inc.	443
Mobile Computing Corporation	351	Saskatchewan Research Council, The	446
Monarch Communications Inc.	353	Saskatoon, City of	448
Moosehead Breweries Limited	354	Saskferco Products Inc.	448
Morrison Hershfield Limited	354	SaskTel	449
MOSAID Technologies Inc.	355	SC Infrastructure Inc.	449
Motorola Canada Ltd.	356	Scarborough General Hospital	450
Mustang Survival Corp.	358	Schlumberger Canada Ltd.	450
Natco Canada Ltd.	360	SCIEX MDS Health Group	452
National Manufacturing of Canada Inc.	361	Seprotech Systems Incorporated	454
Neles Automation, Scada Solutions Ltd.	362	Shaw Communications	455
Nestle Canada Inc.	364	Shermag Inc.	457
New Brunswick Telephone Company	366	Siemens Electric Ltd.	460
Newfoundland and Labrador Hydro	367	Silicon Graphics Canada Inc.	461
NLK Consultants Inc.	372	SolutionInc Limited	465
Northwestel Inc.	376	Sony Music Canada	465
Nova Scotia Power Corp.	377	Spar Aerospace Limited	467
Oetiker Limited	381	Spectra Premium Industries	468
Oland Breweries Limited	382	Spectrum Signal Processing Inc.	468
Omstead Foods Limited	383	Sportsco International	469
Oracle Corp. Canada Inc.	386	St. Lawrence Seaway Mgmt. Corp., The	473
Ottawa Hospital	386	Standen's Limited	474
Overlander Hospital	387	Stantec Consulting Ltd.	475
PavCo	391	Star Data Systems Inc.	476
PCL Constructors Inc.	392	Steelcraft Industries Ltd.	477
Peel Regional Police	394	Steelpipe Ltd.	477
Pelmorex Inc.	395	Sudbury Regional Hospital	480
Phillips & Tempro Industries Ltd.	398	Sun Rype Products Ltd.	481
Pine Falls Paper Company Limited	400	Supreme Tooling Group	483

The Canada Student Employment Guide

College Index

Surrey, City of	484
Talisman Energy Inc.	487
Teklogix Inc.	489
The Garland Group	494
The McElhanney Group Ltd.	494
Thunder Bay Regional Hospital	497
Toronto and Region Conservation Authority	501
Toronto Catholic District School Board	502
Toronto General Hospital	505
Toronto Hydro	505
Toronto, City of	508
Toshiba of Canada Ltd.	508
TransAlta	509
Triumf	510
Trojan Technologies Inc.	511
Trow Consulting Engineers Ltd.	511
Union Gas Ltd.	513
Unisys Canada Inc.	514
University College of Cape Breton	516
Urban Systems Ltd.	516
US Filter BCP	517
USF WaterGroup	517
Vancouver International Airport	520
Visteon Canada Inc.	522
Wegu Canada Inc.	526
Weldco-Beales Manufacturing Inc.	527
West Coast Apparel	528
West Kootenay Power Ltd.	528
Westcliff Management Ltd.	529
Westcoast Energy Inc.	530
Western Glove Works	530
Westinghouse Canada Inc.	532
WestJet Airlines	532
Westport Innovations Inc.	534
Westshore Terminals Ltd.	534
Weyerhaeuser Company Limited	535
Wilson Auto Electric Ltd.	538
Windsor, City of	538
Winpak Ltd.	539
Wire Rope Industries Ltd.	540
Yamaha Motor Canada Ltd.	542
Yellowknife, City of	544
Zenastra	547
Zenon Environmental Inc.	547

Faculty Management

A.G. Simpson Co. Ltd.	75
Banff Centre for Continuing Education, The	120
Calgary Co-operative Association Limited	157
Calgary, City of	158
Centre de Santé de St-Henri Inc.	182
CKF Inc.	192

David Thompson Health Region	212
Duha Color Services	220
Entreprises Premier Canadien Ltée	232
Foyer Valade Inc.	245
Gimbel Eye Centre	252
Glaxo Wellcome Canada	253
Grenville Management Ltd.	259
Hasbro Canada Inc.	266
Hippodrome de Montréal	270
Hôtel Dieu de Montréal	276
Imprimerie Interweb Inc.	287
Intercon Security Ltd.	292
James Richardson International Limited	300
Leduc, City of	313
Les Centres Jeunesse de Montréal	316
Liberty Health	318
MAAX Inc.	324
Metro Richelieu Inc.	342
Metro Toronto Convention Centre	342
Michaels of Canada Inc.	345
Midland Walwyn Inc.	345
North West Company Inc.	374
Prince Albert, City of	410
Prince George, City of	410
Recochem Inc.	420
Saan Stores Ltd.	441
Shaw Communications	455
Shorewood Packaging Corp. of Canada Ltd.	459
Sodexho Marriott Services Canada	464
Sony Music Canada	465
Toronto General Hospital	505
Westminster Savings Credit Union	533

Forestry

Abitibi-Consolidated Inc.	77
Arbor Care Tree Service Ltd.	106
BC Research Inc.	126
Bowater Mersey Paper Company Limited	146
Bugbusters Pest Management Inc.	152
Coquitlam, City of	204
Domtar Inc.	218
Entreprises Premier Canadien Ltée	232
Federated Co-operatives Limited	239
Flakeboard Company Limited	242
Groupe Savoie Inc.	260
H A Simmons Ltd.	261
Interforest Ltd.	292
J.D. Irving Limited	298
Kitchener, City of	309
Mississauga, City of	349
Niagara Parks Commission, The	369
Norbord Industries	372

The Canada Student Employment Guide

College Index 577

Nova Scotia Power Corp.	377
Pine Falls Paper Company Limited	400
Premdor Inc.	408
Science North	452
Toronto and Region Conservation Authority	501
Toronto, City of	508
Weyerhaeuser Company Limited	535
White Rose Crafts and Nursery Sales Limited	536

General

ACE INI Insurance	79
ADI Group Inc.	82
Akita Drilling Ltd.	87
Alberta Gaming & Liquor Commission	90
Allianz Canada	95
Amram's Distributing Ltd.	100
Anthony Insurance Inc.	102
Apex Land Corp.	103
Armor Personnel	107
Atlantic Lottery Corporation Inc.	113
Atlas Van Lines (Canada) Ltd.	115
Aurum Ceramic Dental Laboratories Ltd.	117
Ballard Power Systems Inc.	120
Banff Centre for Continuing Education, The	120
BASF Canada Inc.	122
Bayer Inc.	124
BC Telecom Inc.	126
Bell Mobility	131
Bio-Research Laboratories Ltd.	137
Birks Jewelry	138
Black Photo Corporation	139
Bloorview MacMillan Centre, The	140
British Columbia Ferry Corporation	149
Brookfield Properties Corporation	150
Burger King Restaurants of Canada Inc.	153
Cabre Exploration Ltd.	156
Cadith Entertainment Ltd.	156
Calgary Co-operative Association Limited	157
Canadian Cancer Society	164
Canadian National Institute For The Blind	167
Canbra Foods Ltd.	170
CancerCare Manitoba	171
Cape Breton Development Corporation	174
Casa Loma	177
Century Sales and Service Limited	182
Chapters Inc.	186
Charlottetown Driving Park	187
Christian Horizons	190
COBI Foods Inc.	194
Coca Cola Foods Canada Inc.	195
Columbia House	197
Comtronic Computer Inc.	202

Coquitlam, City of	204
Cornwall Electric	206
Credit Union Central of Canada	208
Culinar Inc.	209
D.A. Stuart Inc.	210
D.H. Howden	211
Degussa - Huls Canada Inc.	214
Directwest Publishers Ltd.	217
Druxy's Inc.	219
Dynasty Furniture Manufacturing Ltd.	224
Economical Insurance Group, The	227
Eddie Bauer Inc.	227
Eli Lilly Canada Inc.	230
EMJ Data Systems Ltd.	231
Federated Co-operatives Limited	239
Fisher Scientific Limited	241
FM Global	243
Forzani Group Ltd., The	244
Gienow Building Products Ltd.	251
Gilbey Canada Inc.	252
Gimbel Eye Centre	252
Gisborne Design Services Ltd.	253
Glentel Inc.	254
Goepel McDermid Securities	254
Goodman and Carr	255
Goodwill Industries of Toronto	256
Goodyear Canada Inc.	256
Great-West Life Assurance Company, The	259
Grenville Management Ltd.	259
Groupe Savoie Inc.	260
Grouse Mountain Resorts Ltd.	260
Halifax Water Commission	264
Hasbro Canada Inc.	266
Holiday Inn Select Toronto Airport	272
Hydro Electric Commission of Thunder Bay	281
Indalex Limited	288
Industrial-Alliance Life Insurance Company	289
ING Canada Financial Services International	291
Insurance Corp. of B.C.	291
Intercon Security Ltd.	292
Jim Pattison Group	301
Kitchener, City of	309
La Confiserie Comete Ltee	311
Leduc, City of	313
Lego Canada Inc.	314
Leica Geosystems Canada Inc.	314
Les Centres Jeunesse de Montréal	316
Liberty Health	318
M. McGrawth Canada Limited	324
Manitoba Public Insurance Corporation	329
Mark Anthony Group Inc.	332
Marks & Spencer Canada Inc.	332
McBee Systems of Canada Inc.	336
Metro Richelieu Inc.	342

The Canada Student Employment Guide

578 College Index

Metro Toronto Convention Centre	342
Metropolitan Life Insurance Company	344
Midland Walwyn Inc.	345
Midwest Food Products Inc.	346
Milne & Craighead Inc.	347
Ministry of Northern Develop. and Mines	348
Montreal Trust Co.	353
MOSAID Technologies Inc.	355
Motorola Canada Ltd.	356
National Grocers Co. Ltd.	360
National Life	361
New Brunswick Power Corporation	365
Newfoundland and Labrador Credit Union	367
News Marketing Canada	368
Nichirin Inc.	370
Norwich Union Life Insurance Society	376
Novartis Consumer Health Canada Inc.	378
Novotel Canada Inc.	378
Ontario Legislative Offices	384
Ontario March of Dimes	385
Oracle Corp. Canada Inc.	386
Paramount Canada's Wonderland Inc.	389
Patheon Inc.	390
PavCo	391
Peel Board of Education	393
PennCorp Life Insurance Company	396
Pharma Plus Drugmarts Ltd.	398
Pilot Insurance Company	399
Pine Falls Paper Company Limited	400
Pitney Bowes of Canada Ltd.	401
Poco Petroleums Ltd.	402
Pollack Rentals Limited	403
Potacan Mining Company	405
Public Utilities of Kingston	413
Purolator Courier Ltd.	413
Ramada Inn	416
Raylo Chemicals Inc.	417
Regal Constellation Hotel Ltd.	422
Revenue Properties Company Limited	429
Royal & Sun Alliance Insurance Co. of Cda	437
Sandman Hotels and Inns	443
Sara Lee Corporation of Canada Limited	444
Saskatchewan Government Insurance	445
Scarborough General Hospital	450
Science North	452
Sharp Electronics of Canada Ltd.	454
Shaw Communications	455
Sheraton Fallsview Hotel	456
Shorewood Packaging Corp. of Canada Ltd.	459
Siemens Electric Ltd.	460
Signature Vacations Inc.	460
Sony Music Canada	465
Stanley Canada Inc.	475
State Farm Insurance Companies	476

Supreme Tooling Group	483
TD Waterhouse Investor Services (Canada)	488
Teklogix Inc.	489
Thomas & Betts Ltée	495
Thomas Cook Group (Canada) Ltd.	495
Ticketmaster Canada Inc.	498
Tiger Brand Knitting Company Limited	498
Today's Business Products Ltd.	500
Toronto Cricket Skating & Curling	502
Toronto Hydro	505
Toronto Police Service	506
Toronto Sun Publishing Corp., The	507
Toshiba of Canada Ltd.	508
Toyota Canada Ltd.	509
TSC Stores Ltd.	512
Union Pacific Resources Group	514
University College of Cape Breton	516
Valley First Credit Union	518
Vancouver International Airport	520
VIA Rail Canada Inc.	521
Volvo Cars of Canada Ltd.	523
Waverly & York Corporation	525
West Coast Apparel	528
Weston Produce Inc.	533
White Rose Crafts and Nursery Sales Limited	536
Winpak Ltd.	539
Yanke Group of Companies	543
Yellowknife, City of	544
Zellers Inc.	546

Graphic Arts

Air Canada	85
Alberta Blue Cross	88
Allmar Distributors Ltd.	95
ATCO Gas Services Ltd.	112
Atlantic Blue Cross Care	113
Atlantic Lottery Corporation Inc.	113
Atlantic Packaging Products Ltd.	114
Atlantic Wholesalers Ltd.	114
Banff Centre for Continuing Education, The	120
Bargain Finder Press Ltd.	121
Benwell Atkins Ltd.	132
Camp Hill Hospital	160
Canadian Museum of Civilization Corp.	167
Carlson Marketing Group Canada Ltd.	176
Chevron Canada Resources Ltd.	188
Cineplex Odeon Corporation	191
Columbia House	197
Co-op Atlantic	203
Cotton Ginny Ltd.	207
David Thompson Health Region	212
Duha Color Services	220

College Index

Dynapro Systems Inc.	223	Surrey, City of	484
Economical Insurance Group, The	227	Symantec Corporation	486
Electronics Arts (Canada) Inc.	229	The Co-operators	493
EMJ Data Systems Ltd.	231	Transcontinental Digital Services Inc.	510
EnerFlex Systems Ltd.	232	WebCanada	526
Federated Co-operatives Limited	239	Westbury Life	529
Future Shop Ltd.	246	Whistler Blackcomb Mountain	535
Grand & Toy Ltd.	257	Winpak Ltd.	539
Grant MacEwen Community College	258	YFactor	544
Grenville Management Ltd.	259		
HB Studios Multimedia Ltd.	266		

Hospitality

Health Sciences Centre	268		
I P L Plastics Ltd.	284		
Jostens Canada Ltd.	303	Air Nova Inc.	86
Keyano College	306	Assiniboine Community College	109
Kitchener, City of	309	Best Western Carlton Place Hotel	133
Les Modes Smart Inc.	318	Burger King Restaurants of Canada Inc.	153
Lifetouch Canada Inc.	319	Cadith Entertainment Ltd.	156
Manitoba Hydro	328	Capilano Suspension Bridge	174
Manitoba Pool Elevators	328	Casa Loma	177
Mark Anthony Group Inc.	332	Central Park Lodges Ltd.	181
Matrox Electronic Systems Ltd.	335	Columbia House	197
McGraw Hill Ryerson Ltd.	337	Delta Hotels	215
McLaren-McCann Advertising of Canada Ltd.	338	Delta Toronto Airport Hotel	216
McMillan & Associates Inc.	339	Druxy's Inc.	219
Metroland Printing, Publishing & Dist. Ltd.	343	Economic Development Edmonton	226
Michaels of Canada Inc.	345	Grouse Mountain Resorts Ltd.	260
Ministry of Northern Develop. and Mines	348	Halifax Regional Municipality	263
N B S Card Services	359	Helijet Airways Inc.	268
Neles Automation, Scada Solutions Ltd.	362	Holiday Inn Select Toronto Airport	272
North West Company Inc.	374	Horseshoe Resort Corporation	275
Paperboard Industries International Inc.	389	Lick's Ice Cream & Burger Shops Inc.	319
Paramount Canada's Wonderland Inc.	389	Marine Atlantic Inc.	331
Peel Board of Education	393	Metro Toronto Convention Centre	342
PennCorp Life Insurance Company	396	Metropolitan Life Insurance Company	344
Pizza Pizza Ltd.	401	Michaels of Canada Inc.	345
Polygram Group Canada Inc.	403	Novotel Canada Inc.	378
Reader's Digest Association of Canada Ltd.	419	Paladin Security & Investigations Limited	388
Regal Greeting and Gifts	423	Panorama Mountain Village	388
Regis Pictures and Frames Ltd.	425	Paramount Canada's Wonderland Inc.	389
Saskatchewan Government Insurance	445	PavCo	391
Saskatoon, City of	448	Pizza Pizza Ltd.	401
Scholastic Canada Ltd.	451	Ramada Inn	416
Science North	452	Regal Constellation Hotel Ltd.	422
Shaw Communications	455	Richmond, City of	431
Shorewood Packaging Corp. of Canada Ltd.	459	Rimrock Resort Hotel	432
Signature Vacations Inc.	460	Sandman Hotels and Inns	443
Sony Music Canada	465	Science North	452
Southam Inc.	466	Sheraton Fallsview Hotel	456
Spectra Premium Industries	468	Sheraton Toronto East Hotel and Towers	456
Spectrum Signal Processing Inc.	468	Signature Vacations Inc.	460
Steelpipe Ltd.	477	Skiing Louise Ltd.	461
Sterling Marking Products Inc.	478	Sportsco International	469
Stitches	478	St. Lawrence Parks Commission	472

The Canada Student Employment Guide

Sun Peaks Resort Corporation	481	Athabasca, Town of	112
Thomas Cook Group (Canada) Ltd.	495	Atlantic Blue Cross Care	113
Toronto and Region Conservation Authority	501	Atlantic Lottery Corporation Inc.	113
Toronto Cricket Skating & Curling	502	Atlantic Packaging Products Ltd.	114
University College of Cape Breton	516	Atlantic Wholesalers Ltd.	114
Versa Services Ltd.	521	Atlas Ideal Metals Inc.	115
VIA Rail Canada Inc.	521	ATS Automation Tooling Systems Inc.	116
Waterloo Inn	525	Aurum Ceramic Dental Laboratories Ltd.	117
Wendy's Restaurants of Canada Inc.	527	AXA Insurance (Canada)	118
Westin Bayshore Resort and Marina, The	531	Axidata Inc.	118
Westin Prince Hotel, The	531	Babcock and Wilcox Canada	119
WestJet Airlines	532	Ballard Power Systems Inc.	120
Whistler Blackcomb Mountain	535	Banff Centre for Continuing Education, The	120
White Spot Limited	536	BASF Canada Inc.	122
Windsor, City of	538	Basic Technologies Corporation	122
World of Vacations Ltd.	541	Battlefords Health District	123
		Baycrest Centre for Geriatric Care	123
		BBM Bureau of Measurement	125

Human Resources

		BC Research Inc.	126
		Bearskin Lake Air Service Ltd.	128
1-800-GOT-JUNK?	74	Bechtel Canada Co.	128
A C A Cooperative Limited	74	Bell Mobility	131
A.G. Simpson Co. Ltd.	75	Belleville General Hospital	132
Aar-Kel Moulds Ltd.	76	Best Western Carlton Place Hotel	133
ABC Group	76	Bethesda Hospital	134
Aberdeen Hospital	77	Bettis Canada Ltd.	135
Abitibi-Consolidated Inc.	77	BFGoodrich Landing Gear Division	135
Acadia University	78	Bic Inc.	136
Access Communications	78	Black Photo Corporation	139
Accucaps Industries Limited	79	Blaney McMurty LLP	139
ACE INI Insurance	79	Bloorview Childrens Hospital	140
Acklands-Grainger Inc.	80	Bloorview MacMillan Centre, The	140
Addictions Foundation of Manitoba, The	81	Bonus Resource Services Corp.	144
ADT Canada Inc.	82	BOVAR Waste Management	145
AGF Management Limited	83	Bowater Mersey Paper Company Limited	146
Agricultural Credit Corp. of Saskatchewan	84	Brandon, City of	146
Air Ontario Inc.	86	Brewers Retail Inc.	148
Alberta Blue Cross	88	British Columbia Ferry Corporation	149
Alberta Energy & Utilities Board	89	Buckeye Canada Inc.	151
Alberta Gaming & Liquor Commission	90	Budd Canada Inc.	152
Algoma District Home For The Aged	92	Bullock Associates Design Consultants Inc.	153
Allianz Canada	95	C.S.T. Consultants Inc.	155
Allmar Distributors Ltd.	95	Cabre Exploration Ltd.	156
Amcan Castings Limited	98	Cadith Entertainment Ltd.	156
Amcor Twinpak North America Inc.	98	Calgary Co-operative Association Limited	157
AMEC Inc.	99	Calgary, City of	158
Amram's Distributing Ltd.	100	Camp Hill Hospital	160
Apex Land Corp.	103	Canada Post Corporation	162
Arctic Co-operatives Limited	107	Canada Safeway Limited	163
Armor Personnel	107	Canada Starch Company Inc.	163
ArvinMeritor	108	Canadian Cancer Society	164
Assiniboine Community College	109	Canadian Commercial Corp.	165
ATCO Electric	111	Canadian Dairy Commission	165
ATCO Frontec Corp.	111	Canadian Depository for Securities Ltd.	166

College Index 581

Canadian Museum of Civilization Corp.	167	Domtar Inc.	218
Canadian Western Bank	169	Drug Trading Company Ltd.	219
Cancarb Limited	170	Dun & Bradstreet Canada	221
CancerCare Manitoba	171	Dylex Limited	222
Canon Canada Inc.	172	Dynapro Systems Inc.	223
Canpar Transport Ltd.	173	Echo Bay Mines Ltd.	226
Cape Breton Development Corporation	174	Economic Development Edmonton	226
Capilano Suspension Bridge	174	Economical Insurance Group, The	227
Carbone of America (LCL) Ltd.	175	Eli Lilly Canada Inc.	230
Carte International Inc.	176	Emco Limited	230
Casa Loma	177	EMJ Data Systems Ltd.	231
Cassels Brock & Blackwell	177	EnerFlex Systems Ltd.	232
CCL Industries Inc.	178	Exfo	235
Centra Gas British Columbia Inc.	180	Exide Canada Inc.	235
Centra Gas Manitoba Inc.	181	Explorer Hotel, The	236
Central Park Lodges Ltd.	181	Extendicare (Canada) Inc.	237
Centre de Santé de St-Henri Inc.	182	FAG Bearings Limited	237
Ceridian Canada	183	Farm Credit Corp. Canada	238
CFCN Communications Inc.	184	Finning	240
Chapters Inc.	186	Fisher Scientific Limited	241
Christian Horizons	190	Fishery Products International	241
Cineplex Odeon Corporation	191	Flint Energy Services Ltd.	243
Citibank Canada	191	Foremost Industries Inc.	244
CKF Inc.	192	Forzani Group Ltd., The	244
COBI Foods Inc.	194	Foyer Valade Inc.	245
Cobourg District General Hospital	194	Friesens Corporation	246
Coca Cola Foods Canada Inc.	195	Future Shop Ltd.	246
Columbia House	197	Gay Lea Foods Co-Operative Ltd.	247
COM DEV International	197	Gendis Inc.	248
Comcare Health Services	198	General Chemical Canada Ltd.	249
Communications & Power Industries Canada	198	George Jeffrey Children's Treatment Centre	250
Community Savings Credit Union	199	Giffels Associates Limited	251
Computalog Ltd.	200	Gilbey Canada Inc.	252
Computer Associates Canada Ltd.	201	Gimbel Eye Centre	252
Connors Bros, Limited	203	Glaxo Wellcome Canada	253
Co-op Atlantic	203	Goodman and Carr	255
Coppley Apparel Group	204	Goodwill Industries of Toronto	256
Coquitlam, City of	204	Grand & Toy Ltd.	257
Corner Brook, City of	205	Grant MacEwen Community College	258
Cornwall Electric	206	Great-West Life Assurance Company, The	259
Cotton Ginny Ltd.	207	Groupe Savoie Inc.	260
Cougar Helicopters Inc.	208	Haley Industries Limited	262
Credit Union Central of Canada	208	Halifax Regional Municipality	263
Culinar Inc.	209	Halifax Water Commission	264
Custom Trim Ltd.	210	Hasbro Canada Inc.	266
D.A. Stuart Inc.	210	Health Authority 5	267
DaimlerChrysler Canada Ltd.	211	Helijet Airways Inc.	268
David Thompson Health Region	212	Hermes Electronics Inc.	269
Deer Lodge Centre Inc.	213	Hill & Knowlton Canada Ltd.	270
Degussa - Huls Canada Inc.	214	Hippodrome de Montréal	270
Dell Computer Corporation	214	Hoffman-La Roche Limited	272
Delphi Solutions Inc.	215	Holiday Inn Select Toronto Airport	272
Delta Hotels	215	Home Oil Co. Ltd.	273
Delta Toronto Airport Hotel	216	Homewood Corp.	274

The Canada Student Employment Guide

582 College Index

Honda Canada Inc.	274	Midland Walwyn Inc.	345
Hôtel Dieu de Montréal	276	Midwest Food Products Inc.	346
Hudon & Deaudelin Ltée	279	Milne & Craighead Inc.	347
Hudson's Bay Company, The	279	Ministry of Northern Develop. and Mines	348
Humber River Regional Hospital	280	Misericordia General Hospital	348
Huronia Regional Centre	280	Mississauga, City of	349
Hydro Electric Commission of Thunder Bay	281	Mitel Corporation	350
I M P Group International Inc.	283	Mitsubishi Electric Sales Canada	351
Indalex Limited	288	Moen Inc.	352
Industries Lassonde Inc.	289	Montreal Trust Co.	353
ING Canada Financial Services International	291	Moosehead Breweries Limited	354
Insurance Corp. of B.C.	291	Mortice Kern Systems Inc.	355
Intercon Security Ltd.	292	MOSAID Technologies Inc.	355
Interior Savings Credit Union	293	Motorola Canada Ltd.	356
InterOne Marketing Group	293	Mountain Equipment Co-op	356
IWK Grace Health Centre	297	Mustang Survival Corp.	358
Izaak Walton Killam Hospital, The	297	N B S Card Services	359
James Richardson International Limited	300	Nanaimo Credit Union	359
John P. Robarts Research Institute	302	National Grocers Co. Ltd.	360
Johnson Incorporated	303	National Life	361
Kawneer Company Canada Limited	304	National Manufacturing of Canada Inc.	361
Kennametal Ltd.	305	National Sports Centre	362
Keyano College	306	Neles Automation, Scada Solutions Ltd.	362
Kings Regional Rehabilitation Centre	308	Nelvana Limited	363
Kitchener, City of	309	Neptune Food Suppliers Ltd.	363
Kodak Canada Inc.	309	Nesbitt Burns Inc.	364
Laidlaw Inc.	312	Nestle Canada Inc.	364
Leduc, City of	313	Newfoundland and Labrador Credit Union	367
Lenbrook Industries Limited	315	Newness Machine Ltd.	368
Les Centres Jeunesse de Montréal	316	News Marketing Canada	368
Les Modes Smart Inc.	318	Nichirin Inc.	370
Liberty Health	318	Nike Canada Ltd.	371
Lifetouch Canada Inc.	319	Nissan Canada Inc.	371
London Goodwill Industries Association	322	Norbord Industries	372
M M Industra Ltd.	323	Norcen Energy Resources Ltd.	373
MAAX Inc.	324	North American Life Assurance Company	373
Magna International Inc.	327	North West Company Inc.	374
Manitoba Agriculture and Food	327	Northern Lights Regional Health Centre	375
Manitoba Public Insurance Corporation	329	Northwestel Inc.	376
Maple Leaf Consumer Foods	330	Norwich Union Life Insurance Society	376
Marine Atlantic Inc.	331	Nova Scotia Liquor Commission	377
Maritime Life Assurance Company, The	331	Nova Scotia Power Corp.	377
Mark Anthony Group Inc.	332	Novartis Consumer Health Canada Inc.	378
Marystown Shipyard Limited	334	Novotel Canada Inc.	378
Matrox Electronic Systems Ltd.	335	Numac Energy Inc.	379
McBee Systems of Canada Inc.	336	Nygard International Ltd.	380
McGraw Hill Ryerson Ltd.	337	Ocelot Energy Inc.	381
McMillan & Associates Inc.	339	Oetiker Limited	381
Mediacom Inc.	340	Oland Breweries Limited	382
Metro Toronto Convention Centre	342	Omstead Foods Limited	383
Metroland Printing, Publishing & Dist. Ltd.	343	Ontario Jockey Club, The	384
Metropolitan Life Insurance Company	344	Ontario Legislative Offices	384
Meyers Norris Penny & Co.	344	Ontario March of Dimes	385
Michaels of Canada Inc.	345	Oracle Corp. Canada Inc.	386

The Canada Student Employment Guide

College Index

Ottawa Hospital	386
Paramount Canada's Wonderland Inc.	389
Patheon Inc.	390
Peacock Inc.	392
Pearson Education Canada	393
Peel Board of Education	393
Peel Children's Centre	394
Peel Regional Police	394
Pelmorex Inc.	395
PennCorp Life Insurance Company	396
Pharma Plus Drugmarts Ltd.	398
Phoenix International	399
Pilot Insurance Company	399
Pine Falls Paper Company Limited	400
Pitney Bowes of Canada Ltd.	401
Pizza Pizza Ltd.	401
Poco Petroleums Ltd.	402
Polygram Group Canada Inc.	403
Pool People Ltd.	404
Potacan Mining Company	405
PPG Canada Inc.	407
Pricewaterhouse Coopers	409
Prince George, City of	410
Providence Centre	412
Prudential Insurance Co. of America, The	412
Public Utilities of Kingston	413
Purolator Courier Ltd.	413
QEII Health Sciences Centre	414
Québéc Cartier Mining Company	415
Quebecor Inc.	415
Ramada Inn	416
Rasco Specialty Metals Inc.	417
Raymond Industrial Equipment Ltd.	418
Raymond Rebar Inc.	418
Regal Capital Planners Ltd.	422
Regal Constellation Hotel Ltd.	422
Regina Health District	423
Regional Municipality of Niagara	424
Regis Pictures and Frames Ltd.	425
Rehabilitation Institute of Toronto	425
Replicon Inc.	428
Rhone-Poulenc Canada Inc.	430
Richmond, City of	431
Rimrock Resort Hotel	432
Riverside Fabricating Ltd.	433
Rogers AT&T Wireless Inc.	436
Rogers Media, Publishing	436
Rothmans, Benson and Hedges Inc.	437
Royal & Sun Alliance Insurance Co. of Cda	437
Royal Bank of Canada	438
Royal Canadian Mint	438
Royal Philips Electronics	439
Ryerson Polytechnic University	441
Saan Stores Ltd.	441
Salisbury House of Canada Ltd.	442
Sandman Hotels and Inns	443
Saskatchewan Economic Development	445
Saskatchewan Government Insurance	445
Saskatchewan Transportation Company	446
Saskatoon, City of	448
Saskferco Products Inc.	448
Scarborough General Hospital	450
Schlumberger Canada Ltd.	450
Schneider Electric Canada Inc.	451
SCIEX MDS Health Group	452
Sharp Electronics of Canada Ltd.	454
Shaw Communications	455
Shaw Industries Ltd.	455
Sheraton Fallsview Hotel	456
Sherwood Credit Union	458
Shopping Channel, The	459
Shorewood Packaging Corp. of Canada Ltd.	459
Siemens Electric Ltd.	460
Signature Vacations Inc.	460
Silicon Graphics Canada Inc.	461
Skiing Louise Ltd.	461
Slocan Forest Products Ltd.	462
Sobeys Inc.	463
Sony Music Canada	465
Southam Inc.	466
Spectra Premium Industries	468
Sportsco International	469
Sprint Canada	470
St. Joseph's Care Group	472
St. Lawrence Parks Commission	472
St. Vincent's Hospitals	473
Standard Knitting Limited	474
Star Data Systems Inc.	476
State Farm Insurance Companies	476
Steelcraft Industries Ltd.	477
Steelpipe Ltd.	477
Stitches	478
Sudbury Regional Hospital	480
Sun Peaks Resort Corporation	481
Sun Rype Products Ltd.	481
Sundog Printing Limited	482
Supreme Tooling Group	483
Surrey Memorial Hospital	483
Surrey, City of	484
Swift Current Health District	485
Sydney Steel Corporation	485
Symantec Corporation	486
TCT Logistics	488
TD Waterhouse Investor Services (Canada)	488
Teck Corp.	489
Teklogix Inc.	489
Telus Corporation	492
The Barn Fruit Markets Inc.	493

The Canada Student Employment Guide

College Index

The Co-operators	493	Atlantic Packaging Products Ltd.	114
The Garland Group	494	Babcock and Wilcox Canada	119
Thomas & Betts Ltée	495	Basic Technologies Corporation	122
Thomas Cook Group (Canada) Ltd.	495	Bettis Canada Ltd.	135
Thomson - CSF Systems Canada Inc.	497	Biovail Corporation International	137
Thunder Bay Regional Hospital	497	CancerCare Manitoba	171
Ticketmaster Canada Inc.	498	CCL Industries Inc.	178
Timmins, City of	499	Centra Gas Manitoba Inc.	181
Today's Business Products Ltd.	500	CKF Inc.	192
Toronto Catholic District School Board	502	Connors Bros, Limited	203
Toronto District School Board	503	Coquitlam, City of	204
Toronto East General Hospital	503	Corner Brook, City of	205
Toronto General Hospital	505	DDM Plastics Inc.	213
Toronto Hydro	505	Entreprises Premier Canadien Ltée	232
Toronto Police Service	506	Espial Group Incorporated	234
Toronto Sun Publishing Corp., The	507	Exfo	235
Toshiba of Canada Ltd.	508	Giffels Associates Limited	251
Toyota Canada Ltd.	509	Groupe Savoie Inc.	260
Uni Select Inc.	513	Health Care Corporation of St. John's	267
Union Pacific Resources Group	514	Ilco Unican Inc.	286
Universal Rehabilitation Service Agency	515	Industries Lassonde Inc.	289
Vancouver International Airport	520	Ivaco Inc.	296
W C I Canada Inc.	524	Lambert Somec Inc.	313
Waterloo Furniture Components Ltd.	524	MAAX Inc.	324
West Kootenay Power Ltd.	528	MacViro Consultants Inc.	326
Westbury Life	529	Magna International Inc.	327
Westcoast Energy Inc.	530	Maple Leaf Consumer Foods	330
Western Glove Works	530	Natco Canada Ltd.	360
Westin Prince Hotel, The	531	Nichirin Inc.	370
WestJet Airlines	532	Ottawa Hospital	386
Westminster Savings Credit Union	533	Phillips & Tempro Industries Ltd.	398
Westport Innovations Inc.	534	Positron Industries Inc.	404
Westshore Terminals Ltd.	534	Proctor and Redfern Ltd.	411
Weyerhaeuser Company Limited	535	Québec Cartier Mining Company	415
Whistler Blackcomb Mountain	535	Raymond Industrial Equipment Ltd.	418
Wilson Auto Electric Ltd.	538	Raymond Rebar Inc.	418
Winners Apparel Ltd.	539	Reid Crowther	426
Winpak Ltd.	539	Roctest Ltée	435
World of Vacations Ltd.	541	Royal Canadian Mint	438
Yamaha Motor Canada Ltd.	542	Sandwell Inc.	443
Yanke Group of Companies	543	Seprotech Systems Incorporated	454
Yellowknife, City of	544	Shermag Inc.	457
Zellers Inc.	546	Siemens Electric Ltd.	460
Zenon Environmental Inc.	547	Standard Knitting Limited	474
Zurich Canada	548	Standen's Limited	474
		Steelcraft Industries Ltd.	477
		Steelpipe Ltd.	477
		Thomas & Betts Ltée	495

Industrial Design

		Toronto Hydro	505
		Toronto Sun Publishing Corp., The	507
		Toyota Canada Ltd.	509
Aar-Kel Moulds Ltd.	76	Waterloo Furniture Components Ltd.	524
Alcan Aluminium Limited	91	Weldco-Beales Manufacturing Inc.	527
Alias	Wavefront	94	Wire Rope Industries Ltd.	540
Aquatic Sciences Inc.	105		
ArvinMeritor	108		

The Canada Student Employment Guide

College Index 585

Zenon Environmental Inc.	547

Information Systems

ABC Group	76
Algoma Steel Inc.	93
Alias | Wavefront	94
Assure Health Inc.	110
ATCO Frontec Corp.	111
Atlantic Blue Cross Care	113
Atlantic Packaging Products Ltd.	114
Atlas Ideal Metals Inc.	115
Basic Technologies Corporation	122
Bearskin Lake Air Service Ltd.	128
Behlen Industries	130
BFGoodrich Landing Gear Division	135
Brandon, City of	146
Capilano Suspension Bridge	174
Carlson Marketing Group Canada Ltd.	176
Central Park Lodges Ltd.	181
CGU Group Canada Ltd.	185
Challenger Motor Freight Inc.	186
Cognos Incorporated	196
Compaq Canada Inc.	199
Connors Bros, Limited	203
Coquitlam, City of	204
Cotton Ginny Ltd.	207
Cougar Helicopters Inc.	208
DaimlerChrysler Canada Ltd.	211
DDM Plastics Inc.	213
Deer Lodge Centre Inc.	213
Domtar Inc.	218
Echo Bay Mines Ltd.	226
Economical Insurance Group, The	227
Exfo	235
FAG Bearings Limited	237
Farm Credit Corp. Canada	238
Finning	240
Flint Energy Services Ltd.	243
Gencorp Vehicle Sealing	248
Haliburton Energy Services	262
Halliburton Energy Services	264
Health Authority 5	267
Humber River Regional Hospital	280
IDEA Associates Inc.	285
Ilco Unican Inc.	286
Information Gateway Services	290
Interior Savings Credit Union	293
IWK Grace Health Centre	297
John P. Robarts Research Institute	302
Leon's Manufacturing Company Inc.	316
Les Modes Smart Inc.	318
Lifetouch Canada Inc.	319
Maritime Life Assurance Company, The	331
Marshall Macklin Monaghan Ltd.	333
Matrox Electronic Systems Ltd.	335
Maxxam Analytics Inc.	335
McInnes Cooper & Robertson	337
Mediasynergy	340
Meyers Norris Penny & Co.	344
Mortice Kern Systems Inc.	355
Neles Automation, Scada Solutions Ltd.	362
News Marketing Canada	368
North York Community Care Access Centre	374
Northwestel Inc.	376
Nygard International Ltd.	380
Ottawa Hospital	386
PPG Canada Inc.	407
QEII Health Sciences Centre	414
Raymond Rebar Inc.	418
Regal Greeting and Gifts	423
Regina Health District	423
Regional Municipality of Niagara	424
Royal Canadian Mint	438
Seprotech Systems Incorporated	454
Slocan Forest Products Ltd.	462
Sobeys Inc.	463
Spectra Premium Industries	468
Sportsco International	469
SRI Homes Inc.	470
Standard Knitting Limited	474
Steelcraft Industries Ltd.	477
Steelpipe Ltd.	477
Swift Current Health District	485
The Co-operators	493
Trojan Technologies Inc.	511
Uni Select Inc.	513
Westcliff Management Ltd.	529
Western Glove Works	530
WestJet Airlines	532
Weyerhaeuser Company Limited	535
Whitehill Technologies Inc.	537
Winners Apparel Ltd.	539
YFactor	544

Insurance

ACE INI Insurance	79
Allianz Canada	95
Allstate Insurance Co. of Canada	96
AMEC Inc.	99
Anthony Insurance Inc.	102
Aon Reed Stenhouse Inc.	103
Assure Health Inc.	110
Atlantic Blue Cross Care	113
AXA Insurance (Canada)	118

The Canada Student Employment Guide

586 College Index

Boréal Assurances Inc.	144	Casa Loma	177
Buck Consultants Limited	151	CFCN Communications Inc.	184
CGU Group Canada Ltd.	185	Charlottetown Driving Park	187
Compu-Quote Inc.	200	Columbia House	197
Dun & Bradstreet Canada	221	Co-op Atlantic	203
Economical Insurance Group, The	227	Credit Union Central of Canada	208
Finning	240	Economical Insurance Group, The	227
FM Global	243	Extendicare (Canada) Inc.	237
Grant MacEwen Community College	258	Farm Credit Corp. Canada	238
Great-West Life Assurance Company, The	259	Foremost Industries Inc.	244
Hippodrome de Montréal	270	Gimbel Eye Centre	252
Industrial-Alliance Life Insurance Company	289	Glaxo Wellcome Canada	253
ING Canada Financial Services International	291	Goodwill Industries of Toronto	256
Insurance Corp. of B.C.	291	Grant MacEwen Community College	258
Interior Savings Credit Union	293	Health Care Corporation of St. John's	267
Johnson Incorporated	303	Hill & Knowlton Canada Ltd.	270
Liberty Health	318	Homewood Corp.	274
Lifetouch Canada Inc.	319	Lifetouch Canada Inc.	319
Manitoba Public Insurance Corporation	329	Magna International Inc.	327
Maritime Life Assurance Company, The	331	Manitoba Hydro	328
Metropolitan Life Insurance Company	344	Manitoba Public Insurance Corporation	329
Midland Walwyn Inc.	345	Maritime Life Assurance Company, The	331
Nanaimo Credit Union	359	Metroland Printing, Publishing & Dist. Ltd.	343
National Life	361	Monarch Communications Inc.	353
North American Life Assurance Company	373	Moosehead Breweries Limited	354
Norwich Union Life Insurance Society	376	National Life	361
Paul Revere Life Insurance Company, The	391	Okanagan Skeena Group Limited	382
PennCorp Life Insurance Company	396	Ontario March of Dimes	385
Pilot Insurance Company	399	Paladin Security & Investigations Limited	388
Progressive Financial Strategy	411	Peel Regional Police	394
Prudential Insurance Co. of America, The	412	Pelmorex Inc.	395
Royal & Sun Alliance Insurance Co. of Cda	437	Polygram Group Canada Inc.	403
Saskatchewan Government Insurance	445	Quebecor Inc.	415
SSQ Life	471	Reader's Digest Association of Canada Ltd.	419
State Farm Insurance Companies	476	Rogers Media, Publishing	436
TD Waterhouse Investor Services (Canada)	488	Sandman Hotels and Inns	443
Toronto Sun Publishing Corp., The	507	Saskatchewan Economic Development	445
Westbury Life	529	Saskatchewan Government Insurance	445
Zurich Canada	548	Scholastic Canada Ltd.	451
		Shaw Communications	455
		Signature Vacations Inc.	460

Journalism

		Sony Music Canada	465
		Southam Inc.	466
1-800-GOT-JUNK?	74	St. Lawrence Parks Commission	472
Air Canada	85	Surrey, City of	484
Alberta Blue Cross	88	Telus Corporation	492
Alberta Energy & Utilities Board	89	The Co-operators	493
ATCO Gas Services Ltd.	112	Toronto General Hospital	505
Atlantic Blue Cross Care	113	Toronto Sun Publishing Corp., The	507
Babcock and Wilcox Canada	119	West Kootenay Power Ltd.	528
Banff Centre for Continuing Education, The	120	Westbury Life	529
British Columbia Ferry Corporation	149	Westminster Savings Credit Union	533
Calgary Co-operative Association Limited	157	Weyerhaeuser Company Limited	535
Canadian Cancer Society	164		

The Canada Student Employment Guide

Laboratory Tech.

A C A Cooperative Limited	74
A E McKenzie Co. Inc.	75
Aberdeen Hospital	77
ADI Group Inc.	82
Alberta Cancer Board	88
ArvinMeritor	108
ATCO Gas Services Ltd.	112
Aurum Ceramic Dental Laboratories Ltd.	117
Aventis Pasteur Limited	117
Ballard Power Systems Inc.	120
Battlefords Health District	123
Baycrest Centre for Geriatric Care	123
BC Research Inc.	126
Beckman Coulter Canada Inc.	129
Belleville General Hospital	132
Bethesda Hospital	134
Bic Inc.	136
Bio-Research Laboratories Ltd.	137
Biovail Corporation International	137
BJ Services Company	138
Calgary, City of	158
Cambridge Memorial Hospital	159
Cameco Corporation	160
Camp Hill Hospital	160
Canadian General Tower Limited	166
Cancarb Limited	170
CH2M Gore and Storrie Limited	185
Children's Hospital of Eastern Ontario	189
Chilliwack General Hospital	189
Cobourg District General Hospital	194
Cognis Canada Corporation	195
Co-op Atlantic	203
Cosmair Canada Inc.	206
Culinar Inc.	209
D.A. Stuart Inc.	210
David Thompson Health Region	212
Degussa - Huls Canada Inc.	214
Dynacare Laboratories	223
Entreprises Premier Canadien Ltée	232
Flakeboard Company Limited	242
Fletcher's Fine Foods	242
General Chemical Canada Ltd.	249
Glaxo Wellcome Canada	253
Halifax Water Commission	264
Health Authority 5	267
Health Care Corporation of St. John's	267
Health Sciences Centre	268
Hôtel Dieu de Montréal	276
Humber River Regional Hospital	280
Hydro One Inc.	282
Industries Lassonde Inc.	289
IPL Energy Inc.	294
IWK Grace Health Centre	297
Kelowna, City of	305
Laidlaw Inc.	312
Les Forges de Sorel Inc.	317
Liberty Health	318
Manitoba Agriculture and Food	327
Manitoba Hydro	328
Maxxam Analytics Inc.	335
Midwest Food Products Inc.	346
Ministry of Northern Develop. and Mines	348
Mitsubishi Electric Sales Canada	351
Moosehead Breweries Limited	354
Nestle Canada Inc.	364
Oland Breweries Limited	382
Patheon Inc.	390
Petromont & Co. Ltd. Partnership	397
Phoenix International	399
Powertech Labs Inc.	406
Providence Centre	412
QEII Health Sciences Centre	414
QIT-Fer et Titane Inc.	414
Québéc Cartier Mining Company	415
Raylo Chemicals Inc.	417
Recochem Inc.	420
Regina Health District	423
Rhone-Poulenc Canada Inc.	430
Riverside Hospital of Ottawa, The	434
Rothmans, Benson and Hedges Inc.	437
Royal Inland Hospital	439
Ryerson Polytechnic University	441
Saskatchewan Research Council, The	446
Saskatoon, City of	448
Saskferco Products Inc.	448
SC Infrastructure Inc.	449
Scarborough General Hospital	450
Seprotech Systems Incorporated	454
Shaw Industries Ltd.	455
Société des Alcools du Québec	464
St. Vincent's Hospitals	473
Sudbury Regional Hospital	480
Sun Rype Products Ltd.	481
Swift Current Health District	485
Syncrude Canada Ltd.	486
Thomas J. Lipton	496
Toronto East General Hospital	503
Yarmouth Regional Hospital	543

Law

Air Canada	85
AMEC Inc.	99
Anthony Insurance Inc.	102
Bayer Inc.	124

The Canada Student Employment Guide

College Index

Blaney McMurty LLP	139	Allmar Distributors Ltd.	95
BNP PARIBAS (Canada)	143	Amcor Twinpak North America Inc.	98
Bratty & Partners LLP	147	American Airlines Inc.	99
Canadian Broadcasting Corporation	164	Amram's Distributing Ltd.	100
Canadian Commercial Corp.	165	Anthony Insurance Inc.	102
Canadian Depository for Securities Ltd.	166	Apple Canada Inc.	104
Comstock Canada	201	Aqua-Power Cleaners Ltd.	105
Coquitlam, City of	204	Aquatic Sciences Inc.	105
Emco Limited	230	Arbor Memorial Services Inc.	106
Goodman and Carr	255	Armor Personnel	107
Hudon & Deaudelin Ltée	279	ArvinMeritor	108
Hydro Québec	283	Assiniboine Community College	109
Ivaco Inc.	296	Atlantic Lottery Corporation Inc.	113
Kitchener, City of	309	Atlantic Packaging Products Ltd.	114
Leduc, City of	313	Atlantic Wholesalers Ltd.	114
Les Centres Jeunesse de Montréal	316	Atlas Ideal Metals Inc.	115
Manitoba Hydro	328	Atlas Van Lines (Canada) Ltd.	115
Maritime Life Assurance Company, The	331	Aurum Ceramic Dental Laboratories Ltd.	117
Matrox Electronic Systems Ltd.	335	Axidata Inc.	118
McInnes Cooper & Robertson	337	Banff Centre for Continuing Education, The	120
Metro Richelieu Inc.	342	BASF Canada Inc.	122
Metropolitan Life Insurance Company	344	Basic Technologies Corporation	122
Midland Walwyn Inc.	345	BBM Bureau of Measurement	125
Neles Automation, Scada Solutions Ltd.	362	BC Telecom Inc.	126
Pizza Pizza Ltd.	401	Bearskin Lake Air Service Ltd.	128
Polygram Group Canada Inc.	403	Bell & Howell Ltd.	130
Regional Municipality of Niagara	424	Bell Mobility	131
Revenue Properties Company Limited	429	Best Western Carlton Place Hotel	133
Sandman Hotels and Inns	443	Bettis Canada Ltd.	135
Saskatchewan Government Insurance	445	Bic Inc.	136
Surrey, City of	484	Biovail Corporation International	137
TD Waterhouse Investor Services (Canada)	488	Black Photo Corporation	139
The Co-operators	493	Blaney McMurty LLP	139
Toronto, City of	508	Bonus Resource Services Corp.	144
University College of Cape Breton	516	BOVAR Waste Management	145
Westbury Life	529	British Columbia Ferry Corporation	149
Westcliff Management Ltd.	529	Bullock Associates Design Consultants Inc.	153
Weyerhaeuser Company Limited	535	Calgary Co-operative Association Limited	157
		Calgary, City of	158
		Canada Post Corporation	162

Marketing/Sales

		Canada Safeway Limited	163
		Canadian Commercial Corp.	165
A C A Cooperative Limited	74	Canadian Dairy Commission	165
A E McKenzie Co. Inc.	75	Canadian Museum of Civilization Corp.	167
Aar-Kel Moulds Ltd.	76	Canadian Thermos Products Inc.	168
Access Communications	78	Canadian Western Bank	169
Accucaps Industries Limited	79	Cancarb Limited	170
Acklands-Grainger Inc.	80	Cancore Industries Inc.	171
Advanta Seeds	83	Canon Canada Inc.	172
Air Canada	85	Canpar Transport Ltd.	173
Air Ontario Inc.	86	Capilano Suspension Bridge	174
Alberta Blue Cross	88	Carbone of America (LCL) Ltd.	175
Alberta Gaming & Liquor Commission	90	Carte International Inc.	176
Allianz Canada	95	Casa Loma	177

College Index 589

Cassels Brock & Blackwell	177	Goodwill Industries of Toronto	256
Centra Gas British Columbia Inc.	180	Grand & Toy Ltd.	257
Central Park Lodges Ltd.	181	Grant MacEwen Community College	258
Century Sales and Service Limited	182	Great-West Life Assurance Company, The	259
Ceridian Canada	183	Groupe Savoie Inc.	260
CFCN Communications Inc.	184	Grouse Mountain Resorts Ltd.	260
CKF Inc.	192	Haley Industries Limited	262
Coca Cola Foods Canada Inc.	195	Harry Rosen Inc.	265
Columbia House	197	Helijet Airways Inc.	268
Community Savings Credit Union	199	Hermes Electronics Inc.	269
Compu-Quote Inc.	200	Homewood Corp.	274
Connors Bros, Limited	203	Honda Canada Inc.	274
Coppley Apparel Group	204	Hub Meat Packers Ltd.	278
Corner Brook, City of	205	Hubbell Canada Inc.	278
Cosmair Canada Inc.	206	Hudon & Deaudelin Ltée	279
Cougar Helicopters Inc.	208	Hydro Mississauga Corporation	282
Credit Union Central of Canada	208	Industrial Equipment Co. Ltd.	288
Culinar Inc.	209	Industrial-Alliance Life Insurance Company	289
DaimlerChrysler Canada Ltd.	211	Information Gateway Services	290
Degussa - Huls Canada Inc.	214	Intercon Security Ltd.	292
Dell Computer Corporation	214	Interior Savings Credit Union	293
Delphi Solutions Inc.	215	Island Savings Credit Union	295
Delta Hotels	215	James Richardson International Limited	300
Directwest Publishers Ltd.	217	Johnson Incorporated	303
Domtar Inc.	218	Jostens Canada Ltd.	303
Dylex Limited	222	Kimberly-Clark Inc.	307
Dynasty Furniture Manufacturing Ltd.	224	Kitchener, City of	309
Economic Development Edmonton	226	Kodak Canada Inc.	309
Economical Insurance Group, The	227	Laidlaw Inc.	312
EDS of Canada Ltd.	228	Lego Canada Inc.	314
Elco	229	Lenbrook Industries Limited	315
EMJ Data Systems Ltd.	231	Leon's Manufacturing Company Inc.	316
Espial Group Incorporated	234	Les Modes Smart Inc.	318
Exfo	235	Liberty Health	318
Exide Canada Inc.	235	Lifetouch Canada Inc.	319
Extendicare (Canada) Inc.	237	London Goodwill Industries Association	322
Farm Credit Corp. Canada	238	M M Industra Ltd.	323
Federated Co-operatives Limited	239	MAAX Inc.	324
Finning	240	Mactac Canada Ltd.	326
Fishery Products International	241	Magna International Inc.	327
Flakeboard Company Limited	242	Maritime Life Assurance Company, The	331
Fletcher's Fine Foods	242	Mark Anthony Group Inc.	332
Foremost Industries Inc.	244	Marks & Spencer Canada Inc.	332
Forzani Group Ltd., The	244	Matrox Electronic Systems Ltd.	335
Friesens Corporation	246	McBee Systems of Canada Inc.	336
Future Shop Ltd.	246	McGraw Hill Ryerson Ltd.	337
Gay Lea Foods Co-Operative Ltd.	247	McLaren-McCann Advertising of Canada Ltd.	338
Gendis Inc.	248	Mediacom Inc.	340
Gienow Building Products Ltd.	251	Mediasynergy	340
Gilbey Canada Inc.	252	Metro Toronto Convention Centre	342
Gimbel Eye Centre	252	Metroland Printing, Publishing & Dist. Ltd.	343
Gisborne Design Services Ltd.	253	Metropolitan Life Insurance Company	344
Glaxo Wellcome Canada	253	Meyers Norris Penny & Co.	344
Goodman and Carr	255	Michaels of Canada Inc.	345

The Canada Student Employment Guide

College Index

Midland Walwyn Inc.	345
Mitsubishi Electric Sales Canada	351
Moen Inc.	352
Monarch Communications Inc.	353
Moosehead Breweries Limited	354
Mortice Kern Systems Inc.	355
MOSAID Technologies Inc.	355
Mustang Survival Corp.	358
Nanaimo Credit Union	359
National Grocers Co. Ltd.	360
National Life	361
National Manufacturing of Canada Inc.	361
Neles Automation, Scada Solutions Ltd.	362
Neptune Food Suppliers Ltd.	363
Nesbitt Burns Inc.	364
Nestle Canada Inc.	364
Newfoundland and Labrador Credit Union	367
Newness Machine Ltd.	368
News Marketing Canada	368
Nielsen Marketing Research	370
Nike Canada Ltd.	371
Norbord Industries	372
Norcen Energy Resources Ltd.	373
North West Company Inc.	374
Northwestel Inc.	376
Norwich Union Life Insurance Society	376
Nova Scotia Liquor Commission	377
Novartis Consumer Health Canada Inc.	378
Novotel Canada Inc.	378
Oetiker Limited	381
Okanagan Skeena Group Limited	382
Oland Breweries Limited	382
Ontario Jockey Club, The	384
Oracle Corp. Canada Inc.	386
Panorama Mountain Village	388
Paramount Canada's Wonderland Inc.	389
PavCo	391
Peacock Inc.	392
Peel Regional Police	394
Pelmorex Inc.	395
Pharma Plus Drugmarts Ltd.	398
Phoenix International	399
Pitney Bowes of Canada Ltd.	401
Pizza Pizza Ltd.	401
Poco Petroleums Ltd.	402
Pollack Rentals Limited	403
Polygram Group Canada Inc.	403
PPG Canada Inc.	407
Prince Albert Credit Union	409
Prince George, City of	410
Progressive Financial Strategy	411
Public Utilities of Kingston	413
Purolator Courier Ltd.	413
Ramada Inn	416
Rasco Specialty Metals Inc.	417
Raymond Rebar Inc.	418
Reader's Digest Association of Canada Ltd.	419
Regal Capital Planners Ltd.	422
Regal Constellation Hotel Ltd.	422
Regal Greeting and Gifts	423
Reliable Engine Services Ltd.	426
Renaissance Energy Ltd.	427
Rentway Inc.	427
Replicon Inc.	428
Rogers AT&T Wireless Inc.	436
Rogers Media, Publishing	436
Rothmans, Benson and Hedges Inc.	437
Royal & Sun Alliance Insurance Co. of Cda	437
Royal Bank of Canada	438
Royal Canadian Mint	438
Royal Philips Electronics	439
Saan Stores Ltd.	441
Sales & Merchandising Group	442
Salisbury House of Canada Ltd.	442
Sandman Hotels and Inns	443
Saskatchewan Centre of the Arts	444
Saskatchewan Transportation Company	446
Saskatoon, City of	448
SaskTel	449
Schlumberger Canada Ltd.	450
Science North	452
Seprotech Systems Incorporated	454
Sharp Electronics of Canada Ltd.	454
Shaw Communications	455
Sheraton Fallsview Hotel	456
Shermag Inc.	457
Sherwood Credit Union	458
Shoppers Drug Mart Limited	458
Shopping Channel, The	459
Shorewood Packaging Corp. of Canada Ltd.	459
Siemens Electric Ltd.	460
Signature Vacations Inc.	460
Skiing Louise Ltd.	461
Slocan Forest Products Ltd.	462
Sobeys Inc.	463
Sony Music Canada	465
Southam Inc.	466
Spectra Premium Industries	468
Speedware Corp. Inc.	469
Sportsco International	469
SRI Homes Inc.	470
St. Lawrence Parks Commission	472
Standard Knitting Limited	474
Stanley Canada Inc.	475
State Farm Insurance Companies	476
Steelcraft Industries Ltd.	477
Stitches	478
Sun Peaks Resort Corporation	481

The Canada Student Employment Guide

Sun Rype Products Ltd.	481	A.G. Simpson Co. Ltd.	75
Sundog Printing Limited	482	ABC Group	76
Surrey, City of	484	Alberta Energy Company Ltd.	89
TCT Logistics	488	Alcan Aluminium Limited	91
TD Waterhouse Investor Services (Canada)	488	Algoma Steel Inc.	93
Telus Corporation	492	Aquatic Sciences Inc.	105
The Arthritis Society	492	Armor Personnel	107
The Barn Fruit Markets Inc.	493	Armtec Limited	108
Thomas & Betts Ltée	495	ArvinMeritor	108
Thomas Cook Group (Canada) Ltd.	495	Assumption Mutual Life Insurance	109
Thompson's Moving and Storage	496	ATCO Electric	111
Today's Business Products Ltd.	500	ATCO Frontec Corp.	111
Top Producers Systems Inc.	500	Atlas Ideal Metals Inc.	115
Toronto and Region Conservation Authority	501	ATS Automation Tooling Systems Inc.	116
Toronto Sun Publishing Corp., The	507	Babcock and Wilcox Canada	119
Toshiba of Canada Ltd.	508	Ballard Power Systems Inc.	120
Toyota Canada Ltd.	509	Banff Centre for Continuing Education, The	120
Trojan Technologies Inc.	511	Basic Technologies Corporation	122
TSC Stores Ltd.	512	BCG Services	127
Uni Select Inc.	513	Bell & Howell Ltd.	130
University College of Cape Breton	516	Bettis Canada Ltd.	135
US Filter BCP	517	BFGoodrich Landing Gear Division	135
Vacances Air Transat Inc.	518	Black Photo Corporation	139
Vancouver International Airport	520	Blue Wave Seafoods Inc.	142
W C I Canada Inc.	524	Bosal Canada Inc.	145
Waterloo Furniture Components Ltd.	524	BOVAR Waste Management	145
Waterloo Inn	525	Bowater Mersey Paper Company Limited	146
Wegu Canada Inc.	526	Brantcorp Inc.	147
Weldco-Beales Manufacturing Inc.	527	Buckeye Canada Inc.	151
West Coast Apparel	528	Budd Canada Inc.	152
Western Glove Works	530	C MAC Industries Inc.	155
Westin Prince Hotel, The	531	Canadian General Tower Limited	166
WestJet Airlines	532	Canadian Museum of Civilization Corp.	167
Westminster Savings Credit Union	533	Canadian Thermos Products Inc.	168
Weyerhaeuser Company Limited	535	CancerCare Manitoba	171
Whistler Blackcomb Mountain	535	Canon Canada Inc.	172
Whitehill Technologies Inc.	537	Cape Breton Development Corporation	174
Wilson Auto Electric Ltd.	538	Carbone of America (LCL) Ltd.	175
Winners Apparel Ltd.	539	Carte International Inc.	176
Wire Rope Industries Ltd.	540	Centra Gas Manitoba Inc.	181
World of Vacations Ltd.	541	CH2M Gore and Storrie Limited	185
XCAN Grain Pool Ltd.	541	CKF Inc.	192
Yamaha Motor Canada Ltd.	542	COM DEV International	197
Yanke Group of Companies	543	Communications & Power Industries Canada	198
YFactor	544	Computalog Ltd.	200
Zellers Inc.	546	Conair Aviation Ltd.	202
Zenastra	547	Connors Bros, Limited	203
Zenon Environmental Inc.	547	Coquitlam, City of	204
Zurich Canada	548	Corner Brook, City of	205
		Custom Trim Ltd.	210
		D.A. Stuart Inc.	210
Mechanical Tech.		DDM Plastics Inc.	213
		Dofasco Inc.	218
A C A Cooperative Limited	74	Domtar Inc.	218

The Canada Student Employment Guide

College Index

Echo Bay Mines Ltd.	226
EnerFlex Systems Ltd.	232
Entreprises Premier Canadien Ltée	232
Exfo	235
Finning	240
Fishery Products International	241
Flakeboard Company Limited	242
Fletcher's Fine Foods	242
Flint Energy Services Ltd.	243
Foremost Industries Inc.	244
Gencorp Vehicle Sealing	248
General Chemical Canada Ltd.	249
Giffels Associates Limited	251
Groupe Savoie Inc.	260
Haley Industries Limited	262
Haliburton Energy Services	262
Halliburton Energy Services	264
Hallmark Tools	265
Helijet Airways Inc.	268
Hermes Electronics Inc.	269
Hudon & Deaudelin Ltée	279
Huronia Regional Centre	280
Hydro One Inc.	282
Hydro Québec	283
Ilco Unican Inc.	286
Imprimerie Interweb Inc.	287
INCO Limited	287
Industrial Equipment Co. Ltd.	288
Industries Lassonde Inc.	289
IPL Energy Inc.	294
Ivaco Inc.	296
J.D. Irving Limited	298
Jo-Ann Trucking Ltd.	301
Kawneer Company Canada Limited	304
Leduc, City of	313
Les Forges de Sorel Inc.	317
Litton Systems Canada Ltd.	320
Lovat Inc.	323
M M Industra Ltd.	323
MAAX Inc.	324
MacViro Consultants Inc.	326
Magna International Inc.	327
Manitoba Hydro	328
McBee Systems of Canada Inc.	336
MDS Nordion	339
Minas Basin Pulp and Power Company Ltd.	347
Mississauga, City of	349
Mobile Computing Corporation	351
Morrison Hershfield Limited	354
Mustang Survival Corp.	358
New Brunswick Power Corporation	365
Newfoundland and Labrador Hydro	367
Norbord Industries	372
Northern Lights Regional Health Centre	375
Novartis Consumer Health Canada Inc.	378
Omstead Foods Limited	383
Ottawa Hospital	386
Paramount Canada's Wonderland Inc.	389
Patheon Inc.	390
PavCo	391
Peel Regional Police	394
Petromont & Co. Ltd. Partnership	397
Phillips & Tempro Industries Ltd.	398
Pitney Bowes of Canada Ltd.	401
Prince George, City of	410
Proctor and Redfern Ltd.	411
Public Utilities of Kingston	413
QEII Health Sciences Centre	414
Raymond Industrial Equipment Ltd.	418
Raymond Rebar Inc.	418
Recochem Inc.	420
Regional Municipality of Niagara	424
Reid Crowther	426
Richmond, City of	431
Rimrock Resort Hotel	432
Riverside Fabricating Ltd.	433
Roctest Ltée	435
Royal Canadian Mint	438
Ryerson Polytechnic University	441
Sandman Hotels and Inns	443
Sandwell Inc.	443
Saskatchewan Government Insurance	445
Saskferco Products Inc.	448
SCIEX MDS Health Group	452
Seprotech Systems Incorporated	454
Siemens Electric Ltd.	460
Sony Music Canada	465
Spectra Premium Industries	468
Sportsco International	469
St. Lawrence Parks Commission	472
St. Lawrence Seaway Mgmt. Corp., The	473
Standard Knitting Limited	474
Standen's Limited	474
Stantec Consulting Ltd.	475
Steelcraft Industries Ltd.	477
Steelpipe Ltd.	477
Sudbury Regional Hospital	480
Sun Peaks Resort Corporation	481
Supreme Tooling Group	483
Sydney Steel Corporation	485
The Garland Group	494
Thomson - CSF Systems Canada Inc.	497
Toronto Catholic District School Board	502
Trojan Technologies Inc.	511
Union Gas Ltd.	513
University College of Cape Breton	516
Visteon Canada Inc.	522
Westcoast Energy Inc.	530

The Canada Student Employment Guide

College Index 593

Western Glove Works	530	Grant MacEwen Community College	258
Westinghouse Canada Inc.	532	Halifax County Regional Rehabilitation Centre	263
Westport Innovations Inc.	534	Health Authority 5	267
Weyerhaeuser Company Limited	535	Health Care Corporation of St. John's	267
Wilson Auto Electric Ltd.	538	Health Sciences Centre	268
Windsor, City of	538	Homewood Corp.	274
Wire Rope Industries Ltd.	540	Hôtel Dieu de Montréal	276
Zenastra	547	Humber River Regional Hospital	280
		Huronia Regional Centre	280
		Hydro Québec	283

Nursing (RN/RNA)

		Ivaco Inc.	296
		IWK Grace Health Centre	297
Aberdeen Hospital	77	Kelowna Home Support	304
Alberta Alcohol and Drug Abuse Commission	87	Kennedy Lodge Nursing Home Inc.	306
Alberta Blue Cross	88	Kings Regional Rehabilitation Centre	308
Algoma District Home For The Aged	92	Les Centres Jeunesse de Montréal	316
Altona Community Memorial Health Centre	97	Liberty Health	318
Assiniboine Community College	109	Magna International Inc.	327
Atlantic Blue Cross Care	113	Medical Laboratories of Windsor Limited	341
Aurizon Mines Ltd.	116	Metro Toronto West Detention Centre	343
Barton Place Long Term Care Facility	121	Misericordia General Hospital	348
Battlefords Health District	123	Northern Lights Regional Health Centre	375
Belleville General Hospital	132	Novartis Consumer Health Canada Inc.	378
Bethania Mennonite Personal Care Home Inc.	134	Omstead Foods Limited	383
Bethesda Hospital	134	Ottawa Hospital	386
BFGoodrich Landing Gear Division	135	Overlander Hospital	387
Biovail Corporation International	137	Paramount Canada's Wonderland Inc.	389
Bowater Mersey Paper Company Limited	146	Phoenix International	399
Cambridge Memorial Hospital	159	Pioneer Village Special Care Corp.	400
Camp Hill Hospital	160	Pool People Ltd.	404
CancerCare Manitoba	171	Providence Centre	412
Cangene Corporation	172	QEII Health Sciences Centre	414
Cape Breton Development Corporation	174	Reena	421
Central Park Lodges Ltd.	181	Regina Health District	423
Centre de Santé de St-Henri Inc.	182	Regional Municipality of Niagara	424
Children's Hospital of Eastern Ontario	189	Rehabilitation Institute of Toronto	425
Chilliwack General Hospital	189	Riverside Hospital of Ottawa, The	434
Chinook Health Region	190	Royal Inland Hospital	439
CKF Inc.	192	Royal Victoria Hospital	440
Cobourg District General Hospital	194	Sandman Hotels and Inns	443
Comcare Health Services	198	Saskatchewan Government Insurance	445
Custom Trim Ltd.	210	Scarborough General Hospital	450
David Thompson Health Region	212	Sherbrooke Community Centre	457
Deer Lodge Centre Inc.	213	Skills Training & Support Services Association	462
Edmonton Home Services Ltd.	228	SSQ Life	471
Endpoint Research Ltd.	231	St. Amant Centre Inc.	471
EnerFlex Systems Ltd.	232	St. Vincent's Hospitals	473
Extendicare (Canada) Inc.	237	Steelpipe Ltd.	477
Fisher Scientific Limited	241	Sudbury Regional Hospital	480
Foyer Valade Inc.	245	Surrey Memorial Hospital	483
Gencorp Vehicle Sealing	248	Surrey Place Centre	484
Gimbel Eye Centre	252	Surrey, City of	484
Glaxo Wellcome Canada	253	Swift Current Health District	485
Goodwill Industries of Toronto	256	Thunder Bay Regional Hospital	497

The Canada Student Employment Guide

/ College Index

Timmins, City of	499
Toronto East General Hospital	503
Toronto General Hospital	505
Toronto Police Service	506
Toronto, City of	508
Universal Rehabilitation Service Agency	515
Villa Providence Shediac Inc.	522
Westbury Life	529
Windsor, City of	538
Yarmouth Regional Hospital	543

Performing Arts

Banff Centre for Continuing Education, The	120
Canadian Museum of Civilization Corp.	167
Casa Loma	177
Grant MacEwen Community College	258
Metropolitan Life Insurance Company	344
Nelvana Limited	363
Paramount Canada's Wonderland Inc.	389
Surrey, City of	484

Plumbing

BCG Services	127
Blue Mountain Resorts Limited	141
BOVAR Waste Management	145
Coquitlam, City of	204
DaimlerChrysler Canada Ltd.	211
Deer Lodge Centre Inc.	213
EnerFlex Systems Ltd.	232
Flint Energy Services Ltd.	243
Ottawa Hospital	386
QEII Health Sciences Centre	414
Regional Municipality of Niagara	424
Sportsco International	469
Sudbury Regional Hospital	480
Sun Peaks Resort Corporation	481
Western Glove Works	530

Radiology Tech.

Aberdeen Hospital	77
Belleville General Hospital	132
Bethesda Hospital	134
Cambridge Memorial Hospital	159
Camp Hill Hospital	160
CancerCare Manitoba	171
Children's Hospital of Eastern Ontario	189
Chilliwack General Hospital	189
Chinook Health Region	190

Cobourg District General Hospital	194
David Thompson Health Region	212
Health Authority 5	267
Health Care Corporation of St. John's	267
Health Sciences Centre	268
Hôtel Dieu de Montréal	276
Humber River Regional Hospital	280
IWK Grace Health Centre	297
Kodak Canada Inc.	309
Northern Lights Regional Health Centre	375
Ottawa Hospital	386
QEII Health Sciences Centre	414
Regina Health District	423
Rehabilitation Institute of Toronto	425
Riverside Hospital of Ottawa, The	434
Royal Inland Hospital	439
Royal Victoria Hospital	440
Scarborough General Hospital	450
Siemens Electric Ltd.	460
St. Vincent's Hospitals	473
Sudbury Regional Hospital	480
Swift Current Health District	485
Thunder Bay Regional Hospital	497
Toronto East General Hospital	503
Toronto General Hospital	505
Yarmouth Regional Hospital	543

Recreation Studies

Alberta Alcohol and Drug Abuse Commission	87
Altona Community Memorial Health Centre	97
Athabasca, Town of	112
Banff Centre for Continuing Education, The	120
Barton Place Long Term Care Facility	121
Belleville General Hospital	132
Betel Home Foundation	133
Bethania Mennonite Personal Care Home Inc.	134
Bethesda Hospital	134
Bloorview Childrens Hospital	140
Bloorview MacMillan Centre, The	140
Blue Mountain Resorts Limited	141
Brandon, City of	146
Camp Hill Hospital	160
Casa Loma	177
Central Park Lodges Ltd.	181
Christian Horizons	190
Coquitlam, City of	204
Corner Brook, City of	205
David Thompson Health Region	212
Deer Lodge Centre Inc.	213
Extendicare (Canada) Inc.	237
Foyer Valade Inc.	245
George Jeffrey Children's Treatment Centre	250

The Canada Student Employment Guide

College Index 595

Halifax Regional Municipality	263	Alcan Aluminium Limited	91
Health Authority 5	267	Algoma Steel Inc.	93
Health Care Corporation of St. John's	267	Allianz Canada	95
Homewood Corp.	274	Allstate Insurance Co. of Canada	96
Huronia Regional Centre	280	Alpine Oil Service Corporation	96
Kings Regional Rehabilitation Centre	308	Amcor Twinpak North America Inc.	98
Kitchener, City of	309	Anjura Services Inc.	101
Leduc, City of	313	Antamex International Inc.	102
Metro Toronto West Detention Centre	343	Anthony Insurance Inc.	102
Metropolitan Life Insurance Company	344	Armor Personnel	107
Pool People Ltd.	404	Assiniboine Community College	109
Prince Albert, City of	410	Assumption Mutual Life Insurance	109
Prince George, City of	410	AstraZeneca	110
Providence Centre	412	ATCO Electric	111
QEII Health Sciences Centre	414	ATCO Frontec Corp.	111
Regal Constellation Hotel Ltd.	422	ATCO Gas Services Ltd.	112
Regional Residential Services Society	424	Atlantic Blue Cross Care	113
Rehabilitation Institute of Toronto	425	Atlantic Lottery Corporation Inc.	113
Richmond, City of	431	Atlas Ideal Metals Inc.	115
Saskatoon, City of	448	ATS Automation Tooling Systems Inc.	116
Scarborough General Hospital	450	Aurizon Mines Ltd.	116
Sherbrooke Community Centre	457	Aurum Ceramic Dental Laboratories Ltd.	117
Skiing Louise Ltd.	461	Aventis Pasteur Limited	117
Skills Training & Support Services Association	462	AXA Insurance (Canada)	118
St. Lawrence Parks Commission	472	Axidata Inc.	118
Sudbury Regional Hospital	480	Ballard Power Systems Inc.	120
Surrey, City of	484	Bargain Finder Press Ltd.	121
Timmins, City of	499	Barton Place Long Term Care Facility	121
Toronto and Region Conservation Authority	501	BASF Canada Inc.	122
Toronto Cricket Skating & Curling	502	Basic Technologies Corporation	122
Toronto, City of	508	Baytex Energy Limited	124
Universal Rehabilitation Service Agency	515	BBM Bureau of Measurement	125
Yellowknife, City of	544	BC Research Inc.	126
		Bell Canada	131
		Bell Mobility	131

Science (General)

		Belleville General Hospital	132
		Bettis Canada Ltd.	135
A C A Cooperative Limited	74	BFGoodrich Landing Gear Division	135
A E McKenzie Co. Inc.	75	Biomira Inc.	136
A.G. Simpson Co. Ltd.	75	Bio-Research Laboratories Ltd.	137
ABC Group	76	BJ Services Company	138
Aberdeen Hospital	77	Black Photo Corporation	139
Access Communications	78	Bloorview MacMillan Centre, The	140
Accucaps Industries Limited	79	Blue Wave Seafoods Inc.	142
ACE INI Insurance	79	BNP PARIBAS (Canada)	143
Acklands-Grainger Inc.	80	BOVAR Waste Management	145
ADI Group Inc.	82	Bowater Mersey Paper Company Limited	146
ADT Canada Inc.	82	Brandon, City of	146
Air Ontario Inc.	86	Bratty & Partners LLP	147
Alberta Blue Cross	88	Brewers Retail Inc.	148
Alberta Cancer Board	88	Brookfield Properties Corporation	150
Alberta Energy & Utilities Board	89	Buck Consultants Limited	151
Alberta Energy Company Ltd.	89	Buckeye Canada Inc.	151
Alberta Gaming & Liquor Commission	90	Budd Canada Inc.	152

The Canada Student Employment Guide

College Index

C B C L Limited	154	Crestar Energy Inc.	209
C MAC Industries Inc.	155	Culinar Inc.	209
Cabre Exploration Ltd.	156	Custom Trim Ltd.	210
Calgary Co-operative Association Limited	157	D.A. Stuart Inc.	210
Calgary, City of	158	D.H. Howden	211
Cambridge Memorial Hospital	159	DaimlerChrysler Canada Ltd.	211
Camp Hill Hospital	160	David Thompson Health Region	212
Canadian Cancer Society	164	Degussa - Huls Canada Inc.	214
Canadian Commercial Corp.	165	Dell Computer Corporation	214
Canadian Dairy Commission	165	Directwest Publishers Ltd.	217
Canadian Depository for Securities Ltd.	166	Dofasco Inc.	218
Canadian General Tower Limited	166	Domtar Inc.	218
Canadian Occidental Petroleum Ltd.	168	Dun & Bradstreet Canada	221
Canadian Thermos Products Inc.	168	Dynapro Systems Inc.	223
Canadian Tire Corporation Ltd.	169	Economic Development Edmonton	226
Canadian Western Bank	169	Economical Insurance Group, The	227
Canbra Foods Ltd.	170	EDS of Canada Ltd.	228
CancerCare Manitoba	171	Electronics Arts (Canada) Inc.	229
Cangene Corporation	172	EMJ Data Systems Ltd.	231
Canon Canada Inc.	172	EnerFlex Systems Ltd.	232
Cape Breton Development Corporation	174	Entreprises Premier Canadien Ltée	232
Cargill Limited	175	Espial Group Incorporated	234
Carte International Inc.	176	Exfo	235
Centra Gas British Columbia Inc.	180	Exide Canada Inc.	235
Centra Gas Manitoba Inc.	181	Extendicare (Canada) Inc.	237
Centre de Santé de St-Henri Inc.	182	Farm Credit Corp. Canada	238
Ceridian Canada	183	Farmers Co-operative Dairy Limited	239
CGI	184	Federated Co-operatives Limited	239
CGU Group Canada Ltd.	185	Fisher Scientific Limited	241
CH2M Gore and Storrie Limited	185	Fishery Products International	241
Chevron Canada Resources Ltd.	188	Flakeboard Company Limited	242
Children's Hospital of Eastern Ontario	189	Flint Energy Services Ltd.	243
Citibank Canada	191	Foremost Industries Inc.	244
CKF Inc.	192	Foyer Valade Inc.	245
Clarica	192	Friesens Corporation	246
COBI Foods Inc.	194	Future Shop Ltd.	246
Cobourg District General Hospital	194	General Chemical Canada Ltd.	249
Cognos Incorporated	196	General Electric Canada Inc.	249
Columbia House	197	George Jeffrey Children's Treatment Centre	250
Comcare Health Services	198	Gienow Building Products Ltd.	251
Community Savings Credit Union	199	Giffels Associates Limited	251
Compu-Quote Inc.	200	Gilbey Canada Inc.	252
Computalog Ltd.	200	Gimbel Eye Centre	252
Comtronic Computer Inc.	202	Glaxo Wellcome Canada	253
Conair Aviation Ltd.	202	Glentel Inc.	254
Connors Bros, Limited	203	Goodman and Carr	255
Co-op Atlantic	203	Goodwill Industries of Toronto	256
Coquitlam, City of	204	Goodyear Canada Inc.	256
Corel Corporation	205	Gov't of Newfoundland – Dept. of Finance	257
Corner Brook, City of	205	Grand & Toy Ltd.	257
Cornwall Electric	206	Grant MacEwen Community College	258
Cotton Ginny Ltd.	207	Great-West Life Assurance Company, The	259
Cougar Helicopters Inc.	208	H A Simmons Ltd.	261
Credit Union Central of Canada	208	Halifax Regional Municipality	263

The Canada Student Employment Guide

College Index

Halifax Water Commission	264
HB Studios Multimedia Ltd.	266
Health Care Corporation of St. John's	267
Health Sciences Centre	268
Hippodrome de Montréal	270
Holland College	273
Home Oil Co. Ltd.	273
Homewood Corp.	274
Honeywell Ltd.	275
Hôtel Dieu de Montréal	276
Household Movers & Shippers Limited	276
HSBC Bank Canada	277
Hubbell Canada Inc.	278
Hudon & Deaudelin Ltée	279
Hudson's Bay Company, The	279
Huronia Regional Centre	280
Husky Energy Inc.	281
Hydro Electric Commission of Thunder Bay	281
Hydro One Inc.	282
Hydro Québec	283
I M P Group International Inc.	283
IBM Canada Ltd.	284
Industrial Equipment Co. Ltd.	288
Industrial-Alliance Life Insurance Company	289
Industries Lassonde Inc.	289
InfoInterActive Inc.	290
ING Canada Financial Services International	291
InterOne Marketing Group	293
IPL Energy Inc.	294
IST Group Inc.	296
Ivaco Inc.	296
IWK Grace Health Centre	297
J.D. Irving Limited	298
James Richardson International Limited	300
Jim Pattison Group	301
Johnson Controls Ltd.	302
Johnson Incorporated	303
Jostens Canada Ltd.	303
Kelowna, City of	305
Kitchener, City of	309
Kodak Canada Inc.	309
La Confiserie Comete Ltee	311
Laidlaw Inc.	312
Leduc, City of	313
Lenbrook Industries Limited	315
Les Centres Jeunesse de Montréal	316
Les Forges de Sorel Inc.	317
Liberty Health	318
Lifetouch Canada Inc.	319
Linmor Technologies	320
Litton Systems Canada Ltd.	320
MAAX Inc.	324
MacDonald Dettwiler and Associates Ltd.	325
MacDonald Steel Ltd.	325
Manitoba Agriculture and Food	327
Manitoba Hydro	328
Manitoba Pool Elevators	328
Manitoba Public Insurance Corporation	329
Manitoba Telecom Services Inc.	329
Maple Leaf Consumer Foods	330
Marcam Canada	330
Marine Atlantic Inc.	331
Maritime Life Assurance Company, The	331
Mark Anthony Group Inc.	332
Marshall Macklin Monaghan Ltd.	333
Marystown Shipyard Limited	334
Matrox Electronic Systems Ltd.	335
McBee Systems of Canada Inc.	336
McKay-Cocker Construction Limited	338
MDS Nordion	339
Mediasynergy	340
Metro Richelieu Inc.	342
Metro Toronto West Detention Centre	343
Meyers Norris Penny & Co.	344
Michaels of Canada Inc.	345
Midland Walwyn Inc.	345
Midwest Food Products Inc.	346
Minas Basin Pulp and Power Company Ltd.	347
Ministry of Northern Develop. and Mines	348
Mississauga, City of	349
Mitel Corporation	350
Mitra Imaging Inc.	350
Mitsubishi Electric Sales Canada	351
Mobile Computing Corporation	351
Moen Inc.	352
Monarch Communications Inc.	353
Montreal Trust Co.	353
Moosehead Breweries Limited	354
Mortice Kern Systems Inc.	355
MOSAID Technologies Inc.	355
Motorola Canada Ltd.	356
Multitech Electronics Inc.	358
Mustang Survival Corp.	358
N B S Card Services	359
Natco Canada Ltd.	360
National Grocers Co. Ltd.	360
National Life	361
National Manufacturing of Canada Inc.	361
National Sports Centre	362
Neles Automation, Scada Solutions Ltd.	362
Nelvana Limited	363
Nesbitt Burns Inc.	364
Nestle Canada Inc.	364
New Brunswick Power Corporation	365
Newfoundland and Labrador Credit Union	367
News Marketing Canada	368
NewTel Communications	369
Nielsen Marketing Research	370

The Canada Student Employment Guide

598 College Index

North West Company Inc.	374
Northern Lights Regional Health Centre	375
Northwestel Inc.	376
Norwich Union Life Insurance Society	376
Nova Scotia Liquor Commission	377
Nova Scotia Power Corp.	377
NPS Alleix Corp.	379
Numac Energy Inc.	379
Nygard International Ltd.	380
Okanagan Skeena Group Limited	382
Oland Breweries Limited	382
Ontario Jockey Club, The	384
Ontario Legislative Offices	384
Oracle Corp. Canada Inc.	386
Ottawa Hospital	386
Paramount Canada's Wonderland Inc.	389
Patheon Inc.	390
Paul Revere Life Insurance Company, The	391
PavCo	391
PCL Constructors Inc.	392
Pearson Education Canada	393
Peel Board of Education	393
Peel Regional Police	394
Pelmorex Inc.	395
Petromont & Co. Ltd. Partnership	397
Pharma Plus Drugmarts Ltd.	398
Phoenix International	399
Pine Falls Paper Company Limited	400
Pitney Bowes of Canada Ltd.	401
Placer Dome Inc.	402
Pollack Rentals Limited	403
Polygram Group Canada Inc.	403
Potacan Mining Company	405
Powertech Labs Inc.	406
Premdor Inc.	408
PRI Automation	408
Prince George, City of	410
Prudential Insurance Co. of America, The	412
Public Utilities of Kingston	413
Purolator Courier Ltd.	413
QEII Health Sciences Centre	414
QIT-Fer et Titane Inc.	414
Québéc Cartier Mining Company	415
Quebecor Inc.	415
Raylo Chemicals Inc.	417
Raytheon Systems Canada Ltd.	419
Reader's Digest Association of Canada Ltd.	419
Recochem Inc.	420
Regal Capital Planners Ltd.	422
Regal Constellation Hotel Ltd.	422
Rehabilitation Institute of Toronto	425
Replicon Inc.	428
Revenue Properties Company Limited	429
Reynolds and Reynolds (Canada) Limited	430
Richmond, City of	431
Riverside Hospital of Ottawa, The	434
Rivtow Marine Ltd.	434
Rockwell Automation	435
Rogers AT&T Wireless Inc.	436
Rothmans, Benson and Hedges Inc.	437
Royal & Sun Alliance Insurance Co. of Cda	437
Royal Bank of Canada	438
Saan Stores Ltd.	441
Salisbury House of Canada Ltd.	442
Sandman Hotels and Inns	443
Saskatchewan Economic Development	445
Saskatchewan Government Insurance	445
Saskatchewan Wheat Pool	447
Saskatoon, City of	448
Saskferco Products Inc.	448
SaskTel	449
SC Infrastructure Inc.	449
Scarborough General Hospital	450
Schneider Electric Canada Inc.	451
Science North	452
SCIEX MDS Health Group	452
SED Systems	453
Shaw Communications	455
Sherwood Credit Union	458
Shorewood Packaging Corp. of Canada Ltd.	459
Siemens Electric Ltd.	460
Signature Vacations Inc.	460
Silicon Graphics Canada Inc.	461
Société des Alcools du Québec	464
SolutionInc Limited	465
Sony Music Canada	465
Southam Inc.	466
Spar Aerospace Limited	467
Spectra Premium Industries	468
Spectrum Signal Processing Inc.	468
Speedware Corp. Inc.	469
Sprint Canada	470
SSQ Life	471
St. Lawrence Seaway Mgmt. Corp., The	473
St. Vincent's Hospitals	473
Standen's Limited	474
Stanley Canada Inc.	475
Star Data Systems Inc.	476
State Farm Insurance Companies	476
Sterling Marking Products Inc.	478
Stitches	478
StorageTek Canada Inc.	479
Sun Rype Products Ltd.	481
Sundog Printing Limited	482
Sunoco Inc.	482
Surrey Memorial Hospital	483
Surrey Place Centre	484
Surrey, City of	484

The Canada Student Employment Guide

College Index 599

Symantec Corporation	486
Syncrude Canada Ltd.	486
TCG International Inc.	487
TCT Logistics	488
TD Waterhouse Investor Services (Canada)	488
Teck Corp.	489
Telebec Ltée	490
Telegraph Journal	491
The Garland Group	494
Thomas J. Lipton	496
Thompson's Moving and Storage	496
Thomson - CSF Systems Canada Inc.	497
Thunder Bay Regional Hospital	497
Tiger Brand Knitting Company Limited	498
Timmins, City of	499
Top Producers Systems Inc.	500
Toronto Catholic District School Board	502
Toronto District School Board	503
Toronto East General Hospital	503
Toronto General Hospital	505
Toronto Hydro	505
Toronto Police Service	506
Toronto Sun Publishing Corp., The	507
Toronto, City of	508
Toshiba of Canada Ltd.	508
Toyota Canada Ltd.	509
TransAlta	509
Trojan Technologies Inc.	511
TSC Stores Ltd.	512
Turnbull & Turnbull Ltd.	512
Union Pacific Resources Group	514
Unisys Canada Inc.	514
University College of Cape Breton	516
US Filter BCP	517
Vancouver International Airport	520
W C I Canada Inc.	524
WebCanada	526
Weldco-Beales Manufacturing Inc.	527
West Coast Apparel	528
Westbury Life	529
Westcoast Energy Inc.	530
Westinghouse Canada Inc.	532
WestJet Airlines	532
Westminster Savings Credit Union	533
Westport Innovations Inc.	534
Westshore Terminals Ltd.	534
Weyerhaeuser Company Limited	535
Whistler Blackcomb Mountain	535
Whitehill Technologies Inc.	537
Windsor, City of	538
Winners Apparel Ltd.	539
Winpak Ltd.	539
Wire Rope Industries Ltd.	540
XCAN Grain Pool Ltd.	541
xwave solutions	542
Yanke Group of Companies	543
Yellowknife, City of	544
Zellers Inc.	546
Zurich Canada	548

Secretarial

A E McKenzie Co. Inc.	75
A.G. Simpson Co. Ltd.	75
ABC Group	76
Aberdeen Hospital	77
Abitibi-Consolidated Inc.	77
Acadia University	78
Access Communications	78
ACE INI Insurance	79
Acier Leroux Inc.	80
Acklands-Grainger Inc.	80
ADI Group Inc.	82
ADT Canada Inc.	82
AGF Management Limited	83
Agricultural Credit Corp. of Saskatchewan	84
Air Canada	85
Air Nova Inc.	86
Air Ontario Inc.	86
Alberta Blue Cross	88
Alberta Cancer Board	88
Alberta Energy & Utilities Board	89
Alberta Gaming & Liquor Commission	90
Alcan Aluminium Limited	91
Algoma District Home For The Aged	92
Amcor Twinpak North America Inc.	98
Anthony Insurance Inc.	102
Aon Reed Stenhouse Inc.	103
Apex Land Corp.	103
Arctic Co-operatives Limited	107
Armor Personnel	107
Assiniboine Community College	109
Assumption Mutual Life Insurance	109
Athabasca, Town of	112
Atlantic Blue Cross Care	113
Atlantic Packaging Products Ltd.	114
Atlantic Wholesalers Ltd.	114
Atlas Ideal Metals Inc.	115
Aurizon Mines Ltd.	116
AXA Insurance (Canada)	118
Babcock and Wilcox Canada	119
BASF Canada Inc.	122
Basic Technologies Corporation	122
Battlefords Health District	123
Baycrest Centre for Geriatric Care	123
Bayer Inc.	124
BCG Services	127

The Canada Student Employment Guide

College Index

Beckman Coulter Canada Inc.	129
Bell Mobility	131
Belleville General Hospital	132
Best Western Carlton Place Hotel	133
Bethesda Hospital	134
BFGoodrich Landing Gear Division	135
Bic Inc.	136
Biovail Corporation International	137
Bloorview Childrens Hospital	140
Bloorview MacMillan Centre, The	140
Bluewater District School Board	142
BNP PARIBAS (Canada)	143
Bonus Resource Services Corp.	144
Boréal Assurances Inc.	144
Bowater Mersey Paper Company Limited	146
Brandon, City of	146
British Columbia Ferry Corporation	149
Brookfield Properties Corporation	150
C.S.T. Consultants Inc.	155
Calgary Co-operative Association Limited	157
Calgary, City of	158
Cambridge Memorial Hospital	159
Cameco Corporation	160
Camp Hill Hospital	160
Canada Post Corporation	162
Canada Safeway Limited	163
Canadian Cancer Society	164
Canadian Depository for Securities Ltd.	166
Canadian General Tower Limited	166
Canadian Museum of Civilization Corp.	167
Canadian Occidental Petroleum Ltd.	168
Canadian Western Bank	169
Canbra Foods Ltd.	170
Cancarb Limited	170
CancerCare Manitoba	171
Cancore Industries Inc.	171
Cangene Corporation	172
Canon Canada Inc.	172
Cape Breton Development Corporation	174
Carbone of America (LCL) Ltd.	175
Carlson Marketing Group Canada Ltd.	176
Cassels Brock & Blackwell	177
CCL Industries Inc.	178
Central Park Lodges Ltd.	181
CFCF Inc.	183
CFCN Communications Inc.	184
CGU Group Canada Ltd.	185
Challenger Motor Freight Inc.	186
Charlottetown Driving Park	187
Cheticamp Packers Ltd.	187
Children's Hospital of Eastern Ontario	189
Chilliwack General Hospital	189
Cineplex Odeon Corporation	191
CKF Inc.	192
COBI Foods Inc.	194
Cobourg District General Hospital	194
Coca Cola Foods Canada Inc.	195
COM DEV International	197
Comcare Health Services	198
Community Savings Credit Union	199
Compu-Quote Inc.	200
Comstock Canada	201
Connors Bros, Limited	203
Co-op Atlantic	203
Coppley Apparel Group	204
Coquitlam, City of	204
Cornwall Electric	206
Cosyn Technology	207
Cougar Helicopters Inc.	208
Credit Union Central of Canada	208
Crestar Energy Inc.	209
Culinar Inc.	209
Custom Trim Ltd.	210
D.A. Stuart Inc.	210
David Thompson Health Region	212
Delphi Solutions Inc.	215
Directwest Publishers Ltd.	217
Domtar Inc.	218
Ducks Unlimited Canada	220
Dun & Bradstreet Canada	221
Economic Development Edmonton	226
Economical Insurance Group, The	227
Emco Limited	230
EMJ Data Systems Ltd.	231
Endpoint Research Ltd.	231
EnerFlex Systems Ltd.	232
Entreprises Premier Canadien Ltée	232
Exfo	235
Extendicare (Canada) Inc.	237
Family Day Care Service	238
Farm Credit Corp. Canada	238
Federated Co-operatives Limited	239
FedEx Express	240
Finning	240
Fishery Products International	241
Flakeboard Company Limited	242
Fletcher's Fine Foods	242
Foremost Industries Inc.	244
Foyer Valade Inc.	245
Friesens Corporation	246
Future Shop Ltd.	246
Gendis Inc.	248
Gienow Building Products Ltd.	251
Giffels Associates Limited	251
Gilbey Canada Inc.	252
Glaxo Wellcome Canada	253
Goodman and Carr	255
Goodwill Industries of Toronto	256

The Canada Student Employment Guide

College Index 601

Grand & Toy Ltd.	257	Les Centres Jeunesse de Montréal	316
Grant MacEwen Community College	258	Les Modes Smart Inc.	318
Great-West Life Assurance Company, The	259	Liberty Health	318
Halifax Regional Municipality	263	Loewen Windows	321
Halifax Water Commission	264	London Goodwill Industries Association	322
Harry Rosen Inc.	265	M M Industra Ltd.	323
Health Authority 5	267	MAAX Inc.	324
Health Care Corporation of St. John's	267	Manitoba Hydro	328
Health Sciences Centre	268	Manitoba Pool Elevators	328
Helijet Airways Inc.	268	Manitoba Public Insurance Corporation	329
Hoffman-La Roche Limited	272	Maritime Life Assurance Company, The	331
Holiday Inn Select Toronto Airport	272	Marshall Macklin Monaghan Ltd.	333
Holland College	273	Marystown Shipyard Limited	334
Home Oil Co. Ltd.	273	McGraw Hill Ryerson Ltd.	337
Homewood Corp.	274	McInnes Cooper & Robertson	337
Honda Canada Inc.	274	McKay-Cocker Construction Limited	338
Honeywell Ltd.	275	Mediacom Inc.	340
Horseshoe Resort Corporation	275	Metro Toronto Convention Centre	342
Hôtel Dieu de Montréal	276	Michaels of Canada Inc.	345
Housesitters Canada, The	277	Midland Walwyn Inc.	345
Hub Meat Packers Ltd.	278	Minas Basin Pulp and Power Company Ltd.	347
Hubbell Canada Inc.	278	Ministry of Northern Develop. and Mines	348
Hudon & Deaudelin Ltée	279	Mississauga, City of	349
Hudson's Bay Company, The	279	Mitel Corporation	350
Huronia Regional Centre	280	Moosehead Breweries Limited	354
Husky Energy Inc.	281	Mustang Survival Corp.	358
Hydro Electric Commission of Thunder Bay	281	National Grocers Co. Ltd.	360
Hydro Mississauga Corporation	282	National Life	361
Hydro Québec	283	National Sports Centre	362
I M P Group International Inc.	283	Neles Automation, Scada Solutions Ltd.	362
ICI Canada Inc.	285	Nelvana Limited	363
Ilco Unican Inc.	286	Nesbitt Burns Inc.	364
Imprimerie Interweb Inc.	287	Nestle Canada Inc.	364
Industrial-Alliance Life Insurance Company	289	Newfoundland and Labrador Credit Union	367
Industries Lassonde Inc.	289	Nissan Canada Inc.	371
ING Canada Financial Services International	291	North American Life Assurance Company	373
InterOne Marketing Group	293	North West Company Inc.	374
IPL Energy Inc.	294	North York Community Care Access Centre	374
Island Telecom Inc.	295	Northern Lights Regional Health Centre	375
Ivaco Inc.	296	Northwestel Inc.	376
IWK Grace Health Centre	297	Norwich Union Life Insurance Society	376
Izaak Walton Killam Hospital, The	297	Nova Scotia Liquor Commission	377
J.D. Irving Limited	298	Nova Scotia Power Corp.	377
John P. Robarts Research Institute	302	Novartis Consumer Health Canada Inc.	378
Johnson Incorporated	303	Numac Energy Inc.	379
Kelowna, City of	305	Oceanis Seafoods Ltd.	380
Keyano College	306	Ocelot Energy Inc.	381
Kitchener, City of	309	Omstead Foods Limited	383
Kodak Canada Inc.	309	Ontario Jockey Club, The	384
La Confiserie Comete Ltee	311	Ontario March of Dimes	385
Laidlaw Inc.	312	Oracle Corp. Canada Inc.	386
Leduc, City of	313	Ottawa Hospital	386
Leica Geosystems Canada Inc.	314	Owen Bird	387
Leon's Manufacturing Company Inc.	316	Paramount Canada's Wonderland Inc.	389

The Canada Student Employment Guide

College Index

PavCo	391	Siemens Electric Ltd.	460
PCL Constructors Inc.	392	Signature Vacations Inc.	460
Pearson Education Canada	393	Skiing Louise Ltd.	461
Peel Board of Education	393	Slocan Forest Products Ltd.	462
Peel Children's Centre	394	Sodexho Marriott Services Canada	464
Peel Regional Police	394	Southam Inc.	466
Pembina Pipeline Corporation	395	Spar Aerospace Limited	467
PennCorp Life Insurance Company	396	Spectra Premium Industries	468
Petromont & Co. Ltd. Partnership	397	Speedware Corp. Inc.	469
Pharma Plus Drugmarts Ltd.	398	St. Amant Centre Inc.	471
Pitney Bowes of Canada Ltd.	401	St. Joseph's Care Group	472
Pizza Pizza Ltd.	401	St. Lawrence Seaway Mgmt. Corp., The	473
Poco Petroleums Ltd.	402	Standard Knitting Limited	474
Polygram Group Canada Inc.	403	Stanley Canada Inc.	475
Positron Industries Inc.	404	Steelcraft Industries Ltd.	477
Providence Centre	412	Sterling Marking Products Inc.	478
Prudential Insurance Co. of America, The	412	Stone Consolidated Inc.	479
QEII Health Sciences Centre	414	Sudbury Regional Hospital	480
QIT-Fer et Titane Inc.	414	Sun Peaks Resort Corporation	481
Raymond Rebar Inc.	418	Sun Rype Products Ltd.	481
Reader's Digest Association of Canada Ltd.	419	Sundog Printing Limited	482
Recochem Inc.	420	Surrey, City of	484
Regal Constellation Hotel Ltd.	422	Sydney Steel Corporation	485
Regina Health District	423	Symantec Corporation	486
Rehabilitation Institute of Toronto	425	TD Waterhouse Investor Services (Canada)	488
Revenue Properties Company Limited	429	Telus Corporation	492
Rhone-Poulenc Canada Inc.	430	The Garland Group	494
Richmond, City of	431	Thomas & Betts Ltée	495
Riverside Fabricating Ltd.	433	Thompson's Moving and Storage	496
Riverside Hospital of Ottawa, The	434	Timmins, City of	499
Rogers AT&T Wireless Inc.	436	Today's Business Products Ltd.	500
Rothmans, Benson and Hedges Inc.	437	Toronto and Region Conservation Authority	501
Royal & Sun Alliance Insurance Co. of Cda	437	Toronto Catholic District School Board	502
Royal Canadian Mint	438	Toronto Cricket Skating & Curling	502
Royal Inland Hospital	439	Toronto General Hospital	505
Royal Philips Electronics	439	Toronto Police Service	506
Ryerson Polytechnic University	441	Toronto Sun Publishing Corp., The	507
Saan Stores Ltd.	441	Toshiba of Canada Ltd.	508
Salisbury House of Canada Ltd.	442	Toyota Canada Ltd.	509
Sandman Hotels and Inns	443	Trow Consulting Engineers Ltd.	511
Saskatchewan Economic Development	445	TSC Stores Ltd.	512
Saskatchewan Government Insurance	445	University College of Cape Breton	516
Saskatchewan Wheat Pool	447	VIA Rail Canada Inc.	521
SaskTel	449	Waverly & York Corporation	525
Scarborough General Hospital	450	Weldco-Beales Manufacturing Inc.	527
SCIEX MDS Health Group	452	West Coast Apparel	528
Seprotech Systems Incorporated	454	West Kootenay Power Ltd.	528
Shaw Communications	455	Westbury Life	529
Shaw Industries Ltd.	455	Westcliff Management Ltd.	529
Sheraton Fallsview Hotel	456	Westcoast Energy Inc.	530
Sherbrooke Community Centre	457	Western Glove Works	530
Shermag Inc.	457	Westin Prince Hotel, The	531
Shoppers Drug Mart Limited	458	Westinghouse Canada Inc.	532
Shorewood Packaging Corp. of Canada Ltd.	459	WestJet Airlines	532

The Canada Student Employment Guide

College Index   603

Weyerhaeuser Company Limited	535	National Grocers Co. Ltd.	360
Whistler Blackcomb Mountain	535	National Sports Centre	362
Windsor, City of	538	Nelvana Limited	363
Winners Apparel Ltd.	539	Northern Lights Regional Health Centre	375
Winpak Ltd.	539	Ontario Jockey Club, The	384
Yarmouth Regional Hospital	543	Paladin Security & Investigations Limited	388
Yellowknife, City of	544	Paramount Canada's Wonderland Inc.	389
Zellers Inc.	546	Peel Regional Police	394
Zenastra	547	Pool People Ltd.	404
Zenon Environmental Inc.	547	Regional Municipality of Niagara	424
		Ryerson Polytechnic University	441
		Sandman Hotels and Inns	443

Security/Law Enforcement

		Sheraton Toronto East Hotel and Towers	456
		Skiing Louise Ltd.	461
Acadia University	78	St. Lawrence Parks Commission	472
Alberta Gaming & Liquor Commission	90	State Farm Insurance Companies	476
AMEC Inc.	99	Surrey, City of	484
Apex Land Corp.	103	Sydney Steel Corporation	485
Atlantic Wholesalers Ltd.	114	The Barn Fruit Markets Inc.	493
Baycrest Centre for Geriatric Care	123	Tiger Brand Knitting Company Limited	498
Bell Mobility	131	Toronto General Hospital	505
Brandon, City of	146	Toronto Police Service	506
Brookfield Properties Corporation	150	Toronto Sun Publishing Corp., The	507
Burns International Security Services Ltd.	154	Toronto Zoo	507
Cadith Entertainment Ltd.	156	Toronto, City of	508
Canada Post Corporation	162	Winners Apparel Ltd.	539
Canadian Broadcasting Corporation	164	York Regional Police	545
Canadian Depository for Securities Ltd.	166		
Canadian Museum of Civilization Corp.	167		
Canadian Western Bank	169	## Social Work	
Cape Breton Development Corporation	174		
Carte International Inc.	176	1-800-GOT-JUNK?	74
Casa Loma	177	Addictions Foundation of Manitoba, The	81
Children's Hospital of Eastern Ontario	189	Alberta Alcohol and Drug Abuse Commission	87
Columbia House	197	Atlantic Blue Cross Care	113
Coquitlam, City of	204	Central Park Lodges Ltd.	181
Corner Brook, City of	205	Christian Horizons	190
DaimlerChrysler Canada Ltd.	211	Coquitlam, City of	204
Economical Insurance Group, The	227	Deer Lodge Centre Inc.	213
Grant MacEwen Community College	258	Peel Children's Centre	394
Health Sciences Centre	268	QEII Health Sciences Centre	414
Holiday Inn Select Toronto Airport	272	Reena	421
Homewood Corp.	274	Regional Municipality of Niagara	424
Hydro Québec	283	Sudbury Regional Hospital	480
Intercon Security Ltd.	292	Swift Current Health District	485
IWK Grace Health Centre	297	Weyerhaeuser Company Limited	535
Jim Pattison Group	301		
Kitchener, City of	309		
Leduc, City of	313	## Statistics	
Litton Systems Canada Ltd.	320		
Metro Toronto Convention Centre	342	ABC Group	76
Metro Toronto West Detention Centre	343	Acklands-Grainger Inc.	80
Minas Basin Pulp and Power Company Ltd.	347	AGF Management Limited	83
Mitel Corporation	350	BBM Bureau of Measurement	125

The Canada Student Employment Guide

College Index

Bloorview MacMillan Centre, The	140	Michaels of Canada Inc.	345
Calgary, City of	158	Monarch Communications Inc.	353
Canada Safeway Limited	163	Nielsen Marketing Research	370
Canadian Dairy Commission	165	Okanagan Skeena Group Limited	382
CH2M Gore and Storrie Limited	185	Ontario Jockey Club, The	384
Columbia House	197	Paramount Canada's Wonderland Inc.	389
Coquitlam, City of	204	Peel Regional Police	394
Corner Brook, City of	205	Pelmorex Inc.	395
David Thompson Health Region	212	Polygram Group Canada Inc.	403
Gienow Building Products Ltd.	251	Shaw Communications	455
Hasbro Canada Inc.	266	Shopping Channel, The	459
Home Oil Co. Ltd.	273	Sony Music Canada	465
Kodak Canada Inc.	309	Sportsco International	469
Liberty Health	318	Toronto Sun Publishing Corp., The	507
Maritime Life Assurance Company, The	331	YTV Canada Inc.	545
National Life	361		
News Marketing Canada	368		
Nielsen Marketing Research	370	## Travel/Tourism	
Paramount Canada's Wonderland Inc.	389		
Peel Regional Police	394	Air Canada	85
Pricewaterhouse Coopers	409	Air Nova Inc.	86
Reader's Digest Association of Canada Ltd.	419	Air Ontario Inc.	86
Richmond, City of	431	American Airlines Inc.	99
Rogers AT&T Wireless Inc.	436	Arctic Co-operatives Limited	107
Royal & Sun Alliance Insurance Co. of Cda	437	Atlantic Blue Cross Care	113
Saan Stores Ltd.	441	Banff Centre for Continuing Education, The	120
Saskatchewan Government Insurance	445	Bearskin Lake Air Service Ltd.	128
Sherwood Credit Union	458	Best Western Carlton Place Hotel	133
Signature Vacations Inc.	460	Blue Mountain Resorts Limited	141
Thompson's Moving and Storage	496	Cambridge Suites	159
Toronto Hydro	505	Capilano Suspension Bridge	174
Toronto Sun Publishing Corp., The	507	Carlson Marketing Group Canada Ltd.	176
Toyota Canada Ltd.	509	Casa Loma	177
Westbury Life	529	Corner Brook, City of	205
Weyerhaeuser Company Limited	535	Delta Hotels	215
Winners Apparel Ltd.	539	Economic Development Edmonton	226
		Explorer Hotel, The	236
		Federated Co-operatives Limited	239
## Television/Radio		Grant MacEwen Community College	258
		Grouse Mountain Resorts Ltd.	260
Access Communications	78	Halifax Regional Municipality	263
Assiniboine Community College	109	Helijet Airways Inc.	268
Banff Centre for Continuing Education, The	120	Holiday Inn Select Toronto Airport	272
BBM Bureau of Measurement	125	Horseshoe Resort Corporation	275
Canadian Broadcasting Corporation	164	Housesitters Canada, The	277
Casa Loma	177	Metro Toronto Convention Centre	342
CFCF Inc.	183	National Grocers Co. Ltd.	360
CFCN Communications Inc.	184	Niagara Parks Commission, The	369
Columbia House	197	Panorama Mountain Village	388
Gimbel Eye Centre	252	Paramount Canada's Wonderland Inc.	389
Hasbro Canada Inc.	266	Regal Constellation Hotel Ltd.	422
Hill & Knowlton Canada Ltd.	270	Rimrock Resort Hotel	432
Jim Pattison Group	301	Sandman Hotels and Inns	443
McLaren-McCann Advertising of Canada Ltd.	338	Science North	452

The Canada Student Employment Guide

Sheraton Fallsview Hotel	456	Behlen Industries	130
Sheraton Toronto East Hotel and Towers	456	Blue Mountain Resorts Limited	141
Signature Vacations Inc.	460	Bonus Resource Services Corp.	144
Skiing Louise Ltd.	461	Bosal Canada Inc.	145
St. Lawrence Parks Commission	472	Brandon, City of	146
Sun Peaks Resort Corporation	481	Coquitlam, City of	204
Surrey, City of	484	DaimlerChrysler Canada Ltd.	211
Thomas Cook Group (Canada) Ltd.	495	EnerFlex Systems Ltd.	232
Toronto and Region Conservation Authority	501	Farmers Co-operative Dairy Limited	239
Toronto Cricket Skating & Curling	502	Finning	240
Vacances Air Transat Inc.	518	Flint Energy Services Ltd.	243
Waterloo Inn	525	MDS Nordion	339
Westin Prince Hotel, The	531	Raymond Rebar Inc.	418
WestJet Airlines	532	Regional Municipality of Niagara	424
Whistler Blackcomb Mountain	535	Spectra Premium Industries	468
World of Vacations Ltd.	541	Sportsco International	469
		Steelcraft Industries Ltd.	477
		Steelpipe Ltd.	477
		The Garland Group	494

Urban Planning

Calgary Co-operative Association Limited	157
Calgary, City of	158
Canadian Western Bank	169
CH2M Gore and Storrie Limited	185
Coquitlam, City of	204
Corner Brook, City of	205
Giffels Associates Limited	251
Goodman and Carr	255
Halifax Regional Municipality	263
Kitchener, City of	309
Leduc, City of	313
Marshall Macklin Monaghan Ltd.	333
National Grocers Co. Ltd.	360
Peel Board of Education	393
Prince Albert, City of	410
Prince George, City of	410
Proctor and Redfern Ltd.	411
Public Utilities of Kingston	413
Richmond, City of	431
SaskTel	449
St. Lawrence Seaway Mgmt. Corp., The	473
Surrey, City of	484
Timmins, City of	499
Toronto and Region Conservation Authority	501
Toronto, City of	508
Urban Systems Ltd.	516
Yellowknife, City of	544

Welding

Yellowknife, City of	544
Air Liquide Canada Inc.	85
Basic Technologies Corporation1	22

University Index

Below are some of the most popular University Degree Programs in Canada. Use the University Index to find employers listed by the academic areas they consider important in the selection of candidates. The corresponding page number of the firm's profile is also shown.

Bachelor of Arts

Business	607
Criminology	611
Economics	611
English	613
Fine Arts	614
General	614
Gerontology	616
History	616
Journalism	617
Languages	617
Music	618
Philosophy	618
Political Science	618
Psychology	618
Public Relations	620
Recreation Studies	621
Sociology/Social Work	622
Statistics	623
Urban Geography	623

Bachelor of Commerce/Admin.

Accounting	624
Finance	629
General	634
Human Resources	637
Marketing	638
Information Management	642
Public Administration	646

Bachelor of Science

Actuarial	646
Agriculture	647
Biology	647
Chemistry	648
Computer Science	650
Environmental Studies	653
Food Science	655
Forestry	655
General	656
Geography	657
Health Science	657
Horticulture	658
Kinesiology	658
Mathematics	659
Microbiology	660
Nursing (RN)	660
Occupational Therapy	661
Pharmacy	662
Physics	663
Physiotherapy	663
Psychology	664
Zoology	665

Bachelor of Laws

Corporate	665
General	666
Real Estate	666

Bachelor of Engineering

Biomedical	666
Chemical	667
Civil	668
Computer Systems	669
Design	672
Electrical	673
Environmental Studies	676
General	677
Geotechnical	678
Industrial	678
Materials Science	680
Mechanical	680
Mining	683
Transportaton	683

University Index

Water Resources	684
Bachelor of Architecture	684
Bachelor of Landscape Architecture	684

Bachelor of Education

Adult Education	685
Childhood	685
General	686
Physical	686
Special	686

Masters

Arts	687
Business Administration	687
Education	691
Engineering	691
Library Science	694
Science	694

Doctorate 696

Bachelor of Arts

Business

1-800-GOT-JUNK?	74
A E McKenzie Co. Inc.	75
ABC Group	76
Aberdeen Hospital	77
Abitibi-Consolidated Inc.	77
Accucaps Industries Limited	79
ACE INI Insurance	79
Acklands-Grainger Inc.	80
ADT Canada Inc.	82
AGF Management Limited	83
Air Nova Inc.	86
Akita Drilling Ltd.	87
Alberta Blue Cross	88
Alberta Energy & Utilities Board	89
Alberta Gaming & Liquor Commission	90
Alberto Culver Canada Inc.	90
Alexandra Hospital	91
Algoma Steel Inc.	93
Allianz Canada	95
Allstate Insurance Co. of Canada	96
Alpine Oil Service Corporation	96
Amcan Castings Limited	98
Amcor Twinpak North America Inc.	98
American Airlines Inc.	99
Amram's Distributing Ltd.	100
Andersen Consulting	101
Anthony Insurance Inc.	102
Apex Land Corp.	103
Arbor Memorial Services Inc.	106
Armor Personnel	107
Assiniboine Community College	109
ATCO Frontec Corp.	111
ATCO Gas Services Ltd.	112
Atlantic Blue Cross Care	113
Atlantic Lottery Corporation Inc.	113
Atlantic Packaging Products Ltd.	114
Atlantic Wholesalers Ltd.	114
Atlas Ideal Metals Inc.	115
Atlas Van Lines (Canada) Ltd.	115
ATS Automation Tooling Systems Inc.	116
Aurum Ceramic Dental Laboratories Ltd.	117
AXA Insurance (Canada)	118
Axidata Inc.	118
Banff Centre for Continuing Education, The	120
Barton Place Long Term Care Facility	121
BASF Canada Inc.	122
Bayer Inc.	124
BBM Bureau of Measurement	125
BC Hydro	125
BC Telecom Inc.	126
BCG Services	127
Bell Mobility	131
Belleville General Hospital	132
Best Western Carlton Place Hotel	133
Bethesda Hospital	134
Bettis Canada Ltd.	135
BFGoodrich Landing Gear Division	135
Bic Inc.	136
Birks Jewelry	138
Black Photo Corporation	139
Blue Giant Equipment of Canada Ltd.	141
Blue Mountain Resorts Limited	141
Blue Wave Seafoods Inc.	142
Boréal Assurances Inc.	144
BOVAR Waste Management	145
Bowater Mersey Paper Company Limited	146
Brandon, City of	146
Brewers Retail Inc.	148
British Columbia Ferry Corporation	149
Brookfield Properties Corporation	150
Browning Harvey Limited	150
Buckeye Canada Inc.	151
Burger King Restaurants of Canada Inc.	153
C.S.T. Consultants Inc.	155
Cabre Exploration Ltd.	156
Cadith Entertainment Ltd.	156

The Canada Student Employment Guide

University Index

Calgary Co-operative Association Limited	157	Directwest Publishers Ltd.	217
Canada Games Aquatic Centre	162	Druxy's Inc.	219
Canada Post Corporation	162	Duha Color Services	220
Canada Safeway Limited	163	Dun & Bradstreet Canada	221
Canadian Cancer Society	164	Dylex Limited	222
Canadian Commercial Corp.	165	Dynasty Furniture Manufacturing Ltd.	224
Canadian Dairy Commission	165	Economic Development Edmonton	226
Canadian Depository for Securities Ltd.	166	Economical Insurance Group, The	227
Canadian General Tower Limited	166	EDS of Canada Ltd.	228
Canadian National Institute For The Blind	167	Eli Lilly Canada Inc.	230
Canadian Tire Corporation Ltd.	169	Emco Limited	230
Canadian Western Bank	169	EMJ Data Systems Ltd.	231
Cancarb Limited	170	Endpoint Research Ltd.	231
CancerCare Manitoba	171	EnerFlex Systems Ltd.	232
Cancore Industries Inc.	171	Entreprises Premier Canadien Ltée	232
Canon Canada Inc.	172	Exfo	235
Capilano Suspension Bridge	174	Exide Canada Inc.	235
Carbone of America (LCL) Ltd.	175	Explorer Hotel, The	236
Carte International Inc.	176	Export Development Corporation	236
Casa Loma	177	Extendicare (Canada) Inc.	237
CCL Industries Inc.	178	Farm Credit Corp. Canada	238
Celestica International Inc.	179	Farmers Co-operative Dairy Limited	239
Centra Gas British Columbia Inc.	180	Federated Co-operatives Limited	239
CFCF Inc.	183	Finning	240
CGU Group Canada Ltd.	185	Fishery Products International	241
Charlottetown Driving Park	187	Flakeboard Company Limited	242
Chilliwack General Hospital	189	Flint Energy Services Ltd.	243
Christian Horizons	190	Forzani Group Ltd., The	244
Cineplex Odeon Corporation	191	Friesens Corporation	246
Citibank Canada	191	Future Shop Ltd.	246
CKF Inc.	192	Gallup Canada Inc.	247
Cobourg District General Hospital	194	Gay Lea Foods Co-Operative Ltd.	247
Coca Cola Foods Canada Inc.	195	General Chemical Canada Ltd.	249
Cognis Canada Corporation	195	General Electric Canada Inc.	249
Columbia House	197	Gienow Building Products Ltd.	251
COM DEV International	197	Gilbey Canada Inc.	252
Comcare Health Services	198	Gimbel Eye Centre	252
Community Savings Credit Union	199	Glaxo Wellcome Canada	253
Compaq Canada Inc.	199	Glentel Inc.	254
Compu-Quote Inc.	200	Goodman and Carr	255
Computer Associates Canada Ltd.	201	Goodwill Industries of Toronto	256
Connors Bros, Limited	203	Goodyear Canada Inc.	256
Coquitlam, City of	204	Grand & Toy Ltd.	257
Corner Brook, City of	205	Grant MacEwen Community College	258
Cornwall Electric	206	Grant Thornton	258
Cotton Ginny Ltd.	207	Great-West Life Assurance Company, The	259
Cougar Helicopters Inc.	208	Groupe Savoie Inc.	260
Credit Union Central of Canada	208	Halifax County Regional Rehabilitation Centre	263
Culinar Inc.	209	Halifax Regional Municipality	263
Custom Trim Ltd.	210	Halifax Water Commission	264
D.H. Howden	211	Hasbro Canada Inc.	266
David Thompson Health Region	212	Health Care Corporation of St. John's	267
Dell Computer Corporation	214	Hoffman-La Roche Limited	272
Delta Toronto Airport Hotel	216	Holiday Inn Select Toronto Airport	272

The Canada Student Employment Guide

University Index

Home Oil Co. Ltd.	273
Homewood Corp.	274
Honda Canada Inc.	274
Honeywell Ltd.	275
HSBC Bank Canada	277
Hubbell Canada Inc.	278
Hudon & Deaudelin Ltée	279
Hudson's Bay Company, The	279
Huronia Regional Centre	280
Hydro Electric Commission of Thunder Bay	281
Hydro One Inc.	282
I M P Group International Inc.	283
IBM Canada Ltd.	284
Indalex Limited	288
Industrial Equipment Co. Ltd.	288
Industrial-Alliance Life Insurance Company	289
ING Canada Financial Services International	291
Insurance Corp. of B.C.	291
Intercon Security Ltd.	292
Interforest Ltd.	292
Interior Savings Credit Union	293
InterOne Marketing Group	293
Island Savings Credit Union	295
Island Telecom Inc.	295
J.D. Irving Limited	298
James Richardson International Limited	300
Jim Pattison Group	301
Johnson Incorporated	303
Jostens Canada Ltd.	303
Kelowna, City of	305
Kennametal Ltd.	305
KFC Canada	307
Kimberly-Clark Inc.	307
Kitchener, City of	309
Kodak Canada Inc.	309
Kraft Canada Inc.	310
Krug Inc.	310
La Confiserie Comete Ltee	311
Laidlaw Inc.	312
Leduc, City of	313
Lego Canada Inc.	314
Leica Geosystems Canada Inc.	314
Lenbrook Industries Limited	315
Leo Burnett Co. Ltd.	315
Les Distilleries Corby Ltée	317
Les Modes Smart Inc.	318
Liberty Health	318
Lick's Ice Cream & Burger Shops Inc.	319
Lifetouch Canada Inc.	319
M. McGrawth Canada Limited	324
Mactac Canada Ltd.	326
Magna International Inc.	327
Manitoba Hydro	328
Manitoba Public Insurance Corporation	329
Marcam Canada	330
Marine Atlantic Inc.	331
Maritime Life Assurance Company, The	331
Mark Anthony Group Inc.	332
Marks & Spencer Canada Inc.	332
McBee Systems of Canada Inc.	336
McCarney Greenwood	336
McInnes Cooper & Robertson	337
McLaren-McCann Advertising of Canada Ltd.	338
MDS Nordion	339
Mediasynergy	340
Metro Toronto Convention Centre	342
Metroland Printing, Publishing & Dist. Ltd.	343
Metropolitan Life Insurance Company	344
Meyers Norris Penny & Co.	344
Michaels of Canada Inc.	345
Midland Walwyn Inc.	345
Midwest Food Products Inc.	346
Minas Basin Pulp and Power Company Ltd.	347
Moen Inc.	352
Moffat Communications Limited	352
Montreal Trust Co.	353
Morrison Hershfield Limited	354
MOSAID Technologies Inc.	355
Motorola Canada Ltd.	356
Mountain Equipment Co-op	356
MSM Transportation Inc.	357
N B S Card Services	359
Nanaimo Credit Union	359
National Grocers Co. Ltd.	360
National Life	361
National Sports Centre	362
Neles Automation, Scada Solutions Ltd.	362
Nelvana Limited	363
Nesbitt Burns Inc.	364
Nestle Canada Inc.	364
New Holland Canada Ltd.	366
Newfoundland and Labrador Credit Union	367
Newfoundland and Labrador Hydro	367
News Marketing Canada	368
Nielsen Marketing Research	370
Nissan Canada Inc.	371
Norbord Industries	372
North American Life Assurance Company	373
North West Company Inc.	374
Northern Mountain Helicopters Inc.	375
Northwestel Inc.	376
Norwich Union Life Insurance Society	376
Novartis Consumer Health Canada Inc.	378
Novotel Canada Inc.	378
Numac Energy Inc.	379
Nygard International Ltd.	380
Ocelot Energy Inc.	381
Oland Breweries Limited	382

The Canada Student Employment Guide

610 University Index

Omstead Foods Limited	383	Salisbury House of Canada Ltd.	442
Ontario Guard Services Inc.	383	Sandman Hotels and Inns	443
Ontario Jockey Club, The	384	Sara Lee Corporation of Canada Limited	444
Ontario Legislative Offices	384	Saskatchewan Centre of the Arts	444
Oracle Corp. Canada Inc.	386	Saskatchewan Government Insurance	445
Paramount Canada's Wonderland Inc.	389	Saskatchewan Wheat Pool	447
Paul Revere Life Insurance Company, The	391	Saskatoon, City of	448
PavCo	391	Saskferco Products Inc.	448
PCL Constructors Inc.	392	SaskTel	449
Peacock Inc.	392	Scarborough General Hospital	450
Pearson Education Canada	393	Schlumberger Canada Ltd.	450
Peel Board of Education	393	Sharp Electronics of Canada Ltd.	454
Peel Regional Police	394	Shaw Communications	455
Pelmorex Inc.	395	Sheraton Fallsview Hotel	456
PennCorp Life Insurance Company	396	Shoppers Drug Mart Limited	458
Pharma Plus Drugmarts Ltd.	398	Shorewood Packaging Corp. of Canada Ltd.	459
Pilot Insurance Company	399	Siemens Electric Ltd.	460
Pine Falls Paper Company Limited	400	Signature Vacations Inc.	460
Pitney Bowes of Canada Ltd.	401	Silicon Graphics Canada Inc.	461
Pizza Pizza Ltd.	401	Skiing Louise Ltd.	461
Poco Petroleums Ltd.	402	Slocan Forest Products Ltd.	462
Pollack Rentals Limited	403	Sobeys Inc.	463
Polygram Group Canada Inc.	403	Sony Music Canada	465
Potacan Mining Company	405	Southam Inc.	466
Power Measurement Ltd.	406	Southern Railway of British Columbia Ltd.	466
PPG Canada Inc.	407	Southland Canada	467
Premdor Inc.	408	Spectrum Signal Processing Inc.	468
Progressive Financial Strategy	411	Sportsco International	469
Prudential Insurance Co. of America, The	412	St. Joseph's Care Group	472
Public Utilities of Kingston	413	St. Lawrence Parks Commission	472
Purolator Courier Ltd.	413	St. Lawrence Seaway Mgmt. Corp., The	473
QEII Health Sciences Centre	414	St. Vincent's Hospitals	473
Quesnel River Pulp Company	416	Stanley Canada Inc.	475
Rasco Specialty Metals Inc.	417	State Farm Insurance Companies	476
Raymond Industrial Equipment Ltd.	418	Sterling Marking Products Inc.	478
Ready Bake Foods Inc.	420	Stitches	478
Red Deer Co-op Limited	421	Sudbury Regional Hospital	480
Regal Constellation Hotel Ltd.	422	Sun Rype Products Ltd.	481
Regal Greeting and Gifts	423	Sundog Printing Limited	482
Revenue Properties Company Limited	429	Sunoco Inc.	482
Reynolds and Reynolds (Canada) Limited	430	Supreme Tooling Group	483
Rhone-Poulenc Canada Inc.	430	Surrey, City of	484
Richmond, City of	431	Symantec Corporation	486
Richter Usher & Vineberg	432	Talisman Energy Inc.	487
Rimrock Resort Hotel	432	TCG International Inc.	487
Riverside Fabricating Ltd.	433	TCT Logistics	488
Rogers AT&T Wireless Inc.	436	TD Waterhouse Investor Services (Canada)	488
Rogers Media, Publishing	436	Teck Corp.	489
Rothmans, Benson and Hedges Inc.	437	Teklogix Inc.	489
Royal & Sun Alliance Insurance Co. of Cda	437	Teldon International Inc.	490
Royal Bank of Canada	438	Telebec Ltée	490
Royal Victoria Hospital	440	Telegraph Journal	491
Ryerson Polytechnic University	441	Telus Corporation	492
Sales & Merchandising Group	442	The Arthritis Society	492

University Index

The Barn Fruit Markets Inc.	493
The Co-operators	493
The Garland Group	494
Thomas & Betts Ltée	495
Thompson's Moving and Storage	496
Ticketmaster Canada Inc.	498
Tiger Brand Knitting Company Limited	498
Today's Business Products Ltd.	500
Toronto East General Hospital	503
Toronto General Hospital	505
Toronto Police Service	506
Toronto Sun Publishing Corp., The	507
Toronto, City of	508
Toshiba of Canada Ltd.	508
Toyota Canada Ltd.	509
TSC Stores Ltd.	512
Unisys Canada Inc.	514
University College of Cape Breton	516
US Filter BCP	517
Valley First Credit Union	518
Vancouver International Airport	520
Vancouver Sun	520
VIA Rail Canada Inc.	521
Volvo Cars of Canada Ltd.	523
W C I Canada Inc.	524
Waterloo Furniture Components Ltd.	524
Wendy's Restaurants of Canada Inc.	527
West Kootenay Power Ltd.	528
Westbury Life	529
Westcliff Management Ltd.	529
Westcoast Energy Inc.	530
Western Glove Works	530
Westinghouse Canada Inc.	532
WestJet Airlines	532
Westminster Savings Credit Union	533
Weston Produce Inc.	533
Weyerhaeuser Company Limited	535
Whistler Blackcomb Mountain	535
White Rose Crafts and Nursery Sales Limited	536
Wilson Auto Electric Ltd.	538
Windsor, City of	538
Winners Apparel Ltd.	539
Winpak Ltd.	539
XCAN Grain Pool Ltd.	541
Yanke Group of Companies	543
Yellowknife, City of	544
YFactor	544
YTV Canada Inc.	545
Zellers Inc.	546
Zenon Environmental Inc.	547

Criminology

Brandon, City of	146
Calgary, City of	158
CGU Group Canada Ltd.	185
Columbia House	197
Grant MacEwen Community College	258
Insurance Corp. of B.C.	291
Intercon Security Ltd.	292
Les Centres Jeunesse de Montréal	316
Loss Prevention Group Inc.	322
M. McGrawth Canada Limited	324
McInnes Cooper & Robertson	337
News Marketing Canada	368
Niagara Parks Commission, The	369
Ontario Guard Services Inc.	383
Paladin Security & Investigations Limited	388
Paramount Canada's Wonderland Inc.	389
Peel Regional Police	394
Pharma Plus Drugmarts Ltd.	398
Saskatchewan Government Insurance	445
Saskatoon, City of	448
State Farm Insurance Companies	476
Toronto Police Service	506
Yellowknife, City of	544
York Regional Police	545

Economics

1-800-GOT-JUNK?	74
A E McKenzie Co. Inc.	75
Abitibi-Consolidated Inc.	77
Acklands-Grainger Inc.	80
AGF Management Limited	83
Agricultural Credit Corp. of Saskatchewan	84
Alberta Blue Cross	88
Alberta Energy & Utilities Board	89
Alberta Gaming & Liquor Commission	90
Algoma Steel Inc.	93
Allstate Insurance Co. of Canada	96
Amcan Castings Limited	98
Amcor Twinpak North America Inc.	98
American Airlines Inc.	99
Assiniboine Community College	109
Atlantic Blue Cross Care	113
Atlantic Packaging Products Ltd.	114
Atlas Ideal Metals Inc.	115
ATS Automation Tooling Systems Inc.	116
AXA Insurance (Canada)	118
Barton Place Long Term Care Facility	121
BASF Canada Inc.	122
Bell Mobility	131
BFGoodrich Landing Gear Division	135

The Canada Student Employment Guide

612 University Index

Black Photo Corporation	139	Island Telecom Inc.	295
Blue Giant Equipment of Canada Ltd.	141	Jim Pattison Group	301
British Columbia Ferry Corporation	149	Kimberly-Clark Inc.	307
Budd Canada Inc.	152	Kitchener, City of	309
Cabre Exploration Ltd.	156	Kraft Canada Inc.	310
Cadith Entertainment Ltd.	156	La Confiserie Comete Ltee	311
Canada Post Corporation	162	Laidlaw Inc.	312
Canadian Commercial Corp.	165	Les Distilleries Corby Ltée	317
Canadian Dairy Commission	165	Liberty Health	318
Canadian Depository for Securities Ltd.	166	Lifetouch Canada Inc.	319
Canadian Occidental Petroleum Ltd.	168	M. McGrawth Canada Limited	324
Canadian Western Bank	169	Manitoba Hydro	328
Canon Canada Inc.	172	McCarney Greenwood	336
Cineplex Odeon Corporation	191	McLaren-McCann Advertising of Canada Ltd.	338
Citibank Canada	191	Metropolitan Life Insurance Company	344
Cobourg District General Hospital	194	Meyers Norris Penny & Co.	344
Columbia House	197	Michaels of Canada Inc.	345
Compaq Canada Inc.	199	Midland Walwyn Inc.	345
Computer Associates Canada Ltd.	201	Ministry of Northern Develop. and Mines	348
Coquitlam, City of	204	Montreal Trust Co.	353
Corner Brook, City of	205	Motorola Canada Ltd.	356
Credit Union Central of Canada	208	Nanaimo Credit Union	359
Crestar Energy Inc.	209	National Life	361
Dun & Bradstreet Canada	221	Neles Automation, Scada Solutions Ltd.	362
Dylex Limited	222	Neptune Food Suppliers Ltd.	363
Economic Development Edmonton	226	Nesbitt Burns Inc.	364
Economical Insurance Group, The	227	Newfoundland and Labrador Credit Union	367
Eli Lilly Canada Inc.	230	News Marketing Canada	368
EMJ Data Systems Ltd.	231	Nielsen Marketing Research	370
EnerFlex Systems Ltd.	232	North American Life Assurance Company	373
Exfo	235	Norwich Union Life Insurance Society	376
Extendicare (Canada) Inc.	237	Numac Energy Inc.	379
Fishery Products International	241	Ocelot Energy Inc.	381
Friesens Corporation	246	Paul Revere Life Insurance Company, The	391
Future Shop Ltd.	246	Pitney Bowes of Canada Ltd.	401
Gay Lea Foods Co-Operative Ltd.	247	Poco Petroleums Ltd.	402
Goodman and Carr	255	Powell Equipment Ltd.	405
Grant MacEwen Community College	258	PPG Canada Inc.	407
Grant Thornton	258	Premdor Inc.	408
Great-West Life Assurance Company, The	259	Progressive Financial Strategy	411
Hasbro Canada Inc.	266	Prudential Insurance Co. of America, The	412
Home Oil Co. Ltd.	273	Rasco Specialty Metals Inc.	417
Honda Canada Inc.	274	Regal Capital Planners Ltd.	422
Honeywell Ltd.	275	Reuters Information Services (Canada) Ltd.	428
Household Movers & Shippers Limited	276	Rhone-Poulenc Canada Inc.	430
HSBC Bank Canada	277	Rogers AT&T Wireless Inc.	436
Hydro One Inc.	282	Royal & Sun Alliance Insurance Co. of Cda	437
Hydro Québec	283	Royal Bank of Canada	438
IBM Canada Ltd.	284	Saskatchewan Centre of the Arts	444
Information Gateway Services	290	Saskatchewan Economic Development	445
ING Canada Financial Services International	291	Saskatchewan Government Insurance	445
Insurance Corp. of B.C.	291	SaskTel	449
Interior Savings Credit Union	293	Shaw Communications	455
Island Savings Credit Union	295	Signature Vacations Inc.	460

The Canada Student Employment Guide

University Index

Slocan Forest Products Ltd.	462	Economical Insurance Group, The	227
Southland Canada	467	EMJ Data Systems Ltd.	231
Spectra Premium Industries	468	Exfo	235
St. Lawrence Seaway Mgmt. Corp., The	473	Gimbel Eye Centre	252
State Farm Insurance Companies	476	Goodwill Industries of Toronto	256
Steelpipe Ltd.	477	Goodyear Canada Inc.	256
Sunoco Inc.	482	Grant MacEwen Community College	258
Supreme Tooling Group	483	Great-West Life Assurance Company, The	259
Symantec Corporation	486	Harry Rosen Inc.	265
TD Waterhouse Investor Services (Canada)	488	Honeywell Ltd.	275
The Co-operators	493	Information Gateway Services	290
Toronto Catholic District School Board	502	InterOne Marketing Group	293
Toronto French School, The	504	Island Telecom Inc.	295
Toronto General Hospital	505	Keyano College	306
Toronto Hydro	505	Kitchener, City of	309
Toronto Sun Publishing Corp., The	507	Lego Canada Inc.	314
Toyota Canada Ltd.	509	Liberty Health	318
TSC Stores Ltd.	512	Matrox Electronic Systems Ltd.	335
University College of Cape Breton	516	McGraw Hill Ryerson Ltd.	337
Vancouver Sun	520	Metro Toronto Convention Centre	342
W C I Canada Inc.	524	Metropolitan Life Insurance Company	344
Wendy's Restaurants of Canada Inc.	527	Mitel Corporation	350
West Kootenay Power Ltd.	528	Montreal Trust Co.	353
Westcliff Management Ltd.	529	Multi-Languages	357
Westcoast Energy Inc.	530	News Marketing Canada	368
Westminster Savings Credit Union	533	Norwich Union Life Insurance Society	376
Weyerhaeuser Company Limited	535	Oracle Corp. Canada Inc.	386
Winners Apparel Ltd.	539	Pearson Education Canada	393
Yamaha Motor Canada Ltd.	542	Peel Board of Education	393
Yellowknife, City of	544	Pelmorex Inc.	395
		Phoenix International	399
		Power Measurement Ltd.	406

English

		Prudential Insurance Co. of America, The	412
		Reader's Digest Association of Canada Ltd.	419
1-800-GOT-JUNK?	74	Rogers AT&T Wireless Inc.	436
Acklands-Grainger Inc.	80	Rogers Media, Publishing	436
Alberta Blue Cross	88	Sandman Hotels and Inns	443
Allstate Insurance Co. of Canada	96	Saskatchewan Government Insurance	445
Anthony Insurance Inc.	102	Scholastic Canada Ltd.	451
Assiniboine Community College	109	Shorewood Packaging Corp. of Canada Ltd.	459
Aurum Ceramic Dental Laboratories Ltd.	117	Southam Inc.	466
Banff Centre for Continuing Education, The	120	Spar Aerospace Limited	467
Black Photo Corporation	139	State Farm Insurance Companies	476
C.S.T. Consultants Inc.	155	Stitches	478
Calgary Co-operative Association Limited	157	Symantec Corporation	486
Casa Loma	177	TD Waterhouse Investor Services (Canada)	488
CFCF Inc.	183	Thompson's Moving and Storage	496
Chapters Inc.	186	Toronto District School Board	503
Charlottetown Driving Park	187	Toronto French School, The	504
Columbia House	197	Toronto General Hospital	505
Coquitlam, City of	204	Toronto Sun Publishing Corp., The	507
Credit Union Central of Canada	208	University College of Cape Breton	516
Dun & Bradstreet Canada	221	WestJet Airlines	532
Dynapro Systems Inc.	223		

The Canada Student Employment Guide

614   University Index

Fine Arts

American Airlines Inc.	99
Aurum Ceramic Dental Laboratories Ltd.	117
Banff Centre for Continuing Education, The	120
Bargain Finder Press Ltd.	121
Black Photo Corporation	139
Bullock Associates Design Consultants Inc.	153
Canadian Museum of Civilization Corp.	167
Casa Loma	177
CFCF Inc.	183
Electronics Arts (Canada) Inc.	229
Grant MacEwen Community College	258
Harry Rosen Inc.	265
HB Studios Multimedia Ltd.	266
McBee Systems of Canada Inc.	336
Nelvana Limited	363
News Marketing Canada	368
Paramount Canada's Wonderland Inc.	389
Polygram Group Canada Inc.	403
Regis Pictures and Frames Ltd.	425
Richmond, City of	431
Saskatoon, City of	448
Shopping Channel, The	459
Shorewood Packaging Corp. of Canada Ltd.	459
Sony Music Canada	465
State Farm Insurance Companies	476
Surrey, City of	484
Toronto French School, The	504
Toronto Sun Publishing Corp., The	507
University College of Cape Breton	516
WebCanada	526
Western Glove Works	530

General

1-800-GOT-JUNK?	74
Accucaps Industries Limited	79
ACE INI Insurance	79
Acklands-Grainger Inc.	80
ADT Canada Inc.	82
Akita Drilling Ltd.	87
Alberta Blue Cross	88
Alberta Gaming & Liquor Commission	90
Allianz Canada	95
Allstate Insurance Co. of Canada	96
Amcan Castings Limited	98
Amram's Distributing Ltd.	100
Anthony Insurance Inc.	102
Apple Canada Inc.	104
Arbor Memorial Services Inc.	106
Armor Personnel	107
Assiniboine Community College	109

Atlantic Blue Cross Care	113
Atlas Ideal Metals Inc.	115
Atlas Van Lines (Canada) Ltd.	115
Aurum Ceramic Dental Laboratories Ltd.	117
Axidata Inc.	118
Banff Centre for Continuing Education, The	120
Bayer Inc.	124
BC Telecom Inc.	126
Bearskin Lake Air Service Ltd.	128
Behlen Industries	130
Bell Mobility	131
Belleville General Hospital	132
Best Western Carlton Place Hotel	133
BFGoodrich Landing Gear Division	135
Birks Jewelry	138
Black Photo Corporation	139
Blue Mountain Resorts Limited	141
Brandon, City of	146
Brewers Retail Inc.	148
British Columbia Ferry Corporation	149
Brookfield Properties Corporation	150
Buckeye Canada Inc.	151
Bullock Associates Design Consultants Inc.	153
Burns International Security Services Ltd.	154
C.S.T. Consultants Inc.	155
Cabre Exploration Ltd.	156
Cadith Entertainment Ltd.	156
Calgary Co-operative Association Limited	157
Canada Safeway Limited	163
Canadian Cancer Society	164
Canadian Museum of Civilization Corp.	167
Canadian National Institute For The Blind	167
Canadian Western Bank	169
Capilano Suspension Bridge	174
Cargill Limited	175
Casa Loma	177
Central Park Lodges Ltd.	181
CGU Group Canada Ltd.	185
Charlottetown Driving Park	187
Christian Horizons	190
Columbia House	197
Compu-Quote Inc.	200
Computer Associates Canada Ltd.	201
Comtronic Computer Inc.	202
Corner Brook, City of	205
Cotton Ginny Ltd.	207
Credit Union Central of Canada	208
Culinar Inc.	209
D.H. Howden	211
Delta Toronto Airport Hotel	216
Directwest Publishers Ltd.	217
Druxy's Inc.	219
Dynapro Systems Inc.	223
Dynasty Furniture Manufacturing Ltd.	224

The Canada Student Employment Guide

University Index

Economic Development Edmonton	226
Economical Insurance Group, The	227
Eddie Bauer Inc.	227
EDS of Canada Ltd.	228
Eli Lilly Canada Inc.	230
EMJ Data Systems Ltd.	231
Exfo	235
Exide Canada Inc.	235
Extendicare (Canada) Inc.	237
Gay Lea Foods Co-Operative Ltd.	247
Gilbey Canada Inc.	252
Gimbel Eye Centre	252
Glaxo Wellcome Canada	253
Glentel Inc.	254
Goepel McDermid Securities	254
Goodman and Carr	255
Goodyear Canada Inc.	256
Great-West Life Assurance Company, The	259
Grenville Management Ltd.	259
Grouse Mountain Resorts Ltd.	260
Halifax County Regional Rehabilitation Centre	263
Halifax Water Commission	264
Harry Rosen Inc.	265
Hasbro Canada Inc.	266
Hoffman-La Roche Limited	272
Holiday Inn Select Toronto Airport	272
Honda Canada Inc.	274
HSBC Bank Canada	277
Huronia Regional Centre	280
Hydro Electric Commission of Thunder Bay	281
Hydro Mississauga Corporation	282
Insurance Corp. of B.C.	291
Intercon Security Ltd.	292
IPL Energy Inc.	294
Island Telecom Inc.	295
Jim Pattison Group	301
Johnson Incorporated	303
Jostens Canada Ltd.	303
Kitchener, City of	309
Laidlaw Inc.	312
Leduc, City of	313
Lego Canada Inc.	314
Leica Geosystems Canada Inc.	314
Leo Burnett Co. Ltd.	315
Liberty Health	318
Lifetouch Canada Inc.	319
M. McGrawth Canada Limited	324
Manitoba Public Insurance Corporation	329
Mark Anthony Group Inc.	332
McBee Systems of Canada Inc.	336
McCarney Greenwood	336
McLaren-McCann Advertising of Canada Ltd.	338
Metro Toronto Convention Centre	342
Metropolitan Life Insurance Company	344
Midland Walwyn Inc.	345
Midwest Food Products Inc.	346
Milne & Craighead Inc.	347
Ministry of Northern Develop. and Mines	348
Moen Inc.	352
Montreal Trust Co.	353
MOSAID Technologies Inc.	355
Motorola Canada Ltd.	356
Mountain Equipment Co-op	356
Multi-Languages	357
Nanaimo Credit Union	359
National Grocers Co. Ltd.	360
National Life	361
Nelvana Limited	363
Newfoundland and Labrador Credit Union	367
News Marketing Canada	368
Niagara Parks Commission, The	369
Nike Canada Ltd.	371
Nissan Canada Inc.	371
North American Life Assurance Company	373
North West Company Inc.	374
Norwich Union Life Insurance Society	376
Oland Breweries Limited	382
Ontario Guard Services Inc.	383
Ontario Jockey Club, The	384
Ontario Legislative Offices	384
Oracle Corp. Canada Inc.	386
Paramount Canada's Wonderland Inc.	389
Pearson Education Canada	393
PennCorp Life Insurance Company	396
Pharma Plus Drugmarts Ltd.	398
Pilot Insurance Company	399
Pitney Bowes of Canada Ltd.	401
Pizza Pizza Ltd.	401
Poco Petroleums Ltd.	402
Pollack Rentals Limited	403
Potacan Mining Company	405
Powell Equipment Ltd.	405
Progressive Financial Strategy	411
Providence Centre	412
Purolator Courier Ltd.	413
QEII Health Sciences Centre	414
Regal Constellation Hotel Ltd.	422
Regis Pictures and Frames Ltd.	425
Revenue Properties Company Limited	429
Reynolds and Reynolds (Canada) Limited	430
Rogers AT&T Wireless Inc.	436
Royal & Sun Alliance Insurance Co. of Cda	437
Royal Bank of Canada	438
Sandman Hotels and Inns	443
Saskatchewan Economic Development	445
Saskatchewan Government Insurance	445
Scarborough General Hospital	450
Sharp Electronics of Canada Ltd.	454

The Canada Student Employment Guide

616 University Index

Shaw Communications	455
Shorewood Packaging Corp. of Canada Ltd.	459
Signature Vacations Inc.	460
Skiing Louise Ltd.	461
Slocan Forest Products Ltd.	462
Sony Music Canada	465
Southam Inc.	466
Southern Railway of British Columbia Ltd.	466
Sportsco International	469
Sprint Canada	470
Stanley Canada Inc.	475
State Farm Insurance Companies	476
Steelpipe Ltd.	477
Stitches	478
Sundog Printing Limited	482
Sunoco Inc.	482
Supreme Tooling Group	483
TD Waterhouse Investor Services (Canada)	488
Teklogix Inc.	489
Thomas & Betts Ltée	495
Thomas Cook Group (Canada) Ltd.	495
Thompson's Moving and Storage	496
Ticketmaster Canada Inc.	498
Tiger Brand Knitting Company Limited	498
Today's Business Products Ltd.	500
Toronto Catholic District School Board	502
Toronto French School, The	504
Toronto General Hospital	505
Toronto Hydro	505
Toronto Police Service	506
Toronto Sun Publishing Corp., The	507
Toronto, City of	508
Toshiba of Canada Ltd.	508
Toyota Canada Ltd.	509
TSC Stores Ltd.	512
University College of Cape Breton	516
Valley First Credit Union	518
Vancouver Sun	520
VIA Rail Canada Inc.	521
Volvo Cars of Canada Ltd.	523
Wendy's Restaurants of Canada Inc.	527
Westbury Life	529
Western Glove Works	530
WestJet Airlines	532
Weston Produce Inc.	533
Whistler Blackcomb Mountain	535
White Rose Crafts and Nursery Sales Limited	536
Wilson Auto Electric Ltd.	538
Winners Apparel Ltd.	539
Winpak Ltd.	539
Yellowknife, City of	544
Zellers Inc.	546
Zenon Environmental Inc.	547

Gerontology

Barton Place Long Term Care Facility	121
Belleville General Hospital	132
Betel Home Foundation	133
Bethania Mennonite Personal Care Home Inc.	134
Cambridge Memorial Hospital	159
Canadian National Institute For The Blind	167
Central Park Lodges Ltd.	181
Chilliwack General Hospital	189
Christian Horizons	190
Cobourg District General Hospital	194
Coquitlam, City of	204
David Thompson Health Region	212
Extendicare (Canada) Inc.	237
Foyer Valade Inc.	245
Gimbel Eye Centre	252
Grant MacEwen Community College	258
Halifax County Regional Rehabilitation Centre	263
Kennedy Lodge Nursing Home Inc.	306
Kitchener, City of	309
Metropolitan Life Insurance Company	344
Misericordia General Hospital	348
News Marketing Canada	368
Providence Centre	412
Reena	421
Regional Residential Services Society	424
Rehabilitation Institute of Toronto	425
St. Vincent's Hospitals	473
Sudbury Regional Hospital	480
Swift Current Health District	485
Timmins, City of	499
Toronto General Hospital	505
Toronto, City of	508

History

1-800-GOT-JUNK?	74
American Airlines Inc.	99
Canadian Museum of Civilization Corp.	167
Casa Loma	177
Columbia House	197
Grant MacEwen Community College	258
Harry Rosen Inc.	265
Island Telecom Inc.	295
McGraw Hill Ryerson Ltd.	337
News Marketing Canada	368
Pearson Education Canada	393
Reader's Digest Association of Canada Ltd.	419
Regis Pictures and Frames Ltd.	425
St. Lawrence Parks Commission	472
State Farm Insurance Companies	476
Surrey, City of	484

The Canada Student Employment Guide

University Index   617

Toronto District School Board	503	Metropolitan Life Insurance Company	344
Toronto French School, The	504	Moosehead Breweries Limited	354
Toronto General Hospital	505	National Life	361
Toronto Sun Publishing Corp., The	507	News Marketing Canada	368
University College of Cape Breton	516	Ontario March of Dimes	385
		Pearson Education Canada	393
		Peel Regional Police	394

Journalism

		Pelmorex Inc.	395
		Quebecor Inc.	415
1-800-GOT-JUNK?	74	Reader's Digest Association of Canada Ltd.	419
Acklands-Grainger Inc.	80	Rogers Media, Publishing	436
Air Canada	85	Ryerson Polytechnic University	441
Alberta Blue Cross	88	Saskatchewan Economic Development	445
Assiniboine Community College	109	Saskatchewan Government Insurance	445
ATCO Electric	111	Saskatchewan Wheat Pool	447
ATCO Gas Services Ltd.	112	Saskatoon, City of	448
Atlantic Blue Cross Care	113	Scholastic Canada Ltd.	451
Babcock and Wilcox Canada	119	Shaw Communications	455
Banff Centre for Continuing Education, The	120	Sony Music Canada	465
British Columbia Ferry Corporation	149	Southam Inc.	466
Calgary Co-operative Association Limited	157	St. Lawrence Parks Commission	472
Canadian Broadcasting Corporation	164	State Farm Insurance Companies	476
Canadian Commercial Corp.	165	Surrey, City of	484
Casa Loma	177	Symantec Corporation	486
CFCF Inc.	183	Teldon International Inc.	490
CFCN Communications Inc.	184	Telegraph Journal	491
Chapters Inc.	186	Toronto General Hospital	505
Charlottetown Driving Park	187	Toronto Sun Publishing Corp., The	507
Columbia House	197	Toyota Canada Ltd.	509
Co-op Atlantic	203	Vancouver Sun	520
Coquitlam, City of	204	Weyerhaeuser Company Limited	535
Economical Insurance Group, The	227		
Extendicare (Canada) Inc.	237		
Farm Credit Corp. Canada	238	## Languages	
Foremost Industries Inc.	244		
Gimbel Eye Centre	252	American Airlines Inc.	99
Glaxo Wellcome Canada	253	Axidata Inc.	118
Goodwill Industries of Toronto	256	Bell Mobility	131
Grant MacEwen Community College	258	Brookfield Properties Corporation	150
Halifax Regional Municipality	263	Casa Loma	177
Hill & Knowlton Canada Ltd.	270	Chapters Inc.	186
Homewood Corp.	274	Columbia House	197
Honeywell Ltd.	275	Corner Brook, City of	205
Island Telecom Inc.	295	Dell Computer Corporation	214
IWK Grace Health Centre	297	Exfo	235
Liberty Health	318	Explorer Hotel, The	236
Manitoba Pool Elevators	328	Hasbro Canada Inc.	266
Manitoba Public Insurance Corporation	329	InterOne Marketing Group	293
Marine Atlantic Inc.	331	Island Telecom Inc.	295
Maritime Life Assurance Company, The	331	Ivaco Inc.	296
Matrox Electronic Systems Ltd.	335	Mactac Canada Ltd.	326
McLaren-McCann Advertising of Canada Ltd.	338	Maritime Life Assurance Company, The	331
Metro Toronto Convention Centre	342	Matrox Electronic Systems Ltd.	335
Metroland Printing, Publishing & Dist. Ltd.	343	McGraw Hill Ryerson Ltd.	337

The Canada Student Employment Guide

618 University Index

Metropolitan Life Insurance Company	344
Multi-Languages	357
National Life	361
Nelvana Limited	363
News Marketing Canada	368
Niagara Parks Commission, The	369
Nissan Canada Inc.	371
North American Life Assurance Company	373
PennCorp Life Insurance Company	396
Premdor Inc.	408
Reader's Digest Association of Canada Ltd.	419
Regal Constellation Hotel Ltd.	422
Rogers AT&T Wireless Inc.	436
Sandman Hotels and Inns	443
Sheraton Fallsview Hotel	456
Signature Vacations Inc.	460
St. Lawrence Parks Commission	472
State Farm Insurance Companies	476
Stitches	478
Ticketmaster Canada Inc.	498
Toronto District School Board	503
Toronto French School, The	504
Toronto Sun Publishing Corp., The	507
Toshiba of Canada Ltd.	508
Toyota Canada Ltd.	509
University College of Cape Breton	516
Vancouver Sun	520
Westbury Life	529
WestJet Airlines	532

Music

Banff Centre for Continuing Education, The	120
Barton Place Long Term Care Facility	121
Bloorview MacMillan Centre, The	140
Casa Loma	177
Columbia House	197
Foyer Valade Inc.	245
Grant MacEwen Community College	258
Keyano College	306
Nelvana Limited	363
News Marketing Canada	368
Paramount Canada's Wonderland Inc.	389
Pelmorex Inc.	395
Polygram Group Canada Inc.	403
Science North	452
Sheraton Fallsview Hotel	456
Shorewood Packaging Corp. of Canada Ltd.	459
Sony Music Canada	465
St. Lawrence Parks Commission	472
Toronto District School Board	503
Toronto French School, The	504

Philosophy

1-800-GOT-JUNK?	74
Bell Mobility	131
Columbia House	197
Harry Rosen Inc.	265
Island Telecom Inc.	295
Metropolitan Life Insurance Company	344
News Marketing Canada	368
Toronto French School, The	504
University College of Cape Breton	516

Political Science

1-800-GOT-JUNK?	74
Accucaps Industries Limited	79
AGF Management Limited	83
AXA Insurance (Canada)	118
Black Photo Corporation	139
Canadian Western Bank	169
CFCF Inc.	183
Columbia House	197
Computer Associates Canada Ltd.	201
Environics Research Group Ltd.	233
Gimbel Eye Centre	252
Goodman and Carr	255
Grant MacEwen Community College	258
ING Canada Financial Services International	291
Keyano College	306
Kitchener, City of	309
Laidlaw Inc.	312
Leduc, City of	313
Loss Prevention Group Inc.	322
Metropolitan Life Insurance Company	344
Multi-Languages	357
News Marketing Canada	368
Ontario Legislative Offices	384
Pearson Education Canada	393
Rogers Media, Publishing	436
Royal & Sun Alliance Insurance Co. of Cda	437
State Farm Insurance Companies	476
Surrey, City of	484
TD Waterhouse Investor Services (Canada)	488
Toronto District School Board	503
Toronto Hydro	505
Toronto Sun Publishing Corp., The	507
University College of Cape Breton	516
Vancouver Sun	520

Psychology

1-800-GOT-JUNK?	74

The Canada Student Employment Guide

University Index

Accucaps Industries Limited	79	Kennametal Ltd.	305
ACE INI Insurance	79	Keyano College	306
Acklands-Grainger Inc.	80	Kitchener, City of	309
Addictions Foundation of Manitoba, The	81	Kodak Canada Inc.	309
AGF Management Limited	83	Leduc, City of	313
Alberta Alcohol and Drug Abuse Commission	87	Les Centres Jeunesse de Montréal	316
Alcan Aluminium Limited	91	Liberty Health	318
Allstate Insurance Co. of Canada	96	London Goodwill Industries Association	322
Amram's Distributing Ltd.	100	Loss Prevention Group Inc.	322
Andersen Consulting	101	Marine Atlantic Inc.	331
Anthony Insurance Inc.	102	Maryvale Adolescent and Family Services	334
Assiniboine Community College	109	Metro Toronto Convention Centre	342
Aurum Ceramic Dental Laboratories Ltd.	117	Metro Toronto West Detention Centre	343
Barton Place Long Term Care Facility	121	Metropolitan Life Insurance Company	344
Belleville General Hospital	132	Meyers Norris Penny & Co.	344
BFGoodrich Landing Gear Division	135	Neptune Food Suppliers Ltd.	363
Bic Inc.	136	News Marketing Canada	368
Biovail Corporation International	137	North American Life Assurance Company	373
Black Photo Corporation	139	Ontario March of Dimes	385
Bloorview MacMillan Centre, The	140	Peel Children's Centre	394
Boréal Assurances Inc.	144	Pitney Bowes of Canada Ltd.	401
Brandon, City of	146	Poco Petroleums Ltd.	402
Brookfield Properties Corporation	150	QEII Health Sciences Centre	414
Buckeye Canada Inc.	151	Reena	421
Cadith Entertainment Ltd.	156	Regional Residential Services Society	424
Calgary Co-operative Association Limited	157	Sandman Hotels and Inns	443
Canadian National Institute For The Blind	167	Saskatoon, City of	448
Canon Canada Inc.	172	Scarborough General Hospital	450
Casa Loma	177	Shaw Communications	455
Central Park Lodges Ltd.	181	Shorewood Packaging Corp. of Canada Ltd.	459
Christian Horizons	190	Skills Training & Support Services Association	462
Cobourg District General Hospital	194	Sony Music Canada	465
Cognos Incorporated	196	St. Amant Centre Inc.	471
Columbia House	197	St. Lawrence Seaway Mgmt. Corp., The	473
Computer Associates Canada Ltd.	201	State Farm Insurance Companies	476
David Thompson Health Region	212	Sudbury Regional Hospital	480
Dylex Limited	222	Sun Rype Products Ltd.	481
Economical Insurance Group, The	227	Supreme Tooling Group	483
FedEx Express	240	Surrey Place Centre	484
Gay Lea Foods Co-Operative Ltd.	247	Swift Current Health District	485
Goodman and Carr	255	Toronto Association For Community Living	501
Goodwill Industries of Toronto	256	Toronto East General Hospital	503
Grant MacEwen Community College	258	Toronto General Hospital	505
Great-West Life Assurance Company, The	259	Toronto Sun Publishing Corp., The	507
Halifax County Regional Rehabilitation Centre	263	Toyota Canada Ltd.	509
Harry Rosen Inc.	265	Universal Rehabilitation Service Agency	515
Health Authority 5	267	University College of Cape Breton	516
Health Care Corporation of St. John's	267	Vancouver Sun	520
Homewood Corp.	274	Wendy's Restaurants of Canada Inc.	527
Huronia Regional Centre	280	Yanke Group of Companies	543
Insurance Corp. of B.C.	291	Yarmouth Regional Hospital	543
Interior Savings Credit Union	293		
IWK Grace Health Centre	297		
Izaak Walton Killam Hospital, The	297		

The Canada Student Employment Guide

University Index

Public Relations

1-800-GOT-JUNK?	74
Accucaps Industries Limited	79
ADT Canada Inc.	82
AGF Management Limited	83
Agricultural Credit Corp. of Saskatchewan	84
Air Canada	85
Air Nova Inc.	86
Alberta Blue Cross	88
Alberta Energy & Utilities Board	89
Alcan Aluminium Limited	91
American Airlines Inc.	99
Amram's Distributing Ltd.	100
Apex Land Corp.	103
Assiniboine Community College	109
Assumption Mutual Life Insurance	109
ATCO Gas Services Ltd.	112
Atlantic Blue Cross Care	113
Atlantic Lottery Corporation Inc.	113
Atlantic Wholesalers Ltd.	114
Atlas Van Lines (Canada) Ltd.	115
Aurizon Mines Ltd.	116
Aurum Ceramic Dental Laboratories Ltd.	117
Axidata Inc.	118
Banff Centre for Continuing Education, The	120
Barton Place Long Term Care Facility	121
Bayer Inc.	124
BC Hydro	125
Bettis Canada Ltd.	135
Bic Inc.	136
Biovail Corporation International	137
Black Photo Corporation	139
Boréal Assurances Inc.	144
Bowater Mersey Paper Company Limited	146
Brandon, City of	146
British Columbia Ferry Corporation	149
Calgary Co-operative Association Limited	157
Calgary, City of	158
Canada Safeway Limited	163
Canadian Cancer Society	164
Canadian National Institute For The Blind	167
Canadian Western Bank	169
Canon Canada Inc.	172
Capilano Suspension Bridge	174
Carbone of America (LCL) Ltd.	175
Casa Loma	177
Centra Gas British Columbia Inc.	180
Centra Gas Manitoba Inc.	181
Charlottetown Driving Park	187
Cobourg District General Hospital	194
Columbia House	197
Comcare Health Services	198
Co-op Atlantic	203
Coquitlam, City of	204
Corner Brook, City of	205
Culinar Inc.	209
David Thompson Health Region	212
Delta Hotels	215
Dun & Bradstreet Canada	221
Dynapro Systems Inc.	223
Dynatek Automation Systems Inc.	224
Economic Development Edmonton	226
Economical Insurance Group, The	227
Eli Lilly Canada Inc.	230
Environics Research Group Ltd.	233
Exfo	235
Farm Credit Corp. Canada	238
FedEx Express	240
Foremost Industries Inc.	244
Foyer Valade Inc.	245
Friesens Corporation	246
Future Shop Ltd.	246
Gay Lea Foods Co-Operative Ltd.	247
Gimbel Eye Centre	252
Gisborne Design Services Ltd.	253
Glaxo Wellcome Canada	253
Goodman and Carr	255
Goodwill Industries of Toronto	256
Grant MacEwen Community College	258
Grouse Mountain Resorts Ltd.	260
Halifax County Regional Rehabilitation Centre	263
Halifax Regional Municipality	263
Hasbro Canada Inc.	266
Health Care Corporation of St. John's	267
Hill & Knowlton Canada Ltd.	270
Hippodrome de Montréal	270
Holiday Inn Select Toronto Airport	272
Home Oil Co. Ltd.	273
Homewood Corp.	274
Housesitters Canada, The	277
Humber River Regional Hospital	280
Hydro Electric Commission of Thunder Bay	281
IBM Canada Ltd.	284
Interior Savings Credit Union	293
InterOne Marketing Group	293
Island Telecom Inc.	295
IWK Grace Health Centre	297
Izaak Walton Killam Hospital, The	297
J.D. Irving Limited	298
Johnson Incorporated	303
Kitchener, City of	309
La Confiserie Comete Ltee	311
Leduc, City of	313
Lenbrook Industries Limited	315
Liberty Health	318
Magna International Inc.	327
Manitoba Hydro	328

The Canada Student Employment Guide

University Index 621

Manitoba Public Insurance Corporation	329	Saskatchewan Government Insurance	445
Marine Atlantic Inc.	331	Saskatchewan Transportation Company	446
Maritime Life Assurance Company, The	331	Saskferco Products Inc.	448
Marks & Spencer Canada Inc.	332	Science North	452
Matrox Electronic Systems Ltd.	335	Shaw Communications	455
McMillan & Associates Inc.	339	Sheraton Fallsview Hotel	456
Mediasynergy	340	Shopping Channel, The	459
Metropolitan Life Insurance Company	344	Siemens Electric Ltd.	460
Michaels of Canada Inc.	345	Signature Vacations Inc.	460
Ministry of Northern Develop. and Mines	348	Skiing Louise Ltd.	461
Mitel Corporation	350	Sobeys Inc.	463
Moosehead Breweries Limited	354	Société des Alcools du Québec	464
National Life	361	Sportsco International	469
Neles Automation, Scada Solutions Ltd.	362	Sprint Canada	470
Nelvana Limited	363	St. Lawrence Parks Commission	472
Nestle Canada Inc.	364	State Farm Insurance Companies	476
News Marketing Canada	368	Stitches	478
NewTel Communications	369	Sun Peaks Resort Corporation	481
Niagara Parks Commission, The	369	Sun Rype Products Ltd.	481
Nike Canada Ltd.	371	Surrey, City of	484
Northern Lights Regional Health Centre	375	TD Waterhouse Investor Services (Canada)	488
Northwestel Inc.	376	Telus Corporation	492
Nova Scotia Liquor Commission	377	The Co-operators	493
Nova Scotia Power Corp.	377	Thompson's Moving and Storage	496
Novartis Consumer Health Canada Inc.	378	Ticketmaster Canada Inc.	498
Oetiker Limited	381	Today's Business Products Ltd.	500
Ontario Guard Services Inc.	383	Toronto General Hospital	505
Ontario Jockey Club, The	384	Toronto Sun Publishing Corp., The	507
Ontario Legislative Offices	384	Toronto, City of	508
Ontario March of Dimes	385	Toshiba of Canada Ltd.	508
Oracle Corp. Canada Inc.	386	Toyota Canada Ltd.	509
Paramount Canada's Wonderland Inc.	389	US Filter BCP	517
Peel Regional Police	394	Vancouver Sun	520
Pelmorex Inc.	395	Volvo Cars of Canada Ltd.	523
PennCorp Life Insurance Company	396	Wendy's Restaurants of Canada Inc.	527
Phoenix International	399	West Kootenay Power Ltd.	528
Pine Falls Paper Company Limited	400	Westcliff Management Ltd.	529
Pitney Bowes of Canada Ltd.	401	WestJet Airlines	532
Pizza Pizza Ltd.	401	Weyerhaeuser Company Limited	535
Pool People Ltd.	404	Whistler Blackcomb Mountain	535
Prince Albert, City of	410	Wilson Auto Electric Ltd.	538
Prince George, City of	410	Yellowknife, City of	544
Prudential Insurance Co. of America, The	412	YFactor	544
Public Utilities of Kingston	413	Zurich Canada	548
QEII Health Sciences Centre	414		
Regal Capital Planners Ltd.	422		
Regal Constellation Hotel Ltd.	422		
Regis Pictures and Frames Ltd.	425		
Rehabilitation Institute of Toronto	425		
Riverside Hospital of Ottawa, The	434		
Rogers AT&T Wireless Inc.	436		
Rogers Media, Publishing	436		
Royal Canadian Mint	438		
Sandman Hotels and Inns	443		

Recreation Studies

Athabasca, Town of	112
Banff Centre for Continuing Education, The	120
Barton Place Long Term Care Facility	121
Belleville General Hospital	132
Betel Home Foundation	133
Bethania Mennonite Personal Care Home Inc.	134

622   University Index

Bethesda Hospital	134	Addictions Foundation of Manitoba, The	81
Bloorview Childrens Hospital	140	Alberta Alcohol and Drug Abuse Commission	87
Bloorview MacMillan Centre, The	140	Algoma Child & Youth Services Inc.	92
Canada Games Aquatic Centre	162	Armor Personnel	107
Canadian Museum of Civilization Corp.	167	Assiniboine Community College	109
Canadian National Institute For The Blind	167	Atlantic Blue Cross Care	113
Corner Brook, City of	205	Aurum Ceramic Dental Laboratories Ltd.	117
David Thompson Health Region	212	Banff Centre for Continuing Education, The	120
Extendicare (Canada) Inc.	237	Barton Place Long Term Care Facility	121
Foyer Valade Inc.	245	Battlefords Health District	123
Grant MacEwen Community College	258	Bayer Inc.	124
Grouse Mountain Resorts Ltd.	260	Belleville General Hospital	132
Halifax County Regional Rehabilitation Centre	263	Betel Home Foundation	133
Halifax Regional Municipality	263	Bethania Mennonite Personal Care Home Inc.	134
Health Care Corporation of St. John's	267	Biovail Corporation International	137
Health Sciences Centre	268	Black Photo Corporation	139
Homewood Corp.	274	Bloorview MacMillan Centre, The	140
Horseshoe Resort Corporation	275	Brandon, City of	146
Huronia Regional Centre	280	Brookfield Properties Corporation	150
Izaak Walton Killam Hospital, The	297	Cambridge Memorial Hospital	159
Kelowna, City of	305	Canadian Commercial Corp.	165
Kitchener, City of	309	CancerCare Manitoba	171
Leduc, City of	313	Casa Loma	177
Metropolitan Life Insurance Company	344	Catholic Children's Aid Society Foundation	178
Misericordia General Hospital	348	Centra Gas British Columbia Inc.	180
Ontario March of Dimes	385	Central Park Lodges Ltd.	181
Pool People Ltd.	404	Children's Aid Society of Metro Toronto	188
Prince George, City of	410	Chilliwack General Hospital	189
Regal Constellation Hotel Ltd.	422	Christian Horizons	190
Rehabilitation Institute of Toronto	425	Cobourg District General Hospital	194
Richmond, City of	431	Columbia House	197
Ryerson Polytechnic University	441	Computer Associates Canada Ltd.	201
Saskatoon, City of	448	Coquitlam, City of	204
Scarborough General Hospital	450	David Thompson Health Region	212
Science North	452	Deer Lodge Centre Inc.	213
Sherbrooke Community Centre	457	Environics Research Group Ltd.	233
Skills Training & Support Services Association	462	Foyer Valade Inc.	245
St. Joseph's Care Group	472	Gay Lea Foods Co-Operative Ltd.	247
St. Lawrence Parks Commission	472	George Jeffrey Children's Treatment Centre	250
State Farm Insurance Companies	476	Gimbel Eye Centre	252
Surrey, City of	484	Goodwill Industries of Toronto	256
Toronto and Region Conservation Authority	501	Grant MacEwen Community College	258
Toronto Cricket Skating & Curling	502	Great-West Life Assurance Company, The	259
Toronto General Hospital	505	Halifax County Regional Rehabilitation Centre	263
Toronto, City of	508	Health Care Corporation of St. John's	267
Universal Rehabilitation Service Agency	515	Health Sciences Centre	268
Whistler Blackcomb Mountain	535	Homewood Corp.	274
Yellowknife, City of	544	Huronia Regional Centre	280
		Izaak Walton Killam Hospital, The	297
		Kennedy Lodge Nursing Home Inc.	306
Sociology/Social Work		Kitchener, City of	309
		Leduc, City of	313
1-800-GOT-JUNK?	74	Les Centres Jeunesse de Montréal	316
Acklands-Grainger Inc.	80	London Goodwill Industries Association	322

The Canada Student Employment Guide

University Index

Loss Prevention Group Inc.	322
Manitoba Hydro	328
Maryvale Adolescent and Family Services	334
Metro Toronto West Detention Centre	343
Metropolitan Life Insurance Company	344
News Marketing Canada	368
North American Life Assurance Company	373
Ontario March of Dimes	385
Peel Children's Centre	394
Pitney Bowes of Canada Ltd.	401
QEII Health Sciences Centre	414
Reena	421
Regina Health District	423
Regional Residential Services Society	424
Richmond, City of	431
Riverside Hospital of Ottawa, The	434
Royal Inland Hospital	439
Sandman Hotels and Inns	443
Scarborough General Hospital	450
Sherbrooke Community Centre	457
Shorewood Packaging Corp. of Canada Ltd.	459
Skills Training & Support Services Association	462
St. Amant Centre Inc.	471
St. Joseph's Care Group	472
State Farm Insurance Companies	476
Sudbury Regional Hospital	480
Supreme Tooling Group	483
Surrey Place Centre	484
Swift Current Health District	485
The Arthritis Society	492
The Barn Fruit Markets Inc.	493
The Co-operators	493
Thompson's Moving and Storage	496
Timmins, City of	499
Toronto Association For Community Living	501
Toronto District School Board	503
Toronto General Hospital	505
Toronto Hydro	505
Toronto Sun Publishing Corp., The	507
Universal Rehabilitation Service Agency	515
Vancouver Sun	520
Weyerhaeuser Company Limited	535
Windsor, City of	538

Statistics

ABC Group	76
Acklands-Grainger Inc.	80
Alberta Blue Cross	88
BBM Bureau of Measurement	125
BFGoodrich Landing Gear Division	135
Biovail Corporation International	137
Calgary Co-operative Association Limited	157

Canada Safeway Limited	163
Canadian Dairy Commission	165
Citibank Canada	191
Columbia House	197
Coquitlam, City of	204
Corner Brook, City of	205
David Thompson Health Region	212
Economic Development Edmonton	226
Environics Research Group Ltd.	233
Gallup Canada Inc.	247
Hasbro Canada Inc.	266
Home Oil Co. Ltd.	273
Hydro Québec	283
ING Canada Financial Services International	291
La Confiserie Comete Ltee	311
Liberty Health	318
Manitoba Hydro	328
Marine Atlantic Inc.	331
Maritime Life Assurance Company, The	331
Meyers Norris Penny & Co.	344
Moosehead Breweries Limited	354
National Life	361
Nesbitt Burns Inc.	364
Newfoundland and Labrador Credit Union	367
News Marketing Canada	368
Nielsen Marketing Research	370
North American Life Assurance Company	373
Paramount Canada's Wonderland Inc.	389
Prudential Insurance Co. of America, The	412
Reader's Digest Association of Canada Ltd.	419
Richmond, City of	431
Rogers AT&T Wireless Inc.	436
Royal & Sun Alliance Insurance Co. of Cda	437
Saskatchewan Government Insurance	445
Signature Vacations Inc.	460
State Farm Insurance Companies	476
Thompson's Moving and Storage	496
Toronto District School Board	503
Toronto French School, The	504
Toronto General Hospital	505
Toronto Hydro	505
Toyota Canada Ltd.	509
University College of Cape Breton	516
Vancouver Sun	520
Weyerhaeuser Company Limited	535
Winners Apparel Ltd.	539
Yanke Group of Companies	543

Urban Geography

Canada Safeway Limited	163
CH2M Gore and Storrie Limited	185
Coquitlam, City of	204

The Canada Student Employment Guide

624 University Index

Corner Brook, City of	205	Allcolour Paint Limited	94
Goodman and Carr	255	Allianz Canada	95
Halifax Regional Municipality	263	Alpine Oil Service Corporation	96
Kelowna, City of	305	Amcor Twinpak North America Inc.	98
Kitchener, City of	309	American Airlines Inc.	99
Leduc, City of	313	Anthony Insurance Inc.	102
Marshall Macklin Monaghan Ltd.	333	Apex Land Corp.	103
Mississauga, City of	349	Apple Canada Inc.	104
News Marketing Canada	368	Aqua-Power Cleaners Ltd.	105
Pelmorex Inc.	395	Arbor Memorial Services Inc.	106
Richmond, City of	431	Arctic Co-operatives Limited	107
Signature Vacations Inc.	460	Armor Personnel	107
Southam Inc.	466	Assiniboine Community College	109
Toronto and Region Conservation Authority	501	Assumption Mutual Life Insurance	109
Toronto Hydro	505	AstraZeneca	110
Vancouver Sun	520	ATCO Electric	111
White Rose Crafts and Nursery Sales Limited	536	ATCO Frontec Corp.	111
Yanke Group of Companies	543	ATCO Gas Services Ltd.	112
Yellowknife, City of	544	Athabasca, Town of	112

Bachelor of Commerce/Administration

Accounting

Atlantic Blue Cross Care	113
Atlantic Lottery Corporation Inc.	113
Atlantic Packaging Products Ltd.	114
Atlas Ideal Metals Inc.	115
Atlas Van Lines (Canada) Ltd.	115
Aurizon Mines Ltd.	116
Aurum Ceramic Dental Laboratories Ltd.	117
Aventis Pasteur Limited	117

A C A Cooperative Limited	74	AXA Insurance (Canada)	118
A.G. Simpson Co. Ltd.	75	Axidata Inc.	118
ABC Group	76	Babcock and Wilcox Canada	119
Aberdeen Hospital	77	Bakemark Ingredients Ltd.	119
Abitibi-Consolidated Inc.	77	Banff Centre for Continuing Education, The	120
Acadia University	78	Barton Place Long Term Care Facility	121
Access Communications	78	BASF Canada Inc.	122
Accucaps Industries Limited	79	Basic Technologies Corporation	122
ACE INI Insurance	79	Bayer Inc.	124
Acklands-Grainger Inc.	80	Baytex Energy Limited	124
Addictions Foundation of Manitoba, The	81	BBM Bureau of Measurement	125
ADI Group Inc.	82	BCG Services	127
ADT Canada Inc.	82	BDO Dunwoody	127
AGF Management Limited	83	Becker Milk Company Ltd., The	129
Agricultural Credit Corp. of Saskatchewan	84	Beckman Coulter Canada Inc.	129
Air Canada	85	Bell Mobility	131
Air Liquide Canada Inc.	85	Belleville General Hospital	132
Air Nova Inc.	86	Best Western Carlton Place Hotel	133
Air Ontario Inc.	86	Bethesda Hospital	134
Akita Drilling Ltd.	87	Bettis Canada Ltd.	135
Alberta Blue Cross	88	BFGoodrich Landing Gear Division	135
Alberta Energy & Utilities Board	89	Bic Inc.	136
Alberta Energy Company Ltd.	89	Bio-Research Laboratories Ltd.	137
Alberta Gaming & Liquor Commission	90	BJ Services Company	138
Alcan Aluminium Limited	91	Black Photo Corporation	139
Algoma Steel Inc.	93	Bloorview MacMillan Centre, The	140
Aliant Telecom Inc.	93	Blue Mountain Resorts Limited	141

The Canada Student Employment Guide

University Index

Blue Wave Seafoods Inc.	142	Chevron Canada Resources Ltd.	188
BNP PARIBAS (Canada)	143	Children's Hospital of Eastern Ontario	189
Boréal Assurances Inc.	144	Chilliwack General Hospital	189
BOVAR Waste Management	145	Christian Horizons	190
Bowater Mersey Paper Company Limited	146	Cineplex Odeon Corporation	191
Brewers Retail Inc.	148	Citibank Canada	191
British Columbia Ferry Corporation	149	CKF Inc.	192
Brookfield Properties Corporation	150	Cobourg District General Hospital	194
Budd Canada Inc.	152	Coca Cola Foods Canada Inc.	195
C MAC Industries Inc.	155	COM DEV International	197
C.S.T. Consultants Inc.	155	Community Savings Credit Union	199
Cabre Exploration Ltd.	156	Compaq Canada Inc.	199
Cadith Entertainment Ltd.	156	Computalog Ltd.	200
Calgary Co-operative Association Limited	157	Computer Associates Canada Ltd.	201
Calgary, City of	158	Comtronic Computer Inc.	202
Cambior Inc.	158	Conair Aviation Ltd.	202
Cambridge Memorial Hospital	159	Connors Bros, Limited	203
Camp Hill Hospital	160	Co-op Atlantic	203
Canada Post Corporation	162	Coppley Apparel Group	204
Canada Safeway Limited	163	Coquitlam, City of	204
Canada Starch Company Inc.	163	Corner Brook, City of	205
Canadian Cancer Society	164	Cornwall Electric	206
Canadian Dairy Commission	165	Cosmair Canada Inc.	206
Canadian Depository for Securities Ltd.	166	Cotton Ginny Ltd.	207
Canadian General Tower Limited	166	Cougar Helicopters Inc.	208
Canadian Museum of Civilization Corp.	167	Credit Union Central of Canada	208
Canadian National Institute For The Blind	167	Crestar Energy Inc.	209
Canadian Occidental Petroleum Ltd.	168	Culinar Inc.	209
Canadian Tire Corporation Ltd.	169	Custom Trim Ltd.	210
Canadian Western Bank	169	D.A. Stuart Inc.	210
Canbra Foods Ltd.	170	Dana Corporation - Long Manufacturing	212
Cancarb Limited	170	David Thompson Health Region	212
CancerCare Manitoba	171	DDM Plastics Inc.	213
Canon Canada Inc.	172	Deer Lodge Centre Inc.	213
Canpar Transport Ltd.	173	Degussa - Huls Canada Inc.	214
Cape Breton Development Corporation	174	Dell Computer Corporation	214
Capilano Suspension Bridge	174	Delphi Solutions Inc.	215
Carbone of America (LCL) Ltd.	175	Delta Hotels	215
Cargill Limited	175	Delta Toronto Airport Hotel	216
Carte International Inc.	176	Derlan Industries Limited	216
Cassels Brock & Blackwell	177	Directwest Publishers Ltd.	217
Catholic Children's Aid Society Foundation	178	Dofasco Inc.	218
Celestica International Inc.	179	Domtar Inc.	218
CenAlta Energy Services Inc.	180	Drug Trading Company Ltd.	219
Centra Gas British Columbia Inc.	180	Dun & Bradstreet Canada	221
Centra Gas Manitoba Inc.	181	DuPont Canada Inc.	221
Central Park Lodges Ltd.	181	Dura Automotive Systems (Canada) Ltd.	222
Centre de Santé de St-Henri Inc.	182	Dynacare Laboratories	223
Ceridian Canada	183	Dynapro Systems Inc.	223
CFCF Inc.	183	Dynasty Furniture Manufacturing Ltd.	224
CGI	184	Dynatek Automation Systems Inc.	224
CGU Group Canada Ltd.	185	Echo Bay Mines Ltd.	226
Chapters Inc.	186	Economical Insurance Group, The	227
Charlottetown Driving Park	187	Eli Lilly Canada Inc.	230

The Canada Student Employment Guide

626 University Index

Emco Limited	230	Honda Canada Inc.	274
EMJ Data Systems Ltd.	231	Honeywell Ltd.	275
Entreprises Premier Canadien Ltée	232	Horseshoe Resort Corporation	275
Ernst & Young	234	Hôtel Dieu de Montréal	276
Exfo	235	Household Movers & Shippers Limited	276
Exide Canada Inc.	235	Housesitters Canada, The	277
Explorer Hotel, The	236	HSBC Bank Canada	277
Export Development Corporation	236	Hub Meat Packers Ltd.	278
Extendicare (Canada) Inc.	237	Hubbell Canada Inc.	278
Farm Credit Corp. Canada	238	Hudon & Deaudelin Ltée	279
Farmers Co-operative Dairy Limited	239	Hudson's Bay Company, The	279
Federated Co-operatives Limited	239	Humber River Regional Hospital	280
Finning	240	Huronia Regional Centre	280
Fisher Scientific Limited	241	Husky Energy Inc.	281
Fishery Products International	241	Hydro Electric Commission of Thunder Bay	281
Fletcher's Fine Foods	242	Hydro Mississauga Corporation	282
Flint Energy Services Ltd.	243	Hydro Québec	283
Foremost Industries Inc.	244	I M P Group International Inc.	283
Forzani Group Ltd., The	244	ICI Canada Inc.	285
Foyer Valade Inc.	245	Ilco Unican Inc.	286
Friesens Corporation	246	Imperial Oil Limited	286
Future Shop Ltd.	246	INCO Limited	287
Gendis Inc.	248	Indalex Limited	288
General Chemical Canada Ltd.	249	Industrial Equipment Co. Ltd.	288
General Electric Canada Inc.	249	Industrial-Alliance Life Insurance Company	289
George Jeffrey Children's Treatment Centre	250	Industries Lassonde Inc.	289
Gienow Building Products Ltd.	251	InfoInterActive Inc.	290
Giffels Associates Limited	251	Information Gateway Services	290
Gilbey Canada Inc.	252	ING Canada Financial Services International	291
Gimbel Eye Centre	252	Insurance Corp. of B.C.	291
Glaxo Wellcome Canada	253	Intercon Security Ltd.	292
Glentel Inc.	254	IPL Energy Inc.	294
Goodman and Carr	255	Island Savings Credit Union	295
Goodwill Industries of Toronto	256	Island Telecom Inc.	295
Goodyear Canada Inc.	256	IWK Grace Health Centre	297
Gov't of Newfoundland - Dept. of Finance	257	Izaak Walton Killam Hospital, The	297
Grant Thornton	258	J.D. Irving Limited	298
Great-West Life Assurance Company, The	259	J.S. Redpath Limited	299
Grenville Management Ltd.	259	Jacques Whitford Consulting Engineers	299
Groupe Savoie Inc.	260	James Richardson International Limited	300
Grouse Mountain Resorts Ltd.	260	Jim Pattison Group	301
Halifax County Regional Rehabilitation Centre	263	John P. Robarts Research Institute	302
Halifax Regional Municipality	263	Johnson Incorporated	303
Halifax Water Commission	264	Jostens Canada Ltd.	303
Hasbro Canada Inc.	266	Kawneer Company Canada Limited	304
Health Authority 5	267	Kelowna, City of	305
Health Care Corporation of St. John's	267	Kennametal Ltd.	305
Helijet Airways Inc.	268	Kennedy Lodge Nursing Home Inc.	306
Hemosol Inc.	269	Keyano College	306
Hermes Electronics Inc.	269	KFC Canada	307
Hippodrome de Montréal	270	Kitchener, City of	309
Hoffman-La Roche Limited	272	La Confiserie Comete Ltee	311
Holiday Inn Select Toronto Airport	272	Laidlaw Inc.	312
Home Oil Co. Ltd.	273	Leduc, City of	313

The Canada Student Employment Guide

University Index

Lego Canada Inc.	314	Motorola Canada Ltd.	356
Lenbrook Industries Limited	315	Mountain Equipment Co-op	356
Leon's Manufacturing Company Inc.	316	Mustang Survival Corp.	358
Les Centres Jeunesse de Montréal	316	N B S Card Services	359
Les Distilleries Corby Ltée	317	Nanaimo Credit Union	359
Les Modes Smart Inc.	318	Natco Canada Ltd.	360
Liberty Health	318	National Grocers Co. Ltd.	360
Lifetouch Canada Inc.	319	National Life	361
Linmor Technologies	320	National Manufacturing of Canada Inc.	361
Litton Systems Canada Ltd.	320	National Sports Centre	362
London Goodwill Industries Association	322	Neles Automation, Scada Solutions Ltd.	362
M M Industra Ltd.	323	Nelvana Limited	363
MAAX Inc.	324	Neptune Food Suppliers Ltd.	363
MacDonald Dettwiler and Associates Ltd.	325	Nesbitt Burns Inc.	364
Mactac Canada Ltd.	326	Nestle Canada Inc.	364
Magna International Inc.	327	New Brunswick Power Corporation	365
Manitoba Agriculture and Food	327	New Holland Canada Ltd.	366
Manitoba Hydro	328	Newfoundland and Labrador Credit Union	367
Manitoba Pool Elevators	328	Newfoundland and Labrador Hydro	367
Manitoba Public Insurance Corporation	329	Newness Machine Ltd.	368
Marine Atlantic Inc.	331	News Marketing Canada	368
Maritime Life Assurance Company, The	331	Niagara Parks Commission, The	369
Mark Anthony Group Inc.	332	Nike Canada Ltd.	371
Marystown Shipyard Limited	334	Nissan Canada Inc.	371
Matrox Electronic Systems Ltd.	335	Norbord Industries	372
McBee Systems of Canada Inc.	336	Norcen Energy Resources Ltd.	373
McCarney Greenwood	336	North American Life Assurance Company	373
McGraw Hill Ryerson Ltd.	337	North West Company Inc.	374
McInnes Cooper & Robertson	337	Northern Lights Regional Health Centre	375
McKay-Cocker Construction Limited	338	Northern Mountain Helicopters Inc.	375
Mediacom Inc.	340	Northwestel Inc.	376
Medical Laboratories of Windsor Limited	341	Norwich Union Life Insurance Society	376
Memotec Communications Inc.	341	Nova Scotia Liquor Commission	377
Metro Richelieu Inc.	342	Nova Scotia Power Corp.	377
Metro Toronto Convention Centre	342	Novartis Consumer Health Canada Inc.	378
Metroland Printing, Publishing & Dist. Ltd.	343	Novotel Canada Inc.	378
Metropolitan Life Insurance Company	344	NPS Allelix Corp.	379
Meyers Norris Penny & Co.	344	Numac Energy Inc.	379
Michaels of Canada Inc.	345	Nygard International Ltd.	380
Midland Walwyn Inc.	345	Ocelot Energy Inc.	381
Midwest Food Products Inc.	346	Oland Breweries Limited	382
Milne & Craighead Inc.	347	Omstead Foods Limited	383
Minas Basin Pulp and Power Company Ltd.	347	Ontario Jockey Club, The	384
Ministry of Northern Develop. and Mines	348	Ontario Legislative Offices	384
Misericordia General Hospital	348	Oracle Corp. Canada Inc.	386
Mitel Corporation	350	Ottawa Hospital	386
Mitsubishi Electric Sales Canada	351	Paramount Canada's Wonderland Inc.	389
Mobile Computing Corporation	351	Patheon Inc.	390
Moen Inc.	352	PavCo	391
Moffat Communications Limited	352	PCL Constructors Inc.	392
Monarch Communications Inc.	353	Peacock Inc.	392
Montreal Trust Co.	353	Pearson Education Canada	393
Moosehead Breweries Limited	354	Peel Board of Education	393
MOSAID Technologies Inc.	355	Pelmorex Inc.	395

The Canada Student Employment Guide

University Index

Pembina Pipeline Corporation	395
PennCorp Life Insurance Company	396
Petro-Canada	397
Pharma Plus Drugmarts Ltd.	398
Phoenix International	399
Pilot Insurance Company	399
Pine Falls Paper Company Limited	400
Pitney Bowes of Canada Ltd.	401
Pizza Pizza Ltd.	401
Placer Dome Inc.	402
Poco Petroleums Ltd.	402
Polygram Group Canada Inc.	403
Positron Industries Inc.	404
Potacan Mining Company	405
Power Measurement Ltd.	406
PPG Canada Inc.	407
Pratt & Whitney Canada Inc.	407
Premdor Inc.	408
PRI Automation	408
Pricewaterhouse Coopers	409
Prince Albert Credit Union	409
Prince Albert, City of	410
Prince George, City of	410
Public Utilities of Kingston	413
Purolator Courier Ltd.	413
QEII Health Sciences Centre	414
QIT-Fer et Titane Inc.	414
Québec Cartier Mining Company	415
Quebecor Inc.	415
Quesnel River Pulp Company	416
Rasco Specialty Metals Inc.	417
Raymond Industrial Equipment Ltd.	418
Raymond Rebar Inc.	418
Reader's Digest Association of Canada Ltd.	419
Ready Bake Foods Inc.	420
Recochem Inc.	420
Red Deer Co-op Limited	421
Regal Capital Planners Ltd.	422
Regal Constellation Hotel Ltd.	422
Regal Greeting and Gifts	423
Regina Health District	423
Reid Crowther	426
Reuters Information Services (Canada) Ltd.	428
Reynolds and Reynolds (Canada) Limited	430
Richter Usher & Vineberg	432
Rio Algom Limited	433
Rivtow Marine Ltd.	434
Rogers AT&T Wireless Inc.	436
Rothmans, Benson and Hedges Inc.	437
Royal & Sun Alliance Insurance Co. of Cda	437
Royal Bank of Canada	438
Royal Canadian Mint	438
Royal Inland Hospital	439
Royal Philips Electronics	439

Royal Victoria Hospital	440
Ryerson Polytechnic University	441
Saan Stores Ltd.	441
Salisbury House of Canada Ltd.	442
Sandman Hotels and Inns	443
Sara Lee Corporation of Canada Limited	444
Saskatchewan Economic Development	445
Saskatchewan Government Insurance	445
Saskatchewan Wheat Pool	447
Saskatoon, City of	448
Saskferco Products Inc.	448
SaskTel	449
SC Infrastructure Inc.	449
Schlumberger Canada Ltd.	450
Seprotech Systems Incorporated	454
Sharp Electronics of Canada Ltd.	454
Shaw Communications	455
Sheraton Fallsview Hotel	456
Shermag Inc.	457
Sherwood Credit Union	458
Shopping Channel, The	459
Shorewood Packaging Corp. of Canada Ltd.	459
Siemens Electric Ltd.	460
Signature Vacations Inc.	460
Silicon Graphics Canada Inc.	461
Skiing Louise Ltd.	461
Slocan Forest Products Ltd.	462
Sobeys Inc.	463
Sony Music Canada	465
Southam Inc.	466
Southern Railway of British Columbia Ltd.	466
Southland Canada	467
Spar Aerospace Limited	467
Spectra Premium Industries	468
Spectrum Signal Processing Inc.	468
Sportsco International	469
Sprint Canada	470
SRI Homes Inc.	470
SSQ Life	471
St. Joseph's Care Group	472
St. Lawrence Seaway Mgmt. Corp., The	473
Standard Knitting Limited	474
Star Data Systems Inc.	476
Steelcraft Industries Ltd.	477
Steelpipe Ltd.	477
Stitches	478
Stone Consolidated Inc.	479
Sudbury Regional Hospital	480
Sun Rype Products Ltd.	481
Sundog Printing Limited	482
Sunoco Inc.	482
Supreme Tooling Group	483
Surrey, City of	484
Swift Current Health District	485

The Canada Student Employment Guide

University Index

Sydney Steel Corporation	485	Western Glove Works	530
Symantec Corporation	486	Westinghouse Canada Inc.	532
Syncrude Canada Ltd.	486	WestJet Airlines	532
Talisman Energy Inc.	487	Westport Innovations Inc.	534
TCG International Inc.	487	Westshore Terminals Ltd.	534
TCT Logistics	488	Weyerhaeuser Company Limited	535
TD Waterhouse Investor Services (Canada)	488	Whistler Blackcomb Mountain	535
Teck Corp.	489	Whitehill Technologies Inc.	537
Teklogix Inc.	489	Wilson Auto Electric Ltd.	538
Telus Corporation	492	Windsor, City of	538
The Barn Fruit Markets Inc.	493	Winners Apparel Ltd.	539
The Co-operators	493	Winpak Ltd.	539
The Garland Group	494	Wire Rope Industries Ltd.	540
Thomas & Betts Ltée	495	World of Vacations Ltd.	541
Thomas Cook Group (Canada) Ltd.	495	XCAN Grain Pool Ltd.	541
Thomas J. Lipton	496	Yamaha Motor Canada Ltd.	542
Thompson's Moving and Storage	496	Yarmouth Regional Hospital	543
Thunder Bay Regional Hospital	497	Yellowknife, City of	544
Tiger Brand Knitting Company Limited	498	YFactor	544
Today's Business Products Ltd.	500	Zellers Inc.	546
Toronto District School Board	503	Zenon Environmental Inc.	547
Toronto East General Hospital	503		
Toronto General Hospital	505		
Toronto Police Service	506		

Finance

Toronto Sun Publishing Corp., The	507
Toronto, City of	508
Toshiba of Canada Ltd.	508
Toyota Canada Ltd.	509
TransAlta	509
Trojan Technologies Inc.	511
TSC Stores Ltd.	512
Turnbull & Turnbull Ltd.	512
Uni Select Inc.	513
Union Gas Ltd.	513
University College of Cape Breton	516
US Filter BCP	517
USF WaterGroup	517
Vacances Air Transat Inc.	518
Valley First Credit Union	518
VanCity Credit Union	519
Vancouver International Airport	520
Vancouver Sun	520
Volkswagen Canada Inc.	523
Volvo Cars of Canada Ltd.	523
W C I Canada Inc.	524
Waterloo Furniture Components Ltd.	524
Waverly & York Corporation	525
Wegu Canada Inc.	526
Weldco-Beales Manufacturing Inc.	527
Wendy's Restaurants of Canada Inc.	527
West Kootenay Power Ltd.	528
Westbury Life	529
Westcliff Management Ltd.	529
Westcoast Energy Inc.	530

A C A Cooperative Limited	74
Aar-Kel Moulds Ltd.	76
Aberdeen Hospital	77
Abitibi-Consolidated Inc.	77
Access Communications	78
Accucaps Industries Limited	79
ACE INI Insurance	79
Acklands-Grainger Inc.	80
ADT Canada Inc.	82
AGF Management Limited	83
Agricultural Credit Corp. of Saskatchewan	84
Aimtronics	84
Air Canada	85
Air Liquide Canada Inc.	85
Air Ontario Inc.	86
Akita Drilling Ltd.	87
Alberta Blue Cross	88
Alberta Energy & Utilities Board	89
Alberta Energy Company Ltd.	89
Alberta Gaming & Liquor Commission	90
Alcan Aluminium Limited	91
Algoma Steel Inc.	93
Aliant Telecom Inc.	93
Allcolour Paint Limited	94
Allianz Canada	95
Allstate Insurance Co. of Canada	96
Alpine Oil Service Corporation	96
Amcor Twinpak North America Inc.	98
Anthony Insurance Inc.	102

The Canada Student Employment Guide

630 University Index

Aon Reed Stenhouse Inc.	103
Apex Land Corp.	103
Aqua-Power Cleaners Ltd.	105
Armor Personnel	107
Assumption Mutual Life Insurance	109
AstraZeneca	110
ATCO Electric	111
ATCO Frontec Corp.	111
ATCO Gas Services Ltd.	112
Athabasca, Town of	112
Atlantic Blue Cross Care	113
Atlantic Packaging Products Ltd.	114
Atlantic Wholesalers Ltd.	114
Atlas Ideal Metals Inc.	115
Atlas Van Lines (Canada) Ltd.	115
Aventis Pasteur Limited	117
AXA Insurance (Canada)	118
Axidata Inc.	118
Babcock and Wilcox Canada	119
Ballard Power Systems Inc.	120
Banff Centre for Continuing Education, The	120
Barton Place Long Term Care Facility	121
BASF Canada Inc.	122
Basic Technologies Corporation	122
Bayer Inc.	124
BBM Bureau of Measurement	125
Bell Mobility	131
Bettis Canada Ltd.	135
BFGoodrich Landing Gear Division	135
Bic Inc.	136
Black Photo Corporation	139
Bloorview MacMillan Centre, The	140
BNP PARIBAS (Canada)	143
Boréal Assurances Inc.	144
BOVAR Waste Management	145
Bowater Mersey Paper Company Limited	146
Brewers Retail Inc.	148
British Columbia Ferry Corporation	149
Brookfield Properties Corporation	150
Buckeye Canada Inc.	151
Budd Canada Inc.	152
C MAC Industries Inc.	155
C.S.T. Consultants Inc.	155
Cabre Exploration Ltd.	156
Cadith Entertainment Ltd.	156
Calgary Co-operative Association Limited	157
Cambior Inc.	158
Cambridge Memorial Hospital	159
Camp Hill Hospital	160
Canada Post Corporation	162
Canada Safeway Limited	163
Canada Starch Company Inc.	163
Canadian Cancer Society	164
Canadian Dairy Commission	165
Canadian Depository for Securities Ltd.	166
Canadian Museum of Civilization Corp.	167
Canadian Occidental Petroleum Ltd.	168
Canadian Tire Corporation Ltd.	169
Canadian Western Bank	169
Cancarb Limited	170
CancerCare Manitoba	171
Canon Canada Inc.	172
Canpar Transport Ltd.	173
Cape Breton Development Corporation	174
Carbone of America (LCL) Ltd.	175
Carte International Inc.	176
CCL Industries Inc.	178
Celestica International Inc.	179
Centra Gas British Columbia Inc.	180
Centra Gas Manitoba Inc.	181
Central Park Lodges Ltd.	181
Ceridian Canada	183
CGU Group Canada Ltd.	185
Chapters Inc.	186
Chevron Canada Resources Ltd.	188
Christian Horizons	190
Cineplex Odeon Corporation	191
Citibank Canada	191
CKF Inc.	192
Cobourg District General Hospital	194
Coca Cola Foods Canada Inc.	195
COM DEV International	197
Communications & Power Industries Canada	198
Community Savings Credit Union	199
Compaq Canada Inc.	199
Computalog Ltd.	200
Computer Associates Canada Ltd.	201
Connors Bros, Limited	203
Co-op Atlantic	203
Coppley Apparel Group	204
Coquitlam, City of	204
Corner Brook, City of	205
Cornwall Electric	206
Cotton Ginny Ltd.	207
Cougar Helicopters Inc.	208
Credit Union Central of Canada	208
Culinar Inc.	209
Custom Trim Ltd.	210
D.A. Stuart Inc.	210
David Thompson Health Region	212
DDM Plastics Inc.	213
Deer Lodge Centre Inc.	213
Dell Computer Corporation	214
Delphi Solutions Inc.	215
Delta Hotels	215
Derlan Industries Limited	216
Directwest Publishers Ltd.	217
Dofasco Inc.	218

The Canada Student Employment Guide

University Index

Domtar Inc.	218
Dun & Bradstreet Canada	221
DuPont Canada Inc.	221
Dura Automotive Systems (Canada) Ltd.	222
Dylex Limited	222
Dynapro Systems Inc.	223
Dynasty Furniture Manufacturing Ltd.	224
Dynatek Automation Systems Inc.	224
Echo Bay Mines Ltd.	226
Economical Insurance Group, The	227
EDS of Canada Ltd.	228
Eli Lilly Canada Inc.	230
Emco Limited	230
EMJ Data Systems Ltd.	231
EnerFlex Systems Ltd.	232
Exfo	235
Exide Canada Inc.	235
Explorer Hotel, The	236
Export Development Corporation	236
Extendicare (Canada) Inc.	237
Farm Credit Corp. Canada	238
Farmers Co-operative Dairy Limited	239
Federated Co-operatives Limited	239
FedEx Express	240
Finning	240
Fishery Products International	241
Fletcher's Fine Foods	242
Flint Energy Services Ltd.	243
Forzani Group Ltd., The	244
Foyer Valade Inc.	245
Friesens Corporation	246
Future Shop Ltd.	246
Gendis Inc.	248
General Chemical Canada Ltd.	249
General Electric Canada Inc.	249
George Jeffrey Children's Treatment Centre	250
Gienow Building Products Ltd.	251
Gilbey Canada Inc.	252
Gimbel Eye Centre	252
Glaxo Wellcome Canada	253
Goodman and Carr	255
Goodwill Industries of Toronto	256
Goodyear Canada Inc.	256
Gov't of Newfoundland - Dept. of Finance	257
Grant Thornton	258
Great-West Life Assurance Company, The	259
Groupe Savoie Inc.	260
Halifax County Regional Rehabilitation Centre	263
Halifax Regional Municipality	263
Halifax Water Commission	264
Hasbro Canada Inc.	266
Health Authority 5	267
Health Sciences Centre	268
Helijet Airways Inc.	268

Hermes Electronics Inc.	269
Hippodrome de Montréal	270
Hoffman-La Roche Limited	272
Holiday Inn Select Toronto Airport	272
Home Oil Co. Ltd.	273
Homewood Corp.	274
Honda Canada Inc.	274
Honeywell Ltd.	275
Horseshoe Resort Corporation	275
Household Movers & Shippers Limited	276
HSBC Bank Canada	277
Hub Meat Packers Ltd.	278
Hudon & Deaudelin Ltée	279
Hudson's Bay Company, The	279
Humber River Regional Hospital	280
Huronia Regional Centre	280
Hydro Electric Commission of Thunder Bay	281
Hydro Mississauga Corporation	282
Hydro Québec	283
I M P Group International Inc.	283
IBM Canada Ltd.	284
ICI Canada Inc.	285
Ilco Unican Inc.	286
Imperial Oil Limited	286
Industrial-Alliance Life Insurance Company	289
Industries Lassonde Inc.	289
InfoInterActive Inc.	290
ING Canada Financial Services International	291
Insurance Corp. of B.C.	291
Intercon Security Ltd.	292
Interior Savings Credit Union	293
IPL Energy Inc.	294
Island Savings Credit Union	295
Island Telecom Inc.	295
Ivaco Inc.	296
IWK Grace Health Centre	297
J.D. Irving Limited	298
James Richardson International Limited	300
Jim Pattison Group	301
John P. Robarts Research Institute	302
Johnson Incorporated	303
Jostens Canada Ltd.	303
Kawneer Company Canada Limited	304
Kelowna, City of	305
Kennametal Ltd.	305
Keyano College	306
KFC Canada	307
Kitchener, City of	309
Kodak Canada Inc.	309
Kraft Canada Inc.	310
Laidlaw Inc.	312
Leduc, City of	313
Lego Canada Inc.	314
Leon's Manufacturing Company Inc.	316

The Canada Student Employment Guide

University Index

Les Centres Jeunesse de Montréal	316	New Brunswick Power Corporation	365
Les Distilleries Corby Ltée	317	New Holland Canada Ltd.	366
Les Modes Smart Inc.	318	Newfoundland and Labrador Credit Union	367
Liberty Health	318	Newfoundland and Labrador Hydro	367
Lifetouch Canada Inc.	319	News Marketing Canada	368
Linmor Technologies	320	Niagara Parks Commission, The	369
Litton Systems Canada Ltd.	320	Nike Canada Ltd.	371
Loewen Windows	321	Nissan Canada Inc.	371
M M Industra Ltd.	323	Norbord Industries	372
MacDonald Dettwiler and Associates Ltd.	325	North American Life Assurance Company	373
Magna International Inc.	327	North West Company Inc.	374
Manitoba Agriculture and Food	327	Northern Lights Regional Health Centre	375
Manitoba Hydro	328	Northwestel Inc.	376
Manitoba Pool Elevators	328	Norwich Union Life Insurance Society	376
Manitoba Public Insurance Corporation	329	Nova Scotia Power Corp.	377
Maple Leaf Consumer Foods	330	Novartis Consumer Health Canada Inc.	378
Marine Atlantic Inc.	331	Numac Energy Inc.	379
Maritime Life Assurance Company, The	331	Oland Breweries Limited	382
Mark Anthony Group Inc.	332	Omstead Foods Limited	383
Marystown Shipyard Limited	334	Ontario Jockey Club, The	384
McBee Systems of Canada Inc.	336	Ontario Legislative Offices	384
McCarney Greenwood	336	Ottawa Hospital	386
McGraw Hill Ryerson Ltd.	337	Paramount Canada's Wonderland Inc.	389
Medical Laboratories of Windsor Limited	341	Patheon Inc.	390
Memotec Communications Inc.	341	PavCo	391
Metro Richelieu Inc.	342	Peacock Inc.	392
Metropolitan Life Insurance Company	344	Pearson Education Canada	393
Meyers Norris Penny & Co.	344	Peel Board of Education	393
Michaels of Canada Inc.	345	Peel Regional Police	394
Midland Walwyn Inc.	345	Pelmorex Inc.	395
Midwest Food Products Inc.	346	PennCorp Life Insurance Company	396
Milne & Craighead Inc.	347	Pharma Plus Drugmarts Ltd.	398
Ministry of Northern Develop. and Mines	348	Pine Falls Paper Company Limited	400
Misericordia General Hospital	348	Pitney Bowes of Canada Ltd.	401
Mitel Corporation	350	Pizza Pizza Ltd.	401
Mitsubishi Electric Sales Canada	351	Poco Petroleums Ltd.	402
Mobile Computing Corporation	351	Polygram Group Canada Inc.	403
Moen Inc.	352	Positron Industries Inc.	404
Moffat Communications Limited	352	Potacan Mining Company	405
Montreal Trust Co.	353	Power Measurement Ltd.	406
Moosehead Breweries Limited	354	Pratt & Whitney Canada Inc.	407
MOSAID Technologies Inc.	355	Premdor Inc.	408
Motorola Canada Ltd.	356	Pricewaterhouse Coopers	409
Mountain Equipment Co-op	356	Prince Albert Credit Union	409
Mustang Survival Corp.	358	Prince George, City of	410
Nanaimo Credit Union	359	Progressive Financial Strategy	411
National Grocers Co. Ltd.	360	Prudential Insurance Co. of America, The	412
National Life	361	Public Utilities of Kingston	413
National Manufacturing of Canada Inc.	361	Purolator Courier Ltd.	413
National Sports Centre	362	QIT-Fer et Titane Inc.	414
Neles Automation, Scada Solutions Ltd.	362	Quebecor Inc.	415
Neptune Food Suppliers Ltd.	363	Rasco Specialty Metals Inc.	417
Nesbitt Burns Inc.	364	Raymond Rebar Inc.	418
Nestle Canada Inc.	364	Reader's Digest Association of Canada Ltd.	419

The Canada Student Employment Guide

University Index

Recochem Inc.	420
Red Deer Co-op Limited	421
Regal Capital Planners Ltd.	422
Regal Constellation Hotel Ltd.	422
Regal Greeting and Gifts	423
Regina Health District	423
Renaissance Energy Ltd.	427
Rentway Inc.	427
Reuters Information Services (Canada) Ltd.	428
Richter Usher & Vineberg	432
Rio Algom Limited	433
Riverside Hospital of Ottawa, The	434
Rivtow Marine Ltd.	434
Rogers AT&T Wireless Inc.	436
Rogers Media, Publishing	436
Rothmans, Benson and Hedges Inc.	437
Royal & Sun Alliance Insurance Co. of Cda	437
Royal Bank of Canada	438
Royal Canadian Mint	438
Royal Philips Electronics	439
Ryerson Polytechnic University	441
Saan Stores Ltd.	441
Salisbury House of Canada Ltd.	442
Sara Lee Corporation of Canada Limited	444
Saskatchewan Economic Development	445
Saskatchewan Government Insurance	445
Saskatchewan Transportation Company	446
Saskatchewan Wheat Pool	447
Saskatoon, City of	448
Saskferco Products Inc.	448
SaskTel	449
Schlumberger Canada Ltd.	450
Science North	452
Seprotech Systems Incorporated	454
Sharp Electronics of Canada Ltd.	454
Shaw Communications	455
Shermag Inc.	457
Sherwood Credit Union	458
Shopping Channel, The	459
Shorewood Packaging Corp. of Canada Ltd.	459
Siemens Electric Ltd.	460
Signature Vacations Inc.	460
Silicon Graphics Canada Inc.	461
Skiing Louise Ltd.	461
Slocan Forest Products Ltd.	462
Sobeys Inc.	463
Sony Music Canada	465
Southam Inc.	466
Southland Canada	467
Spar Aerospace Limited	467
Spectra Premium Industries	468
Spectrum Signal Processing Inc.	468
Sportsco International	469
Sprint Canada	470
SRI Homes Inc.	470
SSQ Life	471
St. Lawrence Parks Commission	472
Standard Knitting Limited	474
Stanley Canada Inc.	475
Star Data Systems Inc.	476
Steelcraft Industries Ltd.	477
Sudbury Regional Hospital	480
Sun Rype Products Ltd.	481
Sundog Printing Limited	482
Sunoco Inc.	482
Supreme Tooling Group	483
Surrey, City of	484
Swift Current Health District	485
Sydney Steel Corporation	485
Symantec Corporation	486
Talisman Energy Inc.	487
TCG International Inc.	487
TCT Logistics	488
TD Waterhouse Investor Services (Canada)	488
Teklogix Inc.	489
Telus Corporation	492
The Barn Fruit Markets Inc.	493
The Co-operators	493
The Garland Group	494
Thomas Cook Group (Canada) Ltd.	495
Thomas J. Lipton	496
Thompson's Moving and Storage	496
Thomson - CSF Systems Canada Inc.	497
Tiger Brand Knitting Company Limited	498
Today's Business Products Ltd.	500
Toronto District School Board	503
Toronto East General Hospital	503
Toronto General Hospital	505
Toronto Police Service	506
Toronto Sun Publishing Corp., The	507
Toronto, City of	508
Toshiba of Canada Ltd.	508
Toyota Canada Ltd.	509
TransAlta	509
TSC Stores Ltd.	512
Turnbull & Turnbull Ltd.	512
Uni Select Inc.	513
Union Gas Ltd.	513
University College of Cape Breton	516
Vacances Air Transat Inc.	518
Valley First Credit Union	518
VanCity Credit Union	519
Vancouver International Airport	520
Vancouver Sun	520
Visteon Canada Inc.	522
Volvo Cars of Canada Ltd.	523
W C I Canada Inc.	524
Waterloo Furniture Components Ltd.	524

The Canada Student Employment Guide

634 University Index

Waverly & York Corporation	525	ArvinMeritor	108
Weldco-Beales Manufacturing Inc.	527	Assiniboine Community College	109
West Kootenay Power Ltd.	528	Atlantic Blue Cross Care	113
Westbury Life	529	Atlas Ideal Metals Inc.	115
Westcliff Management Ltd.	529	Atlas Van Lines (Canada) Ltd.	115
Westcoast Energy Inc.	530	Aurum Ceramic Dental Laboratories Ltd.	117
Western Glove Works	530	Axidata Inc.	118
Westinghouse Canada Inc.	532	Banff Centre for Continuing Education, The	120
WestJet Airlines	532	BASF Canada Inc.	122
Westminster Savings Credit Union	533	Basic Technologies Corporation	122
Westport Innovations Inc.	534	BBM Bureau of Measurement	125
Westshore Terminals Ltd.	534	BCG Services	127
Weyerhaeuser Company Limited	535	Bearskin Lake Air Service Ltd.	128
Whistler Blackcomb Mountain	535	Behlen Industries	130
Wilson Auto Electric Ltd.	538	Bell Mobility	131
Windsor, City of	538	Bettis Canada Ltd.	135
Winners Apparel Ltd.	539	BFGoodrich Landing Gear Division	135
Winpak Ltd.	539	Birks Jewelry	138
Wire Rope Industries Ltd.	540	Black Photo Corporation	139
World of Vacations Ltd.	541	Blue Giant Equipment of Canada Ltd.	141
XCAN Grain Pool Ltd.	541	Blue Mountain Resorts Limited	141
Yellowknife, City of	544	BNP PARIBAS (Canada)	143
YFactor	544	Boréal Assurances Inc.	144
Zellers Inc.	546	Bowater Mersey Paper Company Limited	146
		British Columbia Ferry Corporation	149
		Brookfield Properties Corporation	150
General		Buckeye Canada Inc.	151
		Burger King Restaurants of Canada Inc.	153
1-800-GOT-JUNK?	74	C.S.T. Consultants Inc.	155
Aberdeen Hospital	77	Cabre Exploration Ltd.	156
Acadia University	78	Cadith Entertainment Ltd.	156
Access Communications	78	Calgary Co-operative Association Limited	157
ACE INI Insurance	79	Canada Safeway Limited	163
Acklands-Grainger Inc.	80	Canada Starch Company Inc.	163
ADT Canada Inc.	82	Canadian Cancer Society	164
Akita Drilling Ltd.	87	Canadian Dairy Commission	165
Alberta Blue Cross	88	Canadian Depository for Securities Ltd.	166
Alberta Energy & Utilities Board	89	Canadian Museum of Civilization Corp.	167
Alberta Gaming & Liquor Commission	90	Canadian Occidental Petroleum Ltd.	168
Aliant Telecom Inc.	93	Canadian Western Bank	169
Allianz Canada	95	Canbra Foods Ltd.	170
Allmar Distributors Ltd.	95	Cangene Corporation	172
Allstate Insurance Co. of Canada	96	Canon Canada Inc.	172
Amcan Castings Limited	98	Capilano Suspension Bridge	174
Amcor Twinpak North America Inc.	98	Cargill Limited	175
American Airlines Inc.	99	Centra Gas Manitoba Inc.	181
Amram's Distributing Ltd.	100	Central Park Lodges Ltd.	181
Andersen Consulting	101	Century Sales and Service Limited	182
Antamex International Inc.	102	CFCF Inc.	183
Anthony Insurance Inc.	102	CGU Group Canada Ltd.	185
Apex Land Corp.	103	Chapters Inc.	186
Arbor Memorial Services Inc.	106	Charlottetown Driving Park	187
Arctic Co-operatives Limited	107	Chevron Canada Resources Ltd.	188
Armor Personnel	107	Christian Horizons	190

The Canada Student Employment Guide

University Index

Citibank Canada	191	Halifax Regional Municipality	263
Cobourg District General Hospital	194	Halifax Water Commission	264
Coca Cola Foods Canada Inc.	195	Hasbro Canada Inc.	266
Cognos Incorporated	196	Health Care Corporation of St. John's	267
Columbia House	197	Helijet Airways Inc.	268
COM DEV International	197	Hermes Electronics Inc.	269
Compaq Canada Inc.	199	Hippodrome de Montréal	270
Computer Associates Canada Ltd.	201	Holiday Inn Select Toronto Airport	272
Co-op Atlantic	203	Holland College	273
Coppley Apparel Group	204	Home Oil Co. Ltd.	273
Coquitlam, City of	204	Honeywell Ltd.	275
Corner Brook, City of	205	Horseshoe Resort Corporation	275
Cosmair Canada Inc.	206	Household Movers & Shippers Limited	276
Cotton Ginny Ltd.	207	HSBC Bank Canada	277
Credit Union Central of Canada	208	Hub Meat Packers Ltd.	278
Culinar Inc.	209	Hudson's Bay Company, The	279
David Thompson Health Region	212	Hydro Electric Commission of Thunder Bay	281
Degussa - Huls Canada Inc.	214	I M P Group International Inc.	283
Dell Computer Corporation	214	ICI Canada Inc.	285
Delta Toronto Airport Hotel	216	INCO Limited	287
Directwest Publishers Ltd.	217	InfoInterActive Inc.	290
Domtar Inc.	218	ING Canada Financial Services International	291
Drug Trading Company Ltd.	219	Insurance Corp. of B.C.	291
Duha Color Services	220	Intercon Security Ltd.	292
Dynapro Systems Inc.	223	Interforest Ltd.	292
Dynasty Furniture Manufacturing Ltd.	224	Interior Savings Credit Union	293
Economic Development Edmonton	226	Intertape Polymer Group Inc.	294
Economical Insurance Group, The	227	IPL Energy Inc.	294
Eli Lilly Canada Inc.	230	Island Savings Credit Union	295
EMJ Data Systems Ltd.	231	Island Telecom Inc.	295
Endpoint Research Ltd.	231	J.D. Irving Limited	298
Epson Canada Limited	233	Jim Pattison Group	301
Exfo	235	Johnson Incorporated	303
Extendicare (Canada) Inc.	237	Jostens Canada Ltd.	303
Farm Credit Corp. Canada	238	KFC Canada	307
Farmers Co-operative Dairy Limited	239	Kitchener, City of	309
Federated Co-operatives Limited	239	Laidlaw Inc.	312
Finning	240	Leduc, City of	313
Future Shop Ltd.	246	Lego Canada Inc.	314
Gay Lea Foods Co-Operative Ltd.	247	Leon's Manufacturing Company Inc.	316
Gendis Inc.	248	Les Centres Jeunesse de Montréal	316
General Electric Canada Inc.	249	Les Distilleries Corby Ltée	317
Gienow Building Products Ltd.	251	Liberty Health	318
Gilbey Canada Inc.	252	Lick's Ice Cream & Burger Shops Inc.	319
Glaxo Wellcome Canada	253	Lifetouch Canada Inc.	319
Glentel Inc.	254	Manitoba Agriculture and Food	327
Goepel McDermid Securities	254	Manitoba Public Insurance Corporation	329
Goodman and Carr	255	Maple Leaf Consumer Foods	330
Goodwill Industries of Toronto	256	Maritime Life Assurance Company, The	331
Goodyear Canada Inc.	256	Mark Anthony Group Inc.	332
Grant Thornton	258	Matrox Electronic Systems Ltd.	335
Great-West Life Assurance Company, The	259	McBee Systems of Canada Inc.	336
Groupe Savoie Inc.	260	McCarney Greenwood	336
Halifax County Regional Rehabilitation Centre	263	McInnes Cooper & Robertson	337

The Canada Student Employment Guide

University Index

McLaren-McCann Advertising of Canada Ltd.	338
Metro Richelieu Inc.	342
Metro Toronto Convention Centre	342
Metropolitan Life Insurance Company	344
Midland Walwyn Inc.	345
Midwest Food Products Inc.	346
Milne & Craighead Inc.	347
Minas Basin Pulp and Power Company Ltd.	347
Ministry of Northern Develop. and Mines	348
Mitel Corporation	350
Mitsubishi Electric Sales Canada	351
Mobile Computing Corporation	351
Moen Inc.	352
Montreal Trust Co.	353
Morrison Hershfield Limited	354
MOSAID Technologies Inc.	355
Motorola Canada Ltd.	356
Nanaimo Credit Union	359
National Grocers Co. Ltd.	360
National Life	361
Neles Automation, Scada Solutions Ltd.	362
Nelvana Limited	363
New Brunswick Power Corporation	365
New Brunswick Telephone Company	366
Newfoundland and Labrador Credit Union	367
News Marketing Canada	368
Niagara Parks Commission, The	369
Nielsen Marketing Research	370
Nissan Canada Inc.	371
Norbord Industries	372
North American Life Assurance Company	373
North West Company Inc.	374
Northern Mountain Helicopters Inc.	375
Northwestel Inc.	376
Norwich Union Life Insurance Society	376
Novartis Consumer Health Canada Inc.	378
Nygard International Ltd.	380
Ontario Jockey Club, The	384
Ontario Legislative Offices	384
Paperboard Industries International Inc.	389
Paramount Canada's Wonderland Inc.	389
Paul Revere Life Insurance Company, The	391
PavCo	391
Pearson Education Canada	393
Peel Board of Education	393
PennCorp Life Insurance Company	396
Pharma Plus Drugmarts Ltd.	398
Pilot Insurance Company	399
Pitney Bowes of Canada Ltd.	401
Pizza Pizza Ltd.	401
Poco Petroleums Ltd.	402
Pollack Rentals Limited	403
Potacan Mining Company	405
PPG Canada Inc.	407
Prince Albert, City of	410
Prince George, City of	410
Progressive Financial Strategy	411
QEII Health Sciences Centre	414
Raymond Rebar Inc.	418
Red Deer Co-op Limited	421
Regal Capital Planners Ltd.	422
Regal Constellation Hotel Ltd.	422
Regal Greeting and Gifts	423
Renaissance Energy Ltd.	427
Rentway Inc.	427
Replicon Inc.	428
Reynolds and Reynolds (Canada) Limited	430
Rhone-Poulenc Canada Inc.	430
Rio Algom Limited	433
Rogers AT&T Wireless Inc.	436
Rothmans, Benson and Hedges Inc.	437
Royal & Sun Alliance Insurance Co. of Cda	437
Royal Bank of Canada	438
Sales & Merchandising Group	442
Sandman Hotels and Inns	443
Saskatchewan Economic Development	445
Saskatchewan Government Insurance	445
SCIEX MDS Health Group	452
Sharp Electronics of Canada Ltd.	454
Shaw Communications	455
Shermag Inc.	457
Sherwood Credit Union	458
Shoppers Drug Mart Limited	458
Shopping Channel, The	459
Shorewood Packaging Corp. of Canada Ltd.	459
Siemens Electric Ltd.	460
Signature Vacations Inc.	460
Skiing Louise Ltd.	461
Slocan Forest Products Ltd.	462
Sodexho Marriott Services Canada	464
Sony Music Canada	465
Southam Inc.	466
Southern Railway of British Columbia Ltd.	466
Spar Aerospace Limited	467
Sportsco International	469
Sprint Canada	470
SSQ Life	471
Stanley Canada Inc.	475
Star Data Systems Inc.	476
State Farm Insurance Companies	476
Steelpipe Ltd.	477
Supreme Tooling Group	483
TCG International Inc.	487
TCT Logistics	488
TD Waterhouse Investor Services (Canada)	488
Teck Corp.	489
Teklogix Inc.	489
Teldon International Inc.	490

The Canada Student Employment Guide

University Index

Telus Corporation	492
Thomas & Betts Ltée	495
Thompson's Moving and Storage	496
Ticketmaster Canada Inc.	498
Tiger Brand Knitting Company Limited	498
Today's Business Products Ltd.	500
Toronto General Hospital	505
Toronto Sun Publishing Corp., The	507
Toshiba of Canada Ltd.	508
Toyota Canada Ltd.	509
TSC Stores Ltd.	512
Turnbull & Turnbull Ltd.	512
Union Gas Ltd.	513
University College of Cape Breton	516
Valley First Credit Union	518
Vancouver Sun	520
VIA Rail Canada Inc.	521
Volvo Cars of Canada Ltd.	523
Waverly & York Corporation	525
Wendy's Restaurants of Canada Inc.	527
Western Glove Works	530
Westinghouse Canada Inc.	532
WestJet Airlines	532
Weston Produce Inc.	533
Westshore Terminals Ltd.	534
Weyerhaeuser Company Limited	535
Whistler Blackcomb Mountain	535
Wilson Auto Electric Ltd.	538
Windsor, City of	538
Winners Apparel Ltd.	539
Winpak Ltd.	539
xwave solutions	542
Yamaha Motor Canada Ltd.	542
Yanke Group of Companies	543
Yellowknife, City of	544
Zellers Inc.	546
Zenon Environmental Inc.	547

Human Resources

1-800-GOT-JUNK?	74
A C A Cooperative Limited	74
ABC Group	76
Addictions Foundation of Manitoba, The	81
Alberta Energy & Utilities Board	89
Aliant Telecom Inc.	93
Aqua-Power Cleaners Ltd.	105
ATCO Frontec Corp.	111
Atlantic Blue Cross Care	113
Atlantic Packaging Products Ltd.	114
Atlas Ideal Metals Inc.	115
ATS Automation Tooling Systems Inc.	116
AXA Insurance (Canada)	118

Babcock and Wilcox Canada	119
Bearskin Lake Air Service Ltd.	128
BFGoodrich Landing Gear Division	135
Blaney McMurty LLP	139
Bonus Resource Services Corp.	144
BOVAR Waste Management	145
Budd Canada Inc.	152
Capilano Suspension Bridge	174
Central Park Lodges Ltd.	181
COM DEV International	197
Connors Bros, Limited	203
Coppley Apparel Group	204
Coquitlam, City of	204
Cosyn Technology	207
Cotton Ginny Ltd.	207
Cougar Helicopters Inc.	208
David Thompson Health Region	212
DDM Plastics Inc.	213
Deer Lodge Centre Inc.	213
Domtar Inc.	218
Echo Bay Mines Ltd.	226
Economical Insurance Group, The	227
EnerFlex Systems Ltd.	232
Exfo	235
Farm Credit Corp. Canada	238
Farmers Co-operative Dairy Limited	239
Finning	240
Flint Energy Services Ltd.	243
Halifax County Regional Rehabilitation Centre	263
Health Authority 5	267
Hemosol Inc.	269
Humber River Regional Hospital	280
Ilco Unican Inc.	286
Interior Savings Credit Union	293
IWK Grace Health Centre	297
J.D. Irving Limited	298
John P. Robarts Research Institute	302
Kawneer Company Canada Limited	304
Leduc, City of	313
Leon's Manufacturing Company Inc.	316
Les Modes Smart Inc.	318
Lifetouch Canada Inc.	319
Manitoba Hydro	328
Maple Leaf Consumer Foods	330
Maritime Life Assurance Company, The	331
Matrox Electronic Systems Ltd.	335
MDS Nordion	339
Meyers Norris Penny & Co.	344
Mortice Kern Systems Inc.	355
Neles Automation, Scada Solutions Ltd.	362
News Marketing Canada	368
Northwestel Inc.	376
Omstead Foods Limited	383
Ottawa Hospital	386

The Canada Student Employment Guide

638   University Index

Patheon Inc.	390	Air Ontario Inc.	86
Peel Children's Centre	394	Akita Drilling Ltd.	87
Phoenix International	399	Alberta Blue Cross	88
PPG Canada Inc.	407	Alberta Energy Company Ltd.	89
Progressive Financial Strategy	411	Alberto Culver Canada Inc.	90
QEII Health Sciences Centre	414	Algoma Steel Inc.	93
Raymond Rebar Inc.	418	Aliant Telecom Inc.	93
Regina Health District	423	Allcolour Paint Limited	94
Rimrock Resort Hotel	432	Allmar Distributors Ltd.	95
Rogers AT&T Wireless Inc.	436	Amcor Twinpak North America Inc.	98
Royal Canadian Mint	438	American Airlines Inc.	99
Saskferco Products Inc.	448	Amram's Distributing Ltd.	100
Sherwood Credit Union	458	Anthony Insurance Inc.	102
Skiing Louise Ltd.	461	Apex Land Corp.	103
Slocan Forest Products Ltd.	462	Aquatic Sciences Inc.	105
Sobeys Inc.	463	Armor Personnel	107
Spectra Premium Industries	468	Assiniboine Community College	109
Spectrum Signal Processing Inc.	468	Assumption Mutual Life Insurance	109
Sportsco International	469	AstraZeneca	110
Sprint Canada	470	Atlantic Blue Cross Care	113
Standard Knitting Limited	474	Atlantic Lottery Corporation Inc.	113
Steelcraft Industries Ltd.	477	Atlantic Packaging Products Ltd.	114
Sudbury Regional Hospital	480	Atlantic Wholesalers Ltd.	114
Swift Current Health District	485	Atlas Ideal Metals Inc.	115
The Co-operators	493	Atlas Van Lines (Canada) Ltd.	115
The Garland Group	494	Aurum Ceramic Dental Laboratories Ltd.	117
TransAlta	509	Axidata Inc.	118
Trojan Technologies Inc.	511	Babcock and Wilcox Canada	119
Uni Select Inc.	513	Ballard Power Systems Inc.	120
Visteon Canada Inc.	522	Banff Centre for Continuing Education, The	120
Volvo Cars of Canada Ltd.	523	Barton Place Long Term Care Facility	121
Western Glove Works	530	BASF Canada Inc.	122
WestJet Airlines	532	BBM Bureau of Measurement	125
Westport Innovations Inc.	534	BC Telecom Inc.	126
Weyerhaeuser Company Limited	535	Bell Canada	131
Winners Apparel Ltd.	539	Bell Mobility	131
		Bettis Canada Ltd.	135
		Bic Inc.	136
Marketing		Bio-Research Laboratories Ltd.	137
		Black Photo Corporation	139
1-800-GOT-JUNK?	74	Blue Mountain Resorts Limited	141
A C A Cooperative Limited	74	Blue Wave Seafoods Inc.	142
A.G. Simpson Co. Ltd.	75	Bonus Resource Services Corp.	144
Abitibi-Consolidated Inc.	77	Boréal Assurances Inc.	144
Access Communications	78	BOVAR Waste Management	145
Accucaps Industries Limited	79	British Columbia Ferry Corporation	149
Acklands-Grainger Inc.	80	Browning Harvey Limited	150
ADI Group Inc.	82	Buckeye Canada Inc.	151
ADT Canada Inc.	82	C.S.T. Consultants Inc.	155
AGF Management Limited	83	Cabre Exploration Ltd.	156
Agricultural Credit Corp. of Saskatchewan	84	Calgary Co-operative Association Limited	157
Air Canada	85	Canada Post Corporation	162
Air Liquide Canada Inc.	85	Canada Safeway Limited	163
Air Nova Inc.	86	Canada Starch Company Inc.	163

The Canada Student Employment Guide

University Index

Canadian Cancer Society	164	Economical Insurance Group, The	227
Canadian Dairy Commission	165	Elco	229
Canadian General Tower Limited	166	Eli Lilly Canada Inc.	230
Canadian Museum of Civilization Corp.	167	EMJ Data Systems Ltd.	231
Canadian Thermos Products Inc.	168	EnerFlex Systems Ltd.	232
Canadian Western Bank	169	Entreprises Premier Canadien Ltée	232
Cancarb Limited	170	Epson Canada Limited	233
Cancore Industries Inc.	171	Exfo	235
Cangene Corporation	172	Exide Canada Inc.	235
Canon Canada Inc.	172	Explorer Hotel, The	236
Canpar Transport Ltd.	173	Farm Credit Corp. Canada	238
Capilano Suspension Bridge	174	Farmers Co-operative Dairy Limited	239
Carbone of America (LCL) Ltd.	175	Federated Co-operatives Limited	239
Cargill Limited	175	FedEx Express	240
Carte International Inc.	176	Finning	240
Celestica International Inc.	179	Fishery Products International	241
CenAlta Energy Services Inc.	180	Fletcher's Fine Foods	242
Centra Gas British Columbia Inc.	180	Forzani Group Ltd., The	244
Central Park Lodges Ltd.	181	Friesens Corporation	246
Century Sales and Service Limited	182	Future Shop Ltd.	246
Ceridian Canada	183	Gallup Canada Inc.	247
Chapters Inc.	186	Gay Lea Foods Co-Operative Ltd.	247
Cineplex Odeon Corporation	191	Gendis Inc.	248
CKF Inc.	192	General Chemical Canada Ltd.	249
Colgate-Palmolive Canada Inc.	196	General Electric Canada Inc.	249
COM DEV International	197	Gienow Building Products Ltd.	251
Comcare Health Services	198	Gilbey Canada Inc.	252
Community Savings Credit Union	199	Gimbel Eye Centre	252
Compu-Quote Inc.	200	Glaxo Wellcome Canada	253
Computer Associates Canada Ltd.	201	Goodman and Carr	255
Comtronic Computer Inc.	202	Goodwill Industries of Toronto	256
Conair Aviation Ltd.	202	Goodyear Canada Inc.	256
Connors Bros, Limited	203	Grand & Toy Ltd.	257
Co-op Atlantic	203	Grant MacEwen Community College	258
Coppley Apparel Group	204	Great-West Life Assurance Company, The	259
Coquitlam, City of	204	Groupe Savoie Inc.	260
Corel Corporation	205	Grouse Mountain Resorts Ltd.	260
Corner Brook, City of	205	Hasbro Canada Inc.	266
Cosmair Canada Inc.	206	Helijet Airways Inc.	268
Cosyn Technology	207	Hemosol Inc.	269
Cotton Ginny Ltd.	207	Hermes Electronics Inc.	269
Cougar Helicopters Inc.	208	Hill & Knowlton Canada Ltd.	270
Credit Union Central of Canada	208	Holiday Inn Select Toronto Airport	272
Crestar Energy Inc.	209	Holland College	273
Culinar Inc.	209	Home Oil Co. Ltd.	273
Dell Computer Corporation	214	Homewood Corp.	274
Directwest Publishers Ltd.	217	Honda Canada Inc.	274
Dofasco Inc.	218	Household Movers & Shippers Limited	276
Domtar Inc.	218	Housesitters Canada, The	277
Drug Trading Company Ltd.	219	HSBC Bank Canada	277
Dylex Limited	222	Hubbell Canada Inc.	278
Dynasty Furniture Manufacturing Ltd.	224	Hudson's Bay Company, The	279
Dynatek Automation Systems Inc.	224	Hydro Mississauga Corporation	282
Economic Development Edmonton	226	Hydro One Inc.	282

The Canada Student Employment Guide

University Index

IBM Canada Ltd.	284
Ilco Unican Inc.	286
Imperial Oil Limited	286
Industrial-Alliance Life Insurance Company	289
Industries Lassonde Inc.	289
InfoInterActive Inc.	290
Insurance Corp. of B.C.	291
Intercon Security Ltd.	292
Interior Savings Credit Union	293
Island Savings Credit Union	295
Island Telecom Inc.	295
J.D. Irving Limited	298
James Richardson International Limited	300
Jim Pattison Group	301
Johnson Incorporated	303
Jostens Canada Ltd.	303
Kennametal Ltd.	305
Keyano College	306
KFC Canada	307
Kimberly-Clark Inc.	307
Kitchener, City of	309
Kodak Canada Inc.	309
Kraft Canada Inc.	310
La Confiserie Comete Ltee	311
Laidlaw Inc.	312
Lego Canada Inc.	314
Lenbrook Industries Limited	315
Leon's Manufacturing Company Inc.	316
Les Distilleries Corby Ltée	317
Les Modes Smart Inc.	318
Lifetouch Canada Inc.	319
Linmor Technologies	320
Litton Systems Canada Ltd.	320
Loewen Windows	321
M M Industra Ltd.	323
MAAX Inc.	324
MacDonald Dettwiler and Associates Ltd.	325
Magna International Inc.	327
Manitoba Agriculture and Food	327
Manitoba Hydro	328
Manitoba Pool Elevators	328
Manitoba Telecom Services Inc.	329
Maple Leaf Consumer Foods	330
Maritime Life Assurance Company, The	331
Mark Anthony Group Inc.	332
Marks & Spencer Canada Inc.	332
Matrox Electronic Systems Ltd.	335
McBee Systems of Canada Inc.	336
McGraw Hill Ryerson Ltd.	337
McLaren-McCann Advertising of Canada Ltd.	338
McMillan & Associates Inc.	339
MDS Nordion	339
Mediasynergy	340
Memotec Communications Inc.	341
Metro Richelieu Inc.	342
Metro Toronto Convention Centre	342
Metropolitan Life Insurance Company	344
Meyers Norris Penny & Co.	344
Michaels of Canada Inc.	345
Midland Walwyn Inc.	345
Milne & Craighead Inc.	347
Mitel Corporation	350
Mitsubishi Electric Sales Canada	351
Mobile Computing Corporation	351
Moen Inc.	352
Monarch Communications Inc.	353
Moosehead Breweries Limited	354
Mortice Kern Systems Inc.	355
MOSAID Technologies Inc.	355
Motorola Canada Ltd.	356
Mustang Survival Corp.	358
Nanaimo Credit Union	359
National Grocers Co. Ltd.	360
National Life	361
National Sports Centre	362
Neles Automation, Scada Solutions Ltd.	362
Neptune Food Suppliers Ltd.	363
Nestle Canada Inc.	364
New Brunswick Telephone Company	366
Newfoundland and Labrador Credit Union	367
News Marketing Canada	368
NewTel Communications	369
Niagara Parks Commission, The	369
Nielsen Marketing Research	370
Nike Canada Ltd.	371
Norbord Industries	372
Norcen Energy Resources Ltd.	373
North American Life Assurance Company	373
North West Company Inc.	374
Northern Mountain Helicopters Inc.	375
Northwestel Inc.	376
Norwich Union Life Insurance Society	376
Nova Scotia Liquor Commission	377
Nova Scotia Power Corp.	377
Novartis Consumer Health Canada Inc.	378
Numac Energy Inc.	379
Oetiker Limited	381
Oland Breweries Limited	382
Ontario Guard Services Inc.	383
Ontario Jockey Club, The	384
Oracle Corp. Canada Inc.	386
Paramount Canada's Wonderland Inc.	389
PavCo	391
Peacock Inc.	392
Pearson Education Canada	393
Peel Regional Police	394
Pelmorex Inc.	395
PennCorp Life Insurance Company	396

The Canada Student Employment Guide

Pitney Bowes of Canada Ltd.	401		Skiing Louise Ltd.	461
Pizza Pizza Ltd.	401		Slocan Forest Products Ltd.	462
Poco Petroleums Ltd.	402		Sobeys Inc.	463
Pollack Rentals Limited	403		Sodexho Marriott Services Canada	464
Polygram Group Canada Inc.	403		Sony Music Canada	465
Positron Industries Inc.	404		Southern Railway of British Columbia Ltd.	466
Power Measurement Ltd.	406		Spectra Premium Industries	468
PPG Canada Inc.	407		Spectrum Signal Processing Inc.	468
Premdor Inc.	408		Speedware Corp. Inc.	469
Pricewaterhouse Coopers	409		Sportsco International	469
Prince Albert Credit Union	409		Sprint Canada	470
Prince George, City of	410		SRI Homes Inc.	470
Progressive Financial Strategy	411		St. Lawrence Parks Commission	472
Prudential Insurance Co. of America, The	412		St. Lawrence Seaway Mgmt. Corp., The	473
Public Utilities of Kingston	413		Standard Knitting Limited	474
Purolator Courier Ltd.	413		Stanley Canada Inc.	475
Rasco Specialty Metals Inc.	417		Steelcraft Industries Ltd.	477
Raymond Rebar Inc.	418		Sterling Marking Products Inc.	478
Reader's Digest Association of Canada Ltd.	419		Stitches	478
Regal Capital Planners Ltd.	422		Sun Rype Products Ltd.	481
Regal Constellation Hotel Ltd.	422		Sunoco Inc.	482
Regal Greeting and Gifts	423		Surrey, City of	484
Renaissance Energy Ltd.	427		Symantec Corporation	486
Rentway Inc.	427		Talisman Energy Inc.	487
Replicon Inc.	428		TCG International Inc.	487
Reynolds and Reynolds (Canada) Limited	430		TCT Logistics	488
Rich Products of Canada Limited	431		TD Waterhouse Investor Services (Canada)	488
Rogers AT&T Wireless Inc.	436		Teklogix Inc.	489
Rothmans, Benson and Hedges Inc.	437		Teldon International Inc.	490
Royal & Sun Alliance Insurance Co. of Cda	437		Telebec Ltée	490
Royal Bank of Canada	438		Telus Corporation	492
Royal Canadian Mint	438		The Barn Fruit Markets Inc.	493
Saan Stores Ltd.	441		The Co-operators	493
Sales & Merchandising Group	442		Thomas & Betts Ltée	495
Sandman Hotels and Inns	443		Thomas Cook Group (Canada) Ltd.	495
Sara Lee Corporation of Canada Limited	444		Thomas J. Lipton	496
Saskatchewan Centre of the Arts	444		Thompson's Moving and Storage	496
Saskatchewan Economic Development	445		Tiger Brand Knitting Company Limited	498
Saskatchewan Government Insurance	445		Today's Business Products Ltd.	500
Saskatchewan Wheat Pool	447		Top Producers Systems Inc.	500
Saskatoon, City of	448		Toronto Sun Publishing Corp., The	507
SaskTel	449		Toshiba of Canada Ltd.	508
Schlumberger Canada Ltd.	450		Toyota Canada Ltd.	509
Science North	452		Trojan Technologies Inc.	511
Sharp Electronics of Canada Ltd.	454		TSC Stores Ltd.	512
Shaw Communications	455		Uni Select Inc.	513
Shermag Inc.	457		Union Gas Ltd.	513
Sherwood Credit Union	458		University College of Cape Breton	516
Shoppers Drug Mart Limited	458		US Filter BCP	517
Shopping Channel, The	459		Vacances Air Transat Inc.	518
Shorewood Packaging Corp. of Canada Ltd.	459		VanCity Credit Union	519
Siemens Electric Ltd.	460		Vancouver International Airport	520
Signature Vacations Inc.	460		Vancouver Sun	520
Silicon Graphics Canada Inc.	461		Volvo Cars of Canada Ltd.	523

University Index

W C I Canada Inc.	524	Armor Personnel	107
Waterloo Furniture Components Ltd.	524	Assiniboine Community College	109
WebCanada	526	ATCO Frontec Corp.	111
Weldco-Beales Manufacturing Inc.	527	Atlantic Blue Cross Care	113
West Kootenay Power Ltd.	528	Atlantic Lottery Corporation Inc.	113
Westcliff Management Ltd.	529	Atlantic Wholesalers Ltd.	114
Western Glove Works	530	Atlas Ideal Metals Inc.	115
WestJet Airlines	532	Atlas Van Lines (Canada) Ltd.	115
Westminster Savings Credit Union	533	Aventis Pasteur Limited	117
Weyerhaeuser Company Limited	535	Axidata Inc.	118
Whistler Blackcomb Mountain	535	Babcock and Wilcox Canada	119
Whitehill Technologies Inc.	537	Bakemark Ingredients Ltd.	119
Wilson Auto Electric Ltd.	538	Ballard Power Systems Inc.	120
Winners Apparel Ltd.	539	Banff Centre for Continuing Education, The	120
Winpak Ltd.	539	Bargain Finder Press Ltd.	121
Wire Rope Industries Ltd.	540	Barton Place Long Term Care Facility	121
World of Vacations Ltd.	541	Baytex Energy Limited	124
XCAN Grain Pool Ltd.	541	BBM Bureau of Measurement	125
Yamaha Motor Canada Ltd.	542	BC Telecom Inc.	126
YFactor	544	Becker Milk Company Ltd., The	129
YTV Canada Inc.	545	Beckman Coulter Canada Inc.	129
Zellers Inc.	546	Bell Mobility	131
Zenon Environmental Inc.	547	Belleville General Hospital	132
		Bettis Canada Ltd.	135
Information Management		BFGoodrich Landing Gear Division	135
		Bio-Research Laboratories Ltd.	137
		Biovail Corporation International	137
A C A Cooperative Limited	74	Black Photo Corporation	139
Aberdeen Hospital	77	BNP PARIBAS (Canada)	143
Abitibi-Consolidated Inc.	77	Boréal Assurances Inc.	144
Acadia University	78	BOVAR Waste Management	145
Access Communications	78	Bowater Mersey Paper Company Limited	146
Accucaps Industries Limited	79	Brewers Retail Inc.	148
ACE INI Insurance	79	British Columbia Ferry Corporation	149
Acklands-Grainger Inc.	80	Buckeye Canada Inc.	151
ADT Canada Inc.	82	Budd Canada Inc.	152
AGF Management Limited	83	C.S.T. Consultants Inc.	155
Agricultural Credit Corp. of Saskatchewan	84	Cabre Exploration Ltd.	156
Aimtronics	84	Cadith Entertainment Ltd.	156
Air Canada	85	Calgary Co-operative Association Limited	157
Air Ontario Inc.	86	Cambridge Memorial Hospital	159
Alberta Blue Cross	88	Camp Hill Hospital	160
Alberta Cancer Board	88	Canada Post Corporation	162
Alberta Energy Company Ltd.	89	Canadian Cancer Society	164
Alberta Gaming & Liquor Commission	90	Canadian Dairy Commission	165
Alcan Aluminium Limited	91	Canadian General Tower Limited	166
Algoma Steel Inc.	93	Canadian Thermos Products Inc.	168
Aliant Telecom Inc.	93	Canadian Western Bank	169
Allianz Canada	95	Canbra Foods Ltd.	170
Allstate Insurance Co. of Canada	96	CancerCare Manitoba	171
Alpine Oil Service Corporation	96	Canon Canada Inc.	172
Amcor Twinpak North America Inc.	98	Cape Breton Development Corporation	174
Anthony Insurance Inc.	102	Capilano Suspension Bridge	174
Apex Land Corp.	103	Carbone of America (LCL) Ltd.	175

The Canada Student Employment Guide

University Index

Cargill Limited	175		Exfo	235
Cassels Brock & Blackwell	177		Exide Canada Inc.	235
Celestica International Inc.	179		Explorer Hotel, The	236
CenAlta Energy Services Inc.	180		Export Development Corporation	236
Centra Gas British Columbia Inc.	180		Extendicare (Canada) Inc.	237
Centra Gas Manitoba Inc.	181		Farm Credit Corp. Canada	238
Central Park Lodges Ltd.	181		Farmers Co-operative Dairy Limited	239
CGU Group Canada Ltd.	185		Federated Co-operatives Limited	239
CH2M Gore and Storrie Limited	185		FedEx Express	240
Chapters Inc.	186		Fishery Products International	241
Children's Hospital of Eastern Ontario	189		Fletcher's Fine Foods	242
Chilliwack General Hospital	189		Flint Energy Services Ltd.	243
Citibank Canada	191		Foremost Industries Inc.	244
CKF Inc.	192		Forzani Group Ltd., The	244
Coca Cola Foods Canada Inc.	195		Foyer Valade Inc.	245
Cognos Incorporated	196		Friesens Corporation	246
COM DEV International	197		Future Shop Ltd.	246
Comcare Health Services	198		Gendis Inc.	248
Community Savings Credit Union	199		General Electric Canada Inc.	249
Compaq Canada Inc.	199		Gienow Building Products Ltd.	251
Conair Aviation Ltd.	202		Giffels Associates Limited	251
Connors Bros, Limited	203		Gilbey Canada Inc.	252
Co-op Atlantic	203		Gimbel Eye Centre	252
Coquitlam, City of	204		Glentel Inc.	254
Corner Brook, City of	205		Goodman and Carr	255
Cotton Ginny Ltd.	207		Goodwill Industries of Toronto	256
Cougar Helicopters Inc.	208		Grand & Toy Ltd.	257
Credit Union Central of Canada	208		Halifax Regional Municipality	263
Crestar Energy Inc.	209		Halifax Water Commission	264
Culinar Inc.	209		Hasbro Canada Inc.	266
D.A. Stuart Inc.	210		Health Care Corporation of St. John's	267
David Thompson Health Region	212		Health Sciences Centre	268
DDM Plastics Inc.	213		Helijet Airways Inc.	268
Deer Lodge Centre Inc.	213		Hippodrome de Montréal	270
Dell Computer Corporation	214		Hoffman-La Roche Limited	272
Delphi Solutions Inc.	215		Homewood Corp.	274
Delta Hotels	215		Honda Canada Inc.	274
Directwest Publishers Ltd.	217		Household Movers & Shippers Limited	276
Dofasco Inc.	218		HSBC Bank Canada	277
Domtar Inc.	218		Hub Meat Packers Ltd.	278
Drug Trading Company Ltd.	219		Hudon & Deaudelin Ltée	279
DuPont Canada Inc.	221		Humber River Regional Hospital	280
Dylex Limited	222		Huronia Regional Centre	280
Dynacare Laboratories	223		Hydro Electric Commission of Thunder Bay	281
Dynapro Systems Inc.	223		Hydro Mississauga Corporation	282
Dynasty Furniture Manufacturing Ltd.	224		Hydro One Inc.	282
Dynatek Automation Systems Inc.	224		Hydro Québec	283
Echo Bay Mines Ltd.	226		I M P Group International Inc.	283
Economic Development Edmonton	226		IBM Canada Ltd.	284
Economical Insurance Group, The	227		Imperial Oil Limited	286
EDS of Canada Ltd.	228		Indalex Limited	288
Eli Lilly Canada Inc.	230		Industrial-Alliance Life Insurance Company	289
EMJ Data Systems Ltd.	231		Industries Lassonde Inc.	289
Entreprises Premier Canadien Ltée	232		Information Gateway Services	290

The Canada Student Employment Guide

University Index

ING Canada Financial Services International	291	MOSAID Technologies Inc.	355
Insurance Corp. of B.C.	291	Motorola Canada Ltd.	356
Interforest Ltd.	292	Mountain Equipment Co-op	356
Interior Savings Credit Union	293	Mustang Survival Corp.	358
IPL Energy Inc.	294	N B S Card Services	359
IWK Grace Health Centre	297	National Life	361
J.D. Irving Limited	298	National Manufacturing of Canada Inc.	361
James Richardson International Limited	300	National Sports Centre	362
Jim Pattison Group	301	Neles Automation, Scada Solutions Ltd.	362
Johnson Incorporated	303	Nelvana Limited	363
Jostens Canada Ltd.	303	Neptune Food Suppliers Ltd.	363
Kelowna, City of	305	Nesbitt Burns Inc.	364
Keyano College	306	Netron Inc.	365
KFC Canada	307	New Brunswick Power Corporation	365
Kitchener, City of	309	New Brunswick Telephone Company	366
Kodak Canada Inc.	309	Newfoundland and Labrador Credit Union	367
Kraft Canada Inc.	310	Newfoundland and Labrador Hydro	367
La Confiserie Comete Ltee	311	News Marketing Canada	368
Laidlaw Inc.	312	NewTel Communications	369
Leduc, City of	313	Nielsen Marketing Research	370
Lego Canada Inc.	314	Norbord Industries	372
Lenbrook Industries Limited	315	North American Life Assurance Company	373
Leon's Manufacturing Company Inc.	316	North West Company Inc.	374
Les Centres Jeunesse de Montréal	316	Northern Mountain Helicopters Inc.	375
Les Distilleries Corby Ltée	317	Northwestel Inc.	376
Les Forges de Sorel Inc.	317	Norwich Union Life Insurance Society	376
Les Modes Smart Inc.	318	Nova Scotia Liquor Commission	377
Liberty Health	318	Nova Scotia Power Corp.	377
Lifetouch Canada Inc.	319	Novartis Consumer Health Canada Inc.	378
MAAX Inc.	324	Nygard International Ltd.	380
Marine Atlantic Inc.	331	Oetiker Limited	381
Mark Anthony Group Inc.	332	Ontario Jockey Club, The	384
Marystown Shipyard Limited	334	Ontario Legislative Offices	384
Matrox Electronic Systems Ltd.	335	Ontario March of Dimes	385
McGraw Hill Ryerson Ltd.	337	Oracle Corp. Canada Inc.	386
McInnes Cooper & Robertson	337	Ottawa Hospital	386
MDS Nordion	339	Panorama Mountain Village	388
Mediasynergy	340	Paramount Canada's Wonderland Inc.	389
Memotec Communications Inc.	341	PavCo	391
Metro Richelieu Inc.	342	Peacock Inc.	392
Metro Toronto Convention Centre	342	Pearson Education Canada	393
Meyers Norris Penny & Co.	344	Peel Board of Education	393
Michaels of Canada Inc.	345	Pelmorex Inc.	395
Midwest Food Products Inc.	346	PennCorp Life Insurance Company	396
Milne & Craighead Inc.	347	Pharma Plus Drugmarts Ltd.	398
Minas Basin Pulp and Power Company Ltd.	347	Phoenix International	399
Ministry of Northern Develop. and Mines	348	Pitney Bowes of Canada Ltd.	401
Misericordia General Hospital	348	Pizza Pizza Ltd.	401
Mitel Corporation	350	Polygram Group Canada Inc.	403
Mitsubishi Electric Sales Canada	351	Power Measurement Ltd.	406
Mobile Computing Corporation	351	PPG Canada Inc.	407
Moen Inc.	352	Pricewaterhouse Coopers	409
Moosehead Breweries Limited	354	Prince George, City of	410
Mortice Kern Systems Inc.	355	Progressive Financial Strategy	411

The Canada Student Employment Guide

Prudential Insurance Co. of America, The	412	StorageTek Canada Inc.	479
Public Utilities of Kingston	413	Sudbury Regional Hospital	480
Purolator Courier Ltd.	413	Sun Rype Products Ltd.	481
QIT-Fer et Titane Inc.	414	Surrey Place Centre	484
Québéc Cartier Mining Company	415	Swift Current Health District	485
Quebecor Inc.	415	Sydney Steel Corporation	485
Quesnel River Pulp Company	416	Symantec Corporation	486
Rasco Specialty Metals Inc.	417	TCG International Inc.	487
Reader's Digest Association of Canada Ltd.	419	TCT Logistics	488
Recochem Inc.	420	TD Waterhouse Investor Services (Canada)	488
Regal Greeting and Gifts	423	Teklogix Inc.	489
Rehabilitation Institute of Toronto	425	Telebec Ltée	490
Reuters Information Services (Canada) Ltd.	428	Telesat Canada	491
Riverside Hospital of Ottawa, The	434	The Barn Fruit Markets Inc.	493
Rogers AT&T Wireless Inc.	436	Thomas & Betts Ltée	495
Rogers Media, Publishing	436	Thomas Cook Group (Canada) Ltd.	495
Rothmans, Benson and Hedges Inc.	437	Thunder Bay Regional Hospital	497
Royal & Sun Alliance Insurance Co. of Cda	437	Today's Business Products Ltd.	500
Royal Bank of Canada	438	Toronto East General Hospital	503
Royal Philips Electronics	439	Toronto General Hospital	505
Saan Stores Ltd.	441	Toronto Sun Publishing Corp., The	507
Saskatchewan Government Insurance	445	Toronto, City of	508
Saskatchewan Transportation Company	446	Toshiba of Canada Ltd.	508
Saskatchewan Wheat Pool	447	Toyota Canada Ltd.	509
Saskatoon, City of	448	Trojan Technologies Inc.	511
SaskTel	449	TSC Stores Ltd.	512
Scholastic Canada Ltd.	451	Uni Select Inc.	513
SCIEX MDS Health Group	452	Unisys Canada Inc.	514
Seprotech Systems Incorporated	454	University College of Cape Breton	516
Sharp Electronics of Canada Ltd.	454	Vancouver International Airport	520
Shaw Communications	455	Vancouver Sun	520
Shermag Inc.	457	Volvo Cars of Canada Ltd.	523
Sherwood Credit Union	458	W C I Canada Inc.	524
Shopping Channel, The	459	Waterloo Furniture Components Ltd.	524
Shorewood Packaging Corp. of Canada Ltd.	459	Westbury Life	529
Siemens Electric Ltd.	460	Westcliff Management Ltd.	529
Signature Vacations Inc.	460	Western Glove Works	530
Silicon Graphics Canada Inc.	461	Westminster Savings Credit Union	533
Slocan Forest Products Ltd.	462	Westshore Terminals Ltd.	534
Sobeys Inc.	463	Weyerhaeuser Company Limited	535
Sony Music Canada	465	Whistler Blackcomb Mountain	535
Spectra Premium Industries	468	Whitehill Technologies Inc.	537
Speedware Corp. Inc.	469	Wilson Auto Electric Ltd.	538
Sportsco International	469	Windsor, City of	538
Sprint Canada	470	Winners Apparel Ltd.	539
SSQ Life	471	Yamaha Motor Canada Ltd.	542
St. Joseph's Care Group	472	Yanke Group of Companies	543
St. Lawrence Parks Commission	472	Yellowknife, City of	544
St. Vincent's Hospitals	473	YFactor	544
Standard Knitting Limited	474	Zellers Inc.	546
Stanley Canada Inc.	475	Zurich Canada	548
Star Data Systems Inc.	476		
Steelcraft Industries Ltd.	477		
Steelpipe Ltd.	477		

646   University Index

Public Administration

1-800-GOT-JUNK?	74
Acadia University	78
Addictions Foundation of Manitoba, The	81
Alberta Gaming & Liquor Commission	90
Armor Personnel	107
Athabasca, Town of	112
Axidata Inc.	118
Barton Place Long Term Care Facility	121
Bettis Canada Ltd.	135
Biovail Corporation International	137
British Columbia Ferry Corporation	149
Calgary Co-operative Association Limited	157
Canadian Broadcasting Corporation	164
Canadian Cancer Society	164
Canadian Dairy Commission	165
Canadian Western Bank	169
CancerCare Manitoba	171
Central Park Lodges Ltd.	181
Cobourg District General Hospital	194
Coquitlam, City of	204
Corner Brook, City of	205
Credit Union Central of Canada	208
Culinar Inc.	209
David Thompson Health Region	212
Deer Lodge Centre Inc.	213
Dynasty Furniture Manufacturing Ltd.	224
Economic Development Edmonton	226
Explorer Hotel, The	236
Federated Co-operatives Limited	239
Finning	240
Foyer Valade Inc.	245
Future Shop Ltd.	246
Gendis Inc.	248
Gienow Building Products Ltd.	251
Halifax County Regional Rehabilitation Centre	263
Halifax Water Commission	264
Health Sciences Centre	268
Holland College	273
Homewood Corp.	274
Hôtel Dieu de Montréal	276
HSBC Bank Canada	277
Hydro Electric Commission of Thunder Bay	281
Island Telecom Inc.	295
Kelowna, City of	305
Kitchener, City of	309
Leduc, City of	313
Les Centres Jeunesse de Montréal	316
Liberty Health	318
Manitoba Agriculture and Food	327
Metropolitan Life Insurance Company	344
Michaels of Canada Inc.	345
News Marketing Canada	368
North West Company Inc.	374
Ontario Legislative Offices	384
Paramount Canada's Wonderland Inc.	389
PavCo	391
Peel Board of Education	393
Peel Regional Police	394
Pelmorex Inc.	395
PennCorp Life Insurance Company	396
Prince George, City of	410
Public Utilities of Kingston	413
Royal Bank of Canada	438
Saskatchewan Government Insurance	445
Shaw Communications	455
Sherwood Credit Union	458
Signature Vacations Inc.	460
Sony Music Canada	465
Spectra Premium Industries	468
Sprint Canada	470
Sudbury Regional Hospital	480
Surrey, City of	484
Thompson's Moving and Storage	496
Today's Business Products Ltd.	500
Toronto General Hospital	505
Toronto Sun Publishing Corp., The	507
Toronto, City of	508
University College of Cape Breton	516
Vancouver Sun	520
Waverly & York Corporation	525
Weyerhaeuser Company Limited	535
Yanke Group of Companies	543
Yellowknife, City of	544
YFactor	544

Bachelor of Science

Acturial

Acklands-Grainger Inc.	80
Alcan Aluminium Limited	91
Allianz Canada	95
Assumption Mutual Life Insurance	109
Atlantic Blue Cross Care	113
AXA Insurance (Canada)	118
Boréal Assurances Inc.	144
Buck Consultants Limited	151
Calgary, City of	158
Cambior Inc.	158
CGU Group Canada Ltd.	185
Dun & Bradstreet Canada	221
Economical Insurance Group, The	227
Great-West Life Assurance Company, The	259
Home Oil Co. Ltd.	273

The Canada Student Employment Guide

University Index   647

Industrial-Alliance Life Insurance Company	289
ING Canada Financial Services International	291
Insurance Corp. of B.C.	291
InterOne Marketing Group	293
Liberty Health	318
Maritime Life Assurance Company, The	331
Metropolitan Life Insurance Company	344
Moffat Communications Limited	352
Montreal Trust Co.	353
National Life	361
North American Life Assurance Company	373
Norwich Union Life Insurance Society	376
Oracle Corp. Canada Inc.	386
Paul Revere Life Insurance Company, The	391
Pricewaterhouse Coopers	409
Prudential Insurance Co. of America, The	412
Rogers AT&T Wireless Inc.	436
Royal & Sun Alliance Insurance Co. of Cda	437
Sprint Canada	470
SSQ Life	471
State Farm Insurance Companies	476
TD Waterhouse Investor Services (Canada)	488
The Co-operators	493
Toronto Hydro	505
Toronto Sun Publishing Corp., The	507
Turnbull & Turnbull Ltd.	512
Westbury Life	529

Agriculture

A C A Cooperative Limited	74
Advanta Seeds	83
Agricultural Credit Corp. of Saskatchewan	84
Arbor Care Tree Service Ltd.	106
Assiniboine Community College	109
BASF Canada Inc.	122
Brandon, City of	146
Canbra Foods Ltd.	170
Cangene Corporation	172
Cargill Limited	175
Charlottetown Driving Park	187
COBI Foods Inc.	194
Connors Bros, Limited	203
Co-op Atlantic	203
Ducks Unlimited Canada	220
DuPont Canada Inc.	221
Entreprises Premier Canadien Ltée	232
Farm Credit Corp. Canada	238
Federated Co-operatives Limited	239
Gay Lea Foods Co-Operative Ltd.	247
James Richardson International Limited	300
Lakeside Farm Industries Ltd.	312
Manitoba Agriculture and Food	327

Manitoba Pool Elevators	328
Meyers Norris Penny & Co.	344
Midwest Food Products Inc.	346
New Holland Canada Ltd.	366
Niagara Parks Commission, The	369
Novartis Consumer Health Canada Inc.	378
Omstead Foods Limited	383
Powell Equipment Ltd.	405
Rhone-Poulenc Canada Inc.	430
Royal Bank of Canada	438
Saskatchewan Wheat Pool	447
Saskferco Products Inc.	448
Sun Rype Products Ltd.	481
Surrey, City of	484
Toronto, City of	508
Vancouver Sun	520
White Rose Crafts and Nursery Sales Limited	536
XCAN Grain Pool Ltd.	541

Biology

A E McKenzie Co. Inc.	75
Aberdeen Hospital	77
Abitibi-Consolidated Inc.	77
Acadia University	78
Accucaps Industries Limited	79
Adherex Technologies Inc.	81
ADI Group Inc.	82
Advanta Seeds	83
Alberta Energy & Utilities Board	89
Alberto Culver Canada Inc.	90
Apotex Fermentation Inc.	104
Assiniboine Community College	109
AstraZeneca	110
Aurum Ceramic Dental Laboratories Ltd.	117
Aventis Pasteur Limited	117
Bayer Inc.	124
BC Hydro	125
BC Research Inc.	126
Becker Milk Company Ltd., The	129
Biomira Inc.	136
Bio-Research Laboratories Ltd.	137
Biovail Corporation International	137
Blue Wave Seafoods Inc.	142
Canadian Cancer Society	164
CancerCare Manitoba	171
Cangene Corporation	172
CH2M Gore and Storrie Limited	185
COBI Foods Inc.	194
Cobourg District General Hospital	194
Connors Bros, Limited	203
D.A. Stuart Inc.	210
David Thompson Health Region	212

The Canada Student Employment Guide

University Index

Ducks Unlimited Canada	220
Dynacare Laboratories	223
Eli Lilly Canada Inc.	230
Endpoint Research Ltd.	231
Entreprises Premier Canadien Ltée	232
Farmers Co-operative Dairy Limited	239
Fisher Scientific Limited	241
Gay Lea Foods Co-Operative Ltd.	247
Glaxo Wellcome Canada	253
Golder Associates Ltd.	255
Grant MacEwen Community College	258
Halifax Water Commission	264
Hemosol Inc.	269
Humber River Regional Hospital	280
Hydro Québec	283
IWK Grace Health Centre	297
J.D. Irving Limited	298
Jacques Whitford Consulting Engineers	299
John P. Robarts Research Institute	302
Keyano College	306
KFC Canada	307
Kraft Canada Inc.	310
Manitoba Agriculture and Food	327
Maple Leaf Consumer Foods	330
Marshall Macklin Monaghan Ltd.	333
Maxxam Analytics Inc.	335
MDS Nordion	339
Medical Laboratories of Windsor Limited	341
Midwest Food Products Inc.	346
Moosehead Breweries Limited	354
Nestle Canada Inc.	364
Newfoundland and Labrador Hydro	367
Nova Scotia Power Corp.	377
Novartis Consumer Health Canada Inc.	378
NPS Allelix Corp.	379
Oland Breweries Limited	382
Omstead Foods Limited	383
Ottawa Hospital	386
Patheon Inc.	390
Peel Board of Education	393
Pine Falls Paper Company Limited	400
Prudential Insurance Co. of America, The	412
QEII Health Sciences Centre	414
Raylo Chemicals Inc.	417
Regina Health District	423
Rothmans, Benson and Hedges Inc.	437
Royal Inland Hospital	439
Saskatchewan Research Council, The	446
Scarborough General Hospital	450
Science North	452
SCIEX MDS Health Group	452
Société des Alcools du Québec	464
State Farm Insurance Companies	476
StressGen Biotechnologies Corp.	480
Sudbury Regional Hospital	480
Sun Rype Products Ltd.	481
Surrey, City of	484
Toronto and Region Conservation Authority	501
Toronto District School Board	503
Toronto General Hospital	505
Trojan Technologies Inc.	511
University College of Cape Breton	516
Weyerhaeuser Company Limited	535
Windsor, City of	538

Chemistry

Abitibi-Consolidated Inc.	77
Acadia University	78
Accucaps Industries Limited	79
Adherex Technologies Inc.	81
ADI Group Inc.	82
Advanta Seeds	83
Alberta Energy & Utilities Board	89
Alberta Energy Company Ltd.	89
Alberto Culver Canada Inc.	90
Alcan Aluminium Limited	91
Algoma Steel Inc.	93
Amcor Twinpak North America Inc.	98
Apotex Fermentation Inc.	104
Assiniboine Community College	109
AstraZeneca	110
Aurum Ceramic Dental Laboratories Ltd.	117
Aventis Pasteur Limited	117
AXA Insurance (Canada)	118
Ballard Power Systems Inc.	120
BASF Canada Inc.	122
Bayer Inc.	124
BC Research Inc.	126
Beckman Coulter Canada Inc.	129
Biomira Inc.	136
Bio-Research Laboratories Ltd.	137
Biovail Corporation International	137
BJ Services Company	138
BOVAR Waste Management	145
Bowater Mersey Paper Company Limited	146
Browning Harvey Limited	150
Buckeye Canada Inc.	151
Budd Canada Inc.	152
Cambior Inc.	158
Canada Safeway Limited	163
Canadian General Tower Limited	166
Canbra Foods Ltd.	170
Cancarb Limited	170
CancerCare Manitoba	171
Cangene Corporation	172
CCL Industries Inc.	178

The Canada Student Employment Guide

University Index   649

Celestica International Inc.	179	Nova Scotia Power Corp.	377
CH2M Gore and Storrie Limited	185	Novartis Consumer Health Canada Inc.	378
Citibank Canada	191	NPS Allelix Corp.	379
CKF Inc.	192	Oland Breweries Limited	382
Cobourg District General Hospital	194	Omstead Foods Limited	383
Cognis Canada Corporation	195	Patheon Inc.	390
Communications & Power Industries Canada	198	Peel Board of Education	393
Culinar Inc.	209	Phoenix International	399
D.A. Stuart Inc.	210	Pine Falls Paper Company Limited	400
David Thompson Health Region	212	Powertech Labs Inc.	406
DDM Plastics Inc.	213	PPG Canada Inc.	407
Degussa - Huls Canada Inc.	214	Pricewaterhouse Coopers	409
Domtar Inc.	218	Public Utilities of Kingston	413
Duha Color Services	220	QEII Health Sciences Centre	414
DuPont Canada Inc.	221	QIT-Fer et Titane Inc.	414
Dynacare Laboratories	223	Québéc Cartier Mining Company	415
Eli Lilly Canada Inc.	230	Raylo Chemicals Inc.	417
Endpoint Research Ltd.	231	Recochem Inc.	420
Entreprises Premier Canadien Ltée	232	Rhone-Poulenc Canada Inc.	430
Federated Co-operatives Limited	239	Rio Algom Limited	433
Fisher Scientific Limited	241	Rothmans, Benson and Hedges Inc.	437
Flakeboard Company Limited	242	Royal Inland Hospital	439
Gencorp Vehicle Sealing	248	Ryerson Polytechnic University	441
General Chemical Canada Ltd.	249	Sandwell Inc.	443
Gilbey Canada Inc.	252	Saskatchewan Research Council, The	446
Glaxo Wellcome Canada	253	Saskferco Products Inc.	448
Grant MacEwen Community College	258	Scarborough General Hospital	450
Haliburton Energy Services	262	SCIEX MDS Health Group	452
Halifax Water Commission	264	Seprotech Systems Incorporated	454
Hemosol Inc.	269	Shaw Industries Ltd.	455
Hydro One Inc.	282	State Farm Insurance Companies	476
Hydro Québec	283	StressGen Biotechnologies Corp.	480
IBM Canada Ltd.	284	Sudbury Regional Hospital	480
INCO Limited	287	Sun Rype Products Ltd.	481
Intertape Polymer Group Inc.	294	Sydney Steel Corporation	485
J.D. Irving Limited	298	Syncrude Canada Ltd.	486
Jim Pattison Group	301	Thunder Bay Regional Hospital	497
John P. Robarts Research Institute	302	Tiger Brand Knitting Company Limited	498
Keyano College	306	Toronto District School Board	503
KFC Canada	307	Toronto French School, The	504
Kinross Gold Corp.	308	Toronto General Hospital	505
Kodak Canada Inc.	309	Toronto Sun Publishing Corp., The	507
La Confiserie Comete Ltee	311	Trojan Technologies Inc.	511
Litton Systems Canada Ltd.	320	University College of Cape Breton	516
MAAX Inc.	324	Vancouver Sun	520
Manitoba Hydro	328	Westcoast Energy Inc.	530
Maple Leaf Consumer Foods	330	Weyerhaeuser Company Limited	535
Maxxam Analytics Inc.	335	Windsor, City of	538
MDS Nordion	339	Winpak Ltd.	539
Medical Laboratories of Windsor Limited	341	Zenon Environmental Inc.	547
Minas Basin Pulp and Power Company Ltd.	347		
Ministry of Northern Develop. and Mines	348		
Moosehead Breweries Limited	354		
National Manufacturing of Canada Inc.	361		

The Canada Student Employment Guide

Computer Science

A C A Cooperative Limited	74
A.G. Simpson Co. Ltd.	75
ABC Group	76
Aberdeen Hospital	77
Abitibi-Consolidated Inc.	77
Acadia University	78
Access Communications	78
Acklands-Grainger Inc.	80
ADT Canada Inc.	82
Air Canada	85
Alberta Blue Cross	88
Alberta Energy & Utilities Board	89
Alberta Energy Company Ltd.	89
Alberta Gaming & Liquor Commission	90
Alcan Aluminium Limited	91
Algoma Steel Inc.	93
Aliant Telecom Inc.	93
Alias	Wavefront	94
Allianz Canada	95
Alpine Oil Service Corporation	96
Amcor Twinpak North America Inc.	98
Andersen Consulting	101
Anjura Services Inc.	101
Anthony Insurance Inc.	102
Arbor Memorial Services Inc.	106
Assiniboine Community College	109
Assumption Mutual Life Insurance	109
Assure Health Inc.	110
AstraZeneca	110
ATCO Electric	111
ATCO Frontec Corp.	111
Atlantic Blue Cross Care	113
Atlantic Lottery Corporation Inc.	113
ATS Automation Tooling Systems Inc.	116
Aventis Pasteur Limited	117
Axidata Inc.	118
Barton Place Long Term Care Facility	121
BASF Canada Inc.	122
Basic Technologies Corporation	122
Baycrest Centre for Geriatric Care	123
BBM Bureau of Measurement	125
BC Telecom Inc.	126
BDO Dunwoody	127
Bell Mobility	131
Belleville General Hospital	132
Bettis Canada Ltd.	135
BFGoodrich Landing Gear Division	135
Bic Inc.	136
Bio-Research Laboratories Ltd.	137
Biovail Corporation International	137
Black Photo Corporation	139
Blaney McMurty LLP	139
Bloorview Childrens Hospital	140
BNP PARIBAS (Canada)	143
Boréal Assurances Inc.	144
BOVAR Waste Management	145
Bowater Mersey Paper Company Limited	146
Brandon, City of	146
Brewers Retail Inc.	148
British Columbia Ferry Corporation	149
Buck Consultants Limited	151
Buckeye Canada Inc.	151
Budd Canada Inc.	152
C MAC Industries Inc.	155
Cabre Exploration Ltd.	156
Calgary Co-operative Association Limited	157
Calgary, City of	158
Cambior Inc.	158
Camp Hill Hospital	160
Canada Post Corporation	162
Canadian Broadcasting Corporation	164
Canadian General Tower Limited	166
Canadian Thermos Products Inc.	168
Canadian Tire Corporation Ltd.	169
Canadian Western Bank	169
Canbra Foods Ltd.	170
CancerCare Manitoba	171
Canon Canada Inc.	172
Cape Breton Development Corporation	174
Cargill Limited	175
Carlson Marketing Group Canada Ltd.	176
Carte International Inc.	176
Catholic Children's Aid Society Foundation	178
Celestica International Inc.	179
Centra Gas British Columbia Inc.	180
Ceridian Canada	183
CFCF Inc.	183
CGI	184
CGU Group Canada Ltd.	185
CH2M Gore and Storrie Limited	185
Chevron Canada Resources Ltd.	188
Children's Aid Society of Metro Toronto	188
Children's Hospital of Eastern Ontario	189
Citibank Canada	191
CKF Inc.	192
Clarica	192
Cognos Incorporated	196
Columbia House	197
COM DEV International	197
Communications & Power Industries Canada	198
Community Savings Credit Union	199
Compaq Canada Inc.	199
Compu-Quote Inc.	200
Computalog Ltd.	200
Computer Associates Canada Ltd.	201
Comtronic Computer Inc.	202

University Index 651

Conair Aviation Ltd.	202	Goodwill Industries of Toronto	256
Connors Bros, Limited	203	Gov't of Newfoundland - Dept. of Finance	257
Co-op Atlantic	203	Grand & Toy Ltd.	257
Coquitlam, City of	204	Grant MacEwen Community College	258
Cornwall Electric	206	Great-West Life Assurance Company, The	259
Cotton Ginny Ltd.	207	Halifax Regional Municipality	263
Credit Union Central of Canada	208	Halifax Water Commission	264
Crestar Energy Inc.	209	HB Studios Multimedia Ltd.	266
Culinar Inc.	209	Health Care Corporation of St. John's	267
D.A. Stuart Inc.	210	Health Sciences Centre	268
DaimlerChrysler Canada Ltd.	211	Hermes Electronics Inc.	269
Deer Lodge Centre Inc.	213	Holland College	273
Dell Computer Corporation	214	Home Oil Co. Ltd.	273
Develcon Electronics Ltd.	217	Homewood Corp.	274
Directwest Publishers Ltd.	217	Honda Canada Inc.	274
Dofasco Inc.	218	Honeywell Ltd.	275
Domtar Inc.	218	Housesitters Canada, The	277
Ducks Unlimited Canada	220	HSBC Bank Canada	277
Dun & Bradstreet Canada	221	Hudon & Deaudelin Ltée	279
DuPont Canada Inc.	221	Hudson's Bay Company, The	279
Dylex Limited	222	Humber River Regional Hospital	280
Dynapro Systems Inc.	223	Hydro Electric Commission of Thunder Bay	281
Dynatek Automation Systems Inc.	224	Hydro One Inc.	282
Economic Development Edmonton	226	I M P Group International Inc.	283
Economical Insurance Group, The	227	IBM Canada Ltd.	284
EDS of Canada Ltd.	228	Ilco Unican Inc.	286
Electronics Arts (Canada) Inc.	229	Imperial Oil Limited	286
Eli Lilly Canada Inc.	230	INCO Limited	287
EMJ Data Systems Ltd.	231	Industrial Equipment Co. Ltd.	288
EnerFlex Systems Ltd.	232	Industrial-Alliance Life Insurance Company	289
Entreprises Premier Canadien Ltée	232	InfoInterActive Inc.	290
Environics Research Group Ltd.	233	Information Gateway Services	290
Espial Group Incorporated	234	ING Canada Financial Services International	291
Exfo	235	Interior Savings Credit Union	293
Exide Canada Inc.	235	InterOne Marketing Group	293
Extendicare (Canada) Inc.	237	IPL Energy Inc.	294
FAG Bearings Limited	237	Island Telecom Inc.	295
Farm Credit Corp. Canada	238	IWK Grace Health Centre	297
Farmers Co-operative Dairy Limited	239	Izaak Walton Killam Hospital, The	297
Federated Co-operatives Limited	239	J.D. Irving Limited	298
FedEx Express	240	James Richardson International Limited	300
Fishery Products International	241	Jim Pattison Group	301
Flint Energy Services Ltd.	243	John P. Robarts Research Institute	302
Foremost Industries Inc.	244	Johnson Controls Ltd.	302
Foyer Valade Inc.	245	Johnson Incorporated	303
Friesens Corporation	246	Jostens Canada Ltd.	303
Future Shop Ltd.	246	Kelowna, City of	305
Gencorp Vehicle Sealing	248	Keyano College	306
General Chemical Canada Ltd.	249	KFC Canada	307
General Electric Canada Inc.	249	Kitchener, City of	309
Gienow Building Products Ltd.	251	Kodak Canada Inc.	309
Giffels Associates Limited	251	Kraft Canada Inc.	310
Gilbey Canada Inc.	252	La Confiserie Comete Ltee	311
Glaxo Wellcome Canada	253	Laidlaw Inc.	312

The Canada Student Employment Guide

652 University Index

Lambert Somec Inc.	313	Nike Canada Ltd.	371
Leduc, City of	313	Norcen Energy Resources Ltd.	373
Lego Canada Inc.	314	North American Life Assurance Company	373
Leica Geosystems Canada Inc.	314	North West Company Inc.	374
Lenbrook Industries Limited	315	Northern Lights Regional Health Centre	375
Les Centres Jeunesse de Montréal	316	Norwich Union Life Insurance Society	376
Les Distilleries Corby Ltée	317	Nova Scotia Liquor Commission	377
Liberty Health	318	Nova Scotia Power Corp.	377
Litton Systems Canada Ltd.	320	NPS Allelix Corp.	379
MAAX Inc.	324	Numac Energy Inc.	379
MacDonald Dettwiler and Associates Ltd.	325	Oland Breweries Limited	382
Manitoba Agriculture and Food	327	Ontario Jockey Club, The	384
Manitoba Hydro	328	Oracle Corp. Canada Inc.	386
Manitoba Pool Elevators	328	Ottawa Hospital	386
Manitoba Public Insurance Corporation	329	Paramount Canada's Wonderland Inc.	389
Manitoba Telecom Services Inc.	329	PCL Constructors Inc.	392
Maple Leaf Consumer Foods	330	Peel Board of Education	393
Marcam Canada	330	Peel Regional Police	394
Marine Atlantic Inc.	331	Pelmorex Inc.	395
Maritime Life Assurance Company, The	331	Pembina Pipeline Corporation	395
Marystown Shipyard Limited	334	Phoenix International	399
Matrox Electronic Systems Ltd.	335	Pine Falls Paper Company Limited	400
McBee Systems of Canada Inc.	336	Pizza Pizza Ltd.	401
McLaren-McCann Advertising of Canada Ltd.	338	Polygram Group Canada Inc.	403
MDS Nordion	339	Positron Industries Inc.	404
Mediasynergy	340	Potacan Mining Company	405
Medical Laboratories of Windsor Limited	341	Power Measurement Ltd.	406
Metro Richelieu Inc.	342	PPG Canada Inc.	407
Meyers Norris Penny & Co.	344	Pratt & Whitney Canada Inc.	407
Michaels of Canada Inc.	345	Premdor Inc.	408
Midland Walwyn Inc.	345	Pricewaterhouse Coopers	409
Midwest Food Products Inc.	346	Prince Albert Credit Union	409
Minas Basin Pulp and Power Company Ltd.	347	Prince Albert, City of	410
Ministry of Northern Develop. and Mines	348	Prince George, City of	410
Mississauga, City of	349	Prudential Insurance Co. of America, The	412
Mitel Corporation	350	Public Utilities of Kingston	413
Mitsubishi Electric Sales Canada	351	QEII Health Sciences Centre	414
Mobile Computing Corporation	351	Quebecor Inc.	415
Monarch Communications Inc.	353	Quesnel River Pulp Company	416
Montreal Trust Co.	353	Raymond Industrial Equipment Ltd.	418
Moosehead Breweries Limited	354	Raytheon Systems Canada Ltd.	419
Mortice Kern Systems Inc.	355	Reader's Digest Association of Canada Ltd.	419
MOSAID Technologies Inc.	355	Recochem Inc.	420
Multitech Electronics Inc.	358	Regina Health District	423
National Grocers Co. Ltd.	360	Rehabilitation Institute of Toronto	425
National Life	361	Reid Crowther	426
Neles Automation, Scada Solutions Ltd.	362	Reynolds and Reynolds (Canada) Limited	430
Nesbitt Burns Inc.	364	Richmond, City of	431
Nestle Canada Inc.	364	Riverside Hospital of Ottawa, The	434
Netron Inc.	365	Rogers AT&T Wireless Inc.	436
New Brunswick Power Corporation	365	Rothmans, Benson and Hedges Inc.	437
New Brunswick Telephone Company	366	Royal & Sun Alliance Insurance Co. of Cda	437
NewTel Communications	369	Royal Bank of Canada	438
Nielsen Marketing Research	370	Royal Victoria Hospital	440

The Canada Student Employment Guide

University Index

Salisbury House of Canada Ltd.	442
Sandwell Inc.	443
Saskatchewan Economic Development	445
Saskatchewan Government Insurance	445
Saskatchewan Wheat Pool	447
Saskatoon, City of	448
Saskferco Products Inc.	448
SaskTel	449
Scarborough General Hospital	450
Schneider Electric Canada Inc.	451
Scholastic Canada Ltd.	451
SCIEX MDS Health Group	452
SED Systems	453
Sharp Electronics of Canada Ltd.	454
Shaw Communications	455
Sherwood Credit Union	458
Siemens Electric Ltd.	460
Signature Vacations Inc.	460
Silicon Graphics Canada Inc.	461
Skiing Louise Ltd.	461
Société des Alcools du Québec	464
SolutionInc Limited	465
Southam Inc.	466
Spar Aerospace Limited	467
Spectrum Signal Processing Inc.	468
Speedware Corp. Inc.	469
Sprint Canada	470
SSQ Life	471
St. Lawrence Seaway Mgmt. Corp., The	473
St. Vincent's Hospitals	473
Stantec Consulting Ltd.	475
Star Data Systems Inc.	476
State Farm Insurance Companies	476
Steelpipe Ltd.	477
Sterling Marking Products Inc.	478
Stitches	478
Stone Consolidated Inc.	479
StorageTek Canada Inc.	479
StressGen Biotechnologies Corp.	480
Sudbury Regional Hospital	480
Sun Rype Products Ltd.	481
Sundog Printing Limited	482
Sunoco Inc.	482
Surrey, City of	484
Sydney Steel Corporation	485
Symantec Corporation	486
Syncrude Canada Ltd.	486
Teck Corp.	489
Teklogix Inc.	489
Telegraph Journal	491
Telesat Canada	491
The Co-operators	493
Thomas J. Lipton	496
Thompson's Moving and Storage	496

Thomson - CSF Systems Canada Inc.	497
Thunder Bay Regional Hospital	497
Tiger Brand Knitting Company Limited	498
Timmins, City of	499
Today's Business Products Ltd.	500
Top Producers Systems Inc.	500
Toronto District School Board	503
Toronto East General Hospital	503
Toronto French School, The	504
Toronto General Hospital	505
Toronto Hydro	505
Toronto Police Service	506
Toronto Sun Publishing Corp., The	507
Toronto, City of	508
Toshiba of Canada Ltd.	508
Toyota Canada Ltd.	509
Triumf	510
Trojan Technologies Inc.	511
Union Gas Ltd.	513
Unisys Canada Inc.	514
University College of Cape Breton	516
US Filter BCP	517
Vacances Air Transat Inc.	518
Vancouver Sun	520
Versa Services Ltd.	521
WebCanada	526
West Kootenay Power Ltd.	528
Westbury Life	529
Westcoast Energy Inc.	530
Westinghouse Canada Inc.	532
WestJet Airlines	532
Weyerhaeuser Company Limited	535
Whistler Blackcomb Mountain	535
Whitehill Technologies Inc.	537
Wilson Auto Electric Ltd.	538
Windsor, City of	538
Winners Apparel Ltd.	539
Wire Rope Industries Ltd.	540
Workfire Development Corp.	540
Yamaha Motor Canada Ltd.	542
Yanke Group of Companies	543
Yarmouth Regional Hospital	543
Yellowknife, City of	544
Zellers Inc.	546
Zurich Canada	548

Environmental Studies

A.G. Simpson Co. Ltd.	75
ACE INI Insurance	79
ADI Group Inc.	82
Alberta Energy & Utilities Board	89
Alcan Aluminium Limited	91

654 University Index

Aquatic Sciences Inc.	105	J.D. Irving Limited	298
ArvinMeritor	108	Jacques Whitford Consulting Engineers	299
AstraZeneca	110	Jim Pattison Group	301
Banff Centre for Continuing Education, The	120	Kelowna, City of	305
Barton Place Long Term Care Facility	121	Leduc, City of	313
BC Hydro	125	Magna International Inc.	327
BC Research Inc.	126	Manitoba Hydro	328
Bell Mobility	131	Marine Atlantic Inc.	331
Biovail Corporation International	137	Marshall Macklin Monaghan Ltd.	333
BOVAR Waste Management	145	Maxxam Analytics Inc.	335
Bowater Mersey Paper Company Limited	146	Ministry of Northern Develop. and Mines	348
Budd Canada Inc.	152	Mississauga, City of	349
Cabre Exploration Ltd.	156	National Manufacturing of Canada Inc.	361
Calgary, City of	158	Newfoundland and Labrador Hydro	367
Cameco Corporation	160	Niagara Parks Commission, The	369
Canadian General Tower Limited	166	Norbord Industries	372
Cangene Corporation	172	Norcen Energy Resources Ltd.	373
Cape Breton Development Corporation	174	North West Company Inc.	374
Casa Loma	177	Northern Lights Regional Health Centre	375
CCL Industries Inc.	178	Nova Scotia Power Corp.	377
Centra Gas British Columbia Inc.	180	Novartis Consumer Health Canada Inc.	378
CH2M Gore and Storrie Limited	185	Pelmorex Inc.	395
CKF Inc.	192	Pembina Pipeline Corporation	395
Cognis Canada Corporation	195	Pine Falls Paper Company Limited	400
Co-op Atlantic	203	Placer Dome Inc.	402
Coquitlam, City of	204	PPG Canada Inc.	407
D.A. Stuart Inc.	210	Prince George, City of	410
DaimlerChrysler Canada Ltd.	211	QIT-Fer et Titane Inc.	414
Domtar Inc.	218	Royal Canadian Mint	438
Duha Color Services	220	Sandwell Inc.	443
Echo Bay Mines Ltd.	226	Saskatoon, City of	448
Emco Limited	230	Saskferco Products Inc.	448
Entreprises Premier Canadien Ltée	232	SC Infrastructure Inc.	449
Environics Research Group Ltd.	233	Science North	452
Exide Canada Inc.	235	Signature Vacations Inc.	460
Extendicare (Canada) Inc.	237	Skiing Louise Ltd.	461
Federated Co-operatives Limited	239	Southam Inc.	466
Fisher Scientific Limited	241	St. Lawrence Parks Commission	472
Flakeboard Company Limited	242	Stantec Consulting Ltd.	475
Foyer Valade Inc.	245	State Farm Insurance Companies	476
General Chemical Canada Ltd.	249	Sun Peaks Resort Corporation	481
Giffels Associates Limited	251	Surrey, City of	484
Glaxo Wellcome Canada	253	Sydney Steel Corporation	485
Golder Associates Ltd.	255	Talisman Energy Inc.	487
Grant MacEwen Community College	258	Timmins, City of	499
Haley Industries Limited	262	Toronto and Region Conservation Authority	501
Halifax Regional Municipality	263	Toronto French School, The	504
Home Oil Co. Ltd.	273	Toronto Hydro	505
Homewood Corp.	274	Toronto Sun Publishing Corp., The	507
Hydro Electric Commission of Thunder Bay	281	Toronto Zoo	507
Hydro One Inc.	282	Toronto, City of	508
Hydro Québec	283	Trow Consulting Engineers Ltd.	511
Imperial Oil Limited	286	University College of Cape Breton	516
Island Telecom Inc.	295	Vancouver Sun	520

The Canada Student Employment Guide

University Index 655

Waterloo Furniture Components Ltd.	524	Izaak Walton Killam Hospital, The	297
Westcoast Energy Inc.	530	KFC Canada	307
Westshore Terminals Ltd.	534	Kraft Canada Inc.	310
Weyerhaeuser Company Limited	535	La Confiserie Comete Ltee	311
White Rose Crafts and Nursery Sales Limited	536	Maple Leaf Consumer Foods	330
Windsor, City of	538	Midwest Food Products Inc.	346
		Moosehead Breweries Limited	354
		Nestle Canada Inc.	364

Food Science

		Northern Lights Regional Health Centre	375
		Oland Breweries Limited	382
Aberdeen Hospital	77	Omstead Foods Limited	383
Assiniboine Community College	109	Ottawa Hospital	386
AstraZeneca	110	Paramount Canada's Wonderland Inc.	389
Bakemark Ingredients Ltd.	119	Patheon Inc.	390
Banff Centre for Continuing Education, The	120	Pioneer Village Special Care Corp.	400
Barton Place Long Term Care Facility	121	Providence Centre	412
Becker Milk Company Ltd., The	129	QEII Health Sciences Centre	414
Belleville General Hospital	132	Ready Bake Foods Inc.	420
Bethesda Hospital	134	Red Deer Co-op Limited	421
Biovail Corporation International	137	Rhone-Poulenc Canada Inc.	430
Bloorview Childrens Hospital	140	Rich Products of Canada Limited	431
Bloorview MacMillan Centre, The	140	Rimrock Resort Hotel	432
Blue Wave Seafoods Inc.	142	Royal Inland Hospital	439
Cambridge Memorial Hospital	159	Ryerson Polytechnic University	441
Camp Hill Hospital	160	Sherbrooke Community Centre	457
Canbra Foods Ltd.	170	Sodexho Marriott Services Canada	464
Cangene Corporation	172	St. Amant Centre Inc.	471
Central Park Lodges Ltd.	181	St. Joseph's Care Group	472
Centre de Santé de St-Henri Inc.	182	St. Vincent's Hospitals	473
Children's Hospital of Eastern Ontario	189	Sudbury Regional Hospital	480
Chilliwack General Hospital	189	Sun Rype Products Ltd.	481
COBI Foods Inc.	194	Surrey Memorial Hospital	483
Cobourg District General Hospital	194	Swift Current Health District	485
Connors Bros, Limited	203	Thomas J. Lipton	496
Culinar Inc.	209	Toronto District School Board	503
David Thompson Health Region	212	Toronto East General Hospital	503
Extendicare (Canada) Inc.	237	Toronto General Hospital	505
Farmers Co-operative Dairy Limited	239	Versa Services Ltd.	521
Federated Co-operatives Limited	239	Whistler Blackcomb Mountain	535
Fishery Products International	241	Windsor, City of	538
Fletcher's Fine Foods	242	Winpak Ltd.	539
Foyer Valade Inc.	245	XCAN Grain Pool Ltd.	541
Gay Lea Foods Co-Operative Ltd.	247		
Gilbey Canada Inc.	252		
Halifax County Regional Rehabilitation Centre	263	## Forestry	
Health Authority 5	267		
Health Care Corporation of St. John's	267	Abitibi-Consolidated Inc.	77
Homewood Corp.	274	Arbor Care Tree Service Ltd.	106
Hôtel Dieu de Montréal	276	BC Research Inc.	126
Hub Meat Packers Ltd.	278	Bowater Mersey Paper Company Limited	146
Hudon & Deaudelin Ltée	279	Bugbusters Pest Management Inc.	152
Humber River Regional Hospital	280	Casa Loma	177
Huronia Regional Centre	280	Coquitlam, City of	204
IWK Grace Health Centre	297	Domtar Inc.	218

The Canada Student Employment Guide

656   University Index

Entreprises Premier Canadien Ltée	232	Columbia House	197
Federated Co-operatives Limited	239	Credit Union Central of Canada	208
Flakeboard Company Limited	242	D.A. Stuart Inc.	210
Groupe Savoie Inc.	260	Economic Development Edmonton	226
H A Simmons Ltd.	261	Economical Insurance Group, The	227
Halifax Water Commission	264	Eddie Bauer Inc.	227
Horseshoe Resort Corporation	275	Eli Lilly Canada Inc.	230
J.D. Irving Limited	298	EMJ Data Systems Ltd.	231
Jacques Whitford Consulting Engineers	299	Endpoint Research Ltd.	231
Kitchener, City of	309	Exfo	235
Mississauga, City of	349	Foremost Industries Inc.	244
Niagara Parks Commission, The	369	Gienow Building Products Ltd.	251
Norbord Industries	372	Glaxo Wellcome Canada	253
Nova Scotia Power Corp.	377	Goepel McDermid Securities	254
Premdor Inc.	408	Goodwill Industries of Toronto	256
Science North	452	Goodyear Canada Inc.	256
Slocan Forest Products Ltd.	462	Halifax County Regional Rehabilitation Centre	263
St. Lawrence Parks Commission	472	Hoffman-La Roche Limited	272
Sun Peaks Resort Corporation	481	Honda Canada Inc.	274
Toronto and Region Conservation Authority	501	HSBC Bank Canada	277
Toronto, City of	508	Insurance Corp. of B.C.	291
Weyerhaeuser Company Limited	535	InterOne Marketing Group	293
White Rose Crafts and Nursery Sales Limited	536	Island Telecom Inc.	295
Windsor, City of	538	Izaak Walton Killam Hospital, The	297
		Jim Pattison Group	301
		KFC Canada	307

General

		Leduc, City of	313
		Lego Canada Inc.	314
1-800-GOT-JUNK?	74	Liberty Health	318
Accucaps Industries Limited	79	Mark Anthony Group Inc.	332
Acklands-Grainger Inc.	80	McBee Systems of Canada Inc.	336
Alberta Gaming & Liquor Commission	90	McCarney Greenwood	336
Arbor Memorial Services Inc.	106	Metropolitan Life Insurance Company	344
Armor Personnel	107	Ministry of Northern Develop. and Mines	348
AstraZeneca	110	Mitel Corporation	350
Atlantic Blue Cross Care	113	Montreal Trust Co.	353
Aurum Ceramic Dental Laboratories Ltd.	117	MSM Transportation Inc.	357
Bayer Inc.	124	Newfoundland and Labrador Credit Union	367
BBM Bureau of Measurement	125	News Marketing Canada	368
Behlen Industries	130	Norwich Union Life Insurance Society	376
Bell Mobility	131	Novartis Consumer Health Canada Inc.	378
BFGoodrich Landing Gear Division	135	Ontario March of Dimes	385
Black Photo Corporation	139	Paramount Canada's Wonderland Inc.	389
Bloorview MacMillan Centre, The	140	Peel Board of Education	393
Brandon, City of	146	Pitney Bowes of Canada Ltd.	401
British Columbia Ferry Corporation	149	Pizza Pizza Ltd.	401
Brookfield Properties Corporation	150	Poco Petroleums Ltd.	402
Burger King Restaurants of Canada Inc.	153	Pollack Rentals Limited	403
Calgary Co-operative Association Limited	157	Providence Centre	412
Canadian Cancer Society	164	QEII Health Sciences Centre	414
Canadian General Tower Limited	166	Royal & Sun Alliance Insurance Co. of Cda	437
Canadian Occidental Petroleum Ltd.	168	Royal Bank of Canada	438
Cangene Corporation	172	Sandman Hotels and Inns	443
Cobourg District General Hospital	194	Saskatchewan Economic Development	445

The Canada Student Employment Guide

Saskatchewan Government Insurance	445
Scarborough General Hospital	450
Science North	452
Shaw Communications	455
Signature Vacations Inc.	460
Sony Music Canada	465
State Farm Insurance Companies	476
Supreme Tooling Group	483
Thomas & Betts Ltée	495
Thomas J. Lipton	496
Thompson's Moving and Storage	496
Toronto General Hospital	505
Toronto Hydro	505
Toronto Sun Publishing Corp., The	507
Toronto, City of	508
University College of Cape Breton	516
US Filter BCP	517
Vancouver Sun	520
Wendy's Restaurants of Canada Inc.	527
WestJet Airlines	532
Weston Produce Inc.	533
Weyerhaeuser Company Limited	535
Winners Apparel Ltd.	539
Winpak Ltd.	539
xwave solutions	542
Yanke Group of Companies	543
Yellowknife, City of	544

Geography

Coquitlam, City of	204
Environics Research Group Ltd.	233
Halifax Regional Municipality	263
Hydro Québec	283
Jacques Whitford Consulting Engineers	299
Kitchener, City of	309
Leduc, City of	313
Leica Geosystems Canada Inc.	314
McGraw Hill Ryerson Ltd.	337
Mississauga, City of	349
Norcen Energy Resources Ltd.	373
Peel Board of Education	393
Pelmorex Inc.	395
Saskatchewan Research Council, The	446
Signature Vacations Inc.	460
State Farm Insurance Companies	476
Surrey, City of	484
Toronto and Region Conservation Authority	501
Toronto District School Board	503
Toronto French School, The	504
Toronto Hydro	505
Vacances Air Transat Inc.	518
Weyerhaeuser Company Limited	535

Yanke Group of Companies	543

Health Science

Aberdeen Hospital	77
Addictions Foundation of Manitoba, The	81
AstraZeneca	110
Atlantic Blue Cross Care	113
Aurum Ceramic Dental Laboratories Ltd.	117
Aventis Pasteur Limited	117
AXA Insurance (Canada)	118
Barton Place Long Term Care Facility	121
Battlefords Health District	123
Bayer Inc.	124
Belleville General Hospital	132
Bethesda Hospital	134
Bio-Research Laboratories Ltd.	137
Bloorview Childrens Hospital	140
Bloorview MacMillan Centre, The	140
Calgary Co-operative Association Limited	157
Cambridge Memorial Hospital	159
Camp Hill Hospital	160
Canadian Cancer Society	164
CancerCare Manitoba	171
Cape Breton Development Corporation	174
Central Park Lodges Ltd.	181
Centre de Santé de St-Henri Inc.	182
Children's Hospital of Eastern Ontario	189
Chilliwack General Hospital	189
Chinook Health Region	190
Cobourg District General Hospital	194
Comcare Health Services	198
Endpoint Research Ltd.	231
Fisher Scientific Limited	241
Foyer Valade Inc.	245
George Jeffrey Children's Treatment Centre	250
Glaxo Wellcome Canada	253
Halifax County Regional Rehabilitation Centre	263
Health Authority 5	267
Health Care Corporation of St. John's	267
Health Sciences Centre	268
Hemosol Inc.	269
Homewood Corp.	274
Hôtel Dieu de Montréal	276
Humber River Regional Hospital	280
Huronia Regional Centre	280
IWK Grace Health Centre	297
Izaak Walton Killam Hospital, The	297
Kennedy Lodge Nursing Home Inc.	306
Kodak Canada Inc.	309
Leduc, City of	313
Liberty Health	318
MDS Nordion	339

658 University Index

Medical Laboratories of Windsor Limited	341	Kitchener, City of	309
Metropolitan Life Insurance Company	344	Leduc, City of	313
National Grocers Co. Ltd.	360	Manitoba Agriculture and Food	327
Nestle Canada Inc.	364	Mississauga, City of	349
Northern Lights Regional Health Centre	375	Niagara Parks Commission, The	369
Nova Scotia Power Corp.	377	Prince Albert, City of	410
Novartis Consumer Health Canada Inc.	378	Prince George, City of	410
Patheon Inc.	390	Saskatoon, City of	448
PennCorp Life Insurance Company	396	Slocan Forest Products Ltd.	462
Phoenix International	399	St. Lawrence Parks Commission	472
Pool People Ltd.	404	Sun Peaks Resort Corporation	481
Providence Centre	412	Toronto and Region Conservation Authority	501
QEII Health Sciences Centre	414	Toronto, City of	508
Reena	421	White Rose Crafts and Nursery Sales Limited	536
Regina Health District	423	Windsor, City of	538
Rimrock Resort Hotel	432		
Royal Inland Hospital	439		
Royal Victoria Hospital	440	**Kinesiology**	
Saskatchewan Government Insurance	445		
Scarborough General Hospital	450	Aberdeen Hospital	77
Science North	452	AstraZeneca	110
Sherbrooke Community Centre	457	Atlantic Blue Cross Care	113
St. Amant Centre Inc.	471	AXA Insurance (Canada)	118
Sudbury Regional Hospital	480	Barton Place Long Term Care Facility	121
Surrey Place Centre	484	BC Research Inc.	126
Swift Current Health District	485	Bloorview MacMillan Centre, The	140
Thompson's Moving and Storage	496	Budd Canada Inc.	152
Thunder Bay Regional Hospital	497	Calgary Co-operative Association Limited	157
Timmins, City of	499	Canada Games Aquatic Centre	162
Toronto Cricket Skating & Curling	502	Cobourg District General Hospital	194
Toronto East General Hospital	503	Cognos Incorporated	196
Toronto General Hospital	505	David Thompson Health Region	212
Toronto Hydro	505	Endpoint Research Ltd.	231
Toronto Sun Publishing Corp., The	507	Glaxo Wellcome Canada	253
Toronto, City of	508	Health Authority 5	267
Universal Rehabilitation Service Agency	515	Health Sciences Centre	268
Vancouver Sun	520	Hoffman-La Roche Limited	272
Whistler Blackcomb Mountain	535	Horseshoe Resort Corporation	275
Windsor, City of	538	Humber River Regional Hospital	280
Yarmouth Regional Hospital	543	Huronia Regional Centre	280
		Metropolitan Life Insurance Company	344
		Mustang Survival Corp.	358
Horticulture		Ontario March of Dimes	385
		Pitney Bowes of Canada Ltd.	401
A E McKenzie Co. Inc.	75	Pool People Ltd.	404
Arbor Memorial Services Inc.	106	QEII Health Sciences Centre	414
Assiniboine Community College	109	Rimrock Resort Hotel	432
Brandon, City of	146	Science North	452
Calgary Co-operative Association Limited	157	Steelpipe Ltd.	477
Casa Loma	177	Sudbury Regional Hospital	480
Co-op Atlantic	203	Surrey, City of	484
Federated Co-operatives Limited	239	Toronto General Hospital	505
Homewood Corp.	274	Toronto Hydro	505
Horseshoe Resort Corporation	275	Universal Rehabilitation Service Agency	515

Mathematics

Abitibi-Consolidated Inc.	77
Acklands-Grainger Inc.	80
Alberta Blue Cross	88
Algoma Steel Inc.	93
Allianz Canada	95
Amcor Twinpak North America Inc.	98
Andersen Consulting	101
Assiniboine Community College	109
Axidata Inc.	118
BASF Canada Inc.	122
BDO Dunwoody	127
BFGoodrich Landing Gear Division	135
Buck Consultants Limited	151
CAE Newness	157
Canadian Tire Corporation Ltd.	169
Canadian Western Bank	169
Canon Canada Inc.	172
Centra Gas British Columbia Inc.	180
CH2M Gore and Storrie Limited	185
Citibank Canada	191
CKF Inc.	192
Cognos Incorporated	196
Compu-Quote Inc.	200
Co-op Atlantic	203
Dun & Bradstreet Canada	221
Dylex Limited	222
Economical Insurance Group, The	227
Electronics Arts (Canada) Inc.	229
EMJ Data Systems Ltd.	231
Environics Research Group Ltd.	233
Exfo	235
Export Development Corporation	236
Extendicare (Canada) Inc.	237
Gallup Canada Inc.	247
Gienow Building Products Ltd.	251
Glaxo Wellcome Canada	253
Grant MacEwen Community College	258
Great-West Life Assurance Company, The	259
Halifax Regional Municipality	263
Hallmark Tools	265
HB Studios Multimedia Ltd.	266
Home Oil Co. Ltd.	273
Honda Canada Inc.	274
IBM Canada Ltd.	284
Imperial Oil Limited	286
InfoInterActive Inc.	290
Information Gateway Services	290
ING Canada Financial Services International	291
IPL Energy Inc.	294
John P. Robarts Research Institute	302
Keyano College	306
Kitchener, City of	309
Kodak Canada Inc.	309
Leica Geosystems Canada Inc.	314
Lenbrook Industries Limited	315
Les Distilleries Corby Ltée	317
Liberty Health	318
Magna International Inc.	327
Manitoba Hydro	328
Marcam Canada	330
Maritime Life Assurance Company, The	331
McGraw Hill Ryerson Ltd.	337
Mediasynergy	340
Mitel Corporation	350
Montreal Trust Co.	353
Mortice Kern Systems Inc.	355
National Life	361
Neles Automation, Scada Solutions Ltd.	362
Nesbitt Burns Inc.	364
Netron Inc.	365
Newness Machine Ltd.	368
Nielsen Marketing Research	370
North American Life Assurance Company	373
Norwich Union Life Insurance Society	376
Nova Scotia Power Corp.	377
Novartis Consumer Health Canada Inc.	378
Oracle Corp. Canada Inc.	386
Peel Board of Education	393
Pitney Bowes of Canada Ltd.	401
Pricewaterhouse Coopers	409
Prudential Insurance Co. of America, The	412
Raytheon Systems Canada Ltd.	419
Reader's Digest Association of Canada Ltd.	419
Reuters Information Services (Canada) Ltd.	428
Rogers AT&T Wireless Inc.	436
Royal Bank of Canada	438
Sandwell Inc.	443
Saskatchewan Government Insurance	445
Signature Vacations Inc.	460
Silicon Graphics Canada Inc.	461
Speedware Corp. Inc.	469
Sprint Canada	470
Star Data Systems Inc.	476
State Farm Insurance Companies	476
Steelpipe Ltd.	477
Symantec Corporation	486
TD Waterhouse Investor Services (Canada)	488
Teklogix Inc.	489
Telesat Canada	491
Thompson's Moving and Storage	496
Top Producers Systems Inc.	500
Toronto District School Board	503
Toronto French School, The	504
Toronto Sun Publishing Corp., The	507
Union Gas Ltd.	513
University College of Cape Breton	516

The Canada Student Employment Guide

University Index

US Filter BCP	517
Vancouver Sun	520
Westbury Life	529
Westcoast Energy Inc.	530
Weyerhaeuser Company Limited	535
Whitehill Technologies Inc.	537
Winners Apparel Ltd.	539
Workfire Development Corp.	540

Microbiology

Aberdeen Hospital	77
Accucaps Industries Limited	79
Apotex Fermentation Inc.	104
AstraZeneca	110
Aventis Pasteur Limited	117
Bayer Inc.	124
Becker Milk Company Ltd., The	129
Biomira Inc.	136
Bio-Research Laboratories Ltd.	137
Biovail Corporation International	137
CancerCare Manitoba	171
Cangene Corporation	172
CH2M Gore and Storrie Limited	185
COBI Foods Inc.	194
Cobourg District General Hospital	194
Connors Bros, Limited	203
David Thompson Health Region	212
Dynacare Laboratories	223
Eli Lilly Canada Inc.	230
Endpoint Research Ltd.	231
Entreprises Premier Canadien Ltée	232
Farmers Co-operative Dairy Limited	239
Fisher Scientific Limited	241
Gay Lea Foods Co-Operative Ltd.	247
Glaxo Wellcome Canada	253
Grant MacEwen Community College	258
Hemosol Inc.	269
Humber River Regional Hospital	280
IWK Grace Health Centre	297
John P. Robarts Research Institute	302
KFC Canada	307
Kraft Canada Inc.	310
Manitoba Agriculture and Food	327
Maple Leaf Consumer Foods	330
Maxxam Analytics Inc.	335
MDS Nordion	339
Medical Laboratories of Windsor Limited	341
Midwest Food Products Inc.	346
Moosehead Breweries Limited	354
Nestle Canada Inc.	364
Novartis Consumer Health Canada Inc.	378
NPS Allelix Corp.	379
Oland Breweries Limited	382
Omstead Foods Limited	383
Patheon Inc.	390
Regina Health District	423
Royal Inland Hospital	439
Saskatchewan Research Council, The	446
Scarborough General Hospital	450
Société des Alcools du Québec	464
State Farm Insurance Companies	476
StressGen Biotechnologies Corp.	480
Sudbury Regional Hospital	480
Sun Rype Products Ltd.	481
Toronto General Hospital	505

Nursing (RN)

Aberdeen Hospital	77
Addictions Foundation of Manitoba, The	81
Alberta Alcohol and Drug Abuse Commission	87
Alberta Cancer Board	88
Altona Community Memorial Health Centre	97
Assiniboine Community College	109
Assumption Mutual Life Insurance	109
AstraZeneca	110
Atlantic Blue Cross Care	113
Aventis Pasteur Limited	117
Barton Place Long Term Care Facility	121
Battlefords Health District	123
Baycrest Centre for Geriatric Care	123
Belleville General Hospital	132
Bethania Mennonite Personal Care Home Inc.	134
Bethesda Hospital	134
BFGoodrich Landing Gear Division	135
Biovail Corporation International	137
Bloorview Childrens Hospital	140
Bloorview MacMillan Centre, The	140
Budd Canada Inc.	152
Calgary Co-operative Association Limited	157
Cambridge Memorial Hospital	159
Camp Hill Hospital	160
Cangene Corporation	172
Cape Breton Development Corporation	174
Catholic Children's Aid Society Foundation	178
Central Park Lodges Ltd.	181
Centre de Santé de St-Henri Inc.	182
Children's Hospital of Eastern Ontario	189
Chilliwack General Hospital	189
Chinook Health Region	190
CKF Inc.	192
Cobourg District General Hospital	194
Comcare Health Services	198
Custom Trim Ltd.	210
DaimlerChrysler Canada Ltd.	211

The Canada Student Employment Guide

University Index 661

David Thompson Health Region	212
Deer Lodge Centre Inc.	213
Dynacare Laboratories	223
Edmonton Home Services Ltd.	228
Eli Lilly Canada Inc.	230
Endpoint Research Ltd.	231
Extendicare (Canada) Inc.	237
Fisher Scientific Limited	241
Fishery Products International	241
Foyer Valade Inc.	245
Glaxo Wellcome Canada	253
Goodwill Industries of Toronto	256
Grant MacEwen Community College	258
Great-West Life Assurance Company, The	259
Halifax County Regional Rehabilitation Centre	263
Health Authority 5	267
Health Care Corporation of St. John's	267
Health Sciences Centre	268
Hoffman-La Roche Limited	272
Homewood Corp.	274
Hôtel Dieu de Montréal	276
Humber River Regional Hospital	280
Huronia Regional Centre	280
Hydro Québec	283
Ivaco Inc.	296
IWK Grace Health Centre	297
Izaak Walton Killam Hospital, The	297
Kelowna Home Support	304
Kennedy Lodge Nursing Home Inc.	306
Keyano College	306
Kings Regional Rehabilitation Centre	308
Les Centres Jeunesse de Montréal	316
Liberty Health	318
Magna International Inc.	327
Medical Laboratories of Windsor Limited	341
Metro Toronto West Detention Centre	343
Metropolitan Life Insurance Company	344
Misericordia General Hospital	348
National Grocers Co. Ltd.	360
North York Community Care Access Centre	374
Northern Lights Regional Health Centre	375
Ottawa Hospital	386
Overlander Hospital	387
Paramount Canada's Wonderland Inc.	389
Phoenix International	399
Pioneer Village Special Care Corp.	400
Pool People Ltd.	404
Potacan Mining Company	405
Providence Centre	412
QEII Health Sciences Centre	414
Regina Health District	423
Rehabilitation Institute of Toronto	425
Riverside Hospital of Ottawa, The	434
Royal Inland Hospital	439

Royal Victoria Hospital	440
Sandman Hotels and Inns	443
Saskatchewan Government Insurance	445
Scarborough General Hospital	450
Sherbrooke Community Centre	457
SSQ Life	471
St. Amant Centre Inc.	471
St. Joseph's Care Group	472
St. Vincent's Hospitals	473
Sudbury Regional Hospital	480
Surrey Memorial Hospital	483
Surrey Place Centre	484
Surrey, City of	484
Swift Current Health District	485
Thunder Bay Regional Hospital	497
Timmins, City of	499
Toronto East General Hospital	503
Toronto General Hospital	505
Toronto Police Service	506
Toronto, City of	508
Turnbull & Turnbull Ltd.	512
Vancouver Sun	520
Villa Providence Shediac Inc.	522
Westbury Life	529
Windsor, City of	538
Yarmouth Regional Hospital	543

Occupational Therapy

Aberdeen Hospital	77
Aliant Telecom Inc.	93
Atlantic Blue Cross Care	113
Barton Place Long Term Care Facility	121
Battlefords Health District	123
Baycrest Centre for Geriatric Care	123
Belleville General Hospital	132
Bethesda Hospital	134
BFGoodrich Landing Gear Division	135
Biovail Corporation International	137
Bloorview Childrens Hospital	140
Bloorview MacMillan Centre, The	140
Calgary Co-operative Association Limited	157
Cambridge Memorial Hospital	159
Camp Hill Hospital	160
Centre de Santé de St-Henri Inc.	182
Children's Hospital of Eastern Ontario	189
Chilliwack General Hospital	189
Chinook Health Region	190
Christian Horizons	190
Cobourg District General Hospital	194
Comcare Health Services	198
David Thompson Health Region	212
Deer Lodge Centre Inc.	213

The Canada Student Employment Guide

662 University Index

Extendicare (Canada) Inc.	237	Toronto General Hospital	505
Foyer Valade Inc.	245	Toronto, City of	508
George Jeffrey Children's Treatment Centre	250	Universal Rehabilitation Service Agency	515
Glaxo Wellcome Canada	253	Vancouver Sun	520
Grant MacEwen Community College	258	Yarmouth Regional Hospital	543
Great-West Life Assurance Company, The	259		
Halifax County Regional Rehabilitation Centre	263		
Health Authority 5	267		

Pharmacy

Health Care Corporation of St. John's	267		
Health Sciences Centre	268	Aberdeen Hospital	77
Hermes Electronics Inc.	269	Accucaps Industries Limited	79
Homewood Corp.	274	Adherex Technologies Inc.	81
Hôtel Dieu de Montréal	276	Alberta Blue Cross	88
Humber River Regional Hospital	280	Alberta Cancer Board	88
Huronia Regional Centre	280	Assure Health Inc.	110
IWK Grace Health Centre	297	AstraZeneca	110
Izaak Walton Killam Hospital, The	297	Atlantic Blue Cross Care	113
KFC Canada	307	Battlefords Health District	123
Kings Regional Rehabilitation Centre	308	Bayer Inc.	124
Liberty Health	318	Belleville General Hospital	132
Magna International Inc.	327	Bethesda Hospital	134
Maritime Life Assurance Company, The	331	Biomira Inc.	136
Metropolitan Life Insurance Company	344	Bio-Research Laboratories Ltd.	137
Midwest Food Products Inc.	346	Biovail Corporation International	137
Misericordia General Hospital	348	Bloorview Childrens Hospital	140
North York Community Care Access Centre	374	Calgary Co-operative Association Limited	157
Northern Lights Regional Health Centre	375	Cambridge Memorial Hospital	159
Ontario March of Dimes	385	Camp Hill Hospital	160
Ottawa Hospital	386	Canada Safeway Limited	163
Overlander Hospital	387	CancerCare Manitoba	171
Providence Centre	412	Cangene Corporation	172
QEII Health Sciences Centre	414	Centre de Santé de St-Henri Inc.	182
Regina Health District	423	Children's Hospital of Eastern Ontario	189
Rehabilitation Institute of Toronto	425	Chilliwack General Hospital	189
Riverside Hospital of Ottawa, The	434	Cobourg District General Hospital	194
Royal Inland Hospital	439	David Thompson Health Region	212
Royal Victoria Hospital	440	Deer Lodge Centre Inc.	213
Sandman Hotels and Inns	443	Drug Trading Company Ltd.	219
Scarborough General Hospital	450	Eli Lilly Canada Inc.	230
Sherbrooke Community Centre	457	Federated Co-operatives Limited	239
Skills Training & Support Services Association	462	Fisher Scientific Limited	241
St. Amant Centre Inc.	471	Glaxo Wellcome Canada	253
St. Joseph's Care Group	472	Halifax County Regional Rehabilitation Centre	263
St. Vincent's Hospitals	473	Health Authority 5	267
Steelpipe Ltd.	477	Health Care Corporation of St. John's	267
Sudbury Regional Hospital	480	Health Sciences Centre	268
Surrey Memorial Hospital	483	Hoffman-La Roche Limited	272
Surrey Place Centre	484	Homewood Corp.	274
Surrey, City of	484	Hôtel Dieu de Montréal	276
Swift Current Health District	485	Humber River Regional Hospital	280
The Arthritis Society	492	Huronia Regional Centre	280
The Co-operators	493	IWK Grace Health Centre	297
Thunder Bay Regional Hospital	497	Izaak Walton Killam Hospital, The	297
Toronto East General Hospital	503	John P. Robarts Research Institute	302

The Canada Student Employment Guide

University Index   663

Kings Regional Rehabilitation Centre	308
Liberty Health	318
National Grocers Co. Ltd.	360
Northern Lights Regional Health Centre	375
Novartis Consumer Health Canada Inc.	378
Ottawa Hospital	386
Patheon Inc.	390
Pharma Plus Drugmarts Ltd.	398
Phoenix International	399
Providence Centre	412
QEII Health Sciences Centre	414
Regina Health District	423
Rehabilitation Institute of Toronto	425
Riverside Hospital of Ottawa, The	434
Royal Inland Hospital	439
Scarborough General Hospital	450
Shoppers Drug Mart Limited	458
Sobeys Inc.	463
St. Amant Centre Inc.	471
St. Joseph's Care Group	472
St. Vincent's Hospitals	473
Sudbury Regional Hospital	480
Surrey Memorial Hospital	483
Swift Current Health District	485
Thunder Bay Regional Hospital	497
Toronto East General Hospital	503
Toronto General Hospital	505
Yarmouth Regional Hospital	543

Physics

Alberta Energy Company Ltd.	89
Alcan Aluminium Limited	91
Assiniboine Community College	109
Ballard Power Systems Inc.	120
Camp Hill Hospital	160
CancerCare Manitoba	171
CH2M Gore and Storrie Limited	185
COM DEV International	197
Communications & Power Industries Canada	198
Duha Color Services	220
Dynapro Systems Inc.	223
Exfo	235
Fisher Scientific Limited	241
Glaxo Wellcome Canada	253
Grant MacEwen Community College	258
Haliburton Energy Services	262
Halliburton Energy Services	264
Hallmark Tools	265
HB Studios Multimedia Ltd.	266
Hydro Québec	283
IBM Canada Ltd.	284
IWK Grace Health Centre	297

JDS Uniphase Corporation	300
John P. Robarts Research Institute	302
Keyano College	306
Lenbrook Industries Limited	315
Liberty Health	318
Litton Systems Canada Ltd.	320
MacDonald Dettwiler and Associates Ltd.	325
MDS Nordion	339
Mitel Corporation	350
Mitra Imaging Inc.	350
Mustang Survival Corp.	358
Netron Inc.	365
Newness Machine Ltd.	368
Peel Board of Education	393
Powertech Labs Inc.	406
QEII Health Sciences Centre	414
Raytheon Systems Canada Ltd.	419
Science North	452
SCIEX MDS Health Group	452
Toronto District School Board	503
Toronto French School, The	504
Toronto Sun Publishing Corp., The	507
Triumf	510
University College of Cape Breton	516
Zenastra	547

Physiotherapy

Aberdeen Hospital	77
AstraZeneca	110
AXA Insurance (Canada)	118
Barton Place Long Term Care Facility	121
Battlefords Health District	123
Baycrest Centre for Geriatric Care	123
Belleville General Hospital	132
Bethesda Hospital	134
Bloorview Childrens Hospital	140
Cambridge Memorial Hospital	159
Camp Hill Hospital	160
Chilliwack General Hospital	189
Chinook Health Region	190
Christian Horizons	190
Cobourg District General Hospital	194
Comcare Health Services	198
David Thompson Health Region	212
Deer Lodge Centre Inc.	213
Extendicare (Canada) Inc.	237
George Jeffrey Children's Treatment Centre	250
Halifax County Regional Rehabilitation Centre	263
Health Authority 5	267
Health Care Corporation of St. John's	267
Health Sciences Centre	268
Humber River Regional Hospital	280

The Canada Student Employment Guide

664　University Index

Huronia Regional Centre	280
IWK Grace Health Centre	297
Izaak Walton Killam Hospital, The	297
Kings Regional Rehabilitation Centre	308
Magna International Inc.	327
Metropolitan Life Insurance Company	344
Misericordia General Hospital	348
North York Community Care Access Centre	374
Northern Lights Regional Health Centre	375
Ottawa Hospital	386
Overlander Hospital	387
Providence Centre	412
QEII Health Sciences Centre	414
Regina Health District	423
Rehabilitation Institute of Toronto	425
Riverside Hospital of Ottawa, The	434
Royal Inland Hospital	439
Royal Victoria Hospital	440
Scarborough General Hospital	450
Sherbrooke Community Centre	457
St. Amant Centre Inc.	471
St. Joseph's Care Group	472
St. Vincent's Hospitals	473
Sudbury Regional Hospital	480
Surrey Memorial Hospital	483
Swift Current Health District	485
The Arthritis Society	492
Thunder Bay Regional Hospital	497
Toronto East General Hospital	503
Toronto General Hospital	505
Toronto Hydro	505
Universal Rehabilitation Service Agency	515
Yarmouth Regional Hospital	543

Psychology

1-800-GOT-JUNK?	74
Aberdeen Hospital	77
Acklands-Grainger Inc.	80
Alberta Alcohol and Drug Abuse Commission	87
Alcan Aluminium Limited	91
Andersen Consulting	101
Assiniboine Community College	109
AXA Insurance (Canada)	118
Barton Place Long Term Care Facility	121
Battlefords Health District	123
Belleville General Hospital	132
Biovail Corporation International	137
Bloorview MacMillan Centre, The	140
Buckeye Canada Inc.	151
Calgary Co-operative Association Limited	157
Camp Hill Hospital	160
Children's Hospital of Eastern Ontario	189

Christian Horizons	190
Cobourg District General Hospital	194
Co-op Atlantic	203
David Thompson Health Region	212
Endpoint Research Ltd.	231
Environics Research Group Ltd.	233
FedEx Express	240
Gallup Canada Inc.	247
Goodwill Industries of Toronto	256
Grant MacEwen Community College	258
Halifax County Regional Rehabilitation Centre	263
Health Authority 5	267
Health Care Corporation of St. John's	267
Homewood Corp.	274
Hôtel Dieu de Montréal	276
Huronia Regional Centre	280
Island Telecom Inc.	295
IWK Grace Health Centre	297
Izaak Walton Killam Hospital, The	297
Kings Regional Rehabilitation Centre	308
Kodak Canada Inc.	309
Les Centres Jeunesse de Montréal	316
Liberty Health	318
Marine Atlantic Inc.	331
Metropolitan Life Insurance Company	344
Montreal Trust Co.	353
National Grocers Co. Ltd.	360
North American Life Assurance Company	373
Northern Lights Regional Health Centre	375
Ontario March of Dimes	385
Ottawa Hospital	386
Peel Children's Centre	394
Pitney Bowes of Canada Ltd.	401
QEII Health Sciences Centre	414
Reena	421
Regional Residential Services Society	424
Scarborough General Hospital	450
Signature Vacations Inc.	460
St. Amant Centre Inc.	471
St. Joseph's Care Group	472
State Farm Insurance Companies	476
Sudbury Regional Hospital	480
Supreme Tooling Group	483
Surrey Place Centre	484
Symantec Corporation	486
Toronto Association For Community Living	501
Toronto General Hospital	505
University College of Cape Breton	516
Yanke Group of Companies	543
Yarmouth Regional Hospital	543

The Canada Student Employment Guide

University Index   665

Zoology

Blue Wave Seafoods Inc.	142
Brandon, City of	146
Grant MacEwen Community College	258
Paramount Canada's Wonderland Inc.	389
Toronto French School, The	504
Toronto Zoo	507
University College of Cape Breton	516

Bachelor of Laws

Corporate

1-800-GOT-JUNK?	74
Abitibi-Consolidated Inc.	77
Acier Leroux Inc.	80
Acklands-Grainger Inc.	80
Alcan Aluminium Limited	91
AMEC Inc.	99
Anthony Insurance Inc.	102
Assiniboine Community College	109
Assumption Mutual Life Insurance	109
Aventis Pasteur Limited	117
Babcock and Wilcox Canada	119
Biovail Corporation International	137
Blaney McMurty LLP	139
Blue Wave Seafoods Inc.	142
BNP PARIBAS (Canada)	143
Boréal Assurances Inc.	144
BOVAR Waste Management	145
Cabre Exploration Ltd.	156
Canadian Commercial Corp.	165
Canadian Western Bank	169
Chevron Canada Resources Ltd.	188
Cobourg District General Hospital	194
Coquitlam, City of	204
Credit Union Central of Canada	208
DaimlerChrysler Canada Ltd.	211
Domtar Inc.	218
Emco Limited	230
Exfo	235
Explorer Hotel, The	236
Federated Co-operatives Limited	239
FedEx Express	240
Fishery Products International	241
Glaxo Wellcome Canada	253
Grant MacEwen Community College	258
Great-West Life Assurance Company, The	259
Home Oil Co. Ltd.	273
Honda Canada Inc.	274
Hydro Québec	283

I M P Group International Inc.	283
Industrial-Alliance Life Insurance Company	289
Ivaco Inc.	296
J.D. Irving Limited	298
Jim Pattison Group	301
Kitchener, City of	309
Lenbrook Industries Limited	315
Magna International Inc.	327
Manitoba Agriculture and Food	327
Manitoba Hydro	328
Marine Atlantic Inc.	331
Matrox Electronic Systems Ltd.	335
McInnes Cooper & Robertson	337
Metropolitan Life Insurance Company	344
Meyers Norris Penny & Co.	344
Michaels of Canada Inc.	345
Mitel Corporation	350
Moffat Communications Limited	352
Montreal Trust Co.	353
MOSAID Technologies Inc.	355
National Grocers Co. Ltd.	360
National Life	361
Neles Automation, Scada Solutions Ltd.	362
Nelvana Limited	363
Nesbitt Burns Inc.	364
NewTel Communications	369
Northwestel Inc.	376
Nova Scotia Power Corp.	377
Novartis Consumer Health Canada Inc.	378
Ocelot Energy Inc.	381
Oland Breweries Limited	382
Pembina Pipeline Corporation	395
Polygram Group Canada Inc.	403
Public Utilities of Kingston	413
Purolator Courier Ltd.	413
Quebecor Inc.	415
Rio Algom Limited	433
Royal Philips Electronics	439
Saskatchewan Government Insurance	445
Saskatoon, City of	448
SaskTel	449
Shaw Communications	455
Sony Music Canada	465
Sprint Canada	470
Steelpipe Ltd.	477
Surrey, City of	484
Talisman Energy Inc.	487
Today's Business Products Ltd.	500
Toronto, City of	508
Vancouver Sun	520
Waverly & York Corporation	525
Westbury Life	529
Westcliff Management Ltd.	529
Weyerhaeuser Company Limited	535

The Canada Student Employment Guide

666 University Index

General

1-800-GOT-JUNK?	74
Abitibi-Consolidated Inc.	77
Alberta Energy & Utilities Board	89
Assiniboine Community College	109
Blaney McMurty LLP	139
BNP PARIBAS (Canada)	143
Canadian Commercial Corp.	165
Canadian Western Bank	169
Catholic Children's Aid Society Foundation	178
Columbia House	197
Coquitlam, City of	204
DaimlerChrysler Canada Ltd.	211
Dun & Bradstreet Canada	221
Dylex Limited	222
Exfo	235
Federated Co-operatives Limited	239
Future Shop Ltd.	246
Goepel McDermid Securities	254
Goodman and Carr	255
Grant MacEwen Community College	258
Great-West Life Assurance Company, The	259
Insurance Corp. of B.C.	291
Kitchener, City of	309
Leduc, City of	313
Loss Prevention Group Inc.	322
Manitoba Public Insurance Corporation	329
Maritime Life Assurance Company, The	331
Matrox Electronic Systems Ltd.	335
McInnes Cooper & Robertson	337
Mississauga, City of	349
Montreal Trust Co.	353
National Grocers Co. Ltd.	360
National Life	361
Nelvana Limited	363
New Brunswick Power Corporation	365
Northwestel Inc.	376
Ontario Guard Services Inc.	383
Ontario Legislative Offices	384
Paramount Canada's Wonderland Inc.	389
Prince Albert, City of	410
Progressive Financial Strategy	411
Sandman Hotels and Inns	443
Saskatchewan Government Insurance	445
Saskatoon, City of	448
SaskTel	449
Shaw Communications	455
SSQ Life	471
State Farm Insurance Companies	476
Surrey, City of	484
Toronto, City of	508
Turnbull & Turnbull Ltd.	512
Westbury Life	529
Weston Produce Inc.	533

Real Estate

Abitibi-Consolidated Inc.	77
Acier Leroux Inc.	80
Acklands-Grainger Inc.	80
Blaney McMurty LLP	139
Brandon, City of	146
Brookfield Properties Corporation	150
Canadian Western Bank	169
Centra Gas British Columbia Inc.	180
Coquitlam, City of	204
Future Shop Ltd.	246
Housesitters Canada, The	277
Hudon & Deaudelin Ltée	279
Kitchener, City of	309
McInnes Cooper & Robertson	337
Michaels of Canada Inc.	345
Mississauga, City of	349
National Grocers Co. Ltd.	360
Prince George, City of	410
Sprint Canada	470
Surrey, City of	484
Waverly & York Corporation	525
Westcliff Management Ltd.	529

Bachelor of Engineering

Biomedical

AstraZeneca	110
Biomira Inc.	136
Bio-Research Laboratories Ltd.	137
Biovail Corporation International	137
Cambridge Memorial Hospital	159
Camp Hill Hospital	160
Chilliwack General Hospital	189
Cobourg District General Hospital	194
Health Care Corporation of St. John's	267
Health Sciences Centre	268
Hôtel Dieu de Montréal	276
IWK Grace Health Centre	297
Izaak Walton Killam Hospital, The	297
John P. Robarts Research Institute	302
MDS Nordion	339
Ottawa Hospital	386
QEII Health Sciences Centre	414
Regina Health District	423
Royal Inland Hospital	439
SCIEX MDS Health Group	452

The Canada Student Employment Guide

University Index   667

Siemens Electric Ltd.	460
Sudbury Regional Hospital	480
Toronto General Hospital	505
Toronto, City of	508
Windsor, City of	538

Chemical

A.G. Simpson Co. Ltd.	75
Accucaps Industries Limited	79
ADI Group Inc.	82
Air Liquide Canada Inc.	85
Alberta Energy & Utilities Board	89
Alcan Aluminium Limited	91
Algoma Steel Inc.	93
Amcor Twinpak North America Inc.	98
Andersen Consulting	101
Apotex Fermentation Inc.	104
Aquatic Sciences Inc.	105
AstraZeneca	110
Aventis Pasteur Limited	117
Ballard Power Systems Inc.	120
BASF Canada Inc.	122
Baytex Energy Limited	124
BC Research Inc.	126
BFGoodrich Landing Gear Division	135
Bio-Research Laboratories Ltd.	137
Biovail Corporation International	137
BJ Services Company	138
BOVAR Waste Management	145
Bowater Mersey Paper Company Limited	146
Buckeye Canada Inc.	151
Calgary, City of	158
Cameco Corporation	160
Canadian General Tower Limited	166
Canadian Thermos Products Inc.	168
Cancarb Limited	170
Cangene Corporation	172
CCL Industries Inc.	178
Centra Gas Manitoba Inc.	181
CH2M Gore and Storrie Limited	185
Chevron Canada Resources Ltd.	188
CKF Inc.	192
Cognis Canada Corporation	195
Computalog Ltd.	200
Cosyn Technology	207
Crestar Energy Inc.	209
D.A. Stuart Inc.	210
DaimlerChrysler Canada Ltd.	211
Dana Corporation - Long Manufacturing	212
DDM Plastics Inc.	213
Degussa - Huls Canada Inc.	214
Dofasco Inc.	218

Domtar Inc.	218
DuPont Canada Inc.	221
Dynasty Furniture Manufacturing Ltd.	224
Entreprises Premier Canadien Ltée	232
Flakeboard Company Limited	242
Gencorp Vehicle Sealing	248
General Chemical Canada Ltd.	249
General Electric Canada Inc.	249
Gienow Building Products Ltd.	251
Giffels Associates Limited	251
Gilbey Canada Inc.	252
Glaxo Wellcome Canada	253
Haliburton Energy Services	262
Halifax Regional Municipality	263
Halliburton Energy Services	264
Home Oil Co. Ltd.	273
Honeywell Ltd.	275
Hydro One Inc.	282
Hydro Québec	283
IBM Canada Ltd.	284
Imperial Oil Limited	286
INCO Limited	287
Industries Lassonde Inc.	289
J.D. Irving Limited	298
Jim Pattison Group	301
Keyano College	306
Kimberly-Clark Inc.	307
Kodak Canada Inc.	309
Kraft Canada Inc.	310
Litton Systems Canada Ltd.	320
MAAX Inc.	324
MacViro Consultants Inc.	326
Magna International Inc.	327
Manitoba Hydro	328
MDS Nordion	339
Minas Basin Pulp and Power Company Ltd.	347
Moosehead Breweries Limited	354
Natco Canada Ltd.	360
National Grocers Co. Ltd.	360
Nestle Canada Inc.	364
Netron Inc.	365
New Brunswick Power Corporation	365
NLK Consultants Inc.	372
Norcen Energy Resources Ltd.	373
Nova Scotia Power Corp.	377
Novartis Consumer Health Canada Inc.	378
NPS Allelix Corp.	379
Numac Energy Inc.	379
Ocelot Energy Inc.	381
Oland Breweries Limited	382
Omstead Foods Limited	383
Oracle Corp. Canada Inc.	386
Pembina Pipeline Corporation	395
Petro-Canada	397

The Canada Student Employment Guide

668 University Index

Petromont & Co. Ltd. Partnership	397	ATCO Frontec Corp.	111
Pine Falls Paper Company Limited	400	ATCO Gas Services Ltd.	112
Placer Dome Inc.	402	BC Hydro	125
Poco Petroleums Ltd.	402	Bechtel Canada Co.	128
PPG Canada Inc.	407	Behlen Industries	130
Pricewaterhouse Coopers	409	Belleville General Hospital	132
QIT-Fer et Titane Inc.	414	Boréal Assurances Inc.	144
Raylo Chemicals Inc.	417	BOVAR Waste Management	145
Recochem Inc.	420	Bowater Mersey Paper Company Limited	146
Rhone-Poulenc Canada Inc.	430	Brandon, City of	146
Royal Canadian Mint	438	British Columbia Ferry Corporation	149
Ryerson Polytechnic University	441	C B C L Limited	154
Sandwell Inc.	443	Calgary, City of	158
Saskatchewan Research Council, The	446	Cambior Inc.	158
Saskatoon, City of	448	Canadian Commercial Corp.	165
Saskferco Products Inc.	448	Canadian Occidental Petroleum Ltd.	168
SCIEX MDS Health Group	452	Centra Gas British Columbia Inc.	180
Seprotech Systems Incorporated	454	Centra Gas Manitoba Inc.	181
Shaw Industries Ltd.	455	CH2M Gore and Storrie Limited	185
Sony Music Canada	465	Chevron Canada Resources Ltd.	188
Stantec Consulting Ltd.	475	Connors Bros, Limited	203
State Farm Insurance Companies	476	Coquitlam, City of	204
Stone Consolidated Inc.	479	Corner Brook, City of	205
Sun Rype Products Ltd.	481	Cosyn Technology	207
Sunoco Inc.	482	Crestar Energy Inc.	209
Supreme Tooling Group	483	DaimlerChrysler Canada Ltd.	211
Syncrude Canada Ltd.	486	DDM Plastics Inc.	213
Talisman Energy Inc.	487	Dofasco Inc.	218
Toronto General Hospital	505	Dynasty Furniture Manufacturing Ltd.	224
Toronto, City of	508	E B A Engineering Consultants Ltd.	225
TransAlta	509	Earth Tech Canada Inc.	225
Trojan Technologies Inc.	511	Entreprises Premier Canadien Ltée	232
Trow Consulting Engineers Ltd.	511	Flakeboard Company Limited	242
Union Gas Ltd.	513	Flint Energy Services Ltd.	243
Vancouver Sun	520	General Chemical Canada Ltd.	249
Wegu Canada Inc.	526	Gienow Building Products Ltd.	251
Westcoast Energy Inc.	530	Giffels Associates Limited	251
Westport Innovations Inc.	534	Gilbey Canada Inc.	252
Weyerhaeuser Company Limited	535	Gisborne Design Services Ltd.	253
Windsor, City of	538	Glaxo Wellcome Canada	253
Winpak Ltd.	539	Golder Associates Ltd.	255
		Halifax Regional Municipality	263
		Halifax Water Commission	264

Civil

		Home Oil Co. Ltd.	273
		I M P Group International Inc.	283
ADI Group Inc.	82	I P L Plastics Ltd.	284
Alberta Energy & Utilities Board	89	Imperial Oil Limited	286
Aliant Telecom Inc.	93	INCO Limited	287
Alumicor Limited	97	IPL Energy Inc.	294
Andersen Consulting	101	J.D. Barnes Limited	298
Apex Land Corp.	103	J.D. Irving Limited	298
Aquatic Sciences Inc.	105	J.S. Redpath Limited	299
Arbor Memorial Services Inc.	106	Jacques Whitford Consulting Engineers	299
Armtec Limited	108	Kelowna, City of	305

The Canada Student Employment Guide

University Index 669

Keyano College	306	Talisman Energy Inc.	487
Kitchener, City of	309	TCT Logistics	488
Kraft Canada Inc.	310	The Garland Group	494
Kvaerner Metals	311	The McElhanney Group Ltd.	494
Leduc, City of	313	Timmins, City of	499
Leica Geosystems Canada Inc.	314	Toronto and Region Conservation Authority	501
MacViro Consultants Inc.	326	Toronto District School Board	503
Manitoba Hydro	328	Toronto Hydro	505
Marine Atlantic Inc.	331	Toronto, City of	508
Marshall Macklin Monaghan Ltd.	333	TransAlta	509
Mississauga, City of	349	Trojan Technologies Inc.	511
Morrison Hershfield Limited	354	Trow Consulting Engineers Ltd.	511
National Grocers Co. Ltd.	360	Union Gas Ltd.	513
Netron Inc.	365	University College of Cape Breton	516
New Brunswick Power Corporation	365	Urban Systems Ltd.	516
Newfoundland and Labrador Hydro	367	Vancouver International Airport	520
NLK Consultants Inc.	372	Vancouver Sun	520
Norcen Energy Resources Ltd.	373	West Kootenay Power Ltd.	528
Northwestel Inc.	376	Westcoast Energy Inc.	530
Nova Scotia Liquor Commission	377	Whitehill Technologies Inc.	537
Nova Scotia Power Corp.	377	Windsor, City of	538
Oland Breweries Limited	382	Wire Rope Industries Ltd.	540
PCL Constructors Inc.	392	Yellowknife, City of	544
Pembina Pipeline Corporation	395		
Peter Kiewit Sons Co.	396		
Poco Petroleums Ltd.	402	## Computer Systems	
Powertech Labs Inc.	406		
Prince Albert, City of	410	A E McKenzie Co. Inc.	75
Prince George, City of	410	A.G. Simpson Co. Ltd.	75
Proctor and Redfern Ltd.	411	Abitibi-Consolidated Inc.	77
Public Utilities of Kingston	413	Accucaps Industries Limited	79
Purolator Courier Ltd.	413	Air Canada	85
Québec Cartier Mining Company	415	Air Liquide Canada Inc.	85
Reid Crowther	426	Alberta Gaming & Liquor Commission	90
Richmond, City of	431	Alcan Aluminium Limited	91
Roctest Ltée	435	Algoma Steel Inc.	93
Rogers AT&T Wireless Inc.	436	Aliant Telecom Inc.	93
Ryerson Polytechnic University	441	Amcor Twinpak North America Inc.	98
Sandwell Inc.	443	Andersen Consulting	101
Saskatchewan Economic Development	445	Anjura Services Inc.	101
Saskatoon, City of	448	Anthony Insurance Inc.	102
SaskTel	449	Apple Canada Inc.	104
SC Infrastructure Inc.	449	Armor Personnel	107
Seprotech Systems Incorporated	454	AstraZeneca	110
SNC-Lavalin	463	Atlantic Lottery Corporation Inc.	113
Sobeys Inc.	463	ATS Automation Tooling Systems Inc.	116
St. Lawrence Parks Commission	472	Aventis Pasteur Limited	117
St. Lawrence Seaway Mgmt. Corp., The	473	Babcock and Wilcox Canada	119
Stantec Consulting Ltd.	475	BASF Canada Inc.	122
State Farm Insurance Companies	476	Basic Technologies Corporation	122
Stone Consolidated Inc.	479	Baycrest Centre for Geriatric Care	123
Sudbury Regional Hospital	480	BBM Bureau of Measurement	125
Surrey, City of	484	BC Telecom Inc.	126
Sydney Steel Corporation	485	Bell Mobility	131

The Canada Student Employment Guide

670 University Index

Belleville General Hospital	132	EMJ Data Systems Ltd.	231
Bettis Canada Ltd.	135	Entreprises Premier Canadien Ltée	232
BFGoodrich Landing Gear Division	135	Exfo	235
Biovail Corporation International	137	FAG Bearings Limited	237
Bloorview MacMillan Centre, The	140	FedEx Express	240
Boréal Assurances Inc.	144	Fishery Products International	241
BOVAR Waste Management	145	Flakeboard Company Limited	242
Bowater Mersey Paper Company Limited	146	Friesens Corporation	246
Brandon, City of	146	Future Shop Ltd.	246
Brantcorp Inc.	147	General Electric Canada Inc.	249
Bratty & Partners LLP	147	Gienow Building Products Ltd.	251
Brookfield Properties Corporation	150	Giffels Associates Limited	251
Budd Canada Inc.	152	Gimbel Eye Centre	252
C MAC Industries Inc.	155	Goodwill Industries of Toronto	256
CAE Newness	157	Gov't of Newfoundland – Dept. of Finance	257
Calgary, City of	158	Grand & Toy Ltd.	257
Cambridge Memorial Hospital	159	Grant MacEwen Community College	258
Camp Hill Hospital	160	Great-West Life Assurance Company, The	259
Canada Post Corporation	162	Health Care Corporation of St. John's	267
Canadian Commercial Corp.	165	Health Sciences Centre	268
Canadian Depository for Securities Ltd.	166	Honda Canada Inc.	274
Canadian Occidental Petroleum Ltd.	168	Honeywell Ltd.	275
Canadian Western Bank	169	Husky Energy Inc.	281
Canbra Foods Ltd.	170	Hydro Electric Commission of Thunder Bay	281
Cangene Corporation	172	Hydro One Inc.	282
Canon Canada Inc.	172	Hydro Québec	283
Canpar Transport Ltd.	173	I M P Group International Inc.	283
CCL Industries Inc.	178	IBM Canada Ltd.	284
Cegelec Enterprises Ltée	179	Ilco Unican Inc.	286
CH2M Gore and Storrie Limited	185	Imperial Oil Limited	286
Children's Hospital of Eastern Ontario	189	Industrial-Alliance Life Insurance Company	289
Christian Horizons	190	Industries Lassonde Inc.	289
Citibank Canada	191	InfoInterActive Inc.	290
CKF Inc.	192	Information Gateway Services	290
Clarica	192	ING Canada Financial Services International	291
Cognos Incorporated	196	IPL Energy Inc.	294
Comcare Health Services	198	Island Telecom Inc.	295
Community Savings Credit Union	199	IST Group Inc.	296
Compaq Canada Inc.	199	IWK Grace Health Centre	297
Compu-Quote Inc.	200	J.D. Irving Limited	298
Computalog Ltd.	200	John P. Robarts Research Institute	302
Connors Bros, Limited	203	Johnson Controls Ltd.	302
Coquitlam, City of	204	Johnson Incorporated	303
Corel Corporation	205	Jostens Canada Ltd.	303
Cougar Helicopters Inc.	208	Keyano College	306
Credit Union Central of Canada	208	Kitchener, City of	309
David Thompson Health Region	212	Kraft Canada Inc.	310
Dofasco Inc.	218	La Confiserie Comete Ltee	311
Domtar Inc.	218	Leduc, City of	313
DuPont Canada Inc.	221	Lenbrook Industries Limited	315
Dynapro Systems Inc.	223	Liberty Health	318
Dynatek Automation Systems Inc.	224	Lifetouch Canada Inc.	319
EDS of Canada Ltd.	228	Litton Systems Canada Ltd.	320
Electronics Arts (Canada) Inc.	229	MAAX Inc.	324

The Canada Student Employment Guide

University Index

MacDonald Dettwiler and Associates Ltd.	325	Power Measurement Ltd.	406
MacDonald Steel Ltd.	325	Pratt & Whitney Canada Inc.	407
MacViro Consultants Inc.	326	PRI Automation	408
Manitoba Hydro	328	Pricewaterhouse Coopers	409
Marcam Canada	330	Prince George, City of	410
Maritime Life Assurance Company, The	331	Proctor and Redfern Ltd.	411
Marystown Shipyard Limited	334	Prudential Insurance Co. of America, The	412
Matrox Electronic Systems Ltd.	335	Public Utilities of Kingston	413
McBee Systems of Canada Inc.	336	Purolator Courier Ltd.	413
MDS Nordion	339	QIT-Fer et Titane Inc.	414
Mediasynergy	340	Quebecor Inc.	415
Michaels of Canada Inc.	345	Raymond Industrial Equipment Ltd.	418
Midland Walwyn Inc.	345	Raymond Rebar Inc.	418
Midwest Food Products Inc.	346	Raytheon Systems Canada Ltd.	419
Mississauga, City of	349	Regal Constellation Hotel Ltd.	422
Mitel Corporation	350	Rehabilitation Institute of Toronto	425
Mitsubishi Electric Sales Canada	351	Replicon Inc.	428
Mobile Computing Corporation	351	Reuters Information Services (Canada) Ltd.	428
Monarch Communications Inc.	353	Richmond, City of	431
Montreal Trust Co.	353	Rogers AT&T Wireless Inc.	436
Mortice Kern Systems Inc.	355	Royal & Sun Alliance Insurance Co. of Cda	437
MOSAID Technologies Inc.	355	Royal Bank of Canada	438
Motorola Canada Ltd.	356	Saskatoon, City of	448
Multitech Electronics Inc.	358	SaskTel	449
Natco Canada Ltd.	360	Scarborough General Hospital	450
National Grocers Co. Ltd.	360	Schneider Electric Canada Inc.	451
National Life	361	SCIEX MDS Health Group	452
Neles Automation, Scada Solutions Ltd.	362	Seprotech Systems Incorporated	454
Nesbitt Burns Inc.	364	Shermag Inc.	457
Nestle Canada Inc.	364	Siemens Electric Ltd.	460
Netron Inc.	365	Silicon Graphics Canada Inc.	461
New Brunswick Power Corporation	365	SolutionInc Limited	465
New Brunswick Telephone Company	366	Sony Music Canada	465
Newness Machine Ltd.	368	Spar Aerospace Limited	467
NewTel Communications	369	Spectrum Signal Processing Inc.	468
Norbord Industries	372	Speedware Corp. Inc.	469
Norcen Energy Resources Ltd.	373	Sprint Canada	470
Northern Lights Regional Health Centre	375	SSQ Life	471
Nova Scotia Power Corp.	377	Standard Knitting Limited	474
Novartis Consumer Health Canada Inc.	378	Stantec Consulting Ltd.	475
Numac Energy Inc.	379	Star Data Systems Inc.	476
Ontario Legislative Offices	384	State Farm Insurance Companies	476
Oracle Corp. Canada Inc.	386	Steelpipe Ltd.	477
Ottawa Hospital	386	Stone Consolidated Inc.	479
Paramount Canada's Wonderland Inc.	389	StorageTek Canada Inc.	479
Peacock Inc.	392	Sudbury Regional Hospital	480
Pelmorex Inc.	395	Sundog Printing Limited	482
Phoenix International	399	Surrey Memorial Hospital	483
Pine Falls Paper Company Limited	400	Surrey, City of	484
Pitney Bowes of Canada Ltd.	401	Sydney Steel Corporation	485
Poco Petroleums Ltd.	402	Symantec Corporation	486
Polygram Group Canada Inc.	403	Syncrude Canada Ltd.	486
Positron Industries Inc.	404	TCT Logistics	488
Potacan Mining Company	405	Teklogix Inc.	489

The Canada Student Employment Guide

672 University Index

Teldon International Inc.	490	Bloorview MacMillan Centre, The	140
Telebec Ltée	490	Blue Giant Equipment of Canada Ltd.	141
Telegraph Journal	491	BOVAR Waste Management	145
The Co-operators	493	Brandon, City of	146
Thompson's Moving and Storage	496	Brantcorp Inc.	147
Thomson - CSF Systems Canada Inc.	497	C B C L Limited	154
Thunder Bay Regional Hospital	497	CAE Newness	157
Timmins, City of	499	Calgary Co-operative Association Limited	157
Today's Business Products Ltd.	500	Cameco Corporation	160
Toronto Catholic District School Board	502	Canadian Commercial Corp.	165
Toronto General Hospital	505	CancerCare Manitoba	171
Toronto Police Service	506	Celestica International Inc.	179
Toronto Sun Publishing Corp., The	507	CenAlta Energy Services Inc.	180
Toronto, City of	508	CH2M Gore and Storrie Limited	185
Toshiba of Canada Ltd.	508	COM DEV International	197
Unisys Canada Inc.	514	Connors Bros, Limited	203
US Filter BCP	517	Coquitlam, City of	204
Vancouver Sun	520	Corner Brook, City of	205
Visteon Canada Inc.	522	Cougar Helicopters Inc.	208
WebCanada	526	Custom Trim Ltd.	210
Westcoast Energy Inc.	530	Dofasco Inc.	218
Westinghouse Canada Inc.	532	Dynapro Systems Inc.	223
Westminster Savings Credit Union	533	EnerFlex Systems Ltd.	232
Weyerhaeuser Company Limited	535	Entreprises Premier Canadien Ltée	232
Whitehill Technologies Inc.	537	Federated Co-operatives Limited	239
Wilson Auto Electric Ltd.	538	Foremost Industries Inc.	244
Windsor, City of	538	General Electric Canada Inc.	249
Wire Rope Industries Ltd.	540	Gienow Building Products Ltd.	251
Workfire Development Corp.	540	Giffels Associates Limited	251
xwave solutions	542	Gisborne Design Services Ltd.	253
Yanke Group of Companies	543	Halifax Water Commission	264
Yarmouth Regional Hospital	543	Husky Energy Inc.	281
Zellers Inc.	546	Hydro Electric Commission of Thunder Bay	281
		I M P Group International Inc.	283
		IBM Canada Ltd.	284

Design

		Industrial Equipment Co. Ltd.	288
		Intercon Security Ltd.	292
ABC Group	76	Island Telecom Inc.	295
Abitibi-Consolidated Inc.	77	John P. Robarts Research Institute	302
Accucaps Industries Limited	79	KFC Canada	307
Alumicor Limited	97	Leduc, City of	313
Amcan Castings Limited	98	Lenbrook Industries Limited	315
Andersen Consulting	101	Leon's Manufacturing Company Inc.	316
Armor Personnel	107	Litton Systems Canada Ltd.	320
Armtec Limited	108	MacViro Consultants Inc.	326
ArvinMeritor	108	Magna International Inc.	327
Atlantic Packaging Products Ltd.	114	Maple Leaf Consumer Foods	330
ATS Automation Tooling Systems Inc.	116	McKay-Cocker Construction Limited	338
Aurizon Mines Ltd.	116	Memotec Communications Inc.	341
Babcock and Wilcox Canada	119	Michaels of Canada Inc.	345
Ballard Power Systems Inc.	120	Midland Walwyn Inc.	345
Bechtel Canada Co.	128	Mitsubishi Electric Sales Canada	351
Bettis Canada Ltd.	135	Mobile Computing Corporation	351
BFGoodrich Landing Gear Division	135	Morrison Hershfield Limited	354

The Canada Student Employment Guide

University Index 673

MOSAID Technologies Inc.	355	**Electrical**		
Motorola Canada Ltd.	356			
Natco Canada Ltd.	360	A.G. Simpson Co. Ltd.	75	
Neles Automation, Scada Solutions Ltd.	362	Access Communications	78	
Netron Inc.	365	Accucaps Industries Limited	79	
New Holland Canada Ltd.	366	ADI Group Inc.	82	
Newness Machine Ltd.	368	Aimtronics	84	
Nichirin Inc.	370	Air Canada	85	
Norcen Energy Resources Ltd.	373	Air Liquide Canada Inc.	85	
Oetiker Limited	381	Akita Drilling Ltd.	87	
Ottawa Hospital	386	Alberta Energy Company Ltd.	89	
Peel Board of Education	393	Alcan Aluminium Limited	91	
Positron Industries Inc.	404	Algoma Steel Inc.	93	
Pricewaterhouse Coopers	409	Aliant Telecom Inc.	93	
Prince Albert, City of	410	Andersen Consulting	101	
Purolator Courier Ltd.	413	Apotex Fermentation Inc.	104	
Raylo Chemicals Inc.	417	Apple Canada Inc.	104	
Raymond Industrial Equipment Ltd.	418	Armor Personnel	107	
Raymond Rebar Inc.	418	ArvinMeritor	108	
Reid Crowther	426	Assiniboine Community College	109	
Revy Home Centres Inc.	429	ATCO Electric	111	
Richmond, City of	431	ATCO Frontec Corp.	111	
Sandwell Inc.	443	ATS Automation Tooling Systems Inc.	116	
Saskatchewan Wheat Pool	447	Aurizon Mines Ltd.	116	
Saskatoon, City of	448	Aventis Pasteur Limited	117	
SaskTel	449	Babcock and Wilcox Canada	119	
SC Infrastructure Inc.	449	Ballard Power Systems Inc.	120	
SCIEX MDS Health Group	452	Banff Centre for Continuing Education, The	120	
Seprotech Systems Incorporated	454	BC Hydro	125	
Shermag Inc.	457	BC Telecom Inc.	126	
Siemens Electric Ltd.	460	Bechtel Canada Co.	128	
SNC-Lavalin	463	Bell Canada	131	
Spectra Premium Industries	468	Bell Mobility	131	
Sprint Canada	470	BFGoodrich Landing Gear Division	135	
St. Lawrence Seaway Mgmt. Corp., The	473	Bic Inc.	136	
Stantec Consulting Ltd.	475	Biovail Corporation International	137	
State Farm Insurance Companies	476	Black Photo Corporation	139	
Steelcraft Industries Ltd.	477	Bloorview Childrens Hospital	140	
Supreme Tooling Group	483	Blue Giant Equipment of Canada Ltd.	141	
Surrey, City of	484	Blue Wave Seafoods Inc.	142	
Teklogix Inc.	489	BOVAR Waste Management	145	
The Garland Group	494	Bowater Mersey Paper Company Limited	146	
Thomson - CSF Systems Canada Inc.	497	British Columbia Ferry Corporation	149	
Toshiba of Canada Ltd.	508	Brookfield Properties Corporation	150	
Trojan Technologies Inc.	511	Buckeye Canada Inc.	151	
Trow Consulting Engineers Ltd.	511	C B C L Limited	154	
US Filter BCP	517	C MAC Industries Inc.	155	
Weldco-Beales Manufacturing Inc.	527	CAE Newness	157	
West Kootenay Power Ltd.	528	Calgary, City of	158	
Westport Innovations Inc.	534	Cambior Inc.	158	
Windsor, City of	538	Cameco Corporation	160	
Zellers Inc.	546	Canada Post Corporation	162	
Zenon Environmental Inc.	547	Canada Starch Company Inc.	163	
		Canadian General Tower Limited	166	

The Canada Student Employment Guide

University Index

Canadian Museum of Civilization Corp.	167	General Chemical Canada Ltd.	249
Canbra Foods Ltd.	170	General Electric Canada Inc.	249
Cape Breton Development Corporation	174	Giffels Associates Limited	251
Carte International Inc.	176	Gimbel Eye Centre	252
Cegelec Enterprises Ltée	179	Glaxo Wellcome Canada	253
Celestica International Inc.	179	H A Simmons Ltd.	261
Centra Gas British Columbia Inc.	180	H.H. Angus & Associates Ltd.	261
CH2M Gore and Storrie Limited	185	Halifax Regional Municipality	263
Chevron Canada Resources Ltd.	188	Health Sciences Centre	268
Chilliwack General Hospital	189	Hermes Electronics Inc.	269
Citibank Canada	191	Honda Canada Inc.	274
CKF Inc.	192	Honeywell Ltd.	275
Cobourg District General Hospital	194	Hubbell Canada Inc.	278
Cognos Incorporated	196	Husky Energy Inc.	281
COM DEV International	197	Hydro Electric Commission of Thunder Bay	281
Communications & Power Industries Canada	198	Hydro Mississauga Corporation	282
Compaq Canada Inc.	199	Hydro One Inc.	282
Computalog Ltd.	200	Hydro Québec	283
Computer Associates Canada Ltd.	201	IBM Canada Ltd.	284
Comstock Canada	201	IDEA Associates Inc.	285
Conair Aviation Ltd.	202	Ilco Unican Inc.	286
Connors Bros, Limited	203	Imperial Oil Limited	286
Cornwall Electric	206	INCO Limited	287
Cosyn Technology	207	Industries Lassonde Inc.	289
Cougar Helicopters Inc.	208	IPL Energy Inc.	294
Crestar Energy Inc.	209	Island Telecom Inc.	295
Culinar Inc.	209	J.D. Irving Limited	298
DaimlerChrysler Canada Ltd.	211	JDS Uniphase Corporation	300
Delphi Solutions Inc.	215	John P. Robarts Research Institute	302
Delta Hotels	215	Johnson Controls Ltd.	302
Derlan Industries Limited	216	Jostens Canada Ltd.	303
Develcon Electronics Ltd.	217	Kelowna, City of	305
Dofasco Inc.	218	Keyano College	306
Domtar Inc.	218	Kimberly-Clark Inc.	307
DuPont Canada Inc.	221	Kraft Canada Inc.	310
Dynapro Systems Inc.	223	Kvaerner Metals	311
Dynasty Furniture Manufacturing Ltd.	224	Lambert Somec Inc.	313
Dynatek Automation Systems Inc.	224	Leduc, City of	313
Earth Tech Canada Inc.	225	Lenbrook Industries Limited	315
EDS of Canada Ltd.	228	Lifetouch Canada Inc.	319
Elco	229	Litton Systems Canada Ltd.	320
EnerFlex Systems Ltd.	232	Lovat Inc.	323
Entreprises Premier Canadien Ltée	232	MAAX Inc.	324
Epson Canada Limited	233	MacDonald Dettwiler and Associates Ltd.	325
Exfo	235	MacViro Consultants Inc.	326
Exide Canada Inc.	235	Magna International Inc.	327
FAG Bearings Limited	237	Manitoba Hydro	328
Federated Co-operatives Limited	239	Manitoba Telecom Services Inc.	329
Finning	240	Marshall Macklin Monaghan Ltd.	333
Flakeboard Company Limited	242	Marystown Shipyard Limited	334
Fletcher's Fine Foods	242	Matrox Electronic Systems Ltd.	335
Flint Energy Services Ltd.	243	MDS Nordion	339
FM Global	243	Memotec Communications Inc.	341
Foyer Valade Inc.	245	Midwest Food Products Inc.	346

The Canada Student Employment Guide

University Index 675

Minas Basin Pulp and Power Company Ltd.	347	Sandwell Inc.	443
Mississauga, City of	349	Saskatchewan Research Council, The	446
Mitel Corporation	350	Saskatoon, City of	448
Mitsubishi Electric Sales Canada	351	Saskferco Products Inc.	448
Mobile Computing Corporation	351	SaskTel	449
Monarch Communications Inc.	353	SC Infrastructure Inc.	449
Moosehead Breweries Limited	354	Schlumberger Canada Ltd.	450
Morrison Hershfield Limited	354	Schneider Electric Canada Inc.	451
MOSAID Technologies Inc.	355	SCIEX MDS Health Group	452
Motorola Canada Ltd.	356	SCL Technologies Inc.	453
National Grocers Co. Ltd.	360	SED Systems	453
Neles Automation, Scada Solutions Ltd.	362	Seprotech Systems Incorporated	454
Netron Inc.	365	Shaw Communications	455
New Brunswick Power Corporation	365	Shaw Industries Ltd.	455
New Brunswick Telephone Company	366	Shermag Inc.	457
New Holland Canada Ltd.	366	Siemens Electric Ltd.	460
Newfoundland and Labrador Hydro	367	Silicon Graphics Canada Inc.	461
Newness Machine Ltd.	368	Skiing Louise Ltd.	461
NewTel Communications	369	SNC-Lavalin	463
NLK Consultants Inc.	372	SolutionInc Limited	465
Norbord Industries	372	Sony Music Canada	465
Norcen Energy Resources Ltd.	373	Spar Aerospace Limited	467
Northwestel Inc.	376	Spectra Premium Industries	468
Nova Scotia Power Corp.	377	Spectrum Signal Processing Inc.	468
Oetiker Limited	381	Sportsco International	469
Oland Breweries Limited	382	Sprint Canada	470
Omstead Foods Limited	383	St. Lawrence Seaway Mgmt. Corp., The	473
Ontario Legislative Offices	384	Stantec Consulting Ltd.	475
Paramount Canada's Wonderland Inc.	389	Star Data Systems Inc.	476
Pelmorex Inc.	395	State Farm Insurance Companies	476
Petromont & Co. Ltd. Partnership	397	Steelpipe Ltd.	477
Phillips & Tempro Industries Ltd.	398	Stone Consolidated Inc.	479
Pine Falls Paper Company Limited	400	Sunoco Inc.	482
Placer Dome Inc.	402	Supreme Tooling Group	483
Positron Industries Inc.	404	Surrey, City of	484
Potacan Mining Company	405	Sydney Steel Corporation	485
Power Measurement Ltd.	406	Symantec Corporation	486
Powertech Labs Inc.	406	Syncrude Canada Ltd.	486
Pricewaterhouse Coopers	409	Teklogix Inc.	489
Prince George, City of	410	Telebec Ltée	490
Proctor and Redfern Ltd.	411	Telesat Canada	491
Public Utilities of Kingston	413	The Garland Group	494
QIT-Fer et Titane Inc.	414	Thomas & Betts Ltée	495
Québec Cartier Mining Company	415	Thomson - CSF Systems Canada Inc.	497
Raymond Industrial Equipment Ltd.	418	Toronto District School Board	503
Raymond Rebar Inc.	418	Toronto Hydro	505
Raytheon Systems Canada Ltd.	419	Toshiba of Canada Ltd.	508
Reid Crowther	426	TransAlta	509
Replicon Inc.	428	Triumf	510
Rockwell Automation	435	Trojan Technologies Inc.	511
Roctest Ltée	435	Trow Consulting Engineers Ltd.	511
Rogers AT&T Wireless Inc.	436	Union Gas Ltd.	513
Royal Philips Electronics	439	University College of Cape Breton	516
Ryerson Polytechnic University	441	US Filter BCP	517

The Canada Student Employment Guide

676   University Index

Vancouver Sun	520		FM Global	243
Visteon Canada Inc.	522		Foyer Valade Inc.	245
West Kootenay Power Ltd.	528		General Chemical Canada Ltd.	249
Westcoast Energy Inc.	530		Giffels Associates Limited	251
Westinghouse Canada Inc.	532		Golder Associates Ltd.	255
Westport Innovations Inc.	534		H.H. Angus & Associates Ltd.	261
Westshore Terminals Ltd.	534		Haley Industries Limited	262
Weyerhaeuser Company Limited	535		Halifax Water Commission	264
Wilson Auto Electric Ltd.	538		Husky Energy Inc.	281
Windsor, City of	538		Hydro One Inc.	282
Wire Rope Industries Ltd.	540		Hydro Québec	283
Workfire Development Corp.	540		Imperial Oil Limited	286
Zenastra	547		Industries Lassonde Inc.	289
Zenon Environmental Inc.	547		Ivaco Inc.	296
			Jacques Whitford Consulting Engineers	299
			Kelowna, City of	305
Environmental Studies			Kitchener, City of	309
			Leduc, City of	313
A.G. Simpson Co. Ltd.	75		MacViro Consultants Inc.	326
ACE INI Insurance	79		Magna International Inc.	327
ADI Group Inc.	82		Manitoba Agriculture and Food	327
Air Canada	85		Manitoba Hydro	328
Alberta Energy Company Ltd.	89		Marshall Macklin Monaghan Ltd.	333
Apex Land Corp.	103		Mississauga, City of	349
Aquatic Sciences Inc.	105		Norbord Industries	372
ArvinMeritor	108		Norcen Energy Resources Ltd.	373
ATCO Frontec Corp.	111		Nova Scotia Power Corp.	377
BASF Canada Inc.	122		Oland Breweries Limited	382
BC Research Inc.	126		Pembina Pipeline Corporation	395
Bell Mobility	131		Pine Falls Paper Company Limited	400
BOVAR Waste Management	145		Placer Dome Inc.	402
Bowater Mersey Paper Company Limited	146		Prince George, City of	410
Budd Canada Inc.	152		Proctor and Redfern Ltd.	411
C B C L Limited	154		Reid Crowther	426
Calgary, City of	158		Rhone-Poulenc Canada Inc.	430
Cameco Corporation	160		Saskatoon, City of	448
Canadian General Tower Limited	166		Saskferco Products Inc.	448
CCL Industries Inc.	178		SC Infrastructure Inc.	449
Centra Gas British Columbia Inc.	180		Science North	452
CH2M Gore and Storrie Limited	185		SNC-Lavalin	463
CKF Inc.	192		St. Lawrence Parks Commission	472
Coquitlam, City of	204		Stantec Consulting Ltd.	475
Corner Brook, City of	205		Sunoco Inc.	482
DaimlerChrysler Canada Ltd.	211		Surrey, City of	484
Dofasco Inc.	218		Sydney Steel Corporation	485
Domtar Inc.	218		Timmins, City of	499
Earth Tech Canada Inc.	225		Toronto and Region Conservation Authority	501
Echo Bay Mines Ltd.	226		Toronto Hydro	505
Emco Limited	230		Toronto, City of	508
Entreprises Premier Canadien Ltée	232		TransAlta	509
Extendicare (Canada) Inc.	237		Trow Consulting Engineers Ltd.	511
Federated Co-operatives Limited	239		University College of Cape Breton	516
Fisher Scientific Limited	241		Urban Systems Ltd.	516
Flakeboard Company Limited	242		Westcoast Energy Inc.	530

The Canada Student Employment Guide

University Index

Weyerhaeuser Company Limited	535
Windsor, City of	538
Zenon Environmental Inc.	547

General

A.G. Simpson Co. Ltd.	75
ACE INI Insurance	79
Acklands-Grainger Inc.	80
Akita Drilling Ltd.	87
Alberta Energy & Utilities Board	89
Alberta Energy Company Ltd.	89
Alberta Gaming & Liquor Commission	90
Amcan Castings Limited	98
Andersen Consulting	101
Apex Land Corp.	103
ArvinMeritor	108
Banff Centre for Continuing Education, The	120
BASF Canada Inc.	122
Basic Technologies Corporation	122
Baytex Energy Limited	124
BC Telecom Inc.	126
Behlen Industries	130
Bell Mobility	131
BFGoodrich Landing Gear Division	135
Brantcorp Inc.	147
British Columbia Ferry Corporation	149
Brookfield Properties Corporation	150
Cabre Exploration Ltd.	156
Calgary Co-operative Association Limited	157
Cambior Inc.	158
Canadian Occidental Petroleum Ltd.	168
Canbra Foods Ltd.	170
Cangene Corporation	172
Cegelec Enterprises Ltée	179
Centra Gas Manitoba Inc.	181
CH2M Gore and Storrie Limited	185
Charlottetown Driving Park	187
COBI Foods Inc.	194
Connors Bros, Limited	203
Coquitlam, City of	204
Corner Brook, City of	205
Credit Union Central of Canada	208
Culinar Inc.	209
DaimlerChrysler Canada Ltd.	211
Earth Tech Canada Inc.	225
Eli Lilly Canada Inc.	230
EMJ Data Systems Ltd.	231
Exfo	235
Extendicare (Canada) Inc.	237
Federated Co-operatives Limited	239
Flint Energy Services Ltd.	243
FM Global	243

Foremost Industries Inc.	244
Gencorp Vehicle Sealing	248
Gienow Building Products Ltd.	251
Gilbey Canada Inc.	252
Glaxo Wellcome Canada	253
Goepel McDermid Securities	254
Goodyear Canada Inc.	256
Groupe Savoie Inc.	260
Halifax Regional Municipality	263
Holiday Inn Select Toronto Airport	272
Home Oil Co. Ltd.	273
Honda Canada Inc.	274
HSBC Bank Canada	277
Intercon Security Ltd.	292
Jim Pattison Group	301
Kraft Canada Inc.	310
Laidlaw Inc.	312
Lambert Somec Inc.	313
Leduc, City of	313
Lenbrook Industries Limited	315
Liberty Health	318
MAAX Inc.	324
MacDonald Steel Ltd.	325
Marcam Canada	330
Mark Anthony Group Inc.	332
McKay-Cocker Construction Limited	338
Metro Richelieu Inc.	342
Metropolitan Life Insurance Company	344
Midwest Food Products Inc.	346
Mobile Computing Corporation	351
National Manufacturing of Canada Inc.	361
Neles Automation, Scada Solutions Ltd.	362
New Brunswick Power Corporation	365
News Marketing Canada	368
Nichirin Inc.	370
Norcen Energy Resources Ltd.	373
Northwestel Inc.	376
Numac Energy Inc.	379
Oetiker Limited	381
Paramount Canada's Wonderland Inc.	389
Peel Board of Education	393
Phillips & Tempro Industries Ltd.	398
Potacan Mining Company	405
PPG Canada Inc.	407
Pricewaterhouse Coopers	409
Proctor and Redfern Ltd.	411
Progressive Financial Strategy	411
Providence Centre	412
Public Utilities of Kingston	413
QEII Health Sciences Centre	414
Quebecor Inc.	415
Raylo Chemicals Inc.	417
Regal Constellation Hotel Ltd.	422
Rimrock Resort Hotel	432

The Canada Student Employment Guide

678   University Index

Royal & Sun Alliance Insurance Co. of Cda	437
Sandman Hotels and Inns	443
Saskatchewan Economic Development	445
SCIEX MDS Health Group	452
Shaw Communications	455
Signature Vacations Inc.	460
Sony Music Canada	465
Sportsco International	469
Stantec Consulting Ltd.	475
State Farm Insurance Companies	476
Sundog Printing Limited	482
Supreme Tooling Group	483
Surrey, City of	484
Teklogix Inc.	489
The Garland Group	494
Thomas J. Lipton	496
Thompson's Moving and Storage	496
Toronto East General Hospital	503
Toronto Hydro	505
Toshiba of Canada Ltd.	508
Trow Consulting Engineers Ltd.	511
Union Gas Ltd.	513
University College of Cape Breton	516
US Filter BCP	517
Vancouver Sun	520
Western Glove Works	530
Weston Produce Inc.	533
Weyerhaeuser Company Limited	535
Windsor, City of	538
Wire Rope Industries Ltd.	540
xwave solutions	542
Yellowknife, City of	544

Geotechnical

ADI Group Inc.	82
Alberta Energy Company Ltd.	89
Apex Land Corp.	103
Cabre Exploration Ltd.	156
Cape Breton Development Corporation	174
Centra Gas British Columbia Inc.	180
CH2M Gore and Storrie Limited	185
Coquitlam, City of	204
Crestar Energy Inc.	209
Echo Bay Mines Ltd.	226
Fisher Scientific Limited	241
Giffels Associates Limited	251
Golder Associates Ltd.	255
Haliburton Energy Services	262
Halliburton Energy Services	264
Home Oil Co. Ltd.	273
Husky Energy Inc.	281
Hydro Québec	283

Jacques Whitford Consulting Engineers	299
Kinross Gold Corp.	308
Leica Geosystems Canada Inc.	314
Manitoba Hydro	328
Ministry of Northern Develop. and Mines	348
Norcen Energy Resources Ltd.	373
Numac Energy Inc.	379
Pembina Pipeline Corporation	395
Placer Dome Inc.	402
Rio Algom Limited	433
Roctest Ltée	435
SNC-Lavalin	463
Stantec Consulting Ltd.	475
Surrey, City of	484
Syncrude Canada Ltd.	486
Toronto and Region Conservation Authority	501
Trow Consulting Engineers Ltd.	511
Westcoast Energy Inc.	530
Weyerhaeuser Company Limited	535
Windsor, City of	538

Industrial

A C A Cooperative Limited	74
A.G. Simpson Co. Ltd.	75
ABC Group	76
Acklands-Grainger Inc.	80
Air Liquide Canada Inc.	85
Air Nova Inc.	86
Alcan Aluminium Limited	91
Aliant Telecom Inc.	93
Alumicor Limited	97
Ancast Industries Ltd.	100
Andersen Consulting	101
Apotex Fermentation Inc.	104
Armor Personnel	107
ArvinMeritor	108
Atlantic Packaging Products Ltd.	114
ATS Automation Tooling Systems Inc.	116
Babcock and Wilcox Canada	119
Ballard Power Systems Inc.	120
BCG Services	127
Bettis Canada Ltd.	135
BFGoodrich Landing Gear Division	135
Blue Giant Equipment of Canada Ltd.	141
Blue Wave Seafoods Inc.	142
Bosal Canada Inc.	145
BOVAR Waste Management	145
Buckeye Canada Inc.	151
C MAC Industries Inc.	155
CAE Newness	157
Camp Hill Hospital	160
Canada Brick Limited	161

The Canada Student Employment Guide

University Index 679

Canada Post Corporation	162	Kodak Canada Inc.	309
Canadian Commercial Corp.	165	Krug Inc.	310
Canadian Thermos Products Inc.	168	La Confiserie Comete Ltee	311
Canadian Tire Corporation Ltd.	169	Lambert Somec Inc.	313
Carte International Inc.	176	Les Forges de Sorel Inc.	317
Centra Gas Manitoba Inc.	181	Les Modes Smart Inc.	318
CKF Inc.	192	Loewen Windows	321
Connors Bros, Limited	203	MacDonald Steel Ltd.	325
Coppley Apparel Group	204	Magna International Inc.	327
Coquitlam, City of	204	Maple Leaf Consumer Foods	330
Culinar Inc.	209	Marine Atlantic Inc.	331
Custom Trim Ltd.	210	McBee Systems of Canada Inc.	336
D.A. Stuart Inc.	210	Midwest Food Products Inc.	346
DaimlerChrysler Canada Ltd.	211	Minas Basin Pulp and Power Company Ltd.	347
DDM Plastics Inc.	213	Mobile Computing Corporation	351
Dofasco Inc.	218	Mustang Survival Corp.	358
Domtar Inc.	218	Natco Canada Ltd.	360
Duha Color Services	220	National Grocers Co. Ltd.	360
Dynapro Systems Inc.	223	National Manufacturing of Canada Inc.	361
Elco	229	Nestle Canada Inc.	364
Eli Lilly Canada Inc.	230	Netron Inc.	365
Emco Limited	230	New Brunswick Telephone Company	366
Entreprises Premier Canadien Ltée	232	New Holland Canada Ltd.	366
Exfo	235	Newness Machine Ltd.	368
Farmers Co-operative Dairy Limited	239	Nichirin Inc.	370
Federated Co-operatives Limited	239	Norcen Energy Resources Ltd.	373
FedEx Express	240	Nova Scotia Power Corp.	377
Fletcher's Fine Foods	242	Oetiker Limited	381
FM Global	243	Paperboard Industries International Inc.	389
Foremost Industries Inc.	244	Paramount Canada's Wonderland Inc.	389
Friesens Corporation	246	Petromont & Co. Ltd. Partnership	397
Gencorp Vehicle Sealing	248	Phillips & Tempro Industries Ltd.	398
General Chemical Canada Ltd.	249	Pratt & Whitney Canada Inc.	407
Gienow Building Products Ltd.	251	Premdor Inc.	408
Giffels Associates Limited	251	Pricewaterhouse Coopers	409
Gisborne Design Services Ltd.	253	Proctor and Redfern Ltd.	411
Groupe Savoie Inc.	260	Purolator Courier Ltd.	413
Health Care Corporation of St. John's	267	Reid Crowther	426
Hermes Electronics Inc.	269	Royal Canadian Mint	438
Honda Canada Inc.	274	Rubbermaid Canada Inc.	440
I M P Group International Inc.	283	Sandwell Inc.	443
I P L Plastics Ltd.	284	Saskatchewan Research Council, The	446
Ilco Unican Inc.	286	Saskferco Products Inc.	448
Imperial Oil Limited	286	Schlumberger Canada Ltd.	450
Indalex Limited	288	SCL Technologies Inc.	453
Industries Lassonde Inc.	289	Seprotech Systems Incorporated	454
Island Telecom Inc.	295	Siemens Electric Ltd.	460
Ivaco Inc.	296	Skiing Louise Ltd.	461
J.D. Irving Limited	298	SNC-Lavalin	463
JDS Uniphase Corporation	300	Sony Music Canada	465
Jim Pattison Group	301	Spectra Premium Industries	468
Kawneer Company Canada Limited	304	St. Lawrence Parks Commission	472
Kennametal Ltd.	305	Standard Knitting Limited	474
Keyano College	306	Standen's Limited	474

The Canada Student Employment Guide

University Index

Stantec Consulting Ltd.	475
State Farm Insurance Companies	476
Steelcraft Industries Ltd.	477
Steelpipe Ltd.	477
Sun Rype Products Ltd.	481
TCT Logistics	488
Teklogix Inc.	489
Thomas & Betts Ltée	495
Thompson's Moving and Storage	496
Today's Business Products Ltd.	500
Toronto Catholic District School Board	502
Toyota Canada Ltd.	509
Vancouver Sun	520
Visteon Canada Inc.	522
West Coast Apparel	528
Western Glove Works	530
Westport Innovations Inc.	534
Westshore Terminals Ltd.	534
Weyerhaeuser Company Limited	535
Wilson Auto Electric Ltd.	538
Windsor, City of	538
Winpak Ltd.	539
Wire Rope Industries Ltd.	540

Materials Science

A.G. Simpson Co. Ltd.	75
Algoma Steel Inc.	93
Babcock and Wilcox Canada	119
Ballard Power Systems Inc.	120
BASF Canada Inc.	122
Bettis Canada Ltd.	135
BFGoodrich Landing Gear Division	135
Biovail Corporation International	137
Budd Canada Inc.	152
Canada Brick Limited	161
Canadian Tire Corporation Ltd.	169
COM DEV International	197
Dofasco Inc.	218
Giffels Associates Limited	251
Honeywell Ltd.	275
I M P Group International Inc.	283
Jacques Whitford Consulting Engineers	299
Litton Systems Canada Ltd.	320
MDS Nordion	339
MOSAID Technologies Inc.	355
Neles Automation, Scada Solutions Ltd.	362
New Holland Canada Ltd.	366
Rasco Specialty Metals Inc.	417
Siemens Electric Ltd.	460
Standard Knitting Limited	474
Standen's Limited	474
Thompson's Moving and Storage	496

Westport Innovations Inc.	534
Wire Rope Industries Ltd.	540
Zeidler Roberts Partnership Architects	546

Mechanical

A E McKenzie Co. Inc.	75
A.G. Simpson Co. Ltd.	75
ABC Group	76
Abitibi-Consolidated Inc.	77
Accucaps Industries Limited	79
ADI Group Inc.	82
Aimtronics	84
Air Liquide Canada Inc.	85
Akita Drilling Ltd.	87
Alberta Energy & Utilities Board	89
Alberta Energy Company Ltd.	89
Alcan Aluminium Limited	91
Algoma Steel Inc.	93
Alpine Oil Service Corporation	96
Amcan Castings Limited	98
Amcor Twinpak North America Inc.	98
Ancast Industries Ltd.	100
Andersen Consulting	101
Apotex Fermentation Inc.	104
Aquatic Sciences Inc.	105
Armor Personnel	107
Armtec Limited	108
ArvinMeritor	108
ATCO Electric	111
ATCO Frontec Corp.	111
ATCO Gas Services Ltd.	112
Atlantic Packaging Products Ltd.	114
Atlas Ideal Metals Inc.	115
ATS Automation Tooling Systems Inc.	116
Aventis Pasteur Limited	117
Babcock and Wilcox Canada	119
Ballard Power Systems Inc.	120
Banff Centre for Continuing Education, The	120
BASF Canada Inc.	122
Basic Technologies Corporation	122
BC Hydro	125
BC Research Inc.	126
Bechtel Canada Co.	128
Bettis Canada Ltd.	135
BFGoodrich Landing Gear Division	135
Bic Inc.	136
Biovail Corporation International	137
BJ Services Company	138
Black Photo Corporation	139
Bloorview MacMillan Centre, The	140
Blue Giant Equipment of Canada Ltd.	141
Blue Wave Seafoods Inc.	142

The Canada Student Employment Guide

University Index 681

Bosal Canada Inc.	145	Dynapro Systems Inc.	223
BOVAR Waste Management	145	Dynasty Furniture Manufacturing Ltd.	224
Bowater Mersey Paper Company Limited	146	Earth Tech Canada Inc.	225
Brantcorp Inc.	147	Echo Bay Mines Ltd.	226
British Columbia Ferry Corporation	149	EDS of Canada Ltd.	228
Brookfield Properties Corporation	150	Elco	229
Buckeye Canada Inc.	151	EnerFlex Systems Ltd.	232
Budd Canada Inc.	152	Entreprises Premier Canadien Ltée	232
C B C L Limited	154	Exfo	235
C MAC Industries Inc.	155	Exide Canada Inc.	235
CAE Newness	157	FAG Bearings Limited	237
Cambior Inc.	158	Federated Co-operatives Limited	239
Cameco Corporation	160	Finning	240
Camp Hill Hospital	160	Fishery Products International	241
Canada Post Corporation	162	Flakeboard Company Limited	242
Canada Starch Company Inc.	163	Fletcher's Fine Foods	242
Canadian General Tower Limited	166	Flint Energy Services Ltd.	243
Canadian Museum of Civilization Corp.	167	Foster Wheeler Limited	245
Canadian Occidental Petroleum Ltd.	168	Gencorp Vehicle Sealing	248
Canadian Thermos Products Inc.	168	General Chemical Canada Ltd.	249
Canbra Foods Ltd.	170	General Electric Canada Inc.	249
CancerCare Manitoba	171	Gienow Building Products Ltd.	251
Cancore Industries Inc.	171	Giffels Associates Limited	251
Cangene Corporation	172	Gisborne Design Services Ltd.	253
Cape Breton Development Corporation	174	Glaxo Wellcome Canada	253
Carbone of America (LCL) Ltd.	175	Groupe Savoie Inc.	260
Carte International Inc.	176	H A Simmons Ltd.	261
Cegelec Enterprises Ltée	179	H.H. Angus & Associates Ltd.	261
Centra Gas British Columbia Inc.	180	Haley Industries Limited	262
Centra Gas Manitoba Inc.	181	Haliburton Energy Services	262
CH2M Gore and Storrie Limited	185	Halliburton Energy Services	264
CKF Inc.	192	Hallmark Tools	265
Cognis Canada Corporation	195	Health Sciences Centre	268
COM DEV International	197	Hermes Electronics Inc.	269
Communications & Power Industries Canada	198	Home Oil Co. Ltd.	273
Computalog Ltd.	200	Honda Canada Inc.	274
Comstock Canada	201	Honeywell Ltd.	275
Conair Aviation Ltd.	202	Hubbell Canada Inc.	278
Connors Bros, Limited	203	Hydro One Inc.	282
Coquitlam, City of	204	Hydro Québec	283
Cosyn Technology	207	I P L Plastics Ltd.	284
Crestar Energy Inc.	209	IBM Canada Ltd.	284
Culinar Inc.	209	Ilco Unican Inc.	286
Custom Trim Ltd.	210	Imperial Oil Limited	286
D.A. Stuart Inc.	210	INCO Limited	287
Dana Corporation - Long Manufacturing	212	Indalex Limited	288
DDM Plastics Inc.	213	Industries Lassonde Inc.	289
Delta Hotels	215	Intertape Polymer Group Inc.	294
Derlan Industries Limited	216	IPL Energy Inc.	294
Dofasco Inc.	218	J.D. Irving Limited	298
Domtar Inc.	218	JDS Uniphase Corporation	300
Duha Color Services	220	Jim Pattison Group	301
DuPont Canada Inc.	221	Johnson Controls Ltd.	302
Dura Automotive Systems (Canada) Ltd.	222	Jostens Canada Ltd.	303

The Canada Student Employment Guide

University Index

Kawneer Company Canada Limited	304	Petromont & Co. Ltd. Partnership	397
Kennametal Ltd.	305	Phillips & Tempro Industries Ltd.	398
Kimberly-Clark Inc.	307	Pine Falls Paper Company Limited	400
Kitchener, City of	309	Poco Petroleums Ltd.	402
Kodak Canada Inc.	309	Positron Industries Inc.	404
Kraft Canada Inc.	310	Potacan Mining Company	405
Kvaerner Metals	311	Power Measurement Ltd.	406
Lambert Somec Inc.	313	Powertech Labs Inc.	406
Leduc, City of	313	PPG Canada Inc.	407
Les Forges de Sorel Inc.	317	Pratt & Whitney Canada Inc.	407
Litton Systems Canada Ltd.	320	Premdor Inc.	408
Loewen Windows	321	Pricewaterhouse Coopers	409
Lovat Inc.	323	Prince George, City of	410
M M Industra Ltd.	323	Proctor and Redfern Ltd.	411
MAAX Inc.	324	Public Utilities of Kingston	413
MacDonald Steel Ltd.	325	QIT-Fer et Titane Inc.	414
Magna International Inc.	327	Quebecor Inc.	415
Manitoba Hydro	328	Quesnel River Pulp Company	416
Marshall Macklin Monaghan Ltd.	333	Raylo Chemicals Inc.	417
Marystown Shipyard Limited	334	Raymond Industrial Equipment Ltd.	418
McBee Systems of Canada Inc.	336	Raytheon Systems Canada Ltd.	419
MDS Nordion	339	Recochem Inc.	420
Midwest Food Products Inc.	346	Reid Crowther	426
Minas Basin Pulp and Power Company Ltd.	347	Rich Products of Canada Limited	431
Mississauga, City of	349	Rimrock Resort Hotel	432
Mobile Computing Corporation	351	Rockwell Automation	435
Moosehead Breweries Limited	354	Roctest Ltée	435
Morrison Hershfield Limited	354	Royal Canadian Mint	438
Mustang Survival Corp.	358	Rubbermaid Canada Inc.	440
N B S Card Services	359	Sandwell Inc.	443
National Grocers Co. Ltd.	360	Saskatchewan Research Council, The	446
National Manufacturing of Canada Inc.	361	Saskatoon, City of	448
Nestle Canada Inc.	364	Saskferco Products Inc.	448
Netron Inc.	365	SC Infrastructure Inc.	449
New Brunswick Power Corporation	365	Schneider Electric Canada Inc.	451
New Holland Canada Ltd.	366	SCIEX MDS Health Group	452
Newfoundland and Labrador Hydro	367	Seprotech Systems Incorporated	454
Newness Machine Ltd.	368	Shaw Industries Ltd.	455
Nichirin Inc.	370	Siemens Electric Ltd.	460
NLK Consultants Inc.	372	SNC-Lavalin	463
Norbord Industries	372	Sony Music Canada	465
Norcen Energy Resources Ltd.	373	Southern Railway of British Columbia Ltd.	466
Northwestel Inc.	376	Spar Aerospace Limited	467
Nova Scotia Power Corp.	377	Spectra Premium Industries	468
Novartis Consumer Health Canada Inc.	378	Spectrum Signal Processing Inc.	468
Numac Energy Inc.	379	St. Lawrence Parks Commission	472
Oetiker Limited	381	St. Lawrence Seaway Mgmt. Corp., The	473
Paperboard Industries International Inc.	389	Standard Knitting Limited	474
Paramount Canada's Wonderland Inc.	389	Standen's Limited	474
PCL Constructors Inc.	392	Stantec Consulting Ltd.	475
Peacock Inc.	392	State Farm Insurance Companies	476
Pembina Pipeline Corporation	395	Steelcraft Industries Ltd.	477
Peter Kiewit Sons Co.	396	Steelpipe Ltd.	477
Petro-Canada	397	Sun Rype Products Ltd.	481

The Canada Student Employment Guide

University Index

Sundog Printing Limited	482	Echo Bay Mines Ltd.	226
Sunoco Inc.	482	Finning	240
Supreme Tooling Group	483	General Chemical Canada Ltd.	249
Surrey, City of	484	Golder Associates Ltd.	255
Sydney Steel Corporation	485	H A Simmons Ltd.	261
Syncrude Canada Ltd.	486	INCO Limited	287
Talisman Energy Inc.	487	J.S. Redpath Limited	299
Teklogix Inc.	489	Kinross Gold Corp.	308
Thomas & Betts Ltée	495	Kvaerner Metals	311
Thomas J. Lipton	496	Ministry of Northern Develop. and Mines	348
Thompson's Moving and Storage	496	Peter Kiewit Sons Co.	396
Thomson - CSF Systems Canada Inc.	497	Placer Dome Inc.	402
Toronto Catholic District School Board	502	Potacan Mining Company	405
Toronto District School Board	503	Pricewaterhouse Coopers	409
Toronto East General Hospital	503	QIT-Fer et Titane Inc.	414
Toronto General Hospital	505	Québec Cartier Mining Company	415
Toronto Sun Publishing Corp., The	507	Rio Algom Limited	433
TransAlta	509	Sandwell Inc.	443
Triumf	510	Siemens Electric Ltd.	460
Trojan Technologies Inc.	511	Syncrude Canada Ltd.	486
Trow Consulting Engineers Ltd.	511	Teck Corp.	489
Union Gas Ltd.	513	TransAlta	509
Unisys Canada Inc.	514	Trow Consulting Engineers Ltd.	511
USF WaterGroup	517	Westshore Terminals Ltd.	534
Vancouver Sun	520		
Visteon Canada Inc.	522		
Waterloo Furniture Components Ltd.	524	**Transportation**	
Wegu Canada Inc.	526		
Weldco-Beales Manufacturing Inc.	527	ADI Group Inc.	82
West Kootenay Power Ltd.	528	Air Liquide Canada Inc.	85
Westcoast Energy Inc.	530	Air Nova Inc.	86
Western Glove Works	530	Atlas Van Lines (Canada) Ltd.	115
Westinghouse Canada Inc.	532	BFGoodrich Landing Gear Division	135
Westport Innovations Inc.	534	C B C L Limited	154
Westshore Terminals Ltd.	534	Calgary, City of	158
Weyerhaeuser Company Limited	535	Canpar Transport Ltd.	173
Wilson Auto Electric Ltd.	538	Centra Gas British Columbia Inc.	180
Windsor, City of	538	Coquitlam, City of	204
Winpak Ltd.	539	Corner Brook, City of	205
Wire Rope Industries Ltd.	540	Earth Tech Canada Inc.	225
Zenastra	547	Giffels Associates Limited	251
Zenon Environmental Inc.	547	Halifax Regional Municipality	263
		Honda Canada Inc.	274
		I M P Group International Inc.	283
Mining		Kelowna, City of	305
		Marine Atlantic Inc.	331
Alberta Energy & Utilities Board	89	Marshall Macklin Monaghan Ltd.	333
Aurizon Mines Ltd.	116	Mississauga, City of	349
Bechtel Canada Co.	128	Mobile Computing Corporation	351
Cambior Inc.	158	Moosehead Breweries Limited	354
Cameco Corporation	160	Morrison Hershfield Limited	354
Cape Breton Development Corporation	174	Pricewaterhouse Coopers	409
Cosyn Technology	207	Proctor and Redfern Ltd.	411
D.A. Stuart Inc.	210	Public Utilities of Kingston	413

The Canada Student Employment Guide

684 University Index

Purolator Courier Ltd.	413
Renaissance Energy Ltd.	427
Rentway Inc.	427
Richmond, City of	431
Sandman Hotels and Inns	443
Sandwell Inc.	443
Saskatoon, City of	448
SC Infrastructure Inc.	449
Siemens Electric Ltd.	460
Southern Railway of British Columbia Ltd.	466
Stantec Consulting Ltd.	475
Surrey, City of	484
TCT Logistics	488
The McElhanney Group Ltd.	494
Thompson's Moving and Storage	496
Today's Business Products Ltd.	500
Trow Consulting Engineers Ltd.	511
Urban Systems Ltd.	516
Weyerhaeuser Company Limited	535
Windsor, City of	538
Yanke Group of Companies	543

Water Resources

ADI Group Inc.	82
Aquatic Sciences Inc.	105
Brandon, City of	146
Calgary, City of	158
Cameco Corporation	160
CH2M Gore and Storrie Limited	185
Coquitlam, City of	204
Corner Brook, City of	205
Domtar Inc.	218
Earth Tech Canada Inc.	225
Echo Bay Mines Ltd.	226
Giffels Associates Limited	251
Golder Associates Ltd.	255
Halifax Regional Municipality	263
Halifax Water Commission	264
Jacques Whitford Consulting Engineers	299
Kelowna, City of	305
MacViro Consultants Inc.	326
Manitoba Hydro	328
Marshall Macklin Monaghan Ltd.	333
Midwest Food Products Inc.	346
Mississauga, City of	349
Paramount Canada's Wonderland Inc.	389
Prince Albert, City of	410
Prince George, City of	410
Proctor and Redfern Ltd.	411
Public Utilities of Kingston	413
QIT-Fer et Titane Inc.	414
Reid Crowther	426

Sandwell Inc.	443
Saskatoon, City of	448
Seprotech Systems Incorporated	454
Stantec Consulting Ltd.	475
Steelpipe Ltd.	477
Surrey, City of	484
Toronto and Region Conservation Authority	501
Trojan Technologies Inc.	511
Urban Systems Ltd.	516
Windsor, City of	538
Zenon Environmental Inc.	547

Bachelor of Architecture

ADI Group Inc.	82
Coquitlam, City of	204
Cosyn Technology	207
Giffels Associates Limited	251
Kelowna, City of	305
LM Architectural Group	321
Morrison Hershfield Limited	354
Peel Board of Education	393
Pizza Pizza Ltd.	401
Revy Home Centres Inc.	429
Sandman Hotels and Inns	443
Saskatoon, City of	448
Stantec Consulting Ltd.	475
Surrey, City of	484
Toronto District School Board	503
Toronto, City of	508
Zeidler Roberts Partnership Architects	546

Bachelor of Landscape Architecture

Arbor Memorial Services Inc.	106
Banff Centre for Continuing Education, The	120
BCG Services	127
Coquitlam, City of	204
Corner Brook, City of	205
Kitchener, City of	309
Marshall Macklin Monaghan Ltd.	333
Paramount Canada's Wonderland Inc.	389
Prince George, City of	410
Ryerson Polytechnic University	441
Sandman Hotels and Inns	443
Skiing Louise Ltd.	461
St. Lawrence Parks Commission	472
Stantec Consulting Ltd.	475
Surrey, City of	484
Toronto, City of	508
Urban Systems Ltd.	516

Bachelor of Education

Adult Education

1-800-GOT-JUNK?	74
A.G. Simpson Co. Ltd.	75
Addictions Foundation of Manitoba, The	81
Alberta Blue Cross	88
Anthony Insurance Inc.	102
Armor Personnel	107
Assiniboine Community College	109
Atlantic Blue Cross Care	113
Banff Centre for Continuing Education, The	120
Bic Inc.	136
Boréal Assurances Inc.	144
Calgary Co-operative Association Limited	157
Camp Hill Hospital	160
Canada Games Aquatic Centre	162
Canada Safeway Limited	163
Canadian National Institute For The Blind	167
Central Park Lodges Ltd.	181
COM DEV International	197
Co-op Atlantic	203
Credit Union Central of Canada	208
Dylex Limited	222
Federated Co-operatives Limited	239
Goodwill Industries of Toronto	256
Grant MacEwen Community College	258
Halifax County Regional Rehabilitation Centre	263
Holland College	273
Homewood Corp.	274
Humber River Regional Hospital	280
Insurance Corp. of B.C.	291
IWK Grace Health Centre	297
J.D. Irving Limited	298
Jostens Canada Ltd.	303
Kennedy Lodge Nursing Home Inc.	306
Keyano College	306
Liberty Health	318
Manitoba Agriculture and Food	327
Manitoba Hydro	328
Marine Atlantic Inc.	331
Metropolitan Life Insurance Company	344
Midwest Food Products Inc.	346
National Grocers Co. Ltd.	360
New Brunswick Power Corporation	365
Ontario Legislative Offices	384
Ontario March of Dimes	385
Oracle Corp. Canada Inc.	386
Ottawa Hospital	386
Peel Board of Education	393
Pitney Bowes of Canada Ltd.	401
Pizza Pizza Ltd.	401
Progressive Financial Strategy	411
Providence Centre	412
Purolator Courier Ltd.	413
Red Deer Co-op Limited	421
Regional Municipality of Niagara	424
Regional Residential Services Society	424
Rogers AT&T Wireless Inc.	436
Royal Bank of Canada	438
Saskatchewan Wheat Pool	447
Sherwood Credit Union	458
Signature Vacations Inc.	460
Surrey, City of	484
The Co-operators	493
Toronto District School Board	503
Toronto General Hospital	505
Toyota Canada Ltd.	509
Universal Rehabilitation Service Agency	515
Western Glove Works	530
Whitehill Technologies Inc.	537
Wilson Auto Electric Ltd.	538
Yanke Group of Companies	543

Childhood

1-800-GOT-JUNK?	74
Bluewater District School Board	142
Canada Games Aquatic Centre	162
Canadian Museum of Civilization Corp.	167
Canadian National Institute For The Blind	167
Chapters Inc.	186
Children's Hospital of Eastern Ontario	189
Grant MacEwen Community College	258
Horseshoe Resort Corporation	275
Huronia Regional Centre	280
IWK Grace Health Centre	297
Peel Board of Education	393
Peel Children's Centre	394
Pool People Ltd.	404
Regional Residential Services Society	424
Royal Victoria Hospital	440
Scholastic Canada Ltd.	451
Skills Training & Support Services Association	462
Sudbury Regional Hospital	480
Surrey, City of	484
Timmins, City of	499
Toronto District School Board	503
Toronto French School, The	504
Toronto Zoo	507
Universal Rehabilitation Service Agency	515
Whistler Blackcomb Mountain	535

686 University Index

General

1-800-GOT-JUNK?	74
Alberta Alcohol and Drug Abuse Commission	87
Alberta Energy & Utilities Board	89
Alberta Gaming & Liquor Commission	90
Anthony Insurance Inc.	102
Banff Centre for Continuing Education, The	120
Bluewater District School Board	142
Brookfield Properties Corporation	150
Cabre Exploration Ltd.	156
Cadith Entertainment Ltd.	156
Canadian Museum of Civilization Corp.	167
Canadian Western Bank	169
Charlottetown Driving Park	187
Coca Cola Foods Canada Inc.	195
Columbia House	197
Computer Associates Canada Ltd.	201
Deer Lodge Centre Inc.	213
Dun & Bradstreet Canada	221
Extendicare (Canada) Inc.	237
Federated Co-operatives Limited	239
Gencorp Vehicle Sealing	248
Gimbel Eye Centre	252
Goepel McDermid Securities	254
Great-West Life Assurance Company, The	259
Halifax County Regional Rehabilitation Centre	263
Health Care Corporation of St. John's	267
Holland College	273
Insurance Corp. of B.C.	291
Island Telecom Inc.	295
Lego Canada Inc.	314
Liberty Health	318
M. McGrawth Canada Limited	324
Maryvale Adolescent and Family Services	334
Metropolitan Life Insurance Company	344
Midwest Food Products Inc.	346
National Grocers Co. Ltd.	360
New Brunswick Power Corporation	365
Newfoundland and Labrador Credit Union	367
News Marketing Canada	368
Oland Breweries Limited	382
Paramount Canada's Wonderland Inc.	389
Patheon Inc.	390
Pearson Education Canada	393
Peel Board of Education	393
Pitney Bowes of Canada Ltd.	401
Pizza Pizza Ltd.	401
Providence Centre	412
Regional Residential Services Society	424
Royal & Sun Alliance Insurance Co. of Cda	437
Sandman Hotels and Inns	443
Saskatchewan Government Insurance	445
Signature Vacations Inc.	460

Sony Music Canada	465
State Farm Insurance Companies	476
Steelpipe Ltd.	477
Supreme Tooling Group	483
Thompson's Moving and Storage	496
Toronto Catholic District School Board	502
Toronto District School Board	503
Toronto French School, The	504
Toronto Police Service	506
Toronto Sun Publishing Corp., The	507
Toronto Zoo	507
Whistler Blackcomb Mountain	535
XCAN Grain Pool Ltd.	541

Physical

Canada Games Aquatic Centre	162
Grant MacEwen Community College	258
Halifax County Regional Rehabilitation Centre	263
Health Care Corporation of St. John's	267
Metro Toronto West Detention Centre	343
Metropolitan Life Insurance Company	344
Pool People Ltd.	404
Ryerson Polytechnic University	441
Skills Training & Support Services Association	462
Sudbury Regional Hospital	480
Surrey, City of	484
Toronto Cricket Skating & Curling	502
Toronto District School Board	503
Whistler Blackcomb Mountain	535

Special

Bluewater District School Board	142
Canadian National Institute For The Blind	167
Grant MacEwen Community College	258
Halifax County Regional Rehabilitation Centre	263
Les Centres Jeunesse de Montréal	316
Maryvale Adolescent and Family Services	334
Metropolitan Life Insurance Company	344
Peel Board of Education	393
Pool People Ltd.	404
Reena	421
Regional Residential Services Society	424
Skills Training & Support Services Association	462
St. Amant Centre Inc.	471
Steelpipe Ltd.	477
Surrey, City of	484
Toronto District School Board	503
Universal Rehabilitation Service Agency	515

University Index 687

Masters

Arts

1-800-GOT-JUNK?	74
Amcor Twinpak North America Inc.	98
Anthony Insurance Inc.	102
Assiniboine Community College	109
Banff Centre for Continuing Education, The	120
Bloorview Childrens Hospital	140
C.S.T. Consultants Inc.	155
Canadian Broadcasting Corporation	164
Canadian Western Bank	169
Computer Associates Canada Ltd.	201
Cotton Ginny Ltd.	207
EMJ Data Systems Ltd.	231
Environics Research Group Ltd.	233
Gallup Canada Inc.	247
Grant MacEwen Community College	258
Hill & Knowlton Canada Ltd.	270
HSBC Bank Canada	277
Hydro Electric Commission of Thunder Bay	281
Island Telecom Inc.	295
Keyano College	306
McBee Systems of Canada Inc.	336
McLaren-McCann Advertising of Canada Ltd.	338
Michaels of Canada Inc.	345
Mitsubishi Electric Sales Canada	351
Multi-Languages	357
Newfoundland and Labrador Credit Union	367
North American Life Assurance Company	373
Peel Board of Education	393
Pine Falls Paper Company Limited	400
PPG Canada Inc.	407
Reader's Digest Association of Canada Ltd.	419
Red Deer Co-op Limited	421
Rogers AT&T Wireless Inc.	436
Royal Bank of Canada	438
Saskatchewan Government Insurance	445
Signature Vacations Inc.	460
St. Joseph's Care Group	472
State Farm Insurance Companies	476
Symantec Corporation	486
TD Waterhouse Investor Services (Canada)	488
Toronto French School, The	504
Toronto Sun Publishing Corp., The	507
Urban Systems Ltd.	516
Vancouver Sun	520
YFactor	544

Business Administration

1-800-GOT-JUNK?	74
A E McKenzie Co. Inc.	75
A.G. Simpson Co. Ltd.	75
Aberdeen Hospital	77
Abitibi-Consolidated Inc.	77
Accucaps Industries Limited	79
ACE INI Insurance	79
Acklands-Grainger Inc.	80
Air Canada	85
Air Liquide Canada Inc.	85
Alberta Blue Cross	88
Alberta Energy & Utilities Board	89
Alberta Energy Company Ltd.	89
Alberta Gaming & Liquor Commission	90
Alcan Aluminium Limited	91
Alexandra Hospital	91
Aliant Telecom Inc.	93
Allianz Canada	95
Amcan Castings Limited	98
Amcor Twinpak North America Inc.	98
American Airlines Inc.	99
Andersen Consulting	101
Anthony Insurance Inc.	102
Apex Land Corp.	103
Apple Canada Inc.	104
ArvinMeritor	108
Assiniboine Community College	109
Assumption Mutual Life Insurance	109
AstraZeneca	110
ATCO Electric	111
ATCO Frontec Corp.	111
ATCO Gas Services Ltd.	112
Atlantic Blue Cross Care	113
Atlantic Lottery Corporation Inc.	113
Atlantic Wholesalers Ltd.	114
ATS Automation Tooling Systems Inc.	116
Aventis Pasteur Limited	117
Ballard Power Systems Inc.	120
Banff Centre for Continuing Education, The	120
Barton Place Long Term Care Facility	121
BASF Canada Inc.	122
Battlefords Health District	123
BC Hydro	125
BC Telecom Inc.	126
Bell Mobility	131
Belleville General Hospital	132
Bettis Canada Ltd.	135
BFGoodrich Landing Gear Division	135
Bic Inc.	136
Biovail Corporation International	137
Bloorview Childrens Hospital	140
Blue Mountain Resorts Limited	141

The Canada Student Employment Guide

University Index

BNP PARIBAS (Canada)	143	Culinar Inc.	209
Boréal Assurances Inc.	144	DaimlerChrysler Canada Ltd.	211
Bosal Canada Inc.	145	David Thompson Health Region	212
BOVAR Waste Management	145	Deer Lodge Centre Inc.	213
British Columbia Ferry Corporation	149	Degussa - Huls Canada Inc.	214
Brookfield Properties Corporation	150	Delphi Solutions Inc.	215
Buckeye Canada Inc.	151	Directwest Publishers Ltd.	217
C.S.T. Consultants Inc.	155	Dofasco Inc.	218
Cabre Exploration Ltd.	156	Domtar Inc.	218
Cadith Entertainment Ltd.	156	Drug Trading Company Ltd.	219
Calgary, City of	158	Duha Color Services	220
Cambior Inc.	158	Dun & Bradstreet Canada	221
Cambridge Memorial Hospital	159	Dylex Limited	222
Cameco Corporation	160	Dynapro Systems Inc.	223
Camp Hill Hospital	160	Economic Development Edmonton	226
Canada Post Corporation	162	Economical Insurance Group, The	227
Canada Starch Company Inc.	163	Eli Lilly Canada Inc.	230
Canadian Broadcasting Corporation	164	Emco Limited	230
Canadian Dairy Commission	165	EMJ Data Systems Ltd.	231
Canadian Depository for Securities Ltd.	166	EnerFlex Systems Ltd.	232
Canadian General Tower Limited	166	Environics Research Group Ltd.	233
Canadian Occidental Petroleum Ltd.	168	Exfo	235
Canadian Tire Corporation Ltd.	169	Export Development Corporation	236
Canadian Western Bank	169	Extendicare (Canada) Inc.	237
CancerCare Manitoba	171	Farm Credit Corp. Canada	238
Canon Canada Inc.	172	Farmers Co-operative Dairy Limited	239
Canpar Transport Ltd.	173	Federated Co-operatives Limited	239
Carbone of America (LCL) Ltd.	175	FedEx Express	240
Carte International Inc.	176	Finning	240
CCL Industries Inc.	178	Fisher Scientific Limited	241
Centra Gas British Columbia Inc.	180	Fishery Products International	241
Centra Gas Manitoba Inc.	181	Flint Energy Services Ltd.	243
Ceridian Canada	183	Foremost Industries Inc.	244
CFCF Inc.	183	Friesens Corporation	246
CGU Group Canada Ltd.	185	Future Shop Ltd.	246
Children's Hospital of Eastern Ontario	189	Gallup Canada Inc.	247
Cineplex Odeon Corporation	191	Gay Lea Foods Co-Operative Ltd.	247
Citibank Canada	191	Gendis Inc.	248
CKF Inc.	192	General Chemical Canada Ltd.	249
Cobourg District General Hospital	194	General Electric Canada Inc.	249
Coca Cola Foods Canada Inc.	195	General Mills Canada Inc.	250
Colgate-Palmolive Canada Inc.	196	Gienow Building Products Ltd.	251
Columbia House	197	Giffels Associates Limited	251
COM DEV International	197	Gilbey Canada Inc.	252
Compaq Canada Inc.	199	Gimbel Eye Centre	252
Compu-Quote Inc.	200	Glaxo Wellcome Canada	253
Computer Associates Canada Ltd.	201	Goodman and Carr	255
Connors Bros, Limited	203	Goodwill Industries of Toronto	256
Co-op Atlantic	203	Goodyear Canada Inc.	256
Coquitlam, City of	204	Gov't of Newfoundland - Dept. of Finance	257
Corner Brook, City of	205	Grand & Toy Ltd.	257
Cornwall Electric	206	Grant MacEwen Community College	258
Cosmair Canada Inc.	206	Grant Thornton	258
Cotton Ginny Ltd.	207	Great-West Life Assurance Company, The	259

The Canada Student Employment Guide

University Index 689

Groupe Savoie Inc.	260	Leica Geosystems Canada Inc.	314
Haley Industries Limited	262	Lenbrook Industries Limited	315
Halifax County Regional Rehabilitation Centre	263	Leo Burnett Co. Ltd.	315
Halifax Regional Municipality	263	Leon's Manufacturing Company Inc.	316
Halifax Water Commission	264	Les Centres Jeunesse de Montréal	316
Hasbro Canada Inc.	266	Les Distilleries Corby Ltée	317
Health Authority 5	267	Lifetouch Canada Inc.	319
Health Care Corporation of St. John's	267	Linmor Technologies	320
Health Sciences Centre	268	Magna International Inc.	327
Helijet Airways Inc.	268	Manitoba Agriculture and Food	327
Hermes Electronics Inc.	269	Manitoba Hydro	328
Hill & Knowlton Canada Ltd.	270	Manitoba Public Insurance Corporation	329
Hoffman-La Roche Limited	272	Maple Leaf Consumer Foods	330
Home Oil Co. Ltd.	273	Marine Atlantic Inc.	331
Honda Canada Inc.	274	Maritime Life Assurance Company, The	331
Honeywell Ltd.	275	McBee Systems of Canada Inc.	336
Horseshoe Resort Corporation	275	McCarney Greenwood	336
Hôtel Dieu de Montréal	276	McKay-Cocker Construction Limited	338
HSBC Bank Canada	277	McLaren-McCann Advertising of Canada Ltd.	338
Hudson's Bay Company, The	279	MDS Nordion	339
Humber River Regional Hospital	280	Mediasynergy	340
Hydro Electric Commission of Thunder Bay	281	Memotec Communications Inc.	341
Hydro Mississauga Corporation	282	Metro Richelieu Inc.	342
Hydro One Inc.	282	Metropolitan Life Insurance Company	344
Hydro Québec	283	Meyers Norris Penny & Co.	344
I M P Group International Inc.	283	Michaels of Canada Inc.	345
IBM Canada Ltd.	284	Midland Walwyn Inc.	345
Ilco Unican Inc.	286	Midwest Food Products Inc.	346
Imperial Oil Limited	286	Ministry of Northern Develop. and Mines	348
Indalex Limited	288	Mitel Corporation	350
Industrial Equipment Co. Ltd.	288	Mitsubishi Electric Sales Canada	351
Industrial-Alliance Life Insurance Company	289	Mobile Computing Corporation	351
Industries Lassonde Inc.	289	Monarch Communications Inc.	353
InfoInterActive Inc.	290	Montreal Trust Co.	353
Insurance Corp. of B.C.	291	MOSAID Technologies Inc.	355
Intercon Security Ltd.	292	Motorola Canada Ltd.	356
Intertape Polymer Group Inc.	294	N B S Card Services	359
IPL Energy Inc.	294	Nanaimo Credit Union	359
Island Telecom Inc.	295	National Grocers Co. Ltd.	360
IWK Grace Health Centre	297	National Life	361
Izaak Walton Killam Hospital, The	297	Neles Automation, Scada Solutions Ltd.	362
J.D. Irving Limited	298	Neptune Food Suppliers Ltd.	363
James Richardson International Limited	300	Nesbitt Burns Inc.	364
Jim Pattison Group	301	Nestle Canada Inc.	364
Johnson Incorporated	303	New Brunswick Power Corporation	365
Jostens Canada Ltd.	303	New Brunswick Telephone Company	366
Kennametal Ltd.	305	New Holland Canada Ltd.	366
Keyano College	306	Newfoundland and Labrador Credit Union	367
Kimberly-Clark Inc.	307	Newfoundland and Labrador Hydro	367
Kodak Canada Inc.	309	News Marketing Canada	368
Kraft Canada Inc.	310	NewTel Communications	369
La Confiserie Comete Ltee	311	Nichirin Inc.	370
Leduc, City of	313	Nielsen Marketing Research	370
Lego Canada Inc.	314	Nike Canada Ltd.	371

The Canada Student Employment Guide

University Index

Norbord Industries	372	Replicon Inc.	428
North American Life Assurance Company	373	Rich Products of Canada Limited	431
North West Company Inc.	374	Richmond, City of	431
Northern Lights Regional Health Centre	375	Richter Usher & Vineberg	432
Northwestel Inc.	376	Rio Algom Limited	433
Norwich Union Life Insurance Society	376	Riverside Hospital of Ottawa, The	434
Nova Scotia Liquor Commission	377	Rogers AT&T Wireless Inc.	436
Nova Scotia Power Corp.	377	Rogers Media, Publishing	436
Novartis Consumer Health Canada Inc.	378	Rothmans, Benson and Hedges Inc.	437
Numac Energy Inc.	379	Royal & Sun Alliance Insurance Co. of Cda	437
Oetiker Limited	381	Royal Bank of Canada	438
Oland Breweries Limited	382	Royal Canadian Mint	438
Omstead Foods Limited	383	Royal Inland Hospital	439
Ontario Jockey Club, The	384	Royal Philips Electronics	439
Ontario Legislative Offices	384	Royal Victoria Hospital	440
Oracle Corp. Canada Inc.	386	Ryerson Polytechnic University	441
Ottawa Hospital	386	Saan Stores Ltd.	441
Paperboard Industries International Inc.	389	Sandman Hotels and Inns	443
Paramount Canada's Wonderland Inc.	389	Saskatchewan Economic Development	445
PCL Constructors Inc.	392	Saskatchewan Government Insurance	445
Pearson Education Canada	393	Saskatchewan Research Council, The	446
Peel Board of Education	393	Saskatchewan Wheat Pool	447
Peel Regional Police	394	SaskTel	449
PennCorp Life Insurance Company	396	Scarborough General Hospital	450
Petro-Canada	397	Schneider Electric Canada Inc.	451
Pharma Plus Drugmarts Ltd.	398	Seprotech Systems Incorporated	454
Phoenix International	399	Shaw Communications	455
Pine Falls Paper Company Limited	400	Shaw Industries Ltd.	455
Pitney Bowes of Canada Ltd.	401	Sheraton Fallsview Hotel	456
Pizza Pizza Ltd.	401	Shorewood Packaging Corp. of Canada Ltd.	459
Placer Dome Inc.	402	Siemens Electric Ltd.	460
Poco Petroleums Ltd.	402	Signature Vacations Inc.	460
Polygram Group Canada Inc.	403	Silicon Graphics Canada Inc.	461
Potacan Mining Company	405	Skiing Louise Ltd.	461
PPG Canada Inc.	407	Slocan Forest Products Ltd.	462
Pratt & Whitney Canada Inc.	407	SNC-Lavalin	463
PRI Automation	408	Sobeys Inc.	463
Pricewaterhouse Coopers	409	Sodexho Marriott Services Canada	464
Progressive Financial Strategy	411	Southam Inc.	466
Providence Centre	412	Southern Railway of British Columbia Ltd.	466
Prudential Insurance Co. of America, The	412	Spar Aerospace Limited	467
Public Utilities of Kingston	413	Spectrum Signal Processing Inc.	468
Purolator Courier Ltd.	413	Sportsco International	469
QIT-Fer et Titane Inc.	414	Sprint Canada	470
Québec Cartier Mining Company	415	St. Lawrence Parks Commission	472
Quebecor Inc.	415	Stanley Canada Inc.	475
Rasco Specialty Metals Inc.	417	State Farm Insurance Companies	476
Raymond Rebar Inc.	418	Stitches	478
Reader's Digest Association of Canada Ltd.	419	Stone Consolidated Inc.	479
Red Deer Co-op Limited	421	StorageTek Canada Inc.	479
Regal Capital Planners Ltd.	422	Sun Rype Products Ltd.	481
Regal Constellation Hotel Ltd.	422	Sundog Printing Limited	482
Renaissance Energy Ltd.	427	Sunoco Inc.	482
Rentway Inc.	427	Supreme Tooling Group	483

The Canada Student Employment Guide

Surrey, City of	484
Swift Current Health District	485
Symantec Corporation	486
Talisman Energy Inc.	487
TCT Logistics	488
TD Waterhouse Investor Services (Canada)	488
Telebec Ltée	490
Telesat Canada	491
Telus Corporation	492
Thomas J. Lipton	496
Thompson's Moving and Storage	496
Thunder Bay Regional Hospital	497
Tiger Brand Knitting Company Limited	498
Timmins, City of	499
Today's Business Products Ltd.	500
Toronto East General Hospital	503
Toronto General Hospital	505
Toronto Police Service	506
Toronto Sun Publishing Corp., The	507
Toshiba of Canada Ltd.	508
Toyota Canada Ltd.	509
TSC Stores Ltd.	512
Uni Select Inc.	513
Union Gas Ltd.	513
University College of Cape Breton	516
Urban Systems Ltd.	516
VanCity Credit Union	519
Vancouver Sun	520
Visteon Canada Inc.	522
Waverly & York Corporation	525
Westbury Life	529
Westcliff Management Ltd.	529
Westcoast Energy Inc.	530
Westin Prince Hotel, The	531
WestJet Airlines	532
Westminster Savings Credit Union	533
Westshore Terminals Ltd.	534
Weyerhaeuser Company Limited	535
Whistler Blackcomb Mountain	535
Whitehill Technologies Inc.	537
Wilson Auto Electric Ltd.	538
Windsor, City of	538
Winners Apparel Ltd.	539
Winpak Ltd.	539
Wire Rope Industries Ltd.	540
XCAN Grain Pool Ltd.	541
xwave solutions	542
Yellowknife, City of	544
YFactor	544
Zellers Inc.	546

Education

Anthony Insurance Inc.	102
Assiniboine Community College	109
Banff Centre for Continuing Education, The	120
Baycrest Centre for Geriatric Care	123
Bethania Mennonite Personal Care Home Inc.	134
Bloorview Childrens Hospital	140
Camp Hill Hospital	160
Deer Lodge Centre Inc.	213
Grant MacEwen Community College	258
Halifax County Regional Rehabilitation Centre	263
Humber River Regional Hospital	280
IWK Grace Health Centre	297
Keyano College	306
Metropolitan Life Insurance Company	344
National Grocers Co. Ltd.	360
Ontario Legislative Offices	384
Oracle Corp. Canada Inc.	386
Pearson Education Canada	393
Peel Board of Education	393
Pitney Bowes of Canada Ltd.	401
Purolator Courier Ltd.	413
Regional Municipality of Niagara	424
Rehabilitation Institute of Toronto	425
Royal & Sun Alliance Insurance Co. of Cda	437
Royal Bank of Canada	438
Sandman Hotels and Inns	443
Scarborough General Hospital	450
Signature Vacations Inc.	460
St. Lawrence Parks Commission	472
State Farm Insurance Companies	476
Sudbury Regional Hospital	480
Surrey, City of	484
Toronto Catholic District School Board	502
Toronto District School Board	503
Toronto French School, The	504
Vancouver Sun	520
Weyerhaeuser Company Limited	535

Engineering

A E McKenzie Co. Inc.	75
A.G. Simpson Co. Ltd.	75
ABC Group	76
Abitibi-Consolidated Inc.	77
Acklands-Grainger Inc.	80
ADI Group Inc.	82
Air Canada	85
Air Liquide Canada Inc.	85
Akita Drilling Ltd.	87
Alberta Energy & Utilities Board	89
Alberta Energy Company Ltd.	89

University Index

Alcan Aluminium Limited	91	Cornwall Electric	206
Alias | Wavefront	94	Cosyn Technology	207
Amcor Twinpak North America Inc.	98	D.A. Stuart Inc.	210
Andersen Consulting	101	DaimlerChrysler Canada Ltd.	211
Apex Land Corp.	103	Dana Corporation - Long Manufacturing	212
Apple Canada Inc.	104	Delphi Solutions Inc.	215
ArvinMeritor	108	Dofasco Inc.	218
Assiniboine Community College	109	Domtar Inc.	218
ATCO Electric	111	Dynapro Systems Inc.	223
ATS Automation Tooling Systems Inc.	116	Dynatek Automation Systems Inc.	224
Aventis Pasteur Limited	117	E B A Engineering Consultants Ltd.	225
Babcock and Wilcox Canada	119	Earth Tech Canada Inc.	225
Ballard Power Systems Inc.	120	Echo Bay Mines Ltd.	226
Baytex Energy Limited	124	Emco Limited	230
BC Hydro	125	EnerFlex Systems Ltd.	232
BC Research Inc.	126	Exfo	235
Bechtel Canada Co.	128	Exide Canada Inc.	235
Bell Mobility	131	Extendicare (Canada) Inc.	237
Bettis Canada Ltd.	135	Federated Co-operatives Limited	239
BFGoodrich Landing Gear Division	135	FedEx Express	240
Biomira Inc.	136	Finning	240
Biovail Corporation International	137	Fishery Products International	241
BJ Services Company	138	Foremost Industries Inc.	244
Bloorview MacMillan Centre, The	140	Friesens Corporation	246
Blue Mountain Resorts Limited	141	Gencorp Vehicle Sealing	248
Bosal Canada Inc.	145	General Chemical Canada Ltd.	249
BOVAR Waste Management	145	General Electric Canada Inc.	249
Buckeye Canada Inc.	151	Giffels Associates Limited	251
Budd Canada Inc.	152	Groupe Savoie Inc.	260
C B C L Limited	154	Halifax Regional Municipality	263
Cabre Exploration Ltd.	156	Halifax Water Commission	264
CAE Newness	157	Hermes Electronics Inc.	269
Calgary, City of	158	Home Oil Co. Ltd.	273
Cambior Inc.	158	Honeywell Ltd.	275
Canadian General Tower Limited	166	Hydro Electric Commission of Thunder Bay	281
Canadian Occidental Petroleum Ltd.	168	Hydro Québec	283
Canadian Tire Corporation Ltd.	169	I M P Group International Inc.	283
CancerCare Manitoba	171	IBM Canada Ltd.	284
Carbone of America (LCL) Ltd.	175	IDEA Associates Inc.	285
Carte International Inc.	176	Ilco Unican Inc.	286
Centra Gas British Columbia Inc.	180	Imperial Oil Limited	286
CGI	184	Indalex Limited	288
CH2M Gore and Storrie Limited	185	InfoInterActive Inc.	290
Chevron Canada Resources Ltd.	188	Intertape Polymer Group Inc.	294
Citibank Canada	191	IPL Energy Inc.	294
CKF Inc.	192	Island Telecom Inc.	295
COM DEV International	197	IWK Grace Health Centre	297
Communications & Power Industries Canada	198	J.D. Irving Limited	298
Compaq Canada Inc.	199	Jacques Whitford Consulting Engineers	299
Computalog Ltd.	200	JDS Uniphase Corporation	300
Comtronic Computer Inc.	202	Johnson Controls Ltd.	302
Coquitlam, City of	204	Kelowna, City of	305
Corel Corporation	205	Kennametal Ltd.	305
Corner Brook, City of	205	Keyano College	306

The Canada Student Employment Guide

University Index

Kvaerner Metals	311	Pine Falls Paper Company Limited	400
Leduc, City of	313	Pitney Bowes of Canada Ltd.	401
Lenbrook Industries Limited	315	Poco Petroleums Ltd.	402
Linmor Technologies	320	Potacan Mining Company	405
Litton Systems Canada Ltd.	320	Powertech Labs Inc.	406
MacDonald Dettwiler and Associates Ltd.	325	PPG Canada Inc.	407
Magna International Inc.	327	PRI Automation	408
Manitoba Agriculture and Food	327	Pricewaterhouse Coopers	409
Manitoba Hydro	328	Prince George, City of	410
Marcam Canada	330	Proctor and Redfern Ltd.	411
Marine Atlantic Inc.	331	Public Utilities of Kingston	413
Marshall Macklin Monaghan Ltd.	333	QIT-Fer et Titane Inc.	414
Matrox Electronic Systems Ltd.	335	Rasco Specialty Metals Inc.	417
MDS Nordion	339	Recochem Inc.	420
Mediasynergy	340	Rhone-Poulenc Canada Inc.	430
Memotec Communications Inc.	341	Richmond, City of	431
Michaels of Canada Inc.	345	Rio Algom Limited	433
Midland Walwyn Inc.	345	Roctest Ltée	435
Midwest Food Products Inc.	346	Rogers AT&T Wireless Inc.	436
Ministry of Northern Develop. and Mines	348	Royal Philips Electronics	439
Mitel Corporation	350	Sandwell Inc.	443
Mitra Imaging Inc.	350	Saskatchewan Research Council, The	446
Mitsubishi Electric Sales Canada	351	SaskTel	449
Mobile Computing Corporation	351	SC Infrastructure Inc.	449
Moosehead Breweries Limited	354	Schneider Electric Canada Inc.	451
Morrison Hershfield Limited	354	SED Systems	453
Mortice Kern Systems Inc.	355	Seprotech Systems Incorporated	454
MOSAID Technologies Inc.	355	Shaw Communications	455
N B S Card Services	359	Shaw Industries Ltd.	455
National Grocers Co. Ltd.	360	Siemens Electric Ltd.	460
National Manufacturing of Canada Inc.	361	Silicon Graphics Canada Inc.	461
Neles Automation, Scada Solutions Ltd.	362	Southern Railway of British Columbia Ltd.	466
Nestle Canada Inc.	364	Spectrum Signal Processing Inc.	468
Netron Inc.	365	Sprint Canada	470
New Brunswick Power Corporation	365	Stantec Consulting Ltd.	475
New Brunswick Telephone Company	366	State Farm Insurance Companies	476
New Holland Canada Ltd.	366	Steelcraft Industries Ltd.	477
Nichirin Inc.	370	Sun Rype Products Ltd.	481
NLK Consultants Inc.	372	Supreme Tooling Group	483
Norbord Industries	372	Surrey, City of	484
Northwestel Inc.	376	Symantec Corporation	486
Nova Scotia Power Corp.	377	Talisman Energy Inc.	487
Novartis Consumer Health Canada Inc.	378	Telebec Ltée	490
NPS Allelix Corp.	379	Telesat Canada	491
Numac Energy Inc.	379	Thomson - CSF Systems Canada Inc.	497
Ocelot Energy Inc.	381	Timmins, City of	499
Oland Breweries Limited	382	Toshiba of Canada Ltd.	508
Omstead Foods Limited	383	Trojan Technologies Inc.	511
Oracle Corp. Canada Inc.	386	University College of Cape Breton	516
Paramount Canada's Wonderland Inc.	389	Urban Systems Ltd.	516
Patheon Inc.	390	US Filter BCP	517
PCL Constructors Inc.	392	Vancouver Sun	520
Peel Regional Police	394	Visteon Canada Inc.	522
Petro-Canada	397	Weldco-Beales Manufacturing Inc.	527

The Canada Student Employment Guide

694 University Index

West Kootenay Power Ltd.	528	University College of Cape Breton	516
Westcoast Energy Inc.	530	Vancouver Sun	520
Westport Innovations Inc.	534	Westcoast Energy Inc.	530
Westshore Terminals Ltd.	534	Yarmouth Regional Hospital	543
Weyerhaeuser Company Limited	535	Yellowknife, City of	544
Whitehill Technologies Inc.	537		
Windsor, City of	538		
Workfire Development Corp.	540		
Zenastra	547		
Zenon Environmental Inc.	547		

Science

1-800-GOT-JUNK?	74
Aberdeen Hospital	77
Acklands-Grainger Inc.	80

Library Science

		Adherex Technologies Inc.	81
		Advanta Seeds	83
Alberta Energy & Utilities Board	89	Alberta Cancer Board	88
Assiniboine Community College	109	Alberta Energy & Utilities Board	89
Aventis Pasteur Limited	117	Alcan Aluminium Limited	91
Banff Centre for Continuing Education, The	120	Amcor Twinpak North America Inc.	98
Baycrest Centre for Geriatric Care	123	Andersen Consulting	101
Bloorview Childrens Hospital	140	Apotex Fermentation Inc.	104
Calgary, City of	158	Assiniboine Community College	109
Camp Hill Hospital	160	Assumption Mutual Life Insurance	109
Canadian Broadcasting Corporation	164	AstraZeneca	110
Canadian Cancer Society	164	Aventis Pasteur Limited	117
Canadian Museum of Civilization Corp.	167	Ballard Power Systems Inc.	120
Canadian National Institute For The Blind	167	Banff Centre for Continuing Education, The	120
Cassels Brock & Blackwell	177	Barton Place Long Term Care Facility	121
Coquitlam, City of	204	BASF Canada Inc.	122
Deer Lodge Centre Inc.	213	Baycrest Centre for Geriatric Care	123
Dynapro Systems Inc.	223	BC Research Inc.	126
Glaxo Wellcome Canada	253	BC Telecom Inc.	126
Goodman and Carr	255	BFGoodrich Landing Gear Division	135
Grant MacEwen Community College	258	Bic Inc.	136
Humber River Regional Hospital	280	Bio-Research Laboratories Ltd.	137
Hydro Québec	283	Bloorview Childrens Hospital	140
IWK Grace Health Centre	297	Bloorview MacMillan Centre, The	140
Keyano College	306	BOVAR Waste Management	145
Manitoba Hydro	328	Calgary, City of	158
NPS Allelix Corp.	379	Cambridge Memorial Hospital	159
Ontario Legislative Offices	384	Camp Hill Hospital	160
Peel Board of Education	393	Canadian Broadcasting Corporation	164
Regina Health District	423	Canadian Cancer Society	164
Rehabilitation Institute of Toronto	425	Canadian General Tower Limited	166
Richmond, City of	431	Canadian Museum of Civilization Corp.	167
Ryerson Polytechnic University	441	Canadian National Institute For The Blind	167
Southam Inc.	466	Canadian Occidental Petroleum Ltd.	168
Sudbury Regional Hospital	480	CancerCare Manitoba	171
Surrey Memorial Hospital	483	Cangene Corporation	172
Surrey, City of	484	Cassels Brock & Blackwell	177
Teck Corp.	489	Centra Gas British Columbia Inc.	180
Toronto District School Board	503	Chevron Canada Resources Ltd.	188
Toronto French School, The	504	Cobourg District General Hospital	194
Toronto Public Library Board	506	Cognis Canada Corporation	195
Toronto Sun Publishing Corp., The	507	Cognos Incorporated	196

The Canada Student Employment Guide

COM DEV International	197
Comtronic Computer Inc.	202
Coquitlam, City of	204
Corel Corporation	205
D.A. Stuart Inc.	210
David Thompson Health Region	212
Deer Lodge Centre Inc.	213
Degussa - Huls Canada Inc.	214
Domtar Inc.	218
Ducks Unlimited Canada	220
Dynapro Systems Inc.	223
Echo Bay Mines Ltd.	226
Electronics Arts (Canada) Inc.	229
Eli Lilly Canada Inc.	230
EMJ Data Systems Ltd.	231
Endpoint Research Ltd.	231
Entreprises Premier Canadien Ltée	232
Exfo	235
Fishery Products International	241
Friesens Corporation	246
Glaxo Wellcome Canada	253
Goodman and Carr	255
Grant MacEwen Community College	258
Halifax Water Commission	264
Hermes Electronics Inc.	269
Humber River Regional Hospital	280
Hydro Québec	283
IBM Canada Ltd.	284
InfoInterActive Inc.	290
Intertape Polymer Group Inc.	294
IWK Grace Health Centre	297
JDS Uniphase Corporation	300
John P. Robarts Research Institute	302
Keyano College	306
Kings Regional Rehabilitation Centre	308
Litton Systems Canada Ltd.	320
MacDonald Dettwiler and Associates Ltd.	325
Manitoba Agriculture and Food	327
Manitoba Hydro	328
Manitoba Pool Elevators	328
Marcam Canada	330
Maxxam Analytics Inc.	335
MDS Nordion	339
Mediasynergy	340
Memotec Communications Inc.	341
Midwest Food Products Inc.	346
Ministry of Northern Develop. and Mines	348
Mitra Imaging Inc.	350
Mitsubishi Electric Sales Canada	351
Mobile Computing Corporation	351
Moosehead Breweries Limited	354
Mortice Kern Systems Inc.	355
National Grocers Co. Ltd.	360
Netron Inc.	365
North West Company Inc.	374
Nova Scotia Power Corp.	377
Novartis Consumer Health Canada Inc.	378
NPS Allelix Corp.	379
Numac Energy Inc.	379
Oland Breweries Limited	382
Omstead Foods Limited	383
Ontario Legislative Offices	384
Patheon Inc.	390
Peel Board of Education	393
Phoenix International	399
Pine Falls Paper Company Limited	400
Powertech Labs Inc.	406
PPG Canada Inc.	407
Reader's Digest Association of Canada Ltd.	419
Recochem Inc.	420
Regina Health District	423
Rehabilitation Institute of Toronto	425
Richmond, City of	431
Rogers AT&T Wireless Inc.	436
Royal Victoria Hospital	440
Ryerson Polytechnic University	441
Saskatchewan Economic Development	445
Saskatchewan Government Insurance	445
Saskatchewan Research Council, The	446
Scarborough General Hospital	450
Seprotech Systems Incorporated	454
Shaw Industries Ltd.	455
Siemens Electric Ltd.	460
Signature Vacations Inc.	460
Silicon Graphics Canada Inc.	461
Southam Inc.	466
State Farm Insurance Companies	476
StorageTek Canada Inc.	479
Sudbury Regional Hospital	480
Sun Rype Products Ltd.	481
Surrey Memorial Hospital	483
Surrey Place Centre	484
Surrey, City of	484
Symantec Corporation	486
Talisman Energy Inc.	487
Teck Corp.	489
Thompson's Moving and Storage	496
Toronto District School Board	503
Toronto East General Hospital	503
Toronto French School, The	504
Toronto General Hospital	505
Toronto Public Library Board	506
Toronto Sun Publishing Corp., The	507
Trojan Technologies Inc.	511
University College of Cape Breton	516
Urban Systems Ltd.	516
Vancouver Sun	520
Westcoast Energy Inc.	530

696 University Index

Weyerhaeuser Company Limited	535
Workfire Development Corp.	540
Yarmouth Regional Hospital	543
Yellowknife, City of	544
Zenastra	547
Zenon Environmental Inc.	547

Doctorate

Adherex Technologies Inc.	81
Aventis Pasteur Limited	117
Ballard Power Systems Inc.	120
Biomira Inc.	136
Bio-Research Laboratories Ltd.	137
Bloorview Childrens Hospital	140
Bloorview MacMillan Centre, The	140
CancerCare Manitoba	171
Cangene Corporation	172
Citibank Canada	191
David Thompson Health Region	212
Entreprises Premier Canadien Ltée	232
Environics Research Group Ltd.	233
Exfo	235
Gallup Canada Inc.	247
Hill & Knowlton Canada Ltd.	270
I M P Group International Inc.	283
IBM Canada Ltd.	284
Imperial Oil Limited	286
IWK Grace Health Centre	297
John P. Robarts Research Institute	302
KFC Canada	307
Litton Systems Canada Ltd.	320
Manitoba Agriculture and Food	327
Maxxam Analytics Inc.	335
Morrison Hershfield Limited	354
MOSAID Technologies Inc.	355
NPS Allelix Corp.	379
Peel Board of Education	393
Powertech Labs Inc.	406
Raylo Chemicals Inc.	417
Regina Health District	423
Rogers AT&T Wireless Inc.	436
St. Amant Centre Inc.	471
Surrey Place Centre	484
Talisman Energy Inc.	487
Toronto French School, The	504
Triumf	510
Workfire Development Corp.	540
Zenastra	547

The Canada Student Employment Guide

Chartered Accounting Index

Below is a list of employers that consider the designations of Charted Accountants (CA), Certified Management Accountants (CMA), and Certified General Accountants (CGA) important in the selection of candidates. The corresponding page number of the firm's profile is also shown.

CA-General	697
CA-Finance	700
CMA-General	703
CMA-Finance	706
CGA-General	709
CGA-Finance	711

CA-General

Aberdeen Hospital	77
Accucaps Industries Limited	79
Acklands-Grainger Inc.	80
ADI Group Inc.	82
Agricultural Credit Corp. of Saskatchewan	84
Air Ontario Inc.	86
Akita Drilling Ltd.	87
Alberta Energy & Utilities Board	89
Alberta Energy Company Ltd.	89
Algoma Steel Inc.	93
Allianz Canada	95
Allmar Distributors Ltd.	95
Allstate Insurance Co. of Canada	96
Alpine Oil Service Corporation	96
Amcan Castings Limited	98
Amcor Twinpak North America Inc.	98
Anthony Insurance Inc.	102
Apex Land Corp.	103
Arbor Memorial Services Inc.	106
Armor Personnel	107
Assiniboine Community College	109
Atlantic Lottery Corporation Inc.	113
Aurizon Mines Ltd.	116
Aurum Ceramic Dental Laboratories Ltd.	117
Ballard Power Systems Inc.	120
Banff Centre for Continuing Education, The	120
Barton Place Long Term Care Facility	121
BBM Bureau of Measurement	125
BC Hydro	125

Bechtel Canada Co.	128
Behlen Industries	130
Bell Mobility	131
Benwell Atkins Ltd.	132
Bettis Canada Ltd.	135
BFGoodrich Landing Gear Division	135
Blaney McMurty LLP	139
Bloorview MacMillan Centre, The	140
Blue Wave Seafoods Inc.	142
BNP PARIBAS (Canada)	143
Bonus Resource Services Corp.	144
Boréal Assurances Inc.	144
BOVAR Waste Management	145
Brandon, City of	146
British Columbia Ferry Corporation	149
Brookfield Properties Corporation	150
C MAC Industries Inc.	155
C.S.T. Consultants Inc.	155
Cabre Exploration Ltd.	156
Cadith Entertainment Ltd.	156
Calgary Co-operative Association Limited	157
Calgary, City of	158
Cambior Inc.	158
Cambridge Memorial Hospital	159
Cameco Corporation	160
Camp Hill Hospital	160
Canada Safeway Limited	163
Canada Starch Company Inc.	163
Canadian Cancer Society	164
Canadian Commercial Corp.	165
Canadian Depository for Securities Ltd.	166
Canadian Museum of Civilization Corp.	167
Canadian National Institute For The Blind	167
Canadian Occidental Petroleum Ltd.	168
Canadian Tire Corporation Ltd.	169
Canadian Western Bank	169
Cape Breton Development Corporation	174
Cargill Limited	175
Centra Gas Manitoba Inc.	181
Central Park Lodges Ltd.	181
Centre de Santé de St-Henri Inc.	182
Chapters Inc.	186
Charlottetown Driving Park	187
Chevron Canada Resources Ltd.	188
Christian Horizons	190
Cineplex Odeon Corporation	191
Citibank Canada	191
CKF Inc.	192
COBI Foods Inc.	194

The Canada Student Employment Guide

698　Chartered Accounting Index

Coca Cola Foods Canada Inc.	195
Columbia House	197
Comcare Health Services	198
Connors Bros, Limited	203
Co-op Atlantic	203
Corner Brook, City of	205
Cotton Ginny Ltd.	207
Credit Union Central of Canada	208
Culinar Inc.	209
Custom Trim Ltd.	210
D.A. Stuart Inc.	210
D.H. Howden	211
DaimlerChrysler Canada Ltd.	211
Dell Computer Corporation	214
Delta Hotels	215
Delta Toronto Airport Hotel	216
Derlan Industries Limited	216
Directwest Publishers Ltd.	217
Dofasco Inc.	218
Domtar Inc.	218
Dylex Limited	222
Dynapro Systems Inc.	223
Echo Bay Mines Ltd.	226
Economical Insurance Group, The	227
Eli Lilly Canada Inc.	230
EMJ Data Systems Ltd.	231
Entreprises Premier Canadien Ltée	232
Exfo	235
Exide Canada Inc.	235
Export Development Corporation	236
Extendicare (Canada) Inc.	237
Farm Credit Corp. Canada	238
Farmers Co-operative Dairy Limited	239
Federated Co-operatives Limited	239
Finning	240
Fisher Scientific Limited	241
Flint Energy Services Ltd.	243
Future Shop Ltd.	246
Gay Lea Foods Co-Operative Ltd.	247
Gendis Inc.	248
General Chemical Canada Ltd.	249
Gienow Building Products Ltd.	251
Giffels Associates Limited	251
Gilbey Canada Inc.	252
Gimbel Eye Centre	252
Glaxo Wellcome Canada	253
Goepel McDermid Securities	254
Goodman and Carr	255
Goodwill Industries of Toronto	256
Goodyear Canada Inc.	256
Gov't of Newfoundland - Dept. of Finance	257
Grant Thornton	258
Great-West Life Assurance Company, The	259
Groupe Savoie Inc.	260
Grouse Mountain Resorts Ltd.	260
Halifax County Regional Rehabilitation Centre	263
Halifax Water Commission	264
Health Care Corporation of St. John's	267
Health Sciences Centre	268
Hill & Knowlton Canada Ltd.	270
Hippodrome de Montréal	270
Honeywell Ltd.	275
Horseshoe Resort Corporation	275
Hôtel Dieu de Montréal	276
Household Movers & Shippers Limited	276
Hudon & Deaudelin Ltée	279
Humber River Regional Hospital	280
Hydro Electric Commission of Thunder Bay	281
ICI Canada Inc.	285
Imprimerie Interweb Inc.	287
ING Canada Financial Services International	291
Insurance Corp. of B.C.	291
Intercon Security Ltd.	292
Interior Savings Credit Union	293
Intertape Polymer Group Inc.	294
IPL Energy Inc.	294
Island Savings Credit Union	295
Island Telecom Inc.	295
IWK Grace Health Centre	297
J.D. Irving Limited	298
James Richardson International Limited	300
Jim Pattison Group	301
Johnson Incorporated	303
Jostens Canada Ltd.	303
Kelowna Home Support	304
Kitchener, City of	309
Laidlaw Inc.	312
Lakeside Farm Industries Ltd.	312
Leduc, City of	313
Lego Canada Inc.	314
Lenbrook Industries Limited	315
Les Centres Jeunesse de Montréal	316
Liberty Health	318
Litton Systems Canada Ltd.	320
MAAX Inc.	324
Manitoba Agriculture and Food	327
Manitoba Hydro	328
Manitoba Public Insurance Corporation	329
Marine Atlantic Inc.	331
Maritime Life Assurance Company, The	331
Mediacom Inc.	340
Metro Richelieu Inc.	342
Metro Toronto Convention Centre	342
Metropolitan Life Insurance Company	344
Michaels of Canada Inc.	345
Midland Walwyn Inc.	345
Midwest Food Products Inc.	346
Ministry of Northern Develop. and Mines	348

The Canada Student Employment Guide

Chartered Accounting Index 699

Misericordia General Hospital	348	Rich Products of Canada Limited	431
Mitel Corporation	350	Richmond, City of	431
Mitsubishi Electric Sales Canada	351	Richter Usher & Vineberg	432
Mobile Computing Corporation	351	Rimrock Resort Hotel	432
Moffat Communications Limited	352	Rivtow Marine Ltd.	434
Montreal Trust Co.	353	Rothmans, Benson and Hedges Inc.	437
Motorola Canada Ltd.	356	Royal & Sun Alliance Insurance Co. of Cda	437
Mountain Equipment Co-op	356	Royal Bank of Canada	438
National Grocers Co. Ltd.	360	Sandman Hotels and Inns	443
National Life	361	Sara Lee Corporation of Canada Limited	444
Nelvana Limited	363	Saskatchewan Centre of the Arts	444
Nesbitt Burns Inc.	364	Saskatchewan Government Insurance	445
New Brunswick Telephone Company	366	Saskatchewan Research Council, The	446
Newfoundland and Labrador Credit Union	367	Saskatchewan Wheat Pool	447
Newness Machine Ltd.	368	Saskatoon, City of	448
News Marketing Canada	368	Saskferco Products Inc.	448
Nike Canada Ltd.	371	Scarborough General Hospital	450
Norbord Industries	372	Schlumberger Canada Ltd.	450
North American Life Assurance Company	373	Seprotech Systems Incorporated	454
Northwestel Inc.	376	Sharp Electronics of Canada Ltd.	454
Norwich Union Life Insurance Society	376	Shaw Communications	455
Novartis Consumer Health Canada Inc.	378	Shaw Industries Ltd.	455
NPS Allelix Corp.	379	Sheraton Fallsview Hotel	456
Okanagan Skeena Group Limited	382	Shermag Inc.	457
Ontario Jockey Club, The	384	Shorewood Packaging Corp. of Canada Ltd.	459
Ontario Legislative Offices	384	Siemens Electric Ltd.	460
Ontario March of Dimes	385	Signature Vacations Inc.	460
Ottawa Hospital	386	Skills Training & Support Services Association	462
Paperboard Industries International Inc.	389	Société des Alcools du Québec	464
Parkland Industries Ltd.	390	Sodexho Marriott Services Canada	464
Patheon Inc.	390	Sony Music Canada	465
PavCo	391	Southam Inc.	466
PCL Constructors Inc.	392	Spar Aerospace Limited	467
Peacock Inc.	392	Sportsco International	469
Peel Board of Education	393	Sprint Canada	470
PennCorp Life Insurance Company	396	SRI Homes Inc.	470
Pharma Plus Drugmarts Ltd.	398	SSQ Life	471
Pitney Bowes of Canada Ltd.	401	St. Vincent's Hospitals	473
Placer Dome Inc.	402	State Farm Insurance Companies	476
Poco Petroleums Ltd.	402	Steelpipe Ltd.	477
Polygram Group Canada Inc.	403	Stitches	478
Positron Industries Inc.	404	Stone Consolidated Inc.	479
Potacan Mining Company	405	Supreme Tooling Group	483
Premdor Inc.	408	Surrey Memorial Hospital	483
Pricewaterhouse Coopers	409	Surrey, City of	484
Progressive Financial Strategy	411	Sydney Steel Corporation	485
Providence Centre	412	Talisman Energy Inc.	487
Prudential Insurance Co. of America, The	412	TCT Logistics	488
Public Utilities of Kingston	413	TD Waterhouse Investor Services (Canada)	488
Purolator Courier Ltd.	413	Teklogix Inc.	489
Raymond Rebar Inc.	418	Telus Corporation	492
Reader's Digest Association of Canada Ltd.	419	The Co-operators	493
Regal Constellation Hotel Ltd.	422	Tiger Brand Knitting Company Limited	498
Revenue Properties Company Limited	429	Today's Business Products Ltd.	500

The Canada Student Employment Guide

700 Chartered Accounting Index

Toronto District School Board	503
Toronto General Hospital	505
Toronto Police Service	506
Toronto Sun Publishing Corp., The	507
Toronto, City of	508
Toshiba of Canada Ltd.	508
Toyota Canada Ltd.	509
Trojan Technologies Inc.	511
TSC Stores Ltd.	512
Uni Select Inc.	513
Union Gas Ltd.	513
University College of Cape Breton	516
Vancouver Sun	520
Versa Services Ltd.	521
Waverly & York Corporation	525
Westbury Life	529
Westcliff Management Ltd.	529
Westcoast Energy Inc.	530
Western Glove Works	530
WestJet Airlines	532
Weston Produce Inc.	533
Westport Innovations Inc.	534
Westshore Terminals Ltd.	534
Weyerhaeuser Company Limited	535
Whistler Blackcomb Mountain	535
Wilson Auto Electric Ltd.	538
Windsor, City of	538
Winners Apparel Ltd.	539
Winpak Ltd.	539
World of Vacations Ltd.	541
Yellowknife, City of	544
Zellers Inc.	546

CA-Finance

A C A Cooperative Limited	74
A.G. Simpson Co. Ltd.	75
ABC Group	76
Accucaps Industries Limited	79
ADI Group Inc.	82
Agricultural Credit Corp. of Saskatchewan	84
Air Ontario Inc.	86
Akita Drilling Ltd.	87
Allianz Canada	95
Allstate Insurance Co. of Canada	96
Altona Community Memorial Health Centre	97
Amcan Castings Limited	98
Amcor Twinpak North America Inc.	98
AMEC Inc.	99
Anthony Insurance Inc.	102
Apex Land Corp.	103
Assumption Mutual Life Insurance	109
ATCO Gas Services Ltd.	112

Aurizon Mines Ltd.	116
Aventis Pasteur Limited	117
Ballard Power Systems Inc.	120
Banff Centre for Continuing Education, The	120
BBM Bureau of Measurement	125
BC Hydro	125
Bechtel Canada Co.	128
Bell Mobility	131
Bethesda Hospital	134
BFGoodrich Landing Gear Division	135
Bloorview Childrens Hospital	140
Bloorview MacMillan Centre, The	140
BNP PARIBAS (Canada)	143
BOVAR Waste Management	145
British Columbia Ferry Corporation	149
Brookfield Properties Corporation	150
C MAC Industries Inc.	155
C.S.T. Consultants Inc.	155
Cabre Exploration Ltd.	156
Cadith Entertainment Ltd.	156
Calgary Co-operative Association Limited	157
Calgary, City of	158
Camp Hill Hospital	160
Canada Post Corporation	162
Canada Starch Company Inc.	163
Canadian Cancer Society	164
Canadian Commercial Corp.	165
Canadian Depository for Securities Ltd.	166
Canadian Museum of Civilization Corp.	167
Canadian Occidental Petroleum Ltd.	168
Canadian Tire Corporation Ltd.	169
Canadian Western Bank	169
Cancarb Limited	170
CancerCare Manitoba	171
Cangene Corporation	172
Cape Breton Development Corporation	174
Carbone of America (LCL) Ltd.	175
Catholic Children's Aid Society Foundation	178
CenAlta Energy Services Inc.	180
Centra Gas British Columbia Inc.	180
Centra Gas Manitoba Inc.	181
Central Park Lodges Ltd.	181
Ceridian Canada	183
Chapters Inc.	186
Chevron Canada Resources Ltd.	188
Christian Horizons	190
Cineplex Odeon Corporation	191
Citibank Canada	191
CKF Inc.	192
Cobourg District General Hospital	194
Coca Cola Foods Canada Inc.	195
Columbia House	197
Communications & Power Industries Canada	198
Computer Associates Canada Ltd.	201

The Canada Student Employment Guide

Connors Bros, Limited	203		Hudon & Deaudelin Ltée	279
Co-op Atlantic	203		Hudson's Bay Company, The	279
Corner Brook, City of	205		Humber River Regional Hospital	280
Credit Union Central of Canada	208		Husky Energy Inc.	281
Culinar Inc.	209		Hydro Electric Commission of Thunder Bay	281
Custom Trim Ltd.	210		Hydro One Inc.	282
Delta Hotels	215		Hydro Québec	283
Delta Toronto Airport Hotel	216		IBM Canada Ltd.	284
Derlan Industries Limited	216		ICI Canada Inc.	285
Directwest Publishers Ltd.	217		Imprimerie Interweb Inc.	287
Dofasco Inc.	218		Industries Lassonde Inc.	289
Domtar Inc.	218		ING Canada Financial Services International	291
Dura Automotive Systems (Canada) Ltd.	222		Intercon Security Ltd.	292
Dynapro Systems Inc.	223		Interior Savings Credit Union	293
Echo Bay Mines Ltd.	226		Intertape Polymer Group Inc.	294
Economic Development Edmonton	226		IPL Energy Inc.	294
Eli Lilly Canada Inc.	230		Island Savings Credit Union	295
Emco Limited	230		IWK Grace Health Centre	297
EMJ Data Systems Ltd.	231		James Richardson International Limited	300
EnerFlex Systems Ltd.	232		Jim Pattison Group	301
Exfo	235		Johnson Incorporated	303
Export Development Corporation	236		Jostens Canada Ltd.	303
Extendicare (Canada) Inc.	237		Kitchener, City of	309
Federated Co-operatives Limited	239		Kodak Canada Inc.	309
FedEx Express	240		Laidlaw Inc.	312
Finning	240		Lakeside Farm Industries Ltd.	312
Fisher Scientific Limited	241		Leduc, City of	313
Fishery Products International	241		Lego Canada Inc.	314
Foyer Valade Inc.	245		Les Distilleries Corby Ltée	317
Friesens Corporation	246		Les Modes Smart Inc.	318
Future Shop Ltd.	246		Liberty Health	318
Gay Lea Foods Co-Operative Ltd.	247		Litton Systems Canada Ltd.	320
Gendis Inc.	248		Magna International Inc.	327
General Chemical Canada Ltd.	249		Manitoba Agriculture and Food	327
Gienow Building Products Ltd.	251		Manitoba Hydro	328
Giffels Associates Limited	251		Manitoba Public Insurance Corporation	329
Gilbey Canada Inc.	252		Manitoba Telecom Services Inc.	329
Gimbel Eye Centre	252		Maritime Life Assurance Company, The	331
Glaxo Wellcome Canada	253		Marystown Shipyard Limited	334
Goodman and Carr	255		McGraw Hill Ryerson Ltd.	337
Goodwill Industries of Toronto	256		Memotec Communications Inc.	341
Goodyear Canada Inc.	256		Metro Richelieu Inc.	342
Gov't of Newfoundland - Dept. of Finance	257		Metroland Printing, Publishing & Dist. Ltd.	343
Grant Thornton	258		Metropolitan Life Insurance Company	344
Great-West Life Assurance Company, The	259		Michaels of Canada Inc.	345
Groupe Savoie Inc.	260		Midland Walwyn Inc.	345
Halifax County Regional Rehabilitation Centre	263		Midwest Food Products Inc.	346
Halifax Water Commission	264		Mitel Corporation	350
Health Sciences Centre	268		Mitsubishi Electric Sales Canada	351
Hippodrome de Montréal	270		Mobile Computing Corporation	351
Honda Canada Inc.	274		Montreal Trust Co.	353
Horseshoe Resort Corporation	275		MOSAID Technologies Inc.	355
Hôtel Dieu de Montréal	276		Motorola Canada Ltd.	356
Household Movers & Shippers Limited	276		Mountain Equipment Co-op	356

The Canada Student Employment Guide

702 Chartered Accounting Index

Nanaimo Credit Union	359	Rothmans, Benson and Hedges Inc.	437
National Grocers Co. Ltd.	360	Royal & Sun Alliance Insurance Co. of Cda	437
National Life	361	Royal Bank of Canada	438
National Manufacturing of Canada Inc.	361	Saan Stores Ltd.	441
Neptune Food Suppliers Ltd.	363	Sara Lee Corporation of Canada Limited	444
Nesbitt Burns Inc.	364	Saskatchewan Government Insurance	445
Nestle Canada Inc.	364	Saskatchewan Research Council, The	446
New Brunswick Telephone Company	366	Saskatchewan Research Council, The	446
Newfoundland and Labrador Credit Union	367	Saskatchewan Transportation Company	446
Nike Canada Ltd.	371	Saskatoon, City of	448
Norbord Industries	372	Saskferco Products Inc.	448
Norcen Energy Resources Ltd.	373	SaskTel	449
North American Life Assurance Company	373	SC Infrastructure Inc.	449
Northern Lights Regional Health Centre	375	Scarborough General Hospital	450
Northwestel Inc.	376	Schlumberger Canada Ltd.	450
Norwich Union Life Insurance Society	376	Sharp Electronics of Canada Ltd.	454
NPS Allelix Corp.	379	Shaw Communications	455
Nygard International Ltd.	380	Shaw Industries Ltd.	455
Okanagan Skeena Group Limited	382	Sheraton Fallsview Hotel	456
Omstead Foods Limited	383	Shorewood Packaging Corp. of Canada Ltd.	459
Ontario Jockey Club, The	384	Siemens Electric Ltd.	460
Ontario Legislative Offices	384	Signature Vacations Inc.	460
Oracle Corp. Canada Inc.	386	Silicon Graphics Canada Inc.	461
Ottawa Hospital	386	Slocan Forest Products Ltd.	462
Patheon Inc.	390	SNC-Lavalin	463
PavCo	391	Société des Alcools du Québec	464
Pearson Education Canada	393	Sony Music Canada	465
Peel Board of Education	393	Southam Inc.	466
Pelmorex Inc.	395	Sportsco International	469
PennCorp Life Insurance Company	396	Sprint Canada	470
Pharma Plus Drugmarts Ltd.	398	SRI Homes Inc.	470
Pitney Bowes of Canada Ltd.	401	SSQ Life	471
Poco Petroleums Ltd.	402	St. Vincent's Hospitals	473
Polygram Group Canada Inc.	403	Stone Consolidated Inc.	479
Positron Industries Inc.	404	Sudbury Regional Hospital	480
Potacan Mining Company	405	Sunoco Inc.	482
Pratt & Whitney Canada Inc.	407	Surrey Memorial Hospital	483
Pricewaterhouse Coopers	409	Surrey, City of	484
Progressive Financial Strategy	411	Symantec Corporation	486
Providence Centre	412	Talisman Energy Inc.	487
Prudential Insurance Co. of America, The	412	TCT Logistics	488
Public Utilities of Kingston	413	TD Waterhouse Investor Services (Canada)	488
Purolator Courier Ltd.	413	Teck Corp.	489
QIT-Fer et Titane Inc.	414	Teklogix Inc.	489
Québéc Cartier Mining Company	415	Telus Corporation	492
Quebecor Inc.	415	The Barn Fruit Markets Inc.	493
Raymond Rebar Inc.	418	Today's Business Products Ltd.	500
Reader's Digest Association of Canada Ltd.	419	Toronto District School Board	503
Recochem Inc.	420	Toronto East General Hospital	503
Regina Health District	423	Toronto General Hospital	505
Rehabilitation Institute of Toronto	425	Toronto Police Service	506
Richmond, City of	431	Toronto Sun Publishing Corp., The	507
Rio Algom Limited	433	Toronto, City of	508
Rivtow Marine Ltd.	434	Toyota Canada Ltd.	509

The Canada Student Employment Guide

TSC Stores Ltd.	512	Babcock and Wilcox Canada	119
Uni Select Inc.	513	Bakemark Ingredients Ltd.	119
Union Gas Ltd.	513	Banff Centre for Continuing Education, The	120
Vacances Air Transat Inc.	518	Bargain Finder Press Ltd.	121
Vancouver Sun	520	BASF Canada Inc.	122
Volvo Cars of Canada Ltd.	523	Baytex Energy Limited	124
Waverly & York Corporation	525	BBM Bureau of Measurement	125
Westbury Life	529	BC Hydro	125
Westcoast Energy Inc.	530	Bechtel Canada Co.	128
Westshore Terminals Ltd.	534	Beckman Coulter Canada Inc.	129
Weyerhaeuser Company Limited	535	Behlen Industries	130
Whistler Blackcomb Mountain	535	Bell Mobility	131
Wilson Auto Electric Ltd.	538	Belleville General Hospital	132
Windsor, City of	538	Bethania Mennonite Personal Care Home Inc.	134
Winners Apparel Ltd.	539	Bettis Canada Ltd.	135
Winpak Ltd.	539	BFGoodrich Landing Gear Division	135
Wire Rope Industries Ltd.	540	Bio-Research Laboratories Ltd.	137
World of Vacations Ltd.	541	BJ Services Company	138
XCAN Grain Pool Ltd.	541	Blue Giant Equipment of Canada Ltd.	141
Yellowknife, City of	544	Bluewater District School Board	142
Zellers Inc.	546	Bonus Resource Services Corp.	144
		BOVAR Waste Management	145
		Brandon, City of	146

CMA-General

		Brewers Retail Inc.	148
		British Columbia Ferry Corporation	149
Abitibi-Consolidated Inc.	77	Brookfield Properties Corporation	150
Acklands-Grainger Inc.	80	Buckeye Canada Inc.	151
ADI Group Inc.	82	C MAC Industries Inc.	155
ADT Canada Inc.	82	C.S.T. Consultants Inc.	155
AGF Management Limited	83	Cabre Exploration Ltd.	156
Agricultural Credit Corp. of Saskatchewan	84	Cadith Entertainment Ltd.	156
Air Canada	85	Calgary Co-operative Association Limited	157
Air Ontario Inc.	86	Calgary, City of	158
Alberta Blue Cross	88	Cambior Inc.	158
Alberta Energy & Utilities Board	89	Cameco Corporation	160
Alcan Aluminium Limited	91	Canada Post Corporation	162
Algoma Steel Inc.	93	Canada Starch Company Inc.	163
Allcolour Paint Limited	94	Canadian Cancer Society	164
Allianz Canada	95	Canadian Dairy Commission	165
Allmar Distributors Ltd.	95	Canadian Depository for Securities Ltd.	166
Allstate Insurance Co. of Canada	96	Canadian National Institute For The Blind	167
Alpine Oil Service Corporation	96	Canadian Occidental Petroleum Ltd.	168
Amcan Castings Limited	98	Canadian Tire Corporation Ltd.	169
Amcor Twinpak North America Inc.	98	Canadian Western Bank	169
Apex Land Corp.	103	Canbra Foods Ltd.	170
Arbor Memorial Services Inc.	106	Cancarb Limited	170
Armor Personnel	107	Cancore Industries Inc.	171
Assiniboine Community College	109	Canon Canada Inc.	172
Assumption Mutual Life Insurance	109	Cape Breton Development Corporation	174
ATCO Electric	111	Cargill Limited	175
ATCO Gas Services Ltd.	112	Centra Gas Manitoba Inc.	181
Atlantic Wholesalers Ltd.	114	Central Park Lodges Ltd.	181
Aurum Ceramic Dental Laboratories Ltd.	117	CFCF Inc.	183
AXA Insurance (Canada)	118	CFCN Communications Inc.	184

704 Chartered Accounting Index

CGI	184	Gimbel Eye Centre	252
Christian Horizons	190	Glaxo Wellcome Canada	253
Cineplex Odeon Corporation	191	Glentel Inc.	254
Citibank Canada	191	Goodman and Carr	255
CKF Inc.	192	Goodwill Industries of Toronto	256
Coca Cola Foods Canada Inc.	195	Goodyear Canada Inc.	256
Cognis Canada Corporation	195	Gov't of Newfoundland - Dept. of Finance	257
Columbia House	197	Grand & Toy Ltd.	257
COM DEV International	197	Grant MacEwen Community College	258
Comcare Health Services	198	Great-West Life Assurance Company, The	259
Compaq Canada Inc.	199	Grouse Mountain Resorts Ltd.	260
Computer Associates Canada Ltd.	201	Halifax County Regional Rehabilitation Centre	263
Connors Bros, Limited	203	Halifax Water Commission	264
Co-op Atlantic	203	Health Care Corporation of St. John's	267
Cosmair Canada Inc.	206	Hippodrome de Montréal	270
Cosyn Technology	207	Hoffman-La Roche Limited	272
Credit Union Central of Canada	208	Honda Canada Inc.	274
Crestar Energy Inc.	209	Honeywell Ltd.	275
Culinar Inc.	209	Horseshoe Resort Corporation	275
Custom Trim Ltd.	210	Household Movers & Shippers Limited	276
D.A. Stuart Inc.	210	HSBC Bank Canada	277
Dell Computer Corporation	214	Hubbell Canada Inc.	278
Delta Hotels	215	Hudon & Deaudelin Ltée	279
Delta Toronto Airport Hotel	216	Hudson's Bay Company, The	279
Derlan Industries Limited	216	Humber River Regional Hospital	280
Directwest Publishers Ltd.	217	Hydro Electric Commission of Thunder Bay	281
Dofasco Inc.	218	Hydro Québec	283
Domtar Inc.	218	IBM Canada Ltd.	284
Ducks Unlimited Canada	220	Imperial Oil Limited	286
Duha Color Services	220	INCO Limited	287
DuPont Canada Inc.	221	Indalex Limited	288
Dylex Limited	222	Industrial-Alliance Life Insurance Company	289
Dynapro Systems Inc.	223	Industries Lassonde Inc.	289
Dynatek Automation Systems Inc.	224	ING Canada Financial Services International	291
Emco Limited	230	Intercon Security Ltd.	292
EMJ Data Systems Ltd.	231	Interior Savings Credit Union	293
Entreprises Premier Canadien Ltée	232	IPL Energy Inc.	294
Exfo	235	Island Savings Credit Union	295
Export Development Corporation	236	IWK Grace Health Centre	297
Extendicare (Canada) Inc.	237	J.D. Irving Limited	298
Family Day Care Service	238	James Richardson International Limited	300
Farm Credit Corp. Canada	238	Jim Pattison Group	301
Farmers Co-operative Dairy Limited	239	Jostens Canada Ltd.	303
Federated Co-operatives Limited	239	Kawneer Company Canada Limited	304
Finning	240	Kelowna, City of	305
Fisher Scientific Limited	241	Kennametal Ltd.	305
Fishery Products International	241	Keyano College	306
Flint Energy Services Ltd.	243	KFC Canada	307
Future Shop Ltd.	246	Kitchener, City of	309
Gay Lea Foods Co-Operative Ltd.	247	Laidlaw Inc.	312
Gendis Inc.	248	Lakeside Farm Industries Ltd.	312
General Chemical Canada Ltd.	249	Leduc, City of	313
Gienow Building Products Ltd.	251	Lego Canada Inc.	314
Gilbey Canada Inc.	252	Lenbrook Industries Limited	315

The Canada Student Employment Guide

Chartered Accounting Index 705

Les Centres Jeunesse de Montréal	316	Patheon Inc.	390
Liberty Health	318	PavCo	391
Litton Systems Canada Ltd.	320	PCL Constructors Inc.	392
Loewen Windows	321	Peacock Inc.	392
London Goodwill Industries Association	322	Pearson Education Canada	393
Lovat Inc.	323	Peel Board of Education	393
M M Industra Ltd.	323	Petro-Canada	397
MAAX Inc.	324	Pharma Plus Drugmarts Ltd.	398
Manitoba Agriculture and Food	327	Pitney Bowes of Canada Ltd.	401
Manitoba Hydro	328	Poco Petroleums Ltd.	402
Manitoba Pool Elevators	328	PPG Canada Inc.	407
Manitoba Public Insurance Corporation	329	Premdor Inc.	408
Marine Atlantic Inc.	331	PRI Automation	408
Maritime Life Assurance Company, The	331	Pricewaterhouse Coopers	409
McKay-Cocker Construction Limited	338	Prince George, City of	410
Metro Richelieu Inc.	342	Progressive Financial Strategy	411
Metropolitan Life Insurance Company	344	Prudential Insurance Co. of America, The	412
Michaels of Canada Inc.	345	Public Utilities of Kingston	413
Midwest Food Products Inc.	346	Purolator Courier Ltd.	413
Mitsubishi Electric Sales Canada	351	Québéc Cartier Mining Company	415
Mobile Computing Corporation	351	Quesnel River Pulp Company	416
Moen Inc.	352	Rasco Specialty Metals Inc.	417
Moffat Communications Limited	352	Raymond Industrial Equipment Ltd.	418
Moosehead Breweries Limited	354	Raymond Rebar Inc.	418
MOSAID Technologies Inc.	355	Reader's Digest Association of Canada Ltd.	419
Motorola Canada Ltd.	356	Recochem Inc.	420
Mustang Survival Corp.	358	Red Deer Co-op Limited	421
National Grocers Co. Ltd.	360	Regal Constellation Hotel Ltd.	422
National Life	361	Reid Crowther	426
Nesbitt Burns Inc.	364	Reliable Engine Services Ltd.	426
Nestle Canada Inc.	364	Rimrock Resort Hotel	432
New Brunswick Power Corporation	365	Riverside Hospital of Ottawa, The	434
New Brunswick Telephone Company	366	Rivtow Marine Ltd.	434
Newfoundland and Labrador Credit Union	367	Roctest Ltée	435
News Marketing Canada	368	Rothmans, Benson and Hedges Inc.	437
Nike Canada Ltd.	371	Royal & Sun Alliance Insurance Co. of Cda	437
Nissan Canada Inc.	371	Royal Bank of Canada	438
Norbord Industries	372	Ryerson Polytechnic University	441
Norcen Energy Resources Ltd.	373	Saan Stores Ltd.	441
North American Life Assurance Company	373	Salisbury House of Canada Ltd.	442
North West Company Inc.	374	Saskatchewan Government Insurance	445
Northern Mountain Helicopters Inc.	375	Saskatchewan Wheat Pool	447
Northwestel Inc.	376	Saskatoon, City of	448
Norwich Union Life Insurance Society	376	Saskferco Products Inc.	448
Nova Scotia Liquor Commission	377	SaskTel	449
Nova Scotia Power Corp.	377	Scarborough General Hospital	450
Novotel Canada Inc.	378	Schlumberger Canada Ltd.	450
NPS Allelix Corp.	379	Scholastic Canada Ltd.	451
Ocelot Energy Inc.	381	Seprotech Systems Incorporated	454
Oetiker Limited	381	Sharp Electronics of Canada Ltd.	454
Ontario Legislative Offices	384	Shaw Communications	455
Oracle Corp. Canada Inc.	386	Shaw Industries Ltd.	455
Ottawa Hospital	386	Sheraton Fallsview Hotel	456
Parkland Industries Ltd.	390	Sherwood Credit Union	458

The Canada Student Employment Guide

706 Chartered Accounting Index

Shopping Channel, The	459
Shorewood Packaging Corp. of Canada Ltd.	459
Siemens Electric Ltd.	460
Signature Vacations Inc.	460
Sobeys Inc.	463
Société des Alcools du Québec	464
Sony Music Canada	465
Southam Inc.	466
Spar Aerospace Limited	467
Speedware Corp. Inc.	469
Sportsco International	469
Sprint Canada	470
SRI Homes Inc.	470
St. Lawrence Seaway Mgmt. Corp., The	473
St. Vincent's Hospitals	473
State Farm Insurance Companies	476
Steelpipe Ltd.	477
Stone Consolidated Inc.	479
Sun Rype Products Ltd.	481
Supreme Tooling Group	483
Surrey Place Centre	484
Surrey, City of	484
Syncrude Canada Ltd.	486
Talisman Energy Inc.	487
TCT Logistics	488
TD Waterhouse Investor Services (Canada)	488
The Barn Fruit Markets Inc.	493
The Co-operators	493
Thomas J. Lipton	496
Timmins, City of	499
Today's Business Products Ltd.	500
Toronto General Hospital	505
Toronto Police Service	506
Toronto Sun Publishing Corp., The	507
Toronto, City of	508
Toshiba of Canada Ltd.	508
Toyota Canada Ltd.	509
TSC Stores Ltd.	512
Turnbull & Turnbull Ltd.	512
Uni Select Inc.	513
Union Gas Ltd.	513
US Filter BCP	517
USF WaterGroup	517
Vacances Air Transat Inc.	518
Vancouver International Airport	520
Volkswagen Canada Inc.	523
Volvo Cars of Canada Ltd.	523
Wegu Canada Inc.	526
Weldco-Beales Manufacturing Inc.	527
Westbury Life	529
Westcliff Management Ltd.	529
Westcoast Energy Inc.	530
Western Glove Works	530
Westinghouse Canada Inc.	532
WestJet Airlines	532
Westminster Savings Credit Union	533
Westport Innovations Inc.	534
Westshore Terminals Ltd.	534
Weyerhaeuser Company Limited	535
Whistler Blackcomb Mountain	535
Wilson Auto Electric Ltd.	538
Windsor, City of	538
Winners Apparel Ltd.	539
Winpak Ltd.	539
Wire Rope Industries Ltd.	540
XCAN Grain Pool Ltd.	541
Yamaha Motor Canada Ltd.	542
Yellowknife, City of	544
YTV Canada Inc.	545
Zellers Inc.	546
Zenon Environmental Inc.	547

CMA-Finance

A C A Cooperative Limited	74
A.G. Simpson Co. Ltd.	75
ABC Group	76
Abitibi-Consolidated Inc.	77
ADI Group Inc.	82
Agricultural Credit Corp. of Saskatchewan	84
Air Liquide Canada Inc.	85
Air Nova Inc.	86
Air Ontario Inc.	86
Alberta Gaming & Liquor Commission	90
Alberto Culver Canada Inc.	90
Alcan Aluminium Limited	91
Algoma District Home For The Aged	92
Allcolour Paint Limited	94
Allianz Canada	95
Allstate Insurance Co. of Canada	96
Amcan Castings Limited	98
Amcor Twinpak North America Inc.	98
Anthony Insurance Inc.	102
Apex Land Corp.	103
ATCO Electric	111
ATCO Frontec Corp.	111
Atlantic Wholesalers Ltd.	114
Aventis Pasteur Limited	117
Babcock and Wilcox Canada	119
Banff Centre for Continuing Education, The	120
BASF Canada Inc.	122
Baycrest Centre for Geriatric Care	123
Bayer Inc.	124
Baytex Energy Limited	124
BBM Bureau of Measurement	125
BC Hydro	125
Bechtel Canada Co.	128

The Canada Student Employment Guide

Chartered Accounting Index 707

Bell Mobility	131	Credit Union Central of Canada	208
BFGoodrich Landing Gear Division	135	Custom Trim Ltd.	210
Bic Inc.	136	Delphi Solutions Inc.	215
Biovail Corporation International	137	Delta Hotels	215
Black Photo Corporation	139	Delta Toronto Airport Hotel	216
Bloorview Childrens Hospital	140	Derlan Industries Limited	216
BNP PARIBAS (Canada)	143	Directwest Publishers Ltd.	217
Bowater Mersey Paper Company Limited	146	Dofasco Inc.	218
Brewers Retail Inc.	148	Domtar Inc.	218
British Columbia Ferry Corporation	149	Dun & Bradstreet Canada	221
Brookfield Properties Corporation	150	DuPont Canada Inc.	221
C MAC Industries Inc.	155	Dura Automotive Systems (Canada) Ltd.	222
C.S.T. Consultants Inc.	155	Dynapro Systems Inc.	223
Cabre Exploration Ltd.	156	Economic Development Edmonton	226
Cadith Entertainment Ltd.	156	EDS of Canada Ltd.	228
Calgary Co-operative Association Limited	157	Emco Limited	230
Calgary, City of	158	EMJ Data Systems Ltd.	231
Cambridge Memorial Hospital	159	EnerFlex Systems Ltd.	232
Canada Post Corporation	162	Exfo	235
Canada Starch Company Inc.	163	Exide Canada Inc.	235
Canadian Cancer Society	164	Export Development Corporation	236
Canadian Dairy Commission	165	Extendicare (Canada) Inc.	237
Canadian Depository for Securities Ltd.	166	Federated Co-operatives Limited	239
Canadian General Tower Limited	166	FedEx Express	240
Canadian Occidental Petroleum Ltd.	168	Finning	240
Canadian Tire Corporation Ltd.	169	Fisher Scientific Limited	241
Canadian Western Bank	169	Fishery Products International	241
Cancarb Limited	170	Flakeboard Company Limited	242
CancerCare Manitoba	171	Flint Energy Services Ltd.	243
Cangene Corporation	172	Foremost Industries Inc.	244
Canpar Transport Ltd.	173	Friesens Corporation	246
Cargill Limited	175	Future Shop Ltd.	246
CCL Industries Inc.	178	Gay Lea Foods Co-Operative Ltd.	247
Centra Gas British Columbia Inc.	180	Gendis Inc.	248
Centra Gas Manitoba Inc.	181	General Chemical Canada Ltd.	249
Central Park Lodges Ltd.	181	General Mills Canada Inc.	250
Ceridian Canada	183	Gienow Building Products Ltd.	251
CFCN Communications Inc.	184	Giffels Associates Limited	251
Christian Horizons	190	Gimbel Eye Centre	252
Cineplex Odeon Corporation	191	Glaxo Wellcome Canada	253
Citibank Canada	191	Goodman and Carr	255
CKF Inc.	192	Goodyear Canada Inc.	256
Cobourg District General Hospital	194	Great-West Life Assurance Company, The	259
Coca Cola Foods Canada Inc.	195	Halifax County Regional Rehabilitation Centre	263
Cognis Canada Corporation	195	Halifax Regional Municipality	263
Columbia House	197	Halifax Water Commission	264
Comcare Health Services	198	Harry Rosen Inc.	265
Communications & Power Industries Canada	198	Hermes Electronics Inc.	269
Compaq Canada Inc.	199	Hoffman-La Roche Limited	272
Computalog Ltd.	200	Home Oil Co. Ltd.	273
Computer Associates Canada Ltd.	201	Horseshoe Resort Corporation	275
Connors Bros, Limited	203	Household Movers & Shippers Limited	276
Co-op Atlantic	203	HSBC Bank Canada	277
Cornwall Electric	206	Hudon & Deaudelin Ltée	279

The Canada Student Employment Guide

708 Chartered Accounting Index

Humber River Regional Hospital	280
Hydro Electric Commission of Thunder Bay	281
Hydro Mississauga Corporation	282
Hydro Québec	283
I M P Group International Inc.	283
IBM Canada Ltd.	284
Industries Lassonde Inc.	289
ING Canada Financial Services International	291
Interior Savings Credit Union	293
InterOne Marketing Group	293
IPL Energy Inc.	294
Island Savings Credit Union	295
Ivaco Inc.	296
IWK Grace Health Centre	297
J.D. Irving Limited	298
James Richardson International Limited	300
Jim Pattison Group	301
Jostens Canada Ltd.	303
Kelowna, City of	305
Keyano College	306
Kitchener, City of	309
Kraft Canada Inc.	310
Laidlaw Inc.	312
Lakeside Farm Industries Ltd.	312
Leduc, City of	313
Lego Canada Inc.	314
Les Distilleries Corby Ltée	317
Les Forges de Sorel Inc.	317
Les Modes Smart Inc.	318
Liberty Health	318
Litton Systems Canada Ltd.	320
Loewen Windows	321
London Goodwill Industries Association	322
Mactac Canada Ltd.	326
Magna International Inc.	327
Manitoba Agriculture and Food	327
Manitoba Hydro	328
Manitoba Public Insurance Corporation	329
Maritime Life Assurance Company, The	331
Mediacom Inc.	340
Metro Richelieu Inc.	342
Metroland Printing, Publishing & Dist. Ltd.	343
Metropolitan Life Insurance Company	344
Michaels of Canada Inc.	345
Midland Walwyn Inc.	345
Mitsubishi Electric Sales Canada	351
Mobile Computing Corporation	351
Moen Inc.	352
Moosehead Breweries Limited	354
Nanaimo Credit Union	359
National Grocers Co. Ltd.	360
National Life	361
National Manufacturing of Canada Inc.	361
Nesbitt Burns Inc.	364
New Brunswick Telephone Company	366
Newfoundland and Labrador Credit Union	367
Nike Canada Ltd.	371
Norbord Industries	372
Norcen Energy Resources Ltd.	373
North American Life Assurance Company	373
North West Company Inc.	374
Northern Lights Regional Health Centre	375
Northwestel Inc.	376
Norwich Union Life Insurance Society	376
Nova Scotia Power Corp.	377
Novartis Consumer Health Canada Inc.	378
NPS Allelix Corp.	379
Nygard International Ltd.	380
Oland Breweries Limited	382
Omstead Foods Limited	383
Ontario Legislative Offices	384
Ottawa Hospital	386
Patheon Inc.	390
Peel Board of Education	393
Peel Regional Police	394
Pelmorex Inc.	395
Pharma Plus Drugmarts Ltd.	398
Pitney Bowes of Canada Ltd.	401
Poco Petroleums Ltd.	402
Pratt & Whitney Canada Inc.	407
PRI Automation	408
Pricewaterhouse Coopers	409
Prince Albert, City of	410
Prince George, City of	410
Progressive Financial Strategy	411
Prudential Insurance Co. of America, The	412
Public Utilities of Kingston	413
Purolator Courier Ltd.	413
QIT-Fer et Titane Inc.	414
Raymond Rebar Inc.	418
Reader's Digest Association of Canada Ltd.	419
Recochem Inc.	420
Regal Constellation Hotel Ltd.	422
Revenue Properties Company Limited	429
Rio Algom Limited	433
Riverside Hospital of Ottawa, The	434
Rivtow Marine Ltd.	434
Rogers Media, Publishing	436
Rothmans, Benson and Hedges Inc.	437
Royal & Sun Alliance Insurance Co. of Cda	437
Royal Bank of Canada	438
Royal Philips Electronics	439
Saskatchewan Government Insurance	445
Saskatchewan Research Council, The	446
Saskatchewan Transportation Company	446
Saskatchewan Wheat Pool	447
Saskatoon, City of	448
Saskferco Products Inc.	448

The Canada Student Employment Guide

Chartered Accounting Index   709

SaskTel	449	Vancouver Sun	520
Scarborough General Hospital	450	Volvo Cars of Canada Ltd.	523
Schlumberger Canada Ltd.	450	W C I Canada Inc.	524
Sharp Electronics of Canada Ltd.	454	Weldco-Beales Manufacturing Inc.	527
Shaw Communications	455	West Kootenay Power Ltd.	528
Shaw Industries Ltd.	455	Westcoast Energy Inc.	530
Sheraton Fallsview Hotel	456	Westinghouse Canada Inc.	532
Sherwood Credit Union	458	Westminster Savings Credit Union	533
Shorewood Packaging Corp. of Canada Ltd.	459	Westshore Terminals Ltd.	534
Signature Vacations Inc.	460	Weyerhaeuser Company Limited	535
Slocan Forest Products Ltd.	462	Whistler Blackcomb Mountain	535
Société des Alcools du Québec	464	Windsor, City of	538
Sony Music Canada	465	Winners Apparel Ltd.	539
Southam Inc.	466	Winpak Ltd.	539
Southern Railway of British Columbia Ltd.	466	Wire Rope Industries Ltd.	540
Spar Aerospace Limited	467	XCAN Grain Pool Ltd.	541
Speedware Corp. Inc.	469	Yellowknife, City of	544
Sportsco International	469	Zellers Inc.	546
Sprint Canada	470		
SRI Homes Inc.	470		
St. Vincent's Hospitals	473		

CGA-General

Stanley Canada Inc.	475		
Star Data Systems Inc.	476	Abitibi-Consolidated Inc.	77
State Farm Insurance Companies	476	Acklands-Grainger Inc.	80
Stone Consolidated Inc.	479	ADT Canada Inc.	82
Sudbury Regional Hospital	480	Advanta Seeds	83
Sun Rype Products Ltd.	481	AGF Management Limited	83
Sunoco Inc.	482	Alberta Blue Cross	88
Surrey, City of	484	Alberta Energy & Utilities Board	89
Talisman Energy Inc.	487	Algoma Steel Inc.	93
TCG International Inc.	487	Allcolour Paint Limited	94
TCT Logistics	488	Allmar Distributors Ltd.	95
TD Waterhouse Investor Services (Canada)	488	Alpine Oil Service Corporation	96
Teck Corp.	489	Anthony Insurance Inc.	102
Teklogix Inc.	489	Arbor Memorial Services Inc.	106
Telus Corporation	492	Arctic Co-operatives Limited	107
The Barn Fruit Markets Inc.	493	Armor Personnel	107
Thomas & Betts Ltée	495	Assiniboine Community College	109
Thomas J. Lipton	496	Assumption Mutual Life Insurance	109
Timmins, City of	499	ATCO Electric	111
Today's Business Products Ltd.	500	ATCO Gas Services Ltd.	112
Toronto Catholic District School Board	502	Atlantic Packaging Products Ltd.	114
Toronto General Hospital	505	Aurum Ceramic Dental Laboratories Ltd.	117
Toronto Police Service	506	AXA Insurance (Canada)	118
Toronto Sun Publishing Corp., The	507	Babcock and Wilcox Canada	119
Toronto, City of	508	Bakemark Ingredients Ltd.	119
Toshiba of Canada Ltd.	508	Barton Place Long Term Care Facility	121
Toyota Canada Ltd.	509	BASF Canada Inc.	122
TSC Stores Ltd.	512	Basic Technologies Corporation	122
Turnbull & Turnbull Ltd.	512	Baycrest Centre for Geriatric Care	123
Uni Select Inc.	513	Beckman Coulter Canada Inc.	129
Union Gas Ltd.	513	Behlen Industries	130
Vacances Air Transat Inc.	518	Belleville General Hospital	132
Vancouver International Airport	520	Bethania Mennonite Personal Care Home Inc.	134

The Canada Student Employment Guide

710 Chartered Accounting Index

Bettis Canada Ltd.	135	Humber River Regional Hospital	280
Blaney McMurty LLP	139	INCO Limited	287
Bluewater District School Board	142	Indalex Limited	288
Bonus Resource Services Corp.	144	Industrial-Alliance Life Insurance Company	289
BOVAR Waste Management	145	IWK Grace Health Centre	297
Brandon, City of	146	J.D. Irving Limited	298
Buckeye Canada Inc.	151	Johnson Incorporated	303
Cambior Inc.	158	Kelowna Home Support	304
Cameco Corporation	160	Kennedy Lodge Nursing Home Inc.	306
Canadian Dairy Commission	165	Keyano College	306
Canadian National Institute For The Blind	167	KFC Canada	307
Canadian Occidental Petroleum Ltd.	168	Kvaerner Metals	311
Canadian Thermos Products Inc.	168	Lenbrook Industries Limited	315
Canbra Foods Ltd.	170	Lifetouch Canada Inc.	319
Cancarb Limited	170	Lovat Inc.	323
Cape Breton Development Corporation	174	M M Industra Ltd.	323
Central Park Lodges Ltd.	181	MAAX Inc.	324
CFCF Inc.	183	MacDonald Steel Ltd.	325
CGU Group Canada Ltd.	185	Manitoba Pool Elevators	328
Chilliwack General Hospital	189	Metro Toronto Convention Centre	342
Cognis Canada Corporation	195	Moen Inc.	352
COM DEV International	197	Moffat Communications Limited	352
Compaq Canada Inc.	199	MOSAID Technologies Inc.	355
Computer Associates Canada Ltd.	201	Mustang Survival Corp.	358
Connors Bros, Limited	203	National Sports Centre	362
Cosmair Canada Inc.	206	Nestle Canada Inc.	364
Cosyn Technology	207	New Brunswick Power Corporation	365
Cotton Ginny Ltd.	207	News Marketing Canada	368
Culinar Inc.	209	Nissan Canada Inc.	371
D.A. Stuart Inc.	210	North West Company Inc.	374
Dofasco Inc.	218	Northern Mountain Helicopters Inc.	375
Domtar Inc.	218	Northwestel Inc.	376
Ducks Unlimited Canada	220	Novotel Canada Inc.	378
Duha Color Services	220	Ocelot Energy Inc.	381
Dylex Limited	222	Ontario March of Dimes	385
Dynacare Laboratories	223	Oracle Corp. Canada Inc.	386
Economical Insurance Group, The	227	Parkland Industries Ltd.	390
Exfo	235	Patheon Inc.	390
Export Development Corporation	236	PavCo	391
Farm Credit Corp. Canada	238	PCL Constructors Inc.	392
Finning	240	PennCorp Life Insurance Company	396
Fishery Products International	241	Petro-Canada	397
Foyer Valade Inc.	245	Pizza Pizza Ltd.	401
Giffels Associates Limited	251	Polygram Group Canada Inc.	403
Gilbey Canada Inc.	252	PPG Canada Inc.	407
Grant MacEwen Community College	258	Premdor Inc.	408
Groupe Savoie Inc.	260	PRI Automation	408
Grouse Mountain Resorts Ltd.	260	Prince Albert Credit Union	409
Harry Rosen Inc.	265	Progressive Financial Strategy	411
Health Care Corporation of St. John's	267	Quebecor Inc.	415
Honeywell Ltd.	275	Quesnel River Pulp Company	416
HSBC Bank Canada	277	Rasco Specialty Metals Inc.	417
Hubbell Canada Inc.	278	Raymond Industrial Equipment Ltd.	418
Hudson's Bay Company, The	279	Raymond Rebar Inc.	418

The Canada Student Employment Guide

Chartered Accounting Index   711

Reader's Digest Association of Canada Ltd.	419	Advanta Seeds	83
Red Deer Co-op Limited	421	Aimtronics	84
Regal Greeting and Gifts	423	Air Canada	85
Rehabilitation Institute of Toronto	425	Air Liquide Canada Inc.	85
Reid Crowther	426	Alberta Gaming & Liquor Commission	90
Richmond, City of	431	Alberto Culver Canada Inc.	90
Rimrock Resort Hotel	432	Allcolour Paint Limited	94
Riverside Hospital of Ottawa, The	434	Anthony Insurance Inc.	102
Roctest Ltée	435	Arctic Co-operatives Limited	107
Ryerson Polytechnic University	441	ATCO Electric	111
Saan Stores Ltd.	441	ATCO Frontec Corp.	111
Salisbury House of Canada Ltd.	442	Aventis Pasteur Limited	117
Sandman Hotels and Inns	443	Babcock and Wilcox Canada	119
Scholastic Canada Ltd.	451	Bakemark Ingredients Ltd.	119
Seprotech Systems Incorporated	454	BASF Canada Inc.	122
Sobeys Inc.	463	Bayer Inc.	124
Spar Aerospace Limited	467	Bic Inc.	136
SRI Homes Inc.	470	Biovail Corporation International	137
SSQ Life	471	Black Photo Corporation	139
St. Lawrence Seaway Mgmt. Corp., The	473	Bloorview Childrens Hospital	140
Steelpipe Ltd.	477	BNP PARIBAS (Canada)	143
Sterling Marking Products Inc.	478	Cambridge Memorial Hospital	159
Sundog Printing Limited	482	Canadian Dairy Commission	165
Supreme Tooling Group	483	Canadian General Tower Limited	166
The Co-operators	493	Canadian Occidental Petroleum Ltd.	168
Thomas & Betts Ltée	495	Canadian Thermos Products Inc.	168
Thomas J. Lipton	496	Cancarb Limited	170
Tiger Brand Knitting Company Limited	498	CancerCare Manitoba	171
Trojan Technologies Inc.	511	Cangene Corporation	172
Turnbull & Turnbull Ltd.	512	Canpar Transport Ltd.	173
Uni Select Inc.	513	CCL Industries Inc.	178
Vacances Air Transat Inc.	518	Centra Gas British Columbia Inc.	180
Vancouver International Airport	520	Central Park Lodges Ltd.	181
Versa Services Ltd.	521	Ceridian Canada	183
Volkswagen Canada Inc.	523	CGU Group Canada Ltd.	185
Westbury Life	529	Cobourg District General Hospital	194
Westcliff Management Ltd.	529	Cognis Canada Corporation	195
Western Glove Works	530	Community Savings Credit Union	199
Westinghouse Canada Inc.	532	Compaq Canada Inc.	199
WestJet Airlines	532	Computalog Ltd.	200
Westport Innovations Inc.	534	Computer Associates Canada Ltd.	201
Whitehill Technologies Inc.	537	Connors Bros, Limited	203
Wire Rope Industries Ltd.	540	Delphi Solutions Inc.	215
YTV Canada Inc.	545	Dofasco Inc.	218
Zenon Environmental Inc.	547	Domtar Inc.	218
		Dun & Bradstreet Canada	221
		Dura Automotive Systems (Canada) Ltd.	222
CGA-Finance		Dynacare Laboratories	223
		Economical Insurance Group, The	227
A C A Cooperative Limited	74	EDS of Canada Ltd.	228
A E McKenzie Co. Inc.	75	EnerFlex Systems Ltd.	232
A.G. Simpson Co. Ltd.	75	Exfo	235
ABC Group	76	Export Development Corporation	236
Abitibi-Consolidated Inc.	77	Finning	240

The Canada Student Employment Guide

712 Chartered Accounting Index

Fishery Products International	241	Progressive Financial Strategy	411
Foremost Industries Inc.	244	QIT-Fer et Titane Inc.	414
Foyer Valade Inc.	245	Raymond Rebar Inc.	418
Friesens Corporation	246	Reader's Digest Association of Canada Ltd.	419
General Mills Canada Inc.	250	Rehabilitation Institute of Toronto	425
Gisborne Design Services Ltd.	253	Richmond, City of	431
Gov't of Newfoundland – Dept. of Finance	257	Rio Algom Limited	433
Grand & Toy Ltd.	257	Riverside Hospital of Ottawa, The	434
Groupe Savoie Inc.	260	Rogers Media, Publishing	436
Halifax Regional Municipality	263	Royal Philips Electronics	439
Helijet Airways Inc.	268	Saskatchewan Research Council, The	446
Hermes Electronics Inc.	269	Slocan Forest Products Ltd.	462
Honda Canada Inc.	274	SNC-Lavalin	463
Hôtel Dieu de Montréal	276	Southern Railway of British Columbia Ltd.	466
HSBC Bank Canada	277	Spar Aerospace Limited	467
Humber River Regional Hospital	280	SRI Homes Inc.	470
Hydro Mississauga Corporation	282	SSQ Life	471
I M P Group International Inc.	283	St. Lawrence Parks Commission	472
Industrial Equipment Co. Ltd.	288	Stanley Canada Inc.	475
InterOne Marketing Group	293	Star Data Systems Inc.	476
Ivaco Inc.	296	Sundog Printing Limited	482
IWK Grace Health Centre	297	Sunoco Inc.	482
J.D. Irving Limited	298	TCG International Inc.	487
Keyano College	306	Teck Corp.	489
Kraft Canada Inc.	310	Teklogix Inc.	489
Les Distilleries Corby Ltée	317	Telus Corporation	492
Les Modes Smart Inc.	318	Thomas J. Lipton	496
Mactac Canada Ltd.	326	Thomson - CSF Systems Canada Inc.	497
Magna International Inc.	327	Thunder Bay Regional Hospital	497
McGraw Hill Ryerson Ltd.	337	Turnbull & Turnbull Ltd.	512
Mediacom Inc.	340	Uni Select Inc.	513
Metroland Printing, Publishing & Dist. Ltd.	343	Vancouver International Airport	520
Midland Walwyn Inc.	345	Vancouver Sun	520
Moen Inc.	352	Wegu Canada Inc.	526
N B S Card Services	359	West Kootenay Power Ltd.	528
Nanaimo Credit Union	359	Westbury Life	529
Neptune Food Suppliers Ltd.	363	Westin Prince Hotel, The	531
Newness Machine Ltd.	368	Westinghouse Canada Inc.	532
North West Company Inc.	374	Wire Rope Industries Ltd.	540
Northern Lights Regional Health Centre	375		
Northwestel Inc.	376		
Novartis Consumer Health Canada Inc.	378		
Nygard International Ltd.	380		
Oland Breweries Limited	382		
Omstead Foods Limited	383		
Ontario March of Dimes	385		
Patheon Inc.	390		
Peacock Inc.	392		
Pearson Education Canada	393		
Pelmorex Inc.	395		
Pizza Pizza Ltd.	401		
Pratt & Whitney Canada Inc.	407		
PRI Automation	408		
Prince Albert Credit Union	409		

The Canada Student Employment Guide

Part Time/Summer Index

The following employers have indicated they occasionally or regularly hire candidates for part time and summer employment. Firms that potentially hire part time employees have been listed first, and companies that potentially hire employees for the summer have been listed second. The corresponding page number of the firm's profile is also shown.

Part Time

1-800-GOT-JUNK?	74
A C A Cooperative Limited	74
A.G. Simpson Co. Ltd.	75
Aar-Kel Moulds Ltd.	76
Abitibi-Consolidated Inc.	77
Acadia University	78
Access Communications	78
Acier Leroux Inc.	80
Acklands-Grainger Inc.	80
Addictions Foundation of Manitoba, The	81
ADI Group Inc.	82
ADT Canada Inc.	82
Advanta Seeds	83
AGF Management Limited	83
Agricultural Credit Corp. of Saskatchewan	84
Air Canada	85
Air Liquide Canada Inc.	85
Air Nova Inc.	86
Air Ontario Inc.	86
Akita Drilling Ltd.	87
Alberta Alcohol and Drug Abuse Commission	87
Alberta Blue Cross	88
Alberta Cancer Board	88
Alberta Gaming & Liquor Commission	90
Alcan Aluminium Limited	91
Algoma Child & Youth Services Inc.	92
Algoma District Home For The Aged	92
Algoma Steel Inc.	93
Aliant Telecom Inc.	93
Allcolour Paint Limited	94
Allianz Canada	95
Allmar Distributors Ltd.	95
Allstate Insurance Co. of Canada	96
Alpine Oil Service Corporation	96
Altona Community Memorial Health Centre	97
Amcan Castings Limited	98
Amcor Twinpak North America Inc.	98
AMEC Inc.	99
American Airlines Inc.	99
Ancast Industries Ltd.	100
Anjura Services Inc.	101
Antamex International Inc.	102
Anthony Insurance Inc.	102
Aon Reed Stenhouse Inc.	103
Apotex Fermentation Inc.	104
Apple Canada Inc.	104
Aqua-Power Cleaners Ltd.	105
Aquatic Sciences Inc.	105
Arbor Memorial Services Inc.	106
Arctic Co-operatives Limited	107
Armor Personnel	107
Assiniboine Community College	109
Assumption Mutual Life Insurance	109
Assure Health Inc.	110
AstraZeneca	110
ATCO Electric	111
ATCO Frontec Corp.	111
ATCO Gas Services Ltd.	112
Athabasca, Town of	112
Atlantic Blue Cross Care	113
Atlantic Lottery Corporation Inc.	113
Atlantic Wholesalers Ltd.	114
Atlas Ideal Metals Inc.	115
Atlas Van Lines (Canada) Ltd.	115
Aurizon Mines Ltd.	116
Aurum Ceramic Dental Laboratories Ltd.	117
Aventis Pasteur Limited	117
Axidata Inc.	118
Babcock and Wilcox Canada	119
Ballard Power Systems Inc.	120
Banff Centre for Continuing Education, The	120
Bargain Finder Press Ltd.	121

The Canada Student Employment Guide

Part Time/Summer Index

Barton Place Long Term Care Facility	121
BASF Canada Inc.	122
Basic Technologies Corporation	122
Battlefords Health District	123
Baycrest Centre for Geriatric Care	123
Bayer Inc.	124
BBM Bureau of Measurement	125
BC Hydro	125
BC Research Inc.	126
BC Telecom Inc.	126
Bearskin Lake Air Service Ltd.	128
Bechtel Canada Co.	128
Becker Milk Company Ltd., The	129
Bell & Howell Ltd.	130
Bell Canada	131
Bell Mobility	131
Belleville General Hospital	132
Benwell Atkins Ltd.	132
Best Western Carlton Place Hotel	133
Betel Home Foundation	133
Bethania Mennonite Personal Care Home Inc.	134
Bethesda Hospital	134
BFGoodrich Landing Gear Division	135
Bic Inc.	136
Biomira Inc.	136
Bio-Research Laboratories Ltd.	137
Birks Jewelry	138
BJ Services Company	138
Black Photo Corporation	139
Bloorview Childrens Hospital	140
Bloorview MacMillan Centre, The	140
Blue Mountain Resorts Limited	141
Blue Wave Seafoods Inc.	142
Bluewater District School Board	142
BNP PARIBAS (Canada)	143
Bonus Resource Services Corp.	144
Boréal Assurances Inc.	144
Bosal Canada Inc.	145
BOVAR Waste Management	145
Bowater Mersey Paper Company Limited	146
Brandon, City of	146
Brewers Retail Inc.	148
British Columbia Ferry Corporation	149
British Columbia Transit	149
Brookfield Properties Corporation	150
Browning Harvey Limited	150
Bugbusters Pest Management Inc.	152
Bullock Associates Design Consultants Inc.	153
Burger King Restaurants of Canada Inc.	153
Burns International Security Services Ltd.	154
C B C L Limited	154
C MAC Industries Inc.	155
C.S.T. Consultants Inc.	155
Cabre Exploration Ltd.	156
Cadith Entertainment Ltd.	156
CAE Newness	157
Calgary Co-operative Association Limited	157
Calgary, City of	158
Cambior Inc.	158
Cambridge Memorial Hospital	159
Cambridge Suites	159
Camp Hill Hospital	160
Canada Brick Limited	161
Canada Catering Co. Ltd.	161
Canada Games Aquatic Centre	162
Canada Safeway Limited	163
Canada Starch Company Inc.	163
Canadian Broadcasting Corporation	164
Canadian Cancer Society	164
Canadian Commercial Corp.	165
Canadian Dairy Commission	165
Canadian Depository for Securities Ltd.	166
Canadian Museum of Civilization Corp.	167
Canadian National Institute For The Blind	167
Canadian Occidental Petroleum Ltd.	168
Canadian Thermos Products Inc.	168
Canadian Tire Corporation Ltd.	169
Canadian Western Bank	169
Canbra Foods Ltd.	170
Cancarb Limited	170
CancerCare Manitoba	171
Cancore Industries Inc.	171
Cangene Corporation	172
Canpar Transport Ltd.	173
CanWel Distribution Ltd.	173
Capilano Suspension Bridge	174
Carlson Marketing Group Canada Ltd.	176
Casa Loma	177
Cassels Brock & Blackwell	177
Catholic Children's Aid Society Foundation	178
CCL Industries Inc.	178
Cegelec Enterprises Ltée	179
Celestica International Inc.	179
CenAlta Energy Services Inc.	180

The Canada Student Employment Guide

Part Time/Summer Index 715

Centra Gas Manitoba Inc.	181	D.H. Howden	211
Central Park Lodges Ltd.	181	DaimlerChrysler Canada Ltd.	211
Centre de Santé de St-Henri Inc.	182	Dana Corporation - Long Manufacturing	212
Century Sales and Service Limited	182	David Thompson Health Region	212
Ceridian Canada	183	Deer Lodge Centre Inc.	213
CFCF Inc.	183	Dell Computer Corporation	214
CFCN Communications Inc.	184	Delphi Solutions Inc.	215
CGI	184	Delta Hotels	215
CGU Group Canada Ltd.	185	Delta Toronto Airport Hotel	216
CH2M Gore and Storrie Limited	185	Derlan Industries Limited	216
Challenger Motor Freight Inc.	186	Directwest Publishers Ltd.	217
Chapters Inc.	186	Drug Trading Company Ltd.	219
Charlottetown Driving Park	187	Druxy's Inc.	219
Chevron Canada Resources Ltd.	188	Ducks Unlimited Canada	220
Children's Aid Society of Metro Toronto	188	Duha Color Services	220
Children's Hospital of Eastern Ontario	189	Dun & Bradstreet Canada	221
Chilliwack General Hospital	189	DuPont Canada Inc.	221
Chinook Health Region	190	Dylex Limited	222
Christian Horizons	190	Dynacare Laboratories	223
Cineplex Odeon Corporation	191	Dynapro Systems Inc.	223
Citibank Canada	191	Dynasty Furniture Manufacturing Ltd.	224
Club Monaco International	193	Economic Development Edmonton	226
Coast Mountain Bus Company Ltd.	193	Economical Insurance Group, The	227
Cobourg District General Hospital	194	Eddie Bauer Inc.	227
Coca Cola Foods Canada Inc.	195	Edmonton Home Services Ltd.	228
Cognos Incorporated	196	EDS of Canada Ltd.	228
Colgate-Palmolive Canada Inc.	196	Electronics Arts (Canada) Inc.	229
Columbia House	197	Eli Lilly Canada Inc.	230
Comcare Health Services	198	Emco Limited	230
Communications & Power Industries Canada	198	EMJ Data Systems Ltd.	231
Community Savings Credit Union	199	Endpoint Research Ltd.	231
Compu-Quote Inc.	200	EnerFlex Systems Ltd.	232
Computalog Ltd.	200	Entreprises Premier Canadien Ltée	232
Comstock Canada	201	Environics Research Group Ltd.	233
Connors Bros, Limited	203	Epson Canada Limited	233
Co-op Atlantic	203	Ernst & Young	234
Coquitlam, City of	204	Espial Group Incorporated	234
Corner Brook, City of	205	Exide Canada Inc.	235
Cornwall Electric	206	Explorer Hotel, The	236
Cosyn Technology	207	Extendicare (Canada) Inc.	237
Cotton Ginny Ltd.	207	FAG Bearings Limited	237
Cougar Helicopters Inc.	208	Family Day Care Service	238
Credit Union Central of Canada	208	Farm Credit Corp. Canada	238
Crestar Energy Inc.	209	Farmers Co-operative Dairy Limited	239
Culinar Inc.	209	Federated Co-operatives Limited	239
Custom Trim Ltd.	210	FedEx Express	240
D.A. Stuart Inc.	210	Finning	240

The Canada Student Employment Guide

Part Time/Summer Index

Fisher Scientific Limited	241	Health Sciences Centre	268
Fishery Products International	241	Helijet Airways Inc.	268
Flakeboard Company Limited	242	Hermes Electronics Inc.	269
Fletcher's Fine Foods	242	Hill & Knowlton Canada Ltd.	270
Flint Energy Services Ltd.	243	Hippodrome de Montréal	270
Foremost Industries Inc.	244	HMV Canada	271
Forzani Group Ltd., The	244	Hockey Hall of Fame	271
Foster Wheeler Limited	245	Holiday Inn Select Toronto Airport	272
Foyer Valade Inc.	245	Holland College	273
Friesens Corporation	246	Home Oil Co. Ltd.	273
Future Shop Ltd.	246	Homewood Corp.	274
Gallup Canada Inc.	247	Honda Canada Inc.	274
Gay Lea Foods Co-Operative Ltd.	247	Honeywell Ltd.	275
Gendis Inc.	248	Horseshoe Resort Corporation	275
General Chemical Canada Ltd.	249	Hôtel Dieu de Montréal	276
General Electric Canada Inc.	249	Household Movers & Shippers Limited	276
General Mills Canada Inc.	250	Housesitters Canada, The	277
George Jeffrey Children's Treatment Centre	250	HSBC Bank Canada	277
Gienow Building Products Ltd.	251	Hub Meat Packers Ltd.	278
Giffels Associates Limited	251	Hudon & Deaudelin Ltée	279
Gilbey Canada Inc.	252	Hudson's Bay Company, The	279
Gimbel Eye Centre	252	Humber River Regional Hospital	280
Glentel Inc.	254	Husky Energy Inc.	281
Golder Associates Ltd.	255	Hydro Electric Commission of Thunder Bay	281
Goodman and Carr	255	Hydro Mississauga Corporation	282
Goodwill Industries of Toronto	256	Hydro One Inc.	282
Goodyear Canada Inc.	256	I M P Group International Inc.	283
Gov't of Newfoundland – Dept. of Finance	257	I P L Plastics Ltd.	284
Grand & Toy Ltd.	257	IBM Canada Ltd.	284
Grant MacEwen Community College	258	ICI Canada Inc.	285
Grant Thornton	258	Imprimerie Interweb Inc.	287
Great-West Life Assurance Company, The	259	Indalex Limited	288
Grenville Management Ltd.	259	Industrial Equipment Co. Ltd.	288
Groupe Savoie Inc.	260	Industrial-Alliance Life Insurance Company	289
Grouse Mountain Resorts Ltd.	260	Industries Lassonde Inc.	289
H A Simmons Ltd.	261	ING Canada Financial Services International	291
Haley Industries Limited	262	Insurance Corp. of B.C.	291
Haliburton Energy Services	262	Intercon Security Ltd.	292
Halifax County Regional Rehabilitation Centre	263	Interforest Ltd.	292
Halifax Regional Municipality	263	Interior Savings Credit Union	293
Halifax Water Commission	264	InterOne Marketing Group	293
Halliburton Energy Services	264	Island Savings Credit Union	295
Harry Rosen Inc.	265	Ivaco Inc.	296
Hasbro Canada Inc.	266	IWK Grace Health Centre	297
HB Studios Multimedia Ltd.	266	Izaak Walton Killam Hospital, The	297
Health Authority 5	267	J.D. Irving Limited	298
Health Care Corporation of St. John's	267	J.S. Redpath Limited	299

The Canada Student Employment Guide

Part Time/Summer Index 717

Jacques Whitford Consulting Engineers	299	Magna International Inc.	327
James Richardson International Limited	300	Manitoba Agriculture and Food	327
JDS Uniphase Corporation	300	Manitoba Hydro	328
Jim Pattison Group	301	Manitoba Pool Elevators	328
John P. Robarts Research Institute	302	Manitoba Public Insurance Corporation	329
Johnson Controls Ltd.	302	Manitoba Telecom Services Inc.	329
Johnson Incorporated	303	Maple Leaf Consumer Foods	330
Jostens Canada Ltd.	303	Marcam Canada	330
Kelowna Home Support	304	Marine Atlantic Inc.	331
Kelowna, City of	305	Maritime Life Assurance Company, The	331
Kennametal Ltd.	305	Mark Anthony Group Inc.	332
Kennedy Lodge Nursing Home Inc.	306	Marks & Spencer Canada Inc.	332
Keyano College	306	Mark's Work Warehouse	333
KFC Canada	307	Marshall Macklin Monaghan Ltd.	333
Kings Regional Rehabilitation Centre	308	Marystown Shipyard Limited	334
Kinross Gold Corp.	308	Maryvale Adolescent and Family Services	334
Kitchener, City of	309	Matrox Electronic Systems Ltd.	335
Kodak Canada Inc.	309	Maxxam Analytics Inc.	335
Kraft Canada Inc.	310	McBee Systems of Canada Inc.	336
Krug Inc.	310	McGraw Hill Ryerson Ltd.	337
Kvaerner Metals	311	McKay-Cocker Construction Limited	338
La Confiserie Comete Ltee	311	McLaren-McCann Advertising of Canada Ltd.	338
Laidlaw Inc.	312	MDS Nordion	339
Lakeside Farm Industries Ltd.	312	Mediasynergy	340
Lambert Somec Inc.	313	Medical Laboratories of Windsor Limited	341
Leduc, City of	313	Memotec Communications Inc.	341
Lego Canada Inc.	314	Metro Richelieu Inc.	342
Leica Geosystems Canada Inc.	314	Metroland Printing, Publishing & Dist. Ltd.	343
Lenbrook Industries Limited	315	Meyers Norris Penny & Co.	344
Leo Burnett Co. Ltd.	315	Michaels of Canada Inc.	345
Les Centres Jeunesse de Montréal	316	Midland Walwyn Inc.	345
Les Distilleries Corby Ltée	317	Millwork & Building Supplies Limited	346
Les Forges de Sorel Inc.	317	Minas Basin Pulp and Power Company Ltd.	347
Liberty Health	318	Misericordia General Hospital	348
Lick's Ice Cream & Burger Shops Inc.	319	Mississauga, City of	349
Lifetouch Canada Inc.	319	Mitel Corporation	350
Linmor Technologies	320	Mitsubishi Electric Sales Canada	351
Litton Systems Canada Ltd.	320	Moen Inc.	352
LM Architectural Group	321	Moffat Communications Limited	352
London Goodwill Industries Association	322	Monarch Communications Inc.	353
Loss Prevention Group Inc.	322	Montreal Trust Co.	353
M M Industra Ltd.	323	Moosehead Breweries Limited	354
M. McGrawth Canada Limited	324	Morrison Hershfield Limited	354
MAAX Inc.	324	Mortice Kern Systems Inc.	355
MacDonald Dettwiler and Associates Ltd.	325	MOSAID Technologies Inc.	355
MacDonald Steel Ltd.	325	Motorola Canada Ltd.	356
MacViro Consultants Inc.	326	Mountain Equipment Co-op	356

The Canada Student Employment Guide

Part Time/Summer Index

MSM Transportation Inc.	357	Ontario Guard Services Inc.	383
Multi-Languages	357	Ontario Jockey Club, The	384
Multitech Electronics Inc.	358	Ontario Legislative Offices	384
Mustang Survival Corp.	358	Ontario March of Dimes	385
N B S Card Services	359	Opinion Search Inc.	385
Nanaimo Credit Union	359	Oracle Corp. Canada Inc.	386
Natco Canada Ltd.	360	Ottawa Hospital	386
National Grocers Co. Ltd.	360	Overlander Hospital	387
National Life	361	Paladin Security & Investigations Limited	388
National Sports Centre	362	Panorama Mountain Village	388
Nelvana Limited	363	Paramount Canada's Wonderland Inc.	389
Neptune Food Suppliers Ltd.	363	Parkland Industries Ltd.	390
Nesbitt Burns Inc.	364	Paul Revere Life Insurance Company, The	391
Nestle Canada Inc.	364	PavCo	391
New Brunswick Power Corporation	365	PCL Constructors Inc.	392
New Brunswick Telephone Company	366	Peacock Inc.	392
New Holland Canada Ltd.	366	Pearson Education Canada	393
Newfoundland and Labrador Credit Union	367	Peel Board of Education	393
Newfoundland and Labrador Hydro	367	Peel Children's Centre	394
Newness Machine Ltd.	368	Peel Regional Police	394
News Marketing Canada	368	Pelmorex Inc.	395
NewTel Communications	369	Pembina Pipeline Corporation	395
Niagara Parks Commission, The	369	PennCorp Life Insurance Company	396
Nichirin Inc.	370	Peter Kiewit Sons Co.	396
Nielsen Marketing Research	370	Petro-Canada	397
Nike Canada Ltd.	371	Pharma Plus Drugmarts Ltd.	398
Nissan Canada Inc.	371	Phoenix International	399
NLK Consultants Inc.	372	Pine Falls Paper Company Limited	400
Norcen Energy Resources Ltd.	373	Pioneer Village Special Care Corp.	400
North American Life Assurance Company	373	Pitney Bowes of Canada Ltd.	401
North West Company Inc.	374	Pizza Pizza Ltd.	401
North York Community Care Access Centre	374	Placer Dome Inc.	402
Northern Lights Regional Health Centre	375	Poco Petroleums Ltd.	402
Northern Mountain Helicopters Inc.	375	Pollack Rentals Limited	403
Northwestel Inc.	376	Polygram Group Canada Inc.	403
Nova Scotia Liquor Commission	377	Pool People Ltd.	404
Nova Scotia Power Corp.	377	Positron Industries Inc.	404
Novartis Consumer Health Canada Inc.	378	Potacan Mining Company	405
Novotel Canada Inc.	378	Powell Equipment Ltd.	405
NPS Allelix Corp.	379	Power Measurement Ltd.	406
Numac Energy Inc.	379	Powertech Labs Inc.	406
Nygard International Ltd.	380	PPG Canada Inc.	407
Oceanis Seafoods Ltd.	380	Pratt & Whitney Canada Inc.	407
Ocelot Energy Inc.	381	Premdor Inc.	408
Oetiker Limited	381	PRI Automation	408
Okanagan Skeena Group Limited	382	Pricewaterhouse Coopers	409
Oland Breweries Limited	382	Prince Albert Credit Union	409

The Canada Student Employment Guide

Prince Albert, City of	410	Royal Bank of Canada	438
Prince George, City of	410	Royal Canadian Mint	438
Providence Centre	412	Royal Inland Hospital	439
Prudential Insurance Co. of America, The	412	Royal Philips Electronics	439
Public Utilities of Kingston	413	Royal Victoria Hospital	440
Purolator Courier Ltd.	413	Ryerson Polytechnic University	441
QEII Health Sciences Centre	414	Saan Stores Ltd.	441
QIT-Fer et Titane Inc.	414	Sales & Merchandising Group	442
Quebecor Inc.	415	Salisbury House of Canada Ltd.	442
Ramada Inn	416	Sandman Hotels and Inns	443
Rasco Specialty Metals Inc.	417	Sandwell Inc.	443
Raylo Chemicals Inc.	417	Sara Lee Corporation of Canada Limited	444
Raymond Rebar Inc.	418	Saskatchewan Centre of the Arts	444
Reader's Digest Association of Canada Ltd.	419	Saskatchewan Economic Development	445
Ready Bake Foods Inc.	420	Saskatchewan Government Insurance	445
Recochem Inc.	420	Saskatchewan Research Council, The	446
Red Deer Co-op Limited	421	Saskatchewan Transportation Company	446
Reena	421	Saskatchewan Wheat Pool	447
Regal Capital Planners Ltd.	422	Saskatoon Co-operative Association Limited	447
Regal Constellation Hotel Ltd.	422	Saskatoon, City of	448
Regal Greeting and Gifts	423	SaskTel	449
Regina Health District	423	Scarborough General Hospital	450
Regional Municipality of Niagara	424	Schlumberger Canada Ltd.	450
Regional Residential Services Society	424	Schneider Electric Canada Inc.	451
Regis Pictures and Frames Ltd.	425	Scholastic Canada Ltd.	451
Rehabilitation Institute of Toronto	425	Science North	452
Reid Crowther	426	SCIEX MDS Health Group	452
Reliable Engine Services Ltd.	426	SCL Technologies Inc.	453
Renaissance Energy Ltd.	427	Seprotech Systems Incorporated	454
Rentway Inc.	427	Shaw Communications	455
Revenue Properties Company Limited	429	Shaw Industries Ltd.	455
Revy Home Centres Inc.	429	Sheraton Fallsview Hotel	456
Rhone-Poulenc Canada Inc.	430	Sheraton Toronto East Hotel and Towers	456
Rich Products of Canada Limited	431	Sherbrooke Community Centre	457
Richmond, City of	431	Shermag Inc.	457
Richter Usher & Vineberg	432	Sherwood Credit Union	458
Rimrock Resort Hotel	432	Shoppers Drug Mart Limited	458
Rio Algom Limited	433	Shopping Channel, The	459
Riverside Fabricating Ltd.	433	Siemens Electric Ltd.	460
Riverside Hospital of Ottawa, The	434	Signature Vacations Inc.	460
Rivtow Marine Ltd.	434	Silicon Graphics Canada Inc.	461
Rockwell Automation	435	Skiing Louise Ltd.	461
Roctest Ltée	435	Skills Training & Support Services Association	462
Rogers AT&T Wireless Inc.	436	Slocan Forest Products Ltd.	462
Rogers Media, Publishing	436	Sobeys Inc.	463
Rothmans, Benson and Hedges Inc.	437	Société des Alcools du Québec	464
Royal & Sun Alliance Insurance Co. of Canada	437	Sodexho Marriott Services Canada	464

The Canada Student Employment Guide

Part Time/Summer Index

Southam Inc.	466
Southern Railway of British Columbia Ltd.	466
Southland Canada	467
Spar Aerospace Limited	467
Spectrum Signal Processing Inc.	468
Speedware Corp. Inc.	469
Sportsco International	469
Sprint Canada	470
SSQ Life	471
St. Amant Centre Inc.	471
St. Joseph's Care Group	472
St. Lawrence Parks Commission	472
St. Lawrence Seaway Mgmt. Corp., The	473
St. Vincent's Hospitals	473
Standard Knitting Limited	474
Standen's Limited	474
Stanley Canada Inc.	475
Stantec Consulting Ltd.	475
State Farm Insurance Companies	476
Steelcraft Industries Ltd.	477
Sterling Marking Products Inc.	478
Stitches	478
Stone Consolidated Inc.	479
StorageTek Canada Inc.	479
StressGen Biotechnologies Corp.	480
Sudbury Regional Hospital	480
Sun Peaks Resort Corporation	481
Sun Rype Products Ltd.	481
Sundog Printing Limited	482
Sunoco Inc.	482
Supreme Tooling Group	483
Surrey Place Centre	484
Surrey, City of	484
Swift Current Health District	485
Syncrude Canada Ltd.	486
Talisman Energy Inc.	487
TCG International Inc.	487
TCT Logistics	488
TD Waterhouse Investor Services (Canada)	488
Teck Corp.	489
Teklogix Inc.	489
Teldon International Inc.	490
Telebec Ltée	490
Telegraph Journal	491
Telesat Canada	491
Telus Corporation	492
The Arthritis Society	492
The Barn Fruit Markets Inc.	493
The Co-operators	493
Thomas & Betts Ltée	495
Thomas Cook Group (Canada) Ltd.	495
Thomas J. Lipton	496
Thompson's Moving and Storage	496
Thomson - CSF Systems Canada Inc.	497
Thunder Bay Regional Hospital	497
Ticketmaster Canada Inc.	498
Tiger Brand Knitting Company Limited	498
Timmins, City of	499
Tippet-Richardson Ltd.	499
Today's Business Products Ltd.	500
Top Producers Systems Inc.	500
Toronto and Region Conservation Authority	501
Toronto Association For Community Living	501
Toronto Cricket Skating & Curling	502
Toronto District School Board	503
Toronto East General Hospital	503
Toronto French School, The	504
Toronto General Hospital	505
Toronto Police Service	506
Toronto Public Library Board	506
Toronto Sun Publishing Corp., The	507
Toronto Zoo	507
Toyota Canada Ltd.	509
TransAlta	509
Transcontinental Digital Services Inc.	510
Triumf	510
Trojan Technologies Inc.	511
TSC Stores Ltd.	512
Turnbull & Turnbull Ltd.	512
Uni Select Inc.	513
Union Gas Ltd.	513
Union Pacific Resources Group	514
Unisys Canada Inc.	514
United Parcel Service Canada Ltd.	515
Universal Rehabilitation Service Agency	515
University College of Cape Breton	516
Urban Systems Ltd.	516
US Filter BCP	517
USF WaterGroup	517
Vacances Air Transat Inc.	518
Valley First Credit Union	518
Value Village Stores	519
VanCity Credit Union	519
Vancouver International Airport	520

The Canada Student Employment Guide

Vancouver Sun	520	**Summer**	
Versa Services Ltd.	521		
VIA Rail Canada Inc.	521	1-800-GOT-JUNK?	74
Villa Providence Shediac Inc.	522	A C A Cooperative Limited	74
Volkswagen Canada Inc.	523	A.G. Simpson Co. Ltd.	75
Volvo Cars of Canada Ltd.	523	Aar-Kel Moulds Ltd.	76
W C I Canada Inc.	524	ABC Group	76
Waterloo Furniture Components Ltd.	524	Aberdeen Hospital	77
Waterloo Inn	525	Abitibi-Consolidated Inc.	77
Waverly & York Corporation	525	Acadia University	78
WebCanada	526	Access Communications	78
Wegu Canada Inc.	526	Accucaps Industries Limited	79
Weldco-Beales Manufacturing Inc.	527	ACE INI Insurance	79
Wendy's Restaurants of Canada Inc.	527	Acier Leroux Inc.	80
West Coast Apparel	528	Acklands-Grainger Inc.	80
West Kootenay Power Ltd.	528	Addictions Foundation of Manitoba, The	81
Westcliff Management Ltd.	529	Adherex Technologies Inc.	81
Westcoast Energy Inc.	530	ADI Group Inc.	82
Western Glove Works	530	ADT Canada Inc.	82
Westin Bayshore Resort and Marina, The	531	Advanta Seeds	83
Westin Prince Hotel, The	531	AGF Management Limited	83
WestJet Airlines	532	Agricultural Credit Corp. of Saskatchewan	84
Westminster Savings Credit Union	533	Air Canada	85
Weston Produce Inc.	533	Air Liquide Canada Inc.	85
Westshore Terminals Ltd.	534	Air Ontario Inc.	86
Weyerhaeuser Company Limited	535	Akita Drilling Ltd.	87
Whistler Blackcomb Mountain	535	Alberta Alcohol and Drug Abuse Commission	87
White Rose Crafts and Nursery Sales Limited	536	Alberta Blue Cross	88
White Spot Limited	536	Alberta Cancer Board	88
Whitehill Technologies Inc.	537	Alberta Energy & Utilities Board	89
Wilderness Reforestation	537	Alberta Energy Company Ltd.	89
Wilson Auto Electric Ltd.	538	Alberta Gaming & Liquor Commission	90
Winners Apparel Ltd.	539	Alberto Culver Canada Inc.	90
Winpak Ltd.	539	Alcan Aluminium Limited	91
Workfire Development Corp.	540	Alexandra Hospital	91
XCAN Grain Pool Ltd.	541	Algoma Child & Youth Services Inc.	92
xwave solutions	542	Algoma District Home For The Aged	92
Yamaha Motor Canada Ltd.	542	Algoma Steel Inc.	93
Yarmouth Regional Hospital	543	Aliant Telecom Inc.	93
Yellowknife, City of	544	Allcolour Paint Limited	94
YFactor	544	Allianz Canada	95
Zeidler Roberts Partnership Architects	546	Allmar Distributors Ltd.	95
Zellers Inc.	546	Allstate Insurance Co. of Canada	96
Zenastra	547	Alpine Oil Service Corporation	96
Zenon Environmental Inc.	547	Altona Community Memorial Health Centre	97
		Alumicor Limited	97
		Amcan Castings Limited	98

The Canada Student Employment Guide

Part Time/Summer Index

Amcor Twinpak North America Inc.	98	Baycrest Centre for Geriatric Care	123
AMEC Inc.	99	Bayer Inc.	124
American Airlines Inc.	99	Baytex Energy Limited	124
Amram's Distributing Ltd.	100	BC Hydro	125
Ancast Industries Ltd.	100	BC Research Inc.	126
Andersen Consulting	101	BC Telecom Inc.	126
Antamex International Inc.	102	BCG Services	127
Anthony Insurance Inc.	102	BDO Dunwoody	127
Aon Reed Stenhouse Inc.	103	Bearskin Lake Air Service Ltd.	128
Apotex Fermentation Inc.	104	Bechtel Canada Co.	128
Apple Canada Inc.	104	Becker Milk Company Ltd., The	129
Aqua-Power Cleaners Ltd.	105	Beckman Coulter Canada Inc.	129
Aquatic Sciences Inc.	105	Behlen Industries	130
Arbor Care Tree Service Ltd.	106	Bell & Howell Ltd.	130
Arbor Memorial Services Inc.	106	Bell Canada	131
Arctic Co-operatives Limited	107	Bell Mobility	131
Armor Personnel	107	Belleville General Hospital	132
ArvinMeritor	108	Benwell Atkins Ltd.	132
Assiniboine Community College	109	Best Western Carlton Place Hotel	133
Assumption Mutual Life Insurance	109	Betel Home Foundation	133
Assure Health Inc.	110	Bethania Mennonite Personal Care Home Inc.	134
AstraZeneca	110	Bethesda Hospital	134
ATCO Electric	111	Bettis Canada Ltd.	135
ATCO Frontec Corp.	111	Bic Inc.	136
ATCO Gas Services Ltd.	112	Biomira Inc.	136
Athabasca, Town of	112	Bio-Research Laboratories Ltd.	137
Atlantic Blue Cross Care	113	Birks Jewelry	138
Atlantic Lottery Corporation Inc.	113	BJ Services Company	138
Atlantic Packaging Products Ltd.	114	Black Photo Corporation	139
Atlantic Wholesalers Ltd.	114	Blaney McMurty LLP	139
Atlas Ideal Metals Inc.	115	Bloorview Childrens Hospital	140
Atlas Van Lines (Canada) Ltd.	115	Bloorview MacMillan Centre, The	140
ATS Automation Tooling Systems Inc.	116	Blue Giant Equipment of Canada Ltd.	141
Aurizon Mines Ltd.	116	Blue Mountain Resorts Limited	141
Aurum Ceramic Dental Laboratories Ltd.	117	Blue Wave Seafoods Inc.	142
Aventis Pasteur Limited	117	Bluewater District School Board	142
AXA Insurance (Canada)	118	BNP PARIBAS (Canada)	143
Axidata Inc.	118	Bombardier Aerospace	143
Babcock and Wilcox Canada	119	Bonus Resource Services Corp.	144
Bakemark Ingredients Ltd.	119	Boréal Assurances Inc.	144
Ballard Power Systems Inc.	120	Bosal Canada Inc.	145
Banff Centre for Continuing Education, The	120	BOVAR Waste Management	145
Bargain Finder Press Ltd.	121	Bowater Mersey Paper Company Limited	146
Barton Place Long Term Care Facility	121	Brandon, City of	146
BASF Canada Inc.	122	Brantcorp Inc.	147
Basic Technologies Corporation	122	Bratty & Partners LLP	147
Battlefords Health District	123	British Columbia Assessment	148

The Canada Student Employment Guide

Part Time/Summer Index   723

British Columbia Ferry Corporation	149	Capilano Suspension Bridge	174
British Columbia Transit	149	Carbone of America (LCL) Ltd.	175
Brookfield Properties Corporation	150	Cargill Limited	175
Browning Harvey Limited	150	Carlson Marketing Group Canada Ltd.	176
Buck Consultants Limited	151	Carte International Inc.	176
Buckeye Canada Inc.	151	Casa Loma	177
Bugbusters Pest Management Inc.	152	Cassels Brock & Blackwell	177
Bullock Associates Design Consultants Inc.	153	Catholic Children's Aid Society Foundation	178
Burger King Restaurants of Canada Inc.	153	CCL Industries Inc.	178
Burns International Security Services Ltd.	154	Cegelec Enterprises Ltée	179
C B C L Limited	154	Celestica International Inc.	179
C MAC Industries Inc.	155	CenAlta Energy Services Inc.	180
C.S.T. Consultants Inc.	155	Centra Gas British Columbia Inc.	180
Cabre Exploration Ltd.	156	Centra Gas Manitoba Inc.	181
CAE Newness	157	Central Park Lodges Ltd.	181
Calgary Co-operative Association Limited	157	Centre de Santé de St-Henri Inc.	182
Calgary, City of	158	Century Sales and Service Limited	182
Cambior Inc.	158	Ceridian Canada	183
Cambridge Memorial Hospital	159	CFCF Inc.	183
Cambridge Suites	159	CGI	184
Cameco Corporation	160	CGU Group Canada Ltd.	185
Camp Hill Hospital	160	CH2M Gore and Storrie Limited	185
Canada Brick Limited	161	Challenger Motor Freight Inc.	186
Canada Catering Co. Ltd.	161	Chapters Inc.	186
Canada Games Aquatic Centre	162	Charlottetown Driving Park	187
Canada Post Corporation	162	Cheticamp Packers Ltd.	187
Canada Safeway Limited	163	Chevron Canada Resources Ltd.	188
Canada Starch Company Inc.	163	Children's Aid Society of Metro Toronto	188
Canadian Broadcasting Corporation	164	Children's Hospital of Eastern Ontario	189
Canadian Cancer Society	164	Chilliwack General Hospital	189
Canadian Commercial Corp.	165	Chinook Health Region	190
Canadian Dairy Commission	165	Christian Horizons	190
Canadian Depository for Securities Ltd.	166	Cineplex Odeon Corporation	191
Canadian General Tower Limited	166	Citibank Canada	191
Canadian Museum of Civilization Corp.	167	CKF Inc.	192
Canadian National Institute For The Blind	167	Clarica	192
Canadian Occidental Petroleum Ltd.	168	Club Monaco International	193
Canadian Thermos Products Inc.	168	Coast Mountain Bus Company Ltd.	193
Canadian Tire Corporation Ltd.	169	COBI Foods Inc.	194
Canadian Western Bank	169	Cobourg District General Hospital	194
Canbra Foods Ltd.	170	Coca Cola Foods Canada Inc.	195
Cancarb Limited	170	Cognos Incorporated	196
CancerCare Manitoba	171	Colgate-Palmolive Canada Inc.	196
Cancore Industries Inc.	171	Columbia House	197
Cangene Corporation	172	COM DEV International	197
Canpar Transport Ltd.	173	Comcare Health Services	198
CanWel Distribution Ltd.	173	Communications & Power Industries Canada	198

The Canada Student Employment Guide

724 Part Time/Summer Index

Community Savings Credit Union	199	Economical Insurance Group, The	227
Compaq Canada Inc.	199	Eddie Bauer Inc.	227
Compu-Quote Inc.	200	Edmonton Home Services Ltd.	228
Computalog Ltd.	200	EDS of Canada Ltd.	228
Comstock Canada	201	Elco	229
Connors Bros, Limited	203	Electronics Arts (Canada) Inc.	229
Co-op Atlantic	203	Eli Lilly Canada Inc.	230
Coppley Apparel Group	204	Emco Limited	230
Coquitlam, City of	204	EMJ Data Systems Ltd.	231
Corel Corporation	205	Endpoint Research Ltd.	231
Corner Brook, City of	205	EnerFlex Systems Ltd.	232
Cornwall Electric	206	Entreprises Premier Canadien Ltée	232
Cosmair Canada Inc.	206	Environics Research Group Ltd.	233
Cosyn Technology	207	Epson Canada Limited	233
Cotton Ginny Ltd.	207	Ernst & Young	234
Cougar Helicopters Inc.	208	Espial Group Incorporated	234
Credit Union Central of Canada	208	Exfo	235
Crestar Energy Inc.	209	Exide Canada Inc.	235
Culinar Inc.	209	Explorer Hotel, The	236
Custom Trim Ltd.	210	Export Development Corporation	236
D.A. Stuart Inc.	210	Extendicare (Canada) Inc.	237
D.H. Howden	211	FAG Bearings Limited	237
DaimlerChrysler Canada Ltd.	211	Family Day Care Service	238
Dana Corporation - Long Manufacturing	212	Farm Credit Corp. Canada	238
David Thompson Health Region	212	Farmers Co-operative Dairy Limited	239
DDM Plastics Inc.	213	FedEx Express	240
Deer Lodge Centre Inc.	213	Finning	240
Degussa - Huls Canada Inc.	214	Fisher Scientific Limited	241
Dell Computer Corporation	214	Fishery Products International	241
Delphi Solutions Inc.	215	Flakeboard Company Limited	242
Delta Hotels	215	Fletcher's Fine Foods	242
Delta Toronto Airport Hotel	216	Flint Energy Services Ltd.	243
Domtar Inc.	218	Foremost Industries Inc.	244
Drug Trading Company Ltd.	219	Forzani Group Ltd., The	244
Druxy's Inc.	219	Foster Wheeler Limited	245
Ducks Unlimited Canada	220	Foyer Valade Inc.	245
Duha Color Services	220	Friesens Corporation	246
Dun & Bradstreet Canada	221	Future Shop Ltd.	246
DuPont Canada Inc.	221	Gay Lea Foods Co-Operative Ltd.	247
Dura Automotive Systems (Canada) Ltd.	222	Gendis Inc.	248
Dylex Limited	222	General Chemical Canada Ltd.	249
Dynacare Laboratories	223	General Electric Canada Inc.	249
Dynapro Systems Inc.	223	General Mills Canada Inc.	250
Dynasty Furniture Manufacturing Ltd.	224	Gienow Building Products Ltd.	251
E B A Engineering Consultants Ltd.	225	Giffels Associates Limited	251
Echo Bay Mines Ltd.	226	Gilbey Canada Inc.	252
Economic Development Edmonton	226	Gimbel Eye Centre	252

The Canada Student Employment Guide

Part Time/Summer Index

Gisborne Design Services Ltd.	253	Hubbell Canada Inc.	278
Glaxo Wellcome Canada	253	Hudon & Deaudelin Ltée	279
Glentel Inc.	254	Humber River Regional Hospital	280
Goepel McDermid Securities	254	Huronia Regional Centre	280
Golder Associates Ltd.	255	Husky Energy Inc.	281
Goodman and Carr	255	Hydro Electric Commission of Thunder Bay	281
Goodwill Industries of Toronto	256	Hydro Mississauga Corporation	282
Goodyear Canada Inc.	256	Hydro One Inc.	282
Gov't of Newfoundland – Dept. of Finance	257	I M P Group International Inc.	283
Grand & Toy Ltd.	257	I P L Plastics Ltd.	284
Grant MacEwen Community College	258	IBM Canada Ltd.	284
Grant Thornton	258	ICI Canada Inc.	285
Great-West Life Assurance Company, The	259	Ilco Unican Inc.	286
Grenville Management Ltd.	259	Imperial Oil Limited	286
Groupe Savoie Inc.	260	Imprimerie Interweb Inc.	287
Grouse Mountain Resorts Ltd.	260	INCO Limited	287
H A Simmons Ltd.	261	Indalex Limited	288
H.H. Angus & Associates Ltd.	261	Industrial-Alliance Life Insurance Company	289
Haley Industries Limited	262	Industries Lassonde Inc.	289
Halifax County Regional Rehabilitation Centre	263	InfoInterActive Inc.	290
Halifax Regional Municipality	263	Information Gateway Services	290
Halifax Water Commission	264	ING Canada Financial Services International	291
Harry Rosen Inc.	265	Insurance Corp. of B.C.	291
Hasbro Canada Inc.	266	Intercon Security Ltd.	292
HB Studios Multimedia Ltd.	266	Interforest Ltd.	292
Health Authority 5	267	Interior Savings Credit Union	293
Health Care Corporation of St. John's	267	InterOne Marketing Group	293
Health Sciences Centre	268	Intertape Polymer Group Inc.	294
Helijet Airways Inc.	268	IPL Energy Inc.	294
Hemosol Inc.	269	Island Savings Credit Union	295
Hermes Electronics Inc.	269	Island Telecom Inc.	295
Hill & Knowlton Canada Ltd.	270	IST Group Inc.	296
Hippodrome de Montréal	270	Ivaco Inc.	296
HMV Canada	271	IWK Grace Health Centre	297
Hockey Hall of Fame	271	Izaak Walton Killam Hospital, The	297
Hoffman-La Roche Limited	272	J.D. Barnes Limited	298
Holland College	273	J.D. Irving Limited	298
Home Oil Co. Ltd.	273	J.S. Redpath Limited	299
Homewood Corp.	274	Jacques Whitford Consulting Engineers	299
Honda Canada Inc.	274	James Richardson International Limited	300
Honeywell Ltd.	275	JDS Uniphase Corporation	300
Horseshoe Resort Corporation	275	Jim Pattison Group	301
Hôtel Dieu de Montréal	276	Jo-Ann Trucking Ltd.	301
Household Movers & Shippers Limited	276	John P. Robarts Research Institute	302
Housesitters Canada, The	277	Johnson Controls Ltd.	302
HSBC Bank Canada	277	Johnson Incorporated	303
Hub Meat Packers Ltd.	278	Jostens Canada Ltd.	303

The Canada Student Employment Guide

726 Part Time/Summer Index

Kawneer Company Canada Limited	304
Kelowna Home Support	304
Kelowna, City of	305
Kennedy Lodge Nursing Home Inc.	306
KFC Canada	307
Kimberly-Clark Inc.	307
Kings Regional Rehabilitation Centre	308
Kinross Gold Corp.	308
Kitchener, City of	309
Kraft Canada Inc.	310
Krug Inc.	310
Kvaerner Metals	311
La Confiserie Comete Ltee	311
Laidlaw Inc.	312
Lakeside Farm Industries Ltd.	312
Lambert Somec Inc.	313
Leduc, City of	313
Leica Geosystems Canada Inc.	314
Lenbrook Industries Limited	315
Leo Burnett Co. Ltd.	315
Leon's Manufacturing Company Inc.	316
Les Centres Jeunesse de Montréal	316
Les Distilleries Corby Ltée	317
Les Forges de Sorel Inc.	317
Les Modes Smart Inc.	318
Liberty Health	318
Lick's Ice Cream & Burger Shops Inc.	319
Lifetouch Canada Inc.	319
Linmor Technologies	320
Litton Systems Canada Ltd.	320
LM Architectural Group	321
Loewen Windows	321
London Goodwill Industries Association	322
Loss Prevention Group Inc.	322
Lovat Inc.	323
M M Industra Ltd.	323
M. McGrawth Canada Limited	324
MAAX Inc.	324
MacDonald Dettwiler and Associates Ltd.	325
MacDonald Steel Ltd.	325
MacViro Consultants Inc.	326
Magna International Inc.	327
Manitoba Agriculture and Food	327
Manitoba Hydro	328
Manitoba Pool Elevators	328
Manitoba Public Insurance Corporation	329
Manitoba Telecom Services Inc.	329
Maple Leaf Consumer Foods	330
Marcam Canada	330
Marine Atlantic Inc.	331
Maritime Life Assurance Company, The	331
Mark Anthony Group Inc.	332
Marks & Spencer Canada Inc.	332
Mark's Work Warehouse	333
Marshall Macklin Monaghan Ltd.	333
Marystown Shipyard Limited	334
Maryvale Adolescent and Family Services	334
Matrox Electronic Systems Ltd.	335
Maxxam Analytics Inc.	335
McBee Systems of Canada Inc.	336
McGraw Hill Ryerson Ltd.	337
McInnes Cooper & Robertson	337
McKay-Cocker Construction Limited	338
McLaren-McCann Advertising of Canada Ltd.	338
MDS Nordion	339
Mediacom Inc.	340
Mediasynergy	340
Medical Laboratories of Windsor Limited	341
Memotec Communications Inc.	341
Metro Richelieu Inc.	342
Metro Toronto West Detention Centre	343
Metroland Printing, Publishing & Dist. Ltd.	343
Meyers Norris Penny & Co.	344
Michaels of Canada Inc.	345
Midland Walwyn Inc.	345
Midwest Food Products Inc.	346
Millwork & Building Supplies Limited	346
Milne & Craighead Inc.	347
Minas Basin Pulp and Power Company Ltd.	347
Ministry of Northern Develop. and Mines	348
Misericordia General Hospital	348
Mississauga, City of	349
Mitchell's Gourmet Foods	349
Mitel Corporation	350
Mitra Imaging Inc.	350
Mitsubishi Electric Sales Canada	351
Mobile Computing Corporation	351
Moen Inc.	352
Moffat Communications Limited	352
Monarch Communications Inc.	353
Montreal Trust Co.	353
Moosehead Breweries Limited	354
Morrison Hershfield Limited	354
Mortice Kern Systems Inc.	355

The Canada Student Employment Guide

Part Time/Summer Index

MOSAID Technologies Inc.	355	Nygard International Ltd.	380
Motorola Canada Ltd.	356	Oceanis Seafoods Ltd.	380
Mountain Equipment Co-op	356	Ocelot Energy Inc.	381
MSM Transportation Inc.	357	Oetiker Limited	381
Multi-Languages	357	Oland Breweries Limited	382
Multitech Electronics Inc.	358	Ontario Guard Services Inc.	383
Mustang Survival Corp.	358	Ontario Jockey Club, The	384
N B S Card Services	359	Ontario Legislative Offices	384
Nanaimo Credit Union	359	Ontario March of Dimes	385
Natco Canada Ltd.	360	Opinion Search Inc.	385
National Grocers Co. Ltd.	360	Oracle Corp. Canada Inc.	386
National Life	361	Owen Bird	387
National Manufacturing of Canada Inc.	361	Paladin Security & Investigations Limited	388
National Sports Centre	362	Panorama Mountain Village	388
Neles Automation, Scada Solutions Ltd.	362	Paperboard Industries International Inc.	389
Nelvana Limited	363	Paramount Canada's Wonderland Inc.	389
Neptune Food Suppliers Ltd.	363	Parkland Industries Ltd.	390
Nesbitt Burns Inc.	364	Patheon Inc.	390
Nestle Canada Inc.	364	Paul Revere Life Insurance Company, The	391
New Brunswick Power Corporation	365	PavCo	391
New Brunswick Telephone Company	366	PCL Constructors Inc.	392
New Holland Canada Ltd.	366	Peacock Inc.	392
Newfoundland and Labrador Credit Union	367	Pearson Education Canada	393
Newfoundland and Labrador Hydro	367	Peel Children's Centre	394
Newness Machine Ltd.	368	Peel Regional Police	394
News Marketing Canada	368	Pembina Pipeline Corporation	395
NewTel Communications	369	PennCorp Life Insurance Company	396
Niagara Parks Commission, The	369	Peter Kiewit Sons Co.	396
Nichirin Inc.	370	Petro-Canada	397
Nielsen Marketing Research	370	Petromont & Co. Ltd. Partnership	397
Nike Canada Ltd.	371	Pharma Plus Drugmarts Ltd.	398
Nissan Canada Inc.	371	Phillips & Tempro Industries Ltd.	398
NLK Consultants Inc.	372	Phoenix International	399
Norbord Industries	372	Pine Falls Paper Company Limited	400
Norcen Energy Resources Ltd.	373	Pioneer Village Special Care Corp.	400
North American Life Assurance Company	373	Pitney Bowes of Canada Ltd.	401
North West Company Inc.	374	Pizza Pizza Ltd.	401
North York Community Care Access Centre	374	Placer Dome Inc.	402
Northern Lights Regional Health Centre	375	Poco Petroleums Ltd.	402
Northern Mountain Helicopters Inc.	375	Pollack Rentals Limited	403
Northwestel Inc.	376	Polygram Group Canada Inc.	403
Norwich Union Life Insurance Society	376	Pool People Ltd.	404
Nova Scotia Power Corp.	377	Positron Industries Inc.	404
Novartis Consumer Health Canada Inc.	378	Potacan Mining Company	405
Novotel Canada Inc.	378	Powell Equipment Ltd.	405
NPS Allelix Corp.	379	Power Measurement Ltd.	406
Numac Energy Inc.	379	Powertech Labs Inc.	406

The Canada Student Employment Guide

728 Part Time/Summer Index

PPG Canada Inc.	407
Pratt & Whitney Canada Inc.	407
Premdor Inc.	408
PRI Automation	408
Pricewaterhouse Coopers	409
Prince Albert Credit Union	409
Prince Albert, City of	410
Prince George, City of	410
Proctor and Redfern Ltd.	411
Providence Centre	412
Prudential Insurance Co. of America, The	412
Public Utilities of Kingston	413
Purolator Courier Ltd.	413
QEII Health Sciences Centre	414
QIT-Fer et Titane Inc.	414
Québec Cartier Mining Company	415
Quebecor Inc.	415
Quesnel River Pulp Company	416
Ramada Inn	416
Rasco Specialty Metals Inc.	417
Raylo Chemicals Inc.	417
Raymond Industrial Equipment Ltd.	418
Raymond Rebar Inc.	418
Reader's Digest Association of Canada Ltd.	419
Ready Bake Foods Inc.	420
Recochem Inc.	420
Red Deer Co-op Limited	421
Reena	421
Regal Capital Planners Ltd.	422
Regal Constellation Hotel Ltd.	422
Regina Health District	423
Regional Municipality of Niagara	424
Regional Residential Services Society	424
Regis Pictures and Frames Ltd.	425
Rehabilitation Institute of Toronto	425
Reid Crowther	426
Reliable Engine Services Ltd.	426
Renaissance Energy Ltd.	427
Rentway Inc.	427
Revenue Properties Company Limited	429
Revy Home Centres Inc.	429
Rhone-Poulenc Canada Inc.	430
Rich Products of Canada Limited	431
Richmond, City of	431
Richter Usher & Vineberg	432
Rimrock Resort Hotel	432
Rio Algom Limited	433
Riverside Fabricating Ltd.	433
Riverside Hospital of Ottawa, The	434
Rivtow Marine Ltd.	434
Rockwell Automation	435
Roctest Ltée	435
Rogers AT&T Wireless Inc.	436
Rogers Media, Publishing	436
Rothmans, Benson and Hedges Inc.	437
Royal & Sun Alliance Insurance Co. of Cda	437
Royal Bank of Canada	438
Royal Canadian Mint	438
Royal Inland Hospital	439
Royal Philips Electronics	439
Royal Victoria Hospital	440
Rubbermaid Canada Inc.	440
Ryerson Polytechnic University	441
Saan Stores Ltd.	441
Sales & Merchandising Group	442
Salisbury House of Canada Ltd.	442
Sandman Hotels and Inns	443
Sara Lee Corporation of Canada Limited	444
Saskatchewan Centre of the Arts	444
Saskatchewan Economic Development	445
Saskatchewan Government Insurance	445
Saskatchewan Research Council, The	446
Saskatchewan Transportation Company	446
Saskatchewan Wheat Pool	447
Saskatoon Co-operative Association Limited	447
Saskatoon, City of	448
Saskferco Products Inc.	448
SaskTel	449
SC Infrastructure Inc.	449
Scarborough General Hospital	450
Schlumberger Canada Ltd.	450
Schneider Electric Canada Inc.	451
Science North	452
SCIEX MDS Health Group	452
SCL Technologies Inc.	453
SED Systems	453
Seprotech Systems Incorporated	454
Sharp Electronics of Canada Ltd.	454
Shaw Communications	455
Shaw Industries Ltd.	455
Sheraton Fallsview Hotel	456
Sheraton Toronto East Hotel and Towers	456
Sherbrooke Community Centre	457
Shermag Inc.	457

The Canada Student Employment Guide

Part Time/Summer Index

Sherwood Credit Union	458	Supreme Tooling Group	483
Shoppers Drug Mart Limited	458	Surrey Memorial Hospital	483
Shopping Channel, The	459	Surrey Place Centre	484
Shorewood Packaging Corp. of Canada Ltd.	459	Surrey, City of	484
Siemens Electric Ltd.	460	Symantec Corporation	486
Signature Vacations Inc.	460	Syncrude Canada Ltd.	486
Silicon Graphics Canada Inc.	461	Talisman Energy Inc.	487
Skiing Louise Ltd.	461	TCG International Inc.	487
Skills Training & Support Services Association	462	TCT Logistics	488
Slocan Forest Products Ltd.	462	Teck Corp.	489
SNC-Lavalin	463	Teklogix Inc.	489
Sobeys Inc.	463	Teldon International Inc.	490
Société des Alcools du Québec	464	Telebec Ltée	490
Sodexho Marriott Services Canada	464	Telegraph Journal	491
SolutionInc Limited	465	Telesat Canada	491
Sony Music Canada	465	Telus Corporation	492
Southam Inc.	466	The Arthritis Society	492
Southern Railway of British Columbia Ltd.	466	The Barn Fruit Markets Inc.	493
Southland Canada	467	The Co-operators	493
Spar Aerospace Limited	467	The Garland Group	494
Spectrum Signal Processing Inc.	468	The McElhanney Group Ltd.	494
Speedware Corp. Inc.	469	Thomas & Betts Ltée	495
Sprint Canada	470	Thomas Cook Group (Canada) Ltd.	495
SRI Homes Inc.	470	Thomas J. Lipton	496
SSQ Life	471	Thompson's Moving and Storage	496
St. Amant Centre Inc.	471	Thomson - CSF Systems Canada Inc.	497
St. Joseph's Care Group	472	Thunder Bay Regional Hospital	497
St. Lawrence Parks Commission	472	Tiger Brand Knitting Company Limited	498
St. Lawrence Seaway Mgmt. Corp., The	473	Timmins, City of	499
St. Vincent's Hospitals	473	Tippet-Richardson Ltd.	499
Standard Knitting Limited	474	Today's Business Products Ltd.	500
Standen's Limited	474	Top Producers Systems Inc.	500
Stanley Canada Inc.	475	Toronto and Region Conservation Authority	501
Stantec Consulting Ltd.	475	Toronto Association For Community Living	501
Star Data Systems Inc.	476	Toronto Catholic District School Board	502
State Farm Insurance Companies	476	Toronto Cricket Skating & Curling	502
Steelcraft Industries Ltd.	477	Toronto District School Board	503
Steelpipe Ltd.	477	Toronto East General Hospital	503
Sterling Marking Products Inc.	478	Toronto French School, The	504
Stitches	478	Toronto General Hospital	505
Stone Consolidated Inc.	479	Toronto Hydro	505
StorageTek Canada Inc.	479	Toronto Police Service	506
StressGen Biotechnologies Corp.	480	Toronto Public Library Board	506
Sudbury Regional Hospital	480	Toronto Sun Publishing Corp., The	507
Sun Peaks Resort Corporation	481	Toronto Zoo	507
Sun Rype Products Ltd.	481	Toronto, City of	508
Sunoco Inc.	482	Toshiba of Canada Ltd.	508

The Canada Student Employment Guide

Part Time/Summer Index

Toyota Canada Ltd.	509
TransAlta	509
Transcontinental Digital Services Inc.	510
Triumf	510
Trojan Technologies Inc.	511
Trow Consulting Engineers Ltd.	511
TSC Stores Ltd.	512
Turnbull & Turnbull Ltd.	512
Uni Select Inc.	513
Union Gas Ltd.	513
Union Pacific Resources Group	514
Unisys Canada Inc.	514
Universal Rehabilitation Service Agency	515
University College of Cape Breton	516
Urban Systems Ltd.	516
US Filter BCP	517
USF WaterGroup	517
Vacances Air Transat Inc.	518
Valley First Credit Union	518
Value Village Stores	519
VanCity Credit Union	519
Vancouver International Airport	520
Vancouver Sun	520
Versa Services Ltd.	521
VIA Rail Canada Inc.	521
Villa Providence Shediac Inc.	522
Visteon Canada Inc.	522
Volkswagen Canada Inc.	523
Volvo Cars of Canada Ltd.	523
W C I Canada Inc.	524
Waterloo Furniture Components Ltd.	524
Waverly & York Corporation	525
WebCanada	526
Wegu Canada Inc.	526
Weldco-Beales Manufacturing Inc.	527
Wendy's Restaurants of Canada Inc.	527
West Coast Apparel	528
West Kootenay Power Ltd.	528
Westbury Life	529
Westcliff Management Ltd.	529
Westcoast Energy Inc.	530
Western Glove Works	530
Westin Bayshore Resort and Marina, The	531
Westin Prince Hotel, The	531
Westinghouse Canada Inc.	532
Westminster Savings Credit Union	533
Weston Produce Inc.	533
Westport Innovations Inc.	534
Westshore Terminals Ltd.	534
Weyerhaeuser Company Limited	535
Whistler Blackcomb Mountain	535
White Rose Crafts and Nursery Sales Limited	536
White Spot Limited	536
Whitehill Technologies Inc.	537
Wilderness Reforestation	537
Wilson Auto Electric Ltd.	538
Windsor, City of	538
Winners Apparel Ltd.	539
Winpak Ltd.	539
Wire Rope Industries Ltd.	540
Workfire Development Corp.	540
xwave solutions	542
Yamaha Motor Canada Ltd.	542
Yanke Group of Companies	543
Yarmouth Regional Hospital	543
Yellowknife, City of	544
YFactor	544
YTV Canada Inc.	545
Zeidler Roberts Partnership Architects	546
Zellers Inc.	546
Zenastra	547
Zenon Environmental Inc.	547
Zurich Canada	548

The Canada Student Employment Guide

Co-op/Internship Index

The following employers have indicated they offer co-op or internship opportunities. The corresponding page number of the firm's profile is also shown.

Addictions Foundation of Manitoba, The	81
Alberta Energy & Utilities Board	89
Alias | Wavefront	94
AMEC Inc.	99
Andersen Consulting	101
Assure Health Inc.	110
ATCO Frontec Corp.	111
ATS Automation Tooling Systems Inc.	116
Barton Place Long Term Care Facility	121
Bearskin Lake Air Service Ltd.	128
Behlen Industries	130
Blaney McMurty LLP	139
Bombardier Aerospace	143
Bosal Canada Inc.	145
BOVAR Waste Management	145
British Columbia Assessment	148
CAE Newness	157
Calgary, City of	158
Canadian General Tower Limited	166
Cangene Corporation	172
Cargill Limited	175
Challenger Motor Freight Inc.	186
CKF Inc.	192
Club Monaco International	193
Cognos Incorporated	196
COM DEV International	197
Communications & Power Industries Canada	198
Corel Corporation	205
Cosyn Technology	207
David Thompson Health Region	212
Dofasco Inc.	218
Domtar Inc.	218
Dura Automotive Systems (Canada) Ltd.	222
Earth Tech Canada Inc.	225
Electronics Arts (Canada) Inc.	229
Endpoint Research Ltd.	231
EnerFlex Systems Ltd.	232

Ernst & Young	234
Espial Group Incorporated	234
Exfo	235
Export Development Corporation	236
FAG Bearings Limited	237
Farm Credit Corp. Canada	238
Finning	240
Forzani Group Ltd., The	244
General Chemical Canada Ltd.	249
General Electric Canada Inc.	249
Gimbel Eye Centre	252
Haliburton Energy Services	262
Halifax County Regional Rehabilitation Centre	263
Hudson's Bay Company, The	279
Ilco Unican Inc.	286
Indalex Limited	288
InfoInterActive Inc.	290
Island Telecom Inc.	295
IWK Grace Health Centre	297
J.D. Irving Limited	298
JDS Uniphase Corporation	300
Johnson Controls Ltd.	302
Kawneer Company Canada Limited	304
Kimberly-Clark Inc.	307
Kraft Canada Inc.	310
Linmor Technologies	320
MacViro Consultants Inc.	326
Manitoba Agriculture and Food	327
Maritime Life Assurance Company, The	331
Matrox Electronic Systems Ltd.	335
McCarney Greenwood	336
McGraw Hill Ryerson Ltd.	337
Meyers Norris Penny & Co.	344
Ministry of Northern Develop. and Mines	348
Mississauga, City of	349
Mitra Imaging Inc.	350
Morrison Hershfield Limited	354
Mortice Kern Systems Inc.	355
Motorola Canada Ltd.	356
Multi-Languages	357
Neles Automation, Scada Solutions Ltd.	362
Pelmorex Inc.	395

The Canada Student Employment Guide

Co-op/Internship Index

Raytheon Systems Canada Ltd.	419
Replicon Inc.	428
Rimrock Resort Hotel	432
Rogers AT&T Wireless Inc.	436
Royal & Sun Alliance Insurance Co. of Cda	437
Schlumberger Canada Ltd.	450
SED Systems	453
Shoppers Drug Mart Limited	458
Sobeys Inc.	463
SolutionInc Limited	465
Sony Music Canada	465
Spectrum Signal Processing Inc.	468
St. Joseph's Care Group	472
Stantec Consulting Ltd.	475
Steelcraft Industries Ltd.	477
StressGen Biotechnologies Corp.	480
Sun Peaks Resort Corporation	481
The Arthritis Society	492
The Co-operators	493
Transcontinental Digital Services Inc.	510
Trojan Technologies Inc.	511
Uni Select Inc.	513
Urban Systems Ltd.	516
Vancouver International Airport	520
Visteon Canada Inc.	522
Western Glove Works	530
WestJet Airlines	532
Westport Innovations Inc.	534
Whitehill Technologies Inc.	537
Winners Apparel Ltd.	539
Winpak Ltd.	539
Workfire Development Corp.	540

Notes

Notes

Notes

THREE GREAT PUBLICATIONS!

Ten Ways To Straight A's

A brand new book that offers valuable insight into the secrets of succeeding in school and beyond. Learn how to get your mind set on school success, how to write effective essays, survive exam time, and much more! The author, an average student herself at the beginning, has developed a formula that has helped her achieve school success. Now, she is a student at Harvard Law School!

188 pages
ISBN 1-896324-36-3
$19.95

The Canada Student Employment Guide (2001 Edition)

Now fully updated and expanded! This year the book contains almost 1,000 employer profiles with contact info, academic fields and skills companies seek, and part time and summer employment information. New this year is a section on co-op and internship opportunities! This book is the most valuable employment reference guide for students!

720 pages
ISBN 1-896324-34-7
$26.95

The Canadian Job Directory (Year 2000/2001 Edition)

A popular resource for both adults and students that contains hundreds of profiles on every imaginable source of employment including: Firms and Organizations; Recruiters; Trade Assoc.; Career Resources on the Internet; and Human Resource Canada Centres. It is an essential job seeker's guide!

462 pages
ISBN 1-896324-30-4
$ 24.95

To Order

Please send me ____ copy(s) of **Ten Ways to Straight A's**

Please send me ____ copy(s) of **The Canada Student Employment Guide (2000 Ed.)**

Please send me ____ copy(s) of **The Canadian Job Directory (2000/2001 Ed.)**

Enclosed is a cheque/money order for $ _____ (payable to SEN)

Please add $6.00 Shipping plus 7% GST to all orders (HST & QST where applicable).

Name: _____

Address: _____ City: _____

Prov: _____   Postal Code: _____   Tel: _____

Student Employment Network
117 Gerrard Street East, Suite 1002, Toronto, ON, M5B 2L4
Tel: (416) 971-5090   Fax: (416) 977-3782
Internet: www.studentjobs.com   E-mail: sen@studentjobs.com

Discounts are available for larger orders. Contact the publisher above for more information.